P9-DEW-771

IMPORTANT

HERE IS YOUR REGISTRATION CODE TO ACCESS MCGRAW-HILL PREMIUM CONTENT AND MCGRAW-HILL ONLINE RESOURCES

For key premium online resources you need THIS CODE to gain access. Once the code is entered, you will be able to use the web resources for the length of your course.

Access is provided only if you have purchased a new book.

If the registration code is missing from this book, the registration screen on our website, and within your WebCT or Blackboard course will tell you how to obtain your new code. Your registration code can be used only once to establish access. It is not transferable

To gain access to these online resources

1. USE your web browser to go to: **http://www.mhhe.com/thompson**

2. CLICK on "First Time User"

3. ENTER the Registration Code printed on the tear-off bookmark on the right

4. After you have entered your registration code, click on "Register"

5. FOLLOW the instructions to setup your personal UserID and Password

6. WRITE your UserID and Password down for future reference. Keep it in a safe place.

If your course is using WebCT or Blackboard, you'll be able to use this code to access the McGraw-Hill content within your instructor's online course.

To gain access to the McGraw-Hill content in your instructor's WebCT or Blackboard course simply log into the course with the user ID and Password provided by your instructor. Enter the registration code exactly as it appears to the right when prompted by the system. You will only need to use this code the first time you click on McGraw-Hill content.

These instructions are specifically for student access. Instructors are not required to register via the above instructions.

The McGraw-Hill Companies

McGraw-Hill Irwin

Thank you, and welcome to your McGraw-Hill/Irwin Online Resources.

Thompson/Strickland/Gamble

Crafting & Executing Strategy: The Quest for Competitive Advantage: Concepts & Cases. 15/e
Crafting & Executing Strategy: Text and Readings. 15/e

ISBN 13: 978-0-07-326939-9; ISBN 10: 0-07-326939-5

THE PREMIMUM CONTENT INCLUDES:

- **Case-TUTOR**—Downloadable software w/assignment questions for all 35 cases in the text, plus analytically-structured exercises for 11 of the cases

- **PowerWeb**—Articles, Weekly Update Archive, and News Feeds

- **Build Your Management Skills**—Interactive self-assessment and concept review exercises

Crafting and Executing Strategy

Text and Readings

NC WESLEYAN COLLEGE LIBRARY
ROCKY MOUNT, NC 27804

North Carolina Wesleyan College Library

Scurry - Drum Collection

Given by:
Dr. Frank Scurry and Carolina Evangelical Divinity School

CGSD LIBRARY

Crafting and Executing Strategy

Text and Readings

15th Edition

CGSD LIBRARY Arthur A. Thompson, Jr.
University of Alabama

A. J. Strickland III
University of Alabama

John E. Gamble
University of South Alabama

McGraw-Hill
Irwin

Boston   Burr Ridge, IL   Dubuque, IA   Madison, WI   New York
San Francisco   St. Louis   Bangkok   Bogotá   Caracas   Kuala Lumpur
Lisbon   London   Madrid   Mexico City   Milan   Montreal   New Delhi
Santiago   Seoul   Singapore   Sydney   Taipei   Toronto

The McGraw·Hill Companies

McGraw-Hill
Irwin

CRAFTING AND EXECUTING STRATEGY: TEXT AND READINGS

Published by McGraw-Hill/Irwin, a business unit of The McGraw-Hill Companies, Inc., 1221 Avenue of the Americas, New York, NY, 10020. Copyright © 2007 by The McGraw-Hill Companies, Inc. All rights reserved. No part of this publication may be reproduced or distributed in any form or by any means, or stored in a database or retrieval system, without the prior written consent of The McGraw-Hill Companies, Inc., including, but not limited to, in any network or other electronic storage or transmission, or broadcast for distance learning.

Some ancillaries, including electronic and print components, may not be available to customers outside the United States.

This book is printed on acid-free paper.

2 3 4 5 6 7 8 9 0 DOW/DOW 0 9 8 7

ISBN-13: 978-0-07-313721-6
ISBN-10: 0-07-313721-9

Editorial director: *John E. Biernat*
Executive editor: *John Weimeister*
Managing developmental editor: *Laura Hurst Spell*
Marketing director: *Ellen Cleary*
Media producer: *Benjamin Curless*
Project manager: *Harvey Yep*
Lead production supervisor: *Rose Hepburn*
Designer: *Cara David*
Photo research coordinator: *Lori Kramer*
Media project manager: *Joyce J. Chappetto*
Cover design: *Cara David*
Interior design: *Cara David*
Typeface: *10.5/12 Times New Roman*
Compositor: *Laserwords Private Limited*
Printer: *R. R. Donnelley*
Cover Image: ©Stockbyte

Library of Congress Cataloging-in-Publication Data

Thompson, Arthur A., 1940-
   Crafting and executing strategy : text and readings / Arthur A. Thompson, A. J. Strickland, John E. Gamble.—15th ed.
      p. cm.
   Includes bibliographical references and index.
   ISBN-13: 978-0-07-313721-6 (alk. paper)
   ISBN-10: 0-07-313721-9 (alk. paper)
   1. Strategic planning. 2. Business planning. I. Strickland, A. J. (Alonzo J.) II. Gamble, John (John E.) III. Title.
HD30.28.T525 2007
658.4' 012—dc22

2006011852

www.mhhe.com

To our families and especially our wives:
Hasseline, Kitty, and Debra

About the Authors

Arthur A. Thompson, Jr., earned his B.S. and Ph.D. degrees in economics from The University of Tennessee, spent three years on the economics faculty at Virginia Tech, and served on the faculty of The University of Alabama's College of Commerce and Business Administration for 24 years. In 1974 and again in 1982, Dr. Thompson spent semester-long sabbaticals as a visiting scholar at the Harvard Business School.

His areas of specialization are business strategy, competition and market analysis, and the economics of business enterprises. In addition to publishing over 30 articles in some 25 different professional and trade publications, he has authored or co-authored five textbooks and six computer-based simulation exercises that are used in colleges and universities worldwide.

Dr. Thompson spends much of his off-campus time giving presentations, putting on management development programs, working with companies, and helping operate a business simulation enterprise in which he is a major partner.

Dr. Thompson and his wife of 45 years have two daughters, two grandchildren, and two Yorkshire terriers.

Dr. A. J. (Lonnie) Strickland, a native of North Georgia, attended the University of Georgia, where he received a bachelor of science degree in math and physics in 1965. Afterward he entered the Georgia Institute of Technology, where he received a master of science in industrial management. He earned a Ph.D. in business administration from Georgia State University in 1969. He currently holds the title of Professor of Strategic Management in the Graduate School of Business at The University of Alabama.

Dr. Strickland's experience in consulting and executive development is in the strategic management area, with a concentration in industry and competitive analysis. He has developed strategic planning systems for such firms as the Southern Company, BellSouth, South Central Bell, American Telephone and Telegraph, Gulf States Paper, Carraway Methodist Medical Center, Delco Remy, Mark IV Industries, Amoco Oil Company, USA Group, General Motors, and Kimberly Clark Corporation (Medical Products). He is a very popular speaker on the subject of implementing strategic change and serves on several corporate boards.

John E. Gamble is currently Associate Dean and Professor of Management in the Mitchell College of Business at the University of South Alabama. His teaching specialty at USA is strategic management and he also conducts a course in strategic management in Germany, which is sponsored by the University of Applied Sciences in Worms.

Dr. Gamble's research interests center on strategic issues in entrepreneurial, health care, and manufacturing settings. His work has been published in various scholarly journals and he is the author or co-author of more than 30 case studies published in an assortment of strategic management and strategic marketing texts. He has done consulting on industry and market analysis for clients in a diverse mix of industries.

Professor Gamble received his Ph.D. in management from The University of Alabama in 1995. Dr. Gamble also has a Bachelor of Science degree and a Master of Arts degree from The University of Alabama.

The Preface

The objective of this text is to effectively and interestingly cover what every senior-level or MBA student needs to know about crafting and executing business strategies. It features a *substantive* presentation of core concepts and analytical techniques and a collection of timely and recently published readings that amplify important topics in managing a company's strategy-making, strategy-executing process. The text–readings content works quite well for courses where the instructor wishes to provide students with a foundation in the core concepts and analytical tools of strategic management and a taste of the literature of strategic management before having them tackle a customized set of cases and/or a simulation exercise. Two state-of-the-art online strategy simulations, *The Business Strategy Game* and *GLO-BUS,* were created expressly as accompanying supplements to this book; either simulation will prove to be an excellent fit with the 13 chapters of this text and the collection of readings.

As you would expect, we believe this edition represents a solid improvement over the 14th edition. A bigger portion of each chapter has been revised and rewritten than in any previous edition. Coverage was trimmed in some areas, expanded in others. Every paragraph on every page of the 14th edition was revisited, producing a host of both major and minor changes in exposition. Pains were taken to improve and enliven the explanations of core concepts and analytical tools. The latest research findings from the literature and cutting-edge strategic practices of companies have been incorporated to keep in step with both theory and practice. Scores of new examples have been added to complement the new and updated Illustration Capsules. More chapter-end exercises have been included. The result is a text treatment with more punch, greater clarity, and improved classroom effectiveness. But none of the changes have altered the fundamental character that has driven the text's success over the years. The chapter content continues to be solidly mainstream and balanced, mirroring *both* the best academic thinking and the pragmatism of real-world strategic management.

Complementing the 13-chapter text presentation is an appealing lineup of 21 readings—all new to this edition. All appeared in the 2004–2005 time frame and were chosen to amplify important topics covered in the text chapters. And the 15th edition has a comprehensive package of support materials that are a breeze to use, highly effective, and flexible enough to fit most any course design.

A TEXT WITH ON-TARGET CONTENT

In our view, for a senior/MBA-level strategy text to qualify as having on-target content, it must:

- Explain core concepts in language that students can grasp and provide examples of their relevance and use by actual companies.
- Take care to thoroughly describe the tools of strategic analysis, how they are used, and where they fit into the managerial process of crafting and executing strategy.

- Be up-to-date and comprehensive, with solid coverage of the landmark changes in competitive markets and company strategies being driven by globalization and Internet technology.
- Focus squarely on what every student needs to know about crafting, implementing, and executing business strategies in today's market environments.

We believe this 15th edition measures up on all four criteria. Chapter discussions cut straight to the chase about what students really need to know. Explanations of core concepts and analytical tools are comprehensive enough to make them understandable and usable, the rationale being that a shallow explanation carries little punch and has almost no instructional value. All the chapters are flush with convincing examples that students can easily relate to. There's a straightforward, integrated flow from one chapter to the next. The latest research findings pertinent to a first course in strategy have been woven into each chapter. And we have deliberately adopted a pragmatic, down-to-earth writing style, not only to better communicate to an audience of students (who, for the most part, will soon be practicing managers) but also to convince readers that the subject matter deals directly with what managers and companies do in the real world.

ORGANIZATION, CONTENT, AND FEATURES OF THE TEXT CHAPERS

The 13 chapters in this edition are arranged in the same order as the 14th edition and cover essentially the same topics. But every chapter has been given a refreshing facelift that includes the latest thinking and evidence from the literature, more refined presentations, and a greater number of current examples. The latest developments in the theory and practice of strategic management have been ingrained in every chapter to keep the content solidly in the mainstream of contemporary strategic thinking. You'll find up-to-date coverage of the continuing march of industries and companies to wider globalization, the growing scope and strategic importance of collaborative alliances, the spread of high-velocity change to more industries and company environments, and how online technology is driving fundamental changes in both strategy and internal operations in companies across the world.

No other leading strategy text comes close to matching our coverage of the resource-based theory of the firm. The resource-based view of the firm is prominently and comprehensively integrated into our coverage of crafting both single-business and multibusiness strategies. Chapters 3 through 9 emphasize that a company's strategy must be matched *both* to its external market circumstances and to its internal resources and competitive capabilities. Moreover, Chapters 11, 12, and 13, on various aspects of executing strategy, have a strong resource-based perspective that makes it unequivocally clear how and why the tasks of assembling intellectual capital and building core competencies and competitive capabilities are absolutely critical to successful strategy execution and operating excellence.

No other leading strategy text comes close to matching our coverage of business ethics, values, and social responsibility. We have embellished the highly important Chapter 10, "Strategy, Ethics, and Social Responsibility," with new discussions and material so that it can better fulfill the important functions of (1) alerting students to the role and importance of incorporating business ethics and social responsibility into decision making and (2) addressing the accreditation requirements of the AACSB that business ethics be visibly and thoroughly embedded in the core curriculum. Moreover, there are discussions of the roles of values and ethics in Chapters 1, 2, 11, and 13, thus providing you with a meaty, comprehensive treatment of business ethics and socially responsible behavior as they apply to crafting and executing company strategies.

The following rundown summarizes the noteworthy chapter features and topical emphasis in this edition:

- Chapter 1 continues to focus on the central questions of "What is strategy?" and "Why is it important?" It defines what is meant by the term *strategy*, identifies the different elements of a company's strategy, and explains why management efforts to craft a company's strategy entail a quest for competitive advantage. Following Henry Mintzberg's pioneering research, we stress how and why a company's strategy is partly planned and partly reactive, and why a company's strategy tends to evolve over time. There's an enhanced discussion of what is meant by the term *business model* and how it relates to the concept of strategy. The thrust of this first chapter is to convince students that good strategy + good strategy execution = good management. The chapter is a perfect accompaniment for your opening-day lecture on what the course is all about and why it matters.

- Chapter 2 delves into the managerial process of actually crafting and executing a strategy—it makes a great assignment for the second day of class and is a perfect follow-on to your first day's lecture. The focal point of the chapter is the five-step managerial process of crafting and executing strategy: (1) forming a strategic vision of where the company is headed and why, (2) setting objectives and performance targets that measure the company's progress, (3) crafting a strategy to achieve these targets and move the company toward its market destination, (4) implementing and executing the strategy, and (5) monitoring progress and making corrective adjustments as needed. Students are introduced to such core concepts as strategic visions, mission statements, strategic versus financial objectives, and strategic intent. There's a section underscoring that *all managers are on a company's strategy-making, strategy-executing team* and that a company's strategic plan is a collection of strategies devised by different managers at different levels in the organizational hierarchy. The chapter winds up with a substantially expanded section on corporate governance.

- Chapter 3 sets forth the now-familiar analytical tools and concepts of industry and competitive analysis and demonstrates the importance of tailoring strategy to fit the circumstances of a company's industry and competitive environment. The standout feature of this chapter is a presentation of Michael E. Porter's "five-forces model of competition" that we think is the clearest, most straightforward discussion of any text in the field. Globalization and Internet technology are treated as potent driving forces capable of reshaping industry competition—their roles as change agents have become factors that most companies in most industries must reckon with in forging winning strategies.

- Chapter 4 establishes the equal importance of doing solid company situation analysis as a basis for matching strategy to organizational resources, competencies, and competitive capabilities. The roles of core competencies and organizational resources and capabilities in creating customer value and helping build competitive advantage are *center stage* in the discussions of company resource strengths and weaknesses. SWOT analysis is cast as a simple, easy-to-use way to assess a company's resources and overall situation. There is much clearer coverage of value chain analysis, benchmarking, and competitive strength assessments—standard tools for appraising a company's relative cost position and market standing vis-à-vis rivals. *An important addition to this chapter is a table showing how key financial and operating ratios are calculated and how to interpret them;* students will find this table handy in doing the number-crunching needed to evaluate whether a company's strategy is delivering good financial performance.

- Chapter 5 deals with a company's quest for competitive advantage and is framed around the five generic competitive strategies—low-cost leadership, differentiation, best-cost provider, focused differentiation, and focused low-cost provider.

- Chapter 6 extends the coverage of the previous chapter and deals with what *other strategic actions* a company can take to complement its choice of a basic competitive strategy. The chapter features sections on what use to make of strategic alliances and collaborative partnerships; merger and acquisition strategies; vertical integration strategies; outsourcing strategies; offensive and defensive strategies; and the different types of Web site strategies that companies can employ to position themselves in the marketplace. The discussion of offensive strategies has been totally overhauled and features a new section on blue ocean strategy. The concluding section of this chapter provides a much-enhanced treatment of first-mover advantages and disadvantages.

- Chapter 7 explores the full range of strategy options for competing in foreign markets: export strategies; licensing; franchising; multicountry strategies; global strategies; and collaborative strategies involving heavy reliance on strategic alliances and joint ventures. The spotlight is trained on two strategic issues unique to competing multinationally: (1) whether to customize the company's offerings in each different country market to match the tastes and preferences of local buyers or whether to offer a mostly standardized product worldwide, and (2) whether to employ essentially the same basic competitive strategy in the markets of all countries where it operates or whether to modify the company's competitive approach country by country as needed to fit the specific market conditions and competitive circumstances it encounters. There's also coverage of the concepts of profit sanctuaries and cross-market subsidization, the ways to achieve competitive advantage by operating multinationally, the special issues of competing in the markets of emerging countries; and the strategies that local companies in emerging countries can use to defend against global giants.

- The role of Chapter 8 is to hammer home the points made in Chapters 3 and 4 that winning strategies have to be matched both to industry and competitive conditions and to company resources and capabilities. The first portion of the chapter covers the broad strategy options for companies competing in six representative industry and competitive situations: (1) emerging industries; (2) rapid-growth industries; (3) mature, slow-growth industries; (4) stagnant or declining industries; (5) turbulent, high-velocity industries; and (6) fragmented industries. The second portion of the chapter looks at matching strategy to the resources and capabilities of four representative types of companies: (1) companies pursuing rapid growth, (2) companies in industry-leading positions, (3) companies in runner-up positions, and (4) companies in competitively weak positions or plagued by crisis conditions. The detail with which these 10 concrete examples are covered in Chapter 8 should enable you to convince students why it is management's job to craft a strategy that is tightly matched to a company's internal and external circumstances.

- Our rather meaty treatment of diversification strategies for multibusiness enterprises in Chapter 9 begins by laying out the various paths for becoming diversified, explains how a company can use diversification to create or compound competitive advantage for its business units, and examines the strategic options an already-diversified company has to improve its overall performance. In the middle part of the chapter, the analytical spotlight is on the techniques and procedures for assessing the strategic attractiveness of a diversified company's business portfolio—the relative attractiveness of the various businesses the company has diversified into, a multi-industry company's competitive strength in each of its lines of business, and the *strategic fits* and *resource fits* among a diversified company's different businesses. The chapter concludes with a brief survey of a company's four main postdiversification strategy alternatives: (1) broadening the diversification base, (2) divesting some businesses and retrenching to a narrower diversification base, (3) restructuring the makeup of the company's business lineup, and (4) multinational diversification.

- Chapter 10 reflects the very latest in the literature on (1) whether and why a company has a *duty* to operate according to ethical standards and (2) whether and why a company has a *duty* or *obligation* to contribute to the betterment of society independent of the needs and preferences of the customers it serves. Is there a credible business case for operating ethically and/or operating in a socially responsible manner? The opening section of the chapter addresses whether ethical standards are universal (as maintained by the school of ethical universalism) or dependent on local norms and situational circumstances (as maintained by the school of ethical relativism) or a combination of both (as maintained by integrative social contracts theory). Following this is a section on the three categories of managerial morality (moral, immoral, and amoral), a section on the drivers of unethical strategies and shady business behavior, a section on the approaches to managing a company's ethical conduct, a section on linking a company's strategy to its ethical principles and core values, a section on the concept of a "social responsibility strategy," and sections that explore the business case for ethical and socially responsible behavior. The chapter will give students some serious ideas to chew on and, hopefully, will make them far more ethically conscious. It has been written as a stand-alone chapter that can be assigned in the early, middle, or late part of the course.

- The three-chapter module on executing strategy (Chapters 11–13) is anchored around a pragmatic, compelling conceptual framework: (1) building the resource strengths and organizational capabilities needed to execute the strategy in competent fashion; (2) allocating ample resources to strategy-critical activities; (3) ensuring that policies and procedures facilitate rather than impede strategy execution; (4) instituting best practices and pushing for continuous improvement in how value chain activities are performed; (5) installing information and operating systems that enable company personnel to better carry out their strategic roles proficiently; (6) tying rewards and incentives directly to the achievement of performance targets and good strategy execution; (7) shaping the work environment and corporate culture to fit the strategy; and (8) exerting the internal leadership needed to drive execution forward.

We have reworked and refreshed the content all three chapters. You will see thoroughly overhauled discussions of staffing the organization, building capabilities, instilling a corporate culture, leading the strategy-execution process, and adopting best practices and Six Sigma in facilitating the drive for operating excellence.

As with the 14th edition, the recurring theme of these Chapters 11–13 is that implementing and executing strategy entails figuring out the specific actions, behaviors, and conditions that are needed for a smooth strategy-supportive operation and then following through to get things done and deliver results—the goal here is to ensure that students understand the strategy-implementing/strategy-executing phase is a make-things-happen and make-them-happen-right kind of managerial exercise.

We have done our best to ensure that the 13 chapters hit the bull's-eye in covering the essentials of a senior/MBA course in strategy and convey the best thinking of academics and practitioners. The number of examples in each chapter has been dramatically expanded. There are new and updated "strategy in action" capsules in each chapter that tie core concepts to real-world management practice. We've provided a host of interesting chapter-end exercises that you can use as a basis for class discussion or written assignments or team presentations. We are confident you'll find this 13-chapter presentation superior to our prior editions as concerns coverage, readability, and convincing examples. The ultimate test of the text, of course, is the positive pedagogical impact it has in the classroom. If this edition sets a more effective stage for your lectures and does a better job of helping you persuade students that the discipline of strategy merits their rapt attention, then it will have fulfilled its purpose.

THE COLLECTION OF READINGS

In selecting a set of readings to accompany the chapter presentations, we opted for readings that (1) were current (most appeared in 2004 and 2005), (2) extended the chapter coverage and expanded on a topic of strategic importance, and (3) were quite readable and relatively short. At the same time, we endeavored to be highly selective, deciding that a manageable number of on-target readings was a better fit with the teaching/learning objectives of most senior and MBA courses in strategy than a more sweeping collection of readings. The 21 readings we chose came from recent issues of the *Business Strategy Review, Strategy & Leadership, Harvard Business Review, MIT Sloan Management Review, Business Horizons, Academy of Management Executive, Business Ethics Quarterly, Business and Society Review, Journal of Business Strategy, The TQM Magazine,* and *Ivey Business Journal.*

Aside from providing an introductory look at the literature of strategic management literature, the readings offer nice variety. The first reading by well-known and much-published Costas Markides, "What Is Strategy and How Do You Know If You Have One?," expands on the various notions of what strategy is, the conflicting definitions that exist, and why strategy is mainly about making some very difficult decisions on a *few* parameters. Mark Lipton's essay, "Walking the Talk (Really!): Why Visions Fail," describes why it is important for company executives to move beyond articulating a vision and actually push company personnel to weave the vision into the fabric of how the company conducts its operations. The article by Scott M. Shafer, H. Jeff Smith, and Jane E. Linder, "The Power of Business Models," tackles some of the vagueness about what business models are, how they can be used, and why they have a powerful role in corporate management. The article "The Balanced Scorecard: To Adopt or Not to Adopt?" looks at the factors that prompt companies to adopt the balanced scorecard approach and provides six lessons for managers considering this approach to measuring performance. Stan Abraham's essay, "Stretching Strategic Thinking," makes a solid case for why strategic thinking is an important part of every manager's job and explains what the strategic thinking process involves. All five of these articles tie tightly to the material in Chapters 1 and 2.

There are seven articles appropriate for use with Chapters 3 through 9. The article entitled "A New Tool for Strategy Analysis: The Opportunity Model" provides a valuable extension of SWOT analysis covered in Chapter 4. George Stalk's article, "Playing Hardball: Why Strategy Still Matters," is must reading and will open eyes about how companies play competitive hardball in the marketplace. The piece by W. Chan Kim and Renée Mauborgne, "Value Innovation: A Leap into the Blue Ocean," expands on the coverage of blue ocean strategy in Chapter 6. Don Potter's article, "Confronting Low-End Competition," offers strategy options for competing effectively against low-cost, low-price competitors. Peter J. Williamson's essay, "Strategies for Asia's New Competitive Game," is a perfect companion to the material in Chapter 7. Costas Markides and Paul A. Geroski's article, "Racing to Be 2nd: Conquering the Industries of the Future," provides excellent insight into first-mover disadvantages and fast follower advantages (topics covered in Chapter 6). The timely reading "Outsourcing Strategies: Opportunities and Risks" provides useful perspectives on when outsourcing makes strategic sense and when it doesn't. Gerry Kerr and James Darroch's reading, "Insights from the New Conglomerates," looks at four ways that diversified companies can try to add shareholder value via a multibusiness strategy; it is best used in conjunction with Chapter 9.

Six readings were chosen for use with the three chapters on executing strategy (Chapters 11–13). Michael C. Mankius and Richard Steele's "Turning Great Strategy into Great Performance," from the *Harvard Business Review,* is a splendid treatise on how to avoid breakdowns in strategy execution; it provides an excellent lead-in to your coverage of the managerial tasks of implementing and executing the chosen strategy. Lynda Gratton and Sumantra Ghoshal's article, "Beyond Best Practice," describes how high-performing companies embrace "signature processes" that reflect their values; this article works quite well with either Chapter 12 or Chapter 13. Edward D. Arnheiter and John Maleyeff's reading, "The Integration of Lean Manufacturing and Six Sigma," describes each system and the key concepts and techniques that underlie their implementation—it will work nicely as part of your coverage of the material in Chapter 12. The Edwin A. Locke reading, "Linking Goals to Monetary Incentives," reinforces and expands the discussion in Chapter 12 on how to use incentives to further the cause of good strategy execution. Brian Leavy's article, "A Leader's Guide to Creating an Innovation Culture," adds significantly to the much-revised coverage of corporate culture in Chapter 13. This group of readings concludes with a very provocative article by Sidney Finkelstein entitled "The Seven Habits of Spectacularly Unsuccessful Executives."

There are two readings that complement the Chapter 10 coverage of strategy, ethics, and social responsibility. Bert van de Ven and Ronald Jeurissen's reading, "Competing Responsibly" examines the effect of different competitive conditions on the extent of a company's investment in corporate social responsibility. Jacquelyn B. Gates's article, "The Ethics Commitment Process: Sustainability through Value-Based Ethics," delves into role of corporate values in achieving compliance with a company's code of ethics.

TWO ACCOMPANYING ONLINE, FULLY-AUTOMATED SIMULATION EXERCISES—*THE BUSINESS STRATEGY GAME* AND *GLO-BUS*

The Business Strategy Game and *GLO-BUS: Developing Winning Competitive Strategies*—two competition-based strategy simulations that are delivered online and that feature automated processing of decisions and grading of performance—are being marketed by the publisher as companion supplements for use with this and other texts in the field. *The Business Strategy Game* is the world's leading strategy simulation, having been played by well over 400,000 students at universities across the world. *GLO-BUS,* a relatively new and somewhat simpler online simulation introduced in 2004, has been played by over 15,000 students at more than 125 universities across the world.

We think there are compelling reasons for using a simulation as a cornerstone, if not a centerpiece, of strategy courses for seniors and MBA students:

- Assigning students to run a company that competes head-to-head against companies run by other class members *gives students immediate opportunity to experiment with various strategy options and to gain proficiency in applying the core concepts and analytical tools that they have been reading about in the chapters.* The whole teaching/learning enterprise is facilitated when what the chapters have to say about the managerial tasks of crafting and executing strategy matches up with the strategy-making challenges that students confront in the simulation.

- *Most students desperately need the experience of actively managing a close-to-real-life company where they can practice and hone their skills* in thinking strategically, evaluating changing industry and competitive conditions, assessing a company's financial and competitive condition, and crafting and executing a strategy that delivers good results and produces sustainable competitive advantage. Strategy simulations put students through a drill where they can improve (1) their business acumen, (2) their ability to make good bottom-line decisions in the face of uncertain market and competitive conditions, and (3) their proficiency in weaving functional area decisions into a cohesive strategy. *Such skills building is the essence of senior and MBA courses in business strategy.*

- Students are *more motivated* to buckle down and figure out what strategic moves will make their simulation company perform better than they are to wrestle with the strategic issues posed in an assigned case (which entails reading the case thoroughly, diagnosing the company's situation, and proposing well-reasoned action recommendations). In a strategy simulation, students have to take the analysis of market conditions, the strategies and actions of competitors, and the condition of their company *seriously*—they are held fully accountable for their decisions and their company's performance. It is to students' advantage to avoid faulty analysis and flawed strategies—*nothing gets students' attention quicker than the adverse grade consequences of a decline in their company's performance or the loss of an industry position.* And no other type of assignment does a better job of spurring students to fully exercise their strategic wits and analytical prowess—*company co-managers have a strong grade incentive to spend quality time debating and deciding how best to boost the performance of their company.*

In class discussions of cases, however, students take on the more passive and detached role of outside observers providing their thoughts about a company's situation. It is sometimes hard to get students to think long and hard about the company in the assigned case or what needs to be done to improve its future performance. They may well not see an immediate or alarming impact on their grade if their case preparation is skimpy or their analysis of the company's situation is deficient or their recommendations about what the company should do are suboptimal or even off-the-wall. Thus, while case analysis absolutely needs to be an essential part of senior/MBA courses in strategy, case assignments fall short of strategy simulations in their capacity to motivate students to do first-rate strategic analysis and come up with insightful action recommendations.

- *A competition-based strategy simulation adds an enormous amount of student interest and excitement*—a head-to-head competitive battle for market share and industry leadership *stirs students' competitive juices and emotionally engages them in the subject matter.* Being an active manager in running a company in which they have a stake makes their task of learning about crafting and executing winning strategies more enjoyable. Their company becomes "real" and takes on a life of its own as the simulation unfolds—and it doesn't take long for students to establish a healthy rivalry with other class members that are running rival companies. Because the competition in the simulation typically gets very personal, most students become immersed in what's going on in their industry—as compared to the more impersonal engagement that occurs when they are assigned a case to analyze.

- A first-rate simulation produces a "Wow! Not only is this fun, but I am learning a lot" reaction from students. *The element of competition ingrained in strategy simulations stirs students' competitive juices and emotionally engages them in the subject matter.* Most students will thoroughly enjoy the *learn-by-doing* character of a simulation, recognize the practical value of having to make all kinds of decisions and run a whole company, and gain confidence from working with all the financial and operating statistics—all of which tends to (1) make the strategy course *a livelier, richer learning experience* and (b) result in higher instructor evaluations at the end of the course.

- Strategy simulations like *The Business Strategy Game* or *GLO-BUS* that have exceptionally close ties between the industry and company circumstances in the simulation and the topics covered in the text chapters *provide instructors with a host of first-rate examples of how the material in the text applies both to the experience that students are having in running their companies and to real-world management.* Since *students can easily relate to these examples,* they are much more apt to say "Aha! Now I see how this applies and why I need to know about it and use it." The host of examples the simulation experience provides to create this "Aha!" effect thus adds real value. (There is information posted in the Instructor Centers for both *The Business Strategy Game* and *GLO-BUS* showing specific links between the pages of this text and the simulation.)

- Because a simulation involves making decisions relating to production operations, worker compensation and training, sales and marketing, distribution, customer service, and finance and requires analysis of company financial statements and market data, *the simulation helps students synthesize the knowledge gained in a variety of different business courses. The cross-functional, integrative nature of a strategy simulation helps make courses in strategy much more of a true capstone experience.*

In sum, *a three-pronged text–case–simulation course model has significantly more teaching/learning power than the traditional text–case combination.* Indeed, a very convincing argument can be made that a competition-based strategy simulation is *the single most powerful vehicle that instructors can use to effectively teach the discipline of business and competitive strategy and to build student proficiencies in crafting and executing a winning strategy.* Mounting instructor recognition of the teaching/learning effectiveness of a good strategy simulation accounts for why strategy simulations have earned a prominent place in so many of today's strategy courses.

And, happily, there's another positive side benefit to using a simulation—*it lightens the grading burden for instructors.* Since a simulation can entail 20 or more hours of student time over the course of a term (depending on the number of decisions and the extent of accompanying assignments), most adopters compensate by trimming the total number of assigned cases or substituting the simulation for one (or two) written cases and/or an hour exam. This results in less time spent grading, because both *The Business Strategy Game* and *GLO-BUS* have built-in grading features that require no instructor effort (beyond setting the grading weights).

A *Bird's-Eye View of* The Business Strategy Game

The setting for *The Business Strategy Game* (*BSG*) is the global athletic footwear industry (there can be little doubt in today's world that a globally competitive strategy simulation is *vastly superior* to a simulation with a domestic-only setting). Global market demand for footwear grows at the rate of 7–9 percent annually for the first five years and 5–7 percent annually for the second five years. However, market growth rates vary by geographic region—North America, Latin America, Europe-Africa, and Asia-Pacific.

Companies begin the simulation producing branded and private-label footwear in two plants, one in North America and one in Asia. They have the option to establish production facilities in Latin America and Europe-Africa, either by constructing new plants or buying previously constructed plants that have been sold by competing companies. Company co-managers exercise control over production costs based on the styling and quality they opt to manufacture, plant location (wages and incentive compensation vary from region to region), the use of best practices and Six Sigma programs to reduce the production of defective footwear and to boost worker productivity, and compensation practices.

All newly produced footwear is shipped in bulk containers to one of four geographic distribution centers. All sales in a geographic region are made from footwear inventories in that region's distribution center. Costs at the four regional distribution centers are a function of inventory storage costs, packing and shipping fees, import tariffs paid on incoming pairs shipped from foreign plants, and exchange rate impacts. At the start of the simulation, import tariffs average $4 per pair in Europe-Africa, $6 per pair in Latin America, and $8 in the Asia-Pacific region. However, the Free Trade Treaty of the Americas allows tariff-free movement of footwear between North America and Latin America. Instructors have the option to alter tariffs as the game progresses.

Companies market their brand of athletic footwear to footwear retailers worldwide and to individuals buying online at the company's Web site. Each company's sales and market share in the branded footwear segments hinge on its competitiveness on 11 factors: attractive pricing, footwear styling and quality, product-line breadth, advertising, the use of mail-in rebates, the appeal of celebrities endorsing a company's brand, success in convincing footwear retailers dealers to carry its brand, the number of weeks it takes to fill retailer orders, the effectiveness of a company's online sales effort at its Web site, and customer loyalty. Sales of private-label footwear hinge solely on being the low-price bidder.

All told, company co-managers make 47 types of decisions each period that cut across production operations (up to 10 decisions each plant, with a maximum of 4 plants), plant capacity additions/sales/upgrades (up to 6 decisions per plant), worker compensation and training (3 decisions per plant), shipping (up to 8 decisions each plant), pricing and marketing (up to 10 decisions in 4 geographic regions), bids to sign celebrities (2 decision entries per bid), and financing of company operations (up to 8 decisions).

Each time company co-managers make a decision entry, an assortment of on-screen calculations instantly shows the projected effects on unit sales, revenues, market shares, unit costs, profit, earnings per share, ROE, and other operating statistics. The on-screen calculations help team members evaluate the relative merits of one decision entry versus another and put together a promising strategy.

Companies can employ any of the five generic competitive strategy options in selling branded footwear—low-cost leadership, differentiation, best-cost provider, focused low-cost, and focused differentiation. They can pursue essentially the same strategy worldwide or craft slightly or very different strategies for the Europe-Africa, Asia-Pacific, Latin America, and North America markets. They can strive for competitive advantage based on more advertising or a wider selection of models or more appealing styling/quality, or bigger rebates, and so on.

Any well-conceived, well-executed competitive approach is capable of succeeding, provided it is not overpowered by the strategies of competitors or defeated by the presence of too many copycat strategies that dilute its effectiveness. The challenge for each company's management team is to craft and execute a competitive strategy that produces good performance on five measures: earnings per share, return on equity investment, stock price appreciation, credit rating, and brand image.

All activity for *The Business Strategy Game* takes place at www.bsg-online.com.

A Bird's-Eye View of GLO-BUS

The industry setting for *GLO-BUS* is the digital camera industry. Global market demand grows at the rate of 8–10 percent annually for the first five years and 4–6 percent annually for the second five years. Retail sales of digital cameras are seasonal, with about 20 percent of consumer demand coming in each of the first three quarters of each calendar year and 40 percent coming during the big fourth-quarter retailing season.

Companies produce entry-level and upscale, multifeatured cameras of varying designs and quality in a Taiwan assembly facility and ship assembled cameras directly to retailers in North America, Asia-Pacific, Europe-Africa, and Latin America. All cameras are assembled as retail orders come in and shipped immediately upon completion of the assembly process—companies maintain no finished-goods inventories, and all parts and components are delivered on a just-in-time basis (which eliminates the need to track inventories and simplifies the accounting for plant operations and costs). Company co-managers exercise control over production costs based on the designs and components they specify for their cameras, workforce compensation and training, the length of warranties offered (which affects warranty costs), the amount spent for technical support provided to buyers of the company's cameras, and their management of the assembly process.

Competition in each of the two product market segments (entry-level and multifeatured digital cameras) is based on 10 factors: price, camera performance and quality, number of quarterly sales promotions, length of promotions in weeks, the size of the promotional discounts offered, advertising, the number of camera models, size of retail dealer network, warranty period, and the amount/caliber of technical support provided to camera buyers. Low-cost leadership, differentiation strategies, best-cost provider strategies, and focus strategies are all viable competitive options. Rival companies can strive to be the clear market leader in either entry-level cameras, upscale multifeatured cameras, or both. They can focus on one or two geographic regions or strive for geographic balance. They can pursue essentially the same strategy worldwide or craft slightly or very different strategies for the Europe-Africa, Asia-Pacific, Latin America, and North America markets. Just as with *The Business Strategy Game,* most any well-conceived, well-executed competitive approach is capable of succeeding, *provided it is not overpowered by the strategies of competitors or defeated by the presence of too many copycat strategies that dilute its effectiveness.*

Company co-managers make 44 types of decisions each period, ranging from R&D, camera components, and camera performance (10 decisions) to production operations and worker compensation (15 decisions) to pricing and marketing (15 decisions) to the financing of company operations (4 decisions). Each time participants make a decision entry, an assortment of on-screen calculations instantly shows the projected effects on unit sales, revenues, market shares, unit costs, profit, earnings per share, ROE, and other operating statistics. These on-screen calculations help team members evaluate the relative merits of one decision entry versus another and stitch the separate decisions into a cohesive and promising strategy. Company performance is judged on five criteria: earnings per share, return on equity investment, stock price, credit rating and brand image.

All activity for *GLO-BUS* occurs at www.glo-bus.com.

Administration and Operating Features of the Two Simulations

The online delivery and user-friendly designs of both *BSG* and *GLO-BUS* make them incredibly easy to administer, even for first-time users. And the menus and controls are so similar that you can readily switch between the two simulations or use one in your undergraduate class and the other in a graduate class. If you have not yet used either of the two simulations, you may find the following of particular interest:

- Time requirements for instructors are minimal. Setting up the simulation for your course is done online and takes about 10–15 minutes. Once setup is completed, no other administrative actions are required beyond that of moving participants to a different team (should the need arise) and monitoring the progress of the simulation (to whatever extent desired).

- There's no software for students or administrators to download and no disks to fool with. All work must be done online and the speed for participants using dial-up modems is quite satisfactory. The servers dedicated to hosting the two simulations have appropriate back-up capability and are maintained by a prominent Web-hosting service that guarantees 99.99 percent reliability on a 24/7/365 basis—as long as students or instructors are connected to the Internet, the servers are virtually guaranteed to be operational.

- Participant's Guides are delivered at the Web site—students can read the Guide on their monitors or print out a copy, as they prefer.

- There are extensive built-in "Help" screens explaining (1) each decision entry, (2) the information on each page of the Industry Reports, and (3) the numbers presented in the Company Reports. *The Help screens allow company co-managers to figure things out for themselves, thereby curbing the need for students to always run to the instructor with questions about "how things work."*

- The results of each decision are processed automatically and are typically available to all participants *15 minutes* after the decision deadline specified by the instructor/game administrator.

- Participants and instructors are notified via e-mail when the results are ready.

- Decision schedules are instructor-determined. Decisions can be made once per week, twice per week, or even twice daily, depending on how instructors want to conduct the exercise. One popular decision schedule involves 1 or 2 practice decisions, 6–10 regular decisions, and weekly decisions across the whole term. A second popular schedule is 1 or 2 practice decisions, 6–8 regular decisions, and biweekly decisions, all made during the last 4 to 6 weeks of the course (when it can be assumed that students have pretty much digested the contents of Chapters 1–6, gotten somewhat comfortable with what is involved in crafting strategy for a single-business company situation, and have prepared several assigned cases). A third popular schedule is to use the simulation as a "final exam" for the course, with daily decisions (Monday through Friday) for the last two weeks of the term.

- Instructors have the flexibility to prescribe 0, 1, or 2 practice decisions and from 3 to 10 regular decisions.

- Company teams can be composed of 1 to 5 players each and the number of companies in a single industry can range from 4 to 12. If your class size is too large for a single industry, then it is a simple matter to create two or more industries for a single class section.

- Following each decision, participants are provided with a complete set of reports—a six-page Industry Report, a one-page Competitive Intelligence report for each geographic region that includes strategic group maps and bulleted lists of competitive strengths and weaknesses, and a set of Company Reports (income statement, balance sheet, cash flow statement, and assorted production, marketing, and cost statistics).

- Two "open-book" multiple-choice tests of 20 questions (optional, but strongly recommended) are included as part of each of the two simulations. The quizzes are taken online and automatically graded, with scores reported instantaneously to participants and automatically recorded in the instructor's electronic gradebook. Students are automatically provided with three sample questions for each test.

- Both simulations contain a three-year strategic plan option that you can assign. Scores on the plan are automatically recorded in the instructor's online gradebook.
- At the end of the simulation, you can have students complete online peer evaluations. (Again, the scores are automatically recorded in your online gradebook.)
- Both simulations have a Company Presentation feature that enables students to easily prepare PowerPoint slides for use in describing their strategy and summarizing their company's performance in a presentation either to the class, the instructor, or an "outside" board of directors.

For more details on either simulation, please consult the Instructor's Manual or visit the simulation Web sites (www.bsg-online.com and www.glo-bus.com). The Web sites provide a wealth of information, including a "Guided Tour" link that takes about five minutes. Once you register (there's no obligation), you'll be able to access the Instructor's Guide and a set of PowerPoint Presentation slides that you can skim to preview the two simulations in some depth. The simulation authors will be glad to provide you with a personal tour of either or both Web sites (while you are on your PC) and walk you through the many features that are built into the simulations. We think you'll be quite impressed with the capabilities that have been programmed into *The Business Strategy Game and GLO-BUS,* the simplicity with which both simulations can be administered, and their exceptionally tight connection to the text chapters, core concepts, and standard analytical tools.

Adopters of the text who also want to incorporate use of either of the two simulation supplements should instruct their bookstores to order the "book-simulation package"—the publisher has a special ISBN for new texts that contain a special card shrink-wrapped with each text; printed on the enclosed card is a prepaid access code that students can use to register for either simulation and gain full access to the student portion of the Web site.

STUDENT SUPPORT MATERIALS FOR THE 15TH EDITION

Key Points Summaries

At the end of each chapter is a synopsis of the core concepts, analytical tools, and other key points discussed in the chapter. These chapter-end synopses, along with the margin notes scattered throughout each chapter, help students focus on basic strategy principles, digest the messages of each chapter, and prepare for tests.

Chapter-End Exercises

Each chapter contains a much-embellished set of exercises that you can use as the basis for class discussion, oral presentation assignments, and/or short written reports. A few of the exercises (and many of the Illustration Capsules) qualify as "mini-cases"; these can be used to round out the rest of a 75-minute class period should your lecture on a chapter only last for 50 minutes.

A Value-Added Web Site

Students use the code that comes on the inside page of each new copy of the text to gain access to the publisher's Web site for the 15th edition; students having a used text can purchase access to the site for a very modest fee. The student section of www.mhhe.com/thompson contains a number of helpful aids:

- Self-scoring 20-question chapter tests that students can take to measure their grasp of the material presented in each of the 13 chapters.
- A "Guide to Case Analysis" containing sections on what a case is, why cases are a standard part of courses in strategy, preparing a case for class discussion, doing a written case analysis, doing an oral presentation, and using financial ratio analysis to assess a company's financial condition. We suggest having students read this Guide prior to the first class discussion of a case.
- A select number of PowerPoint slides for each chapter.

PowerWeb

With each new book, students gain access to the publisher's PowerWeb site offering current news, articles from 6,300 premium sources, a Web research guide, current readings from annual editions, and links to related sites.

INSTRUCTOR SUPPORT MATERIALS FOR THE 15TH EDITION

Instructor's Manual

The accompanying Instructor's Manual contains a section on suggestions for organizing and structuring your course, sample syllabi and course outlines, a set of lecture notes on each chapter, a copy of the test bank, and comprehensive teaching notes for each of the cases.

Test Bank

There is a test bank prepared by the co-authors containing over 1,200 multiple-choice questions and short-answer/essay questions.

EZ-Test

A computerized version of the test bank, EZ-Test allows you to generate tests quite conveniently and to add in your own questions.

PowerPoint Slides

To facilitate delivery preparation of your lectures and to serve as chapter outlines, you'll have access to approximately 500 colorful and professional-looking slides displaying core concepts, analytical procedures, key points, and all the figures in the text chapters. The slides are the creation of Professor Jana Kuzmicki of Troy State University.

The Business Strategy Game *and* GLO-BUS *Online Simulations*

Using one of the two companion simulations is a powerful and constructive way of emotionally connecting students to the subject matter of the course. We know of no more effective and interesting way to stimulate the competitive energy of students and prepare them for the rigors of real-world business decision making than to have them match strategic wits with classmates in running a company in head-to-head competition for global market leadership.

Instructor's Resource CD-ROM

The complete Instructor's Manual and the PowerPoint slides accompanying the chapters have been installed on an Instructor's Resource CD that the publisher provides to adopters.

Resources for Assembling a Set of Custom Cases

Using the capabilities of McGraw-Hill's Primis division, instructors can go online to www.mhhe.com/primis, browse the cases that have appeared in our last four editions (as well as other sources), and quickly assemble a customized collection of cases that can be delivered in either printed copy or e-book form. Teaching notes for all these cases are available.

ACKNOWLEDGMENTS

A great number of colleagues and students at various universities, business acquaintances, and people at McGraw-Hill provided inspiration, encouragement, and counsel during the course of this project. Like all text authors in the strategy field, we are intellectually indebted to the many academics whose research and writing have blazed new trails and advanced the discipline of strategic management. The following reviewers provided seasoned advice and splendid suggestions for improving the chapters in this 15th edition:

Lynne Patten, *Clark Atlanta University*

Nancy E. Landrum, *Morehead State University*

Jim Goes, *Walden University*

Jon Kalinowski, *Minnesota State University–Mankato*

Rodney M. Walter Jr., *Western Illinois University*

Judith D. Powell, *Virginia Union University*

We also express our thanks to Seyda Deligonul, David Flanagan, Esmerelda Garbi, Mohsin Habib, Kim Hester, Jeffrey E. McGee, Diana J. Wong, F. William Brown, Anthony F. Chelte, Gregory G. Dess, Alan B. Eisner, John George, Carle M. Hunt, Theresa Marron-Grodsky, Sarah Marsh, Joshua D. Martin, William L. Moore, Donald Neubaum, George M. Puia, Amit Shah, Lois M. Shelton, Mark Weber, Steve Barndt, J. Michael Geringer, Ming-Fang Li, Richard Stackman, Stephen Tallman, Gerardo R. Ungson, James Boulgarides, Betty Diener, Daniel F. Jennings, David Kuhn, Kathryn Martell, Wilbur Mouton, Bobby Vaught, Tuck Bounds, Lee Burk, Ralph Catalanello,

William Crittenden, Vince Luchsinger, Stan Mendenhall, John Moore, Will Mulvaney, Sandra Richard, Ralph Roberts, Thomas Turk, Gordon VonStroh, Fred Zimmerman, S. A. Billion, Charles Byles, Gerald L. Geisler, Rose Knotts, Joseph Rosenstein, James B. Thurman, Ivan Able, W. Harvey Hegarty, Roger Evered, Charles B. Saunders, Rhae M. Swisher, Claude I. Shell, R. Thomas Lenz, Michael C. White, Dennis Callahan, R. Duane Ireland, William E. Burr II, C. W. Millard, Richard Mann, Kurt Christensen, Neil W. Jacobs, Louis W. Fry, D. Robley Wood, George J. Gore, and William R. Soukup. These reviewers provided valuable guidance in steering our efforts to improve earlier editions.

As always, we value your recommendations and thoughts about the book. Your comments regarding coverage and contents will be taken to heart, and we always are grateful for the time you take to call our attention to printing errors, deficiencies, and other shortcomings. Please e-mail us at athompso@cba.ua.edu, astrickl@cba.ua.edu, or jgamble@usouthal.edu; fax us at (205) 348-6695; or write us at P.O. Box 870225, Department of Management and Marketing, The University of Alabama, Tuscaloosa, Alabama 35487-0225.

Arthur A. Thompson

A. J. Strickland

John E. Gamble

Guided Tour

Chapter Structure and Organization

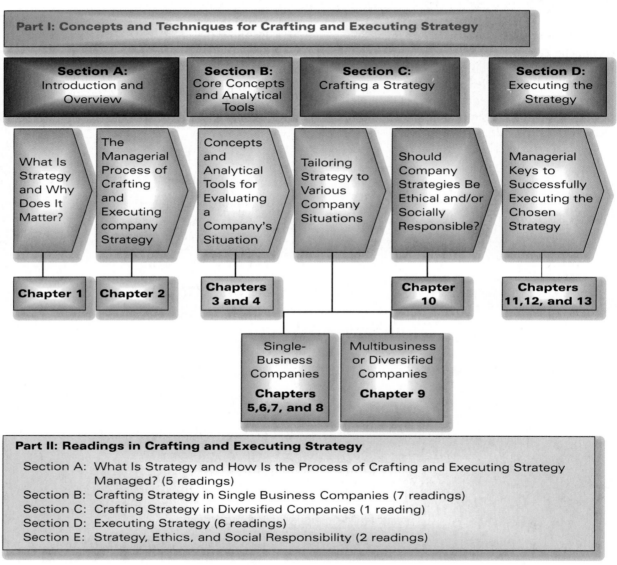

Part I: Concepts and Techniques for Crafting and Executing Strategy

Section A: Introduction and Overview	Section B: Core Concepts and Analytical Tools	Section C: Crafting a Strategy	Section D: Executing the Strategy

What Is Strategy and Why Does It Matter?

The Managerial Process of Crafting and Executing company Strategy

Concepts and Analytical Tools for Evaluating a Company's Situation

Tailoring Strategy to Various Company Situations

Should Company Strategies Be Ethical and/or Socially Responsible?

Managerial Keys to Successfully Executing the Chosen Strategy

Chapter 1

Chapter 2

Chapters 3 and 4

Chapter 10

Chapters 11,12, and 13

Single-Business Companies
Chapters 5,6,7, and 8

Multibusiness or Diversified Companies
Chapter 9

Part II: Readings in Crafting and Executing Strategy

Section A: What Is Strategy and How Is the Process of Crafting and Executing Strategy Managed? (5 readings)
Section B: Crafting Strategy in Single Business Companies (7 readings)
Section C: Crafting Strategy in Diversified Companies (1 reading)
Section D: Executing Strategy (6 readings)
Section E: Strategy, Ethics, and Social Responsibility (2 readings)

chapter one

What Is Strategy and Why Is It Important?

Managers face three central questions in evaluating their company's business prospects: What's the company's present situation? Where does the company need to go from here? How should it get there? Arriving at a probing answer to the question "What's the company's present situation?" prompts managers to evaluate industry conditions and competitive pressures, the company's current performance and market standing, its resource strengths and capabilities, and its competitive weaknesses. The question "Where does the company need to go from here?" pushes managers to make choices about the direction the company should be headed—what new or different customer groups and customer needs it should endeavor to satisfy, what market positions it should be staking out, what changes in its business makeup are needed. The question "How should it get there?" challenges managers to craft and execute a strategy capable of moving the company in the intended direction, growing its business, and improving its financial and market performance.

In this opening chapter, we define the concept of strategy and describe its many facets. We shall indicate the kinds of actions that determine what a company's strategy is, why strategies are partly proactive and partly reactive, and why company strategies tend to evolve over time. We will look at what sets a winning strategy apart from ho-hum or flawed strategies and why the caliber of a company's strategy determines whether it will enjoy a competitive advantage or be burdened by competitive disadvantage. By the end of this chapter, you will have a pretty clear idea of why the tasks of crafting and executing strategy are core management functions and why excellent execution of an excellent strategy is the most reliable recipe for turning a company into a standout performer.

WHAT DO WE MEAN BY *STRATEGY*?

A company's **strategy** is management's action plan for running the business and conducting operations. The crafting of a strategy represents a managerial *commitment to pursue a particular set of actions* in growing the business, attracting and pleasing customers, competing successfully, conducting operations, and improving the company's financial and market performance. Thus a company's strategy is all about *how*—*how* management intends to grow the business, *how* it will build a loyal clientele and outcompete rivals, *how* each functional piece of the business (research and development,

---

Strategy means making clear-cut choices about how to compete.
—**Jack Welch**
Former CEO, General Electric

A strategy is a commitment to undertake one [set of ac]tions rather than another.
—**Sharon Oster**
Professor, Yale University

The process of developing superior strategies is part planning, part trial and error, until you hit upon something that works.
—**Costas Markides**
Professor, London Business School

Without a strategy the organization is like a ship without a rudder.
—**Joel Ross and Michael Kami**
Authors and Consultants

Each chapter begins with a series of pertinent **quotes** and an introductory preview of its contents.

Illustration Capsule 1.2

Microsoft and Red Hat: Two Contrasting Business Models

The strategies of rival companies are often predicated on strikingly different business models. Consider, for example, the business models for Microsoft and Red Hat in operating system software for personal computers (PCs).

Microsoft's business model for making money from its Windows operating system products is based on the following revenue-cost-profit economics:

• Employ a cadre of highly skilled programmers to develop proprietary code; keep the source code hidden so as to keep the inner workings of the software proprietary.

• Sell the resulting operating system and software package to PC makers and to PC users at relatively attractive prices (around $75 to PC makers and about $100 at retail to PC users); strive to maintain a 90 percent or more market share of the 150 million PCs sold annually worldwide.

• Strive for big-volume sales. Most of Microsoft's costs arise on the front end in developing the software and are thus fixed; the variable costs of producing and packaging the CDs provided to users are only a couple of dollars per copy—once the break-even volume is reached, Microsoft's revenues from additional sales are almost pure profit.

• Provide a modest level of technical support to users at no cost.

• Keep rejuvenating revenues by periodically introducing next-generation software versions with features that will induce PC users to upgrade the operating system on previously purchased PCs to the new version.

Red Hat, a company formed to market its own version of the Linux open-source operating system, employs a business model based on sharply different revenue-cost-profit economics:

• Rely on the collaborative efforts of volunteer programmers from all over the world who contribute bits and pieces of code to improve and polish the Linux system. The global community of thousands of programmers who work on Linux in their spare time do what they do because they love it, because they are fervent believers that all software should be free (as in free speech), and in some cases because they are anti-Microsoft and want to have a part in undoing what they see as a Microsoft monopoly.

• Collect and test enhancements and new applications submitted by the open-source community of volunteer programmers. Linux's originator, Linus Torvalds, and a team of 300-plus Red Hat engineers and software developers evaluate which incoming submissions merit inclusion in new releases of Linux—the evaluation and integration of new submissions are Red Hat's only upfront product development costs.

• Market the upgraded and tested family of Red Hat products to large enterprises and charge them a subscription fee that includes 24/7 support within one hour in seven languages. Provide subscribers with updated versions of Linux every 12–18 months to maintain the subscriber base.

• Make the source code open and available to all users, allowing them to create a customized version of Linux.

• Capitalize on the specialized expertise required to use Linux in multiserver, multiprocessor applications by providing fees-based training, consulting, software customization, and client-directed engineering to Linux users. Red Hat offers Linux certification training programs at all skill levels at more than 60 global locations—Red Hat certification in the use of Linux is considered the best in the world.

Microsoft's business model—sell proprietary code software and give service away free—is a proven moneymaker that generates billions in profits annually. In contrast, the jury is still out on Red Hat's business model of selling subscriptions to open-source software to large corporations and deriving substantial revenues from the sales of technical support (included in the subscription cost), training, consulting, software customization, and engineering to generate revenues sufficient to cover costs and yield a profit. Red Hat posted losses of $140 million on revenues of $79 million in fiscal year 2002 and losses of $6.6 million on revenues of $91 million in fiscal year 2003, but it earned $14 million on revenues of $126 million in fiscal 2004. The profits came from a shift in Red Hat's business model that involved putting considerably more emphasis on getting large corporations to purchase subscriptions to the latest Linux updates. In 2005, about 75 percent of Red Hat's revenues came from large enterprise subscriptions, compared to about 53 percent in 2003.

Source: Company documents and information posted on www.microsoft.com and www.redhat.com. (accessed August 10, 2005).

In-depth examples– **Illustration Capsules**– appear in boxes throughout each chapter to illustrate important chapter topics, connect the text presentation to real world companies, and convincingly demonstrate "strategy in action." Some can be used as "mini-cases" for purposes of class discussion.

Margin notes define core concepts and call attention to important ideas and principles.

Strategy and the Quest for Competitive Advantage

The heart and soul of any strategy are the actions and moves in the marketplace that managers are taking to improve the company's financial performance, strengthen its long-term competitive position, and gain a competitive edge over rivals. A creative, distinctive strategy that sets a company apart from rivals and yields a competitive advantage is a company's most reliable ticket for earning above-average profits. Competing in the marketplace with a competitive advantage tends to be more profitable than competing with no advantage. And a company is almost certain to earn significantly higher profits when it enjoys a competitive advantage as opposed to when it is hamstrung by competitive disadvantage. Furthermore, if a company's competitive edge holds promise for being durable and sustainable (as opposed to just temporary), then so much the better for both the strategy and the company's future profitability. It's nice when a company's strategy produces at least a temporary competitive edge, but a **sustainable competitive advantage** is plainly much better. What makes a competitive advantage sustainable as opposed to temporary are actions and elements in the strategy that cause an attractive number of buyers to have a *lasting preference* for a company's products or services as compared to the offerings of competitors. Competitive advantage is the key to above-average profitability and financial performance because strong buyer preferences for the company's product offering translate into higher sales volumes (Wal-Mart) and/or the ability to command a higher price (Häagen-Dazs), thus driving up earnings, return on investment, and other measures of financial performance.

Four of the most frequently used and dependable strategic approaches to setting a company apart from rivals, building strong customer loyalty, and winning a sustainable competitive advantage are:

Core Concept
A company achieves **sustainable competitive advantage** when an attractive number of buyers prefer its products or services over the offerings of competitors and when the basis for this preference is durable.

Figures scattered throughout the chapters provide conceptual and analytical frameworks.

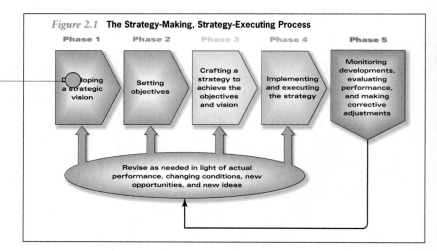

Figure 2.1   **The Strategy-Making, Strategy-Executing Process**

Phase 1	Phase 2	Phase 3	Phase 4	Phase 5
Developing a strategic vision	Setting objectives	Crafting a strategy to achieve the objectives and vision	Implementing and executing the strategy	Monitoring developments, evaluating performance, and making corrective adjustments

Revise as needed in light of actual performance, changing conditions, new opportunities, and new ideas ist and poet Ralph Waldo Emerson: "Commerce is a game of skill which many people play, but which few play well." If the content of this book helps you become a more savvy player and equips you to succeed in business, then your journey through these pages will indeed be time well spent.

Key Points

The tasks of crafting and executing company strategies are the heart and soul of managing a business enterprise and winning in the marketplace. A company's strategy is the game plan management is using to stake out a market position, conduct its operations, attract and please customers, compete successfully, and achieve organizational objectives. The central thrust of a company's strategy is undertaking moves to build and strengthen the company's long-term competitive position and financial performance and, ideally, gain a competitive advantage over rivals that then becomes a company's ticket to above-average profitability. A company's strategy typically evolves and re-forms over time, emerging from a blend of (1) proactive and purposeful actions on the part of company managers and (2) as-needed reactions to unanticipated developments and fresh market conditions.

Key Points sections at the end of each chapter provide a handy summary of essential ideas and things to remember.

the company's product offerings and competitive approaches will generate a revenue stream and have an associated cost structure that produces attractive earnings and return on investment—in effect, a company's business model sets forth the economic logic for making money in a particular business, given the company's current strategy.

A winning strategy fits the circumstances of a company's external situation and its internal resource strengths and competitive capabilities, builds competitive advantage, and boosts company performance.

Crafting and executing strategy are core management functions. Whether a company wins or loses in the marketplace is directly attributable to the caliber of a company's strategy and the proficiency with which the strategy is executed.

Exercises

1. Go to Red Hat's Web site (www.redhat.com) and check whether the company's recent financial reports indicate that its business model is working. Is the company sufficiently profitable to validate its business model and strategy? Is its revenue stream from selling training, consulting, and engineering services growing or declining as a percentage of total revenues? Does your review of the company's recent financial performance suggest that its business model and strategy are changing? Read the company's latest statement about its business model and about why it is pursuing the subscription approach (as compared to Microsoft's approach of selling copies of its operating software directly to PC manufacturers

Value-added **exercises** at the end of each chapter provide a basis for class discussion, oral presentations, and written assignments. Several chapters have exercises that qualify as "mini-cases."

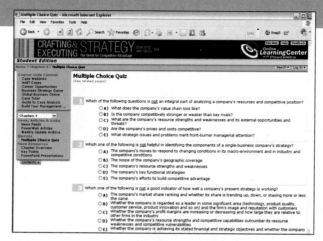

Web site: www.mhhe.com/thompson
The student portion of the Web site features 20-question self-scoring chapter tests, a guide to Case Analysis, and a select number of PowerPoint slides for each chapter.

PowerWeb With each new book, students gain access to publisher's PowerWeb site offering current news, articles from 6,300 premium sources, a Web research guide, current readings from annual editions, and links to related sites.

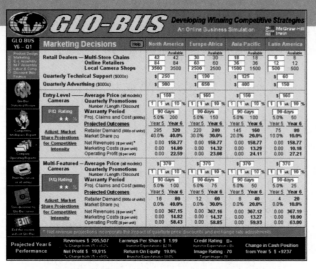

The Business Strategy Game or *GLO-BUS* *Simulation Exercises*

Either one of these text supplements involves teams of students managing companies in a head-to-head contest for global market leadership. Company co-managers have to make decisions relating to product quality, production, workforce compensation and training, pricing and marketing, and financing of company operations. The challenge is to craft and execute a strategy that is powerful enough to deliver good financial performance despite the competitive efforts of rival companies. Each company competes in North America, Latin America, Europe-Africa, and Asia-Pacific.

Brief Contents

Part One Concepts and Techniques for Crafting and Executing Strategy

Section A: Introduction and Overview

1. What Is Strategy and Why Is It Important?   2
2. The Managerial Process of Crafting and Executing Strategy   18

Section B: Core Concepts and Analytical Tools

3. Evaluating a Company's External Environment   48
4. Evaluating a Company's Resources and Competitive Position   94

Section C: Crafting a Strategy

5. The Five Generic Competitive Strategies: Which One to Employ?   132
6. Supplementing the Chosen Competitive Strategy: *Other Important Strategy Choices*   160
7. Competing in Foreign Markets   194
8. Tailoring Strategy to Fit Specific Industry and Company Situations   230
9. Diversification: *Strategies for Managing a Group of Businesses*   266
10. Strategy, Ethics, and Social Responsibility   316

Section D: Executing the Strategy

11. Building an Organization Capable of Good Strategy Execution   358
12. Managing Internal Operations: Actions that Promote Good Strategy Execution   388
13. Corporate Culture and Leadership: Keys to Good Strategy Execution   414

Part Two Readings in Crafting and Executing Strategy

Section A: What Is Strategy and How Is the Process of Crafting and Executing Strategy Managed?

1. What Is Strategy and How Do You Know If You Have One?   452
2. Walking the Talk (Really!): Why Visions Fail   459
3. The Power of Business Models   465

4. The Balanced Scorecard: To Adopt or Not to Adopt?   475

5. Stretching Strategic Thinking   482

Section B: Crafting Strategy in Single Business Companies

6. A New Tool for Strategy Analysis: The Opportunity Model   489

7. Playing Hardball: Why Strategy Still Matters   496

8. Value Innovation: A Leap into the Blue Ocean   502

9. Confronting the Low-End Competition   508

10. Strategies for Asia's New Competitive Game   515

11. Racing to Be 2nd: Conquering the Industries of the Future   521

12. Outsourcing Strategies: Opportunities and Risks   528

Section C: Crafting Strategy in Diversified Companies

13. Insights from the New Conglomerates   534

Section D: Executing Strategy

14. Turning Great Strategy into Great Performance   551

15. Beyond Best Practice   561

16. The Integration of Lean Management and Six Sigma   571

17. Linking Goals to Monetary Incentives   582

18. A Leader's Guide to Creating an Innovation Culture   587

19. The Seven Habits of Spectacularly Unsuccessful Executives   594

Section E: Strategy, Ethics, and Social Responsibility

20. Competing Responsibly   600

21. The Ethics Commitment Process: Sustainability through Value-Based Ethics   614

Endnotes   EN-1

Indexes

Organization   I-1

Name   I-5

Subject   I-9

Table of Contents

Part One   Concepts and Techniques for Crafting
and Executing Strategy   1

Section A: Introduction and Overview

1. What Is Strategy and Why Is It Important?   2

What Do We Mean by *Strategy?*   3
    Strategy and the Quest for Competitive Advantage   6
    Identifying a Company's Strategy   7
    Why a Company's Strategy Evolves over Time   8
    A Company's Strategy Is Partly Proactive and Partly Reactive   9
Strategy and Ethics: Passing the Test of Moral Scrutiny   10
The Relationship between a Company's Strategy and Its Business Model   12
What Makes a Strategy a Winner?   13
Why Are Crafting and Executing Strategy Important?   15
    Good Strategy + Good Strategy Execution = Good Management   15

Illustration Capsules

1.1. Comcast's Strategy to Revolutionize the Cable Industry   5
1.2. Microsoft and Red Hat: Two Contrasting Business Models   14

2. The Managerial Process of Crafting and
Executing Strategy   18

What Does the Strategy-Making, Strategy-Executing Process Entail?   19
Developing a Strategic Vision: Phase 1 of the Strategy-Making,
Strategy-Executing Process   20
    A Strategic Vision Covers Different Ground than the Typical
    Mission Statement   23
    Communicating the Strategic Vision   25
    Linking the Vision/Mission with Company Values   27
Setting Objectives: Phase 2 of the Strategy-Making, Strategy-Executing
Process   29
    What Kinds of Objectives to Set: The Need for a Balanced Scorecard   31
Crafting a Strategy: Phase 3 of the Strategy-Making, Strategy-Executing
Process   35
    Who Participates in Crafting a Company's Strategy?   35
    A Company's Strategy-Making Hierarchy   37
    Uniting the Strategy-Making Effort   40
    A Strategic Vision + Objectives + Strategy = A Strategic Plan   41

Implementing and Executing the Strategy: Phase 4 of the Strategy-Making, Strategy-Executing Process   42

Evaluating Performance and Initiating Corrective Adjustments: Phase 5 of the Strategy-Making, Strategy-Executing Process   43

Corporate Governance: The Role of the Board of Directors in the Strategy-Making, Strategy-Executing Process   44

Illustration Capsules

2.1. Examples of Strategic Visions—How Well Do They Measure Up?   23
2.2. Intel's Two Strategic Inflection Points   27
2.3. The Connection between Yahoo's Mission and Core Values   30
2.4. Examples of Company Objectives   33

Section B: Core Concepts and Analytical Tools

3. Evaluating a Company's External Environment   48

The Strategically Relevant Components of a Company's External Environment   49

Thinking Strategically about a Company's Industry and Competitive Environment   51

Question 1: What Are the Industry's Dominant Economic Features?   52

Question 2: What Kinds of Competitive Forces Are Industry Members Facing?   54

Competitive Pressures Associated with Jockeying among Rival Sellers   55

Competitive Pressures Associated with the Threat of New Entrants   60

Competitive Pressures from the Sellers of Substitute Products   64

Competitive Pressures Stemming from Supplier Bargaining Power and Supplier–Seller Collaboration   66

Competitive Pressures Stemming from Buyer Bargaining Power and Seller–Buyer Collaboration   69

Is the Collective Strength of the Five Competitive Forces Conducive to Good Profitability?   72

Question 3: What Factors Are Driving Industry Change and What Impacts Will They Have?   74

The Concept of Driving Forces   74

Identifying an Industry's Driving Forces   74

Assessing the Impact of the Driving Forces   80

Developing a Strategy That Takes the Impacts of the Driving Forces into Account   81

Question 4: What Market Positions Do Rivals Occupy—Who Is Strongly Positioned and Who Is Not?   81

Using Strategic Group Maps to Assess the Market Positions of Key Competitors   82

What Can Be Learned from Strategic Group Maps?   83

Question 5: What Strategic Moves Are Rivals Likely to Make Next?   85

Identifying Competitors' Strategies and Resource Strengths and Weaknesses   85

Predicting Competitors' Next Moves   86

Question 6: What Are the Key Factors for Future Competitive Success?   87

Question 7: Does the Outlook for the Industry Present the Company
with an Attractive Opportunity? 89

Illustration Capsules

3.1. Comparative Market Positions of Selected Retail Chains: A Strategic
Group Map Application 83

4. Evaluating a Company's Resources and Competitive
Position 94

Question 1: How Well Is the Company's Present Strategy Working? 95
Question 2: What Are the Company's Resource Strengths and Weaknesses,
and Its External Opportunities and Threats? 97
Identifying Company Resource Strengths and Competitive Capabilities 97
Identifying Company Resource Weaknesses and Competitive Deficiencies 104
Identifying a Company's Market Opportunities 104
Identifying the External Threats to a Company's Future Profitability 106
What Do the SWOT Listings Reveal? 107
Question 3: Are the Company's Prices and Costs Competitive? 109
The Concept of a Company Value Chain 110
Why the Value Chains of Rival Companies Often Differ 112
The Value Chain System for an Entire Industry 113
*Activity-Based Costing: A Tool for Assessing a
Company's Cost Competitiveness 114*
*Benchmarking: A Tool for Assessing Whether a Company's
Value Chain Costs Are in Line 116*
Strategic Options for Remedying a Cost Disadvantage 117
*Translating Proficient Performance of Value Chain
Activities into Competitive Advantage 120*
Question 4: Is the Company Competitively Stronger or Weaker
Than Key Rivals? 122
Interpreting the Competitive Strength Assessments 124
Question 5: What Strategic Issues and Problems Merit Front-Burner
Managerial Attention? 125

Illustration Capsules

4.1. Estimated Value Chain Costs for Recording and Distributing Music CDs
through Traditional Music Retailers 115
4.2. Benchmarking and Ethical Conduct 118

Section C: Crafting a Strategy

5. The Five Generic Competitive Strategies: Which One
to Employ? 132

The Five Generic Competitive Strategies 134
Low-Cost Provider Strategies 135
The Two Major Avenues for Achieving a Cost Advantage 135
The Keys to Success in Achieving Low-Cost Leadership 142

When a Low-Cost Provider Strategy Works Best   143

The Pitfalls of a Low-Cost Provider Strategy   144

Broad Differentiation Strategies   144

Types of Differentiation Themes   145

Where along the Value Chain to Create the Differentiating Attributes   145

The Four Best Routes to Competitive Advantage via a Broad Differentiation Strategy   146

The Importance of Perceived Value and Signaling Value   147

When a Differentiation Strategy Works Best   148

The Pitfalls of a Differentiation Strategy   148

Best-Cost Provider Strategies   150

When a Best-Cost Provider Strategy Works Best   151

The Big Risk of a Best-Cost Provider Strategy   151

Focused (or Market Niche) Strategies   151

A Focused Low-Cost Strategy   153

A Focused Differentiation Strategy   153

When a Focused Low-Cost or Focused Differentiation Strategy Is Attractive   154

The Risks of a Focused Low-Cost or Focused Differentiation Strategy   156

The Contrasting Features of the Five Generic Competitive Strategies: A Summary   156

Illustration Capsules

5.1. Nucor Corporation's Low-Cost Provider Strategy   136

5.2. How Wal-Mart Managed Its Value Chain to Achieve a Huge Low-Cost Advantage over Rival Supermarket Chains   141

5.3. Toyota's Best-Cost Producer Strategy for Its Lexus Line   152

5.4. Motel 6's Focused Low-Cost Strategy   154

5.5. Progressive Insurance's Focused Differentiation Strategy in Auto Insurance   155

6. Supplementing the Chosen Competitive Strategy: *Other Important Strategy Choices*   160

Collaborative Strategies: Alliances and Partnerships   163

Why and How Strategic Alliances Are Advantageous   164

Capturing the Benefits of Strategic Alliances   166

Why Many Alliances Are Unstable or Break Apart   167

The Strategic Dangers of Relying Heavily on Alliances and Collaborative Partnerships   167

Merger and Acquisition Strategies   168

Vertical Integration Strategies: Operating across More Stages of the Industry Value Chain   171

The Advantages of a Vertical Integration Strategy   172

The Disadvantages of a Vertical Integration Strategy   173

Outsourcing Strategies: Narrowing the Boundaries of the Business   175

When Outsourcing Strategies Are Advantageous   175

The Big Risk of an Outsourcing Strategy   177

Offensive Strategies: Improving Market Position and Building Competitive Advantage   177

   Blue Ocean Strategy: A Special Kind of Offensive   180

   Choosing Which Rivals to Attack   181

   Choosing the Basis for Competitive Attack   181

Defensive Strategies: Protecting Market Position and Competitive Advantage   182

   Blocking the Avenues Open to Challengers   182

   Signaling Challengers That Retaliation Is Likely   182

Web Site Strategies   183

   Product Information–Only Web Strategies: Avoiding Channel Conflict   183

   Web Site e-Stores as a Minor Distribution Channel   184

   Brick-and-Click Strategies   184

   Strategies for Online Enterprises   185

Choosing Appropriate Functional-Area Strategies   187

First-Mover Advantages and Disadvantages   188

   The Potential for Late-Mover Advantages or First-Mover Disadvantages   189

   To Be a First-Mover or Not   189

Illustration Capsules

6.1. Clear Channel Communications: Using Mergers and Acquisitions to Become a Global Market Leader   170

6.2. Brick-and-Click Strategies in the Office Supplies Industry   186

6.3. The Battle in Consumer Broadband: First-Movers versus Late-Movers   190

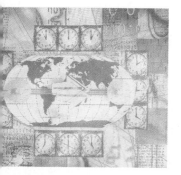

7. Competing in Foreign Markets   194

Why Companies Expand into Foreign Markets   196

   The Difference between Competing Internationally and Competing Globally   196

Cross-Country Differences in Cultural, Demographic, and Market Conditions   197

   Gaining Competitive Advantage Based on Where Activities Are Located   198

   The Risks of Adverse Exchange Rate Shifts   199

   Host Governments' Policies   200

The Concepts of Multicountry Competition and Global Competition   201

Strategy Options for Entering and Competing in Foreign Markets   202

   Export Strategies   203

   Licensing Strategies   203

   Franchising Strategies   204

   Localized Multicountry Strategies or a Global Strategy?   204

The Quest for Competitive Advantage in Foreign Markets   209

   Using Location to Build Competitive Advantage   209

   Using Cross-Border Transfers of Competencies and Capabilities to Build Competitive Advantage   211

   Using Cross-Border Coordination to Build Competitive Advantage   212

Profit Sanctuaries, Cross-Market Subsidization, and Global Strategic
Offensives   213

    *Using Cross-Market Subsidization to Wage a Strategic
Offensive   214*

    Offensive Strategies Suitable for Competing in Foreign Markets   215

Strategic Alliances and Joint Ventures with Foreign Partners   217

    The Risks of Strategic Alliances with Foreign Partners   218

    When a Cross-Border Alliance May Be Unnecessary   220

Strategies That Fit the Markets of Emerging Countries   220

    Strategy Options   222

    *Defending against Global Giants: Strategies for Local Companies
in Emerging Markets   224*

Illustration Capsules

7.1. Multicountry Strategies at Electronic Arts and Coca-Cola   209

7.2. Six Examples of Cross-Border Strategic Alliances   219

7.3. Coca-Cola's Strategy for Growing Its Sales in China and India   221

8. Tailoring Strategy to Fit Specific Industry and Company Situations   230

Strategies for Competing in Emerging Industries   231

    The Unique Characteristics of an Emerging Industry   232

    Strategy Options for Emerging Industries   233

Strategies for Competing in Rapidly Growing Markets   234

Strategies for Competing in Maturing Industries   236

    How Slowing Growth Alters Market Conditions   236

    Strategies That Fit Conditions in Maturing Industries   237

    Strategic Pitfalls in Maturing Industries   238

Strategies for Competing in Stagnant or Declining Industries   239

    End-Game Strategies for Declining Industries   241

Strategies for Competing in Turbulent, High-Velocity Markets   241

    Ways to Cope with Rapid Change   242

    Strategy Options for Fast-Changing Markets   242

Strategies for Competing in Fragmented Industries   245

    Reasons for Supply-Side Fragmentation   245

    Competitive Conditions in a Fragmented Industry   246

    Strategy Options for Competing in a Fragmented Industry   247

Strategies for Sustaining Rapid Company Growth   249

    The Risks of Pursuing Multiple Strategy Horizons   250

Strategies for Industry Leaders   251

Strategies for Runner-Up Firms   254

    Obstacles for Firms with Small Market Shares   254

    Offensive Strategies to Build Market Share   254

    Other Strategic Approaches for Runner-Up Companies   255

Strategies for Weak and Crisis-Ridden Businesses   257
Turnaround Strategies for Businesses in Crisis   257
Harvest Strategies for Weak Businesses   260
Liquidation— the Strategy of Last Resort   261
10 Commandments for Crafting Successful Business Strategies   261

Illustration Capsules

8.1. Exertris's Focus Strategy in the Fragmented Exercise Equipment
    Industry   248
8.2. ESPN's Strategy to Dominate Sports Entertainment   252
8.3. Sony's Turnaround Strategy—Will It Work?   259

9. Diversification: *Strategies for Managing a Group
   of Businesses*   266

When to Diversify   269
Building Shareholder Value: The Ultimate Justification for Diversifying   269
Strategies for Entering New Businesses   270
Acquisition of an Existing Business   271
Internal Start-Up   271
Joint Ventures   271
Choosing the Diversification Path: Related versus Unrelated Businesses   272
The Case for Diversifying into Related Businesses   272
Identifying Cross-Business Strategic Fits along the Value Chain   274
Strategic Fit, Economies of Scope, and Competitive Advantage   277
The Case for Diversifying into Unrelated Businesses   279
The Merits of an Unrelated Diversification Strategy   280
The Drawbacks of Unrelated Diversification   283
Combination Related–Unrelated Diversification Strategies   284
Evaluating the Strategy of a Diversified Company   285
Step 1: Evaluating Industry Attractiveness   286
Step 2: Evaluating Business-Unit Competitive Strength   289
*Step 3: Checking the Competitive Advantage Potential
of Cross-Business Strategic Fits   294*
Step 4: Checking for Resource Fit   294
*Step 5: Ranking the Performance Prospects of Business Units and Assigning
a Priority for Resource Allocation   298*
*Step 6: Crafting New Strategic Moves to Improve Overall Corporate
Performance   299*
After a Company Diversifies: The Four Main Strategy Alternatives   300
Strategies to Broaden a Diversified Company's Business Base   300
*Divestiture Strategies Aimed at Retrenching to a Narrower
Diversification Base   303*
Strategies to Restructure a Company's Business Lineup   306
Multinational Diversification Strategies   308

Illustration Capsules

9.1. Related Diversification at L'Oréal, Johnson & Johnson, PepsiCo, and Darden Restaurants   277

9.2. Unrelated Diversification at General Electric, United Technologies, American Standard, and Lancaster Colony   281

9.3. Managing Diversification at Johnson & Johnson: The Benefits of Cross-Business Strategic Fits   302

9.4. Lucent Technology's Retrenchment Strategy   304

9.5. The Global Scope of Four Prominent Diversified Multinational Corporations   309

10. Strategy, Ethics, and Social Responsibility   316

What Do We Mean by *Business Ethics?*   317

Where Do Ethical Standards Come From—Are They Universal or Dependent on Local Norms and Situational Circumstances?   318

The School of Ethical Universalism   318

The School of Ethical Relativism   319

Ethics and Integrative Social Contracts Theory   322

The Three Categories of Management Morality   323

Evidence of Managerial Immorality in the Global Business Community   325

Do Company Strategies Need to Be Ethical?   327

What Are the Drivers of Unethical Strategies and Business Behavior?   328

Approaches to Managing a Company's Ethical Conduct   333

Why Should Company Strategies Be Ethical?   338

The Moral Case for an Ethical Strategy   338

The Business Case for an Ethical Strategy   338

Linking a Company's Strategy to Its Ethical Principles and Core Values   341

Strategy and Social Responsibility   342

What Do We Mean by Social Responsibility?   342

Crafting a Social Responsibility Strategy: The Starting Point for Demonstrating a Social Conscience   345

The Moral Case for Corporate Social Responsibility   346

The Business Case for Socially Responsible Behavior   347

The Well-Intentioned Efforts of Do-Good Executives Can Be Controversial   349

How Much Attention to Social Responsibility Is Enough?   351

Linking Social Performance Targets to Executive Compensation   352

Illustration Capsules

10.1. Marsh & McLennan's Ethically Flawed Strategy   329

10.2. Philip Morris USA's Strategy for Marlboro Cigarettes: Ethical or Unethical?   334

10.3. A Test of Your Business Ethics   340

Section D: Executing the Strategy

11. Building an Organization Capable of Good Strategy Execution 358

A Framework for Executing Strategy 361
The Principal Managerial Components of the Strategy Execution Process 361
Building an Organization Capable of Good Strategy Execution 363
Staffing the Organization 364
  Putting Together a Strong Management Team 364
  Recruiting and Retaining Capable Employees 365
Building Core Competencies and Competitive Capabilities 368
  The Three-Stage Process of Developing and Strengthening Competencies and Capabilities 368
  The Strategic Role of Employee Training 371
  From Competencies and Capabilities to Competitive Advantage 373
Execution-Related Aspects of Organizing the Work Effort 373
  Deciding Which Value Chain Activities to Perform Internally and Which to Outsource 373
  Making Strategy-Critical Activities the Main Building Blocks of the Organization Structure 376
  Determining the Degree of Authority and Independence to Give Each Unit and Each Employee 378
  Providing for Internal Cross-Unit Coordination 381
  Providing for Collaboration with Outside Suppliers and Strategic Allies 383
Current Organizational Trends 383

Illustration Capsules

11.1. How General Electric Develops a Talented and Deep Management Team 366
11.2. Toyota's Legendary Production System: A Capability That Translates into Competitive Advantage 372

12. Managing Internal Operations: Actions That Promote Good Strategy Execution 388

Marshaling Resources behind the Drive for Good Strategy Execution 389
Instituting Policies and Procedures That Facilitate Good Strategy Execution 390
Adopting Best Practices and Striving for Continuous Improvement 393
  How the Process of Identifying and Incorporating Best Practices Works 393
  Business Process Reengineering, Six Sigma Quality Programs, and TQM: Tools for Promoting Operating Excellence 395
  Capturing the Benefits of Initiatives to Improve Operations 399
Installing Information and Operating Systems 401
  Instituting Adequate Information Systems, Performance Tracking, and Controls 402
  Exercising Adequate Controls over Empowered Employees 403

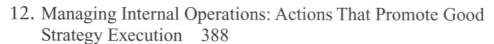

Tying Rewards and Incentives to Good Strategy Execution   404
 Strategy-Facilitating Motivational Practices   404
 Striking the Right Balance between Rewards and Punishment   406
 Linking the Reward System to Strategically Relevant Performance Outcomes   408

Illustration Capsules

12.1. Granite Construction's Short-Pay Policy: An Innovative Way to Drive Better Strategy Execution   392
12.2. Whirlpool's Use of Six Sigma to Promote Operating Excellence   398
12.3. What Companies Do to Motivate and Reward Employees   407
12.4. Nucor and Bank One: Two Companies That Tie Incentives Directly to Strategy Execution   409

13. Corporate Culture and Leadership: Keys to Good Strategy Execution   414

Instilling a Corporate Culture That Promotes Good Strategy Execution   415
 Identifying the Key Features of a Company's Corporate Culture   416
 Strong versus Weak Cultures   420
 Unhealthy Cultures   422
 High-Performance Cultures   424
 Adaptive Cultures   425
 Culture: Ally or Obstacle to Strategy Execution?   426
 Changing a Problem Culture   428
 Grounding the Culture in Core Values and Ethics   434
 Establishing a Strategy–Culture Fit in Multinational and Global Companies   437
Leading the Strategy Execution Process   439
 Staying on Top of How Well Things Are Going   439
 Putting Constructive Pressure on the Organization to Achieve Good Results and Operating Excellence   441
 Leading the Development of Better Competencies and Capabilities   442
 Displaying Ethical Integrity and Leading Social Responsibility Initiatives   443
 Leading the Process of Making Corrective Adjustments   445

Illustration Capsules

13.1. The Corporate Cultures at Google and Alberto-Culver   417
13.2. Changing the Culture in Alberto-Culver's North American Division   433

Part Two   Readings in Crafting and Executing Strategy   451

Section A: What is Strategy and How Is the Process of Crafting and Executing Strategy Managed?

1. What Is Strategy and How Do You Know If You Have One?   452
 Costas Markides, London Business School

2. Walking the Talk (Really!): Why Visions Fail   459
 Mark Lipton, New School University

3. The Power of Business Models   465
   Scott M. Shafer, Wake Forest University
   H. Jeff Smith, Wake Forest University
   Jane E. Linder, Accenture Institute for Strategic Change

4. The Balanced Scorecard: To Adopt or Not to Adopt?   475
   Kevin B. Hendricks, Richard Ivey School of Business
   Larry Menor, Richard Ivey School of Business
   Christine Wiedman, Richard Ivey School of Business

5. Stretching Strategic Thinking   482
   Stan Abraham, California Polytechnic, Pomona

Section B: Crafting Strategy in Single Business Companies

6. A New Tool for Strategy Analysis: The Opportunity Model   489
   Donald Morris, Eastern New Mexico University

7. Playing Hardball: Why Strategy Still Matters   496
   George Stalk, The Boston Consulting Group

8. Value Innovation: A Leap into the Blue Ocean   502
   W. Chan Kim, INSEAD
   Renée Mauborgne, INSEAD

9. Confronting the Low-End Competition   508
   Don Potter, Strategy Street.com

10. Strategies for Asia's New Competitive Game   515
   Peter J. Williamson, INSEAD

11. Racing to Be 2nd: Conquering the Industries of the Future   521
   Costas Markides, London Business School
   Paul A. Geroski, London Business School

12. Outsourcing Strategies: Opportunities and Risks   528
   Brian Leavy, Dublin City University Business School

Section C: Crafting Strategy in Diversified Companies

13. Insights from the New Conglomerates   534
   Gerry Kerr, University of Windsor
   James Durroch, York University

Section D: Executing Strategy

14. Turning Great Strategy into Great Performance   551
   Michael C. Mankins, Marakon Associates
   Richard Steele, Marakon Associates

15. Beyond Best Practice   561
   Lynda Gratton, London Business School
   Sumantra Ghoshal, London Business School

16. The Integration of Lean Management and Six Sigma   571
   Edward D. Arnheiter, Rensselaer Polytechnic Institute
   John Maleyeff, Rensselaer Polytechnic Institute

17. Linking Goals to Monetary Incentives   582
   Edwin A. Locke, University of Maryland

18. A Leader's Guide to Creating an Innovation Culture   587
   Brian Leavy, Dublin City University Business School

19. The Seven Habits of Spectacularly Unsuccessful Executives   594
   Sydney Finkelstein, Dartmouth College

Section E: Strategy, Ethics, and Social Responsibility

20. Competing Responsibly   600
   Bert van de Ven, University of Tilburg
   Ronald Jeurissen, Nyenrode Business University

21. The Ethics Commitment Process: Sustainability through Value-Based Ethics   614
   Jacquelyn B. Gates, Soaring, LLC

Endnotes   EN-1

Indexes

Organization   I-1

Name   I-5

Subject   I-9

part one

1

Concepts and Techniques
for Crafting and
Executing Strategy

What Is Strategy and Why Is It Important?

Strategy means making clear-cut choices about how to compete.
—Jack Welch
Former CEO, General Electric

A strategy is a commitment to undertake one set of actions rather than another.
—Sharon Oster
Professor, Yale University

The process of developing superior strategies is part planning, part trial and error, until you hit upon something that works.
—Costas Markides
Professor, London Business School

Without a strategy the organization is like a ship without a rudder.
—Joel Ross and Michael Kami
Authors and Consultants

Managers face three central questions in evaluating their company's business prospects: What's the company's present situation? Where does the company need to go from here? How should it get there? Arriving at a probing answer to the question "What's the company's present situation?" prompts managers to evaluate industry conditions and competitive pressures, the company's current performance and market standing, its resource strengths and capabilities, and its competitive weaknesses. The question "Where does the company need to go from here?" pushes managers to make choices about the direction the company should be headed—what new or different customer groups and customer needs it should endeavor to satisfy, what market positions it should be staking out, what changes in its business makeup are needed. The question "How should it get there?" challenges managers to craft and execute a strategy capable of moving the company in the intended direction, growing its business, and improving its financial and market performance.

In this opening chapter, we define the concept of strategy and describe its many facets. We shall indicate the kinds of actions that determine what a company's strategy is, why strategies are partly proactive and partly reactive, and why company strategies tend to evolve over time. We will look at what sets a winning strategy apart from ho-hum or flawed strategies and why the caliber of a company's strategy determines whether it will enjoy a competitive advantage or be burdened by competitive disadvantage. By the end of this chapter, you will have a pretty clear idea of why the tasks of crafting and executing strategy are core management functions and why excellent execution of an excellent strategy is the most reliable recipe for turning a company into a standout performer.

WHAT DO WE MEAN BY *STRATEGY?*

A company's **strategy** is management's action plan for running the business and conducting operations. The crafting of a strategy represents a managerial *commitment to pursue a particular set of actions* in growing the business, attracting and pleasing customers, competing successfully, conducting operations, and improving the company's financial and market performance. Thus a company's strategy is all about *how—how* management intends to grow the business, *how* it will build a loyal clientele and outcompete rivals, *how* each functional piece of the business (research and development,

Core Concept
A company's **strategy** consists of the competitive moves and business approaches that managers are employing to grow the business, attract and please customers, compete successfully, conduct operations, and achieve the targeted levels of organizational performance.

supply chain activities, production, sales and marketing, distribution, finance, and human resources) will be operated, *how* performance will be boosted. In choosing a strategy, management is in effect saying, "Among all the many different business approaches and ways of competing we could have chosen, we have decided to employ this particular combination of competitive and operating approaches in moving the company in the intended direction, strengthening its market position and competitiveness, and boosting performance." The strategic choices a company makes are seldom easy decisions, and some of them may turn out to be wrong—but that is not an excuse for not deciding on a concrete course of action.[1]

In most industries companies have considerable freedom in choosing the hows of strategy.[2] Thus, some rivals strive to improve their performance and market standing by achieving lower costs than rivals, while others pursue product superiority or personalized customer service or the development of competencies and capabilities that rivals cannot match. Some target the high end of the market, while others go after the middle or low end; some opt for wide product lines, while others concentrate their energies on a narrow product lineup. Some competitors position themselves in only one part of the industry's chain of production/distribution activities (preferring to be just in manufacturing or wholesale distribution or retailing), while others are partially or fully integrated, with operations ranging from components production to manufacturing and assembly to wholesale distribution or retailing. Some competitors deliberately confine their operations to local or regional markets; others opt to compete nationally, internationally (several countries), or globally (all or most of the major country markets worldwide). Some companies decide to operate in only one industry, while others diversify broadly or narrowly, into related or unrelated industries, via acquisitions, joint ventures, strategic alliances, or internal start-ups.

At companies intent on gaining sales and market share at the expense of competitors, managers typically opt for offensive strategies, frequently launching fresh initiatives of one kind or another to make the company's product offering more distinctive and appealing to buyers. Companies already in a strong industry position are more prone to strategies that emphasize gradual gains in the marketplace, fortifying the company's market position, and defending against the latest maneuvering of rivals and other developments that threaten the company's well-being. Risk-averse companies often prefer conservative strategies, preferring to follow the successful moves of pioneering companies whose managers are more entrepreneurial and willing to take the risks of being first to make a bold and perhaps pivotal move that reshapes the contest among market rivals.

There is no shortage of opportunity to fashion a strategy that both tightly fits a company's own particular situation and is discernibly different from the strategies of rivals. In fact, a company's managers normally attempt to make strategic choices about the key building blocks of its strategy that differ from the choices made by competitors—not 100 percent different but at least different in several important respects. A strategy stands a better chance of succeeding when it is predicated on actions, business approaches, and competitive moves aimed at (1) appealing to buyers in ways that set a company apart from rivals and (2) carving out its own market position. Simply copying what successful companies in the industry are doing and trying to mimic their market position rarely works. Rather, there needs to be some distinctive "aha" element to the strategy that draws in customers and produces a competitive edge. Carbon-copy strategies among companies in the same industry are the exception rather than the rule.

For a concrete example of the actions and approaches that comprise strategy, see Illustration Capsule 1.1, which describes Comcast's strategy to revolutionize the cable TV business.

Comcast's Strategy to Revolutionize the Cable Industry

In 2004–2005 cable TV giant Comcast put the finishing touches on a bold strategy to change the way people watched television and to grow its business by introducing Internet phone service. With revenues of $18 billion and almost 22 million of the 74 million U.S. cable subscribers, Comcast became the industry leader in the U.S. market in 2002 when it acquired AT&T Broadband, along with its 13 million cable subscribers, for about $50 billion. Comcast's strategy had the following elements:

- *Continue to roll out high-speed Internet or broadband service to customers via cable modems.* With more than 8 million customers that generated revenues approaching $5 billion annually, Comcast was already America's number one provider of broadband service. It had recently upgraded its broadband service to allow download speeds of up to six megabits per second—considerably faster than the DSL-type broadband service available over telephone lines.

- *Continue to promote a relatively new video-on-demand service that allowed digital subscribers to watch TV programs whenever they wanted to watch them.* The service allowed customers to use their remotes to choose from a menu of thousands of programs, stored on Comcast's servers as they were first broadcast, and included network shows, news, sports, and movies. Viewers with a Comcast DVR set-top box had the ability to pause, stop, restart, and save programs, without having to remember to record them when they were broadcast. Comcast had signed up more than 10 million of its cable customers for digital service, and it was introducing enhanced digital and high-definition television (HDTV) service in additional geographic markets at a brisk pace.

- *Promote a video-on-demand service whereby digital customers with a set-top box could order and watch pay-per-view movies using a menu on their remote.* Comcast's technology enabled viewers to call up the programs they wanted with a few clicks of the remote. In 2005, Comcast had almost 4000 program choices and customers were viewing about 120 million videos per month.

- *Partner with Sony, MGM, and others to expand Comcast's library of movie offerings.* In 2004, Comcast agreed to develop new cable channels using MGM and Sony libraries, which had a combined 7,500 movies and 42,000 TV shows—it took about 300 movies to feed a 24-hour channel for a month.

- *Use Voice over Internet Protocol (VoIP) technology to offer subscribers Internet-based phone service at a fraction of the cost charged by other providers.* VoIP is an appealing low-cost technology widely seen as the most significant new communication technology since the invention of the telephone. Comcast was on track to make its Comcast Digital Voice (CDV) service available to 41 million homes by year-end 2006. CDV had many snazzy features, including call forwarding, caller ID, and conferencing, thus putting Comcast in position to go after the customers of traditional telephone companies.

- *Use its video-on-demand and CDV offerings to combat mounting competition from direct-to-home satellite TV providers.* Satellite TV providers such as EchoStar and DIRECTV had been using the attraction of lower monthly fees to steal customers away from cable TV providers. Comcast believed that the appeal of video-on-demand and low-cost CDV service would overcome its higher price. And satellite TV providers lacked the technological capability to provide either two-way communications connection to homes (necessary to offer video-on-demand) or reliable high-speed Internet access.

- *Employ a sales force (currently numbering about 3,200 people) to sell advertising to businesses that were shifting some of their advertising dollars from sponsoring network programs to sponsoring cable programs.* Ad sales generated revenues of about $1.6 billion, and Comcast had cable operations in 21 of the 25 largest markets in the United States.

- *Significantly improve Comcast's customer service.* Most cable subscribers were dissatisfied with the caliber of customer service offered by their local cable companies. Comcast management believed that service would be a big issue given the need to support video-on-demand, cable modems, HDTV, phone service, and the array of customer inquiries and problems such services entailed. In 2004, Comcast employed about 12,500 people to answer an expected volume of 200 million phone calls. Newly hired customer service personnel were given five weeks of classroom training, followed by three weeks of taking calls while a supervisor listened in—it cost Comcast about $7 to handle each call. The company's goal was to answer 90 percent of calls within 30 seconds.

Sources: Information posted at www.comcast.com (accessed August 6, 2005); Marc Gunter, "Comcast Wants to Change the World, But Can It Learn to Answer the Phone?" *Fortune,* October 16, 2004, pp. 140–56; and Stephanie N. Mehta, "The Future Is on the Line," *Fortune,* July 26, 2004, pp. 121–30.

Strategy and the Quest for Competitive Advantage

The heart and soul of any strategy are the actions and moves in the marketplace that managers are taking to improve the company's financial performance, strengthen its long-term competitive position, and gain a competitive edge over rivals. A creative, distinctive strategy that sets a company apart from rivals and yields a competitive advantage is a company's most reliable ticket for earning above-average profits. Competing in the marketplace with a competitive advantage tends to be more profitable than competing with no advantage. And a company is almost certain to earn significantly higher profits when it enjoys a competitive advantage as opposed to when it is hamstrung by competitive disadvantage. Furthermore, if a company's competitive edge holds promise for being durable and sustainable (as opposed to just temporary), then so much the better for both the strategy and the company's future profitability. It's nice when a company's strategy produces at least a temporary competitive edge, but a **sustainable competitive advantage** is plainly much better. What makes a competitive advantage sustainable as opposed to temporary are actions and elements in the strategy that cause an attractive number of buyers to have a *lasting preference* for a company's products or services as compared to the offerings of competitors. Competitive advantage is the key to above-average profitability and financial performance because strong buyer preferences for the company's product offering translate into higher sales volumes (Wal-Mart) and/or the ability to command a higher price (Häagen-Dazs), thus driving up earnings, return on investment, and other measures of financial performance.

> **Core Concept**
> A company achieves *sustainable competitive advantage* when an attractive number of buyers prefer its products or services over the offerings of competitors and when the basis for this preference is durable.

Four of the most frequently used and dependable strategic approaches to setting a company apart from rivals, building strong customer loyalty, and winning a sustainable competitive advantage are:

1. *Striving to be the industry's low-cost provider, thereby aiming for a cost-based competitive advantage over rivals.* Wal-Mart and Southwest Airlines have earned strong market positions because of the low-cost advantages they have achieved over their rivals and their consequent ability to underprice competitors. Achieving lower costs than rivals can produce a durable competitive edge when rivals find it hard to match the low-cost leader's approach to driving costs out of the business. Despite years of trying, discounters like Kmart and Target have struck out trying to match Wal-Mart's frugal operating practices, super-efficient distribution systems, and its finely honed supply chain approaches that allow it to obtain merchandise from manufacturers at super-low prices.

2. *Outcompeting rivals based on such differentiating features as higher quality, wider product selection, added performance, value-added services, more attractive styling, technological superiority, or unusually good value for the money.* Successful adopters of differentiation strategies include Johnson & Johnson in baby products (product reliability), Harley-Davidson (bad-boy image and king-of-the-road styling), Chanel and Rolex (top-of-the-line prestige), Mercedes-Benz and BMW (engineering design and performance), L. L. Bean (good value), and Amazon.com (wide selection and convenience). Differentiation strategies can be powerful so long as a company is sufficiently innovative to thwart clever rivals in finding ways to copy or closely imitate the features of a successful differentiator's product offering.

3. *Focusing on a narrow market niche and winning a competitive edge by doing a better job than rivals of serving the special needs and tastes of buyers comprising*

the niche. Prominent companies that enjoy competitive success in a specialized market niche include eBay in online auctions, Jiffy Lube International in quick oil changes, McAfee in virus protection software, Starbucks in premium coffees and coffee drinks, Whole Foods Market in natural and organic foods, CNBC and The Weather Channel in cable TV.

4. *Developing expertise and resource strengths that give the company competitive capabilities that rivals can't easily imitate or trump with capabilities of their own.* FedEx has superior capabilities in next-day delivery of small packages. Walt Disney has hard-to-beat capabilities in theme park management and family entertainment. Over the years, Toyota has developed a sophisticated production system that allows it to produce reliable, largely defect-free vehicles at low cost. IBM has wide-ranging expertise in helping corporate customers develop and install cutting-edge information systems. Ritz-Carlton and Four Seasons have uniquely strong capabilities in providing their hotel guests with an array of personalized services. Very often, winning a durable competitive edge over rivals hinges more on building competitively valuable expertise and capabilities than it does on having a distinctive product. Clever rivals can nearly always copy the attributes of a popular or innovative product, but for rivals to match experience, know-how, and specialized competitive capabilities that a company has developed and perfected over a long period of time is substantially harder to duplicate and takes much longer.

The tight connection between competitive advantage and profitability means that the quest for sustainable competitive advantage always ranks center stage in crafting a strategy. The key to successful strategy making is to come up with one or more differentiating strategy elements that act as a magnet to draw customers and yield a lasting competitive edge. Indeed, what separates a powerful strategy from a run-of-the-mill or ineffective one is management's ability to forge a series of moves, both in the marketplace and internally, that sets the company apart from its rivals, tilts the playing field in the company's favor by giving buyers reason to prefer its products or services, and produces a sustainable competitive advantage over rivals. The bigger and more sustainable the competitive advantage, the better the company's prospects for winning in the marketplace and earning superior long-term profits relative to its rivals. Without a strategy that leads to competitive advantage, a company risks being outcompeted by stronger rivals and/or locked in to mediocre financial performance. Hence, company managers deserve no gold stars for coming up with a ho-hum strategy that results in ho-hum financial performance and a ho-hum industry standing.

Identifying a Company's Strategy

The best indicators of a company's strategy are its actions in the marketplace and the statements of senior managers about the company's current business approaches, future plans, and efforts to strengthen its competitiveness and performance. Figure 1.1 shows what to look for in identifying the key elements of a company's strategy.

Once it is clear what to look for, the task of identifying a company's strategy is mainly one of researching information about the company's actions in the marketplace and business approaches. In the case of publicly owned enterprises, the strategy is often openly discussed by senior executives in the company's annual report and 10-K report, in press releases and company news (posted on the company's Web site), and in the information provided to investors at the company's Web site. To maintain the confidence of investors and Wall Street, most public companies have to be fairly open about their strategies. Company executives typically lay out key elements of their strategies in

Figure 1.1   **Identifying a Company's Strategy—What to Look for**

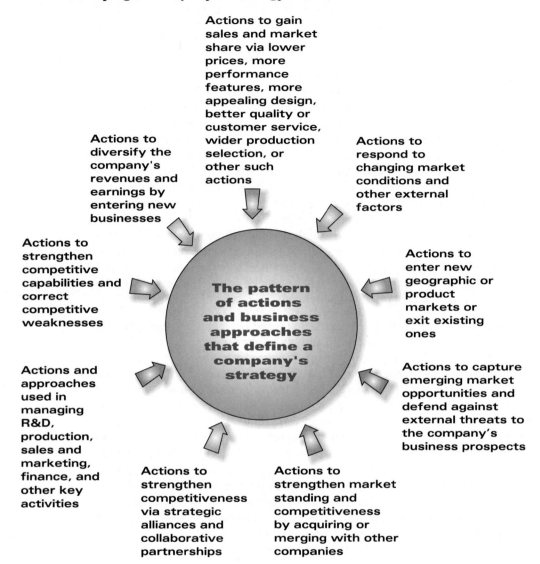

presentations to securities analysts (the accompanying PowerPoint slides are sometimes posted in the investor relations section of the company's Web site), and stories in the business media about the company often include aspects of the company's strategy. Hence, except for some about-to-be-launched moves and changes that remain under wraps and in the planning stage, there's usually nothing secret or undiscoverable about a company's present strategy.

Why a Company's Strategy Evolves over Time

Irrespective of where the strategy comes from—be it the product of top executives or the collaborative product of numerous company personnel—it is unlikely that the strategy, as originally conceived, will prove entirely suitable over time. Every company must be willing and ready to modify its strategy in response to changing market conditions, advancing technology, the fresh moves of competitors, shifting buyer needs and preferences, emerging market opportunities, new ideas for improving the strategy, and mounting evidence that the strategy is not working well. Thus, *a company's strategy is always a work in progress.*

> **Core Concept**
> Changing circumstances and ongoing management efforts to improve the strategy cause a company's strategy to evolve over time—a condition that makes the task of crafting a strategy a work in progress, not a one-time event.

Most of the time a company's strategy evolves incrementally from management's ongoing efforts to fine-tune this or that piece of the strategy and to adjust certain strategy elements in response to unfolding events. But, on occasion, major strategy shifts are called for, such as when a strategy is clearly failing and the company faces a financial crisis, when market conditions or buyer preferences change significantly, or when important technological breakthroughs occur. In some industries, conditions change at a fairly slow pace, making it feasible for the major components of a good strategy to remain in place for long periods. But in industries where industry and competitive conditions change frequently and in sometimes dramatic ways, the life cycle of a given strategy is short. Industry environments characterized by *high-velocity change* require companies to rapidly adapt their strategies.[3] For example, companies in industries with rapid-fire advances in technology—like medical equipment, electronics, and wireless devices—often find it essential to adjust one or more key elements of their strategies several times a year, sometimes even finding necessary to reinvent their approach to providing value to their customers. Companies in online retailing and the travel and resort industries find it necessary to adapt their strategies to accommodate sudden bursts of new spending or sharp drop-offs in demand, often updating their market prospects and financial projections every few months.

> A company's strategy is shaped partly by management analysis and choice and partly by the necessity of adapting and learning by doing.

But regardless of whether a company's strategy changes gradually or swiftly, the important point is that a company's present strategy is always temporary and on trial, pending new ideas for improvement from management, changing industry and competitive conditions, and any other new developments that management believes warrant strategy adjustments. Thus, a company's strategy at any given point is fluid, representing the temporary outcome of an ongoing process that, on the one hand, involves reasoned and creative management efforts to craft an effective strategy and, on the other hand, involves ongoing responses to market change and constant experimentation and tinkering. Adapting to new conditions and constantly learning what is working well enough to continue and what needs to be improved is consequently a normal part of the strategy-making process and results in an evolving strategy.

A Company's Strategy Is Partly Proactive and Partly Reactive

The evolving nature of a company's strategy means that the typical company strategy is a blend of (1) proactive actions to improve the company's financial performance and secure a competitive edge and (2) as-needed reactions to unanticipated developments and fresh market conditions (see Figure 1.2).[4] The biggest portion of a company's current strategy flows from previously initiated actions and business approaches that are working well enough to merit continuation and newly launched initiatives aimed at boosting financial performance and edging out rivals. Typically, managers proactively modify this or that aspect of their strategy as new learning emerges about which pieces of the strategy are working well and which aren't, and as they hit upon new ideas for strategy improvement. This part of management's action plan for running the company is deliberate and proactive, standing as the current product of management's latest and best strategy ideas.

Figure 1.2   **A Company's Strategy Is a Blend of Proactive Initiatives and Reactive Adjustments**

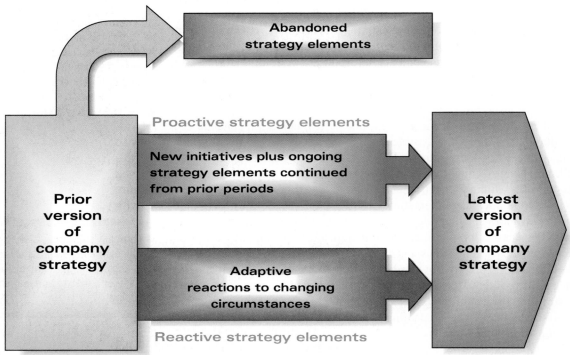

But managers must always be willing to supplement or modify all the proactive strategy elements with as-needed reactions to unanticipated developments. Inevitably, there will be occasions when market and competitive conditions take an unexpected turn that calls for some kind of strategic reaction or adjustment. Hence, a portion of a company's strategy is always developed on the fly, coming as a response to fresh strategic maneuvers on the part of rival firms, unexpected shifts in customer requirements and expectations, fast-changing technological developments, newly appearing market opportunities, a changing political or economic climate, or other unanticipated happenings in the surrounding environment. These adaptive strategy adjustments form the reactive strategy elements.

As shown in Figure 1.2, a company's strategy evolves from one version to the next as managers abandon obsolete or ineffective strategy elements, settle upon a set of *proactive/intended strategy elements*, and then adapt the strategy as new circumstances unfold, thus giving rise to *reactive/adaptive strategy elements*. A company's strategy thus tends to be a *combination* of proactive and reactive elements. In the process, some strategy elements end up being abandoned because they have become obsolete or ineffective.

STRATEGY AND ETHICS: PASSING THE TEST OF MORAL SCRUTINY

In choosing from among strategic alternatives, company managers are well advised to embrace actions that are aboveboard and can pass the test of moral scrutiny. Just keeping a company's strategic actions within the bounds of what is legal does not mean the strategy is ethical. Ethical and moral standards are not governed by what is legal. Rather, they involve issues of both right versus wrong and *duty*—what one *should* do. A strategy is ethical only if (1) it does not entail actions and behaviors that cross the line from "should do" to "should not do" (because such actions are unsavory, unconscionable, or injurious to other people or unnecessarily harmful to the environment) and (2) it allows management to fulfill its ethical duties to all stakeholders— owners/shareholders, employees, customers, suppliers, the communities in which it operates, and society at large.

> **Core Concept**
> A strategy cannot be considered ethical just because it involves actions that are legal. To meet the standard of being ethical, a strategy must entail actions that can pass moral scrutiny and that are aboveboard in the sense of not being shady, unconscionable, injurious to others, or unnecessarily harmful to the environment.

Admittedly, it is not always easy to categorize a given strategic behavior as definitely ethical or definitely unethical. Many strategic actions fall in a gray zone in between, and whether they are deemed ethical or unethical hinges on how clearly the boundaries are defined. For example, is it ethical for advertisers of alcoholic products to place ads in media having an audience of as much as 50 percent underage viewers? (In 2003, growing concerns about underage drinking prompted some beer and distilled spirits companies to agree to place ads in media with an audience at least 70 percent adult, up from a standard of 50 percent adult.) Is it ethical for an apparel retailer attempting to keep prices attractively low to source clothing from foreign manufacturers who pay substandard wages, use child labor, or subject workers to unsafe working conditions? Many people would say no, but some might argue that a company is not unethical simply because it does not police the business practices of its suppliers. Is it ethical for the makers of athletic uniforms, shoes, and other sports equipment to pay coaches large sums of money to induce them to use the manufacturer's products in their sport? (The compensation contracts of many college coaches include substantial payments from sportswear and sports equipment manufacturers, and the teams subsequently end up wearing the uniforms and using the products of those manufacturers.) Is it ethical for manufacturers of life-saving drugs to charge higher prices in some countries than they charge in others? (This is a fairly common practice that has recently come under scrutiny because it raises the costs of health care for consumers who are charged higher prices.) Is it ethical for a company to turn a blind eye to the damage its operations do to the environment even though its operations are in compliance with current environmental regulations—especially if it has the know-how and the means to alleviate some of the environmental impacts by making relatively inexpensive changes in its operating practices?

Senior executives with strong ethical convictions are generally proactive in linking strategic action and ethics: They forbid the pursuit of ethically questionable business opportunities and insist that all aspects of company strategy reflect high ethical standards.[5] They make it clear that all company personnel are expected to act with integrity, and they put organizational checks and balances into place to monitor behavior, enforce ethical codes of conduct, and provide guidance to employees regarding any gray areas. Their commitment to conducting the company's business in an ethical manner is genuine, not hypocritical.

Instances of corporate malfeasance, ethical lapses, and fraudulent accounting practices at Enron, WorldCom, Tyco, Adelphia, HealthSouth, and other companies leave no room to doubt the damage to a company's reputation and business that can result from ethical misconduct, corporate misdeeds, and even criminal behavior on the part of company personnel. Aside from just the embarrassment and black marks that accompany headline exposure of a company's unethical practices, the hard fact is that many customers and many suppliers are wary of doing business with a company that engages in sleazy practices or that turns a blind eye to illegal or unethical behavior on the part of employees. They are turned off by unethical strategies or behavior and, rather than become victims or get burned themselves, wary customers will quickly take their business elsewhere and wary suppliers will tread carefully. Moreover, employees with character and integrity do not want to work for a company whose strategies are shady or whose executives lack character and integrity. There's little lasting benefit to unethical strategies and behavior, and the downside risks can be substantial. Besides, such actions are plain wrong.

THE RELATIONSHIP BETWEEN A COMPANY'S STRATEGY AND ITS BUSINESS MODEL

Core Concept
A company's *business model* explains the rationale for why its business approach and strategy will be a moneymaker. Absent the ability to deliver good profitability, the strategy is not viable and the survival of the business is in doubt.

Closely related to the concept of strategy is the concept of a company's **business model.** While the word *model* conjures up images of ivory-tower ideas that may be loosely connected to the real world, such images do not apply here. A company's business model is management's story line for how the strategy will be a moneymaker. The story line sets forth the key components of the enterprise's business approach, indicates how revenues will be generated, and makes a case for why the strategy can deliver value to customers in a profitable manner.[6] A company's business model thus explains why its business approach and strategy will generate ample revenues to cover costs and capture a profit.

The nitty-gritty issue surrounding a company's business model is whether the chosen strategy makes good business sense. Why is there convincing reason to believe that the strategy is capable of producing a profit? How will the business generate its revenues? Will those revenues be sufficient to cover operating costs? Will customers see enough value in what the business does for them to pay a profitable price? The concept of a company's business model is, consequently, more narrowly focused than the concept of a company's business strategy. A company's strategy *relates broadly to its competitive initiatives and action plan for running the business* (but it may or may not lead to profitability). However, a company's business model zeros in on *how and why the business will generate revenues sufficient to cover costs and produce attractive profits and return on investment.* Absent the ability to deliver good profits, the strategy is not viable, the business model is flawed, and the business itself is in jeopardy of failing.

Companies that have been in business for a while and are making acceptable profits have a proven business model—because there is hard evidence that their strategies are capable of profitability. Companies that are in a start-up mode or that are losing money have questionable business models; their strategies have yet to produce good bottom-line results, putting their story line about how they intend to make money and their viability as business enterprises in doubt.

Magazines and newspapers employ a business model based on generating sufficient subscriptions and advertising to cover the costs of delivering their products to readers. Cable TV companies, cell-phone providers, record clubs, satellite radio companies, and Internet service providers also employ a subscription-based business model. The business model of network TV and radio broadcasters entails providing free programming to audiences but charging advertising fees based on audience size. McDonald's invented the business model for fast food—economical quick-service meals at clean, convenient locations. Wal-Mart has perfected the business model for big-box discount retailing—a model also used by Home Depot, Costco, and Target. Gillette's business model in razor blades involves selling a "master product"—the razor—at an attractively low price and then making money on repeat purchases— the razor blades. Printer manufacturers like Hewlett-Packard, Lexmark, and Epson pursue much the same business model as Gillette—selling printers at a low (virtually break-even) price and making large profit margins on the repeat purchases of printer supplies, especially ink cartridges. Companies like Dell and Avon employ a direct sales business model that helps keep prices low by cutting out the costs of reaching consumers through distributors and retail dealers. Illustration Capsule 1.2 discusses the contrasting business models of Microsoft and Red Hat.

WHAT MAKES A STRATEGY A WINNER?

Three questions can be used to test the merits of one strategy versus another and distinguish a winning strategy from a so-so or flawed strategy:

1. *How well does the strategy fit the company's situation?* To qualify as a winner, a strategy has to be well matched to industry and competitive conditions, a company's best market opportunities, and other aspects of the enterprise's external environment. At the same time, it has to be tailored to the company's resource strengths and weaknesses, competencies, and competitive capabilities. Unless a strategy exhibits tight fit with both the external and internal aspects of a company's overall situation, it is likely to produce less than the best possible business results.

   > **Core Concept**
   > A winning strategy must fit the enterprise's external and internal situation, build sustainable competitive advantage, and improve company performance.

2. *Is the strategy helping the company achieve a sustainable competitive advantage?* Winning strategies enable a company to achieve a competitive advantage that is durable. The bigger and more durable the competitive edge that a strategy helps build, the more powerful and appealing it is.

3. *Is the strategy resulting in better company performance?* A good strategy boosts company performance. Two kinds of performance improvements tell the most about the caliber of a company's strategy: (*a*) gains in profitability and financial strength, and (*b*) gains in the company's competitive strength and market standing.

Once a company commits to a particular strategy and enough time elapses to assess how well it fits the situation and whether it is actually delivering competitive advantage and better performance, then one can determine what grade to assign that strategy. Strategies that come up short on one or more of the above questions are plainly less appealing than strategies that pass all three test questions with flying colors.

Managers can also use the same questions to pick and choose among alternative strategic actions. A company evaluating which of several strategic options to employ can evaluate how well each option measures up against each of the three questions. The strategic option with the highest prospective passing scores on all three questions can be regarded as the best or most attractive strategic alternative.

Other criteria for judging the merits of a particular strategy include internal consistency and unity among all the pieces of strategy, the degree of risk the strategy poses as compared to alternative strategies, and the degree to which it is flexible and adaptable to changing circumstances. These criteria are relevant and merit consideration, but they seldom override the importance of the three test questions posed above.

Illustration Capsule 1.2

Microsoft and Red Hat: Two Contrasting Business Models

The strategies of rival companies are often predicated on strikingly different business models. Consider, for example, the business models for Microsoft and Red Hat in operating system software for personal computers (PCs).

Microsoft's business model for making money from its Windows operating system products is based on the following revenue-cost-profit economics:

- Employ a cadre of highly skilled programmers to develop proprietary code; keep the source code hidden so as to keep the inner workings of the software proprietary.

- Sell the resulting operating system and software package to PC makers and to PC users at relatively attractive prices (around $75 to PC makers and about $100 at retail to PC users); strive to maintain a 90 percent or more market share of the 150 million PCs sold annually worldwide.

- Strive for big-volume sales. Most of Microsoft's costs arise on the front end in developing the software and are thus fixed; the variable costs of producing and packaging the CDs provided to users are only a couple of dollars per copy—once the break-even volume is reached, Microsoft's revenues from additional sales are almost pure profit.

- Provide a modest level of technical support to users at no cost.

- Keep rejuvenating revenues by periodically introducing next-generation software versions with features that will induce PC users to upgrade the operating system on previously purchased PCs to the new version.

Red Hat, a company formed to market its own version of the Linux open-source operating system, employs a business model based on sharply different revenue-cost-profit economics:

- Rely on the collaborative efforts of volunteer programmers from all over the world who contribute bits and pieces of code to improve and polish the Linux system. The global community of thousands of programmers who work on Linux in their spare time do what they do because they love it, because they are fervent believers that all software should be free (as in free speech), and in some cases because they are anti-Microsoft and want to have a part in undoing what they see as a Microsoft monopoly.

- Collect and test enhancements and new applications submitted by the open-source community of volunteer programmers. Linux's originator, Linus Torvalds, and a team of 300-plus Red Hat engineers and software developers evaluate which incoming submissions merit inclusion in new releases of Linux—the evaluation and integration of new submissions are Red Hat's only upfront product development costs.

- Market the upgraded and tested family of Red Hat products to large enterprises and charge them a subscription fee that includes 24/7 support within one hour in seven languages. Provide subscribers with updated versions of Linux every 12–18 months to maintain the subscriber base.

- Make the source code open and available to all users, allowing them to create a customized version of Linux.

- Capitalize on the specialized expertise required to use Linux in multiserver, multiprocessor applications by providing fees-based training, consulting, software customization, and client-directed engineering to Linux users. Red Hat offers Linux certification training programs at all skill levels at more than 60 global locations—Red Hat certification in the use of Linux is considered the best in the world.

Microsoft's business model—sell proprietary code software and give service away free—is a proven money-maker that generates billions in profits annually. In contrast, the jury is still out on Red Hat's business model of selling subscriptions to open-source software to large corporations and deriving substantial revenues from the sales of technical support (included in the subscription cost), training, consulting, software customization, and engineering to generate revenues sufficient to cover costs and yield a profit. Red Hat posted losses of $140 million on revenues of $79 million in fiscal year 2002 and losses of $6.6 million on revenues of $91 million in fiscal year 2003, but it earned $14 million on revenues of $126 million in fiscal 2004. The profits came from a shift in Red Hat's business model that involved putting considerably more emphasis on getting large corporations to purchase subscriptions to the latest Linux updates. In 2005, about 75 percent of Red Hat's revenues came from large enterprise subscriptions, compared to about 53 percent in 2003.

Source: Company documents and information posted on www.microsoft.com and www.redhat.com. (accessed August 10, 2005).

WHY ARE CRAFTING AND EXECUTING STRATEGY IMPORTANT?

Crafting and executing strategy are top-priority managerial tasks for two very big reasons. First, there is a compelling need for managers to *proactively shape*, or *craft*, how the company's business will be conducted. A clear and reasoned strategy is management's prescription for doing business, its road map to competitive advantage, its game plan for pleasing customers and improving financial performance. Winning in the marketplace requires a well-conceived, opportunistic strategy, usually one characterized by strategic offensives to outinnovate and outmaneuver rivals and secure sustainable competitive advantage, then using this market edge to achieve superior financial performance. A powerful strategy that delivers a home run in the marketplace can propel a firm from a trailing position into a leading one, clearing the way for its products/services to become the industry standard. High-achieving enterprises are nearly always the product of astute, creative, proactive strategy making that sets a company apart from its rivals. Companies don't get to the top of the industry rankings or stay there with imitative strategies or with strategies built around timid actions to try to do better. And only a handful of companies can boast of strategies that hit home runs in the marketplace due to lucky breaks or the good fortune of having stumbled into the right market at the right time with the right product. There can be little argument that a company's strategy matters—and matters a lot.

Second, a *strategy-focused enterprise* is more likely to be a strong bottom-line performer than a company whose management views strategy as secondary and puts its priorities elsewhere. There's no escaping the fact that the quality of managerial strategy making and strategy execution has a highly positive impact on revenue growth, earnings, and return on investment. A company that lacks clear-cut direction, has vague or undemanding performance targets, has a muddled or flawed strategy, or can't seem to execute its strategy competently is a company whose financial performance is probably suffering, whose business is at long-term risk, and whose management is sorely lacking. In contrast, when crafting and executing a winning strategy drive management's whole approach to operating the enterprise, the odds are much greater that the initiatives and activities of different divisions, departments, managers, and work groups will be unified into a *coordinated, cohesive effort*. Mobilizing the full complement of company resources in a total team effort behind good execution of the chosen strategy and achievement of the targeted performance allows a company to operate at full power. The chief executive officer of one successful company put it well when he said:

> In the main, our competitors are acquainted with the same fundamental concepts and techniques and approaches that we follow, and they are as free to pursue them as we are. More often than not, the difference between their level of success and ours lies in the relative thoroughness and self-discipline with which we and they develop and execute our strategies for the future.

Good Strategy + Good Strategy Execution = Good Management

Crafting and executing strategy are core management functions. Among all the things managers do, nothing affects a company's ultimate success or failure more fundamentally than how well its management team charts the company's direction, develops

Core Concept

Excellent execution of an excellent strategy is the best test of managerial excellence—and the most reliable recipe for turning companies into standout performers.

competitively effective strategic moves and business approaches, and pursues what needs to be done internally to produce good day-in, day-out strategy execution and operating excellence. Indeed, *good strategy and good strategy execution are the most trustworthy signs of good management.* Managers don't deserve a gold star for designing a potentially brilliant strategy but failing to put the organizational means in place to carry it out in high-caliber fashion—weak implementation and execution undermine the strategy's potential and pave the way for shortfalls in customer satisfaction and company performance. Competent execution of a mediocre strategy scarcely merits enthusiastic applause for management's efforts either. The rationale for using the twin standards of good strategy making and good strategy execution to determine whether a company is well managed is therefore compelling: *The better conceived a company's strategy and the more competently it is executed, the more likely that the company will be a standout performer in the marketplace.*

Throughout the text chapters to come and the accompanying case collection, the spotlight is trained on the foremost question in running a business enterprise: What must managers do, and do well, to make a company a winner in the marketplace? The answer that emerges, and that becomes the message of this book, is that doing a good job of managing inherently requires good strategic thinking and good management of the strategy-making, strategy-executing process.

The mission of this book is to provide a solid overview of what every business student and aspiring manager needs to know about crafting and executing strategy. This requires exploring what good strategic thinking entails; presenting the core concepts and tools of strategic analysis; describing the ins and outs of crafting and executing strategy; and, through the cases, helping you build your skills both in diagnosing how well the strategy-making, strategy-executing task is being performed in actual companies and in prescribing actions for how the companies in question can improve their approaches to crafting and executing their strategies. At the very least, we hope to convince you that capabilities in crafting and executing strategy are basic to managing successfully and merit a place in a manager's tool kit.

As you tackle the following pages, ponder the following observation by the essayist and poet Ralph Waldo Emerson: "Commerce is a game of skill which many people play, but which few play well." If the content of this book helps you become a more savvy player and equips you to succeed in business, then your journey through these pages will indeed be time well spent.

Key Points

The tasks of crafting and executing company strategies are the heart and soul of managing a business enterprise and winning in the marketplace. A company's strategy is the game plan management is using to stake out a market position, conduct its operations, attract and please customers, compete successfully, and achieve organizational objectives. The central thrust of a company's strategy is undertaking moves to build and strengthen the company's long-term competitive position and financial performance and, ideally, gain a competitive advantage over rivals that then becomes a company's ticket to above-average profitability. A company's strategy typically evolves and reforms over time, emerging from a blend of (1) proactive and purposeful actions on the part of company managers and (2) as-needed reactions to unanticipated developments and fresh market conditions.

Closely related to the concept of strategy is the concept of a company's business model. A company's business model is management's story line for how and why the company's product offerings and competitive approaches will generate a revenue stream and have an associated cost structure that produces attractive earnings and return on investment—in effect, a company's business model sets forth the economic logic for making money in a particular business, given the company's current strategy.

A winning strategy fits the circumstances of a company's external situation and its internal resource strengths and competitive capabilities, builds competitive advantage, and boosts company performance.

Crafting and executing strategy are core management functions. Whether a company wins or loses in the marketplace is directly attributable to the caliber of a company's strategy and the proficiency with which the strategy is executed.

Exercises

1. Go to Red Hat's Web site (www.redhat.com) and check whether the company's recent financial reports indicate that its business model is working. Is the company sufficiently profitable to validate its business model and strategy? Is its revenue stream from selling training, consulting, and engineering services growing or declining as a percentage of total revenues? Does your review of the company's recent financial performance suggest that its business model and strategy are changing? Read the company's latest statement about its business model and about why it is pursuing the subscription approach (as compared to Microsoft's approach of selling copies of its operating software directly to PC manufacturers and individuals).

2. From your perspective as a cable or satellite service consumer, does Comcast's strategy as described in Illustration Capsule 1.1 seem to be well matched to industry and competitive conditions? Does the strategy seem to be keyed to maintaining a cost advantage, offering differentiating features, serving the unique needs of a niche, or developing resource strengths and competitive capabilities rivals can't imitate or trump (or a mixture of these)? Do you think Comcast's strategy has evolved in recent years? Why or why not? What is there about Comcast's strategy that can lead to sustainable competitive advantage?

3. In 2003, Levi Strauss & Company announced it would close its two remaining U.S. apparel plants to finalize its transition from a clothing manufacturer to a marketing, sales, and design company. Beginning in 2004, all Levi's apparel would be produced by contract manufacturers located in low-wage countries. As recently as 1990, Levi Strauss had produced 90 percent of its apparel in company-owned plants in the United States employing over 20,000 production workers. With every plant closing, Levi Strauss & Company provided severance and job retraining packages to affected workers and cash payments to small communities where its plants were located. However, the economies of many small communities had yet to recover and some employees had found it difficult to match their previous levels of compensation and benefits.

    Review Levi Strauss & Company's discussion of its Global Sourcing and Operating Guidelines at www.levistrauss.com/responsibility/conduct. Does the company's strategy fulfill the company's ethical duties to all stakeholders—owners/shareholders, employees, customers, suppliers, the communities in which it operates, and society at large? Does Levi Strauss's strategy to outsource all of its manufacturing operations to low-wage countries pass the moral scrutiny test given that 20,000 workers lost their jobs?

chapter 2 two

The Managerial Process of Crafting and Executing Strategy

Unless we change our direction we are likely to end up where we are headed.

—Ancient Chinese proverb

If we can know where we are and something about how we got there, we might see where we are trending—and if the outcomes which lie naturally in our course are unacceptable, to make timely change.

—Abraham Lincoln

If you don't know where you are going, any road will take you there.

—The Koran

Management's job is not to see the company as it is . . . but as it can become.

—John W. Teets
Former CEO

rafting and executing strategy are the heart and soul of managing a business enterprise. But exactly what is involved in developing a strategy and executing it proficiently? What are the various components of the strategy-making, strategy-executing process? And to what extent are company personnel—aside from top executives—involved in the process? In this chapter we present an overview of the managerial ins and outs of crafting and executing company strategies. Special attention will be given to management's direction-setting responsibilities—charting a strategic course, setting performance targets, and choosing a strategy capable of producing the desired outcomes. We will also examine which kinds of strategic decisions are made at which levels of management and the roles and responsibilities of the company's board of directors in the strategy-making, strategy-executing process.

WHAT DOES THE STRATEGY-MAKING, STRATEGY-EXECUTING PROCESS ENTAIL?

The managerial process of crafting and executing a company's strategy consists of five interrelated and integrated phases:

1. *Developing a strategic vision* of where the company needs to head and what its future product/market/customer technology focus should be.
2. *Setting objectives* and using them as yardsticks for measuring the company's performance and progress.
3. *Crafting a strategy to achieve the objectives* and move the company along the strategic course that management has charted.
4. *Implementing and executing the chosen strategy efficiently and effectively.*
5. *Evaluating performance and initiating corrective adjustments* in the company's long-term direction, objectives, strategy, or execution in light of actual experience, changing conditions, new ideas, and new opportunities.

Figure 2.1 displays this five-phase process. Let's examine each phase in enough detail to set the stage for the forthcoming chapters and give you a bird's-eye view of what this book is about.

Figure 2.1 **The Strategy-Making, Strategy-Executing Process**

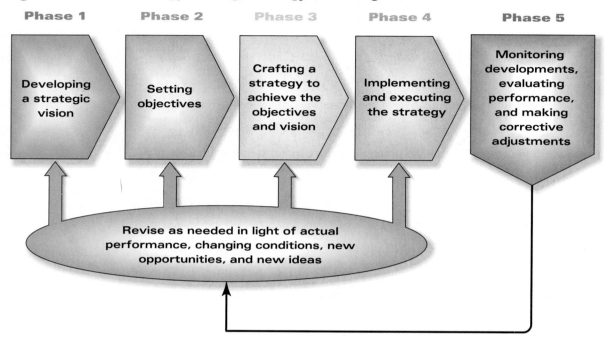

DEVELOPING A STRATEGIC VISION: PHASE 1 OF THE STRATEGY-MAKING, STRATEGY-EXECUTING PROCESS

Very early in the strategy-making process, a company's senior managers must wrestle with the issue of what path the company should take and what changes in the company's product/market/customer/technology focus would improve its market position and future prospects. Deciding to commit the company to one path versus another pushes managers to draw some carefully reasoned conclusions about how to modify the company's business makeup and what market position it should stake out. A number of direction-shaping factors need to be considered in deciding where to head and why such a direction makes good business sense—see Table 2.1.

Top management's views and conclusions about the company's direction and future product/market/customer/technology focus constitute a **strategic vision** for the company. A strategic vision delineates management's aspirations for the business, providing a panoramic view of "where we are going" and a convincing rationale for

Core Concept

A *strategic vision* describes the route a company intends to take in developing and strengthening its business. It lays out the company's strategic course in preparing for the future.

why this makes good business sense for the company. A strategic vision thus points an organization in a particular direction, charts a strategic path, and molds organizational identity.A clearly articulated strategic vision communicates management's aspirations to stakeholders and helps steer the energies of company personnel in a common direction. For instance, Henry Ford's vision of a car in every garage had power because it captured the imagination of others, aided internalefforts to mobilize the Ford Motor Company's resources, and served as a reference point for gauging the merits of the company's strategic actions.

Table 2.1   **Factors to Consider in Deciding to Commit the Company to One Path versus Another**

External Considerations	Internal Considerations
• Is the outlook for the company promising if it simply maintains its product/market/customer/technology focus? Does sticking with the company's current strategic course present attractive growth opportunities? • Are changes under way in the market and competitive landscape acting to enhance or weaken the company's prospects? • What, if any, new customer groups and/or geographic markets should the company get in position to serve? • Which emerging market opportunities should the company pursue? Which ones should not be pursued? • Should the company plan to abandon any of the markets, market segments, or customer groups it is currently serving?	• What are the company's ambitions? What industry standing should the company have? • Will the company's present business generate sufficient growth and profitability in the years ahead to please shareholders? • What organizational strengths ought to be leveraged in terms of adding new products or services and getting into new businesses? • Is the company stretching its resources too thin by trying to compete in too many markets or segments, some of which are unprofitable? • Is the company's technological focus too broad or too narrow? Are any changes needed?

Well-conceived visions are *distinctive* and *specific* to a particular organization; they avoid generic feel-good statements like "We will become a global leader and the first choice of customers in every market we choose to serve"—which could apply to any of hundreds of organizations.[1] And they are not the product of a committee charged with coming up with an innocuous but well-meaning one-sentence vision that wins consensus approval from various stakeholders. Nicely worded vision statements with no specifics about the company's product/market/customer/technology focus fall well short of what it takes for a vision to measure up. A strategic vision proclaiming management's quest "to be the market leader" or "to be the first choice of customers" or "to be the most innovative" or "to be recognized as the best company in the industry" offers scant guidance about a company's direction and what changes and challenges lie on the road ahead.

For a strategic vision to function as a valuable managerial tool, it must (1) provide understanding of what management wants its business to look like and (2) provide managers with a reference point in making strategic decisions and preparing the company for the future. It must say something definitive about how the company's leaders intend to position the company beyond where it is today. A good vision always needs to be a bit beyond a company's reach, but progress toward the vision is what unifies the efforts of company personnel. Table 2.2 lists some characteristics of an effectively worded strategic vision.

A sampling of strategic visions currently in use shows a range from strong and clear to overly general and generic. A surprising number of the visions found on company Web sites and in annual reports are vague and unrevealing, saying very little about the company's future product/market/customer/technology focus. Some are nice-sounding but say little. Others read like something written by a committee to win the support of different stakeholders. And some are so short on specifics as to apply to most any company in any industry. Many read like a public relations statement—high-sounding words that someone came up with because it is fashionable for companies to have an official vision statement.[2] Table 2.3 provides a list of the most

Table 2.2   **Characteristics of an Effectively Worded Strategic Vision**

Graphic	Paints a picture of the kind of company that management is trying to create and the market position(s) the company is striving to stake out.
Directional	Is forward-looking; describes the strategic course that management has charted and the kinds of product/market/customer/technology changes that will help the company prepare for the future.
Focused	Is specific enough to provide managers with guidance in making decisions and allocating resources.
Flexible	Is not a once-and-for-all-time statement—the directional course that management has charted may have to be adjusted as product/market/customer/technology circumstances change.
Feasible	Is within the realm of what the company can reasonably expect to achieve in due time.
Desirable	Indicates why the chosen path makes good business sense and is in the long-term interests of stakeholders (especially shareowners, employees, and customers).
Easy to communicate	Is explainable in 5–10 minutes and, ideally, can be reduced to a simple, memorable slogan (like Henry Ford's famous vision of "a car in every garage").

Source: Based partly on John P. Kotter, *Leading Change* (Boston: Harvard Business School Press, 1996), p. 72.

common shortcomings in strategic vision statements. The one- or two-sentence vision statements most companies make available to the public, of course, provide only a glimpse of what company executives are really thinking and the strategic course they have charted—company personnel nearly always have a much better understanding of where the company is headed and why that is revealed in the official vision. But the real purpose of a strategic vision is to serve as a management tool for giving the organization a sense of direction. Like any tool, it can be used properly or improperly, either clearly conveying a company's strategic course or not.

Table 2.3   **Common Shortcomings in Company Vision Statements**

Vague or incomplete	Is short on specifics about where the company is headed or what the company is doing to prepare for the future.
Not forward-looking	Does not indicate whether or how management intends to alter the company's current product/market/customer/technology focus.
Too broad	Is so umbrella-like and all-inclusive that the company could head in most any direction, pursue most any opportunity, or enter most any business.
Bland or uninspiring	Lacks the power to motivate company personnel or inspire shareholder confidence about the company's direction or future prospects.
Not distinctive	Provides no unique company identity; could apply to companies in any of several industries (or at least several rivals operating in the same industry or market arena).
Too reliant on superlatives	Does not say anything specific about the company's strategic course beyond the pursuit of such lofty accolades as *best, most successful, recognized leader, global or worldwide leader,* or *first choice of customers.*

Sources: Based on information in Hugh Davidson, *The Committed Enterprise: How to Make Vision and Values Work* (Oxford: Butterworth Heinemann, 2002), Chapter 2, and Michel Robert, *Strategy Pure and Simple II* (New York: McGraw-Hill, 1992), Chapters 2, 3, and 6.

Illustration Capsule 2.1
Examples of Strategic Visions—How Well Do They Measure Up?

Using the information in Tables 2.2 and 2.3, critique the following strategic visions and rank them from 1 (best) to 7 (in need of substantial improvement).

RED HAT

To extend our position as the most trusted Linux and open source provider to the enterprise. We intend to grow the market for Linux through a complete range of enterprise Red Hat Linux software, a powerful Internet management platform, and associated support and services.

WELLS FARGO

We want to satisfy all of our customers' financial needs, help them succeed financially, be the premier provider of financial services in every one of our markets, and be known as one of America's great companies.

HILTON HOTELS CORPORATION

Our vision is to be the first choice of the world's travelers. Hilton intends to build on the rich heritage and strength of our brands by:

- Consistently delighting our customers
- Investing in our team members
- Delivering innovative products and services
- Continuously improving performance
- Increasing shareholder value

- Creating a culture of pride
- Strengthening the loyalty of our constituents

THE DENTAL PRODUCTS DIVISION OF 3M CORPORATION

Become THE supplier of choice to the global dental professional markets, providing world-class quality and innovative products.
[*Note:* All employees of the division wear badges bearing these words, and whenever a new product or business procedure is being considered, management asks "Is this representative of THE leading dental company?"]

CATERPILLAR

Be the global leader in customer value.

eBAY

Provide a global trading platform where practically anyone can trade practically anything.

H. J. HEINZ COMPANY

Be the world's premier food company, offering nutritious, superior tasting foods to people everywhere. Being the premier food company does not mean being the biggest but it does mean being the best in terms of consumer value, customer service, employee talent, and consistent and predictable growth.

Sources: Company documents and Web sites.

Illustration Capsule 2.1 provides examples of strategic visions of several prominent companies. See if you can tell which ones are mostly meaningless or nice-sounding and which ones are managerially useful in communicating "where we are headed and the kind of company we are trying to become".

A Strategic Vision Covers Different Ground than the Typical Mission Statement

The defining characteristic of a well-conceived *strategic vision* is what it says about the company's *future strategic course*—"the direction we are headed and what our future product/market/customer/technology focus will be."

In contrast, the *mission statements* that one finds in company annual reports or posted on company Web sites typically provide a brief overview of the company's *present* business purpose and raison d'être, and sometimes its geographic coverage or standing as a market leader. They may or may not single out the company's present products/services, the buyer needs it is seeking to satisfy, the customer groups it serves, or its technological and business capabilities. But rarely do company mission statements say anything about where the company is headed, the anticipated changes in its business, or its aspirations; hence, they lack the essential forward-looking quality of a strategic vision in specifying a company's direction and *future* product/market/customer/technology focus.

Consider, for example, the mission statement of Trader Joe's (a specialty grocery chain):

> The mission of Trader Joe's is to give our customers the best food and beverage values that they can find anywhere and to provide them with the information required for informed buying decisions. We provide these with a dedication to the highest quality of customer satisfaction delivered with a sense of warmth, friendliness, fun, individual pride, and company spirit.

Note that Trader Joe's mission statement does a good job of conveying "who we are, what we do, and why we are here," but provides no sense of "where we are headed." (Some companies use the term *business purpose* instead of *mission statement* in describing themselves; in practice, there seems to be no meaningful difference between the terms *mission statement* and *business purpose*—which one is used is a matter of preference.)

> The distinction between a strategic vision and a mission statement is fairly clear-cut: A strategic vision portrays a company's *future* business scope ("where we are going"), whereas a company's mission typically describes its *present* business and purpose ("who we are, what we do, and why we are here").

There is value in distinguishing between the forward-looking concept of a strategic vision and the here-and-now theme of the typical mission statement. Thus, to mirror actual practice, we will use the term *mission statement* to refer to an enterprise's description of its *present* business and its purpose for existence. Ideally, a company mission statement is sufficiently descriptive to *identify the company's products/services and specify the buyer needs it seeks to satisfy, the customer groups or markets it is endeavoring to serve, and its approach to pleasing customers.* Not many company mission statements fully reveal *all* of these facets (and a few companies have worded their mission statements so obscurely as to mask what they are about), but most company mission statements do a decent job of indicating "who we are, what we do, and why we are here."

An example of a well-formed mission statement with ample specifics is that of the U.S. government's Occupational Safety and Health Administration (OSHA): "to assure the safety and health of America's workers by setting and enforcing standards; providing training, outreach, and education; establishing partnerships; and encouraging continual improvement in workplace safety and health." Google's mission statement, while short, still captures the essence of the company: "to organize the world's information and make it universally accessible and useful." Likewise, Blockbuster has a brief mission statement that cuts right to the chase: "To help people transform ordinary nights into BLOCKBUSTER nights by being their complete source for movies and games."

An example of a not-so-revealing mission statement is that of the present-day Ford Motor Company: "We are a global family with a proud heritage passionately committed to providing personal mobility for people around the world. We anticipate consumer need and deliver outstanding products and services that improve people's lives." A person who has never heard of Ford would not know from reading the company's mission statement that it is a global producer of motor vehicles. Similarly, Microsoft's mission statement—"to help people and businesses throughout the world realize their full potential"—says nothing about its products or business makeup and could apply to many companies in many different industries. Coca-Cola, which markets nearly 400 beverage brands in over 200 countries, also has an overly general mission statement: "to benefit and refresh everyone it touches." A mission statement that provides scant indication of "who we are and what we do" has no substantive value.

Occasionally, companies couch their mission statements in terms of making a profit. This is misguided. Profit is more correctly an *objective* and a *result* of what a company does. Moreover, earning a profit is the obvious intent of every commercial enterprise. Such companies as BMW, McDonald's, Shell Oil, Procter & Gamble, Nintendo, and Nokia are each striving to earn a profit for shareholders; but plainly the fundamentals of their businesses are substantially different when it comes to "who we are and what we do." It is management's answer to "Make a profit doing what and for whom?" that reveals a company's true substance and business purpose. *A well-conceived mission statement distinguishes a company's business makeup from that of other profit-seeking enterprises in language specific enough to give the company its own identity.*

Communicating the Strategic Vision

Effectively communicating the strategic vision down the line to lower-level managers and employees is as important as choosing a strategically sound long-term direction. Not only do people have a need to believe that senior management knows where it's trying to take the company and understand what changes lie ahead both externally and internally, but unless and until frontline employees understand why the strategic course that management has charted is reasonable and beneficial, they are unlikely to rally behind managerial efforts to get the organization moving in the intended direction.

Winning the support of organization members for the vision nearly always means putting "where we are going and why" in writing, distributing the written vision organizationwide, and having executives personally explain the vision and its rationale to as many people as feasible. Ideally, executives should present their vision for the company in a manner that reaches out and grabs people. An engaging and convincing strategic vision has enormous motivational value—for the same reason that a stonemason is more inspired by "building a great cathedral for the ages" than by "laying stones to create floors and walls." When managers articulate a vivid and compelling case for where the company is headed, organization members begin to say, "This is interesting and has a lot of merit. I want to be involved and do my part to helping make it happen." The more that a vision evokes positive support and excitement, the greater its impact in terms of arousing a committed organizational effort and getting company personnel to move in a common direction.[3] Thus executive ability to paint a convincing and inspiring picture of a company's journey and destination is an important element of effective strategic leadership.

> **Core Concept**
> An effectively communicated vision is a valuable management tool for enlisting the commitment of company personnel to actions that get the company moving in the intended direction.

Expressing the Essence of the Vision in a Slogan   The task of effectively conveying the vision to company personnel is assisted when management can capture the vision of where to head in a catchy or easily remembered slogan. A number of organizations have summed up their vision in a brief phrase:

- Levi Strauss & Company: "We will clothe the world by marketing the most appealing and widely worn casual clothing in the world."
- Nike: "To bring innovation and inspiration to every athlete in the world."

NC WESLEYAN COLLEGE LIBRARY
ROCKY MOUNT, NC 27804

- Mayo Clinic: "The best care to every patient every day."
- Scotland Yard: "To make London the safest major city in the world."
- Greenpeace: "To halt environmental abuse and promote environmental solutions."
- Charles Schwab: "To provide customers with the most useful and ethical financial services in the world."

Strategic visions become real only when the vision statement is imprinted in the minds of organization members and then translated into hard objectives and strategies.

Creating a short slogan to illuminate an organization's direction and purpose and then using it repeatedly as a reminder of "where we are headed and why" helps rally organization members to hurdle whatever obstacles lie in the company's path and maintain their focus.

Breaking Down Resistance to a New Strategic Vision   It is particularly important for executives to provide a compelling rationale for a dramatically *new* strategic vision and company direction. When company personnel don't understand or accept the need for redirecting organizational efforts, they are prone to resist change. Hence, reiterating the basis for the new direction, addressing employee concerns head-on, calming fears, lifting spirits, and providing updates and progress reports as events unfold all become part of the task of mobilizing support for the vision and winning commitment to needed actions.

Just stating the case for a new direction once is not enough. Executives must repeat the reasons for the new direction often and convincingly at company gatherings and in company publications, and they must reinforce their pronouncements with updates about how the latest information confirms the choice of direction and the validity of the vision. Unless and until more and more people are persuaded of the merits of management's new vision and the vision gains wide acceptance, it will be a struggle to move the organization down the newly chosen path.

Recognizing Strategic Inflection Points   Sometimes there's an order-of-magnitude change in a company's environment that dramatically alters its prospects and mandates radical revision of its strategic course. Intel's former chairman Andrew Grove has called such occasions *strategic inflection points*—Illustration Capsule 2.2 relates Intel's two encounters with strategic inflection points and the resulting alterations in its strategic vision. As the Intel example forcefully demonstrates, when a company reaches a strategic inflection point, management has some tough decisions to make about the company's course. Often it is a question of what to do to sustain company success, not just how to avoid possible disaster. Responding quickly to unfolding changes in the marketplace lessens a company's chances of becoming trapped in a stagnant or declining business or letting attractive new growth opportunities slip away.

Understanding the Payoffs of a Clear Vision Statement   In sum, a well-conceived, forcefully communicated strategic vision pays off in several respects: (1) it crystallizes senior executives' own views about the firm's long-term direction; (2) it reduces the risk of rudderless decision making; (3) it is a tool for winning the support of organizational members for internal changes that will help make the vision a reality; (4) it provides a beacon for lower-level managers in forming departmental missions, setting departmental objectives, and crafting functional and departmental strategies that are in sync with the company's overall strategy; and (5) it helps an organization prepare for the future. When management is able to demonstrate significant progress in achieving these five benefits, the first step in organizational direction setting has been successfully completed.

Illustration Capsule 2.2
Intel's Two Strategic Inflection Points

Intel Corporation has encountered two strategic inflection points within the past 20 years. The first came in the mid-1980s, when memory chips were Intel's principal business and Japanese manufacturers, intent on dominating the memory chip business, began cutting their prices 10 percent below the prices charged by Intel and other U.S. memory chip manufacturers. Each time U.S. companies matched the Japanese price cuts, the Japanese manufacturers responded with another 10 percent price cut. Intel's management explored a number of strategic options to cope with the aggressive pricing of its Japanese rivals—building a giant memory chip factory to overcome the cost advantage of Japanese producers, investing in research and development (R&D) to come up with a more advanced memory chip, and retreating to niche markets for memory chips that were not of interest to the Japanese.

At the time, Gordon Moore, Intel's chairman and cofounder, and Andrew Grove, Intel's chief executive officer (CEO), jointly concluded that none of these options offered much promise and that the best long-term solution was to abandon the memory chip business even though it accounted for 70 percent of Intel's revenue. Grove, with the concurrence of both Moore and the board of directors, then proceeded to commit Intel's full energies to the business of developing ever more powerful microprocessors for personal computers. Intel had invented microprocessors in the early 1970s but had recently been concentrating on memory chips because of strong competition and excess capacity in the market for microprocessors.

Grove's bold decision to withdraw from memory chips, absorb a $173 million write-off in 1986, and go all out in microprocessors produced a new strategic vision for Intel—becoming the preeminent supplier of microprocessors to the personal computing industry, making the personal computer (PC) the central appliance in the workplace and the home, and being the undisputed leader in driving PC technology forward. Grove's new vision for Intel and the strategic course he charted in 1985 produced spectacular results. Since 1996, over 80 percent of the world's PCs have been made with Intel microprocessors and Intel has become the world's most profitable chip maker.

Intel encountered a second inflection point in 1998, opting to refocus on becoming the preeminent building-block supplier to the Internet economy and spurring efforts to make the Internet more useful. Starting in early 1998 and responding to the mushrooming importance of the Internet, Intel's senior management launched major new initiatives to direct attention and resources to expanding the capabilities of both the PC platform and the Internet. It was this strategic inflection point that led to Intel's latest strategic vision of playing a major role in getting a billion computers connected to the Internet worldwide, installing millions of servers, and building an Internet infrastructure that would support trillions of dollars of e-commerce and serve as a worldwide communication medium.

Source: Andrew S. Grove, *Only the Paranoid Survive* (New York: Doubleday-Currency, 1996), company documents and press releases, and information posted at www.intel.com.

Linking the Vision/Mission with Company Values

Many companies have developed a statement of values to guide the company's pursuit of its vision/mission, strategy, and ways of operating. By **values** (or *core values,* as they are often called*),* we mean the beliefs, traits, and ways of doing things that management has determined should guide the pursuit of its vision and strategy, the conduct of company's operations, and the behavior of company personnel.

Values, good and bad, exist in every organization. They relate to such things as fair treatment, integrity, ethical behavior, innovation, teamwork, top-notch quality, superior customer service, social responsibility, and community citizenship. Most companies have built their statements of values around four to eight traits that company personnel are expected to display and that are supposed to be mirrored in how the company conducts its business.

> **Core Concept**
> A company's **values** are the beliefs, traits, and behavioral norms that company personnel are expected to display in conducting the company's business and pursuing its strategic vision and strategy.

At Kodak, the core values are respect for the dignity of the individual, uncompromising integrity, unquestioned trust, constant credibility, continual improvement and personal renewal, and open celebration of individual and team achievements. Home Depot embraces eight values (entrepreneurial spirit, excellent customer service, giving back to the community, respect for all people, doing the right thing, taking care of people, building strong relationships, and creating shareholder value) in its quest to be the world's leading home improvement retailer by operating warehouse stores filled with a wide assortment of products at the lowest prices with trained associates giving absolutely the best customer service in the industry. Toyota preaches respect for and development of its employees, teamwork, getting quality right the first time, learning, continuous improvement, and embracing change in its pursuit of low-cost, top-notch manufacturing excellence in motor vehicles.[4] DuPont stresses four values—safety, ethics, respect for people, and environmental stewardship; the first three have been in place since the company was founded 200 years ago by the DuPont family. Heinz uses the acronym PREMIER to identify seven values that "define to the world and to ourselves who we are and what we stand for":

- *P*assion . . . to be passionate about winning and about our brands, products and people, thereby delivering superior value to our shareholders.
- *R*isk Tolerance . . . to create a culture where entrepreneurship and prudent risk taking are encouraged and rewarded.
- *E*xcellence . . . to be the best in quality and in everything we do.
- *M*otivation . . . to celebrate success, recognizing and rewarding the achievements of individuals and teams.
- *I*nnovation . . . to innovate in everything, from products to processes.
- *E*mpowerment . . . to empower our talented people to take the initiative and to do what's right.
- *R*espect . . . to act with integrity and respect towards all.

Do companies practice what they preach when it comes to their professed values? Sometimes no, sometimes yes—at runs the gamut. At one extreme are companies with window-dressing values; the values statement is merely a collection of nice words and phrases that may be given lip service by top executives but have little discernible impact on either how company personnel behave or how the company operates. Such companies have values statements because such statements are in vogue and are seen as making the company look good. At the other extreme are companies whose executives take the stated values very seriously—the values are widely adopted by company personnel, are ingrained in the corporate culture, and are mirrored in how company personnel conduct themselves and the company's business on a daily basis. Top executives at companies on this end of the values-statement gamut genuinely believe in the importance of grounding company operations on sound values and ways of doing business. In their view, holding company personnel accountable for displaying the stated values is a way of infusing the company with the desired character, identity, and behavioral norms—the values become the company's equivalent of DNA.

At companies where the stated values are real rather than cosmetic, managers connect values to the pursuit of the strategic vision and mission in one of two ways. In companies with long-standing values that are deeply entrenched in the corporate culture, senior managers are careful to craft a vision, mission, and strategy that match established values, and they reiterate how the values-based behavioral norms contribute to the company's business success. If the company changes to a different vision or strategy, executives take care to explain how and why the core values continue to be relevant. Few companies with sincere commitment to established core values ever undertake strategic moves that conflict with ingrained values.

In new companies or companies with weak or incomplete sets of values, top management considers what values, behaviors, and business conduct should characterize the company and that will help drive the vision and strategy forward. Then values and behaviors that complement and support vision are drafted and circulated among managers and employees for discussion and possible modification. A final values statement that incorporates the desired behaviors and traits and that connects to the vision/mission is then officially adopted. Some companies combine their vision and values into a single statement or document, circulate it to all organization members, and in many instances post the vision/mission and values statement on the company's Web site. Illustration Capsule 2.3 describes the connection between Yahoo's mission and its core values.

Of course, a wide gap sometimes opens between a company's stated values and its actual business practices. Enron, for example, touted four corporate values—respect, integrity, communication, and excellence—but some top officials engaged in dishonest and fraudulent maneuvers that were concealed by "creative" accounting; the lack of integrity on the part of Enron executives and their deliberate failure to accurately communicate with shareholders and regulators in the company's financial filings led directly to the company's dramatic bankruptcy and implosion over a six-week period, along with criminal indictments, fines, or jail terms for over a dozen Enron executives. Once one of the world's most distinguished public accounting firms, Arthur Andersen was renowned for its commitment to the highest standards of audit integrity, but its high-profile audit failures and ethical lapses at Enron, WorldCom, and other companies led to Andersen's demise—in 2002, it was indicted for destroying Enron-related documents to thwart investigators.

SETTING OBJECTIVES: PHASE 2 OF THE STRATEGY-MAKING, STRATEGY-EXECUTING PROCESS

The managerial purpose of setting **objectives** is to convert the strategic vision into specific performance targets—results and outcomes the company's management wants to achieve. Objectives represent a managerial commitment to achieving particular results and outcomes. Well-stated objectives are *quantifiable,* or *measurable,* and contain a *deadline for achievement.* As Bill Hewlett, cofounder of Hewlett-Packard, shrewdly observed, "You cannot manage what you cannot measure. . . . And what gets measured gets done."[5] Concrete, measurable objectives are managerially valuable because they serve as yardsticks for tracking a company's performance and progress—a company that consistently meets or beats its performance targets is generally a better overall performer than a company that frequently falls short of achieving its objectives. Indeed, the experiences of countless companies and managers teach that precisely spelling out *how much* of *what kind* of performance *by when* and then pressing forward with actions and incentives calculated to help achieve the targeted outcomes greatly improve a company's actual performance. Such an approach definitely beats setting vague targets like "maximize profits," "reduce costs," "become more efficient," or "increase sales," which specify neither how much nor when. Similarly, exhorting

> **Core Concept**
> **Objectives** are an organization's performance targets—the results and outcomes management wants to achieve. They function as yardsticks for measuring how well the organization is doing.

Illustration Capsule 2.3

The Connection between Yahoo's Mission and Core Values

Our mission is to be the most essential global Internet service for consumers and businesses. How we pursue that mission is influenced by a set of core values—the standards that guide interactions with fellow Yahoos, the principles that direct how we service our customers, the ideals that drive what we do and how we do it. Many of our values were put into practice by two guys in a trailer some time ago; others reflect ambitions as our company grows. All of them are what we strive to achieve every day.

EXCELLENCE

We are committed to winning with integrity. We know leadership is hard won and should never be taken for granted. We aspire to flawless execution and don't take shortcuts on quality. We seek the best talent and promote its development. We are flexible and learn from our mistakes.

INNOVATION

We thrive on creativity and ingenuity. We seek the innovations and ideas that can change the world. We anticipate market trends and move quickly to embrace them. We are not afraid to take informed, responsible risk.

CUSTOMER FIXATION

We respect our customers above all else and never forget that they come to us by choice. We share a personal responsibility to maintain our customers' loyalty and trust. We listen and respond to our customers and seek to exceed their expectations.

TEAMWORK

We treat one another with respect and communicate openly. We foster collaboration while maintaining individual accountability. We encourage the best ideas to surface from anywhere within the organization. We appreciate the value of multiple perspectives and diverse expertise.

COMMUNITY

We share an infectious sense of mission to make an impact on society and empower consumers in ways never before possible. We are committed to serving both the Internet community and our own communities.

FUN

We believe humor is essential to success. We applaud irreverence and don't take ourselves too seriously. We celebrate achievement. We yodel.

WHAT YAHOO DOESN'T VALUE

At the end of its values statement, Yahoo made a point of singling out 54 things that it did not value, including bureaucracy, losing, good enough, arrogance, the status quo, following, formality, quick fixes, passing the buck, micromanaging, Monday morning quarterbacks, 20/20 hindsight, missing the boat, playing catch-up, punching the clock, and "shoulda coulda woulda."

Source: http://docs.yahoo.com/info/values (accessed August 20, 2005).

company personnel to try hard or do the best they can, and then living with whatever results they deliver, is clearly inadequate.

The Imperative of Setting Stretch Objectives   Ideally, managers ought to use the objective-setting exercise as a tool for *stretching an organization to perform at its full potential and deliver the best possible results.* Challenging company personnel to go all out and deliver "stretch" gains in performance pushes an enterprise to be more inventive, to exhibit more urgency in improving both its financial performance and its business position, and to be more intentional and focused in its actions. Stretch objectives spur exceptional performance and help companies guard against contentment with modest gains in organizational performance. As Mitchell Leibovitz, former CEO of the auto parts and service retailer Pep Boys, once said, "If you want to have ho-hum results, have ho-hum objectives." *There's no better way to avoid ho-hum results than by setting stretch objectives and*

Setting stretch objectives is an effective tool for avoiding ho-hum results.

using compensation incentives to motivate organization members to achieve the stretch performance targets.

What Kinds of Objectives to Set: The Need for a Balanced Scorecard

Two very distinct types of performance yardsticks are required: those relating to *financial performance* and those relating to *strategic performance*—outcomes that indicate a company is strengthening its marketing standing, competitive vitality, and future business prospects. Examples of commonly used **financial objectives** and **strategic objectives** include the following:

> **Core Concept**
> *Financial objectives* relate to the financial performance targets management has established for the organization to achieve. *Strategic objectives* relate to target outcomes that indicate a company is strengthening its market standing, competitive vitality, and future business prospects.

Financial Objectives	Strategic Objectives
• An *x* percent increase in annual revenues • Annual increases in after-tax profits of *x* percent • Annual increases in earnings per share of *x* percent • Annual dividend increases • Larger profit margins • An *x* percent return on capital employed (ROCE) or return on equity (ROE) • Increased shareholder value—in the form of an upward trending stock price and annual dividend increases • Strong bond and credit ratings • Sufficient internal cash flows to fund new capital investment • Stable earnings during periods of recession	• Winning an *x* percent market share • Achieving lower overall costs than rivals • Overtaking key competitors on product performance or quality or customer service • Deriving *x* percent of revenues from the sale of new products introduced within the past five years • Achieving technological leadership • Having better product selection than rivals • Strengthening the company's brand-name appeal • Having stronger national or global sales and distribution capabilities than rivals • Consistently getting new or improved products to market ahead of rivals

Achieving acceptable financial results is a must. Without adequate profitability and financial strength, a company's pursuit of its strategic vision, as well as its long-term health and ultimate survival, is jeopardized. Furthermore, subpar earnings and a weak balance sheet not only alarm shareholders and creditors but also put the jobs of senior executives at risk. However, good financial performance, by itself, is not enough. Of equal or greater importance is a company's strategic performance—outcomes that indicate whether a company's market position and competitiveness are deteriorating, holding steady, or improving.

The Case for a Balanced Scorecard: Improved Strategic Performance Fosters Better Financial Performance

A company's financial performance measures are really *lagging indicators* that reflect the results of past decisions and organizational activities.[6] But a company's past or current financial performance is not a reliable indicator of its future prospects—poor financial performers often turn things around and do better, while good financial performers can fall on hard times. The best and most reliable *leading indicators* of a company's future financial performance and business prospects are strategic outcomes that indicate whether the

> **Core Concept**
> A company that pursues and achieves strategic outcomes that boost its competitiveness and strength in the marketplace is in much better position to improve its future financial performance.

company's competitiveness and market position are stronger or weaker. For instance, if a company has set aggressive strategic objectives and is achieving them—such that its competitive strength and market position are on the rise, then there's reason to expect that its *future* financial performance will be better than its current or past performance. If a company is losing ground to competitors and its market position is slipping—outcomes that reflect weak strategic performance (and, very likely, failure to achieve its strategic objectives), then its ability to maintain its present profitability is highly suspect. Hence, the degree to which a company's managers set, pursue, and achieve stretch strategic objectives tends to be a reliable leading indicator of whether its future financial performance will improve or stall.

Consequently, a *balanced scorecard* for measuring company performance—one that tracks the achievement of both financial objectives and strategic objectives—is optimal.[7] Just tracking a company's financial performance overlooks the fact that what ultimately enables a company to deliver better financial results from its operations is the achievement of strategic objectives that improve its competitiveness and market strength. Indeed, *the surest path to boosting company profitability quarter after quarter and year after year is to relentlessly pursue strategic outcomes that strengthen the company's market position and produce a growing competitive advantage over rivals.*

Roughly 36 percent of global companies and over 100 nonprofit and governmental organizations used the balanced scorecard approach in 2001.[8] A more recent survey of 708 companies on five continents found that 62 percent were using a balanced scorecard to track performance.[9] Organizations that have adopted the balanced scorecard approach to setting objectives and measuring performance include Exxon Mobil, CIGNA, United Parcel Service, Sears, Nova Scotia Power, BMW, AT&T Canada, Chemical Bank, DaimlerChrysler, DuPont, Motorola, Siemens, Wells Fargo, Wendy's, Saatchi & Saatchi, Duke Children's Hospital, U.S. Department of the Army, Tennessee Valley Authority, the United Kingdom's Ministry of Defense, the University of California at San Diego, and the City of Charlotte, North Carolina.[10]

Illustration Capsule 2.4 shows selected objectives of five prominent companies—all employ a combination of strategic and financial objectives.

Both Short-Term and Long-Term Objectives Are Needed   As a rule, a company's set of financial and strategic objectives ought to include both near-term and longer-term performance targets. Having quarterly and annual objectives focuses attention on delivering immediate performance improvements. Targets to be achieved within three to five years prompt considerations of what to do *now* to put the company in position to perform better later. A company that has an objective of doubling its sales within five years can't wait until the third or fourth year to begin growing its sales and customer base. By spelling out annual (or perhaps quarterly) performance targets, management indicates the *speed* at which longer range targets are to be approached. Long-term objectives take on particular importance because it is generally in the best interest of shareholders for companies to be managed for optimal long-term performance. When trade-offs have to be made between achieving long-run objectives and achieving short-run objectives, long-run objectives should take precedence (unless the achievement of one or more short-run performance targets have unique importance). Shareholders are seldom well-served by repeated management actions that sacrifice better long-term performance in order to make quarterly or annual targets.

Strategic Intent: Relentless Pursuit of an Ambitious Strategic Objective
Very ambitious companies often establish a long-term strategic objective that clearly

Illustration Capsule 2.4
Examples of Company Objectives

NISSAN

Increase sales to 4.2 million cars and trucks by 2008 (up from 3 million in 2003); cut purchasing costs 20% and halve the number of suppliers; have zero net debt; maintain a return on invested capital of 20%; maintain a 10% or better operating margin.

McDONALD'S

Place more emphasis on delivering an exceptional customer experience; add approximately 350 net new McDonald's restaurants; reduce general and administrative spending as a percent of total revenues; achieve systemwide sales and revenue growth of 3% to 5%, annual operating income growth of 6% to 7%, and annual returns on incremental invested capital in the high teens.

H. J. HEINZ COMPANY

Achieve 4–6% sales growth, 7–10% growth in operating income, EPS in the range of $2.35 to $2.45, and operating free cash flow of $900 million to $1 billion in fiscal 2006; pay dividends equal to 45–50 percent of earnings; increase the focus on the company's 15 power brands and give top resource priority to those brands with number one and two market positions; continue to introduce new and improved food products; add to the Heinz portfolio of brands by acquiring companies with brands that complement existing brands; increase sales in Russia, Indonesia, China and India by 50 percent in fiscal year 2006 to roughly 6 percent of total sales; and by the end of fiscal 2008, derive approximately 50 percent of sales and profits from North America, 30 percent from Europe, and 20 percent from all other markets.

SEAGATE TECHNOLOGY

Solidify the company's No. 1 position in the overall market for hard-disk drives; get more Seagate drives into popular consumer electronics products; take share away from Western Digital in providing disk drives for Microsoft's Xbox; maintain leadership in core markets and achieve leadership in emerging markets; grow revenues by 10 percent per year; maintain gross margins of 24–26 percent; hold internal operating expenses to 13–13.5 percent of revenue.

3M CORPORATION

To achieve long term sales growth of 5–8% organic plus 2–4% from acquisitions; annual growth in earnings per share of 10% or better, on average; a return on stockholders' equity of 20%–25%; a return on capital employed of 27% or better; double the number of qualified new 3M product ideas and triple the value of products that win in the marketplace; and build the best sales and marketing organization in the world.

Sources: Information posted on company Web sites (accessed August 21, 2005); and "Nissan's Smryna Plant Produces 7 Millionth Vehicle," *Automotive Intelligence News,* August 2, 2005, p. 5.

---

signals **strategic intent** to be a winner in the marketplace, often against long odds.[11] A company's strategic intent can entail unseating the existing industry leader, becoming the dominant market share leader, delivering the best customer service of any company in the industry (or the world), or turning a new technology into products capable of changing the way people work and live. Nike's strategic intent during the 1960s was to overtake Adidas; this intent connected nicely with Nike's core purpose "to experience the emotion of competition, winning, and crushing competitors." Canon's strategic intent in copying equipment was to "beat Xerox." For some years, Toyota has been driving to overtake General Motors as the world's largest motor vehicle producer—and it surpassed Ford Motor Company in total vehicles sold in 2003, to move into second place. Toyota has expressed its strategic intent in the form of a global market share objective of 15 percent by 2010, up from 5 percent in 1980 and 10 percent in 2003. Starbucks' strategic intent is to make the Starbucks brand the world's most recognized and respected brand.

> **Core Concept**
> A company exhibits *strategic intent* when it relentlessly pursues an ambitious strategic objective, concentrating the full force of its resources and competitive actions on achieving that objective.

Ambitious companies that establish exceptionally bold strategic objectives and have an unshakable commitment to achieving them almost invariably begin with strategic intents that are out of proportion to their immediate capabilities and market grasp. But they pursue their strategic target relentlessly, sometimes even obsessively. They rally the organization around efforts to make the strategic intent a reality. They go all out to marshal the resources and capabilities to close in on their strategic target (which is often global market leadership) as rapidly as they can. They craft potent offensive strategies calculated to throw rivals off-balance, put them on the defensive, and force them into an ongoing game of catch-up. They deliberately try to alter the market contest and tilt the rules for competing in their favor. As a consequence, capably managed up-and-coming enterprises with strategic intents exceeding their present reach and resources are a force to be reckoned with, often proving to be more formidable competitors over time than larger, cash-rich rivals that have modest strategic objectives and market ambitions.

The Need for Objectives at All Organizational Levels   Objective setting should not stop with top management's establishing of companywide performance targets. Company objectives need to be broken down into performance targets for each of the organization's separate businesses, product lines, functional departments, and individual work units. Company performance can't reach full potential unless each organizational unit sets and pursues performance targets that contribute directly to the desired companywide outcomes and results. Objective setting is thus a top-down process that must extend to the lowest organizational levels. And it means that each organizational unit must take care to set performance targets that support—rather than conflict with or negate—the achievement of companywide strategic and financial objectives.

The ideal situation is a team effort in which each organizational unit strives to produce results in its area of responsibility that contribute to the achievement of the company's performance targets and strategic vision. Such consistency signals that organizational units know their strategic role and are on board in helping the company move down the chosen strategic path and produce the desired results.

Objective Setting Needs to Be Top-Down Rather than Bottom-Up   To appreciate why a company's objective-setting process needs to be more top-down than bottom-up, consider the following example. Suppose the senior executives of a diversified corporation establish a corporate profit objective of $500 million for next year. Suppose further that, after discussion between corporate management and the general managers of the firm's five different businesses, each business is given a stretch profit objective of $100 million by year-end (i.e., if the five business divisions contribute $100 million each in profit, the corporation can reach its $500 million profit objective). A concrete result has thus been agreed on and translated into measurable action commitments at two levels in the managerial hierarchy. Next, suppose the general manager of business unit A, after some analysis and discussion with functional area managers, concludes that reaching the $100 million profit objective will require selling 1 million units at an average price of $500 and producing them at an average cost of $400 (a $100 profit margin times 1 million units equals $100 million profit). Consequently, the general manager and the manufacturing manager settle on a production objective of 1 million units at a unit cost of $400; and the general manager and the marketing manager agree on a sales objective of 1 million units and a target selling price of $500. In turn, the marketing manager, after consultation with regional sales personnel, breaks the sales objective of 1 million units into unit sales targets for each sales territory, each item in the product line, and each salesperson. It is logical for organizationwide objectives and strategy to be established first so they can guide objective setting and strategy making at lower levels.

A top-down process of setting companywide performance targets first and then insisting that the financial and strategic performance targets established for business units, divisions, functional departments, and operating units be directly connected to the achievement of company objectives has two powerful advantages: One, it helps produce *cohesion* among the objectives and strategies of different parts of the organization. Two, it helps *unify internal efforts* to move the company along the chosen strategic path. If top management, desirous of involving many organization members, allows objective setting to start at the bottom levels of an organization without the benefit of companywide performance targets as a guide, then lower-level organizational units have no basis for connecting their performance targets to the company's. Bottom-up objective setting, with little or no guidance from above, nearly always signals an absence of strategic leadership on the part of senior executives.

CRAFTING A STRATEGY: PHASE 3 OF THE STRATEGY-MAKING, STRATEGY-EXECUTING PROCESS

The task of crafting a strategy entails answering a series of hows: *how* to grow the business, *how* to please customers, *how* to outcompete rivals, *how* to respond to changing market conditions, *how* to manage each functional piece of the business and develop needed competencies and capabilities, *how* to achieve strategic and financial objectives. It also means exercising astute entrepreneurship in choosing among the various strategic alternatives—proactively searching for opportunities to do new things or to do existing things in new or better ways.[12] The faster a company's business environment is changing, the more critical the need for its managers to be good entrepreneurs in diagnosing the direction and force of the changes under way and in responding with timely adjustments in strategy. Strategy makers have to pay attention to early warnings of future change and be willing to experiment with dare-to-be-different ways to alter their market position in preparing for new market conditions. When obstacles unexpectedly appear in a company's path, it is up to management to adapt rapidly and innovatively. *Masterful strategies come partly (maybe mostly) by doing things differently from competitors where it counts—outinnovating them, being more efficient, being more imaginative, adapting faster—rather than running with the herd.* Good strategy making is therefore inseparable from good business entrepreneurship. One cannot exist without the other.

Who Participates in Crafting a Company's Strategy?

A company's senior executives obviously have important strategy-making roles. The chief executive officer (CEO) wears the mantles of chief direction setter, chief objective setter, chief strategy maker, and chief strategy implementer for the total enterprise. Ultimate responsibility for *leading* the strategy-making, strategy-executing process rests with the CEO. In some enterprises the CEO functions as strategic visionary and chief architect of strategy, personally deciding what the key elements of the company's strategy will be, although others may well assist with data gathering and analysis, and the CEO may seek the advice of other senior managers and key employees in fashioning an overall strategy and deciding on important strategic moves. A CEO-centered approach to strategy development is characteristic of small owner-managed companies and sometimes large corporations that have been founded by the present CEO or that have CEOs with strong strategic leadership skills. Meg Whitman at eBay, Andrea Jung at Avon, Jeffrey Immelt at General Electric, and Howard Schultz at Starbucks are prominent examples of corporate CEOs who have wielded a heavy hand in shaping their company's strategy.

In most companies, however, strategy is the product of more than just the CEO's handiwork. Typically, other senior executives—business unit heads, the chief financial officer, and vice presidents for production, marketing, human resources, and other functional departments—have influential strategy-making roles and help fashion the chief strategy components. Normally, a company's chief financial officer (CFO) is in charge of devising and implementing an appropriate financial strategy; the production vice president takes the lead in developing the company's production strategy; the marketing vice president orchestrates sales and marketing strategy; a brand manager is in charge of the strategy for a particular brand in the company's product lineup; and so on.

But even here it is a mistake to view strategy making as a *top* management function, the exclusive province of owner-entrepreneurs, CEOs, and other senior executives. The more that a company's operations cut across different products, industries, and geographical areas, the more that headquarters executives have little option but to delegate considerable strategy-making authority to down-the-line managers in charge of particular subsidiaries, divisions, product lines, geographic sales offices, distribution centers, and plants. On-the-scene managers with authority over specific operating units are in the best position to evaluate the local situation in which the strategic choices must be made and can be expected to have detailed familiarity with local market and competitive conditions, customer requirements and expectations, and all the other aspects surrounding the strategic issues and choices in their arena of authority. This gives them an edge over headquarters executives in keeping the local aspects of the company's strategy responsive to local market and competitive conditions.

Take a company like Toshiba, a $43 billion corporation with 300 subsidiaries, thousands of products, and operations extending across the world. While top-level Toshiba executives may well be personally involved in shaping Toshiba's *overall* strategy and fashioning *important* strategic moves, it doesn't follow that a few senior executives at Toshiba headquarters have either the expertise or a sufficiently detailed understanding of all the relevant factors to wisely craft all the strategic initiatives taken for 300 subsidiaries and thousands of products. They simply cannot know enough about the situation in every Toshiba organizational unit to decide upon every strategy detail and direct every strategic move made in Toshiba's worldwide organization. Rather, it takes involvement on the part of Toshiba's whole management team—top executives, subsidiary heads, division heads, and key managers in such geographic units as sales offices, distribution centers, and plants—to craft the thousands of strategic initiatives that end up comprising the whole of Toshiba's strategy. The same can be said for a company like General Electric, which employs 300,000 people in businesses ranging from jet engines to plastics, power generation equipment to appliances, medical equipment to TV broadcasting, and locomotives to financial services (among many others) and that sells to customers in over 100 countries.

While managers farther down in the managerial hierarchy obviously have a narrower, more specific strategy-making role than managers closer to the top, the important understanding here is that in most of today's companies *every company manager typically has a strategy-making role—ranging from minor to major—for the area he or she heads.* Hence, any notion that an organization's strategists are at the top of the management hierarchy and that midlevel and frontline personnel merely carry out the strategic directives of senior managers needs to be cast aside. In companies with wide-ranging operations, it is far more accurate to view strategy making as a *collaborative or team effort* involving managers (and sometimes key employees) down through the whole organizational hierarchy.

> **Core Concept**
> In most companies, crafting and executing strategy is a team effort in which every manager has a role for the area he or she heads. It is flawed thinking to view crafting and executing strategy as something only high-level managers do.

In fact, the necessity of delegating some strategy-making authority to down-the-line managers has resulted in it being fairly common for key pieces of a company's strategy to originate in a company's middle and lower ranks.[13] Electronic Data Systems conducted a yearlong strategy review involving 2,500 of its 55,000 employees and coordinated by a core of 150 managers and staffers from all over the world.[14] J. M. Smucker, best-known for its jams and jellies, formed a team of 140 employees (7 percent of its 2,000-person workforce) who spent 25 percent of their time over a six-month period looking for ways to rejuvenate the company's growth. Involving teams of people to dissect complex situations and come up with strategic solutions is an often-used component of the strategy-making process because many strategic issues are complex or cut across multiple areas of expertise and operating units, thus calling for the contributions of many disciplinary experts and the collaboration of managers from different parts of the organization. A valuable strength of collaborative strategy-making is that the team of people charged with crafting the strategy can easily include the very people who will also be charged with implementing and executing it. Giving people an influential stake in crafting the strategy they must later help implement and execute not only builds motivation and commitment but also means those people can be held accountable for putting the strategy into place and making it work—the excuse of "It wasn't my idea to do this" won't fly.

The Strategy-Making Role of Corporate Intrapreneurs   In some companies, top management makes a regular practice of encouraging individuals and teams to develop and champion proposals for new product lines and new business ventures. The idea is to unleash the talents and energies of promising "corporate intrapreneurs," letting them try out untested business ideas and giving them the room to pursue new strategic initiatives. Executives judge which proposals merit support, give the chosen intrapreneurs the organizational and budgetary support they need, and let them proceed freely. Thus, important pieces of company strategy can originate with those intrapreneurial individuals and teams who succeed in championing a proposal through the approval stage and then end up being charged with the lead role in launching new products, overseeing the company's entry into new geographic markets, or heading up new business ventures. W. L. Gore and Associates, a privately owned company famous for its Gore-Tex waterproofing film, is an avid and highly successful practitioner of the corporate intrapreneur approach to strategy making. Gore expects all employees to initiate improvements and to display innovativeness. Each employee's intrapreneurial contributions are prime considerations in determining raises, stock option bonuses, and promotions. Gore's commitment to intrapreneurship has produced a stream of product innovations and new strategic initiatives that have kept the company vibrant and growing for nearly two decades.

A Company's Strategy-Making Hierarchy

It thus follows that *a company's overall strategy is a collection of strategic initiatives and actions* devised by managers and key employees up and down the whole organizational hierarchy. The larger and more diverse the operations of an enterprise, the more points of strategic initiative it has and the more managers and employees at more levels of management that have a relevant strategy-making role. Figure 2.2 shows who is generally responsible for devising what pieces of a company's overall strategy.

In diversified, multibusiness companies where the strategies of several different businesses have to be managed, the strategy-making task involves four distinct types or levels of strategy, each of which involves different facets of the company's overall strategy:

1. *Corporate strategy* consists of the kinds of initiatives the company uses to establish business positions in different industries, the approaches corporate executives pursue to boost the combined performance of the set of businesses the company has diversified into, and the means of capturing cross-business synergies and turning them into competitive advantage. Senior corporate executives normally have lead responsibility for devising corporate strategy and for choosing from among whatever recommended actions bubble up from the organization below. Key business-unit heads may also be influential, especially in strategic decisions affecting the businesses they head. Major strategic decisions are usually reviewed and approved by the company's board of directors. We will look deeper into the strategy-making process at diversified companies when we get to Chapter 9.

2. *Business strategy* concerns the actions and the approaches crafted to produce successful performance in one specific line of business. The key focus is crafting responses to changing market circumstances and initiating actions to strengthen market position, build competitive advantage, and develop strong competitive capabilities. Orchestrating the development of business-level strategy is the responsibility of the manager in charge of the business. The business head has at least two other strategy-related roles: (*a*) seeing that lower-level strategies are well conceived, consistent, and adequately matched to the overall business strategy, and (*b*) getting major business-level strategic moves approved by corporate-level officers (and sometimes the board of directors) and keeping them informed of emerging strategic issues. In diversified companies, business-unit heads may have the additional obligation of making sure business-level objectives and strategy conform to corporate-level objectives and strategy themes.

3. *Functional-area strategies* concern the actions, approaches, and practices to be employed in managing particular functions or business processes or key activities within a business. A company's marketing strategy, for example, represents the managerial game plan for running the sales and marketing part of the business. A company's product development strategy represents the managerial game plan for keeping the company's product lineup fresh and in tune with what buyers are looking for. Functional strategies add specifics to the hows of business-level strategy. Plus, they aim at establishing or strengthening a business unit's competencies and capabilities in performing strategy-critical activities so as to enhance the business's market position and standing with customers. The primary role of a functional strategy is to *support* the company's overall business strategy and competitive approach.

    Lead responsibility for functional strategies within a business is normally delegated to the heads of the respective functions, with the general manager of

Figure 2.2   **A Company's Strategy-Making Hierarchy**

Orchestrated by the CEO and other senior executives.

Corporate Strategy
The companywide game plan for managing a set of businesses

In the case of a single-business company, these two levels of the strategy-making hierarchy merge into one level—*business strategy*—that is orchestrated by the company's CEO and other top executives.

Two-Way Influence

Orchestrated by the general managers of each of the company's different lines of business, often with advice and input from the heads of functional area activities within each business and other key people.

Business Strategy
(one for each business the company has diversified into)
- How to strengthen market position and build competitive advantage
- Actions to build competitive capabilities

Two-Way Influence

Crafted by the heads of major functional activities within a particular business—often in collaboration with other key people.

Functional-area strategies within each business
- Add relevant detail to the hows of overall business strategy
- Provide a game plan for managing a particular activity in ways that support the overall business strategy

Two-Way Influence

Crafted by brand managers; the operating managers of plants, distribution centers, and geographic units; and the managers of strategically important activities like advertising and Web site operations—often key employees are involved.

Operating strategies within each business
- Add detail and completeness to business and functional strategy
- Provide a game plan for managing specific lower-echelon activities with strategic significance

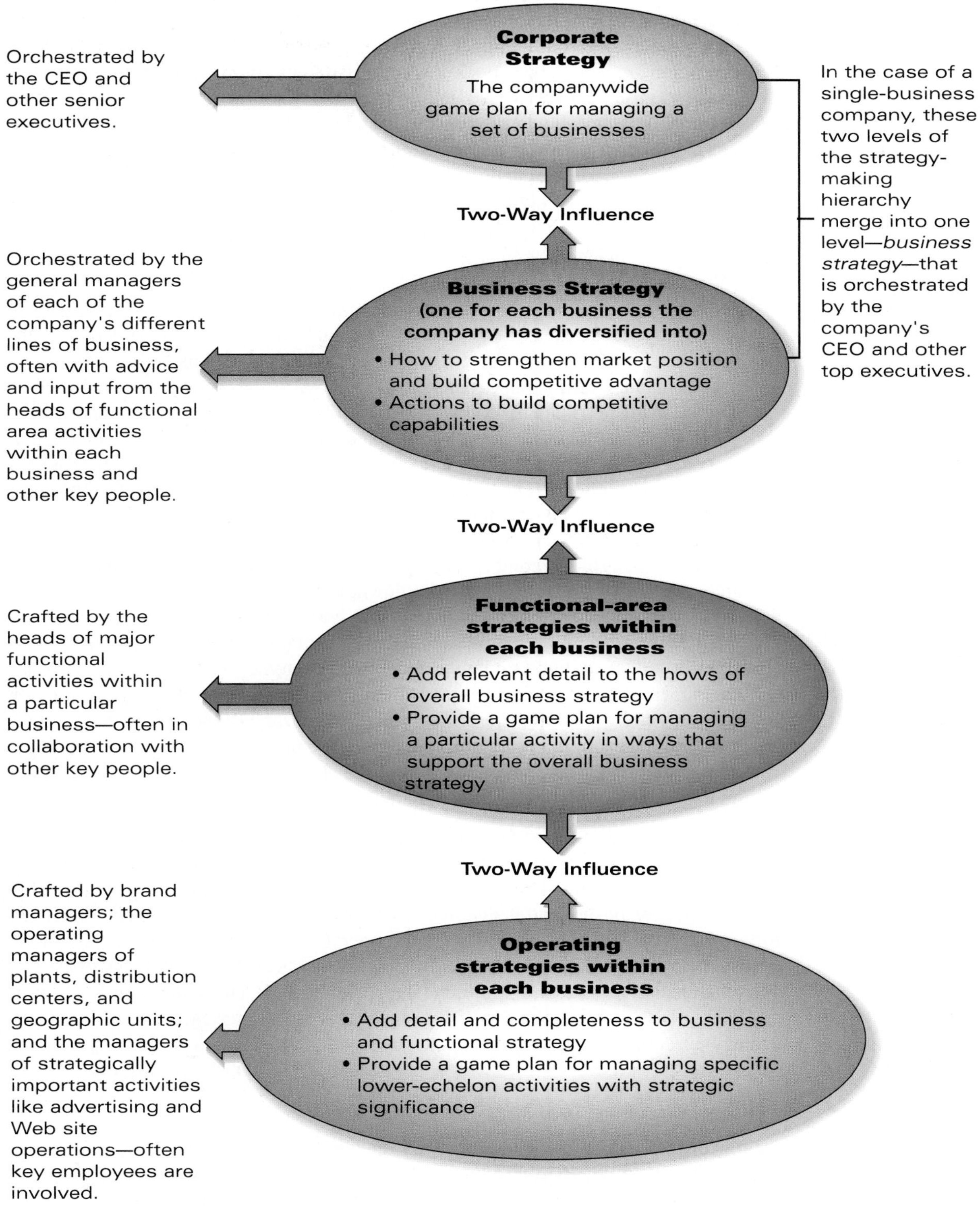

the business having final approval and perhaps even exerting a strong influence over the content of particular pieces of the strategies. To some extent, functional managers have to collaborate and coordinate their strategy-making efforts to avoid uncoordinated or conflicting strategies. For the overall business strategy to have maximum impact, a business's marketing strategy, production strategy, finance strategy, customer service strategy, product development strategy, and human resources strategy should be compatible and mutually reinforcing rather than each serving its own narrower purposes. If inconsistent functional-area strategies are sent up the line for final approval, the business head is responsible for spotting the conflicts and getting them resolved.

4. *Operating strategies* concern the relatively narrow strategic initiatives and approaches for managing key operating units (plants, distribution centers, geographic units) and specific operating activities with strategic significance (advertising campaigns, the management of specific brands, supply chain–related activities, and Web site sales and operations). A plant manager needs a strategy for accomplishing the plant's objectives, carrying out the plant's part of the company's overall manufacturing game plan, and dealing with any strategy-related problems that exist at the plant. A company's advertising manager needs a strategy for getting maximum audience exposure and sales impact from the ad budget. Operating strategies, while of limited scope, add further detail and completeness to functional strategies and to the overall business strategy. Lead responsibility for operating strategies is usually delegated to frontline managers, subject to review and approval by higher-ranking managers.

Even though operating strategy is at the bottom of the strategy-making hierarchy, its importance should not be downplayed. A major plant that fails in its strategy to achieve production volume, unit cost, and quality targets can undercut the achievement of company sales and profit objectives and wreak havoc with strategic efforts to build a quality image with customers. Frontline managers are thus an important part of an organization's strategy-making team because many operating units have strategy-critical performance targets and need to have strategic action plans in place to achieve them. One cannot reliably judge the strategic importance of a given action simply by the strategy level or location within the managerial hierarchy where it is initiated.

In single-business enterprises, the corporate and business levels of strategy making merge into one level—business strategy—because the strategy for the whole company involves only one distinct line of business. Thus, a single-business enterprise has three levels of strategy: business strategy for the company as a whole, functional-area strategies for each main area within the business, and operating strategies undertaken by lower-echelon managers to flesh out strategically significant aspects for the company's business and functional-area strategies. Proprietorships, partnerships, and owner-managed enterprises may have only one or two strategy-making levels since their strategy-making, strategy-executing process can be handled by just a few key people.

Uniting the Strategy-Making Effort

Ideally, the pieces of a company's strategy up and down the strategy hierarchy should be cohesive and mutually reinforcing, fitting together like a jigsaw puzzle. To achieve such unity, the strategizing process requires leadership from the top. It is the responsibility of top executives to provide strategy-making direction and clearly articulate key strategic themes that paint the white lines for lower-level strategy-making efforts. *Mid-level and frontline managers cannot craft unified strategic moves without first understanding the company's long-term direction and knowing the major components of the overall and business strategies that their strategy-making efforts are supposed to support and enhance.* Thus, as a general rule, strategy making must start at the top of the organization and then proceed downward through the hierarchy from the corporate level to the business level and then from the business level to the associated functional and operating levels. Strategy cohesion requires that business-level strategies complement and be compatible with the overall corporate strategy. Likewise, functional and operating strategies have to complement and support the overall business-level strategy of which they are a part. When the strategizing process is mostly top-down, with lower-level strategy-making efforts taking their cues from the higher-level strategy elements they are supposed to complement and support, there's less potential for strategy conflict between different levels. An absence of strong strategic leadership from the top sets the stage for some degree of strategic disunity. The strategic disarray that occurs in an organization when there is weak leadership and too few strategy guidelines coming from top executives is akin to what would happen to a football team's offensive performance if the quarterback decided not to call a play for the team but instead let each player do whatever he/thought would work best at his respective position. In business, as in sports, all the strategy makers in a company are on the same team and the many different pieces of the overall strategy crafted at various organizational levels need to be in sync. *Anything less than a unified collection of strategies weakens the overall strategy and is likely to impair company performance.*

> **Core Concept**
> A company's strategy is at full power only when its many pieces are united.

There are two things that top-level executives can do to drive consistent strategic action down through the organizational hierarchy. One is to effectively communicate the company's vision, objectives, and major strategy components to down-the-line managers and key personnel. The greater the numbers of company personnel who know, understand, and buy into the company's long-term direction and overall strategy, the smaller the risk that organization units will go off in conflicting strategic directions when strategy making is pushed down to frontline levels and many people are given a strategy-making role. The second is to exercise due diligence in reviewing lower-level strategies for consistency and support of higher level strategies. Any strategy conflicts must be addressed and resolved, either by modifying the lower-level strategies with conflicting elements or by adapting the higher-level strategy to accommodate what may be more appealing strategy ideas and initiatives bubbling from below. Thus, the process of synchronizing the strategy initiatives up and down the organizational hierarchy does not necessarily mean that lower-level strategies must be changed whenever conflicts and inconsistencies are spotted. When more attractive strategies ideas originate at lower organizational levels, it makes sense to adapt higher-level strategies to accommodate them.

A Strategic Vision + Objectives + Strategy = A Strategic Plan

Developing a strategic vision and mission, setting objectives, and crafting a strategy are basic direction-setting tasks. They map out where a company is headed, the targeted strategic and financial outcomes, and the competitive moves and internal action approaches to be used in achieving the desired business results. Together, they constitute a **strategic plan** for coping with industry and competitive conditions, the expected actions of the industry's key players, and the challenges and issues that stand as obstacles to the company's success.[15]

> **Core Concept**
> A **strategic plan** lays out the company's future direction, performance targets, and strategy.

In companies that do regular strategy reviews and develop explicit strategic plans, the strategic plan usually ends up as a written document that is circulated to most managers and perhaps selected employees. Near-term performance targets are the part of the strategic plan most often spelled out explicitly and communicated to managers and employees. A number of companies summarize key elements of their strategic plans in the company's annual report to shareholders, in postings on their Web site, or in statements provided to the business media. Other companies, perhaps for reasons of competitive sensitivity, make only vague, general statements about their strategic plans. In small, privately owned companies, it is rare for strategic plans to exist in written form. Small companies' strategic plans tend to reside in the thinking and directives of owners/executives, with aspects of the plan being revealed in meetings and conversations with company personnel, and the understandings and commitments among managers and key employees about where to head, what to accomplish, and how to proceed.

IMPLEMENTING AND EXECUTING THE STRATEGY: PHASE 4 OF THE STRATEGY-MAKING, STRATEGY-EXECUTING PROCESS

Managing the implementation and execution of strategy is an operations-oriented, make-things-happen activity aimed at performing core business activities in a strategy-supportive manner. It is easily the most demanding and time-consuming part of the strategy management process. Converting strategic plans into actions and results tests a manager's ability to direct organizational change, motivate people, build and strengthen company competencies and competitive capabilities, create and nurture a strategy-supportive work climate, and meet or beat performance targets. Initiatives to put the strategy in place and execute it proficiently have to be launched and managed on many organizational fronts.

Management's action agenda for implementing and executing the chosen strategy emerges from assessing what the company will have to do differently or better, given its particular operating practices and organizational circumstances, to execute the strategy competently and achieve the targeted financial and strategic performance. Each company manager has to think through the answer to "What has to be done in my area to execute my piece of the strategic plan, and what actions should I take to get the process under way?" How much internal change is needed depends on how much of the strategy is new, how far internal practices and competencies deviate from what the strategy requires, and how well the present work climate/culture supports good strategy execution. Depending on the amount of internal change involved, full implementation and proficient execution of company strategy (or important new pieces thereof) can take several months to several years.

In most situations, managing the strategy execution process includes the following principal aspects:

- Staffing the organization with the needed skills and expertise, consciously building and strengthening strategy-supportive competencies and competitive capabilities, and organizing the work effort.
- Allocating ample resources to those activities critical to strategic success.
- Ensuring that policies and procedures facilitate rather than impede effective execution.

- Using best practices to perform core business activities and pushing for continuous improvement. Organizational units have to periodically reassess how things are being done and diligently pursue useful changes and improvements.
- Installing information and operating systems that enable company personnel to better carry out their strategic roles day in and day out.
- Motivating people to pursue the target objectives energetically and, if need be, modifying their duties and job behavior to better fit the requirements of successful strategy execution.
- Tying rewards and incentives directly to the achievement of performance objectives and good strategy execution.
- Creating a company culture and work climate conducive to successful strategy execution.
- Exerting the internal leadership needed to drive implementation forward and keep improving on how the strategy is being executed. When stumbling blocks or weaknesses are encountered, management has to see that they are addressed and rectified in timely and effective fashion.

Good strategy execution requires diligent pursuit of operating excellence. It is a job for a company's whole management team. And success hinges on the skills and cooperation of operating managers who can push needed changes in their organization units and consistently deliver good results. Strategy implementation can be considered successful if things go smoothly enough that the company meets or beats its strategic and financial performance targets and shows good progress in achieving management's strategic vision.

EVALUATING PERFORMANCE AND INITIATING CORRECTIVE ADJUSTMENTS: PHASE 5 OF THE STRATEGY-MAKING, STRATEGY-EXECUTING PROCESS

The fifth phase of the strategy management process—monitoring new external developments, evaluating the company's progress, and making corrective adjustments—is the trigger point for deciding whether to continue or change the company's vision, objectives, strategy, or strategy execution methods. So long as the company's direction and strategy seem well matched to industry and competitive conditions, and performance targets are being met, company executives may well decide to stay the course. Simply fine-tuning the strategic plan and continuing with efforts to improve strategy execution are sufficient.

> **Core Concept**
> A company's vision, objectives, strategy, and approach to strategy execution are never final; managing strategy is an ongoing process, not an every-now-and-then task.

But whenever a company encounters disruptive changes in its environment, questions need to be raised about the appropriateness of its direction and strategy. If a company experiences a downturn in its market position or persistent shortfalls in performance, then company managers are obligated to ferret out the causes—do they relate to poor strategy, poor strategy execution, or both?—and take timely corrective action. A company's direction, objectives, and strategy have to be revisited anytime external or internal conditions warrant. It is to be expected that a company will modify its strategic vision, direction, objectives, and strategy over time.

Likewise, it is not unusual for a company to find that one or more aspects of its strategy implementation and execution are not going as well as intended. Proficient strategy execution is always the product of much organizational learning. It is achieved unevenly—coming quickly in some areas and proving nettlesome in others. It is both normal and desirable to periodically assess strategy execution to determine which aspects are working well and which need improving. Successful strategy execution entails vigilantly searching for ways to improve and then making corrective adjustments whenever and wherever it is useful to do so.

CORPORATE GOVERNANCE: THE ROLE OF THE BOARD OF DIRECTORS IN THE STRATEGY-MAKING, STRATEGY-EXECUTING PROCESS

Although senior managers have *lead responsibility* for crafting and executing a company's strategy, it is the duty of the board of directors to exercise *strong oversight* and see that the five tasks of strategic management are done in a manner that benefits shareholders (in the case of investor-owned enterprises) or stakeholders (in the case of not-for-profit organizations). In watching over management's strategy-making, strategy-executing actions and making sure that executive actions are not only proper but also aligned with the interests of stakeholders, a company's board of directors has four important obligations to fulfill:

1. *Be inquiring critics and oversee the company's direction, strategy, and business approaches.* Board members must ask probing questions and draw on their business acumen to make independent judgments about whether strategy proposals have been adequately analyzed and whether proposed strategic actions appear to have greater promise than alternatives. If executive management is bringing well-supported and reasoned strategy proposals to the board, there's little reason for board members to aggressively challenge or pick apart everything put before them. Asking incisive questions is usually sufficient to test whether the case for management's proposals is compelling. However, when the company's strategy is failing or is plagued with faulty execution, and certainly when there is a precipitous collapse in profitability, board members have a duty to express their concerns about the validity of the strategy and/or operating methods, initiate debate about the company's strategic path, hold one-on-one discussions with key executives and other board members, and perhaps directly intervene as a group to alter the company's executive leadership and, ultimately, its strategy and business approaches.

2. *Evaluate the caliber of senior executives' strategy-making and strategy-executing skills.* The board is always responsible for determining whether the current CEO is doing a good job of strategic leadership (as a basis for awarding salary increases and bonuses and deciding on retention or removal). Boards must also exercise due diligence in evaluating the strategic leadership skills of other senior executives in line to succeed the CEO. When the incumbent CEO steps down or leaves for a position elsewhere, the board must elect a successor, either going with an insider or deciding that a better-qualified outsider is needed to perhaps radically change the company's strategic course.

3. *Institute a compensation plan for top executives that rewards them for actions and results that serve stakeholder interests, and most especially those of shareholders.* A basic principle of corporate governance is that the owners of a corporation delegate operating authority and managerial control to top management in return for compensation. In their role as an *agent* of shareholders, top executives have a

clear and unequivocal duty to make decisions and operate the company in accord with shareholder interests (but this does not mean disregarding the interests of other stakeholders, particularly those of employees, with whom they also have an agency relationship). Most boards of directors have a compensation committee, composed entirely of outside directors, to develop a salary and incentive compensation plan that makes it in the self-interest of executives to operate the business in a manner that benefits the owners; the compensation committee's recommendations are presented to the full board for approval. But in addition to creating compensation plans intended to align executive actions with owner interests, the board of directors must put a halt to self-serving executive perks and privileges that simply line the financial pockets of executives. Numerous media reports have recounted instances in which boards of directors have gone along with opportunistic executive efforts to secure excessive, if not downright obscene, compensation of one kind or another (multimillion-dollar interest-free loans, personal use of corporate aircraft, lucrative severance and retirement packages, outsized stock incentive awards, and so on).

4. *Oversee the company's financial accounting and financial reporting practices.* While top managers, particularly the company's CEO and CFO, are primarily responsible for seeing that the company's financial statements fairly and accurately report the results of the company's operations, it is well established that board members have a fiduciary duty to protect shareholders by exercising oversight of the company's financial practices, ensuring that generally accepted accounting principles (GAAP) are properly used in preparing the company's financial statements, and determining whether proper financial controls are in place to prevent fraud and misuse of funds. Virtually all boards of directors monitor the financial reporting activities by appointing an audit committee, always composed entirely of outside directors. The members of the audit committee have lead responsibility for overseeing the company's financial officers and consulting with both internal and external auditors to ensure accurate financial reporting and adequate financial controls.

The number of prominent companies penalized because of the actions of scurrilous or out-of-control CEOs and CFOs, the growing propensity of disgruntled stockholders to file lawsuits alleging director negligence, and the escalating costs of liability insurance for directors all underscore the responsibility that a board of directors has for overseeing a company's strategy-making, strategy-executing process and ensuring that management actions are proper and responsible. Moreover, holders of large blocks of shares (mutual funds and pension funds), regulatory authorities, and the financial press consistently urge that board members, especially outside directors, be active and diligent in their oversight of company strategy and maintain a tight rein on executive actions.

Every corporation should have a strong, independent board of directors that (1) is well informed about the company's performance, (2) guides and judges the CEO and other top executives, (3) has the courage to curb inappropriate or unduly risky management actions, (4) certifies to shareholders that the CEO is doing what the board expects, (5) provides insight and advice to management, and (6) is intensely involved in debating the pros and cons of key decisions and actions.[14] Boards of directors that lack the backbone to challenge a strong-willed or imperial CEO or that rubber-stamp most anything the CEO recommends without probing inquiry and debate (perhaps because the board is stacked with the CEO's cronies) abdicate their duty to represent and protect shareholder interests. The whole fabric of effective corporate governance is undermined when boards of directors shirk their responsibility to maintain ultimate control over the company's strategic direction, the major elements of its strategy, the business approaches management is using to implement and execute the strategy, executive compensation, and the financial reporting process. Thus, even though lead responsibility for crafting and executing strategy falls to top executives, boards of directors have a very important oversight role in the strategy-making, strategy-executing process.

Key Points

The managerial process of crafting and executing a company's strategy consists of five interrelated and integrated phases:

1. *Developing a strategic vision* of where the company needs to head and what its future product/market/customer/technology focus should be. This managerial step provides long-term direction, infuses the organization with a sense of purposeful action, and communicates management's aspirations to stakeholders.

2. *Setting objectives* to spell out for the company *how much* of *what kind* of performance is expected, and *by when.* The objectives need to require a significant amount of organizational stretch. A balanced scorecard approach for measuring company performance entails setting both *financial objectives* and *strategic objectives.*

3. *Crafting a strategy to achieve the objectives* and move the company along the strategic course that management has charted. Crafting strategy is concerned principally with forming responses to changes under way in the external environment, devising competitive moves and market approaches aimed at producing sustainable competitive advantage, building competitively valuable competencies and capabilities, and uniting the strategic actions initiated in various parts of the company. The more that a company's operations cut across different products, industries, and geographical areas, the more that strategy making becomes a *team effort* involving managers and company personnel at many organizational levels. The total strategy that emerges in such companies is really a collection of strategic actions and business approaches initiated partly by senior company executives, partly by the heads of major business divisions, partly by functional-area managers, and partly by frontline operating managers. The larger and more diverse the operations of an enterprise, the more points of strategic initiative it has and the more managers and employees at more levels of management that have a relevant strategy-making role. A single business enterprise has three levels of strategy—business strategy for the company as a whole, functional-area strategies for each main area within the business, and operating strategies undertaken by lower-echelon managers to flesh out strategically significant aspects for the company's business and functional-area strategies. In diversified, multibusiness companies, the strategy-making task involves four distinct types or levels of strategy: corporate strategy for the company as a whole, business strategy (one for each business the company has diversified into), functional-area strategies within each business, and operating strategies. Typically, the strategy-making task is more top-down than bottom-up, with higher-level strategies serving as the guide for developing lower-level strategies.

4. *Implementing and executing the chosen strategy efficiently and effectively.* Managing the implementation and execution of strategy is an operations-oriented, make-things-happen activity aimed at shaping the performance of core business activities in a strategy-supportive manner. Management's handling of the strategy implementation process can be considered successful if things go smoothly

enough that the company meets or beats its strategic and financial performance targets and shows good progress in achieving management's strategic vision.

5. *Evaluating performance and initiating corrective adjustments* in vision, long-term direction, objectives, strategy, or execution in light of actual experience, changing conditions, new ideas, and new opportunities. This phase of the strategy management process is the trigger point for deciding whether to continue or change the company's vision, objectives, strategy, and/or strategy execution methods.

A company's strategic vision, objectives, and strategy constitute a *strategic plan* for coping with industry and competitive conditions, outcompeting rivals, and addressing the challenges and issues that stand as obstacles to the company's success.

Boards of directors have a duty to shareholders to play a vigilant role in overseeing management's handling of a company's strategy-making, strategy-executing process. A company's board is obligated to (1) critically appraise and ultimately approve strategic action plans; (2) evaluate the strategic leadership skills of the CEO and others in line to succeed the incumbent CEO; (3) institute a compensation plan for top executives that rewards them for actions and results that serve stakeholder interests, most especially those of shareholders; and (4) ensure that the company issues accurate financial reports and has adequate financial controls.

Exercises

1. Go to the Investors section of Heinz's Web site (www.heinz.com) and read the letter to the shareholders in the company's fiscal 2003 annual report. Is the vision for Heinz articulated by Chairman and CEO William R. Johnson sufficiently clear and well defined? Why or why not? Are the company's objectives well stated and appropriate? What about the strategy that Johnson outlines for the company? If you were a shareholder, would you be satisfied with what Johnson has told you about the company's direction, performance targets, and strategy?

2. Consider the following mission statement of the American Association of Retired People (AARP):

AARP Mission Statement

- AARP is a nonprofit, nonpartisan membership organization for people age 50 and over.
- AARP is dedicated to enhancing quality of life for all as we age. We lead positive social change and deliver value to members through information, advocacy and service.
- AARP also provides a wide range of unique benefits, special products, and services for our members. These benefits include AARP Web site at www.aarp.org, "AARP The Magazine," the monthly "AARP Bulletin," and a Spanish-language newspaper, "Segunda Juventud."
- Active in every state, the District of Columbia, Puerto Rico, and the U.S. Virgin Islands, AARP celebrates the attitude that age is just a number and life is what you make it.

Is AARP's mission statement well-crafted? Does it do an adequate job of indicating "who we are, what we do, and why we are here"? Why or why not?

3. How would you rewrite/restate the strategic vision for Caterpillar in Illustration Capsule 2.1 so as to better exemplify the characteristics of effective vision statements presented in Tables 2.2 and 2.3? Visit www.caterpillar.com to get more information about Caterpillar and figure out how a more appropriate strategic vision might be worded.

Evaluating a Company's External Environment

Analysis is the critical starting point of strategic thinking.

—Kenichi Ohmae
Consultant and Author

Things are always different—the art is figuring out which differences matter.

—Laszlo Birinyi
Investments Manager

Competitive battles should be seen not as one-shot skirmishes but as a dynamic multiround game of moves and countermoves.

—Anil K. Gupta
Professor

Managers are not prepared to act wisely in steering a company in a different direction or altering its strategy until they have a deep understanding of the pertinent factors surrounding the company's situation. As indicated in the opening paragraph of Chapter 1, one of the three central questions that managers must address in evaluating their company's business prospects is "What's the company's present situation?" Two facets of a company's situation are especially pertinent: (1) the industry and competitive environment in which the company operates and the forces acting to reshape this environment, and (2) the company's own market position and competitiveness—its resources and capabilities, its strengths and weaknesses vis-à-vis rivals, and its windows of opportunity.

Insightful diagnosis of a company's external and internal environment is a prerequisite for managers to succeed in crafting a strategy that is an excellent fit with the company's situation, is capable of building competitive advantage, and holds good prospect for boosting company performance—the three criteria of a winning strategy. As depicted in Figure 3.1, the task of crafting a strategy thus should always begin with an appraisal of the company's external and internal situation (as a basis for developing strategic vision of where the company needs to head), then move toward an evaluation of the most promising alternative strategies and business models, and culminate in choosing a specific strategy.

This chapter presents the concepts and analytical tools for zeroing in on those aspects of a single-business company's external environment that should be considered in making strategic choices. Attention centers on the competitive arena in which a company operates, the drivers of market change, and what rival companies are doing. In Chapter 4 we explore the methods of evaluating a company's internal circumstances and competitiveness.

THE STRATEGICALLY RELEVANT COMPONENTS OF A COMPANY'S EXTERNAL ENVIRONMENT

All companies operate in a "macroenvironment" shaped by influences emanating from the economy at large; population demographics; societal values and lifestyles; governmental legislation and regulation; technological factors; and, closer to home, the

Figure 3.1   **From Thinking Strategically about the Company's Situation to Choosing a Strategy**

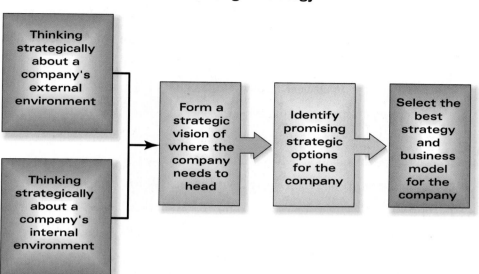

industry and competitive arena in which the company operates (see Figure 3.2). Strictly speaking, a company's macroenvironment includes *all relevant factors and influences* outside the company's boundaries; by relevant, we mean important enough to have a bearing on the decisions the company ultimately makes about its direction, objectives, strategy, and business model. Strategically relevant influences coming from the outer ring of the macroenvironment can sometimes have a high impact on a company's business situation and have a very significant impact on the company's direction and strategy. The strategic opportunities of cigarette producers to grow their business are greatly reduced by antismoking ordinances and the growing cultural stigma attached to smoking. Motor vehicle companies must adapt their strategies (especially as concerns the fuel mileage of their vehicles) to customer concerns about gasoline prices. The demographics of an aging population and longer life expectancies are having a dramatic impact on the business prospects and strategies of health care and prescription drug companies. Companies in most all industries have to craft strategies that are responsive to environmental regulations, growing use of the Internet and broadband technology, and energy prices. Companies in the food-processing, restaurant, sports, and fitness industries have to pay special attention to changes in lifestyles, eating habits, leisure-time preferences, and attitudes toward nutrition and exercise in fashioning their strategies.

Happenings in the outer ring of the macroenvironment may occur rapidly or slowly, with or without advance warning. The impact of outer-ring factors on a company's choice of strategy can range from big to small. But even if the factors in the outer ring of the macroenvironment change slowly or have such a comparatively low impact on a company's situation that only the edges of a company's direction and strategy are affected, there are enough strategically relevant outer-ring trends and events to justify a watchful eye. As company managers scan the external environment, they must be alert for potentially important outer-ring developments, assess their impact and influence, and adapt the company's direction and strategy as needed.

Figure 3.2 **The Components of a Company's Macroenvironment**

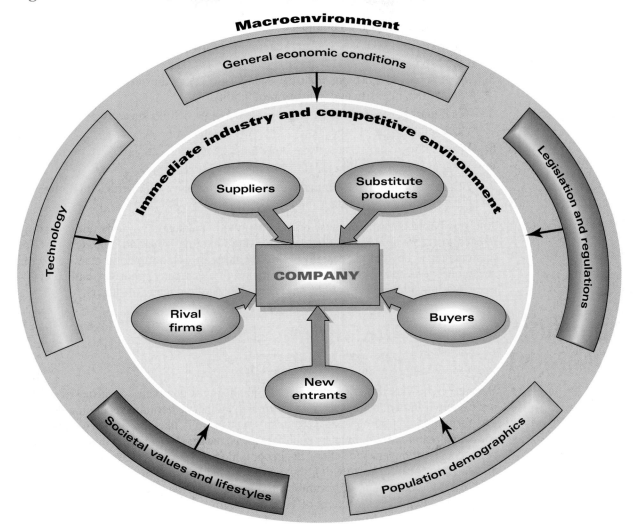

However, the factors and forces in a company's macroenvironment having the *biggest* strategy-shaping impact typically pertain to the company's immediate industry and competitive environment—competitive pressures, the actions of rivals firms, buyer behavior, supplier-related considerations, and so on. Consequently, it is on a company's industry and competitive environment that we concentrate our attention in this chapter.

THINKING STRATEGICALLY ABOUT A COMPANY'S INDUSTRY AND COMPETITIVE ENVIRONMENT

To gain a deep understanding of a company's industry and competitive environment, managers do not need to gather all the information they can find and spend lots of time digesting it. Rather, the task is much more focused. Thinking strategically about a company's industry and competitive environment entails using some well-defined concepts and analytical tools to get clear answers to seven questions:

1. What are the industry's dominant economic features?
2. What kinds of competitive forces are industry members facing and how strong is each force?
3. What forces are driving industry change and what impacts will they have on competitive intensity and industry profitability?
4. What market positions do industry rivals occupy—who is strongly positioned and who is not?
5. What strategic moves are rivals likely to make next?
6. What are the key factors for future competitive success?
7. Does the outlook for the industry present the company with sufficiently attractive prospects for profitability?

Analysis-based answers to these questions provide managers with the understanding needed to craft a strategy that fits the company's external situation. The remainder of this chapter is devoted to describing the methods of obtaining solid answers to the seven questions and explaining how the nature of a company's industry and competitive environment weighs upon the strategic choices of company managers.

QUESTION 1: WHAT ARE THE INDUSTRY'S DOMINANT ECONOMIC FEATURES?

Because industries differ so significantly, analyzing a company's industry and competitive environment begins with identifying an industry's dominant economic features and forming a picture of what the industry landscape is like. An industry's dominant economic features are defined by such factors as market size and growth rate, the number and sizes of buyers and sellers, the geographic boundaries of the market (which can extend from local to worldwide), the degree to which sellers' products are differentiated, the pace of product innovation, market supply/demand conditions, the pace of technological change, the extent of vertical integration, and the extent to which costs are affected by scale economies (i.e., situations in which large-volume operations result in lower unit costs) and learning/experience curve effects (i.e., situations in which costs decline as a company gains knowledge and experience). Table 3.1 provides a convenient summary of what economic features to look at and the corresponding questions to consider in profiling an industry's landscape.

Getting a handle on an industry's distinguishing economic features not only sets the stage for the analysis to come but also promotes understanding of the kinds of strategic moves that industry members are likely to employ. For example, in industries characterized by one product advance after another, companies must invest in research and development (R&D) and develop strong product innovation capabilities—a strategy of continuous product innovation becomes a condition of survival in such industries as video games, mobile phones, and pharmaceuticals. An industry that has recently passed through the rapid-growth stage and is looking at single-digit percentage increases in buyer demand is likely to be experiencing a competitive shake-out and much stronger strategic emphasis on cost reduction and improved customer service.

In industries like semiconductors, strong *learning/experience curve effects* in manufacturing cause unit costs to decline about 20 percent each time *cumulative* production

Table 3.1 **What to Consider in Identifying an Industry's Dominant Economic Features**

Economic Feature	Questions to Answer
Market size and growth rate	• How big is the industry and how fast is it growing? • What does the industry's position in the life cycle (early development, rapid growth and takeoff, early maturity and slowing growth, saturation and stagnation, decline) reveal about the industry's growth prospects?
Number of rivals	• Is the industry fragmented into many small companies or concentrated and dominated by a few large companies? • Is the industry going through a period of consolidation to a smaller number of competitors?
Scope of competitive rivalry	• Is the geographic area over which most companies compete local, regional, national, multinational, or global? • Is having a presence in the foreign country markets becoming more important to a company's long-term competitive success?
Number of buyers	• Is market demand fragmented among many buyers? • Do some buyers have bargaining power because they purchase in large volume?
Degree of product differentiation	• Are the products of rivals becoming more differentiated or less differentiated? • Are increasingly look-alike products of rivals causing heightened price competition?
Product innovation	• Is the industry characterized by rapid product innovation and short product life cycles? • How important is R&D and product innovation? • Are there opportunities to overtake key rivals by being first-to-market with next-generation products?
Supply/demand conditions	• Is a surplus of capacity pushing prices and profit margins down? • Is the industry overcrowded with too many competitors? • Are short supplies creating a sellers' market?
Pace of technological change	• What role does advancing technology play in this industry? • Are ongoing upgrades of facilities/equipment essential because of rapidly advancing production process technologies? • Do most industry members have or need strong technological capabilities?
Vertical integration	• Do most competitors operate in only one stage of the industry (parts and components production, manufacturing and assembly, distribution, retailing) or do some competitors operate in multiple stages? • Is there any cost or competitive advantage or disadvantage associated with being fully or partially integrated?
Economies of scale	• Is the industry characterized by economies of scale in purchasing, manufacturing, advertising, shipping, or other activities? • Do companies with large-scale operations have an important cost advantage over small-scale firms?
Learning/experience curve effects	• Are certain industry activities characterized by strong learning/experience curve effects ("learning by doing") such that unit costs decline as a company's experience in performing the activity builds? • Do any companies have significant cost advantages because of their learning/experience in performing particular activities?

volume doubles. With a 20 percent experience curve effect, if the first 1 million chips cost $100 each, the unit cost would be $80 (80 percent of $100) by a production volume of 2 million, the unit cost would be $64 (80 percent of $80) by a production volume of 4 million, and so on.[1] The bigger the learning/experience curve effect, the bigger the cost advantage of the company with the largest *cumulative* production volume.

Thus, when an industry is characterized by important learning/experience curve effects (or by economies of scale), industry members are strongly motivated to adopt volume-increasing strategies to capture the resulting cost-saving economies and maintain their competitiveness. Unless small-scale firms succeed in pursuing strategic options that allow them to grow sales sufficiently to remain cost-competitive with larger-volume rivals, they are unlikely to survive. The bigger the learning/experience curve effects and/or scale economies in an industry, the more imperative it becomes for competing sellers to pursue strategies to win additional sales and market share—the company with the biggest sales volume gains sustainable competitive advantage as the low-cost producer.

QUESTION 2: WHAT KINDS OF COMPETITIVE FORCES ARE INDUSTRY MEMBERS FACING?

The character, mix, and subtleties of the competitive forces operating in a company's industry are never the same from one industry to another. Far and away the most powerful and widely used tool for systematically diagnosing the principal competitive pressures in a market and assessing the strength and importance of each is the *five-forces model of competition.*[2] This model, depicted in Figure 3.3, holds that the state of competition in an industry is a composite of competitive pressures operating in five areas of the overall market:

1. Competitive pressures associated with the market maneuvering and jockeying for buyer patronage that goes on among *rival sellers* in the industry.
2. Competitive pressures associated with the threat of *new entrants* into the market.
3. Competitive pressures coming from the attempts of companies in other industries to win buyers over to their own *substitute products.*
4. Competitive pressures stemming from *supplier* bargaining power and supplier–seller collaboration.
5. Competitive pressures stemming from *buyer* bargaining power and seller–buyer collaboration.

The way one uses the five-forces model to determine the nature and strength of competitive pressures in a given industry is to build the picture of competition in three steps:

- *Step 1:* Identify the specific competitive pressures associated with each of the five forces.
- *Step 2:* Evaluate how strong the pressures comprising each of the five forces are (fierce, strong, moderate to normal, or weak).
- *Step 3:* Determine whether the collective strength of the five competitive forces is conducive to earning attractive profits.

Figure 3.3   **The Five-Forces Model of Competition: A Key Analytical Tool**

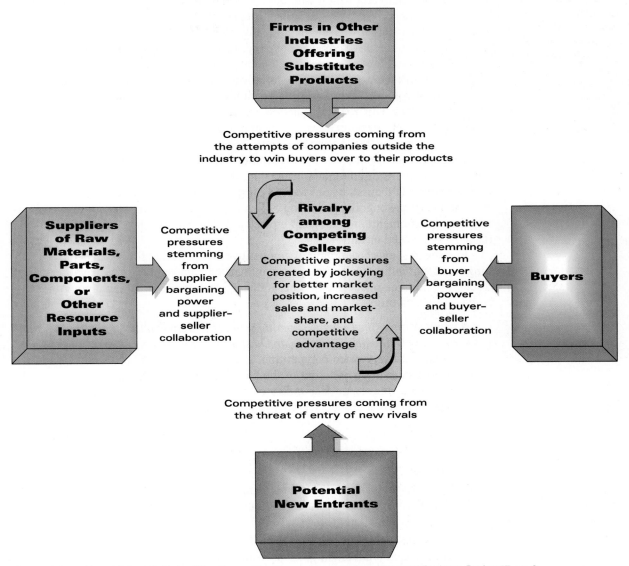

Source: Adapted from Michael E. Porter, "How Competitive Forces Shape Strategy," *Harvard Business Review* 57, no. 2 (March–April 1979), pp. 137–45.

Competitive Pressures Associated with the Jockeying among Rival Sellers

The strongest of the five competitive forces is nearly always the market maneuvering and jockeying for buyer patronage that goes on among rival sellers of a product or service. In effect, *a market is a competitive battlefield* where there's no end to the jockeying for buyer patronage. Rival sellers are prone to employ whatever weapons they

Core Concept

Competitive jockeying among industry rivals is ever changing, as rivals initiate fresh offensive and defensive moves and emphasize first one mix of competitive weapons and then another in efforts to improve their market positions.

have in their business arsenal to improve their market positions, strengthen their market position with buyers, and earn good profits. The challenge is to craft a competitive strategy that, at the very least, allows a company to hold its own against rivals and that, ideally, *produces a competitive edge over rivals.* But competitive contests are ongoing and dynamic. When one firm makes a strategic move that produces good results, its rivals typically respond with offensive or defensive countermoves, shifting their strategic emphasis from one combination of product attributes, marketing tactics, and capabilities to another. This pattern of action and reaction, move and countermove, adjust and readjust produces a continually evolving competitive landscape in which the market battle ebbs and flows, sometimes takes unpredictable twists and turns, and produces winners and losers. But the winners—the current market leaders—have no guarantees of continued leadership; their market success is no more durable than the power of their strategies to fend off the strategies of ambitious challengers. In every industry, the ongoing jockeying of rivals leads to one or another companies gaining or losing momentum in the marketplace according to whether their latest strategic maneuvers succeed or fail.

Figure 3.4 shows a sampling of competitive weapons that firms can deploy in battling rivals and indicates the factors that influence the intensity of their rivalry. A brief discussion of some of the factors that influence the tempo of rivalry among industry competitors is in order:[3]

- *Rivalry intensifies when competing sellers are active in launching fresh actions to boost their market standing and business performance.* One indicator of active rivalry is lively price competition, a condition that puts pressure on industry members to drive costs out of the business and threatens the survival of high-cost companies. Another indicator of active rivalry is rapid introduction of next-generation products—when one or more rivals frequently introduce new or improved products, competitors that lack good product innovation capabilities feel considerable competitive heat to get their own new and improved products into the marketplace quickly. Other indicators of active rivalry among industry members include:

  - Whether industry members are racing to differentiate their products from rivals by offering better performance features or higher quality or improved customer service or a wider product selection.

  - How frequently rivals resort to such marketing tactics as special sales promotions, heavy advertising, rebates, or low-interest-rate financing to drum up additional sales.

  - How actively industry members are pursuing efforts to build stronger dealer networks or establish positions in foreign markets or otherwise expand their distribution capabilities and market presence.

  - How hard companies are striving to gain a market edge over rivals by developing valuable expertise and capabilities that rivals are hard pressed to match.

  Normally, competitive jockeying among rival sellers is active and fairly intense because competing companies are highly motivated to launch whatever fresh actions and creative market maneuvers they can think of to try to strengthen their market positions and business performance.

- *Rivalry intensifies as the number of competitors increases and as competitors become more equal in size and capability.* Rivalry is not as vigorous in microprocessors for PCs, where Advanced Micro Devices (AMD) is one of the few

Figure 3.4   **Weapons for Competing and Factors Affecting the Strength of Rivalry**

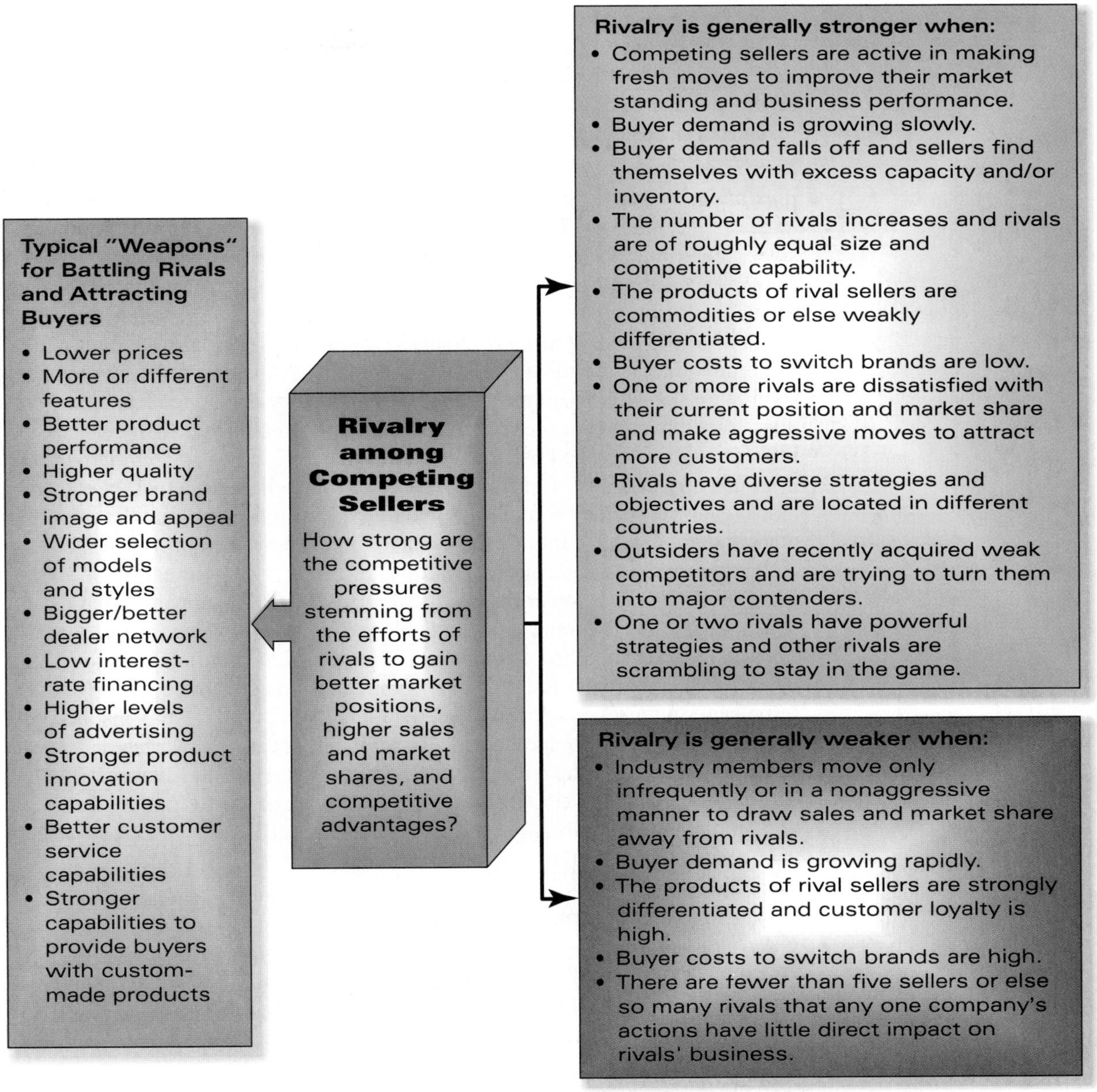

Typical "Weapons" for Battling Rivals and Attracting Buyers

- Lower prices
- More or different features
- Better product performance
- Higher quality
- Stronger brand image and appeal
- Wider selection of models and styles
- Bigger/better dealer network
- Low interest-rate financing
- Higher levels of advertising
- Stronger product innovation capabilities
- Better customer service capabilities
- Stronger capabilities to provide buyers with custom-made products

Rivalry among Competing Sellers

How strong are the competitive pressures stemming from the efforts of rivals to gain better market positions, higher sales and market shares, and competitive advantages?

Rivalry is generally stronger when:

- Competing sellers are active in making fresh moves to improve their market standing and business performance.
- Buyer demand is growing slowly.
- Buyer demand falls off and sellers find themselves with excess capacity and/or inventory.
- The number of rivals increases and rivals are of roughly equal size and competitive capability.
- The products of rival sellers are commodities or else weakly differentiated.
- Buyer costs to switch brands are low.
- One or more rivals are dissatisfied with their current position and market share and make aggressive moves to attract more customers.
- Rivals have diverse strategies and objectives and are located in different countries.
- Outsiders have recently acquired weak competitors and are trying to turn them into major contenders.
- One or two rivals have powerful strategies and other rivals are scrambling to stay in the game.

Rivalry is generally weaker when:

- Industry members move only infrequently or in a nonaggressive manner to draw sales and market share away from rivals.
- Buyer demand is growing rapidly.
- The products of rival sellers are strongly differentiated and customer loyalty is high.
- Buyer costs to switch brands are high.
- There are fewer than five sellers or else so many rivals that any one company's actions have little direct impact on rivals' business.

challengers to Intel, as it is in fast-food restaurants, where numerous sellers are actively jockeying for buyer patronage. Up to a point, the greater the number of competitors, the greater the probability of fresh, creative strategic initiatives. In addition, when rivals are nearly equal in size and capability, they can usually compete on a fairly even footing, making it harder for one or two firms to win commanding market shares and confront weaker market challenges from rivals.

- *Rivalry is usually stronger in slow-growing markets and weaker in fast-growing markets.* Rapidly expanding buyer demand produces enough new business for all industry members to grow. Indeed, in a fast-growing market, a company may find itself stretched just to keep abreast of incoming orders, let alone devote resources to stealing customers away from rivals. But in markets where growth is sluggish or where buyer demand drops off unexpectedly, expansion-minded firms and firms with excess capacity often are quick to cut prices and initiate other sales-increasing tactics, thereby igniting a battle for market share that can result in a shake-out of weak, inefficient firms.

- *Rivalry is usually weaker in industries comprised of so many rivals that the impact of any one company's actions is spread thin across all industry members; likewise, it is often weak when there are fewer than five competitors.* A progressively larger number of competitors can actually begin to weaken head-to-head rivalry once an industry becomes populated with so many rivals that the impact of successful moves by any one company is spread thin across many industry members. To the extent that a company's strategic moves ripple out to have little discernible impact on the businesses of its many rivals, then industry members soon learn that it is not imperative to respond every time one or another rival does something to enhance its market position—an outcome that weakens the intensity of head-to-head battles for market share. Rivalry also *tends* to be weak if an industry consists of just two or three or four sellers. In a market with few rivals, each competitor soon learns that aggressive moves to grow its sales and market share can have immediate adverse impact on rivals' businesses, almost certainly provoking vigorous retaliation and risking an all-out battle for market share that is likely to lower the profits of all concerned. Companies that have a few strong rivals thus come to understand the merits of *restrained* efforts to wrest sales and market share from competitors as opposed to undertaking hard-hitting offensives that escalate into a profit-eroding arms-race or price war. However, some caution must be exercised in concluding that rivalry is weak just because there are only a few competitors. Thus, although occasional warfare can break out (the fierceness of the current battle between Red Hat and Microsoft and the decades-long war between Coca-Cola and Pepsi are prime examples), competition among the few normally produces a live-and-let-live approach to competing because rivals see the merits of restrained efforts to wrest sales and market share from competitors as opposed to undertaking hard-hitting offensives that escalate into a profit-eroding arms race or price war.

- *Rivalry increases when buyer demand falls off and sellers find themselves with excess capacity and/or inventory.* Excess supply conditions create a "buyers' market," putting added competitive pressure on industry rivals to scramble for profitable sales levels (often by price discounting).

- *Rivalry increases as it becomes less costly for buyers to switch brands.* The less expensive it is for buyers to switch their purchases from the seller of one brand to the s eller of another brand, the easier it is for sellers to steal customers away from rivals. But the higher the costs buyers incur to switch brands, the less prone they are to brand switching. Even if consumers view one or more rival brands as more attractive, they may not be inclined to switch because of the added time and inconvenience or the psychological costs of abandoning a familiar brand. Distributors and retailers may not switch to the brands of rival manufacturers because they are hesitant to sever long-standing supplier relationships, incur any technical support costs or retraining expenses in making the switchover, go to the trouble of testing the quality and reliability of the rival brand, or devote resources to marketing the new brand (especially if the brand is lesser known).

Apple Computer, for example, has been unable to convince PC users to switch from Windows-based PCs because of the time burdens and inconvenience associated with learning Apple's operating system and because so many Windows-based applications will not run on a MacIntosh due to operating system incompatibility. Consequently, unless buyers are dissatisfied with the brand they are presently purchasing, high switching costs can significantly weaken the rivalry among competing sellers.

- *Rivalry increases as the products of rival sellers become more standardized and diminishes as the products of industry rivals become more strongly differentiated.* When the offerings of rivals are identical or weakly differentiated, buyers have less reason to be brand-loyal—a condition that makes it easier for rivals to convince buyers to switch to their offering. And since the brands of different sellers have comparable attributes, buyers can shop the market for the best deal and switch brands at will. In contrast, strongly differentiated product offerings among rivals breed high brand loyalty on the part of buyers—because many buyers view the attributes of certain brands as better suited to their needs. Strong brand attachments make it tougher for sellers to draw customers away from rivals. Unless meaningful numbers of buyers are open to considering new or different product attributes being offered by rivals, the high degrees of brand loyalty that accompany strong product differentiation work against fierce rivalry among competing sellers. *The degree of product differentiation also affects switching costs.* When the offerings of rivals are identical or weakly differentiated, it is usually easy and inexpensive for buyers to switch their purchases from one seller to another. Strongly differentiated products raise the probability that buyers will find it costly to switch brands.

- *Rivalry is more intense when industry conditions tempt competitors to use price cuts or other competitive weapons to boost unit volume.* When a product is perishable, seasonal, or costly to hold in inventory, competitive pressures build quickly anytime one or more firms decide to cut prices and dump supplies on the market. Likewise, whenever fixed costs account for a large fraction of total cost, such that unit costs tend to be lowest at or near full capacity, then firms come under significant pressure to cut prices or otherwise try to boost sales whenever they are operating below full capacity. Unused capacity imposes a significant cost-increasing penalty because there are fewer units over which to spread fixed costs. The pressure of high fixed costs can push rival firms into price concessions, special discounts, rebates, low-interest-rate financing, and other volume-boosting tactics.

- *Rivalry increases when one or more competitors become dissatisfied with their market position and launch moves to bolster their standing at the expense of rivals.* Firms that are losing ground or in financial trouble often pursue aggressive (or perhaps desperate) turnaround strategies that can involve price discounts, more advertising, acquisition of or merger with other rivals, or new product introductions—such strategies can turn competitive pressures up a notch.

- *Rivalry becomes more volatile and unpredictable as the diversity of competitors increases in terms of visions, strategic intents, objectives, strategies, resources, and countries of origin.* A diverse group of sellers often contains one or more mavericks willing to try novel or high-risk or rule-breaking market approaches, thus generating a livelier and less predictable competitive environment. Globally competitive markets often contain rivals with different views about where the industry is headed and a willingness to employ perhaps radically different competitive approaches. Attempts by cross-border rivals to gain stronger footholds in each other's domestic markets usually boost the intensity of rivalry, especially when the aggressors have lower costs or products with more attractive features.

- *Rivalry increases when strong companies outside the industry acquire weak firms in the industry and launch aggressive, well-funded moves to transform their newly acquired competitors into major market contenders.* A concerted effort to turn a weak rival into a market leader nearly always entails launching well-financed strategic initiatives to dramatically improve the competitor's product offering, excite buyer interest, and win a much bigger market share—actions that, if successful, put added pressure on rivals to counter with fresh strategic moves of their own.

- *A powerful, successful competitive strategy employed by one company greatly intensifies the competitive pressures on its rivals to develop effective strategic responses or be relegated to also-ran status.*

Rivalry can be characterized as *cutthroat* or *brutal* when competitors engage in protracted price wars or habitually employ other aggressive tactics that are mutually destructive to profitability. Rivalry can be considered *fierce* to *strong* when the battle for market share is so vigorous that the profit margins of most industry members are squeezed to bare-bones levels. Rivalry can be characterized as *moderate* or *normal* when the maneuvering among industry members, while lively and healthy, still allows most industry members to earn acceptable profits. Rivalry is *weak* when most companies in the industry are relatively well satisfied with their sales growth and market shares, rarely undertake offensives to steal customers away from one another, and have comparatively attractive earnings and returns on investment.

Competitive Pressures Associated with the Threat of New Entrants

Several factors determine whether the threat of new companies entering the marketplace poses significant competitive pressure (see Figure 3.5). One factor relates to the size of the pool of likely entry candidates and the resources at their command. As a rule, the bigger the pool of entry candidates, the stronger the threat of potential entry. This is especially true when some of the likely entry candidates have ample resources and the potential to become formidable contenders for market leadership. Frequently, the strongest competitive pressures associated with potential entry come not from outsiders, but from current industry participants looking for growth opportunities. *Existing industry members are often strong candidates for entering market segments or geographic areas where they currently do not have a market presence.* Companies already well established in certain product categories or geographic areas often possess the resources, competencies, and competitive capabilities to hurdle the barriers of entering a different market segment or new geographic area.

A second factor concerns whether the likely entry candidates face high or low entry barriers. High barriers reduce the competitive threat of potential entry, while low barriers make entry more likely, especially if the industry is growing and offers attractive profit opportunities. The most widely encountered barriers that entry candidates must hurdle include:[4]

- *The presence of sizable economies of scale in production or other areas of operation*—When incumbent companies enjoy cost advantages associated with

Figure 3.5   **Factors Affecting the Threat of Entry**

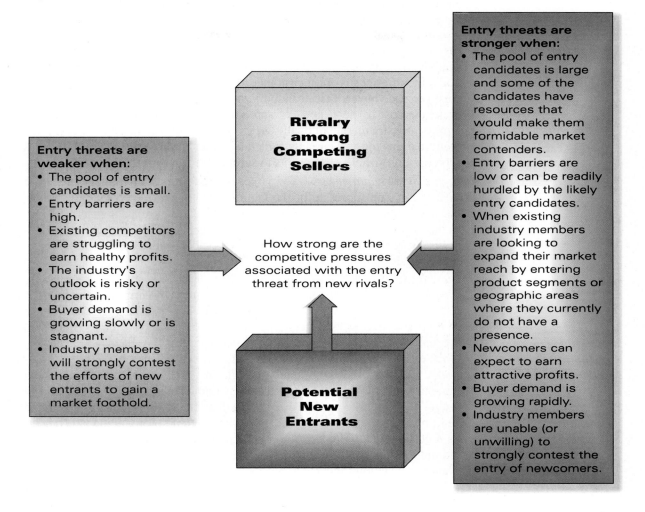

Entry threats are weaker when:
- The pool of entry candidates is small.
- Entry barriers are high.
- Existing competitors are struggling to earn healthy profits.
- The industry's outlook is risky or uncertain.
- Buyer demand is growing slowly or is stagnant.
- Industry members will strongly contest the efforts of new entrants to gain a market foothold.

Rivalry among Competing Sellers

How strong are the competitive pressures associated with the entry threat from new rivals?

Potential New Entrants

Entry threats are stronger when:
- The pool of entry candidates is large and some of the candidates have resources that would make them formidable market contenders.
- Entry barriers are low or can be readily hurdled by the likely entry candidates.
- When existing industry members are looking to expand their market reach by entering product segments or geographic areas where they currently do not have a presence.
- Newcomers can expect to earn attractive profits.
- Buyer demand is growing rapidly.
- Industry members are unable (or unwilling) to strongly contest the entry of newcomers.

large-scale operation, outsiders must either enter on a large scale (a costly and perhaps risky move) or accept a cost disadvantage and consequently lower profitability. Trying to overcome the disadvantages of small size by entering on a large scale at the outset can result in long-term overcapacity problems for the new entrant (until sales volume builds up), and it can so threaten the market shares of existing firms that they launch strong defensive maneuvers (price cuts, increased advertising and sales promotion, and similar blocking actions) to maintain their positions and make things hard on a newcomer.

- *Cost and resource disadvantages not related to scale of operation*—Aside from enjoying economies of scale, there are other reasons why existing firms may have low unit costs that are hard to replicate by newcomers. Industry incumbents can have cost advantages that stem from learning/experience curve effects, the possession of key patents or proprietary technology, partnerships with the best and cheapest suppliers of raw materials and components, favorable locations, and low fixed costs (because they have older facilities that have been mostly depreciated).

- *Strong brand preferences and high degrees of customer loyalty*—The stronger the attachment of buyers to established brands, the harder it is for a newcomer to break into the marketplace. In such cases, a new entrant must have the financial resources to spend enough on advertising and sales promotion to overcome customer loyalties and build its own clientele. Establishing brand recognition and building customer loyalty can be a slow and costly process. In addition, if it is difficult or costly for a customer to switch to a new brand, a new entrant must persuade buyers that its brand is worth the switching costs. To overcome switching-cost barriers, new entrants may have to offer buyers a discounted price or an extra margin of quality or service. All this can mean lower expected profit margins for new entrants, which increases the risk to start-up companies dependent on sizable early profits to support their new investments.

- *High capital requirements*—The larger the total dollar investment needed to enter the market successfully, the more limited the pool of potential entrants. The most obvious capital requirements for new entrants relate to manufacturing facilities and equipment, introductory advertising and sales promotion campaigns, working capital to finance inventories and customer credit, and sufficient cash to cover start-up costs.

- *The difficulties of building a network of distributors or retailers and securing adequate space on retailers' shelves*—A potential entrant can face numerous distribution channel challenges. Wholesale distributors may be reluctant to take on a product that lacks buyer recognition. Retailers have to be recruited and convinced to give a new brand ample display space and an adequate trial period. When existing sellers have strong, well-functioning distributor or retailer networks, a newcomer has an uphill struggle in squeezing its way in. Potential entrants sometimes have to "buy" their way into wholesale or retail channels by cutting their prices to provide dealers and distributors with higher markups and profit margins or by giving them big advertising and promotional allowances. As a consequence, a potential entrant's own profits may be squeezed unless and until its product gains enough consumer acceptance that distributors and retailers are anxious to carry it.

- *Restrictive regulatory policies*—Government agencies can limit or even bar entry by requiring licenses and permits. Regulated industries like cable TV, telecommunications, electric and gas utilities, radio and television broadcasting, liquor retailing, and railroads entail government-controlled entry. In international markets, host governments commonly limit foreign entry and must approve all foreign investment applications. Stringent government-mandated safety regulations and environmental pollution standards are entry barriers because they raise entry costs.

- *Tariffs and international trade restrictions*—National governments commonly use tariffs and trade restrictions (antidumping rules, local content requirements, quotas, etc.) to raise entry barriers for foreign firms and protect domestic producers from outside competition.

- *The ability and inclination of industry incumbents to launch vigorous initiatives to block a newcomer's successful entry*—Even if a potential entrant has or can acquire the needed competencies and resources to attempt entry, it must still worry about the reaction of existing firms.[5] Sometimes, there's little that incumbents can do to throw obstacles in an entrant's path—for instance, existing restaurants have little in their arsenal to discourage a new restaurant from opening or to dissuade people from trying the new restaurant. But there are times when incumbents do all they can to make it difficult for a new entrant, using price cuts, increased advertising, product improvements, and whatever else they can think of to prevent the entrant from building a clientele. Cable TV companies vigorously fight the entry of satellite TV companies; Sony and Nintendo have mounted strong defenses to thwart Microsoft's entry in videogames with its Xbox; existing hotels try to combat the opening of new hotels with loyalty programs, renovations of their own, the addition of new services, and so on. A potential entrant can have second thoughts when financially strong incumbent firms send clear signals that they will give newcomers a hard time.

Whether an industry's entry barriers ought to be considered high or low depends on the resources and competencies possessed by the pool of potential entrants. Companies with sizable financial resources, proven competitive capabilities, and a respected brand name may be able to hurdle an industry's entry barriers rather easily. Small start-up enterprises may find the same entry barriers insurmountable. Thus, how hard it will be for potential entrants to compete on a level playing field is always relative to the financial resources and competitive capabilities of likely entrants. For example, when Honda opted to enter the U.S. lawn-mower market in competition against Toro, Snapper, Craftsman, John Deere, and others, it was easily able to hurdle entry barriers that would have been formidable to other newcomers because it had long-standing expertise in gasoline engines and because its well-known reputation for quality and durability gave it instant credibility with shoppers looking to buy a new lawn mower. Honda had to spend relatively little on advertising to attract buyers and gain a market foothold, distributors and dealers were quite willing to handle the Honda lawn-mower line, and Honda had ample capital to build a U.S. assembly plant.

In evaluating whether the threat of additional entry is strong or weak, company managers must look at (1) how formidable the entry barriers are for each type of potential entrant—start-up enterprises, specific candidate companies in other industries, and current industry participants looking to expand their market reach—and (2) how attractive the growth and profit prospects are for new entrants. Rapidly growing market demand and high potential profits act as magnets, motivating potential entrants to commit the resources needed to hurdle entry barriers.[6] When profits are sufficiently attractive, entry barriers are unlikely to be an effective entry deterrent. At most, they limit the pool of candidate entrants to enterprises with the requisite competencies and resources and with the creativity to fashion a strategy for competing with incumbent firms.

Hence, *the best test of whether potential entry is a strong or weak competitive force in the marketplace is to ask if the industry's growth and profit prospects are strongly attractive to potential entry candidates.* When the answer is no, potential entry is a weak competitive force. When the answer is yes and there are entry candidates with sufficient expertise and resources, then potential entry adds significantly to competitive pressures in the marketplace. The stronger the threat of entry, the more that incumbent firms are driven to seek ways to fortify their positions against newcomers, pursuing strategic moves not only to protect their market shares but also to make entry more costly or difficult.

One additional point: *The threat of entry changes as the industry's prospects grow brighter or dimmer and as entry barriers rise or fall.* For example, in the pharmaceutical industry the expiration of a key patent on a widely prescribed drug virtually guarantees that one or more drug makers will enter with generic offerings of their own. Growing use of the Internet for shopping is making it much easier for Web-based retailers to enter into competition

> High entry barriers and weak entry threats today do not always translate into high entry barriers and weak entry threats tomorrow.

against such well-known retail chains as Sears, Circuit City, and Barnes and Noble. In international markets, entry barriers for foreign-based firms fall as tariffs are lowered, as host governments open up their domestic markets to outsiders, as domestic whole-salers and dealers seek out lower-cost foreign-made goods, and as domestic buyers become more willing to purchase foreign brands.

Competitive Pressures from the Sellers of Substitute Products

Companies in one industry come under competitive pressure from the actions of com-panies in a closely adjoining industry whenever buyers view the products of the two industries as good substitutes. For instance, the producers of sugar experience com-petitive pressures from the sales and marketing efforts of the makers of artificial sweet-eners. Similarly, the producers of eyeglasses and contact lenses are currently facing mounting competitive pressures from growing consumer interest in corrective laser surgery. Newspapers are feeling the competitive force of the general public turning to cable news channels for late-breaking news and using Internet sources to get informa-tion about sports results, stock quotes, and job opportunities. The makers of videotapes and VCRs have watched demand evaporate as more and more consumers have been attracted to substitute use of DVDs and DVD recorders/players. Traditional providers of telephone service like BellSouth, AT&T, Verizon, and Qwest are feeling enormous competitive pressure from cell phone providers, as more and more consumers find cell phones preferable to landline phones.

Just how strong the competitive pressures are from the sellers of substitute prod-ucts depends on three factors:

1. *Whether substitutes are readily available and attractively priced.* The presence of readily available and attractively priced substitutes creates competitive pressure by placing a ceiling on the prices industry members can charge without giving customers an incentive to switch to substitutes and risking sales erosion.[7] This price ceiling, at the same time, puts a lid on the profits that industry members can earn unless they find ways to cut costs. When substitutes are cheaper than an industry's product, industry members come under heavy competitive pressure to reduce their prices and find ways to absorb the price cuts with cost reductions.

2. *Whether buyers view the substitutes as being comparable or better in terms of quality, performance, and other relevant attributes.* The availability of substitutes inevitably invites customers to compare performance, features, ease of use, and other attributes as well as price. For example, ski boat manufacturers are expe-riencing strong competition from personal water-ski craft because water sports enthusiasts see personal water skis as fun to ride and less expensive. The users of paper cartons constantly weigh the performance trade-offs with plastic containers and metal cans. Camera users consider the convenience and performance trade-offs when deciding whether to substitute a digital camera for a film-based camera. Competition from good-performing substitutes unleashes competitive pressures on industry participants to incorporate new performance features and attributes that makes their product offerings more competitive.

3. *Whether the costs that buyers incur in switching to the substitutes are high or low.* High switching costs deter switching to substitutes, while low switching costs make it easier for the sellers of attractive substitutes to lure buyers to their offering.[8] Typical switching costs include the time and inconvenience that may be involved, the costs of additional equipment, the time and cost in testing the quality

Figure 3.6   **Factors Affecting Competition from Substitute Products**

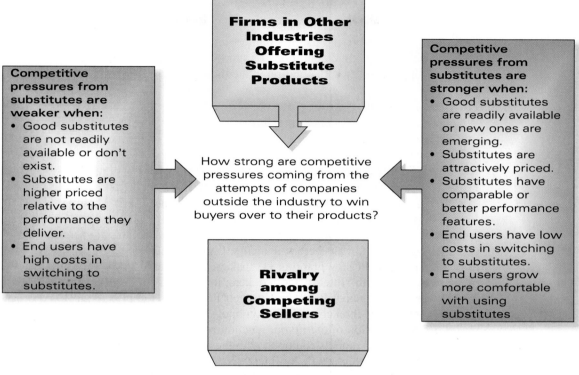

Firms in Other Industries Offering Substitute Products

Competitive pressures from substitutes are weaker when:
- Good substitutes are not readily available or don't exist.
- Substitutes are higher priced relative to the performance they deliver.
- End users have high costs in switching to substitutes.

How strong are competitive pressures coming from the attempts of companies outside the industry to win buyers over to their products?

Competitive pressures from substitutes are stronger when:
- Good substitutes are readily available or new ones are emerging.
- Substitutes are attractively priced.
- Substitutes have comparable or better performance features.
- End users have low costs in switching to substitutes.
- End users grow more comfortable with using substitutes

Rivalry among Competing Sellers

Signs That Competition from Substitutes Is Strong
- Sales of substitutes are growing faster than sales of the industry being analyzed (an indication that the sellers of substitutes are drawing customers away from the industry in question).
- Producers of substitutes are moving to add new capacity.
- Profits of the producers of substitutes are on the rise.

and reliability of the substitute, the psychological costs of severing old supplier relationships and establishing new ones, payments for technical help in making the changeover, and employee retraining costs. High switching costs can materially weaken the competitive pressures that industry members experience from substitutes unless the sellers of substitutes are successful in offsetting the high switching costs with enticing price discounts or additional performance enhancements.

Figure 3.6 summarizes the conditions that determine whether the competitive pressures from substitute products are strong, moderate, or weak.

As a rule, the lower the price of substitutes, the higher their quality and performance, and the lower the user's switching costs, the more intense the competitive pressures posed by substitute products. Other market indicators of the competitive strength of substitute products include (1) whether the sales of substitutes are growing faster than the sales of the industry being analyzed (a sign that the sellers of substitutes may be drawing customers away from the industry in question), (2) whether the producers of substitutes are moving to add new capacity, and (3) whether the profits of the producers of substitutes are on the rise.

Competitive Pressures Stemming from Supplier Bargaining Power and Supplier–Seller Collaboration

Whether supplier–seller relationships represent a weak or strong competitive force depends on (1) whether the major suppliers can exercise sufficient bargaining power to influence the terms and conditions of supply in their favor, and (2) the nature and extent of supplier–seller collaboration in the industry.

How Supplier Bargaining Power Can Create Competitive Pressures

Whenever the major suppliers to an industry have considerable leverage in determining the terms and conditions of the item they are supplying, then they are in a position to exert competitive pressure on one or more rival sellers. For instance, Microsoft and Intel, both of which supply personal computer (PC) makers with products that most PC users consider essential, are known for using their dominant market status not only to charge PC makers premium prices but also to leverage PC makers in other ways. Microsoft pressures PC makers to load only Microsoft products on the PCs they ship and to position the icons for Microsoft software prominently on the screens of new computers that come with factory-loaded software. Intel pushes greater use of Intel microprocessors in PCs by granting PC makers sizable advertising allowances on PC models equipped with "Intel Inside" stickers; it also tends to give PC makers that use the biggest percentages of Intel chips in their PC models top priority in filling orders for newly introduced Intel chips. Being on Intel's list of preferred customers helps a PC maker get an allocation of the first production runs of Intel's latest and greatest chips and thus get new PC models equipped with these chips to market ahead of rivals who are heavier users of chips made by Intel's rivals. The ability of Microsoft and Intel to pressure PC makers for preferential treatment of one kind or another in turn affects competition among rival PC makers.

Several other instances of supplier bargaining power are worth citing. Small-scale retailers must often contend with the power of manufacturers whose products enjoy prestigious and well-respected brand names; when a manufacturer knows that a retailer needs to stock the manufacturer's product because consumers expect to find the product on the shelves of retail stores where they shop, the manufacturer usually has some degree of pricing power and can also push hard for favorable shelf displays. Motor vehicle manufacturers typically exert considerable power over the terms and conditions with which they supply new vehicles to their independent automobile dealerships. The operators of franchised units of such chains as McDonald's, Dunkin' Donuts, Pizza Hut, Sylvan Learning Centers, and Hampton Inns must frequently agree not only to source some of their supplies from the franchisor at prices and terms favorable to that franchisor but also to operate their facilities in a manner largely dictated by the franchisor.

Strong supplier bargaining power is a competitive factor in industries where unions have been able to organize the workforces of some industry members but not others; those industry members that must negotiate wages, fringe benefits, and working conditions with powerful unions (which control the supply of labor) often find themselves with higher labor costs than their competitors with nonunion labor forces. The bigger the gap between union and nonunion labor costs in an industry, the more that unionized industry members must scramble to find ways to relieve the competitive pressure associated with their disadvantage on labor costs. High labor costs are proving a huge competitive liability to unionized supermarket chains like Kroger and Safeway in trying to combat the market share gains being made by Wal-Mart in supermarket retailing—Wal-Mart has a nonunion workforce, and the prices for supermarket items at its Supercenters tend to run 5 to 20 percent lower than those at unionized supermarket chains.

The factors that determine whether any of the suppliers to an industry are in a position to exert substantial bargaining power or leverage are fairly clear-cut:[9]

- *Whether the item being supplied is a commodity that is readily available from many suppliers at the going market price.* Suppliers have little or no bargaining power or leverage whenever industry members have the ability to source their requirements at competitive prices from any of several alternative and eager suppliers, perhaps dividing their purchases among two or more suppliers to promote lively competition for orders. The suppliers of commodity items have market power only when supplies become quite tight and industry members are so eager to secure what they need that they agree to terms more favorable to suppliers.

- *Whether a few large suppliers are the primary sources of a particular item.* The leading suppliers may well have pricing leverage unless they are plagued with excess capacity and are scrambling to secure additional orders for their products. Major suppliers with good reputations and strong demand for the items they supply are harder to wring concessions from than struggling suppliers striving to broaden their customer base or more fully utilize their production capacity.

- *Whether it is difficult or costly for industry members to switch their purchases from one supplier to another or to switch to attractive substitute inputs.* High switching costs signal strong bargaining power on the part of suppliers, whereas low switching costs and ready availability of good substitute inputs signal weak bargaining power. Soft-drink bottlers, for example, can counter the bargaining power of aluminum can suppliers by shifting or threatening to shift to greater use of plastic containers and introducing more attractive plastic container designs.

- *Whether certain needed inputs are in short supply.* Suppliers of items in short supply have some degree of pricing power, whereas a surge in the availability of particular items greatly weakens supplier pricing power and bargaining leverage.

- *Whether certain suppliers provide a differentiated input that enhances the performance or quality of the industry's product.* The more valuable that a particular input is in terms of enhancing the performance or quality of the products of industry members or of improving the efficiency of their production processes, the more bargaining leverage its suppliers are likely to possess.

- *Whether certain suppliers provide equipment or services that deliver valuable cost-saving efficiencies to industry members in operating their production processes.* Suppliers who provide cost-saving equipment or other valuable or necessary production-related services are likely to possess bargaining leverage. Industry members that do not source from such suppliers may find themselves at a cost disadvantage and thus under competitive pressure to do so (on terms that are favorable to the suppliers).

- *Whether suppliers provide an item that accounts for a sizable fraction of the costs of the industry's product.* The bigger the cost of a particular part or component, the more opportunity for the pattern of competition in the marketplace to be affected by the actions of suppliers to raise or lower their prices.

- *Whether industry members are major customers of suppliers.* As a rule, suppliers have less bargaining leverage when their sales to members of this one industry constitute a big percentage of their total sales. In such cases, the well-being of suppliers is closely tied to the well-being of their major customers.

Suppliers then have a big incentive to protect and enhance their customers' competitiveness via reasonable prices, exceptional quality, and ongoing advances in the technology of the items supplied.

- *Whether it makes good economic sense for industry members to integrate backward and self-manufacture items they have been buying from suppliers.* The make-or-buy issue generally boils down to whether suppliers who specialize in the production of a particular part or component and make them in volume for many different customers have the expertise and scale economies to supply as good or better component at a lower cost than industry members could achieve via self-manufacture. Frequently, it is difficult for industry members to self-manufacture parts and components more economically than they can obtain them from suppliers who specialize in making such items. For instance, most producers of outdoor power equipment (lawn mowers, rotary tillers, leaf blowers, etc.) find it cheaper to source the small engines they need from outside manufacturers who specialize in small-engine manufacture rather than make their own engines because the quantity of engines they need is too small to justify the investment in manufacturing facilities, master the production process, and capture scale economies. Specialists in small-engine manufacture, by supplying many kinds of engines to the whole power equipment industry, can obtain a big enough sales volume to fully realize scale economies, become proficient in all the manufacturing techniques, and keep costs low. As a rule, suppliers are safe from the threat of self-manufacture by their customers *until* the volume of parts a customer needs becomes large enough for the customer to justify backward integration into self-manufacture of the component. Suppliers also gain bargaining power when they have the resources and profit incentive to integrate forward into the business of the customers they are supplying and thus become a strong rival.

Figure 3.7 summarizes the conditions that tend to make supplier bargaining power strong or weak.

How Seller–Supplier Partnerships Can Create Competitive Pressures

In more and more industries, sellers are forging strategic partnerships with select suppliers in efforts to (1) reduce inventory and logistics costs (e.g., through just-in-time deliveries), (2) speed the availability of next-generation components, (3) enhance the quality of the parts and components being supplied and reduce defect rates, and (4) squeeze out important cost savings for both themselves and their suppliers. Numerous Internet technology applications are now available that permit real-time data sharing, eliminate paperwork, and produce cost savings all along the supply chain. The many benefits of effective seller–supplier collaboration can translate into competitive advantage for industry members that do the best job of managing supply chain relationships.

Dell Computer has used strategic partnering with key suppliers as a major element in its strategy to be the world's lowest-cost supplier of branded PCs, servers, and workstations. Because Dell has managed its supply chain relationships in ways that contribute to a low-cost, high-quality competitive edge in components supply, it has put enormous pressure on its PC rivals to try to imitate its supply chain management practices. Effective partnerships with suppliers on the part of one or more industry members can thus become a major source of competitive pressure for rival firms.

The more opportunities that exist for win–win efforts between a company and its suppliers, the less their relationship is characterized by who has the upper hand in

Figure 3.7   **Factors Affecting the Bargaining Power of Suppliers**

Supplier bargaining power is stronger when:
- Industry members incurs high costs in switching their purchases to alternative suppliers.
- Needed inputs are in short supply (which gives suppliers more leverage in setting prices).
- A supplier has a differentiated input that enhances the quality or performance of sellers' products or is a valuable or critical part of sellers' production process.
- There are only a few suppliers of a particular input.
- Some suppliers threaten to integrate forward into the business of industry members and perhaps become a powerful rival.

Supplier bargaining power is weaker when:
- The item being supplied is a commodity that is readily available from many suppliers at the going market price.
- Seller switching costs to alternative suppliers are low.
- Good substitute inputs exist or new ones emerge.
- There is a surge in the availability of supplies (thus greatly weakening supplier pricing power).
- Industry members account for a big fraction of suppliers' total sales and continued high volume purchases are important to the well-being of suppliers.
- Industry members are a threat to integrate backward into the business of suppliers and to self-manufacture their own requirements.
- Seller collaboration or partnering with selected suppliers provides attractive win–win opportunities.

bargaining with the other. Collaborative partnerships between a company and a supplier tend to last so long as the relationship is producing valuable benefits for both parties. Only if a supply partner is falling behind alternative suppliers is a company likely to switch suppliers and incur the costs and trouble of building close working ties with a different supplier.

Competitive Pressures Stemming from Buyer Bargaining Power and Seller–Buyer Collaboration

Whether seller–buyer relationships represent a weak or strong competitive force depends on (1) whether some or many buyers have sufficient bargaining leverage to obtain price concessions and other favorable terms and conditions of sale, and (2) the extent and competitive importance of seller–buyer strategic partnerships in the industry.

How Buyer Bargaining Power Can Create Competitive Pressures   As with suppliers, the leverage that certain types of buyers have in negotiating favorable terms can range from weak to strong. Individual consumers, for example, rarely have much bargaining power in negotiating price concessions or other favorable terms with sellers; the primary exceptions involve situations in which price haggling is customary, such as the purchase of new and used motor vehicles, homes, and certain big-ticket items like luxury watches, jewelry, and pleasure boats. For most consumer goods and services, individual buyers have no bargaining leverage—their option is to pay the seller's posted price or take their business elsewhere.

In contrast, large retail chains like Wal-Mart, Best Buy, Staples, and Home Depot typically have considerable negotiating leverage in purchasing products from manufacturers because of manufacturers' need for broad retail exposure and the most appealing shelf locations. Retailers may stock two or three competing brands of a product but rarely all competing brands, so competition among rival manufacturers for visibility on the shelves of popular multistore retailers gives such retailers significant bargaining strength. Major supermarket chains like Kroger, Safeway, and Royal Ahold, which provide access to millions of grocery shoppers, have sufficient bargaining power to demand promotional allowances and lump-sum payments (called slotting fees) from food products manufacturers in return for stocking certain brands or putting them in the best shelf locations. Motor vehicle manufacturers have strong bargaining power in negotiating to buy original equipment tires from Goodyear, Michelin, Bridgestone/Firestone, Continental, and Pirelli not only because they buy in large quantities but also because tire makers believe they gain an advantage in supplying replacement tires to vehicle owners if their tire brand is original equipment on the vehicle. "Prestige" buyers have a degree of clout in negotiating with sellers because a seller's reputation is enhanced by having prestige buyers on its customer list.

Even if buyers do not purchase in large quantities or offer a seller important market exposure or prestige, they gain a degree of bargaining leverage in the following circumstances:[10]

- *If buyers' costs of switching to competing brands or substitutes are relatively low*—Buyers who can readily switch brands or source from several sellers have more negotiating leverage than buyers who have high switching costs. When the products of rival sellers are virtually identical, it is relatively easy for buyers to switch from seller to seller at little or no cost and anxious sellers may be willing to make concessions to win or retain a buyer's business.

- *If the number of buyers is small or if a customer is particularly important to a seller*—The smaller the number of buyers, the less easy it is for sellers to find alternative buyers when a customer is lost to a competitor. The prospect of losing a customer not easily replaced often makes a seller more willing to grant concessions of one kind or another.

- *If buyer demand is weak and sellers are scrambling to secure additional sales of their products*—Weak or declining demand creates a "buyers' market"; conversely, strong or rapidly growing demand creates a "sellers' market" and shifts bargaining power to sellers.

- *If buyers are well informed about sellers' products, prices, and costs*—The more information buyers have, the better bargaining position they are in. The mushrooming availability of product information on the Internet is giving added bargaining power to individuals. Buyers can easily use the Internet to compare prices and features of vacation packages, shop for the best interest rates on mortgages and loans, and find the best prices on big-ticket items such as digital cameras. Bargain-hunting individuals can shop around for the best deal on the Internet and use that information to negotiate a better deal from local retailers; this method is becoming commonplace in buying new and used motor vehicles. Further, the Internet has created opportunities for manufacturers, wholesalers, retailers, and sometimes individuals to join online buying groups to pool their purchasing power and approach vendors for better terms than could be gotten individually. A multinational manufacturer's geographically scattered purchasing groups can use Internet technology to pool their orders with parts and components suppliers and bargain for volume discounts. Purchasing agents at some companies are banding together at third-party Web sites to pool corporate purchases to get better deals or special treatment.

- *If buyers pose a credible threat of integrating backward into the business of sellers*—Companies like Anheuser-Busch, Coors, and Heinz have integrated backward into metal can manufacturing to gain bargaining power in obtaining the balance of their can requirements from otherwise powerful metal can manufacturers. Retailers gain bargaining power by stocking and promoting their own private-label brands alongside manufacturers' name brands. Wal-Mart, for example, has elected to compete against Procter & Gamble (P&G), its biggest supplier, with its own brand of laundry detergent, called Sam's American Choice, which is priced 25 to 30 percent lower than P&G's Tide.

- *If buyers have discretion in whether and when they purchase the product*—Many consumers, if they are unhappy with the present deals offered on major appliances or hot tubs or home entertainment centers, may be in a position to delay purchase until prices and financing terms improve. If business customers are not happy with the prices or security features of bill-payment software systems, they can either delay purchase until next-generation products become available or attempt to develop their own software in-house. If college students believe that the prices of new textbooks are too high, they can purchase used copies.

Figure 3.8 highlights the factors causing buyer bargaining power to be strong or weak.

A final point to keep in mind is that *not all buyers of an industry's product have equal degrees of bargaining power with sellers*, and some may be less sensitive than others to price, quality, or service differences. For example, independent tire retailers have less bargaining power in purchasing tires than do Honda, Ford, and DaimlerChrysler (which buy in much larger quantities), and they are also less sensitive to quality. Motor vehicle manufacturers are very particular about tire quality and tire performance because of the effects on vehicle performance, and they drive a hard bargain with tire manufacturers on both price and quality. Apparel manufacturers confront significant bargaining power when selling to big retailers like JCPenney, Macy's, or L. L. Bean but they can command much better prices selling to small owner-managed apparel boutiques.

How Seller–Buyer Partnerships Can Create Competitive Pressures   Partnerships between sellers and buyers are an increasingly important element of the competitive picture in *business-to-business relationships* (as opposed to business-to-consumer relationships). Many sellers that provide items to business customers have found it in their mutual interest to collaborate closely on such matters as just-in-time deliveries, order processing, electronic invoice payments, and data sharing. Wal-Mart, for example, provides the manufacturers with which it does business (like Procter & Gamble) with daily sales at each of its stores so that the manufacturers can maintain sufficient inventories at Wal-Mart's distribution centers to keep the shelves at each Wal-Mart store amply stocked. Dell has partnered with its largest PC customers to create

Figure 3.8 **Factors Affecting the Bargaining Power of Buyers**

Buyer bargaining power is stronger when:
- Buyer switching costs to competing brands or substitute products are low.
- Buyers are large and can demand concessions when purchasing large quantities.
- Large-volume purchases by buyers are important to sellers.
- Buyer demand is weak or declining.
- There are only a few buyers—so that each one's business is important to sellers.
- Identity of buyer adds prestige to the seller's list of customers.
- Quantity and quality of information available to buyers improves.
- Buyers have the ability to postpone purchases until later if they do not like the present deals being offered by sellers.
- Some buyers are a threat to integrate backward into the business of sellers and become an important competitor.

Buyer bargaining power is weaker when:
- Buyers purchase the item infrequently or in small quantities.
- Buyer switching costs to competing brands are high.
- There is a surge in buyer demand that creates a "sellers' market."
- A seller's brand reputation is important to a buyer.
- A particular seller's product delivers quality or performance that is very important to buyer and that is not matched in other brands.
- Buyer collaboration or partnering with selected sellers provides attractive win–win opportunities.

online systems for over 50,000 corporate customers, providing their employees with information on approved product configurations, global pricing, paperless purchase orders, real-time order tracking, invoicing, purchasing history, and other efficiency tools. Dell loads a customer's software at the factory and installs asset tags so that customer setup time is minimal; it also helps customers upgrade their PC systems to next-generation hardware and software. Dell's partnerships with its corporate customers have put significant competitive pressure on other PC makers.

Is the Collective Strength of the Five Competitive Forces Conducive to Good Profitability?

Scrutinizing each of the five competitive forces one by one provides a powerful diagnosis of what competition is like in a given market. Once the strategist has gained an understanding of the specific competitive pressures comprising each force and determined whether these pressures constitute a strong, moderate, or weak competitive force, the next step is to evaluate the collective strength of the five forces and determine whether the state of competition is conducive to good profitability. Is the collective impact of the five competitive forces stronger than "normal"? Are some of the competitive forces sufficiently strong to undermine industry profitability? Can companies in this industry reasonably expect to earn decent profits in light of the prevailing competitive forces?

Is the Industry Competitively Attractive or Unattractive?   *As a rule, the stronger the collective impact of the five competitive forces, the lower the combined profitability of industry participants.* The most extreme case of a competitively unattractive industry is when all five forces are producing strong competitive pressures: Rivalry among sellers is vigorous, low entry barriers allow new rivals to gain a market foothold, competition from substitutes is intense, and both suppliers and customers are able to exercise considerable bargaining leverage. Fierce to strong competitive pressures coming from all five directions nearly always drive industry profitability to unacceptably low levels, frequently producing losses for many industry members and forcing some out of business. But an industry can be competitively unattractive even when not all five competitive forces are strong. Intense competitive pressures from just two or three of the five forces may suffice to destroy the conditions for good profitability and prompt some companies to exit the business. The manufacture of disk drives, for example, is brutally competitive; IBM recently announced the sale of its disk drive business to Hitachi, taking a loss of over $2 billion on its exit from the business. Especially intense competitive conditions seem to be the norm in tire manufacturing and apparel, two industries where profit margins have historically been thin.

> The stronger the forces of competition, the harder it becomes for industry members to earn attractive profits.

In contrast, when the collective impact of the five competitive forces is moderate to weak, an industry is competitively attractive in the sense that industry members can reasonably expect to earn good profits and a nice return on investment. The ideal competitive environment for earning superior profits is one in which both suppliers and customers are in weak bargaining positions, there are no good substitutes, high barriers block further entry, and rivalry among present sellers generates only moderate competitive pressures. Weak competition is the best of all possible worlds for also-ran companies because even they can usually eke out a decent profit—if a company can't make a decent profit when competition is weak, then its business outlook is indeed grim.

In most industries, the collective strength of the five competitive forces is somewhere near the middle of the two extremes of very intense and very weak, typically ranging from slightly stronger than normal to slightly weaker than normal and typically allowing well-managed companies with sound strategies to earn attractive profits.

Matching Company Strategy to Competitive Conditions   Working through the five-forces model step by step not only aids strategy makers in assessing whether the intensity of competition allows good profitability but also promotes sound strategic thinking about how to better match company strategy to the specific competitive character of the marketplace. Effectively matching a company's strategy to prevailing competitive conditions has two aspects:

> A company's strategy is increasingly effective the more it provides some insulation from competitive pressures and shifts the competitive battle in the company's favor.

1. Pursuing avenues that shield the firm from as many of the different competitive pressures as possible.
2. Initiating actions calculated to produce sustainable competitive advantage, thereby shifting competition in the company's favor, putting added competitive pressure on rivals, and perhaps even defining the business model for the industry.

But making headway on these two fronts first requires identifying competitive pressures, gauging the relative strength of each of the five competitive forces, and gaining a deep enough understanding of the state of competition in the industry to know which strategy buttons to push.

QUESTION 3: WHAT FACTORS ARE DRIVING INDUSTRY CHANGE AND WHAT IMPACTS WILL THEY HAVE?

An industry's present conditions don't necessarily reveal much about the strategically relevant ways in which the industry environment is changing. All industries are characterized by trends and new developments that gradually or speedily produce changes important enough to require a strategic response from participating firms. A popular hypothesis states that industries go through a life cycle of takeoff, rapid growth, early maturity and slowing growth, market saturation, and stagnation or decline. This hypothesis helps explain industry change—but it is far from complete.[11] There are more causes of industry change than an industry's normal progression through the life cycle—these need to be identified and their impacts understood.

The Concept of Driving Forces

Core Concept
Industry conditions change because important forces are *driving* industry participants (competitors, customers, or suppliers) to alter their actions; the **driving forces** in an industry are the *major underlying causes* of changing industry and competitive conditions—they have the biggest influence on how the industry landscape will be altered. Some driving forces originate in the outer ring of macroenvironment and some originate from the inner ring.

While it is important to track where an industry is in the life cycle, there's more analytical value in identifying the other factors that may be even stronger drivers of industry and competitive change. The point to be made here is that industry and competitive conditions change because forces are enticing or pressuring certain industry participants (competitors, customers, suppliers) to alter their actions in important ways.[12] The most powerful of the change agents are called **driving forces** because they have the biggest influences in reshaping the industry landscape and altering competitive conditions. Some driving forces originate in the outer ring of the company's macroenvironment (see Figure 3.2), but most originate in the company's more immediate industry and competitive environment.

Driving-forces analysis has three steps: (1) identifying what the driving forces are; (2) assessing whether the drivers of change are, on the whole, acting to make the industry more or less attractive; and (3) determining what strategy changes are needed to prepare for the impacts of the driving forces. All three steps merit further discussion.

Identifying an Industry's Driving Forces

Many developments can affect an industry powerfully enough to qualify as driving forces. Some drivers of change are unique and specific to a particular industry situation, but most drivers of industry and competitive change fall into one of the following categories:[13]

- *Emerging new Internet capabilities and applications*—Since the late 1990s, the Internet has woven its way into everyday business operations and the social fabric of life all across the world. Mushrooming Internet use, growing acceptance of Internet shopping, the emergence of high-speed Internet service and Voice over Internet Protocol (VoIP) technology, and an ever-growing series of Internet applications and capabilities have been major drivers of change in industry after industry. Companies are increasingly using online technology (1) to collaborate closely with suppliers and streamline their supply chains and (2) to revamp internal operations and squeeze out cost savings. Manufacturers can use their Web sites to access customers directly rather than distribute exclusively through traditional wholesale and retail channels. Businesses of all types can use Web stores to extend their geographic reach and vie for sales in areas where they formerly did not have a presence. The ability of companies to reach consumers via the Internet increases the number of rivals a company faces and often escalates rivalry by pitting pure online sellers against combination brick-and-click sellers against pure brick-and-mortar sellers. The Internet gives buyers unprecedented ability to research the product offerings of competitors and shop the market for the best value. Mounting ability of consumers to download music from the Internet via either file sharing or online music retailers has profoundly and reshaped the music industry and the business of traditional brick-and-mortar music retailers. Widespread use of e-mail has forever eroded the business of providing fax services and the first-class mail delivery revenues of government postal services worldwide. Videoconferencing via the Internet can erode the demand for business travel. Online course offerings at universities have the potential to revolutionize higher education. The Internet of the future will feature faster speeds, dazzling applications, and over a billion connected gadgets performing an array of functions, thus driving further industry and competitive changes. But Internet-related impacts vary from industry to industry. The challenges here are to assess precisely how emerging Internet developments are altering a particular industry's landscape and to factor these impacts into the strategy-making equation.

- *Increasing globalization*—Competition begins to shift from primarily a regional or national focus to an international or global focus when industry members begin seeking out customers in foreign markets or when production activities begin to migrate to countries where costs are lowest. Globalization of competition really starts to take hold when one or more ambitious companies precipitate a race for worldwide market leadership by launching initiatives to expand into more and more country markets. Globalization can also be precipitated by the blossoming of consumer demand in more and more countries and by the actions of government officials in many countries to reduce trade barriers or open up once-closed markets to foreign competitors, as is occurring in many parts of Europe, Latin America, and Asia. Significant differences in labor costs among countries give manufacturers a strong incentive to locate plants for labor-intensive products in low-wage countries and use these plants to supply market demand across the world. Wages in China, India, Singapore, Mexico, and Brazil, for example, are about one-fourth those in the United States, Germany, and Japan. The forces of globalization are sometimes such a strong driver that companies find it highly advantageous, if not necessary, to spread their operating reach into more and more country markets. Globalization is very much a driver of industry change in such industries as credit cards, cell phones, digital cameras, golf and ski equipment, motor vehicles, steel, petroleum, personal computers, video games, public accounting, and textbook publishing.

- *Changes in an industry's long-term growth rate*—Shifts in industry growth up or down are a driving force for industry change, affecting the balance between industry supply and buyer demand, entry and exit, and the character and strength of competition. An upsurge in buyer demand triggers a race among established firms and newcomers to capture the new sales opportunities; ambitious companies with trailing market shares may see the upturn in demand as a golden opportunity to launch offensive strategies to broaden their customer base and move up several notches in the industry standings. A slowdown in the rate at which demand is growing nearly always portends mounting rivalry and increased efforts by some firms to maintain their high rates of growth by taking sales and market share away from rivals. If industry sales suddenly turn flat or begin to shrink after years of rising at double-digit levels, competition is certain to intensify as industry members scramble for the available business and as mergers and acquisitions result in industry consolidation to a smaller number of competitively stronger participants. Stagnating sales usually prompt both competitively weak and growth-oriented companies to sell their business operations to those industry members who elect to stick it out; as demand for the industry's product continues to shrink, the remaining industry members may be forced to close inefficient plants and retrench to a smaller production base—all of which results in a much-changed competitive landscape.

- *Changes in who buys the product and how they use it*—Shifts in buyer demographics and new ways of using the product can alter the state of competition by opening the way to market an industry's product through a different mix of dealers and retail outlets; prompting producers to broaden or narrow their product lines; bringing different sales and promotion approaches into play; and forcing adjustments in customer service offerings (credit, technical assistance, maintenance, and repair). The mushrooming popularity of downloading music from the Internet, storing music files on PC hard drives, and burning custom discs has forced recording companies to reexamine their distribution strategies and raised questions about the future of traditional retail music stores; at the same time, it has stimulated sales of disc burners and blank discs. Longer life expectancies and growing percentages of relatively well-to-do retirees are driving changes in such industries as health care, prescription drugs, recreational living, and vacation travel. The growing percentage of households with PCs and Internet access is opening opportunities for banks to expand their electronic bill-payment services and for retailers to move more of their customer services online.

- *Product innovation*—Competition in an industry is always affected by rivals racing to be first to introduce one new product or product enhancement after another. An ongoing stream of product innovations tends to alter the pattern of competition in an industry by attracting more first-time buyers, rejuvenating industry growth, and/or creating wider or narrower product differentiation among rival sellers. Successful new product introductions strengthen the market positions of the innovating companies, usually at the expense of companies that stick with their old products or are slow to follow with their own versions of the new product. Product innovation has been a key driving force in such industries as digital cameras, golf clubs, video games, toys, and prescription drugs.

- *Technological change and manufacturing process innovation*—Advances in technology can dramatically alter an industry's landscape, making it possible to produce new and better products at lower cost and opening up whole new industry frontiers. For instance, Voice over Internet Protocol (VoIP) technology has spawned low-cost, Internet-based phone networks that are stealing large numbers of customers away from traditional telephone companies worldwide (whose higher cost technology depends on hardwired connections via overhead and underground telephone lines). Flat-screen technology for PC monitors is killing the demand for conventional cathode ray tube (CRT) monitors. Liquid crystal display (LCD), plasma screen technology, and high-definition technology are precipitating a revolution in the television industry and driving use of cathode ray technology (CRT) into the background. MP3 technology is transforming how people listen to music. Digital technology is driving huge changes in the camera and film industries. Satellite radio technology is allowing satellite radio companies with their largely commercial-free programming to draw millions of listeners away from traditional radio stations whose revenue streams from commercials are dependent on audience size. Technological developments can also produce competitively significant changes in capital requirements, minimum efficient plant sizes, distribution channels and logistics, and learning/experience curve effects. In the steel industry, ongoing advances in electric arc minimill technology (which involve recycling scrap steel to make new products) have allowed steelmakers with state-of-the-art minimills to gradually expand into the production of more and more steel products, steadily taking sales and market share from higher-cost integrated producers (which make steel from scratch using iron ore, coke, and traditional blast furnace technology). Nucor Corporation, the leader of the minimill technology revolution in the United States, began operations in 1970 and has ridden the wave of technological advances in minimill technology to become the biggest U.S. steel producer (as of 2004) and rank among the lowest-cost producers in the world. In a space of 30 years, advances in minimill technology have changed the face of the steel industry worldwide.

- *Marketing innovation*—When firms are successful in introducing new ways to *market* their products, they can spark a burst of buyer interest, widen industry demand, increase product differentiation, and lower unit costs—any or all of which can alter the competitive positions of rival firms and force strategy revisions. Online marketing is shaking up competition in electronics (where there are dozens of online electronics retailers, often with deep-discount prices) and office supplies (where Office Depot, Staples, and Office Max are using their Web sites to market office supplies to corporations, small businesses, schools and universities, and government agencies). Increasing numbers of music artists are marketing their recordings at their own Web sites rather than entering into contracts with recording studios that distribute through online and brick-and-mortar music retailers.

- *Entry or exit of major firms*—The entry of one or more foreign companies into a geographic market once dominated by domestic firms nearly always shakes up competitive conditions. Likewise, when an established domestic firm from another industry attempts entry either by acquisition or by launching its own start-up venture, it usually applies its skills and resources in some innovative fashion that pushes competition in new directions. Entry by a major firm thus often produces a new ball game, not only with new key players but also with new rules for competing. Similarly, exit of a major firm changes the competitive structure by reducing the number of market leaders (perhaps increasing the dominance of the leaders who remain) and causing a rush to capture the exiting firm's customers.

- *Diffusion of technical know-how across more companies and more countries—* As knowledge about how to perform a particular activity or execute a particular manufacturing technology spreads, the competitive advantage held by firms originally possessing this know-how erodes. Knowledge diffusion can occur through scientific journals, trade publications, on-site plant tours, word of mouth among suppliers and customers, employee migration, and Internet sources. It can also occur when those possessing technological knowledge license others to use that knowledge for a royalty fee or team up with a company interested in turning the technology into a new business venture. Quite often, technological know-how can be acquired by simply buying a company that has the wanted skills, patents, or manufacturing capabilities. In recent years, *rapid technology transfer across national boundaries has been a prime factor in causing industries to become more globally competitive.* As companies worldwide gain access to valuable technical know-how, they upgrade their manufacturing capabilities in a long-term effort to compete head-on with established companies. Cross-border technology transfer has made the once domestic industries of automobiles, tires, consumer electronics, telecommunications, computers, and others increasingly global.

- *Changes in cost and efficiency—*Widening or shrinking differences in the costs among key competitors tend to dramatically alter the state of competition. The low cost of fax and e-mail transmission has put mounting competitive pressure on the relatively inefficient and high-cost operations of the U.S. Postal Service—sending a one-page fax is cheaper and far quicker than sending a first-class letter; sending e-mail is faster and cheaper still. In the steel industry, the lower costs of companies using electric-arc furnaces to recycle scrap steel into new steel products has forced traditional manufacturers that produce steel from iron ore using blast furnace technology to overhaul their plants and to withdraw totally from making those steel products where they could no longer be cost competitive. Shrinking cost differences in producing multifeatured mobile phones is turning the mobile phone market into a commodity business and causing more buyers to base their purchase decisions on price.

- *Growing buyer preferences for differentiated products instead of a commodity product (or for a more standardized product instead of strongly differentiated products)—*When buyer tastes and preferences start to diverge, sellers can win a loyal following with product offerings that stand apart from those of rival sellers. In recent years, beer drinkers have grown less loyal to a single brand and have begun to drink a variety of domestic and foreign beers; as a consequence, beer manufacturers have introduced a host of new brands and malt beverages with different tastes and flavors. Buyer preferences for motor vehicles are becoming increasingly diverse, with few models generating sales of more than 250,000 units annually. When a shift from standardized to differentiated products occurs, the driver of change is the contest among rivals to cleverly outdifferentiate one another.

  However, buyers sometimes decide that a standardized, budget-priced product suits their requirements as well as or better than a premium-priced product with lots of snappy features and personalized services. Online brokers, for example, have used the lure of cheap commissions to attract many investors willing to place their own buy–sell orders via the Internet; growing acceptance of online trading has put significant competitive pressures on full-service brokers whose business model has always revolved around convincing clients of the value of asking for personalized advice from professional brokers and paying their high commission fees to make trades. Pronounced shifts toward greater product standardization usually spawn lively price competition and force rival sellers to drive down their costs to maintain profitability. The lesson here is that competition is driven partly by whether the market forces in motion are acting to increase or decrease product differentiation.

- *Reductions in uncertainty and business risk*—An emerging industry is typically characterized by much uncertainty over potential market size, how much time and money will be needed to surmount technological problems, and what distribution channels and buyer segments to emphasize. Emerging industries tend to attract only risk-taking entrepreneurial companies. Over time, however, if the business model of industry pioneers proves profitable and market demand for the product appears durable, more conservative firms are usually enticed to enter the market. Often, these later entrants are large, financially strong firms looking to invest in attractive growth industries.

  Lower business risks and less industry uncertainty also affect competition in international markets. In the early stages of a company's entry into foreign markets, conservatism prevails and firms limit their downside exposure by using less risky strategies like exporting, licensing, joint marketing agreements, or joint ventures with local companies to accomplish entry. Then, as experience accumulates and perceived risk levels decline, companies move more boldly and more independently, making acquisitions, constructing their own plants, putting in their own sales and marketing capabilities to build strong competitive positions in each country market, and beginning to link the strategies in each country to create a more globalized strategy.

- *Regulatory influences and government policy changes*—Government regulatory actions can often force significant changes in industry practices and strategic approaches. Deregulation has proved to be a potent pro-competitive force in the airline, banking, natural gas, telecommunications, and electric utility industries. Government efforts to reform Medicare and health insurance have become potent driving forces in the health care industry. In international markets, host governments can drive competitive changes by opening their domestic markets to foreign participation or closing them to protect domestic companies. Note that this driving force is spawned by forces in a company's macroenvironment.

- *Changing societal concerns, attitudes, and lifestyles*—Emerging social issues and changing attitudes and lifestyles can be powerful instigators of industry change. Growing antismoking sentiment has emerged as a major driver of change in the tobacco industry; concerns about terrorism are having a big impact on the travel industry. Consumer concerns about salt, sugar, chemical additives, saturated fat, cholesterol, carbohydrates, and nutritional value have forced food producers to revamp food-processing techniques, redirect R&D efforts into the use of healthier ingredients, and compete in developing nutritious, good-tasting products. Safety concerns have driven product design changes in the automobile, toy, and outdoor power equipment industries, to mention a few. Increased interest in physical fitness has spawned new industries in exercise equipment, biking, outdoor apparel, sports gyms and recreation centers, vitamin and nutrition supplements, and medically supervised diet programs. Social concerns about air and water pollution have forced industries to incorporate expenditures for controlling pollution into their cost structures. Shifting societal concerns, attitudes, and lifestyles alter the pattern of competition, usually favoring those

Table 3.2 **The Most Common Driving Forces**

1. Emerging new Internet capabilities and applications
2. Increasing globalization
3. Changes in an industry's long-term growth rate
4. Changes in who buys the product and how they use it
5. Product innovation
6. Technological change and manufacturing process innovation
7. Marketing innovation
8. Entry or exit of major firms
9. Diffusion of technical know-how across more companies and more countries
10. Changes in cost and efficiency
11. Growing buyer preferences for differentiated products instead of a commodity product (or for a more standardized product instead of strongly differentiated products)
12. Reductions in uncertainty and business risk
13. Regulatory influences and government policy changes
14. Changing societal concerns, attitudes, and lifestyles

players that respond quickly and creatively with products targeted to the new trends and conditions. As with the preceding driving force, this driving force springs from factors at work in a company's macroenvironment.

Table 3.2 lists these 14 most common driving forces.

That there are so many different potential driving forces explains why it is too simplistic to view industry change only in terms of moving through the different stages in an industry's life cycle and why a full understanding of all types of change drivers is a fundamental part of industry analysis. However, while many forces of change may be at work in a given industry, no more than three or four are likely to be true driving forces powerful enough to qualify as the *major determinants* of why and how the industry is changing. Thus company strategists must resist the temptation to label every change they see as a driving force; the analytical task is to evaluate the forces of industry and competitive change carefully enough to separate major factors from minor ones.

Assessing the Impact of the Driving Forces

An important part of driving-forces analysis is to determine whether the collective impact of the driving forces will be to increase or decrease market demand, make competition more or less intense, and lead to higher or lower industry profitability.

Just identifying the driving forces is not sufficient, however. The second, and more important, step in driving-forces analysis is to determine whether the prevailing driving forces are, on the whole, acting to make the industry environment more or less attractive. Answers to three questions are needed here:

1. Are the driving forces collectively acting to cause demand for the industry's product to increase or decrease?

2. Are the driving forces acting to make competition more or less intense?

3. Will the combined impacts of the driving forces lead to higher or lower industry profitability?

Getting a handle on the collective impact of the driving forces usually requires looking at the likely effects of each force separately, since the driving forces may not all be pushing change in the same direction. For example, two driving forces may be acting to spur demand for the industry's product while one driving force may be working to curtail demand. Whether the net effect on industry demand is up or down hinges on which driving forces are the more powerful. The analyst's objective here is to get a good grip on what external factors are shaping industry change and what difference these factors will make.

Developing a Strategy That Takes the Impacts of the Driving Forces into Account

The third step of driving-forces analysis—where the real payoff for strategy making comes—is for managers to draw some conclusions about what strategy adjustments will be needed to deal with the impacts of the driving forces. The real value of doing driving-forces analysis is to gain better understanding of what strategy adjustments will be needed to cope with the drivers of industry change and the impacts they are likely to have on market demand, competitive intensity, and industry profitability. In short, the strategy-making challenge that flows from driving-forces analysis is what to do to prepare for the industry and competitive changes being wrought by the driving forces. Indeed, without understanding the forces driving industry change and the impacts these forces will have on the character of the industry environment and on the company's business over the next one to three years, managers are ill-prepared to craft a strategy tightly matched to emerging conditions. Similarly, if managers are uncertain about the implications of one or more driving forces, or if their views are incomplete or off base, it's difficult for them to craft a strategy that is responsive to the driving forces and their consequences for the industry. So driving-forces analysis is not something to take lightly; it has practical value and is basic to the task of thinking strategically about where the industry is headed and how to prepare for the changes ahead.

> Driving-forces analysis, when done properly, pushes company managers to think about what's around the corner and what the company needs to be doing to get ready for it.

> The real payoff of driving-forces analysis is to help managers understand what strategy changes are needed to prepare for the impacts of the driving forces.

QUESTION 4: WHAT MARKET POSITIONS DO RIVALS OCCUPY—WHO IS STRONGLY POSITIONED AND WHO IS NOT?

Since competing companies commonly sell in different price/quality ranges, emphasize different distribution channels, incorporate product features that appeal to different types of buyers, have different geographic coverage, and so on, it stands to reason that some companies enjoy stronger or more attractive market positions than other companies. Understanding which companies are strongly positioned and which are weakly positioned is an integral part of analyzing an industry's competitive structure. The best technique for revealing the market positions of industry competitors is **strategic group mapping**.[14] This analytical tool is useful for comparing the market positions of each firm separately or for grouping them into like positions when an industry has so many competitors that it is not practical to examine each one in depth.

> **Core Concept**
> **Strategic group mapping** is a technique for displaying the different market or competitive positions that rival firms occupy in the industry.

Using Strategic Group Maps to Assess the Market Positions of Key Competitors

A **strategic group** consists of those industry members with similar competitive approaches and positions in the market.[15] Companies in the same strategic group can resemble one another in any of several ways: They may have comparable product-line breadth, sell in the same price/quality range, emphasize the same distribution channels, use essentially the same product attributes to appeal to similar types of buyers, depend on identical technological approaches, or offer buyers similar services and technical assistance.[16] An industry contains only one strategic group when all sellers pursue essentially identical strategies and have comparable market positions. At the other extreme, an industry may contain as many strategic groups as there are competitors when each rival pursues a distinctively different competitive approach and occupies a substantially different market position.

Core Concept
A **strategic group** is a cluster of industry rivals that have similar competitive approaches and market positions.

The procedure for constructing a *strategic group map* is straightforward:

- Identify the competitive characteristics that differentiate firms in the industry. Typical variables are price/quality range (high, medium, low); geographic coverage (local, regional, national, global); degree of vertical integration (none, partial, full); product-line breadth (wide, narrow); use of distribution channels (one, some, all); and degree of service offered (no-frills, limited, full).
- Plot the firms on a two-variable map using pairs of these differentiating characteristics.
- Assign firms that fall in about the same strategy space to the same strategic group.
- Draw circles around each strategic group, making the circles proportional to the size of the group's share of total industry sales revenues.

This produces a two-dimensional diagram like the one for the retailing industry in Illustration Capsule 3.1.

Several guidelines need to be observed in mapping the positions of strategic groups in the industry's overall strategy space.[17] First, the two variables selected as axes for the map should *not* be highly correlated; if they are, the circles on the map will fall along a diagonal and strategy makers will learn nothing more about the relative positions of competitors than they would by considering just one of the variables. For instance, if companies with broad product lines use multiple distribution channels while companies with narrow lines use a single distribution channel, then looking at broad versus narrow product lines reveals just as much about who is positioned where as looking at single versus multiple distribution channels; that is, one of the variables is redundant. Second, the variables chosen as axes for the map should expose big differences in how rivals position themselves to compete in the marketplace. This, of course, means analysts must identify the characteristics that differentiate rival firms and use these differences as variables for the axes and as the basis for deciding which firm belongs in which strategic group. Third, the variables used as axes don't have to be either quantitative or continuous; rather, they can be discrete variables or defined in terms of distinct classes and combinations. Fourth, drawing the sizes of the circles on the map proportional to the combined sales of the firms in each strategic group allows the map to reflect the relative sizes of each strategic group. Fifth, if more than two good competitive variables can be used as axes for the map, several maps can be drawn to give different exposures to the competitive positioning relationships present

Illustration Capsule 3.1

Comparative Market Positions of Selected Retail Chains: A Strategic Group Map Application

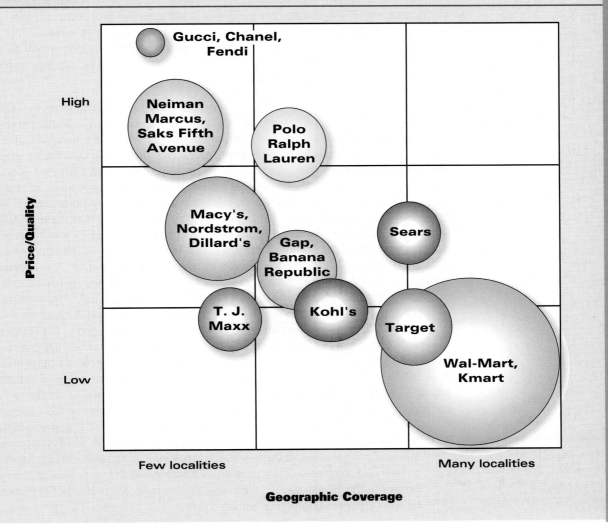

Note: Circles are drawn roughly proportional to the sizes of the chains, based on revenues.

in the industry's structure. Because there is not necessarily one best map for portraying how competing firms are positioned in the market, it is advisable to experiment with different pairs of competitive variables.

What Can Be Learned from Strategic Group Maps?

Strategic group maps are revealing in several respects. The most important has to do with which rivals are similarly positioned and are thus close rivals and which are distant rivals. Generally speaking, *the closer strategic groups are to each other on the*

Strategic group maps reveal which companies are close competitors and which are distant competitors.

map, the stronger the cross-group competitive rivalry tends to be. Although firms in the same strategic group are the closest rivals, the next closest rivals are in the immediately adjacent groups.[18] Often, firms in strategic groups that are far apart on the map hardly compete at all. For instance, Wal-Mart's clientele, merchandise selection, and pricing points are much too different to justify calling them close competitors of Neiman Marcus or Saks Fifth Avenue in retailing. For the same reason, Timex is not a meaningful competitive rival of Rolex, and Subaru is not a close competitor of Lincoln or Mercedes-Benz.

The second thing to be gleaned from strategic group mapping is that *not all positions on the map are equally attractive.* Two reasons account for why some positions can be more attractive than others:

1. *Prevailing competitive pressures and industry driving forces favor some strategic groups and hurt others.*[19] Discerning which strategic groups are advantaged and disadvantaged requires scrutinizing the map in light of what has also been learned from the prior analysis of competitive forces and driving forces. Quite often the strength of competition varies from group to group—there's little reason to believe that all firms in an industry feel the same degrees of competitive pressure, since their strategies and market positions may well differ in important respects. For instance, the competitive battle among Wal-Mart, Target, and Sears/Kmart (Kmart acquired Sears in 2005) is more intense (with consequently smaller profit margins) than the rivalry among Gucci, Chanel, Fendi, and other high-end fashion retailers. Likewise, industry driving forces may be acting to grow the demand for the products of firms in some strategic groups and shrink the demand for the products of firms in other strategic groups—as is the case in the radio broadcasting industry where satellite radio firms like XM and Sirius stand to gain market ground at the expense of commercial-based radio broadcasters due to the impacts of such driving forces as technological advances in satellite broadcasting, growing buyer preferences for more diverse radio programming, and product innovation in satellite radio devices. Firms in strategic groups that are being adversely impacted by intense competitive pressures or driving forces may try to shift to a more favorably situated group. But shifting to a different position on the map can prove difficult when entry barriers for the target strategic group are high. Moreover, attempts to enter a new strategic group nearly always increase competitive pressures in the target strategic group. If certain firms are known to be trying to change their competitive positions on the map, then attaching arrows to the circles showing the targeted direction helps clarify the picture of competitive maneuvering among rivals.

Core Concept
Not all positions on a strategic group map are equally attractive.

2. *The profit potential of different strategic groups varies due to the strengths and weaknesses in each group's market position.* The profit prospects of firms in different strategic groups can vary from good to ho-hum to poor because of differing growth rates for the principal buyer segments served by each group, differing degrees of competitive rivalry within strategic groups, differing degrees of exposure to competition from substitute products outside the industry, and differing degrees of supplier or customer bargaining power from group to group.

Thus, part of strategic group map analysis always entails drawing conclusions about where on the map is the "best" place to be and why. Which companies/strategic groups are destined to prosper because of their positions? Which companies/strategic groups seem destined to struggle because of their positions? What accounts for why some parts of the map are better than others?

QUESTION 5: WHAT STRATEGIC MOVES ARE RIVALS LIKELY TO MAKE NEXT?

Unless a company pays attention to what competitors are doing and knows their strengths and weaknesses, it ends up flying blind into competitive battle. As in sports, scouting the opposition is essential. *Competitive intelligence* about rivals' strategies, their latest actions and announcements, their resource strengths and weaknesses, the efforts being made to improve their situation, and the thinking and leadership styles of their executives is valuable for predicting or anticipating the strategic moves competitors are likely to make next in the marketplace. Having good information to predict the strategic direction and likely moves of key competitors allows a company to prepare defensive countermoves, to craft its own strategic moves with some confidence about what market maneuvers to expect from rivals, and to exploit any openings that arise from competitors' missteps or strategy flaws.

> Good scouting reports on rivals provide a valuable assist in anticipating what moves rivals are likely to make next and outmaneuvering them in the marketplace.

Identifying Competitors' Strategies and Resource Strengths and Weaknesses

Keeping close tabs on a com.petitor's strategy entails monitoring what the rival is doing in the marketplace, what its management is saying in company press releases, information posted on the company's Web site (especially press releases and the presentations management has recently made to securities analysts), and such public documents as annual reports and 10-K filings, articles in the business media, and the reports of securities analysts. (Figure 1.1 in Chapter 1 indicates what to look for in identifying a company's strategy.) Company personnel may be able to pick up useful information from a rival's exhibits at trade shows and from conversations with a rival's customers, suppliers, and former employees.[20] Many companies have a competitive intelligence unit that sifts through the available information to construct up-to-date strategic profiles of rivals—their current strategies, resource strengths and competitive capabilities, competitive shortcomings, press releases, and recent executive pronouncements. Such profiles are typically updated regularly and made available to managers and other key personnel.

Those who gather competitive intelligence on rivals, however, can sometimes cross the fine line between honest inquiry and unethical or even illegal behavior. For example, calling rivals to get information about prices, the dates of new product introductions, or wage and salary levels is legal, but misrepresenting one's company affiliation during such calls is unethical. Pumping rivals' representatives at trade shows is ethical only if one wears a name tag with accurate company affiliation indicated. Avon Products at one point secured information about its biggest rival, Mary Kay Cosmetics (MKC), by having its personnel search through the garbage bins outside MKC's headquarters.[21] When MKC officials learned of the action and sued, Avon claimed it did nothing illegal, since a 1988 Supreme Court case had ruled that trash left on public property (in this case, a sidewalk) was anyone's for the taking. Avon even produced a videotape of its removal of the trash at the MKC site. Avon won the lawsuit—but Avon's action, while legal, scarcely qualifies as ethical.

In sizing up competitors, it makes sense for company strategists to make three assessments:

1. Which competitor has the best strategy? Which competitors appear to have flawed or weak strategies?

2. Which competitors are poised to gain market share, and which ones seem destined to lose ground?

3. Which competitors are likely to rank among the industry leaders five years from now? Do one or more up-and-coming competitors have powerful strategies and sufficient resource capabilities to overtake the current industry leader?

The industry's *current* major players are generally easy to identify, but some of the leaders may be plagued with weaknesses that are causing them to lose ground; other notable rivals may lack the resources and capabilities to remain strong contenders given the superior strategies and capabilities of up-and-coming companies. In evaluating which competitors are favorably or unfavorably positioned to gain market ground, company strategists need to focus on why there is potential for some rivals to do better or worse than other rivals. Usually, a competitor's prospects are a function of whether it is in a strategic group that is being favored or hurt by competitive pressures and driving forces, whether its strategy has resulted in competitive advantage or disadvantage, and whether its resources and capabilities are well suited for competing on the road ahead.

> Today's market leaders don't automatically become tomorrow's.

Predicting Competitors' Next Moves

Predicting the next strategic moves of competitors is the hardest yet most useful part of competitor analysis. Good clues about what actions a specific company is likely to undertake can often be gleaned from how well it is faring in the marketplace, the problems or weaknesses it needs to address, and how much pressure it is under to improve its financial performance. Content rivals are likely to continue their present strategy with only minor fine-tuning. Ailing rivals can be performing so poorly that fresh strategic moves are virtually certain. Ambitious rivals looking to move up in the industry ranks are strong candidates for launching new strategic offensives to pursue emerging market opportunities and exploit the vulnerabilities of weaker rivals.

Since the moves a competitor is likely to make are generally predicated on the views their executives have about the industry's future and their beliefs about their firm's situation, it makes sense to closely scrutinize the public pronouncements of rival company executives about where the industry is headed and what it will take to be successful, what they are saying about their firm's situation, information from the grapevine about what they are doing, and their past actions and leadership styles. Other considerations in trying to predict what strategic moves rivals are likely to make next include the following:

- Which rivals badly need to increase their unit sales and market share? What strategic options are they most likely to pursue: lowering prices, adding new models and styles, expanding their dealer networks, entering additional geographic markets, boosting advertising to build better brand-name awareness, acquiring a weaker competitor, or placing more emphasis on direct sales via their Web site?

- Which rivals have a strong incentive, along with the resources, to make major strategic changes, perhaps moving to a different position on the strategic group map? Which rivals are probably locked in to pursuing the same basic strategy with only minor adjustments?

- Which rivals are good candidates to be acquired? Which rivals may be looking to make an acquisition and are financially able to do so?

- Which rivals are likely to enter new geographic markets?
- Which rivals are strong candidates to expand their product offerings and enter new product segments where they do not currently have a presence?

To succeed in predicting a competitor's next moves, company strategists need to have a good feel for each rival's situation, how its managers think, and what the rival's best strategic options are. Doing the necessary detective work can be tedious and time-consuming, but scouting competitors well enough to anticipate their next moves allows managers to prepare effective countermoves (perhaps even beat a rival to the punch) and to take rivals' probable actions into account in crafting their own best course of action.

> Managers who fail to study competitors closely risk being caught napping when rivals make fresh and perhaps bold strategic moves.

QUESTION 6: WHAT ARE THE KEY FACTORS FOR FUTURE COMPETITIVE SUCCESS?

An industry's **key success factors (KSFs)** are those competitive factors that most affect industry members' ability to prosper in the marketplace—the particular strategy elements, product attributes, resources, competencies, competitive capabilities, and market achievements that spell the difference between being a strong competitor and a weak competitor—and sometimes between profit and loss. KSFs by their very nature are so important to future competitive success that *all firms* in the industry must pay close attention to them or risk becoming an industry also-ran. To indicate the significance of KSFs another way, how well a company's product offering, resources, and capabilities measure up against an industry's KSFs determines just how financially and competitively successful that company will be. Identifying KSFs, in light of the prevailing and anticipated industry and competitive conditions, is therefore always a top-priority analytical and strategy-making consideration. Company strategists need to understand the industry landscape well enough to separate the factors most important to competitive success from those that are less important.

> **Core Concept**
> **Key success factors** are the product attributes, competencies, competitive capabilities, and market achievements with the greatest impact on future competitive success in the marketplace.

In the beer industry, the KSFs are full utilization of brewing capacity (to keep manufacturing costs low), a strong network of wholesale distributors (to get the company's brand stocked and favorably displayed in retail outlets where beer is sold), and clever advertising (to induce beer drinkers to buy the company's brand and thereby pull beer sales through the established wholesale/retail channels). In apparel manufacturing, the KSFs are appealing designs and color combinations (to create buyer interest) and low-cost manufacturing efficiency (to permit attractive retail pricing and ample profit margins). In tin and aluminum cans, because the cost of shipping empty cans is substantial, one of the keys is having can-manufacturing facilities located close to end-use customers. Key success factors thus vary from industry to industry, and even from time to time within the same industry, as driving forces and competitive conditions change. Table 3.3 lists the most common types of industry key success factors.

An industry's key success factors can usually be deduced from what was learned from the previously described analysis of the industry and competitive environment. Which factors are most important to future competitive success flow directly from the industry's dominant characteristics, what competition is like, the impacts of the driving forces, the comparative market positions of industry members, and the likely

Table 3.3   **Common Types of Industry Key Success Factors**

Technology-related KSFs	• Expertise in a particular technology or in scientific research (important in pharmaceuticals, Internet applications, mobile communications, and most high-tech industries) • Proven ability to improve production processes (important in industries where advancing technology opens the way for higher manufacturing efficiency and lower production costs)
Manufacturing-related KSFs	• Ability to achieve scale economies and/or capture learning/experience curve effects (important to achieving low production costs) • Quality control know-how (important in industries where customers insist on product reliability) • High utilization of fixed assets (important in capital-intensive, high-fixed-cost industries) • Access to attractive supplies of skilled labor • High labor productivity (important for items with high labor content) • Low-cost product design and engineering (reduces manufacturing costs) • Ability to manufacture or assemble products that are customized to buyer specifications
Distribution-related KSFs	• A strong network of wholesale distributors/dealers • Strong direct sales capabilities via the Internet and/or having company-owned retail outlets • Ability to secure favorable display space on retailer shelves
Marketing-related KSFs	• Breadth of product line and product selection • A well-known and well-respected brand name • Fast, accurate technical assistance • Courteous, personalized customer service • Accurate filling of buyer orders (few back orders or mistakes) • Customer guarantees and warranties (important in mail-order and online retailing, big-ticket purchases, new product introductions) • Clever advertising
Skills and capability-related KSFs	• A talented workforce (important in professional services like accounting and investment banking) • National or global distribution capabilities • Product innovation capabilities (important in industries where rivals are racing to be first-to-market with new product attributes or performance features) • Design expertise (important in fashion and apparel industries) • Short delivery time capability • Supply chain management capabilities • Strong e-commerce capabilities—a user-friendly Web site and/or skills in using Internet technology applications to streamline internal operations
Other types of KSFs	• Overall low costs (not just in manufacturing) so as to be able to meet customer expectations of low price • Convenient locations (important in many retailing businesses) • Ability to provide fast, convenient after-the-sale repairs and service • A strong balance sheet and access to financial capital (important in newly emerging industries with high degrees of business risk and in capital-intensive industries) • Patent protection

next moves of key rivals. In addition, the answers to three questions help identify an industry's key success factors:

1. On what basis do buyers of the industry's product choose between the competing brands of sellers? That is, what product attributes are crucial?
2. Given the nature of competitive rivalry and the competitive forces prevailing in the marketplace, what resources and competitive capabilities does a company need to have to be competitively successful?
3. What shortcomings are almost certain to put a company at a significant competitive disadvantage?

Only rarely are there more than five or six key factors for future competitive success. And even among these, two or three usually outrank the others in importance. Managers should therefore bear in mind the purpose of identifying key success factors— to determine which factors are most important to future competitive success— and resist the temptation to label a factor that has only minor importance a KSF. To compile a list of every factor that matters even a little bit defeats the purpose of concentrating management attention on the factors truly critical to long-term competitive success.

Correctly diagnosing an industry's KSFs raises a company's chances of crafting a sound strategy. The goal of company strategists should be to design a strategy aimed at stacking up well on all of the industry's future KSFs and trying to be *distinctively better* than rivals on one (or possibly two) of the KSFs. Indeed, companies that stand out or excel on a particular KSF are likely to enjoy a stronger market position—*being distinctively better than rivals on one or two key success factors tends to translate into competitive advantage.* Hence, using the industry's KSFs as *cornerstones* for the company's strategy and trying to gain sustainable competitive advantage by excelling at one particular KSF is a fruitful competitive strategy approach.[22]

Core Concept
A sound strategy incorporates the intent to stack up well on all of the industry's key success factors and to excel on one or two KSFs.

QUESTION 7: DOES THE OUTLOOK FOR THE INDUSTRY PRESENT THE COMPANY WITH AN ATTRACTIVE OPPORTUNITY?

The final step in evaluating the industry and competitive environment is to use the preceding analysis to decide whether the outlook for the industry presents the company with a sufficiently attractive business opportunity. The important factors on which to base such a conclusion include:

- The industry's growth potential.
- Whether powerful competitive forces are squeezing industry profitability to subpar levels and whether competition appears destined to grow stronger or weaker.
- Whether industry profitability will be favorably or unfavorably affected by the prevailing driving forces.
- The degrees of risk and uncertainty in the industry's future.
- Whether the industry as a whole confronts severe problems—regulatory or environmental issues, stagnating buyer demand, industry overcapacity, mounting competition, and so on.

- The company's competitive position in the industry vis-à-vis rivals. (Being a well-entrenched leader or strongly positioned contender in a lackluster industry may present adequate opportunity for good profitability; however, having to fight a steep uphill battle against much stronger rivals may hold little promise of eventual market success or good return on shareholder investment, even though the industry environment is attractive.)

- The company's potential to capitalize on the vulnerabilities of weaker rivals, perhaps converting a relatively unattractive *industry* situation into a potentially rewarding *company* opportunity.

- Whether the company has sufficient competitive strength to defend against or counteract the factors that make the industry unattractive.

- Whether continued participation in this industry adds importantly to the firm's ability to be successful in other industries in which it may have business interests.

Core Concept

The degree to which an industry is attractive or unattractive is not the same for all industry participants and all potential entrants; the attractiveness of the opportunities an industry presents depends heavily on whether a company has the resource strengths and competitive capabilities to capture them.

As a general proposition, *if an industry's overall profit prospects are above average, the industry environment is basically attractive; if industry profit prospects are below average, conditions are unattractive.* However, it is a mistake to think of a particular industry as being equally attractive or unattractive to all industry participants and all potential entrants. Attractiveness is relative, not absolute, and conclusions one way or the other have to be drawn from the perspective of a particular company. Industries attractive to insiders may be unattractive to outsiders. Companies on the outside may look at an industry's environment and conclude that it is an unattractive business for them to get into, given the prevailing entry barriers, the difficulty of challenging current market leaders with their particular resources and competencies, and the opportunities they have elsewhere. Industry environments unattractive to weak competitors may be attractive to strong competitors. A favorably positioned company may survey a business environment and see a host of opportunities that weak competitors cannot capture.

When a company decides an industry is fundamentally attractive and presents good opportunities, a strong case can be made that it should invest aggressively to capture the opportunities it sees and to improve its long-term competitive position in the business. When a strong competitor concludes an industry is relatively unattractive and lacking in opportunity, it may elect to simply protect its present position, investing cautiously if at all and looking for opportunities in other industries. A competitively weak company in an unattractive industry may see its best option as finding a buyer, perhaps a rival, to acquire its business.

Key Points

Thinking strategically about a company's external situation involves probing for answers to the following seven questions:

1. *What are the industry's dominant economic features?* Industries differ significantly on such factors as market size and growth rate, the number and relative sizes of both buyers and sellers, the geographic scope of competitive rivalry, the degree of product differentiation, the speed of product innovation, demand–supply conditions, the extent of vertical integration, and the extent of scale economies and learning-curve effects. In addition to setting the stage for the analysis to come,

identifying an industry's economic features also promotes understanding of the kinds of strategic moves that industry members are likely to employ.

2. *What kinds of competitive forces are industry members facing, and how strong is each force?* The strength of competition is a composite of five forces: (1) competitive pressures stemming from the competitive jockeying and market maneuvering among industry rivals, (2) competitive pressures associated with the market inroads being made by the sellers of substitutes, (3) competitive pressures associated with the threat of new entrants into the market, (4) competitive pressures stemming from supplier bargaining power and supplier–seller collaboration, and (5) competitive pressures stemming from buyer bargaining power and seller–buyer collaboration. The nature and strength of the competitive pressures associated with these five forces have to be examined force by force to identify the specific competitive pressures they each comprise and to decide whether these pressures constitute a strong or weak competitive force. The next step in competition analysis is to evaluate the collective strength of the five forces and determine whether the state of competition is conducive to good profitability. Working through the five-forces model step by step not only aids strategy makers in assessing whether the intensity of competition allows good profitability but also promotes sound strategic thinking about how to better match company strategy to the specific competitive character of the marketplace. Effectively matching a company's strategy to the particular competitive pressures and competitive conditions that exist has two aspects: (1) pursuing avenues that shield the firm from as many of the prevailing competitive pressures as possible, and (2) initiating actions calculated to produce sustainable competitive advantage, thereby shifting competition in the company's favor, putting added competitive pressure on rivals, and perhaps even defining the business model for the industry.

3. *What factors are driving industry change and what impact will they have on competitive intensity and industry profitability?* Industry and competitive conditions change because forces are in motion that create incentives or pressures for change. The first phase is to identify the forces that are driving change in the industry; the most common driving forces include the Internet and Internet technology applications, globalization of competition in the industry, changes in the long-term industry growth rate, changes in buyer composition, product innovation, entry or exit of major firms, changes in cost and efficiency, changing buyer preferences for standardized versus differentiated products or services, regulatory influences and government policy changes, changing societal and lifestyle factors, and reductions in uncertainty and business risk. The second phase of driving-forces analysis is to determine whether the driving forces, taken together, are acting to make the industry environment more or less attractive. Are the driving forces causing demand for the industry's product to increase or decrease? Are the driving forces acting to make competition more or less intense? Will the driving forces lead to higher or lower industry profitability?

4. *What market positions do industry rivals occupy—who is strongly positioned and who is not?* Strategic group mapping is a valuable tool for understanding the similarities, differences, strengths, and weaknesses inherent in the market positions of rival companies. Rivals in the same or nearby strategic groups are close competitors, whereas companies in distant strategic groups usually pose little or no immediate threat. The lesson of strategic group mapping is that some positions on the map are more favorable than others. The profit potential of different strategic groups varies due to strengths and weaknesses in each group's market

position. Often, industry driving forces and competitive pressures favor some strategic groups and hurt others.

5. *What strategic moves are rivals likely to make next?* This analytical step involves identifying competitors' strategies, deciding which rivals are likely to be strong contenders and which are likely to be weak, evaluating rivals' competitive options, and predicting their next moves. Scouting competitors well enough to anticipate their actions can help a company prepare effective countermoves (perhaps even beating a rival to the punch) and allows managers to take rivals' probable actions into account in designing their own company's best course of action. Managers who fail to study competitors risk being caught unprepared by the strategic moves of rivals.

6. *What are the key factors for future competitive success?* An industry's key success factors (KSFs) are the particular strategy elements, product attributes, competitive capabilities, and business outcomes that spell the difference between being a strong competitor and a weak competitor—and sometimes between profit and loss. KSFs by their very nature are so important to competitive success that *all firms* in the industry must pay close attention to them or risk becoming an industry also-ran. Correctly diagnosing an industry's KSFs raises a company's chances of crafting a sound strategy. The goal of company strategists should be to design a strategy aimed at stacking up well on all of the industry KSFs and trying to be *distinctively better* than rivals on one (or possibly two) of the KSFs. Indeed, using the industry's KSFs as *cornerstones* for the company's strategy and trying to gain sustainable competitive advantage by excelling at one particular KSF is a fruitful competitive strategy approach.

7. *Does the outlook for the industry present the company with sufficiently attractive prospects for profitability?* If an industry's overall profit prospects are above average, the industry environment is basically attractive; if industry profit prospects are below average, conditions are unattractive. Conclusions regarding industry attractive are a major driver of company strategy. When a company decides an industry is fundamentally attractive and presents good opportunities, a strong case can be made that it should invest aggressively to capture the opportunities it sees and to improve its long-term competitive position in the business. When a strong competitor concludes an industry is relatively unattractive and lacking in opportunity, it may elect to simply protect its present position, investing cautiously if at all and looking for opportunities in other industries. A competitively weak company in an unattractive industry may see its best option as finding a buyer, perhaps a rival, to acquire its business. On occasion, an industry that is unattractive overall is still very attractive to a favorably situated company with the skills and resources to take business away from weaker rivals.

A competently conducted industry and competitive analysis generally tells a clear, easily understood story about the company's external environment. Different analysts can have varying judgments about competitive intensity, the impacts of driving forces, how industry conditions will evolve, how good the outlook is for industry profitability, and the degree to which the industry environment offers the company an attractive business opportunity. However, while no method can guarantee that all analysts will come to identical conclusions about the state of industry and competitive conditions and an industry's future outlook, this doesn't justify shortcutting hardnosed strategic analysis and relying instead on opinion and casual observation. Managers become better strategists when they know what questions to pose and what tools to use. This is why this chapter has concentrated on suggesting the right questions to ask, explaining concepts and analytical approaches, and indicating the kinds of things to look for. There's no substitute for doing cutting edge strategic thinking about a company's external situation—anything less weakens managers' ability to craft strategies that are well matched to industry and competitive conditions.

Exercises

1. As the owner of a fast-food enterprise seeking a loan from a bank to finance the construction and operation of three new store locations, you have been asked to provide the loan officer with a brief analysis of the competitive environment in fast food. Draw a five-forces diagram for the fast-food industry, and briefly discuss the nature and strength of each of the five competitive forces in fast food. Do whatever Internet research is required to expand your understanding of competition in the fast-food industry and do a competent five-forces analysis.

2. Based on the strategic group map in Illustration Capsule 3.1: Who are Polo Ralph Lauren's closest competitors? Between which two strategic groups is competition the strongest? Why do you think no retailers are positioned in the upper right-hand corner of the map? Which company/strategic group faces the weakest competition from the members of other strategic groups?

3. With regard to the ice cream industry, which of the following factors might qualify as possible driving forces capable of causing fundamental change in the industry's structure and competitive environment?

    a. Increasing sales of frozen yogurt and frozen sorbets.

    b. The potential for additional makers of ice cream to enter the market.

    c. Growing consumer interest in low-calorie/low-fat/low-carb/sugar-free dessert alternatives.

    d. A slowdown in consumer purchases of ice cream products.

    e. Rising prices for milk, sugar, and other ice cream ingredients.

    f. A decision by Häagen-Dazs to increase its prices by 10 percent.

    g. A decision by Ben & Jerry's to add five new flavors to its product line.

chapter four

Evaluating a Company's Resources and Competitive Position

Before executives can chart a new strategy, they must reach common understanding of the company's current position.

**—W. Chan Kim and
Rene Mauborgne**

The real question isn't how well you're doing today against your own history, but how you're doing against your competitors.

—Donald Kress

Organizations succeed in a competitive marketplace over the long run because they can do certain things their customers value better than can their competitors.

—Robert Hayes, Gary Pisano, and David Upton

Only firms who are able to continually build new strategic assets faster and cheaper than their competitors will earn superior returns over the long term.

**—C. C. Markides and
P. J. Williamson**

In Chapter 3 we described how to use the tools of industry and competitive analysis to assess a company's external environment and lay the groundwork for matching a company's strategy to its external situation. In this chapter we discuss the techniques of evaluating a company's resource capabilities, relative cost position, and competitive strength vis-á-vis its rivals. The analytical spotlight will be trained on five questions:

1. How well is the company's present strategy working?

2. What are the company's resource strengths and weaknesses, and its external opportunities and threats?

3. Are the company's prices and costs competitive?

4. Is the company competitively stronger or weaker than key rivals?

5. What strategic issues and problems merit front-burner managerial attention?

We will describe four analytical tools that should be used to probe for answers to these questions—SWOT analysis, value chain analysis, benchmarking, and competitive strength assessment. All four are valuable techniques for revealing a company's competitiveness and for helping company managers match their strategy to the company's own particular circumstances.

QUESTION 1: HOW WELL IS THE COMPANY'S PRESENT STRATEGY WORKING?

In evaluating how well a company's present strategy is working, a manager has to start with what the strategy is. Figure 4.1 shows the key components of a single-business company's strategy. The first thing to pin down is the company's competitive approach. Is the company striving to be a low-cost leader *or* stressing ways to differentiate its product offering from rivals? Is it concentrating its efforts on serving a broad spectrum of customers *or* a narrow market niche? Another strategy-defining consideration is the firm's competitive scope within the industry—what its geographic market coverage is and whether it operates in just a single stage of the industry's production/distribution chain or is vertically integrated across several stages. Another good indication of the company's strategy is whether the company has made moves recently to improve its competitive position and performance—for instance, by cutting prices, improving design, stepping up advertising, entering a new geographic market (domestic or foreign),

Figure 4.1   **Identifying the Components of a Single-Business Company's Strategy**

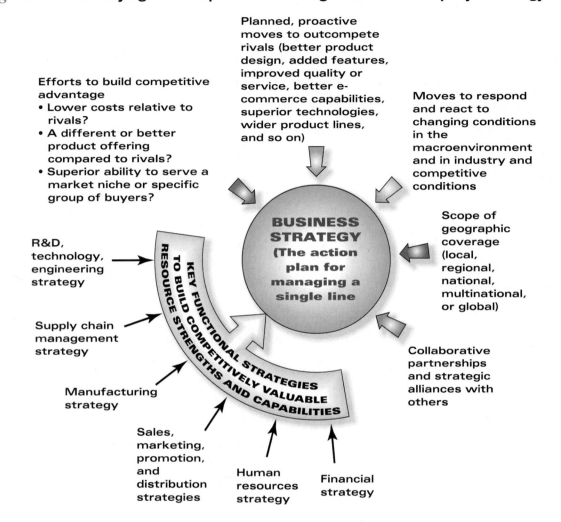

or merging with a competitor. The company's functional strategies in R&D, production, marketing, finance, human resources, information technology, and so on further characterize company strategy.

While there's merit in evaluating the strategy from a *qualitative* standpoint (its completeness, internal consistency, rationale, and relevance), the best *quantitative* evidence of how well a company's strategy is working comes from its results. The two best empirical indicators are (1) whether the company is achieving its stated financial and strategic objectives, and (2) whether the company is an above-average industry performer. Persistent shortfalls in meeting company performance targets and weak performance relative to rivals are reliable warning signs that the company suffers from poor strategy making, less-than-competent strategy execution, or both. Other indicators of how well a company's strategy is working include:

- Whether the firm's sales are growing faster, slower, or about the same pace as the market as a whole, thus resulting in a rising, eroding, or stable market share.

- Whether the company is acquiring new customers at an attractive rate as well as retaining existing customers.
- Whether the firm's profit margins are increasing or decreasing and how well its margins compare to rival firms' margins.
- Trends in the firm's net profits and return on investment and how these compare to the same trends for other companies in the industry.
- Whether the company's overall financial strength and credit rating are improving or on the decline.
- Whether the company can demonstrate continuous improvement in such internal performance measures as days of inventory, employee productivity, unit cost, defect rate, scrap rate, misfilled orders, delivery times, warranty costs, and so on.
- How shareholders view the company based on trends in the company's stock price and shareholder value (relative to the stock price trends at other companies in the industry).
- The firm's image and reputation with its customers.
- How well the company stacks up against rivals on technology, product innovation, customer service, product quality, delivery time, price, getting newly developed products to market quickly, and other relevant factors on which buyers base their choice of brands.

The stronger a company's current overall performance, the less likely the need for radical changes in strategy. The weaker a company's financial performance and market standing, the more its current strategy must be questioned. Weak performance is almost always a sign of weak strategy, weak execution, or both.

> The stronger a company's financial performance and market position, the more likely it has a well-conceived, well-executed strategy.

Table 4.1 provides a compilation of the financial ratios most commonly used to evaluate a company's financial performance and balance sheet strength.

QUESTION 2: WHAT ARE THE COMPANY'S RESOURCE STRENGTHS AND WEAKNESSES AND ITS EXTERNAL OPPORTUNITIES AND THREATS?

Appraising a company's resource strengths and weaknesses and its external opportunities and threats, commonly known as **SWOT analysis,** provides a good overview of whether the company's overall situation is fundamentally healthy or unhealthy. Just as important, a first-rate SWOT analysis provides the basis for crafting a strategy that capitalizes on the company's resources, aims squarely at capturing the company's best opportunities, and defends against the threats to its well-being.

> **Core Concept**
> **SWOT analysis** is a simple but powerful tool for sizing up a company's resource capabilities and deficiencies, its market opportunities, and the external threats to its future well-being.

Identifying Company Resource Strengths and Competitive Capabilities

A *resource strength* is something a company is good at doing or an attribute that enhances its competitiveness in the marketplace. Resource strengths can take any of several forms:

Table 4.1   **Key Financial Ratios: How to Calculate Them and What They Mean**

Ratio	How Calculated	What It Shows
Profitability ratios		
1. Gross profit margin	$\dfrac{\text{Sales} - \text{cost of goods sold}}{\text{Sales}}$	Shows the percentage of revenues available to cover operating expenses and yield a profit. Higher is better, and the trend should be upward.
2. Operating profit margin (or return on sales)	$\dfrac{\text{Sales} - \text{Operating expenses}}{\text{Sales}}$ or $\dfrac{\text{Operating income}}{\text{Sales}}$	Shows the profitability of current operations without regard to interest charges and income taxes. Higher is better, and the trend should be upward.
3. Net profit margin (or net return on sales)	$\dfrac{\text{Profits after taxes}}{\text{Sales}}$	Shows after-tax profits per dollar of sales. Higher is better, and the trend should be upward.
4. Return on total assets	$\dfrac{\text{Profits after taxes} + \text{Interest}}{\text{Total assets}}$	A measure of the return on total investment in the enterprise. Interest is added to after-tax profits to form the numerator since total assets are financed by creditors as well as by stockholders. Higher is better, and the trend should be upward.
5. Return on stockholders' equity	$\dfrac{\text{Profits after taxes}}{\text{Total stockholders' equity}}$	Shows the return stockholders are earning on their investment in the enterprise. A return in the 12–15 percent range is average, and the trend should be upward.
6. Earnings per share	$\dfrac{\text{Profits after taxes}}{\text{Number of shares of common stock outstanding}}$	Shows the earnings for each share of common stock outstanding. The trend should be upward, and the bigger the annual percentage gains, the better.
Liquidity ratios		
1. Current ratio	$\dfrac{\text{Current assets}}{\text{Current liabilities}}$	Shows a firm's ability to pay current liabilities using assets that can be converted to cash in the near term. Ratio should definitely be higher than 1.0; ratios of 2 or higher are better still.
2. Quick ratio (or acid-test ratio)	$\dfrac{\text{Current assets} - \text{Inventory}}{\text{Current liabilities}}$	Shows a firm's ability to pay current liabilities without relying on the sale of its inventories.
3. Working capital	Current assets − Current liabilities	Bigger amounts are better because the company has more internal funds available to (1) pay its current liabilities on a timely basis and (2) finance inventory expansion, additional accounts receivable, and a larger base of operations without resorting to borrowing or raising more equity capital.
Leverage ratios		
1. Debt-to-assets ratio	$\dfrac{\text{Total debt}}{\text{Total assets}}$	Measures the extent to which borrowed funds have been used to finance the firm's operations. Low fractions or ratios are better—high fractions indicate overuse of debt and greater risk of bankruptcy.

(Continued)

Table 4.1   **Continued**

Ratio	How Calculated	What It Shows
2. Debt-to-equity ratio	$\dfrac{\text{Total debt}}{\text{Total stockholders' equity}}$	Should usually be less than 1.0. High ratios (especially above 1.0) signal excessive debt, lower creditworthiness, and weaker balance sheet strength.
3. Long-term debt-to-equity ratio	$\dfrac{\text{Long-term debt}}{\text{Total stockholders' equity}}$	Shows the balance between debt and equity in the firm's *long-term* capital structure. Low ratios indicate greater capacity to borrow additional funds if needed.
4. Times-interest-earned (or coverage) ratio	$\dfrac{\text{Operating income}}{\text{Interest expenses}}$	Measures the ability to pay annual interest charges. Lenders usually insist on a minimum ratio of 2.0, but ratios above 3.0 signal better creditworthiness.
Activity ratios		
1. Days of inventory	$\dfrac{\text{Inventory}}{\text{Cost of goods sold} \div 365}$	Measures inventory management efficiency. Fewer days of inventory are usually better.
2. Inventory turnover	$\dfrac{\text{Cost of goods sold}}{\text{Inventory}}$	Measures the number of inventory turns per year. Higher is better.
3. Average collection period	$\dfrac{\text{Accounts receivable}}{\text{Total sales} \div 365}$ or $\dfrac{\text{Accounts receivable}}{\text{Average daily sales}}$	Indicates the average length of time the firm must wait after making a sale to receive cash payment. A shorter collection time is better.
Other important measures of financial performance		
1. Dividend yield on common stock	$\dfrac{\text{Annual dividends per share}}{\text{Current market price per share}}$	A measure of the return that shareholders receive in the form of dividends. A "typical" dividend yield in 2–3%. The dividend yield for fast-growth companies in often below 1% (may be even 0); the dividend yield for slow-growth companies can run 4–5%.
2. Price/earnings ratio	$\dfrac{\text{Current market price per share}}{\text{Earnings per share}}$	P/E ratios above 20 indicate strong investor confidence in a firm's outlook and earnings growth; firms whose future earnings are at risk or likely to grow slowly typically have ratios below 12.
3. Dividend payout ratio	$\dfrac{\text{Annual dividends per share}}{\text{Earnings per share}}$	Indicates the percentage of after-tax profits paid out as dividends.
4. Internal cash flow	After tax profits + Depreciation	A quick and rough estimate of the cash a company's business is generating after payment of operating expenses, interest, and taxes. Such amounts can be used for dividend payments or funding capital expenditures.

- *A skill, specialized expertise, or competitively important capability*—skills in low-cost operations, technological expertise, expertise in defect-free manufacture, proven capabilities in developing and introducing innovative products, cutting-edge supply chain management capabilities, expertise in getting new products to market quickly, strong e-commerce expertise, expertise in providing consistently good customer service, excellent mass merchandising skills, or unique advertising and promotional talents.

- *Valuable physical assets*—state-of-the-art plants and equipment, attractive real estate locations, worldwide distribution facilities, or ownership of valuable natural resource deposits.

- *Valuable human assets and intellectual capital*—an experienced and capable workforce, talented employees in key areas, cutting-edge knowledge in technology or other important areas of the business, collective learning embedded in the organization and built up over time, or proven managerial know-how.[1]

- *Valuable organizational assets*—proven quality control systems, proprietary technology, key patents, state-of-the-art systems for doing business via the Internet, ownership of important natural resources, a cadre of highly trained customer service representatives, a strong network of distributors or retail dealers, sizable amounts of cash and marketable securities, a strong balance sheet and credit rating (thus giving the company access to additional financial capital), or a comprehensive list of customers' e-mail addresses.

- *Valuable intangible assets*—a powerful or well-known brand name, a reputation for technological leadership, or strong buyer loyalty and goodwill.

- *An achievement or attribute that puts the company in a position of market advantage*—low overall costs relative to competitors, market share leadership, a superior product, a wider product line than rivals, wide geographic coverage, or award-winning customer service.

- *Competitively valuable alliances or cooperative ventures*—fruitful partnerships with suppliers that reduce costs and/or enhance product quality and performance; alliances or joint ventures that provide access to valuable technologies, specialized know-how, or geographic markets.

Core Concept
A company's resource strengths represent *competitive assets* and are big determinants of its competitiveness and ability to succeed in the marketplace.

A company's resource strengths represent its endowment of *competitive assets.* The caliber of a firm's resource strengths is a big determinant of its competitiveness—whether it has the wherewithal to be a strong competitor in the marketplace or whether its capabilities and competitive strengths are modest, thus relegating it to a trailing position in the industry.[2] Plainly, a company's resource strengths may or may not enable it to improve its competitive position and financial performance.

Assessing a Company's Competencies and Capabilities—What Activities Does It Perform Well?   One of the most important aspects of appraising a company's resource strengths has to do with its competence level in performing key pieces of its business—such as supply chain management, research and development (R&D), production, distribution, sales and marketing, and customer service. Which activities does it perform especially well? And are there any activities it performs better than rivals? A company's proficiency in conducting different facets of its operations can range from merely a competence in performing an activity to a core competence to a distinctive competence:

1.   A **competence** is something an organization is good at doing. It is nearly always the product of experience, representing an accumulation of learning and the buildup

of proficiency in performing an internal activity. Usually a company competence originates with deliberate efforts to develop the organizational ability to do something, however imperfectly or inefficiently. Such efforts involve selecting people with the requisite knowledge and skills, upgrading or expanding individual abilities as needed, and then molding the efforts and work products of individuals into a cooperative group effort to create organizational ability. Then, as experience builds, such that the company gains proficiency in performing the activity consistently well and at an acceptable cost, the ability evolves into a true competence and company capability. Some competencies relate to fairly specific skills and expertise (like just-in-time inventory control or low-cost manufacturing efficiency or picking locations for new stores or designing an unusually appealing and user-friendly Web site); they spring from proficiency in a single discipline or function and may be performed in a single department or organizational unit. Other competencies, however, are inherently multidisciplinary and cross-functional—they are the result of effective collaboration among people with different expertise working in different organizational units. A competence in continuous product innovation, for example, comes from teaming the efforts of people and groups with expertise in market research, new product R&D, design and engineering, cost-effective manufacturing, and market testing.

> **Core Concept**
> A **competence** is an activity that a company has learned to perform well.

2. A **core competence** is a proficiently performed internal activity that is *central* to a company's strategy and competitiveness. A core competence is a more valuable resource strength than a competence because of the well-performed activity's core role in the company's strategy and the contribution it makes to the company's success in the marketplace. A core competence can relate to any of several aspects of a company's business: expertise in integrating multiple technologies to create families of new products, know-how in creating and operating systems for cost-efficient supply chain management, the capability to speed new or next-generation products to market, good after-sale service capabilities, skills in manufacturing a high-quality product at a low cost, or the capability to fill customer orders accurately and swiftly. A company may have more than one core competence in its resource portfolio, but rare is the company that can legitimately claim more than two or three core competencies. Most often, *a core competence is knowledge-based, residing in people and in a company's intellectual capital and not in its assets on the balance sheet.* Moreover, a core competence is more likely to be grounded in cross-department combinations of knowledge and expertise rather than being the product of a single department or work group. 3M Corporation has a core competence in product innovation—its record of introducing new products goes back several decades and new product introduction is central to 3M's strategy of growing its business. Ben & Jerry's Homemade, a subsidiary of Unilever, has a core competence in creating unusual flavors of ice cream and marketing them with catchy names like Chunky Monkey, Wavy Gravy, Chubby Hubby, The Gobfather, Dublin Mudslide, and Marsha Marsha Marshmallow.

> **Core Concept**
> A **core competence** is a *competitively important* activity that a company performs better than other internal activities.

3. A **distinctive competence** is a competitively valuable activity that a company *performs better than its rivals.* A distinctive competence thus signifies even greater proficiency than a core competence. But what is especially important about a distinctive competence is that the company enjoys *competitive superiority*

Core Concept

A **distinctive competence** is a competitively important activity that a company performs better than its rivals—it thus represents *a competitively superior resource strength*.

in performing that activity—a distinctive competence represents a level of proficiency that rivals do not have. Because a distinctive competence represents uniquely strong capability relative to rival companies, it qualifies as a *competitively superior resource strength* with competitive advantage potential. This is particularly true when the distinctive competence enables a company to deliver standout value to customers (in the form of lower costs and prices or better product performance or superior service). Toyota has worked diligently over several decades to establish a distinctive competence in low-cost, high-quality manufacturing of motor vehicles; its "lean production" system is far superior to that of any other automaker's, and the company is pushing the boundaries of its production advantage with a new type of assembly line—called the Global Body line—that costs 50 percent less to install and can be changed to accommodate a new model for 70 percent less than its previous production system.[3] Starbucks' distinctive competence in innovative coffee drinks and store ambience has propelled it to the forefront among coffee retailers.

The conceptual differences between a competence, a core competence, and a distinctive competence draw attention to the fact that a company's resource strengths and competitive capabilities are not all equal.[4] Some competencies and competitive capabilities merely enable market survival because most rivals have them—indeed, not having a competence or capability that rivals have can result in competitive disadvantage. If an apparel company does not have the competence to produce its apparel items cost-efficiently, it is unlikely to survive given the intensely price-competitive nature of the apparel industry. Every Web retailer requires a basic competence in designing an appealing and user-friendly Web site.

Core competencies are *competitively* more important resource strengths than competencies because they add power to the company's strategy and have a bigger positive impact on its market position and profitability. Distinctive competencies are even more competitively important. A distinctive competence is a competitively potent resource strength for three reasons: (1) it gives a company competitively valuable capability that is unmatched by rivals, (2) it has potential for being the cornerstone of the company's strategy, and (3) it can produce a competitive edge in the marketplace since it represents a level of proficiency that is superior to rivals. It is always easier for a company to build competitive advantage when it has a distinctive competence in performing an activity important to market success, when rival companies do not have offsetting competencies, and when it is costly and time-consuming for rivals to imitate the competence. A distinctive competence is thus potentially the mainspring of a company's success—unless it is trumped by more powerful resources possessed by rivals.

Core Concept

A distinctive competence is a competitively potent resource strength for three reasons: (1) it gives a company competitively valuable capability that is unmatched by rivals, (2) it can underpin and add real punch to a company's strategy, and (3) it is a basis for sustainable competitive advantage.

What Is the Competitive Power of a Resource Strength?

It is not enough to simply compile a list of a company's resource strengths and competitive capabilities. What is most telling about a company's resource strengths, individually and collectively, is how powerful they are in the marketplace. The competitive power of a resource strength is measured by how many of the following four tests it can pass:[5]

1.   *Is the resource strength hard to copy?* The more difficult and more expensive it is to imitate a company's resource strength, the greater its potential competitive

value. Resources tend to be difficult to copy when they are unique (a fantastic real estate location, patent protection), when they must be built over time in ways that are difficult to imitate (a brand name, mastery of a technology), and when they carry big capital requirements (a cost-effective plant to manufacture cutting-edge microprocessors). Wal-Mart's competitors have failed miserably in their attempts over the past two decades to match Wal-Mart's super-efficient state-of-the-art distribution capabilities. Hard-to-copy strengths and capabilities are valuable competitive assets, adding to a company's market strength and contributing to sustained profitability.

2. *Is the resource strength durable—does it have staying power?* The longer the competitive value of a resource lasts, the greater its value. Some resources lose their clout in the marketplace quickly because of the rapid speeds at which technologies or industry conditions are moving. The value of Eastman Kodak's resources in film and film processing is rapidly being undercut by the growing popularity of digital cameras. The investments that commercial banks have made in branch offices is a rapidly depreciating asset because of growing use of direct deposits, debit cards, automated teller machines, and telephone and Internet banking options.

3. *Is the resource really competitively superior?* Companies have to guard against pridefully believing that their core competencies are distinctive competencies or that their brand name is more powerful than the brand names of rivals. Who can really say whether Coca-Cola's consumer marketing prowess is better than Pepsi-Cola's or whether the Mercedes-Benz brand name is more powerful than that of BMW or Lexus? Although many retailers claim to be quite proficient in product selection and in-store merchandising, a number run into trouble in the marketplace because they encounter rivals whose competencies in product selection and in-store merchandising are better than theirs. Apple's operating system for its MacIntosh PCs is by most accounts a world beater (compared to Windows XP), but Apple has failed miserably in converting its resource strength in operating system design into competitive success in the global PC market—it is an also-ran with a paltry 2–3 percent market share worldwide.

4. *Can the resource strength be trumped by the different resource strengths and competitive capabilities of rivals?* Many commercial airlines have invested heavily in developing the resources and capabilities to offer passengers safe, reliable flights at convenient times, along with an array of in-flight amenities. However, Southwest Airlines and JetBlue in the United States and Ryanair and easyJet in Europe have been quite successful deploying their resources in ways that enable them to provide commercial air services at radically lower fares. Amazon.com's strengths in online retailing of books have put a big dent in the business prospects of brick-and-mortar bookstores. Whole Foods Market has a resource lineup that enables it to merchandise a dazzling array of natural and organic food products in a supermarket setting, thus putting strong competitive pressure on Kroger, Safeway, Albertson's, and other prominent supermarket chains. The prestigious brand names of Cadillac and Lincoln have faded because Mercedes, BMW, Audi, and Lexus have used their resources to design, produce, and market more appealing luxury vehicles.

The vast majority of companies are not well endowed with standout resource strengths, much less with one or more competitively superior resources (or distinctive competencies) capable of passing all four tests with high marks. Most firms have a mixed bag of resources—one or two quite valuable, some good, many satisfactory to mediocre.

Companies in the top tier of their industry may have as many as two core competencies in their resource strength lineup. But only a few companies, usually the strongest industry leaders or up-and-coming challengers, have a resource strength that truly qualifies as a distinctive competence. Even so, a company can still marshal the resource strengths to be competitively successful without having a competitively superior resource or distinctive competence. A company can achieve considerable competitive vitality, maybe even competitive advantage, from a collection of good-to-adequate resource strengths that collectively give it competitive power in the marketplace. A number of fast-food chains—for example, Wendy's, Taco Bell, and Subway—have achieved a respectable market position competing against McDonald's with satisfactory sets of resource strengths and no apparent distinctive competence. The same can be said for Lowe's, which competes against industry leader Home Depot, and such regional banks as Compass, State Street, Keybank, PNC, BB&T, and AmSouth, which increasingly find themselves in competition with the top five U.S. banks—JPMorgan Chase, Bank of America, Citibank, Wachovia, and Wells Fargo.

> **Core Concept**
> A company's ability to succeed in the marketplace hinges to a considerable extent on the competitive power of its resources—the set of competencies, capabilities, and competitive assets at its command.

Identifying Company Resource Weaknesses and Competitive Deficiencies

A *resource weakness,* or *competitive deficiency,* is something a company lacks or does poorly (in comparison to others) or a condition that puts it at a disadvantage in the marketplace. A company's resource weaknesses can relate to (1) inferior or unproven skills, expertise, or intellectual capital in competitively important areas of the business; (2) deficiencies in competitively important physical, organizational, or intangible assets; or (3) missing or competitively inferior capabilities in key areas. *Internal weaknesses are thus shortcomings in a company's complement of resources and represent competitive liabilities.* Nearly all companies have competitive liabilities of one kind or another. Whether a company's resource weaknesses make it competitively vulnerable depends on how much they matter in the marketplace and whether they are offset by the company's resource strengths.

> **Core Concept**
> A company's resource strengths represent competitive assets; its resource weaknesses represent competitive liabilities.

Table 4.2 lists the kinds of factors to consider in compiling a company's resource strengths and weaknesses. Sizing up a company's complement of resource capabilities and deficiencies is akin to constructing a *strategic balance sheet,* where resource strengths represent *competitive assets* and resource weaknesses represent *competitive liabilities.* Obviously, the ideal condition is for the company's competitive assets to outweigh its competitive liabilities by an ample margin—a 50–50 balance is definitely not the desired condition!

Identifying a Company's Market Opportunities

Market opportunity is a big factor in shaping a company's strategy. Indeed, managers can't properly tailor strategy to the company's situation without first identifying its market opportunities and appraising the growth and profit potential each one holds. Depending on the prevailing circumstances, a company's opportunities can be plentiful or scarce, fleeting or lasting, and can range from wildly attractive (an absolute "must" to pursue) to marginally interesting (because the growth and profit potential are questionable) to unsuitable (because there's not a good match with the company's

Table 4.2   **What to Look for in Identifying a Company's Strengths, Weaknesses, Opportunities, and Threats**

Potential Resource Strengths and Competitive Capabilities	Potential Resource Weaknesses and Competitive Deficiencies
• A powerful strategy • Core competencies in _____ • A distinctive competence in _____ • A product that is strongly differentiated from those of rivals • Competencies and capabilities that are well matched to industry key success factors • A strong financial condition; ample financial resources to grow the business • Strong brand-name image/company reputation • An attractive customer base • Economy of scale and/or learning/experience curve advantages over rivals • Proprietary technology/superior technological skills/ important patents • Superior intellectual capital relative to key rivals • Cost advantages over rivals • Strong advertising and promotion • Product innovation capabilities • Proven capabilities in improving production processes • Good supply chain management capabilities • Good customer service capabilities • Better product quality relative to rivals • Wide geographic coverage and/or strong global distribution capability • Alliances/joint ventures with other firms that provide access to valuable technology, competencies, and/or attractive geographic markets	• No clear strategic direction • Resources that are not well matched to industry key success factors • No well-developed or proven core competencies • A weak balance sheet; burdened with too much debt • Higher overall unit costs relative to key competitors • Weak or unproven product innovation capabilities • A product/service with ho-hum attributes or features inferior to those of rivals • Too narrow a product line relative to rivals • Weak brand image or reputation • Weaker dealer network than key rivals and/or lack of adequate global distribution capability • Behind on product quality, R&D, and/or technological know-how • In the wrong strategic group • Losing market share because . . . • Lack of management depth • Inferior intellectual capital relative to leading rivals • Subpar profitability because . . . • Plagued with internal operating problems or obsolete facilities • Behind rivals in e-commerce capabilities • Short on financial resources to grow the business and pursue promising initiatives • Too much underutilized plant capacity
Potential Market Opportunities	**Potential External Threats to a Company's Future Prospects**
• Openings to win market share from rivals • Sharply rising buyer demand for the industry's product • Serving additional customer groups or market segments • Expanding into new geographic markets • Expanding the company's product line to meet a broader range of customer needs • Using existing company skills or technological know-how to enter new product lines or new businesses • Online sales • Integrating forward or backward • Falling trade barriers in attractive foreign markets • Acquiring rival firms or companies with attractive technological expertise or capabilities • Entering into alliances or joint ventures to expand the firm's market coverage or boost its competitive capability • Openings to exploit emerging new technologies	• Increasing intensity of competition among industry rivals—may squeeze profit margins • Slowdowns in market growth • Likely entry of potent new competitors • Loss of sales to substitute products • Growing bargaining power of customers or suppliers • A shift in buyer needs and tastes away from the industry's product • Adverse demographic changes that threaten to curtail demand for the industry's product • Vulnerability to unfavorable industry driving forces • Restrictive trade policies on the part of foreign governments • Costly new regulatory requirements

resource strengths and capabilities). A checklist of potential market opportunities is included in Table 4.2.

While stunningly big or "golden" opportunities appear fairly frequently in volatile, fast-changing markets (typically due to important technological developments or rapidly shifting consumer preferences), they are nonetheless hard to see before most all companies in the industry identify them. The more volatile and thus unpredictable market conditions are, the more limited a company's ability to do market reconnaissance and spot important opportunities much ahead of rivals—there are simply too many variables in play for managers to peer into the fog of the future, identify one or more upcoming opportunities, and get a jump on rivals in pursuing it.[6] In mature markets, unusually attractive market opportunities emerge sporadically, often after long periods of relative calm—but future market conditions may be less foggy, thus facilitating good market reconnaissance and making emerging opportunities easier for industry members to detect. But in both volatile and stable markets, the rise of a golden opportunity is almost never under the control of a single company or manufactured by company executives—rather, it springs from the simultaneous alignment of several external factors. For instance, in China the recent upsurge in demand for motor vehicles was spawned by a convergence of many factors—increased disposable income, rising middle-class aspirations, a major road-building program by the government, the demise of employer-provided housing, and easy credit.[7] But golden opportunities are nearly always seized rapidly—and the companies that seize them are usually those that have been actively waiting, staying alert with diligent market reconnaissance, and preparing themselves to capitalize on shifting market conditions by patiently assembling an arsenal of competitively valuable resources—talented personnel, technical know-how, strategic partnerships, and a war chest of cash to finance aggressive action when the time comes.[8]

A company is well advised to pass on a particular market opportunity unless it has or can acquire the resources to capture it.

In evaluating a company's market opportunities and ranking their attractiveness, managers have to guard against viewing every *industry* opportunity as a *company* opportunity. Not every company is equipped with the resources to successfully pursue each opportunity that exists in its industry. Some companies are more capable of going after particular opportunities than others, and a few companies may be hopelessly outclassed. *The market opportunities most relevant to a company are those that match up well with the company's financial and organizational resource capabilities, offer the best growth and profitability, and present the most potential for competitive advantage.*

Identifying the External Threats to a Company's Future Profitability

Often, certain factors in a company's external environment pose *threats* to its profitability and competitive well-being. Threats can stem from the emergence of cheaper or better technologies, rivals' introduction of new or improved products, the entry of lower-cost foreign competitors into a company's market stronghold, new regulations that are more burdensome to a company than to its competitors, vulnerability to a rise in interest rates, the potential of a hostile takeover, unfavorable demographic shifts, adverse changes in foreign exchange rates, political upheaval in a foreign country where the company has facilities, and the like. A list of potential threats to a company's future profitability and market position is shown in Table 4.2.

External threats may pose no more than a moderate degree of adversity (all companies confront some threatening elements in the course of doing business), or they may be so imposing as to make a company's situation and outlook quite tenuous. On rare occasions, market shocks can give birth to a *sudden-death* threat that throws a company into an immediate crisis and battle to survive. Many of the world's major airlines have been plunged into unprecedented financial crisis by the perfect storm of the September 11, 2001, terrorist attacks, rising prices for jet fuel, mounting competition from low-fare carriers, shifting traveler preferences for low fares as opposed to lots of in-flight amenities, and out-of-control labor costs. It is management's job to identify the threats to the company's future prospects and to evaluate what strategic actions can be taken to neutralize or lessen their impact.

What Do the SWOT Listings Reveal?

SWOT analysis involves more than making four lists. The two most important parts of SWOT analysis are *drawing conclusions* from the SWOT listings about the company's overall situation, and *translating these conclusions into strategic actions* to better match the company's strategy to its resource strengths and market opportunities, to correct the important weaknesses, and to defend against external threats. Figure 4.2 shows the three steps of SWOT analysis.

> Simply making lists of a company's strengths, weaknesses, opportunities, and threats is not enough; the payoff from SWOT analysis comes from the conclusions about a company's situation and the implications for strategy improvement that flow from the four lists.

Just what story the SWOT listings tell about the company's overall situation is often revealed in the answers to the following sets of questions:

- Does the company have an attractive set of resource strengths? Does it have any strong core competencies or a distinctive competence? Are the company's strengths and capabilities well matched to the industry key success factors? Do they add adequate power to the company's strategy, or are more or different strengths needed? Will the company's current strengths and capabilities matter in the future?

- How serious are the company's weaknesses and competitive deficiencies? Are they mostly inconsequential and readily correctable, or could one or more prove fatal if not remedied soon? Are some of the company's weaknesses in areas that relate to the industry's key success factors? Are there any weaknesses that if uncorrected, would keep the company from pursuing an otherwise attractive opportunity? Does the company have important resource gaps that need to be filled for it to move up in the industry rankings and/or boost its profitability?

- Do the company's resource strengths and competitive capabilities (its competitive assets) outweigh its resource weaknesses and competitive deficiencies (its competitive liabilities) by an attractive margin?

- Does the company have attractive market opportunities that are well suited to its resource strengths and competitive capabilities? Does the company lack the resources and capabilities to pursue any of the most attractive opportunities?

- Are the threats alarming, or are they something the company appears able to deal with and defend against?

Figure 4.2   **The Three Steps of SWOT Analysis: Identify, Draw Conclusions, Translate into Strategic Action**

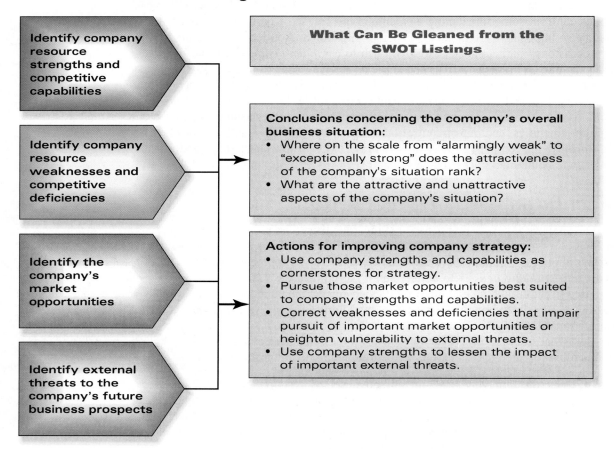

• All things considered, how strong is the company's overall situation? Where on a scale of 1 to 10 (1 being alarmingly weak and 10 exceptionally strong) should the firm's position and overall situation be ranked? What aspects of the company's situation are particularly attractive? What aspects are of the most concern?

The final piece of SWOT analysis is to translate the diagnosis of the company's situation into actions for improving the company's strategy and business prospects. The following questions point to implications the SWOT listings have for strategic action:

• Which competitive capabilities need to be strengthened immediately, so as to add greater power to the company's strategy and boost sales and profitability? Do new types of competitive capabilities need to be put in place to help the company better respond to emerging industry and competitive conditions? Which resources and capabilities need to be given greater emphasis, and which merit less emphasis? Should the company emphasize leveraging its existing resource strengths and capabilities, or does it need to create new resource strengths and capabilities?

• What actions should be taken to reduce the company's competitive liabilities? Which weaknesses or competitive deficiencies are in urgent need of correction?

- Which market opportunities should be top priority in future strategic initiatives (because they are good fits with the company's resource strengths and competitive capabilities, present attractive growth and profit prospects, and/or offer the best potential for securing competitive advantage)? Which opportunities should be ignored, at least for the time being (because they offer less growth potential or are not suited to the company's resources and capabilities)?
- What should the company be doing to guard against the threats to its well-being?

A company's resource strengths should generally form the cornerstones of strategy because they represent the company's best chance for market success.[9] As a rule, strategies that place heavy demands on areas where the company is weakest or has unproven ability are suspect and should be avoided. If a company doesn't have the resources and competitive capabilities around which to craft an attractive strategy, managers need to take decisive remedial action either to upgrade existing organizational resources and capabilities and add others as needed or to acquire them through partnerships or strategic alliances with firms possessing the needed expertise. Plainly, managers have to look toward correcting competitive weaknesses that make the company vulnerable, hold down profitability, or disqualify it from pursuing an attractive opportunity.

At the same time, sound strategy making requires sifting through the available market opportunities and aiming strategy at capturing those that are most attractive and suited to the company's circumstances. Rarely does a company have the resource depth to pursue all available market opportunities simultaneously without spreading itself too thin. How much attention to devote to defending against external threats to the company's market position and future performance hinges on how vulnerable the company is, whether there are attractive defensive moves that can be taken to lessen their impact, and whether the costs of undertaking such moves represent the best use of company resources.

QUESTION 3: ARE THE COMPANY'S PRICES AND COSTS COMPETITIVE?

Company managers are often stunned when a competitor cuts its price to "unbelievably low" levels or when a new market entrant comes on strong with a very low price. The competitor may not, however, be "dumping" (an economic term for selling at prices that are below cost), buying its way into the market with a super-low price, or waging a desperate move to gain sales—it may simply have substantially lower costs. One of the most telling signs of whether a company's business position is strong or precarious is whether its prices and costs are competitive with industry rivals. For a company to compete successfully, its costs must be *in line* with those of close rivals.

> The higher a company's costs are above those of close rivals, the more competitively vulnerable it becomes.

Price–cost comparisons are especially critical in a commodity-product industry where the value provided to buyers is the same from seller to seller, price competition is typically the ruling market force, and low-cost companies have the upper hand. But even in industries where products are differentiated and competition centers on the different attributes of competing brands as much as on price, rival companies have to keep their costs in line and make sure that any added costs they incur, and any price premiums they charge, create ample value that buyers are willing to pay extra for.

While some cost disparity is justified so long as the products or services of closely competing companies are sufficiently differentiated, a high-cost firm's market position becomes increasingly vulnerable the more its costs exceed those of close rivals.

Two analytical tools are particularly useful in determining whether a company's prices and costs are competitive: value chain analysis and benchmarking.

The Concept of a Company Value Chain

Core Concept

A company's *value chain* identifies the primary activities that create customer value and the related support activities.

Every company's business consists of a collection of activities undertaken in the course of designing, producing, marketing, delivering, and supporting its product or service. All of the various activities that a company performs internally combine to form a **value chain**—so called because the underlying intent of a company's activities is to do things that ultimately *create value for buyers*. A company's value chain also includes an allowance for profit because a markup over the cost of performing the firm's value-creating activities is customarily part of the price (or total cost) borne by buyers—unless an enterprise succeeds in creating and delivering sufficient value to buyers to produce an attractive profit, it can't survive for long.

As shown in Figure 4.3, a company's value chain consists of two broad categories of activities: the *primary activities* that are foremost in creating value for customers and the requisite *support activities* that facilitate and enhance the performance of the primary activities.[10] For example, the primary value-creating activities for a maker of bakery goods include supply chain management, recipe development and testing, mixing and baking, packaging, sales and marketing, and distribution; related support activities include quality control, human resource management, and administration. A wholesaler's primary activities and costs deal with merchandise selection and purchasing, inbound shipping and warehousing from suppliers, and outbound distribution to retail customers. The primary activities for a department store retailer include merchandise selection and buying, store layout and product display, advertising, and customer service; its support activities include site selection, hiring and training, and store maintenance, plus the usual assortment of administrative activities. A hotel chain's primary activities and costs are in site selection and construction, reservations, operation of its hotel properties (check-in and check-out, maintenance and housekeeping, dining and room service, and conventions and meetings), and managing its lineup of hotel locations; principal support activities include accounting, hiring and training hotel staff, advertising, building a brand and reputation, and general administration. Supply chain management is a crucial activity for Nissan and Amazon.com but is not a value chain component at Google or a TV and radio broadcasting company. Sales and marketing are dominant activities at Procter & Gamble and Sony but have minor roles at oil drilling companies and natural gas pipeline companies. Delivery to buyers is a crucial activity at Domino's Pizza but comparatively insignificant at Starbucks. Thus, what constitutes a primary or secondary activity varies according to the specific nature of a company's business, meaning that you should view the listing of the primary and support activities in Figure 4.3 as illustrative rather than definitive.

A Company's Primary and Support Activities Identify the Major Components of Its Cost Structure   Segregating a company's operations into different types of primary and support activities is the first step in understanding its cost structure. Each activity in the value chain gives rise to costs and ties up assets.

Figure 4.3   **A Representative Company Value Chain**

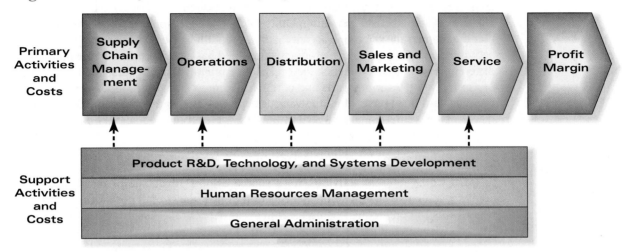

PRIMARY ACTIVITIES
- **Supply chain management**—activities, costs, and assets associated with purchasing fuel, energy, raw materials, parts and components, merchandise, and consumable items from vendors; receiving, storing, and disseminating inputs from suppliers; inspection; and inventory management.

- **Operations**—activities, costs, and assets associated with converting inputs into final product from (production, assembly, packaging, equipment maintenance, facilities, operations, quality assurance, environmental protection).

- **Distribution**—activities, costs, and assets dealing with physically distributing the product to buyers (finished goods warehousing, order processing, order picking and packing, shipping, delivery vehicle operations, establishing and maintaining a network of dealers and distributors).

- **Sales and marketing**—activities, costs, and assets related to sales force efforts, advertising and promotion, market research and planning, and dealer/distributor support.

- **Service**—activities, costs, and assets associated with providing assistance to buyers, such as installation, spare parts delivery, maintenance and repair, technical assistance, buyer inquiries, and complaints.

SUPPORT ACTIVITIES
- **Product R&D, technology, and systems development**—activities, costs, and assets relating to product R&D, process R&D, process design improvement, equipment design, computer software development, telecommunications systems, computer-assisted design and engineering, database capabilities, and development of computerized support systems.

- **Human resources management**—activities, costs, and assets associated with the recruitment, hiring, training, development, and compensation of all types of personnel; labor relations activities; and development of knowledge-based skills and core competencies.

- **General administration**—activities, costs, and assets relating to general management, accounting and finance, legal and regulatory affairs, safety and security, management information systems, forming strategic alliances and collaborating with strategic partners, and other overhead functions.

Source: Based on the discussion in Michael E. Porter, *Competitive Advantage* (New York: Free Press, 1985), pp. 37–43.

Assigning the company's operating costs and assets to each individual activity in the chain provides cost estimates and capital requirements—a process that accountants call activity-based cost accounting. Quite often, there are links between activities such that the manner in which one activity is done can affect the costs of performing other activities. For instance, how a product is designed has a huge impact on the number of different parts and components, their respective manufacturing costs, and the expense of assembling the various parts and components into a finished product.

The combined costs of all the various activities in a company's value chain define the company's internal cost structure. Further, the cost of each activity contributes to whether the company's overall cost position relative to rivals is favorable or unfavorable. The tasks of value chain analysis and benchmarking are to develop the data for comparing a company's costs activity-by-activity against the costs of key rivals and to learn which internal activities are a source of cost advantage or disadvantage. A company's relative cost position is a function of how the overall costs of the activities it performs in conducting business compare to the overall costs of the activities performed by rivals.

Why the Value Chains of Rival Companies Often Differ

A company's value chain and the manner in which it performs each activity reflect the evolution of its own particular business and internal operations, its strategy, the approaches it is using to execute its strategy, and the underlying economics of the activities themselves.[11] Because these factors differ from company to company, the value chains of rival companies sometimes differ substantially—a condition that complicates the task of assessing rivals' relative cost positions. For instance, music retailers like Blockbuster and Musicland, which purchase CDs from recording studios and wholesale distributors and sell them in their own retail store locations, have value chains and cost structures different from those of rival online music stores like Apple's iTunes and Musicmatch, which sell downloadable music files directly to music shoppers. Competing companies may differ in their degrees of vertical integration. The operations component of the value chain for a manufacturer that *makes* all of its own parts and assembles them into a finished product differs from the operations component of a rival producer that *buys* the needed parts from outside suppliers and performs assembly operations only. Likewise, there is legitimate reason to expect value chain and cost differences between a company that is pursuing a low-cost/low-price strategy and a rival that is positioned on the high end of the market. The costs of certain activities along the low-cost company's value chain should indeed be relatively low, whereas the high-end firm may understandably be spending relatively more to perform those activities that create the added quality and extra features of its products.

Moreover, cost and price differences among rival companies can have their origins in activities performed by suppliers or by distribution channel allies involved in getting the product to end users. Suppliers or wholesale/retail dealers may have excessively high cost structures or profit margins that jeopardize a company's cost-competitiveness even though its costs for internally performed activities are competitive. For example, when determining Michelin's cost-competitiveness vis-à-vis Goodyear and Bridgestone in supplying replacement tires to vehicle owners, we have to look at more than whether Michelin's tire manufacturing costs are above or below Goodyear's and Bridgestone's. Let's say that a motor vehicle owner looking for a new set of tires has to pay $400 for a set of Michelin tires and only $350 for a set of Goodyear or Bridgestone tires. Michelin's $50 price disadvantage can stem not only from higher manufacturing costs (reflecting, perhaps, the added costs of Michelin's strategic efforts to build a better-quality tire with more performance features) but also from (1) differences in what the three tire makers pay their suppliers for materials and tire-making components, and (2) differences in the operating efficiencies, costs, and markups of Michelin's wholesale–retail dealer outlets versus those of Goodyear and Bridgestone.

The Value Chain System for an Entire Industry

As the tire industry example makes clear, a company's value chain is embedded in a larger system of activities that includes the value chains of its suppliers and the value chains of whatever distribution channel allies it uses in getting its product or service to end users.[12] Suppliers' value chains are relevant because suppliers perform activities and incur costs in creating and delivering the purchased inputs used in a company's own value-creating activities. The costs, performance features, and quality of these inputs influence a company's own costs and product differentiation capabilities. Anything a company can do to help its suppliers' drive down the costs of their value chain activities or improve the quality and performance of the items being supplied can enhance its own competitiveness—a powerful reason for working collaboratively with suppliers in managing supply chain activities.[13]

The value chains of forward channel partners and/or the customers to whom a company sells are relevant because (1) the costs and margins of a company's distributors and retail dealers are part of the price the ultimate consumer pays, and (2) the activities that distribution allies perform affect customer satisfaction. For these reasons, companies normally work closely with their forward channel allies (who are their direct customers) to perform value chain activities in mutually beneficial ways. For instance, motor vehicle manufacturers work closely with their local automobile dealers to keep the retail prices of their vehicles competitive with rivals' models and to ensure that owners are satisfied with dealers' repair and maintenance services. Some aluminum can producers have constructed plants next to beer breweries and deliver cans on overhead conveyors directly to the breweries' can-filling lines; this has resulted in significant savings in production scheduling, shipping, and inventory costs for both container producers and breweries.[14] Many automotive parts suppliers have built plants near the auto assembly plants they supply to facilitate just-in-time deliveries, reduce warehousing and shipping costs, and promote close collaboration on parts design and production scheduling. Irrigation equipment companies, suppliers of grape-harvesting and winemaking equipment, and firms making barrels, wine bottles, caps, corks, and labels all have facilities in the California wine country to be close to the nearly 700 winemakers they supply.[15] The lesson here is that a company's value chain activities are often closely linked to the value chains of their suppliers and the forward allies or customers to whom they sell.

> A company's cost-competitiveness depends not only on the costs of internally performed activities (its own value chain) but also on costs in the value chains of its suppliers and forward channel allies.

As a consequence, *accurately assessing a company's competitiveness from the perspective of the consumers who ultimately use its products or services thus requires that company managers understand an industry's entire value chain system for delivering a product or service to customers, not just the company's own value chain.* A typical industry value chain that incorporates the value chains of suppliers and forward channel allies (if any) is shown in Figure 4.4. However, industry value chains

Figure 4.4   **Representative Value Chain for an Entire Industry**

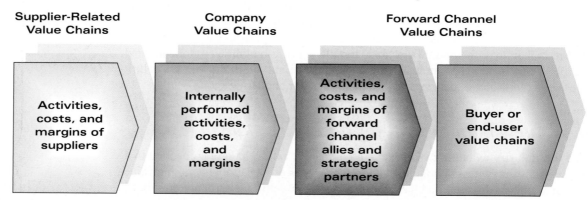

Source: Based in part on the single-industry value chain displayed in Michael E. Porter, *Competitive Advantage* (New York: Free Press, 1985), p. 35.

vary significantly by industry. The primary value chain activities in the pulp and paper industry (timber farming, logging, pulp mills, and papermaking) differ from the primary value chain activities in the home appliance industry (parts and components manufacture, assembly, wholesale distribution, retail sales). The value chain for the soft-drink industry (processing of basic ingredients and syrup manufacture, bottling and can filling, wholesale distribution, advertising, and retail merchandising) differs from that for the computer software industry (programming, disk loading, marketing, distribution). Producers of bathroom and kitchen faucets depend heavily on the activities of wholesale distributors and building supply retailers in winning sales to homebuilders and do-it-yourselfers, but producers of papermaking machines internalize their distribution activities by selling directly to the operators of paper plants. Illustration Capsule 4.1 shows representative costs for various activities performed by the producers and marketers of music CDs.

Activity-Based Costing: A Tool for Assessing a Company's Cost Competitiveness

Once the company has identified its major value chain activities, the next step in evaluating its cost competitiveness involves determining the costs of performing specific value chain activities, using what accountants call activity-based costing.[16] Traditional accounting identifies costs according to broad categories of expenses—wages and salaries, employee benefits, supplies, maintenance, utilities, travel, depreciation, R&D, interest, general administration, and so on. But activity-based cost accounting involves establishing expense categories for specific value chain activities and assigning costs to the activity responsible for creating the cost. An illustrative example is shown in Table 4.3. Perhaps 25 percent of the companies that have explored the feasibility of activity-based costing have adopted this accounting approach.

Illustration Capsule 4.1

Estimated Value Chain Costs for Recording and Distributing Music CDs through Traditional Music Retailers

The following table presents the representative costs and markups associated with producing and distributing a music CD retailing for $15 in music stores (as opposed to Internet sources).

Value Chain Activities and Costs in Producing and Distributing a CD		
1. Record company direct production costs:		$2.40
Artists and repertoire	$0.75	
Pressing of CD and packaging	1.65	
2. Royalties		0.99
3. Record company marketing expenses		1.50
4. Record company overhead		1.50
5. Total record company costs		6.39
6. Record company's operating profit		1.86
7. Record company's selling price to distributor/wholesaler		8.25
8. Average wholesale distributor markup to cover distribution activities and profit margins		1.50
9. Average wholesale price charged to retailer		9.75
10. Average retail markup over wholesale cost		5.25
11. Average price to consumer at retail		$15.00

Source: Developed from information in "Fight the Power," a case study prepared by Adrian Aleyne, Babson College, 1999.

The degree to which a company's costs should be disaggregated into specific activities depends on how valuable it is to develop cross-company cost comparisons for narrowly defined activities as opposed to broadly defined activities. Generally speaking, cost estimates are needed at least for each broad category of primary and secondary activities, but finer classifications may be needed if a company discovers that it has a cost disadvantage vis-à-vis rivals and wants to pin down the exact source or activity causing the cost disadvantage. It can also be necessary to develop cost estimates for activities performed in the competitively relevant portions of suppliers' and customers' value chains—which requires going to outside sources for reliable cost information.

Once a company has developed good cost estimates for each of the major activities in its value chain, and perhaps has cost estimates for subactivities within each primary/secondary value chain activity, then it is ready to see how its costs for these activities compare with the costs of rival firms. This is where benchmarking comes in.

Table 4.3   **The Difference between Traditional Cost Accounting and Activity-Based Cost Accounting: A Supply Chain Activity Example**

Traditional Cost Accounting Categories for Supply Chain Activities		Cost of Performing Specific Supply Chain Activities Using Activity-Based Cost Accounting	
Wages and salaries	$450,000	Evaluate supplier capabilities	$150,000
Employee benefits	95,000	Process purchase orders	92,000
Supplies	21,500	Collaborate with suppliers on just-in-time deliveries	180,000
Travel	12,250		
Depreciation	19,000	Share data with suppliers	69,000
Other fixed charges (office space, utilities)	112,000	Check quality of items purchased	94,000
Miscellaneous operating expenses	40,250	Check incoming deliveries against purchase orders	50,000
	$750,000	Resolve disputes	15,000
		Conduct internal administration	100,000
			$750,000

Source: Developed from information in Terence P. Par, "A New Tool for Managing Costs," *Fortune,* June 14, 1993, pp. 124–29.

Benchmarking: A Tool for Assessing Whether a Company's Value Chain Costs Are in Line

Core Concept

Benchmarking is a potent tool for learning which companies are best at performing particular activities and then using their techniques (or "best practices") to improve the cost and effectiveness of a company's own internal activities.

Many companies today are **benchmarking** their costs of performing a given activity against competitors' costs (and/or against the costs of a non-competitor that efficiently and effectively performs much the same activity in another industry). *Benchmarking is a tool that allows a company to determine whether its performance of a particular function or activity represents the "best practice" when both cost and effectiveness are taken into account.*

Benchmarking entails comparing how different companies perform various value chain activities—how materials are purchased, how suppliers are paid, how inventories are managed, how products are assembled, how fast the company can get new products to market, how the quality control function is performed, how customer orders are filled and shipped, how employees are trained, how payrolls are processed, and how maintenance is performed—and then making cross-company comparisons of the costs of these activities.[17] The objectives of benchmarking are to identify the best practices in performing an activity, to learn how other companies have actually achieved lower costs or better results in performing benchmarked activities, and to take action to improve a company's competitiveness whenever benchmarking reveals that its costs and results of performing an activity are not on a par with what other companies (either competitors or noncompetitors) have achieved.

Xerox became one of the first companies to use benchmarking when, in 1979, Japanese manufacturers began selling midsize copiers in the United States for $9,600 each—less than Xerox's production costs.[18] Xerox management suspected its Japanese competitors were dumping, but it sent a team of line managers to Japan, including the head of manufacturing, to study competitors' business processes and costs. With the aid of Xerox's joint venture partner in Japan, Fuji-Xerox, which knew the competitors well, the team found that Xerox's costs were excessive due to gross inefficiencies in the company's manufacturing processes and business practices. The findings triggered a major internal effort at Xerox to become cost-competitive and prompted Xerox to begin benchmarking 67 of its key work processes against companies identified as employing the best practices. Xerox quickly decided not to restrict its benchmarking efforts to its office equipment rivals but to extend them to any company regarded as world class in performing *any activity* relevant to Xerox's business. Other companies quickly picked up on Xerox's approach. Toyota managers got their idea for just-in-time inventory deliveries by studying how U.S. supermarkets replenished their shelves. Southwest Airlines reduced the turnaround time of its aircraft at each scheduled stop by studying pit crews on the auto racing circuit. Over 80 percent of Fortune 500 companies reportedly use benchmarking for comparing themselves against rivals on cost and other competitively important measures.

The tough part of benchmarking is not whether to do it, but rather how to gain access to information about other companies' practices and costs. Sometimes benchmarking can be accomplished by collecting information from published reports, trade groups, and industry research firms and by talking to knowledgeable industry analysts, customers, and suppliers. Sometimes field trips to the facilities of competing or noncompeting companies can be arranged to observe how things are done, ask questions, compare practices and processes, and perhaps exchange data on productivity, staffing levels, time requirements, and other cost components—but the problem here is that such companies, even if they agree to host facilities tours and answer questions, are unlikely to share competitively sensitive cost information. Furthermore, comparing one company's costs to another's costs may not involve comparing apples to apples if the two companies employ different cost accounting principles to calculate the costs of particular activities.

> Benchmarking the costs of company activities against rivals provides hard evidence of whether a company is cost-competitive.

However, a third and fairly reliable source of benchmarking information has emerged. The explosive interest of companies in benchmarking costs and identifying best practices has prompted consulting organizations (e.g., Accenture, A. T. Kearney, Benchnet—The Benchmarking Exchange, Towers Perrin, and Best Practices) and several councils and associations (e.g., the American Productivity and Quality Center, the Qualserve Benchmarking Clearinghouse, and the Strategic Planning Institute's Council on Benchmarking) to gather benchmarking data, distribute information about best practices, and provide comparative cost data without identifying the names of particular companies. Having an independent group gather the information and report it in a manner that disguises the names of individual companies avoid having the disclosure of competitively sensitive data and lessens the potential for unethical behavior on the part of company personnel in gathering their own data about competitors.Illustration Capsule 4.2 presents a widely recommended code of conduct for engaging in benchmarking that is intended to help companies avoid any improprieties in gathering and using benchmarking data.

Strategic Options for Remedying a Cost Disadvantage

Value chain analysis and benchmarking can reveal a great deal about a firm's cost competitiveness. Examining the costs of a company's own value chain activities and comparing them to rivals' indicates who has how much of a cost advantage or

Illustration Capsule 4.2
Benchmarking and Ethical Conduct

Because discussions between benchmarking partners can involve competitively sensitive data, conceivably raising questions about possible restraint of trade or improper business conduct, many benchmarking organizations urge all individuals and organizations involved in benchmarking to abide by a code of conduct grounded in ethical business behavior. Among the most widely used codes of conduct is the one developed by the American Productivity and Quality Center and advocated by the Qualserve Benchmarking Clearinghouse; it is based on the following principles and guidelines:

- Avoid discussions or actions that could lead to or imply an interest in restraint of trade, market and/or customer allocation schemes, price fixing, dealing arrangements, bid rigging, or bribery. Don't discuss costs with competitors if costs are an element of pricing.

- Refrain from the acquisition of trade secrets from another by any means that could be interpreted as improper including the breach or inducement of a breach of any duty to maintain secrecy. Do not disclose or use any trade secret that may have been obtained through improper means or that was disclosed by another in violation of duty to maintain its secrecy or limit its use.

- Be willing to provide the same type and level of information that you request from your benchmarking partner to your benchmarking partner.

- Communicate fully and early in the relationship to clarify expectations, avoid misunderstanding, and establish mutual interest in the benchmarking exchange.

- Be honest and complete.

- Treat benchmarking interchange as confidential to the individuals and companies involved. Information must not be communicated outside the partnering organizations without the prior consent of the benchmarking partner who shared the information.

- Use information obtained through benchmarking only for purposes stated to the benchmarking partner.

- The use or communication of a benchmarking partner's name with the data obtained or practices observed requires the prior permission of that partner.

- Respect the corporate culture of partner companies and work within mutually agreed-on procedures.

- Use benchmarking contacts designated by the partner company, if that is the company's preferred procedure.

- Obtain mutual agreement with the designated benchmarking contact on any hand-off of communication or responsibility to other parties.

- Make the most of your benchmarking partner's time by being fully prepared for each exchange.

- Help your benchmarking partners prepare by providing them with a questionnaire and agenda prior to benchmarking visits.

- Follow through with each commitment made to your benchmarking partner in a timely manner.

- Understand how your benchmarking partner would like to have the information he or she provides handled and used, and handle and use it in that manner.

Note: Identification of firms, organizations, and contacts visited is prohibited without advance approval from the organization.

Sources: The American Productivity and Quality Center, www.apqc.org, and the Qualserve Benchmarking Clearinghouse, www.awwa.org (accessed September 14, 2005).

disadvantage and which cost components are responsible. Such information is vital in strategic actions to eliminate a cost disadvantage or create a cost advantage. One of the fundamental insights of value chain analysis and benchmarking is that *a company's competitiveness on cost depends on how efficiently it manages its value chain activities relative to how well competitors manage theirs.*[19] There are three main areas in a company's overall value chain where important differences in the costs of competing firms can occur: a company's own activity segments, suppliers' part of the industry value chain, and the forward channel portion of the industry chain.

Remedying an Internal Cost Disadvantage   When a company's cost disadvantage stems from performing internal value chain activities at a higher cost than key rivals, then managers can pursue any of several strategic approaches to restore cost parity:[20]

1. Implement the use of best practices throughout the company, particularly for high-cost activities.

2. Try to eliminate some cost-producing activities altogether by revamping the value chain. Examples include cutting out low-value-added activities or bypassing the value chains and associated costs of distribution allies and marketing directly to end users. Dell has used this approach in PCs, and airlines have begun bypassing travel agents by getting passengers to purchase their tickets directly at airline Web sites.

3. Relocate high-cost activities (such as manufacturing) to geographic areas—such as China, Latin America, or Eastern Europe—where they can be performed more cheaply.

4. See if certain internally performed activities can be outsourced from vendors or performed by contractors more cheaply than they can be done in-house.

5. Invest in productivity-enhancing, cost-saving technological improvements (robotics, flexible manufacturing techniques, state-of-the-art electronic networking).

6. Find ways to detour around the activities or items where costs are high—computer chip makers regularly design around the patents held by others to avoid paying royalties; automakers have substituted lower-cost plastic and rubber for metal at many exterior body locations.

7. Redesign the product and/or some of its components to facilitate speedier and more economical manufacture or assembly.

8. Try to make up the internal cost disadvantage by reducing costs in the supplier or forward channel portions of the industry value chain—usually a last resort.

Remedying a Supplier-Related Cost Disadvantage   Supplier-related cost disadvantages can be attacked by pressuring suppliers for lower prices, switching to lower-priced substitute inputs, and collaborating closely with suppliers to identify mutual cost-saving opportunities.[21] For example, just-in-time deliveries from suppliers can lower a company's inventory and internal logistics costs and may also allow its suppliers to economize on their warehousing, shipping, and production scheduling costs—a win–win outcome for both. In a few instances, companies may find that it is cheaper to integrate backward into the business of high-cost suppliers and make the item in-house instead of buying it from outsiders. If a company strikes out in wringing savings out of its high-cost supply chain activities, then it must resort to finding cost savings either in-house or in the forward channel portion of the industry value chain to offset its supplier-related cost disadvantage.

Remedying a Cost Disadvantage Associated with Activities Performed by Forward Channel Allies   There are three main ways to combat a cost disadvantage in the forward portion of the industry value chain:

1. Pressure dealer-distributors and other forward channel allies to reduce their costs and markups so as to make the final price to buyers more competitive with the prices of rivals.

2. Work closely with forward channel allies to identify win–win opportunities to reduce costs. For example, a chocolate manufacturer learned that by shipping its bulk chocolate in liquid form in tank cars instead of 10-pound molded bars, it could not only save its candy bar manufacturing customers the costs associated with unpacking and melting but also eliminate its own costs of molding bars and packing them.

3. Change to a more economical distribution strategy, including switching to cheaper distribution channels (perhaps direct sales via the Internet) or perhaps integrating forward into company-owned retail outlets.

If these efforts fail, the company can either try to live with the cost disadvantage or pursue cost-cutting earlier in the value chain system.

Translating Proficient Performance of Value Chain Activities into Competitive Advantage

Performing value chain activities in ways that give a company the capabilities to either outmatch the competencies and capabilities of rivals or else beat them on costs are two good ways to secure competitive advantage.

A company that does a *first-rate job* of managing its value chain activities *relative to competitors* stands a good chance of achieving sustainable competitive advantage. As shown in Figure 4.5, outmanaging rivals in performing value chain activities can be accomplished in either or both of two ways: (1) by astutely developing core competencies and maybe a distinctive competence that rivals don't have or can't quite match and that are instrumental in helping it deliver attractive value to customers, and/or (2) by simply doing an overall better job than rivals of lowering its combined costs of performing all the various value chain activities, such that it ends up with a low-cost advantage over rivals.

The first of these two approaches begins with management efforts to build more organizational expertise in performing certain competitively important value chain activities, deliberately striving to develop competencies and capabilities that add power to its strategy and competitiveness. If management begins to make selected competencies and capabilities cornerstones of its strategy and continues to invest resources in building greater and greater proficiency in performing them, then over time one (or maybe several) of the targeted competencies/capabilities may rise to the level of a core competence. Later, following additional organizational learning and investments in gaining still greater proficiency, a core competence could evolve into a distinctive competence, giving the company superiority over rivals in performing an important value chain activity. Such superiority, if it gives the company significant competitive clout in the marketplace, can produce an attractive competitive edge over rivals and, more important, prove difficult for rivals to match or offset with competencies and capabilities of their own making. As a general rule, it is substantially harder for rivals to achieve best-in-industry proficiency in performing a key value chain activity than it is for them to clone the features and attributes of a hot-selling product or service.[22] This is especially true when a company with a distinctive competence avoids becoming complacent and works diligently to maintain its industry-leading expertise and capability. GlaxoSmithKline, one of the world's most competitively capable pharmaceutical companies, has built its business position around expert performance of a few competitively crucial activities: extensive R&D to achieve first discovery of new drugs, a carefully constructed approach to patenting, skill in gaining rapid and thorough clinical clearance through regulatory bodies, and unusually strong distribution and sales-force

Figure 4.5   **Translating Company Performance of Value Chain Activities into Competitive Advantage**

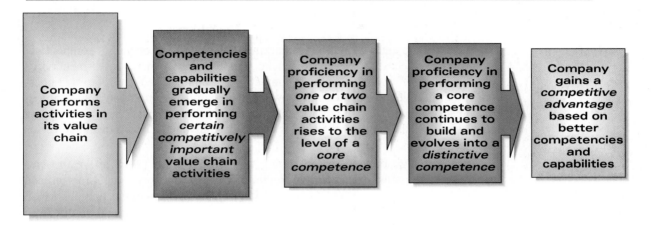

Option 1: Beat rivals in performing value chain activities more proficiently

Company performs activities in its value chain → Competencies and capabilities gradually emerge in performing *certain competitively important* value chain activities → Company proficiency in performing *one or two* value chain activities rises to the level of a *core competence* → Company proficiency in performing a core competence continues to build and evolves into a *distinctive competence* → Company gains a *competitive advantage* based on better competencies and capabilities

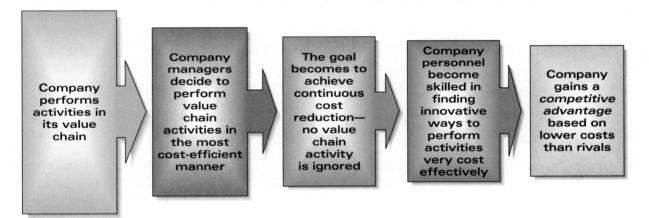

Option 2: Beat rivals in performing value chain activities more cheaply

Company performs activities in its value chain → Company managers decide to perform value chain activities in the most cost-efficient manner → The goal becomes to achieve continuous cost reduction—no value chain activity is ignored → Company personnel become skilled in finding innovative ways to perform activities very cost effectively → Company gains a *competitive advantage* based on lower costs than rivals

capabilities.[23] FedEx's astute management of its value chain has produced unmatched competencies and capabilities in overnight package delivery.

The second approach to building competitive advantage entails determined management efforts to be cost-efficient in performing value chain activities. Such efforts have to be ongoing and persistent, and they have to involve each and every value chain activity. The goal must be continuous cost reduction, not a one-time or on-again/off-again effort. Companies whose managers are truly committed to low-cost performance of value chain activities and succeed in engaging company personnel to discover innovative ways to drive costs out of the business have a real chance of gaining a durable low-cost edge over rivals. It is not as easy as it seems to imitate a company's low-cost practices. Companies like Wal-Mart, Dell, Nucor Steel, Southwest Airlines,

Toyota, and French discount retailer Carrefour have been highly successful in managing their values chains in a low-cost manner.

QUESTION 4: IS THE COMPANY COMPETITIVELY STRONGER OR WEAKER THAN KEY RIVALS?

Using value chain analysis and benchmarking to determine a company's competitiveness on price is necessary but not sufficient. A more comprehensive assessment needs to be made of the company's overall competitive strength. The answers to two questions are of particular interest: First, how does the company rank relative to competitors on each of the important factors that determine market success? Second, all things considered, does the company have a net competitive advantage or disadvantage versus major competitors?

An easy-to-use method for answering the two questions posed above involves developing quantitative strength ratings for the company and its key competitors on each industry key success factor and each competitively pivotal resource capability. Much of the information needed for doing a competitive strength assessment comes from previous analyses. Industry and competitive analysis reveals the key success factors and competitive capabilities that separate industry winners from losers. Benchmarking data and scouting key competitors provide a basis for judging the competitive strength of rivals on such factors as cost, key product attributes, customer service, image and reputation, financial strength, technological skills, distribution capability, and other competitively important resources and capabilities. SWOT analysis reveals how the company in question stacks up on these same strength measures.

Step 1 in doing a competitive strength assessment is to make a list of the industry's key success factors and most telling measures of competitive strength or weakness (6 to 10 measures usually suffice). Step 2 is to rate the firm and its rivals on each factor. Numerical rating scales (e.g., from 1 to 10) are best to use, although ratings of stronger (+), weaker (−), and about equal (=) may be appropriate when information is scanty and assigning numerical scores conveys false precision. Step 3 is to sum the strength ratings on each factor to get an overall measure of competitive strength for each company being rated. Step 4 is to use the overall strength ratings to draw conclusions about the size and extent of the company's net competitive advantage or disadvantage and to take specific note of areas of strength and weakness.

Table 4.5 provides two examples of competitive strength assessment, using the hypothetical ABC Company against four rivals. The first example employs an *unweighted rating system*. With unweighted ratings, each key success factor/competitive strength measure is assumed to be equally important (a rather dubious assumption). Whichever company has the highest strength rating on a given measure has an implied competitive edge on that factor; the size of its edge is mirrored in the margin of difference between its rating and the ratings assigned to rivals—a rating of 9 for one company versus ratings of 5, 4, and 3, respectively, for three other companies indicates a bigger advantage than a rating of 9 versus ratings of 8, 7, and 6. Summing a company's ratings on all the measures produces an overall strength rating. The higher a company's overall strength rating, the stronger its overall competitiveness versus rivals. The bigger the difference between a company's overall rating and the scores of *lower-rated* rivals, the greater its implied *net competitive advantage*. Conversely, the bigger the difference between a company's overall rating and the scores of *higher-rated* rivals, the greater its implied

Table 4.5 Illustrations of Unweighted and Weighted Competitive Strength Assessments

A. An Unweighted Competitive Strength Assessment

Key Success Factor/Strength Measure	Strength Rating (Scale: 1 = Very weak; 10 = Very strong)				
	ABC Co.	Rival 1	Rival 2	Rival 3	Rival 4
Quality/product performance	8	5	10	1	6
Reputation/image	8	7	10	1	6
Manufacturing capability	2	10	4	5	1
Technological skills	10	1	7	3	8
Dealer network/distribution capability	9	4	10	5	1
New product innovation capability	9	4	10	5	1
Financial resources	5	10	7	3	1
Relative cost position	5	10	3	1	4
Customer service capabilities	5	7	10	1	4
Unweighted overall strength rating	61	58	71	25	32

B. A Weighted Competitive Strength Assessment (Rating Scale: 1 = Very weak; 10 = Very strong)

Key Success Factor/ Strength Measure	Importance Weight	ABC Co.		Rival 1		Rival 2		Rival 3		Rival 4	
		Strength Rating	Score	Strength Rating	Score	Strength Rating	Score	Strength Rating	Score	Strength Rating	Score
Quality/product performance	0.10	8	0.80	5	0.50	10	1.00	1	0.10	6	0.60
Reputation/image	0.10	8	0.80	7	0.70	10	1.00	1	0.10	6	0.60
Manufacturing capability	0.10	2	0.20	10	1.00	4	0.40	5	0.50	1	0.10
Technological skills	0.05	10	0.50	1	0.05	7	0.35	3	0.15	8	0.40
Dealer network/distribution capability	0.05	9	0.45	4	0.20	10	0.50	5	0.25	1	0.05
New product innovation capability	0.05	9	0.45	4	0.20	10	0.50	5	0.25	1	0.05
Financial resources	0.10	5	0.50	10	1.00	7	0.70	3	0.30	1	0.10
Relative cost position	0.30	5	1.50	10	3.00	3	0.95	1	0.30	4	1.20
Customer service capabilities	0.15	5	0.75	7	1.05	10	1.50	1	0.15	4	0.60
Sum of importance weights	1.00										
Weighted overall strength rating		61	5.95	58	7.70	71	6.85	25	2.10	32	3.70

net competitive disadvantage. Thus, ABC's total score of 61 (see the top half of Table 4.5) signals a much greater net competitive advantage over Rival 4 (with a score of 32) than over Rival 1 (with a score of 58) but indicates a moderate net competitive disadvantage against Rival 2 (with an overall score of 71).

However, a better method is a *weighted rating system* (shown in the bottom half of Table 4.5) because the different measures of competitive strength are unlikely to be equally important. In an industry where the products/services of rivals are virtually identical, for instance, having low unit costs relative to rivals is nearly always the most important determinant of competitive strength. In an industry with strong product differentiation, the most significant measures of competitive strength

> A weighted competitive strength analysis is conceptually stronger than an unweighted analysis because of the inherent weakness in assuming that all the strength measures are equally important.

may be brand awareness, amount of advertising, product attractiveness, and distribution capability. In a weighted rating system each measure of competitive strength is assigned a weight based on its perceived importance in shaping competitive success. A weight could be as high as 0.75 (maybe even higher) in situations where one particular competitive variable is overwhelmingly decisive, or a weight could be as low as 0.20 when two or three strength measures are more important than the rest. Lesser competitive strength indicators can carry weights of 0.05 or 0.10. No matter whether the differences between the importance weights are big or little, *the sum of the weights must equal 1.0.*

Weighted strength ratings are calculated by rating each competitor on each strength measure (using the 1 to 10 rating scale) and multiplying the assigned rating by the assigned weight (a rating of 4 times a weight of 0.20 gives a weighted rating, or score, of 0.80). Again, the company with the highest rating on a given measure has an implied competitive edge on that measure, with the size of its edge reflected in the difference between its rating and rivals' ratings. The weight attached to the measure indicates how important the edge is. Summing a company's weighted strength ratings for all the measures yields an overall strength rating. Comparisons of the weighted overall strength scores indicate which competitors are in the strongest and weakest competitive positions and who has how big a net competitive advantage over whom.

Note in Table 4.5 that the unweighted and weighted rating schemes produce different orderings of the companies. In the weighted system, ABC Company drops from second to third in strength, and Rival 1 jumps from third to first because of its high strength ratings on the two most important factors. Weighting the importance of the strength measures can thus make a significant difference in the outcome of the assessment.

Interpreting the Competitive Strength Assessments

> High competitive strength ratings signal a strong competitive position and possession of competitive advantage; low ratings signal a weak position and competitive disadvantage.

Competitive strength assessments provide useful conclusions about a company's competitive situation. The ratings show how a company compares against rivals, factor by factor or capability by capability, thus revealing where it is strongest and weakest, and against whom. Moreover, the overall competitive strength scores indicate how all the different factors add up—whether the company is at a net competitive advantage or disadvantage against each rival. The firm with the largest overall competitive strength rating enjoys the strongest competitive position, with the size of its net competitive advantage reflected by how much its score exceeds the scores of rivals.

In addition, the strength ratings provide guidelines for designing wise offensive and defensive strategies. For example, consider the ratings and weighted scores in the bottom half of Table 4.5. If ABC Company wants to go on the offensive to win additional sales and market share, such an offensive probably needs to be aimed directly at winning customers away from Rivals 3 and 4 (which have lower overall strength scores) rather than Rivals 1 and 2 (which have higher overall strength scores). Moreover, while ABC has high ratings for quality/product performance (an 8 rating), reputation/image (an 8 rating), technological skills (a 10 rating), dealer network/distribution capability (a 9 rating), and new product innovation capability (a 9 rating), these strength measures have low importance weights—meaning that ABC has strengths in areas that don't translate into much competitive clout in the marketplace. Even so, it outclasses Rival 3 in all five areas, plus it enjoys lower costs than Rival 3: On relative cost position ABC has a 5 rating versus a 1 rating for Rival 3—and relative cost position carries the highest importance weight of all the strength measures. ABC also has greater competitive strength than Rival 3 as concerns customer service capabilities (which carries the second-highest importance weight). Hence, because ABC's strengths are in the very areas where Rival 3 is weak, ABC is in good position to attack Rival 3—it may well be able to persuade a number of Rival 3's customers to switch their purchases over to ABC's product.

But in mounting an offensive to win customers away from Rival 3, ABC should note that Rival 1 has an excellent relative cost position—its rating of 10, combined with the importance weight of 0.30 for relative cost, means that Rival 1 has meaningfully lower costs in an industry where low costs are competitively important. Rival 1 is thus strongly positioned to retaliate against ABC with lower prices if ABC's strategy offensive ends up drawing customers away from Rival 1. Moreover, Rival 1's very strong relative cost position vis-à-vis all the other companies arms it with the ability to use its lower-cost advantage to underprice all of its rivals and gain sales and market share at their expense. If ABC wants to defend against its vulnerability to potential price cutting by Rival 1, then it needs to aim a portion of its strategy at lowering its costs.

> A company's competitive strength scores pinpoint its strengths and weaknesses against rivals and point directly to the kinds of offensive/defensive actions it can use to exploit its competitive strengths and reduce its competitive vulnerabilities.

The point here is that a competitively astute company should use the strength assessment in deciding what strategic moves to make—which strengths to exploit in winning business away from rivals and which competitive weaknesses to try to correct. When a company has important competitive strengths in areas where one or more rivals are weak, it makes sense to consider offensive moves to exploit rivals' competitive weaknesses. When a company has important competitive weaknesses in areas where one or more rivals are strong, it makes sense to consider defensive moves to curtail its vulnerability.

QUESTION 5: WHAT STRATEGIC ISSUES AND PROBLEMS MERIT FRONT-BURNER MANAGERIAL ATTENTION?

The final and most important analytical step is to zero in on exactly what strategic issues that company managers need to address—and resolve—for the company to be more financially and competitively successful in the years ahead. This step involves drawing on the results of both industry and competitive analysis and the evaluations of the company's own competitiveness. The task here is to get a clear fix on exactly what strategic and competitive challenges confront the company, which of the company's competitive shortcomings need fixing, what obstacles stand in the way of improving the company's competitive position in the marketplace, and what specific problems

Zeroing in on the strategic issues a company faces and compiling a "worry list" of problems and roadblocks creates a strategic agenda of problems that merit prompt managerial attention.

Actually deciding upon a strategy and what specific actions to take is what comes *after* developing the list of strategic issues and problems that merit front-burner management attention.

A good strategy must contain ways to deal with all the strategic issues and obstacles that stand in the way of the company's financial and competitive success in the years ahead.

merit front-burner attention by company managers. *Pinpointing the precise things that management needs to worry about sets the agenda for deciding what actions to take next to improve the company's performance and business outlook.*

The "worry list" of issues and problems that have to be wrestled with can include such things as *how* to stave off market challenges from new foreign competitors, *how* to combat the price discounting of rivals, *how* to reduce the company's high costs and pave the way for price reductions, *how* to sustain the company's present rate of growth in light of slowing buyer demand, *whether* to expand the company's product line, *whether* to correct the company's competitive deficiencies by acquiring a rival company with the missing strengths, *whether* to expand into foreign markets rapidly or cautiously, *whether* to reposition the company and move to a different strategic group, *what to do* about growing buyer interest in substitute products, and *what to do* to combat the aging demographics of the company's customer base. The worry list thus always centers on such concerns as "how to . . .," "what to do about . . .," and "whether to . . ."—the purpose of the worry list is to identify the specific issues/problems that management needs to address, not to figure out what specific actions to take. Deciding what to do—which strategic actions to take and which strategic moves to make—comes later (when it is time to craft the strategy and choose from among the various strategic alternatives).

If the items on the worry list are relatively minor—which suggests the company's strategy is mostly on track and reasonably well matched to the company's overall situation—then company managers seldom need to go much beyond fine-tuning of the present strategy. If, however, the issues and problems confronting the company are serious and indicate the present strategy is not well suited for the road ahead, the task of crafting a better strategy has got to go to the top of management's action agenda.

Key Points

There are five key questions to consider in analyzing a company's own particular competitive circumstances and its competitive position vis-à-vis key rivals:

1. *How well is the present strategy working?* This involves evaluating the strategy from a qualitative standpoint (completeness, internal consistency, rationale, and suitability to the situation) and also from a quantitative standpoint (the strategic and financial results the strategy is producing). The stronger a company's current overall performance, the less likely the need for radical strategy changes. The weaker a company's performance and/or the faster the changes in its external situation (which can be gleaned from industry and competitive analysis), the more its current strategy must be questioned.

2. *What are the company's resource strengths and weaknesses, and its external opportunities and threats?* A SWOT analysis provides an overview of a firm's situation and is an essential component of crafting a strategy tightly matched to the company's situation. The two most important parts of SWOT analysis are (*a*) drawing conclusions about what story the compilation of strengths, weaknesses, opportunities, and threats tells about the company's overall situation, and

(*b*) acting on those conclusions to better match the company's strategy, to its resource strengths and market opportunities, to correct the important weaknesses, and to defend against external threats. A company's resource strengths, competencies, and competitive capabilities are strategically relevant because they are the most logical and appealing building blocks for strategy; resource weaknesses are important because they may represent vulnerabilities that need correction. External opportunities and threats come into play because a good strategy necessarily aims at capturing a company's most attractive opportunities and at defending against threats to its well-being.

3. *Are the company's prices and costs competitive?* One telling sign of whether a company's situation is strong or precarious is whether its prices and costs are competitive with those of industry rivals. Value chain analysis and benchmarking are essential tools in determining whether the company is performing particular functions and activities cost-effectively, learning whether its costs are in line with competitors, and deciding which internal activities and business processes need to be scrutinized for improvement. Value chain analysis teaches that how competently a company manages its value chain activities relative to rivals is a key to building a competitive advantage based on either better competencies and competitive capabilities or lower costs than rivals.

4. *Is the company competitively stronger or weaker than key rivals?* The key appraisals here involve how the company matches up against key rivals on industry key success factors and other chief determinants of competitive success and whether and why the company has a competitive advantage or disadvantage. Quantitative competitive strength assessments, using the method presented in Table 4.5, indicate where a company is competitively strong and weak, and provide insight into the company's ability to defend or enhance its market position. As a rule a company's competitive strategy should be built around its competitive strengths and should aim at shoring up areas where it is competitively vulnerable. When a company has important competitive strengths in areas where one or more rivals are weak, it makes sense to consider offensive moves to exploit rivals' competitive weaknesses. When a company has important competitive weaknesses in areas where one or more rivals are strong, it makes sense to consider defensive moves to curtail its vulnerability.

5. *What strategic issues and problems merit front-burner managerial attention?* This analytical step zeros in on the strategic issues and problems that stand in the way of the company's success. It involves using the results of both industry and competitive analysis and company situation analysis to identify a "worry list" of issues to be resolved for the company to be financially and competitively successful in the years ahead. The worry list always centers on such concerns as "how to . . .," "what to do about . . .," and "whether to . . ."—the purpose of the worry list is to identify the specific issues/problems that management needs to address. Actually deciding upon a strategy and what specific actions to take is what comes after the list of strategic issues and problems that merit front-burner management attention is developed.

Good company situation analysis, like good industry and competitive analysis, is a valuable precondition for good strategy making. A competently done evaluation of a company's resource capabilities and competitive strengths exposes strong and weak points in the present strategy and how attractive or unattractive the company's competitive position is and why. Managers need such understanding to craft a strategy that is well suited to the company's competitive circumstances.

Exercises

1. Review the information in Illustration Capsule 4.1 concerning the costs of the different value chain activities associated with recording and distributing music CDs through traditional brick-and-mortar retail outlets. Then answer the following questions:

   a. Does the growing popularity of downloading music from the Internet give rise to a new music industry value chain that differs considerably from the traditional value chain? Explain why or why not.

   b. What costs are cut out of the traditional value chain or bypassed when *online music retailers* (Apple, Sony, Microsoft, Musicmatch, Napster, Cdigix, and others) sell songs directly to online buyers? (Note: In 2005, online music stores were selling download-only titles for $0.79 to $0.99 per song and $9.99 for most albums.)

   c. What costs would be cut out of the traditional value chain or bypassed in the event that *recording studios* sell downloadable files of artists' recordings directly to online buyers?

   d. What happens to the traditional value chain if more and more music lovers use peer-to-peer file-sharing software to download music from the Internet to play music on their PCs or MP3 players or make their own CDs? (Note: It was estimated that, in 2004, about 1 billion songs were available for online trading and file sharing via such programs as Kazaa, Grokster, Shareaza, BitTorrent, and eDonkey, despite the fact that some 4,000 people had been sued by the Recording Industry Association of America for pirating copyrighted music via peer-to-peer file sharing.)

2. Using the information in Table 4.1 and the following financial statement information for Avon Products, calculate the following ratios for Avon for both 2003 and 2004:

   a. Gross profit margin.

   b. Operating profit margin.

   c. Net profit margin.

   d. Return on total assets.

   e. Return on stockholders' equity.

   f. Debt-to-equity ratio.

   g. Times-interest-earned.

   h. Days of inventory.

   i. Inventory turnover ratio.

   j. Average collection period.

   Based on these ratios, did Avon's financial performance improve, weaken, or remain about the same from 2003 to 2004?

Avon Products Inc., Consolidated Statements of Income
(in millions, except per share data)

| | Years Ended December 31 | |
	2004	2003
Net sales	$7,656.2	$6,773.7
Other revenue	91.6	71.4
Total revenue	7,747.8	6,845.1
Costs, expenses and other:		
Cost of sales	2,911.7	2,611.8
Marketing, distribution and administrative expenses	3,610.3	3,194.4
Special charges, net	(3.2)	(3.9)
Operating profit	1,229.0	1,042.8
Interest expense	33.8	33.3
Interest income	(20.6)	(12.6)
Other expense (income), net	28.3	28.6
Total other expenses	41.5	49.3
Income before taxes and minority interest	1,187.5	993.5
Income taxes	330.6	318.9
Income before minority interest	856.9	674.6
Minority interest	(10.8)	(9.8)
Net income	$ 846.1	$ 664.8
Earnings per share:		
Basic	$ 1.79	$ 1.41
Diluted	$ 1.77	$ 1.39
Weighted-average shares outstanding (in millions):		
Basic	472.35	471.08
Diluted	477.96	483.13

Avon Products Inc. Consolidated Balance Sheets (in millions)

	December 31	
	2004	2003
Current assets		
Cash, including cash equivalents of $401.2 and $373.8	$ 769.6	$ 694.0
Accounts receivable (less allowances of $101.0 and $81.1)	599.1	553.2
Inventories	740.5	653.4
Prepaid expenses and other	397.2	325.5
Total current assets	$2,506.4	$2,226.1
Property, plant and equipment, at cost:		
Land	$ 61.7	$ 58.6
Buildings and improvements	886.8	765.9
Equipment	1,006.7	904.4
	1,955.2	1,728.9
Less accumulated depreciation	(940.4)	(873.3)
	1,014.8	855.6
Other assets	626.9	499.9
Total assets	$4,148.1	$3,581.6
Liabilities and shareholders' equity		
Current liabilities		
Debt maturing within one year	$ 51.7	$ 244.1
Accounts payable	490.1	400.1
Accrued compensation	164.5	149.5
Other accrued liabilities	360.1	332.6
Sales and taxes other than income	154.4	139.5
Income taxes	304.7	341.2
Total current liabilities	$1,525.5	$1,607.0
Long-term debt	$ 866.3	$ 877.7
Employee benefit plans	620.6	502.1
Deferred income taxes	12.1	50.6
Other liabilities (including minority interest of $42.5 and $46.0)	173.4	172.9
Total liabilities	$3,197.9	$3,210.3

(Continued)

	December 31	
	2004	**2003**
Shareholders' equity		
Common stock, par value $.25—authorized 1,500 shares; issued 728.61 and 722.25 shares	182.2	90.3
Additional paid-in capital	1,356.8	1,188.4
Retained earnings	2,693.5	2,202.4
Accumulated other comprehensive loss	(679.5)	(729.4)
Treasury stock, at cost—257.08 and 251.66 shares	(2,602.8)	(2,380.4)
Total shareholders' equity	950.2	371.3
Total liabilities and shareholders' equity	$4,148.1	$3,581.6

Source: Avon Products Inc., 2004 10-K

The Five Generic Competitive Strategies

Which One to Employ?

Competitive strategy is about being different. It means deliberately choosing to perform activities differently or to perform different activities than rivals to deliver a unique mix of value.

—**Michael E. Porter**

Strategy . . . is about first analyzing and then experimenting, trying, learning, and experimenting some more.

—**Ian C. McMillan and Rita Gunther McGrath**

Winners in business play rough and don't apologize for it. The nicest part of playing hardball is watching your competitors squirm.

—**George Stalk Jr. and Rob Lachenauer**

The essence of strategy lies in creating tomorrow's competitive advantages faster than competitors mimic the ones you possess today.

—**Gary Hamel and C. K. Prahalad**

This chapter describes the *five basic competitive strategy options*—which of the five to employ is a company's first and foremost choice in crafting an overall strategy and beginning its quest for competitive advantage. A company's **competitive strategy** deals exclusively with the specifics of management's game plan for competing successfully—its specific efforts to please customers, its offensive and defensive moves to counter the maneuvers of rivals, its responses to whatever market conditions prevail at the moment, its initiatives to strengthen its market position, and its approach to securing a competitive advantage vis-à-vis rivals. Companies the world over are imaginative in conceiving competitive strategies to win customer favor. At most companies the aim, quite simply, is to do a significantly better job than rivals of providing what buyers are looking for and thereby secure an upper hand in the marketplace.

> **Core Concept**
> A *competitive strategy* concerns the specifics of management's game plan for competing successfully and securing a competitive advantage over rivals.

A company achieves competitive advantage whenever it has some type of edge over rivals in attracting buyers and coping with competitive forces. There are many routes to competitive advantage, but they all involve giving buyers what they perceive as superior value compared to the offerings of rival sellers. Superior value can mean a good product at a lower price; a superior product that is worth paying more for; or a best-value offering that represents an attractive combination of price, features, quality, service, and other appealing attributes. Delivering superior value—whatever form it takes—nearly always requires performing value chain activities differently than rivals and building competencies and resource capabilities that are not readily matched.

> **Core Concept**
> The objective of competitive strategy is to knock the socks off rival companies by doing a better job of satisfying buyer needs and preferences.

THE FIVE GENERIC COMPETITIVE STRATEGIES

There are countless variations in the competitive strategies that companies employ, mainly because each company's strategic approach entails custom-designed actions to fit its own circumstances and industry environment. The custom-tailored nature of each company's strategy makes the chances remote that any two companies—even companies in the same industry—will employ strategies that are exactly alike in every detail. Managers at different companies always have a slightly different spin on future market conditions and how to best align their company's strategy with these conditions; moreover, they have different notions of how they intend to outmaneuver rivals and what strategic options make the most sense for their particular company. However, when one strips away the details to get at the real substance, the biggest and most important differences among competitive strategies boil down to (1) whether a company's market target is broad or narrow, and (2) whether the company is pursuing a competitive advantage linked to low costs or product differentiation. Five distinct competitive strategy approaches stand out:[1]

1. *A low-cost provider strategy*—striving to achieve lower overall costs than rivals and appealing to a broad spectrum of customers, usually by underpricing rivals.

2. *A broad differentiation strategy*—seeking to differentiate the company's product offering from rivals' in ways that will appeal to a broad spectrum of buyers.

3. *A best-cost provider strategy*—giving customers more value for their money by incorporating good-to-excellent product attributes at a lower cost than rivals; the target is to have the lowest (best) costs and prices compared to rivals offering products with comparable attributes.

Figure 5.1   **The Five Generic Competitive Strategies: Each Stakes Out a Different Market Position**

Source: This is an author-expanded version of a three-strategy classification discussed in Michael E. Porter, *Competitive Strategy: Techniques for Analyzing Industries and Competitors* (New York: Free Press, 1980), pp. 35–40.

4. *A focused (or market niche) strategy based on low costs*—concentrating on a narrow buyer segment and outcompeting rivals by having lower costs than rivals and thus being able to serve niche members at a lower price.

5. *A focused (or market niche) strategy based on differentiation*—concentrating on a narrow buyer segment and outcompeting rivals by offering niche members customized attributes that meet their tastes and requirements better than rivals' products.

Each of these five generic competitive approaches stakes out a different market position, as shown in Figure 5.1. Each involves distinctively different approaches to competing and operating the business. The remainder of this chapter explores the ins and outs of the five generic competitive strategies and how they differ.

LOW-COST PROVIDER STRATEGIES

Striving to be the industry's overall low-cost provider is a powerful competitive approach in markets with many price-sensitive buyers. A company achieves low-cost leadership when it becomes the industry's lowest-cost provider rather than just being one of perhaps several competitors with comparatively low costs. A low-cost provider's strategic target is meaningfully lower costs than rivals—but not necessarily the absolutely lowest possible cost. In striving for a cost advantage over rivals, managers must take care to include features and services that buyers consider essential—*a product offering that is too frills-free sabotages the attractiveness of the company's product and can turn buyers off even if it is priced lower than competing products.* For maximum effectiveness, companies employing a low-cost provider strategy need to achieve their cost advantage in ways difficult for rivals to copy or match. If rivals find it relatively easy or inexpensive to imitate the leader's low-cost methods, then the leader's advantage will be too short-lived to yield a valuable edge in the marketplace.

> **Core Concept**
> A low-cost leader's basis for competitive advantage is lower overall costs than competitors. Successful low-cost leaders are exceptionally good at finding ways to drive costs out of their businesses.

A company has two options for translating a low-cost advantage over rivals into attractive profit performance. Option 1 is to use the lower-cost edge to underprice competitors and attract price-sensitive buyers in great enough numbers to increase total profits. The trick to profitably underpricing rivals is either to keep the size of the price cut smaller than the size of the firm's cost advantage (thus reaping the benefits of both a bigger profit margin per unit sold and the added profits on incremental sales) or to generate enough added volume to increase total profits despite thinner profit margins (larger volume can make up for smaller margins provided the underpricing of rivals brings in enough extra sales). Option 2 is to maintain the present price, be content with the present market share, and use the lower-cost edge to earn a higher profit margin on each unit sold, thereby raising the firm's total profits and overall return on investment.

Illustration Capsule 5.1 describes Nucor Corporation's strategy for gaining low-cost leadership in manufacturing a variety of steel products.

The Two Major Avenues for Achieving a Cost Advantage

To achieve a low-cost edge over rivals, a firm's cumulative costs across its overall value chain must be lower than competitors' cumulative costs—and the means of achieving

Illustration Capsule 5.1

Nucor Corporation's Low-Cost Provider Strategy

Nucor Corporation is the world's leading minimill producer of such steel products as carbon and alloy steel bars, beams, sheet, and plate; steel joists and joist girders; steel deck; cold finished steel; steel fasteners; metal building systems; and light gauge steel framing. In 2004, it had close to $10 billion in sales, 9,000 employees, and annual production capacity of nearly 22 million tons, making it the largest steel producer in the United States and one of the 10 largest in the world. The company has pursued a strategy that has made it among the world's lowest-cost producers of steel and has allowed the company to consistently outperform its rivals in terms of financial and market performance.

Nucor's low-cost strategy aims to give it a cost and pricing advantage in the commodity-like steel industry and leaves no part of the company's value chain neglected. The key elements of the strategy include the following:

- Using electric arc furnaces where scrap steel and directly reduced iron ore are melted and then sent to a continuous caster and rolling mill to be shaped into steel products, thereby eliminating an assortment of production processes from the value chain used by traditional integrated steel mills. Nucor's minimill value chain makes the use of coal, coke, and iron ore unnecessary; cuts investment in facilities and equipment (eliminating coke ovens, blast furnaces, basic oxygen furnaces, and ingot casters); and requires fewer employees than integrated mills.

- Striving hard for continuous improvement in the efficiency of its plants and frequently investing in state-of-the-art equipment to reduce unit costs. Nucor is known for its technological leadership and its aggressive pursuit of production process innovation.

- Carefully selecting plant sites to minimize inbound and outbound shipping costs and to take advantage of low rates for electricity (electric arc furnaces are heavy users of electricity). Nucor tends to avoid locating new plants in geographic areas where labor unions are a strong influence.

- Hiring a nonunion workforce that uses team-based incentive compensation systems (often opposed by unions). Operating and maintenance employees and supervisors are paid weekly bonuses based on the productivity of their work group. The size of the bonus is based on the capabilities of the equipment employed and ranges from 80 percent to 150 percent of an employee's base pay; no bonus is paid if the equipment is not operating. Nucor's compensation program has boosted the company's labor productivity to levels nearly double the industry average while rewarding productive employees with annual compensation packages that exceed what their union counterparts earn by as much as 20 percent. Nucor has been able to attract and retain highly talented, productive, and dedicated employees. In addition, the company's healthy culture and results-oriented self-managed work teams allow the company to employ fewer supervisors than what would be needed with an hourly union workforce.

- Heavily emphasizing consistent product quality and has rigorous quality systems.

- Minimizing general and administrative expenses by maintaining a lean staff at corporate headquarters (fewer than 125 employees) and allowing only four levels of management between the CEO and production workers. Headquarters offices are modestly furnished and located in an inexpensive building. The company minimizes reports, paperwork, and meetings to keep managers focused on value-adding activities. Nucor is noted not only for its streamlined organizational structure but also for its frugality in travel and entertainment expenses—the company's top managers set the example by flying coach class, avoiding pricey hotels, and refraining from taking customers out for expensive dinners.

In 2001–2003, when many U.S. producers of steel products were in dire economic straits because of weak demand for steel and deep price discounting by foreign rivals, Nucor began acquiring state-of-the-art steelmaking facilities from bankrupt or nearly bankrupt rivals at bargain-basement prices, often at 20 to 25 percent of what it cost to construct the facilities. This has given Nucor much lower depreciation costs than rivals having comparable plants.

Nucor management's outstanding execution of its low-cost strategy and its commitment to drive down costs throughout its value chain has allowed it to compete aggressively on price, earn higher profit margins than rivals, and grow its business at a considerably faster rate than its integrated steel mill rivals.

Source: Company annual reports, news releases, and Web site.

the cost advantage must be durable. There are two ways to accomplish this:[2]

1. Do a better job than rivals of performing value chain activities more cost-effectively.
2. Revamp the firm's overall value chain to eliminate or bypass some cost-producing activities.

Let's look at each of the two approaches to securing a cost advantage.

Cost-Efficient Management of Value Chain Activities   For a company to do a more cost-efficient job of managing its value chain than rivals, managers must launch a concerted, ongoing effort to ferret out cost-saving opportunities in every part of the value chain. No activity can escape cost-saving scrutiny, and all company personnel must be expected to use their talents and ingenuity to come up with innovative and effective ways to keep costs down. All avenues for performing value chain activities at a lower cost than rivals have to be explored. Attempts to outmanage rivals on cost commonly involve such actions as:

1. *Striving to capture all available economies of scale.* Economies of scale stem from an ability to lower unit costs by increasing the scale of operation—there are many occasions when a large plant is more economical to operate than a small or medium-size plant or when a large distribution warehouse is more cost efficient than a small warehouse. Often, manufacturing economies can be achieved by using common parts and components in different models and/or by cutting back on the number of models offered (especially slow-selling ones) and then scheduling longer production runs for fewer models. In global industries, making separate products for each country market instead of selling a mostly standard product worldwide tends to boost unit costs because of lost time in model changeover, shorter production runs, and inability to reach the most economic scale of production for each country model.

2. *Taking full advantage of learning/experience curve effects.* The cost of performing an activity can decline over time as the learning and experience of company personnel builds. Learning/experience curve economies can stem from debugging and mastering newly introduced technologies, using the experiences and suggestions of workers to install more efficient plant layouts and assembly procedures, and the added speed and effectiveness that accrues from repeatedly picking sites for and building new plants, retail outlets, or distribution centers. Aggressively managed low-cost providers pay diligent attention to capturing the benefits of learning and experience and to keeping these benefits proprietary to whatever extent possible.

3. *Trying to operate facilities at full capacity.* Whether a company is able to operate at or near full capacity has a big impact on units costs when its value chain contains activities associated with substantial fixed costs. Higher rates of capacity utilization allow depreciation and other fixed costs to be spread over a larger unit volume, thereby lowering fixed costs per unit. The more capital-intensive the business, or the higher the percentage of fixed costs as a percentage of total costs, the more important that full-capacity operation becomes because there's such a stiff unit-cost penalty for underutilizing existing capacity. In such cases, finding ways to operate close to full capacity year-round can be an important source of cost advantage.

4. *Pursuing efforts to boost sales volumes and thus spread such costs as R&D, advertising, and selling and administrative costs out over more units.* The more units

a company sells, the more it lowers its unit costs for R&D, sales and marketing, and administrative overhead.

5. *Improving supply chain efficiency.* Many companies pursue cost reduction by partnering with suppliers to streamline the ordering and purchasing process via online systems, reduce inventory carrying costs via just-in-time inventory practices, economize on shipping and materials handling, and ferret out other cost-saving opportunities. A company with a core competence (or better still a distinctive competence) in cost-efficient supply chain management can sometimes achieve a sizable cost advantage over less adept rivals.

6. *Substituting the use of low-cost for high-cost raw materials or component parts.* If the costs of raw materials and parts are too high, a company can either substitute the use of lower-cost items or maybe even design the high-cost components out of the product altogether.

7. *Using online systems and sophisticated software to achieve operating efficiencies.* Data sharing, starting with customer orders and going all the way back to components production, coupled with the use of enterprise resource planning (ERP) and manufacturing execution system (MES) software, can make custom manufacturing just as cheap as mass production—and sometimes cheaper. Online systems and software can also greatly reduce production times and labor costs. Lexmark used ERP and MES software to cut its production time for inkjet printers from four hours to 24 minutes. Southwest Airlines uses proprietary software to schedule flights and assign flight crews cost-effectively.

8. *Adopting labor-saving operating methods.* Examples of ways for a company to economize on labor costs include the following: installing labor-saving technology, shifting production from geographic areas where labor costs are high to geographic areas where labor costs are low, avoiding the use of union labor where possible (because of work rules that can stifle productivity and because of union demands for above-market pay scales and costly fringe benefits), and using incentive compensation systems that promote high labor productivity.

9. *Using the company's bargaining power vis-à-vis suppliers to gain concessions.* Many large enterprises (e.g., Wal-Mart, Home Depot, the world's major motor vehicle producers) have used their bargaining clout in purchasing large volumes to wrangle good prices on their purchases from suppliers. Having greater buying power than rivals can be an important source of cost advantage.

10. *Being alert to the cost advantages of outsourcing and vertical integration.* Outsourcing the performance of certain value chain activities can be more economical than performing them in-house if outside specialists, by virtue of their expertise and volume, can perform the activities at lower cost. Indeed, outsourcing has in recent years become a widely used cost-reduction approach. However, there can be times when integrating the activities of either suppliers or distribution channel allies can allow an enterprise to detour suppliers or buyers who have an adverse impact on costs because of their considerable bargaining power.

In addition to the above means of achieving lower costs than rivals, managers can also achieve important cost savings by deliberately opting for an inherently economical strategy keyed to a frills-free product offering. For instance, a company can bolster its attempts to open up a durable cost advantage over rivals by:

- Having lower specifications for purchased materials, parts, and components than rivals do. Thus, a maker of personal computers (PCs) can use the cheapest hard drives, microprocessors, monitors, DVD drives, and other components it can find so as to end up with lower production costs than rival PC makers.

- Distributing the company's product only through low-cost distribution channels and avoiding high-cost distribution channels.
- Choosing to use the most economical method for delivering customer orders (even if it results in longer delivery times).

These strategy-related means of keeping costs low don't really involve "outmanaging" rivals, but they can nonetheless contribute materially to becoming the industry's low-cost leader.

Revamping the Value Chain to Curb or Eliminate Unnecessary Activities

Dramatic cost advantages can emerge from finding innovative ways to cut back on or entirely bypass certain cost-producing value chain activities. There are six primary ways companies can achieve a cost advantage by reconfiguring their value chains:

1. *Cutting out distributors and dealers by selling directly to customers.* Selling directly and bypassing the activities and costs of distributors or dealers can involve (1) having the company's own direct sales force (which adds the costs of maintaining and supporting a sales force but may well be cheaper than accessing customers through distributors or dealers) and/or (2) conducting sales operations at the company's Web site (Web site operations may be substantially cheaper than distributor or dealer channels). Costs in the wholesale/retail portions of the value chain frequently represent 35–50 percent of the price final consumers pay. There are several prominent examples in which companies have instituted a sell-direct approach to cutting costs out of the value chain. Software developers allow customers to download new programs directly from the Internet, eliminating the costs of producing and packaging CDs and cutting out the host of activities, costs, and markups associated with shipping and distributing software through wholesale and retail channels. By cutting all these costs and activities out of the value chain, software developers have the pricing room to boost their profit margins and still sell their products below levels that retailers would have to charge. The major airlines now sell most of their tickets directly to passengers via their Web sites, ticket counter agents, and telephone reservation systems, allowing them to save hundreds of millions of dollars in commissions once paid to travel agents.

2. *Replacing certain value chain activities with faster and cheaper online technology.* In recent years the Internet and Internet technology applications have become powerful and pervasive tools for conducting business and reengineering company and industry value chains. For instance, Internet technology has revolutionized supply chain management, turning many time-consuming and labor-intensive activities into paperless transactions performed instantaneously. Company procurement personnel can—with only a few mouse clicks—check materials inventories against incoming customer orders, check suppliers' stocks, check the latest prices for parts and components at auction and e-sourcing Web sites, and check FedEx delivery schedules. Various e-procurement software packages streamline the purchasing process by eliminating paper documents such as requests for quotations, purchase orders, order acceptances, and shipping notices. There's software that permits the relevant details of incoming customer orders to be instantly shared with the suppliers of needed parts and components. All this facilitates

just-in-time deliveries of parts and components and matching the production of parts and components to assembly plant requirements and production schedules, cutting out unnecessary activities and producing savings for both suppliers and manufacturers. Retailers can install online systems that relay data from cash register sales at the check-out counter back to manufacturers and their suppliers. Manufacturers can use online systems to collaborate closely with parts and components suppliers in designing new products and shortening the time it takes to get them into production. Online systems allow warranty claims and product performance problems involving supplier components to be instantly relayed to the relevant suppliers so that corrections can be expedited. Online systems have the further effect of breaking down corporate bureaucracies and reducing overhead costs. The whole back-office data management process (order processing, invoicing, customer accounting, and other kinds of transaction costs) can be handled fast, accurately, and with less paperwork and fewer personnel.

3. *Streamlining operations by eliminating low-value-added or unnecessary work steps and activities.* Examples include using computer-assisted design techniques, standardizing parts and components across models and styles, having suppliers collaborate to combine parts and components into modules so that products can be assembled in fewer steps, and shifting to an easy-to-manufacture product design. At Wal-Mart, some items supplied by manufacturers are delivered directly to retail stores rather than being routed through Wal-Mart's distribution centers and delivered by Wal-Mart trucks; in other instances, Wal-Mart unloads incoming shipments from manufacturers' trucks arriving at its distribution centers directly onto outgoing Wal-Mart trucks headed to particular stores without ever moving the goods into the distribution center. Many supermarket chains have greatly reduced in-store meat butchering and cutting activities by shifting to meats that are cut and packaged at the meat-packing plant and then delivered to their stores in ready-to-sell form.

4. *Relocating facilities so as to curb the need for shipping and handling activities.* Having suppliers locate facilities adjacent to the company's plant or locating the company's plants or warehouses near customers can help curb or eliminate shipping and handling costs.

5. *Offering a frills-free product.* Deliberately restricting a company's product offering to the essentials can help the company cut costs associated with snazzy attributes and a full lineup of options and extras. Activities and costs can also be eliminated by incorporating fewer performance and quality features into the product and by offering buyers fewer services. Stripping extras like first-class sections, meals, and reserved seating is a favorite technique of budget airlines like Southwest, Ryanair (Europe), easyJet (Europe), and Gol (Brazil).

6. *Offering a limited product line as opposed to a full product line.* Pruning slow-selling items from the product lineup and being content to meet the needs of most buyers rather than all buyers can eliminate activities and costs associated with numerous product versions and wide selection.

Illustration Capsule 5.2 describes how Wal-Mart has managed its value chain in the retail grocery portion of its business to achieve a dramatic cost advantage over rival supermarket chains and become the world's biggest grocery retailer.

Examples of Companies That Revamped Their Value Chains to Reduce Costs Iowa Beef Packers (IBP), now a subsidiary of Tyson Foods, pioneered the

Ilustration Capsule 5.2

How Wal-Mart Managed Its Value Chain to Achieve a Huge Low-Cost Advantage over Rival Supermarket Chains

Wal-Mart has achieved a very substantial cost and pricing advantage over rival supermarket chains both by revamping portions of the grocery retailing value chain and by out-managing its rivals in efficiently performing various value chain activities. Its cost advantage stems from a series of initiatives and practices:

- Instituting extensive information sharing with vendors via online systems that relay sales at its check-out counters directly to suppliers of the items, thereby providing suppliers with real-time information on customer demand and preferences (creating an estimated 6 percent cost advantage). It is standard practice at Wal-Mart to collaborate extensively with vendors on all aspects of the purchasing and store delivery process to squeeze out mutually beneficial cost savings. Procter & Gamble, Wal-Mart's biggest supplier, went so far as to integrate its enterprise resource planning (ERP) system with Wal-Mart's.

- Pursuing global procurement of some items and centralizing most purchasing activities so as to leverage the company's buying power (creating an estimated 2.5 percent cost advantage).

- Investing in state-of-the-art automation at its distribution centers, efficiently operating a truck fleet that makes daily deliveries to Wal-Mart's stores, and putting assorted other cost-saving practices into place at its headquarters, distribution centers, and stores (resulting in an estimated 4 percent cost advantage).

- Striving to optimize the product mix and achieve greater sales turnover (resulting in about a 2 percent cost advantage).

- Installing security systems and store operating procedures that lower shrinkage rates (producing a cost advantage of about 0.5 percent).

- Negotiating preferred real estate rental and leasing rates with real estate developers and owners of its store sites (yielding a cost advantage of 2 percent).

- Managing and compensating its workforce in a manner that produces lower labor costs (yielding an estimated 5 percent cost advantage)

Altogether, these value chain initiatives give Wal-Mart an approximately 22 percent cost advantage over Kroger, Safeway, and other leading supermarket chains. With such a sizable cost advantage, Wal-Mart has been able to under-price its rivals and become the world's leading supermarket retailer in little more than a decade.

Source: Developed by the authors from information at www.wal-mart.com (accessed September 15, 2004) and in Marco Iansiti and Roy Levien, "Strategy as Ecology," *Harvard Business Review* 82, no. 3 (March 2004), p. 70.

development of a cheaper value chain system in the beef-packing industry.[3] The traditional cost chain involved raising cattle on scattered farms and ranches; shipping them live to labor-intensive, unionized slaughtering plants; and then transporting whole sides of beef to grocery retailers whose butcher departments cut them into smaller pieces and packaged them for sale to grocery shoppers. IBP revamped the traditional chain with a radically different strategy: It built large automated plants employing nonunion workers near cattle supplies. Near the plants it arranged to set up large feed lots (or holding pens) where cattle were fed grain for a short time to fatten them up prior to slaughter. The meat was butchered at the processing plant into small, high-yield cuts. Some of the trimmed and boned cuts were vacuum-sealed in plastic casings for further butchering in supermarket meat departments, but others were trimmed and/or boned, put in plastic-sealed ready-to-sell trays, boxed, and shipped to retailers. IBP's strategy was to increase the volume of prepackaged, "case-ready" cuts that retail grocers could unpack from boxes and place directly into the meat case. In addition, IBP provided meat retailers with individually wrapped quick-frozen steaks, as well as precooked roasts, beef tip, and meatloaf selections that could be prepared in a matter of minutes. Iowa Beef's inbound cattle transportation expenses, traditionally a major cost item, were cut significantly by avoiding the weight losses that occurred when live animals were shipped long distances just prior to slaughter. Sizable major outbound shipping cost savings were achieved by not having to ship whole sides of beef, which had a high waste factor. Meat retailers had to do far less butchering to stock their meat cases. IBP value chain revamping was so successful that the company became the largest U.S. meatpacker.

Southwest Airlines has reconfigured the traditional value chain of commercial airlines to lower costs and thereby offer dramatically lower fares to passengers. Its mastery of fast turnarounds at the gates (about 25 minutes versus 45 minutes for rivals) allows its planes to fly more hours per day. This translates into being able to schedule more flights per day with fewer aircraft, allowing Southwest to generate more revenue per plane on average than rivals. Southwest does not offer in-flight meals, assigned seating, baggage transfer to connecting airlines, or first-class seating and service, thereby eliminating all the cost-producing activities associated with these features. The company's fast, user-friendly online reservation system facilitates e-ticketing and reduces staffing requirements at telephone reservation centers and airport counters. Its use of automated check-in equipment reduces staffing requirements for terminal check-in.

Dell has created the best, most cost-efficient value chain in the global personal computer industry. Whereas Dell's major rivals (Hewlett-Packard, Lenovo, Sony, and Toshiba) produce their models in volume and sell them through independent resellers and retailers, Dell has elected to market directly to PC users, building its PCs to customer specifications as orders come in and shipping them to customers within a few days of receiving the order. Dell's value chain approach has proved cost-effective in coping with the PC industry's blink-of-an-eye product life cycle. The build-to-order strategy enables the company to avoid misjudging buyer demand for its various models and being saddled with quickly obsolete excess components and finished-goods inventories—all parts and components are obtained on a just-in-time basis from vendors, many of which deliver their items to Dell assembly plants several times a day in volumes matched to the Dell's daily assembly schedule. Also, Dell's sell-direct strategy slices reseller/retailer costs and margins out of the value chain (although some of these savings are offset by the cost of Dell's direct marketing and customer support activities—functions that would otherwise be performed by resellers and retailers). Partnerships with suppliers that facilitate just-in-time deliveries of components and minimize Dell's inventory costs, coupled with Dell's extensive use of e-commerce technologies further reduce Dell's costs. Dell's value chain approach is widely considered to have made it the global low-cost leader in the PC industry.

The Keys to Success in Achieving Low-Cost Leadership

To succeed with a low-cost-provider strategy, company managers have to scrutinize each cost-creating activity and determine what factors cause costs to be high or low. Then they have to use this knowledge to keep the unit costs of each activity low, exhaustively pursuing cost efficiencies throughout the value chain. They have to be proactive in restructuring the value chain to eliminate nonessential work steps and low-value activities. Normally, low-cost producers work diligently to create cost-conscious corporate cultures that feature broad employee participation in continuous cost improvement efforts and limited perks and frills for executives. They strive to operate with exceptionally small corporate staffs to keep administrative costs to a minimum.

Many successful low-cost leaders also use benchmarking to keep close tabs on how their costs compare with rivals and firms performing comparable activities in other industries.

But while low-cost providers are champions of frugality, they are usually aggressive in investing in resources and capabilities that promise to drive costs out of the business. Wal-Mart, one of the foremost practitioners of low-cost leadership, employs state-of-the-art technology throughout its operations— its distribution facilities are an automated showcase, it uses online systems to order goods from suppliers and manage inventories, it equips its stores with cutting-edge sales-tracking and check-out systems, and it sends daily point-of-sale data to 4,000 vendors. Wal-Mart's information and communications systems and capabilities are more sophisticated than those of virtually any other retail chain in the world.

> Success in achieving a low-cost edge over rivals comes from outmanaging rivals in figuring out how to perform value chain activities most cost effectively and eliminating or curbing non essential value chain activities

Other companies noted for their successful use of low-cost provider strategies include Lincoln Electric in arc welding equipment, Briggs & Stratton in small gasoline engines, Bic in ballpoint pens, Black & Decker in power tools, Stride Rite in footwear, Beaird-Poulan in chain saws, and General Electric and Whirlpool in major home appliances.

When a Low-Cost Provider Strategy Works Best

A competitive strategy predicated on low-cost leadership is particularly powerful when:

1. *Price competition among rival sellers is especially vigorous*—Low-cost providers are in the best position to compete offensively on the basis of price, to use the appeal of lower price to grab sales (and market share) from rivals, to win the business of price-sensitive buyers, to remain profitable in the face of strong price competition, and to survive price wars.

2. *The products of rival sellers are essentially identical and supplies are readily available from any of several eager sellers*—Commodity-like products and/or ample supplies set the stage for lively price competition; in such markets, it is less efficient, higher-cost companies whose profits get squeezed the most.

3. *There are few ways to achieve product differentiation that have value to buyers*—When the differences between brands do not matter much to buyers, buyers are nearly always very sensitive to price differences and shop the market for the best price.

4. *Most buyers use the product in the same ways*—With common user requirements, a standardized product can satisfy the needs of buyers, in which case low selling price, not features or quality, becomes the dominant factor in causing buyers to choose one seller's product over another's.

5. *Buyers incur low costs in switching their purchases from one seller to another*—Low switching costs give buyers the flexibility to shift purchases to lower-priced sellers having equally good products or to attractively priced substitute products. A low-cost leader is well positioned to use low price to induce its customers not to switch to rival brands or substitutes.

6. *Buyers are large and have significant power to bargain down prices*—Low-cost providers have partial profit-margin protection in bargaining with high-volume buyers, since powerful buyers are rarely able to bargain price down past the survival level of the next most cost-efficient seller.

7. *Industry newcomers use introductory low prices to attract buyers and build a customer base*—The low-cost leader can use price cuts of its own to make it harder

A low-cost provider is in the best position to win the business of price-sensitive buyers, set the floor on market price, and still earn a profit.

for a new rival to win customers; the pricing power of the low-cost provider acts as a barrier for new entrants.

As a rule, the more price-sensitive buyers are, the more appealing a low-cost strategy becomes. A low-cost company's ability to set the industry's price floor and still earn a profit erects protective barriers around its market position.

The Pitfalls of a Low-Cost Provider Strategy

Perhaps the biggest pitfall of a low-cost provider strategy is getting carried away with overly aggressive price cutting and ending up with lower, rather than higher, profitability. A low-cost/low-price advantage results in superior profitability only if (1) prices are cut by less than the size of the cost advantage or (2) the added gains in unit sales are large enough to bring in a bigger total profit despite lower margins per unit sold. A company with a 5 percent cost advantage cannot cut prices 20 percent, end up with a volume gain of only 10 percent, and still expect to earn higher profits!

A second big pitfall is not emphasizing avenues of cost advantage that can be kept proprietary or that relegate rivals to playing catch-up. The value of a cost advantage depends on its sustainability. Sustainability, in turn, hinges on whether the company achieves its cost advantage in ways difficult for rivals to copy or match.

A low-cost provider's product offering must always contain enough attributes to be attractive to prospective buyers—low price, by itself, is not always appealing to buyers.

A third pitfall is becoming too fixated on cost reduction. Low cost cannot be pursued so zealously that a firm's offering ends up being too features-poor to generate buyer appeal. Furthermore, a company driving hard to push its costs down has to guard against misreading or ignoring increased buyer interest in added features or service, declining buyer sensitivity to price, or new developments that start to alter how buyers use the product. A low-cost zealot risks losing market ground if buyers start opting for more upscale or features-rich products.

Even if these mistakes are avoided, a low-cost competitive approach still carries risk. Cost-saving technological breakthroughs or the emergence of still-lower-cost value chain models can nullify a low-cost leader's hard-won position. The current leader may have difficulty in shifting quickly to the new technologies or value chain approaches because heavy investments lock it in (at least temporarily) to its present value chain approach.

BROAD DIFFERENTIATION STRATEGIES

Core Concept
The essence of a broad differentiation strategy is to be unique in ways that are valuable to a wide range of customers.

Differentiation strategies are attractive whenever buyers' needs and preferences are too diverse to be fully satisfied by a standardized product or by sellers with identical capabilities. A company attempting to succeed through differentiation must study buyers' needs and behavior carefully to learn what buyers consider important, what they think has value, and what they are willing to pay for. Then the company has to incorporate buyer-desired attributes into its product or service offering that will clearly set it apart from rivals. Competitive advantage results once a sufficient number of buyers become strongly attached to the differentiated attributes.

Successful differentiation allows a firm to:

- Command a premium price for its product, and/or
- Increase unit sales (because additional buyers are won over by the differentiating features), and/or

- Gain buyer loyalty to its brand (because some buyers are strongly attracted to the differentiating features and bond with the company and its products).

Differentiation enhances profitability whenever the extra price the product commands outweighs the added costs of achieving the differentiation. Company differentiation strategies fail when buyers don't value the brand's uniqueness and when a company's approach to differentiation is easily copied or matched by its rivals.

Types of Differentiation Themes

Companies can pursue differentiation from many angles: a unique taste (Dr Pepper, Listerine); multiple features (Microsoft Windows, Microsoft Office); wide selection and one-stop shopping (Home Depot, Amazon.com); superior service (FedEx); spare parts availability (Caterpillar); engineering design and performance (Mercedes, BMW); prestige and distinctiveness (Rolex); product reliability (Johnson & Johnson in baby products); quality manufacture (Karastan in carpets, Michelin in tires, Toyota and Honda in automobiles); technological leadership (3M Corporation in bonding and coating products); a full range of services (Charles Schwab in stock brokerage); a complete line of products (Campbell's soups); and top-of-the-line image and reputation (Ralph Lauren and Starbucks).

The most appealing approaches to differentiation are those that are hard or expensive for rivals to duplicate. Indeed, resourceful competitors can, in time, clone almost any product or feature or attribute. If Coca-Cola introduces a vanilla-flavored soft drink, so can Pepsi; if Ford offers a 50,000-mile bumper-to-bumper warranty on its new vehicles, so can Volkswagen and Nissan. If Nokia introduces cell phones with cameras and Internet capability, so can Motorola and Samsung. As a rule, differentiation yields a longer-lasting and more profitable competitive edge when it is based on product innovation, technical superiority, product quality and reliability, comprehensive customer service, and unique competitive capabilities. Such differentiating attributes tend to be tough for rivals to copy or offset profitably, and buyers widely perceive them as having value.

> Easy-to-copy differentiating features cannot produce sustainable competitive advantage; differentiation based on competencies and capabilities tend to be more sustainable.

Where along the Value Chain to Create the Differentiating Attributes

Differentiation is not something hatched in marketing and advertising departments, nor is it limited to the catchalls of quality and service. Differentiation opportunities can exist in activities all along an industry's value chain; possibilities include the following:

- *Supply chain activities* that ultimately spill over to affect the performance or quality of the company's end product. Starbucks gets high ratings on its coffees partly because it has very strict specifications on the coffee beans purchased from suppliers.

- *Product R&D activities* that aim at improved product designs and performance features, expanded end uses and applications, more frequent first-on-the-market victories, wider product variety and selection, added user safety, greater recycling capability, or enhanced environmental protection.

- *Production R&D and technology-related activities* that permit custom-order manufacture at an efficient cost; make production methods safer for the environment; or improve product quality, reliability, and appearance. Many manufacturers have developed flexible manufacturing systems that allow different models and product versions to be made on the same assembly line. Being able to provide buyers with made-to-order products can be a potent differentiating capability.

- *Manufacturing activities* that reduce product defects, prevent premature product failure, extend product life, allow better warranty coverages, improve economy of use, result in more end-user convenience, or enhance product appearance. The quality edge enjoyed by Japanese automakers stems partly from their distinctive competence in performing assembly-line activities.

- *Distribution and shipping activities* that allow for fewer warehouse and on-the-shelf stockouts, quicker delivery to customers, more accurate order filling, and/or lower shipping costs.

- *Marketing, sales, and customer service activities* that result in superior technical assistance to buyers, faster maintenance and repair services, more and better product information provided to customers, more and better training materials for end users, better credit terms, quicker order processing, or greater customer convenience.

Managers need keen understanding of the sources of differentiation and the activities that drive uniqueness to evaluate various differentiation approaches and design durable ways to set their product offering apart from those of rival brands.

The Four Best Routes to Competitive Advantage via a Broad Differentiation Strategy

While it is easy enough to grasp that a successful differentiation strategy must entail creating buyer value in ways unmatched by rivals, the big issue in crafting a differentiation strategy is which of four basic routes to take in delivering unique buyer value via a broad differentiation strategy. Usually, building a sustainable competitive advantage via differentiation involves pursuing one of four basic routes to delivering superior value to buyers.

One route is to *incorporate product attributes and user features that lower the buyer's overall costs of using the company's product.* Making a company's product more economical for a buyer to use can be done by reducing the buyer's raw materials waste (providing cut-to-size components), reducing a buyer's inventory requirements (providing just-in-time deliveries), increasing maintenance intervals and product reliability so as to lower a buyer's repair and maintenance costs, using online systems to reduce a buyer's procurement and order processing costs, and providing free technical support. Rising costs for gasoline have dramatically spurred the efforts of motor vehicle manufacturers worldwide to introduce models with better fuel economy and reduce operating costs for motor vehicle owners.

A second route is to *incorporate features that raise product performance.*[4] This can be accomplished with attributes that provide buyers greater reliability, ease of use, convenience, or durability. Other performance-enhancing options include making the company's product or service cleaner, safer, quieter, or more maintenance-free than rival brands. Cell phone manufacturrs are in a race to introduce next-generation phones with trendsetting features and options.

A third route to a differentiation-based competitive advantage is to *incorporate features that enhance buyer satisfaction in noneconomic or intangible ways.* Goodyear's Aquatread tire design appeals to safety-conscious motorists wary of slick roads. Rolls Royce, Ralph Lauren, Gucci, Tiffany, Cartier, and Rolex have differentiation-based competitive advantages linked to buyer desires for status, image, prestige, upscale fashion, superior craftsmanship, and the finer things in life. L. L. Bean makes its mail-order customers feel secure in their purchases by providing an unconditional guarantee with no time limit: "All of our products are guaranteed to give 100 percent satisfaction in every way. Return anything purchased from us at any time if it proves otherwise. We will replace it, refund your purchase price, or credit your credit card, as you wish."

> **Core Concept**
> A differentiator's basis for competitive advantage is either a product/service offering whose attributes differ significantly from the offerings of rivals or a set of capabilities for delivering customer value that rivals don't have.

The fourth route is to *deliver value to customers by differentiating on the basis of competencies and competitive capabilities that rivals don't have or can't afford to match.*[5] The importance of cultivating competencies and capabilities that add power to a company's resource strengths and competitiveness comes into play here. Core and/or distinctive competencies not only enhance a company's ability to compete successfully in the marketplace but can also be unique in delivering value to buyers. There are numerous examples of companies that have differentiated themselves on the basis of capabilities. Because Fox News and CNN have the capability to devote more air time to breaking news stories and get reporters on the scene very quickly compared to the major networks, many viewers turn to the cable networks when a major news event occurs. Microsoft has stronger capabilities to design, create, distribute, and advertise an array of software products for PC applications than any of its rivals. Avon and Mary Kay Cosmetics have differentiated themselves from other cosmetics and personal care companies by assembling a sales force numbering in the hundreds of thousands that gives them direct sales capability—their sales associates can demonstrate products to interested buyers, take their orders on the spot, and deliver the items to buyers' homes. Japanese automakers have the capability to satisfy changing consumer preferences for one vehicle style versus another because they can bring new models to market faster than American and European automakers.

The Importance of Perceived Value and Signaling Value

Buyers seldom pay for value they don't perceive, no matter how real the unique extras may be.[6] Thus, the price premium commanded by a differentiation strategy reflects *the value actually delivered* to the buyer and *the value perceived* by the buyer (even if not actually delivered). Actual and perceived value can differ whenever buyers have trouble assessing what their experience with the product will be. Incomplete knowledge on the part of buyers often causes them to judge value based on such signals as price (where price connotes quality), attractive packaging, extensive ad campaigns (i.e., how well-known the product is), ad content and image, the quality of brochures and sales presentations, the seller's facilities, the seller's list of customers, the firm's market share, the length of time the firm has been in business, and the professionalism, appearance, and personality of the seller's employees. Such signals of value may be as important as actual value (1) when the nature of differentiation is subjective or hard to quantify, (2) when buyers are making a first-time purchase, (3) when repurchase is infrequent, and (4) when buyers are unsophisticated.

When a Differentiation Strategy Works Best

Differentiation strategies tend to work best in market circumstances where:

- *Buyer needs and uses of the product are diverse*—Diverse buyer preferences present competitors with a bigger window of opportunity to do things differently and set themselves apart with product attributes that appeal to particular buyers. For instance, the diversity of consumer preferences for menu selection, ambience, pricing, and customer service gives restaurants exceptionally wide latitude in creating a differentiated product offering. Other companies having many ways to strongly differentiate themselves from rivals include the publishers of magazines, the makers of motor vehicles, and the manufacturers of cabinetry and countertops.

- *There are many ways to differentiate the product or service and many buyers perceive these differences as having value*—There is plenty of room for retail apparel competitors to stock different styles and quality of apparel merchandise but very little room for the makers of paper clips, copier paper, or sugar to set their products apart. Likewise, the sellers of different brands of gasoline or orange juice have little differentiation opportunity compared to the sellers of high-definition TVs, patio furniture, or breakfast cereal. Unless different buyers have distinguishably different preferences for certain features and product attributes, profitable differentiation opportunities are very restricted.

- *Few rival firms are following a similar differentiation approach*—The best differentiation approaches involve trying to appeal to buyers on the basis of attributes that rivals are not emphasizing. A differentiator encounters less head-to-head rivalry when it goes its own separate way in creating uniqueness and does not try to outdifferentiate rivals on the very same attributes—when many rivals are all claiming "Ours tastes better than theirs" or "Ours gets your clothes cleaner than theirs," the most likely result is weak brand differentiation and "strategy overcrowding"—a situation in which competitors end up chasing the same buyers with very similar product offerings.

- *Technological change is fast-paced and competition revolves around rapidly evolving product features*—Rapid product innovation and frequent introductions of next-version products not only provide space for companies to pursue separate differentiating paths but also heighten buyer interest. In video game hardware and video games, golf equipment, PCs, cell phones, and MP3 players, competitors are locked into an ongoing battle to set themselves apart by introducing the best next-generation products—companies that fail to come up with new and improved products and distinctive performance features quickly lose out in the marketplace. In network TV broadcasting in the United States, NBC, ABC, CBS, Fox, and several others are always scrambling to develop a lineup of TV shows that will win higher audience ratings and pave the way for charging higher advertising rates and boosting ad revenues.

The Pitfalls of a Differentiation Strategy

Differentiation strategies can fail for any of several reasons. *A differentiation strategy is always doomed when competitors are able to quickly copy most or all of the appealing product attributes a company comes up with.* Rapid imitation means that no rival achieves differentiation, since whenever one firm introduces some aspect of uniqueness that strikes the fancy of buyers, fast-following copycats quickly reestablish similarity. This is why a firm must search out sources of uniqueness that are time-consuming or burdensome for rivals to match if it hopes to use differentiation to win a competitive edge over rivals.

> **Core Concept**
> Any differentiating feature that works well is a magnet for imitators.

*A second pitfall is that the company's differentiation strategy produces a ho-hum market reception because buyers see little value in the unique attributes of a company's produc*t. Thus, even if a company sets the attributes of its brand apart from the brands of rivals, its strategy can fail because of trying to differentiate on the basis of something that does not deliver adequate value to buyers (such as lowering a buyer's cost to use the product or enhancing a buyer's well-being). Anytime many potential buyers look at a company's differentiated product offering and conclude "So what?" the company's differentiation strategy is in deep trouble—buyers will likely decide the product is not worth the extra price, and sales will be disappointingly low.

The third big pitfall of a differentiation strategy is overspending on efforts to differentiate the company's product offering, thus eroding profitability. Company efforts to achieve differentiation nearly always raise costs. The trick to profitable differentiation is either to keep the costs of achieving differentiation below the price premium the differentiating attributes can command in the marketplace (thus increasing the profit margin per unit sold) or to offset thinner profit margins per unit by selling enough additional units to increase total profits. If a company goes overboard in pursuing costly differentiation efforts and then unexpectedly discovers that buyers are unwilling to pay a sufficient price premium to cover the added costs of differentiation, it ends up saddled with unacceptably thin profit margins or even losses. The need to contain differentiation costs is why many companies add little touches of differentiation that add to buyer satisfaction but are inexpensive to institute. Upscale restaurants often provide valet parking. Ski resorts provide skiers with complimentary coffee or hot apple cider at the base of the lifts in the morning and late afternoon. FedEx, UPS, and many catalog and online retailers have installed software capabilities that allow customers to track packages in transit. Some hotels and motels provide free continental breakfasts, exercise facilities, and in-room coffeemaking amenities. Publishers are using their Web sites to deliver supplementary educational materials to the buyers of their textbooks. Laundry detergent and soap manufacturers add pleasing scents to their products.

Other common pitfalls and mistakes in crafting a differentiation strategy include:[7]

- *Overdifferentiating so that product quality or service levels exceed buyers' needs.* Even if buyers like the differentiating extras, they may not find them sufficiently valuable for their purposes to pay extra to get them. Many shoppers shy away from buying top-of-the-line items because they have no particular interest in all the bells and whistles; for them, a less deluxe model or style makes better economic sense.

- *Trying to charge too high a price premium.* Even if buyers view certain extras or deluxe features as nice to have, they may still conclude that the added cost is excessive relative to the value they deliver. A differentiator must guard against turning off would-be buyers with what is perceived as price gouging. Normally, the bigger the price premium for the differentiating extras, the harder it is to keep buyers from switching to the lower-priced offerings of competitors.

- *Being timid and not striving to open up meaningful gaps in quality or service or performance features vis-à-vis the products of rivals.* Tiny differences between rivals' product offerings may not be visible or important to buyers. If a company wants to generate the fiercely loyal customer following needed to earn superior profits and open up a differentiation-based competitive advantage over rivals, then its strategy must result in strong rather than weak product differentiation. In markets where differentiators do no better than achieve weak product differentiation (because the attributes of rival brands are fairly similar in the minds of many buyers), customer loyalty to any one brand is weak, the costs of buyers to switch to rival brands are fairly low, and no one company has enough of a market edge that it can get by with charging a price premium over rival brands.

A low-cost provider strategy can defeat a differentiation strategy when buyers are satisfied with a basic product and don't think extra attributes are worth a higher price.

BEST-COST PROVIDER STRATEGIES

Core Concept
The competitive advantage of a best-cost provider is lower costs than rivals in incorporating upscale attributes, putting the company in a position to underprice rivals whose products have similar upscale attributes.

Best-cost provider strategies aim at giving customers *more value for the money.* The objective is to deliver superior value to buyers by satisfying their expectations on key quality/features/performance/service attributes and beating their expectations on price (given what rivals are charging for much the same attributes). *A company achieves best-cost status from an ability to incorporate attractive or upscale attributes at a lower cost than rivals.* The attractive attributes can take the form of appealing features, good-to-excellent product performance or quality, or attractive customer service. When a company has the resource strengths and competitive capabilities to incorporate these upscale attributes into its product offering *at a lower cost than rivals,* it enjoys best-cost status—it is the low-cost provider *of an upscale product.*

Being a best-cost provider is different from being a low-cost provider because the additional upscale features entail additional costs (that a low-cost provider can avoid by offering buyers a basic product with few frills). As Figure 5.1 indicates, best-cost provider strategies stake out a middle ground between pursuing a low-cost advantage and a differentiation advantage and between appealing to the broad market as a whole and a narrow market niche. From a competitive positioning standpoint, best-cost strategies are thus a *hybrid,* balancing a strategic emphasis on low cost against a strategic emphasis on differentiation (upscale features delivered at a price that constitutes superior value).

The competitive advantage of a best-cost provider is its capability to include upscale attributes at a lower cost than rivals whose products have comparable attributes. A best-cost provider can use its low-cost advantage to underprice rivals whose products have similar upscale attributes—it is usually not difficult to entice customers away from rivals charging a higher price for an item with highly comparable features, quality, performance, and/or customer service attributes. To achieve competitive advantage with a best-cost provider strategy, it is critical that a company have the resources and capabilities to incorporate upscale attributes at a lower cost than rivals. In other words, it must be able to (1) incorporate attractive features at a lower cost than rivals whose products have similar features, (2) manufacture a good-to-excellent quality product at a lower cost than rivals with good-to-excellent product quality, (3) develop a product that delivers good-to-excellent performance at a lower cost than rivals whose products also entail good-to-excellent performance, or (4) provide attractive customer service at a lower cost than rivals who provide comparably attractive customer service.

What makes a best-cost provider strategy so appealing is being able to incorporate upscale attributes at a lower cost than rivals and then using the company's low-cost advantage to underprice rivals whose products have similar upscale attributes.

The target market for a best-cost provider is value-conscious buyers—buyers that are looking for appealing extras at an appealingly low price. Value-hunting buyers (as distinct from buyers looking only for bargain-basement prices) often constitute a very sizable part of the overall market. Normally, value-conscious buyers are willing to pay a fair price for extra features, but they shy away from paying top dollar for items havingall the bells and whistles. It is the desire to cater to *value-conscious buyers* as opposed to *budget-conscious buyers* that sets a best-cost provider apart from a low-cost provider—the two strategies aim at distinguishably different market targets.

When a Best-Cost Provider Strategy Works Best

A best-cost provider strategy works best in markets where buyer diversity makes product differentiation the norm and where many buyers are also sensitive to price and value. This is because a best-cost provider can position itself near the middle of the market with either a medium-quality product at a below-average price or a high-quality product at an average or slightly higher price. Often, substantial numbers of buyers prefer midrange products rather than the cheap, basic products of low-cost producers or the expensive products of top-of-the-line differentiators. But unless a company has the resources, know-how, and capabilities to incorporate upscale product or service attributes at a lower cost than rivals, adopting a best-cost strategy is ill advised—a winning strategy must always be matched to a company's resource strengths and capabilities.

Illustration Capsule 5.3 describes how Toyota has applied the principles of a best-cost provider strategy in producing and marketing its Lexus brand.

The Big Risk of a Best-Cost Provider Strategy

A company's biggest vulnerability in employing a best-cost provider strategy is getting squeezed between the strategies of firms using low-cost and high-end differentiation strategies. Low-cost providers may be able to siphon customers away with the appeal of a lower price (despite their less appealing product attributes). High-end differentiators may be able to steal customers away with the appeal of better product attributes (even though their products carry a higher price tag). Thus, to be successful, a best-cost provider must offer buyers *significantly* better product attributes in order to justify a price above what low-cost leaders are charging. Likewise, it has to achieve *significantly* lower costs in providing upscale features so that it can outcompete high-end differentiators on the basis of a *significantly* lower price.

FOCUSED (OR MARKET NICHE) STRATEGIES

What sets focused strategies apart from low-cost leadership or broad differentiation strategies is concentrated attention on a narrow piece of the total market. The target segment, or niche, can be defined by geographic uniqueness, by specialized requirements in using the product, or by special product attributes that appeal only to niche members. Community Coffee, the largest family-owned specialty coffee retailer in the United States, is a company that focused on a geographic market niche; despite having a national market share of only 1.1 percent, Community has won a 50 percent share of the coffee business in supermarkets in southern Louisiana in competition

Illustration Capsule 5.3

Toyota's Best-Cost Producer Strategy for Its Lexus Line

Toyota Motor Company is widely regarded as a low-cost producer among the world's motor vehicle manufacturers. Despite its emphasis on product quality, Toyota has achieved low-cost leadership because it has developed considerable skills in efficient supply chain management and low-cost assembly capabilities, and because its models are positioned in the low-to-medium end of the price spectrum, where high production volumes are conducive to low unit costs. But when Toyota decided to introduce its new Lexus models to compete in the luxury-car market, it employed a classic best-cost provider strategy. Toyota took the following four steps in crafting and implementing its Lexus strategy:

- Designing an array of high-performance characteristics and upscale features into the Lexus models so as to make them comparable in performance and luxury to other high-end models and attractive to Mercedes, BMW, Audi, Jaguar, Cadillac, and Lincoln buyers.

- Transferring its capabilities in making high-quality Toyota models at low cost to making premium-quality Lexus models at costs below other luxury-car makers. Toyota's supply chain capabilities and low-cost assembly know-how allowed it to incorporate high-tech performance features and upscale quality into Lexus models at substantially less cost than comparable Mercedes and BMW models.

- Using its relatively lower manufacturing costs to underprice comparable Mercedes and BMW models. Toyota believed that with its cost advantage it could price attractively equipped Lexus cars low enough to draw price-conscious buyers away from Mercedes and BMW and perhaps induce dissatisfied Lincoln and Cadillac owners to switch to a Lexus. Lexus's pricing advantage over Mercedes and BMW was sometimes quite significant. For example, in 2006 the Lexus RX 330, a midsized SUV, carried a sticker price in the $36,000–$45,000 range (depending on how it was equipped), whereas variously equipped Mercedes M-class SUVs had price tags in the $50,000–$65,000 range and a BMW X5 SUV could range anywhere from $42,000 to $70,000, depending on the optional equipment chosen.

- Establishing a new network of Lexus dealers, separate from Toyota dealers, dedicated to providing a level of personalized, attentive customer service unmatched in the industry.

Lexus models have consistently ranked first in the widely watched J. D. Power & Associates quality survey, and the prices of Lexus models are typically several thousand dollars below those of comparable Mercedes and BMW models—clear signals that Toyota has succeeded in becoming a best-cost producer with its Lexus brand.

against Starbucks, Folger's, Maxwell House, and asserted specialty coffee retailers. Community Coffee's geographic version of a focus strategy has allowed it to capture sales in excess of $100 million annually by catering to the tastes of coffee drinkers across an 11-state region. Examples of firms that concentrate on a well-defined market niche keyed to a particular product or buyer segment include Animal Planet and the History Channel (in cable TV); Google (in Internet search engines); Porsche (in sports cars); Cannondale (in top-of-the-line mountain bikes); Domino's Pizza (in pizza delivery); Enterprise Rent-a-Car (a specialist in providing rental cars to repair garage customers); Bandag (a specialist in truck tire recapping that promotes its recaps aggressively at over 1,000 truck stops), CGA Inc. (a specialist in providing insurance to cover the cost of lucrative hole-in-one prizes at golf tournaments); Match.com (the world's largest online dating service); and Avid Technology (the world leader in digital technology products to create 3D animation and to edit films, videos, TV broadcasts, video games, and audio recordings). Microbreweries, local bakeries, bed-and-breakfast inns, and local owner-managed retail boutiques are all good examples of enterprises that have scaled their operations to serve narrow or local customer segments.

A Focused Low-Cost Strategy

A focused strategy based on low cost aims at securing a competitive advantage by serving buyers in the target market niche at a lower cost and lower price than rival competitors. This strategy has considerable attraction when a firm can lower costs significantly by limiting its customer base to a well-defined buyer segment. The avenues to achieving a cost advantage over rivals also serving the target market niche are the same as for low-cost leadership—outmanage rivals in keeping the costs of value chain activities contained to a bare minimum and search for innovative ways to reconfigure the firm's value chain and bypass or reduce certain value chain activities. The only real difference between a low-cost provider strategy and a focused low-cost strategy is the size of the buyer group that a company is trying to appeal to—the former involves a product offering that appeals broadly to most all buyer groups and market segments whereas the latter at just meeting the needs of buyers in a narrow market segment.

Focused low-cost strategies are fairly common. Producers of private-label goods are able to achieve low costs in product development, marketing, distribution, and advertising by concentrating on making generic items imitative of name-brand merchandise and selling directly to retail chains wanting a basic house brand to sell to price-sensitive shoppers. Several small printer-supply manufacturers have begun making low-cost clones of the premium-priced replacement ink and toner cartridges sold by Hewlett-Packard, Lexmark, Canon, and Epson; the clone manufacturers dissect the cartridges of the name-brand companies and then reengineer a similar version that won't violate patents. The components for remanufactured replacement cartridges are aquired from various outside sources, and the clones are then marketed at prices as much as 50 percent below the name-brand cartridges. Cartridge remanufacturers have been lured to focus on this market because replacement cartridges constitute a multibillion-dollar business with considerable profit potential given their low costs and the premium pricing of the name-brand companies. Illustration Capsule 5.4 describes how Motel 6 has kept its costs low in catering to budget-conscious travelers.

A Focused Differentiation Strategy

A focused strategy keyed to differentiation aims at securing a competitive advantage with a product offering carefully designed to appeal to the unique preferences and needs of a narrow, well-defined group of buyers (as opposed to a broad differentiation strategy aimed at many buyer groups and market segments). Successful use of a focused differentiation strategy depends on the existence of a buyer segment that is looking for special product attributes or seller capabilities and on a firm's ability to stand apart from rivals competing in the same target market niche.

Companies like Godiva Chocolates, Chanel, Gucci, Rolls-Royce, Häagen-Dazs, and W. L. Gore (the maker of Gore-Tex) employ successful differentiation-based focused strategies targeted at upscale buyers wanting products and services with world-class attributes. Indeed, most markets contain a buyer segment willing to pay a big price premium for the very finest items available, thus opening the strategic window for some competitors to pursue differentiation-based focused strategies aimed at the very top of the market pyramid. Another successful focused differentiator is Trader Joe's, a 150-store East and West Coast "fashion food retailer" that is a combination gourmet deli and grocery warehouse.[8] Customers shop Trader Joe's as much for entertainment as for conventional grocery items—the store stocks out-of-the-ordinary culinary treats like raspberry salsa, salmon burgers, and jasmine fried rice,

Illustration Capsule 5.4
Motel 6's Focused Low-Cost Strategy

Motel 6 caters to price-conscious travelers who want a clean, no-frills place to spend the night. To be a low-cost provider of overnight lodging, Motel 6 (1) selects relatively inexpensive sites on which to construct its units (usually near interstate exits and high-traffic locations but far enough away to avoid paying prime site prices); (2) builds only basic facilities (no restaurant or bar and only rarely a swimming pool); (3) relies on standard architectural designs that incorporate inexpensive materials and low-cost construction techniques; and (4) provides simple room furnishings and decorations. These approaches lower both investment costs and operating costs. Without restaurants,

bars, and all kinds of guest services, a Motel 6 unit can be operated with just front-desk personnel, room cleanup crews, and skeleton building-and-grounds maintenance.

To promote the Motel 6 concept with travelers who have simple overnight requirements, the chain uses unique, recognizable radio ads done by nationally syndicated radio personality Tom Bodett; the ads describe Motel 6's clean rooms, no-frills facilities, friendly atmosphere, and dependably low rates (usually under $40 a night).

Motel 6's basis for competitive advantage is lower costs than competitors in providing basic, economical overnight accommodations to price-constrained travelers.

as well as the standard goods normally found in supermarkets. What sets Trader Joe's apart is not just its unique combination of food novelties and competitively priced grocery items but also its capability to turn an otherwise mundane grocery excursion into a whimsical treasure hunt that is just plain fun.

Illustration Capsule 5.5 describes Progressive Insurance's focused differentiation strategy.

When a Focused Low-Cost or Focused Differentiation Strategy Is Attractive

A focused strategy aimed at securing a competitive edge based on either low cost or differentiation becomes increasingly attractive as more of the following conditions are met:

- The target market niche is big enough to be profitable and offers good growth potential.
- Industry leaders do not see that having a presence in the niche is crucial to their own success—in which case focusers can often escape battling head-to-head against some of the industry's biggest and strongest competitors.
- It is costly or difficult for multisegment competitors to put capabilities in place to meet the specialized needs of buyers comprising the target market niche and at the same time satisfy the expectations of their mainstream customers.
- The industry has many different niches and segments, thereby allowing a focuser to pick a competitively attractive niche suited to its resource strengths and capabilities. Also, with more niches, there is more room for focusers to avoid each other in competing for the same customers.

Illustration Capsule 5.5

Progressive Insurance's Focused Differentiation Strategy in Auto Insurance

Progressive Insurance has fashioned a strategy in auto insurance focused on people with a record of traffic violations who drive high-performance cars, drivers with accident histories, motorcyclists, teenagers, and other so-called high-risk categories of drivers that most auto insurance companies steer away from. Progressive discovered that some of these high-risk drivers are affluent and pressed for time, making them less sensitive to paying premium rates for their car insurance. Management learned that it could charge such drivers high enough premiums to cover the added risks, plus it differentiated Progressive from other insurers by expediting the process of obtaining insurance and decreasing the annoyance that such drivers faced in obtaining insurance coverage. Progressive pioneered the low-cost direct sales model of allowing customers to purchase insurance online and over the phone.

Progressive also studied the market segments for insurance carefully enough to discover that some motorcycle owners were not especially risky (middle-aged suburbanites who sometimes commuted to work or used their motorcycles mainly for recreational trips with their friends). Progressive's strategy allowed it to become a leader in the market for luxury-car insurance for customers who appreciated Progressive's streamlined approach to doing business.

In further differentiating and promoting Progressive policies, management created teams of roving claims adjusters who would arrive at accident scenes to assess claims and issue checks for repairs on the spot. Progressive introduced 24-hour claims reporting, now an industry standard. In addition, it developed a sophisticated pricing system so that it could quickly and accurately assess each customer's risk and weed out unprofitable customers.

By being creative and excelling at the nuts and bolts of its business, Progressive has won a 7 percent share of the $150 billion market for auto insurance and has the highest underwriting margins in the auto-insurance industry.

Sources: www.progressiveinsurance.com; Ian C. McMillan, Alexander van Putten, and Rita Gunther McGrath, "Global Gamesmanship," *Harvard Business Review* 81, no. 5 (May 2003), p. 68; and *Fortune,* May 16, 2005, p. 34.

- Few, if any, other rivals are attempting to specialize in the same target segment—a condition that reduces the risk of segment overcrowding.
- The focuser has a reservoir of customer goodwill and loyalty (accumulated from having catered to the specialized needs and preferences of niche members over many years) that it can draw on to help stave off ambitious challengers looking to horn in on its business.

The advantages of focusing a company's entire competitive effort on a single market niche are considerable, especially for smaller and medium-sized companies that may lack the breadth and depth of resources to tackle going after a broad customer base with a "something for everyone" lineup of models, styles, and product selection. eBay has made a huge name for itself and very attractive profits for shareholders by focusing its attention on online auctions—at one time a very small niche in the overall auction business that eBay's focus strategy turned into the dominant piece of the global auction industry. Google has capitalized on its specialized expertise in Internet search engines to become one of the most spectacular growth companies of the past 10 years. Two hippie entrepreneurs, Ben Cohen and Jerry Greenfield, built Ben & Jerry's Homemade into an impressive business by focusing their energies and resources solely on the superpremium segment of the ice cream market.

The Risks of a Focused Low-Cost or Focused Differentiation Strategy

Focusing carries several risks. One is the chance that competitors will find effective ways to match the focused firm's capabilities in serving the target niche—perhaps by coming up with products or brands specifically designed to appeal to buyers in the target niche or by developing expertise and capabilities that offset the focuser's strengths. In the lodging business, large chains like Marriott and Hilton have launched multibrand strategies that allow them to compete effectively in several lodging segments simultaneously. Marriott has flagship hotels with a full complement of services and amenities that allow it to attract travelers and vacationers going to major resorts, it has J. W. Marriot hotels usually located in downtown metropolitan areas that cater to business travelers; the Courtyard by Marriott brand is for business travelers looking for moderately priced lodging; Marriott Residence Inns are designed as a home away from home for travelers staying five or more nights; and the 530 Fairfield Inn locations cater to travelers looking for quality lodging at an affordable price. Similarly, Hilton has a lineup of brands (Conrad Hotels, Doubletree Hotels, Embassy Suite Hotels, Hampton Inns, Hilton Hotels, Hilton Garden Inns, and Homewood Suites) that enable it to operate in multiple segments and compete head-to-head against lodging chains that operate only in a single segment. Multibrand strategies are attractive to large companies like Marriott and Hilton precisely because they enable a company to enter a market niche and siphon business away from companies that employ a focus strategy.

A second risk of employing a focus strategy is the potential for the preferences and needs of niche members to shift over time toward the product attributes desired by the majority of buyers. An erosion of the differences across buyer segments lowers entry barriers into a focuser's market niche and provides an open invitation for rivals in adjacent segments to begin competing for the focuser's customers. A third risk is that the segment may become so attractive it is soon inundated with competitors, intensifying rivalry and splintering segment profits.

THE CONTRASTING FEATURES OF THE FIVE GENERIC COMPETITIVE STRATEGIES: A SUMMARY

Deciding which generic competitive strategy should serve as the framework for hanging the rest of the company's strategy is not a trivial matter. Each of the five generic competitive strategies positions the company differently in its market and competitive environment. Each establishes a central theme for how the company will endeavor to outcompete rivals. Each creates some boundaries or guidelines for maneuvering as market circumstances unfold and as ideas for improving the strategy are debated. Each points to different ways of experimenting and tinkering with the basic strategy—for example, employing a low-cost leadership strategy means experimenting with ways that costs can be cut and value chain activities can be streamlined, whereas a broad differentiation strategy means exploring ways to add new differentiating features or to perform value chain activities differently if the result is to add value for customers in ways they are willing to pay for. Each entails differences in terms of product line, production emphasis, marketing emphasis, and means of sustaining the strategy—as shown in Table 5.1.

Table 5.1 **Distinguishing Features of the Five Generic Competitive Strategies**

	Low-Cost Provider	Broad Differentiation	Best-Cost Provider	Focused Low-Cost Provider	Focused Differentiation
Strategic target	• A broad cross-section of the market	• A broad cross-section of the market	• Value-conscious buyers	• A narrow market niche where buyer needs and preferences are distinctively different	• A narrow market niche where buyer needs and preferences are distinctively different
Basis of competitive advantage	• Lower overall costs than competitors	• Ability to offer buyers something attractively different from competitors	• Ability to give customers more value for the money	• Lower overall cost than rivals in serving niche members	• Attributes that appeal specifically to niche members
Product line	• A good basic product with few frills (acceptable quality and limited selection)	• Many product variations, wide selection; emphasis on differentiating features	• Items with appealing attributes; assorted upscale features	• Features and attributes tailored to the tastes and requirements of niche members	• Features and attributes tailored to the tastes and requirements of niche members
Production emphasis	• A continuous search for cost reduction without sacrificing acceptable quality and essential features	• Build in whatever differentiating features buyers are willing to pay for; strive for product superiority	• Build in upscale features and appealing attributes at lower cost than rivals	• A continuous search for cost reduction while incorporating features and attributes matched to niche member preferences	• Custom-made products that match the tastes and requirements of niche members
Marketing emphasis	• Try to make a virtue out of product features that lead to low cost	• Tout differentiating features • Charge a premium price to cover the extra costs of differentiating features	• Tout delivery of best value • Either deliver comparable features at a lower price than rivals or else match rivals on prices and provide better features	• Communicate attractive features of a budget-priced product offering that fits niche buyers' expectations	• Communicate how product offering does the best job of meeting niche buyers' expectations
Keys to sustaining the strategy	• Economical prices/good value • Strive to manage costs down, year after year, in every area of the business	• Stress constant innovation to stay ahead of imitative competitors • Concentrate on a few key differentiating features	• Unique expertise in simultaneously managing costs down while incorporating upscale features and attributes	• Stay committed to serving the niche at lowest overall cost; don't blur the firm's image by entering other market segments or adding other products to widen market appeal	• Stay committed to serving the niche better than rivals; don't blur the firm's image by entering other market segments or adding other products to widen market appeal

Thus, a choice of which generic strategy to employ spills over to affect several aspects of how the business will be operated and the manner in which value chain activities must be managed. Deciding which generic strategy to employ is perhaps the most important strategic commitment a company makes—it tends to drive the rest of the strategic actions a company decides to undertake.

One of the big dangers in crafting a competitive strategy is that managers, torn between the pros and cons of the various generic strategies, will opt for *stuck-in-the-middle strategies* that represent compromises between lower costs and greater differentiation and between broad and narrow market appeal. Compromise or middle-ground strategies rarely produce sustainable competitive advantage or a distinctive competitive position—a well-executed best-cost producer strategy is the only compromise between low cost and differentiation that succeeds. Usually, companies with compromise strategies end up with a middle-of-the-pack industry ranking—they have average costs, some but not a lot of product differentiation relative to rivals, an average image and reputation, and little prospect of industry leadership. Having a competitive edge over rivals is the single most dependable contributor to above-average company profitability. Hence, only if a company makes a strong and unwavering commitmentto one of the five generic competitive strategies does it stand much chance of achieving sustainable competitive advantage that such strategies can deliver if properly executed.

Key Points

Early in the process of crafting a strategy company managers have to decide which of the five basic competitive strategies to employ—overall low-cost, broad differentiation, best-cost, focused low-cost, or focused differentiation.

In employing a low-cost provider strategy and trying to achieve a low-cost advantage over rivals, a company must do a better job than rivals of cost-effectively managing value chain activities and/or find innovative ways to eliminate or bypass cost-producing activities. Low-cost provider strategies work particularly well when the products of rival sellers are virtually identical or very weakly differentiated and supplies are readily available from eager sellers, when there are not many ways to differentiate that have value to buyers, when many buyers are price sensitive and shop the market for the lowest price, and when buyer switching costs are low.

Broad differentiation strategies seek to produce a competitive edge by incorporating attributes and features that set a company's product/service offering apart from rivals in ways that buyers consider valuable and worth paying for. Successful differentiation allows a firm to (1) command a premium price for its product, (2) increase unit sales (because additional buyers are won over by the differentiating features), and/or (3) gain buyer loyalty to its brand (because some buyers are strongly attracted to the differentiating features and bond with the company and its products). Differentiation strategies work best in markets with diverse buyer preferences where there are big windows of opportunity to strongly differentiate a company's product offering from those of rival brands, in situations where few other rivals are pursuing a similar differentiation approach, and in circumstances where companies are racing to bring out the most appealing next-generation product. A differentiation strategy is doomed when competitors are able to quickly copy most or all of the appealing product attributes a company comes up with, when a company's differentiation efforts meet with a ho-hum or so what market reception, or when a company erodes profitability by overspending on efforts to differentiate its product offering.

Best-cost provider strategies combine a strategic emphasis on low cost with a strategic emphasis on more than minimal quality, service, features, or performance. The aim is to create competitive advantage by giving buyers more value for the money—an approach that entails matching close rivals on key quality/service/features/performance attributes and beating them on the costs of incorporating such attributes into the product or service. A best-cost provider strategy works best in markets where buyer diversity makes product differentiation the norm and where many buyers are also sensitive to price and value.

A focus strategy delivers competitive advantage either by achieving lower costs than rivals in serving buyers comprising the target market niche or by developing specialized ability to offer niche buyers an appealingly differentiated offering than meets their needs better than rival brands. A focused strategy based on either low cost or differentiation becomes increasingly attractive when the target market niche is big enough to be profitable and offers good growth potential, when it is costly or difficult for multi-segment competitors to put capabilities in place to meet the specialized needs of the target market niche and at the same time satisfy the expectations of their mainstream customers, when there are one or more niches that present a good match with a focuser's resource strengths and capabilities, and when few other rivals are attempting to specialize in the same target segment.

Deciding which generic strategy to employ is perhaps the most important strategic commitment a company makes—it tends to drive the rest of the strategic actions a company decides to undertake and it sets the whole tone for the pursuit of a competitive advantage over rivals.

Exercises

1. Go to www.google.com and do a search for "low-cost producer." See if you can identify five companies that are pursuing a low-cost strategy in their respective industries.

2. Using the advanced search function at www.google.com, enter "best-cost producer" in the exact-phrase box and see if you can locate three companies that indicate they are employing a best-cost producer strategy.

3. Go to BMW's Web site (www.bmw.com) click on the link for BMW Group. The site you find provides an overview of the company's key functional areas, including R&D and production activities. Explore each of the links on the Research & Development page—People & Networks, Innovation & Technology, and Mobility & Traffic—to better understand the company's approach. Also review the statements under Production focusing on vehicle production and sustainable production. How do these activities contribute to BMW's differentiation strategy and the unique position in the auto industry that BMW has achieved?

4. Which of the five generic competitive strategies do you think the following companies are employing (do whatever research at the various company Web sites might be needed to arrive at and support your answer):

   a. The Saturn division of General Motors
   b. Abercrombie & Fitch
   c. Amazon.com
   d. Home Depot
   e. Mary Kay Cosmetics
   f. *USA Today*

chapter six

Supplementing the Chosen Competitive Strategy

Other Important Strategy Choices

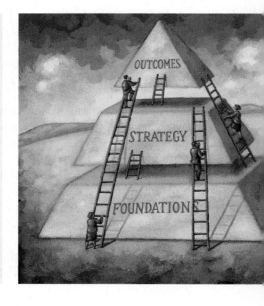

Don't form an alliance to correct a weakness and don't ally with a partner that is trying to correct a weakness of its own. The only result from a marriage of weaknesses is the creation of even more weaknesses.

—Michel Robert

Strategies for taking the hill won't necessarily hold it.

—Amar Bhide

The sure path to oblivion is to stay where you are.

—Bernard Fauber

Successful business strategy is about actively shaping the game you play, not just playing the game you find.

—Adam M. Brandenburger and Barry J. Nalebuff

O nce a company has settled on which of the five generic strategies to employ, attention turns to what other *strategic actions* it can take to complement its choice of a basic competitive strategy. Several decisions have to be made:

- What use to make of strategic alliances and collaborative partnerships.
- Whether to bolster the company's market position via merger or acquisitions.
- Whether to integrate backward or forward into more stages of the industry value chain.
- Whether to outsource certain value chain activities or perform them in-house.
- Whether and when to employ offensive and defensive moves.
- Which of several ways to use the Internet as a distribution channel in positioning the company in the marketplace.

This chapter contains sections discussing the pros and cons of each of the above complementary strategic options. The next-to-last section in the chapter discusses the need for strategic choices in each functional area of a company's business (R&D, production, sales and marketing, finance, and so on) to support its basic competitive approach and complementary strategic moves. The chapter concludes with a brief look at the competitive importance of timing strategic moves—when it is advantageous to be a first-mover and when it is better to be a fast-follower or late-mover.

Figure 6.1 shows the menu of strategic options a company has in crafting a strategy and the order in which the choices should generally be made. The portion of Figure 6.1 below the five generic competitive strategy options illustrates the structure of this chapter and the topics that will be covered.

Figure 6.1   **A Company's Menu of Strategy Options**

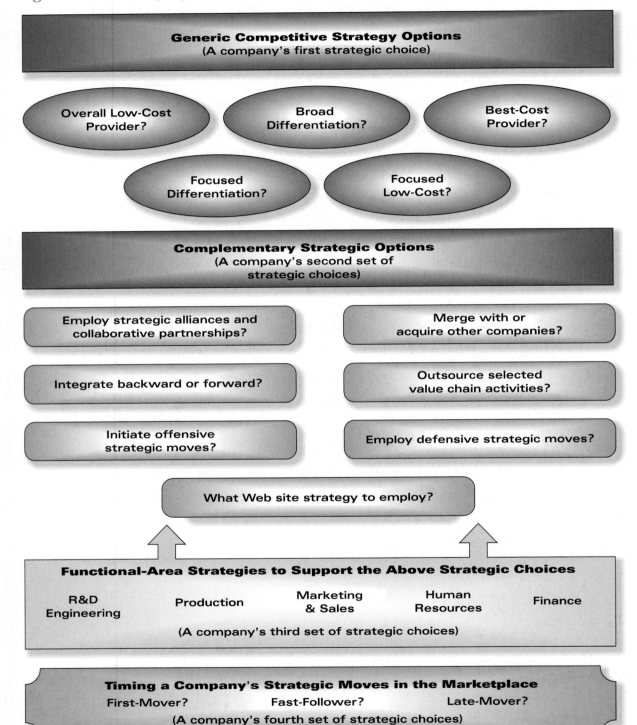

COLLABORATIVE STRATEGIES: ALLIANCES AND PARTNERSHIPS

Companies in all types of industries and in all parts of the world have elected to form strategic alliances and partnerships to complement their own strategic initiatives and strengthen their competitiveness in domestic and international markets. This is an about-face from times past, when the vast majority of companies were content to go it alone, confident that they already had or could independently develop whatever resources and know-how were needed to be successful in their markets. But globalization of the world economy; revolutionary advances in technology across a broad front; and untapped opportunities in Asia, Latin America, and Europe—whose national markets are opening up, deregulating, and/or undergoing privatization—have made strategic partnerships of one kind or another integral to competing on a broad geographic scale.

Many companies now find themselves thrust into two very demanding competitive races: (1) *the global race to build a market presence in many different national markets* and join the ranks of companies recognized as global market leaders, and (2) *the race to seize opportunities on the frontiers of advancing technology* and build the resource strengths and business capabilities to compete successfully in the industries and product markets of the future.[1] Even the largest and most financially sound companies have concluded that simultaneously running the races for global market leadership and for a stake in the industries of the future requires more diverse and expansive skills, resources, technological expertise, and competitive capabilities than they can assemble and manage alone. Such companies, along with others that are missing the resources and competitive capabilities needed to pursue promising opportunities, have determined that the fastest way to fill the gap is often to form alliances with enterprises having the desired strengths. Consequently, these companies form strategic alliances or collaborative partnerships in which two or more companies jointly work to achieve mutually beneficial strategic outcomes. Thus, a **strategic alliance** is a formal agreement between two or more separate companies in which there is strategically relevant collaboration of some sort, joint contribution of resources, shared risk, shared control, and mutual dependence. Often, alliances involve joint marketing, joint sales or distribution, joint production, design collaboration, joint research, or projects to jointly develop new technologies or products. The relationship between the partners may be contractual or merely collaborative; the arrangement commonly stops short of formal ownership ties between the partners (although there are a few strategic alliances where one or more allies have minority ownership in certain of the other alliance members). Five factors make an alliance strategic, as opposed to just a convenient business arrangement:[2]

> **Core Concept**
> ***Strategic alliances*** are collaborative arrangements where two or more companies join forces to achieve mutually beneficial strategic outcomes.

1. It is critical to the company's achievement of an important objective.
2. It helps build, sustain, or enhance a core competence or competitive advantage.
3. It helps block a competitive threat.
4. It helps open up important new market opportunities.
5. It mitigates a significant risk to a company's business.

Strategic cooperation is a much-favored, indeed necessary, approach in industries where new technological developments are occurring at a furious pace along many different paths and where advances in one technology spill over to affect others (often blurring industry boundaries). Whenever industries are experiencing high-velocity technological advances in many areas simultaneously, firms find it virtually essential to have cooperative relationships with other enterprises to stay on the leading edge of technology and product performance even in their own area of specialization.

Companies in many different industries all across the world have made strategic alliances a core part of their overall strategy; U.S. companies alone announced nearly 68,000 alliances from 1996 through 2003.[3] In the personal computer (PC) industry, alliances are pervasive because the different components of PCs and the software to run them are supplied by so many different companies—one set of companies provides the microprocessors, another group makes the motherboards, another the monitors, another the disk drives, another the memory chips, and so on. Moreover, their facilities are scattered across the United States, Japan, Taiwan, Singapore, Malaysia, and parts of Europe. Strategic alliances among companies in the various parts of the PC industry facilitate the close cross-company collaboration required on next-generation product development, logistics, production, and the timing of new product releases.

> Company use of alliances is quite widespread.

Toyota has forged long-term strategic partnerships with many of its suppliers of automotive parts and components, both to achieve lower costs and to improve the quality and reliability of its vehicles. Microsoft collaborates very closely with independent software developers to ensure that their programs will run on the next-generation versions of Windows. Genentech, a leader in biotechnology and human genetics, has a partnering strategy to increase its access to novel biotherapeutics products and technologies and has formed alliances with over 30 companies to strengthen its research and development (R&D) pipeline. During the 1998–2004 period, Samsung Electronics, a South Korean corporation with $54 billion in sales, entered into over 50 major strategic alliances involving such companies as Sony, Yahoo, Hewlett-Packard, Nokia, Motorola, Intel, Microsoft, Dell, Mitsubishi, Disney, IBM, Maytag, and Rockwell Automation; the alliances involved joint investments, technology transfer arrangements, joint R&D projects, and agreements to supply parts and components—all of which facilitated Samsung's strategic efforts to transform itself into a global enterprise and establish itself as a leader in the worldwide electronics industry.

Studies indicate that large corporations are commonly involved in 30 to 50 alliances and that some have hundreds of alliances. One recent study estimated that about 35 percent of corporate revenues in 2003 came from activities involving strategic alliances, up from 15 percent in 1995.[4] Another study reported that the typical large corporation relied on alliances for 15 to 20 percent of its revenues, assets, or income.[5] Companies that have formed a host of alliances have a need to manage their alliances like a portfolio—terminating those that no longer serve a useful purpose or that have produced meager results, forming promising new alliances, and restructuring certain existing alliances to correct performance problems and/or redirect the collaborative effort.[6]

Why and How Strategic Alliances Are Advantageous

The most common reasons why companies enter into strategic alliances are to expedite the development of promising new technologies or products, to overcome deficits in their own technical and manufacturing expertise, to bring together the personnel and expertise needed to create desirable new skill sets and capabilities, to improve supply chain efficiency, to gain economies of scale in production and/or marketing, and to acquire or improve market access through joint marketing agreements.[7] In bringing together firms with different skills and knowledge bases, alliances open up learning opportunities that help partner firms better leverage their own resource strengths.[8] In industries where technology is advancing rapidly, alliances are all about fast cycles of learning, staying abreast of the latest developments, and gaining quick access to the latest round of technological know-how and capability.

> The best alliances are highly selective, focusing on particular value chain activities and on obtaining a particular competitive benefit. They tend to enable a firm to build on its strengths and to learn.

There are several other instances in which companies find strategic alliances particularly valuable. A company that is racing for *global market leadership* needs alliances to:

- Get into critical country markets quickly and accelerate the process of building a potent global market presence.
- *Gain inside knowledge about unfamiliar markets and cultures* through alliances with local partners. For example, U.S., European, and Japanese companies wanting to build market footholds in the fast-growing Chinese market have pursued partnership arrangements with Chinese companies to help in getting products through the tedious and typically corrupt customs process, to help guide them through the maze of government regulations, to supply knowledge of local markets, to provide guidance on adapting their products to better match the buying preferences of Chinese consumers, to set up local manufacturing capabilities, and to assist in distribution, marketing, and promotional activities. The Chinese government has long required foreign companies operating in China to have a state-owned Chinese company as a minority or maybe even 50 percent partner—only recently has it backed off this requirement for foreign companies operating in selected parts of the Chinese economy.
- *Access valuable skills and competencies* that are concentrated in particular geographic locations (such as software design competencies in the United States, fashion design skills in Italy, and efficient manufacturing skills in Japan and China).

A company that is racing to *stake out a strong position in an industry of the future* needs alliances to:

- *Establish a stronger beachhead* for participating in the target industry.
- *Master new technologies and build new expertise and competencies* faster than would be possible through internal efforts.
- *Open up broader opportunities* in the target industry by melding the firm's own capabilities with the expertise and resources of partners.

Allies can learn much from one another in performing joint research, sharing technological know-how, and collaborating on complementary new technologies and products—sometimes enough to enable them to pursue other new opportunities on their own.[9] Manufacturers frequently pursue alliances with parts and components suppliers to gain the efficiencies of better supply chain management and to speed new products to market. By joining forces in components production and/or final assembly, companies may be able to realize cost savings not achievable with their own small volumes—German automakers Volkswagen, Audi, and Porsche formed a strategic alliance to spur mutual development of a gasoline-electric hybrid engine and transmission system that they could each then incorporate into their motor vehicle models; BMW, General

> The competitive attraction of alliances is in allowing companies to bundle competencies and resources that are more valuable in a joint effort than when kept separate.

Motors, and DaimlerChrysler formed a similar partnership. Both alliances were aimed at closing the gap on Toyota, generally said to be the world leader in fuel-efficient hybrid engines. Information systems consultant Accenture has developed strategic alliances with such leading technology providers as SAP, Oracle, Siebel, Microsoft, BEA, and Hewlett-Packard to give it greater capabilities in designing and integrating information systems for its corporate clients. Johnson & Johnson and Merck entered into an alliance to market Pepcid AC; Merck developed the stomach distress remedy, and Johnson & Johnson functioned as marketer—the alliance made Pepcid products the best-selling remedies for acid indigestion and heartburn. United Airlines, American Airlines, Continental, Delta, and Northwest created an alliance to form Orbitz, an Internet travel site to compete head-to-head against Expedia and Travelocity, thereby strengthening their access to travelers and vacationers shopping online for airfares, rental cars, lodging, cruises, and vacation packages.

Capturing the Benefits of Strategic Alliances

The extent to which companies benefit from entering into alliances and collaborative partnerships seems to be a function of six factors:[10]

1. *Picking a good partner*—A good partner not only has the desired expertise and capabilities but also shares the company's vision about the purpose of the alliance. Experience indicates that it is generally wise to avoid a partnership in which there is strong potential of direct competition because of overlapping product lines or other conflicting interests—agreements to jointly market each other's products hold much potential for conflict unless the products are complements rather than substitutes and unless there is good chemistry among key personnel. Experience also indicates that alliances between strong and weak companies rarely work because the alliance is unlikely to provide the strong partner with useful resources or skills and because there's a greater chance of the alliance producing mediocre results.

2. *Being sensitive to cultural differences*—Unless the outsider exhibits respect for the local culture and local business practices, productive working relationships are unlikely to emerge.

3. *Recognizing that the alliance must benefit both sides*—Information must be shared as well as gained, and the relationship must remain forthright and trustful. Many alliances fail because one or both partners grow unhappy with what they are learning. Also, if either partner plays games with information or tries to take advantage of the other, the resulting friction can quickly erode the value of further collaboration.

4. *Ensuring that both parties live up to their commitments*—Both parties have to deliver on their commitments for the alliance to produce the intended benefits. The division of work has to be perceived as fairly apportioned, and the caliber of the benefits received on both sides has to be perceived as adequate.

5. *Structuring the decision-making process so that actions can be taken swiftly when needed*—In many instances, the fast pace of technological and competitive changes dictates an equally fast decision-making process. If the parties get bogged down in discussion or in gaining internal approval from higher-ups, the alliance can turn into an anchor of delay and inaction.

6. *Managing the learning process and then adjusting the alliance agreement over time to fit new circumstances*—One of the keys to long-lasting success is adapting the nature and structure of the alliance to be responsive to shifting market conditions, emerging technologies, and changing customer requirements. Wise allies are quick

to recognize the merit of an evolving collaborative arrangement, where adjustments are made to accommodate changing market conditions and to overcome whatever problems arise in establishing an effective working relationship. Most alliances encounter troubles of some kind within a couple of years—those that are flexible enough to evolve are better able to recover.

Most alliances that aim at technology sharing or providing market access turn out to be temporary, fulfilling their purpose after a few years because the benefits of mutual learning have occurred and because the businesses of both partners have developed to the point where they are ready to go their own ways. In such cases, it is important for each partner to learn thoroughly and rapidly about the other partner's technology, business practices, and organizational capabilities and then promptly transfer valuable ideas and practices into its own operations. Although long-term alliances sometimes prove mutually beneficial, most partners don't hesitate to terminate the alliance and go it alone when the payoffs run out.

Alliances are more likely to be long-lasting when (1) they involve collaboration with suppliers or distribution allies and each party's contribution involves activities in different portions of the industry value chain, or (2) both parties conclude that continued collaboration is in their mutual interest, perhaps because new opportunities for learning are emerging or perhaps because further collaboration will allow each partner to extend its market reach beyond what it could accomplish on its own.

Why Many Alliances Are Unstable or Break Apart

The stability of an alliance depends on how well the partners work together, their success in responding and adapting to changing internal and external conditions, and their willingness to renegotiate the bargain if circumstances so warrant. A successful alliance requires real in-the-trenches collaboration, not merely an arm's-length exchange of ideas. Unless partners place a high value on the skills, resources, and contributions each brings to the alliance and the cooperative arrangement results in valuable win–win outcomes, it is doomed. A surprisingly large number of alliances never live up to expectations. A 1999 study by Accenture, a global business consulting organization, revealed that 61 percent of alliances were either outright failures or "limping along." In 2004, McKinsey & Company estimated that the overall success rate of alliances was around 50 percent, based on whether the alliance achieved the stated objectives.[11] Many alliances are dissolved after a few years. The high "divorce rate" among strategic allies has several causes—diverging objectives and priorities, an inability to work well together (an alliance between Disney and Pixar came apart because of clashes between high-level executives—in 2005, after one of the feuding executives retired, Disney acquired Pixar), changing conditions that render the purpose of the alliance obsolete, the emergence of more attractive technological paths, and marketplace rivalry between one or more allies.[12] Experience indicates that *alliances stand a reasonable chance of helping a company reduce competitive disadvantage, but very rarely have they proved a strategic option for gaining a durable competitive edge over rivals.*

The Strategic Dangers of Relying Heavily on Alliances and Collaborative Partnerships

The Achilles heel of alliances and collaborative partnerships is dependence on another company for *essential* expertise and capabilities. To be a market leader (and perhaps even a serious market contender), a company must ultimately develop its own capabilities in areas where internal strategic control is pivotal to protecting its competitiveness and building competitive advantage. Moreover, some alliances hold only limited potential because the partner guards its most valuable skills and expertise; in such instances, acquiring or merging with a company possessing the desired know-how and resources is a better solution.

MERGER AND ACQUISITION STRATEGIES

Mergers and acquisitions are much-used strategic options—for example, U.S. companies alone made 90,000 acquisitions from 1996 through 2003.[13] Mergers and acquisitions are especially suited for situations in which alliances and partnerships do not go far enough in providing a company with access to needed resources and capabilities.[14] Ownership ties are more permanent than partnership ties, allowing the operations of the merger/acquisition participants to be tightly integrated and creating more in-house control and autonomy. A *merger* is a pooling of equals, with the newly created company often taking on a new name. An *acquisition* is a combination in which one company, the acquirer, purchases and absorbs the operations of another, the acquired. The difference between a merger and an acquisition relates more to the details of ownership, management control, and financial arrangements than to strategy and competitive advantage. The resources, competencies, and competitive capabilities of the newly created enterprise end up much the same whether the combination is the result of acquisition or merger.

> Combining the operations of two companies, via merger or acquisition, is an attractive strategic option for achieving operating economies, strengthening the resulting company's competences and competitiveness, and opening up avenues of new market opportunity.

Many mergers and acquisitions are driven by strategies to achieve any of five strategic objectives:[15]

1. *To create a more cost-efficient operation out of the combined companies*—When a company acquires another company in the same industry, there's usually enough overlap in operations that certain inefficient plants can be closed or distribution activities partly combined and downsized (when nearby centers serve some of the same geographic areas), or sales-force and marketing activities combined and downsized (when each company has salespeople calling on the same customer). The combined companies may also be able to reduce supply chain costs because of buying in greater volume from common suppliers and from closer collaboration with supply chain partners. Likewise, it is usually feasible to squeeze out cost savings in administrative activities, again by combining and downsizing such administrative activities as finance and accounting, information technology, and human resources. The merger that formed DaimlerChrysler was motivated in large part by the fact that the motor vehicle industry had far more production capacity worldwide than was needed; top executives at both Daimler-Benz and Chrysler believed that the efficiency of the two companies could be significantly improved by shutting some plants and laying off workers; realigning which models were produced at which plants; and squeezing out efficiencies by combining supply chain activities, product design, and administration. Quite a number of acquisitions are undertaken with the objective of transforming two or more otherwise high-cost companies into one lean competitor with average or below-average costs.

2. *To expand a company's geographic coverage*—One of the best and quickest ways to expand a company's geographic coverage is to acquire rivals with operations in the desired locations. And if there is some geographic overlap, then a side benefit is being able to reduce costs by eliminating duplicate facilities in those geographic areas where undesirable overlap exists. Banks like Wells Fargo, Bank

of America, Wachovia, and Suntrust have pursued geographic expansion by making a series of acquisitions over the years, enabling them to establish a market presence in an ever-growing number of states and localities. Many companies use acquisitions to expand internationally; for example, food products companies like Nestlé, Kraft, Unilever, and Procter & Gamble—all racing for global market leadership—have made acquisitions an integral part of their strategies to widen their geographic reach.

3.   *To extend the company's business into new product categories*—Many times a company has gaps in its product line that need to be filled. Acquisition can be a quicker and more potent way to broaden a company's product line than going through the exercise of introducing a company's own new product to fill the gap. PepsiCo acquired Quaker Oats chiefly to bring Gatorade into the Pepsi family of beverages. While Coca-Cola has expanded its beverage lineup by introducing its own new products (like Powerade and Dasani), it has also expanded its lineup by acquiring Fanta (carbonated fruit beverages), Minute Maid (juices and juice drinks), Odwalla (juices), and Hi-C (ready-to-drink fruit beverages).

4.   *To gain quick access to new technologies or other resources and competitive capabilities*—Making acquisitions to bolster a company's technological know-how or to fill resource holes is a favorite of companies racing to establish a position in an industry or product category about to be born. Making acquisitions aimed at filling meaningful gaps in technological expertise allows a company to bypass a time-consuming and perhaps expensive R&D effort (which might not succeed). Cisco Systems purchased over 75 technology companies to give it more technological reach and product breadth, thereby buttressing its standing as the world's biggest supplier of systems for building the infrastructure of the Internet. Intel has made over 300 acquisitions in the past five or so years to broaden its technological base, obtain the resource capabilities to produce and market a variety of Internet-related and electronics-related products, and make it less dependent on supplying microprocessors for PCs.

5.   *To try to invent a new industry and lead the convergence of industries whose boundaries are being blurred by changing technologies and new market opportunities*—Such acquisitions are the result of a company's management betting that two or more distinct industries are converging into one and deciding to establish a strong position in the consolidating markets by bringing together the resources and products of several different companies. Examples include the merger of AOL and media giant Time Warner—a move predicated on the belief that entertainment content would ultimately converge into a single industry (much of which would be distributed over the Internet)—and News Corporation's purchase of satellite TV companies to complement its media holdings in TV broadcasting (the Fox network and TV stations in various countries); cable TV (Fox News, Fox Sports, and FX); filmed entertainment (Twentieth Century Fox and Fox Studios); and newspaper, magazine, and book publishing.

Numerous companies have employed an acquisition strategy to catapult themselves from the ranks of the unknown into positions of market leadership. During the 1990s, North Carolina National Bank (NCNB) pursued a series of acquisitions to transform itself into a major regional bank in the Southeast. But NCNB's strategic vision was to become a bank with offices across most of the United States, so the company changed its name to NationsBank. In 1998, NationsBank acquired Bank of America for $66 billion and adopted its name. In 2004, Bank of America acquired Fleet Boston Financial for $48 billion. Then in mid-2005, Bank of America spent $35 billion to acquire MBNA,

Illustration Capsule 6.1

Clear Channel Communications: Using Mergers and Acquisitions to Become a Global Market Leader

Going into 2006, Clear Channel Communications was the world's fourth largest media company, behind Disney, Time Warner, and Viacom/CBS. The company, founded in 1972 by Lowry Mays and Billy Joe McCombs, got its start by acquiring an unprofitable country-music radio station in San Antonio, Texas. Over the next 10 years, Mays learned the radio business and slowly bought other radio stations in a variety of states. Going public in 1984 helped the company raise the equity capital needed to continue acquiring radio stations in additional geographic markets.

In the late 1980s, when the Federal Communications Commission loosened the rules regarding the ability of one company to own both radio and TV stations, Clear Channel broadened its strategy and began acquiring small, struggling TV stations. By 1998, Clear Channel had used acquisitions to build a leading position in radio and television stations. Domestically, it owned, programmed, or sold airtime for 69 AM radio stations, 135 FM stations, and 18 TV stations in 48 local markets in 24 states. Clear Channel's big move was to begin expanding internationally, chiefly by acquiring interests in radio station properties in a variety of countries.

In 1997, Clear Channel used acquisitions to establish a major position in outdoor advertising. Its first acquisition was Phoenix-based Eller Media Company, an outdoor advertising company with over 100,000 billboard facings. This was quickly followed by additional acquisitions of outdoor advertising companies, the most important of which were ABC Outdoor in Milwaukee, Wisconsin; Paxton Communications (with operations in Tampa and Orlando, Florida); Universal Outdoor; the More Group, with outdoor operations and 90,000 displays in 24 countries; and the Ackerley Group.

Then in October 1999, Clear Channel made a major move by acquiring AM-FM Inc. and changed its name to

Clear Channel Communications; the AM-FM acquisition gave Clear Channel operations in 32 countries, including 830 radio stations, 19 TV stations, and more than 425,000 outdoor displays.

Additional acquisitions were completed during the 2000–2003 period. The emphasis was on buying radio, TV, and outdoor advertising properties with operations in many of the same local markets, which made it feasible to (1) cut costs by sharing facilities and staffs, (2) improve programming, and (3) sell advertising to customers in packages for all three media simultaneously. Packaging ads for two or three media not only helped Clear Channel's advertising clients distribute their messages more effectively but also allowed the company to combine its sales activities and have a common sales force for all three media, achieving significant cost savings and boosting profit margins. But in 2000 Clear Channel broadened its media strategy by acquiring SFX Entertainment, one of the world's largest promoters, producers, and presenters of live entertainment events.

At year-end 2005, Clear Channel owned radio and television stations, outdoor displays, and entertainment venues in 66 countries around the world. It operated approximately 1,200 radio and 40 television stations in the United States and had equity interests in over 240 radio stations internationally. It also operated a U.S. radio network of syndicated talk shows with about 180 million weekly listeners. In addition, the company owned or operated over 820,000 outdoor advertising displays, including billboards, street furniture, and transit panels around the world. In late 2005, the company spun off its Clear Channel Entertainment division (which was a leading promoter, producer, and marketer of about 32,000 live entertainment events annually and also owned leading athlete management and sports marketing companies) as a separate entity via an initial public offering of stock.

Sources: Information posted at www.clearchannel.com (accessed September 2005), and *BusinessWeek,* October 19, 1999, p. 56.

a leading credit card company. Going into 2006, Bank of America had a network of 5,900 branch banks in 29 states and the District of Columbia, and was managing $140 billion in credit card balances. It was the largest U.S. bank in terms of deposits, the second largest in terms of assets, and the fifth most profitable company in the world (with 2005 profits of about $17 billion).

Illustration Capsule 6.1 describes how Clear Channel Worldwide has used acquisitions to build a leading global position in outdoor advertising and radio and TV broadcasting.

All too frequently, mergers and acquisitions do not produce the hoped-for outcomes.[16] Cost savings may prove smaller than expected. Gains in competitive capabilities may take substantially longer to realize or, worse, may never materialize at all. Efforts to mesh the corporate cultures can stall due to formidable resistance from organization members. Managers and employees at the acquired company may argue forcefully for continuing to do certain things the way they were done prior to the acquisition. Key employees at the acquired company can quickly become disenchanted and leave; morale can drop to disturbingly low levels because personnel who remain disagree with newly instituted changes. Differences in management styles and operating procedures can prove hard to resolve. The managers appointed to oversee the integration of a newly acquired company can make mistakes in deciding what activities to leave alone and what activities to meld into their own operations and systems.

A number of previously applauded mergers/acquisitions have yet to live up to expectations—the merger of America Online (AOL) and Time Warner, the merger of Daimler-Benz and Chrysler, Hewlett-Packard's acquisition of Compaq Computer, Ford's acquisition of Jaguar, and Kmart's acquisition of Sears are prime examples. The AOL–Time Warner merger has proved to be mostly a disaster, partly because AOL's once-rapid growth has evaporated, partly because of a huge clash of corporate cultures, and partly because most of the expected benefits from industry convergence have yet to materialize. Ford paid a handsome price to acquire Jaguar but has yet to make the Jaguar brand a major factor in the luxury-car segment in competition against Mercedes, BMW, and Lexus. Novell acquired WordPerfect for $1.7 billion in stock in 1994, but the combination never generated enough punch to compete against Microsoft Word and Microsoft Office—Novell sold WordPerfect to Corel for $124 million in cash and stock less than two years later. In 2001 electronics retailer Best Buy paid $685 million to acquire Musicland, a struggling 1,300-store music retailer that included stores operating under the names Musicland, Sam Goody, Suncoast, Media Play, and On Cue. But Musicland's sales, already declining, dropped even further. In June 2003, Best Buy "sold" Musicland to a Florida investment firm—no cash changed hands and the "buyer" received shares of stock in Best Buy in return for assuming Musicland's liabilities.

VERTICAL INTEGRATION STRATEGIES: OPERATING ACROSS MORE STAGES OF THE INDUSTRY VALUE CHAIN

Vertical integration extends a firm's competitive and operating scope within the same industry. It involves expanding the firm's range of activities backward into sources of supply and/or forward toward end users. Thus, if a manufacturer invests in facilities to produce certain component parts that it formerly purchased from outside suppliers, it remains in essentially the same industry as before. The only change is that it has operations in two stages of the industry value chain. Similarly, if a paint manufacturer, Sherwin-Williams for example, elects to integrate forward by opening 100 retail stores to market its paint products directly to consumers, it remains in the paint business even though its competitive scope extends from manufacturing to retailing.

Vertical integration strategies can aim at *full integration* (participating in all stages of the industry value chain) or *partial integration* (building positions in selected stages of the industry's total value chain). A firm can pursue vertical integration by starting its own operations in other stages in the industry's activity chain or by acquiring a company already performing the activities it wants to bring in-house.

The Advantages of a Vertical Integration Strategy

<table>
<tr>
<td>

Core Concept
A vertical integration strategy has appeal *only* if it significantly strengthens a firm's competitive position.

</td>
<td>

The two best reasons for investing company resources in vertical integration are to strengthen the firm's competitive position and/or boost its profitability.[17] Vertical integration has no real payoff profitwise or strategywise unless it produces sufficient cost savings or profit increases to justify the extra investment, adds materially to a company's technological and competitive strengths, or helps differentiate the company's product offering.

</td>
</tr>
</table>

Integrating Backward to Achieve Greater Competitiveness It is harder than one might think to generate cost savings or boost profitability by integrating backward into activities such as manufacturing parts and components (which could otherwise be purchased from suppliers with specialized expertise in making these parts and components). For backward integration to be a viable and profitable strategy, a company must be able to (1) achieve the same scale economies as outside suppliers and (2) match or beat suppliers' production efficiency with no drop-off in quality. Neither outcome is a slam-dunk. To begin with, a company's in-house requirements are often too small to reach the optimum size for low-cost operation—for instance, if it takes a minimum production volume of 1 million units to achieve mass-production economies and a company's in-house requirements are just 250,000 units, then the company falls way short of being able to capture the scale economies of outside suppliers (which may readily find buyers for 1 million or more units). Furthermore, matching the production efficiency of suppliers is fraught with problems when suppliers have considerable production experience of their own, when the technology they employ has elements that are hard to master, or when substantial R&D expertise is required to develop next-version parts and components or keep pace with advancing technology in parts/components production.

But that being said, there are still occasions when a company can improve its cost position and competitiveness by performing a broad range of value chain activities in-house. The best potential for being able to reduce costs via a backward integration strategy exists in situations where suppliers have outsized profit margins, where the item being supplied is a major cost component, and where the requisite technological skills are easily mastered or can be gained by acquiring a supplier with the desired technological know-how. Furthermore, when a company has proprietary know-how that it is beneficial to keep away from rivals, then in-house performance of value chain activities related to this know-how is beneficial even if such activities could be performed by outsiders. For example, Krispy Kreme Doughnuts has successfully employed a backward vertical integration strategy that involves internally producing both the doughnut-making equipment and ready-mixed doughnut ingredients that company-owned and franchised retail stores used in making Krispy Kreme doughnuts—the company earned substantial profits from producing these items internally rather than having them supplied by outsiders. Furthermore, Krispy Kreme's vertical integration strategy made good competitive sense because both its doughnut-making equipment and its doughnut recipe were proprietary; keeping its equipment manufacturing know-how and its secret recipe out of the hands of outside suppliers helped Krispy Kreme protect its doughnut offering from would-be imitators.

Backward vertical integration can produce a differentiation-based competitive advantage when a company, by performing activities internally rather than using outside suppliers, ends up with a better-quality product/service offering, improves the caliber of its customer service, or in other ways enhances the performance of its final product. On occasion, integrating into more stages along the industry value chain can add to a company's differentiation capabilities by allowing the company to build or strengthen its core competencies, better master key skills or strategy-critical technologies, or add features that deliver greater customer value. Other potential advantages of backward integration include sparing a company the uncertainty of being dependent on suppliers for crucial components or support services and lessening a company's vulnerability to powerful suppliers inclined to raise prices at every opportunity.

Integrating Forward to Enhance Competitiveness   The strategic impetus for forward integration is to gain better access to end users and better market visibility. In many industries, independent sales agents, wholesalers, and retailers handle competing brands of the same product; having no allegiance to any one company's brand, they tend to push whatever sells and earns them the biggest profits. An independent insurance agency, for example, represents a number of different insurance companies—in trying to find the best match between a customer's insurance requirements and the policies of alternative insurance companies, there's plenty of opportunity for independent agents to end up promoting certain insurance companies' policies ahead of others'. An insurance company may therefore conclude that it is better off setting up its own local sales offices with its own local agents to exclusively promote its policies. Likewise, a manufacturer can be frustrated in its attempts to win higher sales and market share or get rid of unwanted inventory or maintain steady, near-capacity production if it must distribute its products through distributors and/or retailers who are only halfheartedly committed to promoting and marketing its brand as opposed to those of rivals. In such cases, it can be advantageous for a manufacturer to integrate forward into wholesaling or retailing via company-owned distributorships or a chain of retail stores. For instance, both Goodyear and Bridgestone opted to integrate forward into tire retailing rather than to use independent distributors and retailers that stocked multiple brands because the independent distributors/retailers stressed selling the tire brands on which they earned the highest profit margins. A number of housewares and apparel manufacturers have integrated forward into retailing so as to move seconds, overstocked items, and slow-selling merchandise through their own branded retail outlet stores located in discount malls. Some producers have opted to integrate forward into retailing by selling directly to customers at the company's Web site. Bypassing regular wholesale/retail channels in favor of direct sales and Internet retailing can have appeal if it lowers distribution costs, produces a relative cost advantage over certain rivals, and results in lower selling prices to end users.

The Disadvantages of a Vertical Integration Strategy

Vertical integration has some substantial drawbacks, however.[18] As it boosts a firm's capital investment in the industry, it increases business risk (what if industry growth and profitability go sour?) and increases the company's vested interests in sticking with its vertically integrated value chain (what if some aspects of its technology and production facilities become obsolete before they are worn out or fully depreciated?). Vertically integrated companies that have invested heavily in a particular technology or in parts/components manufacture are often slow to embrace technological advances or more efficient production methods compared to partially integrated or nonintegrated firms. This is because less integrated firms can pressure suppliers to provide only the latest and best parts and components (even going so far as to shift their purchases from one supplier to another if need be), whereas a vertically integrated firm that is saddled with older technology or facilities that make items it no longer needs is looking at the high costs of premature abandonment. Second, integrating forward or backward locks a firm into relying on its own in-house activities and sources of supply (which later may prove more costly than outsourcing) and potentially results in less flexibility in accommodating shifting buyer preferences or a product design that doesn't include parts and components that it makes in-house. *In today's world of close working relationships with suppliers and efficient supply chain management systems, very few businesses can make a case for integrating backward into the business of suppliers to ensure a reliable supply of materials and components or to reduce production costs.* The best materials and components suppliers stay abreast of advancing technology and are adept in boosting their efficiency and keeping their costs and prices as low as possible. A company that pursues a vertical integration strategy and tries to produce many parts and components in-house is likely to find itself hard-pressed to keep up with technological advances and cutting-edge production practices for each part and component used in making its product.

Third, vertical integration poses all kinds of capacity-matching problems. In motor vehicle manufacturing, for example, the most efficient scale of operation for making axles is different from the most economic volume for radiators, and different yet again for both engines and transmissions. Building the capacity to produce just the right number of axles, radiators, engines, and transmissions in-house—and doing so at the lowest unit cost for each—is much easier said than done. If internal capacity for making transmissions is deficient, the difference has to be bought externally. Where internal capacity for radiators proves excessive, customers need to be found for the surplus. And if by-products are generated—as occurs in the processing of many chemical products—they require arrangements for disposal. Consequently, integrating across several production stages in ways that achieve the lowest feasible costs is not as easy as it might seem.

Fourth, integration forward or backward often calls for radical changes in skills and business capabilities. Parts and components manufacturing, assembly operations, wholesale distribution and retailing, and direct sales via the Internet are different businesses with different key success factors. Managers of a manufacturing company should consider carefully whether it makes good business sense to invest time and money in developing the expertise and merchandising skills to integrate forward into wholesaling and retailing. Many manufacturers learn the hard way that company-owned wholesale/retail networks present many headaches, fit poorly with what they do best, and don't always add the kind of value to their core business they thought they would. Selling to customers via the Internet poses still another set of problems—it is usually easier to use the Internet to sell to business customers than to consumers.

Finally, integrating backward into parts and components manufacture can impair a company's operating flexibility when it comes to changing out the use of certain parts and components. It is one thing to design out a component made by a supplier and another to design out a component being made in-house (which can mean laying off employees and writing off the associated investment in equipment and facilities). Companies that alter designs and models frequently in response to shifting buyer preferences often find that outsourcing the needed parts and components is cheaper and less complicated than producing them in-house. Most of the world's automakers, despite their expertise in automotive technology and manufacturing, have concluded that purchasing many of their key parts and components from manufacturing specialists results in higher quality, lower costs, and greater design flexibility than does the vertical integration option.

Weighing the Pros and Cons of Vertical Integration   All in all, therefore, a strategy of vertical integration can have both important strengths and weaknesses. The tip of the scales depends on (1) whether vertical integration can enhance the performance of strategy-critical activities in ways that lower cost, build expertise, protect proprietary know-how, or increase differentiation; (2) the impact of vertical integration on investment costs, flexibility and response times, and the administrative costs of coordinating operations across more value chain activities; and (3) whether vertical integration substantially enhances a company's competitiveness and profitability. *Vertical integration strategies have merit according to which capabilities and value-chain activities truly need to be performed in-house and which can be performed better or cheaper by outsiders.* Absent solid benefits, integrating forward or backward is not likely to be an attractive strategy option.

OUTSOURCING STRATEGIES: NARROWING THE BOUNDARIES OF THE BUSINESS

Outsourcing involves a conscious decision to abandon or forgo attempts to perform certain value chain activities internally and instead to farm them out to outside specialists and strategic allies. The two big drivers for outsourcing are that (1) outsiders can often perform certain activities better or cheaper and (2) outsourcing allows a firm to focus its entire energies on those activities at the center of its expertise (its core competencies) and that are the most critical to its competitive and financial success.

> **Core Concept**
> **Outsourcing** involves farming out certain value chain activities to outside vendors.

The current interest of many companies in making outsourcing a key component of their overall strategy and their approach to supply chain management represents a big departure from the way that companies used to deal with their suppliers and vendors. In years past, it was common for companies to maintain arm's-length relationships with suppliers and outside vendors, insisting on items being made to precise specifications and negotiating long and hard over price.[19] Although a company might place orders with the same supplier repeatedly, there was no expectation that this would be the case; price usually determined which supplier was awarded an order, and companies used the threat of switching suppliers to get the lowest possible prices. To enhance their bargaining power and, to make the threat of switching credible, it was standard practice for companies to source key parts and components from several suppliers as opposed to dealing with only a single supplier. But today most companies are abandoning such approaches in favor of forging alliances and strategic partnerships with a small number of highly capable suppliers. Collaborative relationships are replacing contractual, purely price-oriented relationships because companies have discovered that many of the advantages of performing value chain activities in-house can be captured and many of the disadvantages avoided by forging close, long-term cooperative partnerships with able suppliers and vendors and tapping into the expertise and capabilities that they have painstakingly developed.

When Outsourcing Strategies Are Advantageous

Outsourcing pieces of the value chain to narrow the boundaries of a firm's business makes strategic sense whenever:

- *An activity can be performed better or more cheaply by outside specialists.* Many PC makers, for example, have shifted from assembling units in-house to using contract assemblers because of the sizable scale economies associated with purchasing PC components in large volumes and assembling PCs. German shoemaker Birkenstock, by outsourcing the distribution of shoes made in its two plants in Germany to UPS, cut the time for delivering orders to U.S. footwear retailers from seven weeks to three weeks.[20]

- *The activity is not crucial to the firm's ability to achieve sustainable competitive advantage and won't hollow out its core competencies, capabilities, or technical know-how.* Outsourcing of maintenance services, data processing and data storage, fringe benefit management, Web site operations, and similar administrative support activities to specialists has become commonplace. American Express, for instance, recently entered into a seven-year, $4 billion deal whereby IBM's Services division would host American Express's Web site, network servers, data storage, and help desk; American Express indicated that it would save several hundred million dollars by paying only for the services it needed when it needed them (as opposed to funding its own full-time staff). A number of companies have begun outsourcing their call center operations to foreign-based contractors who have access to lower-cost labor supplies and can employ lower-paid call center personnel to respond to customer inquiries or requests for technical support.

> **Core Concept**
> A company should generally *not* perform any value chain activity internally that can be performed more efficiently or effectively by outsiders—the chief exception is when a particular activity is strategically crucial and internal control over that activity is deemed essential.

  - *It reduces the company's risk exposure to changing technology and/ or changing buyer preferences.* When a company outsources certain parts, components, and services, its suppliers must bear the burden of incorporating state-of-the-art technologies and/or undertaking redesigns and upgrades to accommodate a company's plans to introduce next-generation products. If what a supplier provides falls out of favor with buyers or is designed out of next-generation products, it is the supplier's business that suffers rather than a company's own internal operations.

- *It improves a company's ability to innovate.* Collaborative partnerships with world-class suppliers who have cutting-edge intellectual capital and are early adopters of the latest technology give a company access to ever better parts and components—such supplier-driven innovations, when incorporated into a company's own product offering, fuel a company's ability to introduce its own new and improved products.

- *It streamlines company operations in ways that improve organizational flexibility and cuts the time it takes to get new products into the marketplace.* Outsourcing gives a company the flexibility to switch suppliers in the event that its present supplier falls behind competing suppliers. To the extent that its suppliers can speedily get next-generation parts and components into production, then a company can get its own next-generation product offerings into the marketplace quicker. Moreover, seeking out new suppliers with the needed capabilities already in place is frequently quicker, easier, less risky, and cheaper than hurriedly retooling internal operations to replace obsolete capabilities or try to install and master new technologies.

- *It allows a company to assemble diverse kinds of expertise speedily and efficiently.* A company can nearly always gain quicker access to first-rate capabilities and expertise by partnering with suppliers who already have them in place than it can by trying to build them from scratch with its own company personnel.

- *It allows a company to concentrate on its core business, leverage its key resources, and do even better what it already does best.* A company is better able to build and develop its own competitively valuable competencies and capabilities when it concentrates its full resources and energies on performing those activities internally that it can perform better than outsiders and/or that it needs to have under its direct control. Cisco Systems, for example, devotes its energy to designing new generations of switches, routers, and other Internet-related equipment, opting to outsource the more mundane activities of producing and assembling its routers and switching equipment to contract manufacturers that together operate 37 factories, all closely monitored and overseen by Cisco personnel via online systems. Cisco's contract suppliers work so closely with Cisco that they can ship Cisco products to Cisco customers without a Cisco employee ever touching the gear. This system of alliances saves $500 million to $800 million annually.[21]

Dell Computer's partnerships with the suppliers of PC components have allowed it to operate with only three days of inventory (just a couple of hours of inventory in the case of some components), to realize substantial savings in inventory costs, and to get PCs equipped with next-generation components into the marketplace in less than a week after the newly upgraded components start shipping. Hewlett-Packard, IBM, Silicon Graphics (now SGI), and others have sold plants to suppliers and then contracted to purchase the output. Starbucks has found purchasing coffee beans from independent growers far more advantageous than trying to integrate backward into the coffee-growing business.

The Big Risk of an Outsourcing Strategy

The biggest danger of outsourcing is that a company will farm out too many or the wrong types of activities and thereby hollow out its own capabilities.[22] In such cases, a company loses touch with the very activities and expertise that over the long run determine its success. But most companies are alert to this danger and take actions to protect against being held hostage by outside suppliers. Cisco Systems guards against loss of control and protects its manufacturing expertise by designing the production methods that its contract manufacturers must use. Cisco keeps the source code for its designs proprietary, thereby controlling the initiation of all improvements and safeguarding its innovations from imitation. Further, Cisco uses the Internet to monitor the factory operations of contract manufacturers around the clock and can therefore know immediately when problems arise and whether to get involved.

OFFENSIVE STRATEGIES: IMPROVING MARKET POSITION AND BUILDING COMPETITIVE ADVANTAGE

Most every company must at times go on the offensive to improve its market position and try to build a competitive advantage or widen an existing one. Companies like Dell, Wal-Mart, and Toyota play hardball, aggressively pursuing competitive advantage and trying to reap the benefits a competitive edge offers—a leading market share, excellent profit margins and rapid growth (as compared to rivals), and all the intangibles of being known as a company on the move and one that plays to win.[23] The best offensives tend to incorporate several behaviors and principles: (1) focusing relentlessly on building competitive advantage and then striving to convert competitive advantage into decisive advantage, (2) employing the element of surprise as opposed to doing what rivals expect and are prepared for, (3) applying resources where rivals are least able to defend themselves, and (4) being impatient with the status quo and displaying a strong bias for swift, decisive actions to boost a company's competitive position vis-à-vis rivals.[24]

Offensive strategies are also important when a company has no choice but to try to whittle away at a strong rival's competitive advantage and when it is possible to gain profitable market share at the expense of rivals despite whatever resource strengths and capabilities they have. How long it takes for an offensive to yield good results varies with the competitive circumstances.[25] It can be short if buyers respond immediately (as can occur with a dramatic price cut, an imaginative ad campaign, or an especially appealing new product). Securing a competitive edge can take much longer if winning consumer acceptance of an innovative product will take some time or if the firm may need several years to debug a new technology or put new production capacity in place or develop and perfect new competitive capabilities. Ideally, an offensive move will improve a company's market standing or result in a competitive edge fairly quickly; the longer it takes, the more likely it is that rivals will spot the move, see its potential, and begin a counterresponse.

> **Core Concept**
>
> It takes successful offensive strategies to build competitive advantage—good defensive strategies can help protect competitive advantage but rarely are the basis for creating it.

The principal offensive strategy options include the following:

1. *Offering an equally good or better product at a lower price.* This is the classic offensive for improving a company's market position vis-à-vis rivals. Advanced Micro Devices (AMD), wanting to grow its sales of microprocessors for PCs, has on several occasions elected to attack Intel head-on, offering a faster alternative to Intel's Pentium chips at a lower price. Believing that the company's survival depends on eliminating the performance gap between AMD chips and Intel chips, AMD management has been willing to risk that a head-on offensive might prompt Intel to counter with lower prices of its own and accelerated development of next-generation chips. Lower prices can produce market share gains if competitors don't respond with price cuts of their own and if the challenger convinces buyers that its product is just as good or better. However, such a strategy increases total profits only if the gains in additional unit sales are enough to offset the impact of lower prices and thinner margins per unit sold. Price-cutting offensives generally work best when a company *first achieves a cost advantage and then hits competitors with a lower price.*[26]

2. *Leapfrogging competitors by being the first adopter of next-generation technologies or being first to market with next-generation products.* In 2004–2005, Microsoft waged an offensive to get its next-generation Xbox to market four to six months ahead of Sony's PlayStation 3, anticipating that such a lead time would allow help it convince video gamers to switch to the Xbox rather than wait for the new PlayStation to hit the market in 2006.

3. *Pursuing continuous product innovation to draw sales and market share away from less innovative rivals.* Aggressive and sustained efforts to trump the products of rivals by introducing new or improved products with features calculated to win customers away from rivals can put rivals under tremendous competitive pressure, especially when their new product development capabilities are weak or suspect. But such offensives work only if a company has potent product innovation skills of its own and can keep its pipeline full of ideas that are consistently well received in the marketplace.

4. *Adopting and improving on the good ideas of other companies (rivals or otherwise).*[27] The idea of warehouse-type hardware and home improvement centers did not

originate with Home Depot founders Arthur Blank and Bernie Marcus; they got the big-box concept from their former employer Handy Dan Home Improvement. But they were quick to improve on Handy Dan's business model and strategy and take Home Depot to the next plateau in terms of product line breadth and customer service. Casket maker Hillenbrand greatly improved its market position by adapting Toyota's production methods to casket making. Ryanair has succeeded as a low-cost airline in Europe by imitating many of Southwest Airlines' operating practices and applying them in a different geographic market. Companies that like to play hardball are willing to take any good idea (not nailed down by a patent or other legal protection), make it their own, and then aggressively apply it to create competitive advantage for themselves.[28]

5. *Deliberately attacking those market segments where a key rival makes big profits.*[29] Dell Computer's recent entry into printers and printer cartridges—the market arena where number-two PC maker Hewlett-Packard (HP) enjoys hefty profit margins and makes the majority of its profits—while mainly motivated by Dell's desire to broaden its product line and save its customers money (because of Dell's lower prices), nonetheless represented a hardball offensive calculated to weaken HP's market position in printers. To the extent that Dell might be able to use lower prices to woo away some of HP's printer customers, the move would erode HP's "profit sanctuary," distract HP's attention away from PCs, and reduce the financial resources HP has available for battling Dell in the global market for PCs.

6. *Attacking the competitive weaknesses of rivals.* Offensives aimed at rivals' weaknesses present many options. One is to go after the customers of those rivals whose products lag on quality, features, or product performance. If a company has especially good customer service capabilities, it can make special sales pitches to the customers of those rivals who provide subpar customer service. Aggressors with a recognized brand name and strong marketing skills can launch efforts to win customers away from rivals with weak brand recognition. There is considerable appeal in emphasizing sales to buyers in geographic regions where a rival has a weak market share or is exerting less competitive effort. Likewise, it may be attractive to pay special attention to buyer segments that a rival is neglecting or is weakly equipped to serve.

7. *Maneuvering around competitors and concentrating on capturing unoccupied or less contested market territory.* Examples include launching initiatives to build strong positions in geographic areas where close rivals have little or no market presence and trying to create new market segments by introducing products with different attributes and performance features to better meet the needs of selected buyers.

8. *Using hit-and-run or guerrilla warfare tactics to grab sales and market share from complacent or distracted rivals.* Options for "guerrilla offensives" include occasional lowballing on price (to win a big order or steal a key account from a rival); surprising key rivals with sporadic but intense bursts of promotional activity (offering a 20 percent discount for one week to draw customers away from rival brands); or undertaking special campaigns to attract buyers away from rivals plagued with a strike or problems in meeting buyer demand.[30] Guerrilla offensives are particularly well suited to small challengers who have neither the resources nor the market visibility to mount a full-fledged attack on industry leaders.

9. *Launching a preemptive strike to secure an advantageous position that rivals are prevented or discouraged from duplicating.*[31] What makes a move preemptive

is its one-of-a-kind nature—whoever strikes first stands to acquire competitive assets that rivals can't readily match. Examples of preemptive moves include (1) securing the best distributors in a particular geographic region or country; (2) moving to obtain the most favorable site along a heavily traveled thorough fare, at a new interchange or intersection, in a new shopping mall, in a natural beauty spot, close to cheap transportation or raw material supplies or market outlets, and so on; (3) tying up the most reliable, high-quality suppliers via exclusive partnership, long-term contracts, or even acquisition; and (4) moving swiftly to acquire the assets of distressed rivals at bargain prices. To be successful, a preemptive move doesn't have to totally block rivals from following or copying; it merely needs to give a firm a prime position that is not easily circumvented.

Blue Ocean Strategy: A Special Kind of Offensive

A "blue ocean strategy" seeks to gain a dramatic and durable competitive advantage *by abandoning efforts to beat out competitors in existing markets and, instead, inventing a new industry or distinctive market segment (a wide-open blue ocean of possibility) that renders existing competitors largely irrelevant and allows a company to create and capture altogether new demand.*[32] This strategy views the business universe as consisting of two distinct types of market space. One is where industry boundaries are defined and accepted, the competitive rules of the game are well understood by all industry members, and companies try to outperform rivals by capturing a bigger share of existing demand; in such markets, lively competition constrains a company's prospects for rapid growth and superior profitability since rivals move quickly to either imitate or counter the successes of competitors. In the second type of market space, the industry does not really exist yet, is untainted by competition, and offers wide-open opportunity for profitable and rapid growth if a company can come up with a product offering and strategy that allows it to create new demand rather than fight over existing demand. A terrific example of such a blue ocean market space is the online auction industry that eBay created and now dominates.

Another company that has employed a blue ocean strategy is Cirque du Soleil, which increased its revenues by 22 times during the 1993–2003 period in the circus business, an industry that had been in long-term decline for 20 years. How did Cirque du Soleil pull this off against legendary industry leader Ringling Bros. and Barnum & Bailey? By reinventing the circus, creating a distinctively different market space for its performances (Las Vegas nightclubs and theater-type settings), and pulling in a whole new group of customers—adults and corporate clients—who were noncustomers of traditional circuses and were willing to pay several times more than the price of a conventional circus ticket to have an "entertainment experience" featuring sophisticated clowns and star-quality acrobatic acts in a comfortable big-tent atmosphere. Cirque studiously avoided the use of animals because of costs and because of concerns over their treatment by traditional circus organizations. Cirque's market research led management to conclude that the lasting allure of the traditional circus came down to just three factors: the clowns, classic acrobatic acts, and a tentlike stage. As of 2005, Cirque du Soleil was presenting nine different shows, each with its own theme and story line; was performing before audiences of about 7 million people annually; and had performed 250 engagements in 100 cities before 50 million spectators since its formation in 1984.

Other examples of companies that have achieved competitive advantages by creating blue ocean market spaces include AMC via its pioneering of megaplex movie theaters, The Weather Channel in cable TV, Home Depot in big-box retailing of hardware and building supplies, and FedEx in overnight package delivery. Companies that create blue ocean market spaces can usually sustain their initially won competitive advantage without encountering major competitive challenge for 10 to 15 years because of high barriers to imitation and the strong brand-name awareness that a blue ocean strategy can produce.

Choosing Which Rivals to Attack

Offense-minded firms need to analyze which of their rivals to challenge as well as how to mount that challenge. The following are the best targets for offensive attacks:[33]

- *Market leaders that are vulnerable*—Offensive attacks make good sense when a company that leads in terms of size and market share is not a true leader in terms of serving the market well. Signs of leader vulnerability include unhappy buyers, an inferior product line, a weak competitive strategy with regard to low-cost leadership or differentiation, strong emotional commitment to an aging technology the leader has pioneered, outdated plants and equipment, a preoccupation with diversification into other industries, and mediocre or declining profitability. Offensives to erode the positions of market leaders have real promise when the challenger is able to revamp its value chain or innovate to gain a fresh cost-based or differentiation-based competitive advantage.[34] To be judged successful, attacks on leaders don't have to result in making the aggressor the new leader; a challenger may "win" by simply becoming a stronger runner-up. Caution is well advised in challenging strong market leaders—there's a significant risk of squandering valuable resources in a futile effort or precipitating a fierce and profitless industrywide battle for market share.

- *Runner-up firms with weaknesses in areas where the challenger is strong*—Runner-up firms are an especially attractive target when a challenger's resource strengths and competitive capabilities are well suited to exploiting their weaknesses.

- *Struggling enterprises that are on the verge of going under*—Challenging a hard-pressed rival in ways that further sap its financial strength and competitive position can weaken its resolve and hasten its exit from the market.

- *Small local and regional firms with limited capabilities*—Because small firms typically have limited expertise and resources, a challenger with broader capabilities is well positioned to raid their biggest and best customers—particularly those who are growing rapidly, have increasingly sophisticated requirements, and may already be thinking about switching to a supplier with more full-service capability.

Choosing the Basis for Competitive Attack

As a rule, challenging rivals on competitive grounds where they are strong is an uphill struggle.[35] Offensive initiatives that exploit competitor weaknesses stand a better chance of succeeding than do those that challenge competitor strengths, especially if the weaknesses represent important vulnerabilities and weak rivals can be caught by surprise with no ready defense.[36]

> **Core Concept**
> The best offensives use a company's resource strengths to attack rivals in those competitive areas where they are weak.

Strategic offensives should, as a general rule, be grounded in a company's competitive assets and strong points—its core competencies, competitive capabilities, and such resource strengths as a better-known brand name, a cost advantage in manufacturing or distribution, greater technological capability, or a superior product. If the attacker's resource strengths give it a competitive advantage over the targeted rivals, so much the better. Ignoring the need to tie a strategic offensive to a company's competitive strengths is like going to war with a popgun—the prospects for success are dim. For instance, it is foolish for a company with relatively high costs to employ a price-cutting offensive—price-cutting offensives are best left to financially strong companies whose costs are relatively low in comparison to those of the companies being attacked. Likewise, it is ill advised to pursue a product innovation offensive without having proven expertise in R&D, new product development, and speeding new or improved products to market.

DEFENSIVE STRATEGIES: PROTECTING MARKET POSITION AND COMPETITIVE ADVANTAGE

It is just as important to discern when to fortify a company's present market position with defensive actions as it is to seize the initiative and launch strategic offensives.

In a competitive market, all firms are subject to offensive challenges from rivals. The purposes of defensive strategies are to lower the risk of being attacked, weaken the impact of any attack that occurs, and influence challengers to aim their efforts at other rivals. While defensive strategies usually don't enhance a firm's competitive advantage, they can definitely help fortify its competitive position, protect its most valuable resources and capabilities from imitation, and defend whatever competitive advantage it might have. Defensive strategies can take either of two forms: actions to block challengers and signaling the likelihood of strong retaliation.

Blocking the Avenues Open to Challengers

There are many ways to throw obstacles in the path of would-be challengers.

The most frequently employed approach to defending a company's present position involves actions that restrict a challenger's options for initiating competitive attack. There are any number of obstacles that can be put in the path of would-be challengers.[37] A defender can participate in alternative technologies as a hedge against rivals attacking with a new or better technology. A defender can introduce new features, add new models, or broaden its product line to close off gaps and vacant niches to opportunity-seeking challengers. It can thwart the efforts of rivals to attack with a lower price by maintaining economy-priced options of its own. It can try to discourage buyers from trying competitors' brands by lengthening warranties, offering free training and support services, developing the capability to deliver spare parts to users faster than rivals can, providing coupons and sample giveaways to buyers most prone to experiment, and making early announcements about impending new products or price changes to induce potential buyers to postpone switching. It can challenge the quality or safety of rivals' products. Finally, a defender can grant volume discounts or better financing terms to dealers and distributors to discourage them from experimenting with other suppliers, or it can convince them to handle its product line *exclusively* and force competitors to use other distribution outlets.

Signaling Challengers that Retaliation Is Likely

The goal of signaling challengers that strong retaliation is likely in the event of an attack is either to dissuade challengers from attacking at all or to divert them to less threatening options. Either goal can be achieved by letting challengers know the battle will cost more than it is worth. Would-be challengers can be signaled by:[38]

- Publicly announcing management's commitment to maintain the firm's present market share.
- Publicly committing the company to a policy of matching competitors' terms or prices.
- Maintaining a war chest of cash and marketable securities.
- Making an occasional strong counterresponse to the moves of weak competitors to enhance the firm's image as a tough defender.

WEB SITE STRATEGIES

One of the biggest strategic issues facing company executives across the world is just what role the company's Web site should play in a company's competitive strategy. In particular, to what degree should a company use the Internet as a distribution channel for accessing buyers? Should a company use its Web site *only as a means of disseminating product information* (with traditional distribution channel partners making all sales to end users), as a *secondary or minor channel* for selling directly to buyers of its product, as *one of several important distribution channels* for accessing customers, as *the primary distribution channel* for accessing customers, or as *the exclusive channel* for transacting sales with customers?[39] Let's look at each of these strategic options in turn.

> Companies today must wrestle with the strategic issue of how to use their Web sites in positioning themselves in the marketplace—whether to use their Web sites just to disseminate product information or whether to operate an e-store to sell direct to online shoppers.

Product Information–Only Web Strategies: Avoiding Channel Conflict

Operating a Web site that contains extensive product information but that relies on click-throughs to the Web sites of distribution channel partners for sales transactions (or that informs site users where nearby retail stores are located) is an attractive market positioning option for manufacturers and/or wholesalers that have invested heavily in building and cultivating retail dealer networks and that face nettlesome channel conflict issues if they try to sell online in direct competition with their dealers. A manufacturer or wholesaler that aggressively pursues online sales to end users is signaling both a weak strategic commitment to its dealers and a willingness to cannibalize dealers' sales and growth potential.

To the extent that strong partnerships with wholesale and/or retail dealers are critical to accessing end users, selling directly to end users via the company's Web site is a very tricky road to negotiate. A manufacturer's efforts to use its Web site to sell around its dealers is certain to anger its wholesale distributors and retail dealers, which may respond by putting more effort into marketing the brands of rival manufacturers that don't sell online. In sum, the manufacturer may stand to lose more sales by offending its dealers than it gains from its own online sales effort. Moreover, dealers may be in better position to employ a brick-and-click strategy than a manufacturer is because dealers have a local presence to complement their online sales approach (which consumers may find appealing). Consequently, in industries where the strong support and goodwill of dealer networks is essential, manufacturers may conclude that their Web site should be designed to partner with dealers rather than compete with them—just as the auto manufacturers are doing with their franchised dealers.

Web Site e-Stores as a Minor Distribution Channel

A second strategic option is to use online sales as a relatively minor distribution channel for achieving incremental sales, gaining online sales experience, and doing marketing research. If channel conflict poses a big obstacle to online sales, or if only a small fraction of buyers can be attracted to make online purchases, then companies are well advised to pursue online sales with the strategic intent of gaining experience, learning more about buyer tastes and preferences, testing reaction to new products, creating added market buzz about their products, and boosting overall sales volume a few percentage points. Sony and Nike, for example, sell most all of their products at their Web sites without provoking resistance from their retail dealers since most buyers of their products prefer to do their buying at retail stores rather than online. They use their Web site not so much to make sales as to glean valuable marketing research data from tracking the browsing patterns of Web site visitors. The behavior and actions of Web surfers are a veritable gold mine of information for companies seeking to keep their finger on the market pulse and respond more precisely to buyer preferences and interests.

Despite the channel conflict that exists when a manufacturer sells directly to end users at its Web site in head-to-head competition with its distribution channel allies, manufacturers might still opt to pursue online sales at their Web sites and try to establish online sales as an important distribution channel because (1) their profit margins from online sales are bigger than they earned from selling to their wholesale/retail customers; (2) encouraging buyers to visit the company's Web site helps educate them to the ease and convenience of purchasing online and, over time, prompts more and more buyers to purchase online (where company profit margins are greater)—which makes incurring channel conflict in the short term and competing against traditional distribution allies potentially worthwhile—and (3) selling directly to end users allows a manufacturer to make greater use of build-to-order manufacturing and assembly, which, if met with growing buyer acceptance of and satisfaction, would increase the rate at which sales migrate from distribution allies to the company's Web site—such migration could lead to streamlining the company's value chain and boosting its profit margins.

Brick-and-Click Strategies

Brick-and-click strategies have two big strategic appeals for wholesale and retail enterprises: They are an economic means of expanding a company's geographic reach, and they give both existing and potential customers another choice of how to communicate with the company, shop for product information, make purchases, or resolve customer service problems. Software developers, for example, have come to rely on the Internet as a highly effective distribution channel to complement sales through brick-and-mortar wholesalers and retailers. Selling online directly to end users has the advantage of eliminating the costs of producing and packaging CDs, as well as cutting out the costs and margins of software wholesalers and retailers (often 35 to 50 percent of the retail price). However, software developers are still strongly motivated to continue to distribute their products through wholesalers and retailers (to maintain broad access to existing and potential users who, for whatever reason, may be reluctant to buy online). Chain retailers like Wal-Mart and Circuit City operate online stores for their products primarily as a convenience to customers who want to buy online rather than making a shopping trip to nearby stores.

Many brick-and-mortar companies can enter online retailing at relatively low cost—all they need is a Web store and systems for filling and delivering individual customer orders. Brick-and-mortar distributors and retailers (as well as manufacturers with company-owned retail stores) can employ brick-and-click strategies by using their current distribution centers and/or retail stores for picking orders from on-hand inventories and making deliveries. Blockbuster, the world's largest chain of video and DVD rental stores, uses the inventories at its stores to fill orders for its online subscribers, who pay a monthly fee for unlimited DVDs delivered by mail carrier; using local stores to fill orders typically allows delivery in 24 hours versus 48 hours for shipments made from a regional shipping center. Walgreen's, a leading drugstore chain, allows customers to order a prescription online and then pick it up at the drive-through window or inside counter of a local store. In banking, a brick-and-click strategy allows customers to use local branches and ATMs for depositing checks and getting cash while using online systems to pay bills, check account balances, and transfer funds. Many industrial distributors are finding it efficient for customers to place their orders over the Web rather than phoning them in or waiting for salespeople to call in person. Illustration Capsule 6.2 describes how office supply chains like Office Depot, Staples, and OfficeMax have successfully migrated from a traditional brick-and-mortar distribution strategy to a combination brick-and-click distribution strategy.

Strategies for Online Enterprises

A company that elects to use the Internet as its exclusive channel for accessing buyers is essentially an online enterprise from the perspective of the customer. The Internet becomes the vehicle for transacting sales and delivering customer services; except for advertising, the Internet is the sole point of all buyer–seller contact. Many so-called pure dot-com enterprises have chosen this strategic approach—prominent examples include eBay, Yahoo, Amazon.com, Buy.com, Overstock.com, and Priceline.com. For a company to succeed in using the Internet as its exclusive distribution channel, its product or service must be one for which buying online holds strong appeal.

A company that decides to use online sales as its exclusive method for sales transactions must address several strategic issues:

- *How it will deliver unique value to buyers*—Online businesses must usually attract buyers on the basis of low price, convenience, superior product information, build-to-order options, or attentive online service.

- *Whether it will pursue competitive advantage based on lower costs, differentiation, or better value for the money*—For an online-only sales strategy to succeed in head-to-head competition with brick-and-mortar and brick-and-click rivals, an online seller's value chain approach must hold potential for a low-cost advantage, competitively valuable differentiating attributes, or a best-cost provider advantage. If an online firm's strategy is to attract customers by selling at cut-rate prices, then it must possess cost advantages in those activities it performs, and it must outsource the remaining activities to low-cost specialists. If an online seller is going to differentiate itself on the basis of a superior buying experience and top-notch customer service, then it needs to concentrate on having an easy-to-navigate Web site, an array of functions and conveniences for customers, Web reps who can answer questions online, and logistical capabilities to deliver products quickly and accommodate returned merchandise. If it is going to deliver more value for the money, then it must manage value chain activities so as to deliver upscale products and services at lower costs than rivals.

Illustration Capsule 6.2

Brick-and-Click Strategies in the Office Supplies Industry

Office Depot was in the first wave of retailers to adopt a combination brick-and-click strategy. Management quickly saw the merits of allowing business customers to use the Internet to place orders instead of having to make a call, generate a purchase order, and pay an invoice—while still getting same-day or next-day delivery from one of Office Depot's local stores.

Office Depot already had an existing network of retail stores, delivery centers and warehouses, delivery trucks, account managers, sales offices, and regional call centers that handled large business customers. In addition, it had a solid brand name and enough purchasing power with its suppliers to counter discount-minded online rivals trying to attract buyers of office supplies on the basis of super-low prices. Office Depot's incremental investment to enter the e-commerce arena was minimal since all it needed to add was a Web site where customers could see pictures and descriptions of the 14,000 items it carried, their prices, and in-stock availability. Marketing costs to make customers aware of its Web store option ran less than $10 million.

Office Depot's online prices were the same as its store prices, the strategy being to promote Web sales on the basis of service, convenience, and lower customer costs for order processing and inventories. Customers reported that doing business with Office Depot online cut their transaction costs by up to 80 percent; plus, Office Depot's same-day or next-day delivery capability allowed them to reduce office supply inventories.

The company set up customized Web pages for 37,000 corporate and educational customers that allowed the customer's employees varying degrees of freedom to buy supplies. A clerk might be able to order only copying paper, toner cartridges, computer disks, and paper clips up to a preset dollar limit per order, while a vice president might have carte blanche to order any item Office Depot sold.

Web site sales cost Office Depot less than $1 per $100 of goods ordered, compared with about $2 for phone and fax orders. And since Web sales eliminate the need to key in transactions, order-entry errors were virtually eliminated and product returns cut by 50 percent. Billing is handled electronically.

In 2005, over 50 percent of Office Depot's major customers were ordering most of their supplies online. Online sales accounted for almost $3 billion in 2004 (about 24 percent of Office Depot's total revenues), up from $982 million in 2000 and making Office Depot the third-largest online retailer. Its online operations were profitable from the start.

Office Depot's successful brick-and-click strategy prompted its two biggest rivals—Staples and OfficeMax—to adopt brick-and-click strategies too. In 2005, all three companies were enjoying increasing success with selling online to business customers and using local stores to fill orders and make deliveries.

Sources: Information posted at www.officedepot.com (accessed September 28, 2005); "Office Depot's e-Diva," *BusinessWeek Online* (www.businessweek.com), August 6, 2001; Laura Lorek, "Office Depot Site Picks Up Speed," *Interactive Week* (www.zdnet.com/intweek), June 25, 2001; "Why Office Depot Loves the Net," *BusinessWeek,* September 27, 1999, pp. EB 66, EB 68; and *Fortune,* November 8, 1999, p. 17.

- *Whether it will have a broad or a narrow product offering*—A one-stop shopping strategy like that employed by Amazon.com (which offers over 30 million items for sale at its Web sites in the United States, Britain, France, Germany, Denmark, and Japan) has the appealing economics of helping spread fixed operating costs over a wide number of items and a large customer base. Other e-tailers, such as E-Loan and Hotel.com, have adopted classic focus strategies and cater to a sharply defined target audience shopping for a particular product or product category.

- *Whether to perform order fulfillment activities internally or to outsource them*—Building central warehouses, stocking them with adequate inventories, and developing systems to pick, pack, and ship individual orders all require substantial start-up capital but may result in lower overall unit costs than would paying the fees of order fulfillment specialists who make a business of providing warehouse space, stocking inventories, and shipping orders for e-tailers. However, outsourcing order fulfillment activities is likely to be more economical unless an e-tailer has high unit volume and the capital to invest in its own order fulfillment capabilities. Buy.com, an online superstore consisting of some 30,000 items, obtains products from name-brand manufacturers and uses outsiders to stock and ship those products; thus, its focus is not on manufacturing or order fulfillment but rather on selling.

- *How it will draw traffic to its Web site and then convert page views into revenues*—Web sites have to be cleverly marketed. Unless Web surfers hear about the site, like what they see on their first visit, and are intrigued enough to return again and again, the site is unlikely to generate adequate revenues. Marketing campaigns that result only in heavy site traffic and lots of page views are seldom sufficient; the best test of effective marketing and the appeal of an online company's product offering is the ratio at which page views are converted into revenues (the "look-to-buy" ratio). For example, in 2001 Yahoo's site traffic averaged 1.2 *billion* page views daily but generated only about $2 million in daily revenues; in contrast, the traffic at brokerage firm Charles Schwab's Web site averaged only 40 *million* page views per day but resulted in an average of $5 million daily in online commission revenues.

CHOOSING APPROPRIATE FUNCTIONAL-AREA STRATEGIES

A company's strategy is not complete until company managers have made strategic choices about how the various functional parts of the business—R&D, production, human resources, sales and marketing, finance, and so on—will be managed in support of its basic competitive strategy approach and the other important competitive moves being taken. Normally, functional-area strategy choices rank third on the menu of choosing among the various strategy options, as shown in Figure 6.1 (see p. 162). But whether commitments to particular functional strategies are made before or after the choices of complementary strategic options shown in Figure 6.1 is beside the point—what's really important is what the functional strategies are and how they mesh to enhance the success of the company's higher-level strategic thrusts.

In many respects, the nature of functional strategies is dictated by the choice of competitive strategy. For example, a manufacturer employing a low-cost provider strategy needs an R&D and product design strategy that emphasizes cheap-to-incorporate features and facilitates economical assembly and a production strategy that stresses capture of scale economies and actions to achieve low-cost manufacture (such as high labor productivity, efficient supply chain management, and automated production processes), and a low-budget marketing strategy. A business pursuing a high-end differentiation strategy needs a production strategy geared to top-notch quality and a marketing strategy aimed at touting differentiating features and using advertising and a trusted brand name to "pull" sales through the chosen distribution channels. A company using a focused differentiation strategy needs a marketing strategy that stresses growing the niche. For example, the Missouri-based franchise Panera Bread has been growing its business by getting more people hooked on fresh-baked specialty breads and patronizing its bakery-cafés, keeping buyer interest in Panera's all-natural specialty breads at a high level, and protecting its specialty bread niche against invasion by outsiders.

Beyond very general prescriptions, it is difficult to say just what the content of the different functional-area strategies should be without first knowing what higher-level strategic choices a company has made, the industry environment in which it operates, the resource strengths that can be leveraged, and so on. Suffice it to say here that company personnel—both managers and employees charged with strategy-making responsibility down through the organizational hierarchy—must be clear about which higher-level strategies top management has chosen and then must tailor the company's functional-area strategies accordingly.

FIRST-MOVER ADVANTAGES AND DISADVANTAGES

Core Concept
Because of first-mover advantages and disadvantages, competitive advantage can spring from *when* a move is made as well as from *what* move is made.

When to make a strategic move is often as crucial as *what* move to make. Timing is especially important when *first-mover advantages* or *disadvantages* exist.[40] Being first to initiate a strategic move can have a high payoff when (1) pioneering helps build a firm's image and reputation with buyers; (2) early commitments to new technologies, new-style components, new or emerging distribution channels, and so on can produce an absolute cost advantage over rivals; (3) first-time customers remain strongly loyal to pioneering firms in making repeat purchases; and (4) moving first constitutes a preemptive strike, making imitation extra hard or unlikely. The bigger the first-mover advantages, the more attractive making the first move becomes.[41] In e-commerce, companies like America Online, Amazon.com, Yahoo, eBay, and Priceline.com that were first with a new technology, network solution, or business model enjoyed lasting first-mover advantages in gaining the visibility and reputation needed to remain market leaders. However, other first-movers such as Xerox in fax machines, eToys (an online toy retailer), Webvan and Peapod (in online groceries), and scores of other dot-com companies never converted their first-mover status into any sort of competitive advantage. Sometimes markets are slow to accept the innovative product offering of a first-mover; sometimes, a fast-follower with greater resources and marketing muscle can easily overtake the first-mover (as Microsoft was able to do when it introduced Internet Explorer against Netscape, the pioneer of Internet browsers with the lion's share of the market); and sometimes furious technological change or product innovation makes a first-mover vulnerable to quickly appearing next-generation technology or products. Hence, just being a first-mover by itself is seldom enough to win a sustainable competitive advantage.[42]

To sustain any advantage that may initially accrue to a pioneer, a first-mover needs to be a fast learner and continue to move aggressively to capitalize on any initial pioneering advantage. It helps immensely if the first-mover has deep financial pockets, important competencies and competitive capabilities, and astute managers. If a first-mover's skills, know-how, and actions are easily copied or even surpassed, then fast-followers and even late-movers can catch or overtake the first-mover in a relatively short period. What makes being a first-mover strategically important is not being the first company to do something but rather being the first competitor to put together the precise combination of features, customer value, and sound revenue/cost/profit economics that gives it an edge over rivals in the battle for market leadership.[43] If the marketplace quickly takes to a first-mover's innovative product offering, a first-mover must have large-scale production, marketing, and distribution capabilities if it is to stave off fast-followers who possess these resources capabilities. If technology is advancing at torrid pace, a first-mover cannot hope to sustain its lead without having strong capabilities in R&D, design, and new product development, along with the financial strength to fund these activities.

The Potential for Late-Mover Advantages or First-Mover Disadvantages

There are instances when there are actually *advantages* to being an adept follower rather than a first-mover. Late-mover advantages (or *first-mover disadvantages*) arise in four instances:

- When pioneering leadership is more costly than imitating followership and only negligible learning/experience curve benefits accrue to the leader—a condition that allows a follower to end up with lower costs than the first-mover.

- When the products of an innovator are somewhat primitive and do not live up to buyer expectations, thus allowing a clever follower to win disenchanted buyers away from the leader with better-performing products.

- When the demand side of the marketplace is skeptical about the benefits of a new technology or product being pioneered by a first-mover.

- When rapid market evolution (due to fast-paced changes in either technology or buyer needs and expectations) gives fast-followers and maybe even cautious late-movers the opening to leapfrog a first-mover's products with more attractive next-version products.

To Be a First-Mover or Not

In weighing the pros and cons of being a first-mover versus a fast-follower versus a slow-mover, it matters whether the race to market leadership in a particular industry is a marathon or a sprint. In marathons, a slow-mover is not unduly penalized—first-mover advantages can be fleeting, and there is ample time for fast-followers and sometimes even late-movers to play catch-up.[44] Thus, the speed at which the pioneering innovation is likely to catch on matters considerably as companies struggle with whether to pursue a particular emerging market opportunity aggressively (as a first-mover or fast-follower) or cautiously (as a late-mover). For instance, it took 18 months for 10 million users to sign up for Hotmail, 5.5 years for worldwide mobile phone use to grow from 10 million to 100 million worldwide, 7 years for videocassette recorders to find their way into 1 million U.S. homes, and close to 10 years for the number of at-home broadband subscribers to grow to 100 million worldwide. The lesson here is that there is a market-penetration curve for every emerging opportunity; typically, the curve has an inflection point at which all the pieces of the business model fall into place, buyer demand explodes, and the market takes off. The inflection point can come early on a fast-rising curve (like use of e-mail) or further up on a slow-rising curve (like the use of broadband). Any company that seeks competitive advantage by being a first-mover thus needs to ask some hard questions:

- Does market takeoff depend on the development of complementary products or services that currently are not available?

- Is new infrastructure required before buyer demand can surge?

- Will buyers need to learn new skills or adopt new behaviors? Will buyers encounter high switching costs?

- Are there influential competitors in a position to delay or derail the efforts of a first-mover?

Illustration Capsule 6.3

The Battle in Consumer Broadband: First-Movers versus Late-Movers

In 1988 an engineer at the Bell companies' research labs figured out how to rush signals along ordinary copper wire at high speed using digital technology, thus creating the digital subscriber line (DSL). But the regional Bells, which dominated the local telephone market in the United States, showed little interest over the next 10 years, believing it was more lucrative to rent T-1 lines to businesses that needed fast data transmission capability and rent second phone lines to households wanting an Internet connection that didn't disrupt their regular telephone service. Furthermore, telephone executives were skeptical about DSL technology—there were a host of technical snarls to overcome, and early users encountered annoying glitches. Many executives doubted that it made good sense to invest billions of dollars in the infrastructure needed to roll out DSL to residential and small business customers, given the success they were having with T-1 and second-line rentals. As a consequence, the Bells didn't seriously begin to market DSL until the late 1990s, two years after the cable TV companies began their push to market cable broadband.

Cable companies were more than happy to be the first-movers in marketing broadband service via their copper cable wires, chiefly because their business was threatened by satellite TV technology and they saw broadband as an innovative service they could provide that the satellite companies could not. (Delivering broadband service via satellite has yet to become a factor in the marketplace, winning only a 1 percent share in 2003.) Cable companies were able to deploy broadband on their copper wire economically because during the 1980s and early 1990s most cable operators had spent about $60 billion to upgrade their systems with fiber-optic technology in order to handle two-way traffic rather than just one-way TV signals and thereby make good on their promises to local governments to develop "interactive" cable systems if they were awarded franchises. Although the early interactive services were duds, technicians discovered in the mid-1990s that the two-way systems enabled high-speed Internet hookups.

With Internet excitement surging in the late 1990s, cable executives saw high-speed Internet service as a no-brainer and began rolling it out to customers in 1998, securing about 362,000 customers by year-end versus only about 41,000 for DSL. Part of the early success of cable broadband was due to a cost advantage in modems—cable executives, seeing the potential of cable broadband several years earlier, had asked CableLabs to standardize the technology for cable modems, a move that lowered costs and made cable modems marketable in consumer electronics stores. DSL modems were substantially more complicated, and it took longer to drive the costs down from several hundred dollars each to under $100—in 2004, both cable and phone companies paid about $50 for modems, but cable modems got there much sooner.

As cable broadband began to attract more and more attention in the 1998–2002 period, the regional Bells continued to move slowly on DSL. The technical problems lingered, and early users were disgruntled by a host of annoying and sometimes horrendous installation difficulties and service glitches. Not only did providing users with convenient and reliable service prove to be a formidable challenge, but some regulatory issues stood in the way as well. Even in 2003 phone company executives found it hard to justify multibillion-dollar investments to install the necessary equipment and support systems to offer, market, manage, and maintain DSL service on the vast scale of a regional Bell company. SBC Communications figured it would cost at least $6 billion to roll out DSL to its customers. Verizon estimated that it would take 3.5 to 4 million customers to make DSL economics work, a number it would probably not reach until the end of 2005.

In 2003–2004, high-speed consumer access to the Internet was a surging business with a bright outlook—the number of U.S. Internet users upgrading to high-speed service increased by close to 500,000 monthly. In 2005, cable broadband was the preferred choice—70 percent of U.S. broadband users had opted for cable modems supplied by cable TV companies, with cable modem subscribers outnumbering DSL subscribers 30 million to 10.6 million. Its late start made it questionable whether DSL would be able to catch cable broadband in the U.S. marketplace, although DSL providers added 1.4 million subscribers in the first three months of 2005 compared to 1.2 million new subscribers for cable. In the rest of the world, however, DSL was the broadband connection of choice—there were an estimated 200 million broadband subscribers worldwide at the end of 2005.

Source: Developed from information in Shawn Young and Peter Grant, "How Phone Firms Lost to Cable in Consumer Broadband Market," *The Wall Street Journal,* March 13, 2003, pp. A1, A6, and Cnet's www.news.com site (accessed September 22, 2005).

When the answers to any of these questions are yes, then a company must be careful not to pour too many resources into getting ahead of the market opportunity—the race is likely going to be more of a 10-year marathon than a 2-year sprint. Being first out of the starting block is competitively important only when pioneering early introduction of a technology or product delivers clear and substantial benefits to early adopters and buyers, thus winning their immediate support, perhaps giving the pioneer a reputational head-start advantage, and forcing competitors to quickly follow the pioneer's lead. In the remaining instances where the race is more of a marathon, the companies that end up capturing and dominating new-to-the-world markets are almost never the pioneers that gave birth to those markets—there is time for a company to marshal the needed resources and to ponder its best time and method of entry.[45] Furthermore, being a late-mover into industries of the future has the advantages of being less risky and skirting the costs of pioneering.

But while a company is right to be cautious about quickly entering virgin territory, where all kinds of risks abound, rarely does a company have much to gain from consistently being a late-mover whose main concern is avoiding the mistakes of first-movers. Companies that are habitual late-movers regardless of the circumstances, while often able to survive, can find themselves and scrambling to keep pace with more progressive and innovative rivals and fighting to retain their customers. For a habitual late-mover to catch up, it must count on first-movers to be slow learners and complacent in letting their lead dwindle. It also has to hope that buyers will be slow to gravitate to the products of first-movers, again giving it time to catch up. And it has to have competencies and capabilities that are sufficiently strong to allow it to close the gap fairly quickly once it makes its move. Counting on all first-movers to stumble or otherwise be easily overtaken is usually a bad bet that puts a late-mover's competitive position at risk.

Illustration Capsule 6.3 describes the challenges that late-moving telephone companies have in winning the battle to supply at-home high-speed Internet access and overcoming the first-mover advantages of cable companies.

Key Points

Once a company has selected which of the five basic competitive strategies to employ in its quest for competitive advantage, then it must decide whether to supplement its choice of a basic competitive strategy approach, as shown in Figure 6.1 (p. 162).

Many companies are using strategic alliances and collaborative partnerships to help them in the race to build a global market presence or be a leader in the industries of the future. Strategic alliances are an attractive, flexible, and often cost-effective means by which companies can gain access to missing technology, expertise, and business capabilities.

Mergers and acquisitions are another attractive strategic option for strengthening a firm's competitiveness. When the operations of two companies are combined via merger or acquisition, the new company's competitiveness can be enhanced in any of several ways—lower costs; stronger technological skills; more or better competitive capabilities; a more attractive lineup of products and services; wider geographic coverage; and/or greater financial resources with which to invest in R&D, add capacity, or expand into new areas.

Vertically integrating forward or backward makes strategic sense only if it strengthens a company's position via either cost reduction or creation of a differentiation-based advantage. Otherwise, the drawbacks of vertical integration (increased investment, greater business risk, increased vulnerability to technological changes, and less flexibility in making product changes) are likely to outweigh any advantages.

Outsourcing pieces of the value chain formerly performed in-house can enhance a company's competitiveness whenever an activity (1) can be performed better or more cheaply by outside specialists; (2) is not crucial to the firm's ability to achieve sustainable competitive advantage and won't hollow out its core competencies, capabilities, or technical know-how; (3) reduces the company's risk exposure to changing technology or changing buyer preferences; (4) streamlines company operations in ways that improve organizational flexibility, cut cycle time, speed decision making, and reduce coordination costs; or (5) allows a company to concentrate on its core business and do what it does best.

One of the most pertinent strategic issues that companies face is how to use the Internet in positioning the company in the marketplace—whether to use the Internet as *only a means of disseminating product information* (with traditional distribution channel partners making all sales to end users), as *a secondary or minor channel*, as *one of several important distribution channels*, as *the company's primary distribution channel,* or as *the company's exclusive channel for accessing customers.*

Companies have a number of offensive strategy options for improving their market positions and trying to secure a competitive advantage: offering an equal or better product at a lower price, leapfrogging competitors by being first to adopt next-generation technologies or the first to introduce next-generation products, pursuing sustained product innovation, attacking competitors weaknesses, going after less contested or unoccupied market territory, using hit-and-run tactics to steal sales away from unsuspecting rivals, and launching preemptive strikes. A blue ocean strategy seeks to gain a dramatic and durable competitive advantage by abandoning efforts to beat out competitors in existing markets and, instead, inventing a new industry or distinctive market segment that renders existing competitors largely irrelevant and allows a company to create and capture altogether new demand.

Defensive strategies to protect a company's position usually take the form of making moves that put obstacles in the path of would-be challengers and fortify the company's present position while undertaking actions to dissuade rivals from even trying to attack (by signaling that the resulting battle will be more costly to the challenger than it is worth).

Once all the higher-level strategic choices have been made, company managers can turn to the task of crafting functional and operating-level strategies to flesh out the details of the company's overall business and competitive strategy.

The timing of strategic moves also has relevance in the quest for competitive advantage. Company managers are obligated to carefully consider the advantages or disadvantages that attach to being a first-mover versus a fast-follower versus a late-mover.

Exercises

1. Go to Google or another Internet search engine and do a search on "strategic alliances." Identify at least two companies in different industries that are making a significant use of strategic alliances as a core part of their strategies. In addition, identify who their alliances are with and describe the purpose of the alliances.

2. Go to Google or another Internet search engine and do a search on "acquisition strategy." Identify at least two companies in different industries that are using

acquisitions to strengthen their market positions. Identify some of the companies that have been acquired, and research the purpose behind the acquisitions.

3. Go to www.goodyear.com/investor and read Goodyear's most recent annual report. To what extent is the company vertically integrated? What segments of the industry value chain has the company chosen to perform? Based on the company's discussion of business unit performance, does it appear the company is becoming more vertically integrated or choosing to narrow its range of internally performed activities?

4. Illustration Capsule 6.3 describes how cable companies used fiber-optic networks to gain a first-mover advantage over telephone companies in providing high-speed Internet access to home subscribers. Telephone companies are attempting to catch up with cable companies in the broadband access market with the widespread rollout of DSL to telephone customers. In addition, phone companies are pursuing fiber-to-the-premises (FTTP) and outdoor wireless networks (outdoor WLAN) technologies to supplement or replace DSL. Conduct Web searches on FTTP and outdoor WLAN, and discuss how use of these technologies by telephone companies might offset the first-mover advantage currently held by cable companies in the high-speed Internet market.

5. Go to the Web sites of various companies (such as those appearing on the Fortune 500) and identify two companies using each of the following Web site strategies and explain why the approach is well matched to the company's business model:

    a. Product information only.

    b. E-store as a minor distribution strategy.

    c. Brick-and-click.

    d. Online enterprise.

chapter seven

Competing in Foreign Markets

You have no choice but to operate in a world shaped by globalization and the information revolution. There are two options: Adapt or die.

—Andrew S. Grove
Former Chairman, Intel Corporation

You do not choose to become global. The market chooses for you; it forces your hand.

—Alain Gomez
CEO, Thomson SA

[I]ndustries actually vary a great deal in the pressures they put on a company to sell internationally.

—Niraj Dawar and Tony Frost
Professors, Richard Ivey School of Business

Any company that aspires to industry leadership in the 21st century must think in terms of global, not domestic, market leadership. The world economy is globalizing at an accelerating pace as countries previously closed to foreign companies open up their markets, as the Internet shrinks the importance of geographic distance, and as ambitious growth-minded companies race to build stronger competitive positions in the markets of more and more countries. Companies in industries that are already globally competitive or in the process of becoming so are under the gun to come up with a strategy for competing successfully in foreign markets.

This chapter focuses on strategy options for expanding beyond domestic boundaries and competing in the markets of either a few or a great many countries. The spotlight will be on four strategic issues unique to competing multinationally:

1. Whether to customize the company's offerings in each different country market to match the tastes and preferences of local buyers or to offer a mostly standardized product worldwide.

2. Whether to employ essentially the same basic competitive strategy in all countries or modify the strategy country by country.

3. Where to locate the company's production facilities, distribution centers, and customer service operations so as to realize the greatest location advantages.

4. How to efficiently transfer the company's resource strengths and capabilities from one country to another in an effort to secure competitive advantage.

In the process of exploring these issues, we will introduce a number of core concepts—multicountry competition, global competition, profit sanctuaries, and cross-market subsidization. The chapter includes sections on cross-country differences in cultural, demographic, and market conditions; strategy options for entering and competing in foreign markets; the growing role of alliances with foreign partners; the importance of locating operations in the most advantageous countries; and the special circumstances of competing in such emerging markets as China, India, Brazil, Russia, and Eastern Europe.

WHY COMPANIES EXPAND INTO FOREIGN MARKETS

A company may opt to expand outside its domestic market for any of four major reasons:

1. *To gain access to new customers*—Expanding into foreign markets offers potential for increased revenues, profits, and long-term growth and becomes an especially attractive option when a company's home markets are mature. Firms like Cisco Systems, Dell, Sony, Nokia, Avon, and Toyota, which are racing for global leadership in their respective industries, are moving rapidly and aggressively to extend their market reach into all corners of the world.

2. *To achieve lower costs and enhance the firm's competitiveness*—Many companies are driven to sell in more than one country because domestic sales volume is not large enough to fully capture manufacturing economies of scale or learning/experience curve effects and thereby substantially improve the firm's cost-competitiveness. The relatively small size of country markets in Europe explains why companies like Michelin, BMW, and Nestlé long ago began selling their products all across Europe and then moved into markets in North America and Latin America.

3. *To capitalize on its core competencies*—A company may be able to leverage its competencies and capabilities into a position of competitive advantage in foreign markets as well as just domestic markets. Nokia's competencies and capabilities in mobile phones have propelled it to global market leadership in the wireless telecommunications business. Wal-Mart is capitalizing on its considerable expertise in discount retailing to expand into China, Latin America, and parts of Europe—Wal-Mart executives believe the company has tremendous growth opportunities in China.

4. *To spread its business risk across a wider market base*—A company spreads business risk by operating in a number of different foreign countries rather than depending entirely on operations in its domestic market. Thus, if the economies of certain Asian countries turn down for a period of time, a company with operations across much of the world may be sustained by buoyant sales in Latin America or Europe.

In a few cases, companies in industries based on natural resources (e.g., oil and gas, minerals, rubber, and lumber) often find it necessary to operate in the international arena because attractive raw material supplies are located in foreign countries.

The Difference Between Competing Internationally and Competing Globally

Typically, a company will start to compete internationally by entering just one or maybe a select few foreign markets. Competing on a truly global scale comes later, after the company has established operations on several continents and is racing against rivals for global market leadership. Thus, there is a meaningful distinction between the competitive scope of a company that operates in a few foreign countries (with perhaps modest ambitions to enter several more country markets) and a company that markets its products in 50 to 100 countries and is expanding its operations into additional country markets annually. The former is most accurately termed an *international competitor,* whereas the latter qualifies as a *global competitor.* In the discussion that follows, we'll continue to make a distinction between strategies for competing internationally and strategies for competing globally.

CROSS-COUNTRY DIFFERENCES IN CULTURAL, DEMOGRAPHIC, AND MARKET CONDITIONS

Regardless of a company's motivation for expanding outside its domestic markets, the strategies it uses to compete in foreign markets must be situation-driven. Cultural, demographic, and market conditions vary significantly among the countries of the world.[1] Cultures and lifestyles are the most obvious areas in which countries differ; market demographics and income levels are close behind. Consumers in Spain do not have the same tastes, preferences, and buying habits as consumers in Norway; buyers differ yet again in Greece, Chile, New Zealand, and Taiwan. Less than 20 percent of the populations of Brazil, India, and China have annual purchasing power equivalent to $25,000. Middle-class consumers represent a much smaller portion of the population in these and other emerging countries than in North America, Japan, and much of Western Europe—China's middle class numbers about 125 million out of a population of 1.3 billion.[2]

Sometimes product designs suitable in one country are inappropriate in another—for example, in the United States electrical devices run on 110-volt systems, but in some European countries the standard is a 240-volt system, necessitating the use of different electrical designs and components. In France consumers prefer top-loading washing machines, while in most other European countries consumers prefer front-loading machines. Northern Europeans want large refrigerators because they tend to shop once a week in supermarkets; southern Europeans can get by on small refrigerators because they shop daily. In parts of Asia refrigerators are a status symbol and may be placed in the living room, leading to preferences for stylish designs and colors—in India bright blue and red are popular colors. In other Asian countries household space is constrained and many refrigerators are only four feet high so that the top can be used for storage. In Hong Kong the preference is for compact European-style appliances, but in Taiwan large American-style appliances are more popular. In Italy, most people use automatic washing machines but prefer to hang the clothes out to dry on a clothesline—there is a strongly entrenched tradition and cultural belief that sun-dried clothes are fresher, which virtually shuts down any opportunities for appliance makers to market clothes dryers in Italy. In China, many parents are reluctant to purchase personal computers (PCs) even when they can afford them because of concerns that their children will be distracted from their schoolwork by surfing the Web, playing PC-based video games, and downloading and listening to pop music.

Similarly, market growth varies from country to country. In emerging markets like India, China, Brazil, and Malaysia, market growth potential is far higher than in the more mature economies of Britain, Denmark, Canada, and Japan. In automobiles, for example, the potential for market growth is explosive in China, where 2005 sales of new vehicles amounted to less than 5 million in a country with 1.3 billion people. In India there are efficient, well-developed national channels for distributing trucks, scooters, farm equipment, groceries, personal care items, and other packaged products to the country's 3 million retailers, whereas in China distribution is primarily local and there is no national network for distributing most products. The marketplace is intensely competitive in some countries and only moderately contested in others. Industry driving forces may be one thing in Spain, quite another in Canada, and different yet again in Turkey or Argentina or South Korea.

One of the biggest concerns of companies competing in foreign markets is whether to customize their offerings in each different country market to match the tastes and preferences of local buyers or whether to offer a mostly standardized product worldwide. While making products that are closely matched to local tastes makes them more appealing to local buyers, customizing a company's products country by country may have the effect of raising production and distribution costs due to the greater variety of designs and components, shorter production runs, and the complications of added inventory handling and distribution logistics. Greater standardization of a global company's product offering, however, can lead to scale economies and experience/learning curve effects, thus contributing to the achievement of a low-cost advantage. *The tension between the market pressures to localize a company's product offerings country by country and the competitive pressures to lower costs is one of the big strategic issues that participants in foreign markets have to resolve.*

Aside from the basic cultural and market differences among countries, a company also has to pay special attention to location advantages that stem from country-to-country variations in manufacturing and distribution costs, the risks of adverse shifts in exchange rates, and the economic and political demands of host governments.

Gaining Competitive Advantage Based on Where Activities Are Located

Differences in wage rates, worker productivity, inflation rates, energy costs, tax rates, government regulations, and the like create sizable variations in manufacturing costs from country to country. Plants in some countries have major manufacturing cost advantages because of lower input costs (especially labor), relaxed government regulations, the proximity of suppliers, or unique natural resources. In such cases, the low-cost countries become principal production sites, with most of the output being exported to markets in other parts of the world. Companies that build production facilities in low-cost countries (or that source their products from contract manufacturers in these countries) have a competitive advantage over rivals with plants in countries where costs are higher. The competitive role of low manufacturing costs is most evident in low-wage countries like China, India, Pakistan, Cambodia, Vietnam, Mexico, Brazil, Guatemala, the Philippines, and several countries in Africa that have become production havens for manufactured goods with high labor content (especially textiles and apparel). Labor costs in China averaged about $0.70 an hour in 2004–2005 versus about $1.50 in Russia, $4.60 in Hungary, $4.90 in Portugal, $16.50 in Canada, $21.00 in the United States, $23.00 in Norway, and $25.00 in Germany.[3] China is fast becoming the manufacturing capital of the world—virtually all of the world's major manufacturing companies now have facilities in China, and China attracted more foreign direct investment in 2002 and 2003 than any other country in the world. Likewise, concerns about short delivery times and low shipping costs make some countries better locations than others for establishing distribution centers.

The quality of a country's business environment also offers locational advantages—the governments of some countries are anxious to attract foreign investments and go all out to create a business climate that outsiders will view as favorable. A good example is Ireland, which has one of the world's most pro-business environments. Ireland offers companies very low corporate tax rates, has a government that is responsive to the needs of industry, and aggressively recruits high-tech manufacturing facilities and multinational companies. Such policies were a significant force in making Ireland the most dynamic, fastest-growing nation in Europe during the 1990s. Ireland's policies were a major factor in Intel's decision to choose Leixlip, County Kildare, as the site for a $2.5 billion chip manufacturing plant that employs over 4,000 people. Another locational advantage is the clustering of suppliers of components and capital equipment; infrastructure suppliers (universities, vocational training providers, research enterprises); trade associations; and makers of complementary products in a geographic area—such clustering can be an important source of cost savings in addition to facilitating close collaboration with key suppliers.

The Risks of Adverse Exchange Rate Shifts

The volatility of exchange rates greatly complicates the issue of geographic cost advantages. Currency exchange rates often move up or down 20 to 40 percent annually. Changes of this magnitude can either totally wipe out a country's low-cost advantage or transform a former high-cost location into a competitive-cost location. For instance, in the mid-1980s, when the dollar was strong relative to the Japanese yen (meaning that $1 would purchase, say, 125 yen as opposed to only 100 yen), Japanese heavy-equipment maker Komatsu was able to undercut U.S.-based Caterpillar's prices by as much as 25 percent, causing Caterpillar to lose sales and market share. But starting in 1985, when exchange rates began to shift and the dollar grew steadily weaker against the yen (meaning that $1 was worth fewer and fewer yen, and that a Komatsu product made in Japan at a cost of 20 million yen translated into costs of many more dollars than before), Komatsu had to raise its prices to U.S. buyers six times over two years. With its competitiveness against Komatsu restored because of the weaker dollar and Komatsu's higher prices, Caterpillar regained sales and market share. *The lesson of fluctuating exchange rates is that companies that export goods to foreign countries always gain in competitiveness when the currency of the country in which the goods are manufactured is weak. Exporters are disadvantaged when the currency of the country where goods are being manufactured grows stronger.* Sizable long-term shifts in exchange rates thus shuffle the global cards of which rivals have the upper hand in the marketplace and which countries represent the low-cost manufacturing location.

> **Core Concept**
> Companies with manufacturing facilities in a particular country are more cost-competitive in exporting goods to world markets when the local currency is weak (or declines in value relative to other currencies); their competitiveness erodes when the local currency grows stronger relative to the currencies of the countries to which the locally made goods are being exported.

As a further illustration of the risks associated with fluctuating exchange rates, consider the case of a U.S. company that has located manufacturing facilities in Brazil (where the currency is reals—pronounced *ray-alls*) and that exports most of the Brazilian-made goods to markets in the European Union (where the currency is euros). To keep the numbers simple, assume that the exchange rate is 4 Brazilian reals for 1 euro and that the product being made in Brazil has a manufacturing cost of 4 Brazilian reals (or 1 euro). Now suppose that for some reason the exchange rate shifts from 4 reals per euro to 5 reals per euro (meaning that the real has declined in value and that the euro is stronger). Making the product in Brazil is now more cost-competitive because a Brazilian good costing 4 reals to produce has fallen to only 0.8 euros at the new exchange rate. If, in contrast, the value of the Brazilian real grows stronger in relation to the euro—resulting in an exchange rate of 3 reals to 1 euro—the same good costing 4 reals to produce now has a cost of 1.33 euros. Clearly, the attraction of manufacturing a good in Brazil and selling it in Europe is far greater when the euro is strong (an exchange rate of 1 euro for 5 Brazilian reals) than when the euro is weak and exchanges for only 3 Brazilian reals.

Insofar as U.S.-based manufacturers are concerned, declines in the value of the U.S. dollar against foreign currencies act to reduce or eliminate whatever cost advantage foreign manufacturers might have over U.S. manufacturers and can even prompt foreign companies to establish production plants in the United States. Likewise, a weak euro enhances the cost competitiveness of companies manufacturing goods in Europe for export to foreign markets; a strong euro versus other currencies weakens the cost competitiveness of European plants that manufacture goods for export.

In 2002, when the Brazilian real declined in value by about 25 percent against the dollar, the euro, and several other currencies, the ability of companies with manufacturing plants in Brazil to compete in world markets was greatly enhanced—of course, in the future years this windfall gain in cost advantage might well be eroded by sustained rises in the value of the Brazilian real against these same currencies. Herein lies the risk: *Currency exchange rates are rather unpredictable, swinging first one way and then another way, so the competitiveness of any company's facilities in any country is partly dependent on whether exchange rate changes over time have a favorable or unfavorable cost impact.* Companies producing goods in one country for export abroad always improve their cost competitiveness when the country's currency grows weaker relative to currencies of the countries where the goods are being exported to, and they find their cost competitiveness eroded when the local currency grows stronger. In contrast, domestic companies that are under pressure from lower-cost imported goods become more cost competitive when their currency grows weaker in relation to the currencies of the countries where the imported goods are made—in other words, a U.S. manufacturer views a weaker U.S. dollar as a *favorable exchange rate shift* because such shifts help make its costs more competitive versus those of foreign rivals.

Core Concept

Fluctuating exchange rates pose significant risks to a company's competitiveness in foreign markets. Exporters win when the currency of the country where goods are being manufactured grows weaker, and they lose when the currency grows stronger. Domestic companies under pressure from lower-cost imports are benefited when their government's currency grows weaker in relation to the countries where the imported goods are being made.

Host Governments' Policies

National governments enact all kinds of measures affecting business conditions and the operation of foreign companies in their markets. Host governments may set local content requirements on goods made inside their borders by foreign-based companies, have rules and policies that protect local companies from foreign competition, put restrictions on exports to ensure adequate local supplies, regulate the prices of imported and locally produced goods, enact deliberately burdensome procedures and requirements for imported goods to pass customs inspection, and impose tariffs or quotas on the imports of certain goods—until 2002, when it joined the World Trade Organization, China imposed a 100 percent tariff on motor vehicle imports. The European Union imposes quotas on textile and apparel imports from China, as a measure to protect European producers in southern Europe. India imposed excise taxes on newly purchased motor vehicles in 2005 ranging from 24 to 40 percent—a policy that has significantly dampened the demand for new vehicles in India (though down from as much as 50 percent in prior years). Governments may or may not have burdensome tax structures, stringent environmental regulations, or strictly enforced worker safety standards. Sometimes outsiders face a web of regulations regarding technical standards, product certification, prior approval of capital spending projects, withdrawal of funds from the country, and required minority (sometimes majority) ownership of foreign company operations by local companies or investors. A few governments may be hostile to or suspicious of foreign companies operating within their borders. Some governments provide subsidies and low-interest loans to domestic companies to help them compete against foreign-based companies. Other governments, anxious to obtain new plants and jobs, offer foreign companies a helping hand in the form of subsidies, privileged market access, and technical assistance. All of these possibilities explain why the managers of companies opting to compete in foreign markets have to take a close look at a country's politics and policies toward business in general, and foreign companies in particular, in deciding which country markets to participate in and which ones to avoid.

THE CONCEPTS OF MULTICOUNTRY COMPETITION AND GLOBAL COMPETITION

There are important differences in the patterns of international competition from industry to industry.[4] At one extreme is **multicountry competition,** in which there's so much cross-country variation in market conditions and in the companies contending for leadership that the market contest among rivals in one country is not closely connected to the market contests in other countries. The standout features of multicountry competition are that (1) buyers in different countries are attracted to different product attributes, (2) sellers vary from country to country, and (3) industry conditions and competitive forces in each national market differ in important respects. Take the banking industry in Italy, Brazil, and Japan as an example—the requirements and expectations of banking customers vary among the three countries, the lead banking competitors in Italy differ from those in Brazil or in Japan, and the competitive battle going on among the leading banks in Italy is unrelated to the rivalry taking place in Brazil or Japan. Thus, with multicountry competition, rival firms battle for national championships, and winning in one country does not necessarily signal the ability to fare well in other countries. In multicountry competition, the power of a company's strategy and resource capabilities in one country may not enhance its competitiveness to the same degree in other countries where it operates. Moreover, any competitive advantage a company secures in one country is largely confined to that country; the spillover effects to other countries are minimal to nonexistent. Industries characterized by multicountry competition include radio and TV broadcasting, consumer banking, life insurance, apparel, metals fabrication, many types of food products (coffee, cereals, breads, canned goods, frozen foods), and retailing.

> **Core Concept**
> *Multicountry competition* exists when competition in one national market is not closely connected to competition in another national market—there is no global or world market, just a collection of self-contained country markets.

At the other extreme is **global competition,** in which prices and competitive conditions across country markets are strongly linked and the term *global market* has true meaning. In a globally competitive industry, much the same group of rival companies competes in many different countries, but especially so in countries where sales volumes are large and where having a competitive presence is strategically important to building a strong global position in the industry. Thus, a company's competitive position in one country both affects and is affected by its position in other countries. In global competition, a firm's overall competitive advantage grows out of its entire worldwide operations; the competitive advantage it creates at its home base is supplemented by advantages growing out of its operations in other countries (having plants in low-wage countries, being able to transfer expertise from country to country, having the capability to serve customers who also have multinational operations, and brand-name recognition in many parts of the world). Rival firms in globally competitive industries vie for worldwide leadership. Global competition exists in motor vehicles, television sets, tires, mobile phones, personal computers, copiers, watches, digital cameras, bicycles, and commercial aircraft.

> **Core Concept**
> *Global competition* exists when competitive conditions across national markets are linked strongly enough to form a true international market and when leading competitors compete head to head in many different countries.

An industry can have segments that are globally competitive and segments in which competition is country by country.[5] In the hotel/motel industry, for example, the low- and medium-priced segments are characterized by multicountry competition—competitors serve travelers mainly within the same country. In the business and luxury segments, however, competition is more globalized. Companies like Nikki, Marriott, Sheraton, and Hilton have hotels at many international locations, use worldwide reservation systems, and establish common quality and service standards to gain marketing advantages in serving businesspeople and other travelers who make frequent international trips. In lubricants, the marine engine segment is globally competitive—ships move from port to port and require the same oil everywhere they stop. Brand reputations in marine lubricants have a global scope, and successful marine engine lubricant producers (Exxon Mobil, BP Amoco, and Shell) operate globally. In automotive motor oil, however, multicountry competition dominates—countries have different weather conditions and driving patterns, production of motor oil is subject to limited scale economies, shipping costs are high, and retail distribution channels differ markedly from country to country. Thus, domestic firms—like Quaker State and Pennzoil in the United States and Castrol in Great Britain—can be leaders in their home markets without competing globally.

It is also important to recognize that an industry can be in transition from multicountry competition to global competition. In a number of today's industries—beer and major home appliances are prime examples—leading domestic competitors have begun expanding into more and more foreign markets, often acquiring local companies or brands and integrating them into their operations. As some industry members start to build global brands and a global presence, other industry members find themselves pressured to follow the same strategic path—especially if establishing multinational operations results in important scale economies and a powerhouse brand name. As the industry consolidates to fewer players, such that many of the same companies find themselves in head-to-head competition in more and more country markets, global competition begins to replace multicountry competition.

At the same time, consumer tastes in a number of important product categories are converging across the world. Less diversity of tastes and preferences opens the way for companies to create global brands and sell essentially the same products in most all countries of the world. Even in industries where consumer tastes remain fairly diverse, companies are learning to use "custom mass production" to economically create different versions of a product and thereby satisfy the tastes of people in different countries.

In addition to taking the obvious cultural and political differences between countries into account, a company has to shape its strategic approach to competing in foreign markets according to whether its industry is characterized by multicountry competition, global competition, or a transition from one to the other.

STRATEGY OPTIONS FOR ENTERING AND COMPETING IN FOREIGN MARKETS

There are a host of generic strategic options for a company that decides to expand outside its domestic market and compete internationally or globally:

1. *Maintain a national (one-country) production base and export goods to foreign markets*, using either company-owned or foreign-controlled forward distribution channels.

2. *License foreign firms to use the company's technology or to produce and distribute the company's products.*

3. *Employ a franchising strategy.*

4. *Follow a multicountry strategy,* varying the company's strategic approach (perhaps a little, perhaps a lot) from country to country in accordance with local conditions and differing buyer tastes and preferences.

5. *Follow a global strategy,* using essentially the same competitive strategy approach in all country markets where the company has a presence.

6. *Use strategic alliances or joint ventures with foreign companies as the primary vehicle for entering foreign markets* and perhaps also using them as an ongoing strategic arrangement aimed at maintaining or strengthening its competitiveness.

The following sections discuss the first five options in more detail; the sixth option is discussed in a separate section later in the chapter.

Export Strategies

Using domestic plants as a production base for exporting goods to foreign markets is an excellent initial strategy for pursuing international sales. It is a conservative way to test the international waters. The amount of capital needed to begin exporting is often quite minimal; existing production capacity may well be sufficient to make goods for export. With an export strategy, a manufacturer can limit its involvement in foreign markets by contracting with foreign wholesalers experienced in importing to handle the entire distribution and marketing function in their countries or regions of the world. If it is more advantageous to maintain control over these functions, however, a manufacturer can establish its own distribution and sales organizations in some or all of the target foreign markets. Either way, a home-based production and export strategy helps the firm minimize its direct investments in foreign countries. Such strategies are commonly favored by Chinese, Korean, and Italian companies—products are designed and manufactured at home and then distributed through local channels in the importing countries; the primary functions performed abroad relate chiefly to establishing a network of distributors and perhaps conducting sales promotion and brand awareness activities.

Whether an export strategy can be pursued successfully over the long run hinges on the relative cost competitiveness of the home-country production base. In some industries, firms gain additional scale economies and experience/learning curve benefits from centralizing production in one or several giant plants whose output capability exceeds demand in any one country market; obviously, a company must export to capture such economies. However, an export strategy is vulnerable when (1) manufacturing costs in the home country are substantially higher than in foreign countries where rivals have plants, (2) the costs of shipping the product to distant foreign markets are relatively high, or (3) adverse shifts occur in currency exchange rates. Unless an exporter can both keep its production and shipping costs competitive with rivals and successfully hedge against unfavorable changes in currency exchange rates, its success will be limited.

Licensing Strategies

Licensing makes sense when a firm with valuable technical know-how or a unique patented product has neither the internal organizational capability nor the resources to enter foreign markets. Licensing also has the advantage of avoiding the risks of committing resources to country markets that are unfamiliar, politically volatile, economically unstable, or otherwise risky. By licensing the technology or the production rights to foreign-based firms, the firm does not have to bear the costs and risks of entering foreign markets on its own, yet it is able to generate income from royalties. The big disadvantage of licensing is the risk of providing valuable technological know-how to foreign companies and thereby losing some degree of control over its use; monitoring licensees and safeguarding the company's proprietary know-how can prove quite difficult in some circumstances. But if the royalty potential is considerable and the companies to whom the licenses are being granted are both trustworthy and reputable, then licensing can be a very attractive option. Many software and pharmaceutical companies use licensing strategies.

Franchising Strategies

While licensing works well for manufacturers and owners of proprietary technology, franchising is often better suited to the global expansion efforts of service and retailing enterprises. McDonald's, Yum! Brands (the parent of Pizza Hut, KFC, and Taco Bell), The UPS Store, Jani-King International (the world's largest commercial cleaning franchisor), Roto-Rooter, 7-Eleven, and Hilton Hotels have all used franchising to build a presence in foreign markets. Franchising has much the same advantages as licensing. The franchisee bears most of the costs and risks of establishing foreign locations; a franchisor has to expend only the resources to recruit, train, support, and monitor franchisees. The big problem a franchisor faces is maintaining quality control; foreign franchisees do not always exhibit strong commitment to consistency and standardization, especially when the local culture does not stress the same kinds of quality concerns. Another problem that can arise is whether to allow foreign franchisees to make modifications in the franchisor's product offering so as to better satisfy the tastes and expectations of local buyers. Should McDonald's allow its franchised units in Japan to modify Big Macs slightly to suit Japanese tastes? Should the franchised KFC units in China be permitted to substitute spices that appeal to Chinese consumers? Or should the same menu offerings be rigorously and unvaryingly required of all franchisees worldwide?

Localized Multicountry Strategies or a Global Strategy?

The issue of whether to vary the company's competitive approach to fit specific market conditions and buyer preferences in each host country or whether to employ essentially the same strategy in all countries is perhaps the foremost strategic issue that companies must address when they operate in two or more foreign markets. Figure 7.1 shows a company's options for resolving this issue.

Core Concept

A *localized* or *multicountry strategy* is one where a company varies its product offering and competitive approach from country to country in an effort to be responsive to differing buyer preferences and market conditions.

Think-Local, Act-Local Approaches to Strategy Making   The bigger the differences in buyer tastes, cultural traditions, and market conditions in different countries, the stronger the case for a think-local, act-local approach to strategy-making, in which a company tailors its product offerings and perhaps its basic competitive strategy to fit buyer tastes and market conditions in each country where it opts to compete. The strength of employing a set of *localized* or *multicountry strategies* is that the company's actions and business approaches are deliberately crafted to accommodate the

Figure 7.1 **A Company's Strategic Options for Dealing with Cross-Country Variations in Buyer Preferences and Market Conditions**

Strategic Posturing Options	Ways to Deal with Cross-Country Variations in Buyer Preferences and Market Conditions
Think Local, Act Local	**Employ localized strategies—one for each country market:** ■ Tailor the company's competitive approach and product offering to fit specific market conditions and buyer preferences in each host country. ■ Delegate strategy making to local managers with firsthand knowledge of local conditions.
Think Global, Act Global	**Employ same strategy worldwide:** ■ Pursue *the same basic competitive strategy theme* (low-cost, differentiation, best-cost, or focused) *in all country markets*—a global strategy. ■ Offer the same products worldwide, with only very minor deviations from one country to another when local market conditions so dictate. ■ Utilize the same capabilities, distribution channels, and marketing approaches worldwide. ■ Coordinate strategic actions from central headquarters
Think Global, Act Local	**Employ a combination global-local strategy:** ■ Employ essentially *the same basic competitive strategy theme* (low-cost, differentiation, best-cost, or focused) in *all country markets*. ■ Develop the capability to customize product offerings and sell different product versions in different countries (perhaps even under different brand names). ■ Give local managers the latitude to adapt the global approach as needed to accommodate local buyer preferences and be responsive to local market and competitive conditions.

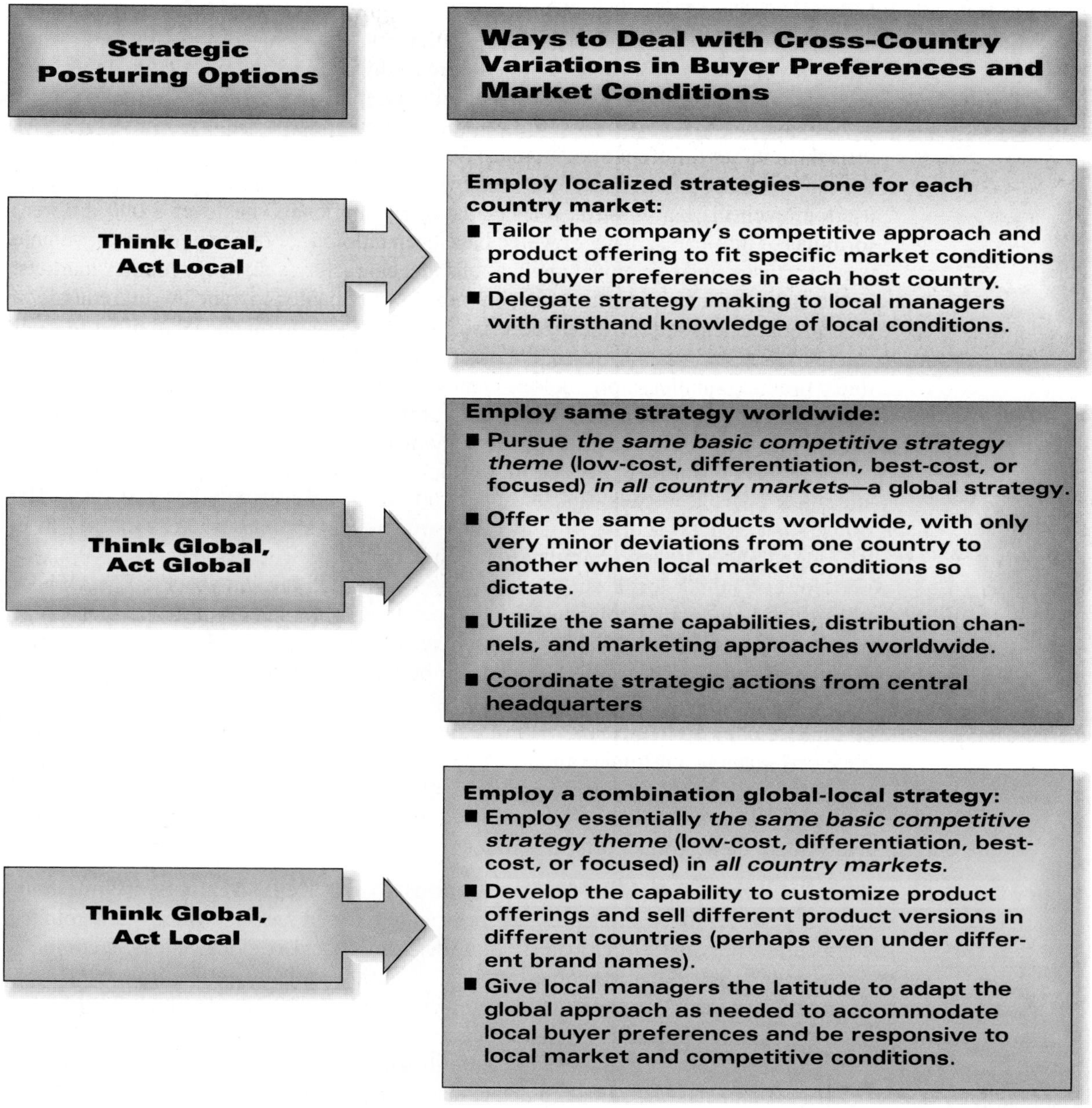

differing tastes and expectations of buyers in each country and to stake out the most attractive market positions vis-à-vis local competitors. A think-local, act-local approach means giving local managers considerable strategy-making latitude. It means having plants produce different product versions for different local markets, and adapting marketing and distribution to fit local customs and cultures. The bigger the country-to-country variations, the more that a company's overall strategy is a collection of its localized country strategies rather than a common or global strategy.

A think-local, act-local approach to strategy making is essential when there are significant country-to-country differences in customer preferences and buying habits, when there are significant cross-country differences in distribution channels and marketing methods, when host governments enact regulations requiring that products sold locally meet strict manufacturing specifications or performance standards, and when the trade restrictions of host governments are so diverse and complicated that they preclude a uniform, coordinated worldwide market approach. With localized strategies, a company often has different product versions for different countries and sometimes sells them under different brand names. Sony markets a different Walkman in Norway than in Sweden to better meet the somewhat different preferences and habits of the users in each market. Castrol, a specialist in oil lubricants, has over 3,000 different formulas of lubricants, many of which have been tailored for different climates, vehicle types and uses, and equipment applications that characterize different country markets. In the food products industry, it is common for companies to vary the ingredients in their products and sell the localized versions under local brand names in order to cater to country-specific tastes and eating preferences. Motor vehicle manufacturers routinely produce smaller, more fuel-efficient vehicles for markets in Europe where roads are often narrower and gasoline prices two or three times higher than they produce for the North American market; the models they manufacture for the Asian market are different yet again. DaimlerChrysler, for example, equips all of the Jeep Grand Cherokees and many of its Mercedes cars sold in Europe with fuel-efficient diesel engines. The Buicks that General Motors sells in China are small compacts, whereas those sold in the United States are large family sedans and SUVs.

However, think-local, act-local strategies have two big drawbacks: They hinder transfer of a company's competencies and resources across country boundaries (since the strategies in different host countries can be grounded in varying competencies and capabilities), and they do not promote building a single, unified competitive advantage—especially one based on low cost. Companies employing highly localized or multicountry strategies face big hurdles in achieving low-cost leadership *unless* they find ways to customize their products and *still* be in position to capture scale economies and experience/learning curve effects. Companies like Dell Computer and Toyota, because they have mass customization production capabilities, can cost effectively adapt their product offerings to local buyer tastes.

Think-Global, Act-Global Approaches to Strategy Making

While multicountry or localized strategies are best suited for industries where multicountry competition dominates and a fairly high degree of local responsiveness is competitively imperative, global strategies are best suited for globally competitive industries. A *global strategy* is one in which the company's approach is predominantly the same in all countries—it sells the same products under the same brand names everywhere, uses much the same distribution channels in all countries, and competes on the basis of the same capabilities and marketing approaches worldwide. Although the company's strategy or product offering may be adapted in very minor ways to accommodate specific situations in a few host countries, the company's fundamental competitive approach (low-cost, differentiation, best-cost, or focused) remains very much intact worldwide, and local managers stick close to the global strategy. A think-global, act-global strategic theme prompts company managers to integrate and coordinate the company's strategic moves worldwide and to expand into most if not all nations where there is significant buyer demand. It puts considerable strategic

Core Concept

A *global strategy* is one where a company employs the same basic competitive approach in all countries where it operates, sells much the same products everywhere, strives to build global brands, and coordinates its actions worldwide.

emphasis on building a *global* brand name and aggressively pursuing opportunities to transfer ideas, new products, and capabilities from one country to another.[6] Indeed, with a think global, act global approach to strategy making, a company's operations in each country can be viewed as experiments that result in learning and in capabilities that may merit transfer to other country markets.

Whenever country-to-country differences are small enough to be accommodated within the framework of a global strategy, a global strategy is preferable to localized strategies because a company can more readily unify its operations and focus on establishing a brand image and reputation that is uniform from country to country. Moreover, with a global strategy a company is better able to focus its full resources on building the resource strengths and capabilities to secure a sustainable low-cost or differentiation-based competitive advantage over both domestic rivals and global rivals racing for world market leadership. Figure 7.2 summarizes the basic differences between a localized or multicountry strategy and a global strategy.

Think-Global, Act-Local Approaches to Strategy Making Often, a company can accommodate cross-country variations in buyer tastes, local customs, and market conditions with a think-global, act-local approach to developing strategy. This middle-ground approach entails using the same basic competitive theme (low-cost, differentiation, best-cost, or focused) in each country but allowing local mangers the latitude to (1) incorporate whatever country-specific variations in product attributes are needed to best satisfy local buyers and (2) make whatever adjustments in production, distribution, and marketing are needed to be responsive to local market conditions and compete successfully against local rivals. Slightly different product versions sold under the same brand name may suffice to satisfy local tastes, and it may be feasible to accommodate these versions rather economically in the course of designing and manufacturing the company's product offerings. The build-to-order component of Dell's strategy in PCs for example, makes it simple for Dell to be responsive to how buyers in different parts of the world want their PCs equipped. However, Dell has not wavered in its strategy to sell directly to customers rather than through local retailers, even though the majority of buyers in countries such as China are concerned about ordering online and prefer to personally inspect PCs at stores before making a purchase.

As a rule, most companies that operate multinationally endeavor to employ as global a strategy as customer needs and market conditions permit. Philips Electronics, the Netherlands-based electronics and consumer products company, operated successfully with localized strategies for many years but has recently begun moving more toward a unified strategy within the European Union and within North America.[7] Whirlpool has been globalizing its low-cost leadership strategy in home appliances for over 15 years, striving to standardize parts and components and move toward worldwide designs for as many of its appliance products as possible. But it has found it necessary to continue producing significantly different versions of refrigerators, washing machines, and cooking appliances for consumers in different regions of the world because the needs and tastes of local buyers for appliances of different sizes and designs have not converged sufficiently to permit standardization of Whirlpool's product offerings worldwide. General Motors began an initiative in 2004 to insist that its worldwide units share basic parts and work together to design vehicles that can be sold, with modest variations, anywhere around the world; by reducing the types of radios used in its cars and trucks from 270 to 50, it expected to save 40 percent in radio costs.

Illustration Capsule 7.1 on page 209 describes how two companies localize their strategies for competing in country markets across the world.

Figure 7.2   **How a Localized or Multicountry Strategy Differs from a Global Strategy**

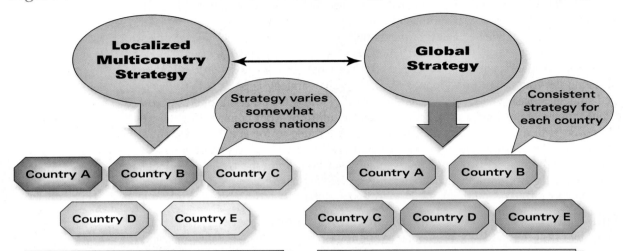

- ■ Customize the company's competitive approach as needed to fit market and business circumstances in each host country—strong responsiveness to local conditions.
- ■ Sell different product versions in different countries under different brand names—adapt product attributes to fit buyer tastes and preferences country by country.
- ■ Scatter plants across many host countries, each producing product versions for local markets.
- ■ Preferably use local suppliers (some local sources may be required by host government).
- ■ Adapt marketing and distribution to local customs and culture of each country.
- ■ Transfer competencies and capabilities from country to country where feasible.
- ■ Give country managers fairly wide strategy-making latitude and autonomy over local operations.

- ■ Pursue same basic competitive strategy worldwide (low-cost, differentiation, best-cost, focused low-cost, focused differentiation), with minimal responsiveness to local conditions.
- ■ Sell same products under same brand name worldwide; focus efforts on building global brands as opposed to strengthening local/regional brands sold in local/regional markets.
- ■ Locate plants on basis of maximum locational advantage, usually in countries where production costs are lowest but plants may be scattered if shipping costs are high or other locational advantages dominate.
- ■ Use best suppliers from anywhere in world.
- ■ Coordinate marketing and distribution worldwide; make minor adaptation to local countries where needed.
- ■ Compete on basis of same technologies, competencies, and capabilities worldwide; stress rapid transfer of new ideas, products, and capabilities to other countries.
- ■ Coordinate major strategic decisions worldwide; expect local managers to stick close to global strategy.

Illustration Capsule 7.1

Multicountry Strategies at Electronic Arts and Coca-Cola

ELECTRONIC ARTS' MULTICOUNTRY STRATEGY IN VIDEO GAMES

Electronic Arts (EA), the world's largest independent developer and marketer of video games, designs games that are suited to the differing tastes of game players in different countries and also designs games in multiple languages. EA has two major design studios—one in Vancouver, British Columbia, and one in Los Angeles—and smaller design studios in San Francisco, Orlando, London, and Tokyo. This dispersion of design studios helps EA to design games that are specific to different cultures—for example, the London studio took the lead in designing the popular FIFA Soccer game to suit European tastes and to replicate the stadiums, signage, and team rosters; the U.S. studio took the lead in designing games involving NFL football, NBA basketball, and NASCAR racing. No other game software company had EA's ability to localize games or to launch games on multiple platforms in multiple countries in multiple languages. EA's game Harry Potter and the Chamber of Secrets was released simultaneously in 75 countries, in 31 languages, and on seven platforms.

COCA-COLA'S MULTICOUNTRY STRATEGY IN BEVERAGES

Coca-Cola strives to meet the demands of local tastes and cultures, offering 300 brands in some 200 countries. Its network of bottlers and distributors is distinctly local, and the company's products and brands are formulated to cater to local tastes. The ways in which Coca-Cola's local operating units bring products to market, the packaging that is used, and the company's advertising messages are all intended to match the local culture and fit in with local business practices. Many of the ingredients and supplies for Coca-Cola's products are sourced locally.

Sources: Information posted at www.ea.com and www.cocacola.com (accessed September 2004).

THE QUEST FOR COMPETITIVE ADVANTAGE IN FOREIGN MARKETS

There are three important ways in which a firm can gain competitive advantage (or offset domestic disadvantages) by expanding outside its domestic market:[8] One, it can use location to lower costs or achieve greater product differentiation. Two, it can transfer competitively valuable competencies and capabilities from its domestic markets to foreign markets. And three, it can use cross-border coordination in ways that a domestic-only competitor cannot.

Using Location to Build Competitive Advantage

To use location to build competitive advantage, a company must consider two issues: (1) whether to concentrate each activity it performs in a few select countries or to disperse performance of the activity to many nations, and (2) in which countries to locate particular activities.[9]

> Companies that compete multi-nationally can pursue competitive advantage in world markets by locating their value chain activities in whatever nations prove most advantageous.

When to Concentrate Activities in a Few Locations   Companies tend to concentrate their activities in a limited number of locations in the following circumstances:

- *When the costs of manufacturing or other activities are significantly lower in some geographic locations than in others*—For example, much of the world's athletic footwear is manufactured in Asia (China and Korea) because of low labor costs; much of the production of motherboards for PCs is located in Taiwan because of both low costs and the high-caliber technical skills of the Taiwanese labor force.

- *When there are significant scale economies*—The presence of significant economies of scale in components production or final assembly means that a company can gain major cost savings from operating a few superefficient plants as opposed to a host of small plants scattered across the world. Important marketing and distribution economies associated with multinational operations can also yield low-cost leadership. In situations where some competitors are intent on global dominance, being the worldwide low-cost provider is a powerful competitive advantage. Achieving low-cost provider status often requires a company to have the largest worldwide manufacturing share, with production centralized in one or a few world-scale plants in low-cost locations. Some companies even use such plants to manufacture units sold under the brand names of rivals. Manufacturing share (as distinct from brand share or market share) is significant because it provides more certain access to production-related scale economies. Japanese makers of VCRs, microwave ovens, TVs, and DVD players have used their large manufacturing share to establish a low-cost advantage.[10]

- *When there is a steep learning curve associated with performing an activity in a single location*—In some industries experience/learning curve effects in parts manufacture or assembly are so great that a company establishes one or two large plants from which it serves the world market. The key to riding down the learning curve is to concentrate production in a few locations to increase the accumulated volume at a plant (and thus the experience of the plant's workforce) as rapidly as possible.

- *When certain locations have superior resources, allow better coordination of related activities, or offer other valuable advantages*—A research unit or a sophisticated production facility may be situated in a particular nation because of its pool of technically trained personnel. Samsung became a leader in memory chip technology by establishing a major R&D facility in Silicon Valley and transferring the know-how it gained back to headquarters and its plants in South Korea. Where just-in-time inventory practices yield big cost savings and/or where an assembly firm has long-term partnering arrangements with its key suppliers, parts manufacturing plants may be clustered around final assembly plants. An assembly plant may be located in a country in return for the host government's allowing freer import of components from large-scale, centralized parts plants located elsewhere. A customer service center or sales office may be opened in a particular country to help cultivate strong relationships with pivotal customers located nearby.

When to Disperse Activities Across Many Locations   There are several instances when dispersing activities is more advantageous than concentrating them. Buyer-related activities—such as distribution to dealers, sales and advertising, and after-sale service—usually must take place close to buyers. This means physically locating the capability to perform such activities in every country market where a global firm has major customers (unless buyers in several adjoining countries can be served quickly from a nearby central location). For example, firms that make mining and oil-drilling equipment maintain operations in many international locations to support customers' needs for speedy equipment repair and technical assistance. The four biggest public accounting firms have numerous international offices to service the foreign operations of their multinational corporate clients. A global competitor that effectively disperses its buyer-related activities can gain a service-based competitive edge in world markets over rivals whose buyer-related activities are more concentrated—this is one reason the Big Four public accounting firms (PricewaterhouseCoopers, KPMG, Deloitte & Touche, and Ernst & Young) have been so successful relative to regional and national firms. Dispersing activities to many locations is also competitively advantageous when high transportation costs, diseconomies of large size, and trade barriers make it too expensive to operate from a central location. Many companies distribute their products from multiple locations to shorten delivery times to customers. In addition, it is strategically advantageous to disperse activities to hedge against the risks of fluctuating exchange rates; supply interruptions (due to strikes, mechanical failures, and transportation delays); and adverse political developments. Such risks are greater when activities are concentrated in a single location.

The classic reason for locating an activity in a particular country is low cost.[11] Even though multinational and global firms have strong reason to disperse buyer-related activities to many international locations, such activities as materials procurement, parts manufacture, finished goods assembly, technology research, and new product development can frequently be decoupled from buyer locations and performed wherever advantage lies. Components can be made in Mexico; technology research done in Frankfurt; new products developed and tested in Phoenix; and assembly plants located in Spain, Brazil, Taiwan, or South Carolina. Capital can be raised in whatever country it is available on the best terms.

Using Cross-Border Transfers of Competencies and Capabilities to Build Competitive Advantage

One of the best ways for a company with valuable competencies and resource strengths to secure competitive advantage is to use its considerable resource strengths to enter additional country markets. A company whose resource strengths prove particularly potent in competing successfully in newly entered country markets not only grows sales and profits but also may find that its competitiveness is sufficiently enhanced to produce competitive advantage over one or more rivals and contend for global market leadership. Transferring competencies, capabilities, and resource strengths from country to country contributes to the development of broader or deeper competencies and capabilities—ideally helping a company achieve dominating depth in some competitively valuable area. Dominating depth in a competitively valuable capability, resource, or value chain activity is a strong basis for sustainable competitive advantage over other multinational or global competitors, and especially so over domestic-only competitors. A one-country customer base is often too small to support the resource buildup needed to achieve such depth; this is particularly true when the market is just emerging and sophisticated resources have not been required.

Whirlpool, the leading global manufacturer of home appliances, with plants in 14 countries and sales in 170 countries, has used the Internet to create a global information technology platform that allows the company to transfer key product innovations and production processes across regions and brands quickly and effectively. Wal-Mart is slowly but forcefully expanding its operations with a strategy that involves transferring its considerable domestic expertise in distribution and discount retailing to store operations recently established in China, Japan, Latin America, and Europe. Its status as the largest, most resource-deep, and most sophisticated user of distribution/retailing know-how has served it well in building its foreign sales and profitability. But Wal-Mart is not racing madly to position itself in many foreign markets; rather, it is establishing a strong presence in select country markets and learning how to be successful in these before tackling entry into other countries well-suited to its business model.

However, cross-border resource transfers are not a guaranteed recipe for success. Philips Electronics sells more color TVs and DVD recorders in Europe than any other company does; its biggest technological breakthrough was the compact disc, which it invented in 1982. Philips has worldwide sales of about 38 billion euros, but as of 2005 Philips had lost money for 17 consecutive years in its U.S. consumer electronics business. In the United States, the company's color TVs and DVD recorders (sold under the Magnavox and Philips brands) are slow sellers. Philips notoriously lags in introducing new products into the U.S. market and has been struggling to develop an able sales force that can make inroads with U.S. electronics retailers and change its image as a low-end brand.

Using Cross-Border Coordination to Build Competitive Advantage

Coordinating company activities across different countries contributes to sustainable competitive advantage in several different ways.[12] Multinational and global competitors can choose where and how to challenge rivals. They may decide to retaliate against an aggressive rival in the country market where the rival has its biggest sales volume or its best profit margins in order to reduce the rival's financial resources for competing in other country markets. They may also decide to wage a price-cutting offensive against weak rivals in their home markets, capturing greater market share and subsidizing any short-term losses with profits earned in other country markets.

If a firm learns how to assemble its product more efficiently at, say, its Brazilian plant, the accumulated expertise can be quickly communicated via the Internet to assembly plants in other world locations. Knowledge gained in marketing a company's product in Great Britain can readily be exchanged with company personnel in New Zealand or Australia. A global or multinational manufacturer can shift production from a plant in one country to a plant in another to take advantage of exchange rate fluctuations, to enhance its leverage with host-country governments, and to respond to changing wage rates, components shortages, energy costs, or changes in tariffs and quotas. Production schedules can be coordinated worldwide; shipments can be diverted from one distribution center to another if sales rise unexpectedly in one place and fall in another.

Using online systems, companies can readily gather ideas for new and improved products from customers and company personnel all over the world, permitting informed decisions about what can be standardized and what should be customized. Likewise, online systems enable multinational companies to involve their best design and engineering personnel (wherever they are located) in collectively coming up with next-generation products—it is easy for company personnel in one location to use the Internet to collaborate closely with personnel in other locations in performing all sorts of strategically relevant activities. Efficiencies can also be achieved by shifting workloads from where they are unusually heavy to locations where personnel are underutilized. Whirlpool's efforts to link its product R&D and manufacturing operations in North America, Latin America, Europe, and Asia allowed it to accelerate the discovery of innovative appliance features, coordinate the introduction of these features in the appliance products marketed in different countries, and create a cost-efficient worldwide supply chain. Whirlpool's conscious efforts to integrate and coordinate its various operations around the world have helped it become a low-cost producer and also speed product innovations to market, thereby giving Whirlpool an edge over rivals in designing and rapidly introducing innovative and attractively priced appliances worldwide.

Furthermore, a multinational company that consistently incorporates the same differentiating attributes in its products worldwide has enhanced potential to build a global brand name with significant power in the marketplace. The reputation for quality that Honda established worldwide first in motorcycles and then in automobiles gave it competitive advantage in positioning Honda lawn mowers at the upper end of the U.S. outdoor power equipment market—the Honda name gave the company immediate credibility with U.S. buyers of power equipment and enabled it to become an instant market contender without all the fanfare and cost of a multimillion-dollar ad campaign to build brand awareness.

PROFIT SANCTUARIES, CROSS-MARKET SUBSIDIZATION, AND GLOBAL STRATEGIC OFFENSIVES

Profit sanctuaries are country markets (or geographic regions) in which a company derives substantial profits because of its strong or protected market position. McDonald's serves about 50 million customers daily at nearly 32,000 locations in 119 countries on five continents; not surprisingly, its biggest profit sanctuary is the United States, which generated 61.2 percent of 2004 profits, despite accounting for just 34.2 percent of 2004 revenues. Nike, which markets its products in 160 countries, has two big profit sanctuaries: the United States (where it earned 41.5 percent of its operating profits in 2005) and Europe, the Middle East, and Africa (where it earned 34.8 percent of 2005 operating profits). Discount retailer Carrefour, which has stores across much of Europe plus stores in Asia and the Americas, also has two principal profit sanctuaries; its biggest is in France (which in 2004 accounted for 49.2 percent of revenues and 60.8 percent of earnings before interest and taxes), and its second biggest is Europe outside of France (which in 2004 accounted for 37.3 percent of revenues and 33.1 percent of earnings before interest and taxes). Japan is the chief profit sanctuary for most Japanese companies because trade barriers erected by the Japanese government effectively block foreign companies from competing for a large share of Japanese sales. Protected from the threat of foreign competition in their home market, Japanese companies can safely charge somewhat higher prices to their Japanese customers and thus earn attractively large profits on sales made in Japan. In most cases, a company's biggest and most strategically crucial profit sanctuary is its home market, but international and global companies may also enjoy profit sanctuary status in other nations where they have a strong competitive position, big sales volume, and attractive profit margins. Companies that compete globally are likely to have more profit sanctuaries than companies that compete in just a few country markets; a domestic-only competitor, of course, can have only one profit sanctuary (see Figure 7.3).

Core Concept
Companies with large, protected *profit sanctuaries* have competitive advantage over companies that don't have a protected sanctuary. Companies with multiple profit sanctuaries have a competitive advantage over companies with a single sanctuary.

Figure 7.3   **Profit Sanctuary Potential of Domestic-Only, International, and Global Competitors**

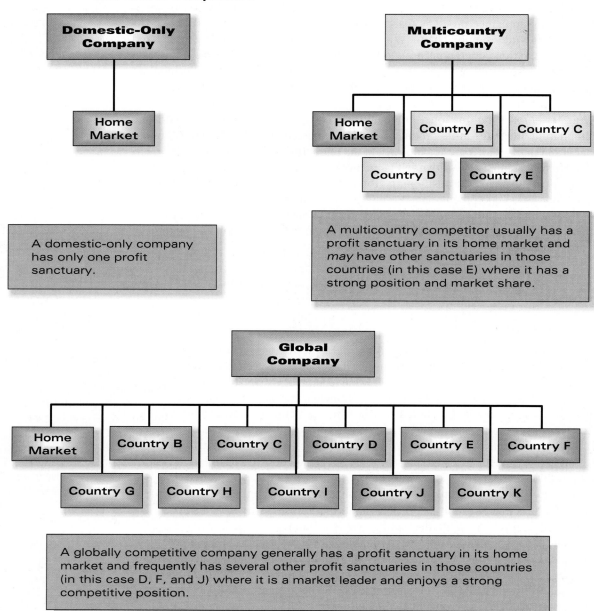

Using Cross-Market Subsidization to Wage a Strategic Offensive

Profit sanctuaries are valuable competitive assets, providing the financial strength to support strategic offensives in selected country markets and fuel a company's race for global market leadership. The added financial capability afforded by multiple profit sanctuaries gives a global or multicountry competitor the financial strength to wage a market offensive against a domestic competitor whose only profit sanctuary is its home market. Consider the case of a purely domestic company in competition with a company that has multiple profit sanctuaries and that is racing for global market leadership. The global company has the flexibility of lowballing its prices in the domestic company's home market and grabbing market share at the domestic company's expense, subsidizing razor-thin margins or even losses with the healthy profits earned in its profit sanctuaries—a practice called **cross-market subsidization.** The global company can adjust the depth of its price cutting to move in and capture market share quickly, or it can shave prices slightly to make gradual market inroads (perhaps over a decade or more) so as not to threaten domestic firms precipitously or trigger protectionist government actions. If the domestic company retaliates with matching price cuts, it exposes its entire revenue and profit base to erosion; its profits can be squeezed substantially and its competitive strength sapped, even if it is the domestic market leader.

> **Core Concept**
> *Cross-market subsidization—*
> supporting competitive offensives in one market with resources and profits diverted from operations in other markets—is a powerful competitive weapon.

Offensive Strategies Suitable for Competing in Foreign Markets

Companies that compete in multiple foreign markets can, of course, fashion an offensive strategy based on any of the approaches discussed in Chapter 6 (pages 160–193)—these types of offensive strategies are universally applicable and are just as suitable for competing in foreign markets as for domestic markets. But there are three additional types of offensive strategies that are suited to companies competing in foreign markets:[13]

- *Attack a foreign rival's profit sanctuaries.* Launching an offensive in a country market where a rival earns its biggest profits can put the rival on the defensive, forcing it to perhaps spend more on marketing/advertising, trim its prices, boost product innovation efforts, or otherwise undertake actions that raise its costs and erode its profits. If a company's offensive succeeds in eroding a rival's profits in its chief profit sanctuary, the rival's financial resources may be sufficiently weakened to enable the attacker to gain the upper hand and build market momentum. While attacking a rival's profit sanctuary violates the principle of attacking competitor weaknesses instead of competitor strengths, it can nonetheless prove valuable when there is special merit in pursuing actions that cut into a foreign rival's profit margins and force it to defend a market that is important to its competitive well-being. This is especially true when the attacker has important resource strengths and profit sanctuaries of its own that it can draw on to support its offensive.

- *Employ cross-market subsidization to win customers and sales away from select rivals in select country markets.* This can be a particularly attractive offensive strategy for companies that compete in multiple country markets with multiple products (several brands of cigarettes or different brands of food products). Competing in multiple country markets gives a company the luxury of drawing upon the resources, profits, and cash flows derived from particular country markets (especially its profit sanctuaries) to support offensives aimed at winning customers away from select rivals in those country markets that it wants either to enter or to boost its sales and market share. Alternatively, a company whose product lineup consists of different items can shift resources from a product category where it is competitively strong and resource deep (say soft drinks) to add firepower to an offensive in those countries with bright growth prospects in another product category (say bottled water or fruit juices).

- *Dump goods at cut-rate prices in the markets of foreign rivals.* A company is said to be dumping when it sells its goods in foreign markets at prices that are (1) well below the prices at which it normally sells in its home market or (2) well below its full costs per unit. Companies that engage in dumping usually keep their selling prices high enough to cover variable costs per unit, thereby limiting their losses on each unit to some percentage of fixed costs per unit. Dumping can be an appealing offensive strategy in either of two instances. One is when dumping drives down the price so far in the targeted country that domestic firms are quickly put in dire financial straits and end up declaring bankruptcy or being driven out of business—for dumping to pay off in this instance, however, the dumping company needs to have deep enough financial pockets to cover any losses from selling at below-market prices, and the targeted domestic companies need to be financially weak. The second instance in which dumping becomes an attractive strategy is when a company with unused production capacity discovers that it is cheaper to keep producing (as long as the selling prices cover average variable costs per unit) than it is to incur the costs associated with idle plant capacity. By keeping its plants operating at or near capacity, a dumping company not only may be able to cover variable costs and earn a contribution to fixed costs but also may be able to use its below-market prices to draw price-sensitive customers away from foreign rivals, then attentively court these new customers and retain their business when prices later begin a gradual rise back to normal market levels. Thus, dumping may prove useful as a way of entering the market of a particular foreign country and establishing a customer base.

Core Concept
Three strategy offensives that are particularly suitable for competing in foreign markets involve (1) attacking a foreign rival's profit sanctuaries, (2) employing cross-market subsidization, and (3) dumping.

However, dumping strategies run a high risk of host government retaliation on behalf of the adversely affected domestic companies. Indeed, as the trade among nations has mushroomed over the past 10 years, most governments have joined the World Trade Organization (WTO), which promotes fair trade practices among nations and actively polices dumping. The WTO allows member governments to take actions against dumping wherever there is material injury to domestic competitors. In 2002, for example, the U.S. government imposed tariffs of up to 30 percent on selected steel products that Asian and European steel manufacturers were said to be selling at ultra-low prices in the U.S. market. Canada recently investigated charges that companies in Austria, Belgium, France, Germany, Poland and China were dumping supplies of laminate flooring in Canada to the detriment of Canadian producers and concluded that companies in France and China were indeed selling such flooring in Canada at unreasonably low prices.[14] Most all governments can be expected to retaliate against dumping by imposing special tariffs on goods being imported from the countries of the guilty companies. Companies deemed guilty of dumping frequently come under pressure from their government to cease and desist, especially if the tariffs adversely affect innocent companies based in the same country or if the advent of special tariffs raises the specter of a trade war.

A company desirous of employing some type of offensive strategy in foreign markets is well advised to observe the principles for employing offensive strategies in general. For instance, it usually wise to attack foreign rivals on grounds that pit the challenger's competitive strengths against the defender's weaknesses and vulnerabilities. As a rule, trying to steal customers away from foreign rivals with strategies aimed at besting rivals where they are strongest stand a lower chance of succeeding than strategies that attack their competitive weaknesses, especially when the challenger has resource strengths that enable it to exploit rivals' weaknesses and when its attack involves an element of surprise.[15] It nearly always makes good strategic sense to use the challenger's core competencies and best competitive capabilities to spearhead the offensive. Furthermore, strategic offensives in foreign markets should, as a general rule, be predicated on exploiting the challenger's core competencies and best competitive capabilities. The ideal condition for a strategic offensive is when the attacker's resource strengths give it a competitive advantage over the targeted foreign rivals. The only two exceptions to these offensive strategy principles come when a competitively strong company with deep financial pockets sees considerable benefit in attacking a foreign rival's profit sanctuary and/or has the ability to employ cross-market subsidization— both of these offensive strategies can involve attacking a foreign rival's strengths (but they also are grounded in important strengths of the challenger and don't fall into the trap of challenging a competitively strong rival with a strategic offensive based on unproven expertise or inferior technology or a relatively unknown brand name or other resource weaknesses).

STRATEGIC ALLIANCES AND JOINT VENTURES WITH FOREIGN PARTNERS

Strategic alliances, joint ventures, and other cooperative agreements with foreign companies are a favorite and potentially fruitful means for entering a foreign market or strengthening a firm's competitiveness in world markets.[16] Historically, export-minded firms in industrialized nations sought alliances with firms in less-developed countries to import and market their products locally—such arrangements were often necessary to win approval for entry from the host country's government. Both Japanese and American companies are actively forming alliances with European companies to strengthen their ability to compete in the 25-nation European Union (and the five countries that are seeking to become EU members) and to capitalize on the opening up of Eastern European markets. Many U.S. and European companies are allying with Asian companies in their efforts to enter markets in China, India, Malaysia, Thailand, and other Asian countries. Companies in Europe, Latin America, and Asia are using alliances and joint ventures as a means of strengthening their mutual ability to compete across a wider geographical area—for instance, all the countries in the European Union or whole continents or most all country markets where there is sizable demand for the industry's product. Many foreign companies, of course, are particularly interested in strategic partnerships that will strengthen their ability to gain a foothold in the U.S. market.

> Cross-border alliances have proved to be popular and viable vehicles for companies to edge their way into the markets of foreign countries.

However, cooperative arrangements between domestic and foreign companies have strategic appeal for reasons besides gaining better access to attractive country markets.[17] A second big appeal of cross-border alliances is to capture economies of scale in production and/or marketing—cost reduction can be the difference that allows a company to be cost-competitive. By joining forces in producing components, assembling models, and marketing their products, companies can realize cost savings not achievable with their own small volumes. A third motivation for entering into a cross-border alliance is to fill gaps in technical expertise and/or knowledge of local markets (buying habits and product preferences of consumers, local customs, and so on). Allies learn much from one another in performing joint research, sharing technological know-how, studying one another's manufacturing methods, and understanding how to tailor sales and marketing approaches to fit local cultures and traditions. Indeed, one of the win–win benefits of an alliance is to learn from the skills, technological know-how, and capabilities of alliance partners and implant the knowledge and know-how of these partners in personnel throughout the company.

A fourth motivation for cross-border alliances is to share distribution facilities and dealer networks, thus mutually strengthening their access to buyers. A fifth benefit is that cross-border allies can direct their competitive energies more toward mutual rivals and less toward one another; teaming up may help them close the gap on leading companies. A sixth driver of cross-border alliances comes into play when companies desirous of entering a new foreign market conclude that alliances with local companies are an effective way to tap into a partner's local market knowledge and help it establish working relationships with key officials in the host-country government.[18] And, finally, alliances can be a particularly useful way for companies across the world to gain agreement on important technical standards—they have been used to arrive at standards for DVD players, assorted PC devices, Internet-related technologies, high-definition televisions, and mobile phones.

> Cross-border alliances enable a growth-minded company to widen its geographic coverage and strengthen its competitiveness in foreign markets while, at the same time, offering flexibility and allowing a company to retain some degree of autonomy and operating control.

What makes cross-border alliances an attractive strategic means of gaining the above types of benefits (as compared to acquiring or merging with foreign-based companies to gain much the same benefits) is that entering into alliances and strategic partnerships to gain market access and/or expertise of one kind or another allows a company to preserve its independence (which is not the case with a merger), retain veto power over how the alliance operates, and avoid using perhaps scarce financial resources to fund acquisitions. Furthermore, an alliance offers the flexibility to readily disengage once its purpose has been served or if the benefits prove elusive, whereas an acquisition is more permanent sort of arrangement (although the acquired company can, of course, be divested).[19]

Illustration Capsule 7.2 provides six examples of cross-border strategic alliances.

The Risks of Strategic Alliances with Foreign Partners

Alliances and joint ventures with foreign partners have their pitfalls, however. Cross-border allies typically have to overcome language and cultural barriers and figure out how to deal with diverse (or perhaps conflicting) operating practices. The communication, trust-building, and coordination costs are high in terms of management time.[20] It is not unusual for there to be little personal chemistry among some of the key people on whom success or failure of the alliance depends—the rapport such personnel need to work well together may never emerge. And even if allies are able to develop productive personal relationships, they can still have trouble reaching mutually agreeable ways to deal with key issues or resolve differences. There is a natural tendency for allies to struggle to collaborate effectively in competitively sensitive areas, thus spawning suspicions on both sides about forthright exchanges of information and expertise. Occasionally, the egos of corporate executives can clash—an alliance between Northwest Airlines and KLM Royal Dutch Airlines resulted in a bitter feud among both companies' top officials (who, according to some reports, refused to speak to each other).[21] In addition, there is the thorny problem of getting alliance partners to sort through issues and reach decisions fast enough to stay abreast of rapid advances in technology or fast-changing market conditions.

Illustration Capsule 7.2

Six Examples of Cross-Border Strategic Alliances

1. Two auto firms, Renault of France and Nissan of Japan, formed a broad-ranging global partnership in 1999 and then strengthened and expanded the alliance in 2002. The initial objective was to gain sales for new Nissan vehicles introduced in the European market, but the alliance now extends to full cooperation in all major areas, including the use of common platforms, joint development and use of engines and transmissions, fuel cell research, purchasing and use of common suppliers, and exchange of best practices. When the alliance was formed in 1999, Renault acquired a 36.8 percent ownership stake in Nissan; this was extended to 44.4 percent in 2002 when the alliance was expanded. Also, in 2002, the partners formed a jointly and equally owned strategic management company, named Renault-Nissan, to coordinate cooperative efforts.

2. Intel, the world's largest chip maker, has formed strategic alliances with leading software application providers and computer hardware providers to bring more innovativeness and expertise to the architecture underlying Intel's family of microprocessors and semiconductors. Intel's partners in the effort to enhance Intel's next-generation products include SAP, Oracle, SAS, BEA, IBM, Hewlett-Packard, Dell, Microsoft, Cisco Systems, and Alcatel. One of the alliances between Intel and Cisco involves a collaborative effort in Hong Kong to build next-generation infrastructure for Electronic Product Code/Radio Frequency Identification (EPC/RFID) solutions used to link manufacturers and logistics companies in the Hong Kong region with retailers worldwide. Intel and France-based Alcatel (a leading provider of fixed and mobile broadband access products, marketed in 130 countries) formed an alliance in 2004 to advance the definition, standardization, development, integration, and marketing of WiMAX broadband services solutions. WiMAX was seen as a cost-effective wireless or mobile broadband solution for deployment in both emerging markets and developed countries when, for either economic or technical reasons, it was not feasible to provide urban or rural customers with hardwired DSL broadband access.

3. Verio, a subsidiary of Japan-based NTT Communications and one of the leading global providers of Web hosting services and IP data transport, operates with the philosophy that in today's highly competitive and challenging technology market, companies must gain and share skills, information, and technology with technology leaders across the world. Believing that no company can be all things to all customers in the Web hosting industry, Verio executives have developed an alliance-oriented business model that combines the company's core competencies with the skills and products of best-of-breed, technology partners. Verio's strategic partners include Accenture, Cisco Systems, Microsoft, Sun Microsystems, Oracle, Arsenal Digital Solutions (a provider of worry-free tape backup, data restore, and data storage services), Internet Security Systems (a provider of firewall and intrusion detection systems), and Mercantec (a developer of storefront and shopping cart software). Verio management believes that its portfolio of strategic alliances allows it to use innovative, best-of-class technologies in providing its customers with fast, efficient, accurate data transport and a complete set of Web hosting services. An independent panel of 12 judges recently selected Verio as the winner of the Best Technology Foresight Award for its efforts in pioneering new technologies.

4. Toyota and First Automotive Works, China's biggest automaker, entered into an alliance in 2002 to make luxury sedans, sport-utility vehicles (SUVs), and minivehicles for the Chinese market. The intent was to make as many as 400,000 vehicles annually by 2010, an amount equal to the number that Volkswagen, the company with the largest share of the Chinese market, was making as of 2002. The alliance envisioned a joint investment of about $1.2 billion. At the time of the announced alliance, Toyota was lagging behind Honda, General Motors, and Volkswagen in setting up production facilities in China. Capturing a bigger share of the Chinese market was seen as crucial to Toyota's success in achieving its strategic objective of having a 15 percent share of the world's automotive market by 2010.

5. Airbus Industrie was formed by an alliance of aerospace companies from Britain, Spain, Germany, and France that included British Aerospace, Daimler-Benz Aerospace, and Aerospatiale. The objective of the alliance was to create a European aircraft company capable of competing with U.S.-based Boeing Corporation. The alliance has proved highly successful, infusing Airbus with the know-how and resources to compete head-to-head with Boeing for world leadership in large commercial aircraft (over 100 passengers).

6. General Motors, DaimlerChrysler, and BMW have entered into an alliance to develop a hybrid gasoline-electric engine that is simpler and less expensive to produce than the hybrid engine technology being pioneered by Toyota. Toyota, the acknowledged world leader in hybrid engines, is endeavoring to establish its design as the industry standard by signing up other automakers to use it. But the technology favored by the General Motors/DaimlerChrysler/BMW alliance is said to be less costly to produce and easier to configure for large trucks and SUVs than Toyota's (although it is also less fuel efficient). Europe's largest automaker, Volkswagen, has allied with Porsche to pursue the development of hybrid engines. Ford Motor and Honda, so far, have elected to go it alone in developing hybrid engine technology.

Sources: Company Web sites and press releases; Yves L. Doz and Gary Hamel, *Alliance Advantage: The Art of Creating Value through Partnering* (Boston, MA: Harvard Business School Press, 1998); and Norihiko Shirouzu and Jathon Sapsford, "As Hybrid Cars Gain Traction, Industry Battles over Designs," *The Wall Street Journal,* October 19, 2005, pp. A1, A9B.

It requires many meetings of many people working in good faith over time to iron out what is to be shared, what is to remain proprietary, and how the cooperative arrangements will work. Often, once the bloom is off the rose, partners discover they have conflicting objectives and strategies, deep differences of opinion about how to proceed, or important differences in corporate values and ethical standards. Tensions build up, working relationships cool, and the hoped-for benefits never materialize.[22]

Even if the alliance becomes a win–win proposition for both parties, there is the danger of becoming overly dependent on foreign partners for essential expertise and competitive capabilities. If a company is aiming for global market leadership and needs to develop capabilities of its own, then at some juncture cross-border merger or acquisition may have to be substituted for cross-border alliances and joint ventures.

> Strategic alliances are more effective in helping establish a beachhead of new opportunity in world markets than in achieving and sustaining global leadership.

One of the lessons about cross-border alliances is that they are more effective in helping a company establish a beachhead of new opportunity in world markets than they are in enabling a company to achieve and sustain global market leadership. Global market leaders, while benefiting from alliances, usually must guard against becoming overly dependent on the assistance they get from alliance partners—otherwise, they are not masters of their own destiny.

When a Cross-Border Alliance May Be Unnecessary

Experienced multinational companies that market in 50 to 100 or more countries across the world find less need for entering into cross-border alliances than do companies in the early stages of globalizing their operations.[23] Multinational companies make it a point to develop senior managers who understand how "the system" works in different countries; these companies can also avail themselves of local managerial talent and know-how by simply hiring experienced local managers and thereby detouring the hazards of collaborative alliances with local companies. If a multinational enterprise with considerable experience in entering the markets of different countries wants to detour the hazards and hassles of allying with local businesses, it can simply assemble a capable management team consisting of both senior managers with considerable international experience and local managers. The responsibilities of its own in-house managers with international business savvy are (1) to transfer technology, business practices, and the corporate culture into the company's operations in the new country market, and (2) to serve as conduits for the flow of information between the corporate office and local operations. The responsibilities of local managers are (1) to contribute needed understanding of the local market conditions, local buying habits, and local ways of doing business, and (2) in many cases, to head up local operations.

Hence, one cannot automatically presume that a company needs the wisdom and resources of a local partner to guide it through the process of successfully entering the markets of foreign countries. Indeed, experienced multinationals often discover that local partners do not always have adequate local market knowledge—much of the so-called experience of local partners can predate the emergence of current market trends and conditions, and sometimes their operating practices can be archaic.[24]

STRATEGIES THAT FIT THE MARKETS OF EMERGING COUNTRIES

Companies racing for global leadership have to consider competing in emerging markets like China, India, Brazil, Indonesia, and Mexico—countries where the business risks are considerable but where the opportunities for growth are huge, especially as their

Illustration Capsule 7.3

Coca-Cola's Strategy for Growing Its Sales in China and India

In 2004, Coca-Cola developed a strategy to dramatically boost its market penetration in such emerging countries as China and India, where annual growth had recently dropped from about 30 percent in 1994–1998 to 10–12 percent in 2001–2003. Prior to 2003, Coca-Cola had focused its marketing efforts in China and India on making its drinks attractive to status-seeking young people in urbanized areas (cities with populations of 500,000 or more), but as annual sales growth steadily declined in these areas during the 1998–2003 period, Coca-Cola's management decided that the company needed a new, bolder strategy aimed at more rural areas of these countries. It began promoting the sales of 6.5-ounce returnable glass bottles of Coke in smaller cities and outlying towns with populations in the 50,000 to 250,000 range. Returnable bottles (which could be reused about 20 times) were much cheaper than plastic bottles or aluminum cans, and the savings in packaging costs were enough to slash the price of single-serve bottles to one yuan in China and about five rupees in India,

the equivalent in both cases of about 12 cents. Initial results were promising. Despite the fact that annual disposable incomes in these rural areas were often less than $1,000, the one-yuan and five-rupee prices proved attractive. Sales of the small bottles of Coke for one local Coca-Cola distributor in Anning, China, soon accounted for two-thirds of the distributor's total sales; a local distributor in India boosted sales from 9,000 cases in 2002 to 27,000 cases in 2003 and was expecting sales of 45,000 cases in 2004. Coca-Cola management expected that greater emphasis on rural sales would boost its growth rate in Asia to close to 20 percent and help boost worldwide volume growth to the 3–5 percent range as opposed to the paltry 1 percent rate experienced in 2003.

However, Pepsi, which had a market share of about 27 percent in China versus Coca-Cola's 55 percent, was skeptical of Coca-Cola's rural strategy and continued with its all-urban strategy of marketing to consumers in China's 165 cities with populations greater than 1 million people.

Sources: Based on information in Gabriel Kahn and Eric Bellman, "Coke's Big Gamble in Asia: Digging Deeper in China, India," *The Wall Street Journal,* August 11, 2004, pp. A1, A4, plus information at www.cocacola.com (accessed September 20, 2004 and October 6, 2005).

economies develop and living standards climb toward levels in the industrialized world.[25] With the world now comprising more than 6 billion people—fully one-third of whom are in India and China, and hundreds of millions more in other less-developed countries of Asia and in Latin America—a company that aspires to world market leadership (or to sustained rapid growth) cannot ignore the market opportunities or the base of technical and managerial talent such countries offer. For example, in 2003 China's population of 1.3 billion people consumed nearly 33 percent of the world's annual cotton production, 51 percent of the world's pork, 35 percent of all the cigarettes, 31 percent of worldwide coal production, 27 percent of the world's steel production, 19 percent of the aluminum, 23 percent of the TVs, 20 percent of the cell phones, and 18 percent of the washing machines.[26] China is the world's largest consumer of copper, aluminum, and cement and the second largest importer of oil; it is the world's biggest market for mobile phones and the second biggest for PCs, and it is on track to become the second largest market for motor vehicles by 2010.

Illustration Capsule 7.3 describes Coca-Cola's strategy to boost its sales and market share in China.

Tailoring products to fit conditions in an emerging-country market, however, often involves more than making minor product changes and becoming more familiar with local cultures.[27] Ford's attempt to sell a Ford Escort in India at a price of $21,000—a luxury-car price, given that India's best-selling Maruti-Suzuki model sold at the time for $10,000 or less, and that fewer than 10 percent of Indian households have annual purchasing power greater than $20,000—met with a less-than-enthusiastic market response. McDonald's has had to offer vegetable burgers in parts of Asia and to rethink its prices, which are often high by local standards and affordable only by the well-to-do. Kellogg has struggled to introduce its cereals successfully because consumers in many less-developed countries do not eat cereal for breakfast—changing habits is difficult and expensive. In several emerging countries, Coca-Cola has found that advertising its world image does not strike a chord with the local populace in a number of emerging-country markets. Single-serving packages of detergents, shampoos, pickles, cough syrup, and cooking oils are very popular in India because they allow buyers to conserve cash by purchasing only what they need immediately. Thus, many companies find that trying to employ a strategy akin to that used in the markets of developed countries is hazardous.[28] Experimenting with some, perhaps many, local twists is usually necessary to find a strategy combination that works.

Strategy Options

Several strategy options for tailoring a company's strategy to fit the sometimes unusual or challenging circumstances presented in emerging-country markets:

- *Prepare to compete on the basis of low price.* Consumers in emerging markets are often highly focused on price, which can give low-cost local competitors the edge unless a company can find ways to attract buyers with bargain prices as well as better products.[29] For example, when Unilever entered the market for laundry detergents in India, it realized that 80 percent of the population could not afford the brands it was selling to affluent consumers there (or the brands it was selling in wealthier countries). To compete against a low-priced detergent made by a local company, Unilever came up with a low-cost formula that was not harsh to the skin, constructed new low-cost production facilities, packaged the detergent (named Wheel) in single-use amounts so that it could be sold very cheaply, distributed the product to local merchants by handcarts, and crafted an economical marketing campaign that included painted signs on buildings and demonstrations near stores—the new brand quickly captured $100 million in sales and was the number one detergent brand in India in 2004 based on dollar sales. Unilever later replicated the strategy with low-priced packets of shampoos and deodorants in India and in South America with a detergent brand named Ala.

- *Be prepared to modify aspects of the company's business model to accommodate local circumstances (but not so much that the company loses the advantage of global scale and global branding).*[30] For instance when Dell entered China, it discovered that individuals and businesses were not accustomed to placing orders through the Internet (in North America, over 50 percent of Dell's sales in 2002–2005 were online). To adapt, Dell modified its direct sales model to rely more heavily on phone and fax orders and decided to be patient in getting Chinese customers to place Internet orders. Further, because numerous Chinese government departments and state-owned enterprises insisted that hardware vendors make their bids through distributors and systems integrators (as opposed to dealing directly with Dell salespeople as did large enterprises in other countries), Dell opted to use third parties in marketing its products to this buyer segment (although it did sell through its own sales force where it could). But Dell was careful not to abandon those parts of its business model that gave it a competitive edge over rivals. When McDonald's moved into Russia in the 1990s, it was forced to alter its practice of obtaining needed supplies from outside vendors because capable local suppliers were not available; to supply its Russian outlets and stay true to its core principle of serving consistent quality fast food, McDonald's set up its own vertically integrated supply chain (cattle were imported from Holland, russet potatoes were imported from the United States); worked with a select number of Russian bakers for its bread; brought in agricultural specialists from Canada and Europe to improve the management practices of Russian farmers; built its own 100,000-square-foot McComplex to produce hamburgers, French fries, ketchup, mustard, and Big Mac sauce; and set up a trucking fleet to move supplies to restaurants.

- *Try to change the local market to better match the way the company does business elsewhere.*[31] A multinational company often has enough market clout to drive major changes in the way a local country market operates. When Hong Kong–based STAR launched its first satellite TV channel in 1991, it profoundly impacted the TV marketplace in India: The Indian government lost its monopoly on TV broadcasts, several other satellite TV channels aimed at Indian audiences quickly emerged, and the excitement of additional channels triggered a boom in TV manufacturing in India. When Japan's Suzuki entered India in 1981, it triggered a quality revolution among Indian auto parts manufacturers. Local parts and components suppliers teamed up with Suzuki's vendors in Japan and worked with Japanese experts to produce higher-quality products. Over the next two decades, Indian companies became very proficient in making top-notch parts and components for vehicles, won more prizes for quality than companies in any country other than Japan, and broke into the global market as suppliers to many automakers in Asia and other parts of the world.

- *Stay away from those emerging markets where it is impractical or uneconomic to modify the company's business model to accommodate local circumstances.*[32] Home Depot has avoided entry into most Latin American countries because its value proposition of good quality, low prices, and attentive customer service relies on (1) good highways and logistical systems to minimize store inventory costs, (2) employee stock ownership to help motivate store personnel to provide good customer service, and (3) high labor costs for housing construction and home repairs to encourage homeowners to engage in do-it-yourself projects. Relying on these factors in the U.S. market has worked spectacularly for Home Depot, but the company has found that it cannot count on these factors in much of Latin America. Thus, to enter the market in Mexico, Home Depot switched to an acquisition strategy; it has acquired two building supply retailers in Mexico with a total of 40-plus stores. But it has not tried to operate them in the style of its U.S. big-box stores, and it doesn't have retail operations in any other developing nations (although it is exploring entry into China).

Company experiences in entering developing markets like China, India, Russia, and Brazil indicate that profitability seldom comes quickly or easily. Building a market for the company's products can often turn into a long-term process that involves reeducation of consumers, sizable investments in advertising and promotion to alter tastes and buying habits, and upgrades of the local infrastructure (the supplier base, transportation systems, distribution channels, labor markets, and capital markets). In such cases, a company must be patient, work within the system to improve the infrastructure, and lay the foundation for generating sizable revenues and profits once conditions are ripe for market takeoff.

> Profitability in emerging markets rarely comes quickly or easily—new entrants have to adapt their business models and strategies to local conditions and be patient in earning a profit.

Figure 7.4   **Strategy Options for Local Companies in Competing Against Global Companies**

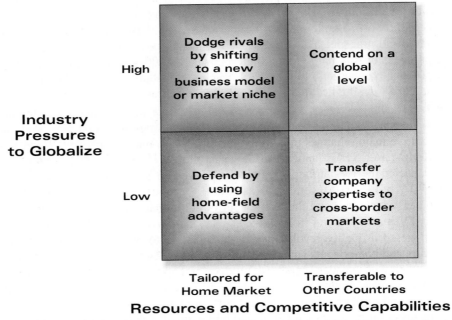

Source: Adapted from Niroj Dawar and Tony Frost, "Competing with Giants: Survival Strategies for Local Companies in Emerging Markets," *Harvard Business Review* 77, no. 1 (January–February 1999), p. 122.

Defending Against Global Giants: Strategies for Local Companies in Emerging Markets

If opportunity-seeking, resource-rich multinational companies are looking to enter emerging markets, what strategy options can local companies use to survive? As it turns out, the prospects for local companies facing global giants are by no means grim. They can employ any of four generic strategic approaches depending on (1) whether their competitive assets are suitable only for the home market or can be transferred abroad, and (2) whether industry pressures to move toward global competition are strong or weak, as shown in Figure 7.4.

Using Home-Field Advantages   When the pressures for competing globally are low and a local firm has competitive strengths well suited to the local market, a good strategy option is to concentrate on the advantages enjoyed in the home market, cater to customers who prefer a local touch, and accept the loss of customers attracted to global brands.[33] A local company may be able to astutely exploit its local orientation—its familiarity with local preferences, its expertise in traditional products, its long-standing customer relationships. In many cases, a local company enjoys a significant cost advantage over global rivals (perhaps because of simpler product design or lower operating and overhead costs), allowing it to compete on the basis of price. Its global competitors often aim their products at upper- and middle-income urban buyers, who tend to be more fashion-conscious, more willing to experiment with new products, and more attracted to global brands.

Another competitive approach is to cater to the local market in ways that pose difficulties for global rivals. A small Middle Eastern cell phone manufacturer competes successfully against industry giants Nokia, Samsung, and Motorola by selling a model designed especially for Muslims—it is loaded with the Koran, alerts people at prayer times, and is equipped with a compass that points them toward Mecca. Several Chinese PC makers have been able to retain customers in competition against global leader Dell because Chinese PC buyers strongly prefer to personally inspect PCs before making a purchase; local PC makers with their extensive retailer networks that allow prospective buyers to check out their offerings in nearby stores have a competitive edge in winning the business of first-time PC buyers vis-à-vis Dell with its build-to-order, sell-direct business strategy (where customers are encouraged to place their orders online or via phone or fax). Bajaj Auto, India's largest producer of scooters, has defended its turf against Honda (which entered the Indian market with local joint venture partner Hero Group to sell scooters, motorcycles, and other vehicles on the basis of its superior technology, quality, and the appeal) by focusing on buyers who wanted low-cost, durable scooters and easy access to maintenance in the countryside. Bajaj designed a rugged, cheap-to-build scooter for India's rough roads, increased its investments in R&D to improve reliability and quality, and created an extensive network of distributors and roadside-mechanic stalls, a strategic approach that allowed it to remain the market leader with a 70–75 percent market share through 2004 despite growing unit sales of Hero Honda motorcycles and scooters.

Transferring the Company's Expertise to Cross-Border Markets   When a company has resource strengths and capabilities suitable for competing in other country markets, launching initiatives to transfer its expertise to cross-border markets becomes a viable strategic option.[34] Televisa, Mexico's largest media company, used its expertise in Spanish culture and linguistics to become the world's most prolific producer of Spanish-language soap operas. Jollibee Foods, a family-owned company with 56 percent of the fast-food business in the Philippines, combated McDonald's entry first by upgrading service and delivery standards and then by using its expertise in seasoning hamburgers with garlic and soy sauce and making noodle and rice meals with fish to open outlets catering to Asian residents in Hong Kong, the Middle East, and California.

Shifting to a New Business Model or Market Niche   When industry pressures to globalize are high, any of the following three options makes the most sense: (1) shift the business to a piece of the industry value chain where the firm's expertise and resources provide competitive advantage, (2) enter into a joint venture with a globally competitive partner, or (3) sell out to (be acquired by) a global entrant into the home market who concludes the company would be a good entry vehicle.[35] When Microsoft entered China, local software developers shifted from cloning Windows products to developing Windows application software customized to the Chinese market. When the Russian PC market opened to IBM, Compaq, and Hewlett-Packard, local Russian PC maker Vist focused on assembling low-cost models, marketing them through exclusive distribution agreements with selected local retailers, and opening company-owned full-service centers in dozens of Russian cities. Vist focused on providing low-cost PCs, giving lengthy warranties, and catering to buyers who felt the need for local service and support. Vist's strategy allowed it to remain the market leader, with a 20 percent share.

An India-based electronics company has been able to carve out a market niche for itself by developing an all-in-one business machine designed especially for India's 1.2 million small shopkeepers that tolerates heat, dust, and power outages and that sells for a modest $180 for the smallest of its three models.[36]

Contending on a Global Level   If a local company in an emerging market has transferable resources and capabilities, it can sometimes launch successful initiatives to meet the pressures for globalization head-on and start to compete on a global level itself.[37] Lenovo, China's biggest PC maker, recently purchased IBM's PC business, moved its headquarters to New York City, put the Lenovo brand on IBM's PCs, and launched initiative to become a global PC maker alongside leaders Dell and Hewlett-Packard. When General Motors (GM) decided to outsource the production of radiator caps for all of its North American vehicles, Sundaram Fasteners of India pursued the opportunity; it purchased one of GM's radiator cap production lines, moved it to India, and became GM's sole supplier of radiator caps in North America—at 5 million units a year. As a participant in GM's supplier network, Sundaram learned about emerging technical standards, built its capabilities, and became one of the first Indian companies to achieve QS 9000 certification, a quality standard that GM now requires for all suppliers. Sundaram's acquired expertise in quality standards enabled it then to pursue opportunities to supply automotive parts in Japan and Europe. Chinese communications equipment maker Huawei has captured a 16 percent share in the global market for Internet routers because its prices are up to 50 percent lower than those of industry leaders like Cisco Systems; Huawei's success in low-priced Internet networking gear has allowed it to expand aggressively outside China, into such country markets as Russia and Brazil, and achieve the number two worldwide market share in broadband networking gear.[38] In 2005 Chinese automakers were laying plans to begin exporting fuel-efficient small cars to the United States and begin the long-term process of competing internationally against the world's leading automakers.

Key Points

Most issues in competitive strategy that apply to domestic companies apply also to companies that compete internationally. But there are four strategic issues unique to competing across national boundaries:

1. Whether to customize the company's offerings in each different country market to match the tastes and preferences of local buyers or offer a mostly standardized product worldwide.

2. Whether to employ essentially the same basic competitive strategy in all countries or modify the strategy country by country to fit the specific market conditions and competitive circumstances it encounters.

3. Where to locate the company's production facilities, distribution centers, and customer service operations so as to realize the greatest locational advantages.

4. Whether and how to efficiently transfer the company's resource strengths and capabilities from one country to another in an effort to secure competitive advantage.

Multicountry competition refers to situations where competition in one national market is largely independent of competition in another national market—there is no "international market," just a collection of self-contained country (or maybe regional) markets. Global competition exists when competitive conditions across national markets are linked strongly enough to form a true world market and when leading competitors compete head-to-head in many different countries.

In posturing to compete in foreign markets, a company has three basic options: (1) a think-local, act-local approach to crafting a strategy, (2) a think-global, act-global approach to crafting a strategy, and (3) a combination think-global, act-local approach. A think-local, act-local, or multicountry, strategy is appropriate for industries where multicountry competition dominates; a localized approach to strategy making calls for a company to vary its product offering and competitive approach from country to country in order to accommodate differing buyer preferences and market conditions. A think-global, act-global approach (or global strategy) works best in markets that are globally competitive or beginning to globalize; global strategies involve employing the same basic competitive approach (low-cost, differentiation, best-cost, focused) in all country markets and marketing essentially the same products under the same brand names in all countries where the company operates. A think-global, act-local approach can be used when it is feasible for a company to employ essentially the same basic competitive strategy in all markets but still customize its product offering and some aspect of its operations to fit local market circumstances.

Other strategy options for competing in world markets include maintaining a national (one-country) production base and exporting goods to foreign markets, licensing foreign firms to use the company's technology or produce and distribute the company's products, employing a franchising strategy, and using strategic alliances or other collaborative partnerships to enter a foreign market or strengthen a firm's competitiveness in world markets.

Strategic alliances with foreign partners have appeal from several angles: gaining wider access to attractive country markets, allowing capture of economies of scale in production and/or marketing, filling gaps in technical expertise and/or knowledge of local markets, saving on costs by sharing distribution facilities and dealer networks, helping gain agreement on important technical standards, and helping combat the impact of alliances that rivals have formed. Cross-border strategic alliances are fast reshaping competition in world markets, pitting one group of allied global companies against other groups of allied global companies.

There are three ways in which a firm can gain competitive advantage (or offset domestic disadvantages) in global markets. One way involves locating various value chain activities among nations in a manner that lowers costs or achieves greater product differentiation. A second way involves efficient and effective transfer of competitively valuable competencies and capabilities from its domestic markets to foreign markets. A third way draws on a multinational or global competitor's ability to deepen or broaden its resource strengths and capabilities and to coordinate its dispersed activities in ways that a domestic-only competitor cannot.

Profit sanctuaries are country markets in which a company derives substantial profits because of its strong or protected market position. They are valuable competitive assets. A company with multiple profit sanctuaries has the financial strength to support competitive offensives in one market with resources and profits diverted from its operations in other markets—a practice called *cross-market subsidization*. The ability of companies with multiple profit sanctuaries to employ cross-subsidization gives them a powerful offensive weapon and a competitive advantage over companies with a single sanctuary.

Companies racing for global leadership have to consider competing in emerging markets like China, India, Brazil, Indonesia, and Mexico—countries where the business risks are considerable but the opportunities for growth are huge. To succeed in these markets, companies often have to (1) compete on the basis of low price, (2) be prepared to modify aspects of the company's business model to accommodate local circumstances (but not so much that the company loses the advantage of global scale and global branding), and/or (3) try to change the local market to better match the way the company does business elsewhere. Profitability is unlikely to come quickly or easily in emerging markets, typically because of the investments needed to alter buying habits and tastes and/or the need for infrastructure upgrades. And there may be times when a company should simply stay away from certain emerging markets until conditions for entry are better suited to its business model and strategy.

Local companies in emerging country markets can seek to compete against multinational companies by (1) defending on the basis of home-field advantages, (2) transferring their expertise to cross-border markets, (3) dodging large rivals by shifting to a new business model or market niche, or (4) launching initiatives to compete on a global level themselves.

Exercises

1. Go to Caterpillar's Web site (www.caterpillar.com) and search for information about the company's strategy in foreign markets. Is Caterpillar pursuing a global strategy or a localized multicountry strategy? Support your answer.

2. Assume you are in charge of developing the strategy for a multinational company selling products in some 50 different countries around the world. One of the issues you face is whether to employ a multicountry strategy or a global strategy.

   a. If your company's product is personal computers, do you think it would make better strategic sense to employ a multicountry strategy or a global strategy? Why?

   b. If your company's product is dry soup mixes and canned soups, would a multicountry strategy seem to be more advisable than a global strategy? Why?

   c. If your company's product is washing machines, would it seem to make more sense to pursue a multicountry strategy or a global strategy? Why?

   d. If your company's product is basic work tools (hammers, screwdrivers, pliers, wrenches, saws), would a multicountry strategy or a global strategy seem to have more appeal? Why?

3. The Hero Group is among the 10 largest corporations in India, with 19 business segments and annual revenues of $2.75 billion in fiscal 2004–2005. Many of the corporation's business units have used strategic alliances with foreign partners to compete in new product and geographic markets. Review the company's statements concerning its alliances and international business operations at www.herogroup.com and prepare a two-page report that outlines Hero's successful use of international strategic alliances.

4. Using this chapter's discussion of strategies for local companies competing against global rivals and Figure 7.4, develop a strategic approach for a manufacturer or service company in your community that might be forced to compete with a global firm. How might the local company exploit a home-field advantage? Would it make sense for the local company to attempt to transfer its capabilities or expertise to cross-border markets? Or change its business model or market niche? Or join the fight on a global level? Explain.

chapter 8 eight

Tailoring Strategy to Fit Specific Industry and Company Situations

Strategy is all about combining choices of what to do and what not to do into a system that creates the requisite fit between what the environment needs and what the company does.

—Costas Markides

Competing in the marketplace is like war. You have injuries and casualties, and the best strategy wins.

—John Collins

It is much better to make your own products obsolete than allow a competitor to do it.

—Michael A. Cusamano and Richard W. Selby

In a turbulent age, the only dependable advantage is reinventing your business model before circumstances force you to.

—Gary Hamel and Liisa Välikangas

P rior chapters have emphasized the analysis and options that go into matching a company's choice of strategy to (1) industry and competitive conditions and (2) its own resource strengths and weaknesses, competitive capabilities, opportunities and threats, and market position. But there's more to be revealed about the hows of matching the choices of strategy to a company's circumstances. This chapter looks at the strategy-making task in 10 commonly encountered situations:

1. Companies competing in emerging industries.
2. Companies competing in rapidly growing markets.
3. Companies competing in maturing industries.
4. Companies competing in stagnant or declining industries.
5. Companies competing in turbulent, high-velocity markets.
6. Companies competing in fragmented industries.
7. Companies striving to sustain rapid growth.
8. Companies in industry leadership positions.
9. Companies in runner-up positions.
10. Companies in competitively weak positions or plagued by crisis conditions.

We selected these situations to shed still more light on the factors that managers need to consider in tailoring a company's strategy. When you finish this chapter, you will have a stronger grasp of the factors that managers have to weigh in choosing a strategy and what the pros and cons are for some of the heretofore unexplored strategic options that are open to a company.

STRATEGIES FOR COMPETING IN EMERGING INDUSTRIES

An emerging industry is one in the formative stage. Examples include Voice over Internet Protocol (VoIP) telephone communications, high-definition TV, assisted living for the elderly, online education, organic food products, e-book publishing, and electronic banking. Many companies striving to establish a strong foothold in an emerging industry are start-up enterprises busily engaged in perfecting technology, gearing up operations, and trying to broaden distribution and gain buyer acceptance. Important product design issues or technological problems may still have to be worked out. The business models and strategies of companies in an emerging industry are unproved—they may look promising but may or may not ever result in attractive profitability.

The Unique Characteristics of an Emerging Industry

Competing in emerging industries presents managers with some unique strategy-making challenges:[1]

- Because the market is in its infancy, there's usually much speculation about how it will function, how fast it will grow, and how big it will get. The little historical information available is virtually useless in making sales and profit projections. There's lots of guesswork about how rapidly buyers will be attracted and how much they will be willing to pay. For example, there is much uncertainty about how many users of traditional telephone service will be inclined to switch over to VoIP telephone technology and how rapidly any such switchovers will occur.

- In many cases, much of the technological know-how underlying the products of emerging industries is proprietary and closely guarded, having been developed in-house by pioneering firms. In such cases, patents and unique technical expertise are key factors in securing competitive advantage. In other cases, numerous companies have access to the requisite technology and may be racing to perfect it, often in collaboration with others. In still other instances, there can be competing technological approaches, with much uncertainty over whether multiple technologies will end up competing alongside one another or whether one approach will ultimately win out because of lower costs or better performance—such a battle is currently under way in the emerging market for gasoline-electric hybrid engines (where demand is mushrooming because of greater fuel efficiency without a loss of power and acceleration). Toyota has pioneered one design; an alliance among General Motors, DaimlerChrysler, and BMW is pursuing another design; a Volkswagen-Porsche alliance is looking at a third technological approach; and Ford and Honda have their own slightly different hybrid engine designs.

- Just as there may be uncertainties surrounding an emerging industry's technology, there may also be no consensus regarding which product attributes will prove decisive in winning buyer favor. Rivalry therefore centers on each firm's efforts to get the market to ratify its own strategic approach to technology, product design, marketing, and distribution. Such rivalry can result in wide differences in product quality and performance from brand to brand.

- Since in an emerging industry all buyers are first-time users, the marketing task is to induce initial purchase and to overcome customer concerns about product features, performance reliability, and conflicting claims of rival firms.

- Many potential buyers expect first-generation products to be rapidly improved, so they delay purchase until technology and product design mature and second- or third-generation products appear on the market.

- Entry barriers tend to be relatively low, even for entrepreneurial start-up companies. Large, well-known, opportunity-seeking companies with ample resources and competitive capabilities are likely to enter if the industry has promise for explosive growth or if its emergence threatens their present business. For instance, many traditional local telephone companies, seeing the potent threat of wireless communications technology and VoIP, have opted to enter the mobile communications business and begin offering landline customers a VoIP option.

- Strong experience/learning curve effects may be present, allowing significant price reductions as volume builds and costs fall.
- Sometimes firms have trouble securing ample supplies of raw materials and components (until suppliers gear up to meet the industry's needs).
- Undercapitalized companies, finding themselves short of funds to support needed R&D and get through several lean years until the product catches on, end up merging with competitors or being acquired by financially strong outsiders looking to invest in a growth market.

Strategy Options for Emerging Industries

The lack of established rules of the game in an emerging industry gives industry participants considerable freedom to experiment with a variety of different strategic approaches. Competitive strategies keyed either to low cost or differentiation are usually viable. Focusing makes good sense when resources and capabilities are limited and the industry has too many technological frontiers or too many buyer segments to pursue at once. Broad or focused differentiation strategies keyed to technological or product superiority typically offer the best chance for early competitive advantage.

> **Core Concept**
> Companies in an emerging industry have wide latitude in experimenting with different strategic approaches.

In addition to choosing a competitive strategy, companies in an emerging industry usually have to fashion a strategy containing one or more of the following actions:[2]

1. Push to perfect the technology, improve product quality, and develop additional attractive performance features. Out-innovating the competition is often one of the best avenues to industry leadership.

2. Consider merging with or acquiring another firm to gain added expertise and pool resource strengths.

3. As technological uncertainty clears and a dominant technology emerges, try to capture any first-mover advantages by adopting it quickly. However, while there's merit in trying to be the industry standard-bearer on technology and to pioneer the dominant product design, firms have to beware of betting too heavily on their own preferred technological approach or product design—especially when there are many competing technologies, R&D is costly, and technological developments can quickly move in surprising new directions.

4. Acquire or form alliances with companies that have related or complementary technological expertise as a means of helping outcompete rivals on the basis of technological superiority.

5. Pursue new customer groups, new user applications, and entry into new geographical areas (perhaps using strategic partnerships or joint ventures if financial resources are constrained).

6. Make it easy and cheap for first-time buyers to try the industry's first-generation product.

7. As the product becomes familiar to a wide portion of the market, shift the advertising emphasis from creating product awareness to increasing frequency of use and building brand loyalty.

8. Use price cuts to attract the next layer of price-sensitive buyers into the market.

9. Form strategic alliances with key suppliers whenever effective supply chain management provides important access to specialized skills, technological capabilities, and critical materials or components.

Young companies in emerging industries face four strategic hurdles: (1) raising the capital to finance initial operations until sales and revenues take off, profits appear, and cash flows turn positive; (2) developing a strategy to ride the wave of industry growth(what market segments and competitive advantages to go after?); (3) managing the rapid expansion of facilities and sales in a manner that positions them to contend for industry leadership; and (4) defending against competitors trying to horn in on their success.[3] Up-and-coming companies can help their cause by selecting knowledgeable members for their boards of directors and by hiring entrepreneurial managers with experience in guiding young businesses through the start-up and takeoff stages. *A firm that develops solid resource capabilities, an appealing business model, and a good strategy has a golden opportunity to shape the rules and establish itself as the recognized industry front-runner.*

But strategic efforts to win the early race for growth and market share leadership in an emerging industry have to be balanced against the longer-range need to build a durable competitive edge and a defendable market position.[4] The initial front-runners in a fast-growing emerging industry that shows signs of good profitability will almost certainly have to defend their positions against ambitious challengers striving to overtake the current market leaders. Well-financed outsiders can be counted on to enter with aggressive offensive strategies once industry sales take off, the perceived risk of investing in the industry lessens, and the success of current industry members becomes apparent. Sometimes a rush of new entrants, attracted by the growth and profit potential, overcrowds the market and forces industry consolidation to a smaller number of players. Resource-rich latecomers, aspiring to industry leadership, may become major players by acquiring and merging the operations of weaker competitors and then using their own perhaps considerable brand name recognition to draw customers and build market share. Hence, the strategies of the early leaders must be aimed at competing for the long haul and making a point of developing the resources, capabilities, and market recognition needed to sustain early successes and stave off competition from capable, ambitious newcomers.

STRATEGIES FOR COMPETING IN RAPIDLY GROWING MARKETS

Companies that have the good fortune to be in an industry growing at double-digit rates have a golden opportunity to achieve double-digit revenues and profit growth. If market demand is expanding 20 percent annually, a company can grow 20 percent annually simply by doing little more than contentedly riding the tide of market growth—it has to simply be aggressive enough to secure enough new customers to realize a 20 percent gain in sales, not a particularly impressive strategic feat. What is more interesting, however, is to craft a strategy that enables sales to grow at 25 or 30 percent when the overall market is growing by 20 percent, such that the company's market share and competitive position improve relative to rivals, on average. Should a company's strategy only deliver sales growth of 12 percent in a market growing at

> In a fast-growing market, a company needs a strategy predicated on growing faster than the market average, so that it can boost its market share and improve its competitive standing vis-à-vis rivals.

20 percent, then it is actually losing ground in the marketplace—a condition that signals a weak strategy and an unappealing product offering. The point here is that, in a rapidly growing market, a company must aim its strategy at producing gains in revenue that exceed the market average; otherwise, the best it can hope for is to maintain its market standing (if it is able to boost sales at a rate equal to the market average) and its market standing may indeed erode if its sales rise by less than the market average.

To be able to grow at a pace exceeding the market average, a company generally must have a strategy that incorporates one or more of the following elements:

- *Driving down costs per unit so as to enable price reductions that attract droves of new customers.* Charging a lower price always has strong appeal in markets where customers are price-sensitive, and lower prices can help push up buyers demand by drawing new customers into the marketplace. But since rivals can lower their prices also, a company must really be able to drive its unit costs down *faster than rivals*, such that it can use its low-cost advantage to underprice rivals. The makers of liquid crystal display (LCD) and high-definition TVs are aggressively pursuing cost reduction to bring the prices of their TV sets down under $1,000 and thus make their products more affordable to more consumers.

- *Pursuing rapid product innovation, both to set a company's product offering apart from rivals and to incorporate attributes that appeal to growing numbers of customers.* Differentiation strategies, when keyed to product attributes that draw in large numbers of new customers, help bolster a company's reputation for product superiority and lay the foundation for sales gains in excess of the overall rate of market growth. If the market is one where technology is advancing rapidly and product life cycles are short, then it becomes especially important to be first-to-market with next-generation products. But product innovation strategies require competencies in R&D and new product development and design, plus organizational agility in getting new and improved products to market quickly. At the same time they are pursuing cost reductions, the makers of LCD and high-definition TVs are pursuing all sorts of product improvements to enhance product quality and performance and boost screen sizes, so as to match or beat the picture quality and reliability of conventional TVs (with old-fashioned cathode-ray tubes) and drive up sales at an even faster clip.

- *Gaining access to additional distribution channels and sales outlets.* Pursuing wider distribution access so as to reach more potential buyers is a particularly good strategic approach for realizing above-average sales gains. But usually this requires a company to be a first-mover in positioning itself in new distribution channels and forcing rivals into playing catch-up.

- *Expanding the company's geographic coverage.* Expanding into areas, either domestic or foreign, where the company does not have a market presence can also be an effective way to reach more potential buyers and pave the way for gains in sales that outpace the overall market average.

- *Expanding the product line to add models/styles that appeal to a wider range of buyers.* Offering buyers a wider selection can be an effective way to draw new customers in numbers sufficient to realize above-average sales gains. Makers of MP3 players and cell phones are adding new models to stimulate buyer demand; Starbucks is adding new drinks and other menu selections to build store traffic; and marketers of VoIP technology are rapidly introducing a wider variety of plans to broaden their appeal to customers with different calling habits and needs.

STRATEGIES FOR COMPETING IN MATURING INDUSTRIES

A *maturing industry* is one that is moving from rapid growth to significantly slower growth. An industry is said to be *mature* when nearly all potential buyers are already users of the industry's products and growth in market demand closely parallels that of the population and the economy as a whole. In a mature market, demand consists mainly of replacement sales to existing users, with growth hinging on the industry's abilities to attract the few remaining new buyers and to convince existing buyers to up their usage. Consumer goods industries that are mature typically have a growth rate under 5 percent—roughly equal to the growth of the customer base or economy as a whole.

How Slowing Growth Alters Market Conditions

An industry's transition to maturity does not begin on an easily predicted schedule. Industry maturity can be forestalled by the emergence of new technological advances, product innovations, or other driving forces that keep rejuvenating market demand. Nonetheless, when growth rates do slacken, the onset of market maturity usually produces fundamental changes in the industry's competitive environment:[5]

1. *Slowing growth in buyer demand generates more head-to-head competition for market share.* Firms that want to continue on a rapid-growth track start looking for ways to take customers away from competitors. Outbreaks of price cutting, increased advertising, and other aggressive tactics to gain market share are common.

2. *Buyers become more sophisticated, often driving a harder bargain on repeat purchases.* Since buyers have experience with the product and are familiar with competing brands, they are better able to evaluate different brands and can use their knowledge to negotiate a better deal with sellers.

3. *Competition often produces a greater emphasis on cost and service.* As sellers all begin to offer the product attributes buyers prefer, buyer choices increasingly depend on which seller offers the best combination of price and service.

4. *Firms have a "topping-out" problem in adding new facilities.* Reduced rates of industry growth mean slowdowns in capacity expansion for manufacturers—adding too much plant capacity at a time when growth is slowing can create oversupply conditions that adversely affect manufacturers' profits well into the future. Likewise, retail chains that specialize in the industry's product have to cut back on the number of new stores being opened to keep from saturating localities with too many stores.

5. *Product innovation and new end-use applications are harder to come by.* Producers find it increasingly difficult to create new product features, find further uses for the product, and sustain buyer excitement.

6. *International competition increases.* Growth-minded domestic firms start to seek out sales opportunities in foreign markets. Some companies, looking for ways to cut costs, relocate plants to countries with lower wage rates. Greater product standardization and diffusion of technological know-how reduce entry barriers and make it possible for enterprising foreign companies to become serious market contenders in more countries. Industry leadership passes to companies that succeed in building strong competitive positions in most of the world's major geographic markets and in winning the biggest global market shares.

7. *Industry profitability falls temporarily or permanently.* Slower growth, increased competition, more sophisticated buyers, and occasional periods of overcapacity put pressure on industry profit margins. Weaker, less-efficient firms are usually the hardest hit.

8. *Stiffening competition induces a number of mergers and acquisitions among former competitors, driving industry consolidation to a smaller number of larger players.* Inefficient firms and firms with weak competitive strategies can achieve respectable results in a fast-growing industry with booming sales. But the intensifying competition that accompanies industry maturity exposes competitive weakness and throws second- and third-tier competitors into a survival-of-the-fittest contest.

Strategies that Fit Conditions in Maturing Industries

As the new competitive character of industry maturity begins to hit full force, any of several strategic moves can strengthen a firm's competitive position: pruning the product line, improving value chain efficiency, trimming costs, increasing sales to present customers, acquiring rival firms, expanding internationally, and strengthening capabilities.[6]

Pruning Marginal Products and Models   A wide selection of models, features, and product options sometimes has competitive value during the growth stage, when buyers' needs are still evolving. But such variety can become too costly as price competition stiffens and profit margins are squeezed. Maintaining many product versions works against achieving design, parts inventory, and production economies at the manufacturing levels and can increase inventory stocking costs for distributors and retailers. In addition, the prices of slow-selling versions may not cover their true costs. Pruning marginal products from the line opens the door for cost savings and permits more concentration on items whose margins are highest and/or where a firm has a competitive advantage. General Motors has been cutting slow-selling models and brands from its lineup of offerings—it has eliminated the entire Oldsmobile division and is said to be looking at whether it can eliminate its Saab lineup. Textbook publishers are discontinuing publication of those books that sell only a few thousand copies annually (where profits are marginal at best) and instead focusing their resources on texts that generate sales of at least 5,000 copies per edition.

Improving Value Chain Efficiency   Efforts to reinvent the industry value chain can have a fourfold payoff: lower costs, better product or service quality, greater capability to turn out multiple or customized product versions, and shorter design-to-market cycles. Manufacturers can mechanize high-cost activities, redesign production lines to improve labor efficiency, build flexibility into the assembly process so that customized product versions can be easily produced, and increase use of advanced technology (robotics, computerized controls, and automated assembly). Suppliers of parts and components, manufacturers, and distributors can collaboratively deploy online systems and product coding techniques to streamline activities and achieve cost savings all along the value chain—from supplier-related activities all the way through distribution, retailing, and customer service.

Trimming Costs   Stiffening price competition gives firms extra incentive to drive down unit costs. Company cost-reduction initiatives can cover a broad front. Some of the most frequently pursued options are pushing suppliers for better prices, implementing tighter supply chain management practices, cutting low-value activities out of the value chain, developing more economical product designs, reengineering internal processes using e-commerce technology, and shifting to more economical distribution arrangements.

Increasing Sales to Present Customers   In a mature market, growing by taking customers away from rivals may not be as appealing as expanding sales to existing customers. Strategies to increase purchases by existing customers can involve adding more sales promotions, providing complementary items and ancillary services, and finding more ways for customers to use the product. Convenience stores, for example, have boosted average sales per customer by adding video rentals, automated teller machines, gasoline pumps, and deli counters.

Acquiring Rival Firms at Bargain Prices   Sometimes a firm can acquire the facilities and assets of struggling rivals quite cheaply. Bargain-priced acquisitions can help create a low-cost position if they also present opportunities for greater operating efficiency. In addition, an acquired firm's customer base can provide expanded market coverage and opportunities for greater scale economies. The most desirable acquisitions are those that will significantly enhance the acquiring firm's competitive strength.

Expanding Internationally   As its domestic market matures, a firm may seek to enter foreign markets where attractive growth potential still exists and competitive pressures are not so strong. Many multinational companies are expanding into such emerging markets as China, India, Brazil, Argentina, and the Philippines, where the long-term growth prospects are quite attractive. Strategies to expand internationally also make sense when a domestic firm's skills, reputation, and product are readily transferable to foreign markets. For example, even though the U.S. market for soft drinks is mature, Coca-Cola has remained a growth company by upping its efforts to penetrate emerging markets where soft-drink sales are expanding rapidly.

Building New or More Flexible Capabilities   The stiffening pressures of competition in a maturing or already mature market can often be combated by strengthening the company's resource base and competitive capabilities. This can mean adding new competencies or capabilities, deepening existing competencies to make them harder to imitate, or striving to make core competencies more adaptable to changing customer requirements and expectations. Microsoft has responded to challenges by such competitors as Google and Linux by expanding its competencies in search engine software and revamping its entire approach to programming next-generation operating systems. Chevron has developed a best-practices discovery team and a best-practices resource map to enhance the speed and effectiveness with which it is able to transfer efficiency improvements from one oil refinery to another.

Strategic Pitfalls in Maturing Industries

Perhaps the biggest strategic mistake a company can make as an industry matures is steering a middle course between low cost, differentiation, and focusing—blending efforts to achieve low cost with efforts to incorporate differentiating features and efforts to focus on a limited target market. Such strategic compromises typically leave the firm *stuck in the middle* with a fuzzy strategy, too little commitment to winning a competitive advantage, an average image with buyers, and little chance of springing into the ranks of the industry leaders.

Other strategic pitfalls include being slow to mount a defense against stiffening competitive pressures, concentrating more on protecting short-term profitability than on building or maintaining long-term competitive position, waiting too long to respond to price cutting by rivals, overexpanding in the face of slowing growth, overspending on advertising and sales promotion efforts in a losing effort to combat the growth slowdown, and failing to pursue cost reduction soon enough or aggressively enough.

STRATEGIES FOR COMPETING IN STAGNANT OR DECLINING INDUSTRIES

Many firms operate in industries where demand is growing more slowly than the economy-wide average or is even declining. The demand for an industry's product can decline for any of several reasons: (1) advancing technology gives rise to better-performing substitute products (slim LCD monitors displace bulky CRT monitors; DVD players replace VCRs; wrinkle-free fabrics replace the need for laundry/dry-cleaning services) or lower costs (cheaper synthetics replace expensive leather); (2) the customer group shrinks (baby foods are in less demand when birthrates fall); (3) changing lifestyles and buyer tastes (cigarette smoking and wearing dress hats go out of vogue); (4) the rising costs of complementary products (higher gasoline prices drive down purchases of gas-guzzling vehicles).[7] The most attractive declining industries are those in which sales are eroding only slowly, there are pockets of stable or even growing demand, and some market niches present good profit opportunities. But in some stagnant or declining industries, decaying buyer demand precipitates a desperate competitive battle among industry members for the available business, replete with price discounting, costly sales promotions, growing amounts of idle plant capacity, and fast-eroding profit margins. It matters greatly whether buyer demand falls gradually or sharply and whether competition proves to be fierce or moderate.

Businesses competing in stagnant or declining industries have to make a fundamental strategic choice—whether to remain committed to the industry for the long term despite the industry's dim prospects or whether to pursue an end-game strategy to withdraw gradually or quickly from the market. Deciding to stick with the industry despite eroding market demand can have considerable merit. Stagnant demand by itself is not enough to make an industry unattractive. Market demand may be decaying slowly. Some segments of the market may still present good profit opportunities. Cash flows from operations may still remain strongly positive. Strong competitors may well be able to grow and boost profits by taking market share from weaker competitors.[8] Furthermore, the acquisition or exit of weaker firms creates opportunities for the remaining companies to capture greater market share. On the one hand, striving to become the market leader and be one of the few remaining companies in a declining industry can lead to above-average profitability even though overall market demand is stagnant or eroding. On the other hand, if the market environment of a declining industry is characterized by bitter warfare for customers and lots of overcapacity, such that companies are plagued with heavy operating losses, then an early exit makes much more strategic sense.

If a company decides to stick with a declining industry—because top management is encouraged by the remaining opportunities or sees merit in striving for market share

> It is erroneous to assume that companies in a declining industry are doomed to having declining revenues and profits.

leadership (or even just being one of the few remaining companies in the industry), then its three best strategic alternatives are usually the following:[9]

1. *Pursue a focused strategy aimed at the fastest-growing or slowest-decaying market segments within the industry.* Stagnant or declining markets, like other markets, are composed of numerous segments or niches. Frequently, one or more of these segments is growing rapidly (or at least decaying much more slowly), despite stagnation in the industry as a whole. An astute competitor who zeros in on fast-growing segments and does a first-rate job of meeting the needs of buyers comprising these segments can often escape stagnating sales and profits and even gain decided competitive advantage. For instance, both Ben & Jerry's and Häagen-Dazs have achieved success by focusing on the growing luxury or superpremium segment of the otherwise stagnant market for ice cream; revenue growth and profit margins are substantially higher for high-end ice creams sold in supermarkets and in scoop shops than is the case in other segments of the ice cream market. Companies that focus on the one or two most attractive market segments in a declining business may well decide to ignore the other segments altogether—withdrawing from them entirely or at least gradually or rapidly disinvesting in them. But the key is to *move aggressively* to establish a strong position in the most attractive parts of the stagnant or declining industry.

2. *Stress differentiation based on quality improvement and product innovation.* Either enhanced quality or innovation can rejuvenate demand by creating important new growth segments or inducing buyers to trade up. Successful product innovation opens up an avenue for competing that bypasses meeting or beating rivals' prices. Differentiation based on successful innovation has the additional advantage of being difficult and expensive for rival firms to imitate. New Covent Garden Soup has met with success by introducing packaged fresh soups for sale in major supermarkets, where the typical soup offerings are canned or dry mixes. Procter & Gamble has rejuvenated sales of its toothbrushes with its new line of Crest battery-powered spin toothbrushes, and it has revitalized interest in tooth care products with a series of product innovations related to teeth whitening. Bread makers are fighting declining sales of white breads that use bleached flour by introducing all kinds of whole-grain breads (which have far more nutritional value).

3. *Strive to drive costs down and become the industry's low-cost leader.* Companies in stagnant industries can improve profit margins and return on investment by pursuing innovative cost reduction year after year. Potential cost-saving actions include (*a*) cutting marginally beneficial activities out of the value chain; (*b*) outsourcing functions and activities that can be performed more cheaply by outsiders; (*c*) redesigning internal business processes to exploit cost-reducing e-commerce technologies; (*d*) consolidating underutilized production facilities; (*e*) adding more distribution channels to ensure the unit volume needed for low-cost production; (*f*) closing low-volume, high-cost retail outlets; and (*g*) pruning marginal products from the firm's offerings. Japan-based Asahi Glass (a low-cost producer of flat glass), PotashCorp and IMC Global (two low-cost leaders in potash production), Alcan Aluminum, Nucor Steel, and Safety Components International (a low-cost producer of air bags for motor vehicles) have all been successful in driving costs down in competitively tough and largely stagnant industry environments.

These three strategic themes are not mutually exclusive.[10] Introducing innovative versions of a product can create a fast-growing market segment. Similarly, relentless pursuit of greater operating efficiencies permits price reductions that create price-conscious growth segments. Note that all three themes are spinoffs of the five generic competitive strategies, adjusted to fit the circumstances of a tough industry environment.

End-Game Strategies for Declining Industries

An *end-game strategy* can take either of two paths: (1) a *slow-exit strategy* that involves a gradual phasing down of operations coupled with an objective of getting the most cash flow from the business even if it means sacrificing market position or profitability and (2) a *fast-exit* or *sell-out-quickly strategy* to disengage from the industry during the early stages of the decline and recover as much of the company's investment as possible for deployment elsewhere.[11]

A Slow-Exit Strategy   With a slow-exit strategy, *the key objective is to generate the greatest possible harvest of cash from the business for as long as possible.* Management either eliminates or severely curtails new investment in the business. Capital expenditures for new equipment are put on hold or given low financial priority (unless replacement needs are unusually urgent); instead, efforts are made to stretch the life of existing equipment and make do with present facilities as long as possible. Old plants with high costs may be retired from service. The operating budget is chopped to a rock-bottom level. Promotional expenses may be cut gradually, quality reduced in not-so-visible ways, nonessential customer services curtailed, and maintenance of facilities held to a bare minimum. The resulting increases in cash flow (and perhaps even bottom-line profitability and return on investment) compensate for whatever declines in sales might be experienced. Withering buyer demand is tolerable if sizable amounts of cash can be reaped in the interim. If and when cash flows dwindle to meager levels as sales volumes decay, the business can be sold or, if no buyer can be found, closed down.

A Fast-Exit Strategy   The challenge of a sell-out-quickly strategy is to find a buyer willing to pay an agreeable price for the company's business assets. Buyers may be scarce since there's a tendency for investors to shy away from purchasing a stagnant or dying business. And even if willing buyers appear, they will be in a strong bargaining position once it's clear that the industry's prospects are permanently waning. How much prospective buyers will pay is usually a function of how rapidly they expect the industry to decline, whether they see opportunities to rejuvenate demand (at least temporarily), whether they believe that costs can be cut enough to still produce attractive profit margins or cash flows, whether there are pockets of stable demand where buyers are not especially price sensitive, and whether they believe that fading market demand will weaken competition (which could enhance profitability) or trigger strong competition for the remaining business (which could put pressure on profit margins). Thus, the expectations of prospective buyers will tend to drive the price they are willing to pay for the business assets of a company wanting to sell out quickly.

STRATEGIES FOR COMPETING IN TURBULENT, HIGH-VELOCITY MARKETS

Many companies operate in industries characterized by rapid technological change, short product life cycles, the entry of important new rivals, lots of competitive maneuvering by rivals, and fast-evolving customer requirements and expectations—all occurring in a manner that creates swirling market conditions. Since news of this or that important competitive development arrives daily, it is an imposing task just to monitor and assess developing events. High-velocity change is plainly the prevailing condition in computer/server hardware and software, video games, networking, wireless telecommunications, medical equipment, biotechnology, prescription drugs, and online retailing.

Ways to Cope with Rapid Change

The central strategy-making challenge in a turbulent market environment is managing change.[12] As illustrated in Figure 8.1, a company can assume any of three strategic postures in dealing with high-velocity change:[13]

- *It can react to change.* The company can respond to a rival's new product with a better product. It can counter an unexpected shift in buyer tastes and buyer demand by redesigning or repackaging its product, or shifting its advertising emphasis to different product attributes. Reacting is a defensive strategy and is therefore unlikely to create fresh opportunity, but it is nonetheless a necessary component in a company's arsenal of options.

- *It can anticipate change.* The company can make plans for dealing with the expected changes and follow its plans as changes occur (fine-tuning them as may be needed). Anticipation entails looking ahead to analyze what is likely to occur and then preparing and positioning for that future. It entails studying buyer behavior, buyer needs, and buyer expectations to get insight into how the market will evolve, then lining up the necessary production and distribution capabilities ahead of time. Like reacting to change, anticipating change is still fundamentally defensive in that forces outside the enterprise are in the driver's seat. Anticipation, however, can open up new opportunities and thus is a better way to manage change than just pure reaction.

- *It can lead change.* Leading change entails initiating the market and competitive forces that others must respond to—it is an offensive strategy aimed at putting a company in the driver's seat. Leading change means being first to market with an important new product or service. It means being the technological leader, rushing next-generation products to market ahead of rivals, and having products whose features and attributes shape customer preferences and expectations. It means proactively seeking to shape the rules of the game.

> A sound way to deal with turbulent market conditions is to try to lead change with proactive strategic moves while at the same time trying to anticipate and prepare for upcoming changes and being quick to react to unexpected developments.

As a practical matter, a company's approach to managing change should, ideally, incorporate all three postures (though not in the same proportion). The best-performing companies in high-velocity markets consistently seek to lead change with proactive strategies that often entail the flexibility to pursue any of several strategic options, depending on how the market actually evolves. Even so, an environment of relentless change makes it incumbent on any company to anticipate and prepare for the future and to react quickly to unpredictable or uncontrollable new developments.

Strategy Options for Fast-Changing Markets

Competitive success in fast-changing markets tends to hinge on a company's ability to improvise, experiment, adapt, reinvent, and regenerate as market and competitive conditions shift rapidly and sometimes unpredictably.[14] It has to constantly reshape its

Figure 8.1   **Meeting the Challenge of High-Velocity Change**

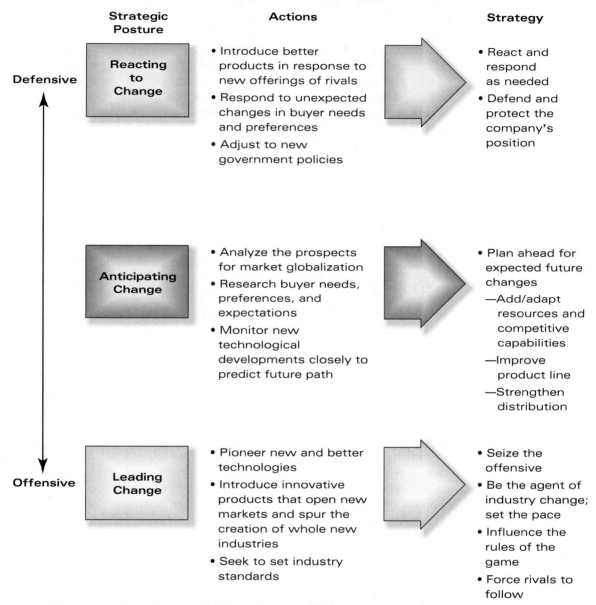

Source: Adapted from Shona L. Brown and Kathleen M. Eisenhardt, *Competing on the Edge: Strategy as Structured Chaos* (Boston, MA: Harvard Business School Press, 1998) p. 5.

strategy and its basis for competitive advantage. While the process of altering offensive and defensive moves every few months or weeks to keep the overall strategy closely matched to changing conditions is inefficient, the alternative—a fast-obsolescing strategy—is worse. The following five strategic moves seem to offer the best payoffs:

1. *Invest aggressively in R&D to stay on the leading edge of technological know-how.* Translating technological advances into innovative new products (and remaining close on the heels of whatever advances and features are pioneered by rivals) is a necessity in industries where technology is the primary driver of change. But it is often desirable to focus the R&D effort on a few critical areas, not only to avoid stretching the company's resources too thin but also to deepen the firm's expertise, master the technology, fully capture experience/learning curve effects, and become the dominant leader in a particular technology or product category.[15] When a fast-evolving market environment entails many technological areas and product categories, competitors have little choice but to employ some type of focus strategy and concentrate on being the leader in a particular product/technology category.

2. *Keep the company's products and services fresh and exciting enough to stand out in the midst of all the change that is taking place.* One of the risks of rapid change is that products and even companies can get lost in the shuffle. The marketing challenge here is to keep the firm's products and services in the limelight and, further, to keep them innovative and well matched to the changes that are occurring in the marketplace.

3. *Develop quick-response capability.* Because no company can predict all of the changes that will occur, it is crucial to have the organizational capability to be able to react quickly, improvising if necessary. This means shifting resources internally, adapting existing competencies and capabilities, creating new competencies and capabilities, and not falling far behind rivals. Companies that are habitual late-movers are destined to be industry also-rans.

4. *Rely on strategic partnerships with outside suppliers and with companies making tie-in products.* In many high-velocity industries, technology is branching off to create so many new technological paths and product categories that no company has the resources and competencies to pursue them all. Specialization (to promote the necessary technical depth) and focus (to preserve organizational agility and leverage the firm's expertise) are desirable strategies. Companies build their competitive position not just by strengthening their own internal resource base but also by partnering with those suppliers making state-of-the-art parts and components and by collaborating closely with both the developers of related technologies and the makers of tie-in products. For example, personal computer companies like Gateway, Dell, Compaq, and Acer rely heavily on the developers and manufacturers of chips, monitors, hard drives, DVD players, and software for innovative advances in PCs. None of the PC makers have done much in the way of integrating backward into parts and components because they have learned that the most effective way to provide PC users with a state-of-the-art product is to outsource the latest, most advanced components from technologically sophisticated suppliers who make it their business to stay on the cutting edge of their specialization and who can achieve economies of scale by mass-producing components for many PC assemblers. An outsourcing strategy also allows a company the flexibility to replace suppliers that fall behind on technology or product features or that cease to be competitive on price. The managerial challenge here is to strike a good balance between building a rich internal resource base that, on the one hand, keeps the firm from being at the mercy of its suppliers and allies and, on the other hand, maintains organizational agility by relying on the resources and expertise of capable (and perhaps best-in-world) outsiders.

5. *Initiate fresh actions every few months, not just when a competitive response is needed.* In some sense, change is partly triggered by the passage of time rather

than solely by the occurrence of events. A company can be proactive by making time-paced moves—introducing a new or improved product every four months, rather than when the market tapers off or a rival introduces a next-generation model.[16] Similarly, a company can expand into a new geographic market every six months rather than waiting for a new market opportunity to present itself; it can also refresh existing brands every two years rather than waiting until their popularity wanes. The keys to successfully using time pacing as a strategic weapon are choosing intervals that make sense internally and externally, establishing an internal organizational rhythm for change, and choreographing the transitions. 3M Corporation has long pursued an objective of having 25 percent of its revenues come from products less than four years old, a force that established the rhythm of change and created a relentless push for new products. Recently, the firm's CEO upped the tempo of change at 3M by increasing the goal from 25 to 30 percent.

Cutting-edge know-how and first-to-market capabilities are very valuable competitive assets in fast-evolving markets. Moreover, action-packed competition demands that a company have quick reaction times and flexible, adaptable resources—organizational agility is a huge competitive asset. Even so, companies will make mistakes and take some actions that do not work out well. When a company's strategy doesn't seem to be working well, it has to quickly regroup—probing, experimenting, improvising, and trying again and again until it finds something that strikes the right chord with buyers and that puts it in sync with market and competitive realities.

STRATEGIES FOR COMPETING IN FRAGMENTED INDUSTRIES

A number of industries are populated by hundreds, even thousands, of small and medium-sized companies, many privately held and none with a substantial share of total industry sales.[17] The standout competitive feature of a fragmented industry is the absence of market leaders with king-sized market shares or widespread buyer recognition. Examples of fragmented industries include book publishing, landscaping and plant nurseries, real estate development, convenience stores, banking, health and medical care, mail order catalog sales, computer software development, custom printing, kitchen cabinets, trucking, auto repair, restaurants and fast food, public accounting, apparel manufacture and apparel retailing, paperboard boxes, hotels and motels, and furniture.

Reasons for Supply-Side Fragmentation

Any of several reasons can account for why the supply side of an industry comprises hundreds or even thousands of companies:

- *The product or service is delivered at neighborhood locations so as to be conveniently accessible to local residents.* Retail and service businesses, for example, are inherently local—gas stations and car washes, pharmacies, dry-cleaning services, nursing homes, auto repair firms, furniture stores, flower shops, and lawn care enterprises. Whenever it takes thousands of locations to adequately serve the market, the way is opened for many enterprises to be engaged in providing products/services to local residents and businesses (and such enterprises can operate at just one location or at multiple locations).

- *Buyer preferences and requirements are so diverse that very large numbers of firms can easily coexist trying to accommodate differing buyer tastes, expectations, and pocketbooks.* This is true in the market for apparel, where there are thousands of apparel manufacturers making garments of various styles and price ranges. There's a host of different hotels and restaurants in places like New York City, London, Buenos Aires, Mexico City, and Tokyo. The software development industry is highly fragmented because there are so many types of software applications and because the needs and expectations of software users are so highly diverse—hence, there's ample market space for a software company to concentrate its attention on serving a particular market niche.

- *Low entry barriers allow small firms to enter quickly and cheaply.* Such tends to be the case in many areas of retailing, residential real estate, insurance sales, beauty shops, and the restaurant business.

- *An absence of scale economies permits small companies to compete on an equal cost footing with larger firms.* The markets for business forms, interior design, kitchen cabinets, and picture framing are fragmented because buyers require relatively small quantities of customized products; since demand for any particular product version is small, sales volumes are not adequate to support producing, distributing, or marketing on a scale that yields cost advantages to a large-scale firm. A locally owned pharmacy can be cost competitive with the pharmacy operations of large drugstore chains like Walgreen's or Rite Aid or CVS. Small trucking companies can be cost-competitive with companies that have huge truck fleets. A local pizzeria is not cost-disadvantaged in competing against such chains as Pizza Hut, Domino's, and Papa John's.

- *The scope of the geographic market for the industry's product or service is transitioning from national to global.* A broadening of geographic scope puts companies in more and more countries in the same competitive market arena (as in the apparel industry, where increasing numbers of garment makers across the world are shifting their production operations to low-wage countries and then shipping their goods to retailers in several countries).

- *The technologies embodied in the industry's value chain are exploding into so many new areas and along so many different paths that specialization is essential just to keep abreast in any one area of expertise.* Technology branching accounts for why the manufacture of electronic parts and components is fragmented and why there's fragmentation in prescription drug research.

- *The industry is young and crowded with aspiring contenders.* In most young industries, no firm has yet developed the resource base, competitive capabilities, and market recognition to command a significant market share (as in online e-tailing).

Competitive Conditions in a Fragmented Industry

Competitive rivalry in fragmented industries can vary from moderately strong to fierce. Low barriers tend to make entry of new competitors an ongoing threat. Competition from substitutes may or may not be a major factor. The relatively small size of companies in fragmented industries puts them in a relatively weak position to bargain with powerful suppliers and buyers, although sometimes they can become members of a cooperative formed for the purpose of using their combined leverage to negotiate better sales and purchase terms. In such an environment, the best a firm can expect is to cultivate a loyal customer base and grow a bit faster than the industry average.

Some fragmented industries consolidate over time as growth slows and the market matures. The stiffer competition that accompanies slower growth produces a shake-out of weak, inefficient firms and a greater concentration of larger, more visible sellers. Others remain atomistic because it is inherent in their businesses. And still others remain stuck in a fragmented state because existing firms lack the resources or ingenuity to employ a strategy powerful enough to drive industry consolidation.

Strategy Options for Competing in a Fragmented Industry

In fragmented industries, firms generally have the strategic freedom to pursue broad or narrow market targets and low-cost or differentiation-based competitive advantages. Many different strategic approaches can exist side by side (unless the industry's product is highly standardized or a commodity—like concrete blocks, sand and gravel, or paperboard boxes). Fragmented industry environments are usually ideal for focusing on a well-defined market niche—a particular geographic area or buyer group or product type. In an industry that is fragmented due to highly diverse buyer tastes or requirements, focusing usually offers more competitive advantage potential than trying to come up with a product offering that has broad market appeal.

Some of the most suitable strategy options for competing in a fragmented industry include:

- *Constructing and operating "formula" facilities*—This strategic approach is frequently employed in restaurant and retailing businesses operating at multiple locations. It involves constructing standardized outlets in favorable locations at minimum cost and then operating them cost-effectively. This is a favorite approach for locally owned fast-food enterprises and convenience stores that have multiple locations serving a geographically limited market area. Major fast-food chains like Yum! Brands—the parent of Pizza Hut, Taco Bell, KFC, Long John Silver's, and A&W restaurants—and big convenience store retailers like 7-Eleven have, of course, perfected the formula facilities strategy.

- *Becoming a low-cost operator*—When price competition is intense and profit margins are under constant pressure, companies can stress no-frills operations featuring low overhead, high-productivity/low-cost labor, lean capital budgets, and dedicated pursuit of total operating efficiency. Successful low-cost producers in a fragmented industry can play the price-discounting game and still earn profits above the industry average. Many e-tailers compete on the basis of bargain prices; so do budget motel chains like Econo Lodge, Super 8, and Days Inn.

- *Specializing by product type*—When a fragmented industry's products include a range of styles or services, a strategy to focus on one product or service category can be effective. Some firms in the furniture industry specialize in only one furniture type such as brass beds, rattan and wicker, lawn and garden, or Early American. In auto repair, companies specialize in transmission repair, body work, or speedy oil changes.

- *Specializing by customer type*—A firm can stake out a market niche in a fragmented industry by catering to those customers who are interested in low prices,

Illustration Capsule 8.1

Exertris's Focus Strategy in the Fragmented Exercise Equipment Industry

The exercise equipment industry is largely fragmented from a global perspective—there are hundreds of companies across the world making exercise and fitness products of one kind or another. The window of opportunity for employing a focus strategy is big. In 2001, three fitness enthusiasts in Great Britain came up with a novel way to make exercise more interesting. Their idea was to create an exercise bike equipped with a video game console, a flat-screen display, and an on-board PC that allowed users to play a video game while doing their workout.

After creating a prototype and forming a company called Exertris, the three fitness entrepreneurs approached a product design company for help in turning the prototype into a marketable product. The design company quickly determined that the task was not trivial and required significant additional product development. But the company was enthusiastic about the product and put up the capital to fund the venture as a minority partner. The partners set a goal of having six prototypes ready in time for a major leisure products trade show scheduled to be held in the United Kingdom in several months. The design company assumed responsibility for engineering the product, finding a contract manufacturer, and managing the supply chain; certain other specialty tasks were outsourced. The three cofounders concentrated on developing gaming software where the exerciser's pedaling performance had direct consequences for particular elements of the game; for example, the exerciser had to pedal harder to power a spaceship's weapon systems or move cards around in a game of Solitaire.

The Exertris bike won the "best new product" award at the trade show. It featured four games (Gems, Orbit, Solitaire, and Space Tripper), and new games and features could be added as they were released. Exercisers could play solo or competitively against other people, with the option of handicapping for multiplayer games. The recommended workout included an automatic warm-up and cool-down period. The bike had an armrest, a monitor, and a seat that optimized posture. The LCD display used the latest 3D graphics, and the on-board PC (positioned under the mounting step) used Microsoft Windows XP Embedded and was compatible with Polar heart rate monitors. Earphones were optional, and the game pad and menu control were sweat-proof and easy to clean.

Production by contract manufacturers started soon after the show. In the ensuing months, the Exertris bike was well received by gyms and fitness enthusiasts (for whom the addictive nature of video games broke the monotony and made exercise time fly by). The first interactive fitness arcade featuring 25 linked Exertris Interactive Bikes opened in Great Britain in April 2003. In 2005, the Exertris exercise bike was being marketed online in Great Britain at Amazon's Web site (www.amazon-leisure.co.uk) at a price of £675 (or about $1,150); it could also be purchased at Broadcast Vision Entertainment's online store. Exertris's strategy of focusing on this one niche product in exercise equipment was, however, producing unexpectedly weak results—sales were much slower than initially expected.

Sources: Information posted at www.betterproductdesign.com (accessed October 14, 2005), www.embedded-resources.com (accessed October 14, 2005), and www.broadcastvision.com (accessed December 31, 2005).

unique product attributes, customized features, carefree service, or other extras. A number of restaurants cater to take-out customers; others specialize in fine dining, and still others cater to the sports bar crowd. Bed-and-breakfast inns cater to a particular type of traveler/vacationer (and also focus on a very limited geographic area).

• *Focusing on a limited geographic area*—Even though a firm in a fragmented industry can't win a big share of total industrywide sales, it can still try to dominate a local or regional geographic area. Concentrating company efforts on a limited territory can produce greater operating efficiency, speed delivery and customer services, promote strong brand awareness, and permit saturation advertising, while avoiding the diseconomies of stretching operations out over a much wider area. Several locally owned banks, drugstores, and sporting goods retailers successfully operate multiple locations within a limited geographic area. Numerous local restaurant operators have pursued operating economies by opening anywhere from 4 to 10 restaurants (each with each its own distinctive theme and menu) scattered across a single metropolitan area like Atlanta or Denver or Houston.

Illustration Capsule 8.1 describes how a new start-up company in Great Britain has employed a product niche type of focus strategy in the fragmented exercise equipment industry.

STRATEGIES FOR SUSTAINING RAPID COMPANY GROWTH

Companies that strive to grow their revenues and earnings at double-digit rates year after year (or at rates exceeding the overall market average so that they are growing faster than rivals and gaining market share) generally have to craft *a portfolio of strategic initiatives* covering three horizons:[18]

- *Horizon 1: "Short-jump" strategic initiatives to fortify and extend the company's position in existing businesses*—Short-jump initiatives typically include adding new items to the company's present product line, expanding into new geographic areas where the company does not yet have a market presence, and launching offensives to take market share away from rivals. The objective is to capitalize fully on whatever growth potential exists in the company's present business arenas.

- *Horizon 2: "Medium-jump" strategic initiatives to leverage existing resources and capabilities by entering new businesses with promising growth potential*—Growth companies have to be alert for opportunities to jump into new businesses where there is promise of rapid growth and where their experience, intellectual capital, and technological know-how will prove valuable in gaining rapid market penetration. While Horizon 2 initiatives may take a back seat to Horizon 1 initiatives as long as there is plenty of untapped growth in the company's present businesses, they move to the front as the onset of market maturity dims the company's growth prospects in its present business(es).

- *Horizon 3: "Long-jump" strategic initiatives to plant the seeds for ventures in businesses that do not yet exist*—Long-jump initiatives can entail pumping funds into long-range R&D projects, setting up an internal venture capital fund to invest in promising start-up companies attempting to create the industries of the future, or acquiring a number of small start-up companies experimenting with technologies and product ideas that complement the company's present businesses. Intel, for example, set up a multibillion-dollar venture fund to invest in over 100 different projects and start-up companies, the intent being to plant seeds for Intel's future, broadening its base as a global leader in supplying building blocks for PCs and the worldwide Internet economy. Royal Dutch/ Shell, with over $140 billion in revenues and over 100,000 employees, spent over $20 million on rule-breaking, game-changing ideas put forth by free-thinking employees; the objective was to inject a new spirit of entrepreneurship into the company and sow the seeds of faster growth.[19]

Figure 8.2   **The Three Strategy Horizons for Sustaining Rapid Growth**

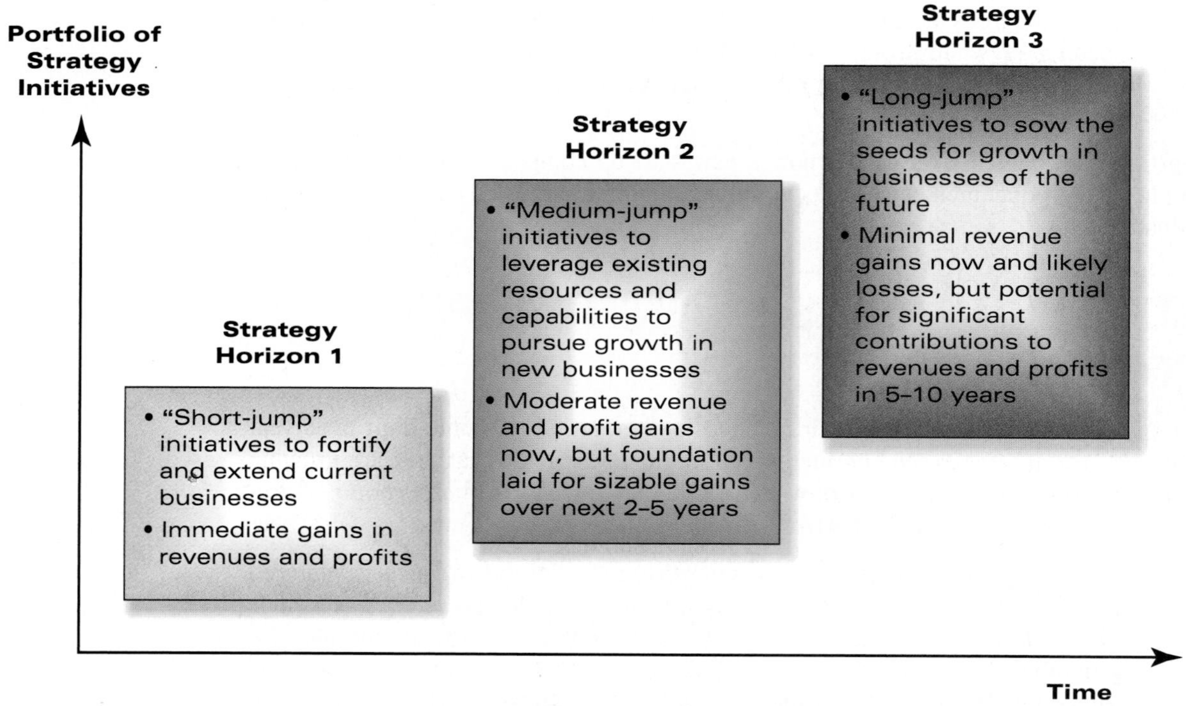

Source: Adapted from Eric D. Beinhocker, "Robust Adaptive Strategies," *Sloan Management Review* 40. No. 3 (Spring 1999), p. 101.

The three strategy horizons are illustrated in Figure 8.2. Managing such a portfolio of strategic initiatives to sustain rapid growth is not easy, however. The tendency of most companies is to focus on Horizon 1 strategies and devote only sporadic and uneven attention to Horizon 2 and 3 strategies. But a recent McKinsey & Company study of 30 of the world's leading growth companies revealed a relatively balanced portfolio of strategic initiatives covering all three horizons. The lesson of successful growth companies is that keeping a company's record of rapid growth intact over the long term entails crafting a diverse population of strategies, ranging from short-jump incremental strategies to grow present businesses to long-jump initiatives with a 5- to 10-year growth payoff horizon.[20] Having a mixture of short-jump, medium-jump, and long-jump initiatives not only increases the odds of hitting a few home runs but also provides some protection against unexpected adversity in present or newly entered businesses.

The Risks of Pursuing Multiple Strategy Horizons

There are, of course, risks to pursuing a diverse strategy portfolio aimed at sustained growth. A company cannot, of course, place bets on every opportunity that appears on its radar screen, lest it stretch its resources too thin. And medium-jump and long-jump initiatives can cause a company to stray far from its core competencies and end up trying to compete in businesses for which it is ill-suited. Moreover, it can be difficult to achieve competitive advantage in medium- and long-jump product families and businesses that prove not to mesh well with a company's present businesses and resource strengths. The payoffs of long-jump initiatives often prove elusive; not all of the seeds a company sows will bear fruit, and only a few may evolve into truly significant contributors to the company's revenue and profit growth. The losses from those long-jump ventures that do not take root may significantly erode the gains from those that do, resulting in disappointingly modest gains in overall profits.

STRATEGIES FOR INDUSTRY LEADERS

The competitive positions of industry leaders normally range from "stronger than average" to "powerful." Leaders typically are well known, and strongly entrenched leaders have proven strategies (keyed either to low-cost leadership or to differentiation). Some of the best-known industry leaders are Anheuser-Busch (beer), Starbucks (coffee drinks), Microsoft (computer software), Callaway (golf clubs), McDonald's (fast food), Procter & Gamble (laundry detergents and soaps), Campbell's (canned soups), Gerber (baby food), Hewlett-Packard (printers), Sony (video game consoles), Black & Decker (power tools), Intel (semiconductors and chip sets), Wal-Mart and Carrefour (discount retailing), Amazon.com (online shopping), eBay (online auctions), Apple (MP3 players), and Ocean Spray (cranberries).

The main strategic concern for a leader revolves around how to defend and strengthen its leadership position, perhaps becoming the dominant leader as opposed to just a leader. However, the pursuit of industry leadership and large market share is primarily important because of the competitive advantage and profitability that accrue to being the industry's biggest company. Three contrasting strategic postures are open to industry leaders:[21]

1. *Stay-on-the-offensive strategy*—The central goal of a stay-on-the-offensive strategy is to be a first-mover and a proactive market leader.[22] It rests on the principle that playing hardball, moving early and frequently, and forcing rivals into a catch-up mode is the surest path to industry prominence and potential market dominance—as the saying goes, the best defense is a good offense. Furthermore, *an offensive-minded industry leader relentlessly concentrates on achieving a competitive advantage over rivals and then widening this advantage over time to achieve extreme competitive advantage.*[23] Being the industry standard setter thus requires being impatient with the status quo, seizing the initiative, and pioneering continuous improvement and innovation—this can mean being first-to-market with technological improvements, new or better products, more attractive performance features, quality enhancements, or customer service improvements. It can mean aggressively seeking out ways to cut operating costs, ways to establish competitive capabilities that rivals cannot match, or ways to make it easier and less costly for potential customers to switch their purchases from runner-up firms to the leader's own products. It can mean aggressively attacking the profit sanctuaries of important rivals, perhaps with bursts of advertising or price-cutting or approaching its customers with special deals.[24]

> The governing principle underlying an industry leader's use of a stay-on-the-offensive strategy is to be an action-oriented first-mover, impatient with the status quo.

A low-cost leader must set the pace for cost reduction, and a differentiator must constantly initiate new ways to keep its product set apart from the brands of imitative rivals in order to be the standard against which rivals' products are judged. The array of options for a potent stay-on-the-offensive strategy can also include initiatives to expand overall industry demand—spurring the creation of new families of products, making the product more suitable for consumers in emerging-country markets, discovering new uses for the product, attracting new users of the product, and promoting more frequent use.

Illustration Capsule 8.2

ESPN's Strategy to Dominate Sports Entertainment

Via a series of offensive initiatives over the past 10 years, ESPN has parlayed its cable TV sports programming franchise into a dominating and pervasive general store of sports entertainment. The thrust of ESPN's strategy has been to stay on the offensive by (1) continually enhancing its program offerings and (2) extending the ESPN brand into a host of cutting-edge sports businesses. Examples of ESPN's enhanced product offering include the ESPY Awards for top achievements in sports, the X Games (an annual extreme sports competition for both winter and summer sports), the addition of *Monday Night Football* (starting in 2006), making new movies to show on ESPN, and producing its own shows (such as *ESPN Hollywood, Cold Pizza,* and *Bound for Glory*). The appeal of ESPN's programming was so powerful that ESPN was able to charge cable operators an estimated $2.80 per subscriber per month—nearly twice as much as the next most popular cable channel (CNN, for instance, was only able to command a monthly fee of roughly $0.40 per subscriber).

But the most important element of ESPN's strategic offensive had been to start up a series of new ESPN-branded businesses—all of which were brainstormed by ESPN's entrepreneurially talented management team. The company's brand extension offensive has produced nine TV channels (the most prominent of which are ESPN, ESPN2, ESPN Classic, ESPNews, and ESPN Desportes); the ESPN radio network, with 700 affiliate stations; ESPN. com (which in 2005 attracted some 16 million unique visitors monthly to view its bazaar of wide-ranging sports stories and information); *ESPN: The Magazine* (with a fast-growing base of 1.8 million subscribers that could in time overtake the barely growing 3.3 million subscriber

base of longtime leader *Sports Illustrated*); ESPN Motion (an online video service); ESPN360 (which offers sports information and video-clip programming tailored for broadband providers—it had 5 million subscribers in 2005 and was available from 14 broadband providers); Mobile ESPN (an ESPN-branded cell phone service provided in partnership with Sprint Nextel); ESPN Zones (nine sports-themed restaurants in various cities); ESPN branded video games (video game developer Electronic Arts has 15-year licensing rights to use the ESPN name for a series of sports-related games), and a business unit that distributes ESPN sports programming in 11 languages in over 180 countries.

In 2005, the empire of ESPN consisted of some 50 different businesses that generated annual revenues in excess of $5 billion and hefty annual operating profits of about $2 billion—about 40 percent of its revenues came from advertising and 60 percent from subscriptions and distribution fees. ESPN, a division of Disney, was one of Disney's most profitable and fastest-growing operations (Disney was also the parent of ABC Broadcasting).

So far, ESPN's stay-a-step-ahead strategy had left lesser rivals in the dust. But Comcast, the largest U.S. cable operator, with 22 million subscribers, was maneuvering to create its own cable TV sports channel; Comcast already owned the Philadelphia 76ers, the Philadelphia Flyers, and a collection of regional sports networks in cities from Philadelphia to Chicago to Los Angeles. And Rupert Murdoch's expansion-minded News Corporation, a worldwide media conglomerate whose many businesses included Fox Broadcasting and DIRECTV, was said to be looking at melding its 15 regional U.S. sports channels into a national sports channel.

Source: Developed from information in Tom Lowry, "ESPN the Zone," *BusinessWeek,* October 17, 2005, pp. 66–78.

A stay-on-the-offensive strategy cannot be considered successful unless it results in growing sales and revenues faster than the industry as a whole and wresting market share from rivals—a leader whose sales growth is only 5 percent in a market growing at 8 percent is losing ground to some of its competitors. Only if an industry's leader's market share is already so dominant that it presents a threat of antitrust action (a market share under 60 percent is usually safe) should an industry leader deliberately back away from aggressively pursuing market share gains.

Illustration Capsule 8.2 describes ESPN's stay-on-the-offensive strategy to dominate the sports entertainment business.

   2. *Fortify-and-defend strategy*—The essence of "fortify and defend" is to make it harder for challengers to gain ground and for new firms to enter. The goals of a strong defense are to hold on to the present market share, strengthen current market position, and protect whatever competitive advantage the firm has. Specific defensive actions can include:

- Attempting to raise the competitive ante for challengers and new entrants via increased spending for advertising, higher levels of customer service, and bigger R&D outlays.
- Introducing more product versions or brands to match the product attributes that challenger brands have or to fill vacant niches that competitors could slip into.
- Adding personalized services and other extras that boost customer loyalty and make it harder or more costly for customers to switch to rival products.
- Keeping prices reasonable and quality attractive.
- Building new capacity ahead of market demand to discourage smaller competitors from adding capacity of their own.
- Investing enough to remain cost-competitive and technologically progressive.
- Patenting the feasible alternative technologies.
- Signing exclusive contracts with the best suppliers and dealer/distributors.

A fortify-and-defend strategy best suits firms that have already achieved industry dominance and don't wish to risk antitrust action. It is also well suited to situations where a firm wishes to milk its present position for profits and cash flow because the industry's prospects for growth are low or because further gains in market share do not appear profitable enough to go after. But a fortify-and-defend strategy always entails trying to grow as fast as the market as a whole (to stave off market-share slippage) and requires reinvesting enough capital in the business to protect the leader's ability to compete.

3. *Muscle-flexing strategy*—Here a dominant leader plays competitive hardball (presumably in an ethical and competitively legal manner) when smaller rivals rock the boat with price cuts or mount new market offensives that directly threaten its position. Specific responses can include quickly matching and perhaps exceeding challengers' price cuts, using large promotional campaigns to counter challengers' moves to gain market share, and offering better deals to their major customers. Dominant leaders may also court distributors assiduously to dissuade them from carrying rivals' products, provide salespersons with documented information about the weaknesses of competing products, or try to fill any vacant positions in their own firms by making attractive offers to the better executives of rivals that get out of line.

The leader may also use various arm-twisting tactics to pressure present customers not to use the products of rivals. This can range from simply forcefully communicating its displeasure should customers opt to use the products of rivals to pushing them to agree to exclusive arrangements in return for better prices to charging them a higher price if they use any competitors' products. As a final resort, a leader may grant certain customers special discounts or preferred treatment if they do not use any products of rivals.

The obvious risks of a muscle-flexing strategy are running afoul of laws prohibiting monopoly practices and unfair competition and using bullying tactics that arouse adverse public opinion. Microsoft paid Real Networks $460 million in 2005 to resolve all of Real Network's antitrust complaints and settle a long-standing feud over Microsoft's repeated bullying of PC makers to include Windows Media Player instead of Real's media player as standard installed software on their PCs. In 2005 AMD filed an antitrust suit against Intel, claiming that Intel unfairly and monopolistically coerced 38 named companies on three continents in efforts to get them to use Intel chips instead of AMD chips in the computer products they manufactured or marketed. Consequently, a company that throws its weight around to protect and enhance its market dominance has got to be judicious, lest it cross the line from allowable muscle-flexing to unethical or illegal competitive bullying.

STRATEGIES FOR RUNNER-UP FIRMS

Runner-up, or second-tier, firms have smaller market shares than first-tier industry leaders. Some runner-up firms are often advancing market challengers, employing offensive strategies to gain market share and build a stronger market position. Other runner-up competitors are focusers, seeking to improve their lot by concentrating their attention on serving a limited portion of the market. There are, of course, always a number of firms in any industry that are destined to be perennial runners-up, either because they are content to follow the trendsetting moves of the market leaders or because they lack the resources and competitive strengths to do much better in the marketplace than they are already doing. But it is erroneous to view runner-up firms as inherently less profitable or unable to hold their own against the biggest firms. Many small and medium-sized firms earn healthy profits and enjoy good reputations with customers.

Obstacles for Firms with Small Market Shares

There are times when runner-up companies face significant hurdles in contending for market leadership. In industries where big size is definitely a key success factor, firms with small market shares have four obstacles to overcome: (1) less access to economies of scale in manufacturing, distribution, or marketing and sales promotion; (2) difficulty in gaining customer recognition (since the products and brands of the market leaders are much better known); (3) less money to spend on mass-media advertising; and (4) limited funds for capital expansion or making acquisitions.[25] Some runner-up companies may be able to surmount these obstacles. Others may not. When significant scale economies give large-volume competitors a dominating cost advantage, small-share firms have only two viable strategic options: initiate offensive moves aimed at building sufficient sales volume to approach the scale economies and lower unit costs enjoyed by larger rivals or withdraw from the business (gradually or quickly) because of the inability to achieve low enough costs to compete effectively against the market leaders.

Offensive Strategies to Build Market Share

A runner-up company desirous of closing in on the market leaders has to make some waves in the marketplace if it wants to make big market share gains—this means coming up with distinctive strategy elements that set it apart from rivals and draw buyer attention. If a challenger has a 5 percent market share and needs a 15 to 20 percent share to contend for leadership and earn attractive profits, it requires a more creative approach to competing than just "Try harder" or "Follow in the footsteps of current industry leaders." Rarely can a runner-up significantly improve its competitive position by imitating the strategies of leading firms. A cardinal rule in offensive strategy is to avoid attacking a leader head-on with an imitative strategy, regardless of the resources and staying power an underdog may have.[26] What an aspiring challenger really needs is a strategy aimed at building a competitive advantage of its own (and certainly a strategy capable of quickly eliminating any important competitive disadvantages).

The best "mover-and-shaker" offensives for a second-tier challenger aiming to join the first-tier ranks usually involve one of the following five approaches:

1. Making a series of acquisitions of smaller rivals to greatly expand the company's market reach and market presence. *Growth via acquisition* is perhaps the most frequently used strategy employed by ambitious runner-up companies to form an enterprise that has greater competitive strength and a larger share of the overall market. For an enterprise to succeed with this strategic approach, senior management must be skilled in quickly assimilating the operations of the acquired companies, eliminating duplication and overlap, generating efficiencies and cost savings, and structuring the combined resources in ways that create substantially stronger competitive capabilities. Many banks and public accounting firms owe their growth during the past decade to acquisition of smaller regional and local banks. Likewise, a number of book publishers have grown by acquiring small publishers, and public accounting firms have grown by acquiring lesser-sized accounting firms with attractive client lists.

2. Finding innovative ways to dramatically drive down costs and then using the attraction of lower prices to win customers from higher-cost, higher-priced rivals. This is a necessary offensive move when a runner-up company has higher costs than larger-scale enterprises (either because the latter possess scale economies or have benefited from experience/learning curve effects). A challenger firm can pursue aggressive cost reduction by eliminating marginal activities from its value chain, streamlining supply chain relationships, improving internal operating efficiency, using various e-commerce techniques, and merging with or acquiring rival firms to achieve the size needed to capture greater scale economies.

3. Crafting an attractive differentiation strategy based on premium quality, technological superiority, outstanding customer service, rapid product innovation, or convenient online shopping options.

4. Pioneering a leapfrog technological breakthrough—an attractive option if an important technological breakthrough is within a challenger's reach and rivals are not close behind.

5. Being first-to-market with new or better products and building a reputation for product leadership. A strategy of product innovation has appeal if the runner-up company possesses the necessary resources—cutting-edge R&D capability and organizational agility in speeding new products to market.

Other possible, but likely less effective, offensive strategy options include (1) outmaneuvering slow-to-change market leaders in adapting to evolving market conditions and customer expectations and (2) forging productive strategic alliances with key distributors, dealers, or marketers of complementary products.

Without a potent offensive strategy to capture added market share, runner-up companies have to patiently nibble away at the lead of market leaders and build sales at a moderate pace over time.

Other Strategic Approaches for Runner-Up Companies

There are five other strategies that runner-up companies can employ.[27] While none of the five is likely to move a company from second-tier to first-tier status, all are capable of producing attractive profits and returns for shareholders.

Vacant-Niche Strategy   A version of a focused strategy, the vacant-niche strategy involves concentrating on specific customer groups or end-use applications that market leaders have bypassed or neglected. An ideal vacant niche is of sufficient size and scope to be profitable, has some growth potential, is well suited to a firm's own capabilities, and for one reason or another is hard for leading firms to serve. Two examples where vacant-niche strategies have worked successfully are (1) regional commuter airlines serving cities with too few passengers to fill the large jets flown by major airlines and (2) health-food producers (like Health Valley, Hain, and Tree of Life) that cater to local health-food stores—a market segment that until recently has been given little attention by such leading companies as Kraft, Nestlé, and Unilever.

Specialist Strategy   A specialist firm trains its competitive effort on one technology, product or product family, end use, or market segment (often one in which buyers have special needs). The aim is to train the company's resource strengths and capabilities on building competitive advantage through leadership in a specific area. Smaller companies that successfully use this focused strategy include Formby's (a specialist in stains and finishes for wood furniture, especially refinishing); Blue Diamond (a California-based grower and marketer of almonds); Cuddledown (a specialty producer and retailer of down and synthetic comforters, featherbeds, and other bedding products); and American Tobacco (a leader in chewing tobacco and snuff). Many companies in high-tech industries concentrate their energies on being the clear leader in a particular technological niche; their competitive advantage is superior technological depth, technical expertise that is highly valued by customers, and the capability to consistently beat out rivals in pioneering technological advances.

Superior Product Strategy   The approach here is to use a differentiation-based focused strategy keyed to superior product quality or unique attributes. Sales and marketing efforts are aimed directly at quality-conscious and performance-oriented buyers. Fine craftsmanship, prestige quality, frequent product innovations, and/or close contact with customers to solicit their input in developing a better product usually undergird the superior product approach. Some examples include Samuel Adams in beer, Tiffany in diamonds and jewelry, Chicago Cutlery in premium-quality kitchen knives, Baccarat in fine crystal, Cannondale in mountain bikes, Bally in shoes, and Patagonia in apparel for outdoor recreation enthusiasts.

Distinctive-Image Strategy   Some runner-up companies build their strategies around ways to make themselves stand out from competitors. A variety of distinctive-image strategies can be used: building a reputation for charging the lowest prices (Dollar General), providing high-end quality at a good price (Orvis, Lands' End, and L. L. Bean), going all out to give superior customer service (Four Seasons hotels), incorporating unique product attributes (Omega-3 enriched eggs), making a product with distinctive styling (General Motors' Hummer), or devising unusually creative advertising (AFLAC's duck ads on TV). Other examples include Dr Pepper's strategy in calling attention to its distinctive taste, Apple Computer's making it easier and more interesting for people to use its Macintosh PCs, and Mary Kay Cosmetics' distinctive use of the color pink.

Content Follower Strategy   Content followers deliberately refrain from initiating trendsetting strategic moves and from aggressive attempts to steal customers away from the leaders. Followers prefer approaches that will not provoke competitive retaliation, often opting for focus and differentiation strategies that keep them out of the leaders' paths. They react and respond rather than initiate and challenge. They prefer defense to offense. And they rarely get out of line with the leaders on price. They are content to simply maintain their market position, albeit sometimes struggling to do so. Followers have no urgent strategic questions to confront beyond "What strategic changes are the leaders initiating and what do we need to do to follow along and maintain our present position?" The marketers of private-label products tend to be followers, imitating many of the newly introduced features of name brand products and content to sell to price-conscious buyers at prices modestly below those of well-known brands.

STRATEGIES FOR WEAK AND CRISIS-RIDDEN BUSINESSES

A firm in an also-ran or declining competitive position has four basic strategic options. If it can come up with the financial resources, it can launch a turnaround strategy keyed either to "low-cost" or "new" differentiation themes, pouring enough money and talent into the effort to move up a notch or two in the industry rankings and become a respectable market contender within five years or so. It can employ a fortify-and-defend strategy, using variations of its present strategy and fighting hard to keep sales, market share, profitability, and competitive position at current levels. It can opt for a fast-exit strategy and get out of the business, either by selling out to another firm or by closing down operations if a buyer cannot be found. Or it can employ an end-game or slow-exit strategy, keeping reinvestment to a bare-bones minimum and taking actions to maximize short-term cash flows in preparation for orderly market withdrawal.

Turnaround Strategies for Businesses in Crisis

Turnaround strategies are needed when a business worth rescuing goes into crisis. The objective is to arrest and reverse the sources of competitive and financial weakness as quickly as possible. Management's first task in formulating a suitable turnaround strategy is to diagnose what lies at the root of poor performance. Is it an unexpected downturn in sales brought on by a weak economy? An ill-chosen competitive strategy? Poor execution of an otherwise viable strategy? High operating costs? Important resource deficiencies? An overload of debt? The next task is to decide whether the business can be saved or whether the situation is hopeless. Understanding what is wrong with the business and how serious its strategic problems are is essential because different diagnoses lead to different turnaround strategies.

Some of the most common causes of business trouble are taking on too much debt, overestimating the potential for sales growth, ignoring the profit-depressing effects of an overly aggressive effort to "buy" market share with deep price cuts, being burdened with heavy fixed costs because weak sales don't permit near-full capacity utilization, betting on R&D efforts but failing to come up with effective innovations, betting on technological long shots, being too optimistic about the ability to penetrate new markets, making frequent changes in strategy (because the previous strategy didn't work out), and being overpowered by more successful rivals. Curing these kinds of problems and achieving a successful business turnaround can involve any of the following actions:

- Selling off assets to raise cash to save the remaining part of the business.
- Revising the existing strategy.
- Launching efforts to boost revenues.

- Pursuing cost reduction.
- Using a combination of these efforts.

Selling Off Assets   Asset-reduction strategies are essential when cash flow is a critical consideration and when the most practical ways to generate cash are (1) through sale of some of the firm's assets (plant and equipment, land, patents, inventories, or profitable subsidiaries) and (2) through retrenchment (pruning of marginal products from the product line, closing or selling older plants, reducing the workforce, withdrawing from outlying markets, cutting back customer service). Sometimes crisis-ridden companies sell off assets not so much to unload losing operations as to raise funds to save and strengthen the remaining business activities. In such cases, the choice is usually to dispose of noncore business assets to support strategy renewal in the firm's core businesses.

Strategy Revision   When weak performance is caused by bad strategy, the task of strategy overhaul can proceed along any of several paths: (1) shifting to a new competitive approach to rebuild the firm's market position; (2) overhauling internal operations and functional-area strategies to better support the same overall business strategy; (3) merging with another firm in the industry and forging a new strategy keyed to the newly merged firm's strengths; and (4) retrenching into a reduced core of products and customers more closely matched to the firm's strengths. The most appealing path depends on prevailing industry conditions, the firm's particular strengths and weaknesses, its competitive capabilities vis-à-vis rival firms, and the severity of the crisis. A situation analysis of the industry, the major competitors, and the firm's own competitive position is a prerequisite for action. As a rule, successful strategy revision must be tied to the ailing firm's strengths and near-term competitive capabilities and directed at its best market opportunities.

Boosting Revenues   Revenue-increasing turnaround efforts aim at generating increased sales volume. The chief revenue-building options include price cuts, increased advertising, a bigger sales force, added customer services, and quickly achieved product improvements. Attempts to increase revenues and sales volumes are necessary (1) when there is little or no room in the operating budget to cut expenses and still break even, and (2) when the key to restoring profitability is increased use of existing capacity. If buyers are not especially price-sensitive (because many are strongly attached to various differentiating features in the company's product offering), the quickest way to boost short-term revenues may be to raise prices rather than opt for volume-building price cuts. A price increase in the 2–4 percent range may well be feasible if the company's prices are already below those of key rivals.

Cutting Costs   Cost-reducing turnaround strategies work best when an ailing firm's value chain and cost structure are flexible enough to permit radical surgery, when operating inefficiencies are identifiable and readily correctable, when the firm's costs are obviously bloated, and when the firm is relatively close to its break-even point. Accompanying a general belt-tightening can be an increased emphasis on paring administrative overheads, elimination of nonessential and low-value-added activities in the firm's value chain, modernization of existing plant and equipment to gain greater productivity, delay of nonessential capital expenditures, and debt restructuring to reduce interest costs and stretch out repayments.

Illustration Capsule 8.3

Sony's Turnaround Strategy—Will It Work?

Electronics was once Sony's star business, but Sony's electronics business was a huge money-loser in 2003–2004, pushing the company's stock price down about 65 percent. Once the clear leader in top-quality TVs, in 2005 Sony lagged miserably behind Samsung, Panasonic, and Sharp in popular flat-panel LCD and plasma TVs, where sales were growing fastest. Apple Computer's iPod players had stolen the limelight in the handheld music market, where Sony's Walkman had long ruled.

In the fall of 2005, Sony management announced a turnaround strategy. Howard Stringer, a dual American and British citizen who was named Sony's CEO in early 2005 and was the first foreigner ever to head Sony, unveiled a plan centered on cutting 10,000 jobs (about 6 percent of Sony's workforce), closing 11 of Sony's 65 manufacturing plants, and shrinking or eliminating 15 unprofitable electronics operations by March 2008 (the unprofitable operations were not identified). These initiatives were projected to reduce costs by $1.8 billion. In addition to the cost cuts, Sony said it would focus on growing its sales of "champion products" like the next-generation Sony PlayStation 3 video game console, a newly introduced line of Bravia LCD TVs, and Walkman MP3 music players.

Analysts were not impressed by the turnaround plan. Standard & Poor's cut its credit rating for Sony, citing doubts about the company's turnaround strategy and forecasting "substantially" lower profitability and cash flow in fiscal 2005. Moody's put Sony on its watch list for a credit rating downgrade. Other analysts said Stringer's strategy lacked vision and creativity because it was in the same mold as most corporate streamlining efforts.

Sources: Company press releases; Yuri Kageyama, "Sony Announcing Turnaround Strategy," www.yahoo.com (accessed October 20, 2005); *Mainichi Daily News*, October 14, 2005 (accessed on Google News, October 20, 2005); and "Sony to Cut 10,000 Jobs," www.cnn.com (accessed October 20, 2005).

Combination Efforts   Combination turnaround strategies are usually essential in grim situations that require fast action on a broad front. Likewise, combination actions frequently come into play when new managers are brought in and given a free hand to make whatever changes they see fit. The tougher the problems, the more likely it is that the solutions will involve multiple strategic initiatives—see the story of turnaround efforts at Sony in Illustration Capsule 8.3.

The Chances of a Successful Turnaround Are Not High   Turnaround efforts tend to be high-risk undertakings; some return a company to good profitability, but most don't. A landmark study of 64 companies found no successful turnarounds among the most troubled companies in eight basic industries.[28] Many of the troubled businesses waited too long to begin a turnaround. Others found themselves short of both the cash and entrepreneurial talent needed to compete in a slow-growth industry characterized by a fierce battle for market share. Better-positioned rivals simply proved too strong to defeat in a long, head-to-head contest. Even when successful, turnaround may involve numerous attempts and management changes before long-term competitive viability and profitability are finally restored. A recent study found that troubled companies that did nothing and elected to wait out hard times had only a 10 percent chance of recovery.[29] This same study also found that, of the companies studied, the chances of recovery were boosted 190 percent if the turnaround strategy involved buying assets that strengthened the company's business in its core markets; companies that both bought assets or companies in their core markets while selling off noncore assets increased their chances of recovery by 250 percent.

Harvest Strategies for Weak Businesses

When a struggling company's chances of pulling off a successful turnaround are poor, the wisest option may be to forget about trying to restore the company's competitiveness and profitability and, instead employ a *harvesting strategy* that aims at generating the largest possible cash flows from the company's operations for as long as possible. A losing effort to transform a competitively weak company into a viable market contender has little appeal when there are opportunities to generate potentially sizable amounts of cash by running the business in a manner calculated to either maintain the status quo or even let the business slowly deteriorate over a long period.

As is the case with a slow-exit strategy, a harvesting strategy entails trimming operating expenses to the bone and spending the minimum amount on capital projects to keep the business going. Internal cash flow becomes the key measure of how well the company is performing, and top priority is given to cash-generating actions. Thus, advertising and promotional costs are kept at minimal levels; personnel who leave for jobs elsewhere or retire may not be replaced; and maintenance is performed with an eye toward stretching the life of existing facilities and equipment. Even though a harvesting strategy is likely to lead to a gradual decline in the company's business over time, the ability to harvest sizable amounts of cash in the interim makes such an outcome tolerable.

> The overriding objective of a harvesting strategy is to maximize short-term cash flows from operations.

The Conditions That Make a Harvesting Strategy Attractive   A strategy of harvesting the cash flows from a weak business is a reasonable option in the following circumstances:[30]

1. *When industry demand is stagnant or declining and there's little hope that either market conditions will improve*—The growing popularity of digital cameras has forever doomed market demand for camera film.

2. *When rejuvenating the business would be too costly or at best marginally profitable*—A struggling provider of dial-up Internet access is likely to realize more benefit from harvesting than from a losing effort to grow its business in the face of the unstoppable shift to high-speed broadband service.

3. *When trying to maintain or grow the company's present sales is becoming increasingly costly*—A money-losing producer of pipe tobacco and cigars is unlikely to make market headway in gaining sales and market share against the top-tier producers (which have more resources to compete for the business that is still available).

4. *When reduced levels of competitive effort will not trigger an immediate or rapid falloff in sales*—the makers of corded telephones will not likely experience much of a decline in sales if they spend all of their R&D and marketing budgets on wireless phone systems.

5. *When the enterprise can redeploy the freed resources in higher-opportunity areas*—The makers of food products with "bad-for-you" ingredients (saturated fats, high transfats, and sugar) are better off devoting their resources to the development, production, and sale of "good-for-you" products (those with no transfats, more fiber, and good types of carbohydrates).

6. *When the business is not a crucial or core component of a diversified company's overall lineup of businesses*—Harvesting a sideline business and perhaps hastening

its decay is strategically preferable to harvesting a mainline or core business (where even a gradual decline may not be a very attractive outcome).

The more of these six conditions that are present, the more ideal the business is for harvesting.

Liquidation: The Strategy of Last Resort

Sometimes a business in crisis is too far gone to be salvaged and presents insufficient harvesting potential to be interesting. Closing down a crisis-ridden business and liquidating its assets is sometimes the best and wisest strategy. But it is also the most unpleasant and painful strategic alternative due to the hardships of job eliminations and the economic effects of business closings on local communities. Nonetheless, in hopeless situations, an early liquidation effort usually serves owner-stockholder interests better than an inevitable bankruptcy. Prolonging the pursuit of a lost cause further erodes an organization's resources and leaves less to salvage, not to mention the added stress and potential career impairment for all the people involved. The problem, of course, is differentiating between when a turnaround is achievable and when it isn't. It is easy for owners or managers to let their emotions and pride overcome sound judgment when a business gets in such deep trouble that a successful turnaround is remote.

10 COMMANDMENTS FOR CRAFTING SUCCESSFUL BUSINESS STRATEGIES

Company experiences over the years prove again and again that disastrous strategies can be avoided by adhering to good strategy-making principles. We've distilled the lessons learned from the strategic mistakes companies most often make into 10 commandments that serve as useful guides for developing sound strategies:

1. *Place top priority on crafting and executing strategic moves that enhance the company's competitive position for the long term.* The glory of meeting one quarter's or one year's financial performance targets quickly fades, but an ever-stronger competitive position pays off year after year. Shareholders are never well served by managers who let short-term financial performance considerations rule out strategic initiatives that will meaningfully bolster the company's longer-term competitive position and competitive strength. The best way to ensure a company's long-term profitability is with a strategy that strengthens the company's long-term competitiveness and market position.

2. *Be prompt in adapting to changing market conditions, unmet customer needs, buyer wishes for something better, emerging technological alternatives, and new initiatives of competitors.* Responding late or with too little often puts a company in the precarious position of having to play catch-up. While pursuit of a consistent strategy has its virtues, adapting strategy to changing circumstances is normal and necessary. Moreover, long-term strategic commitments to achieve top quality or lowest cost should be interpreted relative to competitors' products as well as customers' needs and expectations; the company should avoid singlemindedly striving to make the absolute highest-quality or lowest-cost product no matter what.

3. *Invest in creating a sustainable competitive advantage.* Having a competitive edge over rivals is the single most dependable contributor to above-average profitability.

As a general rule, a company must play aggressive offense to build competitive advantage and aggressive defense to protect it.

4. *Avoid strategies capable of succeeding only in the most optimistic circumstances.* Expect competitors to employ countermeasures and expect times of unfavorable market conditions. A good strategy works reasonably well and produces tolerable results even in the worst of times.

5. *Consider that attacking competitive weakness is usually more profitable and less risky than attacking competitive strength.* Attacking capable, resourceful rivals is likely to fail unless the attacker has deep financial pockets and a solid basis for competitive advantage despite the strengths of the competitor being attacked.

6. *Strive to open up very meaningful gaps in quality or service or performance features when pursuing a differentiation strategy.* Tiny differences between rivals' product offerings may not be visible or important to buyers.

7. *Be wary of cutting prices without an established cost advantage.* Price cuts run the risk that rivals will retaliate with matching or deeper price cuts of their own. The best chance for remaining profitable if the price-cutting contest turns into a price war is to have lower costs than rivals.

8. *Don't underestimate the reactions and the commitment of rival firms.* Rivals are most dangerous when they are pushed into a corner and their well-being is threatened.

9. *Avoid stuck-in-the-middle strategies that represent compromises between lower costs and greater differentiation and between broad and narrow market appeal.* Compromise strategies rarely produce sustainable competitive advantage or a distinctive competitive position—a well-executed best-cost producer strategy is the only exception in which a compromise between low cost and differentiation succeeds. Companies with compromise strategies most usually end up with average costs, an average product, an average reputation, and *no distinctive image in the marketplace*. Lacking any strategy element that causes them to stand out in the minds of buyers, companies with compromise strategies are destined for a middle-of-the-pack industry ranking, with little prospect of ever becoming an industry leader.

10. *Be judicious in employing aggressive moves to wrest market share away from rivals often provoke retaliation in the form of escalating marketing and sales promotion, a furious race to be first-to-market with next-version products or a price war—to the detriment of everyone's profits.* Aggressive moves to capture a bigger market share invite cutthroat competition, especially when many industry members, plagued with high inventories and excess production capacity, are also scrambling for additional sales.

Key Points

The lessons of this chapter are that (1) some strategic options are better suited to certain specific industry and competitive environments than others and (2) some strategic options are better suited to certain specific company situations than others. Crafting a strategy tightly matched to a company's situation thus involves being alert to which strategy alternatives are likely to work well and which alternatives are unlikely to work well. Specifically:

1. What basic type of industry environment (emerging, rapid-growth, mature/slow-growth, stagnant/declining, high-velocity/turbulent, fragmented) does the company operate in? What strategic options and strategic postures are usually best suited to this generic type of environment?

2. What position does the firm have in the industry (leader, runner-up, or weak/distressed)? Given this position, which strategic options merit strong consideration and which options should definitely be ruled out?

In addition, creating a tight strategy-situation fit entails considering all the external and internal situational factors discussed in Chapters 3 and 4 and then revising the list of strategy options accordingly to take account of competitive conditions, industry driving forces, the expected moves of rivals, and the company's own competitive strengths and weaknesses. Listing the pros and cons of the candidate strategies is nearly always a helpful step. In weeding out the least attractive strategic alternatives and weighing the pros and cons of the most attractive ones, the answers to four questions often help point to the best course of action:

1. What kind of competitive edge can the company realistically achieve, given its resource strengths, competencies, and competitive capabilities? Is the company in a position to lead industry change and set the rules by which rivals must compete?

2. Which strategy alternative best addresses all the issues and problems the firm confronts.

3. Are any rivals particularly vulnerable and, if so, what sort of an offensive will it take to capitalize on these vulnerabilities? Will rivals counterattack? What can be done to blunt their efforts?

4. Are any defensive actions needed to protect against rivals' likely moves or other external threats to the company's future profitability?

In picking and choosing among the menu of strategic options, there are four pitfalls to avoid:

1. Designing an overly ambitious strategic plan—one that overtaxes the company's resources and capabilities.

2. Selecting a strategy that represents a radical departure from or abandonment of the cornerstones of the company's prior success—a radical strategy change need not be rejected automatically, but it should be pursued only after careful risk assessment.

3. Choosing a strategy that goes against the grain of the organization's culture.

4. Being unwilling to commit wholeheartedly to one of the five competitive strategies—picking and choosing features of the different strategies usually produces so many compromises between low cost, best cost, differentiation, and focusing that the company fails to achieve any kind of advantage and ends up stuck in the middle.

Table 8.1 provides a generic format for outlining a strategic action plan for a single-business enterprise. It contains all of the pieces of a comprehensive strategic action plan that we discussed at various places in these first eight chapters.

Table 8.1   **Sample Format for a Strategic Action Plan**

1. Strategic Vision and Mission	**5.** Supporting Functional Strategies
	• Production
2. Strategic Objectives	
• Short-term	• Marketing/sales
• Long-term	• Finance
3. Financial Objectives	• Personnel/human resources
• Short-term	
	• Other
• Long-term	
	6. Recommended Actions to Improve Company Performance
4. Overall Business Strategy	• Immediate
	• Longer-range

Exercises

1. Listed below are 10 industries. Classify each one as (*a*) emerging, (*b*) rapid-growth, (*c*) mature/slow-growth, (*d*) stagnant/declining, (*e*) high-velocity/turbulent, and (*f*) fragmented. Do research on the Internet, if needed, to locate information on industry conditions and reach a conclusion on what classification to assign each of the following:

    a. Exercise and fitness industry.

    b. Dry-cleaning industry.

    c. Poultry industry.

    d. Camera film and film-developing industry.

    e. Wine, beer, and liquor retailing.

    f. Watch industry.

    g. Cell-phone industry.

    h. Recorded music industry (DVDs, CDs, tapes).

    i. Computer software industry.

    j. Newspaper industry.

2. Toyota overtook Ford Motor Company in 2003 to become the world's second-largest maker of motor vehicles, behind General Motors. Toyota is widely regarded as having aspirations to overtake General Motors as the global leader in motor vehicles within the next 10 years. Do research on the Internet or in the library to determine what strategy General Motors is pursuing to maintain its status as the industry leader. Then research Toyota's strategy to overtake General Motors.

3. Review the discussion in Illustration Capsule 8.1 concerning the focused differentiation strategy that Exertris has employed in the exercise equipment industry. Then answer the following:

    a. What reasons can you give for why sales of the Exertris exercise bike have not taken off?

    b. What strategic actions would you recommend to the cofounders of Exertris to spark substantially greater sales of its innovative exercise bike and overcome the apparent market apathy for its video-game-equipped exercise bike? Should the company consider making any changes in its product offering? What distribution channels should it emphasize? What advertising and promotional approaches should be considered? How can it get gym owners to purchase or at least try its bikes?

    c. Should the company just give up on its product innovation (because the bike is not ever likely to get good reception in the marketplace)? Or should the cofounders try to sell their fledgling business to another exercise equipment company with a more extensive product line and wider geographic coverage?

4. Review the information in Illustration Capsule 8.3 concerning the turnaround strategy Sony launched in the fall of 2005. Go to the company's Web site and check out other Internet sources to see how Sony's strategy to revitalize its electronics business is coming along. Does your research indicate that Sony's turnaround strategy is a success or a failure, or is it still too early to tell? Explain.

5. Yahoo competes in an industry characterized by high-velocity change. Read the company's press releases at http://yhoo.client.shareholder.com/releases.cfm and answer the following questions:

    a. Does it appear that the company has dealt with change in the industry by reacting to change, anticipating change, or leading change? Explain.

    b. What are its key strategies for competing in fast-changing markets? Describe them.

chapter nine

Diversification

Strategies for Managing a Group of Businesses

To acquire or not to acquire: that is the question.

—Robert J. Terry

Fit between a parent and its businesses is a two-edged sword: a good fit can create value; a bad one can destroy it.

—Andrew Campbell, Michael Goold, and Marcus Alexander

Achieving superior performance through diversification is largely based on relatedness.

—Philippe Very

Make winners out of every business in your company. Don't carry losers.

—Jack Welch
Former CEO, General Electric

We measure each of our businesses against strict criteria: growth, margin, and return-on-capital hurdle rate, and does it have the ability to become number one or two in its industry? We are quite pragmatic. If a business does not contribute to our overall vision, it has to go.

—Richard Wambold
CEO, Pactiv

In this chapter, we move up one level in the strategy-making hierarchy, from strategy making in a single-business enterprise to strategy making in a diversified enterprise. Because a diversified company is a collection of individual businesses, the strategy-making task is more complicated. In a one-business company, managers have to come up with a plan for competing successfully in only a single industry environment—the result is what we labeled in Chapter 2 as *business strategy* (or *business-level strategy*). But in a diversified company, the strategy-making challenge involves assessing multiple industry environments and developing a *set* of business strategies, one for each industry arena in which the diversified company operates. And top executives at a diversified company must still go one step further and devise a company-wide or *corporate strategy* for improving the attractiveness and performance of the company's overall business lineup and for making a rational whole out of its diversified collection of individual businesses.

In most diversified companies, corporate-level executives delegate considerable strategy-making authority to the heads of each business, usually giving them the latitude to craft a business strategy suited to their particular industry and competitive circumstances and holding them accountable for producing good results. But the task of crafting a diversified company's overall or corporate strategy falls squarely in the lap of top-level executives and involves four distinct facets:

1. *Picking new industries to enter and deciding on the means of entry*—The first concerns in diversifying are what new industries to get into and whether to enter by starting a new business from the ground up, acquiring a company already in the target industry, or forming a joint venture or strategic alliance with another company. A company can diversify narrowly into a few industries or broadly into many industries. The choice of whether to enter an industry via a start-up operation; a joint venture; or the acquisition of an established leader, an up-and-coming company, or a troubled company with turnaround potential shapes what position the company will initially stake out for itself.

2. *Initiating actions to boost the combined performance of the businesses the firm has entered*—As positions are created in the chosen industries, corporate strategists typically zero in on ways to strengthen the long-term competitive positions and profits of the businesses the firm has invested in. Corporate parents can help their business subsidiaries by providing financial resources, by supplying missing skills or technological know-how or managerial expertise to better perform key value chain activities, and by providing new avenues for cost reduction. They can also acquire another company in the same industry and merge the two operations into a stronger business, or acquire new businesses that strongly complement existing businesses. Typically, a company will pursue rapid-growth strategies in its most promising businesses, initiate turnaround efforts in weak-performing businesses with potential, and divest businesses that are no longer attractive or that don't fit into management's long-range plans.

3. *Pursuing opportunities to leverage cross-business value chain relationships and strategic fits into competitive advantage*—A company that diversifies into businesses with competitively important value chain matchups (pertaining to technology, supply chain logistics, production, overlapping distribution channels, or common customers) gains competitive advantage potential not open to a company that diversifies into businesses whose value chains are totally unrelated. Capturing this competitive advantage potential requires that corporate strategists spend considerable time trying to capitalize on such cross-business opportunities as transferring skills or technology from one business to another, reducing costs via sharing use of common facilities and resources, and using the company's well-known brand names and distribution muscle to grow the sales of newly acquired products.

4. *Establishing investment priorities and steering corporate resources into the most attractive business units*—A diversified company's different businesses are usually not equally attractive from the standpoint of investing additional funds. It is incumbent on corporate management to (*a*) decide on the priorities for investing capital in the company's different businesses, (*b*) channel resources into areas where earnings potentials are higher and away from areas where they are lower, and (*c*) divest business units that are chronically poor performers or are in an increasingly unattractive industry. Divesting poor performers and businesses in unattractive industries frees up unproductive investments either for redeployment to promising business units or for financing attractive new acquisitions.

The demanding and time-consuming nature of these four tasks explains why corporate executives generally refrain from becoming immersed in the details of crafting and implementing business-level strategies, preferring instead to delegate lead responsibility for business strategy to the heads of each business unit.

In the first portion of this chapter we describe the various means a company can use to become diversified and explore the pros and cons of related versus unrelated diversification strategies. The second part of the chapter looks at how to evaluate the attractiveness of a diversified company's business lineup, decide whether it has a good diversification strategy, and identify ways to improve its future performance. In the chapter's concluding section, we survey the strategic options open to already-diversified companies.

WHEN TO DIVERSIFY

So long as a company has its hands full trying to capitalize on profitable growth opportunities in its present industry, there is no urgency to pursue diversification. The big risk of a single-business company, of course, is having all of the firm's eggs in one industry basket. If demand for the industry's product is eroded by the appearance of alternative technologies, substitute products, or fast-shifting buyer preferences, or if the industry becomes competitively unattractive and unprofitable, then a company's prospects can quickly dim. Consider, for example, what digital cameras have done to erode the revenues of companies dependent on making camera film and doing film processing, what CD and DVD technology have done to business outlook for producers of cassette tapes and 3.5-inch disks, and what cell-phone companies with their no-long-distance-charge plans and marketers of Voice over Internet Protocol (VoIP) are doing to the revenues of such once-dominant long-distance providers as AT&T, British Telecommunications, and NTT in Japan.

Thus, diversifying into new industries always merits strong consideration whenever a single-business company encounters diminishing market opportunities and stagnating sales in its principal business—most landline-based telecommunications companies across the world are quickly diversifying their product offerings to include wireless and VoIP services. But there are four other instances in which a company becomes a prime candidate for diversifying:[1]

1. When it spots opportunities for expanding into industries whose technologies and products complement its present business.

2. When it can leverage existing competencies and capabilities by expanding into businesses where these same resource strengths are key success factors and valuable competitive assets.

3. When diversifying into closely related businesses opens new avenues for reducing costs.

4. When it has a powerful and well-known brand name that can be transferred to the products of other businesses and thereby used as a lever for driving up the sales and profits of such businesses.

The decision to diversify presents wide-open possibilities. A company can diversify into closely related businesses or into totally unrelated businesses. It can diversify its present revenue and earning base to a small extent (such that new businesses account for less than 15 percent of companywide revenues and profits) or to a major extent (such that new businesses produce 30 or more percent of revenues and profits). It can move into one or two large new businesses or a greater number of small ones. It can achieve multibusiness/multi-industry status by acquiring an existing company already in a business/industry it wants to enter, starting up a new business subsidiary from scratch, or forming a joint venture with one or more companies to enter new businesses.

BUILDING SHAREHOLDER VALUE: THE ULTIMATE JUSTIFICATION FOR DIVERSIFYING

Diversification must do more for a company than simply spread its business risk across various industries. In principle, diversification cannot be considered a success unless it results in *added shareholder value*—value that shareholders cannot capture on their own by purchasing stock in companies in different industries or investing in mutual funds so as to spread their investments across several industries.

For there to be reasonable expectations that a company's diversification efforts can produce added value, a move to diversify into a new business must pass three tests:[2]

1. *The industry attractiveness test*—The industry to be entered must be attractive enough to yield consistently good returns on investment. Whether an industry is attractive depends chiefly on the presence of industry and competitive conditions that are conducive to earning as good or better profits and return on investment than the company is earning in its present business(es). It is hard to justify diversifying into an industry where profit expectations are *lower* than in the company's present businesses.

2. *The cost-of-entry test*—The cost to enter the target industry must not be so high as to erode the potential for good profitability. A catch-22 can prevail here, however. The more attractive an industry's prospects are for growth and good long-term profitability, the more expensive it can be to get into. Entry barriers for start-up companies are likely to be high in attractive industries; were barriers low, a rush of new entrants would soon erode the potential for high profitability. And buying a well-positioned company in an appealing industry often entails a high acquisition cost that makes passing the cost-of-entry test less likely. For instance, suppose that the price to purchase a company is $3 million and that the company is earning after-tax profits of $200,000 on an equity investment of $1 million (a 20 percent annual return). Simple arithmetic requires that the profits be tripled if the purchaser (paying $3 million) is to earn the same 20 percent return. Building the acquired firm's earnings from $200,000 to $600,000 annually could take several years—and require additional investment on which the purchaser would also have to earn a 20 percent return. Since the owners of a successful and growing company usually demand a price that reflects their business's profit prospects, it's easy for such an acquisition to fail the cost-of-entry test.

3. *The better-off test*—Diversifying into a new business must offer potential for the company's existing businesses and the new business to perform better together under a single corporate umbrella than they would perform operating as independent, stand-alone businesses. For example, let's say that company A diversifies by purchasing company B in another industry. If A and B's consolidated profits in the years to come prove no greater than what each could have earned on its own, then A's diversification won't provide its shareholders with added value. Company A's shareholders could have achieved the same $1 + 1 = 2$ result by merely purchasing stock in company B. Shareholder value is not created by diversification unless it produces a $1 + 1 = 3$ effect where sister businesses *perform better together* as part of the same firm than they could have performed as independent companies.

Core Concept
Creating added value for shareholders via diversification requires building a multibusiness company where the whole is greater than the sum of its parts.

Diversification moves that satisfy all three tests have the greatest potential to grow shareholder value over the long term. Diversification moves that can pass only one or two tests are suspect.

STRATEGIES FOR ENTERING NEW BUSINESSES

The means of entering new businesses can take any of three forms: acquisition, internal start-up, or joint ventures with other companies.

Acquisition of an Existing Business

Acquisition is the most popular means of diversifying into another industry. Not only is it quicker than trying to launch a brand-new operation, but it also offers an effective way to hurdle such entry barriers as acquiring technological know-how, establishing supplier relationships, becoming big enough to match rivals' efficiency and unit costs, having to spend large sums on introductory advertising and promotions, and securing adequate distribution. Buying an ongoing operation allows the acquirer to move directly to the task of building a strong market position in the target industry, rather than getting bogged down in going the internal start-up route and trying to develop the knowledge, resources, scale of operation, and market reputation necessary to become an effective competitor within a few years.

The big dilemma an acquisition-minded firm faces is whether to pay a premium price for a successful company or to buy a struggling company at a bargain price.[3] If the buying firm has little knowledge of the industry but ample capital, it is often better off purchasing a capable, strongly positioned firm—unless the price of such an acquisition flunks the cost-of-entry test. However, when the acquirer sees promising ways to transform a weak firm into a strong one and has the resources, the know-how, and the patience to do it, a struggling company can be the better long-term investment.

Internal Start-Up

Achieving diversification through *internal start-up* involves building a new business subsidiary from scratch. This entry option takes longer than the acquisition option and poses some hurdles. A newly formed business unit not only has to overcome entry barriers but also has to invest in new production capacity, develop sources of supply, hire and train employees, build channels of distribution, grow a customer base, and so on. Generally, forming a start-up subsidiary to enter a new business has appeal only when (1) the parent company already has in-house most or all of the skills and resources it needs to piece together a new business and compete effectively; (2) there is ample time to launch the business; (3) internal entry has lower costs than entry via acquisition; (4) the targeted industry is populated with many relatively small firms such that the new start-up does not have to compete head-to-head against larger, more powerful rivals; (5) adding new production capacity will not adversely impact the supply–demand balance in the industry; and (6) incumbent firms are likely to be slow or ineffective in responding to a new entrant's efforts to crack the market.[4]

> The biggest drawbacks to entering an industry by forming an internal start-up are the costs of overcoming entry barriers and the extra time it takes to build a strong and profitable competitive position.

Joint Ventures

Joint ventures entail forming a new corporate entity owned by two or more companies, where the purpose of the joint venture is to pursue a mutually attractive opportunity. The terms and conditions of a joint venture concern joint operation of a mutually owned business, which tends to make the arrangement more definitive and perhaps more durable than a strategic alliance—in a strategic alliance, the arrangement between the partners is one of limited collaboration for a limited purpose and a partner can choose to simply walk away or reduce its commitment at any time.

A joint venture to enter a new business can be useful in at least three types of situations.[5] First, a joint venture is a good vehicle for pursuing an opportunity that is too complex, uneconomical, or risky for one company to pursue alone. Second, joint ventures make sense when the opportunities in a new industry require a broader range of competencies and know-how than a company can marshal. Many of the opportunities in satellite-based telecommunications, biotechnology, and network-based systems that blend hardware, software, and services call for the coordinated development of complementary innovations and tackling an intricate web of financial, technical, political, and regulatory factors simultaneously. In such cases, pooling the resources and competencies of two or more companies is a wiser and less risky way to proceed.

Third, companies sometimes use joint ventures to diversify into a new industry when the diversification move entails having operations in a foreign country—several governments require foreign companies operating within their borders to have a local partner that has minority, if not majority, ownership in the local operations. Aside from fulfilling host government ownership requirements, companies usually seek out a local partner with expertise and other resources that will aid the success of the newly established local operation.

However, as discussed in Chapters 6 and 7, partnering with another company—in either a joint venture or a collaborative alliance—has significant drawbacks due to the potential for conflicting objectives, disagreements over how to best operate the venture, culture clashes, and so on. Joint ventures are generally the least durable of the entry options, usually lasting only until the partners decide to go their own ways.

CHOOSING THE DIVERSIFICATION PATH: RELATED VERSUS UNRELATED BUSINESSES

Core Concept
Related businesses possess competitively valuable cross-business value chain matchups; **unrelated businesses** have dissimilar value chains, containing no competitively useful cross-business relationships.

Once a company decides to diversify, its first big strategy decision is whether to diversify into related businesses, unrelated businesses, or some mix of both (see Figure 9.1). *Businesses are said to be related when their value chains possess competitively valuable cross-business relationships that present opportunities for the businesses to perform better under the same corporate umbrella than they could by operating as stand-alone entities.* The big appeal of related diversification is to build shareholder value by leveraging these cross-business relationships into competitive advantage, thus allowing the company as a whole to perform better than just the sum of its individual businesses. *Businesses are said to be unrelated when the activities comprising their respective value chains are so dissimilar that no competitively valuable cross-business relationships are present.*

The next two sections of this chapter explore the ins and outs of related and unrelated diversification.

THE CASE FOR DIVERSIFYING INTO RELATED BUSINESSES

A related diversification strategy involves building the company around businesses whose value chains possess competitively valuable strategic fits, as shown in Figure 9.2. **Strategic fit** exists whenever one or more activities comprising the value chains of different businesses are sufficiently similar as to present opportunities for:[6]

- Transferring competitively valuable expertise, technological know-how, or other capabilities from one business to another.

Figure 9.1   **Strategy Alternatives for a Company Looking to Diversify**

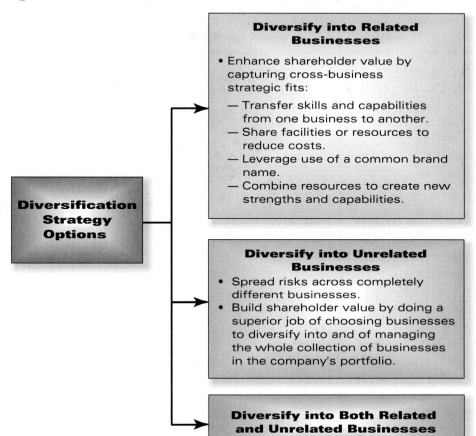

- Combining the related value chain activities of separate businesses into a single operation to achieve lower costs. For instance, it is often feasible to manufacture the products of different businesses in a single plant or use the same warehouses for shipping and distribution or have a single sales force for the products of different businesses (because they are marketed to the same types of customers).

- Exploiting common use of a well-known and potent brand name. For example, Honda's name in motorcycles and automobiles gave it instant credibility and recognition in entering the lawn-mower business, allowing it to achieve a significant market share without spending large sums on advertising to establish a brand identity for its lawn mowers. Canon's reputation in photographic equipment was a competitive asset that facilitated the company's diversification into copying equipment. Sony's name in consumer electronics made it easier and cheaper for Sony to enter the market for video games with its PlayStation console and lineup of PlayStation video games.

- Cross-business collaboration to create competitively valuable resource strengths and capabilities.

Core Concept
Strategic fit exists when the value chains of different businesses present opportunities for cross-business resource transfer, lower costs through combining the performance of related value chain activities, cross-business use of a potent brand name, and cross-business collaboration to build new or stronger competitive capabilities.

Figure 9.2   **Related Businesses Possess Related Value Chain Activities and Competitively Valuable Strategic Fits**

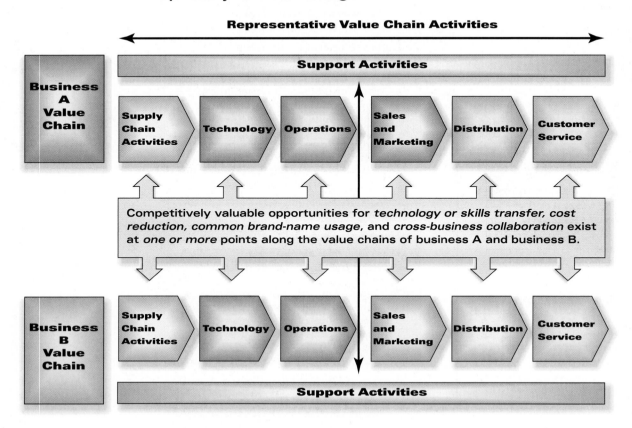

Related diversification thus has strategic appeal from several angles. It allows a firm to reap the competitive advantage benefits of skills transfer, lower costs, a powerful brand name, and/or stronger competitive capabilities and still spread investor risks over a broad business base. Furthermore, the relatedness among the different businesses provides sharper focus for managing diversification and a useful degree of strategic unity across the company's various business activities.

Identifying Cross-Business Strategic Fits along the Value Chain

Cross-business strategic fits can exist anywhere along the value chain—in R&D and technology activities, in supply chain activities and relationships with suppliers, in manufacturing, in sales and marketing, in distribution activities, or in administrative support activities.[7]

Strategic Fits in R&D and Technology Activities   Diversifying into businesses where there is potential for sharing common technology, exploiting the full range of business opportunities associated with a particular technology and its derivatives, or transferring technological know-how from one business to another has considerable appeal. Businesses with technology-sharing benefits can perform better together than apart because of potential cost savings in R&D and potentially shorter times in getting new products to market; also, technological advances in one business can lead to increased sales for both. Technological innovations have been the driver behind the efforts of cable TV companies to diversify into high-speed Internet access (via the use of cable modems) and, further, to explore providing local and long-distance telephone service to residential and commercial customers in either a single wire or using VoIP technology.

Strategic Fits in Supply Chain Activities   Businesses that have supply chain strategic fits can perform better together because of the potential for skills transfer in procuring materials, greater bargaining power in negotiating with common suppliers, the benefits of added collaboration with common supply chain partners, and/or added leverage with shippers in securing volume discounts on incoming parts and components. Dell Computer's strategic partnerships with leading suppliers of microprocessors, motherboards, disk drives, memory chips, flat-panel displays, wireless capabilities, long-life batteries, and other PC-related components have been an important element of the company's strategy to diversify into servers, data storage devices, MP3 players, and LCD TVs—products that include many components common to PCs and that can be sourced from the same strategic partners that provide Dell with PC components.

Manufacturing-Related Strategic Fits   Cross-business strategic fits in manufacturing-related activities can represent an important source of competitive advantage in situations where a diversifier's expertise in quality manufacture and cost-efficient production methods can be transferred to another business. When Emerson Electric diversified into the chain-saw business, it transferred its expertise in low-cost manufacture to its newly acquired Beaird-Poulan business division; the transfer drove Beaird-Poulan's new strategy—to be the low-cost provider of chain-saw products—and fundamentally changed the way Beaird-Poulan chain saws were designed and manufactured. Another benefit of production-related value chain matchups is the ability to consolidate production into a smaller number of plants and significantly reduce overall production costs. When snowmobile maker Bombardier diversified into motorcycles, it was able to set up motorcycle assembly lines in the same manufacturing facility where it was assembling snowmobiles. When Smuckers acquired Procter & Gamble's Jif peanut butter business, it was able to combine the manufacture of its own Smucker's peanut butter products with those of Jif; in addition, it gained greater leverage with vendors in purchasing its peanut supplies.

Distribution-Related Strategic Fits   Businesses with closely related distribution activities can perform better together than apart because of potential cost savings in sharing the same distribution facilities or using many of the same wholesale distributors and retail dealers to access customers. When Sunbeam acquired Mr. Coffee, it was able to consolidate its own distribution centers for small household appliances with those of Mr. Coffee, thereby generating considerable cost savings. Likewise, since Sunbeam products were sold to many of the same retailers as Mr. Coffee products (Wal-Mart, Kmart, Target, department stores, home centers, hardware chains, supermarket chains, and drugstore chains), Sunbeam was able to convince many of the retailers carrying Sunbeam appliances to also take on the Mr. Coffee line and vice versa.

Strategic Fits in Sales and Marketing Activities Various cost-saving opportunities spring from diversifying into businesses with closely related sales and marketing activities. The same distribution centers can be used for warehousing and shipping the products of different businesses. When the products are sold directly to the same customers, sales costs can often be reduced by using a single sales force and avoiding having two different salespeople call on the same customer. The products of related businesses can be promoted at the same Web site, and included in the same media ads and sales brochures. After-sale service and repair organizations for the products of closely related businesses can often be consolidated into a single operation. There may be opportunities to reduce costs by consolidating order processing and billing and using common promotional tie-ins (cents-off couponing, free samples and trial offers, seasonal specials, and the like). When global power-tool maker Black & Decker acquired General Electric's domestic small household appliance business, it was able to use its own global sales force and distribution facilities to sell and distribute the newly acquired GE line of toasters, irons, mixers, and coffeemakers because the types of customers that carried its power tools (discounters like Wal-Mart and Target, home centers, and hardware stores) also stocked small appliances. The economies Black & Decker achieved for both product lines were substantial.

A second category of benefits arises when different businesses use similar sales and marketing approaches; in such cases, there may be competitively valuable opportunities to transfer selling, merchandising, advertising, and product differentiation skills from one business to another. Procter & Gamble's product lineup includes Folgers coffee, Tide laundry detergent, Crest toothpaste, Ivory soap, Charmin toilet tissue, Gillette razors and blades, Duracell batteries, Oral-B toothbrushes, and Head & Shoulders shampoo. All of these have different competitors and different supply chain and production requirements, but they all move through the same wholesale distribution systems, are sold in common retail settings to the same shoppers, are advertised and promoted in much the same ways, and require the same marketing and merchandising skills.

Strategic Fits in Managerial and Administrative Support Activities Often, different businesses require comparable types managerial know-how, thereby allowing know-how in one line of business to be transferred to another. At General Electric (GE), managers who were involved in GE's expansion into Russia were able to expedite entry because of information gained from GE managers involved in expansions into other emerging markets. The lessons GE managers learned in China were passed along to GE managers in Russia, allowing them to anticipate that the Russian government would demand that GE build production capacity in the country rather than enter the market through exporting or licensing. In addition, GE's managers in Russia were better able to develop realistic performance expectations and make tough upfront decisions since experience in China and elsewhere warned them (1) that there would likely be increased short-term costs during the early years of start-up and (2) that if GE committed to the Russian market for the long term and aided the country's economic development it could eventually expect to be given the freedom to pursue profitable penetration of the Russian market.[8]

Likewise, different businesses can often use the same administrative and customer service infrastructure. For instance, an electric utility that diversifies into natural gas, water, appliance sales and repair services, and home security services can use the same customer data network, the same customer call centers and local offices, the same

Illustration Capsule 9.1

Related Diversification at L'Oréal, Johnson & Johnson, PepsiCo, and Darden Restaurants

See if you can identify the value chain relationships that make the businesses of the following companies related in competitively relevant ways. In particular, you should consider whether there are cross-business opportunities for (1) transferring skills/technology, (2) combining related value chain activities to achieve lower costs, (3) leveraging use of a well-respected brand name, and/or (4) establishing cross-business collaboration to create new resource strengths and capabilities.

L'ORÉAL

- Maybelline, Lancôme, Helena Rubenstein, Kiehl's, Garner, and Shu Uemura cosmetics.
- L'Oréal and Soft Sheen/Carson hair care products.
- Redken, Matrix, L'Oréal Professional, and Kerastase Paris professional hair care and skin care products.
- Ralph Lauren and Giorgio Armani fragrances.
- Biotherm skin care products.
- La Roche–Posay and Vichy Laboratories dermocosmetics.

JOHNSON & JOHNSON

- Baby products (powder, shampoo, oil, lotion).
- Band-Aids and other first-aid products.
- Women's health and personal care products (Stayfree, Carefree, Sure & Natural).
- Neutrogena and Aveeno skin care products.

- Nonprescription drugs (Tylenol, Motrin, Pepcid AC, Mylanta, Monistat).
- Prescription drugs.
- Prosthetic and other medical devices.
- Surgical and hospital products.
- Accuvue contact lenses.

PEPSICO

- Soft drinks (Pepsi, Diet Pepsi, Pepsi One, Mountain Dew, Mug, Slice).
- Fruit juices (Tropicana and Dole).
- Sports drinks (Gatorade).
- Other beverages (Aquafina bottled water, SoBe, Lipton ready-to-drink tea, Frappucino—in partnership with Starbucks, international sales of 7UP).
- Snack foods (Fritos, Lay's, Ruffles, Doritos, Tostitos, Santitas, Smart Food, Rold Gold pretzels, Chee-tos, Grandma's cookies, Sun Chips, Cracker Jack, Frito-Lay dips and salsas).
- Cereals, rice, and breakfast products (Quaker oatmeal, Cap'n Crunch, Life, Rice-A-Roni, Quaker rice cakes, Aunt Jemima mixes and syrups, Quaker grits).

DARDEN RESTAURANTS

- Olive Garden restaurant chain (Italian-themed).
- Red Lobster restaurant chain (seafood-themed).
- Bahama Breeze restaurant chain (Caribbean-themed).

Source: Company Web sites, annual reports, and 10-K reports.

billing and customer accounting systems, and the same customer service infrastructure to support all of its products and services.

Illustration Capsule 9.1 lists the businesses of five companies that have pursued a strategy of related diversification.

Strategic Fit, Economies of Scope, and Competitive Advantage

What makes related diversification an attractive strategy is the opportunity to convert cross-business strategic fits into a competitive advantage over business rivals whose operations do not offer comparable strategic-fit benefits. The greater the relatedness among a diversified company's sister businesses, the bigger a company's window for converting strategic fits into competitive advantage via (1) skills transfer, (2) combining related value chain activities to achieve lower costs, (3) leveraging use of a well-respected brand name, and/or (4) cross-business collaboration to create new resource strengths and capabilities.

Economies of Scope: A Path to Competitive Advantage

One of the most important competitive advantages that a related diversification strategy can produce is lower costs than competitors. Related businesses often present opportunities to eliminate or reduce the costs of performing certain value chain activities; such cost savings are termed **economies of scope**—a concept distinct from *economies of scale.* Economies of *scale* are cost savings that accrue directly from a larger-sized operation; for example, unit costs may be lower in a large plant than in a small plant, lower in a large distribution center than in a small one, and lower for large-volume purchases of components than for small-volume purchases. Economies of *scope,* however, stem directly from cost-saving strategic fits along the value chains of related businesses. Such economies are open only to a multibusiness enterprise and are the result of a related diversification strategy that allows sister businesses to share technology, perform R&D together, use common manufacturing or distribution facilities, share a common sales force or distributor/dealer network, use the same established brand name, and/or share the same administrative infrastructure. *The greater the cross-business economies associated with cost-saving strategic fits, the greater the potential for a related diversification strategy to yield a competitive advantage based on lower costs than rivals.*

> **Core Concept**
> **Economies of scope** are cost reductions that flow from operating in multiple businesses; such economies stem directly from strategic fit efficiencies along the value chains of related businesses.

From Competitive Advantage to Added Profitability and Gains in Shareholder Value

The competitive advantage potential that flows from economies of scope and the capture of other strategic-fit benefits is what enables a company pursuing related diversification to achieve $1 + 1 = 3$ financial performance and the hoped-for gains in shareholder value. The strategic and business logic is compelling: Capturing strategic fits along the value chains of its related businesses gives a diversified company a clear path to achieving competitive advantage over undiversified competitors and competitors whose own diversification efforts don't offer equivalent strategic-fit benefits.[9] Such competitive advantage potential provides a company with a dependable basis for earning profits and a return on investment that exceed what the company's businesses could earn as stand-alone enterprises. Converting the competitive advantage potential into greater profitability is what fuels $1 + 1 = 3$ gains in shareholder value—the necessary outcome for satisfying the better-off test and proving the business merit of a company's diversification effort.

> **Core Concept**
> Diversifying into related businesses where competitively valuable strategic fit benefits can be captured puts sister businesses in position to perform better financially as part of the same company than they could have performed as independent enterprises, thus providing a clear avenue for boosting shareholder value.

There are three things to bear in mind here. One, capturing cross-business strategic fits via a strategy of related diversification builds shareholder value in ways that shareholders cannot undertake by simply owning a portfolio of stocks of companies in different industries. Two, the capture of cross-business strategic-fit benefits is possible only via a strategy of related diversification. Three, the benefits of cross-business strategic fits are not automatically realized when a company diversifies into related businesses; *the benefits materialize only after management has successfully pursued internal actions to capture them.*

Figure 9.3   **Unrelated Businesses Have Unrelated Value Chains and No Strategic Fits**

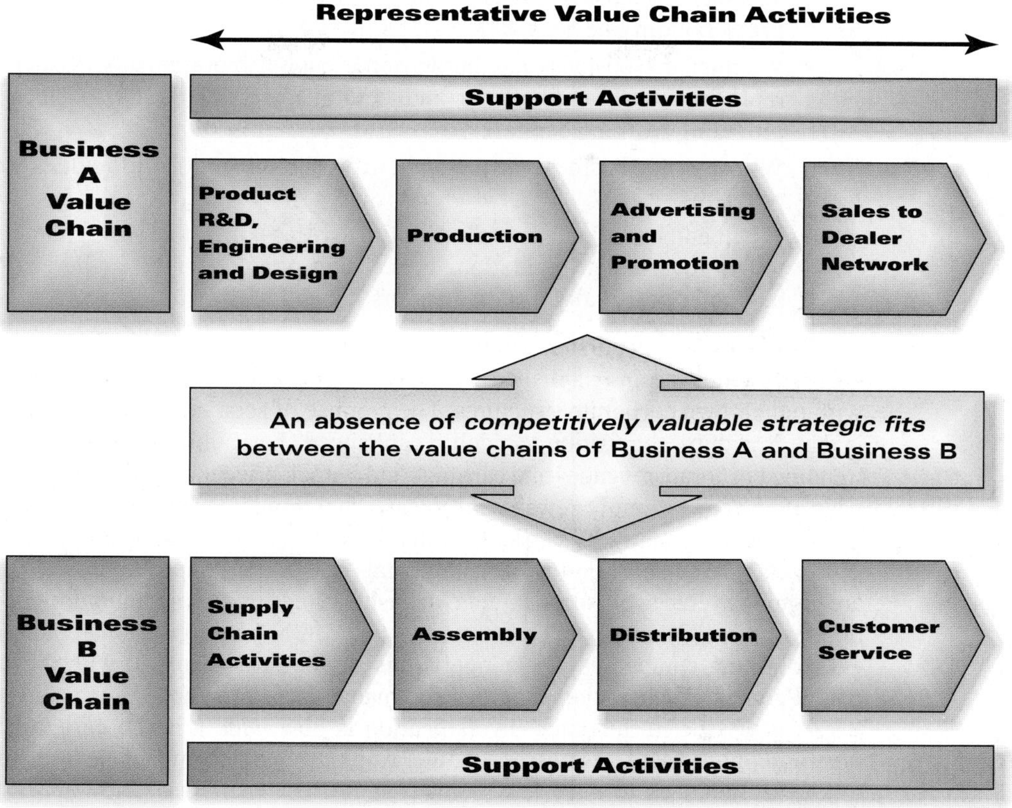

THE CASE FOR DIVERSIFYING INTO UNRELATED BUSINESSES

An unrelated diversification strategy discounts the merits of pursuing cross-business strategic fits and, instead, focuses squarely on entering and operating businesses in industries that allow the company as a whole to grow its revenues and earnings. Companies that pursue a strategy of unrelated diversification generally exhibit a willingness to diversify into *any industry* where senior managers see *opportunity* to realize consistently good financial results—*the basic premise of unrelated diversification is that any company or business that can be acquired on good financial terms and that has satisfactory growth and earnings potential represents a good acquisition and a good business opportunity.* With a strategy of unrelated diversification, the emphasis is on satisfying the attractiveness and cost-of-entry tests and each business's prospects for good financial performance. As indicated in Figure 9.3, there's no deliberate effort to satisfy the better-off test in the sense of diversifying only into businesses having strategic fits with the firm's other businesses.

Thus, with an unrelated diversification strategy, company managers spend much time and effort screening acquisition candidates and evaluating the pros and cons or keeping or divesting existing businesses, using such criteria as:

- Whether the business can meet corporate targets for profitability and return on investment.

- Whether the business is in an industry with attractive growth potential.
- Whether the business is big enough to contribute *significantly* to the parent firm's bottom line.
- Whether the business has burdensome capital requirements (associated with replacing out-of-date plants and equipment, growing the business, and/or providing working capital).
- Whether the business is plagued with chronic union difficulties and labor problems.
- Whether there is industry vulnerability to recession, inflation, high interest rates, tough government regulations concerning product safety or the environment, and other potentially negative factors.

Companies that pursue unrelated diversification nearly always enter new businesses by acquiring an established company rather than by forming a start-up subsidiary within their own corporate structures. The premise of acquisition-minded corporations is that growth by acquisition can deliver enhanced shareholder value through upward-trending corporate revenues and earnings and a stock price that *on average* rises enough year after year to amply reward and please shareholders. Three types of acquisition candidates are usually of particular interest: (1) businesses that have bright growth prospects but are short on investment capital—cash-poor, opportunity-rich businesses are highly coveted acquisition targets for cash-rich companies scouting for good market opportunities; (2) undervalued companies that can be acquired at a bargain price; and (3) struggling companies whose operations can be turned around with the aid of the parent company's financial resources and managerial know-how.

A key issue in unrelated diversification is how wide a net to cast in building a portfolio of unrelated businesses. In other words, should a company pursuing unrelated diversification seek to have few or many unrelated businesses? How much business diversity can corporate executives successfully manage? A reasonable way to resolve the issue of how much diversification comes from answering two questions: "What is the least diversification it will take to achieve acceptable growth and profitability?" and "What is the most diversification that can be managed, given the complexity it adds?"[10] The optimal amount of diversification usually lies between these two extremes.

Illustration Capsule 9.2 lists the businesses of three companies that have pursued unrelated diversification. Such companies are frequently labeled *conglomerates* because their business interests range broadly across diverse industries.

The Merits of an Unrelated Diversification Strategy

A strategy of unrelated diversification has appeal from several angles:

1. Business risk is scattered over a set of truly *diverse* industries. In comparison to related diversification, unrelated diversification more closely approximates *pure* diversification of financial and business risk because the company's investments are spread over businesses whose technologies and value chain activities bear no close relationship and whose markets are largely disconnected.[11]

2. The company's financial resources can be employed to maximum advantage by (*a*) investing in *whatever industries* offer the best profit prospects (as opposed to considering only opportunities in industries with related value chain activities) and (*b*) diverting cash flows from company businesses with lower growth and profit prospects to acquiring and expanding businesses with higher growth and profit potentials.

Illustration Capsule 9.2

Unrelated Diversification at General Electric, United Technologies, American Standard, and Lancaster Colony

The defining characteristic of unrelated diversification is few competitively valuable cross-business relationships. Peruse the business group listings for General Electric, United Technologies, American Standard, and Lancaster Colony and see if you can confirm why these four companies have unrelated diversification strategies.

GENERAL ELECTRIC

- Advanced materials (engineering thermoplastics, silicon-based products and technology platforms, and fused quartz and ceramics)—revenues of $8.3 billion in 2004.
- Commercial and consumer finance (loans, operating leases, financing programs and financial services provided to corporations, retailers, and consumers in 38 countries)—revenues of $39.2 billion in 2004.
- Major appliances, lighting, and integrated industrial equipment, systems and services—revenues of $13.8 billion in 2004.
- Commercial insurance and reinsurance products and services for insurance companies, Fortune 1000 companies, self-insurers, health care providers and other groups—revenues of $23.1 billion in 2004.
- Jet engines for military and civil aircraft, freight and passenger locomotives, motorized systems for mining trucks and drills, and gas turbines for marine and industrial applications—revenues of $15.6 billion in 2004.
- Electric power generation equipment, power transformers, high-voltage breakers, distribution transformers and breakers, capacitors, relays, regulators, substation equipment, metering products—revenues of $17.3 billion in 2004.
- Medical imaging and information technologies, medical diagnostics, patient monitoring systems, disease research, drug discovery and biopharmaceuticals—revenues of $13.5 billion in 2004.
- NBC Universal—owns and operates the NBC television network, a Spanish-language network (Telemundo), several news and entertainment networks (CNBC, MSNBC, Bravo, Sci-Fi Channel, USA Network), Universal Studios, various television production operations, a group of television stations, and theme parks—revenues of $12.9 billion in 2004.
- Chemical treatment programs for water and industrial process systems; precision sensors; security and safety systems for intrusion and fire detection, access and building control, video surveillance, explosives and drug detection; and real estate services—revenues of $3.4 billion in 2004.
- Equipment services, including Penske truck leasing; operating leases, loans, sales, and asset management services for owners of computer networks, trucks, trailers, railcars, construction equipment, and shipping containers—revenues of $8.5 billion in 2004.

UNITED TECHNOLOGIES

- Pratt & Whitney aircraft engines—2005 revenues of $9.3 billion.
- Carrier heating and air-conditioning equipment—2005 revenues of $12.5 billion.
- Otis elevators and escalators—2005 revenues of $9.6 billion.
- Sikorsky helicopters and Hamilton Sunstrand aerospace systems—2005 revenues of $7.2 billion.
- Chubb fire detection and security systems—2005 revenues of $4.3 billion.

AMERICAN STANDARD

- Trane and American Standard furnaces, heat pumps, and air conditioners—2005 revenues of $6.0 billion.
- American Standard, Ideal Standard, Standard, and Porcher lavatories, toilets, bath tubs, faucets, whirlpool baths, and shower basins—2005 revenues of $2.4 billion.
- Commercial and utility vehicle braking and control systems—2005 revenues of $1.8 billion.

LANCASTER COLONY

- Specialty food products: Cardini, Marzetti, Girard's, and Pheiffer salad dressings; Chatham Village croutons; New York Brand, Sister Schubert, and Mamma Bella frozen breads and rolls; Reames and Aunt Vi's frozen noodles and pastas; Inn Maid and Amish dry egg noodles; and Romanoff caviar—fiscal 2005 revenues of $674 million.
- Candles and glassware: Candle-lite candles; Indiana Glass and Fostoria drinkware and tabletop items; Colony giftware; and Brody floral containers—fiscal 2005 revenues of $234 million.
- Automotive products: Rubber Queen automotive floor mats; Dee Zee aluminum accessories and running boards for light trucks; Protecta truck bed mats; and assorted other truck accessories—fiscal 2005 revenues of $224 million.

Source: Company Web sites, annual reports, and 10-K reports.

3. To the extent that corporate managers are exceptionally astute at spotting bargain-priced companies with big upside profit potential, shareholder wealth can be enhanced by buying distressed businesses at a low price, turning their operations around fairly quickly with infusions of cash and managerial know-how supplied by the parent company, and then riding the crest of the profit increases generated by the newly acquired businesses.

4. Company profitability may prove somewhat more stable over the course of economic upswings and downswings because market conditions in all industries don't move upward or downward simultaneously—in a broadly diversified company, there's a chance that market downtrends in some of the company's businesses will be partially offset by cyclical upswings in its other businesses, thus producing somewhat less earnings volatility. (In actual practice, however, there's no convincing evidence that the consolidated profits of firms with unrelated diversification strategies are more stable or less subject to reversal in periods of recession and economic stress than the profits of firms with related diversification strategies.)

Unrelated diversification certainly merits consideration when a firm is trapped in or overly dependent on an endangered or unattractive industry, especially when it has no competitively valuable resources or capabilities it can transfer to an adjacent industry. A case can also be made for unrelated diversification when a company has a strong preference for spreading business risks widely and not restricting itself to investing in a family of closely related businesses.

Building Shareholder Value via Unrelated Diversification   Given the absence of cross-business strategic fits with which to capture added competitive advantage, the task of building shareholder value via unrelated diversification ultimately hinges on the business acumen of corporate executives. To succeed in using a strategy of unrelated diversification to produce companywide financial results above and beyond what the businesses could generate operating as stand-alone entities, corporate executives must:

- Do a superior job of diversifying into new businesses that can produce consistently good earnings and returns on investment (thereby satisfying the attractiveness test).

- Do an excellent job of negotiating favorable acquisition prices (thereby satisfying the cost-of-entry test).

- Do such a good job overseeing the firm's business subsidiaries and contributing to how they are managed—by providing expert problem-solving skills, creative strategy suggestions, and high caliber decision-making guidance to the heads of the various business subsidiaries—that the subsidiaries perform at a higher level than they would otherwise be able to do through the efforts of the business-unit heads alone (a possible way to satisfy the better-off test).

- Be shrewd in identifying when to shift resources out of businesses with dim profit prospects and into businesses with above-average prospects for growth and profitability.

- Be good at discerning when a business needs to be sold (because it is on the verge of confronting adverse industry and competitive conditions and probable declines in long-term profitability) and also finding buyers who will pay a price higher than the company's net investment in the business (so that the sale of divested businesses will result in capital gains for shareholders rather than capital losses).

To the extent that corporate executives are able to craft and execute a strategy of unrelated diversification that produces enough of the above outcomes to result in a stream of dividends and capital gains for stockholders greater than a $1 + 1 = 2$ outcome, a case can be made that shareholder value has truly been enhanced.

The Drawbacks of Unrelated Diversification

Unrelated diversification strategies have two important negatives that undercut the pluses: demanding managerial requirements and limited competitive advantage potential.

Demanding Managerial Requirements Successfully managing a set of fundamentally different businesses operating in fundamentally different industry and competitive environments is an exceptionally challenging proposition for corporate-level managers. It is difficult because key executives at the corporate level, while perhaps having personally worked in one or two of the company's businesses, rarely have the time and expertise to be sufficiently familiar with all the circumstances surrounding each of the company's businesses to be in a position to give high-caliber guidance to business-level managers. Indeed, the greater the number of businesses a company is in and the more diverse they are, the harder it is for corporate managers to (1) stay abreast of what's happening in each industry and each subsidiary and thus judge whether a particular business has bright prospects or is headed for trouble, (2) know enough about the issues and problems facing each subsidiary to pick business-unit heads having the requisite combination of managerial skills and know-how, (3) be able to tell the difference between those strategic proposals of business-unit managers that are prudent and those that are risky or unlikely to succeed, and (4) know what to do if a business unit stumbles and its results suddenly head downhill.[12]

> **Core Concept**
> The two biggest drawbacks to unrelated diversification are the difficulties of competently managing many different businesses and being without the added source of competitive advantage that cross-business strategic fit provides.

In a company like General Electric (see Illustration Capsule 9.2) or Tyco International (which acquired over 1,000 companies during the 1990–2001 period), corporate executives are constantly scrambling to stay on top of fresh industry developments and the strategic progress and plans of each subsidiary, often depending on briefings by business-level managers for many of the details. As a rule, the more unrelated businesses that a company has diversified into, the more corporate executives are dependent on briefings from business unit heads and "managing by the numbers"—that is, keeping a close track on the financial and operating results of each subsidiary and assuming that the heads of the various subsidiaries have most everything under control so long as the latest key financial and operating measures look good. Managing by the numbers works if the heads of the various business units are quite capable and consistently meet their numbers. But the problem comes when things start to go awry in a business despite the best effort of business-unit managers and corporate management has to get deeply involved in turning around a business it does not know all that much about—as the former chairman of a Fortune 500 company advised, "Never acquire a business you don't know how to run." Because every business tends to encounter rough sledding, a good way to gauge the merits of acquiring a company in an unrelated industry is to ask, "If the business got into trouble, is corporate management likely to know how to bail it out?" When the answer is no (or even a qualified yes or maybe), growth via acquisition into unrelated businesses is a chancy strategy.[13] Just one or two unforeseen declines or big strategic mistakes (misjudging the importance of certain competitive forces or the impact of driving forces or key success factors, encountering unexpected problems in a newly acquired business, or being too optimistic about turning around a struggling subsidiary) can cause a precipitous drop in corporate earnings and crash the parent company's stock price.

Hence, competently overseeing a set of widely diverse businesses can turn out to be much harder than it sounds. In practice, comparatively few companies have proved up to the task. There are far more companies whose corporate executives have failed at delivering consistently good financial results with an unrelated diversification strategy than there are companies with corporate executives who have been successful.[14] It is simply very difficult for corporate executives to achieve $1 + 1 = 3$ gains in shareholder value based on their expertise in (*a*) picking which industries to diversify into and which companies in these industries to acquire, (*b*) shifting resources from low-performing businesses into high-performing businesses, and (*c*) giving high-caliber decision-making guidance to the general managers of their business subsidiaries. The odds are that the result of unrelated diversification will be $1 + 1 = 2$ or less.

> Relying solely on the expertise of corporate executives to wisely manage a set of unrelated businesses is *a much weaker foundation for enhancing shareholder value* than is a strategy of related diversification where corporate performance can be boosted by competitively valuable cross-business strategic fits.

Limited Competitive Advantage Potential   The second big negative is that *unrelated diversification offers no potential for competitive advantage beyond what each individual business can generate on its own.* Unlike a related diversification strategy, there are no cross-business strategic fits to draw on for reducing costs, beneficially transferring skills and technology, leveraging use of a powerful brand name, or collaborating to build mutually beneficial competitive capabilities and thereby *adding to any competitive advantage possessed by individual businesses.* Yes, a cash-rich corporate parent pursuing unrelated diversification can provide its subsidiaries with much-needed capital and maybe even the managerial know-how to help resolve problems in particular business units, but otherwise it has little to offer in the way of enhancing the competitive strength of its individual business units. *Without the competitive advantage potential of strategic fits, consolidated performance of an unrelated group of businesses stands to be little or no better than the sum of what the individual business units could achieve if they were independent.*

COMBINATION RELATED–UNRELATED DIVERSIFICATION STRATEGIES

There's nothing to preclude a company from diversifying into both related and unrelated businesses. Indeed, in actual practice the business makeup of diversified companies varies considerably. Some diversified companies are really *dominant-business enterprises*–one major "core" business accounts for 50 to 80 percent of total revenues and a collection of small related or unrelated businesses accounts for the remainder. Some diversified companies are *narrowly diversified* around a few (two to five) related or unrelated businesses. Others are *broadly diversified* around a wide-ranging collection of related businesses, unrelated businesses, or a mixture of both. And a number of multibusiness enterprises have diversified into unrelated areas but have a collection of related businesses within each area—thus giving them a business portfolio consisting of *several unrelated groups of related businesses.* There's ample room for companies to customize their diversification strategies to incorporate elements of both related and unrelated diversification, as may suit their own risk preferences and strategic vision.

Figure 9.4   **Identifying a Diversified Company's Strategy**

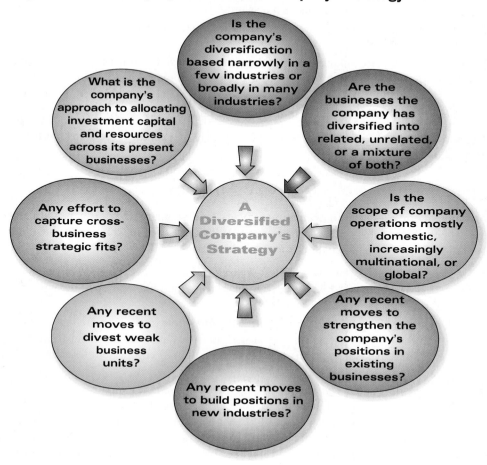

Figure 9.4 indicates what to look for in identifying the main elements of a company's diversification strategy. Having a clear fix on the company's current corporate strategy sets the stage for evaluating how good the strategy is and proposing strategic moves to boost the company's performance.

EVALUATING THE STRATEGY OF A DIVERSIFIED COMPANY

Strategic analysis of diversified companies builds on the concepts and methods used for single-business companies. But there are some additional aspects to consider and a couple of new analytical tools to master. The procedure for evaluating the pluses and minuses of a diversified company's strategy and deciding what actions to take to improve the company's performance involves six steps:

1. Assessing the attractiveness of the industries the company has diversified into, both individually and as a group.

2. Assessing the competitive strength of the company's business units and determining how many are strong contenders in their respective industries.

3. Checking the competitive advantage potential of cross-business strategic fits among the company's various business units.

4. Checking whether the firm's resources fit the requirements of its present business lineup.

5. Ranking the performance prospects of the businesses from best to worst and determining what the corporate parent's priority should be in allocating resources to its various businesses.

6. Crafting new strategic moves to improve overall corporate performance.

The core concepts and analytical techniques underlying each of these steps merit further discussion.

Step 1: Evaluating Industry Attractiveness

A principal consideration in evaluating a diversified company's business makeup and the caliber of its strategy is the attractiveness of the industries in which it has business operations. Answers to several questions are required:

1. *Does each industry the company has diversified into represent a good business for the company to be in?* Ideally, each industry in which the firm operates will pass the attractiveness test.

2. *Which of the company's industries are most attractive and which are least attractive?* Comparing the attractiveness of the industries and ranking them from most to least attractive is a prerequisite to wise allocation of corporate resources across the various businesses.

3. *How appealing is the whole group of industries in which the company has invested?* The answer to this question points to whether the group of industries holds promise for attractive growth and profitability. A company whose revenues and profits come chiefly from businesses in relatively unattractive industries probably needs to look at divesting businesses in unattractive industries and entering industries that qualify as highly attractive.

The more attractive the industries (both individually and as a group) a diversified company is in, the better its prospects for good long-term performance.

Calculating Industry Attractiveness Scores for Each Industry into Which the Company Has Diversified   A simple and reliable analytical tool involves calculating quantitative industry attractiveness scores, which can then be used to gauge each industry's attractiveness, rank the industries from most to least attractive, and make judgments about the attractiveness of all the industries as a group.

The following measures are typically used to gauge an industry's attractiveness:

- *Market size and projected growth rate*—Big industries are more attractive than small industries, and fast-growing industries tend to be more attractive than slow-growing industries, other things being equal.

- *The intensity of competition*—Industries where competitive pressures are relatively weak are more attractive than industries where competitive pressures are strong.

- *Emerging opportunities and threats*—Industries with promising opportunities and minimal threats on the near horizon are more attractive than industries with modest opportunities and imposing threats.

- *The presence of cross-industry strategic fits*—The more the industry's value chain and resource requirements match up well with the value chain activities of other industries in which the company has operations, the more attractive the industry is to a firm pursuing related diversification. However, cross-industry strategic fits may be of no consequence to a company committed to a strategy of unrelated diversification.

- *Resource requirements*—Industries having resource requirements within the company's reach are more attractive than industries where capital and other resource requirements could strain corporate financial resources and organizational capabilities.

- *Seasonal and cyclical factors*—Industries where buyer demand is relatively steady year-round and not unduly vulnerable to economic ups and downs tend to be more attractive than industries where there are wide swings in buyer demand within or across years. However, seasonality may be a plus for a company that is in several seasonal industries, if the seasonal highs in one industry correspond to the lows in another industry, thus helping even out monthly sales levels. Likewise, cyclical market demand in one industry can be attractive if its up-cycle runs counter to the market down-cycles in another industry where the company operates, thus helping reduce revenue and earnings volatility.

- *Social, political, regulatory, and environmental factors*—Industries with significant problems in such areas as consumer health, safety, or environmental pollution or that are subject to intense regulation are less attractive than industries where such problems are not burning issues.

- *Industry profitability*—Industries with healthy profit margins and high rates of return on investment are generally more attractive than industries where profits have historically been low or unstable.

- *Industry uncertainty and business risk*—Industries with less uncertainty on the horizon and lower overall business risk are more attractive than industries whose prospects for one reason or another are quite uncertain, especially when the industry has formidable resource requirements.

After settling on a set of attractiveness measures that suit a diversified company's circumstances, each attractiveness measure is assigned a weight reflecting its relative importance in determining an industry's attractiveness—it is weak methodology to assume that the various attractiveness measures are equally important. The intensity of competition in an industry should nearly always carry a high weight (say, 0.20 to 0.30). Strategic-fit considerations should be assigned a high weight in the case of companies with related diversification strategies; but, for companies with an unrelated diversification strategy, strategic fits with other industries may be given a low weight or even dropped from the list of attractiveness measures altogether. Seasonal and cyclical factors generally are assigned a low weight (or maybe even eliminated from the analysis) unless a company has diversified into industries strongly characterized by seasonal demand and/or heavy vulnerability to cyclical upswings and downswings. The importance weights must add up to 1.0.

Next, each industry is rated on each of the chosen industry attractiveness measures, using a rating scale of 1 to 10 (where a *high* rating signifies *high* attractiveness and a *low* rating signifies *low* attractiveness). *Keep in mind here that the more intensely competitive an industry is, the lower the attractiveness rating for that industry.* Likewise, the higher the capital and resource requirements associated with being in a particular industry, the lower the attractiveness rating. And an industry that is subject

Table 9.1   **Calculating Weighted Industry Attractiveness Scores**

Industry Attractiveness Measure	Importance Weight	Industry A Rating/ Score	Industry B Rating/ Score	Industry C Rating/ Score	Industry D Rating/ Score
Market size and projected growth rate	0.10	8/0.80	5/0.50	7/0.70	3/0.30
Intensity of competition	0.25	8/2.00	7/1.75	3/0.75	2/0.50
Emerging opportunities and threats	0.10	2/0.20	9/0.90	4/0.40	5/0.50
Cross-industry strategic fits	0.20	8/1.60	4/0.80	8/1.60	2/0.40
Resource requirements	0.10	9/0.90	7/0.70	10/1.00	5/0.50
Seasonal and cyclical influences	0.05	9/0.45	8/0.40	10/0.50	5/0.25
Societal, political, regulatory, and environmental factors	0.05	10/1.00	7/0.70	7/0.70	3/0.30
Industry profitability	0.10	5/0.50	10/1.00	3/0.30	3/0.30
Industry uncertainty and business risk	0.05	5/0.25	7/0.35	10/0.50	1/0.05
Sum of the assigned weights	1.00				
Overall industry attractiveness scores		**7.70**	**7.10**	**5.45**	**3.10**

Rating scale: 1 = Very unattractive to company; 10 = Very attractive to company.

to stringent pollution control regulations or that causes societal problems (like cigarettes or alcoholic beverages) should usually be given a low attractiveness rating. Weighted attractiveness scores are then calculated by multiplying the industry's rating on each measure by the corresponding weight. For example, a rating of 8 times a weight of 0.25 gives a weighted attractiveness score of 2.00. The sum of the weighted scores for all the attractiveness measures provides an overall industry attractiveness score. This procedure is illustrated in Table 9.1.

Interpreting the Industry Attractiveness Scores   Industries with a score much below 5.0 probably do not pass the attractiveness test. If a company's industry attractiveness scores are all above 5.0, it is probably fair to conclude that the group of industries the company operates in is attractive as a whole. But the group of industries takes on a decidedly lower degree of attractiveness as the number of industries with scores below 5.0 increases, especially if industries with low scores account for a sizable fraction of the company's revenues.

For a diversified company to be a strong performer, a substantial portion of its revenues and profits must come from business units with relatively high attractiveness scores. It is particularly important that a diversified company's principal businesses be in industries with a good outlook for growth and above-average profitability. Having a big fraction of the company's revenues and profits come from industries with slow growth, low profitability, or intense competition tends to drag overall company performance down. Business units in the least attractive industries are potential candidates for divestiture, unless they are positioned strongly enough to overcome the unattractive aspects of their industry environments or they are a strategically important component of the company's business makeup.

The Difficulties of Calculating Industry Attractiveness Scores   There are two hurdles to calculating industry attractiveness scores. One is deciding on appropriate weights for the industry attractiveness measures. Not only may different analysts have different views about which weights are appropriate for the different attractiveness measures but also different weightings may be appropriate for different companies—based on their strategies, performance targets, and financial circumstances. For instance, placing a low weight on industry resource requirements may be justifiable for a cash-rich company, whereas a high weight may be more appropriate for a financially strapped company. The second hurdle is gaining sufficient command of the industry to assign accurate and objective ratings. Generally, a company can come up with the statistical data needed to compare its industries on such factors as market size, growth rate, seasonal and cyclical influences, and industry profitability. Cross-industry fits and resource requirements are also fairly easy to judge. But the attractiveness measure where judgment weighs most heavily is that of intensity of competition. It is not always easy to conclude whether competition in one industry is stronger or weaker than in another industry because of the different types of competitive influences that prevail and the differences in their relative importance. In the event that the available information is too skimpy to confidently assign a rating value to an industry on a particular attractiveness measure, then it is usually best to use a score of 5, which avoids biasing the overall attractiveness score either up or down.

But despite the hurdles, calculating industry attractiveness scores is a systematic and reasonably reliable method for ranking a diversified company's industries from most to least attractive—numbers like those shown for the four industries in Table 9.1 help pin down the basis for judging which industries are more attractive and to what degree.

Step 2: Evaluating Business-Unit Competitive Strength

The second step in evaluating a diversified company is to appraise how strongly positioned each of its business units are in their respective industry. Doing an appraisal of each business unit's strength and competitive position in its industry not only reveals its chances for industry success but also provides a basis for ranking the units from competitively strongest to competitively weakest and sizing up the competitive strength of all the business units as a group.

Calculating Competitive Strength Scores for Each Business Unit   Quantitative measures of each business unit's competitive strength can be calculated using a procedure similar to that for measuring industry attractiveness. The following factors are using in quantifying the competitive strengths of a diversified company's business subsidiaries:

- *Relative market share*—A business unit's *relative market share* is defined as the ratio of its market share to the market share held by the largest rival firm in the industry, with market share measured in unit volume, not dollars. For instance, if business A has a market-leading share of 40 percent and its largest rival has 30 percent, A's relative market share is 1.33. (Note that only business units that are market share leaders in their respective industries can have relative market shares greater then 1.0.) If business B has a 15 percent market share and B's largest rival has 30 percent, B's relative market share is 0.5. *The further below 1.0 a business unit's relative market share is, the weaker its competitive strength and market position vis-à-vis rivals.* A 10 percent market share, for example, does not signal much competitive strength if the leader's share is 50 percent

> Using relative market share to measure competitive strength is analytically superior to using straight-percentage market share.

(a 0.20 relative market share), but a 10 percent share is actually quite strong if the leader's share is only 12 percent (a 0.83 relative market share)—this is why a company's relative market share is a better measure of competitive strength than a company's market share based on either dollars or unit volume.

- *Costs relative to competitors' costs*—Business units that have low costs relative to key competitors' costs tend to be more strongly positioned in their industries than business units struggling to maintain cost parity with major rivals. Assuming that the prices charged by industry rivals are about the same, there's reason to expect that business units with higher relative market shares have lower unit costs than competitors with lower relative market shares because their greater unit sales volumes offer the possibility of economies from larger-scale operations and the benefits of any experience/learning curve effects. Another indicator of low cost can be a business unit's supply chain management capabilities. The only time when a business unit's competitive strength may not be undermined by having higher costs than rivals is when it has incurred the higher costs to strongly differentiate its product offering and its customers are willing to pay premium prices for the differentiating features.

- *Ability to match or beat rivals on key product attributes*—A company's competitiveness depends in part on being able to satisfy buyer expectations with regard to features, product performance, reliability, service, and other important attributes.

- *Ability to benefit from strategic fits with sister businesses*—Strategic fits with other businesses within the company enhance a business unit's competitive strength and may provide a competitive edge.

- *Ability to exercise bargaining leverage with key suppliers or customers*—Having bargaining leverage signals competitive strength and can be a source of competitive advantage.

- *Caliber of alliances and collaborative partnerships with suppliers and/or buyers*—Well-functioning alliances and partnerships may signal a potential competitive advantage vis-à-vis rivals and thus add to a business's competitive strength. Alliances with key suppliers are often the basis for competitive strength in supply chain management.

- *Brand image and reputation*—A strong brand name is a valuable competitive asset in most industries.

- *Competitively valuable capabilities*—Business units recognized for their technological leadership, product innovation, or marketing prowess are usually strong competitors in their industry. Skills in supply chain management can generate valuable cost or product differentiation advantages. So can unique production capabilities. Sometimes a company's business units gain competitive strength because of their knowledge of customers and markets and/or their proven managerial capabilities. *An important thing to look for here is how well a business unit's competitive assets match industry key success factors.* The more a business unit's resource strengths and competitive capabilities match the industry's key success factors, the stronger its competitive position tends to be.

- *Profitability relative to competitors*—Business units that consistently earn above-average returns on investment and have bigger profit margins than their rivals usually have stronger competitive positions. Moreover, above-average profitability signals competitive advantage, while below-average profitability usually denotes competitive disadvantage.

Table 9.2   **Calculating Weighted Competitive Strength Scores for a Diversified Company's Business Units**

Competitive Strength Measure	Importance Weight	Business A in Industry A Rating/ Score	Business B in Industry B Rating/ Score	Business C in Industry C Rating/ Score	Business D in Industry D Rating/ Score
Relative market share	0.15	10/1.50	1/0.15	6/0.90	2/0.30
Costs relative to competitors' costs	0.20	7/1.40	2/0.40	5/1.00	3/0.60
Ability to match or beat rivals on key product attributes	0.05	9/0.45	4/0.20	8/0.40	4/0.20
Ability to benefit from strategic fits with sister businesses	0.20	8/1.60	4/0.80	8/0.80	2/0.60
Bargaining leverage with suppliers/ buyers; caliber of alliances	0.05	9/0.90	3/0.30	6/0.30	2/0.10
Brand image and reputation	0.10	9/0.90	2/0.20	7/0.70	5/0.50
Competitively valuable capabilities	0.15	7/1.05	2/0.20	5/0.75	3/0.45
Profitability relative to competitors	0.10	5/0.50	1/0.10	4/0.40	4/0.40
Sum of the assigned weights	1.00				
Overall industry attractiveness scores		**8.30**	**2.35**	**5.25**	**3.15**

Rating scale: 1 = Very weak; 10 = Very strong.

After settling on a set of competitive strength measures that are well matched to the circumstances of the various business units, weights indicating each measure's importance need to be assigned. A case can be made for using different weights for different business units whenever the importance of the strength measures differs significantly from business to business, but otherwise it is simpler just to go with a single set of weights and avoid the added complication of multiple weights. As before, the importance weights must add up to 1.0. Each business unit is then rated on each of the chosen strength measures, using a rating scale of 1 to 10 (where a *high* rating signifies competitive *strength* and a *low* rating signifies competitive *weakness*). In the event that the available information is too skimpy to confidently assign a rating value to a business unit on a particular strength measure, then it is usually best to use a score of 5, which avoids biasing the overall score either up or down. Weighted strength ratings are calculated by multiplying the business unit's rating on each strength measure by the assigned weight. For example, a strength score of 6 times a weight of 0.15 gives a weighted strength rating of 0.90. The sum of weighted ratings across all the strength measures provides a quantitative measure of a business unit's overall market strength and competitive standing. Table 9.2 provides sample calculations of competitive strength ratings for four businesses.

Interpreting the Competitive Strength Scores   Business units with competitive strength ratings above 6.7 (on a scale of 1 to 10) are strong market contenders in their industries. Businesses with ratings in the 3.3 to 6.7 range have moderate competitive strength vis-à-vis rivals. Businesses with ratings below 3.3 are in competitively weak market positions. If a diversified company's business units all have competitive strength scores above 5.0, it is fair to conclude that its business units are all fairly strong market contenders in their respective industries. But as the number of business units with scores below 5.0 increases, there's reason to question whether the company can perform well with so many businesses in relatively weak competitive positions. This concern takes on even more importance when business units with low scores account for a sizable fraction of the company's revenues.

Using a Nine-Cell Matrix to Simultaneously Portray Industry Attractiveness and Competitive Strength The industry attractiveness and competitive strength scores can be used to portray the strategic positions of each business in a diversified company. Industry attractiveness is plotted on the vertical axis, and competitive strength on the horizontal axis. A nine-cell grid emerges from dividing the vertical axis into three regions (high, medium, and low attractiveness) and the horizontal axis into three regions (strong, average, and weak competitive strength). As shown in Figure 9.5, high attractiveness is associated with scores of 6.7 or greater on a rating scale of 1 to 10, medium attractiveness to scores of 3.3 to 6.7, and low attractiveness to scores below 3.3. Likewise, high competitive strength is defined as a score greater than 6.7, average strength as scores of 3.3 to 6.7, and low strength as scores below 3.3. *Each business unit is plotted on the nine-cell matrix according to its overall attractiveness score and strength score, and then shown as a bubble.* The size of each bubble is scaled to what percentage of revenues the business generates relative to total corporate revenues. The bubbles in Figure 9.5 were located on the grid using the four industry attractiveness scores from Table 9.1 and the strength scores for the four business units in Table 9.2.

The locations of the business units on the attractiveness–strength matrix provide valuable guidance in deploying corporate resources to the various business units. In general, *a diversified company's prospects for good overall performance are enhanced by concentrating corporate resources and strategic attention on those business units having the greatest competitive strength and positioned in highly attractive industries*—specifically, businesses in the three cells in the upper left portion of the attractiveness–strength matrix, where industry attractiveness and competitive strength/ market position are both favorable. The general strategic prescription for businesses falling in these three cells (for instance, business A in Figure 9.5) is "grow and build," with businesses in the high–strong cell standing first in line for resource allocations by the corporate parent.

Next in priority come businesses positioned in the three diagonal cells stretching from the lower left to the upper right (businesses B and C in Figure 9.5). Such businesses usually merit medium or intermediate priority in the parent's resource allocation ranking. However, some businesses in the medium-priority diagonal cells may have brighter or dimmer prospects than others. For example, a small business in the upper right cell of the matrix (like business B), despite being in a highly attractive industry, may occupy too weak a competitive position in its industry to justify the investment and resources needed to turn it into a strong market contender and shift its position leftward in the matrix over time. If, however, a business in the upper right cell has attractive opportunities for rapid growth and a good potential for winning a much stronger market position over time, it may merit a high claim on the corporate parent's resource allocation ranking and be given the capital it needs to pursue a grow-and-build strategy–the strategic objective here would be to move the business leftward in the attractiveness–strength matrix over time.

Businesses in the three cells in the lower right corner of the matrix (like business D in Figure 9.5) typically are weak performers and have the lowest claim on corporate resources. Most such businesses are good candidates for being divested (sold to other companies) or else managed in a manner calculated to squeeze out the maximum cash flows from operations—the cash flows from low-performing/low-potential businesses

Figure 9.5   **A Nine-Cell Industry Attractiveness–Competitive Strength Matrix**

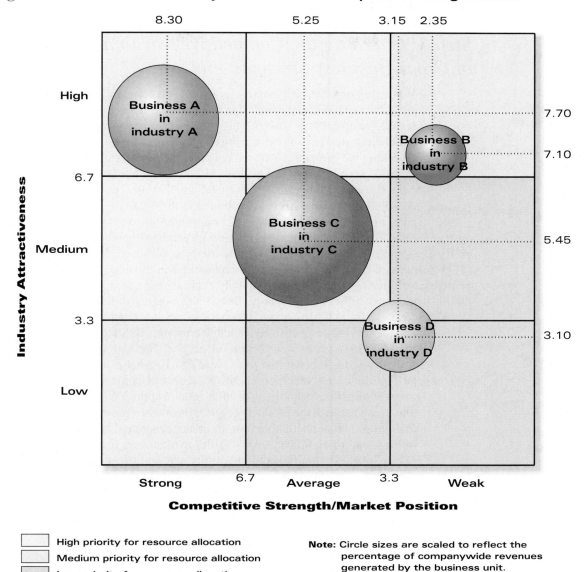

Note: Circle sizes are scaled to reflect the percentage of companywide revenues generated by the business unit.

High priority for resource allocation
Medium priority for resource allocation
Low priority for resource allocation

can then be diverted to financing expansion of business units with greater market opportunities. In exceptional cases where a business located in the three lower right cells is nonetheless fairly profitable (which it might be if it is in the low–average cell) or has the potential for good earnings and return on investment, the business merits retention and the allocation of sufficient resources to achieve better performance.

The nine-cell attractiveness–strength matrix provides clear, strong logic for why a diversified company needs to consider both industry attractiveness and business strength in allocating resources and investment capital to its different businesses. A good case can be made for concentrating resources in those businesses that enjoy higher degrees of attractiveness and competitive strength, being very selective in making investments in businesses with intermediate positions on the grid, and withdrawing resources from businesses that are lower in attractiveness and strength unless they offer exceptional profit or cash flow potential.

Step 3: Checking the Competitive Advantage Potential of Cross-Business Strategic Fits

Core Concept
A company's related diversification strategy derives its power in large part from the presence of competitively valuable strategic fits among its businesses.

While this step can be bypassed for diversified companies whose businesses are all unrelated (since, by design, no strategic fits are present), a high potential for converting strategic fits into competitive advantage is central to concluding just how good a company's related diversification strategy is. Checking the competitive advantage potential of cross-business strategic fits involves searching for and evaluating how much benefit a diversified company can gain from value chain matchups that present (1) opportunities to combine the performance of certain activities, thereby reducing costs and capturing economies of scope; (2) opportunities to transfer skills, technology, or intellectual capital from one business to another, thereby leveraging use of existing resources; (3) opportunities to share use of a well-respected brand name; and (4) opportunities for sister businesses to collaborate in creating valuable new competitive capabilities (such as enhanced supply chain management capabilities, quicker first-to-market capabilities, or greater product innovation capabilities).

Figure 9.6 illustrates the process of comparing the value chains of sister businesses and identifying competitively valuable cross-business strategic fits. *But more than just strategic fit identification is needed. The real test is what competitive value can be generated from these fits.* To what extent can cost savings be realized? How much competitive value will come from cross-business transfer of skills, technology, or intellectual capital? Will transferring a potent brand name to the products of sister businesses grow sales significantly? Will cross-business collaboration to create or strengthen competitive capabilities lead to significant gains in the marketplace or in financial performance? Absent significant strategic fits and dedicated company efforts to capture the benefits, one has to be skeptical about the potential for a diversified company's businesses to perform better together than apart.

Core Concept
The greater the value of cross-business strategic fits in enhancing a company's performance in the marketplace or on the bottom line, the more competitively powerful is its strategy of related diversification.

Step 4: Checking for Resource Fit

Core Concept
Sister businesses possess *resource fit* when they add to a company's overall resource strengths and when a company has adequate resources to support their requirements.

The businesses in a diversified company's lineup need to exhibit good **resource fit.** Resource fit exists when (1) businesses add to a company's overall resource strengths and (2) a company has adequate resources to support its entire group of businesses without spreading itself too thin. One important dimension of resource fit concerns whether a diversified company can generate the internal cash flows sufficient to fund the capital requirements of its businesses, pay its dividends, meet its debt obligations, and otherwise remain financially healthy.

Financial Resource Fits: Cash Cows versus Cash Hogs   Different businesses have different cash flow and investment characteristics. For example, business units in rapidly growing industries are often **cash hogs**—so labeled because the cash flows they are able to generate from internal operations aren't big enough to fund their expansion. To keep pace with rising buyer demand, rapid-growth businesses frequently need sizable annual capital investments—for new facilities and equipment, for

Figure 9.6   **Identifying the Competitive Advantage Potential of Cross-Business Strategic Fits**

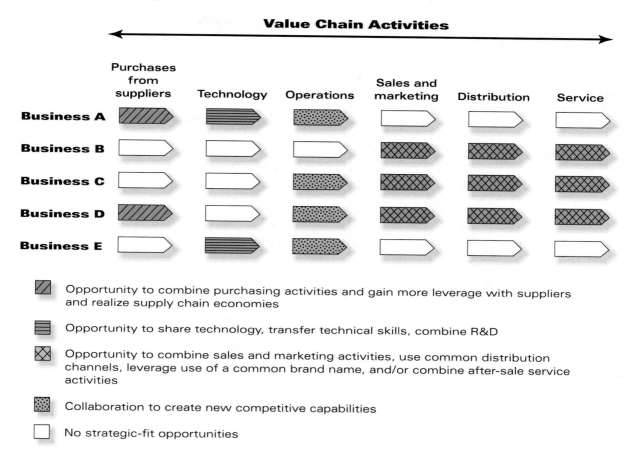

Opportunity to combine purchasing activities and gain more leverage with suppliers and realize supply chain economies

Opportunity to share technology, transfer technical skills, combine R&D

Opportunity to combine sales and marketing activities, use common distribution channels, leverage use of a common brand name, and/or combine after-sale service activities

Collaboration to create new competitive capabilities

No strategic-fit opportunities

new product development or technology improvements, and for additional working capital to support inventory expansion and a larger base of operations. A business in a fast-growing industry becomes an even bigger cash hog when it has a relatively low market share and is pursuing a strategy to become an industry leader. Because a cash hog's financial resources must be provided by the corporate parent, corporate managers have to decide whether it makes good financial and strategic sense to keep pouring new money into a business that continually needs cash infusions.

In contrast, business units with leading market positions in mature industries may, however, be **cash cows**—businesses that generate substantial cash surpluses over what is needed to adequately fund their operations. Market leaders in slow-growth industries often generate sizable positive cash flows *over and above what is needed for growth and reinvestment* because their industry-leading positions tend to give them the sales volumes and reputation to earn attractive profits and because the slow-growth nature of their industry often entails relatively modest annual investment requirements. Cash cows, though not always attractive from a growth standpoint, are valuable businesses from a financial resource perspective. The surplus cash flows they generate can be used to pay corporate dividends, finance acquisitions, and provide

> **Core Concept**
> A **cash hog** generates cash flows that are too small to fully fund its operations and growth; a cash hog requires cash infusions to provide additional working capital and finance new capital investment.

Core Concept
A *cash cow* generates cash flows over and above its internal requirements, thus providing a corporate parent with funds for investing in cash hogs, financing new acquisitions, or paying dividends.

funds for investing in the company's promising cash hogs. It makes good financial and strategic sense for diversified companies to keep cash cows in healthy condition, fortifying and defending their market position so as to preserve their cash-generating capability over the long term and thereby have an ongoing source of financial resources to deploy elsewhere. The cigarette business is one of the world's biggest cash cows. General Electric, whose business lineup is shown in Illustration Capsule 9.2, considers that its advanced materials, equipment services, and appliance and lighting businesses are cash cows.

Viewing a diversified group of businesses as a collection of cash flows and cash requirements (present and future) is a major step forward in understanding what the financial ramifications of diversification are and why having businesses with good financial resource fit is so important. For instance, *a diversified company's businesses exhibit good financial resource fit when the excess cash generated by its cash cows is sufficient to fund the investment requirements of promising cash hogs.* Ideally, investing in promising cash hog businesses over time results in growing the hogs into self-supporting *star businesses* that have strong or market-leading competitive positions in attractive, high-growth markets and high levels of profitability. Star businesses are often the cash cows of the future—when the markets of star businesses begin to mature and their growth slows, their competitive strength should produce self-generated cash flows more than sufficient to cover their investment needs. The "success sequence" is thus cash hog to young star (but perhaps still a cash hog) to self-supporting star to cash cow.

If, however, a cash hog has questionable promise (either because of low industry attractiveness or a weak competitive position), then it becomes a logical candidate for divestiture. Pursuing an aggressive invest-and-expand strategy for a cash hog with an uncertain future seldom makes sense because it requires the corporate parent to keep pumping more capital into the business with only a dim hope of eventually turning the cash hog into a future star and realizing a good return on its investments. Such financially draining businesses fail the resource fit test because they strain the corporate parent's ability to adequately fund its other businesses. Divesting a cash hog is usually the best alternative unless (1) it has valuable strategic fits with other business units or (2) the capital infusions needed from the corporate parent are modest relative to the funds available and there's a decent chance of growing the business into a solid bottom-line contributor yielding a good return on invested capital.

Other Tests of Resource Fit   Aside from cash flow considerations, there are four other factors to consider in determining whether the businesses comprising a diversified company's portfolio exhibit good resource fit:

- *Does the business adequately contribute to achieving companywide performance targets?* A business has good financial fit when it contributes to the achievement of corporate performance objectives (growth in earnings per share, above-average return on investment, recognition as an industry leader, etc.) and when it materially enhances shareholder value via helping drive increases in the company's stock price. A business exhibits poor financial fit if it soaks up a disproportionate share of the company's financial resources, makes subpar or inconsistent bottom-line contributions, is unduly risky and failure would jeopardize the entire enterprise, or remains too small to make a material earnings contribution even though it performs well.

- *Does the company have adequate financial strength to fund its different businesses and maintain a healthy credit rating?* A diversified company's strategy fails the resource fit test when its financial resources are stretched across so many businesses that its credit rating is impaired. Severe financial strain sometimes occurs when a company borrows so heavily to finance new acquisitions that it has to trim way back on capital expenditures for existing businesses and use the big majority of its financial resources to meet interest obligations and to pay down debt. Time Warner, Royal Ahold, and AT&T, for example, have found themselves so financially overextended that they have had to sell off some of their business units to raise the money to pay down burdensome debt obligations and continue to fund essential capital expenditures for the remaining businesses.

- *Does the company have or can it develop the specific resource strengths and competitive capabilities needed to be successful in each of its businesses?*[15] Sometimes the resource strengths a company has accumulated in its core or mainstay business prove to be a poor match with the key success factors and competitive capabilities needed to succeed in one or more businesses it has diversified into. For instance, BTR, a multibusiness company in Great Britain, discovered that the company's resources and managerial skills were quite well suited for parenting industrial manufacturing businesses but not for parenting its distribution businesses (National Tyre Services and Texas-based Summers Group); as a consequence, BTR decided to divest its distribution businesses and focus exclusively on diversifying around small industrial manufacturing.[16] One company with businesses in restaurants and retailing decided that its resource capabilities in site selection, controlling operating costs, management selection and training, and supply chain logistics would enable it to succeed in the hotel business and in property management; but what management missed was that these businesses had some significantly different key success factors—namely, skills in controlling property development costs, maintaining low overheads, product branding (hotels), and ability to recruit a sufficient volume of business to maintain high levels of facility use.[17] Thus, a mismatch between the company's resource strengths and the key success factors in a particular business can be serious enough to warrant divesting an existing business or not acquiring a new business. In contrast, when a company's resources and capabilities are a good match with the key success factors of industries it is not presently in, it makes sense to take a hard look at acquiring companies in these industries and expanding the company's business lineup.

- *Are recently acquired businesses acting to strengthen a company's resource base and competitive capabilities or are they causing its competitive and managerial resources to be stretched too thin?* A diversified company has to guard against overtaxing its resource strengths, a condition that can arise when (1) it goes on an acquisition spree and management is called on to assimilate and oversee many new businesses very quickly or (2) when it lacks sufficient resource depth to do a creditable job of transferring skills and competences from one of its businesses to another (especially, a large acquisition or several lesser ones). The broader the diversification, the greater the concern about whether the company has sufficient managerial depth to cope with the diverse range of operating problems its wide business lineup presents. And the more a company's diversification strategy is tied to transferring its existing know-how or technologies to new businesses, the more it has to develop a big enough and deep enough resource pool to supply these businesses with sufficient capability to create competitive advantage.[18] Otherwise its strengths end up being thinly spread across many businesses and the opportunity for competitive advantage slips through the cracks.

A Cautionary Note About Transferring Resources from One Business to Another   Just because a company has hit a home run in one business doesn't mean it can easily enter a new business with similar resource requirements and hit a second home run.[19] Noted British retailer Marks & Spencer, despite possessing a range of impressive resource capabilities (ability to choose excellent store locations, having a supply chain that gives it both low costs and high merchandise quality, loyal employees, an excellent reputation with consumers, and strong management expertise) that have made it one of Britain's premier retailers for 100 years, has failed repeatedly in its efforts to diversify into department store retailing in the United States. Even though Philip Morris (now named Altria) had built powerful consumer marketing capabilities in its cigarette and beer businesses, it floundered in soft drinks and ended up divesting its acquisition of 7UP after several frustrating years of competing against strongly entrenched and resource-capable rivals like Coca-Cola and PepsiCo. Then in 2002 it decided to divest its Miller Brewing business—despite its long-standing marketing successes in cigarettes and in its Kraft Foods subsidiary—because it was unable to grow Miller's market share in head-to-head competition against the considerable marketing prowess of Anheuser-Busch.

Step 5: Ranking the Performance Prospects of Business Units and Assigning a Priority for Resource Allocation

Once a diversified company's strategy has been evaluated from the perspective of industry attractiveness, competitive strength, strategic fit, and resource fit, the next step is to rank the performance prospects of the businesses from best to worst and determine which businesses merit top priority for resource support and new capital investments by the corporate parent.

The most important considerations in judging business-unit performance are sales growth, profit growth, contribution to company earnings, and return on capital invested in the business. Sometimes cash flow is a big consideration. Information on each business's past performance can be gleaned from a company's financial records. While past performance is not necessarily a good predictor of future performance, it does signal whether a business already has good-to-excellent performance or has problems to overcome.

Furthermore, the industry attractiveness/business strength evaluations provide a solid basis for judging a business's prospects. Normally, strong business units in attractive industries have significantly better prospects than weak businesses in unattractive industries. And, normally, the revenue and earnings outlook for businesses in fast-growing industries is better than for businesses in slow-growing industries—one important exception is when a business in a slow-growing industry has the competitive strength to draw sales and market share away from its rivals and thus achieve much faster growth than the industry as whole. As a rule, the prior analyses, taken together, signal which business units are likely to be strong performers on the road ahead and which are likely to be laggards. And it is a short step from ranking the prospects of business units to drawing conclusions about whether the company as a whole is capable of strong, mediocre, or weak performance in upcoming years.

Figure 9.7   **The Chief Strategic and Financial Options for Allocating a Diversified Company's Financial Resources**

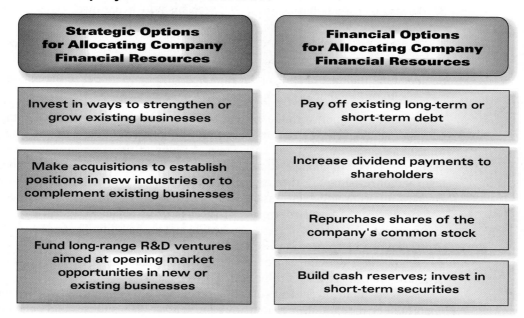

The rankings of future performance generally determine what priority the corporate parent should give to each business in terms of resource allocation. The task here is to decide which business units should have top priority for corporate resource support and new capital investment and which should carry the lowest priority. *Business subsidiaries with the brightest profit and growth prospects and solid strategic and resource fits generally should head the list for corporate resource support.* More specifically, corporate executives need to consider whether and how corporate resources can be used to enhance the competitiveness of particular business units. And they must be diligent in steering resources out of low-opportunity areas and into high-opportunity areas. Divesting marginal businesses is one of the best ways of freeing unproductive assets for redeployment. Surplus funds from cash cows also add to the corporate treasury.

Figure 9.7 shows the chief strategic and financial options for allocating a diversified company's financial resources. Ideally, a company will have enough funds to do what is needed, both strategically and financially. If not, strategic uses of corporate resources should usually take precedence unless there is a compelling reason to strengthen the firm's balance sheet or divert financial resources to pacify shareholders.

Step 6: Crafting New Strategic Moves to Improve Overall Corporate Performance

The diagnosis and conclusions flowing from the five preceding analytical steps set the agenda for crafting strategic moves to improve a diversified company's overall performance. The strategic options boil down to five broad categories of actions:

1. Sticking closely with the existing business lineup and pursuing the opportunities these businesses present.

2. Broadening the company's business scope by making new acquisitions in new industries.

3. Divesting certain businesses and retrenching to a narrower base of business operations.

4. Restructuring the company's business lineup and putting a whole new face on the company's business makeup.

5. Pursuing multinational diversification and striving to globalize the operations of several of the company's business units.

The option of sticking with the current business lineup makes sense when the company's present businesses offer attractive growth opportunities and can be counted on to generate good earnings and cash flows. As long as the company's set of existing businesses puts it in good position for the future and these businesses have good strategic and/or resource fits, then rocking the boat with major changes in the company's business mix is usually unnecessary. Corporate executives can concentrate their attention on getting the best performance from each of its businesses, steering corporate resources into those areas of greatest potential and profitability. The specifics of "what to do" to wring better performance from the present business lineup have to be dictated by each business's circumstances and the preceding analysis of the corporate parent's diversification strategy.

However, in the event that corporate executives are not entirely satisfied with the opportunities they see in the company's present set of businesses and conclude that changes in the company's direction and business makeup are in order, they can opt for any of the four other strategic alternatives listed above. These options are discussed in the following section.

AFTER A COMPANY DIVERSIFIES: THE FOUR MAIN STRATEGY ALTERNATIVES

Diversifying is by no means the final chapter in the evolution of a company's strategy. Once a company has diversified into a collection of related or unrelated businesses and concludes that some overhaul is needed in the company's present lineup and diversification strategy, there are four main strategic paths it can pursue (see Figure 9.8). To more fully understand the strategic issues corporate managers face in the ongoing process of managing a diversified group of businesses, we need to take a brief look at the central thrust of each of the four postdiversification strategy alternatives.

Strategies to Broaden a Diversified Company's Business Base

Diversified companies sometimes find it desirable to build positions in new industries, whether related or unrelated. There are several motivating factors. One is sluggish growth that makes the potential revenue and profit boost of a newly acquired business look attractive. A second is vulnerability to seasonal or recessionary influences or to threats from emerging new technologies. A third is the potential for transferring resources and capabilities to other related or complementary businesses. A fourth is rapidly changing conditions in one or more of a company's core businesses brought on by technological, legislative, or new product innovations that alter buyer requirements and preferences. For instance, the passage of legislation in the United States allowing

Figure 9.8   **A Company's Four Main Strategic Alternatives After It Diversifies**

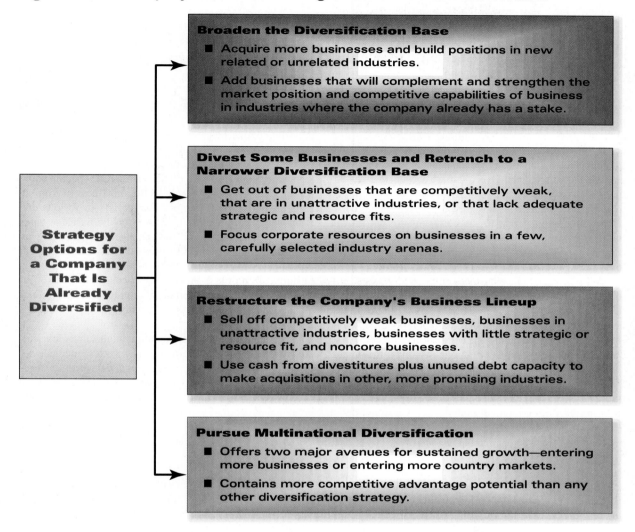

banks, insurance companies, and stock brokerages to enter each other's businesses spurred a raft of acquisitions and mergers to create full-service financial enterprises capable of meeting the multiple financial needs of customers. Citigroup, already the largest U.S. bank, with a global banking franchise, acquired Salomon Smith Barney to position itself in the investment banking and brokerage business and acquired insurance giant Travelers Group to enable it to offer customers insurance products.

A fifth, and often very important, motivating factor for adding new businesses is to complement and strengthen the market position and competitive capabilities of one or more of its present businesses. Procter & Gamble's recent acquisition of Gillette strengthened and extended P&G's reach into personal care and household products—Gillette's businesses included Oral-B toothbrushes, Gillette razors and razor blades, Duracell batteries, Braun shavers and small appliances (coffeemakers, mixers, hair dryers, and electric toothbrushes), and toiletries (Right Guard, Foamy, Soft & Dry, White Rain, and Dry Idea). Unilever, a leading maker of food and personal care products, expanded its business lineup by acquiring SlimFast, Ben & Jerry's Homemade,

Illustration Capsule 9.3

Managing Diversification at Johnson & Johnson: The Benefits of Cross-Business Strategic Fits

Johnson & Johnson (J&J), once a consumer products company known for its Band-Aid line and its baby care products, has evolved into a $42 billion diversified enterprise consisting of some 200-plus operating companies organized into three divisions: drugs, medical devices and diagnostics, and consumer products. Over the past decade J&J has acquired 56 businesses at a cost of about $30 billion; about 10 to 15 percent of J&J's annual growth in revenues has come from acquisitions. Much of the company's recent growth has been in the pharmaceutical division, which in 2004 accounted for 47 percent of J&J's revenues and 57 percent of its operating profits.

While each of J&J's business units sets its own strategies and operates with its own finance and human resource departments, corporate management strongly encourages cross-business cooperation and collaboration, believing that many of the advances in 21st century medicine will come from applying advances in one discipline to another. J&J had 9,300 scientists working in 40 research labs in 2003, and the frequency of cross-disciplinary collaboration was increasing. One of J&J's new drug-coated stents grew out of a discussion between a drug researcher and a

researcher in the company's stent business. (When stents are inserted to prop open arteries following angioplasty, the drug coating helps prevent infection.) A gene technology database compiled by the company's gene research lab was shared with personnel from the diagnostics division, who developed a test that the drug R&D people could use to predict which patients would most benefit from an experimental cancer therapy. J&J experts in various diseases have been meeting quarterly for the past five years to share information, and top management is setting up cross-disciplinary groups to focus on new treatments for particular diseases. J&J's new liquid Band-Aid product (a liquid coating applied to hard-to-cover places like fingers and knuckles) is based on a material used in a wound-closing product sold by the company's hospital products company.

J&J's corporate management maintains that close collaboration among people in its diagnostics, medical devices, and pharmaceuticals businesses—where numerous cross-business strategic fits exist—gives J&J an edge on competitors, most of whom cannot match the company's breadth and depth of expertise.

Sources: Amy Barrett, "Staying on Top," *BusinessWeek,* May 5, 2003, pp. 60–68, and www.jnj.com (accessed October 19, 2005).

and Bestfoods (whose brands included Knorr's soups, Hellman's mayonnaise, Skippy peanut butter, and Mazola cooking oils). Unilever saw these businesses as giving it more clout in competing against such other diversified food and household products companies as Nestlé, Kraft, Procter & Gamble, Campbell Soup, and General Mills.

Usually, expansion into new businesses is undertaken by acquiring companies already in the target industry. Some companies depend on new acquisitions to drive a major portion of their growth in revenues and earnings, and thus are always on the acquisition trail. Cisco Systems built itself into a worldwide leader in networking systems for the Internet by making 95 technology-based acquisitions during 1993–2005 to extend its market reach from routing and switching into Internet Protocol (IP) telephony, home networking, wireless local-area networking (LAN), storage networking, network security, broadband, and optical and broadband systems. Tyco International, now recovering from charges of looting on the part of several top executives, transformed itself from an obscure company in the early 1990s into a $40 billion global manufacturing enterprise with operations in over 100 countries as of 2005 by making over 1,000 acquisitions; the company's far-flung diversification includes businesses in electronics, electrical components, fire and security systems, health care products, valves, undersea telecommunications systems, plastics, and adhesives. Tyco made over 700 acquisitions of small companies in the 1999–2001 period alone. As a group, Tyco's businesses were cash cows, generating a combined free cash flow in 2005 of around $4.4 billion.

Illustration Capsule 9.3 describes how Johnson & Johnson has used acquisitions to diversify far beyond its well-known Band-Aid and baby care businesses and become a major player in pharmaceuticals, medical devices, and medical diagnostics.

Divestiture Strategies Aimed at Retrenching to a Narrower Diversification Base

A number of diversified firms have had difficulty managing a diverse group of businesses and have elected to get out of some of them. Retrenching to a narrower diversification base is usually undertaken when top management concludes that its diversification strategy has ranged too far afield and that the company can improve long-term performance by concentrating on building stronger positions in a smaller number of core businesses and industries. Hewlett-Packard spun off its testing and measurement businesses into a stand-alone company called Agilent Technologies so that it could better concentrate on its PC, workstation, server, printer and peripherals, and electronics businesses. PepsiCo divested its cash-hog group of restaurant businesses, consisting of KFC, Pizza Hut, Taco Bell, and California Pizza Kitchens, to provide more resources for strengthening its soft-drink business (which was losing market share to Coca-Cola) and growing its more profitable Frito-Lay snack foods business. Kmart divested OfficeMax, Sports Authority, and Borders Bookstores in order to refocus management attention and all of the company's resources on restoring luster to its distressed discount retailing business, which was (and still is) being totally outclassed in the marketplace by Wal-Mart and Target. In 2003–2004, Tyco International began a program to divest itself of some 50 businesses, including its entire undersea fiber-optics telecommunications network and an assortment of businesses in its fire and security division; the initiative also involved consolidating 219 manufacturing, sales, distribution, and other facilities and reducing its workforce of some 260,000 people by 7,200. Lucent Technology's retrenchment strategy is described in Illustration Capsule 9.4.

> Focusing corporate resources on a few core and mostly related businesses avoids the mistake of diversifying so broadly that resources and management attention are stretched too thin.

But there are other important reasons for divesting one or more of a company's present businesses. Sometimes divesting a business has to be considered because market conditions in a once-attractive industry have badly deteriorated. A business can become a prime candidate for divestiture because it lacks adequate strategic or resource fit, because it is a cash hog with questionable long-term potential, or because it is weakly positioned in its industry with little prospect the corporate parent can realize a decent return on its investment in the business. Sometimes a company acquires businesses that, down the road, just do not work out as expected even though management has tried all it can think of to make them profitable—mistakes cannot be completely avoided because it is hard to foresee how getting into a new line of business will actually work out. Subpar performance by some business units is bound to occur, thereby raising questions of whether to divest them or keep them and attempt a turnaround. Other business units, despite adequate financial performance, may not mesh as well with the rest of the firm as was originally thought.

Illustration Capsule 9.4
Lucent Technology's Retrenchment Strategy

At the height of the telecommunications boom in 1999–2000, Lucent Technology was a company with $38.3 billion in revenues and 157,000 employees; it was the biggest maker of telecommunications equipment in the United States and a recognized leader worldwide. The company's strategy was to build positions in a number of blossoming technologies and industry arenas and achieve 20 percent annual revenue growth in each of 11 different business groups. But when customers' orders for new equipment began to evaporate in 2000–2001, Lucent's profits vanished and the once-growing company found itself battling to overcome bloated costs, deep price discounting, and customer defaults on the $7.5 billion in loans Lucent had made to finance their purchases. As it became clear that equipment sales and prices would never return to former levels, Lucent executives concluded that the company had overextended itself trying to do too many things and needed to pare its lineup of businesses.

Alongside efforts to curtail lavish spending at the company's fabled Bell Labs research unit, make deep workforce cutbacks, streamline order-taking and billing systems, shore up the balance sheet, and conserve cash by ending dividend payments, management launched a series of retrenchment initiatives:

- Of the 40 businesses Lucent acquired since 1996, 27 were sold, closed, or spun off.
- Lucent ceased all manufacturing operations, opting to outsource everything.
- It stopped making gear for wireless phone networks based on global system for mobile communication (GSM) technology (the dominant technology used in Europe and much of the world) in order to focus more fully on wireless gear using code division multiple access (CDMA) technology (a technology prevalent in the United States and some developing nations). As of 2004 Lucent had an estimated 45 percent share in the CDMA market and the CDMA gear division was the company's chief revenue and profit producer.
- The wireline and wireless business units were combined to form a single, unified organization called Network Solutions.
- All the remaining businesses were grouped into a unit called Lucent Worldwide Services that was engaged in designing, implementing, integrating, and managing sophisticated voice and data networks for service providers in 45 countries.
- The role of Bell Labs was narrowed to supporting the efforts of both the Network Solutions group and the Worldwide Services group.

Lucent's strategic moves to retrench stemmed a string of 13 straight money-losing quarters. In fiscal 2004 Lucent reported profits of $2 billion from continuing operations (equal to EPS of $0.47 but still far below the levels of $0.93 in 2000 and $1.12 in 1999). In May 2004, Lucent announced its first acquisition in four years, buying a maker of Internet transmission technology for $300 million to help it become a leader in Internet telephony technology. Going into 2006, Lucent was a company with sales of about $9 billion (versus $38 billion in 1999) and a workforce of about 30,000 (versus 157,000 in 1999). The company's stock price, which reached a high of $62 in 1999 before crashing to below $1 in 2002, languished in the $3–$4 range for most of 2004–2005, indicating continuing investor skepticism about Lucent's prospects despite its having retreated to businesses where it was strongest.

Sources: Shawn Young, "Less May Be More," *The Wall Street Journal,* October 23, 2004, p. R10, and www.lucent.com (accessed October 19, 2005).

On occasion, a diversification move that seems sensible from a strategic-fit standpoint turns out to be a poor *cultural fit.*[20] Several pharmaceutical companies had just this experience. When they diversified into cosmetics and perfume, they discovered their personnel had little respect for the "frivolous" nature of such products compared to the far nobler task of developing miracle drugs to cure the ill. The absence of shared values and cultural compatibility between the medical research and chemical-compounding expertise of the pharmaceutical companies and the fashion/marketing orientation of the cosmetics business was the undoing of what otherwise was diversification into businesses with technology-sharing potential, product-development fit, and some overlap in distribution channels.

There's evidence indicating that pruning businesses and narrowing a firm's diversification base improves corporate performance.[21] Corporate parents often end up selling off businesses too late and at too low a price, sacrificing shareholder value.[22] A useful guide to determine whether or when to divest a business subsidiary is to ask, "If we were not in this business today, would we want to get into it now?"[23] When the answer is no or probably not, divestiture should be considered. Another signal that a business should become a divestiture candidate is whether it is worth more to another company than to the present parent; in such cases, shareholders would be well served if the company sells the business and collects a premium price from the buyer for whom the business is a valuable fit.[24]

> Diversified companies need to divest low-performing businesses or businesses that don't fit in order to concentrate on expanding existing businesses and entering new ones where opportunities are more promising.

The Two Options for Divesting a Business: Selling It or Spinning It Off as an Independent Company

Selling a business outright to another company is far and away the most frequently used option for divesting a business. But sometimes a business selected for divestiture has ample resource strengths to compete successfully on its own. In such cases, a corporate parent may elect to spin the unwanted business off as a financially and managerially independent company, either by selling shares to the investing public via an initial public offering or by distributing shares in the new company to existing shareholders of the corporate parent. When a corporate parent decides to spin off one of its businesses as a separate company, it must decide whether or not to retain partial ownership. Retaining partial ownership makes sense when the business to be divested has a hot product or technological capabilities that give it good profit prospects. When 3Com elected to divest its PalmPilot business, which investors then saw as having very promising profit potential, it elected to retain a substantial ownership interest so as to provide 3Com shareholders a way of participating in whatever future market success that PalmPilot (now Palm Inc.) might have on its own. In 2001, when Philip Morris (now Altria) became concerned that its popular Kraft Foods subsidiary was suffering because of its affiliation with Philip Morris's cigarette business (antismoking groups were leading a national boycott of Kraft macaroni and cheese, and a Harris poll revealed that about 16 percent of people familiar with Philip Morris had boycotted its products), Philip Morris executives opted to spin Kraft Foods off as an independent public company but retained a controlling ownership interest. R. J. Reynolds Tobacco was also spun off from Nabisco Foods in 1999 in an effort to distance the tobacco operations part of the company from the food operations part. (Nabisco was then acquired by Philip Morris in 2000 and integrated into Kraft Foods.) In 2005, Cendant announced it would split its diversified businesses into four separate publicly traded companies—one for vehicle rental services (which consisted of Avis and Budget car rental companies); one for real estate and mortgage services (which included Century 21, Coldwell Banker, ERA, Sotheby's International Realty, and NRT—a residential real estate brokerage company); one for hospitality and lodging (consisting of such hotels and motel chains as Wyndam, Ramada, Days Inn, Howard Johnson, Travelodge, AmeriHost Inn, and Knights Inn, plus an assortment of time-share resort properties); and one for travel (consisting of various travel agencies, online ticket and vacation travel sites like Orbitz and Cheap Tickets, and vacation rental operations handling some 55,000 villas and condos). Cendant said the reason for the split-up was that shareholders would realize more value from operating the businesses independently—a clear sign that Cendant's diversification strategy had failed to deliver added shareholder value and that the parts were worth more than the whole.

Selling a business outright requires finding a buyer. This can prove hard or easy, depending on the business. As a rule, a company selling a troubled business should not ask, "How can we pawn this business off on someone, and what is the most we can get for it?"[25] Instead, it is wiser to ask, "For what sort of company would this business be a good fit, and under what conditions would it be viewed as a good deal?" Enterprises for which the business is a good fit are likely to pay the highest price. Of course, if a buyer willing to pay an acceptable price cannot be found, then a company must decide whether to keep the business until a buyer appears; spin it off as a separate company; or, in the case of a crisis-ridden business that is losing substantial sums, simply close it down and liquidate the remaining assets. Liquidation is obviously a last resort.

Strategies to Restructure a Company's Business Lineup

Core Concept

Restructuring involves divesting some businesses and acquiring others so as to put a whole new face on the company's business lineup.

Restructuring strategies involve divesting some businesses and acquiring others so as to put a whole new face on the company's business lineup. Performing radical surgery on a company's group of businesses is an appealing strategy alternative when its financial performance is being squeezed or eroded by:

- Too many businesses in slow-growth, declining, low-margin, or otherwise unattractive industries (a condition indicated by the number and size of businesses with industry attractiveness ratings below 5 and located on the bottom half of the attractiveness–strength matrix—see Figure 9.5).
- Too many competitively weak businesses (a condition indicated by the number and size of businesses with competitive strength ratings below 5 and located on the right half of the attractiveness–strength matrix).
- Ongoing declines in the market shares of one or more major business units that are falling prey to more market-savvy competitors.
- An excessive debt burden with interest costs that eat deeply into profitability.
- Ill-chosen acquisitions that haven't lived up to expectations.

Restructuring can also be mandated by the emergence of new technologies that threaten the survival of one or more of a diversified company's important businesses or by the appointment of a new CEO who decides to redirect the company. On occasion, restructuring can be prompted by special circumstances—as when a firm has a unique opportunity to make an acquisition so big and important that it has to sell several existing business units to finance the new acquisition, or when a company needs to sell off some businesses in order to raise the cash for entering a potentially big industry with wave-of-the-future technologies or products.

Candidates for divestiture in a corporate restructuring effort typically include not only weak or up-and-down performers or those in unattractive industries but also business units that lack strategic fit with the businesses to be retained, businesses that are cash hogs or that lack other types of resource fit, and businesses incompatible with the company's revised diversification strategy (even though they may be profitable or in an attractive industry). As businesses are divested, corporate restructuring generally involves aligning the remaining business units into groups with the best strategic fits and then redeploying the cash flows from the divested business to either pay down debt or make new acquisitions to strengthen the parent company's business position in the industries it has chosen to emphasize.[26]

Over the past decade, corporate restructuring has become a popular strategy at many diversified companies, especially those that had diversified broadly into many different industries and lines of business. For instance, one struggling diversified company over a two-year period divested four business units, closed down the operations of four others, and added 25 new lines of business to its portfolio (16 through acquisition and 9 through internal start-up). PerkinElmer used a series of divestitures and new acquisitions to transform itself from a supplier of low-margin services sold to the government agencies into an innovative high-tech company with operations in over 125 countries and businesses in four industry groups—life sciences (drug research and clinical screening), optoelectronics, medical instruments, and fluid control and containment services (for customers in aerospace, power generation, and semiconductors). In 2005, PerkinElmer took a second restructuring step by divesting its entire fluid control and containment business group so that it could concentrate on its higher-growth health sciences and optoelectronics businesses; the company's CEO said, "While fluid services is an excellent business, it does not fit with our long-term strategy."[27] Before beginning a restructuring effort in 1995, British-based Hanson PLC owned companies with more than $20 billion in revenues in industries as diverse as beer, exercise equipment, tools, construction cranes, tobacco, cement, chemicals, coal mining, electricity, hot tubs and whirlpools, cookware, rock and gravel, bricks, and asphalt. By early 1997, Hanson had restructured itself into a $3.8 billion enterprise focused more narrowly on gravel, crushed rock, cement, asphalt, bricks, and construction cranes; the remaining businesses were divided into four groups and divested.

During Jack Welch's first four years as CEO of General Electric (GE), the company divested 117 business units, accounting for about 20 percent of GE's assets; these divestitures, coupled with several important acquisitions, provided GE with 14 major business divisions and led to Welch's challenge to the managers of GE's divisions to become number one or number two in their industry. Ten years after Welch became CEO, GE was a different company, having divested operations worth $9 billion, made new acquisitions totaling $24 billion, and cut its workforce by 100,000 people. Then, during the 1990–2001 period, GE continued to reshuffle its business lineup, acquiring over 600 new companies, including 108 in 1998 and 64 during a 90-day period in 1999. Most of the new acquisitions were in Europe, Asia, and Latin America and were aimed at transforming GE into a truly global enterprise. In 2003, GE's new CEO, Jeffrey Immelt, began a further restructuring of GE's business lineup with three initiatives: (1) spending $10 billion to acquire British-based Amersham and extend GE's Medical Systems business into diagnostic pharmaceuticals and biosciences, thereby creating a $15 billion business designated as GE Healthcare; (2) acquiring the entertainment assets of debt-ridden French media conglomerate Vivendi Universal Entertainment (Universal Studios, five Universal theme parks, USA Network, Sci-Fi Channel, the Trio cable channel, and Spanish-language broadcaster Telemundo) and integrate its operations into GE's NBC division (the owner of NBC, 29 television stations, and cable networks CNBC, MSNBC, and Bravo), thereby creating a broad-based $13 billion media business positioned to compete against Walt Disney, Time Warner, Fox, and Viacom; and (3) beginning a withdrawal from the insurance business by divesting several companies in its insurance division and preparing to spin off its remaining life and mortgage insurance businesses through an initial public offering of stock for a new company called Genworth Financial.

In a study of the performance of the 200 largest U.S. corporations from 1990 to 2000, McKinsey & Company found that those companies that actively managed their business portfolios through acquisitions and divestitures created substantially more shareholder value than those that kept a fixed lineup of businesses.[28]

Multinational Diversification Strategies

The distinguishing characteristics of a multinational diversification strategy are a *diversity of businesses* and a *diversity of national markets.*[29] Such diversity makes multinational diversification a particularly challenging and complex strategy to conceive and execute. Managers have to develop business strategies for each industry (with as many multinational variations as conditions in each country market dictate). Then they have to pursue and manage opportunities for cross-business and cross-country collaboration and strategic coordination in ways calculated to result in competitive advantage and enhanced profitability.

Moreover, the geographic operating scope of individual businesses within a diversified multinational corporation (DMNC) can range from one country only to several countries to many countries to global. Thus, each business unit within a DMNC often competes in a somewhat different combination of geographic markets than the other businesses do—adding another element of strategic complexity, and perhaps an element of opportunity.

Illustration Capsule 9.5 shows the scope of four prominent DMNCs.

The Appeal of Multinational Diversification: More Opportunities for Sustained Growth and Maximum Competitive Advantage Potential

Despite their complexity, multinational diversification strategies have great appeal. They contain *two major avenues* for growing revenues and profits: One is to grow by entering additional businesses, and the other is to grow by extending the operations of existing businesses into additional country markets. Moreover, a strategy of multinational diversification also contains six attractive paths to competitive advantage, *all of which can be pursued simultaneously:*

1. *Full capture of economies of scale and experience/learning curve effects.* In some businesses, the volume of sales needed to realize full economies of scale and/or benefit fully from experience/learning curve effects is rather sizable, often exceeding the volume that can be achieved operating within the boundaries of a single country market, especially a small one. *The ability to drive down unit costs by expanding sales to additional country markets is one reason why a diversified multinational may seek to acquire a business and then rapidly expand its operations into more and more foreign markets.*

2. *Opportunities to capitalize on cross-business economies of scope.* Diversifying into related businesses offering economies of scope can drive the development of a low-cost advantage over less diversified rivals. For example, a DMNC that uses mostly the same distributors and retail dealers worldwide can diversify into new businesses using these same worldwide distribution channels at relatively little incremental expense. The cost savings of piggybacking distribution activities can be substantial. Moreover, with more business selling more products in more countries, a DMNC acquires more bargaining leverage in its purchases from suppliers and more bargaining leverage with retailers in securing attractive display space for its products. Consider, for example, the competitive power that Sony derived

Illustration Capsule 9.5

The Global Scope of Four Prominent Diversified Multinational Corporations

Company	Global Scope	Businesses into Which the Company Has Diversified
Sony	Operations in more than 100 countries and sales offices in more than 200 countries	• Televisions, VCRs, DVD players, Walkman MP3 players, radios, digital cameras and video equipment, Vaio PCs, and Trinitron computer monitors; PlayStation game consoles and video game software; Columbia, Epic, and Sony Classical pre-recorded music; Columbia TriStar motion pictures; syndicated television programs; entertainment complexes, and insurance
Nestlé	Operations in 70 countries and sales offices in more than 200 countries	• Beverages (Nescafé and Taster's Choice coffees, Nestea, Perrier, Arrowhead, & Calistoga mineral and bottled waters); milk products (Carnation, Gloria, Neslac, Coffee Mate, Nestlé ice cream and yogurt); pet foods (Friskies, Alpo, Fancy Feast, Mighty Dog); Contadina, Libby's, and Stouffer's food products and prepared dishes; chocolate and confectionery products (Nestlé Crunch, Smarties, Baby Ruth, Butterfinger, KitKat); and pharmaceuticals (Alcon opthalmic products, Galderma dermatological products)
Siemens	Operations in 160 countries and sales offices in more than 190 countries	• Electrical power generation, transmission, and distribution equipment and products; manufacturing automation systems; industrial motors, machinery, and tools; plant construction and maintenance; corporate communication networks; telephones; PCs, mainframes, computer network products, consulting services; mass transit and light rail systems, rail cars, locomotives, lighting products (bulbs, lamps, theater and television lighting systems); semiconductors; home appliances; vacuum cleaners; and financial, procurement, and logistics services
Samsung	Operations in more than 60 countries and sales in more than 200 countries	• Notebook computers, hard disk drives, CD/DVD-ROM drives, monitors, printers, and fax machines; televisions (big-screen TVs, plasma-screen TVs, and LCD-screen TVs); DVD and MP3 players; Cell phones and various other telecommunications products; compressors; home appliances; DRAM chips, flash memory chips, and graphics memory chips; and optical fibers, fiber-optic cables, and fiber-optic connectors

Source: Company annual reports and Web sites.

from these very sorts of economies of scope when it decided to diversify into the video game business with its PlayStation product line. Sony had in place capability to go after video game sales in all country markets where it presently did business in other electronics product categories (TVs, computers, DVD players, VCRs, radios, CD players, and camcorders). And it had the marketing clout and brand-name credibility to persuade retailers to give Sony's PlayStation products prime shelf space and visibility. These strategic-fit benefits helped Sony quickly overtake long-time industry leaders Nintendo and Sega and defend its market leadership against Microsoft's new Xbox.

3. *Opportunities to transfer competitively valuable resources both from one business to another and from one country to another.* A company pursuing related diversification can gain a competitive edge over less diversified rivals by transferring competitively valuable resources from one business to another; a multinational company can gain competitive advantage over rivals with narrower geographic coverage by transferring competitively valuable resources from one country to another. But a strategy of multinational diversification enables simultaneous pursuit of both sources of competitive advantage.

4. *Ability to leverage use of a well-known and competitively powerful brand name.* Diversified multinational companies whose businesses have brand names that are well known and respected across the world possess a valuable strategic asset with competitive advantage potential. For example, Sony's well-established global brand-name recognition gives it an important marketing and advertising advantage over rivals with lesser-known brands. When Sony goes into a new marketplace with the stamp of the Sony brand on its product families, it can command prominent display space with retailers. It can expect to win sales and market share simply on the confidence that buyers place in products carrying the Sony name. While Sony may spend money to make consumers aware of the availability of its new products, it does not have to spend nearly as much on achieving brand recognition and market acceptance as would a lesser-known competitor looking at the marketing and advertising costs of entering the same new product/business/country markets and trying to go head-to-head against Sony. Further, if Sony moves into a new country market for the first time and does well selling Sony PlayStations and video games, it is easier to sell consumers in that country Sony TVs, digital cameras, PCs, MP3 players, and so on—plus, the related advertising costs are likely to be less than they would be without having already established the Sony brand strongly in the minds of buyers.

5. *Ability to capitalize on opportunities for cross-business and cross-country collaboration and strategic coordination.*[30] A multinational diversification strategy allows competitively valuable cross-business and cross-country coordination of certain value chain activities. For instance, by channeling corporate resources directly into a combined R&D/technology effort for all related businesses, as opposed to letting each business unit fund and direct its own R&D effort however it sees fit, a DMNC can merge its expertise and efforts *worldwide* to advance core technologies, expedite cross-business and cross-country product improvements, speed the development of new products that complement existing products, and pursue promising technological avenues to create altogether new businesses—all significant contributors to competitive advantage and better corporate performance.[31] Honda has been very successful in building R&D expertise in gasoline engines and transferring the resulting technological advances to its businesses in automobiles, motorcycles, outboard engines, snow blowers, lawn mowers, garden tillers, and portable power generators. Further, a DMNC can reduce costs through cross-business and cross-country coordination of purchasing and procurement from suppliers, from collaborative introduction and shared use of e-commerce technologies and online sales efforts, and from coordinated product introductions and promotional campaigns. Firms that are less diversified and less global in scope have less such cross-business and cross-country collaborative opportunities.

6. *Opportunities to use cross-business or cross-country subsidization to outcompete rivals.* A financially successful DMNC has potentially valuable organizational resources and multiple profit sanctuaries in both certain country markets and certain businesses that it can draw on to wage a market offensive. In comparison, a one-business domestic company has only one profit sanctuary—its home market. A diversified one-country competitor may have profit sanctuaries in several businesses, but all are in the same country market. A one-business multinational company may have profit sanctuaries in several country markets, but all are in the same business. All three are vulnerable to an offensive in their more limited profit sanctuaries by an aggressive DMNC willing to lowball its prices or spend extravagantly on advertising to win market share at their expense. A DMNC's ability to keep hammering away at competitors with low prices year after year may reflect either a cost advantage growing out of its related diversification strategy or a willingness to accept low profits or even losses in the market being attacked because it has ample earnings from its other profit sanctuaries. For example, Sony's global-scale diversification strategy gives it unique competitive strengths in outcompeting Nintendo and Sega, neither of which are diversified. If need be, Sony can maintain low prices on its PlayStations or fund high-profile promotions for its latest video game products, using earnings from its other business lines to fund its offensive to wrest market share away from Nintendo and Sega in video games. At the same time, Sony can draw on its considerable resources in R&D, its ability to transfer electronics technology from one electronics product family to another, and its expertise in product innovation to introduce better and better video game players, perhaps players that are multifunctional and do more than just play video games. Such competitive actions not only enhance Sony's own brand image but also make it very tough for Nintendo and Sega to match Sony's prices, advertising, and product development efforts and still earn acceptable profits.

The Combined Effects of These Advantages Is Potent A strategy of diversifying into *related* industries and then competing *globally* in each of these industries thus has great potential for being a winner in the marketplace because of the long-term growth opportunities it offers and the multiple corporate-level competitive advantage opportunities it contains. Indeed, *a strategy of multinational diversification contains more competitive advantage potential* (above and beyond what is achievable through a particular business's own competitive strategy) *than any other diversification strategy.*

> **Core Concept**
> A strategy of multinational diversification has more built-in potential for competitive advantage than any other diversification strategy.

The strategic key to maximum competitive advantage is for a DMNC to concentrate its diversification efforts in those industries where there are resource-sharing and resource-transfer opportunities and where there are important economies of scope and brand-name benefits. The more a company's diversification strategy yields these kinds of strategic-fit benefits, the more powerful a competitor it becomes and the better its profit and growth performance is likely to be.

However, it is important to recognize that while, in theory, a DMNC's cross-subsidization capabilities are a potent competitive weapon, cross-subsidization can, in actual practice, be used only sparingly. It is one thing to *occasionally* divert a portion of the profits and cash flows from existing businesses to help fund entry into a new business or country market or wage a competitive offensive against select rivals. It is quite another thing to *regularly* use cross-subsidization tactics and thereby weaken

Core Concept
Although cross-subsidization is a potent competitive weapon, it must be used sparingly to prevent eroding a DMNC's overall profitability.

overall company performance. A DMNC is under the same pressures as any other company to demonstrate consistently acceptable profitability across its whole operation.[32] At some juncture, every business and every country market needs to make a profit contribution or become a candidate for abandonment. As a general rule, *cross-subsidization tactics are justified only when there is a good prospect that the short-term impairment to corporate profitability will be offset by stronger competitiveness and better overall profitability over the long term.*

Key Points

The purpose of diversification is to build shareholder value. Diversification builds shareholder value when a diversified group of businesses can perform better under the auspices of a single corporate parent than they would as independent, stand-alone businesses—the goal is not to achieve just a $1 + 1 = 2$ result, but rather to realize important $1 + 1 = 3$ performance benefits. Whether getting into a new business has potential to enhance shareholder value hinges on whether a company's entry into that business can pass the attractiveness test, the cost-of-entry test, and the better-off test.

Entry into new businesses can take any of three forms: acquisition, internal start-up, or joint venture/strategic partnership. Each has its pros and cons, but acquisition is the most frequently used; internal start-up takes the longest to produce home-run results, and joint venture/strategic partnership, though used second most frequently, is the least durable.

There are two fundamental approaches to diversification—into related businesses and into unrelated businesses. The rationale for *related* diversification is *strategic*: Diversify into businesses with strategic fits along their respective value chains, capitalize on strategic-fit relationships to gain competitive advantage, and then use competitive advantage to achieve the desired $1 + 1 = 3$ impact on shareholder value.

The basic premise of unrelated diversification is that any business that has good profit prospects and can be acquired on good financial terms is a good business to diversify into. Unrelated diversification strategies surrender the competitive advantage potential of strategic fit in return for such advantages as (1) spreading business risk over a variety of industries and (2) providing opportunities for financial gain (if candidate acquisitions have undervalued assets, are bargain priced and have good upside potential given the right management, or need the backing of a financially strong parent to capitalize on attractive opportunities). However, the greater the number of businesses a company has diversified into and the more diverse these businesses are, the harder it is for corporate executives to select capable managers to run each business, know when the major strategic proposals of business units are sound, or decide on a wise course of recovery when a business unit stumbles.

Analyzing how good a company's diversification strategy is a six-step process:

1. *Evaluate the long-term attractiveness of the industries into which the firm has diversified.* Industry attractiveness needs to be evaluated from three angles: the attractiveness of each industry on its own, the attractiveness of each industry relative to the others, and the attractiveness of all the industries as a group.

2. *Evaluate the relative competitive strength of each of the company's business units.* Again, quantitative ratings of competitive strength are preferable to subjective

judgments. The purpose of rating the competitive strength of each business is to gain clear understanding of which businesses are strong contenders in their industries, which are weak contenders, and the underlying reasons for their strength or weakness. The conclusions about industry attractiveness can be joined with the conclusions about competitive strength by drawing an industry attractiveness–competitive strength matrix that helps identify the prospects of each business and what priority each business should be given in allocating corporate resources and investment capital.

3. *Check for cross-business strategic fits.* A business is more attractive strategically when it has value chain relationships with sister business units that offer potential to (*a*) realize economies of scope or cost-saving efficiencies; (*b*) transfer technology, skills, know-how, or other resource capabilities from one business to another; (*c*) leverage use of a well-known and trusted brand name; and (*d*) to build new or stronger resource strengths and competitive capabilities via cross-business collaboration. Cross-business strategic fits represent a significant avenue for producing competitive advantage beyond what any one business can achieve on its own.

4. *Check whether the firm's resource strengths fit the resource requirements of its present business lineup.* Resource fit exists when (*a*) businesses add to a company's resource strengths, either financially or strategically; (*b*) a company has the resources to adequately support the resource requirements of its businesses as a group without spreading itself too thin; and (*c*) there are close matches between a company's resources and industry key success factors. One important test of financial resource fit involves determining whether a company has ample cash cows and not too many cash hogs.

5. *Rank the performance prospects of the businesses from best to worst and determine what the corporate parent's priority should be in allocating resources to its various businesses.* The most important considerations in judging business-unit performance are sales growth, profit growth, contribution to company earnings, and the return on capital invested in the business. Sometimes, cash flow generation is a big consideration. Normally, strong business units in attractive industries have significantly better performance prospects than weak businesses or businesses in unattractive industries. Business subsidiaries with the brightest profit and growth prospects and solid strategic and resource fits generally should head the list for corporate resource support.

6. *Crafting new strategic moves to improve overall corporate performance.* This step entails using the results of the preceding analysis as the basis for devising actions to strengthen existing businesses, make new acquisitions, divest weak-performing and unattractive businesses, restructure the company's business lineup, expand the scope of the company's geographic reach multinationally or globally, and otherwise steer corporate resources into the areas of greatest opportunity.

Once a company has diversified, corporate management's task is to manage the collection of businesses for maximum long-term performance. There are four different strategic paths for improving a diversified company's performance: (1) broadening the firm's business base by diversifying into additional businesses, (2) retrenching to a narrower diversification base by divesting some of its present businesses, (3) restructuring the company, and (4) diversifying multinationally.

Exercises

1. Consider the business lineup of General Electric (GE) shown in Illustration Capsule 9.2. What problems do you think the top executives at GE encounter in trying to stay on top of all the businesses the company is in? How might they decide the merits of adding new businesses or divesting poorly performing businesses? What types of advice might they be in a position to give to the general managers of each of GE's business units?

2. The Walt Disney Company is in the following businesses:
   - Theme parks.
   - Disney Cruise Line.
   - Resort properties.
   - Movie, video, and theatrical productions (for both children and adults).
   - Television broadcasting (ABC, Disney Channel, Toon Disney, Classic Sports Network, ESPN and ESPN2, E!, Lifetime, and A&E networks).
   - Radio broadcasting (Disney Radio).
   - Musical recordings and sales of animation art.
   - Anaheim Mighty Ducks NHL franchise.
   - Anaheim Angels major league baseball franchise (25 percent ownership).
   - Books and magazine publishing.
   - Interactive software and Internet sites.
   - The Disney Store retail shops.

   Given the above listing, would you say that Walt Disney's business lineup reflects a strategy of related or unrelated diversification? Explain your answer in terms of the extent to which the value chains of Disney's different businesses seem to have competitively valuable cross-business relationships.

3. Newell Rubbermaid is in the following businesses:
   - Cleaning and organizations businesses: Rubbermaid storage, organization, and cleaning products; Blue Ice ice substitute; Roughneck storage itemmms; Stain Shield and TakeAlongs food storage containers; and Brute commercial-grade storage and cleaning products (25 percent of annual revenues).
   - Home and family businesses: Calphalon cookware and bakeware, Cookware Europe, Graco strollers, Little Tikes children's toys and furniture, and Goody hair accessories (20 percent of annual sales).
   - Home fashions: Levolor and Kirsch window blinds, shades, and hardware in the United States; Swish, Gardinia and Harrison Drape home furnishings in Europe (15 percent of annual revenues).
   - Office products businesses: Sharpie markers, Sanford highlighters, Eberhard Faber and Berol ballpoint pens, Paper Mate pens and pencils, Waterman and Parker fine writing instruments, and Liquid Paper (25 percent of annual revenues).

   Would you say that Newell Rubbermaid's strategy is one of related diversification, unrelated diversification or a mixture of both? Explain.

4. Explore the Web sites of the following companies and determine whether the company is pursuing a strategy of related diversification, unrelated diversification, or a mixture of both:

- Berkshire Hathaway
- News Corporation
- Dow Jones & Company
- Kimberly Clark

chapter ten 10

Strategy, Ethics, and Social Responsibility

When morality comes up against profit, it is seldom profit that loses.

—Shirley Chisholm
Former Congresswoman

But I'd shut my eyes in the sentry box so I didn't see nothing wrong.

—Rudyard Kipling
Author

Values can't just be words on a page. To be effective, they must shape action.

—Jeffrey R. Immelt
CEO, General Electric

Leaders must be more than individuals of high character. They must "lead" others to behave ethically.

—Linda K. Treviňo and Michael E. Brown
Professors

Integrity violations are no-brainers. In such cases, you don't need to hesitate for a moment before firing someone or fret about it either. Just do it, and make sure the organization knows why, so that the consequences of breaking the rules are not lost on anyone.

—Jack Welch
Former CEO, General Electric

There is one and only one social responsibility of business—to use its resources and engage in activities designed to increase its profits so long as it stays within the rules of the game, which is to say engages in free and open competition, without deception or fraud.

—Milton Friedman
Nobel Prize–winning economist

Corporations are economic entities, to be sure, but they are also social institutions that must justify their existence by their overall contribution to society.

—Henry Mintzberg, Robert Simons, and Kunal Basu
Professors

Clearly, a company has a responsibility to make a profit and grow the business—in capitalistic, or market, economies, management's fiduciary duty to create value for shareholders is not a matter for serious debate. Just as clearly, a company and its personnel also have a duty to obey the law and play by the rules of fair competition. But does a company have a duty to operate according to the ethical norms of the societies in which it operates—should it be held to some standard of ethical conduct? And does it have a duty or obligation to contribute to the betterment of society independent of the needs and preferences of the customers it serves? Should a company display a social conscience and devote a portion of its resources to bettering society?

The focus of this chapter is to examine what link, if any, there should be between a company's efforts to craft and execute a winning strategy and its duties to (1) conduct its activities ethically and (2) demonstrate socially responsible behavior by being a committed corporate citizen and directing corporate resources to the betterment of employees, the communities in which it operates, and society as a whole.

WHAT DO WE MEAN BY *BUSINESS ETHICS?*

Business ethics is the application of ethical principles and standards to business behavior.[1] Business ethics does not really involve a special set of ethical standards applicable only to business situations. Ethical principles in business are not materially different from ethical principles in general. Why? Because business actions have to be judged in the context of society's standards of right and wrong, not by a special set of rules that businesspeople decide to apply to their own conduct. If dishonesty is considered to be unethical and immoral, then dishonest behavior in business—whether it relates to customers, suppliers, employees or shareholders—qualifies as equally unethical and immoral. If being ethical entails not deliberately harming others, then recalling a defective or unsafe product is ethically necessary and failing to undertake such a recall or correct the problem in future shipments of the product is likewise unethical. If society deems bribery to be unethical, then it is unethical for company personnel to make payoffs to government officials to facilitate business transactions or bestow gifts and other favors on prospective customers to win or retain their business.

Core Concept
Business ethics concerns the application of general ethical principles and standards to the actions and decisions of companies and the conduct of company personnel.

WHERE DO ETHICAL STANDARDS COME FROM—ARE THEY UNIVERSAL OR DEPENDENT ON LOCAL NORMS AND SITUATIONAL CIRCUMSTANCES?

Notions of right and wrong, fair and unfair, moral and immoral, ethical and unethical are present in all societies, organizations, and individuals. But there are three schools of thought about the extent to which the ethical standards travel across cultures and whether multinational companies can apply the same set of ethical standards in any and all of the locations where they operate.

The School of Ethical Universalism

According to the school of **ethical universalism,** some concepts of what is right and what is wrong are *universal*; that is, they transcend all cultures, societies, and religions.[2] For instance, being truthful (or not lying, or not being deliberately deceitful) is considered right by the peoples of all nations. Likewise, demonstrating integrity of character, not cheating, and treating people with dignity and respect are concepts that resonate with people of most cultures and religions. In most societies, people believe that companies should not pillage or degrade the environment in the course of conducting their operations. In most societies, people would concur that it is unethical to knowingly expose workers to toxic chemicals and hazardous materials or to sell products known to be unsafe or harmful to the users. *To the extent that there is common moral agreement about right and wrong actions and behaviors across multiple cultures and countries, there exists a set of universal ethical standards to which all societies, all companies, and all individuals can be held accountable.* These universal ethical principles or norms put limits on what actions and behaviors fall inside the boundaries of what is right and which ones fall outside. They set forth the traits and behaviors that are considered virtuous and that a good person is supposed to believe in and to display.

> **Core Concept**
>
> According to the school of *ethical universalism,* the same standards of what's ethical and what's unethical resonate with peoples of most societies regardless of local traditions and cultural norms; hence, common ethical standards can be used to judge the conduct of personnel at companies operating in a variety of country markets and cultural circumstances.

Many ethicists believe that the most important moral standards travel well across countries and cultures and thus are *universal*—universal norms include honesty or trustworthiness, respecting the rights of others, practicing the Golden Rule, avoiding unnecessary harm to workers or to the users of the company's product or service, and respect for the environment.[3] In all such instances where there is cross-cultural agreement as to what actions and behaviors are inside and outside ethical and moral boundaries, adherents of the school of ethical universalism maintain that the conduct of personnel at companies operating in a variety of country markets and cultural circumstances can be judged against the resulting set of common ethical standards.

The strength of ethical universalism is that it draws on the collective views of multiple societies and cultures to put some clear boundaries on what constitutes ethical business behavior and what constitutes unethical business behavior no matter what country market or culture a company or its personnel are operating in. This means that whenever basic moral standards really do not vary significantly according to local cultural beliefs, traditions, religious convictions, or time and circumstance, a multinational company can apply a code of ethics more or less evenly across its worldwide operations.[4] It can avoid the slippery slope that comes from having different ethical standards for different company personnel depending on where in the world they are working.

The School of Ethical Relativism

Apart from select universal basics—honesty, trustworthiness, fairness, a regard for worker safety, and respect for the environment—there are meaningful variations in what societies generally agree to be right and wrong in the conduct of business activities. Divergent religious beliefs, historic traditions, social customs, and prevailing political and economic doctrines (whether a country leans more toward a capitalistic market economy or one heavily dominated by socialistic or communistic principles) frequently produce ethical norms that vary from one country to another. The school of **ethical relativism** holds that when there are cross-country or cross-cultural differences in what is deemed fair or unfair, what constitutes proper regard for human rights, and what is considered ethical or unethical in business situations, it is appropriate for local moral standards to take precedence over what the ethical standards may be elsewhere—for instance, in a company's home market. The thesis is that whatever a culture thinks is right or wrong really is right or wrong for that culture.[5] Hence, the school of ethical relativism contends that there are important occasions when cultural norms and the circumstances of the situation determine whether certain actions or behaviors are right or wrong. Consider the following examples.

> **Core Concept**
> According to the school of ***ethical relativism*** different societal cultures and customs have divergent values and standards of right and wrong— thus what is ethical or unethical must be judged in the light of local customs and social mores and can vary from culture or nation to another.

The Use of Underage Labor   In industrialized nations, the use of underage workers is considered taboo; social activists are adamant that child labor is unethical and that companies should neither employ children under the age of 18 as full-time employees nor source any products from foreign suppliers that employ underage workers. Many countries have passed legislation forbidding the use of underage labor or, at a minimum, regulating the employment of people under the age of 18. However, in India, Bangladesh, Botswana, Sri Lanka, Ghana, Somalia, Turkey, and 100-plus other countries, it is customary to view children as potential, even necessary, workers.[6] Many poverty-stricken families cannot subsist without the income earned by young family members, and sending their children to school instead of having them participate in the workforce is not a realistic option. In 2000, the International Labor Organization estimated that 211 million children ages 5 to 14 were working around the world.[7] If such children are not permitted to work—due to pressures imposed by activist groups in industrialized nations—they may be forced to seek work in lower-wage jobs in "hidden" parts of the economy of their countries, beg on the street, or even traffic in drugs or engage in prostitution.[8] So if all businesses succumb to the protests of activist groups and government organizations that, based on their values and beliefs, loudly proclaim that underage labor is unethical, then have either businesses or the protesting groups really done something good on behalf of society in general?

The Payment of Bribes and Kickbacks   A particularly thorny area facing multinational companies is the degree of cross-country variability in paying bribes.[9] In many countries in Eastern Europe, Africa, Latin America, and Asia, it is customary to pay bribes to government officials in order to win a government contract, obtain a license or permit, or facilitate an administrative ruling.[10] Senior managers in China often use their power to obtain kickbacks and offer bribes when they purchase materials or other products for their companies.[11] In some developing nations, it is difficult for any company, foreign or domestic, to move goods through customs without paying off low-level officials.[12] Likewise, in many countries it is normal to make payments to prospective customers in order to win or retain their business. A *Wall Street Journal* article reported that 30 to 60 percent of all business transactions in Eastern Europe involved paying bribes, and the costs of bribe payments averaged 2 to 8 percent of revenues.[13] Three recent annual issues of the *Global Corruption Report,* sponsored by Berlin-based Transparency International, provide credible evidence that corruption among public officials and in business transactions is widespread across the world.[14] Some people stretch to justify the payment of bribes and kickbacks on grounds that bribing government officials to get goods through customs or giving kickbacks to customers to retail their business or win an order is simply a payment for services rendered, in the same way that people tip for service at restaurants.[15] But this argument rests on moral quicksand, even though it is a clever and pragmatic way to rationalize why such facilitating payments should be viewed as a normal and maybe unavoidable cost of doing business in some countries.

Companies that forbid the payment of bribes and kickbacks in their codes of ethical conduct and that are serious about enforcing this prohibition face a particularly vexing problem in those countries where bribery and kickback payments have been entrenched as a local custom for decades and are not considered unethical by the local population.[16] Refusing to pay bribes or kickbacks (so as to comply with the company's code of ethical conduct) is very often tantamount to losing business. Frequently, the sales and profits are lost to more unscrupulous companies, with the result that both ethical companies and ethical individuals are penalized. However, winking at the code of ethical conduct and going along with the payment of bribes or kickbacks not only undercuts enforcement of and adherence to the company's code of ethics but can also risk breaking the law. U.S. companies are prohibited by the Foreign Corrupt Practices Act (FCPA) from paying bribes to government officials, political parties, political candidates, or others in all countries where they do business; the FCPA requires U.S. companies with foreign operations to adopt accounting practices that ensure full disclosure of a company's transactions so that illegal payments can be detected. The 35 member countries of the Organization for Economic Cooperation and Development (OECD) in 1997 adopted a convention to combat bribery in international business transactions; the Anti-Bribery Convention obligated the countries to criminalize the bribery of foreign public officials, including payments made to political parties and party officials. So far, however, there has been only token enforcement of the OECD convention and the payment of bribes in global business transactions remains a common practice in many countries.

Ethical Relativism Equates to Multiple Sets of Ethical Standards   The existence of varying ethical norms such as those cited above explains why the adherents of ethical relativism maintain that there are few absolutes when it comes to business ethics and thus few ethical absolutes for consistently judging a company's conduct in various countries and markets. Indeed, the thesis of ethical relativists is that while there are sometimes general moral prescriptions that apply in most every society and business circumstance there are plenty of situations where ethical norms must be contoured to fit the local customs, traditions, and the notions of fairness shared by the parties involved. They argue that a one-size-fits-all template for judging the ethical appropriateness of business actions and the behaviors of company personnel simply does not exist—in other words, ethical problems in business cannot be fully resolved without appealing to the shared convictions of the parties in question.[17] European and American managers may want to impose standards of business conduct that give heavy weight to such core human rights as personal freedom, individual security, political participation, the ownership of property, and the right to subsistence as well as the obligation to respect the dignity of each human person, adequate health and safety standards for all employees, and respect for the environment; managers in China have a much weaker commitment to these kinds of human rights. Japanese managers may prefer ethical standards that show respect for the collective good of society. Muslim managers may wish to apply ethical standards compatible with the teachings of Mohammed. Individual companies may want to give explicit recognition to the importance of company personnel living up to the company's own espoused values and business principles. Clearly, there is merit in the school of ethical relativism's view that what is deemed right or wrong, fair or unfair, moral or immoral, ethical or unethical in business situations depends partly on the context of each country's local customs, religious traditions, and societal norms. Hence, there is a kernel of truth in the argument that businesses need some room to tailor their ethical standards to fit local situations. A company has to be very cautious about exporting its home-country values and ethics to foreign countries where it operates—"photocopying" ethics is disrespectful of other cultures and neglects the important role of moral free space.

> Under ethical relativism, there can be no one-size-fits-all set of authentic ethical norms against which to gauge the conduct of company personnel.

Pushed to Extreme, Ethical Relativism Breaks Down   While the relativistic rule of "When in Rome, do as the Romans do" appears reasonable, it nonetheless presents a big problem—when the envelope starts to be pushed, as will inevitably be the case, *it is tantamount to rudderless ethical standards.* Consider, for instance, the following example: In 1992, the owners of the SS *United States,* an aging luxury ocean liner constructed with asbestos in the 1940s, had the liner towed to Turkey, where a contractor had agreed to remove the asbestos for $2 million (versus a far higher cost in the United States, where asbestos removal safety standards were much more stringent).[18] When Turkish officials blocked the asbestos removal because of the dangers to workers of contracting cancer, the owners had the liner towed to the Black Sea port of Sevastopol, in the Crimean Republic, where the asbestos removal standards were quite lax and where a contractor had agreed to remove more than 500,000 square feet of carcinogenic asbestos for less than $2 million. There are no moral grounds for arguing that exposing workers to carcinogenic asbestos is ethically correct, irrespective of what a country's law allows or the value the country places on worker safety.

A company that adopts the principle of ethical relativism and holds company personnel to local ethical standards necessarily assumes that what prevails as local morality is an adequate guide to ethical behavior. This can be ethically dangerous—it leads to the conclusion that if a country's culture is accepting of bribery or environmental degradation or exposing workers to dangerous conditions (toxic chemicals or bodily harm), then so much the worse for honest people and protection of the environment and safe working conditions. Such a position is morally unacceptable. Even though bribery of government officials in China is a common practice, when Lucent Technologies found that managers in its Chinese operations had bribed government officials, it fired the entire senior management team.[19]

> Managers in multinational enterprises have to figure out how to navigate the gray zone that arises when operating in two cultures with two sets of ethics.

Moreover, from a global markets perspective, ethical relativism results in a maze of conflicting ethical standards for multinational companies wanting to address the very real issue of what ethical standards to enforce companywide. On the one hand, multinational companies need to educate and motivate their employees worldwide to respect the customs and traditions of other nations, and, on the other hand, they must enforce compliance with the company's own particular code of ethical behavior. It is a slippery slope indeed to resolve such ethical diversity without any kind of higher-order moral compass. Imagine, for example, that a multinational company in the name of ethical relativism takes the position that it is okay for company personnel to pay bribes and kickbacks in countries where such payments are customary but forbids company personnel from making such payments in those countries where bribes and kickbacks are considered unethical or illegal. Or that the company says it is ethically fine to use underage labor in its plants in those countries where underage labor is acceptable and ethically inappropriate to employ underage labor at the remainder of its plants. Having thus adopted conflicting ethical standards for operating in different countries, company managers have little moral basis for enforcing ethical standards companywide—rather, the clear message to employees would be that the company has no ethical standards or principles of its own, preferring to let its practices be governed by the countries in which it operates. This is scarcely strong moral ground to stand on.

Ethics and Integrative Social Contracts Theory

Core Concept
According to *integrated social contracts theory,* universal ethical principles or norms based on the collective views of multiple cultures and societies combine to form a "social contract" that all individuals in all situations have a duty to observe. Within the boundaries of this social contract, local cultures or groups can specify other impermissible actions; however, universal ethical norms always take precedence over local ethical norms.

Social contract theory provides a middle position between the opposing views of universalism (that the same set of ethical standards should apply everywhere) and relativism (that ethical standards vary according to local custom).[20] According to **integrative social contracts theory,** the ethical standards a company should try to uphold are governed both by (1) a limited number of universal ethical principles that are widely recognized as putting legitimate ethical boundaries on actions and behavior in *all* situations and (2) the circumstances of local cultures, traditions, and shared values that further prescribe what constitutes ethically permissible behavior and what does not. However, *universal ethical norms take precedence over local ethical norms.* In other words, universal ethical principles apply in those situations where most all societies—endowed with rationality and moral knowledge—have common moral agreement on what is wrong and thereby put limits on what actions and behaviors fall inside the boundaries of what is right and which ones fall outside. *These mostly uniform agreements about what is morally right and wrong form a "social contract" or contract with society that is binding on all individuals, groups, organizations, and businesses in terms of establishing right and wrong and in drawing the line between ethical and unethical behaviors.* But these universal ethical principles or norms nonetheless still leave some moral free space for the people in a particular country (or local culture or even a company) to make specific interpretations of what other actions may or may not be permissible within the bounds defined by universal ethical principles. Hence, while firms, industries, professional associations, and other business-relevant groups are contractually obligated to society to observe universal ethical norms, they have the discretion to go beyond these universal norms and specify other behaviors that are out of bounds and place further limitations on what is considered ethical. Both the legal and medical professions have standards regarding what kinds of advertising are ethically permissible and what kinds are not. Food products companies are beginning to establish ethical guidelines for judging what is and is not appropriate advertising for food products that are inherently unhealthy and may cause dietary or obesity problems for people who eat them regularly or consume them in large quantities.

The strength of integrated social contracts theory is that it accommodates the best parts of ethical universalism and ethical relativism. It is indisputable that cultural differences impact how business is conducted in various parts of the world and that these cultural differences sometimes give rise to different ethical norms. But it is just as indisputable that some ethical norms are more authentic or universally applicable than others, meaning that, in many instances of cross-country differences, one side may be more "ethically correct" or "more right" than another. In such instances, resolving cross-cultural differences entails applying universal, or first-order, ethical norms and overriding the local, or second-order, ethical norms. A good example is the payment of bribes and kickbacks. Yes, bribes and kickbacks seem to be common in some countries, but does this justify paying them? Just because bribery flourishes in a country does not mean that it is an authentic or legitimate ethical norm. Virtually all of the world's major religions (Buddhism, Christianity, Confucianism, Hinduism, Islam, Judaism, Sikhism, and Taoism) and all moral schools of thought condemn bribery and corruption.[21] Bribery is commonplace in India but interviews with Indian CEOs whose companies constantly engaged in payoffs indicated disgust for the practice and they expressed no illusions about its impropriety.[22] Therefore, a multinational company might reasonably conclude that the right ethical standard is one of refusing to condone bribery and kickbacks on the part of company personnel no matter what the local custom is and no matter what the sales consequences are.

Granting an automatic preference to local country ethical norms presents vexing problems to multinational company managers when the ethical standards followed in a foreign country are lower than those in its home country or are in conflict with the company's code of ethics. Sometimes there can be no compromise on what is ethically permissible and what is not. *This is precisely what integrated social contracts theory maintains—universal or first-order ethical norms should always take precedence over local or second-order norms.* Integrated social contracts theory offers managers in multinational companies clear guidance in resolving cross-country ethical differences: Those parts of the company's code of ethics that involve universal ethical norms must be enforced worldwide, but within these boundaries there is room for ethical diversity and opportunity for host country cultures to exert *some* influence in setting their own moral and ethical standards. Such an approach detours the somewhat scary case of a self-righteous multinational company trying to operate as the standard-bearer of moral truth and imposing its interpretation of its code of ethics worldwide no matter what. And it avoids the equally scary case for a company's ethical conduct to be no higher than local ethical norms in situations where local ethical norms permit practices that are generally considered immoral or when local norms clearly conflict with a company's code of ethical conduct. But even with the guidance provided by integrated social contracts theory, there are many instances where cross-country differences in ethical norms create gray areas in which it is tough to draw a line in the sand between right and wrong decisions, actions, and business practices.

THE THREE CATEGORIES OF MANAGEMENT MORALITY

Three categories of managers stand out with regard to ethical and moral principles in business affairs:[23]

- *The moral manager*—Moral managers are dedicated to high standards of ethical behavior, both in their own actions and in their expectations of how the company's business is to be conducted. They see themselves as stewards of ethical behavior and believe it is important to exercise ethical leadership. Moral managers may well be ambitious and have a powerful urge to succeed, but they pursue success in business within the confines of both the letter and the spirit of what is ethical and legal—they typically regard the law as an ethical minimum and have a habit of operating well above what the law requires.

- *The immoral manager*—Immoral managers have no regard for so-called ethical standards in business and pay no attention to ethical principles in making decisions and conducting the company's business. Their philosophy is that good businesspeople cannot spend time watching out for the interests of others and agonizing over "the right thing to do." In the minds of immoral managers, nice guys come in second and the competitive nature of business requires that you either trample on others or get trampled yourself. They believe what really matters is single-minded pursuit of their own best interests—they are living examples of capitalistic greed, caring only about their own or their organization's gains and successes. Immoral managers may even be willing to short-circuit legal and regulatory requirements if they think they can escape detection. And they are always on the lookout for legal loopholes and creative ways to get around rules and regulations that block or constrain actions they deem in their own or their company's self-interest. Immoral managers are thus the bad guys—they have few scruples, little or no integrity, and are willing to do most anything they believe they can get away with. It doesn't bother them much to be seen by others as wearing the black hats.

- *The amoral manager*—Amoral managers appear in two forms: the intentionally amoral manager and the unintentionally amoral manager. Intentionally amoral managers are of the strong opinion that business and ethics are not to be mixed. They are not troubled by failing to factor ethical considerations into their decisions and actions because it is perfectly legitimate for businesses to do anything they wish so long as they stay within legal and regulatory bounds—in other words, if particular actions and behaviors are legal and comply with existing regulations, then they qualify as permissible and should not be seen as unethical. Intentionally amoral managers view the observance of high ethical standards (doing more than what is required by law) as too Sunday-schoolish for the tough competitive world of business, even though observing some higher ethical considerations may be appropriate in life outside of business. Their concept of right and wrong tends to be lawyer-driven—how much can we get by with and can we go ahead even if it is borderline? Thus intentionally amoral managers hold firmly to the view that anything goes, so long as actions and behaviors are not clearly ruled out by prevailing legal and regulatory requirements.

  Core Concept
  Amoral managers believe that businesses ought to be able to do whatever current laws and regulations allow them to do without being shackled by ethical considerations—they think that what is permissible and what is not is governed entirely by prevailing laws and regulations, not by societal concepts of right and wrong.

  Unintentionally amoral managers do not pay much attention to the concept of business ethics either, but for different reasons. They are simply casual about, careless about, or inattentive to the fact that certain kinds of business decisions or company activities are unsavory or may have deleterious effects on others—in short, they go about their jobs as best they can without giving serious thought to the ethical dimension of decisions and business actions. They are ethically unconscious when it comes to business matters, partly or mainly because they have just never stopped to consider whether and to what extent business decisions or company actions sometimes spill over to create adverse impacts on others. Unintentionally amoral managers may even see themselves as people of integrity and as personally ethical. But, like intentionally amoral managers, they are of the firm view that businesses ought to be able to do whatever the current legal and regulatory framework allows them to do without being shackled by ethical considerations.

By some accounts, the population of managers is said to be distributed among all three types in a bell-shaped curve, with immoral managers and moral managers occupying the two tails of the curve, and the amoral managers (especially the intentionally amoral managers) occupying the broad middle ground.[24] Furthermore, within the population of managers, there is experiential evidence to support that while the average manager may be amoral most of the time, he or she may slip into a moral or immoral mode on occasion, based on a variety of impinging factors and circumstances.

Evidence of Managerial Immorality in the Global Business Community

There is considerable evidence that a sizable majority of managers are either amoral or immoral. The *2005 Global Corruption Report,* sponsored by Transparency International, found that corruption among public officials and in business transactions is widespread across the world. Table 10.1 shows some of the countries where corruption is believed to be lowest and highest—even in the countries where business practices are deemed to be least corrupt, there is considerable room for improvement in the extent to which managers observe ethical business practices. Table 10.2 presents data showing the perceived likelihood that companies in the 21 largest exporting countries are paying bribes to win business in the markets of 15 emerging-country markets—Argentina, Brazil, Colombia, Hungary, India, Indonesia, Mexico, Morocco, Nigeria, the Philippines, Poland, Russia, South Africa, South Korea, and Thailand.

Table 10.1   **Corruption Perceptions Index, Selected Countries, 2004**

Country	2004 CPI Score*	High–Low Range	Number of Surveys Used	Country	2004 CPI Score*	High–Low Range	Number of Surveys Used
Finland	9.7	9.2–10.0	9	Taiwan	5.6	4.7–6.0	15
New Zealand	9.6	9.2–9.7	9	Italy	4.8	3.4–5.6	10
Denmark	9.5	8.7–9.8	10	South Africa	4.6	3.4–5.8	11
Sweden	9.2	8.7–9.5	11	South Korea	4.5	2.2–5.8	14
Switzerland	9.1	8.6–9.4	10	Brazil	3.9	3.5–4.8	11
Norway	8.9	8.0–9.5	9	Mexico	3.6	2.6–4.5	11
Australia	8.8	6.7–9.5	15	Thailand	3.6	2.5–4.5	14
Netherlands	8.7	8.3–9.4	10	China	3.4	2.1–5.6	16
United Kingdom	8.6	7.8–9.2	12	Saudi Arabia	3.4	2.0–4.5	5
Canada	8.5	6.5–9.4	12	Turkey	3.2	1.9–5.4	13
Germany	8.2	7.5–9.2	11	India	2.8	2.2–3.7	15
Hong Kong	8.0	3.5–9.4	13	Russia	2.8	2.0–5.0	15
United States	7.5	5.0–8.7	14	Philippines	2.6	1.4–3.7	14
Chile	7.4	6.3–8.7	11	Vietnam	2.6	1.6–3.7	11
France	7.1	5.0–9.0	12	Argentina	2.5	1.7–3.7	11
Spain	7.1	5.6–8.0	11	Venezuela	2.3	2.0–3.0	11
Japan	6.9	3.5–9.0	15	Pakistan	2.1	1.2–3.3	7
Israel	6.4	3.5–8.1	10	Nigeria	1.6	0.9–2.1	9
Uruguay	6.2	5.6–7.3	6	Bangladesh	1.5	0.3–2.4	5

* The CPI scores range between 10 (highly clean) and 0 (highly corrupt); the data were collected between 2002 and 2004 and reflects a composite of 18 data sources from 12 institutions, as indicated in the number of surveys used. The CPI score represents the perceptions of the degree of corruption as seen by businesspeople, academics, and risk analysts. CPI scores were reported for 146 countries.
Source: Transparency International, *2005 Global Corruption Report,* www.globalcorruptionreport.org (accessed October 31, 2005), pp. 235–38.

Table 10.2   **The Degree to Which Companies in Major Exporting Countries Are Perceived to Be Paying Bribes in Doing Business Abroad**

Rank/Country	Bribe-Payer Index (10 = Low; 0 = High)	Rank/Country	Bribe-Payer Index (10 = Low; 0 = High)
1. Australia	8.5	12. France	5.5
2. Sweden	8.4	13. United States	5.3
3. Switzerland	8.4	14. Japan	5.3
4. Austria	8.2	15. Malaysia	4.3
5. Canada	8.1	16. Hong Kong	4.3
6. Netherlands	7.8	17. Italy	4.1
7. Belgium	7.8	18. South Korea	3.9
8. Britain	6.9	19. Taiwan	3.8
9. Singapore	6.3	20. China (excluding Hong Kong)	3.5
10. Germany	6.3	21. Russia	3.2
11. Spain	5.8		

Note: The bribe-payer index is based on a questionnaire developed by Transparency International and a survey of some 835 private-sector leaders in 15 emerging countries accounting for 60 percent of all imports into non-Organization for Economic Cooperation and Development countries—actual polling was conducted by Gallup International.

Source: Transparency International, *2003 Global Corruption Report,* www.globalcorruptionreport.org (accessed November 1, 2005), p. 267.

The *2003 Global Corruption Report* cited data indicating that bribery occurred most often in (1) public works contracts and construction, (2) the arms and defense industry, and (3) the oil and gas industry. On a scale of 1 to 10, where 10 indicates negligible bribery, even the "cleanest" industry sectors—agriculture, light manufacturing, and fisheries—only had "passable" scores of 5.9, indicating that bribes are quite likely a common occurrence in these sectors as well (see Table 10.3).

The corruption, of course, extends beyond just bribes and kickbacks. For example, in 2005, four global chip makers (Samsung and Hynix Semiconductor in South Korea, Infineon Technologies in Germany, and Micron Technology in the United States) pleaded guilty to conspiring to fix the prices of dynamic random access memory (DRAM) chips sold to such companies as Dell, Apple Computer, and Hewlett-Packard—DRAM chips generate annual worldwide sales of around $26 billion and are used in computers, electronics products, and motor vehicles.[25] So far, the probe has resulted in fines of $730 million, jail terms for nine executives, and pending criminal charges for three more employees for their role in the global cartel; the guilty companies face hundreds of millions of dollars more in damage claims from customers and from consumer class-action lawsuits.

A global business community that is apparently so populated with unethical business practices and managerial immorality does not bode well for concluding that many companies ground their strategies on exemplary ethical principles or for the vigor with which company managers try to ingrain ethical behavior into company personnel. And, as many business school professors have noted, there are considerable numbers of amoral business students in our classrooms. So efforts to root out shady and corrupt business practices and implant high ethical principles into the managerial process of crafting and executing strategy is unlikely to produce an ethically strong global business climate anytime in the near future, barring major effort to address and correct the ethical laxness of company managers.

Table 10.3   **Bribery in Different Industries**

Business Sector	Bribery Score (10 = Low; 0 = High)
Agriculture	5.9
Light manufacturing	5.9
Fisheries	5.9
Information technology	5.1
Forestry	5.1
Civilian aerospace	4.9
Banking and finance	4.7
Heavy manufacturing	4.5
Pharmaceuticals/medical care	4.3
Transportation/storage	4.3
Mining	4.0
Power generation/transmission	3.7
Telecommunications	3.7
Real estate/property	3.5
Oil and gas	2.7
Arms and defense	1.9
Public works/construction	1.3

Note: The bribery scores for each industry are based on a questionnaire developed by Transparency International and a survey of some 835 private sector leaders in 15 emerging countries accounting for 60 percent of all imports into non-Organization for Economic Cooperation and Development countries—actual polling was conducted by Gallup International.

Source: Transparency International, *2003 Global Corruption Report,* www.globalcorruption report.org (accessed November 1, 2005), p. 268.

DO COMPANY STRATEGIES NEED TO BE ETHICAL?

Company managers may formulate strategies that are ethical in all respects, or they may decide to employ strategies that, for one reason or another, have unethical or at least gray-area components. While most company managers are usually careful to ensure that a company's strategy is within the bounds of what is legal, the available evidence indicates they are not always so careful to ensure that all elements of their strategies are within the bounds of what is generally deemed ethical. Senior executives with strong ethical convictions are normally proactive in insisting that all aspects of company strategy fall within ethical boundaries. In contrast, senior executives who are either immoral or amoral may use shady strategies and unethical or borderline business practices, especially if they are clever at devising schemes to keep ethically questionable actions hidden from view.

During the past five years, there has been an ongoing series of revelations about managers who have ignored ethical standards, deliberately stepped out of bounds, and been called to account by the media, regulators, and the legal system. Ethical misconduct has occurred at Enron, Tyco International, HealthSouth, Rite Aid, Citicorp, Bristol-Myers, Squibb, Adelphia, Royal Dutch/Shell, Parmalat (an Italy-based food products company), Mexican oil giant Pemex, Marsh & McLennan and other insurance brokers, several leading brokerage houses and investment banking firms, and a host of mutual fund companies. The consequences of crafting strategies that cannot pass the test of moral scrutiny are manifested in the sharp drops in the stock prices of the guilty companies that have cost shareholders billions of dollars; the frequently devastating public relations hits that the accused companies have taken, the sizes of the fines that have been levied (often amounting to several hundred million dollars); the growing legion of criminal indictments and convictions of company executives; and the numbers of executives who have either been dismissed from their jobs, shoved into early retirement, and/or suffered immense public embarrassment. The fallout from all these scandals has resulted in heightened management attention to legal and ethical considerations in crafting strategy. Illustration Capsule 10.1 details the ethically flawed strategy at the world's leading insurance broker, and the consequences to those concerned.

What Are the Drivers of Unethical Strategies and Business Behavior?

The apparent pervasiveness of immoral and amoral businesspeople is one obvious reason why ethical principles are an ineffective moral compass in business dealings and why companies may resort to unethical strategic behavior. But apart from thinking that maintains "The business of business is business, not ethics," three other main drivers of unethical business behavior also stand out:[26]

- Faulty oversight such that overzealous or obsessive pursuit of personal gain, wealth, and other selfish interests is overlooked by or escapes the attention of higher-ups (most usually the board of directors).
- Heavy pressures on company managers to meet or beat performance targets.
- A company culture that puts the profitability and good business performance ahead of ethical behavior.

Overzealous Pursuit of Personal Gain, Wealth, and Selfish Interests
People who are obsessed with wealth accumulation, greed, power, status, and other selfish interests often push ethical principles aside in their quest for self-gain. Driven by their ambitions, they exhibit few qualms in skirting the rules or doing whatever is necessary to achieve their goals. The first and only priority of such corporate bad apples is to look out for their own best interests and if climbing the ladder of success means having few scruples and ignoring the welfare of others, so be it. A general disregard for business ethics can prompt all kinds of unethical strategic maneuvers and behaviors at companies. Top executives, directors, and majority shareholders at cable-TV company Adelphia Communications ripped off the company for amounts totaling well over $1 billion, diverting hundreds of millions of dollars to fund their Buffalo Sabres hockey team, build a private golf course, and buy timber rights—among other things—and driving the company into bankruptcy. Their actions, which represent one of the biggest instances of corporate looting and self-dealing in American business, took place despite the company's public pontifications about the principles it would observe in trying to care for customers, employees, stockholders, and the local communities where it operated. Andrew Fastow, Enron's chief financial officer (CFO), set himself up as the manager of one of Enron's off-the-books partnerships and as the part-owner of another, allegedly earning extra compensation of $30 million for his owner-manager roles in the two partnerships; Enron's board of directors agreed to suspend the company's conflict-of-interest rules designed to protect the company from this very kind of executive self-dealing (but directors and perhaps Fastow's superiors were kept in the dark about how much Fastow was earning on the side).

Illustration Capsule 10.1

Marsh & McLennan's Ethically Flawed Strategy

In October 2004, *Wall Street Journal* headlines trumpeted that a cartel among insurance brokers had been busted. Among the ringleaders was worldwide industry leader Marsh & McLennan Companies Inc., with 2003 revenues of $11.5 billion and a U.S. market share of close to 20 percent. The gist of the brokers' plan was to cheat corporate clients by rigging the bids brokers solicited for insurance policies and thereby collecting big fees (called contingent commissions) from major insurance companies for steering business their way. Two family members of Marsh & McLennan CEO Jeffery Greenberg were CEOs of major insurance companies to which Marsh sometimes steered business. Greenberg's father was CEO of insurance giant AIG (which had total revenues of $81 billion and insurance premium revenues of $28 billion in 2003), and Greenberg's younger brother was CEO of ACE Ltd., the 24th biggest property-casualty insurer in the United States, with 2003 revenues of $10.7 billion and insurance premium revenues of more than $5 billion worldwide. Prior to joining ACE, Greenberg's younger brother had been president and chief operating officer of AIG, headed by his father.

Several months prior to the cartel bust, a Marsh subsidiary, Putnam Investments, had paid a $110 million fine for securities fraud and another Marsh subsidiary, Mercer Consulting, was placed under Securities and Exchange Commission (SEC) investigation for engaging in pay-to-play practices that forced investment managers to pay fees in order to secure Mercer's endorsement of their services when making recommendations to Mercer's pension fund clients.

The cartel scheme arose from the practice of large corporations to hire the services of such brokers as Marsh & McLennan, Aon Corporation, A. J. Gallaher & Company, Wells Fargo, or BB&T Insurance Services to manage their risks and take out appropriate property and casualty insurance on their behalf. The broker's job was to solicit bids from several insurers and obtain the best policies at the lowest prices for the client.

Marsh's insurance brokerage strategy was to solicit artificially high bids from some insurance companies so that it could guarantee that the bid of a preferred insurer on a given deal would win the bid. Marsh brokers called underwriters at various insurers, often including AIG and ACE, and asked for "B" quotes—bids that were deliberately high. Insurers asked for B quotes knew that Marsh wanted another insurer to win the business, but they were willing to participate because on other policy solicitations Marsh could end up steering the business to them via Marsh's same strategy. Sometimes Marsh even asked underwriters that were providing B quotes to attend a meeting with Marsh's client and make a presentation regarding their policy to help bolster the credibility of their inflated bid.

Since it was widespread practice among insurers to pay brokers contingent commissions based on the volume or profitability of the business the broker directed to them, Marsh's B-quote solicitation strategy allowed it to steer business to those insurers paying the largest contingent commissions—these contingent commissions were in addition to the fees the broker earned from the corporate client for services rendered in conducting the bidding process for the client. A substantial fraction of the policies that Marsh unlawfully steered were to two Bermuda-based insurance companies that it helped start up and in which it also had ownership interests (some Marsh executives also indirectly owned shares of stock in one of the companies); indeed, these two insurance companies received 30–40 percent of their total business from policies steered to them by Marsh.

At Marsh, steering business to insurers paying the highest contingent commission was a key component of the company's overall strategy. Marsh's contingent commissions generated revenues of close to $1.5 billion over the 2001–2003 period, including $845 million in 2003. Without these commission revenues, Marsh's $1.5 billion in net profits would have been close to 40 percent lower in 2003.

Within days of headlines about the cartel bust, Marsh's stock price had fallen by 48 percent (costing shareholders about $11.5 billion in market value) and the company was looking down the barrel of a criminal indictment. To stave off the criminal indictment (something no insurance company had ever survived), board members forced Jeffrey Greenberg to resign as CEO. Another top executive was suspended. Criminal charges against several Marsh executives for their roles in the bid-rigging scheme were filed several weeks thereafter.

In an attempt to lead industry reform, Greenberg's successor quickly announced a new business model for Marsh that included not accepting any contingent commissions from insurers. Marsh's new strategy and business model involved charging fees only to its corporate clients for soliciting bids, placing their insurance, and otherwise managing clients' risks and crises. This eliminated Marsh's conflict of interest in earning fees from both sides of the transactions it made on behalf of its corporate clients. Marsh also committed to provide up-front disclosure to clients of the fees it would earn on their business (in the past such fees had been murky and incomplete). Even so, there were indications that close to 10 lawsuits, some involving class action, would soon be filed against the company.

Meanwhile, all major commercial property-casualty insurers were scrambling to determine whether their payment of contingent commissions was ethical, since such arrangements clearly gave insurance brokers a financial incentive to place insurance with companies paying the biggest contingent commissions, not those with the best prices or terms. Prosecutors of the cartel had referred to the contingent commissions as kickbacks.

Sources: Monica Langley and Theo Francis, "Insurers Reel from Bust of a 'Cartel,'" *The Wall Street Journal,* October 18, 2004, pp. A1, A14; Monica Langley and Ian McDonald, "Marsh Averts Criminal Case with New CEO," *The Wall Street Journal,* October 26, 2004, pp. A1, A10; Christopher Oster and Theo Francis, "Marsh and Aon Have Holdings in Two Insurers," *The Wall Street Journal,* November 1, 2004, p. C1; and Marcia Vickers, "The Secret World of Marsh Mac," *BusinessWeek,* November 1, 2004, pp. 78–89.

According to a civil complaint filed by the Securities and Exchange Commission, the CEO of Tyco International, a well-known $35.6 billion manufacturing and services company, conspired with the company's CFO to steal more than $170 million, including a company-paid $2 million birthday party for the CEO's wife held on Sardinia, an island off the coast of Italy; a $7 million Park Avenue apartment for his wife; and secret low-interest and interest-free loans to fund private businesses and investments and purchase lavish artwork, yachts, estate jewelry, and vacation homes in New Hampshire, Connecticut, Massachusetts, and Utah. The CEO allegedly lived rent-free in a $31 million Fifth Avenue apartment that Tyco purchased in his name, directed millions of dollars of charitable contributions in his own name using Tyco funds, diverted company funds to finance his personal businesses and investments, and sold millions of dollars of Tyco stock back to Tyco itself through Tyco subsidiaries located in offshore bank-secrecy jurisdictions. Tyco's CEO and CFO were further charged with conspiring to reap more than $430 million from sales of stock, using questionable accounting to hide their actions, and engaging in deceptive accounting practices to distort the company's financial condition from 1995 to 2002. At the trial on the charges filed by the SEC, the prosecutor told the jury in his opening statement, "This case is about lying, cheating and stealing. These people didn't win the jackpot—they stole it." Defense lawyers countered that "every single transaction . . . was set down in detail in Tyco's books and records" and that the authorized and disclosed multimillion-dollar compensation packages were merited by the company's financial performance and stock price gains. The two Tyco executives were convicted and sentenced to jail.

Prudential Securities paid a total of about $2 billion in the 1990s to settle misconduct charges relating to practices that misled investors on the risks and rewards of limited-partnership investments. Providian Financial Corporation, despite an otherwise glowing record of social responsibility and corporate citizenship, paid $150 million in 2001 to settle claims that its strategy included systematic attempts to cheat credit card holders. Ten prominent Wall Street securities firms in 2003 paid $1.4 billion to settle charges that they knowingly issued misleading stock research to investors in an effort to prop up the stock prices of client corporations. A host of mutual-fund firms made under-the-table arrangements to regularly buy and sell stock for their accounts at special after-hours trading prices that disadvantaged long-term investors and had to pay nearly $2.0 billion in fines and restitution when their unethical practices were discovered by authorities during 2002–2003. Salomon Smith Barney, Goldman Sachs, Credit Suisse First Boston, and several other financial firms were assessed close to $2 billion in fines and restitution for the unethical manner in which they contributed to the scandals at Enron and WorldCom and for the shady practice of allocating shares of hot initial public offering stocks to a select list of corporate executives who either steered or were in a position to steer investment banking business their way.

Heavy Pressures on Company Managers to Meet or Beat Earnings Targets   When companies find themselves scrambling to achieve ambitious earnings growth and meet the quarterly and annual performance expectations of Wall Street analysts and investors, managers often feel enormous pressure to do whatever it takes to sustain the company's reputation for delivering good financial performance. Executives at high-performing companies know that investors will see the slightest sign of a slowdown in earnings growth as a red flag and drive down the company's stock price. The company's credit rating could be downgraded if it has used lots of debt to finance its growth. The pressure to watch the scoreboard and never miss a quarter—so as not to upset the expectations of Wall Street analysts and fickle stock market investors—prompts managers to cut costs wherever savings show up immediately, squeeze extra sales out of early deliveries, and engage in other short-term maneuvers to make the numbers. As the pressure builds to keep performance numbers looking good, company personnel start stretching the rules further and further, until the limits of ethical conduct are overlooked.[27] Once ethical boundaries are crossed in efforts to "meet or beat the numbers," the threshold for making more extreme ethical compromises becomes lower.

Several top executives at WorldCom (the remains of which is now part of Verizon Communications), a company built with scores of acquisitions in exchange for WorldCom stock, allegedly concocted a fraudulent $11 billion accounting scheme to hide costs and inflate revenues and profit over several years; the scheme was said to have helped the company keep its stock price propped up high enough to make additional acquisitions, support its nearly $30 billion debt load, and allow executives to cash in on their lucrative stock options. At Qwest Communications, a company created by the merger of a go-go telecom start-up and U.S. West (one of the regional Bell companies), management was charged with scheming to improperly book $2.4 billion in revenues from a variety of sources and deals, thereby inflating the company's profits and making it appear that the company's strategy to create a telecommunications company of the future was on track when, in fact, it was faltering badly behind the scenes. Top-level Qwest executives were dismissed, and in 2004 new management agreed to $250 million in fines for all the misdeeds.

At Bristol-Myers Squibb, the world's fifth-largest drug maker, management apparently engaged in a series of numbers-game maneuvers to meet earnings targets, including such actions as:

- Offering special end-of-quarter discounts to induce distributors and local pharmacies to stock up on certain prescription drugs—a practice known as channel stuffing.
- Issuing last-minute price increase alerts to spur purchases and beef up operating profits.
- Setting up excessive reserves for restructuring charges and then reversing some of the charges as needed to bolster operating profits.
- Making repeated asset sales small enough that the gains could be reported as additions to operating profit rather than being flagged as one-time gains. (Some accountants have long used a rule of thumb that says a transaction that alters quarterly profits by less than 5 percent is "immaterial" and need not be disclosed in the company's financial reports.)

Such numbers games were said to be a common "earnings management" practice at Bristol-Myers and, according to one former executive, "sent a huge message across the organization that you make your numbers at all costs."[28]

Company executives often feel pressured to hit financial performance targets because their compensation depends heavily on the company's performance. During the late 1990s, it became fashionable for boards of directors to grant lavish bonuses, stock option awards, and other compensation benefits to executives for meeting specified performance targets. So outlandishly large were these rewards that executives had strong personal incentives to bend the rules and engage in behaviors the allowed the targets to be met. Much of the accounting hocus-pocus at the root of recent corporate scandals has entailed situations in which executives benefited enormously from misleading accounting or other shady activities that allowed them to hit the numbers and receive incentive awards ranging from $10 million to $100 million. At Bristol-Myers Squibb, for example, the pay-for-performance link spawned strong rules-bending incentives. About 94 percent of one top executive's $18.5 million in total compensation in 2001 came from stock-option grants, a bonus, and long-term incentive payments linked to corporate performance; about 92 percent of a second executive's $12.9 million of compensation was incentive-based.[29]

The fundamental problem with a "make the numbers and move on" syndrome is that a company doesn't really serve its customers or its shareholders by going overboard in pursuing bottom-line profitability. In the final analysis, shareholder interests are best served by doing a really good job of serving customers (observing the rule that customers are king) and by improving the company's competitiveness in the marketplace—these outcomes are the most reliable drivers of higher profits and added shareholder value. Cutting ethical corners or stooping to downright illegal actions in the name of profits first carries exceptionally high risk for shareholders—the steep stock-price decline and tarnished brand image that accompany the discovery of scurrilous behavior leaves shareholders with a company worth much less than before—and the rebuilding task can be arduous, taking both considerable time and resources.

Company Cultures That Put the Bottom Line Ahead of Ethical Behavior

When a company's culture spawns an ethically corrupt or amoral work climate, people have a company-approved license to ignore what's right and engage in most any behavior or employ most any strategy they think they can get away with. Such cultural norms as "No one expects strict adherence to ethical standards," "Everyone else does it," and "It is politic to bend the rules to get the job done" permeate the work environment.[30] At such companies, ethically immoral or amoral people play down observance of ethical strategic actions and business conduct. Moreover, the pressures to conform to cultural norms can prompt otherwise honorable people to make ethical mistakes and succumb to the many opportunities around them to engage in unethical practices.

A perfect example of a company culture gone awry on ethics is Enron.[31] Enron's leaders encouraged company personnel to focus on the current bottom line and to be innovative and aggressive in figuring out what could be done to grow current revenues and earnings. Employees were expected to pursue opportunities to the utmost. Enron executives viewed the company as a laboratory for innovation; the company hired the best and brightest people and pushed them to be creative, look at problems and opportunities in new ways, and exhibit a sense of urgency in making things happen. Employees were encouraged to make a difference and do their part in creating an entrepreneurial environment in which creativity flourished, people could achieve their full potential, and everyone had a stake in the outcome. Enron employees got the message—pushing the limits and meeting one's numbers were viewed as survival skills. Enron's annual "rank and yank" formal evaluation process, in which the 15 to 20 percent lowest-ranking employees were let go or encouraged to seek other employment, made it abundantly clear that hitting earnings targets and being *the* mover and shaker -in the marketplace were what counted. The name of the game at Enron became devising clever ways to boost revenues and earnings, even if it sometimes meant operating outside established policies and without the knowledge of superiors. In fact, outside-the-lines behavior was celebrated if it generated profitable new business. Enron's energy contracts and its trading and hedging activities grew increasingly more complex and diverse as employees pursued first this avenue and then another to help keep Enron's financial performance looking good.

As a consequence of Enron's well-publicized successes in creating new products and businesses and leveraging the company's trading and hedging expertise into new market arenas, Enron came to be regarded as exceptionally innovative. It was ranked by its corporate peers as the most innovative U.S. company for three consecutive years in *Fortune* magazine's annual surveys of the most-admired companies. A high-performance/high-rewards climate came to pervade the Enron culture, as the best workers (determined by who produced the best bottom-line results) received impressively large incentives and bonuses (amounting to as much as $1 million for traders and even more for senior executives). On Car Day at Enron, an array of luxury sports cars arrived for presentation to the most successful employees. Understandably, employees wanted to be seen as part of Enron's star team and partake in the benefits that being one of Enron's best and smartest employees entailed. The high monetary rewards, the ambitious and hard-driving people that the company hired and promoted, and the competitive, results-oriented culture combined to give Enron a reputation not only for trampling competitors at every opportunity but also for practicing internal ruthlessness. The company's super-aggressiveness and win-at-all-costs mind-set nurtured a culture that gradually and then more rapidly fostered the erosion of ethical standards, eventually making a mockery of the company's stated values of integrity and respect. When it became evident in the fall of 2001 that Enron was a house of cards propped up by deceitful accounting and a myriad of unsavory practices, the company imploded in a matter of weeks—the biggest bankruptcy of all time cost investors $64 billion in losses (between August 2000, when the stock price was at its five-year high, and November 2001), and Enron employees lost their retirement assets, which were almost totally invested in Enron stock.

More recently, a team investigating an ethical scandal at oil giant Royal Dutch/Shell Group that resulted in the payment of $150 million in fines found that an ethically flawed culture was a major contributor to why managers made rosy forecasts that they couldn't meet and why top executives engaged in maneuvers to mislead investors by overstating Shell's oil and gas reserves by 25 percent (equal to 4.5 billion barrels of oil). The investigation revealed that top Shell executives knew that a variety of internal practices, together with unrealistic and unsupportable estimates submitted by overzealous, bonus-conscious managers in Shell's exploration and production group, were being used to overstate reserves. An e-mail written by Shell's top executive for exploration and production (who was caught up in the ethical misdeeds and later forced to resign) said, "I am becoming sick and tired about lying about the extent of our reserves issues and the downward revisions that need to be done because of our far too aggressive/optimistic bookings."[32]

Illustration Capsule 10.2 describes Philip Morris USA's new strategy for growing the sales of its leading Marlboro cigarette brand—judge for yourself whether the strategy is ethical or shady in light of the undisputed medical links between smoking and lung cancer.

Approaches to Managing a Company's Ethical Conduct

The stance a company takes in dealing with or managing ethical conduct at any given point can take any of four basic forms:[33]

- The unconcerned, or nonissue, approach.
- The damage control approach.
- The compliance approach.
- The ethical culture approach.

The differences in these four approaches are discussed briefly below and summarized in Table 10.4 on page 335.

Illustration Capsule 10.2

Philip Morris USA's Strategy for Marlboro Cigarettes: Ethical or Unethical?

In late 2005, Philip Morris USA and its corporate parent, Altria Group Inc., wrapped up a year of promotions and parties to celebrate the 50th year of selling Marlboro cigarettes. Marlboro commanded a 40 percent share of the U.S. market for cigarettes and was also one of the world's top cigarette brands. Despite sharp advertising restrictions agreed to by cigarette marketers in 1998 and a big jump in state excise taxes on cigarettes since 2002, Marlboro's sales and market share were climbing, thanks to a new trailblazing marketing strategy.

Marlboro had become a major brand in the 1960s and 1970s via a classic mass-marketing strategy anchored by annual ad budgets in the millions of dollars. The company's TV, magazine, and billboard ads for Marlboros always featured a rugged cowboy wearing a Stetson, riding a horse in a mountainous area, and smoking a Marlboro—closely connecting the brand with the American West gave Marlboro a distinctive and instantly recognized brand image. The Marlboro ad campaign was a gigantic success, making Marlboro one of the world's best-known and valuable brands.

But following the ad restrictions in 1998, Philip Morris had to shift to a different marketing strategy to grow Marlboro's sales. It opted for an approach aimed at generating all kinds of marketing buzz for the Marlboro brand and creating a larger cadre of loyal Marlboro smokers (who often felt persecuted by social pressures and antismoking ordinances). Philip Morris directed company field reps to set up promotions at local bars where smokers could sign up for promotional offers like price discounts on Marlboro purchases, a Marlboro Miles program that awarded points for each pack purchased, and sweepstakes prizes that included cash, trips, and Marlboro apparel; some prizes could be purchased with Marlboro Miles points. It also began to sponsor live concerts and other events to generate additional sign-ups among attendees. A Web site was created to spur Internet chatter among the Marlboro faithful and to encourage still more sign-ups

for special deals and contests (some with prizes up to a $1 million)—an online community quickly sprang up around the brand. Via all the sign-ups and calls to an 800 number, Philip Morris created a database of Marlboro smokers that by 2005 had grown to 26 million names. Using direct mail and e-mail, the company sent the members of its database a steady stream of messages and offers, ranging from birthday coupons for free breakfasts to price discounts to chances to attend local concerts, enjoy a day at nearby horse tracks, or win a trip to the company's ranch in Montana (where winners got gifts, five-course meals, massages, and free drinks and could go snowmobiling, fly fishing, or horseback riding).

Meanwhile, Philip Morris also became considerably more aggressive in retail stores, launching an offensive initiative to give discounts and incentives to retailers who utilized special aisle displays and signage for its cigarette brands. One 22-store retail chain reported that, by agreeing to a deal to give Philip Morris brands about 66 percent of its cigarette shelf space, it ended up paying about $5.50 per carton less for its Marlboro purchases than it paid for cartons of Camels supplied by rival R. J. Reynolds. Some Wal-Mart stores were said to have awarded Philip Morris as much as 80 percent of its cigarette shelf space.

Thus, despite being besieged by the costs of defending lawsuits and paying out billions to governments as compensation for the increased health care costs associated with smoking, Philip Morris and other cigarette makers were making very healthy profits: operating margins of nearly 28 percent in 2005 (up from 26 percent in 2004) and net income of about $11.4 billion on sales of $66.3 billion in the United States and abroad.

However, health care officials were highly critical of Philip Morris's marketing tactics for Marlboro, and the U.S. Department of Justice had filed a lawsuit claiming, among other things, that the company knowingly marketed Marlboros to underage people in its database, a charge denied by the company.

Source: Based largely on information in Nanette Byrnes, "Leader of the Packs," *BusinessWeek,* October 31, 2005, pp. 56, 58.

The Unconcerned, or Nonissue, Approach The unconcerned approach is prevalent at companies whose executives are immoral and unintentionally amoral. Senior executives at companies using this approach ascribe to the view that notions of right and wrong in matters of business are defined entirely by government via the prevailing laws and regulations. They maintain that trying to enforce ethical standards above and beyond what is legally required is a nonissue because businesses are entitled to conduct their affairs in whatever

Table 10.4   **Four Approaches to Managing Business Ethics**

	Unconcerned, or Nonissue Approach	Damage Control Approach	Compliance Approach	Ethical Culture Approach
Underlying beliefs	• The business of business is business, not ethics. • All that matters is whether an action is legal. • Ethics has no place in the conduct of business. • Companies should not be morally accountable for their actions.	• The company needs to make a token gesture in the direction of ethical standards (a code of ethics).	• The company must be committed to ethical standards and monitoring ethics performance. • Unethical behavior must be prevented and punished if discovered. • It is important to have a reputation for high ethical standards.	• Ethics is basic to the culture. • Behaving ethically must be a deeply held corporate value and become a way of life. • Everyone is expected to walk the talk.
Ethics management approaches	• There's no need to make decisions concerning business ethics—if its legal, it is okay. • No intervention regarding the ethical component of decisions is needed.	• The company must act to protect against the dangers of unethical strategies and behavior. • Ignore unethical behavior or allow it to go unpunished unless the situation is extreme and requires action.	• The company must establish a clear, comprehensive code of ethics. • The company must provide ethics training for all personnel. • Have formal ethics compliance procedures, an ethics compliance office, and a chief ethics officer.	• Ethical behavior is ingrained and reinforced as part of the culture. • Much reliance on co-worker peer pressure—"That's not how we do things here." • Everyone is an ethics watchdog—whistle-blowing is required. • Ethics heroes are celebrated; ethics stories are told.
Challenges	• Financial consequences can become unaffordable. • Some stakeholders are alienated.	• Credibility problems with stakeholders can arise. • The company is susceptible to ethical scandal. • The company has a subpar ethical reputation—executives and company personnel don't walk the talk.	• Organizational members come to rely on the existing rules for moral guidance—fosters a mentality of what is not forbidden is allowed. • Rules and guidelines proliferate. • The locus of moral control resides in the code and in the ethics compliance system rather than in an individual's own moral responsibility for ethical behavior.	• New employees must go through strong ethics induction program. • Formal ethics management systems can be underutilized. • Relying on peer pressures and cultural norms to enforce ethical standards can result in eliminating some or many of the compliance trappings and, over time, induce moral laxness.

Source: Adapted from Gedeon J. Rossouw and Leon J. van Vuuren, "Modes of Managing Morality: A Descriptive Model of Strategies for Managing Ethics," *Journal of Business Ethics* 46, no. 4 (September 2003), pp. 392–93.

manner they wish so long as they comply with the letter of what is legally required. Hence, there is no need to spend valuable management time trying to prescribe and enforce standards of conduct that go above and beyond legal and regulatory requirements. In companies where senior managers are immoral, the prevailing view may well be that under-the-table dealing can be good business if it can be kept hidden or if it can be justified on grounds that others are doing it too. Companies in this mode usually engage in most any business practices they believe they can get away with, and the strategies they employ may well embrace elements that are either borderline from a legal perspective or ethically shady and unsavory.

The Damage Control Approach

The main objective of the damage control approach is to protect against adverse publicity and any damaging consequences brought on by headlines in the media, outside investigation, threats of litigation, punitive government action, or angry or vocal stakeholders.

Damage control is favored at companies whose managers are intentionally amoral but who are wary of scandal and adverse public relations fallout that could cost them their jobs of tarnish their careers. Companies using this approach, not wanting to risk tarnishing the reputations of key personnel or the company, usually make some concession to window-dressing ethics, going so far as to adopt a code of ethics—so that their executives can point to it as evidence of good-faith efforts to prevent unethical strategy making or unethical conduct on the part of company personnel. But the code of ethics exists mainly as nice words on paper, and company personnel do not operate within a strong ethical context—there's a notable gap between talking ethics and walking ethics. Employees quickly get the message that rule bending is tolerated and may even be rewarded if the company benefits from their actions.

Company executives that practice the damage control approach are prone to look the other way when shady or borderline behavior occurs—adopting a kind of "See no evil, hear no evil, speak no evil" stance (except when exposure of the company's actions put executives under great pressure to redress any wrongs that have been done). They may even condone questionable actions that help the company reach earnings targets or bolster its market standing—such as pressuring customers to stock up on the company's product (channel stuffing), making under-the-table payments to win new business, stonewalling the recall of products claimed to be unsafe, bad-mouthing the products of rivals, or trying to keep prices low by sourcing goods from disreputable suppliers in low-wage countries that run sweatshop operations or use child labor. But they are usually careful to do such things in a manner that lessens the risks of exposure or damaging consequences. This generally includes making token gestures to police compliance with codes of ethics and relying heavily on spin to help extricate the company or themselves from claims that the company's strategy has unethical components or that company personnel have engaged in unethical practices.

The Compliance Approach

Anywhere from light to forceful compliance is favored at companies whose managers (1) lean toward being somewhat amoral but are highly concerned about having ethically upstanding reputations or (2) are moral and see strong compliance methods as the best way to impose and enforce ethical rules and high ethical standards. Companies that adopt a compliance mode usually do some or all of the following to display their commitment to ethical conduct: make the code of ethics a visible and regular part of communications with employees, implement ethics training programs, appoint a chief ethics officer or ethics ombudsperson, have ethics committees to give guidance on ethics matters, institute formal procedures for investigating alleged ethics violations, conduct ethics audits to measure and document compliance, give ethics awards to employees for outstanding efforts to create an ethical climate and improve ethical performance, and/or try to deter violations by setting up ethics hotlines for anonymous callers to use in reporting possible violations.

Emphasis here is usually on securing broad compliance and measuring the degree to which ethical standards are upheld and observed. However, violators are disciplined and sometimes subjected to public reprimand and punishment (including dismissal), thereby sending a clear signal to company personnel that complying with ethical standards needs to be taken seriously. The driving force behind the company's commitment to eradicate unethical behavior normally stems from a desire to avoid the cost and damage associated with unethical conduct or else a quest to gain favor from stakeholders (especially ethically conscious customers, employees, and investors) for having a highly regarded reputation for ethical behavior. One of the weaknesses of the compliance approach is that moral control resides in the company's code of ethics and in the ethics compliance system rather than in (1) the strong peer pressures for ethical behavior that come from ingraining a highly ethical corporate culture and (2) an individual's own moral responsibility for ethical behavior.[34]

The Ethical Culture Approach   At some companies, top executives believe that high ethical principles must be deeply ingrained in the corporate culture and function as guides for "how we do things around here." A company using the ethical culture approach seeks to gain employee buy-in to the company's ethical standards, business principles, and corporate values. The ethical principles embraced in the company's code of ethics and/or in its statement of corporate values are seen as integral to the company's identity and ways of operating—they are at the core of the company's soul and are promoted as part of business as usual. The integrity of the ethical culture approach depends heavily on the ethical integrity of the executives who create and nurture the culture—it is incumbent on them to determine how high the bar is to be set and to exemplify ethical standards in their own decisions and behavior. Further, it is essential that the strategy be ethical in all respects and that ethical behavior be ingrained in the means that company personnel employ to execute the strategy. Such insistence on observing ethical standards is what creates an ethical work climate and a workplace where displaying integrity is the norm.

Many of the trappings used in the compliance approach are also manifest in the ethical culture mode, but one other is added—strong peer pressure from coworkers to observe ethical norms. Thus, responsibility for ethics compliance is widely dispersed throughout all levels of management and the rank-and-file. Stories of former and current moral heroes are kept in circulation, and the deeds of company personnel who display ethical values and are dedicated to walking the talk are celebrated at internal company events. The message that ethics matters—and matters a lot—resounds loudly and clearly throughout the organization and in its strategy and decisions. However, one of the challenges to overcome in the ethical culture approach is relying too heavily on peer pressures and cultural norms to enforce ethics compliance rather than on an individual's own moral responsibility for ethical behavior—absent unrelenting peer pressure or strong internal compliance systems, there is a danger that over time company personnel may become lax about its ethical standards. Compliance procedures need to be an integral part of the ethical culture approach to help send the message that management takes the observance of ethical norms seriously and that behavior that falls outside ethical boundaries will have negative consequences.

Why a Company Can Change Its Ethics Management Approach
Regardless of the approach they have used to managing ethical conduct, a company's executives may sense that they have exhausted a particular mode's potential for managing ethics and that they need to become more forceful in their approach to ethics management. Such changes typically occur when the company's ethical failures have made the headlines and created an embarrassing situation for company officials or when the business climate changes. For example, the recent raft of corporate scandals, coupled with aggressive enforcement of anticorruption legislation such as the Sarbanes-Oxley Act of 2002 (which addresses corporate governance and accounting practices), has prompted numerous executives and boards of directors to clean up their acts in accounting and financial reporting, review their ethical standards, and tighten up ethics compliance procedures. Intentionally amoral managers using the unconcerned approach to ethics management may see less risk in shifting to the damage control approach (or, for appearance's sake, maybe a "light" compliance mode). Senior managers who have employed the damage control mode may be motivated by bad experiences to mend their ways and shift to a compliance mode. In the wake of so many corporate scandals, companies in the compliance mode may move closer to the ethical culture approach.

WHY SHOULD COMPANY STRATEGIES BE ETHICAL?

There are two reasons why a company's strategy should be ethical: (1) because a strategy that is unethical in whole or in part is morally wrong and reflects badly on the character of the company personnel involved and (2) because an ethical strategy is good business and in the self-interest of shareholders.

The Moral Case for an Ethical Strategy

Managers do not dispassionately assess what strategic course to steer. Ethical strategy making generally begins with managers who themselves have strong character (i.e., who are honest, have integrity, are ethical, and truly care about how they conduct the company's business). Managers with high ethical principles and standards are usually advocates of a corporate code of ethics and strong ethics compliance, and they are typically genuinely committed to certain corporate values and business principles. They walk the talk in displaying the company's stated values and living up to its business principles and ethical standards. They understand that there is a big difference between adopting values statements and codes of ethics that serve merely as window dressing and those that truly paint the white lines for a company's actual strategy and business conduct. As a consequence, ethically strong managers consciously opt for strategic actions that can pass moral scrutiny—they display no tolerance for strategies with ethically controversial components.

The Business Case for an Ethical Strategy

There are solid business reasons to adopt ethical strategies even if most company managers are not of strong moral character and personally committed to high ethical standards. Pursuing unethical strategies not only damages a company's reputation but can also have costly, wide-ranging consequences. Some of the costs are readily visible; others are hidden and difficult to track down—as shown in Figure 10.1. The costs of

Figure 10.1   **The Business Costs of Ethical Failures**

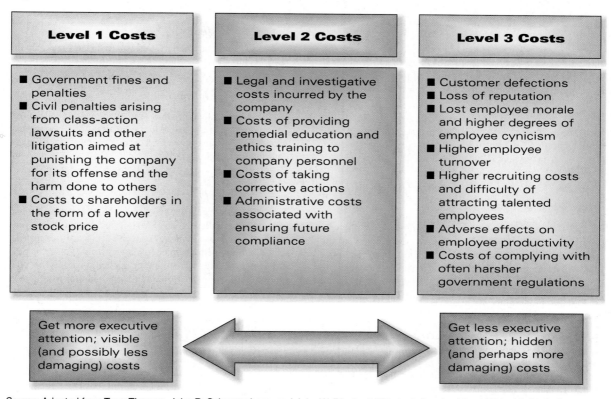

Source: Adapted from Terry Thomas, John R. Schermerhorn, and John W. Dienhart, "Strategic Leadership of Ethical Behavior," *Academy of Management Executive* 18, no. 2 (May 2004), p. 58.

fines and penalties and any declines in the stock price are easy enough to calculate. The administrative cleanup (or Level 2) costs are usually buried in the general costs of doing business and can be difficult to ascribe to any one ethical misdeed. Level 3 costs can be quite difficult to quantify but can sometimes be the most devastating—the aftermath of the Enron debacle left Arthur Andersen's reputation in shreds and led to the once-revered accounting firm's almost immediate demise, and it remains to be seen whether Marsh & McLennan can overcome the problems described in Illustration Capsule 10.1. Merck, once one of the world's most respected pharmaceutical firms, has been struggling against the revelation that senior management deliberately concealed that its Vioxx painkiller, which the company pulled off the market in September 2004, was tied to much greater risk of heart attack and strokes—some 20 million people in the United States had taken Vioxx over the years, and Merck executives had reason to suspect as early as 2000 (and perhaps earlier) that Vioxx had dangerous side effects.[35]

Rehabilitating a company's shattered reputation is time-consuming and costly. Customers shun companies known for their shady behavior. Companies with reputations for unethical conduct have considerable difficulty in recruiting and retaining talented employees. Most hardworking, ethically upstanding people are repulsed by a work environment where unethical behavior is condoned; they don't want to get entrapped in a compromising

Conducting business in an ethical fashion is in a company's enlightened self-interest.

As a gauge of your own ethical and moral standards, take the following quiz and see how you stack up against other members of your class. For the test to be valid, you need to answer the questions candidly, not on the basis of what you think the ethically correct answer is.

1. Do you think that it would be unethical for you to give two Super Bowl tickets to an important customer? Would your answer be different if the customer is likely to place a large order that would qualify you for a large year-end sales bonus?

____Yes ____No ____Unsure (it depends)

____Need more information

2. Would it be wrong to accept a case of fine wine from an important customer? Would your answer be different if you have just convinced your superiors to authorize a special price discount on a big order that the customer has just placed?

____Yes ____No ____Unsure (it depends)

____Need more information

3. Is it unethical for a high school or college coach to accept a "talent fee" or similar type of payment from a maker of sports apparel or sports equipment when the coach has authority to determine which brand of apparel or equipment to use for his or her team and subsequently chooses the brand of the company making the payment? Is it unethical for the maker of the sports apparel or equipment to make such payments in expectation that the coach will reciprocate by selecting the company's brand? (Would you answer be different if everybody else is doing it?)

____Yes ____No ____Unsure (it depends)

____Need more information

4. Is it unethical to accept an invitation from a supplier to spend a holiday weekend skiing at the supplier company's resort home in Colorado? (Would your answer be different if you were presently considering a proposal from that supplier to purchase $1 million worth of components?)

____Yes ____No ____Unsure (it depends)

____Need more information

5. Is it unethical for a food products company to incorporate ingredients that have trans fats in its products, given that trans fats are known to be very unhealthy for consumers and that alternative ingredients (which might be somewhat more expensive) can be used in producing the product?

____Yes ____No ____Unsure (it depends)

____Need more information

6. Would it be wrong to keep quiet if you, as a junior financial analyst, had just calculated that the projected return on a possible project was 18 percent and your boss (a) informed you that no project could be approved without the prospect of a 25 percent return and (b) told you to go back and redo the numbers and "get them right"?

____Yes ____No ____Unsure (it depends)

____Need more information

7. Would it be unethical to allow your supervisor to believe that you were chiefly responsible for the success of a new company initiative if it actually resulted from a team effort or major contributions by a co-worker?

____Yes ____No ____Unsure (it depends)

____Need more information

8. Would it be unethical for you, as the chief company official in India to (a) authorize a $25,000 payment to a local government official to facilitate governmental approval to construct a $200 million petrochemical plant and (b) disguise this payment by instructing accounting personnel to classify the payment as part of the cost of obtaining a building permit? (As you can see from Table 10.1, corruption is the norm in India, and bribes and kickbacks are often a "necessary" cost of doing business there.)

____Yes ____No ____Unsure (it depends)

____Need more information

9. Is it unethical for a motor vehicle manufacturer to resist recalling some of its vehicles when governmental authorities present it with credible evidence that the vehicles have safety defects?

____Yes ____No ____Unsure (it depends)

____Need more information

10. Is it unethical for a credit card company to aggressively try to sign up new accounts when, after an introductory period of interest-free or low-interest charges on unpaid monthly balances, the interest rate on unpaid balances jumps to 1.5 percent or more monthly (even though such high rates of 18 percent or more annually are disclosed in fine print)?

____Yes ____No ____Unsure (it depends)

____Need more information

11. Is it unethical to bolster your résumé with exaggerated claims of your credentials and prior job accomplishments in hopes of improving your chances of gaining employment at another company?

____Yes ____No ____Unsure (it depends)

____Need more information

12. Is it unethical for a company to spend as little as possible on pollution control when, with some extra effort and expenditures, it could substantially reduce the amount of pollution caused by its operations?

____Yes ____No ____Unsure (it depends)

____Need more information

Answers: The answers to questions 1, 2, and 4 probably shift from no/unsure to a definite yes when the second part of the circumstance comes into play. We think a strong case can be made that the answers to the remaining 9 questions are yes, although it can be argued that more information about the circumstances might be needed in responding to questions 5, 7, 9, and 12.

situation, nor do they want their personal reputations tarnished by the actions of an unsavory employer. A 1997 survey revealed that 42 percent of the respondents took into account a company's ethics when deciding whether to accept a job.[36] Creditors are usually unnerved by the unethical actions of a borrower because of the potential business fallout and subsequent risk of default on any loans. To some significant degree, therefore, companies recognize that ethical strategies and ethical conduct are good business. Most companies have strategies that pass the test of being ethical, and most companies are aware that both their reputations and their long-term well-being are tied to conducting their business in a manner that wins the approval of suppliers, employees, investors, and society at large.

As a test your own business ethics and where you stand on the importance of companies having an ethical strategy, take the test on page 340.

LINKING A COMPANY'S STRATEGY TO ITS ETHICAL PRINCIPLES AND CORE VALUES

Many companies have officially adopted a code of ethical conduct and a statement of company values—in the United States, the Sarbannes-Oxley Act, passed in 2002, requires that companies whose stock is publicly traded have a code of ethics or else explain in writing to the Securities and Exchange Commission why they do not. But there's a big difference between having a code of ethics and a values statement that serve merely as a public window dressing and having ethical standards and corporate values that truly paint the white lines for a company's actual strategy and business conduct. If ethical standards and statements of core values are to have more than a cosmetic role, boards of directors and top executives must work diligently to see that they are scrupulously observed in crafting the company's strategy and conducting every facet of the company's business. In other words, living up to the ethical principles and displaying the core values in actions and decisions must become a way of life at the company.

Indeed, the litmus test of whether a company's code of ethics and statement of core values are cosmetic is the extent to which they are embraced in crafting strategy and in operating the business day to day. It is up to senior executives to walk the talk and make a point of considering two sets of questions whenever a new strategic initiative is under review:

- Is what we are proposing to do fully compliant with our code of ethical conduct? Is there anything here that could be considered ethically objectionable?
- Is it apparent that this proposed action is in harmony with our core values? Are any conflicts or concerns evident?

Unless questions of this nature are posed—either in open discussion or by force of habit in the minds of strategy makers, then there's room for strategic initiatives to become disconnected from the company's code of ethics and stated core values. If a company's executives are ethically principled and believe strongly in living up to the company's stated core values, there's a good chance they will pose these types of questions and reject strategic initiatives that don't measure up. There's also a good chance that strategic actions will be scrutinized for their compatibility with ethical standards and core values when the latter are so deeply ingrained in a company's culture and in the

Core Concept
More attention is paid to linking strategy with ethical principles and core values in companies headed by moral executives and in companies where ethical principles and core values are a way of life.

everyday conduct of company personnel that they are automatically taken into account in all that the company does. However, in companies with window-dressing ethics and core values or in companies headed by immoral or amoral managers, any strategy-ethics-values link stems mainly from a desire to avoid the risk of embarrassment, scandal, and possible disciplinary action should strategy makers get called on the carpet and held accountable for approving an unethical strategic initiative.

STRATEGY AND SOCIAL RESPONSIBILITY

The idea that businesses have an obligation to foster social betterment, a much-debated topic in the past 40 years, took root in the 19th century when progressive companies in the aftermath of the industrial revolution began to provide workers with housing and other amenities. The notion that corporate executives should balance the interests of all stakeholders—shareholders, employees, customers, suppliers, the communities in which they operated, and society at large—began to blossom in the 1960s. A group of chief executives of America's 200 largest corporations, calling themselves the Business Roundtable, promoted the concept of corporate social responsibility. In 1981, the Roundtable's "Statement on Corporate Responsibility" said:[37]

> Balancing the shareholder's expectations of maximum return against other priorities is one of the fundamental problems confronting corporate management. The shareholder must receive a good return but the legitimate concerns of other constituencies (customers, employees, communities, suppliers and society at large) also must have the appropriate attention . . . [Leading managers] believe that by giving enlightened consideration to balancing the legitimate claims of all its constituents, a corporation will best serve the interest of its shareholders.

Today, corporate social responsibility is a concept that resonates in Western Europe, the United States, Canada, and such developing nations as Brazil and India.

What Do We Mean by Social Responsibility?

Core Concept
The notion of *social responsibility* as it applies to businesses concerns a company's *duty* to operate in an honorable manner, provide good working conditions for employees, be a good steward of the environment, and actively work to better the quality of life in the local communities where it operates and in society at large.

The essence of socially responsible business behavior is that a company should balance strategic actions to benefit shareholders against the *duty* to be a good corporate citizen. The thesis is that company managers are obligated to display a *social conscience* in operating the business and specifically take into account how management decisions and company actions affect the well-being of employees, local communities, the environment, and society at large. Acting in a socially responsible manner thus encompasses more than just participating in community service projects and donating money to charities and other worthy social causes. Demonstrating social responsibility also entails undertaking actions that earn trust and respect from all stakeholders—operating in an honorable and ethical manner, striving to make the company a great place to work, demonstrating genuine respect for the environment, and trying to make a difference in bettering society. As depicted in Figure 10.2, the menu for demonstrating a social conscience and choosing specific ways to exercise social responsibility includes:

- *Efforts to employ an ethical strategy and observe ethical principles in operating the business*—A sincere commitment to observing ethical principles is

Figure 10.2   **Demonstrating a Social Conscience: The Five Components of Socially Responsible Business Behavior**

Source: Adapted from material in Ronald Paul Hill, Debra Stephens, and Iain Smith, "Corporate Social Responsibility: An Examination of Individual Firm Behavior," *Business and Society Review* 108, no. 3 (September 2003), p. 348.

necessary here simply because unethical strategies and conduct are incompatible with the concept of good corporate citizenship and socially responsible business behavior.

● *Making charitable contributions, donating money and the time of company personnel to community service endeavors, supporting various worthy organizational causes, and reaching out to make a difference in the lives of the disadvantaged*—Some companies fulfill their corporate citizenship and community outreach obligations by spreading their efforts over a multitude of charitable and community activities; for instance, Microsoft and Johnson & Johnson support a broad variety of community art, social welfare, and environmental programs. Others prefer to focus their energies more narrowly. McDonald's, for example, concentrates on sponsoring the Ronald McDonald House program (which provides a home away from home for the families of seriously ill children receiving treatment at nearby hospitals), preventing child abuse and neglect, and participating in local community service activities; in 2004, there were 240 Ronald McDonald Houses in 25 countries and more than 6,000 bedrooms available nightly. British Telecom gives 1 percent of its profits directly to communities, largely for education—teacher training, in-school workshops, and digital technology. Leading prescription drug maker GlaxoSmithKline and other pharmaceutical companies either donate or heavily discount medicines for distribution in the least-developed nations. Numerous health-related businesses take a leading role in community activities that promote effective health care. Many companies work closely with community officials to minimize the impact of hiring large numbers of new employees (which could put a strain on local schools and utility services) and to provide outplacement services for laid-off workers. Companies frequently reinforce their philanthropic efforts by encouraging employees to support charitable causes and participate in community affairs, often through programs to match employee contributions.

- *Actions to protect or enhance the environment and, in particular, to minimize or eliminate any adverse impact on the environment stemming from the company's own business activities*—Social responsibility as it applies to environmental protection means doing more than what is legally required. From a social responsibility perspective, companies have an obligation to be stewards of the environment. This means using the best available science and technology to achieve higher-than-required environmental standards. Even more ideally, it means putting time and money into improving the environment in ways that extend past a company's own industry boundaries— such as participating in recycling projects, adopting energy conservation practices, and supporting efforts to clean up local water supplies. Retailers such as Home Depot in the United States and B&Q in the United Kingdom have pressured their suppliers to adopt stronger environmental protection practices.[38]

> Business leaders who want their companies to be regarded as exemplary corporate citizens must not only see that their companies operate ethically but they must personally display a social conscience in making decisions that affect employees, the environment, the communities in which they operate, and society at large.

- *Actions to create a work environment that enhances the quality of life for employees and makes the company a great place to work*—Numerous companies go beyond providing the ordinary kinds of compensation and exert extra efforts to enhance the quality of life for their employees, both at work and at home. This can include varied and engaging job assignments, career development programs and mentoring, rapid career advancement, appealing compensation incentives, ongoing training to ensure future employability, added decision-making authority, onsite day care, flexible work schedules for single parents, workplace exercise facilities, special leaves to care for sick family members, work-at-home opportunities, gender pay equity, showcase plants and offices, special safety programs, and the like.

- *Actions to build a workforce that is diverse with respect to gender, race, national origin, and perhaps other aspects that different people bring to the workplace*— Most large companies in the United States have established workforce diversity programs, and some go the extra mile to ensure that their workplaces are attractive to ethnic minorities and inclusive of all groups and perspectives. The pursuit of workforce diversity can be good business—Johnson & Johnson, Pfizer, and Coca-Cola believe that a reputation for workforce diversity makes recruiting employees easier (talented employees from diverse backgrounds often seek out such companies). And at Coca-Cola, where strategic success depends on getting people all over the world to become loyal consumers of the company's beverages, efforts to build a public persona of inclusiveness for people of all races, religions, nationalities, interests, and talents has considerable strategic value. Multinational companies are particularly inclined to make workforce diversity a visible strategic component; they recognize that respecting individual differences and promoting inclusiveness resonate well with people all around the world. At a few companies the diversity initiative extends to suppliers—sourcing items from small businesses owned by women or ethnic minorities.

Crafting a Social Responsibility Strategy: The Starting Point for Demonstrating a Social Conscience

While striving to be socially responsible entails choosing from the menu outlined in the preceding section, there's plenty of room for every company to make its own statement about what charitable contributions to make, what kinds of community service projects to emphasize, what environmental actions to support, how to make the company a good place to work, where and how workforce diversity fits into the picture, and what else it will do to support worthy causes and projects that benefit society. The particular combination of socially responsible endeavors a company elects to pursue defines its **social responsibility strategy.** However, unless a company's social responsibility initiatives become part of the way it operates its business every day, the initiatives are unlikely to catch fire and be fully effective. As an executive at Royal Dutch/Shell put it, corporate social responsibility "is not a cosmetic; it must be rooted in our values. It must make a difference to the way we do business."[39] Thus some companies are integrating social responsibility objectives into their missions and overall performance targets—they see social performance and environmental metrics as an essential component of judging the company's overall future performance. Some 2,500 companies around the world are not only articulating their social responsibility strategies and commitments but they are also issuing annual social responsibility reports (much like an annual report) that set forth their commitments and the progress they are making for all the world to see and evaluate.[40]

> **Core Concept**
> A company's *social responsibility strategy* is defined by the specific combination of socially beneficial activities it opts to support with its contributions of time, money, and other resources.

At Starbucks, the commitment to social responsibility is linked to the company's strategy and operating practices via the tag line "Giving back to our communities is the way we do business"; top management makes the theme come alive via the company's extensive community-building activities, efforts to protect the welfare of coffee growers and their families (in particular, making sure they receive a fair price), a variety of recycling and environmental conservation practices, and the financial support it provides to charities and the disadvantaged through the Starbucks Foundation. At Green Mountain Coffee Roasters, social responsibility includes fair dealing with suppliers and trying to do something about the poverty of small coffee growers; in its dealings with suppliers at small farmer cooperatives in Peru, Mexico, and Sumatra, Green Mountain pays "fair trade" prices for coffee beans (in 2002, the fair trade prices were a minimum of $1.26 per pound for conventional coffee and $1.41 for organically grown versus market prices of 24 to 50 cents per pound). Green Mountain also purchases about 25 percent of its coffee direct from farmers so as to cut out intermediaries and see that farmers realize a higher price for their efforts—coffee is the world's second most heavily traded commodity after oil, requiring the labor of some 20 million people, most of whom live at the poverty level.[41] At Whole Foods Market, a $5 billion supermarket chain specializing in organic and natural foods, the social responsibility emphasis is on supporting organic farming and

> Many companies tailor their strategic efforts to operate in a socially responsible manner to fit their core values and business mission, thereby making their own statement about "how we do business and how we intend to fulfill our duties to all stakeholders and society at large."

sustainable agriculture, recycling, sustainable seafood practices, giving employees paid time off to participate in worthy community service endeavors, and donating 5 percent of after-tax profits in cash or products to charitable causes. At General Mills the social responsibility focus is on service to the community and bettering the employment opportunities for minorities and women. Stonyfield Farm, a producer of yogurt and ice cream products, employs a social responsibility strategy focused on wellness, good nutrition, and earth-friendly actions (10 percent of profits are donated to help protect and restore the earth, and yogurt lids are used as miniature billboards to help educate people about environmental issues); in addition, it is stressing the development of an environmentally friendly supply chain, sourcing from farmers that grow organic products and refrain from using artificial hormones in milk production. Chick-Fil-A, an Atlanta-based fast-food chain with over 1,200 outlets in 38 states, has a charitable foundation; supports 14 foster homes and a summer camp (for some 1,600 campers from 22 states and several foreign countries); funds two scholarship programs (including one for employees that has awarded more than $20 million in scholarships); and maintains a closed-on-Sunday policy to ensure that every Chick-Fil-A employee and restaurant operator has an opportunity to worship, spend time with family and friends, or just plain rest from the workweek.[42] Toys "R" Us supports initiatives addressing the issues of child labor and fair labor practices around the world. Community Pride Food Stores is assisting in revitalizing the inner city of Richmond, Virginia, where the company is based.

It is common for companies engaged in natural resource extraction, electric power production, forestry and paper products, motor vehicles, and chemicals production to place more emphasis on addressing environmental concerns than, say, software and electronics firms or apparel manufacturers. Companies whose business success is heavily dependent on high employee morale or attracting and retaining the best and brightest employees are somewhat more prone to stress the well-being of their employees and foster a positive, high-energy workplace environment that elicits the dedication and enthusiastic commitment of employees, thus putting real meaning behind the claim "Our people are our greatest asset." Ernst & Young, one of the four largest global accounting firms, stresses its "People First" workforce diversity strategy, which focuses on respecting differences, fostering individuality, and promoting inclusiveness so that its 105,000 employees in 140 countries can feel valued, engaged, and empowered in developing creative ways to serve the firm's clients.

Thus, while the strategies and actions of all socially responsible companies have a sameness in the sense of drawing on the five categories of socially responsible behavior shown in Figure 10.2, each company's version of being socially responsible is unique.

The Moral Case for Corporate Social Responsibility

Every action a company takes can be interpreted as a statement of what it stands for.

The moral case for why businesses should actively promote the betterment of society and act in a manner that benefits all of the company's stakeholders—not just the interests of shareholders—boils down to the fact that it's the right thing to do. Ordinary decency, civic-mindedness, and contributing to the well-being of society should be expected of any business. In today's social and political climate, most business leaders can be expected to acknowledge that socially responsible actions are important and that businesses have a duty to be good corporate citizens. But there is a complementary school of thought that business operates on the basis of an implied social contract with the members of society. According to this contract, society grants a business the right to conduct its business affairs and agrees not to unreasonably restrain its pursuit of a fair profit for the goods or services it sells; in return for this "license to operate," a business is obligated to act as a responsible citizen and do its fair share to promote the general welfare. Such a view clearly puts a moral burden on a company to take corporate citizenship into consideration and to do what's best for shareholders within the confines of discharging its duties to operate honorably, provide good working conditions to employees, be a good environmental steward, and display good corporate citizenship.

The Business Case for Socially Responsible Behavior

Whatever the merits of the moral case for socially responsible business behavior, it has long been recognized that it is in the enlightened self-interest of companies to be good citizens and devote some of their energies and resources to the betterment of employees, the communities in which they operate, and society in general. In short, there are several reasons why the exercise of social responsibility is good business:

- *It generates internal benefits (particularly as concerns employee recruiting, workforce retention, and training costs)*—Companies with deservedly good reputations for contributing time and money to the betterment of society are better able to attract and retain employees compared to companies with tarnished reputations. Some employees just feel better about working for a company committed to improving society.[43] This can contribute to lower turnover and better worker productivity. Other direct and indirect economic benefits include lower costs for staff recruitment and training. For example, Starbucks is said to enjoy much lower rates of employee turnover because of its full benefits package for both full-time and part-time employees, management efforts to make Starbucks a great place to work, and the company's socially responsible practices. When a U.S. manufacturer of recycled paper, taking eco-efficiency to heart, discovered how to increase its fiber recovery rate, it saved the equivalent of 20,000 tons of waste paper—a factor that helped the company become the industry's lowest-cost producer.[44] Various benchmarking and measurement mechanisms have shown that workforce diversity initiatives promote the success of companies that stay behind them. Making a company a great place to work pays dividends in recruiting talented workers, more creativity and energy on the part of workers, higher worker productivity, and greater employee commitment to the company's business mission/vision and success in the marketplace.

- *It reduces the risk of reputation-damaging incidents and can lead to increased buyer patronage*—Firms may well be penalized by employees, consumers, and shareholders for actions that are not considered socially responsible. When a major oil company suffered damage to its reputation on environmental and social grounds, the CEO repeatedly said that the most negative impact the company suffered—and the one that made him fear for the future of the company—was that bright young graduates were no longer attracted to work for the company.[45] Consumer, environmental, and human rights activist groups are quick to criticize businesses whose behavior they consider to be out of line, and they are adept at getting their message into the media and onto the Internet. Pressure groups can generate widespread adverse publicity, promote boycotts, and influence like-minded or sympathetic buyers to avoid an offender's products.

> The higher the public profile of a company or brand, the greater the scrutiny of its activities and the higher the potential for it to become a target for pressure-group action.

Research has shown that product boycott announcements are associated with a decline in a company's stock price.[46] Outspoken criticism of Royal Dutch/Shell by environmental and human rights groups and associated boycotts were said to be major factors in the company's decision to tune in to its social responsibilities. For many years, Nike received stinging criticism for not policing sweatshop conditions in the Asian factories of its contractors, causing Nike CEO Phil Knight to observe that "Nike has become synonymous with slave wages, forced overtime, and arbitrary abuse."[47] In 1997, Nike began an extensive effort to monitor conditions in the 800 overseas factories from which it outsourced its shoes; Knight said, "Good shoes come from good factories, and good factories have good labor relations." Nonetheless, Nike has continually been plagued by complaints from human rights activists that its monitoring procedures are flawed and that it is not doing enough to correct the plight of factory workers. In contrast, to the extent that a company's socially responsible behavior wins applause from consumers and fortifies its reputation, the company may win additional patronage; Ben & Jerry's, Whole Foods Market, Stonyfield Farm, and the Body Shop have definitely expanded their customer bases because of their visible and well-publicized activities as socially conscious companies. More and more companies are recognizing the strategic value of social responsibility strategies that reach out to people of all cultures and demographics—in the United States, women are said to having buying power of $3.7 trillion, retired and disabled people close to $4.1 trillion, Hispanics nearly $600 billion, African Americans some $500 billion, and Asian Americans about $255 billion.[48] So reaching out in ways that appeal to such groups can pay off at the cash register. Some observers and executives are convinced that a strong, visible social responsibility strategy gives a company an edge in differentiating itself from rivals and in appealing to those consumers who prefer to do business with companies that are solid corporate citizens. Yet there is only limited evidence that consumers go out of their way to patronize socially responsible companies if it means paying a higher price or purchasing an inferior product.[49]

- *It is in the best interest of shareholders*—Well-conceived social responsibility strategies work to the advantage of shareholders in several ways. Socially responsible business behavior helps avoid or preempt legal and regulatory actions that could prove costly and otherwise burdensome. Increasing numbers of mutual funds and pension benefit managers are restricting their stock purchases to companies that meet social responsibility criteria. According to one survey, one out of every eight dollars under professional management in the United States involved socially responsible investing.[50] Moreover, the growth in socially responsible investing and identifying socially responsible companies has led to a substantial increase in the number of companies that publish formal reports on their social and environmental activities.[51] The stock prices of companies that rate high on social and environmental performance criteria have been found to perform 35 to 45 percent better than the average of the 2,500 companies comprising the Dow Jones Global Index.[52] A two-year study of leading companies found that improving environmental compliance and developing environmentally friendly products can enhance earnings per share, profitability, and the likelihood of winning contracts.[53] Nearly 100 studies have examined the relationship between corporate citizenship and corporate financial performance over the past 30 years; the majority point to a positive relationship. Of the 80 studies that examined whether a company's social performance is a good predictor of its financial performance, 42 concluded yes, 4 concluded

> There's little hard evidence indicating shareholders are disadvantaged in any meaningful way by a company's actions to be socially responsible.

no, and the remainder reported mixed or inconclusive findings.[54] To the extent that socially responsible behavior is good business, then, a social responsibility strategy that packs some punch and is more than rhetorical flourish turns out to be in the best interest of shareholders.

In sum, companies that take social responsibility seriously can improve their business reputations and operational efficiency while also reducing their risk exposure and encouraging loyalty and innovation. Overall, companies that take special pains to protect the environment (beyond what is required by law), are active in community affairs, and are generous supporters of charitable causes and projects that benefit society are more likely to be seen as good investments and as good companies to work for or do business with. Shareholders are likely to view the business case for social responsibility as a strong one, even though they certainly have a right to be concerned whether the time and money their company spends to carry out its social responsibility strategy outweighs the benefits and reduces the bottom line by an unjustified amount.

Companies are, of course, sometimes rewarded for bad behavior—a company that is able to shift environmental and other social costs associated with its activities onto society as a whole can reap large short-term profits. The major cigarette producers for many years were able to earn greatly inflated profits by shifting the health-related costs of smoking onto others and escaping any responsibility for the harm their products caused to consumers and the general public. Most companies will, of course, try to evade paying for the social harms of their operations for as long as they can. Calling a halt to such actions usually hinges upon (1) the effectiveness of activist social groups in publicizing the adverse consequences of a company's social irresponsibility and marshaling public opinion for something to be done, (2) the enactment of legislation or regulations to correct the inequity, and (3) widespread actions on the part of socially conscious buyers to take their business elsewhere.

The Well-Intentioned Efforts of Do-Good Executives Can Be Controversial

While there is substantial agreement that businesses have obligations to non-owner stakeholders and to society at large, and that these must be factored into a company's overall strategy and into the conduct of its business operations, there is much less agreement about the extent to which "do-good" executives should pursue their personal vision of a better world using company funds. One view holds that any money executives authorize for so-called social responsibility initiatives is effectively theft from a company's shareholders who can, after all, decide for themselves what and how much to give to charity and other causes they deem worthy. A related school of thought says that companies should be wary of taking on an assortment of societal obligations because doing so diverts valuable resources and weakens a company's competitiveness. Many academics and businesspeople believe that businesses best satisfy their social responsibilities through conventional business activities, primarily producing needed goods and services at prices that people can afford. They further argue that spending shareholders' or customers' money for social causes not only muddies decision making by diluting the focus on the company's business mission but also thrusts business executives into the role of social engineers—a role more appropriately performed by charitable and nonprofit organizations and duly elected government officials. Do we really want corporate executives deciding how to best balance the different interests of stakeholders and functioning as social engineers? Are they competent to make such judgments?

Take the case of Coca-Cola and Pepsi bottlers. Local bottlers of both brands have signed contracts with public school districts that provide millions of dollars of support for local schools in exchange for vending-machine distribution rights in the schools.[55] While such contracts would seem to be a win–win proposition, protests from parents concerned about children's sugar-laden diets and commercialism in the schools make such contracts questionable. Opponents of these contracts claim that it is the role of government to provide adequate school funding and that the learning environment in local schools should be free of commercialism and the self-serving efforts of businesses to hide behind providing support for education.

In September 1997, the Business Roundtable changed its stance from one of support for social responsibility and balanced consideration of stakeholder interests to one of skepticism with regard to such actions:

> The notion that the board must somehow balance the interests of stockholders against the interests of other stakeholders fundamentally misconstrues the role of directors. It is, moreover, an unworkable notion because it would leave the board with no criteria for resolving conflicts between the interest of stockholders and of other stakeholders or among different groups of stakeholders.[56]

The new Business Roundtable view implied that the paramount duty of management and of boards of directors is to the corporation's stockholders. Customers may be "king," and employees may be the corporation's "greatest asset" (at least in the rhetoric), but the interests of shareholders rule.[57]

However, there are real problems with disconnecting business behavior from the well-being of non-owner stakeholders and the well-being of society at large.[58] Isolating business from the rest of society when the two are inextricably intertwined is unrealistic. Many business decisions spill over to impact non-owner stakeholders and society. Furthermore, the notion that businesses must be managed solely to serve the interests of shareholders is something of a stretch. Clearly, a business's first priority must be to deliver value to customers. Unless a company does a creditable job of satisfying buyer needs and expectations of reliable and attractively priced goods and services, it cannot survive. While shareholders provide capital and are certainly entitled to a return on their investment, fewer and fewer shareholders are truly committed to the companies whose stock they own. Shareholders can dispose of their holdings in a moment's whim or at the first sign of a downturn in the stock price. Mutual funds buy and sell shares daily, adding and dropping companies whenever they see fit. Day traders buy and sell within hours. Such buying and selling of shares is nothing more than a financial transaction and results in no capital being provided to the company to fund operations except when it entails the purchase of newly issued shares of stock. So why should shareholders—a group distant from the company's operations and adding little to its operations except when new shares of stock are purchased—lay such a large claim on how a company should be managed? Are most shareholders really interested in or knowledgeable about the companies they own? Or do they just own a stock for whatever financial returns it is expected to provide?

While there is legitimate concern about the use of company resources for do-good purposes and the motives and competencies of business executives in functioning as social engineers, it is tough to argue that businesses have no obligations to nonowner stakeholders or to society at large. If one looks at the category of activities that fall under the umbrella of socially responsible behavior (Figure 10.2), there's really very little for shareholders or others concerned about the do-good attempts of executives to object to in principle. Certainly, it is legitimate for companies to minimize or eliminate any adverse impacts of their operations on the environment. It is hard to argue against efforts to make the company a great place to work or to promote workforce diversity. And with regard to charitable contributions, community service projects, and the like, it would be hard to find a company where spending on such activities is so out of control that shareholders might rightfully complain or that the company's competitiveness is being eroded. What is likely to prove most objectionable in the social responsibility arena are the specific activities a company elects to engage in and/or the manner in which a company carries out its attempts to behave in a socially responsible manner.

How Much Attention to Social Responsibility Is Enough?

What is an appropriate balance between the imperative to create value for shareholders and the obligation to proactively contribute to the larger social good? What fraction of a company's resources ought to be aimed at addressing social concerns and bettering the well-being of society and the environment? A few companies have a policy of setting aside a specified percentage of their profits (typically 5 percent or maybe 10 percent) to fund their social responsibility strategy; they view such percentages as a fair amount to return to the community as a kind of thank-you or a tithe to the betterment of society. Other companies shy away from a specified percentage of profits or revenues because it entails upping the commitment in good times and cutting back on social responsibility initiatives in hard times (even cutting out social responsibility initiatives entirely if profits temporarily turn into losses). If social responsibility is an ongoing commitment rooted in the corporate culture and enlists broad participation on the part of company personnel, then a sizable portion of the funding for the company's social responsibility strategy has to be viewed as simply a regular and ongoing cost of doing business.

But judging how far a particular company should go in pursuing particular social causes is a tough issue. Consider, for example, Nike's commitment to monitoring the workplace conditions of its contract suppliers.[59] The scale of this monitoring task is significant: in 2005, Nike had over 800 contract suppliers employing over 600,000 people in 50 countries. How frequently should sites be monitored? How should it respond to the use of underage labor? If only children above a set age are to be employed by suppliers, should suppliers still be required to provide schooling opportunities? At last count, Nike had some 80 people engaged in site monitoring. Should Nike's monitoring budget be $2 million, $5 million, $10 million, or whatever it takes?

Consider another example: If pharmaceutical manufacturers donate or discount their drugs for distribution to low-income people in less-developed nations, what safeguards should they put in place to see that the drugs reach the intended recipients and are not diverted by corrupt local officials for reexport to markets in other countries? Should drug manufacturers also assist in drug distribution and administration in these less-developed countries? How much should a drug company invest in R&D to develop medicines for tropical diseases commonly occurring in less-developed countries when it is unlikely to recover its costs in the foreseeable future?

And how much should a company allocate to charitable contributions? Is it falling short of its responsibilities if its donations are less than 1 percent of profits? Is a company going too far if it allocates 5 percent or even 10 percent of its profits to worthy causes of one kind or another? The point here is that there is no simple or widely accepted standard for judging when a company has or has not gone far enough in fulfilling its citizenship responsibilities.

Linking Social Performance Targets to Executive Compensation

Perhaps the most surefire way to enlist a genuine commitment to corporate social responsibility initiatives is to link the achievement of social performance targets to executive compensation. If a company's board of directors is serious about corporate citizenship, then it will incorporate measures of the company's social and environmental performance into its evaluation of top executives, especially the CEO. And if the CEO uses compensation incentives to further enlist the support of down-the-line company personnel in effectively crafting and executing a social responsibility strategy, the company will over time build a culture rooted in social responsible and ethical behavior. According to one survey, 80 percent of surveyed CEOs believe that environmental and social performance metrics are a valid part of measuring a company's overall performance. At Verizon Communications, 10 percent of the annual bonus of the company's top 2,500 managers is tied directly to the achievement of social responsibility targets; for the rest of the staff, there are corporate recognition awards in the form of cash for employees who have made big contributions towards social causes. The corporate social responsibility reports being issued annually by 2,500 companies across the world that detail social responsibility initiatives and the results achieved are a good basis for compensating executives and judging the effectiveness of their commitment to social responsibility.

Key Points

Ethics involves concepts of right and wrong, fair and unfair, moral and immoral. Beliefs about what is ethical serve as a moral compass in guiding the actions and behaviors of individuals and organizations. Ethical principles in business are not materially different from ethical principles in general.

There are three schools of thought about ethical standards:

1. According to the *school of ethical universalism*, the same standards of what's ethical and what's unethical resonate with peoples of most societies regardless of local traditions and cultural norms; hence, common ethical standards can be used to judge the conduct of personnel at companies operating in a variety of country markets and cultural circumstances.

2. According to the *school of ethical relativism* different societal cultures and customs have divergent values and standards of right and wrong—thus, what is ethical or unethical must be judged in the light of local customs and social mores and can vary from culture or nation to another.

3. According to *integrated social contracts theory*, universal ethical principles or norms based on the collective views of multiple cultures and societies combine to form a "social contract" that all individuals in all situations have a duty to observe. Within the boundaries of this social contract, local cultures can specify other impermissible actions; however, universal ethical norms always take precedence over local ethical norms.

Three categories of managers stand out as concerns their prevailing beliefs in and commitments to ethical and moral principles in business affairs: the moral manager; the immoral manager, and the amoral manager. By some accounts, the population of managers is said to be distributed among all three types in a bell-shaped curve, with immoral managers and moral managers occupying the two tails of the curve, and the amoral managers, especially the intentionally amoral managers, occupying the broad middle ground.

The apparently large numbers of immoral and amoral businesspeople are one obvious reason why some companies resort to unethical strategic behavior. Three other main drivers of unethical business behavior also stand out:

1. Overzealous or obsessive pursuit of personal gain, wealth, and other selfish interests.
2. Heavy pressures on company managers to meet or beat earnings targets.
3. A company culture that puts the profitability and good business performance ahead of ethical behavior.

The stance a company takes in dealing with or managing ethical conduct at any given time can take any of four basic forms:

1. The unconcerned, or nonissue, approach.
2. The damage control approach.
3. The compliance approach.
4. The ethical culture approach.

There are two reasons why a company's strategy should be ethical: (1) because a strategy that is unethical in whole or in part is morally wrong and reflects badly on the character of the company personnel involved, and (2) because an ethical strategy is good business and in the self-interest of shareholders.

The term *corporate social responsibility* concerns a company's *duty* to operate in an honorable manner, provide good working conditions for employees, be a good steward of the environment, and actively work to better the quality of life in the local communities where it operates and in society at large. The menu of actions and behavior for demonstrating social responsibility includes:

1. Employing an ethical strategy and observing ethical principles in operating the business.
2. Making charitable contributions, donating money and the time of company personnel to community service endeavors, supporting various worthy organizational causes, and making a difference in the lives of the disadvantaged. Corporate commitments are further reinforced by encouraging employees to support charitable and community activities.
3. Protecting or enhancing the environment and, in particular, striving to minimize or eliminate any adverse impact on the environment stemming from the company's own business activities.
4. Creating a work environment that makes the company a great place to work.
5. Employing a workforce that is diverse with respect to gender, race, national origin, and perhaps other aspects that different people bring to the workplace.

There is ample room for every company to tailor its social responsibility strategy to fit its core values and business mission, thereby making their own statement about "how we do business and how we intend to fulfill our duties to all stakeholders and society at large."

The moral case for social responsibility boils down to a simple concept: It's the right thing to do. The business case for social responsibility holds that it is in the enlightened self-interest of companies to be good citizens and devote some of their energies and resources to the betterment of such stakeholders as employees, the communities in which it operates, and society in general.

Exercises

1. Given the description of Marsh & McLennan's strategy presented in Illustration Capsule 10.1, would it be fair to characterize the payment of contingent commissions by property-casualty insurers as nothing more than thinly disguised kickbacks? Why or why not? If you were the manager of a company that hired Marsh & McLennan to provide risk management services, would you see that Marsh had a conflict of interest in steering your company's insurance policies to insurers in which it has an ownership interest? Given Marsh's unethical and illegal foray into rigging the bids on insurance policies for its corporate clients, what sort of fines and penalties would you impose on the company for its misdeeds (assuming you were asked to recommend appropriate penalties by the prosecuting authorities). In arriving at a figure, bear in mind that Prudential Securities paid a total of about $2 billion in the 1990s to settle civil regulatory charges and private lawsuits alleging that it misled investors on the risks and rewards of limited-partnership investments. Ten Wall Street securities firms in 2003 paid $1.4 billion to settle civil charges for issuing misleading stock research to investors. Prominent mutual-fund firms were assessed nearly $2 billion in fines and restitution for engaging in after-hours stock trading at prearranged prices that were contrary to the interests of long-term shareholders. And several well-known financial institutions, including Citigroup, Merrill Lynch, Goldmans Sachs, and Credit Suisse First Boston agreed to pay several billion dollars in fines and restitution for their role in scandals at Enron and WorldCom and for improperly allocating initial public offerings of stock. Using Internet research tools, determine what Marsh & McLennan ended up paying in fines and restitution for its unethical and illegal strategic behavior and assess the extent to which the conduct of company personnel damaged shareholders.

2. Consider the following portrayal of strategies employed by major recording studios:[60]

    Some recording artists and the Recording Artists' Coalition claim that the world's five major music recording studios—Universal, Sony, Time Warner, EMI/Virgin, and Bertelsmann—deliberately employ strategies calculated to take advantage of musicians who record for them. One practice to which they strenuously object is that the major-label record companies frequently require artists to sign contracts committing them to do six to eight albums, an obligation that some artists say can entail an indefinite term of indentured servitude. Further, it is claimed that audits routinely detect unpaid royalties to musicians under contract; according to one music industry attorney, record companies misreport and underpay artist royalties by 10 to 40 percent and are "intentionally fraudulent." One music writer was recently quoted as saying the process was "an entrenched system whose prowess and conniving makes Enron look like amateur hour." Royalty calculations are based on complex formulas that are paid only after artists pay for recording costs and other expenses and after any advances are covered by royalty earnings.

    A *Baffler* magazine article outlined a hypothetical but typical record deal in which a promising young band is given a $250,000 royalty advance on a new album. The album subsequently sells 250,000 copies, earning $710,000 for the record company; but the band, after repaying the record company for $264,000 in expenses ranging from recording fees and video budgets to catering, wardrobe, and bus tour costs for promotional events related to the album, ends up $14,000 in the hole, owes the record company money, and is thus paid no royalties on any of the $710,000 in revenues the recording company receives from the sale of the band's music. It is also standard practice in the music industry for recording studios to sidestep payola laws by hiring independent promoters to lobby and compensate radio stations for playing certain records. Record companies are often entitled to damages for undelivered albums if an artist leaves a recording studio for another label after seven years. Record companies also retain the copyrights in perpetuity on all music recorded under contract, a practice that artists claim is unfair. The Dixie Chicks, after a year-long feud with Sony over contract terms, ended up refusing to do another album; Sony sued for breach of contract, prompting a countersuit by the Dixie Chicks charging "systematic thievery" to cheat them out of royalties. The suits were settled out of court. One artist said, "The record companies are like cartels."

Recording studios defend their strategic practices by pointing out that fewer than 5 percent of the signed artists ever deliver a hit and that they lose money on albums that sell poorly. According to one study, only 1 of 244 contracts signed during 1994–1996 was negotiated without the artists being represented by legal counsel, and virtually all contracts renegotiated after a hit album added terms more favorable to the artist.

a. If you were a recording artist, would you be happy with some of the strategic practices of the recording studios? Would you feel comfortable signing a recording contract with studios engaging in any of the practices?

b. Which, if any, of the practices of the recording studios do you view as unethical?

3. Recently, it came to light that three of the world's four biggest public accounting firms may have overbilled clients for travel-related expenses. Pricewaterhouse Coopers, KPMG, and Ernst & Young were sued for systematically charging their clients full price for airline tickets, hotel rooms and car-rental expenses, even though they received volume discounts and rebates of up to 40 percent under their contracts with various travel companies. Large accounting firms, law firms, and medical practices have in recent years used their size and purchasing volumes to negotiate sizable discounts and rebates on up-front travel costs; some of these contracts apparently required that the discounts not be disclosed to other parties, which seemingly included clients.

However, it has long been the custom for accounting and law firms to bill their clients for actual out-of-pocket expenses. The three accounting firms, so the lawsuit alleges, billed clients for the so-called full prices of the airline tickets, hotel rooms, and car-rental expenses rather than for the out-of-pocket discounted amounts. They pocketed the differences to the tune of several million dollars annually in additional profits. Several clients, upon learning of the full-price billing practices, claimed fraud and sued.

Do you consider the accounting firms' billing practice to be unethical? Why or why not?

4. Suppose you found yourself in the following situation: In preparing a bid for a multimillion-dollar contract in a foreign country, you are introduced to a "consultant" who offers to help you in submitting the bid and negotiating with the customer company. You learn in conversing with the consultant that she is well connected in local government and business circles and knows key personnel in the customer company extremely well. The consultant quotes you a six-figure fee.

Later, your local co-workers tell you that the use of such consultants is normal in this country—and that a large fraction of the fee will go directly to people working for the customer company. They further inform you that bidders who reject the help of such consultants have lost contracts to competitors who employed them. What would you do, assuming your company's code of ethics expressly forbids the payments of bribes or kickbacks in any form?

5. Assume that you are the sales manager at a European company that makes sleepwear products for children. Company personnel discover that the chemicals used to flameproof the company's line of children's pajamas might cause cancer if absorbed through the skin. Following this discovery, the pajamas are then banned from sale in the European Union and the United States, but senior executives of your company learn that the children's pajamas in inventory and the remaining flameproof material can be sold to sleepwear distributors in certain East European countries where there are no restrictions against the material's use. Your superiors instruct you to make the necessary arrangements to sell the inventories of banned pajamas and flameproof materials to East European distributors. Would you comply if you felt that your job would be in jeopardy if you didn't?

6. At Salomon Smith Barney (a subsidiary of Citigroup), Credit Suisse First Boston (CSFB), and Goldman Sachs (three of the world's most prominent investment banking companies), part of the strategy for securing the investment banking business of large corporate clients (to handle the sale of new stock issues or new bond issues or advise on mergers and acquisitions) involved (*a*) hyping the stocks of companies that were actual or prospective customers of their investment banking services, and (*b*) allocating hard-to-get shares of hot new initial public offerings (IPOs) to select executives and directors of existing and potential client companies, who then made millions of dollars in profits when the stocks went up once public trading began.[61] Former WorldCom CEO Bernard Ebbers reportedly made more than $11 million in trading profits over a four-year period on shares of IPOs received from Salomon Smith Barney; Salomon served as WorldCom's investment banker on a variety of deals during this period. Jack Grubman, Salomon's top-paid research analyst at the time, enthusiastically touted WorldCom stock and was regarded as the company's biggest cheerleader on Wall Street.

To help draw in business from new or existing corporate clients, CSFB established brokerage accounts for corporate executives who steered their company's investment banking business to CSFB. Apparently, CSFB's strategy for acquiring more business involved promising the CEO and/or CFO of companies about to go public for the first time or needing to issue new long-term bonds that if CSFB was chosen to handle their company's IPO of common stock or a new bond issue, then CSFB would ensure they would be allocated shares at the initial offering price of all subsequent IPOs in which CSFB was a participant. During 1999–2000, it was common for the stock of a hot new IPO to rise 100 to 500 percent above the initial offering price in the first few days or weeks of public trading; the shares allocated to these executives were then sold for a tidy profit over the initial offering price. According to investigative sources, CSFB increased the number of companies whose executives were allowed to participate in its IPO offerings from 26 companies in January 1999 to 160 companies in early 2000; executives received anywhere from 200 to 1,000 shares each of every IPO in which CSFB was a participant in 2000. CSFB's accounts for these executives reportedly generated profits of about $80 million for the participants. Apparently, it was CSFB's practice to curtail access to IPOs for some executives if their companies didn't come through with additional securities business for CSFB or if CSFB concluded that other securities offerings by these companies would be unlikely.

Goldman Sachs also used an IPO-allocation scheme to attract investment banking business, giving shares to executives at 21 companies—among the participants were the CEOs of eBay, Yahoo, and Ford Motor Company. eBay's CEO was a participant in over 100 IPOs managed by Goldman during the 1996–2000 period and was on Goldman's board of directors part of this time; eBay paid Goldman Sachs $8 million in fees for services during the 1996–2001 period.

a.   If you were a top executive at Salomon Smith Barney, CSFB, or Goldman Sachs, would you be proud to defend your company's actions?

b.   Would you want to step forward and take credit for having been a part of the group who designed or approved of the strategy for gaining new business at any of these three firms?

c.   Is it accurate to characterize the allocations of IPO shares to "favored" corporate executives as bribes or kickbacks?

chapter eleven

Building an Organization Capable of Good Strategy Execution

The best game plan in the world never blocked or tackled anybody.

—Vince Lombardi
Hall of Fame football coach

Strategies most often fail because they aren't executed well.

—Larry Bossidy and Ram Charan
CEO Honeywell International;
author and consultant

A second-rate strategy perfectly executed will beat a first-rate strategy poorly executed every time.

—Richard M. Kovacevich
Chairman and CEO, Wells Fargo

Any strategy, however brilliant, needs to be implemented properly if it is to deliver the desired results.

—Costas Markides
Professor

People are *not* your most important asset. The right people are.

—Jim Collins
Professor and author

Organizing is what you do before you do something, so that when you do it, it is not all mixed up.

—A. A. Milne
Author

Once managers have decided on a strategy, the emphasis turns to converting it into actions and good results. Putting the strategy into place and getting the organization to execute it well call for different sets of managerial skills. Whereas crafting strategy is largely a market-driven activity, implementing and executing strategy is primarily an operations-driven activity revolving around the management of people and business processes. Whereas successful strategy making depends on business vision, solid industry and competitive analysis, and shrewd market positioning, successful strategy execution depends on doing a good job of working with and through others, building and strengthening competitive capabilities, motivating and rewarding people in a strategy-supportive manner, and instilling a discipline of getting things done. Executing strategy is an action-oriented, make-things-happen task that tests a manager's ability to direct organizational change, achieve continuous improvement in operations and business processes, create and nurture a strategy-supportive culture, and consistently meet or beat performance targets.

Experienced managers are emphatic in declaring that it is a whole lot easier to develop a sound strategic plan than it is to execute the plan and achieve the desired outcomes. According to one executive, "It's been rather easy for us to decide where we wanted to go. The hard part is to get the organization to act on the new priorities."[1] *Just because senior managers announce a new strategy doesn't mean that organizational members will agree with it or enthusiastically move forward in implementing it.* Senior executives cannot simply direct immediate subordinates to abandon old ways and take up new ways, and they certainly cannot expect the needed actions and changes to occur in rapid-fire fashion and lead to the desired outcomes. Some managers and employees may be skeptical about the merits of the strategy, seeing it as contrary to the organization's best interests, unlikely to succeed, or threatening to their departments or careers. Moreover, different employees may interpret the new strategy differently or have different ideas about what internal changes are needed to execute it. Long-standing attitudes, vested interests, inertia, and ingrained organizational practices don't melt away when managers decide on a new strategy and begin efforts to implement it—especially when only comparatively few people have been involved in crafting the strategy and when the rationale for strategic change has to be sold to enough organizational members to root out the status quo.

It takes adept managerial leadership to convincingly communicate the new strategy and the reasons for it, overcome pockets of doubt and disagreement, secure the commitment and enthusiasm of concerned parties, identify and build consensus on all the hows of implementation and execution, and move forward to get all the pieces into place. Company personnel have to understand—in their heads and in their hearts—why a new strategic direction is necessary and where the new strategy is taking them.[2] Instituting change is, of course, easier when the problems with the old strategy have become obvious and/or the company has spiraled into a financial crisis.

But the challenge of successfully implementing new strategic initiatives goes well beyond managerial adeptness in overcoming resistance to change. What really makes executing strategy a tougher, more time-consuming management challenge than crafting strategy are the wide array of managerial activities that have to be attended to, the many ways that managers can proceed, and the number of bedeviling issues that must be worked out. It takes first-rate "managerial smarts" to zero in on what exactly needs to be done to put new strategic initiatives in place and, further, how best to get these things done in a timely fashion and in a manner that yields good results. Demanding people-management skills are required. Plus, it takes follow-through and perseverance to get a variety of initiatives launched and moving and to integrate the efforts of many different work groups into a smoothly functioning whole. Depending on how much consensus building and organizational change is involved, the process of implementing strategy changes can take several months to several years. And it takes still longer to achieve *real proficiency* in executing the strategy.

Like crafting strategy, *executing strategy is a job for the whole management team, not just a few senior managers.* While an organization's chief executive officer and the heads of major units (business divisions, functional departments, and key operating units) are ultimately responsible for seeing that strategy is executed successfully, the process typically affects every part of the firm, from the biggest operating unit to the smallest frontline work group. Top-level managers have to rely on the active support and cooperation of middle and lower managers to push strategy changes into functional areas and operating units and to see that the organization actually operates in accordance with the strategy on a daily basis. Middle and lower-level managers not only are responsible for initiating and supervising the execution process in their areas of authority but also are instrumental in getting subordinates to continuously improve on how strategy-critical value chain activities are being performed and in producing the operating results that allow company performance targets to be met—their role on the company's strategy execution team is by no means minimal.

Core Concept
Good strategy execution requires a *team effort.* All managers have strategy-executing responsibility in their areas of authority, and all employees are participants in the strategy execution process.

Strategy execution thus requires every manager to think through the answer to "What does my area have to do to implement its part of the strategic plan, and what should I do to get these things accomplished effectively and efficiently?" The bigger the organization or the more geographically scattered its operating units, the more that successful strategy execution depends on the cooperation and implementing skills of operating managers who can push the needed changes at the lowest organizational levels and, in the process, deliver good results. Only in small organizations can top-level managers get around the need for a team effort on the part of management and personally orchestrate the actions steps required for good strategy execution and operating excellence.

A FRAMEWORK FOR EXECUTING STRATEGY

Implementing and executing strategy entails figuring out all the hows—the specific techniques, actions, and behaviors that are needed for a smooth strategy-supportive operation—and then following through to get things done and deliver results. The idea is to make things happen and make them happen right. The first step in implementing strategic changes is for management to communicate the case for organizational change so clearly and persuasively to organizational members that a determined commitment takes hold throughout the ranks to find ways to put the strategy into place, make it work, and meet performance targets. The ideal condition is for managers to arouse enough enthusiasm for the strategy to turn the implementation process into a companywide crusade. *Management's handling of the strategy implementation process can be considered successful if and when the company achieves the targeted strategic and financial performance and shows good progress in making its strategic vision a reality.*

The specific hows of executing a strategy—the exact items that need to be placed on management's action agenda—always have to be customized to fit the particulars of a company's situation. Making minor changes in an existing strategy differs from implementing radical strategy changes. The hot buttons for successfully executing a low-cost provider strategy are different from those in executing a high-end differentiation strategy. Implementing and executing a new strategy for a struggling company in the midst of a financial crisis is a different job from that of improving strategy execution in a company where the execution is already pretty good. Moreover, some managers are more adept than others at using this or that approach to achieving the desired kinds of organizational changes. Hence, there's no definitive managerial recipe for successful strategy execution that cuts across all company situations and all types of strategies or that works for all types of managers. Rather, the specific hows of implementing and executing a strategy—the to-do list that constitutes management's agenda for action—must always be custom-tailored to fit an individual company's own circumstances and represents management's judgment about how best to proceed.

THE PRINCIPAL MANAGERIAL COMPONENTS OF THE STRATEGY EXECUTION PROCESS

Despite the need to tailor a company's strategy-executing approaches to the particulars of its situation, certain managerial bases have to be covered no matter what the circumstances. Eight managerial tasks crop up repeatedly in company efforts to execute strategy (see Figure 11.1):

1. Building an organization with the competencies, capabilities, and resource strengths to execute strategy successfully.
2. Marshaling sufficient money and people behind the drive for strategy execution.
3. Instituting policies and procedures that facilitate rather than impede strategy execution.
4. Adopting best practices and pushing for continuous improvement in how value chain activities are performed.
5. Installing information and operating systems that enable company personnel to carry out their strategic roles proficiently.

Figure 11.1   **The Eight Components of the Strategy Execution Process**

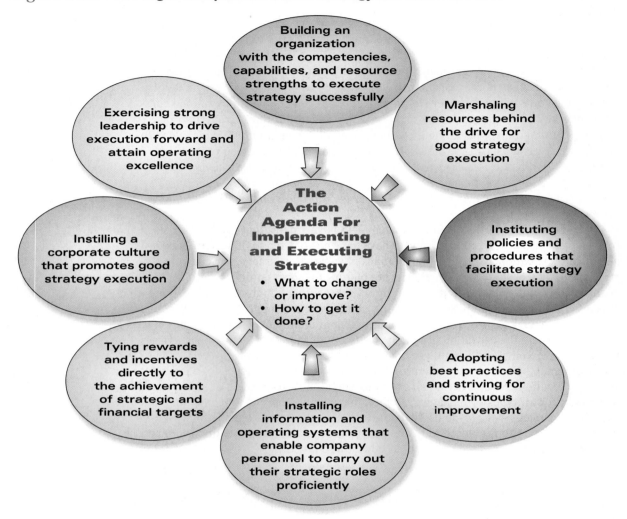

6. Tying rewards directly to the achievement of strategic and financial targets and to good strategy execution.

7. Instilling a corporate culture that promotes good strategy execution.

8. Exercising strong leadership to drive execution forward, keep improving on the details of execution, and achieve operating excellence as rapidly as feasible.

How well managers perform these eight tasks has a decisive impact on whether the outcome is a spectacular success, a colossal failure, or something in between.

In devising an action agenda for implementing and executing strategy, the place for managers to start is with *a probing assessment of what the organization must do differently and better to carry out the strategy successfully.* They should then consider *precisely how to make the necessary internal changes* as rapidly as possible. Successful strategy implementers have a knack for diagnosing what their organizations need to do to execute the chosen strategy well and figuring out how to get things done—they are

When strategies fail, it is often because of poor execution—things that were supposed to get done slip through the cracks.

masters in promoting results-oriented behaviors on the part of company personnel and following through on making the right things happen in a timely fashion.[3]

In big organizations with geographically scattered operating units, the action agenda of senior executives mostly involves communicating the case for change to others, building consensus for how to proceed, installing strong allies in positions where they can push implementation along in key organizational units, urging and empowering subordinates to keep the process moving, establishing measures of progress and deadlines, recognizing and rewarding those who achieve implementation milestones, directing resources to the right places, and personally leading the strategic change process. Thus, the bigger the organization, the more successful strategy execution depends on the cooperation and implementing skills of operating managers who can push needed changes at the lowest organizational levels and deliver results. In small organizations, top managers can deal directly with frontline managers and employees, personally orchestrating the action steps and implementation sequence, observing firsthand how implementation is progressing, and deciding how hard and how fast to push the process along. Regardless of the organization's size and whether implementation involves sweeping or minor changes, the most important leadership traits are a strong, confident sense of what to do and how to do it. Having a strong grip on these two things comes from understanding the circumstances of the organization and the requirements for effective strategy execution. Then it remains for those managers and company personnel in strategy-critical areas to step up to the plate and produce the desired results.

What's Covered in Chapters 11, 12, and 13   In the remainder of this chapter and the next two chapters, we will discuss what is involved in performing the eight key managerial tasks (shown in Figure 11.1) that shape the process of implementing and executing strategy. This chapter explores building an organization with the competencies, capabilities, and resource strengths to execute the strategy successfully. Chapter 12 looks at marshaling resources, instituting strategy-facilitating policies and procedures, adopting best practices, installing operating systems, and tying rewards to the achievement of good results. Chapter 13 deals with creating a strategy-supportive corporate culture and exercising the leadership needed to drive the execution process forward.

BUILDING AN ORGANIZATION CAPABLE OF GOOD STRATEGY EXECUTION

Proficient strategy execution depends heavily on competent personnel, better-than-adequate competitive capabilities, and effective internal organization. Building a capable organization is thus always a top priority in strategy execution. As shown in Figure 11.2, three types of organization-building actions are paramount:

1. *Staffing the organization*—putting together a strong management team, and recruiting and retaining employees with the needed experience, technical skills, and intellectual capital.
2. *Building core competencies and competitive capabilities*—developing proficiencies in performing strategy-critical value chain activities and updating them to match changing market conditions and customer expectations.
3. *Structuring the organization and work effort*—organizing value chain activities and business processes and deciding how much decision-making authority to push down to lower-level managers and frontline employees.

Figure 11.2   **The Three Components of Building an Organization Capable of Proficient Strategy Execution**

Staffing the Organization
- Putting together a strong management team
- Recruiting and retaining talented employees

Building Core Competencies and Competitive Capabilities
- Developing a set of competencies and capabilities suited to the current strategy
- Updating and revising this set as external conditions and strategy change
- Training and retraining employees as needed to maintain skills-based competencies

Matching the Organization Structure to Strategy
- Instituting organizational arrangements that facilitate good strategy execution
- Deciding how much decision-making authority to push down to lower-level managers and front line employees

A Company with the Competencies and Capabilities Needed for Proficient Strategy Execution

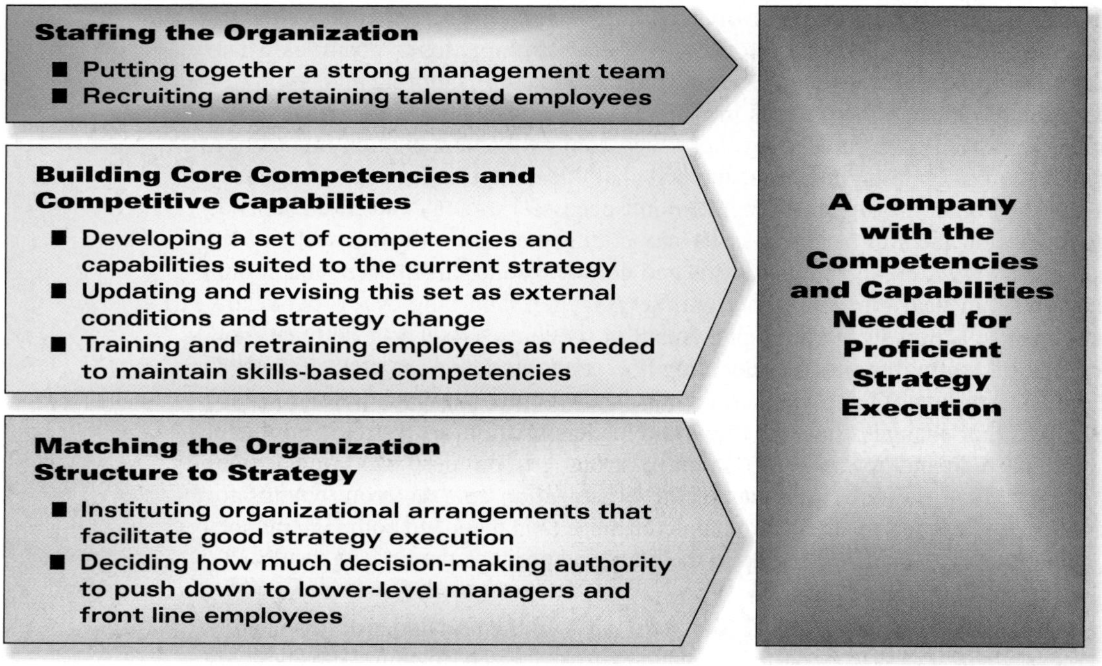

STAFFING THE ORGANIZATION

No company can hope to perform the activities required for successful strategy execution without attracting and retaining talented managers and employees with suitable skills and *intellectual capital.*

Putting Together a Strong Management Team

Assembling a capable management team is a cornerstone of the organization-building task.[4] While different strategies and company circumstances sometimes call for different mixes of backgrounds, experiences, values, beliefs, management styles, and know-how, *the most important consideration is to fill key managerial slots with smart people who are clear thinkers, good at figuring out what needs to be done, and skilled in "making it happen" and delivering good results.*[5] The task of implementing and executing challenging strategic initiatives must be assigned to executives who have the skills and talents to handle them and who can be counted on to turn their decisions and actions into results that meet or beat the established performance targets. It helps enormously when a company's top management team has several people who are particularly good change agents—true believers who champion change, know how to make it happen, and love every second of the process.[6] Without a smart, capable, results-oriented management team, the implementation-execution process ends up being hampered by missed deadlines, misdirected or wasteful efforts, and/or managerial ineptness.[7] Weak executives are serious impediments to getting

Core Concept
Putting together a talented management team with the right mix of experiences, skills, and abilities to get things done is one of the first strategy-implementing steps.

optimal results because they are unable to differentiate between ideas and approaches that have merit and those that are misguided—the caliber of work done under their supervision suffers.[8] In contrast, managers with strong strategy-implementing capabilities have a talent for asking tough, incisive questions. They know enough about the details of the business to be able to challenge and ensure the soundness of the approaches and decisions of the people around them, and they can discern whether the resources people are asking for to put the strategy in place make sense. They are good at getting things done through others, typically by making sure they have the right people under them and that these people are put in the right jobs.[9] They consistently follow through on issues, monitor progress carefully, make adjustments when needed, and not let important details slip through the cracks. In short, they understand how to drive organizational change, and they have the managerial discipline requisite for first-rate strategy execution.

Sometimes a company's existing management team is suitable; at other times it may need to be strengthened or expanded by promoting qualified people from within or by bringing in outsiders whose experiences, talents, and leadership styles better suit the situation. In turnaround and rapid-growth situations, and in instances when a company doesn't have insiders with the requisite know-how, filling key management slots from the outside is a fairly standard organization-building approach. In addition, it is important to ferret out and replace managers who, for whatever reasons, prefer the status quo and who either do not buy into the case for making organizational changes or do not see ways to make things better.[10] For a top management team to be truly effective, it has got to consist of "true believers" who recognize that organizational changes are needed and are ready to get on with the process. Weak executives and diehard resisters have to be replaced or sidelined (by shifting them to positions of lesser influence where they cannot hamper or derail new strategy execution initiatives).

The overriding aim in building a management team should be to assemble a *critical mass* of talented managers who can function as agents of change and further the cause of first-rate strategy execution—every manager's success is enhanced (or limited) by the quality of their managerial colleagues and the degree to which they freely exchange ideas, debate how to improve approaches that have merit, and join forces to tackle issues and solve problems.[11] When a first-rate manager enjoys the help and support of other first-rate managers, it's possible to create a managerial whole that is greater than the sum of individual efforts—talented managers who work well together as a team can produce organizational results that are dramatically better than what one or two star managers acting individually can achieve. The chief lesson here is that *a company needs to get the right executives on the bus—and the wrong executives off the bus—before trying to drive the bus in the desired direction.*[12]

Illustration Capsule 11.1 describes General Electric's widely acclaimed approach to developing a top-caliber management team.

Recruiting and Retaining Capable Employees

Assembling a capable management team is not enough. Staffing the organization with the right kinds of people must go much deeper than managerial jobs in order for value chain activities to be performed competently. *The quality of an organization's people is always an essential ingredient of successful strategy execution—knowledgeable, engaged employees are a company's best source of creative ideas for the nuts-and-bolts operating improvements that lead to operating excellence.* Companies

> **Core Concept**
> In many industries, adding to a company's talent base and building intellectual capital is more important to good strategy execution than additional investments in plants, equipment, and capital projects.

Illustration Capsule 11.1

How General Electric Develops a Talented and Deep Management Team

General Electric (GE) is widely considered to be one of the best-managed companies in the world, partly because of its concerted effort to develop outstanding managers. For starters, GE strives to hire talented people with high potential for executive leadership; it then goes to great lengths to expand the leadership, business, and decision-making capabilities of all its managers. Four key elements undergird GE's efforts to build a talent-rich stable of managers:

- GE makes a practice of transferring managers across divisional, business, or functional lines for sustained periods of time. Such transfers allow managers to develop relationships with colleagues in other parts of the company, help break down insular thinking in business "silos," and promote the sharing of cross-business ideas and best practices. There is an enormous emphasis at GE on transferring ideas and best practices from business to business and making GE a "boundaryless" company.

- In selecting executives for key positions, GE is strongly disposed to candidates who exhibit what are called the four E's—enormous personal *energy,* the ability to motivate and *energize* others, *edge* (a GE code word for instinctive competitiveness and the ability to make tough decisions in a timely fashion, saying yes or no, and not maybe), and *execution* (the ability to carry things through to fruition). Considerable attention is also paid to problem-solving ability, experience in multiple functions or businesses, and experience in driving business growth (as indicated by good market instincts, in-depth knowledge of particular markets, customer touch, and technical understanding).

- All managers are expected to be proficient at what GE calls *workout*—a process in which managers and employees come together to confront issues as soon as they come up, pinpoint the root cause of the issues, and bring about quick resolutions so the business can move forward. Workout is GE's way of training its managers to diagnose what to do and how to do it.

- Each year GE sends about 10,000 newly hired and long-time managers to its Leadership Development Center (generally regarded as one of the best corporate training centers in the world), for a three-week course on the company's Six Sigma quality initiative. Close to 10,000 "master black belt" and "black belt" Six Sigma experts have graduated from the program to drive forward thousands of quality initiatives throughout GE. Six Sigma training is an ironclad requirement for promotion to any professional and managerial position and any stock option award. GE's Leadership Development Center also offers advanced courses for senior managers that may focus on a single management topic for a month. All classes involve managers from different GE businesses and different parts of the world. Some of the most valuable learning comes in between formal class sessions when GE managers from different businesses trade ideas about how to improve processes and better serve the customer. This knowledge sharing not only spreads best practices throughout the organization but also improves each GE manager's knowledge.

All of GE's 85,000 managers and professionals are graded in an annual process that divides them into five tiers: the top 10 percent, the next 15 percent, the middle 50 percent, the next 15 percent, and the bottom 10 percent. Everyone in the top tier gets stock awards, nobody in the fourth tier gets shares of stock, and most of those in the fifth tier become candidates for being weeded out. Business heads are pressured to wean out "C" players. GE's CEO personally reviews the performance of the top 3,000 managers. Senior executive compensation is heavily weighted toward Six Sigma commitment and successful business results.

According to Jack Welch, GE's CEO from 1980 to 2001, "The reality is, we simply cannot afford to field anything but teams of 'A' players."

Sources: General Electric's 1998 and 2003 annual reports; www.ge.com; John A. Byrne, "How Jack Welch Runs GE," *BusinessWeek,* June 8, 1998, p. 90; Miriam Leuchter, "Management Farm Teams," *Journal of Business Strategy,* May 1998, pp. 29–32; and "The House That Jack Built, *The Economist,* September 18, 1999.

like Microsoft, McKinsey & Company, Southwest Airlines, Cisco Systems, Amazon.com, Procter & Gamble, PepsiCo, Nike, Electronic Data Systems, Google, and Intel make a concerted effort to recruit the best and brightest people they can find and then retain them with excellent compensation packages, opportunities for rapid advancement and professional growth, and challenging and interesting assignments. Having a pool of "A players" with strong skill sets and lots of brainpower is essential to their business. Microsoft makes a point of hiring the very brightest and most talented programmers it can find and motivating them with both good monetary incentives and the challenge of working on cutting-edge software design projects. McKinsey & Company, one of the world's premier management consulting companies, recruits only cream-of-the-crop MBAs at the nation's top 10 business schools; such talent is essential to McKinsey's strategy of performing high-level consulting for the world's top corporations. The leading global accounting firms screen candidates not only on the basis of their accounting expertise but also on whether they possess the people skills needed to relate well with clients and colleagues. Southwest Airlines goes to considerable lengths to hire people who can have fun and be fun on the job; it uses special interviewing and screening methods to gauge whether applicants for customer-contact jobs have outgoing personality traits that match its strategy of creating a high-spirited, fun-loving, in-flight atmosphere for passengers; it is so selective that only about 3 percent of the people who apply are offered jobs.

In high-tech companies, the challenge is to staff work groups with gifted, imaginative, and energetic people who can bring life to new ideas quickly and inject into the organization what one Dell Inc. executive calls "hum."[13] The saying "People are our most important asset" may seem hollow, but it fits high-technology companies dead-on. Besides checking closely for functional and technical skills, Dell tests applicants for their tolerance of ambiguity and change, their capacity to work in teams, and their ability to learn on the fly. Companies like Amazon.com, Google, Yahoo, and Cisco Systems have broken new ground in recruiting, hiring, cultivating, developing, and retaining talented employees—most of whom are in their 20s and 30s. Cisco goes after the top 10 percent, raiding other companies and endeavoring to retain key people at the companies it acquires so as to maintain a cadre of star engineers, programmers, managers, salespeople, and support personnel in executing its strategy to remain the world's leading provider of Internet infrastructure products and technology.

In instances where intellectual capital greatly aids good strategy execution, companies have instituted a number of practices aimed at staffing jobs with the best people they can find:

1. Spending considerable effort in screening and evaluating job applicants, selecting only those with suitable skill sets, energy, initiative, judgment, and aptitudes for learning and adaptability to the company's work environment and culture.

2. Putting employees through training programs that continue throughout their careers.

3. Providing promising employees with challenging, interesting, and skill-stretching assignments.

4. Rotating people through jobs that not only have great content but also span functional and geographic boundaries. Providing people with opportunities to gain experience in a variety of international settings is increasingly considered an essential part of career development in multinational or global companies.

5. Encouraging employees to challenge existing ways of doing things, to be creative and innovative in proposing better ways of operating, and to push their ideas for new products or businesses. Progressive companies work hard at creating an environment in which ideas and suggestions bubble up from below and employees are made to feel that their views and suggestions count.

6. Making the work environment stimulating and engaging such that employees will consider the company a great place to work.

7. Striving to retain talented, high-performing employees via promotions, salary increases, performance bonuses, stock options and equity ownership, fringe benefit packages, and other perks.

> The best companies make a point of recruiting and retaining talented employees—the objective is to make the company's entire workforce (managers and rank-and-file employees) a genuine resource strength

8. Coaching average performers to improve their skills and capabilities, while weeding out underperformers and benchwarmers.

It is very difficult for a company to competently execute its strategy and achieve operating excellence without a large band of capable employees who are actively engaged in the process of making ongoing operating improvements.

BUILDING CORE COMPETENCIES AND COMPETITIVE CAPABILITIES

High among the organization-building priorities in the strategy implementing/executing process is the need to build and strengthen competitively valuable core competencies and organizational capabilities. Whereas managers identify the desired competencies and capabilities in the course of crafting strategy, good strategy execution requires putting the desired competencies and capabilities in place, upgrading them as needed, and then modifying them as market conditions evolve. Sometimes a company already has some semblance of the needed competencies and capabilities, in which case managers can concentrate on strengthening and nurturing them to promote better strategy execution. More usually, however, company managers have to significantly broaden or deepen certain capabilities or even add entirely new competencies in order to put strategic initiatives in place and execute them proficiently.

A number of prominent companies have succeeded in establishing core competencies and capabilities that have been instrumental in making them winners in the marketplace. Intel's core competence is in the design and mass production of complex chips for personal computers, servers, and other electronic products. Procter & Gamble's core competencies reside in its superb marketing/distribution skills and its R&D capabilities in five core technologies—fats, oils, skin chemistry, surfactants, and emulsifiers. Ciba Specialty Chemicals has technology-based competencies that allow it to quickly manufacture products for customers wanting customized products relating to coloration, brightening and whitening, water treatment and paper processing, freshness, and cleaning. General Electric has a core competence in developing professional managers with broad problem-solving skills and proven ability to grow global businesses. Disney has core competencies in theme park operation and family entertainment. Dell Inc. has the capabilities to deliver state-of-the-art products to its customers within days of next-generation components coming available—and to do so at attractively low costs (it has leveraged its collection of competencies and capabilities into being the global low-cost leader in PCs). Toyota's success in motor vehicles is due, in large part, to its legendary "production system," which it has honed and perfected and which gives it the capability to produce high-quality vehicles at relatively low costs.

The Three-Stage Process of Developing and Strengthening Competencies and Capabilities

Building core competencies and competitive capabilities is a time-consuming, managerially challenging exercise. While some organization-building assist can be gotten from discovering how best-in-industry or best-in-world companies perform a particular activity, trying to replicate and then improve on the competencies and capabilities of others is, however, much easier said than done—for the same reasons that one is unlikely to ever become a good golfer just by studying what Tiger Woods does. Putting a new capability in place is more complicated than just forming a new team or department and charging it with becoming highly competent in performing the desired activity, using whatever it can learn from other companies having similar competencies or capabilities. Rather, it takes a series of deliberate and well orchestrated organizational steps to achieve mounting proficiency in performing an activity. The capability-building process has three stages:

> **Core Concept**
> Building competencies and capabilities is a multistage process that occurs over a period of months and years, not something that is accomplished overnight.

> *Stage 1*—First, the organization must develop the *ability* to do something, however imperfectly or inefficiently. This entails selecting people with the requisite skills and experience, upgrading or expanding individual abilities as needed, and then molding the efforts and work products of individuals into a collaborative effort to create organizational ability.

> *Stage 2*—As experience grows and company personnel learn how to perform the activity *consistently well and at an acceptable cost*, the ability evolves into a tried-and-true *competence* or *capability*.

> *Stage 3*—Should company personnel continue to polish and refine their know-how and otherwise sharpen their performance of an activity such that the company eventually becomes *better than rivals* at performing the activity, the core competence rises to the rank of a *distinctive competence* (or the capability becomes a competitively superior capability), thus providing a path to competitive advantage.

Many companies are able to get through stages 1 and 2 in performing a strategy-critical activity, but comparatively few achieve sufficient proficiency in performing strategy-critical activities to qualify for the third stage.

Managing the Process   Four traits concerning core competencies and competitive capabilities are important in successfully managing the organization-building process:[14]

1. *Core competencies and competitive capabilities are bundles of skills and know-how that most often grow out of the combined efforts of cross-functional work groups and departments performing complementary activities at different locations in the firm's value chain.* Rarely does a core competence or capability consist of narrow skills attached to the work efforts of a single department. For instance, a core competence in speeding new products to market involves the collaborative efforts of personnel in research and development (R&D), engineering and design, purchasing, production, marketing, and distribution. Similarly, the capability to provide superior customer service is a team effort among people in customer call centers (where orders are taken and inquiries are answered), shipping and delivery, billing and accounts receivable, and after-sale support. Complex activities (like designing and manufacturing a sports-utility vehicle or creating the capability for secure credit card transactions over the Internet) usually involve a number of component skills, technological disciplines, competencies, and capabilities—some performed in-house and some provided by suppliers/allies. An important part of the organization-building function is to think about which activities of which groups need to be linked and made mutually reinforcing and then to forge the necessary collaboration both internally and with outside resource providers.

2. *Normally, a core competence or capability emerges incrementally out of company efforts either to bolster skills that contributed to earlier successes or to respond to customer problems, new technological and market opportunities, and the*

competitive maneuverings of rivals. Migrating from the one-time ability to do something up the ladder to a core competence or competitively valuable capability is usually an organization-building process that takes months and often years to accomplish—it is definitely not an overnight event.

3. *The key to leveraging a core competence into a distinctive competence (or a capability into a competitively superior capability) is concentrating more effort and more talent than rivals on deepening and strengthening the competence or capability, so as to achieve the dominance needed for competitive advantage.* This does not necessarily mean spending more money on such activities than competitors, but it does mean consciously focusing more talent on them and striving for best-in-industry, if not best-in-world, status. To achieve dominance on lean financial resources, companies like Cray in large computers and Honda in gasoline engines have leveraged the expertise of their talent pool by frequently re-forming high-intensity teams and reusing key people on special projects. The experiences of these and other companies indicate that the usual keys to successfully building core competencies and valuable capabilities are superior employee selection, thorough training and retraining, powerful cultural influences, effective cross-functional collaboration, empowerment, motivating incentives, short deadlines, and good databases—not big operating budgets.

4. *Evolving changes in customers' needs and competitive conditions often require tweaking and adjusting a company's portfolio of competencies and intellectual capital to keep its capabilities freshly honed and on the cutting edge.* This is particularly important in high-tech industries and fast-paced markets where important developments occur weekly. As a consequence, wise company managers work at anticipating changes in customer-market requirements and staying ahead of the curve in proactively building a package of competencies and capabilities that can win out over rivals.

Managerial actions to develop core competencies and competitive capabilities generally take one of two forms: either strengthening the company's base of skills, knowledge, and intellect, or coordinating and networking the efforts of the various work groups and departments. Actions of the first sort can be undertaken at all managerial levels, but actions of the second sort are best orchestrated by senior managers who not only appreciate the strategy-executing significance of strong competencies/capabilities but also have the clout to enforce the necessary networking and cooperation among individuals, groups, departments, and external allies.

One organization-building question is whether to develop the desired competencies and capabilities internally or to outsource them by partnering with key suppliers or forming strategic alliances. The answer depends on what can be safely delegated to outside suppliers or allies versus what internal capabilities are key to the company's long-term success. Either way, though, calls for action. Outsourcing means launching initiatives to identify the most attractive providers and to establish collaborative relationships. Developing the capabilities in-house means marshaling personnel with relevant skills and experience, collaboratively networking the individual skills and related cross-functional activities to form organizational capability, and building the desired levels of proficiency through repetition (practice makes perfect).[15]

Sometimes the tediousness of internal organization building can be shortcut by buying a company that has the requisite capability and integrating its competencies into the firm's value chain. Indeed, a pressing need to acquire certain capabilities quickly is one reason to acquire another company—an acquisition aimed at building greater capability can be every bit as competitively valuable as an acquisition aimed at adding new products or services to the company's business lineup. Capabilities-motivated acquisitions are essential (1) when a market opportunity can slip by faster than a needed capability can be created internally, and (2) when industry conditions, technology, or competitors are moving at such a rapid clip that time is of the essence. But usually there's no good substitute for ongoing internal efforts to build and strengthen the company's competencies and capabilities in performing strategy-critical value chain activities.

Updating and Remodeling Competencies and Capabilities as External Conditions and Company Strategy Change   Even after core competencies and competitive capabilities are in place and functioning, company managers can't relax. Competencies and capabilities that grow stale can impair competitiveness unless they are refreshed, modified, or even phased out and replaced in response to ongoing market changes and shifts in company strategy. Indeed, the buildup of knowledge and experience over time, coupled with the imperatives of keeping capabilities in step with ongoing strategy and market changes, makes it appropriate to view a company as *a bundle of evolving competencies and capabilities.* Management's organization-building challenge is one of deciding when and how to recalibrate existing com petencies and capabilities, and when and how to develop new ones. Although the task is formidable, ideally it produces a dynamic organization with "hum" and momentum as well as a distinctive competence. Toyota, aspiring to overtake General Motors as the global leader in motor vehicles, has been aggressively upgrading its capabilities in fuel-efficient hybrid engine technology and is constantly fine-tuning its famed Toyota Production System to enhance its already proficient capabilities in manufacturing top-quality vehicles at relatively low costs—see Illustration Capsule 11.2. Likewise, Honda, which has long had a core competence in gasoline engine technology and small engine design, has accelerated its efforts to broaden its expertise and capabilities in hybrid engines so as to stay close behind Toyota. TV broadcasters are upgrading their capabilities in digital broadcasting technology in readiness for the upcoming switchover from analog to digital signal transmission. Microsoft has totally retooled the manner in which its programmers attack the task of writing code for its new operating systems for PCs and servers (the first wave of which was due out in 2006).

The Strategic Role of Employee Training

Training and retraining are important when a company shifts to a strategy requiring different skills, competitive capabilities, managerial approaches, and operating methods. Training is also strategically important in organizational efforts to build skills-based competencies. And it is a key activity in businesses where technical know-how is changing so rapidly that a company loses its ability to compete unless its skilled people have cutting-edge knowledge and expertise. Successful strategy implementers see to it that the training function is both adequately funded and effective. If the chosen strategy calls for new skills, deeper technological capability, or building and using new capabilities, training should be placed near the top of the action agenda.

The strategic importance of training has not gone unnoticed. Over 600 companies have established internal "universities" to lead the training effort, facilitate continuous organizational learning, and help upgrade company competencies and capabilities. Many companies conduct orientation sessions for new employees, fund an assortment

Illustration Capsule 11.2

Toyota's Legendary Production System: A Capability That Translates into Competitive Advantage

The heart of Toyota's strategy in motor vehicles is to outcompete rivals by manufacturing world-class, quality vehicles at lower costs and selling them at competitive price levels. Executing this strategy requires top-notch manufacturing capability and super-efficient management of people, equipment, and materials. Toyota began conscious efforts to improve its manufacturing competence more than 50 years ago. Through tireless trial and error, the company gradually took what started as a loose collection of techniques and practices and integrated them into a full-fledged process that has come to be known as the Toyota Production System (TPS). The TPS drives all plant operations and the company's supply chain management practices. TPS is grounded in the following principles, practices, and techniques:

- *Deliver parts and components just-in-time to the point of vehicle assembly.* The idea here is to cut out all the bits and pieces of transferring materials from place to place and to discontinue all activities on the part of workers that don't add value (particularly activities where nothing ends up being made or assembled).

- *Develop people who can come up with unique ideas for production improvements.*

- *Emphasize continuous improvement.* Workers are expected to use their heads and develop better ways of doing things, rather than mechanically follow instructions. Toyota managers tell workers that the *T* in TPS also stands for "Thinking." The thesis is that a work environment where people have to think generates the wisdom to spot opportunities for making tasks simpler and easier to perform, increasing the speed and efficiency with which activities are performed, and constantly improving product quality.

- *Empower workers to stop the assembly line when there's a problem or a defect is spotted.* Toyota views worker efforts to purge defects and sort out the problem immediately as critical to the whole concept of building quality

into the production process. According to TPS, "If the line doesn't stop, useless defective items will move on to the next stage. If you don't know where the problem occurred, you can't do anything to fix it." The tool for halting the assembly line is the *andon* electric light board, which is visible to everyone on the production floor.

- *Deal with defects only when they occur.* TPS philosophy holds that when things are running smoothly, they should not be subject to control; if attention is directed to fixing problems that are found, quality control along the assembly line can be handled with fewer personnel.

- *Ask yourself "Why?" five times.* While errors need to be fixed whenever they occur, the value of asking "Why?" five times enables identifying the root cause of the error and correcting it so that the error won't recur.

- *Organize all jobs around human motion to create a production/assembly system with no wasted effort.* Work organized in this fashion is called standardized work, and people are trained to observe standardized work procedures (which include supplying parts to each process on the assembly line at the proper time, sequencing the work in an optimal manner, and allowing workers to do their jobs continuously in a set sequence of subprocesses).

- *Find where a part is made cheaply and use that price as a benchmark.*

The TPS uses unique terms (such as *kanban, takt time, jikoda, kaizen, heijunka, monozukuri, poka yoke,* and *muda*) that facilitate precise discussion of specific TPS elements. In 2003, Toyota established a Global Production Center to efficiently train large numbers of shop-floor experts in the latest TPS methods and better operate an increasing number of production sites worldwide. There's widespread agreement that Toyota's ongoing effort to refine and improve on its renowned TPS gives it important manufacturing capabilities that are the envy of other motor vehicle manufacturers.

Sources: Information posted at www.toyotageorgetown.com, and Taiichi Ohno, *Toyota Production System: Beyond Large-Scale Production* (New York: Sheridan, 1988).

of competence-building training programs, and reimburse employees for tuition and other expenses associated with obtaining additional college education, attending professional development courses, and earning professional certification of one kind or another. A number of companies offer online, just-in-time training courses to employees around the clock. Increasingly, employees at all levels are expected to take an active role in their own professional development, assuming responsibility for keeping their skills and expertise up-to-date and in sync with the company's needs.

From Competencies and Capabilities to Competitive Advantage

While strong core competencies and competitive capabilities are a major assist in executing strategy, they are an equally important avenue for securing a competitive edge over rivals in situations where it is relatively easy for rivals to copy smart strategies. Any time rivals can readily duplicate successful strategy features, making it difficult or impossible to outstrategize rivals and beat them in the marketplace with a superior strategy, the chief way to achieve lasting competitive advantage is to outexecute them (beat them by performing certain value chain activities in a superior fashion). *Building core competencies and competitive capabilities that are very difficult or costly for rivals to emulate and that push a company closer to true operating excellence promotes very proficient strategy execution.* Moreover, because cutting-edge core competencies and competitive capabilities represent resource strengths that are often time-consuming and expensive for rivals to match or trump, any competitive edge they produce tends to be sustainable and pave the way for above-average company performance.

> **Core Concept**
> Building competencies and capabilities that are very difficult or costly for rivals to emulate has a huge payoff—improved strategy execution and a potential for competitive advantage.

It is easy to cite instances where companies have gained a competitive edge based on superior competencies and capabilities. Toyota's production capabilities (see Illustration Capsule 11.2) have given it a decided market edge over such rivals as General Motors, Ford, DaimlerChrysler, and Volkswagen. Dell's competitors have spent years and millions of dollars in what so far is a futile effort to match Dell's cost-efficient supply chain management capabilities. FedEx has unmatched capabilities in reliable overnight delivery of documents and small parcels. Various business news media have been unable to match the competence of Dow-Jones in gathering and reporting business news via *The Wall Street Journal.*

EXECUTION-RELATED ASPECTS OF ORGANIZING THE WORK EFFORT

There are few hard-and-fast rules for organizing the work effort to support good strategy execution. Every firm's organization chart is partly a product of its particular situation, reflecting prior organizational patterns, varying internal circumstances, executive judgments about reporting relationships, and the politics of who gets which assignments. Moreover, every strategy is grounded in its own set of key success factors and value chain activities. But some organizational considerations are common to all companies. These are summarized in Figure 11.3 and discussed in turn in the following sections.

Deciding Which Value Chain Activities to Perform Internally and Which to Outsource

The advantages of a company having an outsourcing component in its strategy were discussed in Chapter 6 (pp. 160–193), but there is also a need to consider the role of outsourcing in executing the strategy. Aside from the fact than an outsider, because of

Figure 11.3   **Structuring the Work Effort to Promote Successful Strategy Execution**

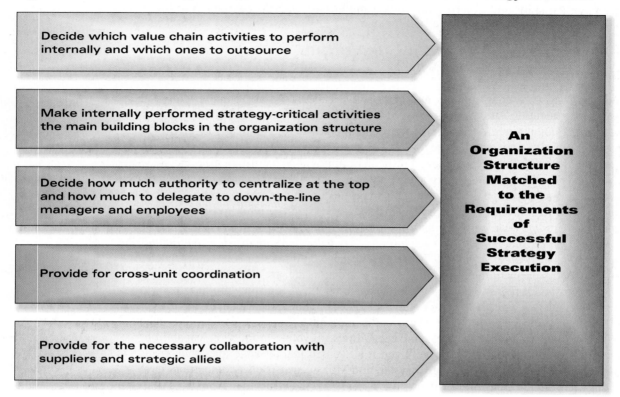

its expertise and specialized know-how, may be able to perform certain value chain activities better or cheaper than a company can perform them internally, outsourcing can also have several organization-related benefits. Managers too often spend inordinate amounts of time, mental energy, and resources haggling with functional support groups and other internal bureaucracies over needed services, leaving less time for them to devote to performing strategy-critical activities in the most proficient manner. One way to reduce such distractions is to outsource the performance of assorted administrative support functions and perhaps even selected core or primary value chain activities to outside vendors, thereby enabling the company to *heighten its strategic focus and concentrate its full energies and resources on even more competently performing those value chain activities that are at the core of its strategy and for which it can create unique value.* For example, E. & J. Gallo Winery outsources 95 percent of its grape production, letting farmers take on the weather and other grape-growing risks while it concentrates its full energies on wine production and sales.[16] A number of personal computer (PC) makers outsource the mundane and highly specialized task of PC assembly, concentrating their energies instead on product design, sales and marketing, and distribution.

When a company uses outsourcing to zero in on ever better performance of those truly strategy-critical activities where its expertise is most needed, then it may be able to realize three very positive benefits:

1. The company improves its chances for outclassing rivals in the performance of strategy-critical activities and turning a core competence into a distinctive competence. At the very least, the heightened focus on performing a select few value chain activities should meaningfully strengthen the company's existing core competences and promote more innovative performance of those activities— either of which could lower costs or materially improve competitive capabilities. Eastman Kodak, Ford, Exxon Mobil, Merrill Lynch, and Chevron have outsourced their data processing activities to computer service firms, believing that outside specialists can perform the needed services at lower costs and equal or better quality. A relatively large number of companies outsource the operation of their Web sites to Web design and hosting enterprises. Many business that get a lot of inquiries from customers or that have to provide 24/7 technical support to users of their products across the world have found that it is considerably less expensive to outsource these functions to specialists (often located in foreign countries where skilled personnel are readily available and worker compensation costs are much lower) than to operate their own call centers.

2. *The streamlining of internal operations that flows from outsourcing often acts to decrease internal bureaucracies, flatten the organization structure, speed internal decision making, and shorten the time it takes to respond to changing market conditions.*[17] In consumer electronics, where advancing technology drives new product innovation, organizing the work effort in a manner that expedites getting next-generation products to market ahead of rivals is a critical competitive capability. Motor vehicle manufacturers have found that they can shorten the cycle time for new models, improve the quality and performance of those models, and lower overall production costs by outsourcing the big majority of their parts and components from independent suppliers and then working closely with their vendors to advance the design and functioning of the items being supplied, to swiftly incorporate new technology, and to better integrate individual parts and components to form engine cooling systems, transmission systems, and electrical systems.

3. *Outsourcing the performance of certain value chain activities to able suppliers can add to a company's arsenal of capabilities and contribute to better strategy execution.* By building, continually improving, and then leveraging its partnerships with able suppliers, a company enhances its overall organizational capabilities and builds resource strengths—strengths that deliver value to customers and consequently pave the way for competitive success. Soft-drink and beer manufacturers all cultivate their relationships with their bottlers and distributors to strengthen access to local markets and build the loyalty, support, and commitment for corporate marketing programs, without which their own sales and growth are weakened. Similarly, fast-food enterprises like McDonald's and Taco Bell find it essential to work hand-in-hand with franchisees on outlet cleanliness, consistency of product quality, in-store ambience, courtesy and friendliness of store personnel, and other aspects of store operations. Unless franchisees continuously deliver sufficient customer satisfaction to attract repeat business, a fast-food chain's sales and competitive standing will suffer quickly. Companies like Boeing, Aerospatiale, Verizon Communications, and Dell have learned that their central R&D groups cannot begin to match the innovative capabilities of a well-managed network of supply chain partners having the ability to advance the technology, lead the development of next-generation parts and components, and supply them at a relatively low price.[18]

As a general rule, companies refrain from outsourcing those value chain activities over which they need direct strategic and operating control in order to build core competencies, achieve competitive advantage, and effectively manage key customer– supplier–distributor relationships. It is the strategically less important activities— like handling customer inquiries and providing technical support, doing the payroll,

Core Concept
Wisely choosing which activities
to perform internally and
which to outsource can lead
to several strategy-executing
advantages—lower costs,
heightened strategic focus, less
internal bureaucracy, speedier
decision making, and a better
arsenal of competencies and
capabilities.

administering employee benefit programs, providing corporate security, managing stockholder relations, maintaining fleet vehicles, operating the company's Web site, conducting employee training, and managing an assortment of information and data processing functions—where outsourcing is most used.

Even so, a number of companies have found ways to successfully rely on outside vendors to perform strategically significant value chain activities.[19] Broadcom, a global leader in chips for broadband communications systems, outsources the manufacture of its chips to Taiwan Semiconductor, thus freeing company personnel to focus their full energies on R&D, new chip design, and marketing. For years Polaroid Corporation bought its film from Eastman Kodak, its electronics from Texas Instruments, and its cameras from Timex and others, while it concentrated on producing its unique self-developing film packets and designing its next-generation cameras and films. Nike concentrates on design, marketing, and distribution to retailers, while outsourcing virtually all production of its shoes and sporting apparel. Cisco Systems outsources virtually all manufacturing of its routers, switches, and other Internet gear, yet it protects its market position by retaining tight internal control over product design and closely monitors the daily operations of its manufacturing vendors. Large numbers of electronics companies outsource the design, engineering, manufacturing, and shipping of their products to such companies as Flextronics and Solectron, both of which have built huge businesses as providers of such services to companies worldwide. So while performing *core* value chain activities in-house normally makes good sense, there can be times when outsourcing some of them works to good advantage.

The Dangers of Excessive Outsourcing   Critics contend that a company can go overboard on outsourcing and so hollow out its knowledge base and capabilities as to leave itself at the mercy of outside suppliers and short of the resource strengths to be a master of its own destiny.[20] The point is well taken, but most companies appear alert to the danger of taking outsourcing to an extreme or failing to maintain control of the work performed by specialist vendors or offshore suppliers. Many companies refuse to source key components from a single supplier, opting to use two or three suppliers as a way of avoiding single supplier dependence or giving one supplier too much bargaining power. Moreover, they regularly evaluate their suppliers, looking not only at the supplier's overall performance but also at whether they should switch to another supplier or even bring the activity back in-house. To avoid loss of control, companies typically work closely with key suppliers, meeting often and setting up online systems to share data and information, collaborate on work in progress, monitor performance, and otherwise document that suppliers' activities are closely integrated with their own requirements and expectations. Indeed, sophisticated online systems permit companies to work in "real time" with suppliers 10,000 miles away, making rapid response possible whenever concerns or problems arise. Hence *the real debate surrounding outsourcing is not about whether too much outsourcing risks loss of control, but about how to use outsourcing in a manner that produces greater competitiveness.*

Making Strategy-Critical Activities the Main Building Blocks of the Organization Structure

In any business, some activities in the value chain are always more critical to strategic success and competitive advantage than others. For instance, hotel/motel enterprises have to be good at fast check-in/check-out, housekeeping and facilities maintenance, food service, and the creation of a pleasant ambience. For a manufacturer of chocolate bars, buying quality cocoa beans at low prices is vital and reducing production costs by a fraction of a cent per bar can mean a seven-figure improvement in the bottom line. In discount stock brokerage, the strategy-critical activities are fast access to information, accurate order execution, efficient record keeping and transactions processing, and good customer service. In specialty chemicals, the critical activities are R&D, product innovation, getting new products onto the market quickly, effective marketing, and expertise in assisting customers. Where such is the case, it is important for management to build its organization structure around proficient performance of these activities, making them the centerpieces or main building blocks on the organization chart.

The rationale for making strategy-critical activities the main building blocks in structuring a business is compelling: If activities crucial to strategic success are to have the resources, decision-making influence, and organizational impact they need, they have to be centerpieces in the organizational scheme. Plainly, implementing a new or changed strategy is likely to entail new or different key activities, competencies, or capabilities and therefore to require new or different organizational arrangements. If workable organizational adjustments are not forthcoming, the resulting mismatch between strategy and structure can open the door to execution and performance problems.[21] Hence, attempting to carry out a new strategy with an old organization structure is usually unwise.

What Types of Organization Structures Fit Which Strategies?   It is generally agreed that some type of functional structure is the best organizational arrangement when a company is in just one particular business (irrespective of which of the five competitive strategies it opts to pursue). The primary organizational building blocks within a business are usually *traditional functional departments* (R&D, engineering and design, production and operations, sales and marketing, information technology, finance and accounting, and human resources) and *process departments* (where people in a single work unit have responsibility for all the aspects of a certain process like supply chain management, new product development, customer service, quality control, or selling direct to customers via the company's Web site). For instance, a technical instruments manufacturer may be organized around research and development, engineering, supply chain management, assembly, quality control, marketing, technical services, and corporate administration. A hotel may have a functional organization based on front-desk operations, housekeeping, building maintenance, food service, convention services and special events, guest services, personnel and training, and accounting. A discount retailer may organize around such functional units as purchasing, warehousing and distribution, store operations, advertising, merchandising and promotion, customer service, and corporate administrative services.

In enterprises with operations in various countries around the world (or with geographically scattered organizational units within a country), the basic building blocks may also include *geographic organizational units,* each of which has profit/loss responsibility for its assigned geographic area. In vertically integrated firms, the major building blocks are *divisional units performing one or more of the major processing steps along the value chain* (raw materials production, components manufacture, assembly, wholesale distribution, retail store operations); each division in the value chain may operate as a profit center for performance measurement purposes. The typical building blocks of a diversified company are its *individual businesses,* with each business unit usually operating as an independent profit center and with corporate headquarters performing assorted support functions for all of its business units. But a divisional business-unit structure can present problems to a company pursuing related diversification.

Determining the Degree of Authority and Independence to Give Each Unit and Each Employee

In executing the strategy and conducting daily operations, companies must decide how much authority to delegate to the managers of each organization unit—especially the heads of business subsidiaries; functional and process departments; and plants, sales offices, distribution centers, and other operating units—and how much decision-making latitude to give individual employees in performing their jobs. The two extremes are to *centralize decision making* at the top (the CEO and a few close lieutenants) or to *decentralize decision making* by giving managers and employees considerable decision-making latitude in their areas of responsibility. As shown in Table 11.1, the two approaches are based on sharply different underlying principles and beliefs, with each having its pros and cons.

Centralized Decision Making: Pros and Cons   *In a highly centralized organization structure, top executives retain authority for most strategic and operating decisions and keep a tight rein on business-unit heads, department heads, and the*

Table 11.1   **Advantages and Disadvantages of Centralized versus Decentralized Decision Making**

Centralized Organizational Structures	Decentralized Organizational Structures
Basic tenets • Decisions on most matters of importance should be pushed to managers up the line who have the experience, expertise, and judgment to decide what is the wisest or best course of action. • Frontline supervisors and rank-and-file employees can't be relied on to make the right decisions—because they seldom know what is best for the organization and because they do not have the time or the inclination to properly manage the tasks they are performing (letting them decide "what to do" is thus risky).	**Basic tenets** • Decision-making authority should be put in the hands of the people closest to and most familiar with the situation and these people should be trained to exercise good judgment. • A company that draws on the combined intellectual capital of all its employees can outperform a command-and-control company.
Chief advantage • Fixes accountability.	**Chief advantages** • Encourages lower level managers and rank-and-file employees to exercise initiative and act responsibly. • Promotes greater motivation and involvement in the business on the part of more company personnel. • Spurs new ideas and creative thinking. • Allows fast response times. • Entails fewer layers of management.
Primary disadvantages • Lengthens response times because management bureaucracy must decide on a course of action. • Does not encourage responsibility among lower level managers and rank-and-file employees. • Discourages lower level managers and rank-and-file employees from exercising any initiative—they are expected to wait to be told what to do.	**Primary disadvantages** • Puts the organization at risk if many bad decisions are made at lower levels—top management lacks full control. • Impedes cross-business coordination and capture of strategic fits in diversified companies.

managers of key operating units; comparatively little discretionary authority is granted to frontline supervisors and rank-and-file employees. The command-and-control paradigm of centralized structures is based on the underlying assumption that frontline personnel have neither the time nor the inclination to direct and properly control the work they are performing, and that they lack the knowledge and judgment to make wise decisions about how best to do it—hence the need for managerially prescribed policies and procedures, close supervision, and tight control. The thesis underlying authoritarian structures is that strict enforcement of detailed procedures backed by rigorous managerial oversight is the most reliable way to keep the daily execution of strategy on track.

The big advantage of an authoritarian structure is tight control by the manager in charge—it is easy to know who is accountable when things do not go well. But there are some serious disadvantages. Hierarchical command-and-control structures make an organization sluggish in responding to changing conditions because of the time it takes for the review/approval process to run up all the layers of the management bureaucracy. Furthermore, to work well, centralized decision making requires top-level managers to gather and process whatever information is relevant to the decision. When the relevant knowledge resides at lower organizational levels (or is technical, detailed, or hard to express in words), it is difficult and time-consuming to get all of the facts and nuances in front of a high-level executive located far from the scene of the action—full understanding of the situation cannot be readily copied from one mind to another. Hence, centralized decision making is often impractical—the larger the company and the more scattered its operations, the more that decision-making authority has to be delegated to managers closer to the scene of the action.

> There are disadvantages to having a small number of top-level managers micromanage the business either by personally making decisions or by requiring lower-level subordinates to gain approval before taking action.

Decentralized Decision Making: Pros and Cons   *In a highly decentralized organization, decision-making authority is pushed down to the lowest organizational level capable of making timely, informed, competent decisions.* The objective is to put adequate decision-making authority in the hands of the people closest to and most familiar with the situation and train them to weigh all the factors and exercise good judgment. Decentralized decision making means that the managers of each organizational unit are delegated lead responsibility for deciding how best to execute strategy (as well as some role in shaping the strategy for the units they head). Decentralization thus requires selecting strong managers to head each organizational unit and holding them accountable for crafting and executing appropriate strategies for their units. Managers who consistently produce unsatisfactory results have to be weeded out.

The case for empowering down-the-line managers and employees to make decisions related to daily operations and executing the strategy is based on the belief that a company that draws on the combined intellectual capital of all its employees can outperform a command-and-control company.[22] Decentralized decision making means, for example, that in a diversified company the various business-unit heads have broad authority to execute the agreed-on business strategy with comparatively little interference from corporate headquarters; moreover, the business-unit heads delegate considerable decision-making latitude to functional and process department heads and the heads of the various operating units (plants, distribution centers, sales offices) in implementing and executing their pieces of the strategy. In turn, work teams may be empowered to manage and improve their assigned value chain activity, and employees with customer contact may be empowered to do what it takes to please customers.

The ultimate goal of decentralized decision making is to put decision-making authority in the hands of those persons or teams closest to and most knowledgeable about the situation.

At Starbucks, for example, employees are encouraged to exercise initiative in promoting customer satisfaction—there's the story of a store employee who, when the computerized cash register system went offline, enthusiastically offered free coffee to waiting customers.[23] *With decentralized decision making, top management maintains control by limiting empowered managers' and employees' discretionary authority and holding people accountable for the decisions they make.*

Decentralized organization structures have much to recommend them. Delegating greater authority to subordinate managers and employees creates a more horizontal organization structure with fewer management layers. Whereas in a centralized vertical structure managers and workers have to go up the ladder of authority for an answer, in a decentralized horizontal structure they develop their own answers and action plans—making decisions in their areas of responsibility and being accountable for results is an integral part of their job. Pushing decision-making authority down to middle and lower-level managers and then further on to work teams and individual employees shortens organizational response times and spurs new ideas, creative thinking, innovation, and greater involvement on the part of subordinate managers and employees. In worker-empowered structures, jobs can be defined more broadly, several tasks can be integrated into a single job, and people can direct their own work. Fewer managers are needed because deciding how to do things becomes part of each person's or team's job. Further, today's online communication systems make it easy and relatively inexpensive for people at all organizational levels to have direct access to data, other employees, managers, suppliers, and customers. They can access information quickly (via the Internet or company intranet), readily check with superiors or coworkers as needed, and take responsible action. Typically, there are genuine gains in morale and productivity when people are provided with the tools and information they need to operate in a self-directed way. Decentralized decision making not only can shorten organizational response times but also can spur new ideas, creative thinking, innovation, and greater involvement on the part of subordinate managers and employees.

The past decade has seen a growing shift from authoritarian, multilayered hierarchical structures to flatter, more decentralized structures that stress employee empowerment. There's strong and growing consensus that authoritarian, hierarchical organization structures are not well suited to implementing and executing strategies in an era when extensive information and instant communication are the norm and when a big fraction of the organization's most valuable assets consists of intellectual capital and resides in the knowledge and capabilities of its employees. Many companies have therefore begun empowering lower-level managers and employees throughout their organizations, giving them greater discretionary authority to make strategic adjustments in their areas of responsibility and to decide what needs to be done to put new strategic initiatives into place and execute them proficiently.

Maintaining Control in a Decentralized Organization Structure

Pushing decision-making authority deep down into the organization structure and empowering employees presents its own organizing challenge: *how to exercise adequate control over the actions of empowered employees so that the business is not put at risk at the same time that the benefits of empowerment are realized.*[24] Maintaining adequate organizational control over empowered employees is generally accomplished by placing limits on the authority that empowered personnel can exercise, holding people accountable for their decisions, instituting compensation incentives that reward people for doing their jobs in a manner that contributes to good company performance, and creating a corporate culture where there's strong peer pressure on individuals to act responsibly.

Capturing Strategic Fits in a Decentralized Structure   Diversified companies striving to capture cross-business strategic fits have to beware of giving business heads full rein to operate independently when cross-business collaboration is essential in order to gain strategic fit benefits. Cross-business strategic fits typically have to be captured either by enforcing close cross-business collaboration or by centralizing performance of functions having strategic fits at the corporate level.[25] For example, if businesses with overlapping process and product technologies have their own independent R&D departments—each pursuing their own priorities, projects, and strategic agendas—it's hard for the corporate parent to prevent duplication of effort, capture either economies of scale or economies of scope, or broaden the company's R&D efforts to embrace new technological paths, product families, end-use applications, and customer groups. Where cross-business R&D fits exist, the best solution is usually to centralize the R&D function and have a coordinated corporate R&D effort that serves both the interests of individual businesses and the company as a whole. Likewise, centralizing the related activities of separate businesses makes sense when there are opportunities to share a common sales force, use common distribution channels, rely on a common field service organization to handle customer requests or provide maintenance and repair services, use common e-commerce systems and approaches, and so on.

The point here is that efforts to decentralize decision making and give organizational units leeway in conducting operations have to be tempered with the need to maintain adequate control and cross-unit coordination—decentralization doesn't mean delegating authority in ways that allow organization units and individuals to do their own thing. There are numerous instances when decision-making authority must be retained at high levels in the organization and ample cross-unit coordination strictly enforced.

Providing for Internal Cross-Unit Coordination

The classic way to coordinate the activities of organizational units is to position them in the hierarchy so that the most closely related ones report to a single person (a functional department head, a process manager, a geographic area head, a senior executive). Managers higher up in the ranks generally have the clout to coordinate, integrate, and arrange for the cooperation of units under their supervision. In such structures, the chief executive officer, chief operating officer, and business-level managers end up as central points of coordination because of their positions of authority over the whole unit. When a firm is pursuing a related diversification strategy, coordinating the related activities of independent business units often requires the centralizing authority of a single corporate-level officer. Also, diversified companies commonly centralize such staff support functions as public relations, finance and accounting, employee benefits, and information technology at the corporate level both to contain the costs of support activities and to facilitate uniform and coordinated performance of such functions within each business unit.

However, close cross-unit collaboration is usually needed to build core competencies and competitive capabilities in strategically important activities—such as speeding new products to market and providing superior customer service—that involve employees scattered across several internal organization units (and perhaps the employees of outside strategic partners or specialty vendors). A big weakness of traditional functionally organized structures is that pieces of strategically relevant activities and capabilities often end up scattered across many departments, with the result that no one group or manager is accountable. Consider, for example, how the following strategy-critical activities cut across different functions:

- *Filling customer orders accurately and promptly*—a process that involves personnel from sales (which wins the order); finance (which may have to check credit terms or approve special financing); production (which must produce the goods and replenish warehouse inventories as needed); warehousing (which has to verify whether the items are in stock, pick the order from the warehouse, and package it for shipping); and shipping (which has to choose a carrier to deliver the goods and release the goods to the carrier).[26]

- *Fast, ongoing introduction of new products*—a cross-functional process involving personnel in R&D, design and engineering, purchasing, manufacturing, and sales and marketing.

- *Improving product quality*—a process that entails the collaboration of personnel in R&D, design and engineering, purchasing, in-house components production, manufacturing, and assembly.

- *Supply chain management*—a collaborative process that cuts across such functional areas as purchasing, inventory management, manufacturing and assembly, and warehousing and shipping.

- *Building the capability to conduct business via the Internet*—a process that involves personnel in information technology, supply chain management, production, sales and marketing, warehousing and shipping, customer service, finance, and accounting.

- *Obtaining feedback from customers and making product modifications to meet their needs*—a process that involves personnel in customer service and after-sale support, R&D, design and engineering, purchasing, manufacturing and assembly, and marketing research.

Handoffs from one department to another lengthen completion time and frequently drive up administrative costs, since coordinating the fragmented pieces can soak up hours of effort on the parts of many people.[27] This is not a fatal flaw of functional organization—organizing around specific functions normally works to good advantage in support activities like finance and accounting, human resource management, and engineering, and in such primary activities as R&D, manufacturing, and marketing. But the tendency for pieces of a strategy-critical activity to be scattered across several functional departments is an important weakness of functional organization and accounts for why a company's competencies and capabilities are typically cross-functional.

Many companies have found that rather than continuing to scatter related pieces of a strategy-critical business process across several functional departments and scrambling to integrate their efforts, it is better to reengineer the work effort and pull the people who performed the pieces in functional departments into a group that works together to perform the whole process, thus creating *process departments* (like customer service or new product development or supply chain management). And sometimes the coordinating mechanisms involve the use of cross-functional task forces, dual reporting relationships, informal organizational networking, voluntary cooperation, incentive compensation tied to measures of group performance, and strong executive-level insistence on teamwork and cross-department cooperation (including removal of recalcitrant managers who stonewall collaborative efforts). At one European-based company, a top executive promptly replaced the managers of several plants who were not fully committed to collaborating closely on eliminating duplication in product development and production efforts among plants in several different countries. Earlier, the executive, noting that negotiations among the managers had stalled on which labs and plants to close, had met with all the managers, asked them to cooperate to find a solution, discussed with them which options were unacceptable, and given them a deadline to find a solution. When the asked-for teamwork wasn't forthcoming, several managers were replaced.

Providing for Collaboration with Outside Suppliers and Strategic Allies

Someone or some group must be authorized to collaborate as needed with each major outside constituency involved in strategy execution. Forming alliances and cooperative relationships presents immediate opportunities and opens the door to future possibilities, but nothing valuable is realized until the relationship grows, develops, and blossoms. Unless top management sees that constructive organizational bridge building with strategic partners occurs and that productive working relationships emerge, the value of alliances is lost and the company's power to execute its strategy is weakened. If close working relationships with suppliers are crucial, then supply chain management must be given formal status on the company's organization chart and a significant position in the pecking order. If distributor/dealer/franchisee relationships are important, someone must be assigned the task of nurturing the relationships with forward channel allies. If working in parallel with providers of complementary products and services contributes to enhanced organizational capability, then cooperative organizational arrangements have to be put in place and managed to good effect.

Building organizational bridges with external allies can be accomplished by appointing "relationship managers" with responsibility for making particular strategic partnerships or alliances generate the intended benefits. Relationship managers have many roles and functions: getting the right people together, promoting good rapport, seeing that plans for specific activities are developed and carried out, helping adjust internal organizational procedures and communication systems, ironing out operating dissimilarities, and nurturing interpersonal cooperation. Multiple cross-organization ties have to be established and kept open to ensure proper communication and coordination.[28] There has to be enough information sharing to make the relationship work and periodic frank discussions of conflicts, trouble spots, and changing situations.[29]

CURRENT ORGANIZATIONAL TRENDS

Many of today's companies are winding up the task of remodeling their traditional hierarchical structures once built around functional specialization and centralized authority. Much of the corporate downsizing movement in the late 1980s and early 1990s was aimed at recasting authoritarian, pyramidal organizational structures into flatter, decentralized structures. The change was driven by growing realization that command-and-control hierarchies were proving a liability in businesses where customer preferences were shifting from standardized products to custom orders and special features, product life cycles were growing shorter, custom mass-production methods were replacing standardized mass-production techniques, customers wanted to be treated as individuals, technological change was ongoing, and market conditions were fluid. Layered management hierarchies with lots of checks and controls that required people to look upward in the organizational structure for answers and approval were failing to deliver responsive customer service and timely adaptations to changing conditions.

The organizational adjustments and downsizing of companies in 2001–2005 brought further refinements and changes to streamline organizational activities and shake out inefficiencies. The goals have been to make companies leaner, flatter, and more responsive to change. Many companies are drawing on five tools of organizational design: (1) managers and workers empowered to act on their own judgments, (2) work process redesign (to achieve greater streamlining and tighter cohesion), (3) self-directed work teams, (4) rapid incorporation of Internet technology applications, and (5) networking with outsiders to improve existing organization capabilities and create new ones. Considerable management attention is being devoted to building a company capable of outcompeting rivals on the basis of superior resource strengths and competitive capabilities—capabilities that are increasingly based on intellectual capital and cross-unit collaboration.

Several other organizational characteristics are emerging:

- Extensive use of Internet technology and e-commerce business practices— real-time data and information systems; greater reliance on online systems for transacting business with suppliers and customers; and Internet-based communication and collaboration with suppliers, customers, and strategic partners.

- Fewer barriers between different vertical ranks, between functions and disciplines, between units in different geographic locations, and between the company and its suppliers, distributors/dealers, strategic allies, and customers—an outcome partly due to pervasive use of online systems.

- Rapid dissemination of information, rapid learning, and rapid response times— also an outcome partly due to pervasive use of online systems.

- Collaborative efforts among people in different functional specialties and geographic locations—essential to create organization competencies and capabilities.

Key Points

Implementing and executing strategy is an operation-driven activity revolving around the management of people and business processes. The managerial emphasis is on converting strategic plans into actions and good results. *Management's handling of the process of implementing and executing the chosen strategy can be considered successful if and when the company achieves the targeted strategic and financial performance and shows good progress in making its strategic vision a reality.* Shortfalls in performance signal weak strategy, weak execution, or both.

The place for managers to start in implementing and executing a new or different strategy is with *a probing assessment of what the organization must do differently and better to carry out the strategy successfully.* They should then consider *precisely how to make the necessary internal changes* as rapidly as possible.

Like crafting strategy, executing strategy is a job for a company's whole management team, not just a few senior managers. Top-level managers have to rely on the active support and cooperation of middle and lower managers to push strategy changes into functional areas and operating units and to see that the organization actually operates in accordance with the strategy on a daily basis.

Eight managerial tasks crop up repeatedly in company efforts to execute strategy:

1. Building an organization with the competencies, capabilities, and resource strengths to execute strategy successfully.

2. Marshaling sufficient money and people behind the drive for strategy execution.

3. Instituting policies and procedures that facilitate rather than impede strategy execution.

4. Adopting best practices and pushing for continuous improvement in how value chain activities are performed.

5. Installing information and operating systems that enable company personnel to carry out their strategic roles proficiently.

6. Tying rewards directly to the achievement of strategic and financial targets and to good strategy execution.

7. Shaping the work environment and corporate culture to fit the strategy.

8. Exercising strong leadership to drive execution forward, keep improving on the details of execution, and achieve operating excellence as rapidly as feasible.

Building an organization capable of good strategy execution entails three types of organization-building actions: (1) *staffing the organization*—assembling a talented, can-do management team, and recruiting and retaining employees with the needed experience, technical skills, and intellectual capital; (2) *building core competencies and competitive capabilities* that will enable good strategy execution and updating them as strategy and external conditions change; and (3) *structuring the organization and work effort*—organizing value chain activities and business processes and deciding how much decision-making authority to push down to lower-level managers and frontline employees.

Building core competencies and competitive capabilities is a time-consuming, managerially challenging exercise that involves three stages: (1) developing the *ability* to do something, however imperfectly or inefficiently, by selecting people with the requisite skills and experience, upgrading or expanding individual abilities as needed, and then molding the efforts and work products of individuals into a collaborative group effort; (2) coordinating group efforts to learn how to perform the activity *consistently well and at an acceptable cost,* thereby transforming the ability into a tried-and-true *competence or capability;* and (3) continuing to polish and refine the organization's know-how and otherwise sharpen performance such that it becomes *better than rivals* at performing the activity, thus raising the core competence (or capability) to the rank of a *distinctive competence* (or competitively superior capability) and opening an avenue to competitive advantage. Many companies manage to get through stages 1 and 2 in performing a strategy-critical activity but comparatively few achieve sufficient proficiency in performing strategy-critical activities to qualify for the third stage.

Strong core competencies and competitive capabilities are an important avenue for securing a competitive edge over rivals in situations where it is relatively easy for rivals to copy smart strategies. Any time rivals can readily duplicate successful strategy features, making it difficult or impossible to *outstrategize* rivals and beat them in the marketplace with a superior strategy, the chief way to achieve lasting competitive advantage is to *outexecute* them (beat them by performing certain value chain activities in superior fashion). *Building core competencies and competitive capabilities that are very difficult or costly for rivals to emulate and that push a company closer to true operating excellence is one of the best and most reliable ways to achieve a durable competitive edge.*

Structuring the organization and organizing the work effort in a strategy-supportive fashion has five aspects: (1) deciding which value chain activities to perform internally and which ones to outsource; (2) making internally performed strategy-critical activities the main building blocks in the organization structure; (3) deciding how much authority to centralize at the top and how much to delegate to down-the-line managers and employees; (4) providing for internal cross-unit coordination and collaboration to build and strengthen internal competencies/capabilities; and (5) providing for the necessary collaboration and coordination with suppliers and strategic allies.

Exercises

1. As the new owner of a local ice cream store located in a strip mall adjacent to a university campus, you are contemplating how to organize your business—whether to make your ice cream in-house or outsource its production to a nearby ice cream manufacturer whose brand is in most of the local supermarkets, and how much authority to delegate to the two assistant store managers and to employees working the counter and the cash register. You plan to sell 20 flavors of ice cream.

    a. What are the pros and cons of contracting with the local company to custom-produce your product line?

    b. Since you do not plan to be in the store during all of the hours it is open, what specific decision-making authority would you delegate to the two assistant store managers?

    c. To what extent, if any, should store employees—many of whom will be university students working part-time—be empowered to make decisions relating to store operations (opening and closing, keeping the premises clean and attractive, keeping the work area behind the counter stocked with adequate supplies of cups, cones, napkins, and so on)?

    d. Should you create a policies and procedures manual for the assistant managers and employees, or should you just give oral instructions and have them learn their duties and responsibilities on the job?

    e. How can you maintain control during the times you are not in the store?

2. Go to Home Depot's corporate home page (www.homedepot.com/corporate) and review the information under the headings About The Home Depot, Investor Relations, and Careers. How does Home Depot go about building core competencies and competitive capabilities? Would any of Home Depot's competencies qualify as a distinctive competence? Please use the chapter's discussion of building core competencies and competitive capabilities as a guide for preparing your answer.

3. Using Google Scholar or your access to EBSCO, InfoTrac, or other online database of journal articles and research in your university's library, do a search for recent writings on self-directed or empowered work teams. According to the articles you found in the various management journals, what are the conditions for the effective use of such teams? Also, how should such teams be organized or structured to better ensure their success?

chapter twelve

Managing Internal Operations

Actions That Promote Good Strategy Execution

Winning companies know how to do their work better.

—Michael Hammer and James Champy

Companies that make best practices a priority are thriving, thirsty, learning organizations. They believe that everyone should always be searching for a better way. Those kinds of companies are filled with energy and curiosity and a spirit of can-do.

—Jack Welch
Former CEO, General Electric

If you want people motivated to do a good job, give them a good job to do.

—Frederick Herzberg

You ought to pay big bonuses for premier performance . . . Be a top payer, not in the middle or low end of the pack.

—Lawrence Bossidy
CEO, Honeywell International

In Chapter 11 we emphasized the importance of building organization capabilities and structuring the work effort so as to perform strategy-critical activities in a coordinated and highly competent manner. In this chapter we discuss five additional managerial actions that promote the success of a company's strategy execution efforts:

1. Marshaling resources behind the drive for good strategy execution.

2. Instituting policies and procedures that facilitate strategy execution.

3. Adopting best practices and striving for continuous improvement in how value chain activities are performed.

4. Installing information and operating systems that enable company personnel to carry out their strategic roles proficiently.

5. Tying rewards and incentives directly to the achievement of strategic and financial targets and to good strategy execution.

MARSHALING RESOURCES BEHIND THE DRIVE FOR GOOD STRATEGY EXECUTION

Early in the process of implementing and executing a new or different strategy, managers need to determine what resources will be needed and then consider whether the current budgets of organizational units are suitable. Plainly, organizational units must have the budgets and resources for executing their parts of the strategic plan effectively and efficiently. Developing a strategy-driven budget requires top management to determine what funding is needed to execute new strategic initiatives and to strengthen or modify the company's competencies and capabilities. This includes careful screening of requests for more people and more or better facilities and equipment, approving those that hold promise for making a cost-justified contribution to strategy execution, and turning down those that don't. Should internal cash flows prove insufficient to fund the planned strategic initiatives, then management must raise additional funds through borrowing or selling additional shares of stock to willing investors.

A company's ability to marshal the resources needed to support new strategic initiatives and steer them to the appropriate organizational units has a major impact on the strategy execution process. Too little funding (stemming either from constrained financial resources or from sluggish management action to adequately increase the budgets of strategy-critical organizational units) slows progress and impedes the efforts of organizational units to execute their pieces of the strategic plan proficiently. Too much funding wastes organizational resources and reduces financial performance. Both outcomes argue for managers to be deeply involved in reviewing budget proposals and directing the proper kinds and amounts of resources to strategy-critical organization units.

Core Concept

The funding requirements of a new strategy must drive how capital allocations are made and the size of each unit's operating budgets. Underfunding organizational units and activities pivotal to strategic success impedes execution and the drive for operating excellence.

A change in strategy nearly always calls for budget reallocations and resource shifting. Units important in the prior strategy but having a lesser role in the new strategy may need downsizing. Units that now have a bigger and more critical strategic role may need more people, new equipment, additional facilities, and above-average increases in their operating budgets. More resources may have to be devoted to quality control or to adding new product features or to building a better brand image or to cutting costs or to employee retraining. Strategy implementers need to be active and forceful in shifting resources, downsizing some functions and upsizing others, not only to amply fund activities with a critical role in the new strategy but also to avoid inefficiency and achieve profit projections. They have to exercise their power to put enough resources behind new strategic initiatives to make things happen, and they have to make the tough decisions to kill projects and activities that are no longer justified.

Visible actions to reallocate operating funds and move people into new organizational units signal a determined commitment to strategic change and frequently are needed to catalyze the implementation process and give it credibility. Microsoft has made a practice of regularly shifting hundreds of programmers to new high-priority programming initiatives within a matter of weeks or even days. At Harris Corporation, where the strategy was to diffuse research ideas into areas that were commercially viable, top management regularly shifted groups of engineers out of government projects and into new commercial venture divisions. Fast-moving developments in many markets are prompting companies to abandon traditional annual or semiannual budgeting and resource allocation cycles in favor of cycles that match the strategy changes a company makes in response to newly developing events.

The bigger the change in strategy (or the more obstacles that lie in the path of good strategy execution), the bigger the resource shifts that will likely be required. Merely fine-tuning the execution of a company's existing strategy seldom requires big movements of people and money from one area to another. The desired improvements can usually be accomplished through above-average budget increases to organizational units launching new initiatives and below-average increases (or even small cuts) for the remaining organizational units. The chief exception occurs where all the strategy changes or new execution initiatives need to be made without adding to total expenses. Then managers have to work their way through the existing budget line-by-line and activity-by-activity, looking for ways to trim costs in some areas and shift the resources to higher priority activities where new execution initiatives are needed.

INSTITUTING POLICIES AND PROCEDURES THAT FACILITATE GOOD STRATEGY EXECUTION

Core Concept

Well-conceived policies and procedures aid strategy execution; out-of-sync ones are barriers.

A company's policies and procedures can either assist the cause of good strategy execution or be a barrier. Anytime a company moves to put new strategy elements in place or improve its strategy execution capabilities, managers are well advised to undertake a careful review of existing policies and procedures, proactively revising or discarding those that are out of sync. A change in strategy or a push for better strategy execution generally requires some changes in work practices and the behavior of company personnel. One way of promoting such changes is by instituting a select set of new policies and procedures deliberately aimed at steering the actions and behavior of company personnel in a direction more conducive to good strategy execution and operating excellence.

Figure 12.1   **How Prescribed Policies and Procedures Facilitate Strategy Execution**

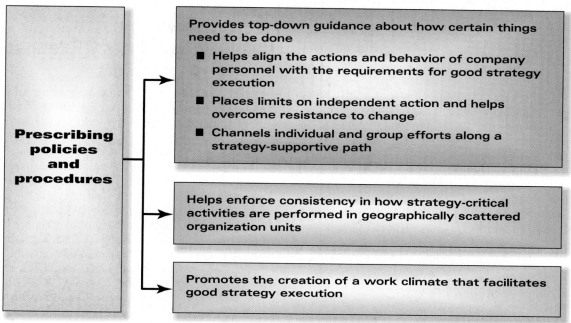

As shown in Figure 12.1, prescribing new policies and operating procedures acts to facilitate strategy execution in three ways:

1. *Instituting new policies and procedures provides top-down guidance regarding how certain things now need to be done.* Asking people to alter established habits and procedures, of course, always upsets the internal order of things. It is normal for pockets of resistance to develop and for people to exhibit some degree of stress and anxiety about how the changes will affect them, especially when the changes may eliminate jobs. But when existing ways of doing things pose a barrier to improving strategy execution, actions and behaviors have to be changed. The managerial role of establishing and enforcing new policies and operating practices is to paint a different set of white lines, place limits on independent behavior, and channel individual and group efforts along a path more conducive to executing the strategy. Policies are a particularly useful way to counteract tendencies for some people to resist change—most people refrain from violating company policy or going against recommended practices and procedures without first gaining clearance or having strong justification.

2. *Policies and procedures help enforce needed consistency in how particular strategy-critical activities are performed in geographically scattered operating units.* Standardization and strict conformity are sometimes desirable components of good strategy execution. Eliminating significant differences in the operating practices of different plants, sales regions, customer service centers, or the individual outlets in a chain operation helps a company deliver consistent product quality and service to customers. Good strategy execution nearly always entails an ability to replicate product quality and the caliber of customer service at every location where the company does business—anything less blurs the company's image and fails to meet customer expectations.

Illustration Capsule 12.1

Granite Construction's Short-Pay Policy: An Innovative Way to Drive Better Strategy Execution

In 1987, the owners of Granite Construction, a 100-plus-year-old supplier of crushed gravel, sand, concrete, and asphalt in Watsonville, California, decided to pursue two strategic targets: total customer satisfaction and a reputation for superior service. To drive the internal efforts to achieve these two objectives and signal both employees and customers that it was deadly serious about these two strategic commitments, top management instituted a short-pay policy that appeared on the bottom of every Granite Construction invoice:

> If you are not satisfied for any reason, don't pay us for it. Simply scratch out the line item, write a brief note about the problem, and return a copy of this invoice along with your check for the balance.

Customers did not have to call and complain and were not expected to return the product. They were given complete discretionary power to decide whether and how much to pay based on their satisfaction level. Management believed that empowering customers not to pay for items or service they found lacking would provide unmistakable feedback and spur company personnel to correct any problems quickly in order to avoid repeated short payments.

The short-pay policy had the desired impact, focusing the attention of company personnel on avoiding short payments by customers and boosting customer satisfaction significantly. Granite has enjoyed compound annual sales gains of 12.2 percent since 2000, while charging a 6 percent price premium for its commodity products in competition against larger rivals.

In addition to its short-pay policy, Granite employs two other policies to help induce company personnel to do their very best to satisfy the company's customers. It has a no-lay-off policy (no employees have been laid off in over 80 years), and it sends positive customer comments about employees home for families to read. To make sure its workforce force is properly trained, company employees go through training programs averaging 43 hours per employee annually. And compensation is attractive: Entry-level employees, called job owners, start at $16 an hour and progress to such positions as "accomplished job owner" and "improvement champion" (base pay of $26 an hour); all employees are entitled to 12 company-paid massages annually.

Granite won the prestigious Malcolm Baldrige National Quality Award in 1992, about five years after instituting the short-pay policy. *Fortune* rated Granite as one of the 100 best companies to work for in America in eight of the nine years from 1998 to 2006 (its highest ranking was 16th in 2002, and its lowest was 90th in 2004). The company was on *Fortune*'s "Most Admired Companies" list in 2005 and 2006.

Source: Based on information in Jim Collins, "Turning Goals into Results: The Power of Catalytic Mechanisms," *Harvard Business Review* 77, no. 4 (July–August 1999), pp. 72–73; Robert Levering and Milton Moskowitz, "The 100 Best Companies to Work For," *Fortune,* February 4, 2004, p. 73; Robert Levering and Milton Moskowitz, "The 100 Best Companies to Work For," *Fortune,* January 12, 2005, p. 78; and www.fortune.com (accessed November 11, 2005).

3. Well-conceived policies and procedures promote the creation of a work climate that facilitates good strategy execution. Because discarding old policies and procedures in favor of new ones invariably alters the internal work climate, managers can use the policy-changing process as a powerful lever for changing the corporate culture in ways that produce a stronger fit with the new strategy. The trick here, obviously, is to hit upon a new policy that will catch the immediate attention of the whole organization, quickly shift their actions and behavior, and then become embedded in how things are done—as with Granite Construction's short-pay policy discussed in Illustration Capsule 12.1.

In an attempt to steer "crew members" into stronger quality and service behavior patterns, McDonald's policy manual spells out detailed procedures that personnel in each McDonald's unit are expected to observe; for example, "Cooks must turn, never flip, hamburgers," "If they haven't been purchased, Big Macs must be discarded in 10 minutes after being cooked and French fries in 7 minutes," and "Cashiers must make eye contact with and smile at every customer."

Nordstrom's strategic objective is to make sure that each customer has a pleasing shopping experience in its department stores and returns time and again; to get store personnel to dedicate themselves to outstanding customer service, Nordstrom has a policy of promoting only those people whose personnel records contain evidence of "heroic acts" to please customers—especially customers who may have made "unreasonable requests" that require special efforts. To keep its R&D activities responsive to customer needs and expectations, Hewlett-Packard (HP) requires R&D people to make regular visits to customers to learn about their problems and learn their reactions to HP's latest new products.

One of the big policymaking issues concerns what activities need to be rigidly prescribed and what activities ought to allow room for independent action on the part of empowered personnel. Few companies need thick policy manuals to direct the strategy execution process or prescribe exactly how daily operations are to be conducted. Too much policy can erect as many obstacles as wrong policy or be as confusing as no policy. There is wisdom in a middle approach: *Prescribe enough policies to give organization members clear direction in implementing strategy and to place desirable boundaries on their actions; then empower them to act within these boundaries however they think makes sense.* Allowing company personnel to act anywhere between the "white lines" is especially appropriate when individual creativity and initiative are more essential to good strategy execution than standardization and strict conformity. Instituting strategy-facilitating policies can therefore mean more policies, fewer policies, or different policies. It can mean policies that require things to be done a certain way or policies that give employees leeway to do activities the way they think best.

ADOPTING BEST PRACTICES AND STRIVING FOR CONTINUOUS IMPROVEMENT

Company managers can significantly advance the cause of competent strategy execution by pushing organization units and company personnel to identify and adopt the best practices for performing value chain activities and, further, insisting on continuous improvement in how internal operations are conducted. One of the most widely used and effective tools for gauging how well a company is executing pieces of its strategy entails benchmarking the company's performance of particular activities and business processes against best-in-industry and best-in-world performers.[1] It can also be useful to look at best-in-company performers of an activity if a company has a number of different organizational units performing much the same function at different locations. Identifying, analyzing, and understanding how top companies or individuals perform particular value chain activities and business processes provides useful yardsticks for judging the effectiveness and efficiency of internal operations and setting performance standards for organization units to meet or beat.

> **Core Concept**
> Managerial efforts to identify and adopt best practices are a powerful tool for promoting operating excellence and better strategy execution.

How the Process of Identifying and Incorporating Best Practices Works

A **best practice** is a technique for performing an activity or business process that at least one company has demonstrated works particularly well. To qualify as a legitimate best practice, the technique must have a proven record in significantly lowering costs, improving quality or performance, shortening time requirements, enhancing safety, or

Core Concept
A ***best practice*** is any practice that at least one company has proved works particularly well.

delivering some other highly positive operating outcome. Best practices thus identify a path to operating excellence. For a best practice to be valuable and transferable, it must demonstrate success over time, deliver quantifiable and highly positive results, and be repeatable.

Benchmarking is the backbone of the process of identifying, studying, and implementing outstanding practices. A company's benchmarking effort looks outward to find best practices and then proceeds to develop the data for measuring how well a company's own performance of an activity stacks up against the best-practice standard. Informally, benchmarking involves being humble enough to admit that others have come up with world-class ways to perform particular activities yet wise enough to try to learn how to match, and even surpass, them. But, as shown in Figure 12.2, the payoff of benchmarking comes from adapting the top-notch approaches pioneered by other companies in the company's own operation and thereby boosting, perhaps dramatically, the proficiency with which value chain tasks are performed.

However, benchmarking is more complicated than simply identifying which companies are the best performers of an activity and then trying to imitate their approaches—especially if these companies are in other industries. Normally, the outstanding practices of other organizations have to be *adapted* to fit the specific circumstances of a company's own business and operating requirements. Since most companies believe their work is unique, the telling part of any best-practice initiative is how well the company puts its own version of the best practice into place and makes it work.

Indeed, a best practice remains little more than another company's interesting success story unless company personnel buy into the task of translating what can be learned from other companies into real action and results. The agents of change must be frontline employees who are convinced of the need to abandon the old ways of doing things and switch to a best-practice mind-set. *The more that organizational units use best practices in performing their work, the closer a company moves toward performing its value chain activities as effectively and efficiently as possible.* This is what operational excellence is all about.

Legions of companies across the world now engage in benchmarking to improve their strategy execution efforts and, ideally, gain a strategic, operational, and financial advantage over rivals. Scores of trade associations and special interest organizations have undertaken efforts to collect best-practice data relevant to a particular industry or business function and make their databases available online to members—good

Figure 12.2   **From Benchmarking and Best-Practice Implementation to Operating Excellence**

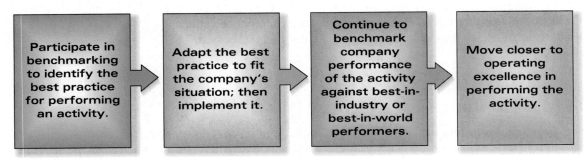

examples include The Benchmarking Exchange's BenchNet (www.benchnet.com), Best Practices LLC (www.best-in-class.com), and the American Productivity and Quality Center (www.apqc.org). Benchmarking and best-practice implementation have clearly emerged as legitimate and valuable managerial tools for promoting operational excellence.

Business Process Reengineering, Six Sigma Quality Programs, and TQM: Tools for Promoting Operating Excellence

In striving for operating excellence, many companies have also come to rely on three other potent management tools: business process reengineering, Six Sigma quality control techniques, and total quality management (TQM) programs. Indeed, these three tools have become globally pervasive techniques for implementing strategies keyed to cost reduction, defect-free manufacture, superior product quality, superior customer service, and total customer satisfaction. The following sections describe how business process reengineering, Six Sigma, and TQM can contribute to operating excellence and better strategy execution.

Business Process Reengineering   Companies scouring for ways to improve their operations have sometimes discovered that the execution of strategy-critical activities is hindered by an organizational arrangement where pieces of the activity are performed in several different functional departments, with no one manager or group being accountable for optimum performance of the entire activity. This can easily occur in such inherently cross-functional activities as customer service (which can involve personnel in order filling, warehousing and shipping, invoicing, accounts receivable, after-sale repair, and technical support), new product development (which can typically involve personnel in R&D, design and engineering, purchasing, manufacturing, and sales and marketing), and supply chain management (which cuts across such areas as purchasing, inventory management, manufacturing and assembly, warehousing, and shipping). Even if personnel in all the different departments and functional areas are inclined to collaborate closely, the activity may not end up being performed optimally or cost-efficiently, such that performance is adversely affected.

To address such shortcomings in strategy execution, many companies during the past decade have opted to *reengineer the work effort* by pulling the pieces of strategy-critical activities out of different departments and unifying their performance in a single department or cross-functional work group. Reorganizing the people who performed the pieces in functional departments into a close-knit group that has charge over the whole process and that can be held accountable for performing the activity in a cheaper, better, and/or more strategy-supportive fashion is called *business process reengineering.*[2]

When done properly, business process reengineering can produce dramatic operating benefits. In the order-processing section of General Electric's circuit breaker division, elapsed time from order receipt to delivery was cut from three weeks to three days by consolidating six production units into one, reducing a variety of former inventory and handling steps, automating the design system to replace a human custom-design process, and cutting the organizational layers between managers and workers from three to one. Productivity rose 20 percent in one year, and unit manufacturing costs dropped 30 percent. Northwest Water, a British utility, used business process reengineering to eliminate 45 work depots that served as home bases to crews who installed and repaired water and sewage lines and equipment. Now crews work directly from their vehicles, receiving assignments and reporting work completion from computer terminals in their trucks. Crew members are no longer employees but rather contractors to Northwest Water. These reengineering efforts not only eliminated the need for the work depots but also allowed Northwest Water to eliminate a big percentage of the bureaucratic personnel and supervisory organization that managed the crews.[3]

Since the early 1990s, reengineering of value chain activities has been undertaken at many companies in many industries all over the world, with excellent results being achieved at some companies.[4] While reengineering has produced only modest results in some instances, usually because of ineptness or lack of wholehearted commitment, reengineering has nonetheless proved itself as a useful tool for streamlining a company's work effort and moving closer to operational excellence.

Total Quality Management Programs   Total quality management (TQM) is a philosophy of managing a set of business practices that emphasizes continuous improvement in all phases of operations, 100 percent accuracy in performing tasks, involvement and empowerment of employees at all levels, team-based work design, benchmarking, and total customer satisfaction.[5] While TQM concentrates on the production of quality goods and fully satisfying customer expectations, it achieves its biggest successes when it is also extended to employee efforts in *all departments*—human resources, billing, R&D, engineering, accounting and records, and information systems—that may lack pressing, customer-driven incentives to improve. It involves reforming the corporate culture and shifting to a total quality/continuous improvement business philosophy that permeates every facet of the organization.[6] TQM aims at instilling enthusiasm and commitment to doing things right from the top to the bottom of the organization. Management's job is to kindle an companywide search for ways to improve, a search that involves all company personnel exercising initiative and using their ingenuity. TQM doctrine preaches that there's no such thing as "good enough" and that everyone has a responsibility to participate in continuous improvement. TQM is thus a race without a finish. Success comes from making little steps forward each day, a process that the Japanese call *kaizen*.

> **Core Concept**
> TQM entails creating a total quality culture bent on continuously improving the performance of every task and value chain activity.

TQM takes a fairly long time to show significant results—very little benefit emerges within the first six months. The long-term payoff of TQM, if it comes, depends heavily on management's success in implanting a culture within which TQM philosophies and practices can thrive. TQM is a managerial tool that has attracted numerous users and advocates over several decades, and it can deliver good results when used properly.

Six Sigma Quality Control   Six Sigma quality control consists of a disciplined, statistics-based system aimed at producing not more than 3.4 defects per million iterations for any business process—from manufacturing to customer transactions.[7] The Six Sigma process of define, measure, analyze, improve, and control (DMAIC) is an improvement system for existing processes falling below specification and needing incremental improvement. The Six Sigma process of define, measure, analyze, design, and verify (DMADV) is used to develop *new* processes or products at Six Sigma quality levels. Both Six Sigma processes are executed by personnel who have earned Six Sigma "green belts" and Six Sigma "black belts," and are overseen by personnel who have completed Six Sigma "master black belt" training. According to the Six Sigma Academy, personnel with black belts can save companies approximately $230,000 per project and can complete four to six projects a year.[8]

The statistical thinking underlying Six Sigma is based on the following three principles: All work is a process, all processes have variability, and all processes create data that explains variability.[9] To illustrate how these three principles drive the metrics of DMAIC, consider the case of a janitorial company that wants to improve the caliber of work done by its cleaning crews and thereby boost customer satisfaction. The janitorial company's Six Sigma team can pursue quality enhancement and continuous improvement via the DMAIC process as follows:

- *Define.* Because Six Sigma is aimed at reducing defects, the first step is to define what constitutes a defect. Six Sigma team members might decide that leaving streaks on windows is a defect because it is a source of customer dissatisfaction.

- *Measure.* The next step is to collect data to find out why, how, and how often this defect occurs. This might include a process flow map of the specific ways that cleaning crews go about the task of cleaning a commercial customer's windows. Other metrics may include recording what tools and cleaning products the crews use to clean windows.

- *Analyze.* After the data are gathered and the statistics analyzed, the company's Six Sigma team discovers that the tools and window-cleaning techniques of certain employees are better than those of other employees because their tools and procedures leave no streaked windows—a "best practice" for avoiding window streaking is thus identified and documented.

- *Improve.* The Six Sigma team implements the documented best practice as a standard way of cleaning windows.

- *Control.* The company teaches new and existing employees the best practice technique for window cleaning. Over time, there's significant improvement in customer satisfaction and increased business.

Six Sigma's DMAIC process is a particularly good vehicle for improving performance when there are *wide variations* in how well an activity is performed.[10] For instance, airlines striving to improve the on-time performance of their flights have more to gain from actions to curtail the number of flights that are late by more then 30 minutes than from actions to reduce the number of flights that are late by less than 5 minutes. Likewise, an overnight delivery service might have a 16-hour average delivery time, but if the actual delivery time varies around the 16-hour average from a low of 12 hours to a high of 26 hours such that 10 percent of its packages are delivered more than 6 hours late, then the company has a huge *reliability* problem.

Since the mid-1990s, thousands of companies and nonprofit organizations around the world have begun using Six Sigma programs to promote operating excellence. Such manufacturers as Motorola, Allied Signal, Caterpillar, DuPont, Xerox, Alcan Aluminum, BMW, Volkswagen, Nokia, Owens Corning, and Emerson Electric have employed Six Sigma techniques to good advantage in improving production quality. General Electric (GE), one of the most successful companies implementing Six Sigma training and pursuing Six Sigma perfection, estimated benefits on the order of $10 billion during the first five years of implementation. GE first began Six Sigma in 1995 after Motorola and Allied Signal blazed the Six Sigma trail. One of GE's successes was in its Lighting division, where Six Sigma was used to cut invoice defects and disputes by 98 percent, a particular benefit to Wal-Mart, the division's largest customer. GE Capital Mortgage improved the chances of a caller reaching a "live" GE person from 76 to 99 percent.[11] Illustration Capsule 12.2 describes Whirlpool's use of Six Sigma in its appliance business.

Illustration Capsule 12.2

Whirlpool's Use of Six Sigma to Promote Operating Excellence

Top management at Whirlpool Corporation, the leading global manufacturer and marketer of home appliances in 2005 with 50 manufacturing and technology centers aound the globe and sales in some 170 countries, has a vision of Whirlpool appliances in "Every Home, Everywhere." One of management's chief objectives in pursuing this vision is to build unmatched customer loyalty to the Whirlpool brand. Whirlpool's strategy to win the hearts and minds of appliance buyers the world over has been to produce and market appliances with top-notch quality and innovative features that users will find appealing. In addition, Whirlpool's strategy has been to offer a wide selection of models (recognizing that buyer tastes and needs differ) and to strive for low-cost production efficiency, thereby enabling Whirlpool to price its products competitively. Executing this strategy at Whirlpool's operations in North America (where it is the market leader), Latin America (where it is also the market leader), Europe (where it is ranks third), and Asia (where it is number one in India and has a foothold with huge growth opportunities elsewhere) has involved a strong focus on continuous improvement, lean manufacturing capabilities, and a drive for operating excellence. To marshal the efforts of Whirlpool's 68,000 employees in executing the strategy successfully, management developed a comprehensive Operational Excellence program with Six Sigma as one of the centerpieces.

The Operational Excellence initiative, which began in the 1990s, incorporated Six Sigma techniques to improve the quality of Whirlpool products, while at the same time lowering costs and trimming the time it took to get product innovations into the marketplace. The Six Sigma program helped Whirlpool save $175 million in manufacturing costs in its first three years.

To sustain the productivity gains and cost savings, Whirlpool embedded Six Sigma practices within each of its manufacturing facilities worldwide and instilled a culture based on Six Sigma and lean manufacturing skills and capabilities. Beginning in 2002, each of Whirlpool's operating units began taking the Six Sigma initiative to a higher level by first placing the needs of the customer at the center of every function—R&D, technology, manufacturing, marketing, and administrative support—and then striving to consistently improve quality levels while eliminating all unnecessary costs. The company systematically went through every aspect of its business with the view that company personnel should perform every activity at every level in a manner that delivers value to the customer and that leads to continuous improvement on how things are done.

Whirlpool management believes that the company's Operational Excellence process has been a major contributor in sustaining the company's global leadership in appliances.

Source: Information posted at www.whirlpool.com (accessed September 25, 2003, and November 15, 2005).

Six Sigma is, however, not just a quality-enhancing tool for manufacturers. At one company, product sales personnel typically wined and dined customers to close their deals.[12] But the costs of such entertaining were viewed as excessively high in many instances. A Six Sigma project that examined sales data found that although face time with customers was important, wining, dining, and other types of entertainment were not. The data showed that regular face time helped close sales, but that time could be spent over a cup of coffee instead of golfing at a resort or taking clients to expensive restaurants. In addition, analysis showed that too much face time with customers was counterproductive. A regularly scheduled customer picnic was found to be detrimental to closing sales because it was held at a busy time of year, when customers preferred not to be away from their offices. Changing the manner in which prospective customers were wooed resulted in a 10 percent increase in sales.

A Milwaukee hospital used Six Sigma to map the process as prescriptions originated with a doctor's writeup, were filled by the hospital pharmacy, and then administered by nurses. DMAIC analysis revealed that most mistakes came from misreading the doctor's handwriting.[13] The hospital implemented a program requiring doctors to type the prescription into a computer, which slashed the number of errors dramatically.

A problem tailor-made for Six Sigma occurs in the insurance industry, where it is common for top agents to outsell poor agents by a factor of 10 to 1 or more. If insurance executives offer a trip to Hawaii in a monthly contest to motivate low-performing agents, the typical result is to motivate top agents to be even more productive and make the performance gap even wider. A DMAIC Six Sigma project to reduce the variation in the performance of agents and correct the problem of so many low-performing agents would begin by measuring the performance of all agents, perhaps discovering that the top 20 percent sell 7 times more policies than the bottom 40 percent. Six Sigma analysis would then consider such steps as mapping how top agents spend their day, investigating the factors that distinguish top performers from low performers, learning what techniques training specialists have employed in converting low-performing agents into high performers, and examining how the hiring process could be improved to avoid hiring underperformers in the first place. The next step would be to *test* proposed solutions—better training methods or psychological profiling to identify and weed out candidates likely to be poor performers—to identify and measure which alternative solutions really work, which don't, and why. Only those actions that prove statistically beneficial are then introduced on a wide scale. The DMAIC method thus entails empirical analysis to diagnose the problem (*design, measure, analyze*), test alternative solutions (*improve*) and then *control* the variability in how well the activity is performed by implementing actions shown to truly fix the problem.

A company that systematically applies Six Sigma methods to its value chain, activity by activity, can make major strides in improving the proficiency with which its strategy is executed. As is the case with TQM, obtaining managerial commitment, establishing a quality culture, and fully involving employees are the three most intractable challenges encountered in the implementation of Six Sigma quality programs.[14]

The Difference between Business Process Reengineering and Continuous Improvement Programs Like Six Sigma and TQM   Business process reengineering and continuous improvement efforts like TQM and Six Sigma both aim at improved efficiency and reduced costs, better product quality, and greater customer satisfaction. The essential difference between business process reengineering and continuous improvement programs is that reengineering aims at *quantum gains* on the order of 30 to 50 percent or more whereas total quality programs stress *incremental progress,* striving for inch-by-inch gains again and again in a never-ending stream. The two approaches to improved performance of value chain activities and operating excellence are not mutually exclusive; it makes sense to use them in tandem. Reengineering can be used first to produce a good basic design that yields quick, dramatic improvements in performing a business process. Total quality programs can then be used as a follow-on to reengineering and/or best-practice implementation, delivering gradual improvements. Such a two-pronged approach to implementing operational excellence is like a marathon race in which you run the first four miles as fast as you can, then gradually pick up speed the remainder of the way.

> Business process reengineering aims at one-time quantum improvement; continuous improvement programs like TQM and Six Sigma aim at ongoing incremental improvements.

Capturing the Benefits of Initiatives to Improve Operations

Usually, the biggest beneficiaries of benchmarking and best-practice initiatives, reengineering, TQM, and Six Sigma are companies that view such programs not as ends in themselves but as tools for implementing and executing company strategy more effectively. The skimpiest payoffs occur when company managers seize them as something worth trying—novel ideas that could improve things. In most such instances, they result in strategy-blind efforts to simply manage better. There's an important lesson here. Best practices, TQM, Six Sigma quality, and reengineering all need to be seen and used as part of a bigger-picture effort to execute strategy proficiently. Only strategy can point to which value chain activities matter and what performance targets make the most sense. Absent a strategic framework, managers lack the context in which to fix things that really matter to business-unit performance and competitive success.

> **Core Concept**
>
> The purpose of using benchmarking, best practices, business process reengineering, TQM, Six Sigma, or other operational improvement programs is to improve the performance of strategy-critical activities and enhance strategy execution.

To get the most from initiative to better execute strategy, managers must have a clear idea of what specific outcomes really matter. Is it a Six Sigma or lower defect rate, high on-time delivery percentages, low overall costs relative to rivals, high percentages of pleased customers and few customer complaints, shorter cycle times, a higher percentage of revenues coming from recently introduced products, or what? Benchmarking best-in-industry and best-in-world performance of most or all value chain activities provides a realistic basis for setting internal performance milestones and longer-range targets.

Then comes the managerial task of building a total quality culture genuinely committed to achieving the performance outcomes that strategic success requires.[15] Managers can take the following action steps to realize full value from TQM or Six Sigma initiatives:[16]

1. Visible, unequivocal, and unyielding commitment to total quality and continuous improvement, including a quality vision and specific, measurable objectives for boosting quality and making continuous improvement.

2. Nudging people toward quality-supportive behaviors by:

    a. Screening job applicants rigorously and hiring only those with attitudes and aptitudes right for quality-based performance.

    b. Providing quality training for most employees.

    c. Using teams and team-building exercises to reinforce and nurture individual effort (the creation of a quality culture is facilitated when teams become more cross-functional, multitask-oriented, and increasingly self-managed).

    d. Recognizing and rewarding individual and team efforts regularly and systematically.

    e. Stressing prevention (doing it right the first time), not inspection (instituting ways to correct mistakes).

3. Empowering employees so that authority for delivering great service or improving products is in the hands of the doers rather than the overseers—*improving quality has to be seen as part of everyone's job.*

4. Using online systems to provide all relevant parties with the latest best practices and actual experiences with them, thereby speeding the diffusion and adoption of best practices throughout the organization and also allowing them to exchange data and opinions about how to upgrade the prevailing best practices.

5. Preaching that performance can, and must, be improved because competitors are not resting on their laurels and customers are always looking for something better.

If the targeted performance measures are appropriate to the strategy and if all organizational members (top executives, middle managers, professional staff, and line employees) buy into a culture of operating excellence, then a company's work climate becomes decidedly more conducive to proficient strategy execution. Benchmarking, best-practice implementation, reengineering, TQM, and Six Sigma initiatives can greatly enhance a company's product design, cycle time, production costs, product quality, service, customer satisfaction, and other operating capabilities—and they can even deliver competitive advantage.[17] Not only do improvements from such initiatives add up over time and strengthen organizational capabilities, but the benefits they produce have hard-to-imitate aspects. While it is relatively easy for rivals to undertake benchmarking, process improvement, and quality training, it is much more difficult and time-consuming for them to instill a deeply ingrained culture of operating excellence (as occurs when such techniques are religiously employed) and top management exhibits lasting commitment to operational excellence throughout the organization.

INSTALLING INFORMATION AND OPERATING SYSTEMS

Company strategies can't be executed well without a number of internal systems for business operations. Southwest, American, Northwest, Delta, and other major airlines cannot hope to provide passenger-pleasing service without a user-friendly online reservation system, an accurate and speedy baggage handling system, and a strict aircraft maintenance program that minimizes equipment failures requiring at-the-gate service and delaying plane departures. FedEx has internal communication systems that allow it to coordinate its over 70,000 vehicles in handling an average of 5.5 million packages a day. Its leading-edge flight operations systems allow a single controller to direct as many as 200 of FedEx's 650 aircraft simultaneously, overriding their flight plans should weather or other special emergencies arise. In addition, FedEx has created a series of e-business tools for customers that allow them to ship and track packages online (either at FedEx's Web site or on their own company intranets or Web sites), create address books, review shipping history, generate custom reports, simplify customer billing, reduce internal warehousing and inventory management costs, purchase goods and services from suppliers, and respond quickly to changing customer demands. All of FedEx's systems support the company's strategy of providing businesses and individuals with a broad array of package delivery services (from premium next-day to economical five-day deliveries) and boosting its competitiveness against United Parcel Service, Airborne Express, and the U.S. Postal Service.

Otis Elevator, the world's largest manufacturer of elevators, has 24-hour communications service centers for customers called OtisLine to coordinate its maintenance efforts for some 1.5 million elevators and escalators it has installed worldwide.[18] Electronic monitors installed on each user's site can detect when an elevator or escalator has any of 325 problems and will automatically place a service call to the nearest service center location. Trained operators take all trouble calls, input critical information on a computer screen, and can dispatch trained mechanics from 325 locations across the world to the local trouble spot when needed. All customers have online access to performance data on each of their Otis elevators. More than 80 percent of mechanics in North America carry Web-enabled phones connected to e*Service that transport needed information quickly and allow mechanics to update data in Otis computers for future reference. The OtisLine system helps keep outage times to less than two and a half hours. All the trouble-call data is relayed to design and manufacturing personnel, allowing them to quickly alter design specifications or manufacturing procedures when needed to correct recurring problems.

Amazon.com ships customer orders from fully computerized, 1,300-by-600-foot warehouses containing about 3 million books, CDs, toys, and houseware items.[19] The warehouses are so technologically sophisticated that they require about as many lines of code to run as Amazon's Web site does. Using complex picking algorithms, computers initiate the order-picking process by sending signals to workers' wireless receivers, telling them which items to pick off the shelves in which order. Computers also generate data on misboxed items, chute backup times, line speed, worker productivity, and shipping weights on orders. Systems are upgraded regularly, and productivity improvements are aggressively pursued. In 2003 Amazon's six warehouses were able to handle three times the volume handled in 1999 at costs averaging 10 percent of revenues (versus 20 percent in 1999); in addition, they turned their inventory over 20 times annually in an industry whose average was 15 turns. Amazon's warehouse efficiency and cost per order filled was so low that one of the fastest-growing and most profitable parts of Amazon's business was using its warehouses to run the e-commerce operations of Toys "R" Us and Target.

Most telephone companies, electric utilities, and TV broadcasting systems have online monitoring systems to spot transmission problems within seconds and increase the reliability of their services. At eBay, there are systems for real-time monitoring of new listings, bidding activity, Web site traffic, and page views. Kaiser Permanente spent $3 billion to digitize the medical records of its 8.2 million members so that it could manage patient care more efficiently.[20] IBM has created a database of 36,000 employee profiles that enable it to better assign the most qualified IBM consultant to the projects it is doing for clients. In businesses such as public accounting and management consulting, where large numbers of professional staff need cutting-edge technical know-how, companies have developed systems that identify when it is time for certain employees to attend training programs to update their skills and know-how. Many companies have cataloged best-practice information on their intranets to promote faster transfer and implementation throughout the organization.[21]

Well-conceived state-of-the-art operating systems not only enable better strategy execution but also strengthen organizational capabilities—perhaps enough to provide a competitive edge over rivals. For example, a company with a differentiation strategy based on superior quality has added capability if it has systems for training personnel in quality techniques, tracking product quality at each production step, and ensuring that all goods shipped meet quality standards. A company striving to be a low-cost provider is competitively stronger if it has a benchmarking system that identifies opportunities to implement best practices and drive costs out of the business. Fast-growing companies get an important assist from having capabilities in place to recruit and train new employees in large numbers and from investing in infrastructure that gives them the capability to handle rapid growth as it occurs. It is nearly always better to put infrastructure and support systems in place before they are actually needed than to have to scramble to catch up to customer demand.

Core Concept

State-of-the-art support systems can be a basis for competitive advantage if they give a firm capabilities that rivals can't match.

Instituting Adequate Information Systems, Performance Tracking, and Controls

Accurate and timely information about daily operations is essential if managers are to gauge how well the strategy execution process is proceeding. Information systems need to cover five broad areas: (1) customer data, (2) operations data, (3) employee data, (4) supplier/partner/collaborative ally data, and (5) financial performance data. All key strategic performance indicators have to be tracked and reported as often as practical. Monthly profit-and-loss statements and monthly statistical summaries, long the norm, are fast being replaced by daily statistical updates and even up-to-the-minute performance monitoring that online technology makes possible. Many retail companies have automated online systems that generate daily sales reports for each store and maintain up-to-the-minute inventory and sales records on each item. Manufacturing plants typically generate daily production reports and track labor productivity on every shift. Many retailers and manufacturers have online data systems connecting them with their suppliers that monitor the status of inventories, track shipments and deliveries, and measure defect rates.

Real-time information systems permit company managers to stay on top of implementation initiatives and daily operations, and to intervene if things seem to be drifting off course. Tracking key performance indicators, gathering information from operating personnel, quickly identifying and diagnosing problems, and taking corrective actions are all integral pieces of the process of managing strategy implementation and execution and exercising adequate organization control. A number of companies have recently begun creating "electronic scorecards" for senior managers that gather daily or weekly statistics from different databases about inventory, sales, costs, and sales trends; such information enables these managers to easily stay abreast of what's happening and make better decisions on a real-time basis.[22] Telephone companies have elaborate information systems to measure signal quality, connection times, interrupts, wrong connections, billing errors, and other measures of reliability that affect customer service and satisfaction. To track and manage the quality of passenger service, airlines have information systems to monitor gate delays, on-time departures and arrivals, baggage handling times, lost baggage complaints, stockouts on meals and drinks, overbookings, and maintenance delays and failures. Continental Airlines has an online system that alerts the company when planes arrive late and assesses whether connecting flights needs to be delayed slightly for late-arriving passengers and carts sent to the gate to shorten the time it will take for passengers to reach their connecting flight. British Petroleum (BP) has outfitted rail cars carrying hazardous materials with sensors and global positioning system (GPS) devices so that it can track the status, location, and other information about these shipments via satellite and relay the data to its corporate intranet. Companies that rely on empowered customer-contact personnel to act promptly and creatively in pleasing customers have installed online information systems that put essential customer data on their computer monitors with a few keystrokes so that they can respond effectively to customer inquiries and deliver personalized customer service.

Statistical information gives managers a feel for the numbers, briefings and meetings provide a feel for the latest developments and emerging issues, and personal contacts add a feel for the people dimension. All are good barometers. Managers have to identify problem areas and deviations from plan before they can take actions to get the organization back on course, by either improving the approaches to strategy execution or fine-tuning the strategy. Jeff Bezos, Amazon's CEO, is an ardent proponent of managing by the numbers—as he puts it, "Math-based decisions always trump opinion and judgment. The trouble with most corporations is that they make judgment-based decisions when data-based decisions could be made."[23]

> **Core Concept**
> Having good information systems and operating data are integral to competent strategy execution and operating excellence.

Exercising Adequate Controls over Empowered Employees

Another important aspect of effectively managing and controlling the strategy execution process is monitoring the performance of empowered workers to see that they are acting within the specified limits.[24] Leaving empowered employees to their own devices in meeting performance standards without appropriate checks and balances can expose an organization to excessive risk.[25] Instances abound of employees' decisions or behavior having gone awry, sometimes costing a company huge sums or producing lawsuits aside from just generating embarrassing publicity.

Managers shouldn't have to devote big chunks of their time to making sure that the decisions and behavior of empowered employees stay between the white lines—this would defeat the major purpose of empowerment and, in effect, lead to the reinstatement of a managerial bureaucracy engaged in constant over-the-shoulder supervision. Yet managers have a clear responsibility to exercise sufficient control over empowered employees to protect the company against out-of-bounds behavior and unwelcome surprises. Scrutinizing daily and weekly operating statistics is one of the important ways in which managers can monitor the results that flow from the actions of empowered subordinates—if the operating results flowing from the actions of empowered employees look good, then it is reasonable to assume that empowerment is working.

But close monitoring of real-time or daily operating performance is only one of the control tools at management's disposal. Another valuable lever of control in companies that rely on empowered employees, especially in those that use self-managed work groups or other such teams, is peer-based control. Most team members feel responsible for the success of the whole team and tend to be relatively intolerant of any team member's behavior that weakens team performance or puts team accomplishments at risk (especially when team performance has a big impact on each team member's compensation). Because peer evaluation is such a powerful control device, companies organized into teams can remove some layers of the management hierarchy and rely on strong peer pressure to keep team members operating between the white lines. This is especially true when a company has the information systems capability to monitor team performance daily or in real time.

TYING REWARDS AND INCENTIVES TO GOOD STRATEGY EXECUTION

It is important for both organization units and individuals to be enthusiastically committed to executing strategy and achieving performance targets. Managers typically use an assortment of motivational techniques and rewards to enlist companywide commitment to executing the strategic plan. A manager has to do more than just talk to everyone about how important new strategic practices and performance targets are to the organization's well-being. No matter how inspiring, talk seldom commands people's best efforts for long. *To get employees' sustained, energetic commitment, management has to be resourceful in designing and using motivational incentives—both monetary and nonmonetary.* The more a manager understands what motivates subordinates and the more he or she relies on motivational incentives as a tool for achieving the targeted strategic and financial results, the greater will be employees' commitment to good day-in, day-out strategy execution and achievement of performance targets.[26]

> **Core Concept**
> A properly designed reward structure is management's most powerful tool for mobilizing organizational commitment to successful strategy execution.

Strategy-Facilitating Motivational Practices

Financial incentives generally head the list of motivating tools for trying to gain wholehearted employee commitment to good strategy execution and operating excellence. Monetary rewards generally include some combination of base pay increases, performance bonuses, profit-sharing plans, stock awards, company contributions to employee

401(k) or retirement plans, and piecework incentives (in the case of production workers). But successful companies and managers normally make extensive use of such nonmonetary carrot-and-stick incentives as frequent words of praise (or constructive criticism), special recognition at company gatherings or in the company newsletter, more (or less) job security, stimulating assignments, opportunities to transfer to attractive locations, increased (or decreased) autonomy, and rapid promotion (or the risk of being sidelined in a routine or dead-end job). In addition, companies use a host of other motivational approaches to make their workplaces more appealing and spur stronger employee commitment to the strategy execution process; the following are some of the most important:[27]

> **Core Concept**
> One of management's biggest strategy-executing challenges is to employ motivational techniques that build wholehearted commitment to operating excellence and winning attitudes among employees.

- *Providing attractive perks and fringe benefits*—The various options here include full coverage of health insurance premiums; full tuition reimbursement for work on college degrees; paid vacation time of three or four weeks; on-site child care at major facilities; on-site gym facilities and massage therapists; getaway opportunities at company-owned recreational facilities (beach houses, ranches, resort condos); personal concierge services; subsidized cafeterias and free lunches; casual dress every day; personal travel services; paid sabbaticals; maternity leaves; paid leaves to care for ill family members; telecommuting; compressed workweeks (four 10-hour days instead of five 8-hour days); reduced summer hours; college scholarships for children; on-the-spot bonuses for exceptional performance; and relocation services.

- *Relying on promotion from within whenever possible*—This practice helps bind workers to their employer and employers to their workers; plus, it is an incentive for good performance. Promotion from within also helps ensure that people in positions of responsibility actually know something about the business, technology, and operations they are managing.

- *Making sure that the ideas and suggestions of employees are valued and that those with merit are promptly acted on*—Many companies find that their best ideas for nuts-and-bolts operating improvements come from the suggestions of employees. Moreover, research indicates that the moves of many companies to push decision making down the line and empower employees increases employee motivation and satisfaction, as well as boosting their productivity. The use of self-managed teams has much the same effect.

- *Creating a work atmosphere in which there is genuine sincerity, caring, and mutual respect among workers and between management and employees*—A "family" work environment in which people are on a first-name basis and there is strong camaraderie promotes teamwork and cross-unit collaboration.

- *Stating the strategic vision in inspirational terms that make employees feel they are a part of doing something very worthwhile in a larger social sense*—There's strong motivating power associated with giving people a chance to be part of something exciting and personally satisfying. Jobs with noble purpose tend to turn employees on. At Pfizer, Merck, and most other pharmaceutical companies, it is the notion of helping sick people get well and restoring patients to full life. At Whole Foods Market (a natural foods grocery chain), it is helping customers discover good eating habits and thus improving human health and nutrition.

- *Sharing information with employees about financial performance, strategy, operational measures, market conditions, and competitors' actions*—Broad disclosure and prompt communication send the message that managers trust their workers. Keeping employees in the dark denies them information useful to performing their job, prevents them from being "students of the business," and usually turns them off.

- *Having knockout facilities*—A workplace with appealing features and amenities usually has decidedly positive effects on employee morale and productivity.
- *Being flexible in how the company approaches people management (motivation, compensation, recognition, recruitment) in multinational, multicultural environments*—There is usually some merit in giving local managers in foreign operations to adapt their motivation, compensation, recognition, and recruitment practices to fit local customs, habits, values, and business practices rather than insisting on consistent people-management practices worldwide. But the one area where consistency is essential is conveying the message that the organization values people of all races and cultural backgrounds and that discrimination of any sort will not be tolerated.

For specific examples of the motivational tactics employed by several prominent companies (many of which appear on *Fortune*'s list of "The 100 Best Companies to Work for in America"), see Illustration Capsule 12.3.

Striking the Right Balance between Rewards and Punishment

While most approaches to motivation, compensation, and people management accentuate the positive, companies also embellish positive rewards with the risk of punishment. At General Electric, McKinsey & Company, several global public accounting firms, and other companies that look for and expect top-notch individual performance, there's an "up-or-out" policy—managers and professionals whose performance is not good enough to warrant promotion are first denied bonuses and stock awards and eventually weeded out. A number of companies deliberately give employees heavy workloads and tight deadlines—personnel are pushed hard to achieve "stretch" objectives and expected to put in long hours (nights and weekends if need be). At most companies, senior executives and key personnel in underperforming units are pressured to boost performance to acceptable levels and keep it there or risk being replaced.

As a general rule, it is unwise to take off the pressure for good individual and group performance or play down the stress, anxiety, and adverse consequences of shortfalls in performance. There is no evidence that a no-pressure/no-adverse-consequences work environment leads to superior strategy execution or operating excellence. As the CEO of a major bank put it, "There's a deliberate policy here to create a level of anxiety. Winners usually play like they're one touchdown behind."[28] *High-performing organizations nearly always have a cadre of ambitious people who relish the opportunity to climb the ladder of success, love a challenge, thrive in a performance-oriented environment, and find some competition and pressure useful to satisfy their own drives for personal recognition, accomplishment, and self-satisfaction.*

However, if an organization's motivational approaches and reward structure induce too much stress, internal competitiveness, job insecurity, and unpleasant consequences, the impact on workforce morale and strategy execution can be counterproductive. Evidence shows that managerial initiatives to improve strategy execution should incorporate more positive than negative motivational elements because when cooperation is

Illustration Capsule 12.3

What Companies Do to Motivate and Reward Employees

Companies have come up with an impressive variety of motivational and reward practices to help create a work environment that energizes employees and promotes better strategy execution. Here's a sampling of what companies are doing:

- Google has a sprawling four-building complex known as the Googleplex where the company's roughly 1,000 employees are provided with free food, unlimited ice cream, pool and Ping-Pong tables, and complimentary massages—management built the Googleplex to be "a dream environment." Moreover, the company gives its employees the ability to spend 20 percent of their work time on any outside activity.

- Lincoln Electric, widely known for its piecework pay scheme and incentive bonus plan, rewards individual productivity by paying workers for each nondefective piece produced. Workers have to correct quality problems on their own time—defects in products used by customers can be traced back to the worker who caused them. Lincoln's piecework plan motivates workers to pay attention to both quality and volume produced. In addition, the company sets aside a substantial portion of its profits above a specified base for worker bonuses. To determine bonus size, Lincoln Electric rates each worker on four equally important performance measures: dependability, quality, output, and ideas and cooperation. The higher a worker's merit rating, the higher the incentive bonus earned; the most highly rated workers in good profit years receive bonuses of as much as 110 percent of their piecework compensation.

- At JM Family Enterprises, a Toyota distributor in Florida, employees get a great lease on new Toyotas and are flown to the Bahamas for cruises on the 172-foot company yacht. The company's office facility has such amenities as a heated lap pool, a fitness center, and a free nail salon. Employees get free prescriptions delivered by a "pharmacy concierge" and professionally made take-home dinners.

- Amazon.com hands out Just Do It awards to employees who do something they think will help Amazon *without* getting their boss's permission. The action has to be well thought through but doesn't have to succeed.

- Nordstrom, widely regarded for its superior in-house customer service experience, typically pays its retail salespeople an hourly wage higher than the prevailing rates paid by other department store chains plus a commission on each sale. Spurred by a culture that encourages salespeople to go all out to satisfy customers and to seek out and promote new fashion ideas, Nordstrom salespeople often earn twice the average incomes of sales employees at competing stores. Nordstrom's rules for employees are simple: "Rule #1: Use your good judgment in all situations. There will be no additional rules."

- At W. L. Gore (the maker of Gore-Tex), employees get to choose what project/team they work on and each team member's compensation is based on other team members' rankings of his or her contribution to the enterprise.

- At Ukrop's Super Markets, a family-owned chain, stores stay closed on Sunday; the company pays out 20 percent of pretax profits to employees in the form of quarterly bonuses; and the company picks up the membership tab for employees if they visit their health club 30 times a quarter.

- At biotech leader Amgen, employees get 16 paid holidays, generous vacation time, tuition reimbursements up to $10,000, on-site massages, a discounted car wash, and the convenience of shopping at on-site farmers' markets.

- At Synovus, a financial services and credit card company, the company adds as much as 20 percent annually to each employee's compensation via a "wealth-building" program that includes a 401(k) and profit sharing; plus, it holds an annual bass fishing tournament.

- At specialty chipmaker Xilinx, new hires receive stock option grants; the CEO responds promptly to employee e-mails, and during hard times management takes a 20 percent pay cut instead of laying off employees.

Sources: Fortune's lists of the 100 best companies to work for in America, 2002, 2004, and 2005 (accessed November 14, 2005); Jefferson Graham, "The Search Engine that Could," *USA Today,* August 26, 2003, p. B3; and Fred Vogelstein, "Winning the Amazon Way," *Fortune* (May 26, 2003), p. 73.

positively enlisted and rewarded, rather than strong-armed by orders and threats (implicit or explicit), people tend to respond with more enthusiasm, dedication, creativity, and initiative. Something of a middle ground is generally optimal—not only handing out decidedly positive rewards for meeting or beating performance targets but also imposing sufficiently negative consequences (if only withholding rewards) when actual performance falls short of the target. But the negative consequences of underachievement should never be so severe or demoralizing as to impede a renewed and determined effort to overcome existing obstacles and hit the targets in upcoming periods.

Linking the Reward System to Strategically Relevant Performance Outcomes

The most dependable way to keep people focused on strategy execution and the achievement of performance targets is to *generously* reward and recognize individuals and groups who meet or beat performance targets and deny rewards and recognition to those who don't. *The use of incentives and rewards is the single most powerful tool management has to win strong employee commitment to diligent, competent strategy execution and operating excellence.* Decisions on salary increases, incentive compensation, promotions, key assignments, and the ways and means of awarding praise and recognition are potent attention-getting, commitment-generating devices.

Core Concept

A properly designed reward system aligns the well-being of organization members with their contributions to competent strategy execution and the achievement of performance targets.

Such decisions seldom escape the closest employee scrutiny, saying more about what is expected and who is considered to be doing a good job than about any other factor. Hence, when meeting or beating strategic and financial targets become *the dominating basis* for designing incentives, evaluating individual and group efforts, and handing out rewards, company personnel quickly grasp that it is in their own self-interest to do their best in executing the strategy competently and achieving key performance targets.[29] Indeed, it is usually through the company's system of incentives and rewards that workforce members emotionally ratify their commitment to the company's strategy execution effort.

Ideally, performance targets should be set for every organization unit, every manager, every team or work group, and perhaps every employee—targets that measure whether strategy execution is progressing satisfactorily. If the company's strategy is to be a low-cost provider, the incentive system must reward actions and achievements that result in lower costs. If the company has a differentiation strategy predicated on superior quality and service, the incentive system must reward such outcomes as Six Sigma defect rates, infrequent need for product repair, low numbers of customer complaints, speedy order processing and delivery, and high levels of customer satisfaction. If a company's growth is predicated on a strategy of new product innovation, incentives should be tied to factors such as the percentages of revenues and profits coming from newly introduced products.

Illustration Capsule 12.4 provides two vivid examples of how companies have designed incentives linked directly to outcomes reflecting good strategy execution.

The Importance of Basing Incentives on Achieving Results, Not on Performing Assigned Duties   To create a strategy-supportive system of rewards and incentives, a company must emphasize rewarding people for accomplishing results, not for just dutifully performing assigned tasks. Focusing jobholders' attention and energy on what to *achieve* as opposed to what to *do* makes the work

Illustration Capsule 12.4

Nucor and Bank One: Two Companies that Tie Incentives Directly to Strategy Execution

The strategy at Nucor Corporation, now the biggest steel producer in the United States, is to be *the* low-cost producer of steel products. Because labor costs are a significant fraction of total cost in the steel business, successful implementation of Nucor's low-cost leadership strategy entails achieving lower labor costs per ton of steel than competitors' costs. Nucor management uses an incentive system to promote high worker productivity and drive labor costs per ton below rivals'. Each plant's workforce is organized into production teams (each assigned to perform particular functions), and weekly production targets are established for each team. Base pay scales are set at levels comparable to wages for similar manufacturing jobs in the local areas where Nucor has plants, but workers can earn a 1 percent bonus for each 1 percent that their output exceeds target levels. If a production team exceeds its weekly production target by 10 percent, team members receive a 10 percent bonus in their next paycheck; if a team exceeds its quota by 20 percent, team members earn a 20 percent bonus. Bonuses, paid every two weeks, are based on the prior two weeks' actual production levels measured against the targets.

Nucor's piece-rate incentive plan has produced impressive results. The production teams put forth exceptional effort; it is not uncommon for most teams to beat their weekly production targets anywhere from 20 to 50 percent. When added to their base pay, the bonuses earned by Nucor workers make Nucor's workforce among the highest-paid in the U.S. steel industry. From a management perspective, the incentive system has resulted in Nucor having labor productivity levels 10 to 20 percent above the average of the unionized workforces at several of its largest rivals, which in turn has given Nucor a significant labor cost advantage over most rivals.

At Bank One (recently acquired by JP Morgan Chase), management believed it was strategically important to boost its customer satisfaction ratings in order to enhance its competitiveness vis-à-vis rivals. Targets were set for customer satisfaction and monitoring systems for measuring customer satisfaction at each branch office were put in place. Then, to motivate branch office personnel to be more attentive in trying to please customers and also to signal that top management was truly committed to achieving higher levels of overall customer satisfaction, top management opted to tie pay scales in each branch office to that branch's customer satisfaction rating—the higher the branch's ratings, the higher that branch's pay scales. Management believed its shift from a theme of equal pay for equal work to one of equal pay for equal performance contributed significantly to its customer satisfaction priority.

environment results-oriented. It is flawed management to tie incentives and rewards to satisfactory performance of duties and activities in hopes that the by-products will be the desired business outcomes and company achievements.[30] In any job, performing assigned tasks is not equivalent to achieving intended outcomes. Diligently showing up for work and attending to one's job assignment does not, by itself, guarantee results. As any student knows, the fact that an instructor teaches and students go to class doesn't necessarily mean that the students are learning. The enterprise of education would no doubt take on a different character if teachers were rewarded for the result of student learning rather than for the activity of teaching.

> It is folly to reward one outcome in hopes of getting another outcome.

Incentive compensation for top executives is typically tied to such financial measures as revenue and earnings growth, stock price performance, return on investment, and creditworthiness and perhaps such strategic measures as market share, product quality, or customer satisfaction. However, incentives for department heads, teams, and individual workers may be tied to performance outcomes more closely related to their strategic area of responsibility. In manufacturing, incentive compensation may be tied to unit manufacturing costs, on-time production and shipping, defect rates,

Core Concept

The role of the reward system is to align the well-being of organization members with realizing the company's vision, so that organization members benefit by helping the company execute its strategy competently and fully satisfy customers.

the number and extent of work stoppages due to labor disagreements and equipment breakdowns, and so on. In sales and marketing, there may be incentives for achieving dollar sales or unit volume targets, market share, sales penetration of each target customer group, the fate of newly introduced products, the frequency of customer complaints, the number of new accounts acquired, and customer satisfaction. Which performance measures to base incentive compensation on depends on the situation—the priority placed on various financial and strategic objectives, the requirements for strategic and competitive success, and what specific results are needed in different facets of the business to keep strategy execution on track.

Guidelines for Designing Incentive Compensation Systems   The concepts and company experiences discussed above yield the following prescriptive guidelines for creating an incentive compensation system to help drive successful strategy execution:

1. *Make the performance payoff a major, not minor, piece of the total compensation package.* Payoffs must be at least 10 to 12 percent of base salary to have much impact. Incentives that amount to 20 percent or more of total compensation are big attention-getters, likely to really drive individual or team effort; incentives amounting to less than 5 percent of total compensation have comparatively weak motivational impact. Moreover, the payoff for high-performing individuals and teams must be meaningfully greater than the payoff for average performers, and the payoff for average performers meaningfully bigger than for below-average performers.

2. *Have incentives that extend to all managers and all workers, not just top management.* It is a gross miscalculation to expect that lower-level managers and employees will work their hardest to hit performance targets just so a few senior executives can get lucrative rewards.

3. *Administer the reward system with scrupulous objectivity and fairness.* If performance standards are set unrealistically high or if individual/group performance evaluations are not accurate and well documented, dissatisfaction with the system will overcome any positive benefits.

4. *Tie incentives to performance outcomes directly linked to good strategy execution and financial performance.* Incentives should never be paid just because people are thought to be "doing a good job" or because they "work hard." Performance evaluation based on factors not tightly related to good strategy execution signal that either the strategic plan is incomplete (because important performance targets were left out) or management's real agenda is something other than the stated strategic and financial objectives.

5. *Make sure that the performance targets each individual or team is expected to achieve involve outcomes that the individual or team can personally affect.* The role of incentives is to enhance individual commitment and channel behavior in beneficial directions. This role is not well served when the performance measures by which company personnel are judged are outside their arena of influence.

6. *Keep the time between achieving the target performance outcome and the payment of the reward as short as possible.* Companies like Nucor and Continental Airlines have discovered that weekly or monthly payments for good performance work much better than annual payments. Nucor pays weekly bonuses based on

prior-week production levels; Continental awards employees a monthly bonus for each month that on-time flight performance meets or beats a specified percentage companywide. Annual bonus payouts work best for higher-level managers and for situations where target outcome relates to overall company profitability or stock price performance.

7. *Make liberal use of nonmonetary rewards; don't rely solely on monetary rewards.* When used properly, money is a great motivator, but there are also potent advantages to be gained from praise, special recognition, handing out plum assignments, and so on.

8. *Absolutely avoid skirting the system to find ways to reward effort rather than results.* Whenever actual performance falls short of targeted performance, there's merit in determining whether the causes are attributable to subpar individual/group performance or to circumstances beyond the control of those responsible. An argument can be made that exceptions should be made in giving rewards to people who've tried hard, gone the extra mile, yet still come up short because of circumstances beyond their control. The problem with making exceptions for unknowable, uncontrollable, or unforeseeable circumstances is that once good excuses start to creep into justifying rewards for subpar results, the door is open for all kinds of reasons why actual performance failed to match targeted performance. A "no excuses" standard is more evenhanded and certainly easier to administer.

Once the incentives are designed, they have to be communicated and explained. Everybody needs to understand how their incentive compensation is calculated and how individual/group performance targets contribute to organizational performance targets. The pressure to achieve the targeted strategic and financial performance and continuously improve on strategy execution should be unrelenting, with few (if any) loopholes for rewarding shortfalls in performance. People at all levels have to be held accountable for carrying out their assigned parts of the strategic plan, and they have to understand their rewards are based on the caliber of results that are achieved. But with the pressure to perform should come meaningful rewards. Without an ample payoff, the system breaks down, and managers are left with the less workable options of barking orders, trying to enforce compliance, and depending on the goodwill of employees.

> **Core Concept**
> The unwavering standard for judging whether individuals, teams, and organizational units have done a good job must be whether they meet or beat performance targets that reflect good strategy execution.

Performance-Based Incentives and Rewards in Multinational Enterprises

In some foreign countries, incentive pay runs counter to local customs and cultural norms. Professor Steven Kerr cites the time he lectured an executive education class on the need for more performance-based pay and a Japanese manager protested, "You shouldn't bribe your children to do their homework, you shouldn't bribe your wife to prepare dinner, and you shouldn't bribe your employees to work for the company."[31] Singling out individuals and commending them for unusually good effort can also be a problem; Japanese culture considers public praise of an individual an affront to the harmony of the group. In some countries, employees have a preference for nonmonetary rewards—more leisure time, important titles, access to vacation villages, and nontaxable perks. Thus, multinational companies have to build some degree of flexibility into the design of incentives and rewards in order to accommodate cross-cultural traditions and preferences.

Key Points

Managers implementing and executing a new or different strategy must identify the resource requirements of each new strategic initiative and then consider whether the current pattern of resource allocation and the budgets of the various subunits are suitable.

Anytime a company alters its strategy, managers should review existing policies and operating procedures, proactively revise or discard those that are out of sync, and formulate new ones to facilitate execution of new strategic initiatives. Prescribing new or freshly revised policies and operating procedures aids the task of strategy execution (1) by providing top-down guidance to operating managers, supervisory personnel, and employees regarding how certain things need to be done and what the boundaries are on independent actions and decisions; (2) by enforcing consistency in how particular strategy-critical activities are performed in geographically scattered operating units; and (3) by promoting the creation of a work climate and corporate culture that promotes good strategy execution.

Competent strategy execution entails visible, unyielding managerial commitment to best practices and continuous improvement. Benchmarking, the discovery and adoption of best practices, reengineering core business processes, and continuous improvement initiatives like total quality management (TQM) or Six Sigma programs, all aim at improved efficiency, lower costs, better product quality, and greater customer satisfaction. *These initiatives are important tools for learning how to execute a strategy more proficiently.*

Company strategies can't be implemented or executed well without a number of support systems to carry on business operations. Well-conceived state-of-the-art support systems not only facilitate better strategy execution but also strengthen organizational capabilities enough to provide a competitive edge over rivals. Real-time information and control systems further aid the cause of good strategy execution.

Strategy-supportive motivational practices and reward systems are powerful management tools for gaining employee commitment. The key to creating a reward system that promotes good strategy execution is to make strategically relevant measures of performance *the dominating basis* for designing incentives, evaluating individual and group efforts, and handing out rewards. Positive motivational practices generally work better than negative ones, but there is a place for both. There's also a place for both monetary and nonmonetary incentives.

For an incentive compensation system to work well (1) the monetary payoff should be a major percentage of the compensation package, (2) the use of incentives should extend to all managers and workers, (3) the system should be administered with care and fairness, (4) the incentives should be linked to performance targets spelled out in the strategic plan, (5) each individual's performance targets should involve outcomes the person can personally affect, (6) rewards should promptly follow the determination of good performance, (7) monetary rewards should be supplemented with liberal use of nonmonetary rewards, and (8) skirting the system to reward nonperformers or subpar results should be scrupulously avoided. Companies with operations in multiple countries often have to build some degree of flexibility into the design of incentives and rewards in order to accommodate cross-cultural traditions and preferences.

Exercises

1. Go to Google or another Internet search engine and, using the advanced search feature, enter "best practices." Browse through the search results to identify at least five organizations that have gathered a set of best practices and are making the best-practice library they have assembled available to members. Explore at least one of the sites to get an idea of the kind of best-practice information that is available.

2. Do an Internet search on "Six Sigma" quality programs. Browse through the search results and (*a*) identify at least three companies that offer Six Sigma training and (*b*) find lists of companies that have implemented Six Sigma programs in their pursuit of operational excellence—you should be able to cite at least 25 companies that are Six Sigma users. Prepare a one-page report to your instructor detailing the experiences and benefits that one company has realized from employing Six Sigma methods in its operations. To learn more about how Six Sigma works, go to www.isixsigma.com and explore the Q&A menu option.

3. Do an Internet search on "total quality management." Browse through the search results and (*a*) identify 10 companies that offer TQM training, (*b*) identify 5 books on TQM programs, and (*c*) find lists of companies that have implemented TQM programs in their pursuit of operational excellence—you should be able to name at least 20 companies that are TQM users.

4. Consult the latest issue of *Fortune* containing the annual "100 Best Companies to Work For" (usually a late-January or early-February issue, or else use a search engine to locate the list online) and identify at least five compensation incentives and work practices that these companies use to enhance employee motivation and reward them for good strategic and financial performance. Choose compensation methods and work practices that are different from those cited in Illustration Capsule 12.3.

5. Review the profiles and applications of the latest Malcolm Baldrige National Quality Award recipients at www.quality.nist.gov. What are the standout features of the companies' approaches to managing operations? What do you find impressive about the companies' policies and procedures, use of best practices, emphasis on continuous improvement, and use of rewards and incentives?

6. Using Google Scholar or your access to online business periodicals in your university's library, search for the term "incentive compensation" and prepare a report of one to two pages to your instructor discussing the successful (or unsuccessful) use of incentive compensation plans by various companies. According to your research, what factors seem to determine whether incentive compensation plans succeed or fail?

13

Corporate Culture and Leadership

Keys to Good Strategy Execution

The biggest levers you've got to change a company are strategy, structure, and culture. If I could pick two, I'd pick strategy and culture.

—Wayne Leonard
CEO, Entergy

An organization's capacity to execute its strategy depends on its "hard" infrastructure—its organizational structure and systems—and on its "soft" infrastructure—its culture and norms.

—Amar Bhide

Weak leadership can wreck the soundest strategy; forceful execution of even a poor plan can often bring victory.

—Sun Zi

Leadership is accomplishing something through other people that wouldn't have happened if you weren't there . . . Leadership is being able to mobilize ideas and values that energize other people . . . Leaders develop a story line that engages other people.

—Noel Tichy

Seeing people in person is a big part of how you drive any change process. You have to show people a positive view of the future and say "we can do it."

—Jeffrey R. Immelt
CEO, General Electric

I n the previous two chapters we examined six of the managerial tasks important to good strategy execution and operating excellence—building a capable organization, marshaling the needed resources and steering them to strategy-critical operating units, establishing policies and procedures that facilitate good strategy execution, adopting best practices and pushing for continuous improvement in how value chain activities are performed, creating internal operating systems that enable better execution, and employing motivational practices and compensation incentives that gain wholehearted employee commitment to the strategy execution process. In this chapter we explore the two remaining managerial tasks that shape the outcome of efforts to execute a company's strategy: creating a strategy-supportive corporate culture and exerting the internal leadership needed to drive the implementation of strategic initiatives forward and achieve higher plateaus of operating excellence.

INSTILLING A CORPORATE CULTURE THAT PROMOTES GOOD STRATEGY EXECUTION

Every company has its own unique culture. The character of a company's culture or work climate is a product of the core values and business principles that executives espouse, the standards of what is ethically acceptable and what is not, the work practices and behaviors that define "how we do things around here," the approach to people management and style of operating, the "chemistry" and the "personality" that permeates the work environment, and the stories that get told over and over to illustrate and reinforce the company's values, business practices, and traditions. The meshing together of stated beliefs, business principles, styles of operating, ingrained behaviors and attitudes, and work climate define a company's **corporate culture.** A company's culture is important because it influences the organization's actions and approaches to conducting business—in a very real sense, the culture is the company's "operating system" or organizational DNA.[1]

> **Core Concept**
> ***Corporate culture*** refers to the character of a company's internal work climate and personality—as shaped by its core values, beliefs, business principles, traditions, ingrained behaviors, work practices, and styles of operating.

The psyche of corporate cultures varies widely. For instance, the bedrock of Wal-Mart's culture is dedication to customer satisfaction, zealous pursuit of low costs and frugal operating practices, a strong work ethic, ritualistic Saturday-morning headquarters meetings to exchange ideas and review problems, and company executives' commitment to visiting stores, listening to customers, and soliciting suggestions from employees. General Electric's culture is founded on a hard-driving, results-oriented atmosphere (where all of the company's business divisions are held to a standard of being number one or two in their industries as well as achieving good business results); extensive cross-business sharing of ideas, best practices, and learning; the reliance on "workout sessions" to identify, debate, and resolve burning issues; a commitment to Six Sigma quality; and globalization of the company. At Occidental Petroleum, the culture is grounded in entrepreneurship on the part of employees; the company's empowered employees are encouraged to be innovative, excel in their fields of specialization, respond quickly to strategic opportunities, and creatively apply state-of-the-art technology in a manner that promotes operating excellence and sets Occidental apart from its competitors. At Nordstrom, the corporate culture is centered on delivering exceptional service to customers; the company's motto is "Respond to unreasonable customer requests"—each out-of-the-ordinary request is seen as an opportunity for a "heroic" act by an employee that can further the company's reputation for a customer-pleasing shopping environment. Nordstrom makes a point of promoting employees noted for their heroic acts and dedication to outstanding service; the company motivates its salespeople with a commission-based compensation system that enables Nordstrom's best salespeople to earn more than double what other department stores pay.

Illustration Capsule 13.1 relates how Google and Alberto-Culver describe their corporate cultures.

Identifying the Key Features of a Company's Corporate Culture

A company's corporate culture is mirrored in the character or "personality" of its work environment—the factors that underlie how the company tries to conduct its business and the behaviors that are held in high esteem. The chief things to look for include the following:

- *The values, business principles, and ethical standards that management preaches and practices.* Actions speak much louder than words here.
- *The company's approach to people management* and the official policies, procedures, and operating practices that paint the white lines for the behavior of company personnel.
- *The spirit and character that pervade the work climate.* Is the workplace vibrant and fun, methodical and all-business, tense and harried, or highly competitive and politicized? Are people excited about their work and emotionally connected to the company's business or are they just there to draw a paycheck? Is there an emphasis on empowered worker creativity or do people have little discretion in how jobs are done?
- *How managers and employees interact and relate to each other.* How much reliance is there on teamwork and open communication? To what extent is there good camaraderie? Are people called by their first names? Do coworkers spend little or lots of time together outside the workplace? What are the dress codes (the accepted styles of attire and whether there are casual days)?
- *The strength of peer pressure to do things in particular ways and conform to expected norms.* What actions and behaviors are approved (and rewarded by management in the form of compensation and promotion) and which ones are frowned on?

Illustration Capsule 13.1

The Corporate Cultures at Google and Alberto-Culver

GOOGLE

Founded in 1998 by Larry Page and Sergey Brin, two Ph.D. students in computer science at Stanford University, Google has beome world-renowned for its search engine technology. Google.com is one of the five most popular sites on the Internet, attracting over 380 million unique visitors monthly from around the world. Google has some unique ways of operating, and its culture is rather quirky. The company describes its culture as follows:

> Though growing rapidly, Google still maintains a small company feel. At the Googleplex headquarters almost everyone eats in the Google café (known as "Charlie's Place"), sitting at whatever table has an opening and enjoying conversations with Googlers from all different departments. Topics range from the trivial to the technical, and whether the discussion is about computer games or encryption or ad serving software, it's not surprising to hear someone say, "That's a product I helped develop before I came to Google."
>
> Google's emphasis on innovation and commitment to cost containment means each employee is a hands-on contributor. There's little in the way of corporate hierarchy and everyone wears several hats. The international webmaster who creates Google's holiday logos spent a week translating the entire site into Korean. The chief operations engineer is also a licensed neurosurgeon. Because everyone realizes they are an equally important part of Google's success, no one hesitates to skate over a corporate officer during roller hockey.
>
> Google's hiring policy is aggressively non-discriminatory and favors ability over experience. The result is a staff that reflects the global audience the search engine serves. Google has offices around the globe and Google engineering centers are recruiting local talent in locations from Zurich to Bangalore. Dozens of languages are spoken by Google staffers, from Turkish to Telugu. When not at work, Googlers pursue interests from cross-country cycling to wine tasting, from flying to Frisbee. As Google expands its development team, it continues to look for those who share an obsessive commitment to creating search perfection and having a great time doing it.

ALBERTO-CULVER

The Alberto-Culver Company, with fiscal 2005 revenues of about $3.5 billion, is the producer and marketer of Alberto VO5, TRESemmé, Consort, and Just for Me hair care products; St. Ives skin care, hair care, and facial care products; and such brands as Molly McButter, Mrs. Dash, Sugar Twin, and Static Guard. Alberto-Culver brands are sold in 120 countries. Its Sally Beauty Company, with over 3,250 stores and 1,250 professional sales consultants, is the largest marketer of professional beauty care products in the world.

At the careers section of its Web site, the company described its culture in the following words:

> Building careers is as important to us as building brands. We believe that passionate people create powerful growth. We believe in a workplace built on values and believe our best people display those same values in their families and their communities. We believe in recognizing and rewarding accomplishment and celebrating our victories.
>
> We believe the best ideas work their way—quickly—up an organization, not down. We believe that we should take advantage of every ounce of your talent on teams and cross-functional activities, not just assign you to a box.
>
> We believe in open communication. We believe that you can improve what you measure, so we survey and spot check all the time. For that same reason, every one has specific goals so that their expectations are in line with their managers' and the company's.
>
> We believe that victory is a team accomplishment. We believe in personal development. We believe if you talk with us you will catch our enthusiasm and want to be a part of the Alberto-Culver team.

Sources: Information posted at www.google.com and www.alberto.com (accessed November 16, 2005).

- *The company's revered traditions and oft-repeated stories.* Do people talk a lot about "heroic acts" and "how we do things around here"?
- *The manner in which the company deals with external stakeholders (particularly vendors and local communities where it has operations).* Does it treat suppliers as business partners or does it prefer

hardnosed, arm's-length business arrangements? How strong and genuine is its commitment to corporate citizenship?

Some of these sociological forces are readily apparent, and others operate quite subtly.

The values, beliefs, and practices that undergird a company's culture can come from anywhere in the organization hierarchy, most often representing the business philosophy and managerial style of influential executives but also resulting from exemplary actions on the part of company personnel and consensus agreement about "how we ought to do things around here."[2] Typically, key elements of the culture originate with a founder or certain strong leaders who articulated them as a set of business principles, company policies, operating approaches, and ways of dealing with employees, customers, vendors, shareholders, and local communities where the company has operations. Over time, these cultural underpinnings take root, become embedded in how the company conducts its business, come to be accepted by company managers and employees alike, and then persist as new employees are encouraged to adopt and follow the professed values, behaviors, and work practices.

The Role of Stories   Frequently, a significant part of a company's culture is captured in the stories that get told over and over again to illustrate to newcomers the importance of certain values and the depth of commitment that various company personnel have displayed. One of the folktales at FedEx, world renowned for the reliability of its next-day package delivery guarantee, is about a deliveryman who had been given the wrong key to a FedEx drop box. Rather than leave the packages in the drop box until the next day when the right key was available, the deliveryman unbolted the drop box from its base, loaded it into the truck, and took it back to the station. There, the box was pried open and the contents removed and sped on their way to their destination the next day. Nordstrom keeps a scrapbook commemorating the heroic acts of its employees and uses it as a regular reminder of the beyond-the-call-of-duty behaviors that employees are encouraged to display. At Frito-Lay, there are dozens of stories about truck drivers who went to extraordinary lengths in overcoming adverse weather conditions in order to make scheduled deliveries to retail customers and keep store shelves stocked with Frito-Lay products. At Microsoft, there are stories of the long hours programmers put in, the emotional peaks and valleys in encountering and overcoming coding problems, the exhilaration of completing a complex program on schedule, the satisfaction of working on cutting-edge projects, the rewards of being part of a team responsible for a popular new software program, and the tradition of competing aggressively. Such stories serve the valuable purpose of illustrating the kinds of behavior the company encourages and reveres. Moreover, each retelling of a legendary story puts a bit more peer pressure on company personnel to display core values and do their part in keeping the company's traditions alive.

Perpetuating the Culture   Once established, company cultures are perpetuated in six important ways: (1) by screening and selecting new employees that will mesh well with the culture, (2) by systematic indoctrination of new members in the culture's fundamentals, (3) by the efforts of senior group members to reiterate core values in daily conversations and pronouncements, (4) by the telling and retelling of company legends, (5) by regular ceremonies honoring members who display desired cultural behaviors, and (6) by visibly rewarding those who display cultural norms and penalizing those who don't.[3] *The more new employees a company is hiring, the more important it becomes to screen job applicants every bit as much for how well their values, beliefs, and personalities match up with the culture as for their technical skills and experience.*

For example, a company that stresses operating with integrity and fairness has to hire people who themselves have integrity and place a high value on fair play. A company whose culture revolves around creativity, product innovation, and leading change has to screen new hires for their ability to think outside the box, generate new ideas, and thrive in a climate of rapid change and ambiguity. Southwest Airlines—whose two core values, "LUV" and fun, permeate the work environment and whose objective is to ensure that passengers have a positive and enjoyable flying experience—goes to considerable lengths to hire flight attendants and gate personnel who are witty, cheery, and outgoing and who display whistle-while-you-work attitudes. Fast-growing companies risk creating a culture by chance rather than by design if they rush to hire employees mainly for their talents and credentials and neglect to screen out candidates whose values, philosophies, and personalities aren't a good fit with the organizational character, vision, and strategy being articulated by the company's senior executives.

As a rule, companies are attentive to the task of hiring people who will fit in and who will embrace the prevailing culture. And, usually, job seekers lean toward accepting jobs at companies where they feel comfortable with the atmosphere and the people they will be working with. Employees who don't hit it off at a company tend to leave quickly, while employees who thrive and are pleased with the work environment stay on, eventually moving up the ranks to positions of greater responsibility. The longer people stay at an organization, the more they come to embrace and mirror the corporate culture—their values and beliefs tend to be molded by mentors, fellow workers, company training programs, and the reward structure. Normally, employees who have worked at a company for a long time play a major role in indoctrinating new employees into the culture.

Forces That Cause a Company's Culture to Evolve   However, even stable cultures aren't static; just like strategy and organization structure, they evolve. New challenges in the marketplace, revolutionary technologies, and shifting internal conditions—especially eroding business prospects, an internal crisis, or top executive turnover—tend to breed new ways of doing things and, in turn, cultural evolution. An incoming CEO who decides to shake up the existing business and take it in new directions often triggers a cultural shift, perhaps one of major proportions. Likewise, diversification into new businesses, expansion into foreign countries, rapid growth, an influx of new employees, and merger with or acquisition of another company can all precipitate cultural changes of one kind or another.

Company Subcultures: The Problems Posed by New Acquisitions and Multinational Operations   Although it is common to speak about corporate culture in the singular, it is not uncommon for companies to have multiple cultures (or subcultures).[4] Values, beliefs, and practices within a company sometimes vary significantly by department, geographic location, division, or business unit. A company's subcultures can clash, or at least not mesh well, if they embrace conflicting business philosophies or operating approaches, if key executives employ different approaches to people management, or if important differences between a company's culture and those of recently acquired companies have not yet been ironed out. *Global and multinational companies tend to be at least partly multicultural* because cross-country organization units have different operating histories and work climates, as well as members who have grown up under different social customs and traditions and who have different sets of values and beliefs. The human resources manager of a global pharmaceutical company who took on an assignment in the Far East discovered, to his surprise, that one of his biggest challenges was to persuade his company's managers in China,

Korea, Malaysia, and Taiwan to accept promotions—their cultural values were such that they did not believe in competing with their peers for career rewards or personal gain, nor did they relish breaking ties to their local communities to assume cross-national responsibilities.[5] Many companies that have merged with or acquired foreign companies have to deal with language- and custom-based cultural differences.

Nonetheless, the existence of subcultures does not preclude important areas of commonality and compatibility. For example, General Electric's cultural traits of boundarylessness, workout, and Six Sigma quality can be implanted and practiced successfully in different countries. AES, a global power company with operations in over 25 countries, has found that the four core values of integrity, fairness, fun, and social responsibility underlying its culture are readily embraced by people in most countries. Moreover, AES tries to define and practice its cultural values the same way in all of its locations while still being sensitive to differences that exist among various people groups across the world; top managers at AES express the views that people across the world are more similar than different and that the company's culture is as meaningful in Buenos Aires or Kazakhstan as in Virginia.

In today's globalizing world, multinational companies are learning how to make strategy-critical cultural traits travel across country boundaries and create a workably uniform culture worldwide. Likewise, company managements are quite alert to the importance of cultural compatibility in making acquisitions and the need to address how to merge and integrate the cultures of newly acquired companies—cultural due diligence is often as important as financial due diligence in deciding whether to go forward on an acquisition or merger. On a number of occasions, companies have decided to pass on acquiring particular companies because of culture conflicts that they believed would be hard to resolve.

Strong versus Weak Cultures

Company cultures vary widely in strength and influence. Some are strongly embedded and have a big impact on a company's practices and behavioral norms. Others are weak and have comparatively little influence on company operations.

Strong-Culture Companies   The hallmark of a strong-culture company is the dominating presence of certain deeply rooted values and operating approaches that "regulate" the conduct of a company's business and the climate of its workplace.[6] Strong cultures emerge over a period of years (sometimes decades) and are never an overnight phenomenon. In strong culture companies, senior managers make a point of reiterating these principles and values to organization members and explaining how they relate to its business environment. But, more important, they make a conscious effort to display these principles in their own actions and behavior—they walk the talk, and they *insist that company values and business principles be reflected in the decisions and actions taken by all company personnel.* An unequivocal expectation that company personnel will act and behave in accordance with the adopted values and ways of doing business leads to two important outcomes: (1) Over time, the values come to be widely shared by rank-and-file employees—people who dislike the culture tend to leave—and (2) individuals encounter strong peer pressure from coworkers to observe the culturally approved norms and behaviors. Hence, a strongly implanted corporate culture ends up having a powerful influence on "how we

> **Core Concept**
>
> In a strong-culture company, culturally-approved behaviors and ways of doing things are nurtured while culturally-disapproved behaviors and work practices get squashed.

do things around here" because so many company personnel are accepting of cultural traditions and because this acceptance is reinforced both by management expectations and coworker peer pressure to conform to cultural norms. Since cultural traditions and norms have such a dominating influence in strong-culture companies, the character of the culture becomes the the company's soul or psyche.

Three factors contribute to the development of strong cultures: (1) a founder or strong leader who establishes values, principles, and practices that are consistent and sensible in light of customer needs, competitive conditions, and strategic requirements; (2) a sincere, long-standing company commitment to operating the business according to these established traditions, thereby creating an internal environment that supports decision making and strategies based on cultural norms; and (3) a genuine concern for the well-being of the organization's three biggest constituencies—customers, employees, and shareholders. Continuity of leadership, small group size, stable group membership, geographic concentration, and considerable organizational success all contribute to the emergence and sustainability of a strong culture.[7]

During the time a strong culture is being implanted, there's nearly always a good strategy–culture fit (which partially accounts for the organization's success). Mismatches between strategy and culture in a strong-culture company tend to occur when a company's business environment undergoes significant change, prompting a drastic strategy revision that clashes with the entrenched culture. A strategy–culture clash can also occur in a strong-culture company whose business has gradually eroded; when a new leader is brought in to revitalize the company's operations, he or she may push the company in a strategic direction that requires substantially different cultural and behavioral norms. In such cases, a major culture-changing effort has to be launched.

In strong-culture companies, values and behavioral norms are so ingrained that they can endure leadership changes at the top—although their strength can erode over time if new CEOs cease to nurture them or move aggressively to institute cultural adjustments. And the cultural norms in a strong-culture company may not change much as strategy evolves and the organization acts to make strategy adjustments, either because the new strategies are compatible with the present culture or because the dominant traits of the culture are somewhat strategy-neutral and compatible with evolving versions of the company's strategy.

> In a strong-culture company, values and behavioral norms are like crabgrass: deeply rooted and hard to weed out.

Weak-Culture Companies   In direct contrast to strong-culture companies, weak-culture companies lack values and principles that are consistently preached or widely shared (usually because the company has had a series of CEOs with differing values and differing views about how the company's business ought to be conducted). As a consequence, the company has few widely revered traditions and few culture-induced norms are evident in operating practices. Because top executives at a weak-culture company don't repeatedly espouse any particular business philosophy, exhibit long-standing commitment to particular values, or extol particular operating practices and behavioral norms, individuals encounter little coworker peer pressure to do things in particular ways. Moreover, a weak company culture breeds no strong employee allegiance to what the company stands for or to operating the business in well-defined ways. While individual employees may well have some bonds of identification with and loyalty toward their department, their colleagues, their union, or their boss, there is neither passion about the company nor emotional commitment to what it is trying to accomplish—a condition that often results in many employees viewing their company as just a place to work and their job as just a way to make a living. Very often, cultural weakness stems from moderately entrenched subcultures that block the emergence of a well-defined companywide work climate.

As a consequence, *weak cultures provide little or no assistance in executing strategy* because there are no traditions, beliefs, values, common bonds, or behavioral norms that management can use as levers to mobilize commitment to executing the chosen strategy. The only plus of a weak culture is that it does not usually pose a strong barrier to strategy execution, but the negative of not providing any support means that culture-building has to be high on management's action agenda. Absent a work climate that channels organizational energy in the direction of good strategy execution, managers are left with the options of either using compensation incentives and other motivational devices to mobilize employee commitment or trying to establish cultural roots that will in time start to nurture the strategy execution process.

Unhealthy Cultures

The distinctive characteristic of an unhealthy corporate culture is the presence of counterproductive cultural traits that adversely impact the work climate and company performance.[8] The following four traits are particularly unhealthy:

1. A highly politicized internal environment in which many issues get resolved and decisions made on the basis of which individuals or groups have the most political clout to carry the day.
2. Hostility to change and a general wariness of people who champion new ways of doing things.
3. An insular "not-invented-here" mind-set that makes company personnel averse to looking outside the company for best practices, new managerial approaches, and innovative ideas.
4. A disregard for high ethical standards and overzealous pursuit of wealth and status on the part of key executives.

Politicized Cultures   What makes a politicized internal environment so unhealthy is that political infighting consumes a great deal of organizational energy, often with the result that what's best for the company takes a backseat to political maneuvering. In companies where internal politics pervades the work climate, empire-building managers jealously guard their decision-making prerogatives. They have their own agendas and operate the work units under their supervision as autonomous "fiefdoms," and the positions they take on issues is usually aimed at protecting or expanding their turf. Collaboration with other organizational units is viewed with suspicion (What are "they" up to? How can "we" protect "our" flanks?), and cross-unit cooperation occurs grudgingly. When an important proposal moves to the front burner, advocates try to ram it through and opponents try to alter it in significant ways or else kill it altogether. The support or opposition of politically influential executives and/or coalitions among departments with vested interests in a particular outcome typically weigh heavily in deciding what actions the company takes. All this maneuvering takes away from efforts to execute strategy with real proficiency and frustrates company personnel who are less political and more inclined to do what is in the company's best interests.

Change-Resistant Cultures   In less-adaptive cultures where skepticism about the importance of new developments and resistance to change are the norm, managers prefer waiting until the fog of uncertainty clears before steering a new course, making fundamental adjustments to their product line, or embracing a major new technology. They believe in moving cautiously and conservatively, preferring to follow others rather than taking decisive action to be in the forefront of change. Change-resistant cultures place a premium on not making mistakes, prompting managers to lean toward safe, don't-rock-the-boat options that will have only a ripple effect on the status quo, protect or advance their own careers, and guard the interests of their immediate work groups.

Change-resistant cultures encourage a number of undesirable or unhealthy behaviors—avoiding risks, not making bold proposals to pursue emerging opportunities, a lax approach to both product innovation and continuous improvement in performing value chain activities, and following rather than leading market change. In change-resistant cultures, word quickly gets around that proposals to do things differently face an uphill battle and that people who champion them may be seen as either something of a nuisance or a troublemaker. Executives who don't value managers or employees with initiative and new ideas put a damper on product innovation, experimentation, and efforts to improve. At the same time, change-resistant companies have little appetite for being first-movers or fast-followers, believing that being in the forefront of change is too risky and that acting too quickly increases vulnerability to costly mistakes. They are more inclined to adopt a wait-and-see posture, carefully analyze several alternative responses, learn from the missteps of early movers, and then move forward cautiously and conservatively with initiatives that are deemed safe. Hostility to change is most often found in companies with multilayered management bureaucracies that have enjoyed considerable market success in years past and that are wedded to the "We have done it this way for years" syndrome.

When such companies encounter business environments with accelerating change, going slow on altering traditional ways of doing things can be become a liability rather than an asset. General Motors, IBM, Sears, and Eastman Kodak are classic examples of companies whose change-resistant bureaucracies were slow to respond to fundamental changes in their markets; clinging to the cultures and traditions that made them successful, they were reluctant to alter operating practices and modify their business approaches. As strategies of gradual change won out over bold innovation and being an early mover, all four lost market share to rivals that quickly moved to institute changes more in tune with evolving market conditions and buyer preferences. These companies are now struggling to recoup lost ground with cultures and behaviors more suited to market success—the kinds of fit that caused them to succeed in the first place.

Insular, Inwardly Focused Cultures   Sometimes a company reigns as an industry leader or enjoys great market success for so long that its personnel start to believe they have all the answers or can develop them on their own. There is a strong tendency to neglect what customers are saying and how their needs and expectations are changing. Such confidence in the correctness of how it does things and in the company's skills and capabilities breeds arrogance—company personnel discount the merits of what outsiders are doing and what can be learned by studying best-in-class performers. Benchmarking and a search for the best practices of outsiders are seen as offering little payoff. Any market share gains on the part of up-and-coming rivals are regarded as temporary setbacks, soon to be reversed by the company's own forthcoming initiatives (which, it is confidently predicted, will be an instant market hit with customers).

Insular thinking, internally driven solutions, and a must-be-invented-here mindset come to permeate the corporate culture. An inwardly focused corporate culture gives rise to managerial inbreeding and a failure to recruit people who can offer fresh thinking and outside perspectives. The big risk of insular cultural thinking is that the company can underestimate the competencies and accomplishments of rival companies and overestimate its own progress—with a resulting loss of competitive advantage over time.

Unethical and Greed-Driven Cultures   Companies that have little regard for ethical standards or that are run by executives driven by greed and ego gratification are scandals waiting to happen. Enron's collapse in 2001 was largely the product of an ethically dysfunctional corporate culture—while the culture embraced the positives of product innovation, aggressive risk taking, and a driving ambition to lead global change in the energy business, its executives exuded the negatives of arrogance, ego, greed, and an ends-justify-the-means mentality in pursuing stretched revenue and profitability targets.[9] A number of Enron's senior managers were all too willing to wink at unethical behavior, to cross over the line to unethical (and sometimes criminal) behavior themselves, and to deliberately stretch generally accepted accounting principles to make Enron's financial performance look far better than it really was. In the end, Enron came unglued because a few top executives chose unethical and illegal paths to pursue corporate revenue and profitability targets—in a company that publicly preached integrity and other notable corporate values but was lax in making sure that key executives walked the talk. Unethical cultures and executive greed have also produced scandals at WorldCom, Qwest, HealthSouth, Adelphia, Tyco, McWane, Parmalat, Rite Aid, Hollinger International, Refco, and Marsh & McLennan, with executives being indicted and/or convicted of criminal behavior. The U.S. Attorney's office elected not to prosecute the accounting firm KPMG with "systematic" criminal acts to market illegal tax shelters to wealthy clients (which KPMG tried mightily to cover up) because a criminal indictment would have resulted in the immediate collapse of KPMG and cut the number of global public accounting firms from four to just three; instead, criminal charges were filed against the company officials deemed most responsible. In 2005, U.S. prosecutors elected not to press criminal charges against Royal Dutch Petroleum (Shell Oil) for repeatedly and knowingly reporting inflated oil reserves to the U.S. Securities and Exchange Commission and not to indict Tommy Hilfiger USA for multiple tax law violations—but both companies agreed to sign nonprosecution agreements, the terms of which were not made public but which almost certainly involved fines and a long-term company commitment to cease and desist.

High-Performance Cultures

Some companies have high-performance cultures, in which the standout cultural traits are a can-do spirit, pride in doing things right, no-excuses accountability, and a pervasive results-oriented work climate in which people go the extra mile to meet or beat stretch objectives. In high-performance cultures, there is a strong sense of involvement on the part of company personnel and emphasis on individual initiative and creativity. Performance expectations are clearly delineated for the company as a whole, for each organizational unit, and for each individual. Issues and problems are promptly addressed—a strong bias exists for being proactive instead of reactive. There is a razor-sharp focus on what needs to be done. The clear and unyielding expectation is that all company personnel, from senior executives to frontline employees will display high-performance behaviors and a passion for making the company successful. There is respect for the contributions of individuals and groups.

A high-performance culture is a valuable contributor to good strategy execution and operating excellence. High performance, results-oriented cultures are permeated with a spirit of achievement and have a good track record in meeting or beating performance targets.

The challenge in creating a high-performance culture is to inspire high loyalty and dedication on the part of employees, such that they are both energized and preoccupied with putting forth their very best efforts to do things right and be unusually productive. Managers have to reinforce constructive behavior, reward top performers, and purge habits and behaviors that stand in the way of high productivity and good results. They must work at knowing the strengths and weaknesses of their subordinates, so as to better match talent with task and enable people to make meaningful contributions by doing what they do best.[10] They have to stress correcting and learning from mistakes, and they must put an unrelenting emphasis on moving forward and making good progress—in effect, there has to be a disciplined, performance-focused approach to managing the organization.

Adaptive Cultures

The hallmark of adaptive corporate cultures is willingness on the part of organizational members to accept change and take on the challenge of introducing and executing new strategies.[11] Company personnel share a feeling of confidence that the organization can deal with whatever threats and opportunities come down the pike; they are receptive to risk taking, experimentation, and innovation. In direct contrast to change-resistant cultures, adaptive cultures are very supportive of managers and employees at all ranks who propose or help initiate useful change. Internal entrepreneurship on the part of individuals and groups is encouraged and rewarded. Senior executives seek out, support, and promote individuals who exercise initiative, spot opportunities for improvement, and display the skills to implement them. Managers openly evaluate ideas and suggestions, fund initiatives to develop new or better products, and take prudent risks to pursue emerging market opportunities. As in high-performance cultures, the adaptive company exhibits a proactive approach to identifying issues, evaluating the implications and options, and quickly moving ahead with workable solutions. Strategies and traditional operating practices are modified as needed to adjust to or take advantage of changes in the business environment.

> **Core Concept**
> In adaptive cultures, there is a spirit of doing what's necessary to ensure long-term organizational success provided the new behaviors and operating practices that management is calling for are seen as legitimate and consistent with the core values and business principles underpinning the culture.

But why is change so willingly embraced in an adaptive culture? Why are organization members not fearful of how change will affect them? Why does an adaptive culture not become unglued with ongoing changes in strategy, operating practices, and behavioral norms? The answers lie in two distinctive and dominant traits of an adaptive culture: (1) Any changes in operating practices and behaviors must *not* compromise core values and long-standing business principles, and (2) the changes that are instituted must satisfy the legitimate interests of stakeholders—customers, employees, shareowners, suppliers, and the communities in which the company operates.[12] In other words, what sustains an adaptive culture is that organization members perceive the changes that management is trying to institute as legitimate and in keeping with the core values and business principles that form the heart and soul of the culture.

Thus, for an adaptive culture to remain intact over time, top management must orchestrate organizational changes in a manner that (1) demonstrates genuine care for the well-being of all key constituencies and (2) tries to satisfy all their legitimate interests simultaneously. Unless fairness to all constituencies is a decision-making principle and a commitment to doing the right thing is evident to organization members, the changes are not likely to be seen as legitimate and thus be readily accepted and implemented wholeheartedly.[13] Making changes that will please customers and that protect, if not enhance, the company's long-term well-being are generally seen as legitimate and are often seen as the best way of looking out for the interests of employees, stockholders, suppliers, and communities where the company operates. At companies with adaptive cultures, management concern for the well-being of employees is nearly always a big factor in gaining employee support for change—company personnel are usually receptive to change as long as employees understand that changes in their job assignments are part of the process of adapting to new conditions and that their employment security will not be threatened unless the company's business unexpectedly reverses direction. In cases where workforce downsizing becomes necessary, management concern for employees dictates that separation be handled humanely, making employee departure as painless as possible. Management efforts to make the process of adapting to change fair and equitable for customers, employees, stockholders, suppliers, and communities where the company operates, keeping adverse impacts to a minimum insofar as possible, breeds acceptance of and support for change among all organization stakeholders.

> Adaptive cultures are exceptionally well suited to companies with fast-changing strategies and market environments.

Technology companies, software companies, and today's dot-com companies are good illustrations of organizations with adaptive cultures. Such companies thrive on change—driving it, leading it, and capitalizing on it (but sometimes also succumbing to change when they make the wrong move or are swamped by better technologies or the superior business models of rivals). Companies like Google, Intel, Cisco Systems, eBay, Nokia, Amazon.com, and Dell cultivate the capability to act and react rapidly. They are avid practitioners of entrepreneurship and innovation, with a demonstrated willingness to take bold risks to create altogether new products, new businesses, and new industries. To create and nurture a culture that can adapt rapidly to changing to shifting business conditions, they make a point of staffing their organizations with people who are proactive, who rise to the challenge of change, and who have an aptitude for adapting.

In fast-changing business environments, a corporate culture that is receptive to altering organizational practices and behaviors is a virtual necessity. However, adaptive cultures work to the advantage of all companies, not just those in rapid-change environments. Every company operates in a market and business climate that is changing to one degree or another and that, in turn, requires internal operating responses and new behaviors on the part of organization members. *As a company's strategy evolves, an adaptive culture is a definite ally in the strategy-implementing, strategy-executing process as compared to cultures that have to be coaxed and cajoled to change.*

Culture: Ally or Obstacle to Strategy Execution?

A company's present culture and work climate may or may not be compatible with what is needed for effective implementation and execution of the chosen strategy. *When a company's present work climate promotes attitudes and behaviors that are well suited to first-rate strategy execution, its culture functions as a valuable ally in the strategy execution process.* When the culture is in conflict with some aspect of the company's direction, performance targets, or strategy, the culture becomes a stumbling block.[14]

How a Company's Culture Can Promote Better Strategy Execution   A culture grounded in strategy-supportive values, practices, and behavioral norms adds significantly to the power and effectiveness of a company's strategy execution effort.

For example, a culture where frugality and thrift are values widely shared by organizational members nurtures employee actions to identify cost-saving opportunities—the very behavior needed for successful execution of a low-cost leadership strategy. A culture built around such business principles as pleasing customers, fair treatment, operating excellence, and employee empowerment promotes employee behaviors and an esprit de corps that facilitate execution of strategies keyed to high product quality and superior customer service. A culture in which taking initiative, challenging the status quo, exhibiting creativity, embracing change, and collaborating with team members pervade the work climate promotes a company's drive to lead market change—outcomes that are conducive to successful execution of product innovation and technological leadership strategies.[15] Good alignment between ingrained cultural norms and the behaviors needed for good strategy execution makes the culture a valuable ally in the strategy-execution process. In a company where strategy and culture are misaligned, some of the very behaviors needed to execute strategy successfully run contrary to the behaviors and values imbedded in the prevailing culture. Such a clash nearly always produces a roadblock from employees whose actions and behaviors are strongly linked to the present culture. Culture-bred resistance to the actions and behaviors needed for good execution, if strong and widespread, poses a formidable hurdle that has to be cleared for strategy execution to get very far.

> **Core Concept**
> The tighter the culture–strategy fit, the more that the culture steers company personnel into displaying behaviors and adopting operating practices that promote good strategy execution.

A tight culture–strategy matchup furthers a company's strategy execution effort in three ways:[16]

1. *A culture that encourages actions, behaviors, and work practices supportive of good strategy execution not only provides company personnel with clear guidance regarding "how we do things around here" but also produces significant peer pressure from coworkers to conform to culturally acceptable norms.* The stronger the admonishments from top executives about "how we need to do things around here" and the stronger the peer pressure from coworkers, the more the culture influences people to display behaviors and observe operating practices that support good strategy execution.

2. *A deeply embedded culture tightly matched to the strategy aids the cause of competent strategy execution by steering company personnel to culturally approved behaviors and work practices and thus makes it far simpler to root out any operating practice that is a misfit.* This is why it is very much in management's best interests to build and nurture a deeply rooted culture where ingrained behaviors and operating practices marshal organizational energy behind the drive for good strategy execution.

3. *A culture imbedded with values and behaviors that facilitate strategy execution promotes strong employee identification with and commitment to the company's vision, performance targets, and strategy.* When a company's culture is grounded in many of the needed strategy-executing behaviors, employees feel genuinely better about their jobs, the company they work for, and the merits of what the company is trying to accomplish. As a consequence, greater numbers of company personnel exhibit some passion about their work and exert their best efforts to execute the strategy and achieve performance targets. All this helps move the company closer to realizing its strategic vision and, from employees' standpoint, makes the company a more engaging place to work.

These aspects of culture–strategy alignment say something important about the task of managing the strategy executing process: *Closely aligning corporate culture with the requirements for proficient strategy execution merits the full attention of senior*

Core Concept
It is in management's best interest to dedicate considerable effort to embedding a corporate culture that encourages behaviors and work practices conducive to good strategy execution—a tight strategy–culture fit automatically nurtures culturally-approved behaviors and squashes culturally disapproved behaviors.

executives. The culture-building objective is to create a work climate and style of operating that mobilize the energy and behavior of company personnel squarely behind efforts to execute strategy competently. The more deeply that management can embed strategy-supportive ways of doing things, the more that management can rely on the culture to automatically steer company personnel toward behaviors and work practices that aid good strategy execution and away from ways of doing things that impede it.

Furthermore, culturally astute managers understand that nourishing the right cultural environment not only adds power to their push for proficient strategy execution but also promotes strong employee identification with and commitment to the company's vision, performance targets, and strategy. A culture–strategy fit prompts employees with emotional allegiance to the culture to feel genuinely better about their jobs, the company they work for, and the merits of what the company is trying to accomplish. As a consequence, their morale is higher and their productivity is higher. In addition, greater numbers of company personnel exhibit passion for their work and exert their best efforts to make the strategy succeed and achieve performance targets. All this helps move the company closer to realizing its strategic vision and, from the employees' standpoint, makes the company a more engaging place to work.

The Perils of Strategy–Culture Conflict   Conflicts between behaviors approved by the culture and behaviors needed for good strategy execution pose a real dilemma for company personnel. Should they be loyal to the culture and company traditions (to which they are likely to be emotionally attached) and thus resist or be indifferent to actions and behaviors that will promote better strategy execution—a choice that will certainly weaken the drive for good strategy execution? Or should they go along with the strategy execution effort and engage in actions and behaviors that run counter to the culture—a choice that will likely impair morale and lead to less-than-wholehearted commitment to management's strategy execution efforts? Neither choice leads to desirable outcomes, and the solution is obvious: eliminate the conflict.

When a company's culture is out of sync with the actions and behaviors needed to execute the strategy successfully, the culture has to be changed as rapidly as can be managed—this, of course, presumes that it is one or more aspects of the culture that are out of whack rather than the strategy executions approaches management wishes to institute. While correcting a strategy–culture conflict can occasionally mean revamping a company's approach to executing the strategy to produce good cultural fit, more usually it means altering aspects of the mismatched culture to ingrain new behaviors and work practices that will enable first-rate strategy execution. The more entrenched the mismatched aspects of the culture, the greater the difficulty of implementing and executing new or different strategies until better strategy–culture alignment emerges. A sizable and prolonged strategy–culture conflict weakens and may even defeat managerial efforts to make the strategy work.

Changing a Problem Culture

Once a culture is established, it is difficult to change.

Changing a company culture that impedes proficient strategy execution is among the toughest management tasks because of the heavy anchor of ingrained behaviors and ways of doing things. It is natural for company personnel to cling to familiar practices and to be wary, if not hostile, to new approaches of how things are to be done. Consequently, it takes concerted management action over a period of time to root out certain unwanted behaviors and replace an out-of-sync culture with different behaviors and ways of doing things deemed more conducive to executing the strategy. *The single most visible factor that distinguishes successful culture-change efforts from failed attempts is competent leadership at the top.* Great power is needed to force major cultural change and overcome the springback resistance of entrenched cultures—and great power is possessed only by the most senior executives, especially the CEO. However, while top management must be out front leading the effort, marshaling support for a new culture and, more important, instilling new cultural behaviors are tasks for the whole management team. Middle managers and frontline supervisors play a key role in implementing the new work practices and operating approaches, helping win rank-and-file acceptance of and support for the changes, and instilling the desired behavioral norms.

As shown in Figure 13.1, the first step in fixing a problem culture is for top management to identify those facets of the present culture that are dysfunctional and pose obstacles to executing new strategic initiatives and meeting or beating company performance targets. Second, managers have to clearly define the desired new behaviors and features of the culture they want to create. Third, managers have to convince company personnel why the present culture poses problems and why and how new behaviors and operating approaches will improve company performance—the case for cultural change and the benefits of a reformed culture have to be persuasive. Finally, and most important, all the talk about remodeling the present culture has to be followed swiftly by visible, forceful actions to promote the desired new behaviors and work practices—actions that company personnel will interpret as a determined top management commitment to alter the culture and instill a different work climate and different ways of operating.

Making a Compelling Case for Culture Change   The place for management to begin a major remodeling of the corporate culture is by selling company personnel on

Figure 13.1   **Changing a Problem Culture**

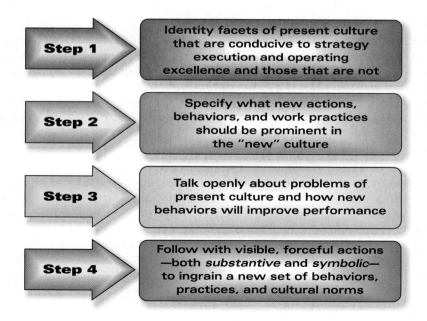

the need for new-style behaviors and work practices. This means making a compelling case for why the company's new strategic direction and culture-remodeling efforts are in the organization's best interests and why company personnel should wholeheartedly join the effort to doing things somewhat differently. Skeptics and opinion leaders have to be convinced that all is not well with the status quo. This can be done by:

- Citing reasons why the current strategy has to be modified and why new strategic initiatives that are being undertaken will bolster the company's competitiveness and performance. The case for altering the old strategy usually needs to be predicated on its shortcomings—why sales are growing slowly, why rivals are doing so much better, why too many customers are opting to go with the products of rivals, why costs are too high, why the company's price has to be lowered, and so on. There may be merit in holding events where managers and other key personnel are forced to listen to dissatisfied customers, the complaints of strategic allies, alienated employees, or disenchanted stockholders
- Citing why and how certain behavioral norms and work practices in the current culture pose obstacles to good execution of new strategic initiatives.
- Explaining how certain new behaviors and work practices that are to be introduced and have important roles in the new culture will be more advantageous and produce better results.

It is essential for the CEO and other top executives to personally talk to company personnel all across the company about the reasons for modifying work practices and culture-related behaviors. Senior officers and department heads have to play the lead role in explaining the behaviors, practices, and operating approaches that are to be introduced and why they are beneficial—and the explanations will likely have to be repeated many times. For the culture-change effort to be successful, frontline supervisors and employee opinion leaders must be won over to the cause, which means convincing them of the merits of *practicing* and *enforcing* cultural norms at the lowest levels in the organization. Until a big majority of employees accept the need for a new culture and agree that different work practices and behaviors are called for, there's more work to be done in selling company personnel on the whys and wherefores of culture change. Building widespread organizational support requires taking every opportunity to repeat the messages of why the new work practices, operating approaches, and behaviors are good for company stakeholders (particularly customers, employees, and shareholders). Effective culture-change leaders are good at telling stories to describe the new values and desired behaviors and connect them to everyday practices.

Management's efforts to make a persuasive case for changing what is deemed to be a problem culture must be *quickly followed* by forceful, high-profile actions across several fronts. The actions to implant the new culture must be both substantive and symbolic.

Substantive Culture-Changing Actions   No culture change effort can get very far with just talk about the need for different actions, behaviors, and work practices. Company executives have to give the culture-change effort some teeth by initiating *a series of actions* that company personnel will see as credible and unmistakably indicative of the seriousness of management's commitment to new strategic initiatives and the associated cultural changes. The strongest signs that management is truly committed to instilling a new culture include:

1. Replacing key executives who are strongly associated with the old culture and are stonewalling needed organizational and cultural changes.

2. Promoting individuals who are known to possess the desired cultural traits, who have stepped forward to advocate the shift to a different culture, and who can serve as role models for the desired cultural behavior.

3. Appointing outsiders with the desired cultural attributes to high-profile positions—bringing in new-breed managers to serve as role models and help drive the culture-change movement sends an unmistakable message that a new era is dawning and acts to reinforce company personnel who have already gotten on board the culture-change effort.

4. Screening all candidates for new positions carefully, hiring only those who appear to fit in with the new culture—this helps build a critical mass of people to help turn the tide in favor of the new culture.

5. Mandating that all company personnel attend culture-training programs to learn more about the new work practices and operating approaches and to better understand the cultured-related actions and behaviors that are expected.

6. Pushing hard to implement new-style work practices and operating procedures.

7. Designing compensation incentives that boost the pay of teams and individuals who display the desired cultural behaviors and hit change resisters in the pocketbook—company personnel are much more inclined to exhibit the desired kinds of actions and behaviors when it is in their financial best interest to do so.

8. Granting generous pay raises to individuals who step out front, lead the adoption of the desired work practices, display the new-style behaviors, and achieve pace-setting results.

9. Revising policies and procedures in ways that will help drive cultural change.

Executives must take care to launch enough companywide culture-change actions at the outset to leave no room for doubt that management is dead serious about changing the present culture and that a cultural transformation is inevitable. To convince doubters and skeptics that they cannot just wait in hopes the culture-change initiative will soon die out, the series of actions initiated by top management must create lots of hallway talk across the whole company, get the change process off to a fast start, and be followed by unrelenting efforts to firmly establish the new work practices and style of operating as standard.

Symbolic Culture-Changing Actions   Symbolic managerial actions are necessary to alter a problem culture and tighten the strategy–culture fit. The most important symbolic actions are those that top executives take to *lead by example.* For instance, if the organization's strategy involves a drive to become the industry's low-cost producer, senior managers must display frugality in their own actions and decisions: inexpensive decorations in the executive suite, conservative expense accounts and entertainment allowances, a lean staff in the corporate office, scrutiny of budget requests, few executive perks, and so on. At Wal-Mart, all the executive offices are simply decorated; executives are habitually frugal in their own actions, and they are zealous in their own efforts to control costs and promote greater efficiency. At Nucor, one of the world's low-cost producers of steel products, executives fly coach class and use taxis at airports rather than limousines. If the culture change imperative is to be more responsive to customers' needs and to pleasing customers, the CEO can instill greater customer awareness by requiring all officers and executives to spend a significant portion of each week talking with customers about their needs. Top executives must be alert to the fact that company personnel will be watching their actions and decisions to see if they are walking the talk. Hence, they need to make sure that their current decisions will be construed as consistent with new-culture values and behaviors.[17]

Another category of symbolic actions includes holding ceremonial events to single out and honor people whose actions and performance exemplify what is called for in the new culture. A point is made of holding events to celebrate each culture-change success (and any other outcome that management would like to see happen again). Executives sensitive to their role in promoting strategy–culture fits make a habit of appearing at ceremonial functions to praise individuals and groups that get with the program. They show up at employee training programs to stress strategic priorities, values, ethical principles, and cultural norms. Every group gathering is seen as an opportunity to repeat and ingrain values, praise good deeds, expound on the merits of the new culture, and cite instances of how the new work practices and operating approaches have worked to good advantage.

The use of symbols in culture building is widespread. Many universities give outstanding teacher awards each year to symbolize their commitment to good teaching and their esteem for instructors who display exceptional classroom talents. Numerous businesses have employee-of-the-month awards. The military has a long-standing custom of awarding ribbons and medals for exemplary actions. Mary Kay Cosmetics awards an array of prizes—from ribbons to pink automobiles—to its beauty consultants for reaching various sales plateaus.

How Long Does It Take to Change a Problem Culture?   Planting and growing the seeds of a new culture require a determined effort by the chief executive and other senior managers. Neither charisma nor personal magnetism is essential. But a sustained and persistent effort to reinforce the culture at every opportunity through both word and deed is very definitely required. Changing a problem culture is never a short-term exercise. It takes time for a new culture to emerge and prevail. Overnight transformations simply don't occur. And it takes even longer for a new culture to become deeply embedded The bigger the organization and the greater the cultural shift needed to produce a strategy–culture fit, the longer it takes. In large companies, fixing a problem culture and instilling a new set of attitudes and behaviors can take two to five years. In fact, it is usually tougher to reform an entrenched problematic culture than it is to instill a strategy-supportive culture from scratch in a brand-new organization. Sometimes executives succeed in changing the values and behaviors of small groups of managers and even whole departments or divisions, only to find the changes eroded over time by the actions of the rest of the organization—what is communicated, praised, supported, and penalized by an entrenched majority undermines the new emergent culture and halts its progress. Executives, despite a series of well-intended actions to reform a problem culture, are likely to fail at weeding out embedded cultural traits when widespread employee skepticism about the company's new directions and culture-change effort spawns covert resistance to the cultural behaviors and operating practices advocated by top management. This is why management must take every opportunity to convince employees of the need for culture change and communicate to them how new attitudes, behaviors, and operating practices will benefit the interests of organizational stakeholders.

A company that succeeded in fixing a problem culture is Alberto-Culver— see Illustration Capsule 13.2.

Illustration Capsule 13.2

Changing the Culture in Alberto-Culver's North American Division

In 1993, Carol Bernick—vice chairperson of Alberto-Culver, president of its North American division, and daughter of the company's founders—concluded that her division's existing culture had four problems: Employees dutifully waited for marching orders from their bosses, workers put pleasing their bosses ahead of pleasing customers, some company policies were not family-friendly, and there was too much bureaucracy and paperwork. What was needed, in Bernick's opinion, was a culture in which company employees had a sense of ownership and an urgency to get things done, welcomed innovation, and were willing to taking risks.

Alberto-Culver's management undertook a series of actions to introduce and ingrain the desired cultural attributes:

- In 1993, a new position, called growth development leader (GDL), was created to help orchestrate the task of fixing the culture deep in the ranks (there were 70 GDLs in Alberto-Culver's North American division). GDLs came from all ranks of the company's managerial ladder and were handpicked for such qualities as empathy, communication skills, positive attitude, and ability to let their hair down and have fun. GDLs performed their regular jobs in addition to taking on the GDL roles; it was considered an honor to be chosen. Each GDL mentored about 12 people from both a career and a family standpoint. GDLs met with senior executives weekly, bringing forward people's questions and issues and then, afterward, sharing with their groups the topics and solutions that were discussed. GDLs brought a group member as a guest to each meeting. One meeting each year is devoted to identifying "macros and irritations"— attendees are divided into four subgroups and given 15 minutes to identify the company's four biggest challenges (the macros) and the four most annoying aspects of life at the company (the irritations); the whole group votes on which four deserve the company's attention. Those selected are then addressed, and assignments made for follow-up and results.

- Changing the culture was made an issue across the company, starting in 1995 with a two-hour State of the Company presentation to employees covering where the company was and where it wanted to be. The State of the Company address then became an annual event.

- Management created ways to measure the gains in changing the culture. One involved an annual all-employee survey to assess progress against cultural goals and to get 360-degree feedback—the 2000 survey had 180 questions, including 33 relating to the performance of each respondent's GDL. A bonfire celebration was held in the company parking lot to announce that paperwork would be cut by 30 percent.

- A list of 10 cultural imperatives was formalized in 1998—honesty, ownership, trust, customer orientation, commitment, fun, innovation, risk taking, speed and urgency, and teamwork. These imperatives came to be known internally as HOT CC FIRST.

- Numerous celebrations and awards programs were instituted. Most celebrations are scheduled, but some are spontaneous (an impromptu thank-you party for a good fiscal year). Business Builder Awards (initiated in 1997) are given to individuals and teams that make a significant impact on the company's growth and profitability. The best-scoring GDLs on the annual employee surveys are awarded shares of company stock. The company notes all work anniversaries and personal milestones with "Alberto-appropriate" gifts; appreciative company employees sometimes give thank-you gifts to their GDLs. According to Carol Bernick, "If you want something to grow, pour champagne on it. We've made a huge effort—maybe even an over-the-top effort—to celebrate our successes and, indeed, just about everything we'd like to see happen again."

The culture change effort at Alberto-Culver North America was viewed as a major contributor to improved performance. From 1993 (when the effort first began) to 2001, the division's sales increased from just under $350 million to over $600 million and pretax profits rose from $20 million to almost $50 million. Carol Bernick was elevated to chairman of Alberto-Culver's board of directors in 2004.

Source: Based on information in Carol Lavin Bernick, "When Your Culture Needs a Makeover," Harvard Business Review 79, no. 6 (June 2001), p. 61 and information posted at the company's Web site, www.alberto.com (accessed November 10, 2005).

Grounding the Culture in Core Values and Ethics

The foundation of a company's corporate culture nearly always resides in its dedication to certain core values and the bar it sets for ethical behavior. The culture-shaping significance of core values and ethical behaviors accounts for why so many companies have developed a formal values statement and a code of ethics—see Table 13.1 for representative core values and the ground usually covered in codes of ethics. Many companies today convey their values and codes of ethics to stakeholders and interested parties in their annual reports and on their Web sites. The trend of making stakeholders aware of a company's commitment to core values and ethical business conduct is attributable to three factors: (1) greater management understanding of the role these statements play in culture building, (2) a renewed focus on ethical standards stemming from the numerous corporate scandals that hit the headlines during 2001–2005, and (3) the sizable fraction of consumers and suppliers who prefer doing business with ethical companies.

Core Concept
A company's culture is grounded in and shaped by its core values and the bar it sets for ethical behavior.

At Darden Restaurants—the world's largest casual dining company, which employs more than 150,000 people and serves 300 million meals annually at 1,400 Red Lobster, Olive Garden, Bahama Breeze, Smokey Bones Barbeque & Grill, and Seasons 52 restaurants in North America—the core values are operating with integrity and fairness, caring and respect, being of service, teamwork, excellence, always learning and teaching, and welcoming and celebrating workforce diversity. Top executives at

Table 13.1   **Representative Content of Company Values Statements and Codes of Ethics**

Typical Core Values	Areas Covered by Codes of Ethics
• Satisfying and delighting customers	• Expecting all company personnel to display honesty and integrity in their actions and avoid conflicts of interest
• Dedication to superior customer service, top-notch quality, product innovation, and/or technological leadership	• Mandating full compliance with all laws and regulations, specifically:
• A commitment to excellence and results	—Antitrust laws prohibiting anticompetitive practices, conspiracies to fix prices, or attempts to monopolize
• Exhibiting such qualities as integrity, fairness, trustworthiness, pride of workmanship, Golden Rule behavior, respect for coworkers, and ethical behavior	—Foreign Corrupt Practices Act
• Creativity, exercising initiative, and accepting responsibility	—Securities laws and prohibitions against insider trading
• Teamwork and cooperative attitudes	—Environmental and workplace safety regulations
• Fair treatment of suppliers	—Discrimination and sexual harassment regulations
• Making the company a great place to work	—Political contributions and lobbying activities
• A commitment to having fun and creating a fun work environment	• Prohibiting giving or accepting bribes, kickbacks, or gifts
• Being stewards of shareholders' investments and remaining committed to profits and growth	• Engaging in fair selling and marketing practices
• Exercising social responsibility and being a good community citizen	• Not dealing with suppliers that employ child labor or engage in other unsavory practices
• Caring about protecting the environment	• Being above-board in acquiring and using competitively sensitive information about rivals and others
• Having a diverse workforce	• Avoiding use of company assets, resources, and property for personal or other inappropriate purposes
	• Responsibility to protect proprietary information and not divulge trade secrets

Darden believe the company's practice of these values has been instrumental in creating a culture characterized by trust, exciting jobs and career opportunities for employees, and a passion to provide "a terrific dining experience to every guest, every time, in every one of our restaurants."[18]

Of course, sometimes a company's stated core values and codes of ethics are cosmetic, existing mainly to impress outsiders and help create a positive company image. But more usually they have been developed to shape the culture. Many executives want the work climate at their companies to mirror certain values and ethical standards, partly because they are personally committed to these values and ethical standards but mainly because they are convinced that adherence to such values and ethical principles will make the company a much better performer *and* improve its image. As discussed earlier, values-related cultural norms promote better strategy execution and mobilize company personnel behind the drive to achieve stretch objectives and the company's strategic vision. Hence, a corporate culture grounded in well-chosen core values and high ethical standards contributes mightily to a company's long-term strategic success.[19] And, not incidentally, strongly ingrained values and ethical standards reduce the likelihood of lapses in ethical and socially-approved behavior that mar a company's reputation and put its financial performance and market standing at risk.

> A company's values statement and code of ethics communicate expectations of how employees should conduct themselves in the workplace.

The Culture-Building Role of Values and Codes of Ethics   At companies where executives believe in the merits of practicing the values and ethical standards that have been espoused, *the stated core values and ethical principles are the cornerstones of the corporate culture.* As depicted in Figure 13.2, a company's stated core values and ethical principles have two roles in the culture-building process. One, a company that works hard at putting its stated core values and ethical principles into practice fosters a work climate where company personnel share common and strongly held convictions about how the company's business is to be conducted. Second, the stated values and ethical principles provide company personnel with guidance about the manner in which

Figure 13.2   **The Two Culture-Building Roles of a Company's Core Values and Ethical Standards**

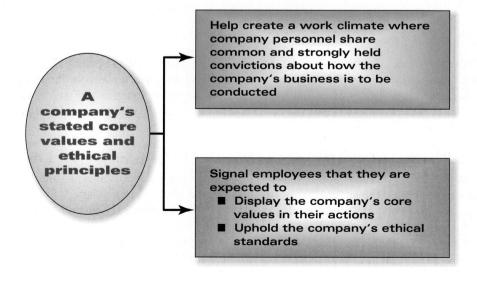

they are to do their jobs—which behaviors and ways of doing things are approved (and expected) and which are out-of-bounds.

Transforming Core Values and Ethical Standards into Cultural Norms
Once values and ethical standards have been formally adopted, they must be institutionalized in the company's policies and practices and embedded in the conduct of company personnel. This can be done in a number of different ways.[20] Tradition-steeped companies with a rich folklore rely heavily on word-of-mouth indoctrination and the power of tradition to instill values and enforce ethical conduct. But most companies employ a variety of techniques to hammer in core values and ethical standards, using some or all of the following:

1. Giving explicit attention to values and ethics in recruiting and hiring to screen out applicants who do not exhibit compatible character traits.
2. Incorporating the statement of values and the code of ethics into orientation programs for new employees and training courses for managers and employees.
3. Having senior executives frequently reiterate the importance and role of company values and ethical principles at company events and internal communications to employees.
4. Using values statements and codes of ethical conduct as benchmarks for judging the appropriateness of company policies and operating practices.
5. Making the display of core values and ethical principles a big factor in evaluating each person's job performance—there's no better way to win the attention and commitment of company personnel than by using the degree to which individuals observe core values and ethical standards as a basis for compensation increases and promotion.
6. Making sure that managers, from the CEO down to frontline supervisors, are diligent in stressing the importance of ethical conduct and observance of core values. Line managers at all levels must give serious and continuous attention to the task of explaining how the values and ethical code apply in their areas.
7. Encouraging everyone to use their influence in helping enforce observance of core values and ethical standards—strong peer pressures to exhibit core values and ethical standards are a deterrent to outside-the-lines behavior.
8. Periodically having ceremonial occasions to recognize individuals and groups who display the values and ethical principles.
9. Instituting ethics enforcement procedures.

To deeply ingrain the stated core values and to high ethical standards, companies must turn them into *strictly enforced cultural norms*. They must put a stake in the ground, making it unequivocally clear that living up to the company's values and ethical standards has to be a way of life at the company and that there will be little toleration of outside-the-lines behavior.

The Benefits of Cultural Norms Grounded in Core Values and Ethical Principles   The more that managers succeed in making the espoused values and ethical principles the main drivers of "how we do things around here," the more that the values and ethical principles function as cultural norms. Over time, a strong culture grounded in the display of core values and ethics may emerge. As shown in Figure 13.3, *cultural norms* rooted in core values and ethical behavior are highly beneficial in three respects.[21] One, the advocated core values and ethical standards accurately

Figure 13.3   **The Benefits of Cultural Norms Strongly Grounded in Core Values and Ethical Principles**

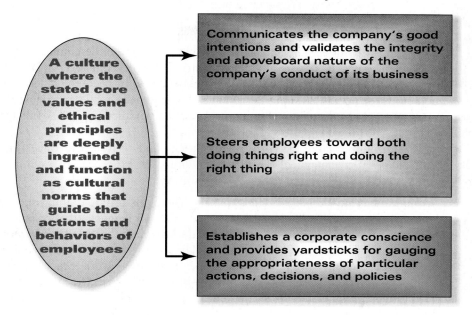

A culture where the stated core values and ethical principles are deeply ingrained and function as cultural norms that guide the actions and behaviors of employees

Communicates the company's good intentions and validates the integrity and aboveboard nature of the company's conduct of its business

Steers employees toward both doing things right and doing the right thing

Establishes a corporate conscience and provides yardsticks for gauging the appropriateness of particular actions, decisions, and policies

communicate the company's good intentions and validate the integrity and above-board character of its business principles and operating methods. There's nothing cosmetic or fake about the company's values statement and code of ethics—company personnel actually strive to practice what is being preached. Second, the values-based and ethics-based cultural norms steer company personnel toward both doing things right and doing the right thing. Third, they establish a "corporate conscience" and provide yardsticks for gauging the appropriateness of particular actions, decisions, and policies.

Establishing a Strategy–Culture Fit in Multinational and Global Companies

In multinational and global companies, establishing a tight strategy–culture fit is complicated by the diverse societal circumstances surrounding the company's operations in different countries. The nature of the local economies, living conditions, per capita incomes, and lifestyles can give rise to considerable cross-border diversity in a company's workforce and to subcultures within the corporate culture. Leading cross-border culture-change initiatives requires sensitivity to prevailing differences in local circumstances; company managers must discern when local subcultures have to be accommodated and when cross-border differences in the company's corporate culture can be and should be narrowed.[22] Cross-border diversity in a multinational enterprise's corporate culture is more tolerable if the company is pursuing a multicountry strategy and if the company's culture in each country is well aligned with its strategy in that country. But significant cross-country differences in a company's culture are likely to impede execution of a global strategy and have to be addressed.

As discussed earlier in this chapter, *the trick to establishing a workable strategy–culture fit in multinational companies is to ground the culture in strategy-supportive values and operating practices that travel well across country borders* and strike a

Core Concept

A multinational company needs to build its corporate culture around values and operating practices that travel well across borders.

chord with managers and workers in many different areas of the world, despite varying local customs and traditions. A multinational enterprise with a misfit between its strategy and culture in certain countries where it operates can attack the problem by rewording its values statement so as to express core values in ways that have universal appeal. The alternative is to allow *some leeway* for certain core values to be reinterpreted or de-emphasized or applied somewhat differently from country to country whenever local customs and traditions in a few countries really need to be accommodated. But such accommodation needs to be done in ways that do not impede good strategy execution. Sometimes certain offending operating styles can be modified to good advantage in all locations where the company operates.

Aside from trying to build the corporate culture around a set of core values that have universal appeal, management can seek to minimize the existence of subcultures and promote greater cross-country cultural uniformity by:

- *Instituting culture training in each country.* The goals of this training should be to (1) communicate the meaning of core values in language that resonates with company personnel in that country and (2) explain the case for common operating approaches and work practices. The use of uniform work practices becomes particularly important when the company's work practices are efficient and aid good strategy execution—in such instances, local managers have to find ways to skirt local preferences and win support for "how we do things around here."

- *Creating a cultural climate where the norm is to adopt best practices, use common work procedures, and pursue operating excellence.* Companies may find that a values-based corporate culture is less crucial to good strategy execution that an operations-based, results-oriented culture in which the dominant cultural norm is an all-out effort to do things in the best possible manner, achieve continuous improvement, and meet or beat performance targets. A results-oriented culture keyed to operating excellence and meeting stretch objectives sidesteps many of the problems with trying to get people from different societies and traditions to embrace common values.

- *Giving local managers the flexibility to modify people management approaches or operating styles.* In some situations, adherence to companywide cultural traditions simply doesn't work well. However, local modifications have to be infrequent and done in a manner that doesn't undermine the establishment of a mostly uniform corporate culture.

- *Giving local managers discretionary authority to use somewhat different motivational and compensation incentives to induce local personnel to adopt and practice the desired cultural behaviors.* Personnel in different countries may respond better to some compensation structures and reward systems than to others.

Generally, a high degree of cross-country homogeneity in a multinational company's corporate culture is desirable and has to be pursued, particularly when it comes to ingraining universal core values and companywide enforcement of such ethical standards as the payment of bribes and kickbacks, the use of underage labor, and environmental stewardship. Having too much variation in the culture from country to country not only makes it difficult to use the culture in helping drive the strategy execution process but also works against the establishment of a one-company mind-set and a consistent corporate identity.

LEADING THE STRATEGY EXECUTION PROCESS

The litany of managing the strategy process is simple enough: Craft a sound strategic plan, implement it, execute it to the fullest, adjust it as needed, and win! But the leadership challenges are significant and diverse. Exerting take-charge leadership, being a "spark plug," ramrodding things through, and achieving results thrusts a manager into a variety of leadership roles in managing the strategy execution process: resource acquirer and allocator, capabilities builder, motivator, policymaker, policy enforcer, head cheerleader, crisis solver, decision maker, and taskmaster, to mention a few. There are times when leading the strategy execution process entails being hard-nosed and authoritarian, times when it is best to be a perceptive listener and a compromising decision maker, times when matters are best delegated to people closest to the scene of the action, and times when mentoring or coaching is appropriate. Many occasions call for the manager in charge to assume a highly visible role and put in long hours guiding the process, while others entail only a brief ceremonial performance with the details delegated to subordinates.

For the most part, leading the strategy execution process is a top-down responsibility driven by mandates to get things on the right track and show good results. It must start with a perceptive diagnosis of the requirements for good strategy execution, given the company's circumstances. Then comes diagnosis of the organization's capabilities and preparedness to execute the necessary strategic initiatives and decisions as to which of several ways to proceed to get things done and achieve the targeted results.[23] In general, leading the drive for good strategy execution and operating excellence calls for five actions on the part of the manager-in-charge:

1. Staying on top of what is happening, closely monitoring progress, ferreting out issues, and learning what obstacles lie in the path of good execution.

2. Putting constructive pressure on the organization to achieve good results and operating excellence.

3. Leading the development of stronger core competencies and competitive capabilities.

4. Displaying ethical integrity and leading social responsibility initiatives.

5. Pushing corrective actions to improve strategy execution and achieve the targeted results.

Staying on Top of How Well Things Are Going

To stay on top of how well the strategy execution process is going, a manager needs to develop a broad network of contacts and sources of information, both formal and informal. The regular channels include talking with key subordinates, attending meetings and quizzing the presenters, reading reviews of the latest operating results, talking to customers, watching the competitive reactions of rival firms, exchanging e-mail and holding telephone conversations with people in outlying locations, making on-site visits, and listening to rank-and-file employees. However, some information is more trustworthy than the rest, and the views and perspectives offered by different people can vary widely. Presentations and briefings by subordinates may be colored by wishful thinking or shoddy analysis rather than representing the unvarnished truth. Bad news is sometimes filtered, minimized, or distorted by people pursuing their own agendas, and in some cases not reported at all as subordinates delay conveying failures and problems in hopes that they can turn things around in time. Hence, managers have to decide which information is trustworthy and get an accurate feel for the existing situation. They have to confirm whether things are on track, identify problems, learn what obstacles lie in the path of good strategy execution, ruthlessly assess whether the organization has the talent and attitude needed to drive the required changes, and develop a basis for determining what, if anything, they can personally do to move the process along.[24]

One of the best ways for executives to stay on top of the strategy execution process is by making regular visits to the field and talking with many different people at many different levels—a technique often labeled **managing by walking around (MBWA).** Wal-Mart executives have had a long-standing practice of spending two to three days every week visiting Wal-Mart's stores and talking with store managers and employees. Sam Walton, Wal-Mart's founder, insisted, "The key is to get out into the store and listen to what the associates have to say." Jack Welch, the highly effective CEO of General Electric (GE) from 1980 to 2001, not only spent several days each month personally visiting GE operations and talking with major customers but also arranged his schedule so that he could spend time exchanging information and ideas with GE managers from all over the world who were attending classes at the company's leadership development center near GE's headquarters.

> **Core Concept**
> **Management by walking around (MBWA)** is one of the techniques that effective leaders use to stay informed about how well the strategy execution process is progressing.

Often, customers and suppliers can provide valuable perspectives on how well a company's strategy execution process is going. Joe Tucci, chief operating officer at data-storage leader EMC, when confronted with an unexpected dropoff in EMC's sales in 2001 and not sure whether the downturn represented a temporary slump or a structural market change went straight to the source for hard information: the chief executive officers and chief financial officers to whom chief information officers at customer companies reported and to the consultants who advised them. The information he got was eye-opening—fundamental market shifts were occurring, and the rules of market engagement now called for major strategy changes at EMC followed by quick implementation.

To keep their fingers on the company's pulse, managers at some companies host weekly get-togethers (often on Friday afternoons) to create a regular opportunity for tidbits of information to flow freely between down-the-line employees and executives. Many manufacturing executives make a point of strolling the factory floor to talk with workers and meeting regularly with union officials. Some managers operate out of open cubicles in big spaces so that they can interact easily and frequently with coworkers. Jeff Bezos, Amazon.com's CEO, is noted for his practice of MBWA, firing off a battery of questions when he tours facilities and insisting that Amazon managers spend time in the trenches with their people to avoid abstract thinking and getting disconnected from the reality of what's happening.[25]

Most managers practice MBWA, attaching great importance to spending time with people at various company facilities and gathering information and opinions firsthand from diverse sources about how well various aspects of the strategy execution process are going. They believe facilities visits and face-to-face contacts give them a good feel for what progress is being made, what problems are being encountered, and whether additional resources or different approaches may be needed. Just as important, MBWA provides opportunities to talk informally to many different people at different organizational levels, give encouragement, lift spirits, shift attention from the old to the new priorities, and create some excitement—all of which generate positive energy and help mobilize organizational efforts behind strategy execution.

Putting Constructive Pressure on the Organization to Achieve Good Results and Operating Excellence

Managers have to be out front in mobilizing organizational energy behind the drive for good strategy execution and operating excellence. Part of the leadership requirement here entails nurturing a results-oriented work climate, where performance standards are high and a spirit of achievement is pervasive. The intended outcome is an organization with a good track record in meeting or beating stretch performance targets. A high-performance culture in which there is constructive pressure to achieve good results is a valuable contributor to good strategy execution and operating excellence. If management wants to drive the strategy execution effort by instilling a results-oriented work climate, then senior executives have to take the lead in promoting certain enabling cultural drivers: a strong sense of involvement on the part of company personnel, emphasis on individual initiative and creativity, respect for the contribution of individuals and groups, and pride in doing things right.

Organizational leaders who succeed in creating a results-oriented work climate typically are intensely people-oriented, and they are skilled users of people-management practices that win the emotional commitment of company personnel and inspire them to do their best.[26] They understand that treating employees well generally leads to increased teamwork, higher morale, greater loyalty, and increased employee commitment to making a contribution. All of these foster an esprit de corps that energizes organizational members to contribute to the drive for operating excellence and proficient strategy execution.

Successfully leading the effort to instill a spirit of high achievement into the culture generally entails such leadership actions and managerial practices as:

- *Treating employees with dignity and respect.* This often includes a strong company commitment to training each employee thoroughly, providing attractive career opportunities, emphasizing promotion from within, and providing a high degree of job security. Some companies symbolize the value of individual employees and the importance of their contributions by referring to them as cast members (Disney), crew members (McDonald's), coworkers (Kinko's and CDW Computer Centers), job owners (Granite Construction), partners (Starbucks), or associates (Wal-Mart, Lenscrafters, W. L. Gore, Edward Jones, Publix Supermarkets, and Marriott International). At a number of companies, managers at every level are held responsible for developing the people who report to them.

- *Making champions out of the people who turn in winning performances.* This must be done in ways that promote teamwork and cross-unit collaboration as opposed to spurring an unhealthy footrace among employees to best one another. Would-be champions who advocate radical or different ideas must not be looked on as disruptive or troublesome. The best champions and change agents are persistent, competitive, tenacious, committed, and fanatic about seeing their idea through to success. It is particularly important that people who champion an unsuccessful idea not be punished or sidelined but rather encouraged to try again—encouraging lots of "tries" is important since many ideas won't pan out.

- *Encouraging employees to use initiative and creativity in performing their work.* Operating excellence requires that everybody be expected to contribute ideas, exercise initiative, and pursue continuous improvement. The leadership trick is to keep a sense of urgency alive in the business so that people see change and innovation as necessities. Moreover, people with maverick ideas or out-of-the-ordinary proposals have to be tolerated and given room to operate; anything less tends to squelch creativity and initiative.

- *Setting stretch objectives.* Managers must clearly communicate an expectation that company personnel are to give their best in achieving performance targets.

- *Using the tools of benchmarking, best practices, business process reengineering, TQM, and Six Sigma quality to focus attention on operating excellence.* These are proven approaches to getting better operating results and facilitating better strategy execution.

- *Using the full range of motivational techniques and compensation incentives to inspire company personnel, nurture a results-oriented work climate, and enforce high-performance standards.* Managers cannot mandate innovative improvements by simply exhorting people to "be creative," nor can they make continuous progress toward operating excellence with directives to "try harder." Rather, they have to foster a culture where innovative ideas and experimentation with new ways of doing things can blossom and thrive. Individuals and groups need to be strongly encouraged to brainstorm, let their imaginations fly in all directions, and come up with proposals for improving how things are done. This means giving company personnel enough autonomy to stand out, excel, and contribute. And it means that the rewards for successful champions of new ideas and operating improvements should be large and visible.

- *Celebrating individual, group, and company successes.* Top management should miss no opportunity to express respect for individual employees and their appreciation of extraordinary individual and group effort.[27] Companies like Mary Kay Cosmetics, Tupperware, and McDonald's actively seek out reasons and opportunities to give pins, buttons, badges, and medals for good showings by average performers—the idea being to express appreciation and give a motivational boost to people who stand out in doing ordinary jobs. General Electric and 3M Corporation make a point of ceremoniously honoring individuals who believe so strongly in their ideas that they take it on themselves to hurdle the bureaucracy, maneuver their projects through the system, and turn them into improved services, new products, or even new businesses.

While leadership efforts to instill a results-oriented, high performance culture usually accentuate the positive, there are negative reinforcers too. Managers whose units consistently perform poorly have to be replaced. Low-performing workers and people who reject the results-oriented cultural emphasis have to be weeded out or at least moved to out-of-the-way positions. Average performers have to be candidly counseled that they have limited career potential unless they show more progress in the form of additional effort, better skills, and improved ability to deliver good results.

Leading the Development of Better Competencies and Capabilities

A third avenue to better strategy execution and operating excellence is proactively strengthening core competencies and competitive capabilities to better perform value chain activities and pave the way for better bottom-line results. This often requires top management intervention for two reasons. One, senior managers are more likely to recognize and appreciate the strategy-executing significance of stronger capabilities; this is especially true in multinational companies where it is top executives are in the best position to spot opportunities to leverage existing competencies and competitive capabilities across geographical borders. Two, senior managers usually have to *lead* the strengthening effort because core competencies and competitive capabilities typically reside in the combined efforts of different work groups, departments, and strategic allies and only senior managers have the organizational clout to enforce the necessary networking and collaboration.

Aside from leading efforts to strengthen *existing* competencies and capabilities, effective strategy leaders try to anticipate changes in customer-market requirements and proactively build *new* competencies and capabilities that offer a competitive edge over rivals. Again, senior managers are in the best position to see the need and potential of new capabilities and then to play a lead role in the capability-building, resource-enhancing process. Proactively building new competencies and capabilities ahead of rivals to gain a competitive edge is strategic leadership of the best kind, but strengthening the company's resource base in reaction to newly developed capabilities of pioneering rivals occurs more frequently.

Displaying Ethical Integrity and Leading Social Responsibility Initiatives

For an organization to avoid the pitfalls of scandal and disgrace and consistently display the intent to conduct its business in a principled manner, the CEO and those around the CEO must be openly and unswervingly committed to ethical conduct and socially redeeming business principles and core values. Leading the effort to operate the company's business in an ethically principled fashion has three pieces. First and foremost, the CEO and other senior executives must set an excellent example in their own ethical behavior, demonstrating character and personal integrity in their actions and decisions. The behavior of senior executives sends a clear message to company personnel regarding what the "real" standards of personal conduct are. Moreover, the company's strategy and operating decisions have to be seen as ethical—actions always speak far louder than the words in a company's code of ethics. Second, top management must declare unequivocal support of the company's ethical code and take an uncompromising stand on expecting all company personnel to conduct themselves in an ethical fashion at all times. This means iterating and reiterating to employees that it is their duty to observe the company's ethical codes. Third, top management must be prepared to act as the final arbiter on hard calls; this means removing people from key positions or terminating them when they are guilty of a violation. It also means reprimanding those who have been lax in monitoring and enforcing ethical compliance. Failure to act swiftly and decisively in punishing ethical misconduct is interpreted as a lack of real commitment.

Establishing an Effective Ethics Compliance and Enforcement Process

If a company's executives truly aspire for company personnel to behave ethically, they must personally see to it that strong and effective procedures for enforcing ethical standards and handling potential violations are put in place. Even in an ethically strong company, there can be bad apples—and some of the bad apples may be executives. So it is rarely enough to rely on either the exhortations of senior executives or an ethically principled culture to produce ethics compliance.

Executive action to institute formal ethics compliance and enforcement mechanisms can entail forming an ethics committee to give guidance on ethics matters, appointing an ethics officers to head the compliance effort, establishing an ethics hotline or Web site that employees can use to either anonymously report a possible violation or get confidential advice on a troubling ethics-related situation, and having an annual ethics audit to measure the extent of ethical behavior and identify problem areas. If senior executives are really serious about enforcing ethical behavior, they probably need to do five things:[28]

1. Have mandatory ethics training programs for employees. Company personnel have to be educated about what is ethical and what is not and given guidance about the gray areas. Special training programs probably are needed for personnel in such ethically vulnerable areas as procurement, sales, and lobbying. Company personnel assigned to subsidiaries in foreign countries can find themselves trapped in ethical dilemmas if bribery and corruption of public officials are common practices or if suppliers or customers are accustomed to kickbacks of one kind or another.

2. Openly encourage company personnel to report possible infractions via anonymous calls to a hotline or e-mails sent to a designated address. Ideally, the company's culture will be sufficiently ethically principled that most company personnel will feel it is their obligation and duty to report possible ethical violations (not so much to get someone in trouble but to prevent further damage and help the company avoid the dire consequences of a debilitating scandal. Furthermore, everyone must be encouraged to raise issues about ethically gray areas and to get confidential advice from the company's ethics specialists.

3. Conduct an annual audit of each manager's efforts to uphold ethical standards and require formal reports on the actions taken by managers to remedy deficient conduct.

4. Require all employees to sign a statement annually certifying that they have complied with the company's code of ethics.

5. Make sure that ethical violations carry appropriate punishment, including dismissal if the violation is sufficiently egregious.

While these actions may seem extreme, they leave little room to doubt the seriousness of executive commitment to ethics compliance. Openly encouraging people to report possible ethical violations heightens awareness of operating within ethical bounds. And while violators have to be disciplined, *the main purpose of the various means of enforcement is to encourage compliance rather than administer punishment.* Most company personnel will think twice about knowingly engaging in unethical conduct when their actions could be reported by watchful coworkers. The same is true when they know their actions will be audited and/or when they have to sign statements certifying compliance with the company's code of ethics.

Top executives in multinational companies face big challenges in enforcing strict ethical standards companywide because what is considered ethical often varies substantially or subtly from country to country. There are shades and variations in what societies generally agree to be right and wrong based on the prevailing circumstances, local customs, and predominant religious convictions. And certainly there are cross-country variations in the *degree* to which certain behaviors are considered unethical.[29] Thus, transnational companies have to make a fundamental decision regarding whether to try to enforce common ethical standards across their operations in all countries or whether to allow some rules to be bent in some cases.

Leading Social Responsibility Initiatives   The exercise of social responsibility, just as with observance of ethical principles, requires top executive leadership. *What separates companies that make a sincere effort to carry their weight in being good corporate citizens from companies that are content to do only what is legally required of them are company leaders who believe strongly that just making a profit is not good enough. Such leaders are committed to a higher standard of performance that includes social and environmental metrics as well as financial and strategic metrics.* Thus, it is up to the CEO and other senior executives to insist that the company go past the rhetoric and cosmetics of corporate citizenship and implement social responsibility initiatives.

> CEOs who are committed to a core value of corporate social responsibility move beyond the rhetorical flourishes and enlist the full support of company personnel behind the execution of social responsibility initiatives.

Among the leadership responsibilities of the CEO and other senior managers, therefore, are to *step out front,* to wave the flag of socially responsible behavior for all to see, to marshal the support of company personnel, and to make social responsibility initiatives an everyday part of how the company conducts its business affairs. Top executives have to use social and environmental metrics in evaluating performance and, ideally, the company's board of directors will elect to tie the company's social and environmental performance to executive compensation—a surefire way to make sure that social responsibility efforts are more than window dressing. To help ensure that it has commitment from senior managers, Verizon Communications ties 10 percent of the annual bonus of the company's top 2,500 managers directly to the achievement of social responsibility targets. One survey found over 60 percent of senior managers believed that a portion of executive compensation should be linked to a company's performance on social and environmental measures. The strength of the commitment from the top—typically a company's CEO and board of directors—ultimately determines whether a company will implement and execute a full-fledged strategy of social responsibility that embraces some customized combination of actions to protect the environment (beyond what is required by law), actively participate in community affairs, be a generous supporter of charitable causes and projects that benefit society, and have a positive impact on workforce diversity and the overall well-being of employees. One of the most reliable signs that company executives are leading an authentic effort to carry out fruitful social responsibility initiatives is whether the company issues an annual report on its social responsibility efforts that cites quantitative and qualitative evidence of the company accomplishments.

Leading the Process of Making Corrective Adjustments

The leadership challenge of making corrective adjustments is twofold: deciding when adjustments are needed and deciding what adjustments to make. Both decisions are a normal and necessary part of managing the strategy execution process, since no scheme for implementing and executing strategy can foresee all the events and problems that will arise. There comes a time at every company when managers have to fine-tune or overhaul the approaches to strategy execution and push for better results. Clearly, when a company's strategy execution effort is not delivering good results and making measurable progress toward operating excellence, it is the leader's responsibility to step forward and push corrective actions.

The *process* of making corrective adjustments varies according to the situation. In a crisis, it is typical for leaders to have key subordinates gather information, identify and evaluate options (crunching whatever numbers may be appropriate), and perhaps prepare a preliminary set of recommended actions for consideration. The organizational leader then usually meets with key subordinates and personally presides over extended discussions of the proposed responses, trying to build a quick consensus among members of the executive inner circle. If no consensus emerges and action is required immediately, the burden falls on the manager in charge to choose the response and urge its support.

When the situation allows managers to proceed more deliberately in deciding when to make changes and what changes to make, most managers seem to prefer a process of incrementally solidifying commitment to a particular course of action.[30] The process that managers go through in deciding on corrective adjustments is essentially the same for both proactive and reactive changes: They sense needs, gather information, broaden and deepen their understanding of the situation, develop options and explore their pros and cons, put forth action proposals, generate partial (comfort-level) solutions, strive for a consensus, and finally formally adopt an agreed-on course of action.[31] Deciding what corrective changes to initiate can take a few hours, a few days, a few weeks, or even a few months if the situation is particularly complicated.

Success in initiating corrective actions usually hinges on thorough analysis of the situation, the exercise of good business judgment in deciding what actions to take, and good implementation of the corrective actions that are initiated. Successful managers are skilled in getting an organization back on track rather quickly; they (and their staffs) are good at discerning what actions to take and in ramrodding them through to a successful conclusion. Managers that struggle to show measurable progress in generating good results and improving the performance of strategy-critical value chain activities are candidates for being replaced.

The challenges of leading a successful strategy execution effort are, without question, substantial.[32] But the job is definitely doable. Because each instance of executing strategy occurs under different organizational circumstances, the managerial agenda for executing strategy always needs to be situation-specific—there's no neat generic procedure to follow. And, as we said at the beginning of Chapter 11, executing strategy is an action-oriented, make-the-right-things-happen task that challenges a manager's ability to lead and direct organizational change, create or reinvent business processes, manage and motivate people, and achieve performance targets. If you now better understand what the challenges are, what approaches are available, which issues need to be considered, and why the action agenda for implementing and executing strategy sweeps across so many aspects of administrative and managerial work, then we will look on our discussion in Chapters 11, 12, and 13 as a success.

A Final Word on Managing the Process of Crafting and Executing Strategy   In practice, it is hard to separate the leadership requirements of executing strategy from the other pieces of the strategy process. As we emphasized in Chapter 1, the job of crafting, implementing, and executing strategy is a five-phase process with much looping and recycling to fine-tune and adjust strategic visions, objectives, strategies, capabilities, implementation approaches, and cultures to fit one another and to fit changing circumstances. The process is continuous, and the conceptually separate acts of crafting and executing strategy blur together in real-world situations. The best tests of good strategic leadership are whether the company has a good strategy and whether the strategy execution effort is delivering the hoped-for results. If these two conditions exist, the chances are excellent that the company has good strategic leadership.

Key Points

The character of a company's culture is a product of the core values and business principles that executives espouse, the standards of what is ethically acceptable and what is not, the work practices and behaviors that define "how we do things around here," its approach to people management and style of operating, the "chemistry" and the "personality" that permeates its work environment, and the stories that get told over and over to illustrate and reinforce the company's values, business practices, and traditions. A company's culture is important because it influences the organization's actions and approaches to conducting business—in a very real sense, the culture is the company's "operating system" or organizational DNA.

The psyche of corporate cultures varies widely. Moreover, company cultures vary widely in strength and influence. Some are strongly embedded and have a big impact on a company's practices and behavioral norms. Others are weak and have comparatively little influence on company operations. There are four types of unhealthy cultures: (1) those that are highly political and characterized by empire building, (2) those that are change resistant, (3) those that are insular and inwardly focused, and (4) those that are ethically unprincipled and are driven by greed. High-performance cultures and adaptive cultures both have positive features that are conducive to good strategy execution.

A culture grounded in values, practices, and behavioral norms that match what is needed for good strategy execution helps energize people throughout the company to do their jobs in a strategy-supportive manner, adding significantly to the power of a company's strategy execution effort and the chances of achieving the targeted results. But when the culture is in conflict with some aspect of the company's direction, performance targets, or strategy, the culture becomes a stumbling block. Thus, an important part of the managing the strategy execution process is establishing and nurturing a good fit between culture and strategy.

A company's present culture and work climate may or may not be compatible with what is needed for effective implementation and execution of the chosen strategy. *When a company's present work climate promotes attitudes and behaviors that are well suited to first-rate strategy execution, its culture functions as a valuable ally in the strategy execution process.* When the culture is in conflict with some aspect of the company's direction, performance targets, or strategy, the culture becomes a stumbling block.

Changing a company's culture, especially a strong one with traits that don't fit a new strategy's requirements, is a tough and often time-consuming challenge. Changing a culture requires competent leadership at the top. It requires symbolic actions and substantive actions that unmistakably indicate serious commitment on the part of top management. The more that culture-driven actions and behaviors fit what's needed for good strategy execution, the less managers have to depend on policies, rules, procedures, and supervision to enforce what people should and should not do.

The taproot of a company's corporate culture nearly always is its dedication to certain core values and the bar it sets for ethical behavior. Of course, sometimes a company's stated core values and codes of ethics are cosmetic, existing mainly to impress outsiders and help create a positive company image. But more usually they have been developed to shape the culture. If management practices what it preaches, a company's core values and ethical standards nurture the corporate culture in three highly positive ways: (1) They communicate the company's good intentions and validate the integrity and above-board character of its business principles and operating methods; (2) they steer company personnel toward both doing the right thing and doing things right; and (3) they establish a corporate conscience that gauges the appropriateness of particular actions, decisions, and policies. Companies that really care about how they conduct their business put a stake in the ground, making it unequivocally clear that company personnel are expected to live up to the company's values and ethical standards—how well individuals display core values and adhere to ethical standards is often part of the job performance evaluations. Peer pressures to conform to cultural norms are quite strong, acting as an important deterrent to outside-the-lines behavior.

Leading the drive for good strategy execution and operating excellence calls for five actions on the part of the manager-in-charge:

1. Staying on top of what is happening, closely monitoring progress, ferreting out issues, and learning what obstacles lie in the path of good execution.

2. Putting constructive pressure on the organization to achieve good results and operating excellence.

3. Leading the development of stronger core competencies and competitive capabilities.

4. Displaying ethical integrity and leading social responsibility initiatives.

5. Pushing corrective actions to improve strategy execution and achieve the targeted results.

Exercises

1. Go to Herman Miller's Web site (www.hermanmiller.com) and read what the company has to say about its corporate culture in its careers sections. Do you think this statement is just public relations, or, based on what else you can learn about the Herman Miller Company from browsing this Web site, is there reason to believe that management has truly built a culture that makes the stated values and principles come alive?

2. Go to the careers section at Qualcomm's Web site (www.qualcomm.com) and see what this company, one of the most prominent companies in mobile communications technology, has to say about life at Qualcomm. Is what's on this Web site just recruiting propaganda, or does it convey the type of work climate that management is actually trying to create? If you were a senior executive at Qualcomm, would you see merit in building and nurturing a culture like what is described in the section "Life at Qualcomm"? Would such a culture represent a tight fit with Qualcomm's high-tech business and strategy? (You can get an overview of the Qualcomm's strategy by exploring the section for investors and some of the recent press releases.) Is your answer consistent with what is presented in the "Awards and Honors" menu selection in the "About Qualcomm" portion of the Web site?

3. Go to the Web site of Johnson & Johnson (www.jnj.com) and read the "J&J Credo," which sets forth the company's responsibilities to customers, employees, the community, and shareholders. Then read the "Our Company" section. Why do you think the credo has resulted in numerous awards and accolades that recognize the company as a good corporate citizen?

4. Do an Internet search or use the resources of your university's library to identify at least five companies that have experienced a failure of strategic leadership on the part of the CEO since 2000. Three candidate companies you might want to research are Adelphia Communications, AIG, and HealthSouth. Then determine which, if any, of the five factors discussed in this chapter's section titled "Leading the Strategy Execution Process" came into play in the CEOs' failure.

5. Dell Inc. has been listed as one of *Fortune*'s most admired companies for several years. Click on the "About Dell" link at www.dell.com. What is your assessment of the company's extensive discussion of accountability, concern for the environment, and community involvement? Does it appear these programs have the support of upper-level management? Is there evidence that this is more than a public relations initiative?

6. Review the material in Illustration Capsule 13.1 on Google's corporate culture; then go to the company's Web site, click on the "About Google" link, then on the "Corporate Info" link and read the "Ten things Google has found to be true" in the "Our Philosophy" section. What relationships do you see between these 10 things and Google's description of its culture? Are the two closely connected? Why or why not? Explain.

part two 2

Readings in Crafting and Executing Strategy

What Is Strategy and How Do You Know If You Have One?

Costas Markides
London Business School

What is strategy, *really?* Despite the obvious importance of a superior strategy to the success of an organization and despite decades of research on the subject, there is little agreement among academics as to what strategy really is. From notions of strategy as positioning to strategy as visioning, several possible definitions are fighting for legitimacy. Lack of an acceptable definition has opened up the field to an invasion of sexy slogans and terms, all of which add to the confusion and state of unease.

Not that the confusion is restricted to academics. If asked, most practicing executives would define strategy as "how I could achieve my company's objectives." Although this definition is technically correct, it is so general that it is practically meaningless.

Needless to say, this state of affairs is unfortunate. Perhaps nothing highlights better the sad (comical?) state of affairs surrounding strategy than the following.

In November 1996, the most prominent strategy academic, Michael Porter of Harvard, published a *Harvard Business Review* article grandly entitled "What Is Strategy?" (*Harvard Business Review,* November–December 1996). This was followed only a few months later by another famous academic, Gary Hamel of London Business School, with an equally impressively titled article, "The Search for

Strategy" (London Business School working paper, 1997). That after 40 years of academic research on the subject, two of the most prominent academics in the field felt the need to go out of their way and start searching for strategy goes to show how much confusion we have managed to create regarding such a crucial business decision.

Although part of the confusion is undoubtedly self-inflicted, a major portion of it also stems from an honest lack of understanding as to the content of strategy. I would like to propose a view of strategy that is based on my research on companies that have strategically innovated in their industries. These are companies that not only developed strategies that are fundamentally different from the strategies of their competitors but whose strategies also turned out to be tremendously successful.

Based on my research on these successful strategists, I'd like to propose that there are certain simple but fundamental principles underlying every successful strategy. When one goes beyond the visible differences among strategies and probes deeper into the roots of these strategies, one cannot fail but notice that all successful strategies share the same underlying principles or building blocks. Thus, the building blocks of Microsoft's successful strategy are the same as the building blocks of the strategy that propelled Sears to industry leadership 100 years ago. My argument is that by understanding what these building blocks are, an organization can use them to develop its own successful strategy. The building blocks are as follows.

"What is the Strategy and How Do You Know If You Have One ?" Costas Markides, *Business Strategy Review,* Vol.15, Issue 2 (Summer 2004), p.5–12. Copyright © 2004 by Blackwell Publishing Ltd. Used by permission.

> *The building blocks of Microsoft's successful strategy are the same as the building blocks of the strategy that propelled Sears to industry leadership 100 years ago*

STRATEGY MUST DECIDE ON A FEW PARAMETERS

In today's uncertain and ever-changing environment strategy is all about making some very difficult decisions on a *few* parameters. It is absolutely essential that the firm decides on these parameters because they become the boundaries within which people are given the freedom and the autonomy to operate and try things out. They also define the company's *strategic position* in its industry. Without clear decisions on these parameters, the company will drift like a rudderless ship in the open seas.

What Are These Parameters?

A company has to decide on three main issues: *who* will be its targeted customers and who it will *not* target; *what* products or services it will offer its chosen customers and what it will *not* offer them; and *how* it will go about achieving all this—what activities it will perform and what activities it will not perform.

> *A company will be successful if it chooses a distinctive (that is, different from competitors) strategic position*

These are not easy decisions to make and each question has many possible answers, all of them *exante* possible and logical. As a result, these kinds of decisions will unavoidably be preceded with debates, disagreements, politicking, and indecision. Yet, at the end of the day, a firm cannot be everything to everybody, so clear and explicit decisions must be made. These choices may turn out to be wrong but that is not an excuse for not deciding.

It is absolutely essential that an organization make clear and explicit choices on these three dimensions because the choices made become the parameters within which people are allowed to operate with autonomy. Without these clear parameters, the end result can be chaos. Seen in another way, it would

be foolish and dangerous to allow people to take initiatives without some clear parameters guiding their actions.

Not only must a company make clear choices on these parameters, it must also attempt to make choices that are different from the choices its competitors have made. A company will be successful if it chooses a *distinctive* (that is, different from competitors) strategic position. Sure, it may be impossible to come up with answers that are 100 percent different from those of competitors, but the ambition should be to create as much differentiation as possible.

Given the importance of coming up with clear answers to these three issues, the question is: Who comes up with possible answers to these questions, who decides what to do out of the many possibilities, and how long do the decisions remain unchanged?

Who Comes Up with Ideas?

Given the right organizational context, strategic ideas (on who to target, what to sell and how to do it) can come from anybody, anywhere, anytime. They may emerge through trial and error or because somebody has a "gut feeling" or because somebody "got lucky" and stumbled across a good idea. They may even emerge out of a formal strategic planning session. (However dismissive we can be of the modern corporation's formal planning process, the possibility still exists that some good ideas can come out of such a process.) No matter how the ideas are conceived, it is unlikely that they will be perfect from the start. The firm must therefore be willing and ready to modify or change its strategic ideas as it receives feedback from the market.

In general, there are numerous tactics at our disposal to enhance creativity at the idea-generation state. Let me list a few of them:

- Encourage everyone in the organization to question the firm's implicit assumptions and beliefs (its sacred cows) as to who our customers really are, what we are really offering to them and how we do these things. Also, encourage a fundamental questioning of the firm's accepted answer to the question "What business are we in?"

- To facilitate this questioning, create a positive crisis. If done correctly, this will galvanize the organization into active thinking. If done incorrectly, it will demoralize everybody and create confusion and disillusionment throughout the organization.

- Develop processes in the organization to collect and utilize ideas from everybody—employees, customers, distributors, and so on. At Lan & Spar Bank, for example, every employee is asked to contribute ideas through a strategy workbook; Schlumberger has an internal venturing unit; Bank One has a specific customer center where all customers are encouraged to phone and express their complaints; at my local supermarket, there is a customer suggestion box. Different organizations have come up with different tactics, but the idea is the same: allow everybody to contribute ideas and make it easy for them to communicate their ideas to the decision makers in the organization.

- Create variety in the thinking that takes place in formal planning processes. This can be achieved not only by using a diverse team of people but by also by utilizing as many thinking approaches as possible.

- Institutionalize a culture of innovation. The organization must create the organizational environment (culture/structure/incentives/people) that promotes and supports innovative behaviors.

This is not an exhaustive list of tactics that could be used to increase creativity in strategy making. I am sure that other tactics and processes exist or can be thought of. The principle, though, remains the same: at this stage of crafting an innovative strategy, the goal must be to generate as many strategic ideas as possible so that we have the luxury of choosing.

Who Decides?

Even though anyone in an organization can come up with new strategic ideas (and everybody should be *encouraged* to do so), it is the responsibility of top management to make the final choices.

There have been many calls lately to make the process of strategy development "democratic" and "flexible"—to bring everybody in the organization into the process. The thinking here is that the odds of conceiving truly innovative ideas are increased if thousands of people rather than just 5 or 10 senior managers put their minds to work. And this much is true.

But the job of choosing the ideas that the firm will actually pursue must be left to top management. Otherwise, the result is chaos, confusion, and ultimately a demotivated workforce. After all is said and done, it is the leaders of an organization, not every single employee, who must choose which ideas will be pursued.

Choosing is difficult. At the time of choosing, no one knows for sure whether a particular idea will work nor does anyone know if the choices made are really the most appropriate ones.

One could reduce the uncertainty at this stage by either evaluating each idea in a rigorous way or by experimenting with the idea in a limited way to see if it works. However, it is crucial to understand that uncertainty can be reduced but not limited. No matter how much experimentation we carry out and no matter how much thinking goes into it, the time will come when a firm must decide one way or another. Choices have to be made, and these choices may turn out to be wrong. However, lack of certainty is no excuse for indecision.

Not only must a firm choose what to do, but it must also make it clear what it will *not* do. The worst strategic mistake possible is to choose something but also keep our options open by doing other things as well. Imagine an organization where the CEO proclaims that "our strategy is crystal clear: we will do ABC" and at the same time the employees of the organization see the firm doing XYZ as well as ABC. In their eyes, this means one of two things: either we don't really have a strategy, or top management is totally confused. Either way, the organization is left demoralized and confidence in senior management is shattered. Organizations that say one thing and then do another are those that have failed to make clear choices about what they will do and what they will not do with their strategy.

The difficult choices made by Canon in attacking Xerox highlight the importance of choosing in an explicit way what to do and what not to do. At the time of the attack, Xerox had a lock on the copier market by following a well-defined and successful strategy, the main elements of which were the following: having segmented the market by volume, Xerox decided to go after the corporate reproduction market by concentrating on copiers designed for high-speed, high-volume needs. This inevitably defined Xerox's customers as big corporations, which in turn determined its distribution method—the direct sales force. At the same time, Xerox decided to lease rather than sell its machines, a strategic choice that had worked well in the company's earlier battles with 3M. Xerox's strategy proved to be so successful that several new competitors, among them IBM and Kodak, tried to enter the market by adopting the same or similar tactics.

> *At this stage of crafting an innovative strategy, the goal must be to generate as many strategic ideas as possible so that we have the luxury of choosing. Unless we take a holistic, big-picture approach in designing the activities of our company, our efforts will backfire*

Canon, on the other hand, chose to play the game differently. Having determined in the early 1960s to diversify out of cameras and into copiers, Canon segmented the market by end user and decided to target small and medium-sized businesses while also producing PC copiers for individuals. At the same time, Canon decided to sell its machines through a dealer network rather than lease them. And while Xerox emphasized the speed of its machines, Canon elected to concentrate on quality and price as its differentiating features.

Cutting the story short, where IBM's and Kodak's assault on the copier market failed, Canon's succeeded. Within 20 years of attacking Xerox, Canon emerged as the market leader in volume terms.

There are many reasons behind the success of Canon. Notice, however, that just as Xerox did 20 years before it, Canon created for itself *a distinctive strategic position* in the industry—a position that was different from Xerox's. Whereas Xerox targeted big corporations as its customers, Canon went after small companies and individuals; while Xerox emphasized the speed of its machines, Canon focused on quality and price; and whereas Xerox used a direct sales force to lease its machines, Canon used its dealer network to sell its copiers. Rather than try to beat Xerox at its own game, Canon triumphed by creating its own unique strategic position.

As in the case of Xerox, these were *not* the only choices available to Canon. Serious debates and disagreements must undoubtedly have taken place

within Canon as to whether these were the right choices to pursue. Yet choices were made and a clear strategy with sharp and well-defined boundaries was put in place. As in the case of Xerox, Canon was successful because it chose a unique and well-defined strategic position in the industry—one with distinctive customers, products, and activities.

STRATEGY MUST PUT ALL OUR CHOICES TOGETHER TO CREATE A REINFORCING MOSAIC

Choosing what to do and what not to do is certainly an important element of strategy. However, strategy is much more than this. Strategy is all about *combining* these choices into a *system* that creates the requisite *fit* between what the environment needs and what the company does. It is the combining of a firm's choices into a well-balanced system that's important, not the individual choices.

The importance of conceptualizing the company *as a combination of activities* cannot be overemphasized. In this perspective, a firm is a complex system of interrelated and interdependent activities, each affecting the other: decisions and actions in one part of the business affect other parts, directly or indirectly. This means that unless we take a holistic, big-picture approach in designing the activities of our company, our efforts will backfire. Even if each individual activity is optimally crafted, the whole may still suffer unless we take interdependencies into consideration. The numerous local optima almost always undermine the global optimum.

The problem is that human beings can never really comprehend all the complexity embedded in our companies. We therefore tend to focus on one or two aspects of the system and try to optimize these subsystems independently. By doing so, we ignore the interdependencies in the system and we are therefore making matters worse. Since it takes time for the effect of our actions to show up, we do not even see that we are the source of our problems. When the long-term effects of our short-sighted actions hit home, we blame other people and especially outside forces for our problems (we had no forecasts, demand is unpredictable, the economy is not growing, and so on).

In designing a company's system of activities, managers must bear four principles in mind:

First, the individual activities we choose to do must be the ones that are demanded by the market.

Second, the activities we decide to perform must fit with each other.

Third, activities must not only fit but must also be in *balance* with each other.

Fourth, in designing these activities, it is important to keep in mind that the collection of these activities will form an interrelated system.

Not only should we pay particular attention to the interrelationships in this system but we should also be aware that the *structure* of this system will drive behavior in it. What people do in a firm is conditioned by this underlying structure. Therefore, if we want to change behavior, we will have to change the structure of the system.

STRATEGY MUST ACHIEVE FIT WITHOUT LOSING FLEXIBILITY

Creating the right fit between what the market needs and what a firm does can backfire if the environment changes and the firm does not respond accordingly. We are all familiar with the story of the frog.

When a frog is put in a pot of boiling water, it jumps out; when, instead, the same frog is put in a pot of cold water and the water is slowly brought to a boil, the frog stays in the pot and boils to death.

In the same manner, if a company does not react to the constant changes taking place in its environment, it will find itself boiled to death.

This implies that a company needs to create the requisite fit with its current environment while remaining flexible enough to respond to (or even create) changes in this environment. But what does it mean when we say that a firm *must remain flexible?*

The way I use the term here, I imply three things: a firm must first be able to identify changes in its environment *early enough;* it must then have the *cultural* readiness to embrace change and respond to it;

and it must have the requisite *skills and competencies* to compete in whatever environment emerges after the change. Thus, flexibility has a cultural element to it (being willing to change) as well as a competence element to it (being able to change).

STRATEGY NEEDS TO BE SUPPORTED BY THE APPROPRIATE ORGANIZATIONAL ENVIRONMENT

Any strategy, however brilliant, needs to be implemented properly if it is to deliver the desired results. However, implementation does not take place in a vacuum. It takes place within an *organizational environment,* which we, as managers, create. It is this organizational environment that produces the behavior that we observe in companies. Therefore, to secure the desired strategic behavior by employees, a firm must first create the appropriate environment—that is, the environment that promotes and supports its chosen strategy.

By environment, I mean four elements: an organization's culture; its incentives; its structure; and its people. (What I call here "environment" is what is widely known as the 7S framework developed by McKinsey and Co. The 7Ss are style, strategy, structure, systems, skills, staff, and superordinate goals.)

A company that wants to put into action a certain strategy must first ask the question "What kind of culture, incentives, structure, and people do we need to implement the strategy?"

In other words, to create a superior strategy, a company must think beyond customers, products, and activities. It must also decide what underlying environment to create and how exactly to create it so as to facilitate the implementation of its strategy.

However, deciding on what kind of culture, structure, incentives, and people to have is not enough. The challenge for strategy is to develop these four elements of organizational environment and then put them together so that on one hand they support and complement each other while on the other they collectively support and promote the chosen strategy. As was the case with the activities I described above, this is the real challenge for strategy: not only to create the correct individual parts but to combine them to create a strong and reinforcing system.

> *A firm must first create the appropriate environment that promotes and supports its chosen strategy*

Achieving internal and external fits will only bring short-term success. Inevitably, fit will create contentment, overconfidence, and inertia. Therefore, while a company aims to achieve fit it must also create enough slack in the system so that, as it grows or as the external environment changes, the organizational environment can remain flexible and responsive.

Finally, if business conditions oblige a strategic change of direction, the internal context of an organization must change them. This is extremely difficult. Not only do we need to change the individual pieces that make up the organizational environment, but we must also put them together to form an overall organizational environment that will again fit with the new strategy.

NO STRATEGY REMAINS UNIQUE FOREVER

There is no question that success stems from the exploitation of a distinctive or unique strategic position. Unfortunately, no position will remain unique or attractive forever. Not only do attractive positions get imitated by aggressive competitors but also—and perhaps more important—*new* strategic positions keep emerging all the time. A new strategic position is simply a new, viable who-what-how combination—perhaps a new customer segment (a new who), or a new value proposition (a new what), or a new way of distributing or manufacturing the product (a new how). Over time, these new positions may grow to challenge the attractiveness of our own position.

You see this happening in industry after industry. Once formidable companies that built their success on what seemed to be unassailable strategic positions find themselves humbled by relatively unknown companies that base their attacks on creating and exploiting new strategic positions in the industry.

New strategic positions—that is, new who-what-how combinations—emerge all around us all the time. As industries change, new strategic positions emerge to challenge existing positions for supremacy. Changing industry conditions, changing customer needs or preferences, countermoves by competitors and a company's own evolving competencies give rise to new opportunities and the potential for new ways of playing the game. Unless a company continuously questions its accepted norms and behaviors, it will never discover what else has become available. It will miss these new combinations and other, more agile, players will jump in and exploit the gaps left behind. Therefore, a company must never settle for what it has. While fighting it out in its current position, it must continuously search for new positions to colonize and new opportunities to take advantage of.

> *If business conditions oblige a strategic change of direction, the internal context of an organization must change.*

Simple as this may sound, it contrasts sharply with the way most companies compete in their industries: most of them take the established rules of the game as given and spend all their time trying to become *better* than each other in their existing positions—usually through cost or differentiation strategies.

Little or no emphasis is placed on becoming *different* from competitors. This is evidenced from the fact that the majority of companies that strategically innovate by breaking the rules of the game tend to be small niche players or new market entrants. It is indeed rare to find a strategic innovator that is also an established industry big player—a fact that hints at the difficulties of risking the sure thing for something uncertain.

There are many reasons why established companies find it hard to become strategic innovators. Compared to new entrants or niche players, leaders are weighed down by *structural* and *cultural* inertia, internal politics, complacency, fear of cannibalizing existing products, fear of destroying existing competencies, satisfaction with the status quo and a general lack of incentives to abandon a certain present for an uncertain future. In addition, since there are fewer industry leaders than potential new entrants, the chances that the innovator will emerge from the ranks of the leaders is inevitably small.

Despite such obstacles, established companies cannot afford not to innovate strategically. As already pointed out, dramatic shifts in company fortunes can only take place if a company succeeds in not only playing its game better than its rivals but in also designing and playing a different game from its competitors.

> *Strategic innovation can take third-rate companies and elevate them to industry leadership; and it can take established industry leaders and destroy them*

Strategic innovation has the potential to take third-rate companies and elevate them to industry leadership status; and it can take established industry leaders and destroy them in a short period of time. Even if established players do not want to innovate strategically (for fear of destroying their existing profitable positions), somebody else will. Established players might as well pre-empt that from happening.

The culture that established players must develop is that *strategies are not cast in concrete.* A company needs to remain flexible and ready to adjust its strategy if the feedback from the market is not favorable. More important, a company needs to continuously question the way it operates in its current position *while* still fighting it out in its current position against existing competitors.

Continuously questioning one's accepted strategic position serves two vital purposes: First, it allows a company to identify early enough whether its current position in the business is losing its attractiveness to others (and so decide what to do about it); second, and more important, it gives the company the opportunity to proactively explore the emerging terrain and hopefully be the first to discover new and attractive strategic positions to take advantage of.

This is no guarantee: Questioning one's accepted answers will not automatically lead to new unexploited gold mines. But a remote possibility of discovering something new will never even come up if the questions are never asked.

Resources

Ansoff, H Igor, *Implanting Strategic Management,* Prentice Hall, 1984, (2nd edition, 1990).

Markides, Costas, *Diversification, Refocusing and Economic Performance,* MIT Press, 1995.

Markides, Costas, *All the Right Moves,* Harvard Business School Press, 1999.

Mintzberg, Henry, *The Rise and Fall of Strategic Planning,* Prentice Hall, 1994.

Nadler, David, and **Tushman, Michael,** *Competing by Design: The Power of Organizational Architecture,* New York: Oxford University Press, 1997.

Markides, Costas, Strategic innovation, *Sloan Management Review,* Spring 1997.

Markides, Costas, "Strategic innovation in established companies," *Sloan Management Review,* Spring 1998.

Slywotzky, Adrian J, *Value Migration: How to Think Several Moves Ahead of the Competition,* Harvard Business School Press, 1996.

Walking the Talk (Really!): Why Visions Fail

Mark Lipton
New School University

Leaders may be able to articulate a vision, but very few actually live the vision each day. However, as this author writes, a leader who lives, breathes and weaves the vision into the fabric of an organization inspires everyone to a higher performance every day.

Some executives are not reluctant to say that vision is a "squishy" concept and nearly impossible to quantify. But research and experiences over the past decade make a nearly incontrovertible case that the vision process has a profound impact on organizational performance. As well, that performance is measurable. So what's the problem? Or, why do so many CEOs *believe* in the need for vision, yet *fail* to carry through on the process to develop and implement one. The reason there is cynicism about "the vision thing" is less about the actual failure of a vision, than it is about a leadership failing I call The Believing-Doing Gap: While there's a lot of talk about vision, few at the helm actually follow through on the work required to bring a vision to life.

The vision process—when fully executed—evokes a considerable amount of emotion, and the Believing-Doing (B-D) Gap exists because executives are ill prepared for the emotional engagement that this process actually demands. Many executives become myopic when it comes to vision. A "successful" vision is not simply a question of crafting a few paragraphs of verbiage that sound as though they were excerpted from a *Dilbert* comic strip. Nor is success how John Rock, once the general manager of General Motors' Oldsmobile division, so eloquently put it, "a bunch of guys taking off their ties and coats, going into a motel room for three days, and putting a bunch of friggen' words on a piece of paper—and then going back to business as usual." A vision is about personal passion. Without substantive ideas and concrete actions, the process becomes a joke, often backfiring on the leader responsible, as others turn into cynics. When the B-D Gap persists, there's rarely a full-range vision that organizational members are able to buy into and use to guide the growth of the firm.

A vision is successful when it "speaks" to a wide audience, tells an engaging story that people want to be a part of, challenges people, and creates a sense of urgency. Success occurs when the vision becomes embedded in the daily decisions and actions taken of those you want to lead. A vision is not merely an extended strategic plan or "mission." When we see a vision that is working, guiding an organization to sustained growth, we know that behind it are leaders who are comfortable leading with their hearts as well as their heads. This article describes what a leader needs to do to sustain a vision—and the growth of an organization.

"Walking the Talk (Really!): Why Visions Fail," Mark Lipton, *Ivey Business Journal* 68, no. 3 (January–February 2004) PP. 358–364. Ivey Management Services prohibits any form of reproduction, storage or transmittal of this material without its written permission. This material is not covered under authorization from any reproduction rights organization. To order copies or request permission to reproduce materials, contact Ivey Publishing, Ivey Management Services, c/o Richard Ivey School of Business, The University of Western Ontario, London, Ontario, Canada, N6A 3K7; phone (519) 661-3208, fax (519) 661-3882, e-mail cases@ivey.uwo.ca. Copyright © 2004, Ivey Management Services. One time Permission to reproduce granted by Ivey Management Services on February 15, 2006.

BELIEVING IS NOT THE PROBLEM; IT'S IN THE DOING

It's worth considering two data points that seem, at first blush, to be contradictory. One study found that 94 percent of CEOs report "a great deal of discomfort working with the vision process." A second study, conducted by The Conference Board, polled 700 global CEOs and found, for the past three years, that the number one marketplace and management issue was "engaging employees in the vision." Perhaps what both studies are saying, from the executive perspective, is that "I believe in the need for vision but I cannot get my 'internal mechanism' in gear to make it happen. I can't connect my desire to create and implement it with the internal energy necessary to get over all the barriers. I'm frustrated!"

At a dinner during the first week of 2004, the chief marketing officer of a Fortune 50 company confided to me how alone he felt at the top:

> We're hitting our revenue targets, we have obscene share of market in most of the areas in which we operate, but our stock price doesn't reflect how well we're doing. The outside world doesn't understand who we are, why we're unique, how all our pieces fit together, and what we stand for. On the inside, we're operating like 60 different silos. My CEO says our vision is to provide shareholder return . . . but that's no vision, shareholder return is something that we get rewarded for as a result of executing against a proper vision. I've got to believe he has some vision of who we are. (long pause) But he can't unlock his thoughts and feelings about it to us. And if he can't begin to get us thinking about a real vision, then I'm afraid of what lies ahead.

BELIEVE IN VISION: IT WORKS

I didn't believe in "the vision thing." A decade ago I considered the notion of organizational vision to be just another fad. I'm inherently skeptical of any new silver bullet that promises to cure a range of organizational ills and, in the late 1980s, vision made the list. Yet, after a few years as a cynical consultant, I found myself intrigued by the paucity of analytic research that would support this gut-level belief. Broad studies analyzing the impact of visions were nonexistent. I, too, thought vision was too "squishy," but I didn't have the data to prove it.

As a management professor, I decided it was time to make the case that vision didn't really matter. After one year into the first leg of the research project on the impact of vision, I began to see some very surprising data. My hypothesis, I realized, was dead wrong.

I found that a well-articulated vision, when implemented throughout an organization, had a profoundly positive impact. The data didn't lie and I found myself a convert from skeptic to born-again believer. Once my research was complete, I began testing some of the best-practices results with a range of organizations in the private, nonprofit and public sectors. Consistently, I found that once senior executives were able to break through the natural barriers of resistance that often bring this process to a screeching halt, they too became believers.

Publicly owned firms that use a vision to guide their growth have significantly higher market-cap, top-line, and bottom-line growth in comparison to their competitors who aren't driven by the vision process. Firms with a vision were twice as profitable as the S&P 500 as a group, and their stock price grew nearly three times the rate of others. An analysis of Average Compounded Total Return found the vision-driven firms earning their investors 17.69 percent more than the S&P 500 overall.

A well-conceived and well-implemented vision doesn't yield this kind of bottom-line performance magically. It comes from the people who are challenged by the vision and remain focused on a clear, yet distant, target. These firms had higher productivity per employee, greater levels of employee commitment, increased loyalty to the firm, greater esprit de corps, clearer departmental and/or organizational values, and a greater sense of pride in their organization.

Vision provides direction and nourishment for sustained growth.

FIND THE APPETITE FOR VISION

Over the past decade, I've found that leaders who overcame the B-D Gap became adept at stretching their time horizons; they also "saw" into and pondered their own thoughts and feelings as the vision evolved. Passion characterized their vision for their organization. They could articulate it to themselves and to others. They were willing to face the reality that, if the vision process at their organization stalled, it was perhaps because they succumbed to a form of inertia. And, most important, they were willing to be true to their own values and refrain from placing blame for inaction on some institutional imperative. They explored the vision not dispassionately from the outside, but with a full-range view of how they thought and felt about that distant future and what would be required of them to implement it.

Ask yourself: "Where does my appetite for vision, with all the risk inherent in its development, come from?"

The "appetite" starts from living. It comes from feeling the bumps and bangs and pain of life that create emotional jolts that stay with us consciously and unconsciously. It comes from living through life-changing events that trigger unique personal insights, and emerging with a new resolve. It comes from finding the passion on a personal level, and harnessing it to hold on to, even before the vision development process gets under way.

Many people have been forced to look inward for meaning in response to an emotionally charged event such as the death or serious illness of a loved one, a divorce, growing up poor or discriminated against, consequences from the September 11 terrorist attack, rejection by a role model—things that are beyond their control.

Some struggle to sort out the meaning of the experience, which may have left them with feelings of profound separateness, perhaps anger and, most likely, disorientation. For these people, what often emerges is the need to examine goals, values, and norms of conduct. The question "Why did this happen to me?" evokes emotional energy, which can either be turned on oneself in a counterproductive way or applied in a creative burst of productive energy.

Two clear examples are Andy Grove and Dave Thomas. Grove is the former CEO and current chairman of Intel. He escaped Nazi Europe with his parents, learned new languages to survive, came to the United States with virtually nothing, worked his way through college and a doctoral program, and waged a winning fight against prostate cancer. Thomas, founder of Wendy's, was an adopted orphan

and high school dropout who ended up leading a chain of six thousand restaurants. He had the audacity to think that square hamburgers would taste better and the commitment to dedicate his life to helping abandoned children.

Theories and research that have tried to explain the success of organizational leaders express a similar theme. Leadership is less about sheer talent than about introspection forged from events that caused great discomfort, if not suffering. It is more than a coincidence that so many people who have successfully built and run complex organizations have had this leadership-shaping experience. At one time or another they have had to let go of something they thought was important.

Now, they seek to clarify for others the "abyss"—the difference between a highly defined and desirable future, matched by dissatisfaction with the status quo. Perhaps they can do this for others because they have had to do it for themselves. They have the capacity to speak to the depths of another person because they are in touch with their own deeper conflicts. They found support along the way through the intensity of their convictions and their awareness of the impressions they left on others.

In 1987, Elisabet Eklind got married and moved to the United States from Stockholm, Sweden, where she had lived all her life. In March 1993, her husband died after a long battle with cancer. As she sat in her home after her husband's death, she told me, she realized that she could either "die" then and there as well—simply continue going through the motions of living—or she could rebuild herself. Start again, in other words, and work through the pain. She chose the latter and, as she says, has emerged "a stronger, better person for the effort":

> A fish doesn't know what water is until it is out of water. And before (those two experiences), I was like a fish. I didn't know what "water" was. I was not aware, in a truly meaningful sense, of how the nuances of my surroundings affected me and how I responded to them.
>
> Now I know what water is. I know when I'm out of it. I am much more aware of my needs, and I believe these experiences also helped me to understand the needs of others—and this includes people in my organization.

Eklind's effort to find a new awareness has shaped her life in ways she never imagined. It has also shaped the way she approaches her work as executive director of HIPPY USA, a nonprofit whose purpose is to enhance the potential for the educational success of low-income children. She realized that to truly realign the values of her organization, she would have to bring the effects of her own very personal journey to bear on the effort.

"You carry significant experiences with you, and they shape the way you look at the world," she said. "And if you let them, they shape the way you approach your work and think about what your organization or company needs. My own personal experiences helped me see HIPPY with greater clarity than I ever could have before."

Those who create and implement visions that serve as engines for guided corporate growth know who they are and what they want their organizations to be. Their articulated vision comes alive from a conviction that not only meets their personal need for action but is also part of a much larger purpose.

VISION FAILURE FROM MYOPIA

When it comes to executing a plan for growth, most CEOs talk the talk. Vision committees crank out visions and post them on their Web sites and on the walls of conference rooms. Usually, however, the process doesn't go far beyond that. And that is where cynicism for the concept of corporate vision takes root. Having a page that articulates a vision is far different from weaving that vision into the daily fabric of organizational life.

When relatively superficial—what I call myopic—visions are used as a rallying cry for the troops, the vision *process* is rarely unleashed with the full force and power it's capable of achieving. Sadly, executive groups take too little advantage of a vision's ability to transform their organizations into one whose actions are driven and directed by that vision.

My experiences with CEOs and executive groups have made me realize that it is difficult for them to stretch their thinking toward the future. They're "grounded," realistic people. They are drawn toward a "mission," which enables them to describe what an organization does now, rather than toward a vision, which forces them to describe why their organization actually engages in these activities.

My Fortune 50 dinner companion commiserated further:

Just because we're so obsessed with planning, tinkering with our plans every year, and holding division leaders accountable for achieving their plan, the executive suite has a collective mentality that we're very strategic. Because the culture has us so focused on planning, they think that's visionary! As head of marketing, I need to position the corporate brand with a far longer horizon but I'm clueless how to do that when everyone's thinking about next year or barely five years out.

Henry Mintzberg, a management professor at McGill University, found that strategic plans invariably fail when there is no overarching vision driving them. Not only do they fail to motivate others to reach further and become innovative, to pull together far-flung units, but they also fail as analytic planning documents (*The Rise and Fall of Strategic Planning,* Free Press: 1994).

Visions, therefore, must describe the desired long-term future of the organization—a future that typically is not quite achievable, but also not so fantastic as to seem like a ridiculous pipe dream. Visioning requires imagination, a mental capacity for synthesis, a trust in intuition, and a deep *emotional* commitment to that desired future. And this is partially why the vision-development process is such a leadership balancing act—and another reason why the B-D Gap exists. Visions need to challenge people, evoke feelings that draw people toward wanting to be a part of something quite special.

When a vision is framed as something that is achievable within a set amount of years, then it falls into the terrain of a strategic plan. That is why the overwhelming majority of organizational visions fail to deliver the impact: they are rational, time-bound, and highly impersonal.

SHRINKING THE BELIEVING-DOING GAP

I have found that there are three particular areas of emotional dissonance in the vision process. Too much time can be lost, and the quality of the final result will be compromised, if each key participant in the process isn't mindful of these three dynamics from the start:

1. *Live in the past, present, and future simultaneously.*

Visions work in part because those who develop them are able to constantly juggle the past, present, and future. A study of firms with rapid, sustained growth found that their senior-most executives seem to stay focused on the state of the firm's desired future. Yet they are also attentive to the day-to-day activities that continually reinforce the vision and the philosophy that guides their internal context (e.g., organizational processes like the structure, culture, and people processes)—what I call the Vision Framework. With a robust vision as their beacon, they modify or supplement existing structures and processes rather than completely replace old techniques that worked well in the past. The overriding characteristic here is their ability to continually analyze and reconcile the firms' recent past with its intended future.

2. *Acknowledge emotion and disorientation.*

Strategic vision depends on the ability *to feel.* It cannot be developed by looking coldly at words and numbers on pieces of paper or computer screens. We have found in our work with the executives who truly desire to create adaptive, growth-oriented organizations that they begin the process first by looking deep within themselves. They need to know who they are and what they want their organizations to be. That way, when they articulate a vision, it comes from a conviction that meets their personal need for action, but is also part of a larger purpose. A deep, visceral commitment signals to themselves and everyone around them that they are open to changing the way they see and think of themselves and the company. This is far from easy and, for most, it can be scary as hell.

After a divisional leader in one of the world's largest consulting firms completed the final outline of his unit's vision, he remarked to me:

> It was like putting together a tough puzzle, only more difficult. You don't see all the pieces, know how many there are, or even where we can go to find them. Then, we found that some of the pieces can change shape as a result of other pieces we were playing around with afterwards. God, I'm glad we went through this, but it was the most nerve-wracking, soul-searching, sobering thing I've ever done professionally.

Leaders who close the B-D Gap don't simply think about themselves in the context of the future

they are defining. They allow themselves to feel enthusiasm, even passion for that future. When this excitement courses through them, it leads in turn to higher levels of commitment and determination. These characteristics make it easier to overcome the often-daunting challenges and roadblocks that prevent the vision from becoming a living reality.

Niall Fitzgerald, co-chairman of Unilever and co-creator of its vision-driven transformation process, spoke openly about the abyss for him: "You feel anticipation, even deep uneasiness, but the excitement of the vision calls on you to take that leap, then build a bridge for others. . . . At Unilever, the bridge we needed to build was all about people: we needed to tap into their passion; we needed them to see their business in entirely new ways; and we needed them to develop very different leadership styles."

Antony Burgmans, Fitzgerald's counterpart as co-chairman, reflected similarly, "As we launched into our growth strategy, I realized that I didn't feel right: something was missing. . . What I saw was that even though we had an excellent change strategy, and an inspiring vision, what was really required to bring about change at Unilever was a new culture, a new leadership mind-set, and new behaviors."

"A new leadership mind-set." In other words, as Burgmans was to discover, what Unilever needed was the passion at the top to fuel the change process throughout the organization. Innovation and the risk taking necessary for closing the abyss, and bringing the vision to life, require the same level of passion for overcoming the Believing-Doing Gap.

Another load of emotional baggage that travels with this process is an executive's comfort level with setting goals and trying to achieve them. Conceptualizing a vision raises goal thinking to a far higher level—one that may easily induce feelings of inadequacy. Visions are like dreams—dreams of the kind of life we want, the things we want to create, or the part of the world we want to change. When the goal-driven executive begins connecting vision to dreams, he or she may relegate it to fantasy. Too often, business is a place reserved only for cold, practical reality and dealing with the problems of the present.

3. *Accept that the process is, by nature, imprecise, frustrating, and sometimes tedious.*

The process of developing a vision runs counter to the way most people in organizations actually operate. Visioning cannot occur without starts, stops, and some confusion. A natural reaction when one's mental map is triggered by new external or unexpected inputs is to be confused. It's a sign that the brain is trying to process new information. Unfortunately, those in senior-most positions too often relate confusion to information not mastered, to not being professional, to something one should avoid doing. Acknowledgment that visioning is not a "clean," easy process will help overcome resistance to a full-range vision.

YOU'RE MAKING PROGRESS WHEN . . .

An organization's vision should provide both movement and direction for shaping the culture, people processes, structure, and how the executive group's decisions will continually reinforce the vision. It should rally energies, galvanize aspirations and commitment from people in the organization, and mobilize them into determined action toward a desired future that includes growth.

As you work through the vision development process, pause frequently and ask yourself if what you're creating will do the following:

- Would it motivate you to join this organization and continue to motivate you once you are there?

- Does it provide a beacon for guiding the kinds of adaptation and change required for continual growth?

- Will it challenge you?

- Can it serve as the basis to formulate strategy that can be acted on?

- Will it serve as the framework to keep all strategic decision making in context?

Well-conceptualized visions, those that come from the heart as well as the head, accomplish all of these. Quantitative, impersonal goals cannot create purpose in a process that has none. Organizations do not become great by having a quest for more of anything, since merely wanting more is inherently unsatisfying. Increasing shareholder return, reaching for other financial metrics, or wanting to be number one falls flat as vision material. It's myopic. If there is no point in what you are doing, if a vision does not evoke emotion, then just measuring your progress can't make it any more worthwhile.

Organizing people around purpose is the most powerful form of leadership. But leaders who create and implement the visions that impact long-run performance can define their organization's raison d'être, a far-reaching strategy that sets its distinctive competencies and competitive advantages apart from others, and the values that give it a soul. These are the leaders who look outward, to a distant future, and declare how their firms will change the world. They can do this because they have also looked inward, to understand how personal discomfort can be converted to commitment, clarity, and courage to create the bridge from believing to doing.

The Power of Business Models

Scott M. Shafer
Wake Forest University

H. Jeff Smith
Wake Forest University

Jane C. Linder
Accenture Institute for Strategic Change

1. BUSINESS MODELS

For many years, Sun Microsystems enjoyed considerable success by bucking the industry trend toward standardized chips and software (Tam, 2003). Sun made the strategic choice to offer more powerful and more expensive computer solutions based on proprietary hardware and software, which worked well as long as Sun was able to maintain a performance advantage. However, standardized chips eventually matched the performance of Sun's proprietary chips, and standardized software offered functionality similar to Sun's. As a result, Sun has seen its quarterly sales drop by more than 40 percent since their peak in 2001, and its stock price decline to under $4 per share from a high of over $60 per share.

In late 2002, after a probing meeting with the head of Sun's low-end server business, Sun's CEO agreed that the firm would add a line of cheaper servers based on Intel chips. This strategic choice marked a clear departure from Sun's existing business model, but there is no evidence that this change has helped the company's business. In fact, revenues for the quarter ending June 30, 2003, were down 13 percent from a year earlier. Indeed, one might reasonably conclude that Sun's "business model" was and remains broken. Certainly, the levels of misdirection and confusion in Sun's engineering and sales organizations, reported recently in *The Wall Street Journal,* suggest that, at a minimum, Sun is experiencing some problems communicating its new model internally.

Reprinted from *Business Horizons* 48, no. 3, (May–June 2005), pp. 199–207. © 2004 Kelley School of Business, Indiana University. Used by permission.

Furthermore, there is little evidence that Sun executives considered issues of internal consistency as they reviewed alternative strategic choices. In particular, the choice to offer less expensive servers needs to be evaluated in terms of the added pressure this will place on Sun's more expensive hardware. In addition, a fundamental element of Sun's traditional strategy has been plowing a significant portion of revenue back into R&D in an effort to maintain its performance advantage. Making the strategic choice to offer less expensive solutions will likely have a significant impact on Sun's ability to maintain its current R&D funding levels, which in turn will have implications regarding its ability to compete on the basis of higher-performing solutions.

It is hard to argue that there is a single "right" strategic answer for Sun. However, it is similarly difficult to believe that all of the cause-and-effect relationships within the new business model have been carefully considered. Based on media reports and customer complaints, it is fairly obvious that Sun's executives have not been successful in explaining their new model. While business models can be powerful tools for analyzing, implementing, and communicating strategic choices, there is no evidence that Sun has successfully harnessed that power.

Over the past few years, "business models" have surged into the management vocabulary. In the mid-1990s, "dot-com" firms pitched business models to attract funding. Now, companies of all sorts in virtually every industry rely on the concept as well; in fact, approximately 27 percent of Fortune 500 firms used the term in their 2001 annual reports. The media have certainly gotten on board also. Within major magazines and journals, only one article in 1990 used the term *business model* three times or more; by 2000, well over 500 articles fell into that category.

While it has become quite fashionable to discuss business models, many executives remain confused about how to use the concept. For example, in a recent Accenture study, in which one of the authors took part, 70 executives from 40 companies were interviewed regarding their company's core logic for creating and capturing value: the basis of a business model. Surprisingly, 62 percent had a difficult time describing succinctly how their own company made money (Linder & Cantrell, 2000), and it appears that Sun's executives may be similarly confused. Strategist Michael Porter (2000) has referred to the phrase "business model" as part of the "Internet's destructive lexicon"; we disagree. We believe that business models can in fact play a positive and powerful role in corporate management. Before exploring that role in more detail, it is first necessary to understand exactly what constitutes a business model.

2. DESPERATELY SEEKING DEFINITION: IDENTITY CRISIS OF THE BUSINESS MODEL

To be sure, many authors have offered definitions of the term *business model.* Our own review of relevant literature uncovered 12 definitions in established publications during the years 1998–2002. None of these definitions, however, appears to have been accepted fully by the business community, and this may be due to emanation from so many different perspectives (i.e., e-business, strategy, technology, and information systems), with the viewpoint of each author driving term definition; by peering through different lenses, authors are seeing different things.

In fact, across these 12 definitions, one can find 42 different business model components: unique building blocks or elements. As Table 1 illustrates, some of these components appear in only one definition, but others are seen time and time again. To gain additional insight, we developed an affinity diagram (Pyzdek, 2003) to categorize the business model components that were cited twice or more (affinity diagrams are a popular "Six Sigma" tool for organizing ideas into categories based on their underlying similarity; affinity diagrams help to

identify patterns and establish related groups that exist in qualitative data sets). The resulting affinity diagram (see Figure 1) identified four major categories: strategic choices, creating value, capturing value, and the value network. To develop the affinity diagram shown in Figure 1, two of the authors, along with a graduate student, worked independently to (*a*) cluster into categories the 20 business model components cited two or more times and (*b*) develop a descriptive name for each category. At that point, the preliminary clusters were shared, and two of the authors discussed the individually developed clusters to reach a final consensus.

Since no generally accepted definition of a business model has emerged to date, we offer a new definition guided by the following two principles. First, the definition should integrate and synthesize the earlier work in this area. Second, the definition should be simple enough so that it can be easily understood, communicated, and remembered.

As a starting point, we began by parsing the term *business model.* More specifically, business is fundamentally concerned with creating value and capturing returns from that value, and a model is simply a representation of reality. Combining these concepts with the results summarized in the affinity diagram shown in Figure 1, we define a business model as a representation of a firm's underlying core logic and strategic choices for creating and capturing value within a value network.

This definition includes four key terms. The first key term, *core logic,* suggests that a properly crafted business model helps articulate and make explicit key assumptions about cause-and-effect relationships and the internal consistency of *strategic choices:* the second key term. In effect, the business model reflects the strategic choices that have been made, a point to which we return in the next section.

The terms *creating* and *capturing value* reflect two fundamental functions that all organizations must perform to remain viable over an extended period of time. Successful firms create substantial value by doing things in ways that differentiate them from the competition. Firms might develop core competencies, capabilities, and positional advantages that are different from those of competitors. They might use those core competencies and capabilities, for example, to perform work activities in a unique way or might combine their work activities into business processes in a way that differentiates them from competitors. They might even have a unique

Table 1 Components of a Business Model

Context / Components	Timmers (1998) E-Business	Hamel (2000) Strategy	Afuah and Tucci (2001) E-Business	Amit and Zott (2001) E-Business	Weill and Vitale (2001) E-Business	Dubosson-Torbay et al. (2002) E-Business	Magretta (2002) Strategy	Rayport and Jaworski (2002) E-Business	Van Der Vorst et al. (2002) E-Business/ SCM[a]	Hoque (2002) Technology	Chesbrough (2003) Strategy	Hedman and Kalling (2003) IS[b] and Strategy
Components												
Value network (suppliers)	X	X			X	X			X	X	X	X
Customer (target market, scope)		X	X			X	X	X		X	X	
Resources/ assets		X		X		X		X		X		X
Value proposition			X			X	X	X	X		X	
Capabilities/ competencies		X	X	X		X						X
Processes/ activities		X	X			X			X			X
Revenue/pricing	X	X	X			X		X		X	X	X
Competitors						X		X			X	
Cost							X					X
Information flows	X			X	X							
Output (offering)		X		X	X	X		X		X		
Product/service flows	X			X		X			X	X		
Strategy		X									X	
Branding		X										
Customer information		X				X						
Customer relationship		X				X				X		
Differentiation		X								X		
Financial aspects				X		X		X				
Mission		X								X		
Profit						X	X					
Business opportunities												

(Continued)

Table 1 **Continued**

Context	Timmers (1998) E-Business	Hamel (2000) Strategy	Afuah and Tucci (2001) E-Business	Amit and Zott (2001) E-Business	Weill and Vitale (2001) E-Business	Dubosson-Torbay et al. (2002) E-Business	Magretta (2002) Strategy	Rayport and Jaworski (2002) E-Business	Van Der Vorst et al. (2002) E-Business/SCMa	Hoque (2002) Technology	Chesbrough (2003) Strategy	Hedman and Kalling (2003) ISb and Strategy
Cash flows					X							
Create value				X								
Culture		X										
Customer benefits										X		
Customer interface								X				
Economic logic							X					
Environment										X		
Firm identity										X		
Firm reputation										X		
Fulfillment and support		X										
Functionalities									X			
Implementation			X			X						
Infrastructure—applications						X			X			
Infrastructure—management												
Management												X
Product innovation									X			
Specific characteristics			X									
Sustainability												
Transaction content				X								
Transaction governance				X								
Transaction structure				X								

a Supply chain management.

b Information systems.

Figure 1   **Components of Business Model Affinity Diagram**

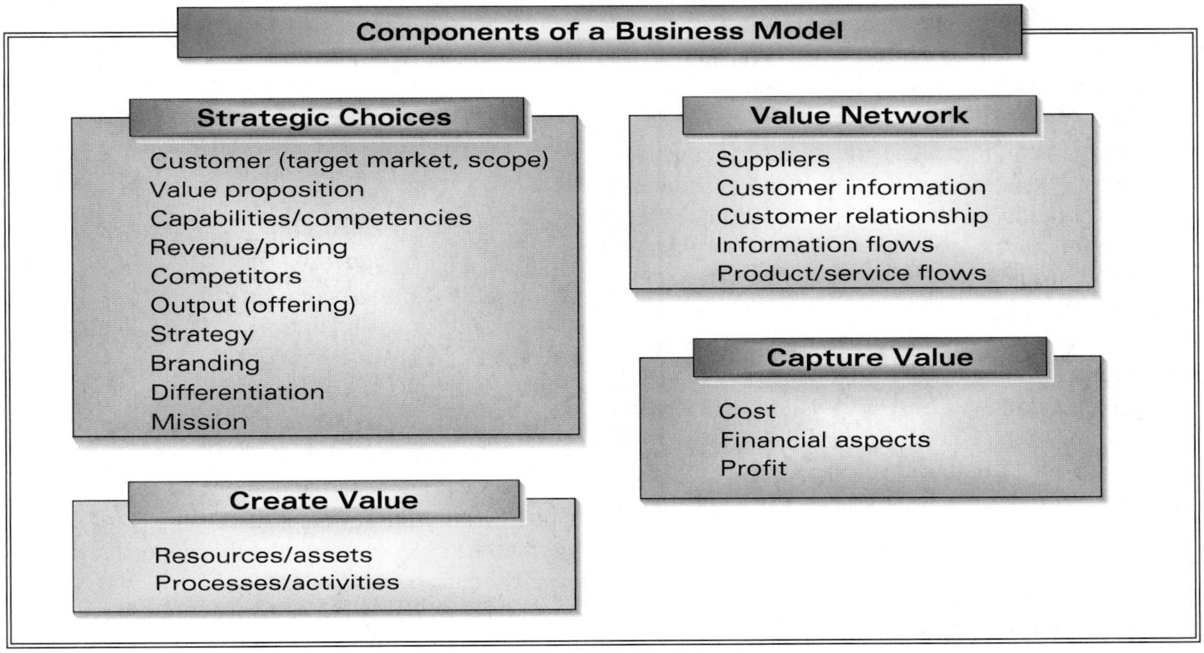

Components of a Business Model

Strategic Choices
- Customer (target market, scope)
- Value proposition
- Capabilities/competencies
- Revenue/pricing
- Competitors
- Output (offering)
- Strategy
- Branding
- Differentiation
- Mission

Value Network
- Suppliers
- Customer information
- Customer relationship
- Information flows
- Product/service flows

Capture Value
- Cost
- Financial aspects
- Profit

Create Value
- Resources/assets
- Processes/activities

approach in securing the capital that is needed to fund the creation of the core competencies, capabilities, and positional advantages. In the end though, for-profit companies must make money to survive; thus, their viability is tied both to the value they create and to the way they capture value and resultantly generate profit.

Neither value creation nor value capture occurs in a vacuum, however. As Hamel (2000) argues, both occur within a value network, which can include suppliers, partners, distribution channels, and coalitions that extend the company's own resources. The firm may be able to create unique relationships with any of these parties or even with its end customers. The role a firm chooses to play within its value network is an important element of its business model.

Note that this definition is in no way restricted to the online world. Of course, it is true that the use of the term *business model* gained momentum during the dot-com era: those bygone days in which sock puppets sold dog food on Web sites. But, as we noted at the outset, the concept is relevant for firms of all sorts. While some refer to "e-business models" (e.g., Chen, 2003; Weill & Vitale, 2001), our definition in no way demands the "e-" prefix.

3. A "BUSINESS MODEL" IS NOT A STRATEGY

With a definition now in hand, we can consider something that a business model is not: a strategy. While a business model does facilitate analysis, testing, and validation of a firm's strategic choices, it is not in itself a strategy.

What exactly is the relationship between a firm's strategy and a business model? To answer this question requires that one first define *strategy,* but unfortunately that is not a trivial task. As Henry Mintzberg (1994) notes in his book *The Rise and Fall of Strategic Planning,* strategy can be viewed in at least four different ways: as a pattern, plan, position, or perspective. Specifically, in a backward-looking context, strategy is sometimes viewed as a pattern of choices made over time. More frequently, however, strategy is considered in a forward-looking sense. Within that forward-looking domain, some see strategy as a plan—a view that relates to choices about paths or courses of action, much like a directional road map. Some, such as leading strategist Michael Porter, see strategy as a position—a view that relates to choices about which products or services are offered in which markets based on differentiating features. Still others, such as management guru Peter Drucker, view, in a grand vision, strategy as perspective—choices about how the business is conceptualized.

Although these views differ in many respects, they all have in common the element regarding making choices. Business models reflect these choices and their operating implications. They facilitate the analysis, testing, and validation of the cause-and-effect relationships that flow from the strategic choices that have been made. In some cases, executives can best effect this by directly translating one set of strategic choices into a single business model, which they then analyze, test, and validate. In other cases, executives may wish to consider a range of business models simultaneously, each representing a different set of strategic choices before drawing a conclusion about the best business model for their organization.

As an illustration of the difference between a strategy and a business model, consider the construction of a custom home. Initially, the architect consults with the future homeowners to understand how they envision the finished home and their life within it. They then consider options in a number of areas (e.g., main level or second-story master bedroom) and create a design to fulfill the vision; this corresponds to the strategy. Next, the architect prepares a detailed floor plan and elevation based on the choices made during the design process; this corresponds to a business model. Just as a business model can be used to help analyze and communicate strategic choices, the floor plan can be used to help understand, analyze, and communicate the design choices that were made. In fact, it could even prod the future homeowners to rethink some of their original strategic choices; for example, as the process moves forward, they might realize their choice of a main-level master bedroom would conflict with the only possible placement of the kitchen, leading them to revisit their original choices and perhaps modification.

Applied in a business context, consider GM's OnStar division (Barabba et al., 2002). In the late 1990s, GM created a project team to develop a business model and strategically analyze opportunities related to the telematics industry (telematics involves the use of wireless communication technologies and global positioning systems to deliver a variety of safety, security, entertainment, and productivity services to individuals while they are traveling

in their cars). The team was unsure how to position the telematics business opportunity. One alternative was to simply treat it as though it was another car feature. From GM's perspective, this was a safer and more conservative approach since it had extensive previous experience in pricing and marketing vehicle options. The other alternative was to position telematics as a new service business. From this perspective, the telematics opportunity entailed greater risk, given the large investment in infrastructure that would be required and GM's lack of experience dealing directly with end consumers (a subset of other strategic decisions and options for each decision are listed in Table 2).

After identifying the relevant strategic decision areas and the options in each, choices are made. A business model embodies a set of choices. Through it, the set can be tested and analyzed to ensure that implicit cause-and-effect relationships are logical and that the choices are mutually supportive and internally consistent.

But how would the OnStar team test the business models that represented different sets of strategic choices? The team had to ensure that implicit and explicit cause-and-effect relationships were logical and reasonable and also had to ensure the choices were internally consistent and mutually supportive. This was not an easy task because no historical data existed for this brand-new industry. Instead, the project team relied on a variety of sophisticated management science methodologies, including systems dynamics, conjoint analysis, dynamic optimization, models

Table 2   **Illustrative Strategic Decision Areas and Options at OnStar**

Strategic Decision	Options
Position	New service business
	New car feature
Installation	Factory
	Field
Internal product scope	Select GM vehicles
	All GM vehicles
External product scope	Only GM vehicles
	Sell to other auto manufactures
Call center	Insource
	Outsource
Application development	Insource
	Outsource

of diffusion, real options valuation, simulation, and game theory. Using simulation techniques, for example, the team was able to analyze how factors, including customer acquisition, customer choice, alliances, customer service, finances, and dealer behavior would impact business performance on multiple dimensions, including market share and cash flow.

As part of this analysis, the team demonstrated that attempting to run the call centers as cost centers would result in business failure. In addition, the team was able to analyze the options of installing OnStar in vehicles both at the factory and in the field and found that factory installation would provide a superior outcome in all parameters.

As a result of these types of analyses, the team ultimately recommended that senior management embrace a more aggressive set of strategic choices and create a new service business. The suggested model included a number of rather aggressive positions, including that OnStar be installed in all new GM cars, that GM recruit and make available OnStar to other auto manufacturers, that one year of service be provided free, and that GM aggressively pursue partnerships with content providers. GM senior management accepted the project team's recommendations and formally acknowledged that the iterative process employed by the team, one in which strategic choices were tested through business models, greatly influenced their decision.

Although the jury is still out regarding OnStar's ability to consistently make money, the results of GM's OnStar initiative have so far been rather impressive. By the fall of 2001, GM had two million OnStar subscribers, representing 80 percent of the telematics market. Alliances with other major auto manufacturers, including Toyota, Honda, VW, Audi, Isuzu, and Subaru, provide OnStar with access to approximately 50 percent of total new vehicle sales. GM has also developed partnerships with important content providers, including Dow Jones and Fidelity Investments. Internal forecasts indicate that the service will break even in 2003 and generate significant positive cash flow thereafter. Based on these results, Merrill Lynch (2002) has valued the OnStar business at between $4 and $12 billion.

We earlier defined a business model as the representation of a firm's underlying core logic and strategic choices for creating and capturing value within a value network. The core logic should be as comprehensive as possible, not simply one or two components, and the business model should reflect

the firm's strategic choices. While executives can use business models to analyze and communicate strategic choices, it is equally important to recognize that misusing the business model concept can lead to problems, a topic to which we now turn.

4. FOUR PROBLEMS OF BUSINESS MODELS

A properly crafted business model has great power and can serve as an essential strategic tool for the firm, but concerns about business models can be traced to four common problems associated with their creation and use. These problems, which follow directly from the key terms in our definition, are the following:

1. Flawed assumptions underlying the core logic.
2. Limitations in the strategic choices considered.
3. Misunderstandings about value creation and value capture.
4. Flawed assumptions about the value network.

4.1. Flawed Assumptions Underlying the Core Logic

A firm moves into a danger zone if its business model's core logic is based on flawed or untested assumptions about the future. Recently, an entrepreneur told us of an exciting opportunity his firm was planning to pursue, providing integrated services over wireless networks in many regions of the United States. His business model seemed to be well formed and internally consistent in that he had a good sense of his core logic for both creating and capturing value. However, when asked about incompatibilities in standards among wireless networks, he told us that he was assuming seamless and interchangeable national service in the near future. While we certainly agree there ought to be such a seamless and standard network across wireless providers, the reality is that such a network does not now exist and likely will not for a number of years; hence, our prediction is that he will face significant challenges in implementing his model.

It is vital that, once a set of strategic choices has been made, the resulting business model be checked to ensure that implicit and explicit cause-and-effect relationships are well grounded as well as logical.

Furthermore, the resulting business model should be scrutinized to ensure that the set of choices is internally consistent and mutually supportive of one another. To illustrate this, consider two of the strategic choices faced by OnStar: its position and its external product scope. One incompatible combination of choices would have been to position OnStar as simply a new car feature and to make OnStar available to other auto manufacturers. If such a combination of choices were embraced, any potential benefits to GM would be quickly negated since the competition would be able to offer the identical feature. Alternatively, choosing to position OnStar as a stand-alone service business and making the service available to other auto manufacturers are choices that are quite compatible. In such a case, the decision to offer the service to other auto manufacturers facilitates penetration of a new market.

4.2. Limitations in the Strategic Choices Considered

A business model should address all of the firm's core logic for creating and capturing value, not just a portion of that logic. Indeed, one of the major mistakes of the "dot-com" era was the assumption that, having defined one portion, one had a business model. When one addresses only a small subset of the rows in Table 1 or only a subset of the categories in Figure 1, one is mistaken in referring to this as a "business model." Definition of a customer set (e.g., families with young children) or a value proposition (e.g., providing much more value at a greater cost), for example, does not constitute a business model. Of course, such an error in nomenclature is problematic in and of itself because it frustrates communication. However, the biggest flaw with such an approach is that it may well delude the executive into overestimating his or her model's probability of success in the marketplace.

eToys serves as a high-profile example of a firm that made this mistake in the dot-com world. In an effort to build its customer base and gain brand awareness in 1999, eToys (and its online competitors, such as KBToys) focused primarily on customer acquisition. Not surprisingly, this led to cut-throat price wars, deep discounts, and offers of free shipping among the toy e-tailers, each of whom was hoping to establish a beachhead in the $23 billion per year toy retailing industry (Bannon,

2000). In fact, eToys' goal of customer acquisition was largely achieved. Four years after opening its virtual doors for business and by spending at times as much as 60 percent of its revenues on marketing, eToys established a base of almost 2 million customers. However, eToys had not developed (or, it appears, even seriously considered) another important component in its business model: the process of fulfilling customer orders. During the 1999 holiday season, eToys received a tremendous amount of bad publicity resulting from its very poor and unreliable delivery performance. In an effort to not repeat this fiasco the following year, the company invested heavily to in-source order fulfillment. But, in the end, eToys was not able to generate the volume of business needed to support its investment in infrastructure and went bankrupt in 2001 (Cox, 2001; eToys, 2001). Its realization that it had never really created a workable business model in that it had been relying on only the single component of customer acquisition came far too late for recovery.

The problem of too limited a set of strategic choices can often be traced to a tendency on the part of senior management to consider strategic decisions in a piecemeal fashion, which is especially likely in a volatile business environment. Sun would certainly fall into this trap if it considered offering low-end servers independent of other strategic decisions. The problem is also exemplified by eToys' initial attention being focused almost exclusively on customer acquisition, with a subsequent shift to order fulfillment.

A business model provides a powerful tool for avoiding this pitfall for two reasons. First, because the business model is a reflection of the strategic choices made, it highlights the need to consider holistically a range of strategic decisions. Second, the business model requires senior management to consider the logic and internal consistency of the strategic decisions collectively.

4.3. Misunderstandings about Value Creation and Value Capture

Many executives have a tendency to focus so much on the value creation part of the model that the value capture portion is ignored or at least downplayed. In these situations, organizations are unable to capture corresponding economic returns in relation to the value they create.

As an example of creating value but not capturing it, consider the online portal Yahoo. For many individuals, Yahoo's continuously expanding range of offerings, including searches of the Web, e-mail accounts, stock quotes and other financial information, greeting cards, maps, driving directions, and so on create a tremendous amount of value. The fact that Yahoo is consistently among the top sites in terms of unique visitors per month is a further indication of its appeal. But, for many years, Yahoo struggled to turn this value into profit; in fact, its net loss more than doubled from its fiscal year ending in 1997 to the one ending in 2001. However, under the hand of CEO Terry S. Semel, who joined Yahoo in May 2001, the company has apparently found a way to capture more of this value, with revenues now coming from "digital music and online games to job listings and premium e-mail accounts with loads of extra storage . . . [Yahoo now] pulls in one-third of revenue from such offerings and hopes to drive it up to 50 percent by 2004," according to a recent *BusinessWeek* report (Elgin & Grover, 2003).

Alternatively, executives can encounter this pitfall when they confuse potential value with actual value. Just a few years ago, professional investment analysts argued that a company's performance ought to be measured by its number of customers, not its free cash flow. It seems silly now, but many capable business leaders have similarly confused potential value with actual value when they design business models. For example, one large commercial bank spent millions acquiring an investment-banking boutique to get into the Wall Street deal flow only to discover that their model did not work. The newly acquired investment bankers refused to share information and resisted the commercial bankers' interference with their clients. They were particularly unenthusiastic about making joint sales calls to help sell commercial banking services with margins that did not support their bonus structure.

4.4. Relying on Flawed Assumptions about the Value Network

Sometimes, a model mistakenly assumes that the existing value network will continue unchanged into the future. For example, oil companies have been accustomed to retailing gasoline through their own branded outlets in the United Kingdom. When supermarket chains, like Tescos and Safeway U.K., began drawing customers into stores with low-priced gasoline, some oil companies simply added food products to their gas station inventories. This choice maintained the current value network. Cagier competitors, like BP, took a different tack. They locked up partnerships with the best grocery chains under the premise that the oil company would manage gas retailing and the grocery company would manage food retailing across all the outlets in their joint network.

In another example, listeners of U.S. commercial radio stations are accustomed to receiving free broadcasts in return for listening to advertisements; in fact, this has been true for several decades. However, building a business model on the long-term assumption that this arrangement will continue may be a mistake. Although only beginning to move from infancy into adolescence, satellite radio (now with two major U.S. providers, XM and Sirius, each offering dozens of commercial-free stations for a fee) may turn the long-standing free-programming-with-commercials structure on its head. Business models that assume a continuation of the current state of affairs, such as one for an intermediary that barters commercial time among local stations in return for services, could well be flawed.

To be sure, some in the broadcast industry have considered the emergence of satellite radio but have downplayed the threat to local stations, arguing that listeners expect to receive local information (e.g., traffic reports, weather, local news), which satellite technology is not well suited to deliver. It should be noted, though, that the XM and Sirius signals are transmitted not just over satellites but also through local signal repeaters that the companies have installed in several U.S. urban areas. Their stated intentions are to use the repeaters to improve reception within crowded city environs, as satellite reception can be unreliable in the midst of tall buildings. At present, these repeaters typically deliver the national feeds without any local customization; however, it is certainly conceivable that these repeaters will allow the satellite companies to someday compete with local programming and carry local advertising (Flynn, 2003).

5. FINAL THOUGHTS

The survival and prosperity of all for-profit organizations is directly linked to their ability to both create and capture value; therefore, business models are applicable to all these. Of course, the strategic decision areas confronting each organization will vary based on numerous factors such as the firm's age, industry, industry concentration, customer type, government regulations, and so on. At the same time, an organization's business model is never complete as the process of making strategic choices and testing business models should be ongoing and iterative. While there are certainly no guarantees, we contend that the probability of long-term success increases with the rigor and formality with which an organization tests its strategic options through business models.

Business models provide a powerful way for executives to analyze and communicate their strategic choices. Although there is some chance that firms with sloppily formulated business models will succeed in the marketplace, the probability is low since the core logic for value creation and capture will not have been clearly thought through. As the old saying suggests, blind squirrels do occasionally find acorns, but, until they do, there is a lot of wasted effort. Just like firms that burn through their working capital, the squirrels may run out of energy before they achieve their prize.

ACKNOWLEDGMENTS

We appreciate constructive comments from Ram Baliga and from the participants in the Research Seminar Series at the Babcock Graduate School of Management. This research was supported by the Babcock Graduate School of Management's Research Fellowship Program.

References

Afuah, A., & Tucci, C. L. (2001). *Internet business models and strategies.* Boston: McGraw-Hill, Irwin.

Amit, R., & Zott, C. (2001). Value creation in e-business. *Strategic Management Journal, 22,* 493–520.

Bannon, L. (2000, October 23). E-commerce (A special report): The lessons we've learned—Toys: Rough play—consumers like buying toys online; but that hasn't made it a great business yet. *The Wall Street Journal,* p. R1.

Barabba, V., Huber, C., Cooke, F., Pudar, N., Smith, J., & Paich, M. (2002). A multimethod approach for creating new business models: The General Motors On-Star project. *Interfaces, 32*(1), 24–34.

Chen, S. (2003). The real value of e-business models. *Business Horizons, 46*(6), 27–33.

Chesbrough, H. (2003). Open innovation. Boston: Harvard Business School Press.

Cox, B. (2001, January 26). eToys on the ropes. www.internetnews.com.

Dubosson-Torbay, M., Osterwalder, A., & Pigneur, Y. (2002). E-business model design, classification, and measurements. *Thunderbird International Business Review, 44*(1), 5–23.

Elgin, B., & Grover, R. (2003, June 2). Yahoo! act two. *BusinessWeek, 3835,* 70–76.

eToys gets approval to sell assets in smaller pieces. *The Wall Street Journal,* p. B11.

Flynn, L. J. (2003, January 7). Investors and local broadcasters watch growth of satellite radio. *New York Times,* p. C7.

Hamel, G. (2000). *Leading the revolution.* New York: Plume.

Hedman, J., & Kalling, T. (2003). The business model concept: theoretical underpinnings and empirical illustrations. *European Journal of Information Systems, 12,* 49–59.

Hoque, F. (2002). *The alignment effect.* Upper Saddle River, NJ: Prentice Hall.

Linder, J., & Cantrell, S. (2000). Carved in water: Changing business models fluidly. *Accenture Institute for strategic change.*

Magretta, J. (2002). Why business models matter. *Harvard Business Review, 80*(5), 86–92.

Merrill Lynch Equity Research. 2002, April. New York: General Motors.

Mintzberg, H. (1994). *The rise and fall of strategic planning.* New York: Free Press.

Porter, M. E. (2000). Strategy and the internet. *Harvard Business Review, 79*(3), 62–78.

Pyzdek, T. (2003). *The six sigma handbook.* New York: McGraw-Hill.

Rayport, J. F., & Jaworski, B. J. (2002). *Cases in e-Commerce.* Boston: McGraw-Hill.

Tam, P. W. (2003, October 16). Cloud over Sun Microsystems: plummeting computer prices. *The Wall Street Journal,* pp. A1–A16.

Timmers, P. (1998). Business models for electronic markets. *Electronic Markets, 8*(2), 3–8.

Van Der Vorst, J. G. A. J., Van Dongen, S., Nouguier, S., & Hilhorst, R. (2002). E-business initiatives in food supply chains; Definition, and typology of electronic business models. *International Journal of Logistics: Research and Applications, 5*(2), 119–138.

Weill, P., & Vitale, M. R. (2001). *Place to space: Migrating to eBusiness models.* Boston: Harvard Business School Press.

The Balanced Scorecard: To Adopt or Not to Adopt?

Kevin B. Hendricks
Richard Ivey School of Business

Larry Menor
Richard Ivey School of Business

Christine Wiedman
Richard Ivey School of Business

Over the past decade, the Balanced Score-card (BSC) has become a widely advocated management tool associated with "best practices." As a management tool, the BSC provides an enhancement to the traditional management planning and control system by looking beyond financial measures to incorporate nonfinancial measures. According to Kaplan and Norton, the developers and staunch advocates of the BSC:

> The name reflected the balance between short- and long-term objectives, between financial and non-financial measures, between lagging and leading indicators, and between external and internal performance perspectives. (Robert S. Kaplan and David P. Norton, *The Balanced Scorecard,* Boston, MA: Harvard Business School Press, 1996, p. viii)

The first BSC-type system, developed by General Electric in the 1950s, was designed to be a performance measurement system, but the BSC has now evolved into a strategic management tool critical to an organization's planning process. The BSC requires that senior management translate the firm's

"The Balances Scorecard: To adopt or not to adopt?" Kevin B. Hendricks, Larry Menor, Christine Wiedman, *Ivey Business Journal,* Vol. 69, No.12 (November/December 2004), p. 1–9. Ivey Management Services prohibits any form of reproduction, storage or transmittal of this material without its written permission. This material is not covered under authorization from any reproduction rights organization. To order copies or request permission to reproduce materials, contact Ivey Publishing, Ivey Management Services, c/o Richard Ivey School of Business, The University of Western Ontario, London, Ontario, Canada, N6A 3K7; Phone (519) 661-3208, fax (519) 661-3882, e-mail cases@ivey.uwo.ca. Copyright @ 2004, Ivey Management Services. One time permission to reproduce granted by Ivey Management Services on February 15, 2006.

vision and strategy into four performance perspectives: financial, customer, internal business, and learning and growth (see Exhibit 1).

A recent Bain & Company survey of more than 708 companies on five continents found that the BSC was used by 62 percent of responding organizations, a higher adoption rate than some other well-known management tools like Total Quality Management, Supply Chain Integration, or Activity Based Management. Key informants from these organizations ranked the BSC eighth overall in satisfaction (again, higher than any of the management tools mentioned above) (Darrell Rigby, "Management Tools Survey 2003: Usage Up as Companies Strive to Make Headway in Tough Times," *Strategy & Leadership,* 31:5, 2003). The appeal of the BSC is also reflected in the widely reported estimate that more than 50 percent of Fortune 1000 firms have used it in some form. Indeed, a number of Canadian companies, from a broad range of industries, have adopted the BSC approach including, among others, Royal Bank of Canada, Molson Inc., Aliant Inc., and Nova Scotia Power Inc. (Balanced Scorecard Collaborative, www.bscol.com).

According to BSC proponents, adopting organizations that also successfully implement an integrated BSC should anticipate a number of benefits, including:

- Better management understanding of the linkages between specific organizational decisions and actions, and the chosen strategic goals.

- A redefinition of relationships with customers.

Exhibit 1   **The Balanced Scorecard**

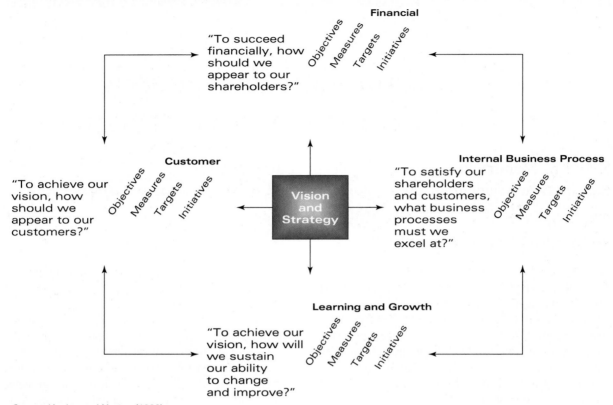

Source: Kaplan and Norton (1996).

- Reengineering of fundamental business processes.
- The emergence of a new corporate culture emphasizing team effort among organizational functions to implement the firm's strategy.

These benefits, while widely touted, have only just begun to be rigorously examined (Steven Salterio and Alan Webb, "The Balanced Scorecard," *CA Magazine,* 136:6, 2003). In contrast, the managerially critical question of whether or not to adopt the BSC has yet to be rigorously examined.

Belief that the BSC represents one of the most significant developments in management accounting, and deserves rigorous research attention, is widespread. However, our review of the extant practitioner and research literatures indicates that (1) there has been little examination of the factors associated with the adoption of the BSC, and (2) there still is the need to demonstrate that the adoption and implementation of the BSC is associated with improved financial performance. We recently completed research specifically examining these two BSC issues.

BSC CONTINGENCY FACTORS

Our BSC investigation was motivated by an observation made in a review of the accounting performance measurement literature:

> The use and performance consequences of these [BSC] measures appear to be affected by organizational strategies and the structural and environmental factors confronting the organization. Future research can make a significant contribution by providing evidence on the contingency variables affecting the predictive ability, adoption and performance consequences of various non-financial measures and balanced scorecards. (Christopher D. Ittner and David F. Larcker, "Innovations in Performance Measurement: Trends and Research Implications," *Journal of Management Accounting Research,* 10, 1998, pp. 223–224)

Specifically, we examined contingency factors including business-level strategy, firm size, environmental uncertainty, and investment in intangible assets. Why do we examine these contingency factors? Our discussions with Canadian business executives who were intimately involved with the adoption and implementation of a BSC at their respective organizations highlight the criticality of many of these factors to the adoption decision. Further, most of these factors have been highlighted in the academic literature as being general considerations underlying decisions to adopt a management control system (Robert H. Chenhall, "Management Control Systems Design Within Its Organizational Context: Findings from Contingency-based Research and Directions for the Future," *Accounting, Organizations and Society,* 28, 2003).

SCOPE OF SURVEY

We surveyed senior executives (primarily CEOs and CFOs) from Canadian organizations to identify whether their firms had adopted the BSC, when they decided to adopt the BSC, when they began using the BSC and whether or not they have since discontinued its use. The final cross-industry sample of organizations in our survey consisted of 579 Canadian firms, chosen from PC Compustat, with annual sales greater than $10 million. We obtained key informant responses from 179 firms, of which 42 (or 23.5 per cent) reported that they had adopted the BSC approach. The BSC adoption year ranged from 1996 through 2003, with the highest number of adoptions (10) occurring in 2002 (Exhibit 2). BSC adoption also covered a wide range of industries, with significantly higher than expected representation in the SIC code range 4000–4999, namely, transportation, communication and utilities.

Employing reliable and valid measures for each of our contingency variables, and controlling for industry effects and the firm's operating performance, we used probit regression to estimate the propensity to adopt a BSC. Our findings are discussed below.

BUSINESS STRATEGY

While it has long been argued in the accounting literature that accounting control systems should be designed according to the business strategy of the firm, this premise has yet to be examined with the BSC. We utilized Miles and Snow's comprehensive, business-level strategic typology that interrelates organizational strategy, structure and process (Raymond E. Miles and Charles C. Snow, *Organizational Strategy, Structure, and Process,* New York: McGraw-Hill, 1978). This typology, which distinguishes distinct firm strategies vis-à-vis the competitive environments in which organizations operate, provides a

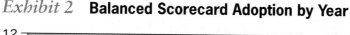

Exhibit 2   **Balanced Scorecard Adoption by Year**

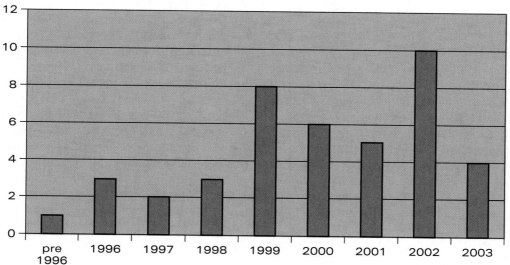

distinct competitive response to the question "How should we compete in a given line of business?" The typology identifies four organizational strategies:

- **Prospectors** who continually search for innovative market opportunities and experiment regularly with new responses to emerging trends.

- **Analyzers** who operate routinely and efficiently through formal structures and processes, while simultaneously watching competitors for promising new ideas which they then rapidly adopt.

- **Defenders** who, given their narrow product-market domains, are highly expert in their organization's area of operation but do little to seek out new opportunities outside their primary domain.

- **Reactors** who are unable to respond effectively to known change and uncertainty in their organization's environment.

Given the broader scope and inclusion of non-financial, forward-looking measures in the BSC, we posited that the use of the BSC would more likely benefit firms that followed a Prospector or Analyzer strategy, and likely not benefit firms that followed a Defender or Reactor strategy. Therefore, we hypothesized that the propensity to adopt the BSC is positively related to the organization's choice of a Prospector or Analyzer strategy. We found that BSC adoption was significantly associated with strategy: firms that followed a Prospector or Analyzer strategy were more likely to adopt the BSC than other firms. One interpretation of this finding is that the BSC may be more useful for some strategy types.

FIRM SIZE

Like business strategy, previous accounting research has suggested that a firm's size can affect the design and use of management control systems. As firms grow, problems in communication and control increase, so these organizations are more likely to adopt complex administration systems. As a result, larger organizations will likely depend on more sophisticated information and control systems that use diverse measures. The BSC represents an integrative management tool that is useful for coordinating cross-function and cross-level decisions and activities. Therefore we hypothesized that the propensity to adopt the BSC was positively related to the firm's

size. We found that BSC adopters were significantly larger than non-adopters. The mean total assets of the adopters was $3.6 billion, compared to mean total assets of $460 million for the non-adopters.

ENVIRONMENTAL UNCERTAINTY

Environmental uncertainty has long been viewed in practice and research as a central problem for organizations. Previous accounting research has found that the uncertainty was related to greater usefulness of broad-scope information, and that the demand for broad-based information systems incorporating non-financial measures was positively associated with perceptions of environmental uncertainty. The BSC, which incorporates both nonfinancial and future-oriented information, would be particularly critical for firms where environmental uncertainty is high. Therefore, we hypothesized that the propensity to adopt the BSC was positively related to the firm's environmental uncertainty. We found that BSC adopters had significantly higher demand volatility (measured as the coefficient of variation in annual sales changes) than non-adopters.

INVESTMENTS IN INTANGIBLE ASSETS

While a definitive classification of intangibles remains to be offered, there is agreement on the importance of effectively managing these assets from a control perspective. Indeed, the effective management of intangible assets—which includes, among others, product innovation, company brand, structural assets, and monopolies (see Baruch Lev, "New Math for a New Economy," *Fast Company*, 31, January 2000)—can be an important driver of business value. The BSC is a notable management tool, since it specifically requires the use of nonfinancial measures directly reflecting the organization's learning and growth decisions, activities, and outcomes. Therefore we hypothesized that the propensity to adopt the BSC was positively related to the firm's investment in intangible assets. However, we did not find support for this hypothesis when we measured intangibles as the ratio of intangible assets to total assets. Given that the financial accounting model is criticized as being overly conservative with regard to the measurement of intangibles, we are currently considering other metrics that might better capture the importance of intangibles to a firm.

BSC AND FINANCIAL PERFORMANCE

Kaplan and Norton propose that the BSC can be used as a strategy map to create value within an organization, through the customer value proposition, internal business processes and the alignment of intangible assets with enterprise strategy. This value should be reflected in improvements in accounting measures such as improved cost structure and increased asset utilization, and ultimately through increased long-term shareholder value (Robert S. Kaplan and David P. Norton, "The Strategy Map: Guide to Aligning Intangible Assets," *Strategy and Leadership*, 32:5, 2004, pp. 10–17). Research can add insight to this area by examining the relation between BSC adoption and implementation and financial performance.

One potential motivation for adopting any new management control system is that the firm's current performance is not meeting the existing expectations of the management team or its shareholders. This was the case in the Group Insurance division of Canada Life in the late 1990s, according to Sandy Richardson, the individual who spearheaded the BSC initiative for the division (see sidebar at the end of this article). The Casualty division had adopted the BSC in 1996—in part because of poor performance—and the Group Insurance division adopted the BSC one year later. The division embraced the BSC for all parts of the management control system. Richardson noted, "It becomes the way you work." While developments and refinements to the BSC were ongoing, Richardson could nevertheless see improvements. Employees better understood linkages between business activities and the unit's strategic objectives, and the BSC encouraged cross-functional communication. Overall, the BSC effort was evaluated as being highly successful.

To examine pre-adoption performance for our sample of 42 BSC adopters, we measured and tested the abnormal financial performance over a three-year period ending in the year of the BSC adoption. Performance was measured as both return on assets (ROA)

and return on sales (ROS). For the BSC adopters that we had the necessary data to perform statistical tests, our results indicated that the mean and median abnormal performance over the three-year period up to the year of the decision to adopt the BSC was negative for both ROA and ROS. However, the statistical significance of these findings was marginal, implying weak evidence that poor performance (measured in terms of increasing costs or declining margins) may be a factor in the decision to adopt the BSC.

We also considered performance following the implementation of a BSC. We measured and tested the abnormal financial performance for adopters up to three years after the BSC was implemented. Our preliminary tests on a subset of the overall sample did not reveal significant performance improvements in ROS or ROA after implementation. However, because a number of adopting firms began implementation after 2003, there was insufficient data to draw any firm conclusions about post-implementation performance. We leave this important question for future research.

BSC MANAGEMENT— FROM ADOPTION TO IMPLEMENTATION

We believe that the adoption of the BSC will continue to grow in the foreseeable future as managers in organizations continue to search for management tools that will spur ongoing improvements in internal and external organizational performance. The practitioner and academic BSC literature continues to grow, as does the list of companies reportedly using the BSC. Our research has begun to address an important shortcoming in the study of management control systems, namely the empirical examination of contingency variables associated with BSC adoption. Focusing on Canadian firms, we provide intriguing evidence about which factors motivate firms to adopt the BSC, and also provide a better profile of the type of organization most likely to adopt a BSC. That said, while we were motivated by the need for a better understanding of BSC adoption, we believe that there has not been enough research effort focused on understanding BSC implementation and performance issues. Our BSC adoption and organizational performance analysis suggests the

The KEY Elements of Balanced Scorecard Success

By Sandy Richardson

Sandy Richardson is Managing Consultant for Strategy Focused Business Solutions Inc. She recently designed and implemented a BSC at Canada Life. Below, she offers her suggestions based on her experience with Canada Life and other organizations. She can be reached at sandyrichardson_bsc@yahoo.ca.

Balanced Scorecard (BSC) initiatives have a mixed track record. However, when you study organizations that have had success, you will notice several recurring themes. These provide six lessons for success for all balanced scorecard practitioners.

SUCCESS ELEMENT 1

Understand that the balanced scorecard is part of a bigger process that starts with strategy.

The balanced scorecard framework forms one (key) component in an integrated business performance management process that revolves around business strategy. This process is really a system where the balanced scorecard plays a critical role in translating business strategy into measurable action. With this in mind, successful BSC organizations define a solid business strategy prior to BSC development. While this may appear obvious to BSC practitioners, many "war stories" exist about organizations that threw themselves into a measurement initiative without spending time on strategy first. Generally, the result of these initiatives is sub-optimization with results that may or may not support business strategy achievement.

When cascaded from strategy, the BSC framework provides an important connection between strategic business performance and individual employee performance. In addition, the BSC helps close the feedback loop in the business-performance management system by providing a means for the business to: monitor and actively manage progress toward the achievement of business strategy, further explore and understand the cause-and-effect relationships within the business, and manage/change business strategy dynamically based on internal insights or shifts in the external operating environment.

Lesson 1: Embedding the BSC in a business-performance management process that begins with business strategy creation starts building strategic alignment from the start.

SUCCESS ELEMENT 2

Senior leadership involvement is **critical!**

Visible and genuine senior leadership involvement is critical to the success of any BSC initiative. That is, you must secure hands-on executive participation in the balanced scorecard development, implementation, and management. Commitment at the top is so important that successful BSC organizations treat it as a "show stopper"—focusing on resolving support issues before moving forward.

The issue of gaining leadership support is the most frequent concern faced by new balanced scorecard practitioners. Most BSC journeys don't begin with executive support from the start—very frequently, the push for a balanced scorecard initiative begins at a grassroots level. The key to "selling" the BSC to executives is to take an individualized approach. That is, first look for the burning platform or key business improvement opportunity that could be addressed by the successful application of a business performance management approach like the balanced scorecard. Then, complete your BSC research (note: there is information out there that can help support your situation!) and build a balanced scorecard business case that clearly demonstrates the benefits required to solve your organization's critical business issue. Keep at it until the executives in your organization get the message.

Lesson 2: Lack of leadership support can destroy your balanced scorecard initiative, so: Do not proceed on your balanced scorecard journey without it.

SUCCESS ELEMENT 3

Start with a clear vision for your balanced scorecard.

A balanced scorecard vision or philosophy is simply a clear statement that describes what your BSC will look like, how it will operate, how it will be built, and how the organization will use it. When created early in the balanced scorecard development process, your BSC vision provides a valuable touchstone going forward, providing focus and facilitating quick consensus when critical balanced scorecard decisions are required.

Lesson 3: Establish your BSC vision early and use it to guide your business performance management road map.

SUCCESS ELEMENT 4

Maximize balanced scorecard utilization by fully deploying it at all levels of the organization.

Successful BSC organizations make their balanced scorecard widely available so that everyone can "make strategy their job." Fully deploying a balanced scorecard across an organization helps develop strategic awareness among employees. This is important because successful strategy implementation requires the active contribution of every employee as they make decisions in their day-to-day work—decisions that can either contribute to or take away from the business strategy. Many business leaders voice concern about sharing their business strategy so broadly across the organization. Worries include the disclosure of critical strategic information to competitors. While these are valid concerns, successful BSC organizations know that the benefits of a broad deployment philosophy and in building employee satisfaction and loyalty levels far outweigh the risk of serious information leaks.

Lesson 4: Implement the BSC at all levels of the organization to maximize organizational alignment and execution.

SUCCESS ELEMENT 5

Communicate, communicate, communicate!

To support BSC implementation and its ongoing use, successful BSC organizations view communication and education on their business strategy and the balanced scorecard as an important internal marketing campaign. As a result, few of these organizations use only a single mode of communication to do the job. In fact, they use almost every type of communication method available, from general communication modes (e.g., large group meetings and mass distribution e-mails) to those that are very personalized with customized messages (e.g., face-to-face discussions) to ensure communication success.

Lesson 5: Be sure to plan and budget for BSC communication activities because experience shows that these activities are critical, they need to happen, and they won't without a solid plan and dedicated funding.

SUCCESS ELEMENT 6

Extend the balanced scorecard and make it "the way we work."

Successful BSC organizations deepen alignment by mirroring their balanced scorecard framework and categories in as many business activities as possible: reward and recognition programs, individual goal plan formats, incentive compensation plan formats, strategic plan categories and format, and almost anything else they can think of! They maximize alignment with the balanced scorecard until it becomes so integral to the business that it is automatic and embedded in everyday work.

Lesson 6: Enhance your integrated business performance management system until the BSC changes from just a measurement framework to the framework by which the business operates.

importance of further examining BSC implementation, as the adopters in our sample may not yet have achieved an effective implementation of their BSC.

A number of guides related to BSC formulation and implementation have been offered in the practitioner literature. Recommendations for effective BSC formulation and implementation include:

- Obtaining senior leadership involvement.

- Articulating the firm's business vision and strategy.

- Identifying the performance categories that link vision and strategy to results.

- Cascading the scorecard to team, division, and functional levels.

- Developing effective measures and meaningful standards (both short- and long-term, leading and lagging).

- Deploying appropriate budgeting, IT, communication and reward systems.

- Viewing the BSC as a continuous process, requiring maintenance, reassessment, and updating.

- Believing in the BSC as a facilitator of organizational and cultural change.

Some of these recommendations are based on anecdotal observations developed during the adoption and implementation of the BSC at specific, individual firms. While there still is little agreement about what constitutes effective BSC implementation, there is consensus around the view that not all BSC tools are created equal. Our continued research efforts will focus on the usage of the BSC following the decision to adopt such a system, developing a more rigorous understanding of formulation and implementation issues.

Stretching Strategic Thinking

Stan Abraham
California Polytechnic, Pomona

Why is strategic thinking such an important part of every manager's job? A company would not need a strategy if it did not have to compete—it could make do simply with a plan. But strategy implies competing and outwitting competitors. It follows that strategic thinking is the process of finding alternative ways of competing and providing customer value. So we can define strategic thinking as identifying alternative viable strategies or business models that deliver customer value.

To stretch company *thinking* about different and better ways of competing, delivering customer value, and growing, top managers can explore five approaches:

- Being successfully different.
- Emulating entrepreneurs.
- Finding new opportunities.
- Being future-oriented.
- Being collaborative.

HOW TO BE SUCCESSFULLY DIFFERENT

Strategy is about being different from your competitors—finding your race to run and winning it. To paraphrase Michael Porter, while becoming better at what you do is desirable, it will not benefit you in the

It is impossible to formulate a strategy, let alone a "best" or preferred strategy, without engaging in strategic thinking. The search for appropriate alternative strategies, often done as part of a strategic-planning process, is actually strategic thinking in action. Coming up with the "right" strategy for a company that might increase stakeholder value, make it a stronger competitor, or find a competitive arena it can dominate is done only through strategic thinking.

long run because it is something other competitors can also do.[1] So long as it is relatively easy for others to imitate or catch up to you, you do not have a sustainable competitive advantage, so you have not crafted a good strategy. Consider concentration, a bona fide strategy, where a company continues to improve its product and expand its market. If other competitors are following the same route to profits, and everyone is playing the same "game"—that is, if they have similar business models—a company might at best achieve a limited or temporary advantage (with a new product or more effective advertising). Porter insists that this is not *strategy*.[2] The exception would be if the company were to successfully differentiate itself in a way that is difficult for competitors to imitate. Differentiating is a means of playing a *different* game or playing the same game differently, one that hopefully only your company can win.

So one challenge in strategic thinking is to find a different way to do what the organization now does or to adopt a business model different from its competitors.

Reprinted from "Stretching Strategic Thinking," Stan Abraham, *Strategy & Leadership* 33, no. 5 (2005), pp. 5–12. © Emerald Group Publishing Limited. Used by permission.

Carmike. In the 1980s, Carmike Cinemas was the fifth largest theater chain in the United States and dominated the Southeast. It grew by acquiring failed theater chains at below market value, remodeling them at low cost, and then managing them by tightly controlling costs. Why did Carmike succeed and eventually become the market leader? Many other large chains had a similar business model—grow through acquisition and remodel single-screen theaters into multiplexes. How did Carmike differentiate itself? It chose to locate in small towns and villages, not urban areas. It found a niche. By so doing, it was often the only theater in town (no competition) and developed a clientele of loyal moviegoers. Yet, as it grew, it also had the buying clout of a large theater chain, ensuring that its theaters could afford to exhibit newly released films.

Trader Joe's. One of the best examples of differentiation is Trader Joe's, the specialty-grocery chain. It grew from a handful of convenience stores in Southern California to 174 stores nationally and $2.4 billion in revenues in 2001. The founder, Joe Coulombe, recognized early on that he could not compete as a convenience store against the likes of the 7-Eleven chain or as a grocery store against such giants as Safeway. He knew he had to be different, so he turned his penchant for traveling to France and enjoying French food and wine into buying trips for his stores. Today, Trader Joe's differentiates itself in five ways: selective products with fast turnover, unique private-label products that sell because the brand is trusted, an intimate "feel" to each store where shopping turns into a social experience, fanatical attention to what customers want and like, and delivering extraordinary value.[3] Trader Joe's is essentially playing its own game by its rules, and winning. Its business model is inimitable. Its brand stands for something solid and unique—and is trusted by its customers. It has, in fact, loyal customers, something that few other grocery stores have. Finally, Trader Joe's chooses the products it stocks and sells, whereas regular supermarkets stock brand name products from other manufacturers who have bargaining power over them. That is why it is also more profitable.

So one challenge in strategic thinking is to find a different way to do what the organization now does or to adopt a business model different from its competitors. Differentiation takes many forms, such as being better than or different from the competition in ways that are valued by customers: better quality, more features, better performance, better reliability, easier to use, stronger, taking up less room, simpler, better looking, and so on. Done correctly, differentiation can enhance a company's brand image, create loyal customers, and help the company achieve above-industry-average profits.

EMULATING ENTREPRENEURS

What is so special about entrepreneurs and being entrepreneurial? The one irrefutable difference between them and everyone else is their ability to see opportunity everywhere they look. They have an innate ability to scan the world for opportunities and look beyond the conventional.

What does seeing opportunities everywhere mean? It means being in a position to notice that something can be done better, quicker, cheaper, differently, more conveniently, faster, more reliably, or _____ (insert your own words). Entrepreneurs resonate with value generation and constantly try to find ways to create and deliver value. Something takes too long to do? There has to be a shorter way. Something breaks down too soon? It could be made more reliable. Some problem too complex? Perhaps there is a simpler solution.

In every case, the level of dissatisfaction is experienced from the customer's point of view, a critical distinction. It is really a customer *need* that is being identified, which the entrepreneur then tries to fill. Literally, it's "walking in the customer's shoes," spotting where value lies, and then organizing to deliver that value.

Strategists, organizational leaders, and marketing people should learn to look at the world with entrepreneurial eyes. Strategic thinking is concerned not only with how to be different but also with identifying alternative possibilities of generating customer value that the organization could deliver.

In high-tech industries, companies have to be eternally vigilant for upstarts that, through new products or better technology, "disrupt" them, that is, take market share from them or knock them from leadership positions. In such cases, other companies found the opportunity before their rivals. The solution, counterintuitively, is to come up with the opportunity *before you really need to.* While companies overtaken or "disrupted" by other companies—such as Digital Equipment Corp. by Compaq, IBM by Oracle, or every computer manufacturer by Dell— were innovative and had good ideas, they lacked "a robust, repeatable process for creating and nurturing new growth businesses."[4] The point is that when you need to be entrepreneurial and need to find a suitable opportunity, it is infinitely easier when you have a process for creating and nurturing new growth businesses already in place. In order for such a process to be used repeatedly, it should be the responsibility of a dedicated group that could apply the acquired learning effectively.

FINDING NEW OPPORTUNITIES

When companies are not doing well, they usually attempt to correct the problem by lowering costs and increasing revenues using their *existing* business model. For some reason, their thinking seldom extends to reexamining their revenue model. Is there a better way of generating revenues? And instead of identifying opportunities only once a year during the strategic-planning process, why not have an *opportunity-finding mechanism* operating all the time? Why not formalize it and use it to generate ideas and worthwhile proposals all the time?

Strategists, organizational leaders, and marketing people should learn to look at the world with entrepreneurial eyes.

Many companies have *new product development committees* through which they screen new product proposals. Such committees encourage promising proposals by asking for more detailed information or requiring a prototype demonstration, and giving increasing support as needed at each stage of development. Such support includes: more time off from the regular job to work on the new project, help forming a multidisciplinary team, and seed money to build prototypes or do market research. Unfortunately, at many firms the prospects for significant growth from new product development are not encouraging.

Why not ask customers for their suggestions and make learning from them a part of company culture? Too few companies do. Why not have everyone in the company participate, instead of just the engineers? And why not broaden the suggestions to embrace any kind of improvement or innovation, not just new product ideas? This way, the ongoing focus of the company would be opportunity recognition, and its revenue model continually refreshed.

The following six opportunity-seeking questions may serve to get a customer-inspired brainstorming process under way:

- What other type of customer could benefit from our product, even if used in a different way?
- What other products or ancillary services could we produce for the same customers?
- What other products could we produce, for any customers, that use the skills, techniques, technologies, and know-how that we have?
- Is there a way of reinventing our business model that would give us a competitive edge?
- What unmet needs do people or companies have that we could meet, even if it means acquiring the necessary know-how and expertise?
- What are the highest-growth industries now and in the foreseeable future that we might enter?

BEING FUTURE-ORIENTED

Methods of looking at or analyzing the future are called *futures research methods.* One useful method is called *scenario planning.* It requires facilitation, the involvement and education of many individuals, and a time period varying from weeks to months.[5] Yet despite the investment, companies that use it benefit from the educational process and shared learning that results and from the pictures of alternative futures that help managers to hone, direct, or change their thinking. Scenario expert Liam Fahey suggests the following scenario-learning principles:

- Scenarios are only a means to an end. They have value only to the extent that they inform decision makers and influence decision making. Scenarios must be relevant to the key issues facing the company and the decisions corporate leaders must contemplate and make.
- Scenarios only add value to decision making when managers and others use them to

systematically shape questions about the present and the future, and to guide how they go about answering them.

- In each step of developing scenarios, the emphasis must be on identifying, challenging, and refining the substance of managers' mind-sets and knowledge—what lies between their ears—and not on refining and perfecting scenario content.

- Alternative projections about some future must challenge managers' current mental models by creating tension about ideas, hypotheses, perspectives, and assumptions.

- The dialogue and discussion spawned by considering alternative futures directly affects managers' tacit knowledge.

- Scenarios are not a one-time event. They generate indicators that allow managers to track how the future is evolving. Thus, learning induced by scenarios never ends.[6]

Scenarios can be used in other ways besides creating a context for making decisions, such as helping to decide among alternative strategies. But the value of the scenario method lies in its ability to stretch participants' thinking, introduce new possibilities, challenge long-held assumptions, update

mental models, form valuable vehicles for learning and shared understanding, and often become the basis for strategic decision making.

WHETHER TO BE COLLABORATIVE: STRATEGIC ALLIANCES, ACQUISITIONS, AND MERGERS

The complexity of change and the imperative of competing more effectively or differently have led firms to consider a number of other opportunities and ways of growing and competing, ones that are collaborative to varying degrees, even with competitors. Such opportunities range from minimally collaborative and not integrative to an acquisition (total integration) of another company. The continuum and principal stages are shown in Figure 1.

The spectrum of strategic alliances includes various strategic alliances, joint ventures (a highly committed strategic alliance), and mergers and

Figure 1   **The Consortium of Strategic Alliances**

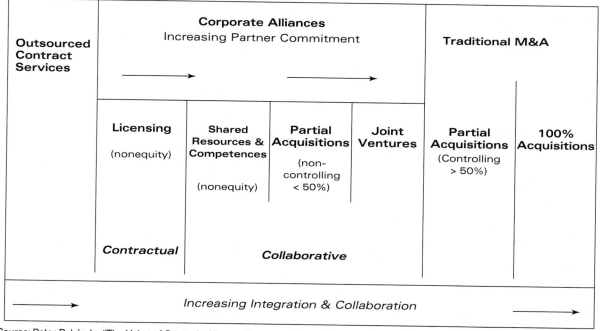

Source: Peter Pekár Jr., "The Value of Strategic Alliances," presentation at the Association for Strategic Planning's first annual conference, *New Strategies for a Rapidly Changing World,* 2001.

acquisitions. While the various forms of strategic alliance and acquisition do not constitute strategic thinking per se, they almost always form the *output* of strategic thinking: coming up with strategic alternatives that involve forming strategic alliances or acquiring another company. For this reason, a brief discussion about them will enable a strategist to consider such alternatives while engaged in strategic thinking.

Outsourcing

Companies can outsource their entire production and manufacturing to another company, their R&D to a university or R&D firm, their marketing and sales function, their financial function, their distribution, and so on. Do these have strategic benefits? Yes, if they make the company a stronger competitor.

Licensing (Nonequity)

This includes licensing the use of another company's technology—or licensing one's own technology or use of a trademark or logo to other companies.

Shared Resources and Competencies (Nonequity)

This includes, for example, sharing the cost of R&D—the way a consortium of semiconductor manufacturers did in the 1980s and 90s when it created Sematech to conduct joint research—or exclusive cross-distribution agreements whereby a company in one country exclusively sells the complementary products of a foreign company, and the foreign company undertakes to sell the products of the first company in that foreign country.

Partial Acquisition, Noncontrolling (< 50 Percent Ownership)

In its most common form, large companies seeking an edge in their industry look for a start-up or emerging company that has a new technology or innovation but that needs capital to develop it and grow. The large company will typically infuse capital into the small one by acquiring a noncontrolling interest. In addition, the investment allows it representation on the board of the small company and first rights

to the technology or innovation being developed. The large company may or may not later acquire a controlling share of the small company with an additional investment.

Joint Ventures

This is a special class of strategic alliance with a high degree of commitment, yet it keeps the two companies that are forming the alliance separate. The high degree of commitment comes in the formation of a separate corporate entity (referred in the literature as "two parents giving birth to a child") through a complex and encompassing agreement between the two parents. The agreement covers the ownership split (50–50, 60–40, etc.), what each parent is contributing to the child such as technology and patents, money, management, distribution, facilities, and the like, the purpose and objectives of the child, the management team for the child, how long the agreement will endure and on what terms either party can terminate the agreement and the joint venture, as well as other legal considerations. Research has shown that joint ventures in which the management team comes from one parent—typically the dominant one—are more likely to succeed than those in which both parents supply managers, especially with international joint ventures in developed countries.[7] Since forming a joint venture is a significant undertaking, it should be considered for major initiatives that need what *both* parents can bring to the venture and that have considerable probability of succeeding.

Acquisitions

Is acquiring another company a strategic move? Yes, if it makes the company a stronger competitor, or enables it to enter another industry or market.

But all too often, acquisitions are not strategic and do not accomplish intended purposes, such as capture significant synergy. The success rate for acquisitions has been abysmal—20 percent is a commonly cited figure. A study of 30 acquisitions made during 1990–2000 found that 24 (80 percent) failed. Over 70 percent of the deals studied failed because the acquirer paid too much.[8]

Mergers combine two companies (also 100 percent integration), and no one company "calls the shots" as in an acquisition. The resulting board of directors comprises representatives from both boards; the chairperson is usually from one company, the

CEO from the other, with other positions going to the best people from both companies.

The strategic questions for which a strategic alliance, acquisition, or merger might be the solution—or output of strategic thinking—include:

- Will we become a stronger competitor?
- Does it fit with our existing strategy?
- Will it improve our situation?
- Will it give us a competitive edge or distinctive competence we lack?
- What is the risk, and is it worth taking?
- Is it a means of acquiring "disruptive" innovation that might sustain the firm in the long term and that we couldn't develop in-house?

COLLABORATING WITH CUSTOMERS

The Internet is responsible for the profound changes experienced by organizations in virtually every kind of customer interaction over the past decade. The power of consumers is growing, because they are "armed" with more information. They are able to make choices that suit them and make them more quickly. In their recent book *The Future of Competition,* C. K. Prahalad and Venkat Ramaswamy characterize consumers as going from "isolated to connected, from unaware to informed, from passive to active."[9] These consumers are developing "thematic consumer communities" (as evidenced by the book reviews and favorite-book lists available for potential consumers on Amazon.com), experimenting (as with MP3 and file sharing), and becoming politically and socially active.

What are some ways of collaborating with customers? Consider the following:

- *In the R&D arena.* About 600,000 people tested the beta version of Windows NT. That translates to $600 million worth of R&D done by consumers—free. It was also consumers, in another example, that co-developed Sony's PlayStation2.
- *In operations.* At one point, FedEx's call center was overloaded with tracking inquiries, resulting in irate customers. Now, its customers can check the status of their own packages. Its call-center costs dropped dramatically, and customer satisfaction went way up. In effect, it became its customers' transportation partner.

The challenge in strategic thinking is to find innovative ways of co-creating value with customers, a technique for finding unique competitive advantage.

- *In creating experiences.* Rather than just providing pacemakers for people with heart problems that need them, medical-equipment manufacturer Medtronic creates value for the patient with the pacemaker *and the information it records.* The value of the pacemaker itself has been increased because it can be constantly monitored by the patient's doctor, or in an emergency could be shared with a hospital and a specialist.
- *In adding value to the experience of using the product.* Consider OnStar, the advanced automotive-communications system of General Motors which, for a fee, can help make reservations, find a place to eat, get weather reports, contact emergency services, get messages to your family, and supply a host of other services. OnStar enables GM to sell a differentiated "experience" rather than just an automobile loaded with features.[10]

To be successful in co-creating value, firms must focus on a new set of practices which Prahalad and Ramaswamy call DART, namely, in-depth **D**ialog with customers, new kinds of **A**ccess to information, the freedom to exchange information to conduct **R**isk assessments, and **T**ransparency to facilitate the interaction. When combined in different ways, the opportunities for customer collaboration skyrocket. Consider:

- Access *and* transparency—as in getting the right kinds of accurate information for stock-investment decisions.
- Dialogue *and* risk assessment—as in the public's increasing ability to influence policy with regard to cigarette smoking.
- Access *and* dialogue—as in New Line Cinema reaching out to the more than 400 unofficial fan Web sites, seeking their feedback on details of the *Lord of the Rings* film trilogy.
- Transparency *and* risk assessment—as in automobile and tire manufacturers disclosing information to the public about the risks associated with vehicle design, tire pressures, and driving conditions.[11]

The challenge in strategic thinking is to find innovative ways of co-creating value with customers, a technique for finding unique competitive advantage.

STRATEGIC THINKING NEVER STOPS

The task of looking for and coming up with better ways of providing customer value and competing—the task of strategic thinking—never ends.

- Are there ways the company can differentiate itself or its products and achieve a competitive advantage? Can it create its own game and rules, and win?

- By "walking in the customers' shoes"—as entrepreneurs do—are there products or services currently offered that one could improve upon? What are customers' dissatisfactions, and could the company provide the solution?

- Is the company's search for opportunities wide-ranging enough? Has it examined every combination of customer needs, current capabilities, and technological advances? Are there opportunities in other growth industries? Can it reinvent its business model? Is the company investing in R&D and experiments now that will, in time, become one of its core businesses?

- What steps is the company taking to address uncertainty in the future? Has it mapped out a number of likely futures? Does it assume a certain future will happen, but has contingencies in case things turn out differently? Is the company dependent on "whatever" the future will bring, or is it trying to "define and design its own future"? Is there a preferred future it would like to bring about?

- Has the company explored taking advantage of opportunities that become feasible only through forming a strategic alliance or merging with—or acquiring—another company? Are there ways in which it could co-create value with its customers?[12]

Whether a company has one person, a group, or everyone doing strategic thinking, the important things are that it is being done continuously and that the opportunities, alternative strategies, or different business models are periodically shared with other key people in the company. Only then is the company in a position to take appropriate action, and only then can it reap the immense benefits of strategic thinking.

Notes

1. Michael Porter, "What Is Strategy?" *Harvard Business Review* 74 (November–December 1996), pp. 61–78.

2. Ibid.

3. Stan Abraham, "Talking Strategy: Dan Bane, CEO of Trader Joe's," *Strategy & Leadership* 30, no. 6 (2002), pp. 30–32.

4. Clayton M. Christensen, Mark W. Johnson, and Darrell K. Rigby, "Foundations for Growth: How to Identify and Build Disruptive New Businesses," *MIT Sloan Management Review* 43 (Spring 2002), p. 30.

5. Peter Schwartz, *The Art of the Long View: Planning for the Future in an Uncertain World,* rev. ed. (New York: Currency Doubleday, 1996), pp. 241–248.

6. Liam Fahey, "How Corporations Learn from Scenarios," *Strategy & Leadership* 31, no. 2 (2003), p. 9. See also these other excellent articles on scenarios in the same issue of *Strategy & Leadership:* Stephen M. Millett, "The Future of Scenarios: Challenges and Opportunities," pp. 16–24; David Mason, "Tailoring Scenario Planning to the Company Culture," pp. 25–28; and Betty S. Flowers, "The Art and Strategy of Scenario Writing," pp. 29–33.

7. J. Peter Killing, *Strategies for Joint Venture Success* (Praeger Publications, 1983), p. 124.

8. Carol Ackatcherian, "Mergers and Acquisitions: Why Do They Fail?" Unpublished MBA Project Final Report, Cal Poly Pomona, May 2001, p. 34.

9. C. K. Prahalad and Venkat Ramaswamy, *The Future of Competition: Co-Creating Unique Value with Customers* (New York: HBS, 2004), pp. 2–5.

10. C. K. Prahalad, Keynote address at the Third Annual Conference of the Association for Strategic Planning on October 14, 2003, in Stan Abraham, "Conference Report—Co-creating Unique Value with Customers: C. K. Prahalad Introduces a Novel Approach to Competitive Advantage," *Strategy & Leadership* 32, no. 3 (2004), pp. 41–45.

11. Ibid.

12. While these questions summarize the different ways in which a firm could go about doing strategic thinking that are discussed in this article, no one should assume the list is complete or that other ways of doing strategic thinking don't exist.

A New Tool for Strategy Analysis: The Opportunity Model

Donald Morris
Eastern New Mexico University

I was seldom able to see an opportunity until it had ceased to be one.
—Mark Twain

In their recent book on leadership and change, the authors report that for many businesses "the biggest obstacle to greater growth is getting employees (including senior executives) to see new opportunities" (Black and Gregersen, 2003, p. 114). Why this is so becomes clear if we spend a little time securing a better grasp on what we mean by opportunity. Like many overused terms, a lack of precision permeates its application. Consider the following example: "Surging demand for telecommunications services, when coupled with deregulation, was seen as an enormous opportunity for new companies to enter the telecom service industry and compete with existing companies for industry revenues" (Hill and Jones, 2004, p. 37). But "Surging demand for telecommunications services . . . coupled with deregulation" is not an opportunity, it is a catalyst. A catalyst performs the function of a midwife in giving birth to an opportunity, but the midwife is not the opportunity. It is a change in the business environment calling for reassessing a company's goals, strategies, and the options for reaching those goals. Calling it an opportunity, according to the model outlined in this article, means it is the solution to a problem; but demand and deregulation are not specific solutions to an organization's problems. They can be considered

solutions to a macro problem in the economy, but opportunities, as I will show, are company specific.

Often, threats to a business are also called opportunities, as are setbacks and catastrophes, but these are problems, not opportunities. An opportunity is a favorable solution to a problem, not the problem itself. Even the options under consideration to solve a problem are often termed opportunities—leading to the search for the best "opportunity" from among the "opportunities." No wonder employees, including senior executives, have difficulty recognizing new opportunities—there is no consensus on the object of the search. To achieve this end the elements that constitute an opportunity must be explicit—so at least we know what we are looking for.

In this paper I present a model for understanding when a circumstance constitutes an opportunity. The model delineates the elements of an opportunity and addresses the uniqueness of opportunity as a sought-after business edge. To illustrate the efficacy of the model in clearing up our thinking, I apply it to opportunity as understood in SWOT (strengths, weaknesses, opportunities, and threats) analysis. I show why, using this strategic tool, the confusion in recognizing opportunity also stymies its application.

When people speak of opportunities they may mean one of three related ideas without distinguishing between them: possible options for solving a problem; a time-constrained decision platform from

Reprinted from "A new tool for Strategy analysis: The opportunity model," Donald Morris, *Journal of Business Strategy* 26, no. 3 (2005), pp. 50–56 © Emerald Group Publishing Limited. Used by permission.

which options are viewed and evaluated; or the solution actually chosen. For example, in 1986 I had an opportunity to run for political office. Hearing this statement, you could reasonably assume that I did run for office, but having an opportunity to run for political office and actually running are different. I may be indicating only that running for office was an option. Alternatively, I may be saying that, for a certain time, I evaluated my options and running for office was among the choices considered. Or, I may have actually selected this option and run.

> *Often, threats to a business are also called opportunities, as are setbacks and catastrophes, but these are problems, not opportunities.*

Analogously, when a manufacturing company speaks of its inventory, it may refer to raw materials, work-in-process or finished goods. They are all called inventory but there is a great deal of difference in what we mean by inventory if we refer to raw materials as opposed to finished products. In the context of opportunities, options are raw materials. They are selected as possible solutions for a problem, but not yet processed through the screening criteria resulting in an ultimate choice, the finished good, or option chosen. An opportunity, as used here, is a time-constrained decision platform from which options are evaluated. That none of the options considered is chosen does not indicate that there was no opportunity. Had I chosen not to run for political office, it would still be true that I had such an opportunity.

Every option is not an opportunity, just as all inventory is not finished product. Opportunity is a confluence of circumstances leading to the choice or rejection of options. In my case running for political office was an option considered and evaluated during the opportunity process, and it was also the end product—I did run for office, although I did not win. An opportunity is not merely a choice, it is a special category of choice. Opportunities are valuable occasions to improve organizational performance in seeking its goals. It is fruitful, it opens the way for additional opportunities because an improved condition contains the seeds for further improvement, more options and future opportunities. A choice that prevents a business from seeking its goals or leads to a dead end is not an opportunity. One way to appreciate this last point is to consider choices or their outcomes that

tend to cut off future opportunities such as a reputation for shoddy products, dishonest business dealings or violations of trust. Conditions such as these narrow the scope of future options and opportunities.

There is something valuable but fleeting about opportunity. Having an opportunity implies that there is nothing hindering or preventing an action or choice. "The company had an opportunity to join a trade association" or "the marketing director had an opportunity to speak her mind freely at the meeting" are examples expressing this freedom from constraint.

THE CONTEXT AND ELEMENTS OF OPPORTUNITY

The context is as follows:

- *Problem.* The fundamental condition for an opportunity is a problem, a challenge, adversity, dissatisfaction, an obstacle, or a threat. A problem may be chronic or acute and is determined by the individual organization and its goals. To limit the discussion, we will focus on problems stemming from the organization's mission or strategic plan.

- *Choice.* An opportunity involves a choice between or among alternatives for solving a problem. The alternatives must be effective solutions to the problem, not mere dreams with no known way of accomplishing them. If only one option exists, there is no opportunity.

- *Value.* Opportunities are scarce occasions during which we seek to improve the organization's condition by finding an advantageous solution to a problem. While opportunities may be everywhere, they are not always apparent, and, once missed, they are gone.

- *Organizational mission.* An organization's mission or strategic plan, or a modification or revamping of those goals, establishes the parameters of opportunity.

The elements are as follows:

- *Time constraint.* When offered an opportunity, an organization has a limited time to make a decision.

- *Sacrifice.* Accepting the need to sacrifice is part of recognizing opportunity. Whether the cost is additional effort, ignoring other goals, exhausting resources (assets or time), or acceding to restrictions placed on actions, we are exchanging what we have for what we want. Economists speak of sacrifice as opportunity cost. In seeking an opportunity there is an exchange, but we expect to receive more value than we relinquish.

- *Risk.* Incurring risk is an integral part of pursuing an opportunity; something can always go wrong. If it is an opportunity we are pursuing, failure must be a possibility.

- *Catalyst.* A catalyst is not within our control but something that prompts us to view a problem in a new light. Change, altered circumstance, disconnects, shifting of the fulcrum, anomaly, unanticipated events, or uncertainty that alters how we evaluate problems and their possible solutions can trigger opportunities.

- *Possibility of regret.* To act on what is believed an opportunity or to fail to recognize or fail to act on an opportunity may lead to regret.

The above characteristics form a model of opportunity and a set of conditions that qualify an occasion as an opportunity.

APPLICATION OF THE MODEL

Early in my career as an accountant I worked for a public accounting firm involved with the building construction and real estate development industries. One day a non-client developer asked if we could meet to talk about his accounting needs. At the meeting it became clear that he did not want to become a client of my employer but wanted me to form my own business with his company as anchor client. Initially I told him "no" and explained the benefits of my employing firm, but he remained adamant. He told me he knew a number of other developers and contractors who were dissatisfied with their present accountants and would likely switch to me—if I ran my own firm. I took up the issue with the managing partner where I worked. He was skeptical, thinking that perhaps I was trying to spirit off the firm's rightful prospects. I agonized and struggled to forge a compromise, but nothing worked. Finally I decided

the situation represented an opportunity for me and I quit my job to form my own CPA firm. I met with the developer and received numerous referrals from him, building up a successful accounting practice. I was also sued by my former employer.

THE ELEMENTS OF THE MODEL

The elements of the model are as follows:

- *Time constraint.* I knew the developer's offer would not be forever—if I kept declining, he would find someone else to do the work.

- *Sacrifice.* I had to give up a steady job where I managed the tax department and was a prospective partner. I had a family and a mortgage and limited savings if things turned out poorly.

- *Risk.* Aside from the obvious risks that my new business might be less successful than I hoped, I had signed an employment agreement with my employer. It stipulated that if I quit, I would not take the firm's clients. I was in an area of potential liability and a court of law might find that I breached this contract by doing work for a client I met while employed by my former firm.

- *Catalyst.* The developer's contact with me asking me to go out on my own was the catalyst, because I had not previously given this option serious thought.

- *Possible regret.* I well knew that a year or two down the road, if my plans didn't work out well, I could be second-guessing my decision and wondering why I left my old job.

APPLYING THE MODEL TO SWOT ANALYSIS— A CRITIQUE

A strategy is a plan for the actions taken to attain one or more organizational goals. "The task of strategy formation is one of achieving a match between the organization's internal skills, capabilities, and resources on the one hand and all of the relevant external considerations on the other hand" (Thompson and Strickland, 1986, p. 74). An institutional goal for a business might be to increase its revenue at a moderate but steady rate or diversify its customer base. The compilation of an organization's institutional goals and the means to reach them forms a strategic plan. SWOT analysis is a frequently used tool to develop a strategic plan. The central focus of a SWOT analysis is to recognize opportunities and avoid threats while weighing an organization's strengths and weaknesses.

In striving to locate opportunities, the organization studies its unique strengths and weaknesses in relation to the competition or to an established ideal. What can it do that its competitors can't; what can the competition do that the organization can't? Strengths for an organization may include the largest market share, strong financial resources, a history of innovative products or a favorable reputation with its customers. Weaknesses may include lack of managerial skill, a poor distribution network, falling behind in research and development or obsolete facilities. Threats are conditions outside the organization's direct control that stand in the way of long-range goals. "Threats arise when conditions in the external environment endanger the integrity and profitability of the company's business" (Hill and Jones, 2004, p. 37). A threat might be the increasing sales of substitute products, cheaper foreign products introduced into the market, or the inability to raise prices as needed to cover costs.

Like threats, the opportunities in a SWOT analysis are external to the business. "The objective [in SWOT analysis] is to select the strategies that ensure the best alignment, or fit, between external environmental opportunities and threats and the internal strengths and weaknesses of the organization" (Hill and Jones, 1989, p. 12; Thompson and Strickland, 1992, p. 89). But opportunities, as the model indicates, are solutions to problems, and restricting our thinking to what is external or internal to an organization is unnecessarily limiting. Without the benefit of the model, it is easy to see why people get confused looking for opportunities and get sidetracked focusing on options and catalysts.

Catalysts are external changes that prompt us to recognize new options, reevaluate existing options or revisit previously discarded options. Believing catalysts are opportunities is what leads the SWOT analyst to assume opportunities are also external. The Internet is an example of this confusion. It is a catalyst, not an opportunity. When businesses began to recognize the potential of the Internet, it was natural, applying the traditional SWOT analysis, to consider the Internet an opportunity. This way of thinking, however, muddies the water because it cuts off more precise analysis regarding the Internet's use to solve an organization's problems. Calling a catalyst an opportunity gives the impression that we have located the solution to a problem. The Internet is an important change in the business environment and such innovation, seen as a catalyst, should prompt an organization to look at new options or reevaluate old ones. "Opportunities arise when a company can take advantage of conditions in its environment to formulate and implement strategies that enable it to become more profitable" (Hill and Jones, 2004, p. 37). The Internet presents new options for marketing, communication, sales, advertising, purchasing, and delivery. Some of these options are solutions to the problems of some organizations; they are not all solutions to every business's problems. A SWOT analysis that includes the Internet as an opportunity simply raises the questions: How can we use the Internet to solve our business's specific problems? What new options does it create? What old options should we revisit?

CONFUSING CATALYSTS WITH OPPORTUNITIES

Confusing catalysts with opportunities is widespread. Peter Drucker, for example, has examined what he calls innovative opportunity. "Purposeful, systematic innovation," he writes, "begins with the analysis of the opportunities. It begins with thinking through . . . sources of innovative opportunity" such as unexpected successes and unexpected failures, incongruities, changes in industry and market structures, changes in demographics, changes in meaning and perception and new knowledge (Drucker, 1993). Others identify opportunities with negative conditions such as failure, disappointment, or cataclysm.

In terms of the opportunity model, these are not opportunities but catalysts, triggering mechanisms in the environment represented by change. They include conflict, new circumstances, disconnect, shifting of the fulcrum, anomaly, unanticipated events, or uncertainties that alter the ways we evaluate possible solutions to a problem. Designating catalysts as opportunities confuses conditions that prompt us to reevaluate our options with the solutions to problems. Much of this obfuscation can be avoided by distinguishing early and clearly between options, catalysts, and opportunities.

CONFUSING OPTIONS WITH OPPORTUNITIES

For a business, major goals are usually expressed in terms such as sustaining a specific growth rate, increasing market share, increasing gross profit percentage, or addressing a changing marketplace. If the goal is to increase its revenue, the organization may consider a number of alternatives, including: entering new markets with existing products, expanding a product line to meet a broader range of customer needs, or diversifying into related products. Although the typical SWOT analysis refers to each of these options as opportunities, they represent an unfiltered list of options, of possible solutions to the problem under consideration. While reviewing the proposed solutions to the problem—in the opportunity process—the organization is determining if any of the options is an opportunity. In making this determination, the organization must apply the opportunity model. Is there a time constraint? What is the sacrifice required to pursue this choice versus another? What are the risks associated with each option that threaten the outcome? Is there a catalyst? And finally, what is the potential for regret?

The opportunity model sheds light on the question "regarding whether the strategy formulation process should begin with an identification of attractive opportunities or with defining the business and setting objectives" (Thompson and Strickland, 1986, pp. 74–75). Since the model views opportunity as arising from a problem, the idea of simply "looking around for opportunities" in a vacuum makes little sense. Someone who appears to locate an opportunity without first determining what business he or she is in has seen the solution to a problem and implicitly determined what kind of business forms the problem's context. Opportunities are generated from problems; problems are needed to anchor opportunities, and they arise from concrete circumstances of business.

UNTANGLING SWOT CONFUSION

The standard SWOT analysis employs two sets of three "kinds of opportunity." In one dimension, opportunities are divided into those relating to the company's strengths, weaknesses, or threats. In another dimension opportunities are divided into those arising at the broad environmental level, at the industry level, or at the company level, including its stakeholders. Strengths are viewed as characteristics of an organization that will allow it to take advantage of the opportunities that are recognized. Weaknesses are seen as characteristics of an organization that stand in the way of an organization's ability to take advantage of its recognized opportunities. Threats are characterized as external conditions that stand in the way of an organization seeking specific opportunities. This way of viewing a SWOT analysis causes two problems.

First, when opportunities are framed in terms of the other three elements in the SWOT analysis, we are left with too many possibilities. We have opportunities to use the organization's strengths, opportunities to overcome the organization's weaknesses, and opportunities to neutralize threats, as well as opportunities that may do two or all three of these at once (Harrison and St. John, 2002, pp. 159–60) The typical analysis holds that in seeking an opportunity we look for a solution that maximizes the organization's strengths, minimizes its weaknesses and avoids possible threats. Since all these types of opportunity can be discovered in the "same opportunity," the types are not different kinds of opportunity but different considerations in our attempt to locate an opportunity. Rather than speaking of an opportunity to use the organization's strengths, it is more helpful to speak of organizational problems best solved by relying on the strengths of an organization. Similarly with weaknesses and threats, an opportunity is the coming together of all the elements of the model resulting in a solution to a problem that improves the organization's condition, utilizing its strengths, minimizing its weaknesses, and avoiding threats.

The second problem with this way of viewing a SWOT analysis is its circularity. How do we know what strengths an organization has? We are told its strengths are what allow it to capitalize on certain opportunities. And how do we recognize these opportunities? By reflecting on the organization's strengths. Strengths are thus seen as characteristics that allow an organization to take advantage of opportunities. This is a circular thought process causing the organization's compass needle to spin aimlessly.

Opportunities are not such in an absolute sense but only in relation to a particular organization's problems at a given time. Opportunities are not generic commodities. The determination that a set of conditions represents an opportunity can only be made by looking at an organization's strengths at that time. Those strengths must be identifiable without reference to the specific opportunities they allow the organization to pursue. Similarly with weaknesses and threats. Each can be defined circularly in terms of opportunity, but this temptation must be avoided if a SWOT analysis is to be effective.

In the second dimension, opportunities are classified into three types based on the source of the opportunity. According to this scheme, one type of opportunity is a response to the widest environmental factors faced by organizations, another to industry specific conditions, and a third to those opportunities arising at the level of the organization and its stakeholders.

The broadest environmental sources of opportunity are variously referred to as the broad environment (Harrison and St. John, 2002, pp. 5–12), the general environment (Coulter, 2002, pp. 81–82) or simply environmental opportunities (Grant and King, 1982, p. 8). This widest category includes such factors as inflation or interest rates, governmental developments such as changes in tariffs or subsidies, and changes in technology not limited to the business's industry (such as the Internet). "The broad environment consists of domestic and global environmental forces such as socio-cultural, technological, political, and economic trends" (Harrison and St. John, 2002, p. 5). In applying the opportunity model, these factors are recognizable as catalysts rather than opportunities. When changes take place on this level it should prompt us to ask: What other factors changed as a result, and what impact they will have on our industry and our business? Recognition of an external catalyst should urge us to look for new options and to reevaluate others put on the shelf at an earlier time.

The industry level is the second category of environmental factors seen as producing opportunities (Thompson and Strickland, 1992, p. 90). "In viewing the role of opportunity in the strategy formation process, it is important to distinguish between industry opportunities and company opportunities" (Thompson and Strickland, 1986, p. 75). These are conditions arising in an organization's industry environment that trigger potential opportunities for the business.

But reflecting on the idea of industry opportunities reveals two problems. First, if we accept that there are industry opportunities distinct from either environ-mental or company level opportunities, they are actually catalysts because they are events occurring in the industry calling for reevaluation at the organizational level. Events that affect an industry or sector of business such as shifts in customer demand or government deregulation are triggers requiring the rethinking of options and strategies by the individual organizations. Second, the belief in industry opportunities is based on a mistaken inference. In logic this is referred to as the fallacy of composition—inferring that what is true of the parts must be true of the whole. An industry is simply a collection of businesses producing the same type of product or service or products that consumers may substitute one for the other. The industry does not itself possess goals or strategies or problems, aside from those of the individual businesses. To speak of problems affecting an industry is an elliptical way of talking about problems faced individually by the organizations in that industry. If we say "The medical profession is facing a crisis," we are speaking of an industry and generalizing the problems faced by the individual participants. But the industry itself has no problems specific to it that are not also the problems of the component members.

The narrowest types of opportunity in this classification dimension are those identified at the level of the business and its stakeholders, sometimes referred to as task opportunities. This is the level where the organization has options and possibly opportunities and where problems occur. An external event at the environmental or industry level may prompt the rethinking of the relationship between the organization and its stakeholders, giving rise to new options. Applying the elements of the opportunity model to these options will determine if any of them is an opportunity.

AVOIDING THE CONFUSION

Since opportunities are ultimately what we seek in a SWOT analysis, the first step in streamlining the process is defining opportunities by applying the opportunity model. Catalysts are an important but unacknowledged part of the SWOT analysis, but, by themselves, catalysts are neither opportunities nor threats, they are neutral. But when considering an organization's independently determined strengths and weaknesses, the occurrence of a catalyst is a signal to evaluate new options and revisit previously discarded ones.

Since the goal of SWOT analysis is recognizing opportunity, it is unfortunate that the O was originally assigned to opportunity rather than to option. This leads to looking for opportunities among the opportunities. Options must first be screened applying the model before meaningful identification as opportunities. If SWOT is viewed as a tool for recognizing opportunity, and its use integrated with the opportunity model, the analysis of an organization's strengths, weaknesses, and threats is seen as an ingredient in analyzing sacrifices and risks associated with individual options. In addition, the appearance of a catalyst is recognized as a call to reevaluate the organization's perceived strengths and weaknesses as well as its options. The opportunity model forms a foundation for effective SWOT analysis and encourages wholeness of thought in its utilization.

References

Black, S. J. and Gregersen, H. B. (2003), *Leading Strategic Change,* Prentice Hall, Upper Saddle River, NJ.

Coulter, M. (2002), *Strategic Management in Action,* 2nd ed., Prentice Hall, Upper Saddle River, NJ.

Drucker, P. F. (1993), *Innovation and Entrepreneurship,* HarperCollins Publishers, Inc., New York, NY.

Grant, J. H. and King, W. R. (1982), *The Logic of Strategic Planning,* Little, Brown & Co., Boston, MA.

Harrison, J. S. and St. John, C. H. (2002), *Foundations in Strategic Management,* 2nd ed., South-Western College Publishing, Cincinnati, OH.

Hill, C. W. L. and Jones, G. R. (1989), *Strategic Management,* 1st ed., Houghton Mifflin Co., Boston, MA.

Hill, C. W. L. and Jones, G. R. (2004), *Strategic Management,* 6th ed., Houghton Mifflin Co., Boston, MA.

Thompson, A. A. Jr. and Strickland, A. J. III (1986), *Strategy Formulation and Implementation,* 3rd ed., Richard D. Irwin, Inc., Homewood, IL.

Thompson, A. A. Jr. and Strickland, A. J. III (1992), *Strategy Formulation and Implementation,* 5th ed., Richard D. Irwin, Inc., Homewood, IL.

Further Reading

Berkeley, G. (1975), *Philosophical Works,* Everyman, London.

Drucker, P. F. (2001), *The Essential Drucker,* HarperCollins Publishers, Inc., New York, NY.

Playing Hardball: Why Strategy Still Matters

George Stalk

The Boston Consulting Group

For a time, it seemed that strategy didn't matter anymore, particularly during the e-commerce boom. The brilliant promise of Web-based business temporarily blinded many managers, academics, and investors to the fundamentals of strategy. Strategy has always been about allocating resources to stimulate customer demand and create competitive advantage. The greater the advantage, the faster a company can grow, the more profitable it can be, and the greater value it can create. But in the first rush of e-commerce, a lot of investment dollars and management talent went into ventures that did not have competitive advantage from the get-go—like Boo.com, BBQ.com, Lifejacketstore.com—and were doomed.

The bust of e-commerce reminded everyone, all too painfully, that strategy always matters. Today, it matters more than ever. Competitive intensity is at an all-time high as a result of globalization, technology, fragmented consumer groups, and shifting power along the supply/demand chain. But while gaining a competitive advantage is harder than ever, strategy is again being pushed off the management agenda—not by e-commerce, but by "managerially correct" demands. Even when managers want to focus on creating and reinforcing competitive advantage, they are being distracted by a plethora of "soft" issues. Not

only must managers cope with the intense scrutiny and burdensome demands of corporate governance, they must deal with the recriminations for outsourcing and offshoring, demands to motivate employees in times of increased uncertainty, and unceasing pressure to produce quick results or face replacement. The time has come to put strategy back on the agenda again. That is why we wrote *Hardball*.

THE FIVE PRINCIPLES OF HARDBALL

Today there are two extremes in business competition. Companies can play softball, relying on weak tactics that look like strategies but do little more than keep the company in the game for the short term. Or they can play hardball, employing tough strategies designed to rout, not simply beat, competitors. Which of today's companies are playing hardball? What strategies are they using to win? And what will it take for firms to adopt and execute these strategies successfully?

1. *Hardball players focus relentlessly on competitive advantage.* Competitive advantage is something I have that you don't. Too bad for you. But too bad for me, too. When I have the advantage, you are forced to accept defeat or find a way around my advantage to build your own. So hardball competitors are never satisfied with today's competitive advantage—they want tomorrow's.

2. *Hardball competitors strive to convert competitive advantage into decisive advantage.* Competitive advantage, as essential as it is, can be fleeting. That's why hardball players seek to put

Reprinted from "Playing Hardball: Why strategy still matters," George Stalk, *Ivey Business Journal*, Vol.69, No.2 (November/December 2004), P.1–8. Ivey Management Services prohibits any form of reproduction, storage or transmittal of this material without its written permission. This material is not covered under authorization from any reproduction rights organization. To order copies or request permission to reproduce materials, contact Ivey Publishing, Ivey Management Services, c/o Richard Ivey School of Business, The University of Western Ontario, London, Ontario, Canada, N6A 3K7: phone (519) 661-3208, fax (519) 661-3882, e-mail cases@ivey.uwo.ca. Copyright © 2004, Ivey Management Services. One time permission to reproduce granted by Ivey Management Services on February 15, 2006.

themselves out of reach of their competitors by building their competitive advantage into decisive, or unassailable, advantage. Decisive advantage is systemically reinforcing. The better you get at it, the harder it is for competitors to compete against it or take it away. And the more likely it is that your competitors will "pick up their marbles" and leave that particular playing field.

3. *Hardball players employ the indirect attack.* When a company makes a direct attack, it does exactly what its opponent expects and is prepared for. The attacker hopes that superior resources and persistence will carry the day. An indirect attack means that you surprise a competitor with your actions and apply resources where the opponent is least able to defend himself.

4. *Hardball players exploit their employees' will to win.* To achieve competitive advantage, people must be action-oriented, and always impatient with the status quo. The will to win can be fostered; softball players can be transformed into hardball players. But as your competitive advantage grows, it gets harder to exploit your employees' will to win.

5. *Hardball players draw a bright line at the edge of the caution zone.* To play hardball means to be aware of when you are entering the "caution zone," that area so rich in possibility that lies between the place where society clearly says you can play the game of business and the place where society clearly says you can't.

Generally, hardball strategies do not require entry into the caution zone. Company leaders are responsible for drawing a bright line that defines the boundary, and for letting everybody know when they're getting close to it.

In rare instances, however, a hardball player will deliberately enter the caution zone. When he does, he must take extra care. Every move must be evaluated in the light of the following questions:

- Will the proposed action break any laws?
- Will the proposed action be bad for the customer?
- Will competitors be directly hurt by an action?
- Will an action hit a nerve with a special interest group in a way that might damage the company?
- Will the action harm the industry or society?

If the answer to any of the questions is "yes," it means the company has ventured too far into the caution zone. The leader must immediately take corrective action.

SIX CLASSIC HARDBALL STRATEGIES

Any strategy that provides a decisive competitive advantage is a hardball strategy. In our book, we describe six classic hardball strategies that have proved, over the decades, to be particularly effective in generating competitive advantage.

1. *Unleash massive and overwhelming force.* Although hardball players prefer the indirect attack, they sometimes surprise and overcome their competitors with a full frontal assault. Massive and overwhelming force must be deployed like the blow of a hammer—accurate, direct, and swift. It must not be used until the company is ready to put all its energy behind it. The company must also be certain that the competitive advantage it believes it has is ready to be deployed.

When a company chooses the direct attack strategy, it may be necessary for it to completely overhaul its business in order to unleash the force. The process can feel like the turnaround of a successful company, a paradoxical situation that is uncomfortable for entrenched leaders. Only those with vision and courage should engage in this bold, and often very public, hardball strategy. And companies must be careful not to put their competitors out of business and into bankruptcy protection, from which they may emerge stronger than ever.

When the president of Frito-Lay, Roger Enrico, had had enough of Eagle Snack's incursion into its market for salty snacks, his first response was to slim down and focus the organization, to reduce costs and concentrate investments. He then launched an all-out attack on Eagle's stronghold, the supermarkets, by increasing promotions and advertising, upping in-store service, and, where necessary, reducing prices. He wrote a check that was larger than Eagle could afford to match. Eagle crumpled under the assault and withdrew.

Hardball executives relish anomalies because they may conceal opportunities that can be exploited.

2. *Exploit anomalies.* Sometimes a growth opportunity lies hidden in a phenomenon that, at first glance, seems irrelevant to the busi-ness or contradictory to current practice. But anomalies—such as idiosyncratic customer pre-ferences, unexpected employee behaviors, or odd insights from another industry—can show the way to competitive advantage, even decisive advantage.

When Rose Marie Bravo took over Burberry, the English manufacturer of raincoats that was dead in the water, she noticed that Burberry's sales in Spain were inexplicably strong. Her interested was piqued because, as she pointed out, "It doesn't rain in Spain." She learned that the country manager had extended the Burberry brand into many other categories. She took this insight to the United States, to Asia, and throughout Europe. Burberry's sales have more than tripled, and its EBITDA has increased sevenfold.

Softball players want to ignore anomalies or to suppress them because they don't conform to standard practice. Hardball executives relish anomalies because they may conceal opportunities that can be exploited.

3. *Threaten your competitor's profit sanctuaries.* Profit sanctuaries are the parts of a business where a company makes the most money and steadily accumulates wealth. In certain circumstances, the hardball player can influence a competitor's behavior and gain competitive advantage by attacking the competitor's profit sanctuaries.

This strategy is risky. It can take you deep into the caution zone, so each use must be considered on its own legal merits. Also, your competitor is likely to retaliate by attacking *your* profit sanctuaries. And he may have greater financial resources than you thought, or a "sugar daddy" waiting in the wings to save his hide.

Toyota has overrun its opponents' sanctuaries. The profit sanctuaries of GM, Ford, and Chrysler are light trucks and SUVs, where they earn between $10,000 and $15,000 per vehicle. Toyota now offers equivalent vehicles and has enough cash that it could give them away. Instead, it is plowing its earnings back into hybrid vehicles and capacity expansions. Toyota effectively controls the strategies of the Big 3 by occupying their profit sanctuaries.

4. *Take it and make it your own.* Softball competitors like to think their bright ideas are sacred. Hardball players know better. They're willing to take any good idea they see (any one that isn't nailed down by a patent or other legal protection), and use it to create competitive advantage for themselves.

This needn't be restricted to borrowing from competitors. You can pick up ideas from one geographic market and transplant them to another. Ideas can also be transplanted between industries. But the "making it your own" part is just as important as the "taking it." Every hardball company finds a way to build on, improve, and customize the borrowed idea so that it's not just a me-too copy.

Batesville Casket is the world-leading manufacturer of welded steel caskets. In the 1970s, Batesville endeavored to reduce its manufacturing costs by transplanting automotive manufacturing techniques to its industry. The impact on Batesville's less sophisticated competitors was stunning. In the 1990s, Batesville set its sights on those competitors with positions in major metropolitan markets. To get at them, Batesville had to offer greater variety and faster response times at affordable prices. Batesville Casket accomplished this with remarkable success by transplanting Toyota's production system.

5. *Entice your competitors into retreat.* Sometimes, through a superior understanding of your business and your industry, you can take actions that confuse your competitors and entice them to behave in ways that they believe will be beneficial to them, but that actually will weaken them. This opportunity hinges on the existence of certain customers that are not worth having because they cost too much to serve. These are the customers you want your competitors to have.

Federal Mogul discovered that smaller engine manufacturers were not as profitable as large OEMs despite having higher gross margins. The cost impact of smaller production runs and higher service needs were hidden from management by the company's standard costing system. Federal Mogul repriced its small OEM business high enough to make money if it won the bid, but low enough to ensure that any competitor who won the bid would not recover its true costs. Over time, the cost position of Federal Mogul's competitors worsened as they continued to win more business with the smaller OEMs.

Enticing your competitors to focus on a business that drives up their costs is one of the most complex strategies of hardball competition. You must have a superb understanding of your own costs and how customers make purchase decisions. For example, you can set prices so your competitors respond by seeking business that they think will be profitable for them, but that will, in fact, drive up their costs and depress their profits. This is a risky, bet-the-company strategy. It works best in complex businesses where costs may be misallocated. There is lots of potential for error. Your analysis of the actual-versus-apparent costs associated with a product, service, or customer—and the strategy that grows out of that analysis—has to be right.

6. *Break compromises.* When a hardball player wants to achieve explosive growth, he looks for a compromise to break. A compromise is a concession that an industry forces on its customers, who often accept it because they have come to believe it is endemic—"just the way things work"?—like the never-changing 3 p.m. check-in time at hotels.

Wausau Paper bet that the standard industry practice of requiring its paper merchants to accept long and unreliable deliveries and large minimum-order quantities was a huge compromise, resulting in higher inventories and greater costs for the merchants. Wausau "retooled" its business to provide merchants with 10 times faster delivery times, three times the variety, and 1/20th the minimum-order quantities. Wausau merchants loved the new model, and Wausau grew like a weed; in the past 15 years, it has created more shareholder value than any other paper company.

If compromises can be identified and businesses altered to create a new model, the result is often fast and profitable growth. Getting rid of a compromise usually confuses your competitors, because they are still locked in the mind-set that generated the compromises.

HARDBALL M&A

Despite their high failure rate, mergers and acquisitions can be a powerful means of pursuing a hardball strategy more quickly, or on a much larger scale, than could be done organically. Mergers made without a strategic rationale, and acquisitions pursued on the whim of the CEO, are softball moves. A good M&A deal creates competitive advantage; a great deal can help a company achieve decisive advantage, enabling it to lock up critical assets or build superior economics.

Companies often pursue M&A to rapidly expand, nationally or globally, or annex a rival and reduce competition. There can be so much strategic benefit in merging or acquiring companies that some hardball players become serial acquirers. Hardball serial acquirers have a clear idea of how to build competitive advantage, and have the capabilities to consummate deals and digest acquisitions for maximum strategic benefit. Companies often begin their M&A activity as a way of pursuing a modest strategic goal, but end up achieving decisive advantage.

The lessons from serial acquirers that use M&A to carry out their hardball strategies are straightforward in concept, but difficult to execute:

- Acquire only if the opportunity fits with the strategy.
- Do not be tempted to step outside your proven process.
- Build an internal M&A capability.
- Seek outside advice and assistance.
- Take a rigorous approach to valuation.
- Invest in post-merger integration capabilities.

CHANGES IN THE FIELD OF PLAY

The strategies in *Hardball* are classics, but "classic" should not be interpreted to mean "static." The game of hardball is dynamic and always evolving. New barriers to achieving competitive advantage emerge, and new roadblocks to building decisive advantage are erected. Several issues will affect the way hardball must be played in the future. They will change the rules for players who wish to be winners, especially on the global field.

Playing the China card. Over the next decade, China will be the biggest and most contentious issue for hardball players, even if they are not global companies themselves. The most important China issue is not that it is a source of low-cost production or even that it is a huge market for companies. The critical China issue today is that this country will be the source of tomorrow's toughest new competitors, who will become a thorn in the side for all Western companies as the Japanese were in the 1980s. Nokia and Motorola know this, and have dramatically intensified their handset investments in China to retain leadership positions there.

Getting stuck in the middle. During the past decade, the U.S. economy has shifted from being producer-driven to consumer-driven. This has become an important issue for companies in virtually every industry and business segment, but many of them have yet to recognize it, or they have leaders that refuse to believe it.

As a result of changes in consumer demographics and behavior, in combination with changes in retailing, the market for consumer goods has become polarized. At the very high end, some luxury brands continue to succeed by selling super-expensive goods at very high margins and in very small quantities.

At the low end, a wide variety of brands of commodities and utilitarian items—including household and office products, food staples, home electronics, toys, and hardware—compete with each other on price and minor product differentiations. These brands, including private-label or generic brands, may grow in volume but must fight ferociously to retain or grow profits.

And then there is the middle, where no consumer or manufacturer wants to be—the territory where hundreds of companies and brands have gotten stuck. Companies like Kmart, Mitsubishi Motors, General Electric appliances, and Samsonite are frozen in the headlights of competitors who are stealing customers at the low and high price points.

The fastest-growing segment in the market is in premium goods that are still affordable for middle-market consumers. These are goods and services, priced from 20 to 200 percent above mid-priced offerings, which offer enough technical differences and performance improvements, along with emotional engagement, that consumers are willing to pay extra for them. These new luxury brands include small, low-priced items such as Aveda personal care, Grey Goose and Belvedere vodka, and Starbucks coffee. They also include more expensive items such as a Viking stove or a set of Callaway golf clubs, and go all the way up to big-ticket purchases, such as a premium sea cruise or a Mercedes C-class sedan.

> *The fastest-growing segment in the market is in premium goods that are still affordable for middle-market consumers. These are goods and services, priced from 20 to 200 percent above mid-priced offerings, which offer enough technical differences and performance improvements, along with emotional engagement, that consumers are willing to pay extra for them.*

Dealing with stranded assets. A nasty side effect of gaining competitive advantage and creating a virtuous cycle that builds into decisive advantage is the stranding of assets. This happens when an asset that was once a contributor to competitive advantage becomes irrelevant or, worse, a drag on competitiveness. Forces such as globalization, technological change and corporate self-interest continuously intensify competition and strand many kinds of assets—including plants and facilities, as well as customers and suppliers.

Softball competitors rally around stranded assets, attempting to delay the day of reckoning when the assets will have to be written off. They seek government aid; they try to push the problem onto the public, as the auto industry is attempting to do with health care costs. The longer the delay, the greater the pain will be in the long run.

As early as the 1970s, both Cadillac and Lincoln faced the problems of an aging and shrinking customer base. Ford flip-flopped: Lincoln was a marketing brand, then it was a company, and then it was part of Ford Division.

In contrast, GM invested in bold, risky new product designs and higher quality, in an attempt to woo new customers and revive the Cadillac customer base. Cadillac's new models have gotten a lot of media attention and are selling well enough that the company has been emboldened to market its vehicles in Europe. Hardball competitors like GM strive to eliminate and, when possible, re-purpose their stranded assets.

Being "Wal-Marted." Wal-Mart is the largest retailer on the planet. Its sales exceed those of the second-largest retailer, Carrefour, by more than three times. Wal-Mart is the largest retailer—or among the top three largest—of goods in many consumer categories. Wal-Mart continues to push into new categories with catastrophic consequences for traditional competitors. Its cost position is so strong that its competitors' attempts to match it on "everyday low prices" end in failure.

For its suppliers, Wal-Mart is a dilemma. It is the most profitable customer for many suppliers, on an absolute basis and often on the basis of percentage. These suppliers are naturally wary of upsetting Wal-Mart.

But there are chinks in the monolith's armor. While customers find great value at Wal-Mart, they are also forced into a compromise when they shop there. They usually have to travel a long distance to get to a store; they have to park in a large, crowded lot; they must roam through acres of retail space, through aisles designed to take them ever deeper into the store. Sales help is scarce, and not always knowledgeable. The prices are dramatically low, but the shopping experience is mediocre at best, and unpleasant at worst.

Internet retailers such as Tesco and Grocerygateway.com are tapping into the willingness of some customers to pay higher prices for a better experience. Internet-savvy consumers who value their time and want competitive prices, but don't need the very lowest prices, find shopping online to be a perfectly acceptable substitute for shopping at Wal-Mart and other big-box retailers. At Grocerygateway.com, shoppers can get groceries at competitive prices; hardware from The Home Depot; liquor; and more, at the click of a mouse. The goods are delivered within an agreed-upon time and unloaded into the house. No driving. No parking. No crowds. No wandering the endless aisles. No lugging packages. No Wal-Mart.

THE HARDBALL MIND-SET

To play the game of hardball to its fullest requires a hardball state of mind. Hardball players possess a number of admirable characteristics. They have an intellectual toughness that enables them to face facts and see reality. They are emotionally aware, which means they know themselves well, and also their people. They are always dissatisfied with the status quo, no matter how fine things may seem. They have the will to catalyze change. They're tough, but not bullies. They're serious about their business. They have such an intense passion for winning that it rubs off on others.

The hardball player needs all of these qualities, and more, in order to accomplish his most important task: to get to the heart of the matter and stay there. The heart of the matter is that set of fundamental, often systemic, issues that is limiting the growth and success of the business. These issues are often so challenging in so many ways that no one in the organization has the guts to take them on, or the ability to actually solve them.

Getting to the heart of the matter is not easy. Organizations do not like addressing heart-of-the-matter issues. These issues are hard, time-consuming, fraught with risks, and prone to defeat individual efforts.

An organization that is unwilling, or not ready, to face the heart of the matter is one doomed to inaction. It will be like a sitting duck in comparison to competitors that are able to face the heart of the matter. It is the job of the hardball leader to compel his organization to face those fundamental issues and then plunge into addressing them.

Hardball leaders succeed in staying at the heart of the matter by keeping their organizations in "perpetual turnaround" mode, no matter how successful they are. They make themselves, and their people, believe that they are in constant danger of losing their advantage because, in fact, they are. A management team in turnaround mode cannot allow itself to be distracted from the central objectives of the turnaround.

Hardball players are often deceptive in appearance and demeanor. They are brave, but not necessarily boastful. They are bold, but never bullying. They may not be flashy; sometimes they may even seem rather bland. But the ones that achieve strong competitive advantage, and especially those that go on to create decisive advantage, tend to have much longer successful runs than their competitors. There is no limit to the duration of advantage, nor are we aware of any average lifespan for advantaged companies. It is the leader that usually causes a company to lose decisive advantage, sometimes as the result of a serious mistake, but most often through complacency and failure to adapt. If a company is aggressive at renewing its competitive advantage, it may enjoy a very long run indeed, and watch as the softball players limp away from the playing field, never to return.

Value Innovation: A Leap into the Blue Ocean

W. Chan Kim
INSEAD

Renée Mauborgne
INSEAD

Corporate strategy is heavily influenced by its military roots. The very language of strategy is imbued with military references—chief executive "officers" in "headquarters," "troops" on the "front lines." Described this way, strategy is about confronting an opponent and fighting over a given piece of land that is both limited and constant. Traditionally, strategy focused on beating the competition, and strategic plans are still couched in warlike terminology. They exhort companies to seize competitive advantage, battle for market share, and fight over price. Competition is a bloody battlefield.

The trouble is that if the opposing army is doing exactly same thing, such strategies often cancel each other out, or trigger immediate tit-for-tat retaliation. Strategy quickly reverts to tactical opportunism. So where should companies turn for a more innovative approach to strategy?

The answer lies with something we call blue ocean strategy. We argue that head-to-head competition results in nothing but a bloody red ocean as rivals fight over shrinking profits. Success comes not from battling competitors, but from making the competition irrelevant by creating "blue oceans" of uncontested market space. The creators of blue oceans don't use the competition as their benchmark. Instead, they follow a different strategic logic that we call value innovation. Value innovation is the cornerstone of blue ocean strategy. We call it value innovation because instead of focusing on beating the competition in existing market space, you focus on getting out of existing market boundaries by creating a leap in value for buyers and your company which leaves the competition behind.

These ideas challenge conventional strategic thinking and are supported by extensive research. Over the past decade, we have created a database that covers more than 30 industries going back over 100 years. So what does all this data show?

We believe that the business world has been overlooking one of the key lessons of wealth creation in history. Our research indicates that the major source of wealth creation over time is not the industry that a company plays in per se. Nor did we find permanently great companies that consistently created and captured wealth.

History reveals that there are neither perpetually excellent companies nor perpetually excellent industries. Companies and industries rise and fall based on the strategic moves that are made. Consider *In Search of Excellence,* the bestselling business book published in 1982. Within just five years, two-thirds of the identified model firms in the book had declined. Likewise for those sample companies in *Built to Last,* another bestselling business book. It was later found that if industry performance was removed from the equation, some of the companies in *Built to Last* were no longer excellent. As Foster and Kaplan point out in their book *Creative Destruction,* while the companies listed certainly outperformed the market, some did not outperform the competition within their entire industries.

So if there is no perpetually high-performing company and if the same company can be brilliant

Reprinted from *Journal of Business Strategy*, Vol. 26, No. 4 (2005), pp. 22–26. Adapted by Permission of Harvard Business School Press. "Blue Ocean Strategy: How to Create Uncontested Market Space and Make the Competition Irrelevant," by W. Chan Kim and Renée Mauborgne. Copyright © 2005 by the Harvard Business School Publishing Corporation; all rights reserved.

The Performance Consequences of Blue Oceans

We set out to quantify the impact of creating blue oceans on a company's growth in both revenues and profits in a study of the business launches of 108 companies (see Figure 1).

We found that 86 percent of the launches were line-extensions, that is, incremental improvement within the red ocean of existing market space. Yet they accounted for only 62 percent of total revenues and a mere 39 percent of total profits. The remaining 14 percent of the launches were aimed at creating new blue oceans. They generated 38 percent of total revenues and 61 percent of total profits.

Given that business launches included the total investments made for creating red and blue oceans (regardless of their subsequent revenue and profit consequences, including failures), the performance benefits of creating blue waters are evident.

at one moment and wrongheaded another, it appears that the company is not the appropriate unit of analysis in exploring the roots of high performance. There are no perpetually excellent industries, either. Five years ago, for example, people envied companies in the IT industry, yet today the reverse is largely true.

Our analysis of industry history shows that the strategic move, and not the company or the industry, is the right unit of analysis for explaining the root of profitable growth. And the strategic move that we found matters centrally is the creation and capturing of blue oceans.

STRATEGIC MOVES

By strategic move, we mean the set of managerial actions and decisions involved in making a major market-creating business offering. The strategic moves we discuss—moves that have delivered products and services that opened and captured new market space, with a significant leap in demand—contain great stories of profitable growth. We built our study around these strategic moves (over 150 from more than 30 industries spanning from 1880 to 2000) to understand the pattern by which blue oceans are created and captured and high performance is achieved.

A snapshot of the auto industry from 1900 to 1940 is instructive. In 1908 Henry Ford created the auto industry as we know it with the Ford Model T. Prior to Ford, consumers had two choices: horse-drawn buggies or expensive custom-made automobiles. Ford created a blue ocean by making the automobile easy to use, reliable, and priced so that the majority of Americans could afford it. Ford's market share went from 9 to 61 percent. The Model T, then, was the strategic move that ignited the automotive industry. But in 1924, it was overtaken by another strategic move, this time by General Motors. Contrary to Ford's functional one-color, one-car, single-model strategy, GM created the new market space of emotional, stylized cars with "a car for every purpose and purse." Not only was the auto industry's growth and profitability again catapulted to new heights, but GM's market share jumped from 20 to 50 percent while Ford's fell from 50 to 20 percent.

Head-to-head competition results in nothing but a bloody red ocean as rivals fight over shrinking profits. Success comes not from battling competitors, but from making the competition irrelevant by creating 'blue oceans' of uncontested market space.

Move forward to the 1970s when Japanese car companies created the blue ocean of small, gas-efficient autos. And then to the 1980s when Chrysler created the blue ocean of minivans. All these companies were incumbents. Moreover, the blue oceans made by incumbents were usually within their core businesses. In fact, most blue oceans are created from within, not beyond, red oceans of existing industries. This challenges the view that new markets are in distant waters. Blue oceans are right next to you in every industry. Issues of perceived cannibalization or creative destruction for established companies also proved to be exaggerated. Blue

Figure 1   **The Profit and Growth Consequences of Blue-Ocean Strategy**

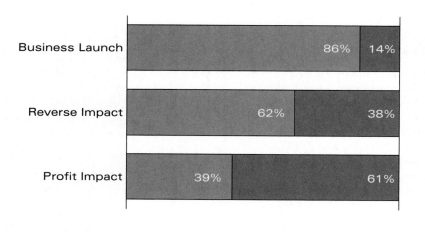

oceans created profitable growth for every company launching them, start-ups and incumbents alike.

Over our study period of more than 100 years, we found a similar pattern in other sectors. In short, the strategic move that matters most to both an industry's long-run profitable growth and that of individual companies is the repeated creation over time of new market space that captured a mass of buyers. Blue ocean strategy is about creating and executing such strategic moves that unlock uncontested market space which render competitors irrelevant. In contrast, red ocean strategy is about how to outcompete in the existing market space.

SAILING INTO A BLUE OCEAN

To understand the power of strategic moves that create blue oceans consider the U.S. wine market. Conventional wisdom caused wineries to compete on the prestige and the quality of wine at a price point—traditional competitive strategy. Prestige and quality were viewed as a function of adding complexity to the wine based on taste profiles shared by wine makers and reinforced by the wine show judging system. The wine experts concur that complexity—layered personality and characteristics that reflect the uniqueness of the soil, season,

and winemaker's skill in tannins, oak, and aging processes—equates with quality.

Then along came Casella Wines, an Australian winery. Casella redefined the problem of the wine industry as how to make a fun and nontraditional wine that's easy to drink. Why? In looking at the demand side of alternatives of beer, spirits, and ready-to-drink cocktails, which captured three times as many consumer alcohol sales as wine, Casella Wines found that the mass of American adults saw wine as a turnoff. It was intimidating and pretentious and the complexity of taste—even though it was where the industry sought to excel—created a challenge to the inexperienced palate. With this insight, Casella was ready to challenge the industry's strategic logic and business model. To do so it considered four key questions outlined in an analytical tool we call the four actions framework.

First, which of the factors that the industry takes for granted should be eliminated? Second, which factors should be reduced well below the industry's standard? Third, which factors should be raised well above the industry's standard? Fourth, which factors should be created that the industry has never offered?

The upshot of this analysis was that Casella Wines created [yellow tail], a wine whose strategic profile broke from the competition and created a blue ocean. Instead of offering wine as wine, Casella created a social drink accessible to everyone. By looking at the alternatives of beer and ready-to-drink cocktails, Casella Wines created three new factors in the U.S. wine industry—easy drinking, easy to select, and fun and adventure. It eliminated or reduced everything else. [yellow tail] was a completely new combination of characteristics that produced an uncomplicated wine structure that was instantly appealing to the mass of alcohol drinkers. The result was an easy drinking wine that did not require years to develop an appreciation for.

This allowed the company to dramatically reduce or eliminate all the factors the wine industry had long competed on—tannins, complexity and aging. With the need for aging reduced, the working capital required was also reduced. The wine industry criticised the sweet fruitiness of [yellow tail] but consumers loved the wine.

Casella also made selection easy by offering only two choices of [yellow tail]—Chardonnay, the most popular white wine in the United States; and a red Shiraz. It removed all technical jargon from the bottle and created instead a striking and instantly recognizable label featuring a kangaroo in vibrant colors. It also scored a home run by making wine shop employees ambassadors of [yellow tail], introducing fun and adventure into the sales process by giving them Australian outback clothing, including bushman hats and oilskin jackets to wear at work. Recommendations to consumers to buy [yellow tail] flew out of their mouths.

From the moment [yellow tail] hit the retail shelves in July 2001, sales took off. In the space of three years. [yellow tail] emerged as the fastest-growing brand in the histories of both the Australian and U.S. wine industries and the number one imported wine into the United States surpassing the wines of France and Italy. By August 2003, it was the number one red wine in a 750 ml bottle sold in America, outstripping California labels. By the end of 2004, [yellow tail's] moving average annual sales were tracking at 11.2 million cases. What's more, whereas large wine companies developed strong brands over decades of marketing investment. [yellow tail] leap-frogged tall competitors with no promotional campaign or mass media or consumer advertising. It didn't just steal sales from competitors it grew the overall market. [yellow tail] brought over 6 million non-wine drinkers—beer and ready-to-drink cocktail drinkers—into the market. Novice table wine drinkers started to drink wine more frequently, jug wine drinkers moved up, and drinkers of more expensive wines moved down to become consumers of [yellow tail].

A MARKET UNIVERSE OF TWO OCEANS

To understand what Casella achieved, imagine a market universe composed of two sorts of oceans—red oceans and blue oceans. Red oceans represent all the industries in existence today. This is the known market space. Blue oceans denote all the industries not in existence today. This is the unknown market space.

In the red oceans, industry boundaries are defined and accepted, and the competitive rules of the game are known. Here, companies try to outperform their rivals to grab a greater share of existing demand. As the market space gets more crowded, prospects for profits and growth are reduced. Products become commodities, and cut-throat competition turns the red ocean bloody.

Blue oceans, in contrast, are defined by untapped market space, demand creation, and the opportunity for highly profitable growth. Although some blue oceans are created well beyond existing industry boundaries, most are created from within red oceans by expanding existing industry boundaries, as [yellow tail] did. In blue oceans, competition is irrelevant because the rules of the game are waiting to be set.

It will always be important to swim successfully in the red ocean by outcompeting rivals. Red oceans will always matter and will always be a fact of business life. But with supply exceeding demand in more industries, competing for a share of contracting markets, while necessary, is not sufficient to sustain high performance. Companies need to go beyond competing. To seize new profit and growth opportunities, they also need to create blue oceans.

> *Our analysis of industry history shows that the strategic move, and not the company or the industry, is the right unit of analysis for explaining the root of profitable growth.*

Unfortunately, blue oceans are largely uncharted. The dominant focus of strategy work over the past 25 years has been on competition-based red ocean strategies. Some discussions around blue oceans exist. But until now there has been little practical guidance on how to create them. That's why in our book *Blue Ocean Strategy,* we provide practical frameworks and analytics for the systematic pursuit and capture of blue oceans.

THE EXPANSION OF BLUE OCEANS

Although the term *blue oceans* is new, their existence is not. They are a feature of business life, past and present. Look back one hundred years and ask, how many of today's industries were then unknown? The answer: many industries as basic as automobiles, music recording, aviation, petrochemicals, health care, and management consulting were unheard of or had just begun to emerge at that time. Now turn the clock back only 30 years. Again, a plethora of multibillion-dollar industries jumps out—mutual funds, mobile phones, gas-fired electricity plants, biotechnology, discount retail, express package delivery, snowboards, coffee bars, and home videos, to name a few. Just three decades ago, none of these industries existed.

Now put the clock forward 20 years—or perhaps 50 years—and ask yourself: How many now unknown industries will likely exist then? If history is any predictor of the future, again the answer is many of them.

The reality is that industries never stand still. They continuously evolve. Operations improve, markets expand, and players come and go. History teaches us that we have a hugely underestimated capacity to create new industries and re-create existing ones.

In fact, the half-century-old Standard Industrial Classification (SIC) system published by the U.S. Census Bureau was replaced in 1997 by the North American Industry Classification Standard (NAICS) system. The new system expanded the 10 SIC industry sectors into 20 sectors to reflect the emerging realities of new industry territories. The service sector under the old system, for example, is now expanded into seven business sectors ranging from information to health care and social assistance. Given that these systems are designed for standardization and continuity, such a replacement shows how significant the expansion of blue oceans has been.

THE IMPORTANCE OF CREATING BLUE OCEANS

There are several driving forces behind a rising imperative to create blue oceans. Accelerated technological advances have substantially improved industrial productivity and have allowed suppliers to produce an unprecedented array of products and services. The result is that in increasing numbers of industries, supply exceeds demand. The trend toward globalization compounds the situation. As trade barriers between nations and regions are dismantled and as information on products and prices becomes instantly and globally available, niche markets and havens for monopoly continue to disappear.

The result has been accelerated commoditization of products and services—something the financial services industry knows all about. The effect is to increase price wars and shrink profit margins. In overcrowded industries, differentiating brands becomes harder in both economic upturns and downturns.

All this suggests that the business environment in which most strategy and management approaches of the 20th century evolved is increasingly disappearing. As red oceans become more and more bloody, management will need to be more concerned with blue oceans than ever before. That is why the future belongs to companies that can create and execute on blue ocean strategy.

The war or competitive battle analogy we have used for strategy so far has its limits. It is based on an assumption that there's only so much territory that exists. So it's been about dividing up that territory by competing against one another. There's been a winner and a loser. But our research shows it's not a zero-sum game. You can create new land. Business history shows us that contrary to perceived wisdom, the number of market spaces that can be created is infinite.

There is, however, a hugely underestimated capacity to create new territory—new industries and markets. The number of industries is ever expanding—and the pace is accelerating. The implications for chief executives and their advisers are profound. Some industries die, some persist. But new industries are constantly being created. It is like a galaxy of stars—infinite. Transpose that onto the future, and the obvious conclusion is that the biggest industries today are unlikely to be the biggest industries 30 years hence.

MINIMIZING RISK AND MAXIMIZING OPPORTUNITY

Some would think that blue ocean strategy may be inherently more risky. Far from it, blue ocean strategy is about risk minimization and not about risk taking. Of course, there is no such thing as a riskless strategy. Any strategy, whether red or blue, will always involve risk. Nonetheless, when it comes to venturing beyond the red ocean to create and capture blue oceans there are six key risks companies face: search risk, planning risk, scope risk, business model risk, organizational risk, and management risk. The first four risks revolve around strategy formulation, and the latter two around strategy execution.

Each of the six principles in *Blue Ocean Strategy* expressly addresses how to mitigate each of these risks. The first blue ocean principle—reconstruct market boundaries—addresses the search risk of how to successfully identify, out of the haystack of possibilities that exist, commercially compelling blue ocean opportunities. The second principle—focus on the big picture, not the numbers—tackles how to mitigate the planning risk of investing lots of effort and lots of time but delivering only tactical red ocean moves. The third principle—reach beyond existing demand—addresses the scope risk of aggregating the greatest demand for a new offering.

The fourth principle—get the strategic sequence right—addresses how to build a robust business model to ensure that you make a healthy profit on your blue ocean idea, thereby mitigating business model risk. The fifth principle—overcome key organizational hurdles—tackles how to knock over organizational hurdles in executing a blue ocean strategy addressing organizational risk. The sixth principle—build execution into strategy—tackles how to motivate people to execute blue ocean strategy to the best of their abilities, overcoming management risk.

These six principles aim to make the formulation and execution of blue ocean strategy as systematic and actionable as competing in the red oceans of existing market space. In creating blue oceans, they guide companies in a way that is both opportunity maximizing and risk minimizing.

BLUE OCEAN STRATEGY IS A DYNAMIC PROCESS

Blue ocean strategy should not be a static process. It must be a dynamic one. Consider The Body Shop. In the 1980s. The Body Shop was highly successful, and rather than compete head-on with large cosmetics companies, it invented a whole new market space for natural beauty products. More recently The Body Shop has struggled. But that does not diminish the brilliance of its original strategic move. The problem was that The Body Shop didn't realize what made it a brilliant strategic move. Its genius lay in creating a new market space in an intensely competitive industry that historically competed on glamour. Once it had created a blue ocean, the company focused on mining that new market space. That was OK while few players imitated it, but as more and more competitors jumped into its blue ocean and it became red, the company became involved in a bruising battle for market share. This was the wrong strategy.

Once a company has created a blue ocean, it should prolong its profit and growth sanctuary by swimming as far as possible in the blue ocean, making itself a moving target, distancing itself from potential imitators, and discouraging them in the process. The aim here is to dominate the blue ocean over imitators for as long as possible. But, as other companies' strategies converge on your market and the blue ocean turns red with intense competition, companies need to reach out to create a new blue ocean to break away from the competition again. This is where The Body Shop stumbled.

Blue ocean strategy shows companies not only how to create and capture blue oceans but also how to monitor when it is time to reach out for a new blue ocean. In this way, blue ocean strategy presents a dynamic iterative process to create uncontested market space across time.

Confronting Low-End Competition

Don Potter
Strategy Street.com

A low-end competitor is like a shark. It can appear unexpectedly from below, churning the waters by offering big savings to customers, taking a bite out of comfortable profits, and disrupting established ways of doing business. And it can leave a wake of destruction: devastated industry leaders, flattened profits, and disgruntled customers.

No company is immune to such an attack, and most managers will face at least one—and possibly many—during their careers. If there is a defense, it lies in knowledge: knowing what form the attack is likely to take and under what conditions. More important, managers should be aware of their different options, including the response that is most likely to restore market calm in the least disruptive way.

THE DYNAMICS OF A LOW-END ATTACK

Every industry has one or more standard leaders: large competitors that set the benchmarks for performance and price. General Motors fills this role in the automotive industry, Hewlett-Packard in personal computers, and Kellogg in breakfast cereals. Typically, a standard leader sells a mix of products that roughly mirrors that of the overall industry, and its price points are followed by other companies to within a narrow range. Together, the standard leaders of a market control a large chunk of the action: usually from 35 to 80 percent of total industry sales.

Reprinted from "Confronting Low-End Competition," Don Potter, MIT Sloan Management Review, Vol. 45, Issue 4, Summer 2004, p. 73–78, by permission of publisher. Copyright © 2004 by Massachusetts Institute of Technology. All rights reserved.

It is these standard leaders—or, more precisely, their sales volume—that the low-end competitor targets, often by offering discounts that are more than 20 percent lower than prevailing price points. In mainframe memory storage, EMC Corp. established itself through price cuts of 25 percent. The successful PC clones of the late 1980s underpriced IBM Corp. by at least 30 percent. Cott sells private-label colas and other soft drinks for prices at least 25 percent below Coca-Cola and Pepsi. When the price discounts are less than 20 percent, low-end competitors usually have to provide other benefits, either in the acquisition of or use of the product or service. In the mid-1980s, for example, Calgary-based Minit Lube Ltd. offered oil changes at a price only slightly below that of service stations, but the service was completed in just 10 minutes, saving customers the inconvenience of dropping off and picking up their cars.

Of course, a low-end competitor almost always has to reduce some customer benefits in order to lower costs (and thereby enable the company to make a profit). There are three types of benefits that can potentially be trimmed—function, convenience, or reliability—but only the first two offer significant opportunities.

Function refers to the characteristics of an offering that affect how the customer uses it. In a manufactured or service product, it includes such aspects as size, power, speed, and styling—think of electronic fuel injection for a marine engine, the processing speed of a PC, an ocean view at a resort. In a retail or distribution business, function includes the choice of products that customers can purchase and the ambience of a physical store. In manufacturing, providing functionality entails the cost of purchased materials, labor, and capital investments. In retail or distribution, it encompasses the cost of the products offered and store improvements to create ambience—all of which can be significant.

Convenience refers to the ease of acquisition and installation, so that customers can move quickly to use a product. To speed that process, companies spend money on advertising to build customer awareness and to differentiate their products from others. They also make their products readily available by maintaining a widespread sales force and specialized distribution or by operating retail outlets close to the customer. Such channels incur significant costs.

Reliability refers to how consistently a company keeps its promises. With manufactured products, the items must be delivered to the distribution channel as promised; they must perform as expected; and the producer must maintain a consistent market presence with end users and channels. In the retail and distribution business, the range of products must be predictably available; stock-outs should be minimal; and returns and credits must be handled efficiently, if not amiably.

A company cannot easily cut the costs of reliability. If it does, it risks losing credibility—a potentially fatal mistake for any business trying to enter a market. A low-cost competitor, then, is most likely to cut costs by reducing functionality, convenience or both. Numerous such strategies exist, with various combinations of price, functionality and convenience. To investigate the different approaches, I analyzed the operations of more than 250 low-end competitors in a number of industries, including high tech, fast food, financial services, and retail. A key result of that research, which included a review of publicly available data for the past 15 years, is that successful low-cost competitors tend to use one of four approaches: stripper, predator, reformer, or transformer.

Strippers

Strippers enter the market with a bare-bones offering, reduced in function and usually in convenience. The substantial price reductions of these products appeal to just the most price-sensitive consumers, and strippers typically achieve only a modest market share. As a group, they rarely capture as much as 30 percent of the market; more often their share falls below 15 percent.

Strippers appear to be most common in service and distribution industries, particularly when the standard leaders are especially committed to traditional ways of doing business. JetBlue Airways Corp. is a case in point. The company offers a very limited choice of flights; it flies into secondary airports in large markets; and it serves only a small portion of the domestic market. Another example is the discount chain Costco Wholesale Corp. The membership-only warehouse stores sell high-quality (primarily nationally branded) merchandise at very low prices, but the product selection is a fraction of that of Wal-Mart Stores Inc. or of even the average supermarket.

Predators

Predators offer products with functions equivalent to those of the standard leader but at lower prices. To do so, they rely on various tactics.

In many cases, predators are able to exploit the opportunities that arise when an industry has tremendous overhead (such as substantial R&D expenses or the high costs of maintaining a brand) or demanding expectations for product profitability. Occasionally, a longtime standard leader may have allowed its prices to rise enough that a relatively unknown company enters the market simply by manufacturing and selling a comparable product under its own brand at significantly lower prices. In the early 1990s, for instance, PC clone makers offered comparable function benefits at prices 25 to 50 percent below standard leader IBM. Current examples include Advanced Micro Devices in semiconductors, Drypers in disposable diapers, and Men's Wearhouse in apparel retailing. Often, a predator will partner with a powerful distributor, thereby saving on advertising and other expenses. Private-label manufacturers such as Dean Foods in dairy, Ralcorp Holdings in breakfast cereals, and Perrigo in nonprescription drugs use this approach. Sometimes, a predator finds a cheaper way to manufacture certain products, especially those at the low end. Throughout the 1980s and 1990s, for example, Nucor Corp. grew into a power in the steel industry by deploying a low-cost manufacturing process that used scrap metal to make basic products, such as reinforcing bars. Other predators rely on third-party or government subsidies to reduce costs below those of the standard leader. And another approach—used by many outsourcing concerns—is to aggregate demand to obtain better economies of scale (and therefore lower costs).

> *Reformers offer a new convenience at the expense of either some functionality or other convenience benefit. The classic example is Amazon.*

The different approaches typically require customers to yield some convenience benefits in exchange for low prices. As such, many predators establish themselves by first targeting the market's weakest (and most price-sensitive) customers, similar to what strippers do. As predators continue to grow, however, they can attract the largest and most valuable customers. For example, by 1987, predator Sprint had already become a serious competitor to AT&T by winning Sears, Roebuck as a customer and by challenging AT&T for GM's business.

Reformers

Unlike strippers or predators, reformers do not compete solely or even primarily on price. Instead, reformers make their mark by offering a new convenience at the expense of either some functionality or another convenience benefit of a standard leader product. The combination of competitive (and usually lower) price plus greater convenience can make reformer products extremely attractive. The term *reformer* refers to the way in which these companies change the way business is done in a particular market segment.

The classic example of a reformer is Amazon.com Inc. At a time when traditional bookstores are offering more functional amenities—reading nooks, coffee bars, and so on—Amazon offers the convenience of buying books and other products over the Web at any hour, literally with the click of a mouse. Other reformers include Jiffy Lube International Inc. and Minit Lube, which pioneered quick-service oil changes in the 1980s. Domino's Pizza Inc. played a similar role in the pizza business. Another example is Dollar General Corp., which pares its product choices to the bare essentials to squeeze them into tiny stores that can be more easily located near its lower-income customers.

Reformers tend to emerge in three situations: when the product can be ordered and delivered online, when the product can be ordered by phone or online and delivered by mail, and when the product can be unbundled into high- and low-cost functional and convenience benefits, and some customers are willing to forgo certain high-cost benefits for greater convenience. Reformers can appeal to current customers as well as to new ones who are attracted by the additional convenience. In such ways, reformers can expand industries by creating new market segments.

Transformers

Like reformers, transformers provide customers with a new benefit, but the advantage is in functionality—not convenience. Often, transformers also offer lower prices, either by using a novel approach to serving the market or by deploying previously unavailable technology. The term *transformer* refers to the way in which these companies can radically alter entire industries.

Most retail chains with "category killer" concepts were originally transformers, including Toys "R" Us, Home Depot, and Staples. The companies' stores offer far greater product selection than the standard leaders, but to keep prices low their locations are less convenient and offer less customer service. Other transformers have created market concepts that reduce the time and cost to sell or purchase products.

Another example of a transformer is Powerwave Technologies Inc. of Santa Ana, California, which sells amplifiers that cell-phone companies use to boost the signals of their broadcast stations. Powerwave's innovative products feature multichannel operation, which is more versatile and efficient than single-channel mode. Powerwave changed the way that power amplification is priced, from a cost per amplifier (which made sense for single-channel products) to a price per power of amplification delivered. As a result, broadcast stations operating near their capacity found that Powerwave amplifiers could help them reduce their per-subscriber costs of power amplification by more than 40 percent, and Powerwave quickly became a leading supplier in the industry.

Transformers like Powerwave have used technology to save customers' time, space, or capacity (think of CD-ROM encyclopedias). Or they may enable people to avoid costly or invasive surgery (consider lithotripsy and arthroscopic surgical techniques). The emergence of such transformers can easily catch a standard leader off-guard because they deploy new technologies that are difficult to foresee.

DEVELOPING A GAME PLAN

For all their advantages, low-end competitors also have their fair share of vulnerabilities. First, a challenger has to create awareness in the customer's mind. Regardless of its strategy—stripper, predator, reformer, or transformer—it will typically have to invest a considerable sum early on to become known and to achieve at least minimal levels of accessibility. And the spending may have to continue for some time. Price-sensitive customers tend to be fickle, jumping quickly to another vendor in pursuit of the industry's lowest price. To the extent that a challenger's appeal is based primarily on price, it must constantly ensure that it has the cheapest offerings and then market that fact. The process can easily incur high marketing expenses, reducing any cost advantage gained in other areas.

Also, many low-end competitors have slim margins and must maintain high sales volumes in order to remain profitable. In other words, they cannot withstand much competition for their price-sensitive customer segments. To make matters worse, their natural market tends to be small. To varying degrees, strippers, predators, reformers, and transformers have all either eliminated or diminished some aspect of function, convenience, or reliability that appeals to the average customer, making it difficult to capture the bulk of the market, where the majority of the purchase volume resides.

Furthermore, until they establish themselves firmly in an industry, low-end competitors appeal primarily to the market's weaker customers, who often need low prices to survive. In contrast, standard leaders tend to win the sales of the largest (and healthiest) customers, who often relegate a low-end competitor to the status of minor supplier until it has achieved the scale and performance record that warrants buyer confidence.

While the challenger has vulnerabilities, the standard leader has inherent advantages. It owns the known brand, which is often a household name.

It has shaped customer expectations for functional benefits and has established its reputation for convenience and reliability. In short, the standard leader offers the product or service that most customers prefer. Furthermore, because standard leaders are typically large and have favorable economies of scale, they can often add a price point or additional benefit (to match a low-end competitor's challenge) while incurring only marginal costs. And some standard leaders can subsidize a battle with a low-end competitor by using profits from other parts of their businesses.

With such advantages, standard leaders appear to be unassailable, and it may seem that the challenger exists only at their forbearance. Yet standard leaders often have a dangerous, sometimes fatal, weakness: an intense desire to protect current profits. So many standard leaders ignore low-end competitors, choosing instead to continue with business as usual. But that only gives challengers the opportunity to grow stronger, posing an even greater threat in the future.

Of course, companies can hardly be faulted for wanting to guard their short-term profits. Nor should they be criticized for hesitating to incur any undue risk in defending against a low-end attack. The challenge, then, is to determine the optimal response that is likely to maximize profits, including those over the long term, while minimizing risks. The strategic alternatives include the following (listed from least to most disruptive to a company's operations): ride out the challenge by ignoring, blocking, or acquiring the low-end competitor; or strengthen your own value proposition by adding price points, increasing benefits, or lowering prices.

Ride Out the Challenge

When a low-end competitor enters the market, the knee-jerk reaction is to fight fire with fire, by matching or even undercutting the discount prices. Often, though, the better (and certainly less risky) response is to ride out the challenge.

Ignore the Low-End Competitor   A standard leader may choose to ignore those low-end competitors that are unlikely to gain significant market share because they lack the resources to expand their product lines. Consider Graymont Inc., a standard leader in the mining industry, which operates in Canada and the United States. A while ago, Graymont was faced with a low-end competitor that sold its lime at cheaper prices. The competitor was a cooperative owned by several customers. It transferred most of its production to its owners' operations at cost and then unloaded the remainder at very low prices. Because the co-op had little potential to move upmarket—the quality of its raw materials was poor—Graymont kept its own prices at an attractive level, accepting a smaller share of the market in return for better profitability.

> *A standard leader can win back all of its customers if it drops prices to the level of the challenger. But few want or need to discount that low.*

In other cases, a low-end competitor has access to the necessary raw materials but lacks the funds required to support expansion. Indeed, many low-end challengers have run into financial difficulties because their operations require a tricky balancing act. A large difference between the discount price and the standard leader price may be attractive to customers, but the resulting profit margins will be thin. However, the smaller the gap between the two prices, the less incentive for customers to switch. That's one reason why the retail grocery industry largely ignored the challenge of online competitors like Webvan Group Inc. Even though Webvan offered a reformer service that allowed consumers to shop from their homes, the company's prices were around the same as those of the standard leader national chains. The result: Webvan was able to attract some enthusiastic consumers but not enough to support its cost structure. It simply couldn't generate an operating profit and ended up exhausting its initial capital.

Block the Low-End Competitor   When a competitor can't be ignored, standard leaders can look for ways to block the company. Often, they can use their sheer size to their advantage by threatening to boycott any supplier or distributor that does business with the low-end competitor. Of course, such tactics should stay within legal bounds, but at the same time standard leaders should not forget the considerable clout they have. Optometrists, for example, account for more than half the market for contact lenses, and the fear of upsetting them is one reason why some contact lens manufacturers have refused to sell their products through stripper direct marketers, such as 1-800-CONTACTS Inc. of Draper, Utah.

Occasionally, the law can be a crucial ally. During the 1980s, the steel industry and several other industries in the United States got the International Trade Commission to declare that certain low-end competitors were dumping products in the domestic market. The result was import tariffs that effectively held foreign competition at bay. Patent and trademark law can also be effective in hampering certain types of low-end competition. Michigan-based Perrigo Co., a predator manufacturer of consumer drugs, has been slowed several times by lawsuits that claimed the company had deliberately copied the look and feel of some branded products.

Acquire the Low-End Competitor   The final approach to ride out a low-end threat is to buy out the challenger. Of course, the standard leader must have sufficient capital, and the acquisition costs should be reasonable. Furthermore, the standard leader needs to have a detailed plan for handling the low-end competitor's business after the buyout. A few years ago, the Shaw Group Inc., a standard leader in the pipe-fabrication industry that is headquartered in Baton Rouge, Louisiana, bought a rival that had been undercutting Shaw's bids for certain jobs. After the acquisition, Shaw renegotiated the company's backlog at higher margins and changed its pricing approach for future bids.

Strengthen Your Value Proposition

Often, riding out the challenge isn't an option, and faced with a strong competitor that is likely to expand, the standard leader must consider other alternatives. The objective is to reduce the sales volume of the low-end competitor so that it loses profitability and cannot continue growing. To achieve this, the standard leader may need to sacrifice some short-term profits to protect its long-term market share and profitability. Again, though, the best response is one that is effective with the minimum risk, so the following approaches are listed beginning with the least disruptive.

Add a New Price Point   Some low-end competitors actually do standard leaders a favor by tapping a hidden source of new customers that can fuel market growth. A standard leader can then introduce its own low-end product, matching the discount price point but offering a higher level of reliability and convenience. In such cases, the standard leader can capture the new customers, adding more revenue than cost.

In the late 1990s, for example, strippers such as San Francisco–based PeoplePC Inc. and eMachines Inc. of Irvine, California, introduced the less than

$1,000 personal computer, which appealed strongly to budget customers, including people who wanted a cheap, second PC in their homes. For two years, the standard leaders Compaq, Dell, and Hewlett-Packard resisted competing at that price point because they wanted to maintain their average selling prices and margins. But eventually, they did enter the low end of the market and discovered that their profits were fatter than the strippers' because they had better economies of scale and were able to charge slightly higher prices for their brand names and convenient distribution outlets.

Increase Your Level of Benefits Suppose, though, that the low-end competitor does not create a new market segment but instead eats into the standard leader's core business. Then the leader may consider adjusting the value proposition of its current product line, beginning with changes in performance. This tactic can be effective especially when the price discounts are less than 20 percent and when the leader can enhance function and convenience benefits that customers will readily notice.

Shopping malls, for example, have faced an assortment of low-end challenges from strippers (such as giant discounters), reformers (e-retailers), and transformers ("category killer" stores). In response, Mills Corp., a regional mall developer based in Arlington, Virginia, devised the concept of *shoppertainment*, which promotes a number of added function benefits. Some of them make shopping easier (for instance, electronic kiosks that enable customers to order hard-to-find items not stocked in a store). But most of the benefits focus on making the shopping experience more entertaining so that, for instance, some sporting goods stores have added archery ranges, fishing ponds, skate parks, or off-road bicycle tracks.

Other standard leaders have countered with function improvements that repackage or reformulate their products, such as H. J. Heinz Co.'s squeezable ketchup container and Procter & Gamble Co.'s thinner disposable diapers. And convenience innovations can also be effective. To stave off competition from Internet discounters, Banana Republic Inc. added free delivery service during the holidays and complimentary rides home for some of its customers.

Drop Your Prices The last bastion of defense is for standard leaders to drop their prices. But how deep do the cuts have to go? Theoretically, a standard leader can win back essentially all of its customers if it drops prices to the level of the challenger, because

it will have superior function, convenience, and reliability. But few standard leaders want—or need—to discount their prices that low. Standard leader Caterpillar Inc. beat back a challenge from Komatsu Ltd. in the 1980s by narrowing the price gap to less than 10 percent. AT&T likewise reduced its prices of long-distance telephone service to within 10 percent of predators MCI and Sprint. But Compaq Computer Corp. had to reduce its prices by more than 30 percent to counter the predator PC manufacturers in the early 1990s.

In all of those cases, the standard leaders were able to stop (if not reverse) the erosion of their businesses without having to match the low-end prices. Sometimes, though, a low-end competitor is too entrenched—customers have already begun to think of the company as equal to the standard leader in terms of function, convenience and reliability. When that happens, the standard leader may have to match the challenger's prices.

WILL YOU LIVE—TO FIGHT AGAIN?

Before a standard leader slashes its prices—or, for that matter, devotes any of its resources in response to a low-end competitor—it should ask a fundamental question: Am I fighting a battle that, even if I prevail, I will only have to fight again?

When Low-End Attacks Are Inevitable

It is entirely possible for standard leaders to beat back a low-end competitor yet leave in place the conditions that allowed it to arise in the first place. Before taking action, then, standard leaders should consider the three basic drivers that lead to a challenge from below.

The first is high industry pricing, which often leads to declining overall demand. With the funeral services business, for example, years of consolidation have resulted in higher prices. As a result, the industry is gradually losing its market share of casket burials in favor of cheaper (and less profitable) cremation. Similarly, the greeting card industry raised prices aggressively throughout the 1990s, and the result has been a steady drop in per capita purchases.

The second driver is a distribution channel in search of a product, particularly if that channel serves the mass market and is in need of a low-cost offering that is unavailable from the standard leader. This situation occurred in the PC market in the early 1990s, when the standard leaders refused to sell their products to mass merchandisers, relying instead on direct sales or specialized computer dealers. That opening was then filled by low-end competitors like now defunct Packard Bell and AST Computer, which were more than willing to provide products to mass-market channels. As a general rule of thumb, a standard leader in consumer products should consider using mass-market channels when an industry is maturing to the point at which an offering's ease of use and affordability have become compatible with the skills and budget of the average consumer.

The final driver is a standard leader's high cost structure. To support that structure, the standard leader has to keep prices high, which in turn raises the value of each individual customer so that the company has to offer more benefits (at additional costs) to satisfy each of them. Costs and prices can continue this upward spiral until strippers and predators emerge to unbundle the benefit package and offer a lower-priced product. This type of situation occurs repeatedly in many consumer packaged-goods businesses: A standard leader develops multiple product line extensions and new consumer and channel benefits, adding costs and pushing prices higher, until a private-label company moves in to capture the bottom of the market.

Different Kinds of Strategic Retreats

Companies faced with any of the above conditions have a number of remedies. To deal with a high internal cost structure, for example, a standard leader can resegment its market to match benefits and product price points to those customers who will pay for them—and reduce benefits and prices for those who will not. Over the long run, though, if the standard leader's costs remain high, the company could find itself continually having to resegment its markets.

To avoid fighting the same battle repeatedly, a standard leader should take a hard look at the industry dynamics as well as its own operations. Often, the self-examination will reveal a fundamental problem that cannot be solved easily. In such cases, rather than fighting back, the standard leader might be better off retreating.

A standard leader may withdraw from just the part of its cost structure that is problematic. In 1999, after years of wrestling with Asian low-end competitors in the bicycle business, standard leader Huffy Corp. closed its manufacturing and outsourced that function to lower-cost providers. Instead, Huffy has focused on its capabilities in design, marketing and distribution.

Another option is to withdraw from only low-end products, especially when they aren't typically purchased by core customers. In the late 1980s, standard leader May Department Stores Co. owned a number of brands, spanning a wide price range from upscale Lord & Taylor to discount houses. Because the profits of two of its cheaper brands—Caldor and Venture—were vulnerable to low-end competitors, the company decided to sell those businesses.

The standard leader can also withdraw from serving a particular customer segment. In the late 1990s, as low-end competitors were gaining in the market for long-distance telephone service, AT&T became weary of pursuing low-use customers. So the company began charging everyone a monthly minimum fee and tried to switch some consumers to prepaid calling cards.

In extreme cases, a standard leader can pull out entirely. In the mid-1980s, Salomon Brothers dominated the market for municipal bonds. Over time, however, the company found itself under increasing pressure from commercial banks that had lower costs and offered cheaper prices. Reluctantly, Salomon Brothers concluded that the banks had a permanent cost advantage, and it completely stopped selling municipal bonds. Amazingly, at that time Salomon Brothers had the largest market share in the industry.

In analyzing more than 400 industries, I have found that fewer than 1 in 10 publicly held corporations have pretax margins above 20 percent of sales, and the average is 9 percent. Thus, few companies can afford simply to drop prices across the board by even 10 percent without wreaking havoc with their financials. In other words, when confronted with low-end competition, standard leaders have to fight wisely and selectively; otherwise they risk incurring substantial damage to their own operations. In particular, they need to be knowledgeable about the different kinds of low-end competition and the conditions that tend to spawn such attacks. Moreover, they should be well versed in the various tactics for combating challenges from below.

Strategies for Asia's New Competitive Game

Peter J. Williamson
INSEAD

A fundamental strategic rethink is now required by Asian companies and Western multinationals operating in Asia alike, because Asia's competitive environment is undergoing a sea change. Repeating what worked in the past is unlikely to succeed in the face of these new realities. Change is being driven by the rapid development of China, the cumulative impact of gradual but sustained deregulation and trade liberalization across Asia, and the implications of a new generation of economic, demographic, and social forces that is beginning to reshape Asia's future. These are all long-term trends, but until now their impact on the Asian competition has been arrested by the fact that many Asian companies have been shackled by the after-effects of the 1997 financial crisis. Only recently have these shackles been removed as debt restructuring is completed or loans finally repaid, giving these Asian corporations the capital and the elbow room to respond to the pent-up pressures for change. Faced with this new economic environment in Asia and reinvigorated Asian competitors, Western multinationals will need to chart new strategies if they are to win a share of the new round of Asian growth that is now under way. Rather than cloning their global strategies or reluctantly adapting them to Asia, successful Western multinationals will adopt innovative strategies in the Asian market that allow them to more accurately pinpoint, and then to fully exploit, their own unique strengths.

This article discusses the fundamental pressures for change in Asia's new competitive game, what

Reprinted from "Strategies for Asia's new competitive game," Peter J. Williamson, *The Journal of Business Strategy* 26, no. 2 (2005), pp. 37–43. © Emerald Group Publishing Limited. Used by permission.

successful new strategies will need to look like. It is about grasping the challenges and exploiting the opportunities that the changing face of Asian competition is bringing in its wake.

FOUR MAJOR SHIFTS IN THE ASIAN COMPETITIVE ENVIRONMENT

Understanding the drivers of change in the Asian environment and what they mean for the way Asian competition will work in the next round is the first step toward creating the new kinds of strategies and companies that will succeed in the future. Four shifts occurring in today's Asia are particularly significant: the demise of asset speculators, China's scattering of the pattern of orderly Asian "flying geese" development, the breakdown of national economic "baronies," and the decay of "me-too" strategies.

The Demise of the Asset Speculators

Profitable strategies are supposed to draw their life-blood from creating new value by finding ways to provide customers with goods and services that either better fit their needs or do so more efficiently than competitors. If we are honest, however, that was not the way a lot of companies in Asia made money during the 1990s boom. Instead, they grew rich through asset speculation: buying assets ranging from real estate to acquiring rival firms or building large manufacturing facilities and letting the rising prices of these assets swell the market value of their companies. Even as they continued to benefit from asset price inflation, too many senior managers in Asian companies were happy to bask in the illusion that they were creating new value through world-beating competitiveness and thriving in a dynamic, open market. The same was true for many of their multinational counterparts operating in the region whose management was more inclined to attribute their success to brilliant strategy and execution, than to favorable market conditions.

The Asian financial crisis of 1997 shattered those illusions because, almost at a stroke, it removed the windfall of rising asset prices that had been the unspoken secret of success in many Asian businesses. Instead of capital gains as asset prices rose year after year, Asian management was faced with a sustained period of asset price deflation. As banks and asset management companies were forced to share in the burden, the impact has been delayed for years. But now, as Asian balance sheets have been reconstructed leaving the investment community chastened, the upper hand is shifting to those who can add the most value to the assets and resources they use and away from simply adding new capacity. The next round will reward those who can do more with less, and do it differently, not those who build the largest corporate empires in Asia or assemble the biggest caches of assets on which to speculate. The drive for sheer volume is being replaced with a drive for value-added.

China Scatters the "Flying Geese"

A second major force of change in Asia's next round of competition is the China factor. Asia's traditional model of economic development was often described as "flying geese" in formation. Each country began by manufacturing and exporting simple, labor-intensive products like garments and shoes and assembly of low-end products. As it accumulated more capital and know-how, it moved through products of intermediate complexity, and then to high-value-added products and services. As one country moved on to the next level of value-added, another developing country would take its place as at the lower-value end. Japan led the flock, followed by Hong Kong, Singapore,

South Korea, and Taiwan. Then came Malaysia, Thailand, the Philippines, Indonesia, and Vietnam in the tail. Albeit somewhat simplistic, this concept of national geese flying in formation underlay many a government policy and corporate strategy. It shaped the pattern of what diversified Asian-owned companies invested in next and where multinationals located their activities in Asia.

Then along came China. *The Economist* magazine aptly summed up the result with a cartoon. It depicted a jet aircraft, piloted by a panda, zooming straight through the flock of Asian geese.[1] China wasn't flying in the cozy formation; by the new millennium it was undertaking activities that ranged from simple manufacturing to design and manufacture of high-technology components and equipment, from making rag dolls and molding plastic toys through to fabrication of semiconductors and specialized machinery. And China is doing this on a scale large enough to redraw the competitive map.

Now that the flying geese model of where to locate low- and high-end operations, respectively, has been exploded and the neat formation is in disarray, companies will have to reevaluate the roles of each of their subsidiaries across Asia. With China now a key part of the Asian game, the winners will be those who can restructure their operations into a more integrated Asian jigsaw where each subsidiary in Asia supplies specialized components or focuses on particular activities within the overall supply chain.

This development represents a fundamental change in the Asian competitive environment. When companies review the footprint of their existing operations through the new lens of a more integrated Asian supply chain, they will often discover that their existing subsidiaries are in the wrong places, with too much vertical integration and possibly specializing in the wrong things.

A fundamental strategic rethink is now required by Asian companies and Western multinationals operating in Asia alike, because Asia's competitive environment is undergoing a sea change.

Semiconductor companies are a good example of the kind of new strategy that will be necessary. Leading companies in this industry have had to abandon the historic setups where they made high-end chips in one country and low-end ones in another.

They have had to replace it with a new structure where a subsidiary in one Asian country does the circuit design, another photolithography, and a different location the so-called "back-end packaging" of the final chip. These kinds of pressures for redrawing the map of Asia have huge implications for the strategies that will succeed in the future.

The Breakdown of National Economic Baronies

Asia's division into highly segregated national markets, separated from each other by a mix of tariff and nontariff barriers, cultural and language differences, divergent choices about local standards, and regulatory differences between countries is legendary. Within this environment it made sense for companies to approach each national market pretty much as a separate competitive playing field. This behavior was reinforced by various forms of preference given by governments to their local companies through the allocation of licenses, preferential access to finance, and other kinds of direct and indirect support. Likewise, multinationals historically approached Asia as a collection of separate national markets.

In this environment, local "country managers" often became local barons: each in charge of a highly autonomous subsidiary within the Asian network. Each baron fought for investment of more resources in their business unit and argued the case against sharing functions from procurement and manufacturing to distribution and marketing on the grounds that any such moves would reduce their ability to respond to the peculiarities of the local market. The result was a set of largely independent subsidiaries spanning Asia under the umbrella of a "global" parent.

Today each of these country subsidiaries is under threat from the rapid growth of cross-border competition in Asia. A potent cocktail of falling trade barriers, deregulation of national markets, and falling costs of transport and communication is now opening the door to new sources of competitive advantage based on cross-border economies of scale and coordination. The results are striking. Trade among Asian countries is now growing more than twice as fast as the area's trade with the rest of the world, reflecting a rapid increase in direct cross-border competition. And perhaps even more significantly, Asian companies have invested an average of almost $50 billion every year in building or acquiring operations in other countries since 1995 (despite the setback of the 1997 financial crisis).[2] Much of this investment is in building beachheads in other Asian markets from which to mount attacks on yesterday's national baronies. In the face of this onslaught, yesterday's fragmented Asian strategies will become untenable.

The Decay of "Me-Too" Strategies

Primary consumer demand—from the first-time purchasers of everything from cars to washing machines and mobile phones—accounts for a large part of the market when economic growth in an economy first takes off. During this phase, consumers are willing to accept standardized, basic consumer goods. If you have never owned a refrigerator before, the most basic box that keeps things cool at reasonable cost is acceptable. But once consumers move on to become second- or third-time purchasers, they look for features such as the exact performance, styling, color, and so on that suits their individual needs. Consumers begin to demand higher product quality and variety, not simply more volume. Whirlpool's experience when it entered the Chinese market for domestic appliances a few years ago is a good example of this change. Contrary to its initial expectations, it quickly found Asian consumers rejected last year's American designs and technologies. Instead, they demanded environmentally friendly CFC-free refrigerators, washing machines with state-of-the-art electronic controls, and integrated, wall-mounted air-conditioners instead of the standard type that hung precariously from a window space.[3]

> *Asian consumers rejected last year's American designs and technologies. Instead, they demanded environmentally friendly CFC-free refrigerators, washing machines with state-of-the-art electronic controls, and integrated, wall-mounted air-conditioners.*

The same is true of fast-moving consumer goods like food or cosmetics and services: once your basic needs are satisfied by the range of products and services you consume, you start to look for particular varieties, flavors, sizes, and presentations or services customized to your individual needs. Even Asia's humble instant noodle now comes in more than 20 different flavors and a range of packaging from paper to styrofoam cups, not to mention pink "Valentine's day" and red and gold "Chinese New Year limited edition" varieties.[4] These trends are a simple fact of life that goes right back to Maslow's hierarchy of needs: as consumers become richer they want better and more customized offerings, not "more of the same."

These trends are now reaching much beyond Asia's wealthy elite. Throughout much of Asia the mass market has now reached a stage of development where consumers are no longer satisfied with reliable but standard, often boring, products and services. Even in China and India, countries with huge rural populations (estimated at 900 million and 700 million, respectively) that have been little touched by consumerism, there are hundreds of millions of urban consumers who are now sophisticated buyers who demand goods and services with the innovative features, variety, and customization that precisely fit their individual needs. Companies unable to provide more innovative, flexible products will literally be left on the shelf.

In parallel, a new generation of Asian consumers is entering the market. Unlike their parents, today's so-called "X" and "Y" generations have never lived through real hardship; they were born into a consumer society. As a result, they take abundance of goods and services largely for granted. Their choices reflect a complex mix of demand for higher quality, fashion, a desire to express more individualism, and a "what's new?" mentality. While the precise implications of serving this new consumer generation will vary by industry, it is safe to say that they will demand even greater variety, customization, and innovation from suppliers than today's mainstream consumers.

Despite all these changes, the Asian consumer is unlikely to abandon his or her traditional nose for value. Nor are Asian business buyers going to forget their historic emphasis on costs. But in the next round of competition in Asia, a strategy based solely on churning out high standard products in high volumes is unlikely to be a winner—even if the price is low. The new environment will demand that winning companies succeed in pursuing a strategy of being different from competitors, as well as better; decisively setting themselves apart from the competition with a wider range of product options, better customer segmentation and more customized offerings and stronger brands to signal differentiation from competitors.

STRATEGIC RESPONSES

The fundamental changes in Asia's competitive environment described above together demand new strategies. Clearly there is no single recipe for winning the new competitive game in Asia. But the new reality of Asia demands that managers stake out their territory based on four core ingredients: improved productivity, local brand and service, innovation, and internationalization that is designed to reshape the Asian playing field and reap cross-border synergies. Figure 1 lays out the strategic options.

Figure 1   **Strategic Choices for Winning in Asia's Next Round of Competition**

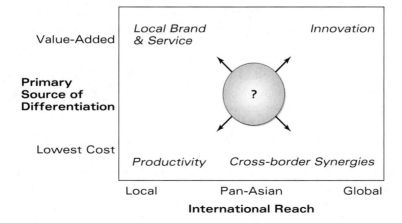

A New Productivity Drive

Given the demise of asset speculation as a way of underpinning Asian profits and increasingly intense competition from local companies in China and cross-border rivalry within Asia, a key element in future Asian strategy must be to enhance efficiency of Asian operations through productivity gains—especially in neglected "overhead" areas beyond the factory gate, like administration, sales, and distribution.

In a recent study I conducted on a sample of consumer-goods multinationals operating in Asia, I found that at an average of $75 million sales their unit overhead was a staggering 300 percent higher than Chinese rivals of comparative size. In fact, in a number of cases the overhead burden a foreign subsidiary expended just in dealing with their foreign headquarters was higher than the total overhead of the local Chinese competitors!

In many multinationals, overhead burdens rose during 1990s when expansion was the name of the game, at almost any cost. Companies recruited armies of staff to make sure support functions such as sales, administration, and distribution did not create bottlenecks or hinder the running of their expensive new factories. But as we enter a new round of Asian competition, it will not be enough for companies to rely on high productivity in manufacturing and routine operations alone. Multinationals will have to be more assiduous about deploying advanced systems—in customer relationship management, logistics, and administration: "soft technologies"—to bring their Asian operations up to world best-practice productivity outside core manufacturing and basic service operations. They will no longer be able to afford to follow the old adage that "Asia's different" as an excuse for inefficient administration and low-productivity support and service activities.

Renewed Focus on Brand Building and Service Quality

As "me-too" strategies decay and Asian consumers demand more variety, customization, and service, there will be a growing need for the capability to deliver an improved product or service experience "on the ground" to each and every individual customer in Asia. Simultaneously there will be a need to signal improved service quality to consumers and to differentiate offerings from competitors by strengthening the equity of the brands in Asia market by market and customer by customer. The need for strategies to strengthen brand differentiation will be given further impetus as local Asian companies start to build or acquire their own brands—a trend that is well under way.

In the next round of competition, multinationals won't be able to take their brand premium for granted. To exploit this potential advantage multinationals will have to increase their investment in brands in Asia. Better localization of branding, marketing, and service will also be required.

Reaping Cross-Border Synergies and Driving Consolidation

The relentless competitive pressure on yesterday's protected national baronies in the new Asian competitive game will demand better exploitation of cross-border synergies between different subsidiaries in Asia. This will mean accelerating pan-Asian and global integration, leaving behind yesterday's scatter of isolated national subsidiaries, and facing up to country barons who resist loss of independence.

As China continues to scatter the flying geese, companies will need to rethink the role of different subsidiaries and locations within the overall Asian jigsaw. Rather than a loosely connected portfolio of largely self-sufficient national companies, each subsidiary will need to be refocused on more specialized sets of activities within a new Asian network that leverages the specific advantages and knowledge within each location.

In many industries succeeding in the new competitive game in Asia will also mean taking advantage of the window of opportunity that is opening up to drive consolidation of Asia's fragmented supply base. This window for industry consolidation is opening because more intense competition from China and the elimination of the protective barriers around national markets are putting increasingly intense pressure on Asian companies to become more efficient and more focused about where they invest their resources in the future. This means that more and more companies will be forced, however reluctantly, to dispose of businesses where they lack the scale and the prospect of building sufficient depth of capabilities to compete in the next round.[5] This will create a new supply of businesses for consolidators to mop up that wasn't there in the past. Here strategies for quickly identifying, assessing, and executing overseas acquisitions and then reshaping these into a fully integrated business will become critical.

Innovating in Asia

With the decay of me-too strategies and the resulting increased emphasis on innovation amongst their local Asian rivals, multinationals will not only have to exploit transfer innovative technologies and products into Asia more rapidly, they will also have to ramp up their own innovation activities in Asia. Rather than just exporting innovations and new technology developed at home, American and European multinationals will need to restructure their innovation processes to benefit from the availability of high-quality researchers and engineers at lower cost, as well as to learn more from their Asian operations.[6]

Too often in the past, multinationals have only seen Asia as a manufacturing base or a source of customers in a growing market. Too few multinational companies have seen the potential of leveraging innovations from their Asian operations across other markets. Even those who have done so frequently fail to recognize Asia as an important, ongoing source of innovation. The primacy of the home base and the "parent" organization as the font of innovation die hard.

Forward-thinking multinationals are, however, beginning to reassess the potential role of Asia in their global innovation strategies. The global drinks group Diageo (owners of Smirnoff Vodka, J&B Scotch, and Bailey's Irish Cream), for example, has an innovation group in Hong Kong whose role is to seek out emerging trends and technologies within the region for global innovations. Johnson & Johnson has begun to deploy innovative manufacturing processes designed in Asia across their subsidiaries in the region, rather than implementing solutions born in the West. Over the last few years, more than 100 global R&D centers have been established in China by leading multinationals such as HP, Microsoft, and Motorola. Others need to follow these pioneers.

> *The new reality of Asia demands that managers stake out their territory based on four core ingredients: improved productivity; local brand and service; innovation; and internationalization that is designed to reshape the Asian playing field and reap cross-border synergies.*

ASIA'S NEW COMPETITIVE GAME

There should be no doubt that it will take a different kind of company to succeed in Asia's next round of competition. Unquestionably this will require determined efforts among multinationals operating in Asia to raise their game in the four key areas of strategy discussed above: a new productivity drive, renewed focus on brand building and service quality, reaping cross-border synergies and driving consolidation, and innovating in Asia. The mix of these strategies will vary by industry and individual company. But whatever route a company chooses to take into Asia's future, the new reality of competition in Asia is unavoidable; Amid renewed opportunity, there will be a sharper divide between the winners and losers. Only one question remains: In which group will your company end up?

Notes

1. See "A panda breaks the formation," *The Economist,* August 25, 2001, p. 65.
2. World Investment report 2003.
3. D. Clyde-Smith and P. J. Williamson, *Whirlpool in China (A): Entering the World's Largest Market.* INSEAD Case No. 08/2001-4950, INSEAD, Paris.
4. S. Donnan, "Indofood wants us to say it with noodles," *Financial Times,* February 14, 2000, p. 24.
5. A. Mody and S. Negishi, "Cross-border mergers and acquisitions in East Asia," *Finance and Development,* March 2001, pp. 6–11.
6. See Y. Doz, J. Santos, and P. Williamson, *From Global to Metanational: How Companies Win in the Knowledge Economy,* Harvard Business School Press, Boston, MA, 2001.

Racing to Be 2nd: Conquering the Industries of the Future

Costas Markides
London Business School

Paul A. Geroski
London Business School

Many ideas have been developed in the last 50 years on how big, established companies could create entirely new markets. This advice has been hungrily consumed by large, established corporations as well as smaller firms. After all, which company does not want to become more innovative and which CEO does not dream about leading his or her organization into virgin territories, discovering in the process exciting new markets?

Yet despite all this advice and good intentions, it is very rare to find a big, established company among the innovators that create radical new markets. Why not?

> *It's virtually impossible to offer proper advice on how to create or colonize radical new markets without first understanding where these kinds of markets come from.*

The simple answer is that the advice given is either inadequate or plainly wrong. What people often forget is that "innovation" is not one entity. There are different kinds of innovations, with different competitive effects. For example, what a firm needs to do to achieve product innovation may be entirely different from what it needs to do to achieve process innovation. Lumping the two kinds of innovation together is like mixing oil with water.

What this implies is that the generic question, "How can the modern corporation be more

innovative and create new markets?" only gets us generic answers—and these answers may or may not help the company achieve the kind of innovation that creates radical new markets. In other words, prescriptions to help a firm become more "innovative" may or may not be the ones that lead to radical new market creation.

It's virtually impossible to offer proper advice on how to create or colonize radical new markets without first understanding where these kinds of markets come from, what they look like, and what it takes to succeed in them. A better opening question is "Where do radical new markets come from, what are their structural characteristics, and what skills are needed to create and compete effectively in them?" This helps us identify the skills and competences needed—and the strategies that must be adopted—if a firm is to be a successful colonizer of radical new markets.

In fact, as we show in our book *Fast Second: How Smart Companies Bypass Radical Innovation to Enter and Dominate New Markets,* the full extent of what established companies need to change to be successful pioneers is such a formidable challenge that many of them are better off not even trying.

WHERE DO RADICAL NEW MARKETS COME FROM?

Radical new markets get created through radical innovation. It's important to appreciate this point because it is only by promoting this specific type of innovation inside a firm that the company can hope to create radical new markets.

Reprinted from "Racing to be 2nd: Conquering the industries of the future," Costas Markides, Paul A. Geroski, *Business Strategy Review*, Vol. 15, Issue 4 (Winter 2004), P. 25–31. Copyright © 2004 by Blackwell Publishing Ltd. Used by permission.

Innovations are considered radical if they meet two conditions: first, they introduce major new value propositions that disrupt existing consumer habits and behaviors—what on earth did our ancestors do in the evenings without television?—and second, the markets they create undermine the competences and complementary assets on which existing competitors have built their success.

Not all innovations are radical. When we classify innovations along the two dimensions mentioned above—disrupting customers' activities and undermining competitors—we get four types of innovation, as shown in Figure 1. The dividing points in the matrix are subjective and our intention is not to defend the boundaries of a particular definition. Rather, our goal is to simply suggest that innovation can mean different things to different people, that different types of innovation exist and that one particular innovation may be more or less radical than another.

We focus on radical innovations here because these are the kind of innovations that give rise to brand new markets. They are innovations that disrupt both customers and producers. They are based on a different set of scientific principles from the prevailing set, create radical new markets, demand new consumer behaviors and present major challenges to the existing competitors. The introduction of the car at the end of the 19th century is an example of radical innovation.

> *Not all innovations are radical. We classify innovations along two dimensions: disrupting customers' activities and undermining competitors.*

Academic researchers have been studying radical innovation for the past 50 years. As a result, we know many things about this kind of innovation. Specifically, we have learned the following about radical innovation over the years:

- Radical innovations that create new-to-the-world markets are disruptive for both customers and producers.
- As a result, these kinds of innovations are rarely driven by demand or immediate customer needs. Instead, they result from a supply-push process that originates from those responsible for developing the new technology.
- Such innovations typically lack champions, either in the form of lead consumers or existing market leaders.
- Supply-push innovations share certain characteristics: They are developed in a haphazard manner without a clear customer need driving

Figure 1 **Different Types of Innovation**

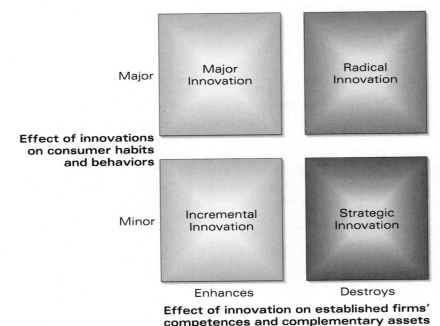

them; they emerge from the efforts of a large number of scientists working independently on totally unrelated research projects who devise the technology for their own uses; and they go through a long gestation process when seemingly nothing happens until they suddenly explode onto the market.

- These kinds of innovation create small niches on the periphery of well-established markets. This makes them unattractive to established firms.

The fact that radical innovations result from a haphazard supply-push process has a serious implication for the modern corporation. Specifically, since this process cannot be easily replicated in the R&D facility of a single firm, it is highly unlikely that brand-new markets will be created by a single firm.

Consider the development of the Internet over the last 40 years. The associated technology, both hardware and software, was developed in a haphazard way without a clear customer need driving it. No one involved with the technology in the early days had any idea that things would end up where they are today; there was no master plan linking the development of new client–server relations between users and mainframe computers to the possibility of booking a hotel room by computer from a mobile phone.

This unplanned, unsystematic development of the underlying technology seems to have largely been a consequence of how the work was done, and by whom—scientists and engineers in research institutes and universities in this case. Even the major

early user, the U.S. Department of Defense, took a remarkably hands-off attitude towards the research work sponsored by DARPA, rarely insisting that it be linked explicitly to defense needs but instead, giving it a blue-skies mandate. Furthermore, the research efforts that "suddenly" culminated in the Internet were undertaken by a host of scientists from a number of institutions and government agencies over a very long period of time. Such a process can hardly be planned or coordinated.

> *These kinds of innovation create small niches on the periphery of well-established markets. This makes them unattractive to established firms.*

SUPPLY-PUSH AND THE EMERGENCE OF NEW MARKETS

Different innovations produce different kinds of markets. Figure 2 lists a number of markets that have been created through innovation. Those on the left came about through radical innovation, while those on the right came about through strategic innovation. Our interest here is with the markets that are created through the supply-push process of radical innovation—how and when they emerge and how firms ought to compete in these markets.

Figure 2   **New Markets Created through Innovation**

New Markets Created through Radical Innovation	New Markets Created through Strategic Innovation
Television	Internet banking
Personal computers	Low-cost flights
Personal digital assistants (PDAs)	Private-label consumer goods
Cars	Screen-based electronic trading systems
Supercomputers	Generic drugs
Semiconductors	Online distribution of groceries
Mobile phones	Catalog retailing
Videocassette recorders (VCRs)	Department stores
Medical diagnostic imaging	Steel minimills
Computer operating systems	Online universities

So what kind of markets do supply-push innovation processes produce? What are their structural characteristics and what skills and competences are needed to compete effectively?

Supply-push innovation processes have one very important property, and this property has a profound impact on how new markets develop. Since the ultimate consumers of the new products or services which embody a new radical technology typically have very little knowledge of what the products have to offer them and how they would feel about them, the race to bring the fruits of the new technology to market is wide open.

No one knows what consumers really want and no one knows just what new technology can do, nor how to produce economically whatever it is that results from the innovation. Your guess is, therefore, as good as ours. Since there are no real barriers to entry into the (as yet) underdeveloped new market, there will not in principle be any shortage of entrepreneurs who are willing to try out their own particular vision of what the new technology has to offer. Anyone who understands the new technology is a potential entrant; anyone sufficiently enthused by what the new technology might ultimately offer will try to become an actual entrant.

This is what happens in all new markets created by radical innovation. Consider the television market. Thirty firms were producing television sets in the United States in 1947, 40 more entered the following year, and another 71 entered between 1949 and 1953. The peak population of television producers in the United States was 71 in 1951, a number larger than the entire number of TV manufacturers that exist today. This massive wave of entry is a phenomenon that always happens in the early days of new markets. Since all of these entrants bring their own product variants to the market, the massive swelling in the population of producers is usually matched by a widening in the range of product variety which is wholly unmatched by anything that happens later on.

Eventually the wave of entry subsides and is in turn followed by what is sometimes a sharp, sudden and very sizable shakeout that leads to the death of most of the early pioneers. The shakeout is associated with the emergence of a dominant design in the market; this is an event that signals the beginning of growth in the industry.

The dominant design is a basic template or core product that defines what the product is and what it does. It is a consensus good that commands the support of a wide range of early consumers (even if it is not their first preference). It is a product standard that sends signals to suppliers upstream, retailers downstream and producers of complementary goods everywhere. Finally, it is a platform good that allows different manufacturers to offer differentiated versions of the product without destroying the consensus or requiring new complementary goods.

The emergence of a dominant design is the decisive step in establishing a new market. It signals the emergence of a standard product that is capable of forming the basis of a mass market. For the many potential consumers who have yet to enter and make a choice, it signals the end of choice and therefore reduces their risk. A successful dominant design almost always triggers massive entry by consumers into the market, and ushers in the early heavy growth phase that most markets undergo.

> *Notice that most of these so-called first-movers were not, in fact, the first into the market. All of them were preceded by many, now forgotten, entrepreneurial start-ups whose work formed the foundation upon which these slightly later entrants built.*

The emergence of a dominant design is important for a second reason. The hundreds of early pioneers who entered the new market on the basis of different product designs die soon after the dominant design emerges. On the other hand, the champion whose product forms the basis of the dominant design often develops substantial and very long-lived first-mover advantages from being the product champion. Notice that most of these so-called first-movers were not, in fact, the first into the market. All of them were preceded by many, now forgotten, entrepreneurial start-ups whose work formed the foundation upon which these slightly later entrants built. These "first-movers" were first only in the sense that they were the first to champion the particular product variant that became the dominant design. They were first when the market, not the product, emerged—and this is why they ended up with most of the profits.

It is important to emphasise three points that emerge from this.

- Very few of the original entrants (the pioneers) survive the consolidation of the market. Most disappear, never to be heard of again.

- The consolidators who ultimately win are rarely the first in the new market. Their success is based precisely on not moving fast—but by choosing the right time to move.

- Consolidators' activities—entering at the right time, standardizing the product, cutting prices, scaling up production, creating distribution networks, segmenting the market, investing in advertising and marketing—are the activities that create what we somewhat inaccurately call "first-mover advantages." Consolidators' shrewd movements create buyer loyalty, obtain pre-emptive control of scarce assets, go down the learning curve, create brands and reputation and enjoy economies of scale benefits—all of which give them advantages that potential new entrants don't have. Thus, even though pioneers are chronologically first to market, consolidators are the "real" first-movers. They are the first to the market that counts—the mass market!

The upshot of all this is that the companies that end up capturing and dominating the new-to-the-world markets are almost never the ones that created these markets. Henry Ford did not create the car market, but his company ended up capturing most of the value in that market in its first century of existence. Procter & Gamble did not create the market for disposable diapers, but it harvested most of the value from the mass market. And General Electric did not create the CAT scanner market, yet it was GE that made most of the money.

It turns out that when it comes to radical new markets, this is more the norm than the exception. So—given this fact—why would any company want to create a new market? Surely, the advice we should be giving companies is how to scale up and consolidate new markets, not how to create them.

HOW TO "CREATE" THE INDUSTRIES OF THE FUTURE

All this has serious implications for big established companies. Specifically:

- The innovation process that creates radical new markets cannot be replicated inside the modern corporation.

- The companies that create brand-new markets are almost never the ones that end up consolidating and dominating these markets.

These two facts suggest to us that big, established firms should leave the task of creation to "the market"—the thousands of small, start-up firms around the world that have the requisite skills and attitudes to succeed at this game. Established firms should, instead, concentrate on what they are good at—which is to consolidate young markets into big mass markets.

They could do this by creating a network of feeder firms—young, entrepreneurial companies that are busy colonizing new niches. Through its business development function, the established company could serve as a venture capitalist to these feeder firms. It may also help them with their own R&D, more to keep close to technological developments than for any other reason. Then, when it is time to consolidate the market, it could build a new mass-market business on the platform that these feeder firms have provided. Since the younger firms do not have the resources, power, marketing, and distribution to scale up their creations, they should—in principle—be happy to subcontract this activity to the bigger firms, subject to a fair division of the spoils.

> *Established firms should, concentrate on what they are good at—which is to consolidate young markets into big mass markets.*

What we are proposing here is for the modern corporation to subcontract the creation of radical new products to the market and for start-up firms to subcontract the consolidation of these products to big established firms. This will strike some people as too radical an idea, but it is in fact a business model that is widely accepted in industries where companies live and die on their ability to bring creative new products continuously to the market. We are talking about creative industries such as movies, plays, art galleries, book publishing, and music publishing.

Think about it. A major book publisher does not try to create any of its "new products" (the books) internally. It could, of course, attempt to do so. It would involve hiring thousands of employees, giving them an office and a computer and asking them to produce new books in return for a fixed salary. But how silly does that sound? An organizational structure like that would be the fastest way to destroy the very creativity and innovation it seeks to generate!

> *What we are proposing here is for the modern corporation to subcontract the creation of radical new products to the market and for start-up firms to subcontract the consolidation of these products to big established firms.*

Instead of attempting to do everything internally, a major book publisher goes out in the market, identifies potential product creators (authors) and signs them up to deliver their product. Once the product is created (outside the bureaucracy of the big firm), the author subcontracts the marketing, promotion, and distribution of his or her creation to the book publisher. Just as it would be silly for the big publisher to attempt to create the new products internally, it would be a similar act of folly for an individual author to attempt to sell and promote his book on his own. The division of labor builds upon the strengths of each participant and is a solution that maximizes the welfare of everyone involved. There may be disagreements and problems between publisher and author, but that's what management is there for.

Professor Richard Caves is to be thanked for this insight. Caves alerted us to the striking similarity between what we are proposing (division of labor between young and established firms) and what he was observing in his study of creative industries. This is an arrangement which appears to be the norm in several creative industries. How many art galleries do you know that create their own "products" (paintings) every year? Equally, how many famous painters do you know who used to be full-time employees of major art houses? The image of Picasso or van Gogh laboring away in the R&D lab of a major gallery, straining to create their next masterpiece is so laughable that no one would take it seriously. Yet this is exactly how we have organized the modern corporation to deliver new radical products.

As a final example, consider the record industry. It would be hard to imagine any famous singers actually working as full-time employees of the big record companies. Professor Caves's research on the subject has shown that there is a very clear division of labor in this market: "Large and small firms play different roles in the recruitment of performers and promotion of their albums. The large companies' distinctive competence lies in promotion and record distribution on a large—increasingly international— scale. The small or independent company performs the gatekeeping function of recruiting new artists and, particularly, identifies and promotes new styles of music and types of performers. The distinction closely parallels that between contemporary art galleries that focus on identifying and developing artists with promise and those devoted to promoting successful artists."

A similar proposition to ours was developed by Reid McRae Watts. In *The Slingshot Syndrome,* he makes the same link between creative industries and the creation of new radical products, showing how the modern corporation could structure itself along the lines that one sees in creative industries. The interested reader is directed to both books.

Some people might object that the division of labor between creators and promoters that we see in creative industries is easy to achieve because the creators of the product are mostly individuals (authors, singers, painters). Therefore, the argument goes, it is easy to allow them to operate as free agents and simply sign them up whenever they have something to offer. By contrast, the creation of a new radical product often requires many scientists to work together, usually in the same laboratory, building upon the knowledge and expertise of the organization. This requires some coordination and supervision of the work.

Although this is a valid concern, we only have to look at the film industry to understand how the division of labor that we are advocating here could be achieved even when there are many people involved in the creation of the product and coordination is necessary. In the film business, a new product (a movie) starts with a screenplay, often written by an independent agent (the writer). The writer approaches several producers to seek financing. The producers may be independent or employed by distribution companies such as Disney, Sony, or Time Warner. Once a producer acquires the rights to the screenplay, it is her job to provide the financing as well as the director and the actors to make the movie.

The image of Picasso or van Gogh laboring away in the R&D lab of a major gallery, straining to create their next masterpiece is so laughable, no one would take it seriously. Yet this is exactly how we have organized the modern corporation to deliver new radical products.

Once again, these are all independent agents, willing to offer their services to a specific project for a specific fee. It is only when the product is finally created that the big established firm—the studio—moves into action. The studio acquires the rights to distribute the new product and uses its massive marketing power and existing distribution infrastructure to sell, promote, and distribute the film.

Therefore, in several creative industries we see a clear separation between those who create the product and those who promote, distribute, and sell it. Needless to say, the "promoters" must be knowledgeable about the latest technology and products so that they can make an intelligent assessment of whether a painting, book, or record is good enough for them to promote. But they do not have to be actively involved in its creation. If this organization of work functions well in creative industries, shouldn't we at least attempt to import it into other industries that aspire to become more creative?

In fact, when we compare the basic economic properties of creative industries with the features that characterise new radical markets, the two types of market are amazingly similar. Given this fact, we would be surprised if the organizational structure that characterizes creative industries cannot be readily imported into any industry that aspires to create radical new markets.

Resources

Markides, Costas, and Geroski, Paul A. (2004), *Fast Second: How Smart Companies Bypass Radical Innovation to Enter and Dominate New Markets,* San Francisco: Jossey Bass.

Caves, Richard (2000), *Creative Industries: Contracts between Art and Commerce,* Harvard University Press.

Watts, Reid McRae (2000), *The Slingshot Syndrome: Why America's Leading Technology Firms Fail at Innovation,* Writers Club Press.

Outsourcing Strategies: Opportunities and Risks

Brian Leavy

Dublin City University Business School

A characteristic of corporate strategy in developed countries in the last 20 years has been an increasing interest in outsourcing as a potential source of competitiveness and value creation. The earliest outsourcing strategies were largely driven by the desire to lower costs in the face of intensifying global competition, typically by moving low-skilled, labor-intensive, activities offshore to Southeast Asia and other low-cost locations. In more recent years, there has been a growing awareness of the potential of outsourcing to support a range of strategies beyond that of lower cost

Corporate strategists may not be fully familiar with four of the most promising opportunities for using outsourcing strategies—focus, scale without mass, disruptive innovation, and strategic repositioning. While assessing the potential of those opportunities in specific corporate situations, strategists also need to look at two of the most significant associated risks—the risk of losing skills that could be key to competing in the future, and the risk of turning to outsourcing at the wrong stage in an industry's evolution. My goal is to widen managers' views of the strategic alternatives that outsourcing can be used to support, while making managers aware of the main risks to be weighed in the balance.

FOUR PROMISING OUTSOURCING STRATEGIES

Focus—Nike and Dell

In intensely competitive environments, many companies see outsourcing as a way to hire "best in class" companies to perform routine business functions and then focus corporate resources on key activities in their value chain where the impact will be felt the most by the customer. This is the strategy that has helped Nike to capture and sustain leadership in the athletic footwear and apparel industry for most of the last three decades.

Nike's business started as a company of athletes selling imported performance Japanese shoes to other athletes, and by the end of its first decade in 1972, sales had reached just $2 million. Despite the relatively slow growth of these early years, the founders continued to experiment with new performance designs and prototypes, based on their intimate knowledge of the market. By the end of their first decade they had already developed the core competencies in brand building and design that were soon to become the foundation for Nike's rapid growth. The company decided to focus primarily on these activities and outsource most of its production and much of its sales and distribution. As a consequence, by the end of its second decade Nike sales had rocketed to $700 million, with gross margins running at nearly 40 percent. Even before the notion of focused outsourcing was generally understood, Nike had demonstrated the potential power of such a strategy. It continues to do so today, retaining a 39 percent share of the $7.8 billion U.S. market for branded athletic footwear, and doing so in the face of very determined competition.

The strategy of focusing corporate resources mainly on those activities where clear differentiation

Reprinted from "Outsourcing Strategies: Opportunities and Risks," Brian Leavy, *Strategy and Leadership* 32, no. 6 (2004), © Emerald Group Publishing Limited. Reprinted with permission of Emerald Group Publishing Ltd.

can be developed and outsourcing much of the rest has also served many other companies well. The key often lies in knowing which of the main value drivers to concentrate on—customer intimacy, product leadership, or operational excellence. All three are key to delivering value to customers, but the organizational capabilities and cultures that promote them are not the same, and often tend to pull in different directions.[1] So, for example, Nike has tended to focus primarily on product leadership and Dell on operational excellence and customer relationship management, and both rely on the competencies of others to help them deliver value in other areas. The appeal of such a strategy continues to widen, even into some of the most traditional sectors. Today, for example, many newspapers now tend to concentrate mainly on the customer relationship area, outsourcing much of their content and most of their printing and distribution.

Scaling Without Mass—Nokia and Nortel

Another attractive feature of outsourcing is that it offers companies the opportunity to grow in market presence without a corresponding expansion in organizational size or bureaucracy. Strategic outsourcing can help a rapidly growing company avoid a premature internal transition from its informal entrepreneurial phase to a more bureaucratic mode of operation. In this way, outsourcing allows firms to retain their entrepreneurial speed and agility, which they would otherwise sacrifice in order to become efficient as they greatly expanded.

This is one of the primary benefits that companies like Nike, opting initially for a focused strategy with extensive outsourcing, tend to enjoy from the outset. For example, over the 1978–82 period, during the steepest phase in Nike's early growth, revenue scaled up nearly tenfold from $71 million to $690 million, while the employee population grew from 720 to 3,600, just half the growth rate of revenue. In fact, Nike continued to retain many of the characteristics of an entrepreneurial firm until it was almost a $1 billion company. It was not until it reached billionaire status that the lack of formal management systems became a serious impediment to the company's further development.

However, the prospect of being able to scale up without a pro-rata increase in organizational mass and complexity is an attractive reason to consider outsourcing at any stage in a company's development, not just at start-up. For example, in early 2000, when employee numbers at Nokia were increasing at the rate of 1,000 per month, and approaching the 60,000 mark, CEO Jorma Ollila decided to outsource a significant portion of its production in both its network equipment and mobile handset businesses in order to help slow down the growth in number of employees without impeding the company's momentum in the marketplace. It was a strategy that helped cushion the effects of a subsequent downturn, but the main consideration was the fear that too-rapid growth would dilute the Nokia spirit and undermine organizational coherence. At the time, Nokia was widely known as one of the least bureaucratic of global corporations, and Ollila embraced outsourcing to keep it that way.

For another large corporate example, at Nortel Networks in 1999 management recognized they were on the cusp of a "once-in-a-lifetime" market shift, with the opportunity to double their company's revenue from $20 billion to $40 billion within 24 months, if they could get their business model right. They also realized that they could not hope to avail themselves of this opportunity by remaining a traditional manufacturer. The realization produced a managerial mantra—"Why do companies fail? They fail because their processes don't scale." This insight led the Nortel management team to conclude that "we'd never be a $40B company with our existing processes" as Frank Dunn, the company's chief financial officer, later recalled. At the time, the company's return on invested capital was running at just about half that of market leader Cisco. Over the 1999–2001 period, Nortel divested 15 manufacturing sites and transferred 9,000 employees to contract manufacturers such as Solectron and Sanmina. This was part of a wider move toward a more customer-centric strategy, outsourcing production while creating in-house supply chain management teams for each major customer. The entire system was dedicated to improving end-to-end fulfillment using Internet-enabled resource management systems.[2]

Disruptive Innovation—IKEA, Canon, and Ryanair

Outsourcing is a key element in many of the most impressive examples of disruptive innovation to date. Typical examples include IKEA's entry into furniture retailing, Canon's into the photocopying market, and Ryanair's into the European airline industry. The primary aim of most disruptive innovation is to create a whole new segment at a price point well below the bottom of the current market and then to dominate this segment as it grows. This usually requires the development of an innovative business model capable of producing overall returns at least as good as those of the leading incumbents, but doing it at significantly lower cost through much higher asset productivity.[3] IKEA, Canon, and Ryanair were all late entrants into their respective industries, but all succeeded in building substantial market positions through such a strategy, and outsourcing was a common element in the development of a distinctive lower-cost/higher-asset productivity formula in all three cases.

At the time of IKEA's founding in the early 1950s, the European furniture industry was highly fragmented geographically. National department stores established exclusive relationships with local manufacturers to allow them to offer distinctive product lines, reflective of local tastes and traditions. Quality new furniture was typically priced beyond the reach of all but the relatively prosperous, and most young people setting out to furnish their first home had to rely on the secondhand market or hand-me-downs from parents. Ingvar Kamprad, and his company IKEA, set out to "democratize" this marketplace by bringing quality new furniture within reach of the many, not just the few. IKEA developed a range of simple, elegant, "modern" designs, using light-colored quality woods. This appealed to young customers of all nations. The key to delivering such attractive furniture at prices well below prevailing norms was designing for manufacturability and transport-ability, not just consumer appeal. IKEA revolutionized the European furniture industry with a novel "production-oriented retailing" business model, the competitiveness of which depended not only on the careful outsourcing of production but also on "outsourcing" final assembly and delivery to the customers themselves. The "production-oriented retailing" principle remains fundamental to the IKEA business model as the company continues to expand internationally, and, no matter how strong the pull at the retail end, the company will only enter new lines of furniture that fit with its production-oriented economics.

Outsourcing has been a prominent feature in the business models of other classic disruptive innovators over the years, not just IKEA. For example, in the case of Canon, outsourcing has always been a major element in the company's strategy in the copier market, with 80 percent of product assembled from purchased parts and only drums and toner manufactured in-house. Outsourcing is also prominent in the business model of Ryanair, the disruptive innovator in the European airline industry (the self-styled "Southwest Airlines of Europe"), where the company contracts out most of its aircraft handling, heavy maintenance, and baggage handling as part of its strategy to avoid complexity, keep cost down, and maintain productivity at levels well above industry norms.

Strategic Repositioning—IBM

Strategic repositioning is rarely easy, especially when you are a longtime industry leader like IBM. Yet one of the biggest strategic bets that Lou Gerstner made as part of the turnaround at IBM in the mid-1990s was that services, not technology, would be the major growth area going forward, particularly in the corporate computing market. As he saw it then: "If customers were going to look to an integrator to help them envision, design, and build end-to-end solutions, then the companies playing that role would exert tremendous influence over the full range of technology decisions—from architecture and applications to hardware and software choices."[4] Traditionally IBM's strategy had always stressed service as a distinguishing feature of its value proposition, but this was service tied to products. What Gerstner had in mind was consultancy and solutions integration services as a major business driver in its own right. In 1992, services was a $9.2 billion business at IBM—within 10 years IBM Global Services had grown into a $30 billion business, employing half the corporation's human resources. Recently, IBM has intensified its commitment to this strategic repositioning, as part of CEO Sam Palmisano's e-business "on-demand" vision.

Outsourcing is central to IBM's repositioning—both as a driver and an enabler. Under the new strategy IBM has become both an extensive provider of outsourcing services to others as part of its offering as a solutions integrator (primarily in the IT area), while at the same time becoming a more extensive user of outsourcing services itself (primarily in the product area from contract manufacturers). For example, IBM's own IT outsourcing services is now one of the main revenue drivers in the company's new e-business on demand strategy and one that generated $13 billion in the European market alone in 2002. Further back its value chain, IBM's decision to outsource a growing share of its own production is helping it accelerate its ongoing migration to a services-led model and reconfigure its resources to support this strategy. Within the last two years the company has entered into a $5 billion outsourcing contract with Sanmina-SCI Corporation to manufacture its NetVista line of desktop computers, later expanded to include a significant portion of its low- to mid-range server and workstation lines, along with some distribution and fulfillment activities. Substantial transfers of assets and overheads have been involved in both of these deals, which the company sees as allowing it to "leverage the skills of the industry where it makes sense to improve our costs, and focus our own investments on areas that deliver the highest value to our customers."[5]

THE RISKS OF OUTSOURCING

Outsourcing also increases certain strategic risks. Two of the most important are the risk of losing skills key to competing for the future and the risk of making the outsourcing move at the least suitable time in an industry's evolution.

Mortgaging the Future: Losing Key Skills and Capabilities

Companies can often be attracted to outsourcing as a means to relieve intensifying competitive pressure. However, if they fail to consider the long-term implications, they may unwittingly mortgage their future opportunities for short-term advantage. For example, not too many years ago Eastman Kodak executives made a decision to exit the camcorder business because the investment challenge at the time looked too steep to stay in the game. Years later, however, they came to recognize that the skills and knowledge they would have developed in the manufacture of the major subcomponents could have been used to support a wider range of applications of the core technologies beyond the consumer market into medical imaging and other areas. In a similar way, Bulova was slow to see the wider applications that the manufacturing

skills developed in the area of miniature tuning fork technology might have beyond the watch market, an insight not lost on Citizen. In contrast, Canon chose to take a longer view and remain in the semiconductor business following its failure to make the hoped-for impact in the calculator market, a decision that in time would leave it well positioned to play in the office products market when electronic imaging later emerged as a key technology.

Like prematurely exiting a market, hasty and near-sighted outsourcing may result in the loss or unintended transfer of critical learning opportunities, as happened to General Electric in its outsourcing arrangement with Samsung in the microwave market. In the early 1980s General Electric was still investing heavily in its own manufacturing capability in Columbia, Maryland, when it decided to outsource the production of some of its models at the small to medium end of the market to Samsung, then just a modest enterprise little known outside of Korea. The initial contract was for just 15,000 units. However, GE quickly found itself on a steep dependence spiral that ultimately saw it ceding most of the investment and skills development initiative in microwave production to its outsourcer within just two years. For Samsung, the arrangement allowed it to scale up its production and engineering to levels that would not have been possible without access to GE's American consumers. This one small outsourcing contract set the stage for Samsung's emergence as a global powerhouse in consumer appliances.[6] The lesson from this and similar examples is that it pays to be mindful that strategic capabilities are rarely synonymous with discrete functions like engineering or production but tend to be deeply embedded in the collective know-how that reflects their integration.[7] That is why many extensive outsourcers like Nike still wish to retain some manufacturing activity and closely tie it to engineering and marketing in order to preserve the multifunctional capabilities they see as key to their future success.

Choosing to Outsource at the Wrong Time in a Market's Evolution

Strategists also need to know when in an industry's evolution and where along its value chain the economics favor outsourcing. They also need to be aware how this tends to change over time, particularly in technology markets. According to disruptive innovation authority, Clayton Christensen, the critical transition is when the market changes from the stage where most customers continue to desire more functionality than is currently offered to the point where the majority of customers come to see themselves as being over-served with features. This is the juncture at which the product rapidly becomes a commodity and where the primary basis of competition shifts to aspects of the value proposition beyond technology—such as price, speed, convenience, and customization.

In the PC market, for example, it is widely recognized today that IBM outsourced too early because of its anxiety to slow down the progress of Apple Computer, and in doing so allowed the initiative at the features-driven stage of the market's evolution to flow mainly to Intel and Microsoft. Later, when the personal computer became a commodity, the market favored the business model of Dell, which focused largely on customer relationship management and efficient fulfillment and used extensive outsourcing. Indeed, in migrating its model to other segments, Dell's success continues to rely on recognizing when a market's evolution has progressed beyond the features-led, technology-driven stage. To date, it has managed to get this right in the personal computer and mid-range server markets. It now believes the time is more than ripe to apply its model to inkjet printers, where market leader Hewlett-Packard continues to place its bets on its superior technological capabilities and on proprietary features. When deciding whether to make such a wager, it is important for managers to recognize that core competence, as understood in many businesses, can be "a dangerously inward-looking notion." Managers are much more likely to win their bet if they understand that competitiveness "is far more about doing what customers value than what you think you are good at."[8] Knowing the difference is one of the secrets to getting the timing of outsourcing strategy right, as the following insight from a senior supply chain executive at Hewlett-Packard makes clear:

> How do you spot early that you are losing your protected differentiation with the customer in terms of product, process or performance? Every company likes to believe that it has a superior product. It takes skill to recognize that others are catching up. In the inkjet printer market we always have to ask ourselves

are we still producing products that the customer values on an ongoing basis? Are things going horizontal? Sooner or later, you get to a point of diminishing returns where the market no longer fully values say an improvement in speed from 25 to 30 pages per minute or where the next improvement in photo quality resolution reaches the point where only a measuring instrument will detect it. When further improvements have a negligible impact on the customer, in terms of perceived value, you are not too far from being commoditized or horizontalized. How do you then operate in a different mode? How do you transition to a different model? This is when outsourcing tends to become a serious option for a business to consider.[9]

KNOW YOUR OPTIONS AND CONSIDER THE TIMING AND RISK

Outsourcing as a strategy has the potential to drive competitiveness and value creation in many ways beyond the narrow goal of cost reduction alone. Achieving greater focus, scaling without mass, fueling disruptive innovation, and enabling strategic repositioning are just four of the many promising options that outsourcing as a strategy can offer and support. However, managers considering any such outsourcing options will always need to ask themselves whether the timing is right and also what strategic skills and capabilities they might be putting at risk.

Notes

1. For a full discussion of these value drivers see Treacy, M. and Wiersema, F. (1993), "Customer intimacy and other value disciplines," *Harvard Business Review,* January–February, pp. 84–93. For a closer look at the inherent tensions among them, see also Hagel, J. and Singer, M. (1999), "Unbundling the corporation," *Harvard Business Review,* March–April, pp. 133–41.

2. For more on the Nortel case see Fisher, L. M. (2001), "From vertical to virtual: how Nortel's supplier alliances extend the enterprise," *Strategy + Business,* Quarter 1.

3. The term disruptive innovation is used here in the sense defined by Clay Christensen—see Christensen, C. M. and Raynor, M. E. (2003), *The Innovator's Solution,* Harvard Business School Press, Boston, MA.

4. Quote from Gerstner, L. V. (2003), *Who Says Elephants Can't Dance?* HarperBusiness, New York, NY.

5. Bob Moffat, general manager of IBM's Personal & Printing Systems Group, quoted in an IBM press release, "IBM signs agreement with Sanmina-SCI to manufacture its NetVista desktop PCs in US and Europe," January 8, 2002.

6. For more on the GE/Samsung case see Magaziner, I. C. and Patinkin, M. (1989), "Fast heat: how Korea won the microwave war," *Harvard Business Review,* January–February, pp. 83–91. For more examples of the risk of losing key skills and learning opportunities, see Lei, D. and Slocum, J. W. (1992), "Global strategy, competence-building and strategic alliances," *California Management Review,* Fall, pp. 81–97.

7. For more on the embedded and integrated nature of core competencies see Prahalad, C. K., Fahey, L. and Randall, R. M. (2001), "Creating and leveraging core competencies," in Fahey, L. and Randall, R. M. (Eds), *The Portable MBA in Strategy,* 2nd ed, Wiley, New York, NY, pp. 236–52.

8. For more on this risk, see Christensen, C. M. and Raynor, M. E. (2003), *The Innovator's Solution,* Harvard Business School Press, Boston, MA (especially chapters 5 and 6—the quote comes from Chapter 6).

9. Maurice O'Connell, Materials Director of Hewlett-Packard's inkjet printer business, in conversation with the author at the HP plant in Dublin, July 2, 2004.

Insights from the New Conglomerates

Gerry Kerr
University of Windsor

James Durroch
York University

1. INVESTIGATING THE CONGLOMERATE

The conglomerate, when it is not being completely ignored in the business and academic presses, is derided as an artifact of old thinking. Because of the high costs of organization, the rationale declares, the widely diversified, multi-industry firm is doomed to destroy value for shareholders. Yet any organization that has been able to master the undeniable challenges of managing such disparate operations offers the chance to uncover insights about what works (and what does not) in corporate strategy. We identified four successful conglomerate archetypes.

In undertaking our analysis, we found that a simple framework facilitated understanding the corporate strategies and the manner in which they were put into action. Corporate strategy is practiced along three dimensions. First, headquarters functions to influence the structure of, and the horizontal relationships within, the portfolio of businesses, including the creation of practices, rules, and regulations. Secondly, headquarters often houses common resources, such as legal and tax advice or merger-and-acquisition expertise, that are shared by the businesses in a vertical relationship. Finally, managing the changing contents of the portfolio forms the third dimension of corporate strategy. The key activities of the head office include acquisitions, the internal creation of new businesses, restructuring, and divestiture.

We discovered that each of the sustainable conglomerate strategies was aimed at different value-adding goals and achieved cohesion along the three dimensions in different ways. Moreover, firms were configured to reach into their environments through contrasting means, seizing disparate opportunities. One of the central identities of strategic management is plainly in evidence among top-performing conglomerates: a "fit" is achieved between the corporate level and its businesses, as well as between the organization and its environment. However, the real story is how the cohesion was achieved, through the archetypes devised by managers to marry organization with opportunities. We were anxious to find out what corporate managers could possibly be doing to add value to such disparate sets of businesses.

The sources and profile of our data were closely controlled in two ways. First, we examined the list of widely diversified companies, called "multi-industry firms," contained in the BusinessWeek Global 1000. The Global 1000 list was published in identical form from 1988 to 2000, representing the previous fiscal years. The group of companies reflects the assessments of conglomerates common to both practitioners and academics, with all firms exhibiting high business diversity and low levels of relatedness in the portfolio. Our focus group includes some of the world's largest companies, as measured by market capitalization. Second, we chose to look only at companies that were classified as multi-industry firms for five or more years, because of the costs of

Reprinted from *Business Horizons* 48, no. 4 (July–August 2005), pp. 347–61. © 2005 Kelley School of Business, Indiana University. Used by permission.

business diversity and the lack of opportunities for synergies. The use of the group allowed us to isolate entities with a sustained commitment to unrelated diversification. As well, we could eliminate the possibility that companies enjoyed short periods of high performance before the costs of bureaucracy set in.

Exactly 100 multi-industry firms appeared on the Global 1000 list between 1988 and 2000. However, 59 of the firms did not remain as multi-industry firms for at least five continuous years, leaving 41 companies for examination. Of these, most of the firms were long-lived conglomerates. Only 4 firms occupied the list for the minimum 5 years, while 24 firms remained for 8 or more years and 7 were there for all 13. The group represents home bases in 11 different countries; however, our focus was trained most consistently on firms based in the United States and Great Britain, because they face the most vigorous competitive landscape and markets for corporate control. Table 1 presents the set of conglomerates, called "multi-industry firms," found in the Global 1000.

2. CORPORATE STRATEGIES AND BUSINESS ENVIRONMENT

Five basic types of corporate strategies were identified in the firms we studied, with four of them linked to at least the possibility of sustained high performance. The five strategies included the *propagation strategy,* which, as the name implies, is directed to supporting the creation of new products and businesses. *Restructuring strategies* guide the purchase and rationalization of underperforming firms, sometimes regardless of industry. (See Michael Porter's [1987] article for a description of restructuring, as well as a discussion of skills transfer and activities sharing as the basis of successful corporate strategy.) The *accretion strategy* is aimed at building mass, and often an international presence, in selected fragmented industries. Mixed strategies were also identified, successfully combining propagation, accretion, and restructuring strategies, as well as subsets of the available archetypes. Finally, the *portfolio strategy* involves the purchase, possession, and divestiture of

businesses as long-term investments (sometimes, as at Loews, after short periods of restructuring or accretion). Table 2 outlines the general characteristics of the five conglomerate strategies, which are more fully examined below.

2.1. Portfolio Strategy

The portfolio strategy, the unpromising member of the group, will be described and disposed of first. The portfolio strategy makes primary reliance on the risk-reducing properties of holding a portfolio of businesses. The strategy, however, seeks benefits that can be more cheaply gained by individual investors, who do not have to pay premiums for acquisitions and who do not bear the costs of organization. Ownership can be partial or full, with the former only making more plain the financial orientation of the strategy. Indeed, many of the firms practicing the portfolio strategy either in its pure form or as the predominant part of a restructuring or accretion strategy contained large banking or insurance divisions. This was especially the case in the less competitive, highly regulated markets in Europe during the 1980s and early 1990s. As well, examples can be found in firms with a controlling group of shares held by the family of the founding entrepreneurs (which was the case at Loews). Whatever the scenario, the narrow opportunities for value additions and the costs of the practice cause poor performance to be strongly associated with the portfolio strategy. Our findings concur with Rumelt's (1974) work and the Porter article previously mentioned, confirming that the passive portfolio strategy contributes little to our understanding of successful corporate strategy, past its avoidance.

2.2. Propagation Strategy

The propagation strategy relies upon the work of corporate entrepreneurs to develop its new products and businesses. Headquarters supports this organic growth by providing strong project support and oversight, and by the creation of a culture that breeds risk taking and forgives the inevitable failures. Over time, the portfolios of propagating firms are filled with sets of ventures resting on a broad platform of research and development expertise. If successful, the central

Table 1 **Multi-Industry Firms**

Company Name	Home Country	"Multi-Industry Firm" in Global 1000	Total Sales ($ mil.)	Total Assets ($ mil.)	Market Value ($ mil.)
CSR	Australia	1988–1997	$ 5,932	$ 4,663	$ 3,703
Pacific Dunlop	Australia	1988–1994	4,760	4,653	3,578
General de Belgique	Belgium	1988–1998	160,901	NA	12,112
Groupe Bruxelles Lambert	Belgium	1988–1995, 1997–2000	5,629	NA	5,846
Tractabel	Belgium	1988–1997	18,824	9,779	6,130
B.A.T. Industries	Great Britain	1992–1998	83,440	24,175	27,951
BET	Great Britain	1988–1992	3,266	4,888	1,951
BTR	Great Britain	1988–1998	12,524	13,194	10,915
Grand Metropolitan	Great Britain	1988–1994	14,144	12,266	13,956
Hanson Trust	Great Britain	1988–1996	36,617	17,328	14,987
Pearson	Great Britain	1988–1993	3,356	2,554	3,745
Siebe	Great Britain	1992–1996	4,034	3,325	6,193
TI Group	Great Britain	1992–1998	2,275	3,050	4,614
Tomkins	Great Britain	1992–1998	5,119	7,483	6,809
Canadian Pacific	Canada	1988–2000	13,566	7,590	7,616
Imasco	Canada	1992–1999	34,890	5,813	9,899
Compagnie de Navigation Mixte	France	1990–1995	8,936	NA	3,001
Suez Lyonnaise des Eaux	France	1991–1995, 1998	79,101	31,828	21,544
Citic Pacific	Hong Kong	1995–2000	8,780	3,391	10,600
Hutchison Whampoa	Hong Kong	1988–2000	48,206	7,115	49,244
Jardine Matheson Holdings	Hong Kong/ Singapore	1990–1997	14,285	11,605	5,018
Jardine Strategic Holdings	Hong Kong/ Singapore	1992–1997	9,501	NA	3,886
Swire Pacific	Hong Kong	1988–2000	11,596	2,164	8,963
Montedison	Italy	1991–1992, 1994–1999	17,242	13,395	4,891
Sime Darby	Malaysia	1988–1994	2,822	2,730	3,950
Compagnie Financiere Richemont	Switzerland	1994–2000	10,417	6,887	12,935
AlliedSignal	U.S.	1988–1999	15,560	15,128	32,090
Berkshire Hathaway	U.S.	1990–1998, 2000	131,416	24,028	89,131
Dover	U.S.	1995–2000	4,132	4,446	9,440
General Electric	U.S.	1988–2000	405,200	111,630	520,247
ITT	U.S.	1988–1995	100,854	23,620	11,822
Loews	U.S.	1988–2000	69,464	15,906	6,986
Minnesota Mining and Manufacturing (3M)	U.S.	1988–2000	13,896	15,659	34,055
Paramount Communications	U.S.	1989–1994	7,054	4,265	5,165

(Continued)

Table 1   **Continued**

Company Name	Home Country	"Multi-Industry Firm" in Global 1000	Total Sales ($ mil.)	Total Assets ($ mil.)	Market Value ($ mil.)
Rockwell International	U.S.	1988–1996	$12,505	$12,981	$12,691
Tenneco	U.S.	1988–1998	8,332	7,220	7,061
Textron	U.S.	1988–2000	13,721	11,579	9,333
TRW	U.S.	1988–1996	5,890	10,172	6,155
Tyco International	U.S.	1990–1991, 1995–2000	32,362	22,497	79,441
Preussag	[West] Germany	1990–2000	7,829	16,667	5,858
Viag	[West] Germany	1988–1996	28,217	27,690	10,230

Source: BusinessWeek Global 1000, 1988–2000. Size data refer to companies' most recent year as a multi-industry firm.

efforts in corporate entrepreneurship can provide solid barriers to competitors and good profits. However, the process takes time and money. Headquarters must strike a tricky balance by containing costs without destroying worthy projects and by speeding time-to-market without expensively rushing duds to unwilling customers. In general terms, the propagation strategy grows more slowly than strategies making use of acquisitions, but also requires less frequent rationalization of the portfolio.

2.3. Restructuring and Accretion Strategies

Restructuring strategies and accretion strategies exhibit similarities, but are clearly differentiated in their value-producing actions and the portfolios they produce. Similarities begin with the heavy use of acquisitions, and include required skills at the head office in target identification, due diligence, and negotiation. Growth profiles are also comparably steep for the two strategies, with pressure building to increase either the pace or proportion of acquisitions as firms grow larger. But, here end the similarities between the two strategies. The restructuring strategy is aimed at returning focus and efficiency to takeover targets, in a wide cross-section of industries. The accretion strategy, by comparison, seeks out targets in a limited number of industries, each imbued with a fragmented structure and opportunities for building

international linkages. Acquisitions are carefully chosen by accretion strategists as a means for building product-line breadth and for increasing manufacturing and/or marketing efficiencies. In short, therefore, the accretion strategy generates value by knitting together clusters of businesses exhibiting a particular profile, while the restructuring strategy pursues profits through the transformation of business assets and by their eventual sale. The portfolios of the restructuring firm are typically more diverse and are subject to many more alterations than those connected to the accretion strategy.

2.4. Mixed Strategy

In using the mixed conglomerate strategy, corporate leadership combines strategies to help broaden organizational competencies and the potential for stable growth. One noteworthy fact is that comparatively few of the conglomerates we studied pursued "pure" versions of the archetypes. The mixed strategy was present in many permutations in the companies we examined, making general statements about the strategy difficult to express; however, a few characteristics were in evidence. In all cases, the mixed strategy required higher investments in people and supporting resources, and involved more challenging oversight. The mixed strategy was found in some of the largest firms and those with the longest commitment to the conglomerate form, like General Electric

Table 2   **Conglomerate Strategy Archetypes**

	Propagation Strategy	Restructuring Strategy	Accretion Strategy	Mixed Strategy	Portfolio Strategy
Primary activity	The successful creation of new products and, especially, new businesses	The improvement, reconfiguration, and sale of business assets	The build-up of mass in selected industries, resulting in market power and superior costs profiles	The combination of the aforementioned strategies	The construction of a diversified portfolio of businesses
Predominant growth mode	Corporate entrepreneurship	Acquisitions	Acquisitions	Acquisitions or mixed	Acquisitions
Role of HQ	Project approval and support; human resource and research formation	Identification of takeover targets and the aims of transformation; deal negotiation; oversight of resource flows and financial goal-setting	Identification of takeover targets and the aims of transformation; deal negotiation; oversight of resource flows and financial goal-setting	Formulation and implementation of the contributing conglomerate strategies	Identification of attractive investments; deal negotiation (as applicable)
Typical portfolio of businesses	Clusters of self-devised businesses, broadly linked by markets and underlying technology; very slow churn of the portfolio	Broad collection of businesses with generally low to medium technology intensity; very high churn rate of the portfolio	Focused collection of businesses, with generally low to medium technology intensity; high rate of disposals after acquisitions, but marked by divisional stability	Broad assortment of businesses often with the full array of technology intensities; varied churn rates	Broad assortment of businesses, with investments ranging from partial to full equity ownership
Vulnerabilities	Cost containment; slow time to market; slow growth profile	High sensitivity to price paid and savings projected; often ungainly portfolios with rationalization dependent on market vagaries for divestiture; difficulty maintaining growth profiles in large firms	High sensitivity to price paid and savings projected; difficulty maintaining growth profiles in large firms	Strategy implementation often requires broad and expensive resource base; implementation is complex and often difficult to understand	Portfolio management is more efficiently accomplished by individual investors; extremely narrow basis for organizational value creation; must consistently "out-guess" the market
Examples	3M	Hanson Trust; BTR	TI Group; Tyco International	General Electric	Loews

and AlliedSignal. Our findings also found agreement with the groundbreaking work of Goold and Campbell (1987): In top-performing firms, headquarters became adept at exerting the correct type of control over the individual businesses in the portfolio. For example, in more staid industrial businesses, financial means of control would be utilized. Conversely, in new or higher-growth businesses (especially in carefully chosen technology-based industries), broader strategic planning or strategic controls would be applied. (For more background on all the conglomerate strategies, please refer to Section 9, entitled "Conglomerate Strategies in Action." The descriptions found there also aid in understanding how the strategies were successfully implemented.)

3. CONTINGENCY AND CONTROL FROM THE CORPORATE LEVEL

How did management meet the challenge of conglomeration? Successful strategy implementation was contingent on achieving widespread cohesion between headquarters and the businesses. The primary concerns were the establishment of dedicated resources at headquarters and a focused, well defined means of interaction with the portfolio. The value-adding interaction was primarily vertical, with headquarters acting in important supporting roles.

Implementation can only be fully understood through a systematic examination of the three dimensions of corporate strategy. The strategic archetypes were implemented through attentive, syncopated control over the relationships among the businesses, the influence of headquarters, and the management of the portfolio of businesses. Through these means, the corporate archetypes were both defined and came to generate value. Tables 3–5 lay out the four major corporate strategies as they directed the relationships among the businesses, the influence of headquarters, and the contents of the corporate portfolio.

To help understand the relationships among the businesses, we include an examination of corporate structure, the presence of activities sharing and/or skills transfer, and the possible occurrence of other types of sharing or coordination (like common brand usage, human resources transfers, etc.). The influence of headquarters is examined through a look at the resources or competencies resident at headquarters and through an investigation of the means of control and coordination commonly exerted from there.

Table 3   **The Relationship among the Businesses**

	Propagation Strategy	Restructuring Strategy	Accretion Strategy	Mixed Strategy
Structure	A simple structure, ensuring divisional presence of technology platforms	A simple, industry-based structure	After rationalization, businesses apportioned simply in product groupings (brand name or industry)	A simple formal structure, arranged mainly by industry and geography
Activities sharing	A focused set of shared services (environmental and information technology, human resources, etc.) led by R&D	Few connections exploited among the businesses	Clear separation of divisions, with very few shared activities	Relatively few shared activities among divisions
Other shared resources	Strong culture invoked, across divisions Brand sharing across divisions Active sharing of management talent	Strong culture invoked, across divisions Active sharing of management talent	Strong culture invoked, across divisions Active sharing of management talent	Strong culture invoked, across divisions Brand sharing across divisions Active sharing of management talent

Table 4   **The Influence of Headquarters**

	Propagation Strategy	Restructuring Strategy	Accretion Strategy	Mixed Strategy
Resources at HQ	Wide range of resources at HQ, attuned to strategic emphases, like goal setting, project direction, and resource control	Small headquarters, with emphasis on M and A support and financial oversight	Small headquarters, with key resources invested in M and A support, financial and management oversight	Highly controlled set of resources at HQ, with key resources invested in M and A support, financial and management oversight
Coordination and Control	Multiple, project-oriented mechanisms for joining organizational levels	Highly decentralized businesses; control exerted through goal-setting, remuneration, culture, and auditing; direct management only by exception	Decentralized businesses (subject to merger with acquisitions), with main control mechanisms being goal-setting, remuneration, and auditing; direct management only by exception	High level of autonomy at the businesses, with HQ overseeing goal-setting and mission creation, culture (through HRM), and M and A activities; direct management only by exception

Portfolio management focuses on the criteria deciding the content of the portfolio, the primary means by which it was built, and the nature of divestiture and restructuring.

4. THE RELATIONSHIPS AMONG THE BUSINESSES

4.1. Structure

Structure in the top-performing firms followed strategy, reflecting another of the key tenets of strategic management. In the case of 3M, the multi-divisional structure is predicated on maintaining access to technological expertise, a natural corollary of a propagation strategy. At Hanson Trust, BTR, TI Group, and General Electric, by comparison, the restructuring, accretion, and mixed strategies demanded simple divisional structures in which the complex tasks of fostering organic growth and

rationalizing mergers and acquisitions can be made independently.

4.2. Activities Sharing or Skills Transfer

The divisional structure at the firms was also closely matched to efforts in activities sharing and skills transfer. At 3M, the heavy use of cross-functional teams to undertake new product research required placing needed resources within each division, to the greatest extent possible. Moreover, creating the large number of line extensions and adapting existing products to new markets put the onus on 3M's management to engage in advanced skills and information transfer. Across divisions, operations at TI Group and General Electric, and especially at Hanson Trust and BTR, were kept much more separated. The corporate center housed key skills for building the depth and breadth of the individual divisions through acquisitions, while the businesses were largely responsible for their own operations.

Table 5 **Portfolio Management**

	Propagation Strategy	Restructuring Strategy	Accretion Strategy	Mixed Strategy
Portfolio content	Widely diverse businesses in consumer, industrial, and international markets	Extremely wide diversification; portfolio composed of groups of restructured assets	Wide diversification, but tightly controlled by industry type and by the application of rigorous acquisition criteria	Often extremely wide diversification, but tightly controlled by industry type and by the application of rigorous acquisition criteria
Portfolio growth	Internally created businesses, through R&D; mostly niche entities predicated on unique designs and technology	Acquisitions the primary tool for building the portfolio	All aspects of M and A internally controlled; organic growth can also be sought	Balance of acquisitions and organic growth
Divestiture and restructuring	Presence of self-developed businesses and constant innovation within business units complicate the divestiture and restructuring processes	Maintenance of size and growth profile (especially in large firms) and culture issues hamper the divestiture process	Maintenance of size and growth profile (especially in large firms) and culture issues hamper the divestiture process	Maintenance of size and growth profile (especially in large firms) and culture issues hamper the divestiture process
		Restructuring can be impeded by the extreme separation of the businesses (if activities sharing or skills transfer are being pursued)	Restructuring can be impeded by the extreme separation of the businesses (if activities sharing or skills transfer are being pursued)	Restructuring can be impeded by the extreme separation of the businesses (if activities sharing or skills transfer are being pursued)

With few exceptions, the business units offered little opportunity for activities sharing, because of substantial differences in their capabilities and operations. All of the firms, however, focused intensely on developing top managers, making use of job rotation and other common training procedures, and on growing a strong culture open to change, innovation, and process improvement.

4.3. Other Sharing/Coordination

Indeed, in more general terms, human resource policies were adapted to support the basic premises for adding value. At 3M, policies were developed to encourage entrepreneurial risk taking and to develop needed skills. An aggressive culture was developed at BTR that heavily rewarded successful risk taking, driving away those who produced repeated failures or who could not work well under such conditions. At TI Group and General Electric, human resource policies were fashioned to achieve two different outcomes. Policies were designed to develop top management talent into fully seasoned managers. A major part of the training was to rotate managers through a number of different jobs. As well, the prominent use of innovation and organic growth at

GE and, to a lesser extent, at TI Group put pressure on management to develop a culture that supported risk taking and experimentation. Human resource policies were shaped to give incentives to successful risk takers and to develop skills throughout the firm in a targeted manner, and to a high degree of sophistication. In firms with so little that could be shared, organizational culture was actively shaped to provide a means of implementing strategy, recognizing and realizing opportunities, lending an identity to work and engendering the meaning of the organization.

5. THE INFLUENCE OF HEADQUARTERS

5.1. Resources and Competencies

In top-performing firms, the intrusions of headquarters into the activities of the businesses were strictly controlled. Goal setting was front-and-center for corporate leaders, notably for connecting universal goals with the mission of the firm. Corporate management usually placed financial goals at the forefront of discussions, but closely connected them with the strategic goals intended to generate value. The example of 3M was perhaps most clear in illustrating the manner in which meeting financial goals was used to prove the worthiness of the company's strategy, but this characteristic can be found at all of the top-performing firms. The prominence of measuring financial outcomes is common to publicly held firms, but its aggressive use at the conglomerates probably best reflects the complexity of their operations and the difficulty in tracking and understanding their parts.

Headquarters also contained key shared resources, again dictated by the needs of the individual strategies. At 3M, key corporate resources included the finances and infrastructure to support the entire product development cycle, from pure science to product launch and beyond. At Hanson Trust and BTR, the key corporate tasks needing support were acquisitions, restructuring, and mergers.

Headquarters thus functioned as an investment bank. After restructuring, strong financial and strategic oversights were exercised. At TI Group and General Electric, the demands of their strategies resulted in larger resource formations at headquarters, with competencies set up to support both the innovation and acquisition processes, and the wide-ranging development of management. In one prominent example, Jack Welch at GE declared the last task most important, devoting the greatest proportion of his time and effort to it.

5.2. Means of Control/ Coordination

All of the top-performing firms accentuated the creation of a particular type of work mode and culture. As stated, 3M made long and extensive use of cross-functional, team-based projects. The multiple technological and skills platforms at 3M placed unique demands on entrepreneurs to cross boundaries. Creative solutions to customers' needs drew from resources throughout the organization. The culture at 3M was therefore influenced by headquarters to be supportive, without encumbering entrepreneurs in a thicket of red tape before their ideas could be realized. Success was celebrated in multiple ways at 3M, while the debilitating effects of failure were largely eliminated. At Hanson Trust and BTR, a successful attempt was made to establish a strong, no-nonsense culture predicated on aggressive cost reduction and margin maintenance. At the same time, prominent efforts were made at BTR to cut across divisions and unite employees in charitable work of a varied nature. A strong culture was therefore created. At both TI Group and General Electric, the fundamental changes underway during the 1980s included a number of activities bent on inciting cultural transformation. At TI Group, headquarters was even moved from Birmingham to London in a calculated effort to reset the orientation of the firm. Simultaneously, remuneration and training were strengthened at both firms so that top recruits could be landed and retained. Power was also heavily decentralized, allowing managers more freedom to pursue ideas.

6. PORTFOLIO MANAGEMENT

6.1. Criteria for Portfolio Content

In terms of their strategies, all of the companies clearly communicated a vision for their portfolios that included a set of interlinked goals, outcomes, and activities. One of the overriding differences between the top performers and the lower performers was the depth to which corporate strategy was communicated. Strategic directions and their expected outcomes at 3M, BTR, Hanson Trust, TI Group, and GE were much more readily available, as was the case at the vast majority of the top performers, through company documents, its leadership, and through sources outside the company.

The overriding logic of the corporate strategies utilized was clear and simple, designed with a long time horizon in mind. Two mechanisms were available for linking environment and organization: firms were developed to innovate and open new markets, and/or to carefully identify and act in specific industries. Firms pursuing mixed strategies sometimes chose to combine the two mechanisms.

The businesses within each division were related by common brand name, as at TI Group during the latter part of the focus period, or by industry or end markets, as was the case at 3M, Hanson Trust, BTR, and GE throughout the period. However, even deeper associations were in evidence within the divisions of the top-performing firms. The businesses were also connected by common developmental processes and technologies, in the example of 3M and the early histories of BTR and GE, or were linked by similar fragmented industry structures in the businesses, as found at TI Group. Except for Hanson Trust and BTR, the businesses making up the portfolios were most often number one or two in their respective industries. In the main, the businesses offered unique products that either did not face strong, direct competition or were supported by vigorous service functions or high switching costs. Each of the top performers expanded the international reach of their portfolios, to some degree. The efforts at GE

and, especially, at 3M were long-standing, extending back decades into the companies' histories. But, TI Group also made great strides in opening its portfolio to global trade, making particularly effective use of its acquisitions to reach new markets and broaden its center of gravity.

6.2. Building the Portfolio

The portfolio of businesses was also grown in ways that both supported and defined the corporate strategies at the top-performing conglomerates. At 3M, growth was accomplished through the creation of new businesses, a process that demanded a flatness of organization and a group- and project-based system of oversight and planning that skillfully brought managerial experience and entrepreneurial genius together. Acquisitions were used very sparingly. Of the remaining firms, only Hanson Trust and BTR made nearly sole use of acquisitions. Management at TI Group utilized a balanced approach to growth, making use of strategic, "bolt-on" acquisitions. These acquisitions were highly disciplined, bringing complementary skills and/or product lines into the portfolio. The belief was that the acquisitions were another method of achieving organic growth. The actions at GE were comparable to those at TI Group, but greater use was made of larger acquisitions, depending upon the overall intent for the group of businesses.

In outcomes that agree broadly with the insightful 2001 work of Joseph Bower, headquarters in the top firms clearly linked the strategic intent of their acquisitions with the demands of integration that followed. Moreover, the types of acquisitions, their strategic intent, and the skills of managing the processes of acquisition and integration were closely coordinated and controlled by headquarters in the top-performing firms. In all cases, companies undertook sophisticated analyses of their acquisition targets, making heavy use of "friendly" takeovers so as to increase the flow of information, compact the time of the operation, ease the forthcoming merger and/or restructuring, and retain core management.

Three types of mergers and acquisitions were emphasized. Even 3M, which completed only a handful of acquisitions during the focus period, utilized the same basic practices of the much more intensive acquirers, Hanson Trust, BTR, TI Group, and GE. The firms successfully undertook well-planned examples of acquisitions as line extensions (in all of the firms), as research and development (BTR, TI Group, and GE), and as a method to achieve geographic consolidation in a fragmented industry (Hanson Trust, BTR, TI Group, and GE).

6.3. Divestiture and Restructuring

The impression should not be conveyed, however, that strategy implementation was always smooth and that continuous challenges did not exist. Of all the concerns of headquarters, divestiture seemed to be subject, even in the top-performing firms, to the most ad hoc strategizing; reaction rather than anticipation. Hanson Trust and GE were the most active in divestment. Hanson notably sold off a parcel of units in 1995, before being broken into four pieces the following year. As well, General Electric was very active, especially early in Jack Welch's tenure. The simple dictum that the businesses be number one or two in their respective industries also provided a clear rationale for selling assets. However, even at GE, divestitures were also completed that were driven by broader strategic and financial concerns, with the controversial sale of the industry-leading small appliances unit serving as a prime example. In most cases, asset sales at all the firms we examined were the results of rationalizing acquisitions, comparatively late moves to restructure the portfolio, or were examples of failed acquisitions.

Indeed, many of the only managerial regrets expressed by the leaders we studied concerned failed takeovers that ended in loss-making divestitures. Many forget the purchase of investment bank Kidder Peabody early in Jack Welch's tenure. However, he did not forget, simply labelling the acquisition "my biggest mistake." The reason for the mistake, according to Welch, began with a lack of due diligence, but also included a misplaced belief in the organization's ability to overcome any challenges in merging operations. At BTR, the problems seemed the most acute. Corporate management did not systematically and deeply cull its portfolio across time and became emotionally attached to some of the member businesses, which allowed the collection to

become increasingly inchoate. Part of the resistance can probably be explained by BTR's central efforts at building a strong culture, which is often incompatible with large-scale divestiture.

The decision to sell key assets was often influenced by the most culturally sensitive issues. As an example, one need look no further than 3M, which, throughout the 1990s, was concerned with their increasingly troubled and strategically mismatched data storage division. In time, cost leadership in a free-standing company, later called Imation, was found to be the solution. However, headquarters spent years and millions of dollars trying to contain costs and defend a premium position in an industry whose pro-ducts were inevitably being turned into commodities. At GE, the heavy negative reaction to the sale of the small appliances unit was largely attributable to the perception of many organizational members that the unit was an integral part of the organization's history and profile. (Broader confirmation and explanation of many of the points developed in this short section, as well as managerial options for developing a more proactive divestiture strategy, can be found in the article by Dranikoff, Koller, and Schneider [2002].)

Organizational crisis or malaise was another feature of the histories of all the firms we studied. BTR's crisis played out through the period. As suggested, the company persisted with a corporate strategy and a group of businesses that gradually became out of step with the economy at large. In reaction, plans were expressed and launched to first create an "international manufacturing and engineering company," and then a "leading global engineering company." Nonetheless, the elements of strong cultural inertia, management resistance, and the immense scale of desired change worked against implementation, and patience quickly wore thin in the markets for debt and warrants that kept the company afloat. A highly decentralized and diversified firm simply could not garner the time and money necessary to become a smaller, focused firm, whose businesses needed to work closely together.

TI Group also experienced enormous external pressures and nearly succumbed to them in the middle 1980s. As a result, a formerly widely diversified portfolio was retrenched in short order, and highly disciplined methods were implemented to stabilize and sustain growth.

Even General Electric, in many ways the quintessential conglomerate, experienced a lengthy phase widely described as "profitless growth." The elements of the transformation eventually led by Jack Welch are famous and celebrated, and will not be repeated here. However, implicit in Welch's actions and their forcefulness was an overriding belief that the company was operating on borrowed time.

7. MANAGING THE NEW CONGLOMERATE

7.1. A Viable Form?

In light of the hostile external opinions and the internal difficulties of managing such widespread, complex operations, does the conglomerate form make sense? After all, capital markets, industry analysts, and the results of a range of research appear to come down overwhelmingly against the practice. Yet the answer to the question of the conglomerate appears to be a highly qualified "yes." The supportable reasons for becoming widely diversified are few in number, including only the superior ability to grow new businesses and/or to transform assets or industries. A variety of resources, abilities, and actions must be combined along the three dimensions described in a mutually enhancing and strategically focused manner. The barriers to successfully developing and integrating the many elements required in mastering unrelated diversification may appear daunting, but the demanding requirements do, once mastered, offer some protection from imitation.

The key tasks for management begin with the clear establishment, communication, and implementation of the means by which the corporate level will add value to the underlying businesses. The method for adding value must orient the top-performing firm's assets and activities, through headquarters, with the external environment, and include opportunities that extend far into the foreseeable future. In the successful firms, changes in the environment, especially relevant industry conditions, were either actively led or were continuously monitored and worked into the strategy, as warranted.

Achieving "fit" cannot be reduced to a reactive posture, no matter how nimble. All of the firms we studied actively influenced their environments. For example, the restructuring strategies of BTR, Hanson Trust, and others were vigorous actors in Great Britain's industrial transformation throughout the 1970s and 1980s. Indeed, the British restructurers were so successful that the pool of viable candidate firms was vastly reduced by the end of the focus period. TI Group and General Electric, in a variety of industries, also actively built up scale and increased their level of international integration. Rather than react to industry concentration and globalization, a far more accurate statement is that a number of firms like TI Group and GE enacted those changes through powerful strategies that also secured their benefits. (The book by Weick [1979] provides a discussion of enactment by organizations, while the article of Smircich and Stubbart [1985] applies the concept to strategic management.) 3M's innovations may provide the clearest examples of a strategy that creates, rather than simply reacts to, the changing features of the business landscape. Entire industries, like data storage, medical diagnostic equipment, and whole areas of business support, have been established or profoundly shaped by 3M's efforts.

The insights provided by our group of conglomerates did not run in only one direction, however. The strengths of the individual strategies also suggested points of weakness. For example, the propagation strategy of 3M seems open to problems with cost containment and speed-to-market. As well, the growth trajectory associated with internal business creation cannot compare favorably with acquisition-led or -dominated strategies. The accretion strategy, especially as practiced by companies like Tyco International, exposed the firm to the nearly crushing pressures of maintaining growth and a no-holds-barred lifestyle which proved difficult to control, and ultimately resulted in criminal charges against its former top management. Rapidly rising numbers of acquisitions were required simply to maintain the historically high rate of expansion. The same problems with sustaining growth were also seen in the restructuring strategy. Hanson Trust and BTR both became wildly diverse while pursuing and improving undermanaged assets. Moreover, the criteria and process for divestiture were neither clearly defined nor consistently applied for a sustained period at either firm. As could reasonably be inferred, a positive relationship exists between the rate of growth and the need to define the strategy for pruning the portfolio. The benefits of balancing acquisitions and organic growth are illustrated through the strategies of both TI Group and G.E. At the same time, however, the breadth of diversity seemed to demand a wider base for corporate-led value-added. The demands placed on managers were also exceptionally broad and exacting. Indeed, the wide expanse of General Electric's businesses incited its model of the "internal economy," demanding that key initiatives and vectors for change were implemented in the businesses in anticipation of their general economic effects. Little room existed for error.

7.2. Do Recent Events Contribute Any New Insights?

One more bit of knowledge about managing conglomerates has emerged during the past few years. The recent histories of our companies (after we acknowledge the shorter period under consideration and, therefore, the scarcer data) provide some evidence that the more robust abilities to weather challenges and determine fates pass to firms that skillfully mix their corporate strategies. For example, the sustained top performance at 3M demonstrates the viability of the propagation strategy. But, the selection of Jay McNerney (a former GE executive), the movement toward greater efficiency (after recent lackluster performance), and the recent limited use of acquisitions are all strongly connected to a profitable blending of the forms of conglomerate strategy. The restructuring strategy at BTR and Hanson Trust undeniably supported a long sustained period of top performance and returns to shareholders. Yet the practice seems to require closely controlled levels of growth and well-developed criteria for maintaining the portfolio. Alternatively, some kind of secondary value-creating activity may also be utilized, like internationalizing the businesses and/or building scale in a fragmented industry. Of course, the developments and results at both Smiths Group (the outcome of TI Group's merger in 2000 with Smiths Industries) and General Electric offer the strongest statement for the efficacy of balanced growth and the mixed corporate strategy, respectively. The stories of AlliedSignal (now Honeywell), Dover, and relative newcomers like Danaher are also worthy of close analysis.

8. ANSWERING THE DEMANDS OF THE CONGLOMERATE FORM

The corporate strategies of today's conglomerates offer some clear directions to managers. The key issues to remember in making corporate strategy in widely diversified firms are to maintain a tight focus and to communicate the plans for the firm as often and effectively as possible. Following that, implementation rests on the effective integration of the three dimensions of corporate strategy (see Table 6).

The effects of entrepreneurial vision at headquarters will be felt through the choice of areas for innovation, the guidance of their requisite skills development, and/or the identification of industries for transformation, each providing numerous target opportunities and strong prospects for a sustained strategy. In all cases, sizeable investments will be required. As well, a steely discipline must be maintained. Broad product-market diversity in the top-performing conglomerates belies the presence of a simple, coordinated system for adding value that emanates from headquarters.

However, a final point should not be lost. Multi-industry firms do offer far more complex subjects than single-industry or narrowly diversified companies, with mixed strategies only adding to the complexity. The critical attention paid by corporate leaders at the top-performing firms to financial returns is an explicit acknowledgement of the difficulty of understanding their strategies and organizations. The shareholders of extremely diversified firms clearly require larger rewards for the added demands of owning them. Our analysis has shown that the expectations were met successfully

Table 6   **Managing the Top-Performing Conglomerate**

Formulating Strategy	
Definition	• Define a compelling, economically viable system for generating value in the businesses.
Strategic premise	• Transform underused or under-performing assets and/or create new products or businesses better than competitors.
Activities focus	• Tightly focus and extensively communicate the types of businesses to be transformed and/or the nature of the build-up of technologies and skills supporting innovation.
Managing implementation	
Focus	• Facilitate a program of value creation for headquarters by developing resources and policies there that are integrated and supportive of it.
Relationship among the businesses	• Establish a simple structure that facilitates the inclusion of acquisitions and/or the sharing of knowledge, production, and people.
	• Tightly control the search for savings from blending businesses.
	• Connect the flow of knowledge, top management personnel, money, and technology as part of the same process of value generation.
The interaction of HQ and the portfolio	• Fix the primary interaction within the organization as vertical, between the businesses and headquarters.
	The well-contained stock of resources and skills at headquarters must nevertheless be deep and a real source of competitive advantage.
Portfolio content management	• Define the parameters for entry, growth, and exit as an explicit part of the overall corporate strategy.

over decades in many of the firms, through a finite number of closely controlled strategies that coordinated environmental effects, the activities of headquarters, and the contents and concerns of the portfolio.

9. CONGLOMERATE STRATEGIES IN ACTION

To understand the strategies in greater depth, a brief reminder of some recent history is useful. We should recall that firms faced three major trends in the industrialized world throughout the period from 1987 to 1999. First, international barriers to trade and investment fell. Second, the focus period contained large increases in international competition and, in some industries, rising consolidation. Connected to the changes, public policy underwent transformation, with a major facet being liberal oversight of mergers and acquisitions. Indeed, mergers and acquisitions took place within an increasingly international and interconnected market for corporate control. Finally, inflation fell throughout the examination period, in a general movement in all of the major industrialized economies.

The Propagation Strategy at 3M

Parts of the 3M story are already widely understood. A group of 30 or so technology platforms, most entirely self-constructed, underpinned all of what 3M produced. Through its innovations, 3M's holdings generated revenues that were geographically dispersed and involved products distributed to a varied cross-section of end users, including both consumer and industrial customers of nearly all types. As well, the businesses included sizeable inflows from less cyclical businesses, like medical technology, and from steady revenue sources, like customer service contracts. The lion's share of 3M's revenues emanated from branded products earning high margins from their unique status and quality.

The propagation strategy practiced by corporate management at 3M fit quite well with the environmental conditions faced by the firm. First, the reduction in international trade barriers facilitated the globalization process, in which the company had been heavily involved since the end of World War II. Second, niche strategies partially insulated 3M from rising industry competitiveness. The company's unique products were difficult to "knock off" in a number of examples, owing to the singularity of the designs and the patents that surrounded many of them. Third, industry consolidation affected the firm less heavily because of the niche positions it held and the large scale to which the products could be produced and distributed. 3M also worked closely with its customers, developing solutions to problems for which customers were often willing to pay extra. On balance, the downward trend in inflation had less effect on 3M. The firm was one of the most admired in American business, maintaining leading positions in a number of prized industries throughout the focus period.

The Restructuring Strategy at Hanson Trust and BTR

The first golden age of the acquisitive conglomerate occurred during the 1960s, centered mainly in the United States. Factors both external and internal to firms helped spur the creation of conglomerates. The phenomenon can be linked, in part, to strong antitrust enforcement and to the new prevalence of "general management" skills being taught in leading business schools.

The more recent period we studied included the second heyday of the conglomerate. This time, the phenomenon was based mainly in Great Britain (but involved sizable investments elsewhere, especially in America) and emerged again after a protracted time of heavy government intervention and stultified competition. The conditions were set for companies aiming at restructuring a large number of undermanaged and undervalued assets.

Two leading lights, Hanson Trust and BTR, dominated the period. Seizing the many available opportunities, both companies racked up decades of revenues and profit growth. Hanson Trust exceeded the returns of Great Britain's top 100 firms by a whopping 368 percent during the 1980s. Performance at BTR was comparable to that at Hanson Trust, with the company routinely counted and awarded among Britain's best-managed firms, well into the 1990s.

Neither Hanson Trust nor BTR remained in restructuring mode through the balance of the decade. Indeed, neither firm was even remotely similar. Hanson Trust broke itself into four pieces in 1996, leaving the Hanson name associated only with the building materials division. The firm did continue its acquisitive ways, however, growing to be included again on the Global 1000 list in 1999. In 1998, BTR fell further, merging from the inferior position with the British engineering firm, Siebe, and eventually forming a new company, Invensys. Management had been heavily pressured by outside stakeholders who lost confidence after an intended retrenchment and strategic reorientation took up a protracted parcel of time.

What had changed? Forces emanating from both inside and outside the firms conspired against them. Internally, the large size of both firms caused managers to undertake either an increasing number of smaller acquisitions or to identify larger and larger targets, merely to maintain historical rates of growth. Simultaneously, divestiture was not pursued as spiritedly as it could have been, especially at BTR. Leadership transition also became an issue for both firms. The restructuring strategy is not, as its detractors have described it, the simple stripping of assets, but is an entrepreneurial action at its core. The results are new combinations of assets that generate greater value more efficiently. Little wonder should therefore surround the fact that both firms were controlled by some of the most talented entrepreneurs of their generation: James Hanson and Gordon White at Hanson Trust, and David Nicholson, Owen Green, and Norman Ireland at BTR. However, by the middle of the 1990s, time had caught up with both groups and viable management succession had not been well worked out.

External pressures also mounted. Competing restructuring firms appeared on the scene. Companies like Tomkins, Wassall, and TT Group squeezed Hanson Trust and BTR, raising prices for targets and eliminating some availability. As well, the strategy gradually came out of phase with some key trends. Neither Hanson Trust nor BTR had been especially aggressive in seeking to internationalize its businesses, thus largely missing out on significant opportunities. The corporate level was also not active in building scale in many of the industries in which its businesses participated. As well, in many cases, corporate management continued to press its industrial businesses to gain margin increases on a short-term basis. The action persisted, despite the fact that many supplier relationships were being developed into long-term relational contracts that relied on much closer working relationships, higher knowledge intensity and joint innovation, and intense communication. In short, the businesses were falling behind by staying the same; at the end of the period under study, many competitors were much larger, designing, producing, and selling their products on a worldwide basis.

In the face of the many changes, does the restructuring strategy remain viable? The fact is that the restructuring strategy was not designed to respond to many of the trends just described. Do the gaps dictate that restructuring be subsumed into accretion or some combination of the other archetypes? The short answer is, not necessarily. Undeniably, restructuring can result in confusing diversity in the portfolio. Moreover, when fully implemented, the restructuring strategy does not allow a conventional interpretation of phrases like "core businesses" or "stick to your knitting." Instead, the strategy entails the process of transformation, beginning with an acquisition and ending in a sale. Sentiments against perceived unrelated diversification and a lack of understanding of the strategy probably contribute to the fact that the most prominent firms practicing the restructuring strategy, companies like Kohlberg Kravis Roberts and Co. (KKR) and the Carlyle Group, are privately held at the present time.

The Accretion Strategy at TI Group

The portfolio at TI Group, another British conglomerate, was a broad collection of engineering-based manufacturing businesses, such as specialized engineering, seals, and tubes. Over time, increasingly commanding positions were developed in the fragmented industries served by the divisions. Each carried a separate, branded identity and included many successful niche products.

TI Group's corporate strategy used portfolio techniques on a number of dimensions to offset the limitations and risks of the niche strategy. Examples included the John Crane Group, which provided seal designs for multiple industrial uses, Bundy group, which supplied specialized tubing to the refrigeration and automobile industries, and the Dowty Group, an extremely varied producer of aerospace applications. Firstly, by their nature, niche products are often constrained with regard to growth and the overall size of the markets to which they appeal. Also, a supplier often encounters a monopsony or oligopsony position if only a single buyer or a handful of large customers use its niche products. In either case, the bargaining power of the customer can be extremely high. Headquarters' decision to hold a portfolio of niche positions, therefore, lessened the risks of individual customer bargaining power and opened the growth potential of the corporate entity to much higher levels. Secondly, the geographic diversity of TI Group's holdings offered less exposure to the fortunes of any single market and raised the ceiling on growth. Thirdly, the company operated three and then four divisions, each exhibiting a diverse cross-section of engineering activities that, in turn, held a remarkable portfolio of niche products. In this way, the portfolio was nested, by virtue of having a "portfolio of portfolios," all with strong positions at the business level. Lastly, the businesses were grown using two distinct means, acquisition and organic growth, that were fitted together to offer a more balanced approach to enlarging the firm.

The actions of corporate management were again closely integrated to take advantage of opportunities extant in the greater environment. The intention of corporate management was to introduce its niche products on an international scale in times of market liberalization, expanding the scope of the opportunities offered by each innovation. As well, relationships between suppliers like TI Group and its largely global customers were more closely structured. In the long term, TI Group's management actively integrated into its strategy the relational contracts that had become the norm in relevant industries, especially automobiles and aerospace.

The company built depth in its product lines and augmented production scale simultaneously. Important examples included the absorption of Dowty's polymer engineering businesses into John Crane in 1992 and the large-scale break-up of the EIS acquisition in 1998. John Crane received the fluid technologies businesses, while Dowty was integrated with the aero-structure units (named Hamble). Acquisitions and innovation were carefully undertaken. Customers valued both the flexibility and capabilities represented in increased product and service depth. At the same time, the expanded scale of production brought on by internationalization and by the larger purchases of growing customers led to lower costs of production. Companies like TI Group mated their strategies with the demands brought on by increased consolidation in their customers, while also leading the trend through their own acquisitions. Thus, TI Group successfully blended aspects of the propagation strategy, through its research efforts and organic growth, with the predominant efforts of its accretion strategy.

The Mixed Corporate Strategy at General Electric

The mixing of strategies reached its zenith with General Electric. The businesses at General Electric were the broadest and most varied of the successful conglomerates, and perhaps the best known. The divisions run the gamut, from financial services and broadcasting to turbines, plastics, and medical products. The twelve businesses were famously required to be number one or two in their respective industries, have achievable plans for gaining those positions, or be sold. At the same time, Jack Welch and his top managers identified and linked key environmental change drivers (globalization; the Internet and e-business; the growth of services; and the search for increased product quality, through six Sigma) to his own plans for every one of their businesses.

The old model of the conglomerate, the "internalized capital market," described how corporate managers made use of the superior reporting information of their divisions, compared with the lower efficiencies of the financial system of the 1970s. In effect, under Welch, top management upped the ante, creating an "internalized economy" in which the salient features of the changing environment were identified and internalized more quickly and efficiently than in the overall economic system.

Rather than simply focusing on the flow of money and maximizing return on investment, which certainly remained important, headquarters at GE also emphasized the movement of people, the efforts in sharing knowledge, and in training workers of all stripes. Headquarters oversaw a vast organizational economy, controlled the development and flow of all key resources, maintained sustainable growth through restructuring, accretion, and propagation, and interjected across the board to stimulate development that matched leading trends before they were universally adopted outside the organization. In the process, the idea of "fit" was being employed at GE at a much more demanding level.

References

Bower, J. L. (2001). Not all M and As are alike, and that matters. *Harvard Business Review, 79*(3), 93–101.

Dranikoff, L., Koller, T., & Schneider, A. (2002). Divestiture: Strategy's missing link. *Harvard Business Review, 80*(5), 74–83.

Goold, M. C., & Campbell, A. (1987). *Strategies and styles.* Oxford, England: Blackwell.

Porter, M. E. (1987). From competitive strategy to corporate advantage. *Harvard Business Review, 65*(3), 43–59.

Rumelt, R. (1974). *Strategy, structure and economic performance.* Cambridge, MA: Harvard Business School Division of Research.

Smircich, L., & Stubbart, C. (1985). Strategic management in an enacted world. *Academy of Management Review, 10*(4), 724–36.

Weick, K. (1979). *The social psychology of organizing* (2nd ed.). Reading, MA: Addison-Wesley.

Turning Great Strategy into Great Performance

Michael C. Mankins
Marakon Associates

Richard Steele
Marakon Associates

Companies typically realize only about 60 percent of their strategies' potential value because of defects and breakdowns in planning and execution. By strictly following seven simple rules, you can get a lot more than that.

Three years ago, the leadership team at a major manufacturer spent months developing a new strategy for its European business. Over the prior half-decade, six new competitors had entered the market, each deploying the latest in low-cost manufacturing technology and slashing prices to gain market share. The performance of the European unit—once the crown jewel of the company's portfolio—had deteriorated to the point that top management was seriously considering divesting it.

To turn around the operation, the unit's leadership team had recommended a bold new "solutions strategy"—one that would leverage the business's installed base to fuel growth in aftermarket services and equipment financing. The financial forecasts were exciting—the strategy promised to restore the business's industry-leading returns and growth. Impressed, top management quickly approved the plan, agreeing to provide the unit with all the resources it needed to make the turnaround a reality.

Today, however, the unit's performance is nowhere near what its management team had projected. Returns, while better than before, remain well below the company's cost of capital. The revenues and profits that managers had expected from services and financing have not materialized, and the business's cost position still lags behind that of its major competitors.

Reprinted by permission of *Harvard Business Review,* from "Turning Great Strategy into Great Performance," by Michael C. Mankins and Richard Steele, July–August 2005, pp. 64–72. © 2005 by the Harvard Business School Publishing Corporation. All rights reserved.

At the conclusion of a recent half-day review of the business's strategy and performance, the unit's general manager remained steadfast and vowed to press on. "It's all about execution," she declared. "The strategy we're pursuing is the right one. We're just not delivering the numbers. All we need to do is work harder, work smarter."

The parent company's CEO was not so sure. He wondered: Could the unit's lackluster performance have more to do with a mistaken strategy than poor execution? More important, what should he do to get better performance out of the unit? Should he do as the general manager insisted and stay the course—focusing the organization more intensely on execution—or should he encourage the leadership team to investigate new strategy options? If execution was the issue, what should he do to help the business improve its game? Or should he just cut his losses and sell the business? He left the operating review frustrated and confused—not at all confident that the business would ever deliver the performance its managers had forecast in its strategic plan.

Talk to almost any CEO, and you're likely to hear similar frustrations. For despite the enormous time and energy that goes into strategy development at most companies, many have little to show for the effort. Our research suggests that companies on average deliver only 63 percent of the financial performance their strategies promise. Even worse, the causes of this strategy-to-performance gap are all but invisible to top management. Leaders then pull the wrong levers in their attempts to turn around performance—pressing for better execution when they actually need a better strategy, or opting to change direction when they really should focus the organization on execution. The result: wasted energy, lost time, and continued underperformance.

But, as our research also shows, a select group of high-performing companies have managed to close the strategy-to-performance gap through better planning *and* execution. These companies—Barclays, Cisco Systems, Dow Chemical, 3M, and Roche, to name a few—develop realistic plans that are solidly grounded in the underlying economics of their markets and then use the plans to drive execution. Their disciplined planning and execution processes make it far less likely that they will face a shortfall in actual performance. And, if they do fall short, their processes enable them to discern the cause quickly and take corrective action. While these companies' practices are broad in scope—ranging from unique forms of planning to integrated processes for deploying and tracking resources—our experience suggests that they can be applied by any business to help craft great plans and turn them into great performance.

THE STRATEGY-TO-PERFORMANCE GAP

In the fall of 2004, our firm, Marakon Associates, in collaboration with the Economist Intelligence Unit, surveyed senior executives from 197 companies worldwide with sales exceeding $500 million. We wanted to see how successful companies are at translating their strategies into performance. Specifically, how effective are they at meeting the financial projections set forth in their strategic plans? And when they fall short, what are the most common causes, and what actions are most effective in closing the strategy-to-performance gap? Our findings were revealing—and troubling.

While the executives we surveyed compete in very different product markets and geographies, they share many concerns about planning and execution. Virtually all of them struggle to produce the financial performance forecasts in their long-range plans. Furthermore, the processes they use to develop plans

and monitor performance make it difficult to discern whether the strategy-to-performance gap stems from poor planning, poor execution, both, or neither. Specifically, we discovered:

Companies Rarely Track Performance against Long-Term Plans

In our experience, less than 15 percent of companies make it a regular practice to go back and compare the business's results with the performance forecast for each unit in its prior years' strategic plans. As a result, top managers can't easily know whether the projections that underlie their capital-investment and portfolio-strategy decisions are in any way predictive of actual performance. More important, they risk embedding the same disconnect between results and forecasts in their future investment decisions. Indeed, the fact that so few companies routinely monitor actual versus planned performance may help explain why so many companies seem to pour good money after bad—continuing to fund losing strategies rather than searching for new and better options.

Multiyear Results Rarely Meet Projections

When companies do track performance relative to projections over a number of years, what commonly emerges is a picture one of our clients recently described as a series of "diagonal venetian blinds," where each year's performance projections, when viewed side by side, resemble venetian blinds hung diagonally. (See Exhibit 1.) If things are going reasonably well, the starting point for each year's new "blind" may be a bit higher than the prior year's starting point, but rarely does performance match the prior year's projection. The obvious implication: year after year of underperformance relative to plan.

The venetian blinds phenomenon creates a number of related problems. First, because the plan's financial forecasts are unreliable, senior management cannot confidently tie capital approval to strategic planning. Consequently, strategy development and resource allocation become decoupled, and the

Exhibit 1 **The Venetian Blinds of Business**

This graphic illustrates a dynamic common to many companies. In January 2001, management approves a strategic plan (Plan 2001) that projects modest performance for the first year and a high rate of performance thereafter, as shown in the first solid line. For beating the first year's projection, the unit management is both commended and handsomely rewarded. A new plan is then prepared, projecting uninspiring results for the first year and once again promising a fast rate of performance improvement thereafter, as shown by the second solid line (Plan 2002). This, too, succeeds only partially, so another plan is drawn up, and so on. The actual rate of performance improvement can be seen by joining the start points of each plan (the dotted line).

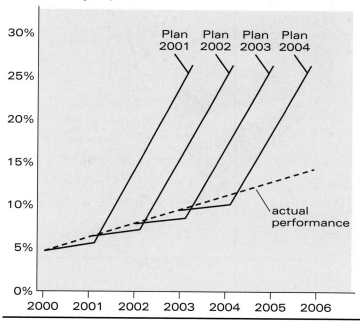

annual operating plan (or budget) ends up driving the company's long-term investments and strategy. Second, portfolio management gets derailed. Without credible financial forecasts, top management cannot know whether a particular business is worth more to the company and its shareholders than to potential buyers. As a result, businesses that destroy shareholder value stay in the portfolio too long (in the hope that their performance will eventually turn around), and value-creating businesses are starved for capital and other resources. Third, poor financial forecasts complicate communications with the investment community. Indeed, to avoid coming up short at the end of the quarter, the CFO and head of investor relations frequently impose a "contingency" or "safety margin" on top of the forecast produced by consolidating the business-unit plans. Because this top-down contingency is wrong just as often as it is right, poor financial forecasts run the risk of damaging a company's reputation with analysts and investors.

A Lot of Value Is Lost in Translation

Given the poor quality of financial forecasts in most strategic plans, it is probably not surprising that most companies fail to realize their strategies' potential value. As we've mentioned, our survey indicates that, on average, most strategies deliver only 63 percent

Exhibit 2   **Where the Performance Goes**

This chart shows the average performance loss implied by the importance ratings that managers in our survey gave to specific breakdowns in the planning and execution process.

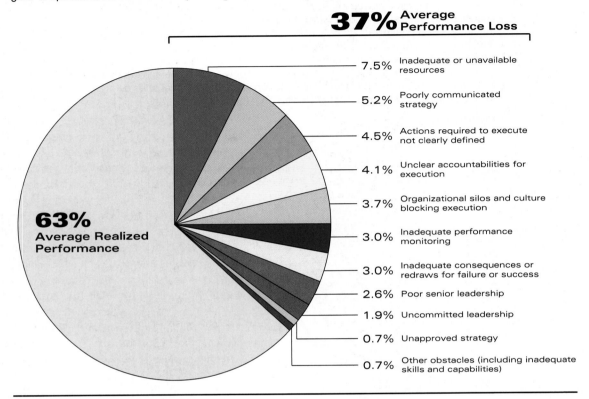

37% Average Performance Loss

- 7.5% Inadequate or unavailable resources
- 5.2% Poorly communicated strategy
- 4.5% Actions required to execute not clearly defined
- 4.1% Unclear accountabilities for execution
- 3.7% Organizational silos and culture blocking execution
- 3.0% Inadequate performance monitoring
- 3.0% Inadequate consequences or redraws for failure or success
- 2.6% Poor senior leadership
- 1.9% Uncommitted leadership
- 0.7% Unapproved strategy
- 0.7% Other obstacles (including inadequate skills and capabilities)

63% Average Realized Performance

of their potential financial performance. And more than one-third of the executives surveyed placed the figure at less than 50 percent. Put differently, if management were to realize the full potential of its current strategy, the increase in value could be as much as 60 to 100 percent!

As illustrated in Exhibit 2, the strategy-to-performance gap can be attributed to a combination of factors, such as poorly formulated plans, misapplied resources, breakdowns in communication, and limited accountability for results. To elaborate, management starts with a strategy it believes will generate a certain level of financial performance and value over time (100 percent, as noted in the exhibit). But, according to the executives we surveyed, the failure to have the right resources in the right place at the right time strips away some 7.5 percent of the strategy's potential value. Some 5.2 percent is lost to poor communications, 4.5 percent to poor action

planning, 4.1 percent to blurred accountabilities, and so on. Of course, these estimates reflect the average experience of the executives we surveyed and may not be representative of every company or every strategy. Nonetheless, they do highlight the issues managers need to focus on as they review their companies' processes for planning and executing strategies.

What emerges from our survey results is a sequence of events that goes something like this: Strategies are approved but poorly communicated. This, in turn, makes the translation of strategy into specific actions and resource plans all but impossible. Lower levels in the organization don't know what they need to do, when they need to do it, or what resources will be required to deliver the performance senior management expects. Consequently, the expected results never materialize. And because no one is held responsible for the shortfall, the cycle of underperformance gets repeated, often for many years.

Performance Bottlenecks Are Frequently Invisible to Top Management

The processes most companies use to develop plans, allocate resources, and track performance whether the strategy-to-performance gap stems from poor planning, poor execution, both, or neither. Because so many plans incorporate overly ambitious projections, companies frequently write off performance shortfalls as "just another hockey-stick forecast." And when plans are realistic and performance falls short, executives have few early warning signals. They often have no way of knowing whether critical actions were carried out as expected, resources were deployed on schedule, competitors responded as anticipated, and so on. Unfortunately, without clear information on how and why performance is falling short, it is virtually impossible for top management to take appropriate corrective action.

The Strategy-to-Performance Gap Fosters a Culture of Underperformance

In many companies, planning and execution breakdowns are reinforced—even magnified—by an insidious shift in culture. In our experience, this change occurs subtly but quickly, and once it has taken root it is very hard to reverse. First, unrealistic plans create the expectation throughout the organization that plans simply will not be fulfilled. Then, as the expectation becomes experience, it becomes the norm that performance commitments won't be kept. So commitments cease to be binding promises with real consequences. Rather than stretching to ensure that commitments are kept, managers, expecting failure, seek to protect themselves from the eventual fallout. They spend time covering their tracks rather than identifying actions to enhance performance. The organization becomes less self-critical and less intellectually honest about its shortcomings. Consequently, it loses its capacity to perform.

CLOSING THE STRATEGY-TO-PERFORMANCE GAP

As significant as the strategy-to-performance gap is at most companies, management can close it. A number of high-performing companies have found ways to realize more of their strategies' potential. Rather than focus on improving their planning and execution processes separately to close the gap, these companies work both sides of the equation, raising standards for both planning and execution simultaneously and creating clear links between them.

Our research and experience in working with many of these companies suggests they follow seven rules that apply to planning and execution. Living by these rules enables them to objectively assess any performance shortfall and determine whether it stems from the strategy, the plan, the execution, or employees' capabilities. And the same rules that allow them to spot problems early also help them prevent performance shortfalls in the first place. These rules may seem simple—even obvious—but when strictly and collectively observed, they can transform both the quality of a company's strategy and its ability to deliver results.

Rule 1: Keep It Simple, Make It Concrete

At most companies, strategy is a highly abstract concept—often confused with vision or aspiration—and is not something that can be easily communicated or translated into action. But without a clear sense of where the company is headed and why, lower levels in the organization cannot put in place executable plans. In short, the link between strategy and performance can't be drawn because the strategy itself is not sufficiently concrete.

To start off the planning and execution process on the right track, high-performing companies avoid long, drawn-out descriptions of lofty goals and instead stick to clear language describing their course of action. Bob Diamond, CEO of Barclays Capital, one of the fastest-growing and best-performing investment banking operations in Europe, puts it this way: "We've been very clear about what we will and will not do. We knew we weren't going to go head-to-head with U.S. bulge bracket firms. We communicated that we wouldn't compete in this way and that we wouldn't play in unprofitable segments within the equity markets but instead would invest to position ourselves for the euro, the burgeoning need for fixed income, and the end of Glass-Steigel. By ensuring everyone knew the strategy and how it was different, we've been able to spend more time on tasks that are key to executing this strategy."

By being clear about what the strategy is and isn't, companies like Barclays keep everyone headed in the same direction. More important, they safeguard the performance their counterparts lose to ineffective communications; their resource and action planning becomes more effective; and accountabilities are easier to specify.

Rule 2: Debate Assumptions, Not Forecasts

At many companies, a business unit's strategic plan is little more than a negotiated settlement—the result of careful bargaining with the corporate center over performance targets and financial forecasts. Planning, therefore, is largely a political process—with unit management arguing for lower near-term profit projections (to secure higher annual bonuses) and top management pressing for more long-term stretch (to satisfy the board of directors and other external constituents). Not surprisingly, the forecasts that emerge from these negotiations almost always understate what each business unit can deliver in the near term and overstate what can realistically be expected in the long-term—the hockey-stick charts with which CEOs are all too familiar.

Even at companies where the planning process is isolated from the political concerns of performance evaluation and compensation, the approach used to generate financial projections often has built-in biases. Indeed, financial forecasting frequently takes place in complete isolation from the marketing or strategy functions. A business unit's finance function prepares a highly detailed line-item forecast whose short-term assumptions may be realistic, if conservative, but whose long-term assumptions are largely uninformed. For example, revenue forecasts

are typically based on crude estimates about average pricing, market growth, and market share. Projections of long-term costs and working capital requirements are based on an assumption about annual productivity gains—expediently tied, perhaps, to some companywide efficiency program. These forecasts are difficult for top management to pick apart. Each line item may be completely defensible, but the overall plan and projections embed a clear upward bias—rendering them useless for driving strategy execution.

High-performing companies view planning altogether differently. They want their forecasts to drive the work they actually do. To make this possible, they have to ensure that the assumptions underlying their long-term plans reflect both the real economics of their markets and the performance experience of the company relative to competitors. Tyco CEO Ed Breen, brought in to turn the company around in July 2002, credits a revamped plan-building process for contributing to Tyco's dramatic recovery. When Breen joined the company, Tyco was a labyrinth of 42 business units and several hundred profit centers, built up over many years through countless acquisitions. Few of Tyco's businesses had complete plans, and virtually none had reliable financial forecasts.

To get a grip on the conglomerate's complex operations, Breen assigned cross-functional teams at each unit, drawn from strategy, marketing, and finance, to develop detailed information on the profitability of Tyco's primary markets as well as the product or service offerings, costs, and price positioning relative to the competition. The teams met with corporate executives biweekly during Breen's first six months to review and discuss the findings. These discussions focused on the assumptions that would drive each unit's long-term financial performance, not on the financial forecasts themselves. In fact, once assumptions about market trends were agreed on, it was relatively easy for Tyco's central finance function to prepare externally oriented and internally consistent forecasts for each unit.

Separating the process of building assumptions from that of preparing financial projections helps to ground the business unit–corporate center dialogue in economic reality. Units can't hide behind specious details, and corporate center executives can't push for unrealistic goals. What's more, the fact-based discussion resulting from this kind of approach builds trust between the top team and each unit and removes barriers to fast and effective execution. "When you understand the fundamentals and performance drivers in a detailed way," says Bob Diamond, "you can then step back, and you don't have to manage the details. The team knows which issues it can get on with, which it needs to flag to me, and which issues we really need to work out together."

Rule 3: Use a Rigorous Framework, Speak a Common Language

To be productive, the dialogue between the corporate center and the business units about market trends and assumptions must be conducted within a rigorous framework. Many of the companies we advise use the concept of profit pools, which draws on the competition theories of Michael Porter and others. In this framework, a business's long-term financial performance is tied to the total profit pool available in each of the markets it serves and its share of each profit pool—which, in turn, is tied to the business's market share and relative profitability versus competitors in each market.

In this approach, the first step is for the corporate center and the unit team to agree on the size and growth of each profit pool. Fiercely competitive markets, such as pulp and paper or commercial airlines, have small (or negative) total profit pools. Less competitive markets, like soft drinks or pharmaceuticals, have large total profit pools. We find it helpful to estimate the size of each profit pool directly—through detailed benchmarking—and then forecast changes in the pool's size and growth. Each business unit then assesses what share of the total profit pool it can realistically capture over time, given its business model and positioning. Competitively advantaged businesses can capture a large share of the profit pool—by gaining or sustaining a high market share, generating above-average profitability, or both. Competitively disadvantaged businesses, by contrast, typically capture a negligible share of the profit pool. Once the unit and the corporate center agree on the likely share of the pool the business will capture over time, the corporate center can easily create the financial projections that will serve as the unit's road map.

In our view, the specific framework a company uses to ground its strategic plans isn't all that important. What is critical is that the framework establish a common language for the dialogue between the corporate center and the units—one that the strategy, marketing, and finance teams all understand and use. Without a rigorous framework to link a business's performance in the product markets with its financial performance over time, it is very difficult for top management to ascertain whether the financial projections that accompany a business unit's strategic plan are reasonable and realistically achievable. As a result, management can't know with confidence whether a performance shortfall stems from poor execution or an unrealistic and ungrounded plan.

Rule 4: Discuss Resource Deployments Early

Companies can create more realistic forecasts and more executable plans if they discuss up front the level and timing of critical resource deployments. At Cisco Systems, for example, a cross-functional team reviews the level and timing of resource deployments early in the planning stage. These teams regularly meet with John Chambers (CEO), Dennis Powell (CFO), Randy Pond (VP of operations), and the other members of Cisco's executive team to discuss their findings and make recommendations. Once agreement is reached on resource allocation and timing at the unit level, those elements are factored into the company's two-year plan. Cisco then monitors each unit's actual resource deployments on a monthly basis (as well as its performance) to make sure things are going according to plan and that the plan is generating the expected results.

Challenging business units about when new resources need to be in place focuses the planning dialogue on what actually needs to happen across the company in order to execute each unit's strategy. Critical questions invariably surface, such as: How long will it take us to change customers' purchase patterns? How fast can we deploy our new sales force? How quickly will competitors respond? These are tough questions. But answering them makes the forecasts and the plans they accompany more feasible.

What's more, an early assessment of resource needs also informs discussions about market trends and drivers, improving the quality of the strategic plan and making it far more executable. In the course of talking about the resources needed to expand in the rapidly growing cable market, for example, Cisco came to realize that additional growth would require more trained engineers to improve existing products and develop new features. So, rather than relying on the functions to provide these resources from the bottom up, corporate management earmarked a specific number of trained engineers to support growth in cable. Cisco's financial-planning organization carefully monitors the engineering head count, the pace of feature development, and revenues generated by the business to make sure the strategy stays on track.

Rule 5: Clearly Identify Priorities

To deliver any strategy successfully, managers must make thousands of tactical decisions and put them into action. But not all tactics are equally important. In most instances, a few key steps must be taken—at the right time and in the right way—to meet planned performance. Leading companies make these priorities explicit so that each executive has a clear sense of where to direct his or her efforts.

At Textron, a $10 billion multi-industrial conglomerate, each business unit identifies "improvement priorities" that it must act upon to realize the performance outlined in its strategic plan. Each improvement priority is translated into action items with clearly defined accountabilities, timetables, and key performance indicators (KPIs) that allow executives to tell how a unit is delivering on a priority. Improvement priorities and action items cascade to every level at the company—from the management committee (consisting of Textron's top five executives) down to the lowest levels in each of the company's ten business units. Lewis Campbell, Textron's CEO, summarizes the company's approach this way: "Everyone needs to know: 'If I have only one hour to work, here's what I'm going to focus on.' Our goal deployment process makes each individual's accountabilities and priorities clear."

The Swiss pharmaceutical giant Roche goes as far as to turn its business plans into detailed performance contracts that clearly specify the steps needed and the risks that must be managed to achieve the plans. These contracts all include a "delivery agenda" that lists the 5 to 10 critical priorities with

the greatest impact on performance. By maintaining a delivery agenda at each level of the company, Chairman and CEO Franz Humer and his leadership team make sure "everyone at Roche understands exactly what we have agreed to do at a strategic level and that our strategy gets translated into clear execution priorities. Our delivery agenda helps us stay the course with the strategy decisions we have made so that execution is actually allowed to happen. We cannot control implementation from HQ, but we can agree on the priorities, communicate relentlessly, and hold managers accountable for executing against their commitments."

Rule 6: Continuously Monitor Performance

Seasoned executives know almost instinctively whether a business has asked for too much, too little, or just enough resources to deliver the goods. They develop this capability over time—essentially through trial and error. High-performing companies use real-time performance tracking to help accelerate this trial-and-error process. They continuously monitor their resource deployment patterns and their results against plan, using continuous feedback to reset planning assumptions and reallocate resources. This real-time information allows management to spot and remedy flaws in the plan and shortfalls in execution—and to avoid confusing one with the other.

At Textron, for example, each KPI is carefully monitored, and regular operating reviews percolate performance shortfalls—or "red light" events—up through the management ranks. This provides CEO Lewis Campbell, CFO Ted French, and the other members of Textron's management committee with the information they need to spot and fix breakdowns in execution.

A similar approach has played an important role in the dramatic revival of Dow Chemical's fortunes. In December 2001, with performance in a free fall, Dow's board of directors asked Bill Stavropoulos (Dow's CEO from 1993 to 1999) to return to the helm. Stavropoulos and Andrew Liveris (the current CEO, then COO) immediately focused Dow's entire top leadership team on execution through a project they called the Performance Improvement Drive. They began by defining clear performance metrics for each of Dow's 79 business units. Performance on these key metrics was tracked against plans on a weekly basis, and the entire leadership team discussed any serious discrepancies first thing every Monday morning. As Liveris told us, the weekly monitoring sessions "forced everyone to live the details of execution" and let "the entire organization know how we were performing."

Continuous monitoring of performance is particularly important in highly volatile industries, where events outside anyone's control can render a plan irrelevant. Under CEO Alan Mulally, Boeing Commercial Airplanes' leadership team holds weekly business performance reviews to track the division's results against its multiyear plan. By tracking the deployment of resources as a leading indicator of whether a plan is being executed effectively, BCA's leadership team can make course corrections each week rather than waiting for quarterly results to roll in.

Furthermore, by proactively monitoring the primary drivers of performance (such as passenger traffic patterns, airline yields and load factors, and new aircraft orders), BCA is better able to develop and deploy effective countermeasures when events throw its plans off course. During the SARS epidemic in late 2002, for example, BCA's leadership team took action to mitigate the adverse consequences of the illness on the business's operating plan within a week of the initial outbreak. The abrupt decline in air traffic to Hong Kong, Singapore, and other Asian business centers signaled that the number of future aircraft deliveries to the region would fall—perhaps precipitously. Accordingly, BCA scaled back its medium-term production plans (delaying the scheduled ramp-up of some programs and accelerating the shutdown of others) and adjusted its multiyear operating plan to reflect the anticipated financial impact.

Rule 7: Reward and Develop Execution Capabilities

No list of rules on this topic would be complete without a reminder that companies have to motivate and develop their staffs; at the end of the day, no process can be better than the people who have to make it work. Unsurprisingly, therefore, nearly all of the companies we studied insisted that the selection and development of management was an essential ingredient in their success. And while improving the capabilities of a company's workforce is no easy task—often taking many years—these capabilities, once built, can drive superior planning and execution for decades.

For Barclays' Bob Diamond, nothing is more important than "ensuring that [the company] hires only A players." In his view, "the hidden costs of bad hiring decisions are enormous, so despite the fact that we are doubling in size, we insist that as a top team we take responsibility for all hiring. The jury of your peers is the toughest judgment, so we vet each others' potential hires and challenge each other to keep raising the bar." It's equally important to make sure that talented hires are rewarded for superior execution. To reinforce its core values of "client," "meritocracy," "team," and "integrity," Barclays Capital has innovative pay schemes that "ring fence" rewards. Stars don't lose out just because the business is entering new markets with lower returns during the growth phase. Says Diamond: "It's so bad for the culture if you don't deliver what you promised to people who have delivered . . . You've got to make sure you are consistent and fair, unless you want to lose your most productive people."

Companies that are strong on execution also emphasize development. Soon after he became CEO of 3M, Jim McNerney and his top team spent 18 months hashing out a new leadership model for the company. Challenging debates among members of the top team led to agreement on six "leadership attributes"—namely, the ability to "chart the course," "energize and inspire others," "demonstrate ethics, integrity, and compliance," "deliver results," "raise the bar," and "innovate resourcefully." 3M's leadership agreed that these six attributes were essential for the company to become skilled at execution and known for accountability. Today, the leaders credit this model with helping 3M to sustain and even improve its consistently strong performance.

The prize for closing the strategy-to-performance gap is huge—an increase in performance of anywhere from 60 to 100 percent for most companies. But this almost certainly understates the true benefits. Companies that create tight links between their strategies, their plans, and, ultimately, their performance often experience a cultural multiplier effect. Over time, as they turn their strategies into great performance, leaders in these organizations become much more confident in their own capabilities and much more willing to make the stretch commitments that inspire and transform large companies. In turn, individual managers who keep their commitments are rewarded—with faster progression and fatter paychecks—reinforcing the behaviors needed to drive any company forward.

> *The prize for closing the strategy-to-performance gap is huge—an increase in performance of anywhere from 60 to 100 percent for most companies.*

Eventually, a culture of overperformance emerges. Investors start giving management the benefit of the doubt when it comes to bold moves and performance delivery. The result is a performance premium on the company's stock—one that further rewards stretch commitments and performance delivery. Before long, the company's reputation among potential recruits rises, and a virtuous circle is created in which talent begets performance, performance begets rewards, and rewards beget even more talent. In short, closing the strategy-to-performance gap is not only a source of immediate performance improvement but also an important driver of cultural change with a large and lasting impact on the organization's capabilities, strategies, and competitiveness.

Beyond Best Practice

Lynda Gratton
London Business School

Sumantra Ghoshal
London Business School

Savvy executives recognize that a company's core organizational and operational processes are crucial to realizing its competitive potential. These organizational processes integrate the goals of the business into its employees' day-to-day activities via routines. Executives also know that a primary route to the development of such processes and practices is the study of best practice. The enterprise's capacity to flourish depends in part on their ability to capture and embed best practices from their own and other companies. Without mechanisms that facilitate the sharing of best-practice knowledge—such as visits to exemplar companies, communities of practice and the use of experts—companies would be consigned to reliving the same mistakes day after day. Searching for and then articulating, refining and embedding best-practice ideas brings companies in a sector to a level playing field. Those companies that fail to adopt best-practice processes rapidly become complacent laggards.[1]

But our research into high-performing companies shows that while the search for and adoption of best-practice processes is indeed necessary, it is not sufficient. (See "About the Research.") Other types of processes, which we call "signature processes," also can be crucial. We find that a unique bundle of signature processes combined with industry best practice ultimately enables a company to prosper and compete.

We use *signature* to describe how these processes embody a company's character and signify their idiosyncratic nature. Signature processes arise from passions and interests *within* the company; by contrast, concepts of best practice arise *outside* the

company. So while one task of every executive is to find and adapt best practice, in a sense *bringing the outside in,* an added critical task of management is to learn to identify and preserve the company's signature processes. This added duty might be thought of as the need to *bring the inside out.*[2]

The distinction between a signature process and an industry best practice is not absolute, however. If a company's signature processes prove especially advantageous, they may be imitated by other companies so often that they eventually become known as best practices. Toyota Motors Corp.'s lean production is an example of a process that began as a signature for the company. It espoused the values and aspirations of Toyota's leaders and has brought the company significant competitive advantage over a long period of time. Many other companies have sought, sometimes with limited success, to adopt the process of lean manufacturing. In this article, we use the term *signature processes* to refer to processes that have evolved internally from executives' values and aspirations, and the term *best practice* for ideas developed outside the boundaries of a business unit or company.

The subtle but crucial differences between standard best-practice processes and unique signature processes first became clear in our research. We found surprising and intriguing practices and processes in many of the high-performing companies. Here are three examples:

- The CEO of a large, fast-moving company requires that all members of the senior executive team meet every morning of the workweek between 9:30 and 10:30 Greenwich Mean Time to discuss the previous day's events. There are about 10 members of this team; those who are not physically present take part via videoconferencing. The meeting is without a prior

Reprinted from "Beyond Best Practice," by Lynda Gratton and Sumantra Ghoshal, *MIT Sloan Management Review* 46, no. 3, (Spring 2005), pp. 49–57. Used by permission. Copyright © 2005 by Massachusetts Institute of Technology. All rights reserved. Sumantra Ghoshal passed away in March 2004, while he was working on this research project.

agreed-upon agenda, instead addressing the issues uppermost in the minds of the executive team.

- Employees of a second multinational company are part of an organizational modular structure that is realigned frequently. These restructurings typically take place over the weekend. While these realignments result in new business groups, they leave intact many of the working relationships that take place within the modular teams.

- The business unit heads of a third large company are required to spend considerable amounts of time supporting the performance of their peers in other businesses, particularly those businesses that are underperforming. A significant proportion of the bonuses of the more successful business unit heads is dependent on improved results by the underperforming businesses.

Each of these processes is highly idiosyncratic. We have not witnessed any of them in scores of other companies we have studied over the last decade. In fact, these processes fly in the face of what is generally accepted as best practice. For example, best practice suggests that the CEO's role is to meet, perhaps on a weekly or even monthly basis, with the executive team and proceed through a previously agreed-upon agenda. So why tie up the whole senior team in daily morning meetings without set agendas? Similarly, best practice in organizational restructuring suggests that restructurings should take place as infrequently as possible in order to create relatively stable organizational structures and minimize confusion. So why restructure frequently? Finally, best practice in performance management requires that managers be responsible for what they can personally affect. So why reward people on the basis of the performance of others who are outside their direct line of accountability?

Yet the three companies in which these processes flourish are not corporate laggards: Each has outperformed many competitors over the last five years. Nor are they clustered in a single sector known for eccentricities, such as a creative industry or IT. The companies in question are in retail banking, high-technology equipment manufacturing and marketing, and oil exploration and distribution. Nor are these processes and practices that top executives would like to be rid of. On the contrary, executives in each company view the practice in question as

unique; its idiosyncrasy is celebrated and seen as a key aspect of the company's success. The procedures in question are believed to serve as one of the crucial links between the processes of the organization and the vision, values and behaviors of top management. They are imbued with energy and passion.

The morning meetings take place in the Edinburgh headquarters of the Royal Bank of Scotland Group with group chief executive Fred Goodwin. Founded by royal charter in 1727, RBS was a small bank until the early 1990s, even by U.K. standards. By 2003, however, RBS had grown to become the fifth-largest bank in the world by market capitalization, ahead of such familiar names as Merrill Lynch, Goldman Sachs and UBS. This was facilitated by a spate of acquisitions, including the acquisition of London-based National Westminster Bank Plc and Citizens Financial Group of Rhode Island. RBS's record organic growth from 1997 to 2002 was the best of all major banks in Europe. At the same time, its cost–income ratio—perhaps the most widely used measure of efficiency and productivity in the banking business—was, at 45 percent, one of the lowest among comparable companies.

Why did three highly successful companies adopt processes that differ significantly from general views of best practice? The answers lie in the idiosyncrasy of the processes.

The frequent restructurings occur at Nokia Corp., whose senior team is led by chairman and CEO Jorma Ollila. The company's history stretches back more than 140 years. Until the early 1990s, Nokia was a conglomerate with businesses as diverse as rubber products, paper, consumer electronics and computers. The company transformed itself during the 1990s into a focused telecommunications business supplying telecommunications network equipment and systems and mobile phones. Nokia's performance from 1997 to 2003 was superior to its competitors, and its brand—practically unknown a decade earlier—has been ranked as one of the 10 most valuable brands in the world by Interbrand Corp., a global branding consultancy based in New York.

The "peer assist" policy exists at BP PLC, the United Kingdom's largest industrial enterprise, under the guidance of group chief executive John Browne.

About the Research

This article is based on our case research over the last five years into how dynamic capabilities lead to competitive advantage. We focused on companies that had demonstrated superior performance from 1997 to 2002, compared to their peers. However, superior performance can be a result of other factors, such as a monopoly, extensive regulations or heavy use of patents. We chose companies whose success was not due to those factors. We studied eight firms and use data from three of them in this article. We collected data in two stages for each company. First, a broad array of secondary sources was used to create a preliminary picture of the company and the industry. Next, we conducted structured interviews with the CEO and 20 to 30 members of the company's executive committee and other significant staff. In addition, we interviewed executives in different functions and at different levels, including the operating-level managers who actually were involved in day-to-day activities connected with the focus area we had chosen.

Both authors were present during all interviews and were supported by a research assistant. Ours was collaborative and participative research. We engaged in discussions with managers as competent and trusted co-researchers, attempting to arrive at a shared interpretation of data. Having identified the key practices, we sought to build a historical perspective and discussed this in depth with the executives.

In 1992, facing rapidly deteriorating business results because of rising debts, rising unit costs and falling oil prices after the Persian Gulf War, BP's board cut the company's dividend and replaced the chief executive. The situation had changed dramatically by 2003. BP had successfully acquired and integrated Amoco, Arco and Castrol, and had achieved the lowest unit cost of operations among comparable firms and the highest return on capital employed. It delivered after-tax profits of more than $1 billion per month.

Why did these three highly successful companies adopt processes that differ significantly from general views of best practice? And, perhaps even more surprisingly, why do the executives involved believe these processes are a key part of their company's success?

The answers lie in the idiosyncrasy of these signature processes and their potential to create the energy to drive high performance. This idiosyncrasy is a direct embodiment, a "signature," of each company's history, values and top executive team. The combination of values, experiences and passion enables these idiosyncratic processes to flourish against all odds.

Adopting best-practice processes gets a company to a level playing field. But the very nature of best practice, drawn as it is from a common pool of industry knowledge, means that the adopters of best practice are always susceptible to being copied by other companies that catch up with them. In contrast, the signature processes at these three companies are so idiosyncratic and so much a part of their organizational heritage and values that competitors would have difficulty replicating them. These signature processes certainly look fascinating to the observer; for example, the peer groups at BP have been widely discussed across the multinational best-practice community. But although they may be the stuff of exciting presentations and intriguing book chapters, the peer-assist process is apparently unpalatable to most companies, and we know of none that have replicated BP's peer groups.

Signature processes are acceptable within the companies in which they develop because very often they have grown as the company grows and are associated with the executive team's passion and values. They are part of the fabric, the way of behaving, the "way we do things around here." So while the task of every executive is to find and adapt best-practice processes from outside the organization to strengthen the company, an added critical task of management is to be able to articulate the company's signature processes.

This is a difficult task. Executives need skills in developing and encouraging best-practice *and* signature processes. However, much of what executives have been schooled to do in developing conventional best practice flies in the face of the creation of signature processes. Our recommendations for creating signature processes actually reverse some of the very prescriptions of best practice. To nurture signature-process development, executives should rediscover their company's heritage and unlock the treasures that have been languishing half-forgotten within their organization rather than search externally, as they do for best-practice processes. Managers should become sensitive to and elaborate on those processes in the company about which people are passionate and should become more in tune with the organization's values and beliefs.

Signature processes developed internally by Nokia, RBS and BP stand in contrast with some of their best-practice processes based on ideas adapted from outside the organization. In all three companies, best-practice processes and signature processes differ in their origins, their development mechanisms and their core. (See Exhibit 1.)

Best-Practice Origins: External Search

One important best-practice process at RBS is the bank's approach to day-to-day management of many of its projects. Over the last decade, its teams have developed their project management approach by an extensive external and internal search of best practice in project management. They have exchanged best practices across the bank, they have occasionally engaged external consultants to add to their knowledge and they have sent executives to external programs on project management. From this sharing of external and internal knowledge, they have developed and documented the RBS way of project management. Project management best practice has been carefully adapted to something more closely aligned with RBS's business goals and context, particularly with respect to conducting projects with increased speed and a larger number of project teams.

This adaptation of project management best practice paid off in the firm's 1999 takeover of NatWest. In 2002, the RBS team announced that the NatWest takeover had been completed and that the 446 systems within NatWest's IT platform had migrated successfully to the RBS platform, which was a quarter of the size. This was the biggest IT integration project of its kind in the financial sector. As analysts at one firm put it, "The integration of NatWest will become a textbook example of how to do deals."

Best-Practice Development: Adaptation

Nokia uses a strategic planning process that follows many of the elements of best practice in strategy creation. Every six months, up to 400 people are hand-picked from across the company and divided into teams. The teams are asked to explore 5 to 15 themes that senior executives believe are most crucial to the company's future. For a two-month period, the team members interview a wide range of internal and external experts. The team members then get together

Exhibit 1 **Understanding Best-Practice and Signature Processes**

Companies need both standard best-practice techniques as well as unique signature processes, which are developed internally. The origin, development and core of the two differ greatly.

	Best Practice	Signature Processes
Origin	*"Bringing the outside in"*: Starts with external and internal search for best-practice processes	*"Bringing the inside out"*: Evolves from a company-specific history
Development	Needs careful adaptation and alignment to the business goal and industry context	Needs championing by executives
Core	Shared knowledge from across the sector	Values

for two days to consolidate their findings and identify any additional information they need. At the end of the second round of research, the teams prepare a report and presentation for the executive board. The information from these reports is incorporated into what Nokia call its "strategy road maps," which are then shared with key employees.

Widely held beliefs about best practice in strategy creation suggest that the process should be both top-down and bottom-up and should include a focus on the short term, as well as consideration of longer-term challenges and scenarios. The plan should be written down and communicated to those assigned to implement it. In other words, the basic elements of Nokia's strategy creation process can be found in textbooks of business strategy and in the practices of companies across the world.

Nokia's strategy creation process has developed and adapted this external understanding of best practice to the firm's business goals. Adaptation has taken place in two key areas, which, as in the case of RBS, are about speed and involvement. First, the norm of best-practice strategy creation is an annual cycle. Nokia adapted this to a six-month cycle because of the fast cycle time of its industry. Second, the best-practice norm for strategy creation suggests the involvement of a relatively small group of people. Nokia involves more than 400 people across the company, an adaptation to the complexity of its technology, which requires multiple technological insights.

Best-Practice Core: Shared Knowledge from across the Sector

BP also has its share of classic best-practice processes. Take, for example, BP's leadership development process. Over the last two decades, BP's senior team systematically has identified high-potential employees and placed them in an "Individual Development Program." Many members of the current senior team, including Browne, have come through the IDP process. IDP participants are given access to exciting and interesting jobs and have opportunities to develop a broad range of competencies and extensive networks. Yet, although this leadership process is important to BP, it is no more than a reflection of industry best practice. The executives responsible for

the leadership process frequently meet with their colleagues from other multinational companies. They attend conferences on leadership development and read some of the books written on the topic. BP has a leadership process that delivers a constant stream of talented young people, as it is designed to. The process is a classic one, almost indistinguishable from leadership programs existing at other large multinational companies.

> *The origin of the morning meetings at Royal Bank of Scotland [can be traced] back to the bank's founding in 1727, [when] banking was a gentlemanly and leisurely business.*

Good companies abound with best-practice processes. RBS's project management process, Nokia's strategic planning process and BP's leadership development process are but single examples of broad portfolios of best practice that each company has developed. These best-practice processes are built from tools and techniques that are valuable in any organization and are crucial to the engine of competition. But they are not unique, and they can be easily replicated by others. In other words, they are not signature processes.

HOW SIGNATURE PROCESSES EVOLVE

In our research, we have discovered that best-practice processes and signature processes develop along rather different paths. The origin of RBS's project management, Nokia's strategy maps and BP's leadership development are all grounded in an external and internal search for best practice. In contrast, we found that the origins of the signature processes—RBS's morning meetings, Nokia's modular structure and BP's peer-assist process—were different. Each of these signature processes was firmly embedded in the history and values of the company and the executives that lead it. At the core of best practice is shared industry knowledge, whether about how strategic plans are created, executives developed or projects managed. At the core of signature processes are the values of each company.[3]

Signature processes are not the same as best practice. Signature processes have the potential to advance the company's competitive position beyond just a level playing field. But to harness this potential, executives have to understand the origin, development and core of signature processes. Managers need, in fact, to develop a whole new way of thinking about processes. (See Exhibit 2.)

Signature Process Origins: A Company-Specific History

When executives at BP, Nokia, and RBS described and mapped how their signature processes developed, the descriptions were deeply rooted in each company's heritage and their own beliefs and values.

Take, for example, the origin of the morning meetings at RBS, which the senior team can trace back to the bank's founding in 1727. The bank originally was one of many regional banks serving local citizens, in this case in the Scottish city of Edinburgh. Banking was a gentlemanly and leisurely business in the 18th and 19th centuries: Bankers typically met with their team in the mornings, and the afternoons were reserved for more leisurely pursuits. The practice of morning meetings died out in the 1930s at most banks, victim of a faster, more dislocated time. However, the practice remained at RBS and has evolved into a signature process.

The origin of Nokia's modular structure can be traced back to the software technology heritage the firm began to develop in the 1980s. At that time, Nokia's software technology was built from two core elements: the software mantra of reusability, and standardization through the creation of a shared common platform. Reusability is considered crucial to software development. When programmers at Nokia built new software programs, up to 75 percent of the program typically was built by reconfiguring modules of previously developed software. This sped up the development process, reduced the cost of making new programs and ensured that knowledge could be rapidly shared. The technological leverage Nokia achieved by reusability and reconfiguration depended on the programmers' skills in slicing and sequencing the modules of previous programming.

This competence and philosophy of reusing modules, which began in the 1980s as an element of its technology, became the design foundation of the modular architecture of the company structure. In the software programs, the modular units that were reconfigured were pieces of written software. In the company architecture, the modular units that were reconfigured were modular teams of people with similar competencies and skills. In the same way that modular reconfigurations ensured that valuable software was not lost, the modular architecture ensured that valuable skills, competencies and team relationships that were held within teams of people were not lost or dissipated. In effect, the signature process of structural modularity has its roots in the software production process of reusability through modularity and reconfiguration.

Nokia's signature process of structural modularity also has its roots in a technology philosophy of shared common platforms and standardization. Reconfiguring different modules of software requires that each module be developed in a similar way with a similar underlying architecture. That is, it requires a high degree of standardization. For more than 20 years, a mind-set, discipline, and philosophy of reusability and standardization had pervaded Nokia. It was well understood that only through common tools, platforms, technologies, and languages could speed be achieved. This became the backdrop to Nokia's signature process: the capacity to build modular corporate structure.

The quality of this signature process was tested in January 2004, when Nokia announced and then implemented what would represent a fundamental organizational shake-up for most companies. In order to focus more closely on changing customer aspirations, Nokia's nine business units were restructured into four. At the same time, in order to ensure speed of innovation and production across the globe, all the customer and market operations, product development operations, and manufacturing, logistics and support activities were reorganized on a companywide basis into three horizontal business units. This organizational change was made fully effective within one week and involved about 100 people assuming new jobs. The rest of the employees had no such change because the modular teams to which they belonged were simply reconfigured. The discipline, philosophy, and mind-set of reconfiguration through standardization and shared platforms, which had initially developed from the company's technology history, ensured that Nokia could skillfully and rapidly reconfigure its human resources to meet changing customer needs.

Signature Process Development: Championing by Executives

Signature processes develop from the heritage and values of the company and are shaped by the philosophy and wisdom of the executive team. BP's peer-assist signature process was not constructed from an amalgam of best practices. Instead, it sprang more than 15 years ago from the mind and philosophy of a young business-unit head who passionately believed that businesses could and should be more focused on cooperation and respect and less on hierarchy and control. This young executive began to put his ideas into practice over the years—initially in his own small part of the business, then in a major business area and, finally, when he became chief executive, across the whole of BP. The signature process of peer assist has its heritage not in industry best practice but in the values and beliefs of chief executive Browne and his team.[4] Browne explained the three core premises of his philosophy: "that people worked better in smaller units . . . that any organization of scale should create proprietary knowledge through learning . . . that there is a very different interaction between people of equal standing."

Peer groups were created by breaking the monolith of the old BP into 150 business units, which enabled people to work in smaller units. The peer-assist process created unprecedented opportunities for learning, as people from different parts of the company shared ideas and knowledge. By creating an organizational structure that was more horizontal than vertical, Browne was able to transform many previous interactions—which would predominantly have been from senior executive to middle manager—to interactions among peers of equal standing.

Browne's philosophy and passion is clearly evident in BP's peer process. The same degree of philosophy and passion is apparent in how Nokia's executive team had talked about and then designed their signature process of structural modularity, which reflects the personal heritage, knowledge, and philosophy of the company's senior team.

> *Nokia's Finnish executives share a heritage of technical education and a "taste for complexity" that enabled a process as complex as Nokia's modular structure to be created.*

Until recently, Nokia's senior management team, all of whom joined Nokia in the late 1970s and early 1980s, were, with one exception, Finnish by birth.

Exhibit 2   **How the Signature Processes Evolved**

Unlike best-practice ideas adopted from outside the organization, signature processes are rooted in a company's history and values.			
Company	**RBS**	**Nokia**	**BP**
Signature Process Origin *(Company-specific)*	Morning meetings Banking tradition dating back to 1727	Modular structure Technology heritage from the 1980s: • Reusability through reconfiguration • Standardization	Peer assistance Initially created in the mid-1990s
Development *(By executive champion)*	• CEO is rigorous manager • Executive team values speed and decision making	Shared education of the senior team: • Technical focus • "Taste for complexity"	Philosophy of CEO John Browne: • Small scale • Learning • Nonhierarchical
Core *(Values)*	Respect Accountability	Renewal Respect	Learning Accountability

(The company has recently added two more non-Finns to its team.) Nokia's Finnish executives share a very similar set of developmental experiences. Most completed a substantial part of their education within the highly respected Finnish education system, and many were trained at either the Helsinki School of Economics or the Helsinki University of Technology, both world-class technical institutions. This shared heritage of technical education created within the executive team a shared experience base from which a vision could be created. Pekka Ala-Pietilä, currently president of Nokia Corp. and head of customer and market operations, described it this way: "What unites the top team is the capacity to think in abstract terms and to digest complex issues and to use pattern recognition. We can understand what is important and what is less important. It is an intellectual challenge. Many have backgrounds in research; there is a taste for complexity."

This "taste for complexity" has enabled a process as complex as Nokia's modular structure to be created. Having similar technological backgrounds, the senior executives understood the need for standardization and common platforms, so they were able to build standard global platforms while other companies built enormous variety across countries. They understood the notion of modularity and the need to keep people within modular teams together over time, even as the organization restructured. Their shared tacit assumptions, drawn from a shared history and way of seeing the world, created the foundation upon which this signature process could develop.

The same deep involvement of the executive team is apparent in RBS's signature process, the morning meetings that have come to embody the characteristics and values of CEO Fred Goodwin and the senior executive team. The practice and discipline of morning meetings is seen as a crucial part of the way in which the senior executives work as a team. It is a process that has meaning to them and enables them to articulate their values about the need for speed and decision making. Of the morning meetings at RBS, Johnny Cameron, a member of the executive team, had this to say: "Fred loves the morning meeting. It is his chance to put his imprint on whatever is happening. . . . Fred is more rigorous as a manager than anyone I have ever met. He is extraordinarily demanding. For example, in the morning meeting he will look at a budget and go straight to page 23 and ask about it. He is very rigorous about apparently small things and this pervades the company. People say, 'If Fred sees this, what would he say?'"

RBS is not alone in having a signature process that expresses the values of the company. In the companies we studied, the values of the CEO and the executive team were at the core of the signature process, and this tight alignment between the values and the process created passion and energy that drove the company forward.

Signature Process Core: Company Values

Learning is a core value at BP. "In order to generate extraordinary value for shareholders," explains Browne, "a company has to learn better than its competitors and apply that knowledge throughout its businesses faster and more widely than they do."[5] For BP, the value of learning is balanced by a second core value: accountability. The idiosyncrasies of the peer-assist process flourish because they enhance that balance.

Peer assist creates the expectation that people will learn from each other across the company. Polly Flinn, a former Amoco employee who is vice president of retail marketing at BP, quickly learned the company's values and philosophy. While serving as the retail business-unit lead in Poland in 1999, Flinn asked for assistance from four BP leaders, who came together in a peer-assist team to look at the strategy for Poland and give Flinn advice. After Flinn implemented the advice, the retail marketing business in Poland became profitable for the first time. She again called on the peer-assist process when faced with the challenging task of masterminding the development and rollout of BP's new retail offering, BP Connect. Flinn recalled that "of the 300 people involved in [the peer assist], only 10 percent actually had performance contract goals related to the rollout of BP Connect, yet because of their desire to share their skills and their expectations of federal behavior, people contributed." The peer-assist process embodies BP's key values. It exemplifies the learning organization and yet ensures that business-unit heads are held accountable for their performance.

Similarly, the morning meetings at RBS exemplify the bank's core values of respect and accountability. These values, which executives see as emanating from the company's Scottish Presbyterian roots, emphasize the virtues of pragmatism, honesty and a respectful egalitarianism that is practical, down-to-earth, straightforward and action-oriented. The morning meetings provide an opportunity for these historical values to become a day-to-day reality; members of the executive team are able to meet with each other daily and engage in straight talk. Respect for the collective team is vital to the smooth running of these meetings. Executives work with each other collaboratively and respectfully, and the meetings reinforce the collective accountability of the senior team. They also reflect the deep concern in the bank's culture for accountability and taking action; when an executive agrees to take action, there is a presumption that the agreement is binding. Actions are discussed and agreed upon, and the meeting moves to the next point. Accountability is at the heart of how the morning meetings are conducted.

> *People participating in signature processes are "in the flow." The energy they exhibit is palpable because, deep down, the process expresses who they are and what they value.*

Nokia's signature process of modularity, like BP's peer-assist process and RBS's morning meetings, essentially embodies the company's values. Company executives say that Finnish cultural values have played a key role in shaping Nokia's environment. Finnish culture historically has sprung from the values of trust, directness and inclusivity in social relationships. Like other Scandinavians, the Finns have an abhorrence of hierarchical authority and a fundamental belief in respect for the individual.[6] At the same time, Finland is a country of renewal. It has one of the highest education rates in the world and one of the most technically literate populations. Finland has renewed itself, and Nokia has attempted to do the same. During Nokia's history, the Finnish values of respect for the individual and renewal have become deeply embedded in a company that has been, in its executive team, essentially Finnish. They permeate Nokia's modular structure, which embodies

a respect for individuals by enabling people to work primarily in collegial teams to which they bring their own competencies. At the same time, the structure's capacity for rapid reconfiguration ensures that renewal can take place.

THE EXECUTIVE ROLE IN SIGNATURE PROCESSES

Three CEOs and their teams are at the heart of BP's peer assistance, RBS's morning meetings and Nokia's modular architecture. Each CEO believes that the signature process in question is key to the organization's longer-term success, and each is committed to maintaining the signature process. What can other executives learn from these companies?

Most executives know that values are important in their day-to-day behavior; few understand that these values can be integrated into their business's goals and individual employee behaviors through a small number of signature processes. What we learned from John Browne, Jorma Ollila and Fred Goodwin is that these exceptional CEOs use processes as a means to communicate their values and the values of their organizations. To do so requires the CEOs to be very clear about what those values are.

The executive role in identifying externally developed best practice is essentially rational and analytical; in contrast, the executive role in signature processes is value-based and insightful. RBS CEO Goodwin "loves" the morning meetings. We could hear the pride in senior executive Mikko Kosonen's voice when he talked of Nokia's modular structure: "One of the distinctive characteristics . . . is the organizational architecture. It is avant-garde." Over hours of discussions, Nokia executives described the structure, their ideas behind it, how it worked and what it meant. Figures were drawn, analogies made and examples given, all with enthusiasm and caring. And at BP there is a huge amount of pride in the philosophy that underpins the peer-assist process. As deputy CEO Rodney Chase remarked, "In our personal lives, we all know how much joy we derive from helping others. As a mother, a brother or a friend, we derive great pleasure from helping those who are close to become successful. Why don't we believe that the same can be true in business? Historically, we didn't. But you can get there—when people in the company can almost derive more pleasure from the success of others than from their own success."

We saw that, when people are participating in the signature processes in these three companies, they are "in the flow." The energy they exhibit is palpable, and they are oblivious to time.[7] When people participate in the signature processes, they feel good precisely because, deep down, the process expresses something they believe in. They feel that what they are doing deeply resonates with who they are and what they value.

Best-practice processes are planned with rigor and built with a clear time frame in mind. By contrast, the creation of signature processes is more serendipitous and is by its nature slower, more complex and more expressive of values. It is this distinction that makes the day-to-day reinforcement of signature processes one of the most valuable opportunities executives have to continually link the goals of a business to its values. This linkage is energizing and can bring meaning to an enterprise in a way that best practices never can.

ACKNOWLEDGMENTS

The authors thank Felipe Monteiro and Michelle Rogan, doctoral candidates at London Business School, as well as Alison Donaldson, Ph.D., for their research assistance. The broader study on which this paper is based was supported by grants from the ESRC/EPSRC Advanced Institute of Management Research.

References

1. Many scholars have considered the development of best-practice processes. See, for example, J. Lowe, R. Delbridge and N. Oliver, "High Performance Manufacturing: Evidence From the Automotive Components Industry," Organizational Studies 18, no. 5 (1997): 783–798. For an overview of the development of best-practice processes such as lean manufacturing, see K. Clark and T. Fujimoto, "Product Development Performance: Strategy, Organization and Management in the World Auto Industry" (Boston: Harvard Business School Press, 1991).

2. Our initial thinking was framed within the concept of dynamic capabilities. For glimpses at the characteristics of dynamic capabilities, see K. M. Eisenhardt and J. A. Martin, "Dynamic Capabilities: What Are They?" Strategic Management Journal 21 (October–November 2000): 1105–1121; and D. J. Teece, G. Pisano and A. Shuen, "Dynamic Capabilities and Strategic Management," Strategic Management Journal 18 (August 1997): 509–533.

3. The idea that culture and values can be a source of competitive advantage has been debated for some time. This is a central thesis of T. E. Deal and A. A. Kennedy, "Corporate Cultures: The Rites and Rituals of Corporate Life" (Reading, Massachusetts: Addison-Wesley, 1982); it was elaborated in E. Schein, "Organizational Culture and Leadership" (San Francisco: Jossey-Bass, 1985). The potential link with performance was argued in the resource-based theory of the firm; see J. B. Barney, "Organizational Culture: Can It Be a Source of Sustained Competitive Advantage?" Academy of Management Review 11, no. 3 (1986): 656–665.

4. We have described peer assist as an integrating mechanism in S. Ghoshal and L. Gratton, "Integrating the Enterprise," MIT Sloan Management Review 44, no. 1 (fall 2002): 31–38. The process also has been described from a learning perspective in M. T. Hansen and B. V. Oetinger, "Introducing T-Shaped Managers: Knowledge Management's Next Generation," Harvard Business Review 79 (March 2001): 107–116.

5. A more detailed description of John Browne's philosophy of learning can be found in S. E. Prokesch, "Unleashing the Power of Learning: An Interview With British Petroleum's John Browne," Harvard Business Review 75 (September–October 1997): 5–19.

6. Finnish values are described in G. Hofstede, "Culture's Consequences: International Differences in Work-Related Values" (Newbury Park, California: Sage, 1980); and A. Laurent, "National and Corporate Cultures: A Study of Six European Countries," INSEAD working paper, Fontainebleau, France, 1982.

7. The idea of "flow" has been described in M. Csikszentmihalyi, "Finding Flow: The Psychology of Engagement With Everyday Life" (New York: Basic Books, 1997).

The Integration of Lean Management and Six Sigma

Edward D. Arnheiter
Rensselaer Polytechnic Institute

John Maleyeff
Rensselaer Polytechnic Institute

INTRODUCTION

Over the last two decades, American industrial organizations have embraced a wide variety of management programs that they hope will enhance competitiveness. Currently, two of the most popular programs are Six Sigma and lean management. Six Sigma was founded by Motorola Corporation and subsequently adopted by many U.S. companies, including GE and AlliedSignal. Lean management originated at Toyota in Japan and has been implemented by many major U.S. firms, including Danaher Corporation and Harley-Davidson. Six Sigma and lean management have diverse roots. The key issue driving the development of Six Sigma was the need for quality improvement when manufacturing complex products having a large number of components, which often resulted in a correspondingly high probability of defective final products. The driving force behind the development of lean management was the elimination of waste, especially in Japan, a country with few natural resources.

Both Six Sigma and lean management have evolved into comprehensive management systems. In each case, their effective implementation involves cultural changes in organizations, new approaches to production and to servicing customers, and a high degree of training and education of employees, from upper management to the shop floor. As such, both systems have come to encompass common features, such as an emphasis on customer satisfaction,

Reprinted from "The integration of lean management and Six Sigma," Edward D. Arnheiter, John Maleyeff, *The TQM Magazine*, Vol. 17, No. 1, 2005. Used by permission of Emerald Group Publishing Ltd.

high quality, and comprehensive employee training and empowerment.

With disparate roots but similar goals, Six Sigma and lean management are both effective on their own. However, some organizations that have embraced either Six Sigma or lean management might find that they eventually reach a point of diminishing returns. That is, after reengineering their operating and supporting systems for improvement by solving major problems and resolving key inefficiencies, further improvements are not easily generated, as illustrated in Figure 1. These organizations have begun to look elsewhere for sources of competitive advantage. Naturally, lean organizations are examining Six Sigma and Six Sigma organizations are exploring lean management. The term *lean Sigma* has recently been used to describe a management system that combines the two systems (Sheridan, 2000). In this paper, the term *lean, Six Sigma (LSS) organization* will be used to describe an entity that integrates the two systems.

The purpose of this paper is to eliminate many misconceptions regarding Six Sigma and lean management by describing each system and the key concepts and techniques that underlie their implementation. Since these misconceptions may tend to discourage the education necessary for proponents of one system to become educated into the key elements of the other system, the misconceptions will be addressed one-by-one. This discussion will be followed by a description of what lean organizations can gain from Six Sigma and what Six Sigma organizations can gain from lean management. Finally, some suggestions will be

Figure 1   **Improvements over Time with Six Sigma or Lean Management Alone**

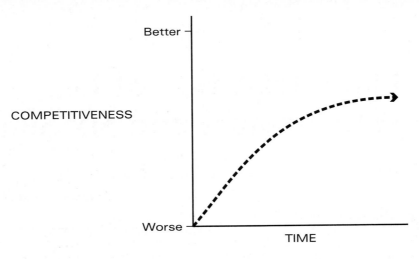

made regarding concepts and methods that would constitute a lean, Six Sigma organization.

OVERVIEW OF SIX SIGMA

The roots of Six Sigma can be traced to two primary sources: total quality management (TQM) and the Six Sigma statistical metric originating at Motorola Corporation. Today, Six Sigma is a broad long-term decision-making business strategy rather than a narrowly focused quality management program.

From TQM, Six Sigma preserved the concept that everyone in an organization is responsible for the quality of goods and services produced by the organization. Other components of Six Sigma that can be traced to TQM include the focus on customer satisfaction when making management decisions, and a significant investment in education and training in statistics, root cause analysis, and other problem solving methodologies. With TQM, quality was the first priority. The main tools of TQM included the seven tools of quality: control charts, histograms, check sheets, scatter plots, cause-and-effect diagrams, flowcharts, and Pareto charts; and the seven management tools of quality: affinity diagrams, interrelationship digraphs, tree diagrams, matrix diagrams, prioritization matrices, process decision program charts, and activity network diagrams (Sower et al., 1999).

The six-sigma metric was developed at Motorola in 1987 in response to substandard product quality traced in many cases to decisions made by engineers when designing component parts. Traditionally,

design engineers used the "three-sigma" rule when evaluating whether or not an acceptable proportion of manufactured components would be expected to meet tolerances. When a component's tolerances were consistent with a spread of six standard deviation units of process variation, about 99.7 percent of the components for a centered process would be expected to conform to tolerances. That is, only 0.3 percent of parts would be nonconforming to tolerances, which translates to about 3,000 nonconforming parts per million (NCPPM).

At Motorola, as products became more complex, defective products were becoming more commonplace while at the same time customers were demanding higher quality. For example, a pager or cell phone included hundreds of components. Each component typically included numerous important quality characteristics. It was not uncommon for a product to include thousands of opportunities for defects (OFDs) in each product sold (Harry and Schroeder, 2000). Traditional three-sigma quality for each OFD was no longer acceptable. For example, consider a product that contains 1,000 OFDs. If, for each OFD, three-sigma quality levels are achieved, only about 5 percent of the products would be defect free. The calculation used to obtain this probability requires raising the fraction conforming (0.997) to the power of 1,000, and is based on the binomial probability distribution (Devore, 2000).

The formula used to determine the probability of defect-free products provides only an approximate guideline for two reasons. Since three-sigma is the

Figure 2   **Process Average Shifting ± 1.5 Sigma Units**

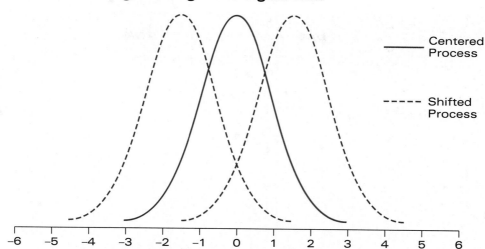

STANDARDIZED PROCESS VARIATION (SIGMA UNITS)

minimum design standard, it would be expected that many products would surpass the three-sigma standard. On the other hand, the 0.997 conformance probability assumes a centered process and it would be expected that many processes would not be centered every time a component is produced. The calculation does, however, effectively illustrate the challenge inherent in producing defect-free products. Assuming 1,000 OFDs, only 37 percent of products will be free of defects if the quality level at each OFD averaged 99.9 percent, and 90 percent of products will be free of defects if the quality level at each OFD averaged 99.99 percent.

Other industries face similar challenges in achieving superior quality. In addition to the consumer electronics industry, other products with a large number of OFDs include automobiles, engines, airframes, and computers. Many industries where products are less complex also face similar challenges. Manufacturers of medical devices and other products where defects in the field may cause harm must achieve almost perfect quality. Companies that manufacture less complex products but sell them in very large volumes also need to be focused on achieving superior quality.

At Motorola, when studying the relationship between component quality and final product quality it was discovered that, from lot to lot, a process tended to shift a maximum of 1.5 sigma units (McFadden, 1993). This concept is shown graphically in Figure 2, which shows a centered process and processes shifted 1.5 sigma units in both directions. Table I provides the relationship between component quality and final product quality, assuming that the full 1.5 sigma shift takes place. In Table I, Sigma level is the standardized process variation (see Figure 2), OFD quality is the NCPPM if the process shifts a full 1.5 sigma units, and the probabilities in the table provide the proportion of final products that will be free of defects. For example, if the company sets a goal for final product quality of 99.7 percent and products include about 1,000 OFDs, then the 3.4 NCPPM corresponding to the Six-Sigma metric would became the standard against which all decisions were made.

In late 1999, Ford Motor Company became the first major automaker to adopt a Six Sigma strategy. At Ford, each car has approximately 20,000 OFDs. Therefore, if Ford were to attain Six Sigma quality, approximately 1 car in every 15 produced would contain a defect (Truby, 2000). It is interesting to note in Table I that if Ford operated at a 5.5 sigma level, about 50 percent of their cars would include at least one defect.

Today, Six Sigma is a combination of the Six Sigma statistical metric and TQM, with additional innovations that enhance the program's effectiveness while expanding its focus. The main components of Six Sigma retained from TQM include a focus on the customer, recognition that quality is the responsibility of all employees, and the emphasis on employee training. The Six Sigma metric is also used, but in an expanded fashion.

With Six Sigma, the value of an organization's output includes not just quality, but availability, reliability, delivery performance, and after-market

Table I **Final Product Quality Level (percentage conforming)**

Sigma Level	OFD Quality (NCPPM)	Number of OFDs per Product				
		100 (%)	500 (%)	1,000 (%)	5,000 (%)	20,000 (%)
2.5	158,655	0.0	0.0	0.0	0.0	0.0
3.0	66,807	0.1	0.0	0.0	0.0	0.0
3.5	22,750	10.0	0.0	0.0	0.0	0.0
4.0	6,210	53.6	4.4	0.2	0.0	0.0
4.5	1,350	87.4	50.9	25.9	0.1	0.0
5.0	233	97.7	89.0	79.2	31.2	1.0
5.5	32	99.7	98.4	96.9	85.3	53.1
6.0	3.4	100.0	99.8	99.7	98.3	93.4
6.5	0.29	100.0	100.0	100.0	99.9	99.4
7.0	0.019	100.0	100.0	100.0	100.0	100.0
7.5	0.0010	100.0	100.0	100.0	100.0	100.0

service. Performance within each of the components of the customer's value equation should be superior. Hence, the Six Sigma metric is applied in a broad fashion, striving for near perfect performance at the lowest level of activity. In addition, Six Sigma programs generally create a structure under which training of employees is formalized and supported to ensure its effectiveness. All employees involved in activities that impact customer satisfaction would be trained in basic problem solving skills. Other employees are provided advanced training and required to act as mentors to others in support of quality improvement projects.

OVERVIEW OF LEAN MANAGEMENT

The concept of lean management can be traced to the Toyota production system (TPS), a manufacturing philosophy pioneered by the Japanese engineers Taiichi Ohno and Shigeo Shingo (Inman, 1999). It is well known, however, that Henry Ford achieved high throughput and low inventories, and practiced short-cycle manufacturing as early as the late 1910s. Ohno greatly admired and studied Ford because of his accomplishments and the overall reduction of waste at early Ford assembly plants (Hopp and Spearman, 2001). The TPS is also credited with being the birthplace of just-in-time (JIT) production methods, a key element of lean production, and for

this reason the TPS remains a model of excellence for advocates of lean management.

By contrast, the traditional U.S. production system was based on the "batch-and-queue" concept. High production volumes, large batch sizes, and long non-value-added queue times between operations characterize batch-and-queue production. Batch-and-queue techniques developed from economy of scale principles, which implicitly assumed that setup and changeover penalties make small batch sizes uneconomical. These methods typically result in lower quality since defects are usually not discovered until subsequent operations or in the finished product.

Lean management emphasizes small batch sizes and, ultimately, single-piece flow (i.e., transfer batch size = 1). The term pull is used to imply that nothing is made until it is needed by the downstream customer, and the application of a make-to-order (MTO) approach whenever possible. In some industries, such as the personal computer business, MTO production has become the de facto business model. The Dell "direct sales model," for example, quickly converts customer orders into finished personal computers ready for shipment (Sheridan, 1999). The initial "pull" on the Dell production line is the telephone or electronic order from the customer. The direct sales model also allows Dell to customize each unit to the customer's specifications.

The lean production goal of eliminating waste (*muda* in Japanese), so that all activities along the value stream create value, is known as perfection.

Efforts focused on the reduction of waste are pursued through continuous improvement or *kaizen* events, as well as radical improvement activities, or *kaikaku.* Both *kaizen* and *kaikaku* reduce *muda,* although the term *kaikaku* is generally reserved for the initial rethinking of a process. Hence, perfection is the goal and the journey to perfection is never ending (Womack and Jones, 1996).

Another element of lean management is the reduction of variability at every opportunity, including demand variability, manufacturing variability, and supplier variability. Manufacturing variability includes not only variation of product quality character istics (e.g., length, width, weight), but also variation present in task time (e.g., downtime, absenteeism, operator skill levels). Lean management attempts to reduce task time variation by establishing standardized work procedures. Supplier variability includes uncertainties in quality and delivery times. The reduction in supplier variability is often achieved through partnerships and other forms of supplier–producer cooperation.

Lean production practices will often reduce lead times so drastically that it becomes feasible to practice MTO production, and still provide on-time deliveries. Even when a make-to-stock (MTS) approach is required (e.g., a high-volume consumer products company filling large supply and distribution channels), reducing lead times improves replenishment times, thereby lowering inventories throughout the supply network, and making the supply chain more respondent to demand uncertainties.

It should be mentioned that individual processes do exist for which batch-and-queue systems are still currently necessary. This is often the case when performing operations such as chrome plating, where large batches are placed in plating tanks. In wrench manufacturing, for example, steel forgings might move in a single-piece flow through a U-shaped machining cell, but then accumulate into a large batch at the end of the cell before being moved to a chrome plating station. In fact, very few lean manufacturers have pure single-piece-flow systems throughout their entire operation.

Lean management also applies to indirect and overhead activities. Any policy or procedure having a goal of optimizing the performance of a single portion of a company risks violating lean management rules. For example, a purchasing manager who is given a reward for cutting costs of component parts may sacrifice quality to achieve his or her goal. Accounting systems that measure efficiency of output for individuals or departments may encourage the generation of products when no demand exists.

Quality management practices in lean production emphasize the concept of zero quality control (ZQC). A ZQC system includes mistake proofing (poka-yoke), source inspection (operators checking their own work), automated 100 percent inspection, stopping operations instantly when a mistake is made, and ensuring setup quality (Shingo, 1986). Typically, inspections are performed quickly using go–no go gages rather than more time consuming variable measurement methods.

Quality practices in batch-and-queue generally emphasize acceptance sampling performed by dedicated inspectors, product quality audits, and statistical process control (SPC). Thus, for equivalent process quality levels, poor quality in a batch-and-queue system would result in high external failure costs, whereas poor quality in a lean production system would cause high internal failure costs (see Figure 3).

MISCONCEPTIONS REGARDING LEAN MANAGEMENT AND SIX SIGMA

It is clear that lean management and Six Sigma were derived from two different points of view. Lean production was derived from the need to increase product flow velocity through the elimination of all non-value-added activities. Six Sigma developed from the need to ensure final product quality by focusing on obtaining very high conformance at the OFD level. In order for proponents of one program to learn from the other program, some common misconceptions should be dispelled. The key misconceptions are described below.

Key Misconceptions Regarding Lean Management

The most common misconception of lean management is lean means layoffs. While this misconception may be due to the term *lean* (especially in the context of *lean and mean*), it is a misinterpretation of the term. In lean management, if an employee were performing non-value-added activities within his or her job, management and the employee would

Figure 3   **Batch-and-Queue Versus Lean Quality Systems**

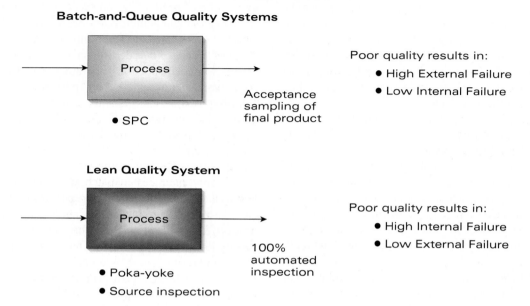

work together to find a better way to perform the job to eliminate the non-value-added activities. Laying off the employee would be counterproductive since a knowledgeable person would no longer be available and the remaining employees would be reluctant to take part in future waste elimination projects. Hence, layoffs cannot take place in the context of lean management, unless it becomes an absolute necessity and every effort to reassign or retrain the employee fails (Emiliani, 2001).

Another misconception is that lean only works in Japan, because of their unique culture. This view is unsubstantiated. In fact, lean management is not a universal system in Japan and some of the most successful lean management implementations have been within non-Japanese companies (Emiliani, 2003). The source of the misconception may be the belief that Japanese workers are by nature more frugal than their international counterparts. Even if this statement were true, eliminating waste and being frugal often conflict, such as when an engineer designs an inferior part to save money.

Another key misconception is that lean is for manufacturing only. Even in a manufacturing environment, lean management views each step in the process as a service step, where customer value is added with minimal waste. Within this framework, processing claims in the insurance industry, evaluating loan applications at a bank, and treating patients in a hospital all involve performing activities synonymous with the lean management viewpoint.

In any business where customers exist and activities take place to satisfy those customers, lean management can be practiced successfully.

A final misconception is that lean only works within certain environments. This view is heard from managers in operations that are traditionally large batch operations as well as from managers of diverse job-shop operations. While these types of operations may never conform to the "lot size of one" principle, lean management encompasses much more than manufacturing process design. If attempts were made to identify and eliminate all non-value-added activities throughout the organization, these companies would be practicing important aspects of lean management. These companies could also pursue other elements of lean management, by continuously attempting to follow lean principles when adopting new manufacturing technologies. For example, new technologies have become available that allow for small lot sizes on processes that traditionally require long setup or cycle times, including semiconductor wafer cleaning (Lester, 2000), coating/laminating (Friedman, 2000), and chemical testing (Anné, 2000).

Key Misconceptions Regarding Six Sigma

The most common misconception of Six Sigma is that it is the new flavor of the month, pushed by quality consultants in a way similar to the way Deming Management, TQM, business process reengineering

(BPR), and ISO 9000 were pushed in the recent past. Unfortunately, there will always be consultants who jump onto any bandwagon, take a seminar and proclaim themselves experts in a program. Six Sigma is no exception to this phenomenon. However, Six Sigma should be considered state-of-the-art in terms of quality management, in that it borrows from previous programs, especially Deming's management philosophies and TQM's focus on the customer, and adds new features such as a comprehensive training structure and a broad definition of value from a customer's perspective to include not only quality, but service and delivery. It is fair to say that while the name of Six Sigma may change in the future, the main features will be carried over to subsequent programs and new and improved versions will emerge.

Another misconception of Six Sigma is that the goal of 3.4 NCPPM is absolute and should be applied to every opportunity tolerance and specification, regardless of its ultimate importance in the customer's value expression. While the 3.4 NCPPM was derived at Motorola based on the characteristics of its products, Six Sigma programs do not use this metric as an absolute goal in all cases. As part of Six Sigma, the Pareto principle is applied so that improvement projects will focus on the "lowest hanging apple" and make improvements where they matter the most. Since no company's business remains static very long, new products and services will generally provide a never-ending source of low-hanging apples. Alternatively, examples can be found where a goal of 3.4 NCPPM will never be good enough and the target must be set at a higher sigma level. For example, the nuclear power, medical device, and aerospace industries all require the pursuit of exceptional quality to prevent catastrophic loss of human life.

As a related point, proponents of ZQC systems may conclude that ZQC is preferred to Six Sigma given that ZQC results in zero NCPPM rather than "settling" for 3.4 NCPPM. This point is invalid for two reasons. First, as shown in Figure 4, the six-sigma metric is applied to the output from a process, before inspection takes place. The "zero" in the ZQC system applies to output from processes after an inspection takes place. Second, many inspection systems are prone to inspection errors. Studies have shown that some inspection systems pass nonconforming items at alarming rates. These inspection errors will be especially prevalent on sensory inspections. For example, a study at an automotive manufacturer found that trained inspectors passed 73 percent of nonconforming items based on a sensory inspection (Burke et al., 1995). Hence, ZQC does not necessarily mean zero defects escaping the inspection.

A final misconception of Six Sigma is that it is a quality only program. As described earlier, the concept of Six Sigma "quality" relates to the entire customer value equation. Its applicability is broad, encompassing manufacturing, delivery, service, and maintenance components.

INTEGRATING LEAN MANAGEMENT AND SIX SIGMA

It was pointed out earlier that companies practicing either lean management or Six Sigma alone might reach a point of diminishing returns. In this section, benefits that may be derived by combining the

Figure 4   **Typical Measurement Points in the Six-Sigma and ZQC Philosophies**

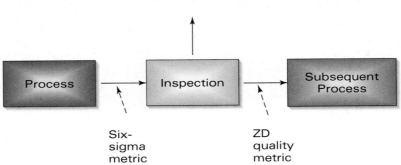

programs are described. In addition, recommendations are made that will help companies practicing one of the programs to integrate the programs via evolutionary, rather than revolutionary, changes.

What Can Lean Organizations Gain from Six Sigma?

Lean organizations should make more use of data in decision making and use methodologies that promote a more scientific approach to quality. For example, when quality problems occur within a lean management system, defects are likely to be identified internally via the ZQC system. When this occurs, waste is incurred in a number of ways. First, there is a loss of opportunity for the production of that component since operation times are synchronized with demand via the pull system of production control. Second, cost is added through rework or scrap. Third, indirect personnel and other overhead must be available to handle the scrap and rework, such as a repair department.

As an example, consider a manufacturing cell with a two-minute cycle time. The cell operates for two 8-hour shifts, resulting in a target production of 480 units per day. Work in the cell consists of 20 individual tasks, and each unit of product possesses a total of 100 OFDs. In this cell, when the 480-unit daily target is not met due to system variations (e.g., defects, machine downtime, power failures), overtime must be utilized. Table II lists the average number of overtime hours that would need to be scheduled per day to accommodate the quality level noted. For example, if component quality at the

OFD level were 1,000 NCPPM (0.1 percent), then on average 1.5 hours of overtime would be required per day. If this were the case, the company could allow for buffer quantities to be preproduced, but this practice also creates waste and is undesirable.

The ZQC system also has the potential to cause reliability and quality problems due to the interaction of tolerances in complex products. An example involving Ford transmissions illustrates the problem caused by relying on tolerance-based pass/fail criteria during inspections. Ford had a problem with warranty claims for automatic transmissions. The transmissions were made at both the Ford Batavia (Ohio, USA) facility and at a Mazda facility in Japan. Data showed that customer satisfaction was higher for the Mazda-built transmissions. Subsequently, samples of both Ford and Mazda transmissions were disassembled and each component part was measured (Gunter, 1987). The Ford transmissions all conformed to tolerances, but exhibited a much higher level of dimensional variation than the Mazda transmissions. With a product as complex as a transmission, the interaction of the parts caused more failures in the Ford transmissions. In order for a lean producer to ensure that this problem is not repeated, less dependence would need to be placed on pass/fail attribute inspections and more on keeping processes on target.

The Ford transmission example illustrates a phenomenon that is likely to occur whenever attribute, or go–no go, inspections are used to judge quality, as is often the case in ZQC systems. By collecting and analyzing variable measurements using control charting methods, processes can be effectively kept on target. In cases where variable measurements are

Table II   **Average Number of Overtime Hours versus Quality Levels**

Sigma Level	OFD-Level Quality (NCPPM)	Percentage Defect-Free Products	Average Overtime Hours/Day
3.8	10,000	36.40	10.1
4.6	1,000	90.48	1.5
5.2	100	99.01	0.2
5.8	10	99.90	0.0
6.0	3.4	99.97	0.0
6.3	1	99.99	0.0

costly or time consuming, narrow limit gauging may be used to keep processes on target (Ott and Schilling, 1990). Alternatively, precontrol, also known as stoplight control, may be used within the context of ZQC (Salvia, 1988). A comparison of control charts and precontrol shows that under most conditions, control charts are better suited for keeping processes on target (Maleyeff and Lewis, 1993).

What Can Six Sigma Companies Gain from Lean Management?

A competitive company must have both high-quality goods and provide a high quality of service. For example, a company that operates in a batch-and-queue mode runs the risk of providing poor service to customers even if quality is at Six Sigma levels. By reducing manufacturing lead times, a company that is producing to order will enhance competitiveness by achieving faster deliveries or by meeting promised due dates a higher proportion of the time. A company that is producing to stock will gain from reduced lead times by decreasing the horizon of their forecasts and by replenishing stocks more often, thereby increasing the company's revenues and inventory turnover rate. Six Sigma organizations should include training in lean management methods that eliminate all forms of waste, such as *kaizen,* reducing setup times, and mapping the value stream. Two examples will be used to show how Six Sigma organizations may get to a point of diminishing returns (illustrated in Figure 1), due to the non-use of certain lean management methodologies.

Consider the following scenario, adapted from a Harvard Business School case study (Wong and Hammond, 1991). A manufacturing company that includes a children's knitwear division is using a process-oriented layout (i.e., the plant is organized by machine type). For this product, the average number of operations is 10 and the average processing time per operation is one minute. Like many companies run in this traditional batch-and-queue mode, processing is done in batches since machine setup times and the reluctance to risk idle machinery cause the company to accumulate large WIP inventories on the shop floor. In the case, it is noted that an average of 30,000 garments of work-in-process inventory exists

on the shop floor and the average manufacturing lead time is 15 days. The 15-day lead time results in a percent value added time of 0.14 percent.

Table III shows that, by reducing WIP inventory, thereby increasing the proportion of value-added time, the lead time can be reduced dramatically. For example, the lead time can be reduced to 17 hours by increasing the value added proportion to just 1 percent. It is within lean management that Six Sigma organizations will learn how to increase the value added time of their operations.

Consider an alternative example involving a typical Six Sigma improvement project where an organization is experiencing too many missed due dates. Efforts to address the problem might begin with the "Five whys" root cause analysis, an appro-ach also often practiced in a lean organization. The result of the "Five whys" series of questions are:

1. Problem is missing due dates—why?
2. Lead times are long—why?
3. Not enough capacity—why?
4. Long setup times—why?
5. Die adjustment is time-consuming.

At this point, two types of decisions are possible:

1. Increase capacity by purchasing additional machinery.
2. Increase capacity by reducing the setup times.

The latter alternative is preferable in terms of cost and would be the obvious choice in a lean organization. In this case, the real root cause in this situation may be that the lack of lean production knowledge

Table III   Effect of Percent Value-Added Time on Manufacturing Lead Time

Percent Value-Added Time	Lead Time (hours)	Lead Time (days)
0.14	119.9	15.0
0.5	33.3	4.2
1	16.7	2.1
5	3.3	0.4
10	1.7	0.2
25	0.7	0.1

within the organization has perpetuated and institutionalized long setup times.

The Intersection of Lean Management and Six Sigma

The performance of a business is determined by the complex interactions of people, materials, equipment, and resources in the context of the program that manages these interactions. It is fair to say that management theory regarding operating systems is still evolving. While both Six Sigma and lean management represent the state of the art, each system gives priority to certain facets of organizational performance. Therefore, in a highly competitive environment, diminishing returns may result when either program is implemented in isolation. A thorough analysis of the two programs provides some likely reasons why the programs alone may fail to achieve absolute perfection.

Figure 5 summarizes the nature of improvements that may occur in organizations that practice lean management or Six Sigma, and the corresponding improvements that an integrated program could offer. The horizontal axis represents the customer's perspective of value, including quality and delivery performance. The vertical axis represents the producer's cost to provide the product or service to the customer. Under either system, improvements will

be made, but these improvements will begin to level off at a certain point in time. With Six Sigma alone, the leveling off of improvements may be due to the emphasis on optimizing measurable quality and delivery metrics, but ignoring changes in the basic operating systems to remove wasteful activities. With lean management alone, the leveling off of improvements may be due to the emphasis on streamlining product flow, but doing so in a less than scientific manner relating to the use of data and statistical quality control methods.

CONCLUSIONS

A lean, Six Sigma (LSS) organization would capitalize on the strengths of both lean management and Six Sigma. A LSS organization would include the following three primary tenets of lean management:

1. It would incorporate an overriding philosophy that seeks to maximize the value-added content of all operations.
2. It would constantly evaluate all incentive systems in place to ensure that they result in global optimization instead of local optimization.
3. It would incorporate a management decision-making process that bases every decision on its relative impact on the customer.

Figure 5   **Nature of Competitive Advantage**

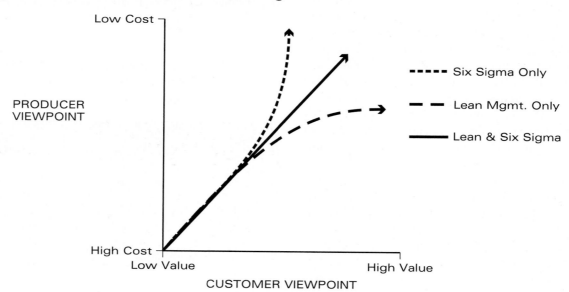

A LSS organization would include the following three primary tenets of Six Sigma:

1. It would stress data-driven methodologies in all decision making, so that changes are based on scientific rather than ad hoc studies.

2. It would promote methodologies that strive to minimize variation of quality characteristics.

3. It would design and implement a companywide and highly structured education and training regimen.

References

Anné, D. C. (2000), "Modern mobile laboratories," *Pollution Engineering,* Vol. 32 No. 8, pp. 37–9.

Burke, R. J., Davis, R. D., Kaminsky, F. C. and Roberts, A. E. P. (1995), "The effect of inspector errors on the true fraction nonconforming: an industrial experiment," *Quality Engineering,* Vol. 7 No. 3, pp. 543–50.

Devore, J. L. (2000), *Probability and Statistics for Engineering and the Sciences,* 5th ed., Duxbury Press, Pacific Grove, CA, pp. 119–26.

Emiliani, M. L. (2001), "Redefining the focus of investment analysts," *The TQM Magazine,* Vol. 13 No. 1, pp. 34–50.

Emiliani, M. L. (2003), *Better Thinking, Better Results,* The Center for Lean Business Management, Kensington, CT.

Friedman, S. (2000), "Where materials and minds meet," *Package Printing and Converting,* Vol. 47 No. 2, pp. 24–5.

Gunter, B. (1987), "A perspective on the Taguchi methods," *Quality Progress,* Vol. 20 No. 6, pp. 44–52.

Harry, M. and Schroeder, R. (2000), *Six Sigma,* Doubleday, New York, NY, p. 65.

Hopp, W. J. and Spearman, M. L. (2001), *Factory Physics,* 2nd ed., Irwin/McGraw-Hill, New York, NY, p. 25.

Inman, R. R. (1999), "Are you implementing a pull system by putting the cart before the horse?," *Production and Inventory Management Journal,* Vol. 40 No. 2, pp. 67–71.

Lester, M. A. (2000), "Quick drying enables single-wafer cleans," *Semiconductor International,* Vol. 23 No. 12, p. 54.

McFadden, F. R. (1993), "Six-Sigma quality programs," *Quality Progress,* Vol. 26 No. 6, pp. 37–42.

Maleyeff, J. and Lewis, D. A. (1993), "Pre-control or X-bar charts: an economic evaluation using alternative cost models," *International Journal of Production Research,* Vol. 31 No. 2, pp. 471–82.

Ott, E. R. and Schilling, E. G. (1990), *Process Quality Control,* Ch. 7, McGraw-Hill, New York, NY.

Salvia, A. A. (1988), "Stoplight control," *Quality Progress,* Vol. 21 No. 9, pp. 39–42.

Sheridan, J. H. (1999), "Focused on flow," *Industry Week,* Vol. 248 No. 19, pp. 46–8.

Sheridan, J. H. (2000), "Lean Sigma synergy," *Industry Week,* Vol. 249 No. 17, pp. 81–2.

Shingo, S. (1986), *Zero Quality Control—Source Inspection and the Poka-yoke System,* Productivity Press, Cambridge, MA.

Sower, V. E., Savoie, M. J. and Renick, S. (1999), *An Introduction to Quality Management and Engineering,* Prentice Hall, Upper Saddle River, NJ, pp. 33–45.

Truby, M. (2000), "Nasser, Ford embrace data-driven quality plan," *Detroit News,* 26 January, p. F1.

Womack, J. P. and Jones, D. T. (1996), *Lean Thinking,* Simon & Schuster, New York, NY, pp. 90–8.

Wong, A. and Hammond, J. H. (1991), *Doré-Doré,* Harvard Business School Publishing, Cambridge, MA.

Linking Goals to Monetary Incentives

Edwin A. Locke
University of Maryland

Every experienced executive knows the importance of rewarding good performance and also how difficult it is to design an incentive system that works as it is supposed to. A recent article in *The Wall Street Journal*[1] reported that Hewitt Associates found that 83 percent of companies with a pay-for-performance system said that their incentive plan was "only some what successful or not working at all."

Consider just some of the ideas that must be addressed in designing an incentive system:

- What should be the form of the incentive plan? That is, how, specifically, should pay be tied to performance?

- How do you keep employees from short-cutting or cheating in order to get their bonus?

- Which actions or outcomes should you pay bonuses for?

- What will be the effect of incentives on actions or outcomes that are not included in the incentive plan?

- How many different actions or outcomes can an employee actually manage?

- If more than one action or outcome is part of the plan, how should they all be combined or weighted?

- What do you do when market conditions change radically and make the incentive system ineffective or meaningless?

It is no accident that most companies constantly tinker with, and often radically overhaul, their in-

Reprinted from "Linking goals to monetary incentives," Edwin A. Locke, *Academy of Management Executive*, Vol. 18, No. 4, 2004, pp. 130–33. Used by permission of the Academy of Management via The Copyright Clearance Center.

centive plans. Many can never seem to get it quite right. This article will try to provide some answers to the above questions, but I will start by addressing one fundamental issue. Hewitt's research indicates that one major cause of the failure of incentive plans is the lack of clear goals.

Goal-setting theory, as summarized by Gary Latham in the previous article, asserts that people must have goals that are both clear and challenging in order to motivate high performance. The question then arises: How do you combine goal setting with incentives?

I will describe four different methods and the pros and cons of each.

METHOD 1: STRETCH GOALS WITH BONUSES FOR SUCCESS

This method involves assigning people difficult or stretch goals, giving them a substantial bonus if they reach them and no bonus if they do not. The respective advantages and disadvantages of this method include the following:

Pros. This method provides a strong incentive to attain the goals. There is a huge difference in reward between attaining the goals and failing, even by a small amount, to attain the goals. Further, it leaves no ambiguity about what is required of the person to receive the bonus.

Cons. A weakness of this method is ironically the result of its strength. Precisely because the motivation for goal attainment is so high, there is considerable temptation for the person to think short range, e.g., pile up excess inventory with customers (which will come back to haunt the company in the next quarter), take short cuts (e.g., lower quality, ignore maintenance, increase risk), and cheat (e.g., exaggerate or make up totally fake results, cook the books) in order to receive the bonus.

To prevent these and other dysfunctional outcomes, the organization needs rules of conduct: ethical norms or standards that are clearly communicated and consistently enforced. The moral atmosphere or climate of an organization is set by the CEO and the senior management team, who must not only be impeccable role models but who must make certain that the company's ethical standards are strictly enforced (e.g., those who flout them must be fired). If the CEO and top managers are not personally honest, it leads to demoralization and cynicism among employees. This, in turn, can lead to a whole culture of dishonesty.

Another downside of this method is that performance which is very high but just misses the goal yields no bonus at all. This can be very demoralizing to competent, hard-working employees. It can lay the seeds for future dishonesty.

METHOD 2: MULTIPLE GOAL LEVELS WITH MULTIPLE BONUS LEVELS

This method avoids some of the problems of method 1. Instead of a single goal level with the bonus being "all or none," there are multiple goal levels (for example, five), and a different bonus level is attached to each—the higher the goal level attained, the higher the reward.

Pros. There is less temptation for employees to short cut or cheat here, because even if they do not attain the top goal level, they can get a bonus for making the next lower level. Highly competent employees who just miss a high-level goal still get rewarded.

Cons. Because there are multiple goal and bonus levels, employees may be less motivated to try for the highest level than in the case of method 1. A problem can occur if employees are content to try for the lowest goal level that is rewarded. For this bonus system to be effective, the CEO or senior management must

set some minimum goal below which performance is considered inadequate. Then the multiple-goal level can start from a level above this minimum. However, this approach still does not push everyone to try for the highest goal. Furthermore, there is no tangible motivation to exceed the top goal because no further bonus would be forthcoming. Of course, pride and recognition are powerful motivators independent of money, but most employees want consistency between tangible and intangible rewards.

METHOD 3: A LINEAR SYSTEM

This method is recommended by Michael Jensen of the Harvard Business School.[2] It is a variation on method 2, which involves increments. Consider five levels of sales goals, e.g., +5 percent, +10 percent, +15 percent, +20 percent, +25 percent. The employee who makes 24.5 percent will get rewarded, but only for reaching the 20 percent goal, so may still feel disappointed at coming close to, but just missing, the 25 percent goal. The simplest solution here is to make this a continuous bonus system, e.g., a 2 percent bonus for every 1 percent increase in sales. (Obviously 1 percent is still an increment but a very small one.)

Pros. This method eliminates two disadvantages of methods 1 and 2. First, there is no "loss" for getting close to a higher goal level and just missing it; an employee gets paid for exactly what is achieved. This, according to Jensen, further decreases the temptation to cheat or take shortcuts. Second, there is no upper limit on the bonus. Under methods 1 and 2 if a person attained the top goal for an increase in sales (say 25 percent), the employee would get the same bonus even if that person achieved a +50 percent or +100 percent sales increase. So there would be little tangible incentive to exceed +25 percent. Under method 3, however, if the person gets a 50 percent sales increase, the bonus would be 2×50 percent or 100 percent.

Cons. There is still the problem inherent in method 2: less pressure for the employee to "stretch." Setting a minimum goal would help as with method 2, but many people might not be financially motivated to go far beyond the minimum. Also some companies could have a problem with unlimited compensation for employees; it might seem unfair to people in other parts of the company (e.g., nonsales jobs) where a meaningful linear system would be hard to design.

METHOD 4: MOTIVATE BY GOALS BUT PAY FOR PERFORMANCE

This method, suggested by Gary Latham of the Rotman Business School (University of Toronto), makes the tie between goals and performance a little looser than under the other methods. The employee is given specific, challenging goals, but the decision about bonus awards is made after the fact so as to take account of the full context in which the goal is pursued. The relevant context factors might include: e.g., how much was actually achieved regardless of what the goals were, how the company as a whole did, how difficult the goals *really* were, in the light of such factors as resources, obstacles, and market conditions, as well as the methods the employee used to attain the goals (e.g., ethical behavior). Often the bonus decisions will be made by a management team because they may have more knowledge than any one executive.

Pros. The main benefit of this method is its flexibility and comprehensiveness. For example, an employee who tries for a hard goal under very difficult circumstances but does not quite reach it can still be well rewarded, whereas an employee who attains an allegedly hard goal which turned out not to be so hard in hindsight would get less (or be penalized or fired if the goal was attained unethically). This method, of course, is similar to what is called "merit based pay," but it would require that clear goals be set for every action or outcome that was important to the organization.

Cons. This method requires the boss to be knowledgeable about the full context and also to be objective in order to minimize favoritism or bias. Many people at the CEO and top-management levels lack these qualities. Of course, with poor quality leadership, the other incentive plans may not work either, because no method is better than the people who use it.

WHICH METHOD IS BEST?

To the author's knowledge, there have been no published field studies or laboratory experiments comparing the effectiveness of the four systems described above or even comparing any two of them. Thus there is no basis for claiming that one is necessarily better than others. Much may depend on the nature of the business and the quality of the management. This topic is ripe for further study and experimentation.

Observe, from the Kerr and Landauer article, that GE decided to make a distinction between goals that were absolutely essential to the organization and goals that were not. Stretch goals, which allowed credit for failure, were used mainly in the latter case. This implies that different incentive rules could be applied to each type of goal.

Cheating or short-cutting can occur under any incentive system; thus, as noted earlier, all companies need a strict (and enforced) code of ethics and well-designed control systems. (GE was known for having excellent control systems).

WHAT ACTIVITIES SHOULD GOALS BE SET FOR?

For whatever is important. This will certainly involve performance outcomes and often goal-setting for the critical actions that lead to those outcomes. For example, sales, specifically repeat sales, depend on customer satisfaction, and there are specific actions that can be taken to satisfy customers (e.g., on-time delivery, high-quality products, changing policies as a result of customer feedback, etc.). Customer satisfaction is a "soft" measure, yet it can be measured quantitatively. Information-sharing with other managers, executives, employees, and so forth is another desirable action that often can benefit the entire company. Information-sharing could be measured by means of peer assessments. Developing subordinates is another important activity required for long-term organizational success.

It is possible to make causal maps that show the relationship between behaviors and outcomes. Consider this example: knowledge sharing within the company and with customers → improved customer service and better products → improved customer satisfaction → improved customer retention and sales → increase in profits. Note that goals can be set for any part or all parts of this sequence. Observe also that the benefit of the causal map is that it forces one to formulate the plan for improving the final outcome: profits. The causal inputs constitute a plan.

Actions and outcomes for which goals are not set and which are not rewarded monetarily will probably get minimum attention unless they are causally connected to the actions and outcomes that are measured and rewarded. A poorly devised bonus system can create "tunnel vision"—a focus only on what gets rewarded to the neglect of other important outcomes. Of course, bonus systems are *supposed* to focus attention and effort in a certain direction to the exclusion of others. Thus it is critical to do a lot of thinking about which actions and outcomes are important before creating a goal and reward system.

> It is critical to do a lot of thinking about which actions and outcomes are important before creating a goal and reward system.

HOW MANY GOALS SHOULD THERE BE?

It is important to avoid cognitive overload. No one manager, for example, could make good progress toward achieving 17 different goals, unless most of them could be delegated, nor would the manager even have the time to track progress. One person alone could probably handle somewhere between three and seven goals, depending on how difficult and complex they were and how much time was allowed for completion.

If employees are trying to achieve multiple goals, this presents a problem with respect to designing the reward system. *Ideal reward systems are simple,* and the simplest system has only one rewarded outcome or goal. The problem is that a one-goal system is usually too narrow in scope for a job. When a one-goal system is not adequate, there is an advantage to method 4, since it can take account of as many goals as the boss or top-management team considers relevant. If methods 1, 2, or 3 are used with multiple goals, then the goals have to be weighted in terms of importance.

GOAL INTEGRATION

In any organization virtually everything that happens affects everything else, for better or for worse. Ideally, goals should be integrated across the entire organization, but this is usually impossible due to time constraints. However, through knowledge sharing within and across organizational levels and departments, it is possible to coordinate essential activities (e.g., sales, marketing, and production all need to be involved if a new product is contemplated). Such coordination is what cross-functional teams are designed to achieve.

Goal integration, including knowledge sharing, may be facilitated if part of the bonus is paid on the basis of peer ratings of knowledge sharing and/or on how well the company as a whole does.

SHOULD GOALS BE CHANGED WHEN CONDITIONS CHANGE?

If goals are changed constantly (e.g., every three months), the danger is that no one will take them seriously. But if the strategic direction of a company changes, the goals need to reflect such changes. For example, when Jack Welch decided that GE would embrace the Six Sigma quality-control process, every executive was given goals to train employees in Six Sigma principles and to initiate Six Sigma projects. Bonuses were based, in part, on performance in relation to those goals.

> If goals are changed constantly (e.g., every three months), the danger is that no one will take them seriously.

What if the economy or industry turns bad? At Nucor, plant workers get paid by team productivity. If steel demand goes down, they get paid less. The same principle holds for Nucor's plant managers and executives. In some years profits drop, and no bonuses are distributed. Nucor's philosophy is: Why should plant employees and executives get bonuses when the stockholders are losing money? At Nucor they have to tough it out until business increases. A business downturn could be a signal to develop better business strategies, to cut costs, and to set new goals.

THE EFFECTIVE INCENTIVE SYSTEM

Effective bonus plans are extraordinarily difficult to set up and to maintain. It has been said that it is better to have no bonus system at all, other than simply merit pay, than to have a bad one. Bad incentive plans encourage people to do the wrong things in the wrong way, and they lead to cynicism, anger, and indifference. The first step that should be taken when considering setting up a bonus system is to ask: What do we really want people to do or accomplish? As Steve Kerr, a former GE executive, said many years ago, there is no point in rewarding A if what you want is B.[3] This issue probably takes more thought than any other aspect of an incentive system.

The second step is to set goals for desired outcomes. Make them clear and challenging. If needed, include goals for the actions that lead to the desired outcomes and not just the outcomes themselves. Make sure the number of goals assigned is doable. And do not change the goals too readily.

The third step is to consider which goals will need to be integrated within and across levels and divisions.

The fourth step is to pick the type of bonus system that is right for your company considering what you came up with in the first three steps, with full awareness of all the pros and cons of each method.

Following these steps will not guarantee that you will devise a successful bonus system, but it will definitely increase the odds.

Endnotes

[1]Chu, K. Firms report lackluster results from pay-for-performance plans. *Wall Street Journal,* 15 June 2004: D-1.

[2]Jensen, M. 2002. Paying people to lie: The truth about the budgeting process. Harvard Business School Working Paper 01-072.

[3]Kerr, S. 1995. On the folly of rewarding A, while hoping for B. *Academy of Management Executive,* 9(1): 7–14.

A Leader's Guide to Creating an Innovation Culture

Brian Leavy

Dublin City University Business School

Today, CEOs are under constant pressure to find new sources of growth in an increasingly demanding and competitive business environment. To meet this challenge, CEOs must learn to inspire their organizations to new levels of inventiveness in everything that they do, not just in marketing or new product development.

Much can be done by most organizations to boost their overall innovation. It starts with learning to tap into the creative potential of all the employees and their knowledge about customers, competitors, and processes, and the key is to establish the right organizational climate. Beyond this, many organizations also need to learn how to make themselves more attractive to more diverse and unconventional talent. Traditionally business organizations have not been the most hospitable to the unusual person with a different view of the world. In seeking to make their organizations become more driven by new ideas and new approaches, however, CEOs should not be tempted to regard innovation and creativity effort as a free-for-all. Turning ideas into commercial reality requires persistence and discipline, and overall effectiveness ultimately depends on top management being able to find the right balance between corporate creativity and efficiency.

GENERATING THE RIGHT ORGANIZATION CLIMATE

Few organizations today come near to mining the full innovative potential already at their disposal.

Reprinted from "A leader's guide to creating an innovation culture," Brain Leavy, *Strategy and Leadership,* Vol. 36, No. 4, 2005, p. 38–45. Used by permission of Emerald Group Publishing Ltd.

They can learn a lot from an example like Wal-Mart. Wal-Mart is particularly good at harnessing the ingenuity of its people and leveraging it to drive growth and competitiveness. Every store is treated as a mini-laboratory, where every day countless small experiments are taking place with pricing, product selection and merchandising displays, as employees are encouraged to look for new ideas to increase throughput. The most promising are quickly taken up and replicated across the Wal-Mart network using the company's state-of-the-art satellite communications system so that their impact is fully amplified throughout the operation. Even in an industry like mass-retailing, not known particularly known for innovation, the power of ideas can be used to drive significant growth by companies that know how leverage it.

Today, as the lure of mergers and acquisitions is fading, many companies like P&G and Glaxo, are returning to innovation as the primary strategy for driving new growth and doing it with impressive effect. At Glaxo, for example, they have begun to restructure their R&D activity into multidisciplinary units on a more "human" scale, and seeing a sharp increase in new candidate compounds emerging from "the same site, staff, people, journals, competitors and largely the same chemical libraries as before." At P&G, the major influence spurring its latest wave of innovation-led growth is the transformation of the work environment and R&D mindset, through its broad "connect and develop" program, to one that encourages a much freer flow of ideas within and beyond company boundaries. (The P&G and Glaxo examples are drawn from Buckley, 2005; Jack, 2005.)

Turning ideas into commercial reality requires persistence and discipline, and overall effectiveness ultimately depends on top management being able to find the right balance between corporate creativity and efficiency.

What many such "born again" innovators are rediscovering are some of the more enduring insights into the link between organizational climate and innovation effectiveness that have long been evident in the practices of some classic exemplars. Few companies have been as effective over the years in tapping into the creative potential of their employees as 3M. Though the company had its problems in the late 1990s, by 2003 it was back to again firing on nearly all cylinders, generating $18 billion in revenues from over 60,000 products based on 34 technological platforms. It is the quintessential ideas-driven company and is still widely recognized as the benchmark for other large corporations seeking to keep the flame of innovation alive at scale. Like 3M, many companies include a commitment to innovation in their mission statements. However, few hold themselves to that aspiration in such concrete and measurable ways. The bedrock value shaping the culture at 3M is an unshakeable belief in the power of ideas and individual initiative. The company also recognizes that entrepreneurial behavior will continue to flourish only if management is willing to accept and even applaud "well-intentioned failure." At 3M the tendency is to ask not why did you fail, but what did you learn? Innovators are continually exhorted to put their knowledge at the service of everyone in the company. At 3M, little is wasted, little forgotten. In the management and leverage of its organizational learning, the company still has few peers.

However, the mistake that many companies have tended to make in looking at 3M is to focus too much on specific innovation practices and policies, and not enough on the philosophy and values underpinning them. At 3M, they have long recognized that "maintaining a climate in which innovation flourishes may be the single biggest factor overall." What 3M and other well-known innovative companies, the likes of design firm IDEO (P&G's new "world-class strategic partner" in helping regenerate its innovative culture)

and Nokia, all share are at least four climate-setting factors that are fundamental to their success:

1. Placing of people and ideas at the heart of the management philosophy.

2. Giving people room to grow, to try things and learn from their mistakes.

3. Building a strong sense of openness, trust, and community across the organization.

4. Facilitating the internal mobility of talent.

All four are key to the development of an internal climate where individual creativity and initiative can flourish, and talent and ideas circulate freely, so that intellectual capital can be leveraged to the maximum.

At 3M, the message that "individual inspiration and effort are the heart and soul" of the company's innovation is real and pervasive, as is the view at Nokia that "this is a meritocracy" and "a place where you are allowed to have a bit of fun, to think unlike the norm, where you are allowed to make a mistake." The emphasis on community, and on the internal mobility of talent as well as ideas, in all three companies helps to foster organizational learning and serendipitous innovation. The sense of community at Nokia means that you can trust your colleagues, peers, and people around you, which "makes it possible to take pretty big risks," while at 3M it means that "ten out of ten" colleagues will respond to calls for help or ideas, promoting the fortuitous collisions of "problems looking for solutions" and "solutions looking for problems," which is a regular feature of innovation at the company. The sense of community, trust and openness also fosters organizational learning at IDEO, where they believe they are successful at innovation less because "of our flawless intellects" than "because we've done thousands of products and we've been mindful." The main considerations in allocating people to projects across IDEO are "who's available, who's the best fit and who needs this kind of experience?," while at Nokia the internal mobility of talent is supported by an intranet-based "flexible open staffing system." (Most of the quotes on 3M, Nokia, and IDEO come from the following sources: Gundling, 2000; Bartlett and Mohammed, 1995; Steinbock, 2001; Fox, 2000; Doornik and Roberts, 2001; Crawford et al., 2003; Thomke and Nimgade, 2000; Nussbaum, 2004; de Geus, 1997.)

Every Wal-Mart store is treated as mini-laboratory, where every day countless small experiments are taking place with pricing, product selection and merchandising displays, as employees are encouraged to look for new ideas to increase throughput.

ATTRACTING AND RETAINING MORE CREATIVE TALENT

One of the most controversial issues among the experts is whether the innovation advantage is primarily rooted in talent or organization. According to Peter Drucker, innovation is "organized, systematic, rational work" in which "everyone who can face up to decision making" can learn to be entrepreneurial, and Andrew Hargadon and Robert Sutton argue that innovation has "everything to do with organization and attitude" and very little to do with nurturing genius. Backing the other argument, Howard Schneiderman, a former vice president of research and development at Monsanto, held the view that "most seminal discoveries are made by a handful of outstanding researchers." Bill Gates echoed this view when he once said: "Take our 20 best people away, and I will tell you that Microsoft will become an unimportant company." (The quotes in this section come from Drucker, 1985; Hargadon and Sutton, 2000; Schneiderman, 1991; Stross, 1996.)

Innovation depends on ideas, and the primary source of ideas is talented individuals. Most organizations still have much to learn about how to make themselves more "hospitable to the unusual person with unusual ideas," and the rewards can be considerable. Sony provides a classic illustration. During his time as leader, the legendary Akio Morita remained on the lookout for potential talent in unusual places, and he persuaded many such individuals to switch careers and join his company. The outstanding example is Noria Ohga, later to succeed Morita as CEO and lead Sony into the video game business against the advice of the board. During Ohga's 13-year tenure at the top, revenues at Sony grew from $15 billion to $45 billion.

As a young undergraduate training to be an opera singer, Ohga first impressed the Sony founders with his ability to critique the pitch and tonal quality of recording equipment the company was trying to sell to Tokyo University. Soon they ordered that no prototypes be put into production before the budding artist had rendered an opinion. Morita quickly came to recognize in the brash young Ohga a rare combination of business savvy and artistic sensibility, and he pursued him relentlessly over the first six years of his career in opera, before finally persuading him to join the company full-time in a very senior capacity for a young man still in his 20s. As Ogha looked back later on his early contribution to Sony, he recalled:

> When I came on the scene, it wasn't really a modern company at all. And I'd been telling Morita for years that what we needed to do was create products that looked smart, stylish, international, and start advertising stylishly, and that's what I undertook to do, and it's amazing that Morita let me do it all, as young as I was. (Nathan, 1999; de Pree, 1989)

In the search for creative talent, leaders need to recognize that creativity and intelligence are not the same. There are many exceptionally intelligent people who are only moderately creative and vice versa. Creative people are marked by a capacity for divergent thinking, characterized by originality, fluency of ideas, flexibility, and the ability to elaborate and refine. They also tend to be "motivated to the point of obsession," according to David Webster of the notably creative design firm IDEO. Most creative production often springs from unresolved emotional undercurrents and the creative drive can often be best understood as the attempt to fashion external symbolic order, whether it be in the form of words, mathematics, music, art, or invention, out of some internal chaos ("One must have chaos in one, to give birth to a dancing star"—Nietzsche). According to the late psychologist Anthony Storr, "some split between the inner world and the outer world is common to all human beings" and "the need to bridge that gap is the source of creative endeavor" (Storr, 1991; Barron et al., 1997). The creative personality is often characterized by deep internal divisions, but also by the emotional strength to channel them to productive purposes.

This notion of the divided self also helps explain how the creative personality works. According to Jungian psychology, we each have two personalities, the one that we show to the world and the one we keep hidden from view, invisible but far from inert. Human development is a process of multiple adaptations to the expectations of parents, teachers, pastors, peers, employers and many others, and a lot of instincts and desires get repressed along the way. Creative people, as they grow and develop, tend to lock less of themselves away in their shadow personalities. According Mihaly Csikszentmihalyi, creative people are typically internally driven, yet relaxed enough to coax and wait on inspiration. They are smart yet naïve, skeptical yet credulous, playful yet disciplined, passionate yet objective. They are a fusion of opposites marked by their ability to draw with ease upon the two polarities of their personalities and to live within "uncertainties, mysteries, doubts," without "any irritable reaching" after fact, reason or premature closure. (For more on the concept of the shadow and the ability of creative people to draw on the polarities of their personalities, see Bly, 1991; Csikszentmihalyi, 1996). This is the kind of quality that Andy Law used to look out for in recruiting creative talent, during his heyday at St Luke's, the award-winning design company:

> I want to feel that people have really reached something dangerous in themselves . . . we all have places like that inside us, and at St Luke's, you have to be able to access them easily . . . Our employees . . . must peel away all levels of their personalities to become who they really are . . . It's terrifying to have no pretences about yourself, yet that's what gives you the psychological resources to question all the rules. (Coutu, 2000)

Much about managing innovation is paradoxical, not least the requirement to find talent with a streak of individualism, that will also function well in organizational settings. However, there are at least three useful guidelines that leaders can draw on when it comes to recruiting and motivating creative talent:

1. Hire individuals with a range of abilities and interests (what they like to call "bandwidth" at Microsoft).

2. Hire people with a variety of backgrounds and personalities.

3. Involve peers heavily in the selection process.

A primary characteristic of innovative companies is that they "love talent and know where to find it" (Bennis and Biederman, 1997), and they typically put much thought and effort into the recruitment process. Just over a decade ago, recruiters at 3M made a systematic attempt to define the profile of the "3M innovator," based on interviews with 25 of their most prolific inventors. Beyond their capacity for divergent thinking as described earlier, the innovators were also characterized by their breadth of interests beyond their disciplines, their eagerness to experiment and tackle the unusual, their passion for what they did, their tenacity and resourcefulness. Recruiters at IDEO also tend to look for individuals with "exceptional skills in their chosen specialties" whose interests are "eclectic and cover a wide range," polymaths not readily definable by conventional occupational labels, the likes of Ade Adekola, an MBA graduate and passionate conceptual artist, or Ilya Prokopoff, a graduate of the U.S. Naval Academy with a BA in history, a master's degree in architecture and a passion for designing furniture and tinkering with antique cars.

Innovation thrives on diversity of talent and outlook, and innovative companies like 3M and IDEO typically seek to leverage this insight even further in the composition of their project teams. Nissan Design International (NDI), another such company, developed a policy of recruiting in "divergent pairs," which grew out of an inspired early experiment. The first two designers that founding CEO, Jerry Hirschberg, selected to help get his organization up and running were very different. Al Flowers tended to approach design as an inventor/engineer, starting with a focus on the major parts and their functional possibilities, whereas Tom Semple tended to approach it more like an artist, with overall aesthetics as his first concern. As Hirshberg later explained:

> Bringing these two individuals together soon after the birth of NDI created an immediate vitality and crackling intensity. Each approached a project with utterly different priorities and work-styles. They pushed and

pulled, inspired and abraded each other . . . As we thought about the rest of our staffing needs, I began to seek out pairs of divergent designers, modelers and engineers who, taken together, would not only meet a wider range of requirements, but also constitute a stimulating and purposefully designed mix. (Hirschberg, 1999)

Making sure the fit is right is one of the most important considerations when adding new creative talent to any existing team. At IDEO, prospective hires go through a dozen or more interviews where both their personalities and skills are carefully scrutinized, and peers are deeply involved in the recruiting process. The process is just as intensive at 3M and at Nokia, where they "marinate" new talent, not just recruit it. However, "fit" at innovative companies is not to be confused with smoothness and affability. People at IDEO are expected to be "cantankerously assertive in their own disciplines," and most such innovative organizations recognize the value in constructive conflict, the clash of ideas and the competitive urge to excel beyond the best to date without or within. In creative organizations, shared obsession and pride of association provide the main cohesion, not amiability. What creative individuals seek most is the opportunity to work with people they regard highly, which is why they need to be involved in the selection process. In organizations like 3M and IDEO, peer recognition tends to be among the most powerful motivators of all.

STRIKING THE RIGHT BALANCE BETWEEN INNOVATION AND EFFICIENCY

Effective innovation also requires a delicate balancing act between play and discipline, practice and process, creativity and efficiency, where firms need to "learn how to walk the fine line between rigidity—which smothers creativity—and chaos—where creativity runs amok and nothing ever gets to market." Business leaders need to establish the right balance on at least three different levels:

1. Within the innovation process itself.
2. Between the primary functions within the organization.

3. In their overall approach to corporate management.

The need to balance creativity and discipline begins with trying to strike the right balance between play and procedure in the innovation process itself. It is widely recognized that innovation is essentially a probabilistic process of "controlled chaos" in which the only sure way to arrive at the best ideas, is to "have a lot of ideas and throw away the bad ones," as Linus Pauling, the Nobel laureate, liked to put it. It is a process that thrives on multiple, diverse, independent, and rapid experimentation, in a failure-tolerant environment that values and accommodates constructive conflict. As Bill Gates of Microsoft describes it:

> You have to listen carefully to all the smart people in the company. That's why a company like ours has to attract a lot of people who think in different ways, it has to allow a lot of dissent and then it has to recognize the right ideas and put some real energy behind them..

The mistake that many companies have tended to make in looking at 3M is to focus too much on specific innovation practices and policies, and not enough on the philosophy and, values underpinning them.

One of the key skills in the leadership of innovative group dynamics is to know when to leave hierarchy out of the process and when to bring it back in again.

One of the most popular metaphors for the creative group is the jazz combo, where leadership often shifts dynamically as different players drive the performance forward at different stages. Different players also tend to excel at different roles, some as highly original thinkers, and others more as idea brokers or promoters. All of these roles need to be recognized and valued. One of the key skills in the leadership of innovative group dynamics is to know when to leave hierarchy out of the process and when to bring it back in again. At Intel they see this as alternating between "letting chaos reign" and then "reining in the chaos." Honda uses a designated forum to generate ideas and legitimize dissent, the *waigaya* session, which anyone can convene, where rank is disregarded. Over time, IDEO has evolved a five-phase methodology (an "IDEO way") with built-in loose-tight balance that has helped produce a steady stream of highly innovative industrial designs and consumer experience solutions. Examples of such practices as these can point the way to others.

Beyond the innovation process itself, companies often need to strike the right balance among the primary functions that are key to its overall operation. This is what Intel has always tried to do, as former Intel CEO, Andy Grove, once colorfully explained:

> Being a manufacturer of high-technology jelly beans, Intel needed a special blend of two types of people. The wild-eyed, bushy-haired boy geniuses that dominate laboratories could never have taken the technology to the mass-production jelly beans stage. But the straight-laced, crew-cut manufacturing operators of conventional industry would never have generated the technology in the first place.

In a growing company, the balancing act must eventually be extended to the level of the corporation itself, when the limits of relative informality in overall coordination sooner or later become exceeded. Microsoft first came to recognize this reality in 1994, when total headcount had risen rapidly to reach the 15,000 mark. Robert Herbold was hired from the then more process-driven Procter & Gamble to become Microsoft's first chief operating officer, with a mission to improve overall profitability by "balancing centralized discipline with individual innovation." Similarly, Nokia came to recognize by 1998 a pressing need to rebalance the ideas-driven culture, which it had carefully crafted during its 1992–1996 entrepreneurial revitalization phase, with more fact-based management in order to take full commercial advantage of its rise to market leadership.

3M's recent decision to appoint its first ever outside CEO, James McNerney, is recognition that as an $18 billion company, it can no longer depend on the bottom-up creation of thousands of niche markets alone to keep on driving corporate growth but must consolidate its franchise into larger and more powerful market positions and secure them with efficiencies, not just innovation. In line with this, the company has adopted a new, more balanced, formulation guiding corporate development (global + speed + innovation = growth), and five main

integrated corporate initiatives linked to make it happen (Six Sigma, 3M Acceleration, eProductivity, Global Sourcing Effectiveness, and Indirect Cost Control). To date, the new CEO has managed to re-ignite 3M's growth through the introduction of greater discipline, sharper focus and astute business portfolio repositioning. What remains to be seen is how his productivity-driven initiatives will impact on 3M's innovative culture over the longer term. As a recent editorial in *BusinessWeek online* put it, McNerney has yet to show that he also "has the DNA for innovation."

Getting the timing right is often the key. Many years ago, Xerox "screwed down the clamps of process" too early following the development of the 914 copier, while more recently Netscape was too late in introducing business discipline in its competition with Microsoft in the browser market. During the dot-com crash, many youthful and exuberant companies paid the ultimate price for putting too much faith in creativity and too little value on traditional business discipline and experience.

Finally, maintaining the balance between innovation and efficiency is a dynamic challenge in most organizations as they continue to grow and develop, with most companies tending to oscillate between the two. At General Electric (GE) the pendulum cycled from tight to loose and back again over the Cordiner, Borch, Jones and Welch eras. The GE that Jack Welch inherited was financially strong, but a company in which procedure was dominant and the culture pervaded by control. Welch spent much of his tenure pruning and simplifying the GE corporate management model as he tried to breathe the soul of the small innovative firm back into the large company body. The biggest payoff from his effort was less the $40 million savings in bureaucratic overhead than "the sudden release of talent and energy that poured out after all the dampers, valves and barriers had been removed," and the emphasis on innovation and risk taking at GE has since been elevated to a whole new level, through corporatewide initiatives such as "imagination breakthrough," in the early years of Jeffrey Immelt's tenure. (The quotes in this section, taken in order, come from Brown and Duguid, 2001; Csikszentmihalyi, 1996; Schlender, 1998; Bartlett and Ashish, 1994; Herbold, 2002; *BusinessWeek online,* 2004; Brown and Duguid, 2001; Lowe, 1998. For more on the importance of idea brokering, see Hargadon, 2003; and Davenport et al., 2003.) Impressive as the recent GE experience has been, and continues to be, any such loosening of the corporate management process will always tend to have its limits. ABB, which under the leadership of Percy Barnevik, enjoyed a similar release of talent and energy, has since been forced to retighten corporate discipline in order to bring back more coherence to its overall corporate development process.

References

Barron, F., Montuori, A. and Barron, A. (1997), *Creators on Creating,* Tarcher-Putnam, New York, NY.

Bartlett, C. A. and Ashish, N. (1994), *Intel Corporation: Leveraging Capabilities for Strategic Renewal,* Case no. 394–141, Harvard Business School, Boston, MA.

Bartlett, C. A. and Mohammed, A. (1995), *3M: Profile of an Innovating Company,* Case study 9-395-016, January, Harvard Business School, Boston, MA.

Bennis, W. and Biederman, P. (1997), *Organizing Genius: The Secrets of Creative Collaboration,* Nicholas Brealey, London.

Bly, R. (1991), "The long bag that we drag behind us," in Zweig, C. and Abrams, J. (Eds), *Meeting the Shadow,* Tarcher-Putnam, New York, NY.

Brown, J. S. and Duguid, P. (2001), "Creativity versus structure: a useful tension," *Sloan Management Review,* Vol. 42 No. 4, pp. 93–4.

Buckley, N. (2005), "The power of original thinking," *Financial Times,* 14 January.

BusinessWeek online (2004), "Innovation is job one," *BusinessWeek online,* 12 April.

Coutu, D. (2000), "Creating the most frightening company on earth: an interview with Andy Law of St Luke's," *Harvard Business Review,* September–October, pp. 143–50.

Crawford, R. J., Boyston, A. and Fischer, B. (2003), *IDEO: An "Idea-Intensive" Organization at Work,* IMD case no. IMD-3-1311, IMD International, Lausanne.

Csikszentmihalyi, M. (1996), *Creativity,* HarperPerennial, New York, NY.

Devenport, T. H., Prusak, L. and Wilson, H. J. (2003), "Who's bringing you hot ideas and how are you responding?," *Harvard Business Review,* Vol. 81 No. 2, pp. 58–64.

de Geus, A. (1997), *The Living Company,* Nicholas Brealey, London.

de Pree, M. (1989), *Leadership Is an Art,* Doubleday, New York, NY.

Doornik, K. and Roberts, J. (2001), *Nokia Corporation: Innovation and Efficiency in a High-Growth Global Firm,* Case no. S-IB-23, Graduate School of Business, Stanford University, Stanford, CA.

Drucker, P. (1985), *Innovation and Entrepreneurship,* William Heinemann, London.

Fox, J. (2000), "Nokia's secret code," *Fortune,* 1 May, pp. 31–8.

Gundling, E. (2000), *The 3M Way to Innovation,* Kodansha International, Tokyo.

Hargadon, A. (2003), *How Breakthroughs Happen,* Harvard Business School Press, Boston, MA.

Hargadon, A. and Sutton, R.I. (2000), "Building an innovation factory," *Harvard Business Review,* May–June, pp. 157–66.

Herbold, R. (2002), "Inside Microsoft: balancing creativity and discipline," *Harvard Business Review,* Vol. 80 No. 1, pp. 72–9.

Hirschberg, J. (1999), *The Creative Priority,* Penguin, London.

Jack, A. (2005), "Glaxo's catalysts for creativity," *Financial Times,* 18 March.

Lowe, J. (1998), *Jack Welch Speaks,* Wiley, New York, NY.

Nathan, J. (1999), *Sony: The Private Life,* Mariner Books, Boston, MA.

Nussbaum, B. (2004), "The power of design," *BusinessWeek online,* 17 May.

Schlender, B. (1998), "In a meeting of incomparable minds, Buffet and Gates muse about taking risks, motivating employees, confronting mistakes and giving back," *Fortune,* 20 July, pp. 41–47.

Schneiderman, H. A. (1991), "Managing R&D: a perspective from the top," *Sloan Management Review,* Summer, pp. 53–8.

Steinbock, D. (2001), *The Nokia Revolution,* Anacom, New York, NY.

Storr, A. (1991), *The Dynamics of Creation,* Penguin, Harmondsworth.

Stross, R. E. (1996), *The Microsoft Way,* Addison-Wesley, Reading, MA.

Thomke, S. and Nimgade, A. (2000), *IDEO Product Development,* Case no. 9-600-143, Harvard Business School, Boston, MA.

The Seven Habits of Spectacularly Unsuccessful Executives

Sydney Finkelstein
Dartmouth College

The past few years have witnessed some admirable business successes—and some exceptional failures. Among the companies that have hit hard times are a few of the most storied names in business—think Arthur Andersen, Rubbermaid, and Schwinn Bicycle—as well as a collection of former high flyers like Enron, Tyco, and WorldCom. Behind each of these failures stands a towering figure, a CEO or business leader who will long be remembered for being spectacularly unsuccessful.

The truth is, it takes some special personal qualities to be spectacularly unsuccessful. I'm talking about people who took world-renowned business operations and made them almost worthless. What's remarkable is that the individuals who possess the personal qualities that make this magnitude of destruction possible usually possess other, genuinely admirable qualities. It makes sense: Hardly anyone gets a chance to destroy so much value without demonstrating the potential for creating it. Most of the great destroyers of value are people of unusual intelligence and talent who display personal magnetism. They are the leaders who appear on the covers of *Fortune* and *Forbes*.

Still, when it comes to the crunch, these people fail—and fail monumentally. What's the secret of their destructive powers? After spending six years studying more than 50 companies and conducting some 200 interviews, I found that spectacularly unsuccessful people had seven characteristics in common. Nearly all of the leaders who preside over major business failures exhibit four or five of these habits. The truly gifted ones exhibit all seven. But here's what's really remarkable: Each of these seven habits represents a quality that is widely admired in the business world. Business not only tolerates the qualities that make these leaders spectacularly unsuccessful, it celebrates them.

Here, then, are seven habits of spectacularly unsuccessful people, along with some warning signs to look out for. These habits are most destructive when a CEO exhibits them, but any manager who has these habits can do terrible harm—including you. Study them. Learn to recognize them. And try to catch these red flags before spectacular failure finds you!

Reprinted from "The Seven Habits of Spectacularly Unsuccessful Executives," Sydney Finkelstein, *Ivey Business Journal,* Vol. 68, No. 3 (Jan/Feb 2004),p. 438–444. Ivey Management Services prohibits any form of reproduction, storage or transmittal of this material without its written permission. This material is not covered under authorization from any reproduction rights organization. To order copies or request permission to reproduce materials, contact Ivey Publishing, Ivey Management Services, c/o Richard Ivey School of Business, The University of Western Ontario, London, Ontario, Canada, N6A 3K7; phone (519) 661-3208, fax (519) 661-3882, e-mail cases@ivey.uwo.ca. Copyright © 2004, Ivey Management Services. One time permission to reproduce granted by Ivey Management Services on February 15, 2006.

HABIT #1: THEY SEE THEMSELVES AND THEIR COMPANIES AS DOMINATING THEIR ENVIRONMENT

This first habit may be the most insidious, since it appears to be highly desirable. Shouldn't a company try to dominate its business environment, shape the future of its markets, and set the pace within them? Yes, but there's a catch. Unlike successful leaders, failed leaders who never question their dominance fail to realize they are at the mercy of changing circumstances. They vastly overestimate the extent to which they actually control events and vastly underestimate the role of chance and circumstance in their success.

CEOs who fall prey to this belief suffer from the illusion of personal preeminence: Like certain film directors, they see themselves as the *auteurs* of their companies. As far as they're concerned, everyone else in the company is there to execute their personal vision for the company. Samsung's CEO Kun-Hee Lee was so successful with electronics that he thought he could repeat this success with automobiles. He invested $5 billion in an already oversaturated auto market. Why? There was no business case. Lee simply loved cars and had dreamed of being in the auto business.

Warning Sign: A Lack of Respect

Leaders who suffer from the illusion of personal preeminence tend to believe that their companies are indispensable to their suppliers and customers. Rather than looking to satisfy customer needs, CEOs who believe they run preeminent companies act as if their customers were the lucky ones. When asked how Johnson & Johnson lost its seemingly insurmountable lead in the medical stent business, cardiologists and hospital administrators pointed to the company's arrogance and lack of respect for customers' ideas. Motorola exhibited the same arrogance when it continued to build fancy analog phones, rather than the digital variety its customers were clamoring for.

HABIT #2: THEY IDENTIFY SO COMPLETELY WITH THE COMPANY THAT THERE IS NO CLEAR BOUNDARY BETWEEN THEIR PERSONAL INTERESTS AND THEIR CORPORATION'S INTERESTS

Like the first habit, this one seems innocuous, perhaps even beneficial. We want business leaders to be completely committed to their companies, with their interests tightly aligned with those of the company. But digging deeper, you find that failed executives weren't identifying too little with the company, but rather too much. Instead of treating companies as enterprises that they needed to nurture, failed leaders treated them as extensions of themselves. And with that, a "private empire" mentality took hold.

CEOs who possess this outlook often use their companies to carry out personal ambitions. The most slippery slope of all for these executives is their tendency to use corporate funds for personal reasons. CEOs who have a long or impressive track record may come to feel that they've made so much money for the company that the expenditures they make on themselves, even if extravagant, are trivial by comparison. This twisted logic seems to have been one of the factors that shaped the behavior of Dennis Kozlowski of Tyco. His pride in his company and his pride in his own extravagance seem to have reinforced each other. This is why he could sound so sincere making speeches about ethics while using corporate funds for personal purposes. Being the CEO of a sizable corporation today is probably the closest thing to being king of your own country, and that's a dangerous title to assume.

Warning Sign: A Question of Character

When it comes right down to it, the biggest warning sign of CEO failure is a question of character.

We might want to believe that leaders at companies like Adelphia, Tyco, and ImClone were trustworthy stewards of those companies, but their behavior suggests otherwise. But questions about character need not be limited to dubious or unethical acts. In fact, most leaders I studied were scrupulously honest. Rather, it is denial and defensiveness that are the critical warning signs. As Tony Galban, a D&O underwriter at Chubb, told me, "Always listen to the analysts' calls because that gives you a sense of how an individual thinks on their feet. They give you a sense of whether they're in denial or whether they're being professional." It gets down to this: Do you really trust this person?

HABIT #3: THEY THINK THEY HAVE ALL THE ANSWERS

Here's the image of executive competence that we've been taught to admire for decades: a dynamic leader making a dozen decisions a minute, dealing with many crises simultaneously, and taking only seconds to size up situations that have stumped everyone else for days. The problem with this picture is that it's a fraud. Leaders who are invariably crisp and decisive tend to settle issues so quickly they have no opportunity to grasp the ramifications. Worse, because these leaders need to feel they have all the answers, they aren't open to learning new ones.

CEO Wolfgang Schmitt of Rubbermaid was fond of demonstrating his ability to sort out difficult issues in a flash. A former colleague remembers that under Schmitt, "the joke went, 'Wolf knows everything about everything.' In one discussion, where we were talking about a particularly complex acquisition we made in Europe, Wolf, without hearing different points of view, just said, 'Well, this is what we are going to do.'" Leaders who need to have all the answers shut out other points of view. When your company or organization is run by someone like this, you'd better hope the answers he comes up with are going to be the right ones. At Rubbermaid they weren't. The company went from being *Fortune*'s most admired company in America in 1993 to being acquired by the conglomerate Newell a few years later.

Warning Sign: A Leader Without Followers

John Keogh, another big-time underwriter of D&O insurance, pointed out what he looks for when CEOs are being interviewed by analysts: "[Was] the management team incredibly arrogant? [Did the CEO or CFO] have all the answers and is [he or she] pretty [much] on top of his or her game?" CEOs who believe they have all the answers don't really need other people, except to do what they want them to do. One of the critical side effects of a CEO's fixation on being right is that opposition can go underground, effectively closing down dissent. As middle management begins to realize that their personal contributions aren't important, an entire organization can grind to a halt. When a leader's perspective and the management team's perspective drastically differ, take note. The difference in perception between Schmitt and his staff at Rubbermaid was striking, and was characteristic of many executives' predicament. He was a leader without followers.

HABIT #4: THEY RUTHLESSLY ELIMINATE ANYONE WHO ISN'T COMPLETELY BEHIND THEM

CEOs who think their job is to instill belief in their vision also think that it is their job to get everyone to buy into it. Anyone who doesn't rally to the cause is undermining the vision. Hesitant managers have a choice: Get with the plan or leave.

The problem with this approach is that it's both unnecessary and destructive. CEOs don't need to have everyone unanimously endorse their vision to have it carried out successfully. In fact, by eliminating all dissenting and contrasting viewpoints, destructive CEOs cut themselves off from their best chance of seeing and correcting problems as they arise. Sometimes CEOs who seek to stifle dissent only drive it underground. Once this happens, the entire organization falters. At Mattel, Jill Barad removed her senior lieutenants if she thought they harbored serious reservations about

Conversations with Myself: Seven Disastrous Thoughts of Unsuccessful Leaders

Habit #1: "Our products are superior and so am I. We're untouchable. My company is successful because of my leadership and intellect—I made it happen."

Habit #2: "I am the sole proprietor. This company is my baby. Obviously, my wants and needs are in the best interest of my company and stockholders."

Habit #3: "I'm a genius. I believe in myself and you should too. Don't worry, I know all the answers. I'm not micromanaging, I'm being attentive. I don't need anyone else, certainly not a team."

Habit #4: "If you're not with me, you're against me! Get with the plan, or get out of the way. Where's your loyalty?"

Habit #5: "I'm the spokesperson. It's all about image. I'm a promotions and public relations genius. I love making public appearances; that's why I star in our commercials. It's my job to be socially visible; that's why I give frequent speeches and have regular media coverage."

Habit #6: "It's just a minor roadblock. Full steam ahead! Let's call that division a partner company so we don't have to show it on our books."

Habit #7: "It has always worked this way in the past. We've done it before, and we can do it again."

---

the way that she was running things. Schmitt created such a threatening atmosphere at Rubbermaid that firings were often unnecessary. When new executives realized that they'd get no support from the CEO, many of them left almost as fast as they'd come on board. Eventually, these CEOs had everyone on their staff completely behind them. But where they were headed was toward disaster. And no one was left to warn them.

Warning Sign: Executive Departures

A revolving door at the top is one of the strongest signals that there has been executive failure at a company. Whether executives leave under false pretenses, or are sent to some distant outpost where they'll have no further influence at headquarters, a pattern of executive departures speaks volumes for what is going on at a company. At Mattel, along with firing senior lieutenants on a moment's notice, Jill Barad drove six direct reports to resign for "personal reasons." The same thing has happened at Sun Microsystems over the last year. A mass exodus may be an indication that the CEO is out to eliminate any contrary opinions, or it may reflect inside information senior executives are acting on. In either case, it's a powerful warning sign. Analysts and many investors regularly track insider sales of stock, but executive departures may provide an even clearer window on the company. After all, what stronger statement can an executive make than to leave his or her job and the company entirely?

HABIT #5: THEY ARE CONSUMMATE SPOKESPERSONS, OBSESSED WITH THE COMPANY IMAGE

You know these CEOs: high-profile executives who are constantly in the public eye. The problem is that amid all the media frenzy and accolades, these leaders' management efforts become shallow and ineffective. Instead of actually accomplishing things, they often settle for the appearance of accomplishing things.

Behind these media darlings is a simple fact of executive life: CEOs don't achieve a high level of media attention without devoting themselves assiduously to public relations. When CEOs are obsessed with their image, they have little time for operational details. Tyco's Dennis Kozlowski sometimes intervened in remarkably minor matters, but left most of the company's day-to-day operations unsupervised.

As a final negative twist, when CEOs make the company's image their top priority, they run the risk of using financial-reporting practices to promote that image. Instead of treating their financial accounts as a control tool, they treat them as a public relations tool. The creative accounting that was apparently practiced by such executives as Enron's Jeffrey Skilling or Tyco's Kozlowski is as much or more an attempt to promote the company's image as it is to deceive the public: In their eyes, everything that the company does is public relations.

Warning Sign: Blatant Attention-Seeking

The types of behavior exhibited by Napoleonic CEOs tend to be so blatant that they can't be missed. Warning signs begin with the executive lifestyle—they may start to run with a very cool crowd, buy expensive art, and hobnob with political dignitaries and celebrities. The CEO will seem to spend more time with PR personnel and making public appearances than doing something as mundane as visiting customers. Other times, a company will build a striking new headquarters, designed to serve as a corporate symbol. In more extreme cases, the CEO will try to acquire the naming rights for a new sports arena or stadium.

HABIT #6: THEY UNDERESTIMATE OBSTACLES

Part of the allure of being a CEO is the opportunity to espouse a vision. Yet, when CEOs become so enamored of their vision, they often overlook or underestimate the difficulty of actually getting there. And when it turns out that the obstacles they casually waved aside are more troublesome than they anticipated, these CEOs have a habit of plunging full-steam into the abyss. For example, when Webvan's core business was racking up huge losses, CEO George Shaheen was busy expanding those operations at an awesome rate.

Why don't CEOs in this situation reevaluate their course of action, or at least hold back for a while until it becomes clearer whether their policies will work? Some feel an enormous need to be right in every important decision they make, because if they admit to being fallible, their position as CEO might seem precarious. Once a CEO admits that he or she made the wrong call, there will always be people who say the CEO wasn't up to the job. These unrealistic expectations make it exceedingly hard for a CEO to pull back from any chosen course of action, which not surprisingly causes them to push that much harder. That's why leaders at Iridium and

Motorola kept investing billions of dollars to launch satellites even after it had become apparent that land-based cell phones were a better alternative.

Warning Sign: Excessive Hype

One of the things we learned from the Internet bubble is the danger of hype, which can hide problems or mask intentions that, if known, would lead people to make different decisions. Simply stated: When something sounds too good to be true . . . it usually is. One of the best signs of a company relying on hype is the missed milestone. Whenever a company announces that its quarterly earnings are below forecast, the market reacts negatively to the news. Another important warning sign to look out for is when companies avoid looking at persuasive market data. When Barneys was planning its doomed geographic expansion, someone suggested that it do a market study to make sure that its offerings could work outside New York. CEO Bob Pressman thought the idea was ludicrous. "Market studies?" he exclaimed, incredulously. "Why do we have to do market studies? We're Barneys!"

HABIT #7: THEY STUBBORNLY RELY ON WHAT WORKED FOR THEM IN THE PAST

Many CEOs on their way to becoming spectacularly unsuccessful accelerate their company's decline by reverting to what they regard as tried-and-true methods. In their desire to make the most of what they regard as their core strengths, they cling to a static business model. They insist on providing a product to a market that no longer exists, or they fail to consider innovations in areas other than those that made the company successful in the past. Instead of considering a range of options that fit new circumstances, they use their own careers as the only point of reference and do the things that made them successful in the past. For example, when Jill Barad was trying to promote educational software at Mattel, she used the promotional techniques that had been effective for her when she was promoting Barbie dolls, despite the fact that software is not distributed or bought the way dolls are.

Frequently, CEOs who fall prey to this habit owe their careers to some "defining moment," a criti-cal decision or policy choice that resulted in their most notable success. It's usually the one thing that they're most known for and the thing that gets them all of their subsequent jobs. The problem is that after people have had the experience of that defining moment, if they become the CEO of a large company, they allow their defining moment to define the company as well—no matter how unrealistic it has become.

Warning Sign: Constantly Referring to What Worked in the Past

When CEOs continually use the same model or repeatedly make the same decision, despite its inappropriateness, it can lead to significant failure. This type of thinking is often evident in the comments of senior executives who focus on similarities across situations while ignoring the sometimes more momentous differences. Take the case of Quaker Oats' acquisition of Snapple. Quaker paid $1.7 billion for Snapple, mistakenly assuming that the drink would be another smash hit like Gatorade. The beverage division president said things such as, "We have an excellent sales and marketing team here at Gatorade. We believe we do know how to build brands; we do know how to advance Snapple as well as Gatorade to the next level." Unfortunately, they didn't realize that Snapple was not a traditional mass-market beverage, but a "quirky, cult" drink. What's more, while Gatorade was distributed via a warehouse system, Snapple relied on family-run distributorships that had little interest in cooperating with Quaker. In 1997, Quaker sold Snapple for a paltry $300 million.

These seven habits of spectacularly unsuccessful people are powerful reminders of how organizational leaders are not only instruments of growth and success, but sometimes also architects of failure. That each of the habits has elements that are valuable for leaders only serves to point out how vigilant people who enter a leader's orbit must be, whether they are other executives, board members, lower-level managers, and employees, regulators, or even suppliers, customers, and competitors. In small doses, each of the habits can be part of a winning formula, but when executives overdose, the habits can quickly become toxic. That is a lesson all leaders and would-be leaders should take to heart.

Competing Responsibly

Bert van de Ven
University of Tilburg

Ronald Jeurissen
Nyenrode Business University

Abstract: In this paper we examine the effects of different competitive conditions on the determination and evaluation of strategies of corporate social responsibility (CSR). Although the mainstream of current thinking in business ethics recognizes that a firm should invest in social responsibility, the normative theory on how specific competitive conditions affect a firm's social responsibility remains underdeveloped. Intensity of competition, risks to reputation, and the regulatory environment determine the competitive conditions of a firm. Our central thesis is that differential strength of competition produces differential moral legitimacy of firm behavior. When competition is fierce or weak, different acts or strategies become morally acceptable, as well as economically rational. A firm has to develop its own strategy of social responsibility, in light of its competitive position, as well as ethical considerations.

1. INTRODUCTION

It is widely accepted in business ethics that a moral evaluation of firm behavior should focus on the impact of the firm on the rights and legitimate interests of its stakeholders.[1] CSR is often defined in stakeholder terms as well. The European Commission, for example, defines CSR as "a concept whereby companies integrate social and environmental concerns in their business operations and in their interaction with their stakeholders on a voluntary basis, as they are increasingly aware that responsible behavior leads to sustainable business success."[2]

When we define the responsibilities of a firm in stakeholder terms, we should realize that the firm itself is a nexus of stakeholders. A firm is a cooperative venture for mutual benefit, a coalition of participants[3] (clients, employees, share owners, suppliers), who are all economic stakeholders of each other, and who all depend on the continuity of the firm for their wealth and well-being. Hence, the ability of a firm to survive is an important *instrumental* moral goal, in view of the legitimate interests and rights of many stakeholders. This means that policies and strategies of companies directed at the continuity of the firm (operationalized in terms of profitability, market share, growth, future cash flows, etc.) must be considered as morally justified activities, prima facie. The continuity of the firm is an important moral value, albeit of an instrumental nature.

This has a bearing on CSR. Contrary to what the European Commission suggests, in the above quotation, there is not always a positive relationship between responsible behavior and sustainable business success. The relationship depends on many factors, important ones of which are the competitive conditions of a firm. Depending on the competitive conditions, some CSR initiatives can be beneficial to a firm, others not. Therefore, not all forms of CSR are feasible for a firm given the actual market in which the firm has to be successful. Competitive conditions are an intervening variable, influencing the relationship between CSR and business success, and even deciding over whether this relationship is positive or negative.

In our view, competitive conditions affect a firm's social responsibility with respect to specific dilemmas, as well as with respect to the CSR strategy a firm can or should adopt. This is so, because competitive conditions are determinants of a firm's

Reprinted from "Competing Responsibly," Bert van de Ven, Ronald Jeurissen, *Business Ethics Quarterly*, Vol. 15, No. 2 (April 2005), p. 299–317. Used by permission of the Philosophy Documentation Center.

survivability, which is an instrumental moral value. In light of the moral value of survivability, managers have a duty to take the competitive conditions of their firm into account in all the strategic decisions that they make, including decisions about CSR. From this, it does not follow, however, that the survivability of the firm should always override other considerations. Sometimes the stakeholders would be better off if a certain business activity were terminated immediately. Take, for instance, the production of CFCs that erode the ozone layer. All living creatures on planet Earth have a high stake in stopping the production of CFCs. So a law that forbids the production of CFCs, as it was actually adopted in, among others, the United States, is morally desirable, even if it means that certain CFC-producing firms would not survive as a result. Furthermore, sometimes the timely liquidation of a firm is legitimate in order to secure the financial interests of stakeholders. Finally, if a certain business violates human rights to stay in business, this could not be legitimized by referring to the instrumental moral value of the firm's survivability. In other words, if the evil of putting the continuance of a firm in jeopardy is the lesser evil, survival of the firm will be overruled by other moral considerations.

Following John Kay, we define business strategy as a firm's scheme for handling the relationships with its environment. Such a scheme includes market entry decisions, product positioning decisions and an approach to relationship building with stakeholders. A scheme may be articulated or implicit, preprogrammed or emergent. The level of conscious design by management of a scheme may vary, since all strategies are based on a mixture of calculation and opportunism, of vision and experiment.[4] CSR as a strategy aims particularly at social and environmental aspects of doing business. Assessing CSR from a strategic perspective, may seem to imply that ethical responsibilities are subordinated to economic imperatives. It may seem as if CSR is not intrinsically valued, but only instrumentally. The suspicion arises that the motivation of firms behind CSR is not truly ethical, since it is in their self-interest. We cannot treat this problem fully within the scope of this paper, because we would then have to deal with the philosophical question what exactly constitutes the moral worth of an action. Is it the respect for the moral law, as Kant suggested? Or are moral sentiments like

empathy and sympathy necessary conditions for a truly ethical motivation? For the purpose of this paper, it suffices to assume that for a strategy of CSR to be qualified as ethical or moral it is not required that self-interested reasons be completely absent. Beyond this, we stress the instrumental moral value of the continuation of a firm with respect to the fulfillment of the legitimate expectations of stakeholders.[5] From the perspective of the social responsibility of a firm, it can only be considered a good thing when ethics contribute to the continuation of the firm, since this way a firm will be able to contribute more to the well-being of stakeholders and of non stakeholders such as the environment. Furthermore, the fact that CSR can serve strategic purposes does not say anything about the motivations behind it. Maybe the members of the board of directors are truly motivated by a sense of moral duty, maybe they are only backing the CSR efforts because it is good for business or for themselves. They will probably have mixed motives to integrate CSR in their corporate strategy. We suggest that the qualification of a strategy as a strategy of CSR should not depend on the motivation of managers, but only on goals and outcomes, just like this is the case for any other business strategy.

CSR should make sense from the perspective of the overall competitive strategy of a firm (and the other way around), and should be treated as an integral part of it; not only because this furthers the long-term survival of a firm, but also because this way the moral claims of stakeholders have the best chance of becoming an accepted part of the firm's decision-making structure and its organizational culture. This way, the relationship between ethics and economics becomes in large measure a matter of strategic choice rather than discovery, as Lynn Sharp Paine has argued.[6]

Many business ethicists agree that, regardless of what a firm does to improve its social performance and to take on its moral responsibilities, it should also be profitable in the long run. Mostly, however, this relationship is discussed only in general terms. Little attention is paid to the relationship between *specific* competitive conditions and the possibilities of a firm to adopt a specific CSR strategy. Sethi and Sama developed a descriptive model of the effect of marketplace competition, industry structure and firm resources on ethical business conduct.[7] It is important to describe how competitive conditions influence ethical business behavior, but this does not tell us to what extent and in what sense it is morally acceptable that market conditions influence the outcomes of the decision-making process. To answer this question, we will have to look more specifically into the relationship between competitive conditions and CSR. This brings us to the following research question:

> How can firms compete in a morally acceptable way, given the fact that they have to survive in an environment where competition is (a) more or less intense, (b) more or less regulated, and (c) more or less susceptible to the scrutiny of influential stakeholders?

By specifying the relationships between specific competitive conditions and CSR strategies, greater justice can be done to the special circumstances that confront a firm that tries to balance its social responsibility with the need to be profitable.

To develop a specifying model of the relationship between CSR and competition, we will first discuss the assumption of perfect competition in economic theory. This assumption totally paralyzes the debate on CSR from an economic perspective, so we will first have to show why, from an ethical perspective, this assumption must be rejected. Next, in section three, we will introduce a conceptualization of competitive forces and competitive strategies, based on the work of Porter. In sections four to six, we will examine what CSR strategies are feasible for firms, under different competitive conditions. In section seven we will draw a number of conclusions.

2. INTENSITY OF COMPETITION AND CSR STRATEGIES

Why should firms pursue profitability? Profits are not the purpose of a business activity, but a means of building the business and rewarding employees, executives, and investors, says Solomon.[8] According to Peter Drucker, profits are not the explanation, cause, or rationale of a firm's behavior and management decisions, but the test of their validity.[9] Steinmann and Löhr express a similar view when they call profitability the formal criterion of success of business activities. This criterion does not say anything as to *how* a firm can or should become profitable.[10] Although the market system functions in such a way that only profitable firms will eventually

survive, this does not tell management which roads will lead to corporate success. As part of the social world, the world of business is socially constructed, rather than economically determined.[11] Corporate strategies are formed in sensemaking processes, which involve a degree of freedom. This implies that a firm can choose to integrate social responsibility into its corporate strategy. If a firm does so, management will probably be convinced that it is good for business. Whether a certain CSR strategy is indeed good for business depends on how the market and other stakeholders will respond.

Ex ante, no one can point to competitive pressures as a condition that completely eliminates the firm's social responsibility. Only the hypothetical case of *perfect competition* would possibly qualify as an excuse for not engaging in CSR. Standard economic theory says that, under the condition of perfect competition, firms do not have the financial means to bear costs that are unilateral, or that cannot be recovered by means of setting a premium price. Therefore, CSR efforts leading to marginal cost increases are simply not a viable option under the condition of perfect competition.[12] When CSR efforts lead to cost savings, or to profitable new business opportunities as they often do, perfect competition not only allows for these kinds of efforts, but they are necessary, since they will lead to the maximization of profits. The tension between profits and morality is therefore limited to those CSR efforts that do not lead to a win–win situation.

But even when CSR efforts do not result in a win–win situation under perfect competition, we would argue that corporate responsibility is not completely eliminated. A firm has the moral duty to prevent posing a serious threat to health, safety or the environment, even when this means that the firm will go bankrupt. Harsh market conditions are no excuse here. Short of unilateral measures, a firm could in this case encourage government regulations or self-regulation of the industry to ensure that every competitor in the business faces the same costs. Firms always have a moral responsibility to (help) counteract a market situation in which immorality leads to a competitive advantage by seeking a solution on a higher institutional level. This is an instance of what De George has called "the principle of ethical displacement."[13] We suggest that this is one of the key ethical principles of CSR, since in this way a firm helps to counter the negative side effects (or the external costs, as economists would say) of the free market system. As one of the players in the market, each firm bears a part of the collective responsibility of all players to promote the ethical functioning of their market.

In a situation of perfect competition, a firm has no room to take on moral responsibilities that involve more costs than benefits relative to the costs and benefits of the competitors. However, since perfect competition is a theoretical ideal type which does not have much in common with most real markets, it is not justified to simply assume that firms have to deal with the extreme conditions of perfect markets.[14] That is why we reject the view of Milton Friedman, who bases part of his criticism of CSR on this ideal description of the market, as is shown by the next quotation: "The participant in a competitive market has no appreciable power to alter terms of exchange; he is hardly visible as a separate entity; hence it is hard to argue that he has any 'social responsibility' except that which is shared by all citizens to obey the law of this land and to live according to his lights."[15] This view of the firm as an entity that is barely visible and has no power to change things for the better or for the worse is clearly flawed as a general theory of the firm. It does not acknowledge that multinational firms in particular are becoming more and more visible to a global public and that in many markets firms have the power to influence the terms of the exchange. Friedman's assumption that most markets could be treated as if they were perfectly competitive is therefore not a methodologically proper one to make for present purposes. Nor is his conclusion acceptable which is based on this assumption, that a firm cannot have any responsibilities other than increasing its profits within the limits of the law and moral custom. Since competition in most real markets is less than perfect, we can conclude that firms in general do have at least some market power and therefore some financial room to enhance CSR.

Although we do not agree with Friedman that in general there is no room for individual firms to engage in CSR efforts that involve more costs than benefits relative to the competitors, we do want to acknowledge that the functioning of markets does put limitations on what a firm can afford with respect to CSR. This leads to a number of ethical questions. Is it morally relevant that some firms have to deal with fierce competition whereas other firms enjoy the comfort of less intense competition, when it comes to determining the moral responsibilities of a firm? Does it make a difference from a moral perspective when a firm bears considerable costs in order to comply with the law, while most

of its competitors do not, because the law is not enforced consistently? Finally, what is the relevance of corporate reputation for CSR? Does reputation as a coordination mechanism always stimulate socially responsible behavior? In the next sections, we set out to answer these questions.

3. COMPETITIVE FORCES AND COMPETITIVE STRATEGIES

We will base our analysis of the relationship between competition and CSR on Porter's seminal research into the competitive strategies of firms. Porter has introduced a distinction between *competitive forces* and *competitive strategies*.[16] Competitive forces determine the degree of competitiveness within an industry. They are: the entry of new competitors, the threat of substitutes, the bargaining power of buyers, the bargaining power of suppliers, and the rivalry among the existing competitors.[17] These five forces influence a firm's prices, costs, and required investments, which are the constituents of return on investment. The entry of new competitors depends on economies of scale, brand identity, and capital requirements. The threat of substitutes is dependent on the relative price performance of substitutes and the buyer's propensity to substitute. The bargaining power of buyers is dependent on buyer concentration versus firm concentration, buyer volume, and the buyer's ability to integrate backward, as well as on the price sensitivity of buyers, among other things. The bargaining power of the supplier is dependent, among other things, on supplier concentration versus firm concentration, the importance of volume to the supplier, and the presence of substitute inputs. Finally, the rivalry among the existing competitors is dependent on things like the growth of the industry, intermittent overcapacity, product differences, brand identity, and switching costs.

For our purpose, it is important to note that, according to Porter, a firm is usually not a prisoner of its industry's structure. "Firms, through their strategies, can influence the five forces. If a firm can shape structure, it can fundamentally change an industry's attractiveness for better or worse. Many successful strategies have shifted the rules of competition in this way."[18] Competitive strategies are ways for a firm to increase its competitiveness within an industry. Porter distinguishes three such strategies, namely cost leadership, differentiation and focus.[19]

In cost leadership, a firm sets out to become *the* low-cost producer in its industry. To achieve the status of low-cost producer, a firm must find and exploit all sources of cost advantage. Typically, low-cost producers sell a standard product and place emphasis on reaping scale or absolute cost advantages. Having a low-cost position yields a firm above average returns in its industry, despite the presence of strong competitive forces. Its cost position gives the firm a defense against rivalry from competitors, because its lower costs mean that it can still earn returns after its competitors have lost their profits through rivalry.

A firm differentiates itself from its competitors if it is unique in something that is widely valued by buyers. It selects one or more attributes that many buyers in an industry perceive as important, and uniquely positions itself to meet these. If a firm pursues forms of uniqueness that buyers do not value, it may be different from its competitors but not differentiated. The best way to learn whether a product is truly differentiated is to see if it is rewarded for its uniqueness with a premium price.

The focus strategy rests on the choice of a narrow competitive scope within an industry. The focuser selects a segment or group of segments in the industry and tailors its strategy to serving them to the exclusion of others. This can be a particular buyer group, a segment of the product line, or a specific market region. The strategy rests on the premise that the firm is thus able to serve its narrow strategic target more effectively or efficiently than competitors who are competing more broadly.

If strategies of CSR do qualify as (part of) a competitive strategy, then we have a sound argument to back up the claim that CSR can contribute to a sustainable competitive advantage and hence to profitability. To investigate this, we will examine a number of markets with varying degrees of competition and briefly explore some ways in which strategies of CSR can lead to a competitive advantage, or are affected by the competitive characteristics of these types of markets. To determine which CSR strategies could succeed, we will also take into account some features of the legal environment and the effect of the strategy on reputation. The combination of these three competitive conditions—intensity of competition, legal environment, and the effect on reputation—determines which strategy of CSR is commercially appropriate.

We will assume that a certain industry structure will result in more or less intense competition,
depending on the five competitive forces. It takes an extensive and laborious analysis to present a complete picture of the competitive forces for an industry. For the theoretical purpose of this study, we do not need such a level of detail. For practical reasons, therefore, we will distinguish between three ideal types, or "frozen moments," of markets, that capture the intensity of the competition for an imaginary firm, at a certain point in time. We will refer to the three levels of competitiveness as "fierce," "strong" and "weak." This distinction is based on stipulations, which are, of course, artificial. Empirically, the intensity of competition varies gradually along the five competitive forces.

For each level of competitiveness, we will investigate the strategic opportunities and limitations for firms to engage in CSR efforts and to deal with moral problems and dilemmas. In general, we can say that a strategy of low costs is the dominant competitive strategy under fierce competition. Only forms of CSR that are reconcilable with a low-cost strategy are competitively feasible under fierce competition. Differentiation is the dominant strategy under strong competition. CSR strategies that help a firm to differentiate itself from its competitors are appropriate under strong competition. Under weak competition, there is no dominant strategy. This market lacks competitive pressure altogether, so that very different strategies can lead to business success. Table 1 outlines the specific CSR strategies that are available to firms under different levels of competitiveness. In sections four to six, we will explain these strategies in greater detail.

4. CSR STRATEGIES UNDER CONDITIONS OF FIERCE COMPETITION

We define fierce competition as a market in which a firm has little or no power to influence prices, because several or all of the following features of the industry structure make the five forces of competition very strong: (i) the entry barriers are low, for instance, because of low capital requirements and because brand identity is not important; (ii) the product can easily be substituted, because there is a high buyer propensity to substitute; (iii) the buyers have a strong bargaining power, because their concentration is relatively high; (iv) the bargaining power of suppliers

Table 1   **Specific CSR Strategies Under Different Levels of Industry Competitiveness**

Intensity of Competition	Fierce	Strong	Weak
Dominant generic competitive strategy	Low-cost strategy	Product-differentiation strategy	Low-cost or product-differentiation
Specific CSR strategy	Ethical displacement strategy: Self-regulation	Compliance with the spirit of the law	All CSR strategies are possible
	Legal compliance	Stakeholder management	
	Reputation protection	Brand reputation management and ethical reporting	
		Ethical product differentiation	

is relatively high, due to a lack of substitute inputs; and (v) the concentration within the industry is low whereas the product is (almost) homogeneous (no product differentiation), causing the rivalry between competitors to be high. In general, one can say that fierce competition leads to low profitability and forces companies to follow a low cost strategy.

Under fierce competition, firms cannot afford to invest in CSR, if this will lead to higher costs than the competitors have to bear, because the buyers will almost immediately switch to a cheaper competitor. Under conditions of fierce competition, a firm has no financial room to bear costs that are structurally higher than those of competitors. Even under these conditions, there are some CSR strategies that are recommendable for firms. These are strategies which, although costly in the short term, are sufficiently beneficial to make them the rational option under fierce competition. We will consider three of them, namely ethical displacement, legal compliance, and reputation protection.

Ethical Displacement

Ethical displacement means that if an ethical conflict cannot be solved at a certain level of social aggregation (the individual, the organization, the industry, or the national/international political level), then one should look for a solution at a level other than that at which the dilemma occurs. Ethical displacement is not only relevant for a market with perfect competition, but also for a market with fierce competition, since individual firms cannot afford high unilateral

investments in CSR. Firms in this situation have a duty to look for competitively neutral means to promote CSR at the industry level. A system of self-regulation of the industry should impose the same costs on all the competitors. This way no individual firm runs the risk of a competitive disadvantage. In a market with fierce competition it is, therefore, a viable form of CSR to take the initiative for industry self-regulation.

Legal Compliance

Under conditions of fierce competition, a firm usually has to set modest goals with respect to its strategy of CSR. It can start by trying to comply with the law. Carroll identifies legal responsibilities as one of the dimensions of CSR.[20] Lynn Sharp Paine considers legal compliance to be an important strategy for ethics management. Both authors agree that obedience to the law is not the highest possible achievement in business ethics, but that it is an important beginning. We would like to stress here that even this beginning can be difficult for firms, and sometimes presents a serious ethical and competitive challenge.

From an ethical perspective (assuming the instrumental moral value of the firm), a firm has to ensure itself that even the legalistic minimum level of CSR will not lead to a competitive disadvantage. To be sure, not all cost disadvantages are a competitive disadvantage. To become a competitive disadvantage the additional costs would have to be so high, or so persistent, that the firm risks losing its business to its competitors. Whether legal compliance will lead to a competitive disadvantage depends for an important part on certain features of the legal environment. Compliance with the law will probably lead to a competitive disadvantage when competitors structurally bear less costs by using loopholes in the law, or when the law is not enforced effectively. In a situation of fierce competition, an acceptable degree of enforcement would have to be determined by the probabilities of detection and conviction, and the size of the fine, compared to the cost advantage resulting from transgression.

Under fierce competition, a firm can be pressured strongly to take advantage of loopholes in the law, when not doing so would lead to a considerable relative cost disadvantage. Likewise, a firm is pressured to break the law when the law is not enforced effectively enough to create a satisfactorily level playing field among the competition.[21] In both cases, compliance with the law could lead to bankruptcy. Hence, if a firm wants to secure its own survival, the competitive condition of fierce competition could force it to choose between its own survival and the duty to comply with the law. Under such extreme circumstances, a firm faces a moral dilemma. As we argued in section one, the continuation of the firm presents an instrumental moral value to all the stakeholders. Securing the survival of the firm is therefore morally desirable, provided that the business itself is not of an immoral nature.[22] On the other hand, securing the continuation of the firm would imply that one breaches the moral and legal duty to comply with the law. How should a firm deal with this dilemma? The *fairness of competitive conditions* provides an important clue to answering this question.

Legal institutions can create circumstances that entail unfair competitive disadvantages for some firms. An example would be legislation which forbids companies to pay bribes to government officials in other countries. The United States has such legislation, under the Foreign Corrupt Practices Act of 1977. Similar legislation has recently been introduced in the Netherlands as well. Until now, the Prosecution Council has only started a few bribery cases. This is not because Dutch managers are so law abiding when it comes to bribery. On the contrary, paying money or giving gifts to government officials in order to get them to do their work (which would be a form of extortion) is widely understood as being an unfortunate but unavoidable part of doing business in some parts of the world. The rather weak enforcement of antibribery laws in the Netherlands creates a cost disadvantage for the compliant firms. The obedient firms are worse off as a result of their legally correct behavior, whereas the firms that violate the law benefit. A lack of law enforcement that creates a competitive disadvantage for compliant firms is an example of unfair competition. If this occurs in a fiercely competitive environment, then we believe the responsibility of firms not to pay bribes might be mitigated to some extent. Here we take recourse to the rule, introduced by Velasquez, that the moral responsibility for an act is mitigated (but not annihilated) by the difficulty to avoid the act, among other things.[23] It is primarily the responsibility of the government to ensure that the legal environment does not create unfair competition. According to the principle of ethical displacement, however, employer organizations and industrial organizations have a responsibility to lobby for legal improvements in this context.

A situation of unfair and fierce competition does not generally justify bribery. Paying bribes, whether one takes the initiative or not, poses a serious moral problem, because it contributes to corruption and makes markets less efficient. Therefore, it is morally better if a firm tries to stay in business without paying bribes. The only point we want to make here is that following the moral duty to comply with the law can take its toll for a firm, when competition is fierce. Managers can be confronted with tough moral choices, when compliance with the law has to be pitted against company survival. Since legal compliance in a fiercely competitive market involves a moral commitment and moral choices from a firm's management, we believe that this strategy can rightly be called a form of CSR.

Reputation Protection

Another possible strategy of CSR in a market with fierce competition is the protection of a good reputation among customers. We call this a form of CSR because reputation protection involves taking care of social aspects of the relationship that cannot be completely captured in a contractual form. Although a firm's reputation is not restricted to the assessment of past performance by customers (both individual and/or industrial), but comprises the assessment by all stakeholders,[24] we will limit ourselves to the reputation of the firm among its customers. This focus on the customer is motivated by the fact that in a fiercely competitive market the relation between corporate reputation and actual buying behavior is very important for the continuation of the firm. We define effect on reputation as the cumulative effect of a certain issue on the customers' beliefs with respect to those features of an organization and its product that influence their buying behavior. The opportunities of firms to use reputation protection as a CSR strategy depend on the interests of the customers. These interests can involve characteristics of the core product, but they can also involve company policies.

The condition of fierce competition involves that brand identity is not so important and the product is almost homogeneous. The customers' interests, as far as the product itself is concerned, are closely related to features of the core product, such as product quality, price, and availability. The product has to be reliable and the price has to be on a level comparable to the prices competitors ask, otherwise the customers will buy a competitor's product next time. In general, we can say that under the condition of fierce competition, reputation will be negatively affected if a certain breach of morality has repercussions for the features of the core product, such as its reliability and safety, and if the customers know about these repercussions. The magnitude of the negative effect will, of course, depend on the perceived importance of the impacts on health or safety. If, for instance, beef is suspected to contain growth hormones, some consumers will look for alternative meat products. Even under fierce competition, such reputational risks can be well worth avoiding.

Company policies, even when they do not affect the quality of products, can cause negative reputational effects among customers, when they perceive the policy as immoral or indecent. This might be a reason for customers to boycott a product or a firm, even if no customer's interest is being hurt directly. Companies like Heineken, Ikea, Nike, and Shell have, each in their own way, experienced what risks a public perception of social irresponsibility can mean to the business, especially when nongovernmental organizations (NGOs) target a firm with their campaign.

Public perceptions of a company's social and environmental performance sometimes strongly influence the buying behavior of consumers, but the pressure of public perception is felt less strongly on the business-to-business market. Here, other consumers come into play, who are often less concerned about social and environmental issues. Business-to-business markets can also be fiercely competitive. Under such conditions, a firm cannot always afford to worry much about a declining reputation in the eyes of the wider public, when their business clients are insensitive to moral issues, or even benefit from them. In business-to-business markets, this parting of public anxiety and consumer interests can be observed frequently. An example of this is the case of the Dutch-based firm IHC Caland in Burma (Myanmar). IHC Caland had agreed to produce an offshore storage and offloading system for oil and gas for Premier Oil, off the coast of Burma. The deal was not illegal under European Union legislation at the time. Like so many other firms, IHC Caland was criticized by pressure groups for its presence in Burma. According to these groups, IHC Caland was supporting the military regime in Burma, by contributing to the economy and hence to the means of existence of the regime. IHC Caland, however, could expect only a few orders of this size each year. Failing one of them could seriously harm their results. Moreover, IHC Caland had already signed a contract with Premier Oil. Leaving Burma would imply a breach of contract which would be detrimental to IHC Caland's reputation within the industry. This would be a threat to the continued existence of IHC Caland, in a market where buyers have great bargaining power. IHC Caland's conclusion on the Burma deal was that they would only pull out if it was forbidden by the government. By taking the matter to a higher (political) level of social organization, IHC Caland in fact invoked the principle of ethical displacement.

We conclude that even under fierce competition, several strategies of CSR are available to firms. Legal compliance is required also under fierce competition, although there should be greater understanding for the costs that legal compliance sometimes poses to companies under fierce competition. Ethical displacement is a CSR strategy that involves relatively low costs, as it aims at equalizing costs between competitors. Inquiring about the problem solving potential of ethical displacement should always be considered morally imperative for firms, when fierce competition makes unilateral CSR initiatives unattractive. Reputation protection, finally, is a means to prevent great costs for companies, which is not only economically feasible but even economically imperative under fierce competition. On the business-to-business market, however, the reputation mechanism may not always make a firm align with the CSR expectations of the larger public. Inevitably, firms under fierce competition will sometimes disappoint the public at large from a CSR perspective. We believe that a competitive analysis helps to understand why these disappointments are not always justified.

5. CSR STRATEGIES UNDER CONDITIONS OF STRONG COMPETITION

The term 'strong competition' refers to markets in which competitors have more financial room to bear costs due to choices made as a result of their moral and social responsibilities. Competition is strong, rather than fierce, if one or two of the five forces of competition are weak, while the other forces remain strong. For instance, the entry barriers are high because of the importance of brand identity and the high costs involved in developing it. Competition is still strong because of the other forces of competition. In these kinds of markets, profit margins need not be as razor-thin as they are in markets with fierce competition. When it comes to exploring the possibilities of the strategies of CSR, strongly competitive markets will be less restrictive.

The dominant generic strategy in a market with strong competition is product differentiation. Firms will try to differentiate their products or services in the eyes of the customers to justify a premium price. The distinctive capabilities of architecture of relational contract, reputation, innovation, as well as the strategic assets of a firm (such as exclusive dealing contracts) are the basis for product differentiation.[25] John Kay defines architecture as a network of relational contracts within, or around, the firm. Architectures depend on the ability of the firm to build and sustain long-term relationships and to establish an environment that penalizes opportunistic behavior.[26]

If a strategy of product differentiation succeeds, the competition in the market becomes less intense than in a market with fierce competition, because product differentiation results in a higher entry barrier. This way a firm can avoid the low-cost strategy which is dominant in a market with fierce competition. CSR initiatives can contribute to a strategy of product differentiation and are therefore appropriate for a market with strong competition. Sometimes, they even lie at the core of the differentiation strategy itself. The chosen strategy of CSR may build on an already developed distinctive capability of the firm, such as reputation or the high-quality of the architecture of relational contracts. A good reputation and high quality architecture can, however, also be the result of a long-term engagement with moral issues and stakeholders' interests in business. Below, we will discuss four ways in which CSR can become an integral part of business strategy, under conditions of strong competition: compliance with the spirit of the law, stakeholder management, brand reputation management and ethical reporting, and ethical product differentiation.

Compliance with the Spirit of the Law

Under conditions of strong competition, a firm has financial room to comply not only with the letter, but also with the spirit of the law. This requires paying attention to the rationale of the law, in order to interpret it correctly and arrive at a proper understanding of how the law should be interpreted in new situations.[27] An example of this is how firms respond to loopholes in tax legislation. If the intention of the legislator is known, but imperfectly expressed in the letter of the law, a firm can consider it its social responsibility to comply with the spirit of the law. Also, a firm has more to gain from this strategy, since distinctive capabilities like a sustainable network of long-term relationships (architecture) and reputation presuppose at least that a firm is able and willing to comply with its contracts in a non-opportunistic way, aimed at establishing long term relationships. Furthermore, the adaptations of the decision-making structure and the organizational culture necessary to enable compliance with the spirit of the law, are first steps in the direction of a full-fledged approach to integrating moral considerations in the decision making of the firm.[28] Stakeholder management is such an approach, and this will be discussed next.

Stakeholder Management

The management and guarding of the interests of stakeholders is essential if a firm wants to strengthen its architecture. According to Kay, architecture is one of the distinctive capabilities on which a competitive advantage can be built. One of the ways in which architecture adds value to individual contributions is through the establishment of a cooperative ethic. In our view, stakeholder management can contribute to building an environment that penalizes opportunistic behavior by monitoring the relationship of the firm with each stakeholder, so that appropriate action can be taken if anything goes wrong. Measures that could be taken to achieve this goal are social and ethical auditing, introducing an ethical committee or ethics officer, and a procedure for dealing with complaints, among other things.

It may seem that presently powerless stakeholders are irrelevant from a strategic perspective. Mitchell, Agle, and Wood have argued, however, that powerless stakeholders who are affected in their interests, will aspire for power vis-à-vis the company, in order to promote their interests.[29] One can never tell in advance whether a stakeholder who has no power at all to act against a certain firm, will not one day find the means to do so. Often, such powerless stakeholders are helped by NGOs to promote their cases. This possibility will always be of some importance to the sustainability of a firm in the long run. Take for example the victims of the Nazi regime's robbery of gold and other possessions during the Second World War. Banks that cooperated with the Nazis during the war had to deal with the claims of Holocaust survivors at a much later date. More recently one can think of the protest of the Ogoni against Shell's activities in Nigeria. The environmentalist movement of the Ogoni did not seem powerful enough to influence Shell's policy. It was only after the killing of Ken Saro-Wiwa by the Nigerian regime that Shell was forced to address the problem of the Ogoni in a new way.

Brand Reputation Management and Ethical Reporting

Another important distinctive capability that can be used widely in strongly competitive markets is brand reputation management. The importance of brand reputation as a distinctive capability can be seen in markets where product quality is important, but it can only be identified through long-term experience.[30] The market for accountancy services provides a good

example. A certified public accountant adds value only if he represents a firm that has an established reputation of independence and trustworthiness. When a public accountancy firm loses its reputation among the users of financial reports, the added value of the audit for the client disappears. Only accountancy firms that succeed in upholding a reputation of independence and trustworthiness will stay in business in the long run. This example shows how the social responsibility of a firm can be addressed at the strategic level of decision making.

Brands can serve several strategic functions. They are a means by which a producer can establish the reputation of a product. They can provide continuity. And the consumption of branded products may be a means by which consumers can express their identity.[31] CSR becomes important from a branding perspective, when many consumers appreciate a corporate image of CSR. Global brands like Motorola, Nike, and Heineken run great financial risks if their brand names become associated with child labor, human rights violations, or discrimination. Consumers seem to be extra critical of the CSR performance of a company when it represents a famous brand.[32] Nevertheless, one should not overestimate the impact of consumer sovereignty on the assessment of the qualities of a product or of ethical issues. Consumers face cognitive and motivational limitations, and limited opportunities to gather information about products or firms.[33]

Some global brands have responded to the greater public scrutiny by setting up a system of ethical and social reporting. For instance, Shell and British Telecom publish independently audited reports, covering issues like environmental impact, health, child labor, and corruption. Reporting can be an important tool of brand management and stakeholder management alike, by gathering information about the needs of stakeholders and about the firm's own performance. By reporting about its ethical and social performance, a firm can at least appear to be making an effort to inform its stakeholders. No matter how imperfect the quality of ethical auditing and reporting may be, the firm will be perceived as being more open and trustworthy. The assurance that the firm is trustworthy already comes from the mere fact that it publishes ethical and social reports. The signal to the stakeholders is clear: a firm that invests in ethical and social reporting not only commits itself to the market, but acknowledges that it has to earn the approval of the public at large by showing that it tries to take on its responsibilities. Whether a firm actually does take its responsibilities seriously is of course not guaranteed by ethical and social reporting as such. To answer this question, independent monitoring of a firm's behavior remains necessary. Social and ethical reporting however, does give stakeholders information about the policies and measures of a firm with respect to CSR. This is at least a good starting point for further dialogue between stakeholders and the firm.

From a strategic point of view, an investment in ethical and social reporting makes sense for global brands in particular. Firstly, they are most likely to become the target of public scrutiny. Secondly, these brands build on their reputation and, therefore, not only have a lot to lose, but also a lot to gain from a reputation of good corporate citizenship.

Ethical Product Differentiation

It is possible to differentiate a product based on some ethical quality or aspect, if the consumer is ready to pay a premium price because he or she values the particular strategy of CSR that a firm intends to follow. There are many examples of such strategies. Take, for instance, the firms that use fair-trade labels to sell coffee or bananas at a premium price, claiming that part of the premium will benefit small farmers who are dependent on such a premium for a "reasonable and fair income." By convincing customers of the social value offered at the premium price, the firms succeed in differentiating their "fair" product form normal, "unfair" trade.

Although the strategy of ethical product differentiation might be appropriate in the case of strong competition, it is also risky. If the customer fails to attach value to the ethical product claim, the firm loses business to competitors. The premium price will be perceived as unjustified. Furthermore, it is risky to claim that a product has some ethical quality to it that is lacking in the products of competitors. As The Body Shop has experienced, a firm that claims to safeguard ethical values in the production process will receive extra critical attention from journalists[34] and consumers. The company was accused of misleading the public, since among other things only a fraction of the product ingredients were actually bought from fair trade supply channels, while the bulk of the ingredients were bought from normal (purportedly unfair) supply channels. To counter this kind of criticism, The Body Shop has invested in social and ethical auditing and reporting.

6. CSR STRATEGIES UNDER CONDITIONS OF WEAK COMPETITION

A market with weak competition has several characteristics that change the strategic importance of CSR. Competition in a market is weak when all five forces of competition are weak or tend to be weak: (i) the threat of entry of new competitors is low, because of economies of scale and well-established brand identity; (ii) the product cannot easily be substituted, because of high switching costs; (iii) the buyers have little bargaining power, because their concentration is relatively low; (iv) the bargaining power of suppliers is relatively low due to the threat of backward integration; and (v) the concentration within the industry is high, causing the rivalry between competitors to be low. Taken together, these five forces of competition lead to weak competition.

Markets with weak competition can be either oligopolistic or monopolistic. Because of the lack of competition in such markets, firms have market power, which means that they can ask higher prices or reduce their quality, without losing too much business. Because of the lack of efficiency and quality in many markets with weak competition, intervention of the government through antitrust legislation and supervisory organs is often undertaken to safeguard the interests of consumers and the public. Market power, however, can have some positive effects as well. It enables a firm to invest in CSR. A firm in a weakly competitive market has the financial and managerial room to choose any of the CSR strategies described in the previous chapters. It is another issue whether all these strategies would be equally wise choices.

Compliance with the spirit of the law makes sense in a market with weak competition, because in this way a firm can prevent or reduce the chance of (further) government intervention. Most firms will consider it in their interests to prevent government intervention, because this way they have more control of the situation. If a firm in a market with weak competition refrains from misusing its market power,it indeed takes away the necessity of government intervention. However, when important interests of consumers or the public at large are at stake, for instance in public transport or energy supply, compliance with the law may not suffice. If important interests are at stake, dissatisfaction of consumers or the public can easily become a political issue. That is why, in these kinds of markets, it is in the interests of a firm to at least keep their key stakeholders satisfied, by using the strategy of stakeholder management or some form of ethical reporting. After all, these tools of ethical management not only benefit the stakeholders but also improve the overall quality of management, by keeping in touch with changing social expectations.

7. CONCLUSIONS

In this paper, we addressed the question of how specific competitive conditions affect CSR, and which CSR strategies are feasible for a firm under different competitive conditions. The competitive condition can be defined by three characteristics: the intensity of competition, the legal environment, and the risks to reputation.

The central moral argument underlying our analysis is that, in general, the continuation of a firm has an instrumental moral value because normally all stakeholders have a legitimate stake in this continuation. If, however, a person or group is better off if a business activity is terminated, management has to balance rights and obligations in such a way that the lesser evil is chosen. If this means that a firm will not be able to survive then this is the lesser evil in such a case. If however, most stakeholders with legitimate claims on a firm have an interest in the continuance of the firm in order to secure their stakes and if this continuation means that the interests of a certain stakeholder or nonstakeholder cannot be secured fully, this could be the lesser evil that should be chosen. It all depends on the nature of what is at stake. From a deontological perspective, for example, the stakes of all stakeholders do not override fundamental rights to liberty, life, and property. Starting from these premises, we conclude that fierce competition can be a morally mitigating factor for making use of loopholes in the law or to violate the law. The latter, of course, depends on the moral issues surrounding a certain law. We conclude that legal compliance can already be an ambitious strategy of CSR, for firms that have to deal with fierce competition.

In the case of strong competition, there is more room for other strategies of CSR that can contribute to product differentiation. We briefly explored the strategies of compliance with the spirit of the law, stakeholder management, brand reputation management and ethical reporting, and ethical product differentiation. To a great extent, these strategies are a necessary response to the demands of different stakeholders who have the option of taking their business to a competitor.

It is a defining characteristic of a market with weak competition that it lacks this kind of competitive pressure altogether. The legal environment, however, does provide a reason for firms in such a market to adopt some form of CSR, because of the risk of government intervention. Other reasons for firms in a market with weak competition to adopt a more ambitious strategy of CSR are of a more intrinsic nature, like the desire of management to be part of a "good" or "well-managed" company.

We analyzed the correspondences between the chosen strategy of CSR and the competitive conditions that confront a firm. From a strategic perspective, this may seem self-evident. From a moral perspective, however, it is anything but self-evident to stress the moral value of a firm's survival. Are we not prioritizing the self-interest of the firm above all other stakeholder interests, and hence, above moral duties that override self-interest? In a way we are, but only in so far as we want to acknowledge that every functioning system has to reproduce itself in order to be able to comply with whatever duty is imposed on it ("ought implies be"). Only if morality is best served by the immediate termination of business activities does this prioritization lose its validity. After all, the reasons for prioritizing a firm's survival are moral reasons.

We have outlined the main features of a normative framework that specifies how firms can compete in a morally acceptable way, given the characteristics of their competitive environment. Further empirical research could provide more detailed insight into the mechanisms through which competitive conditions actually influence the CSR strategies that firms implement. A hypothesis derived from our framework is that the more firms integrate CSR into their corporate strategy, the better they will be able to cater for the legitimate demands of their stakeholders. Also, more in-depth research is needed, from both a moral and strategic perspective, into the strategic potentials of different CSR strategies under different competitive conditions. In this way business ethics could develop a contingency approach to CSR, instead of looking for the one best ethics for all firms.

Notes

1. R. E. Freeman, *Strategic Management: A Stakeholder Approach* (Boston: Pitman, 1984); R. E. Freeman and W. M. Evan, "Corporate Governance: A Stakeholder Approach," *Journal of Behavioral Economics* 19 (1990): 337–59; A. Wicks, D. Gilbert, and E. Freeman, "A Feminist Reinterpretation of the Stakeholder Concept," *Business Ethics Quarterly* 4(4) (October 1994); Th. Donaldson and L. E. Preston, "The Stakeholder Theory of the Corporation: Concepts, Evidence and Implications," *Academy of Management Review* 20(1) (1995): 65–91; N. E. Bowie, *Business Ethics: A Kantian Perspective* (Malden, Mass.: Blackwell, 1999); R. K. Mitchell, B. R. Agle, and D. J. Wood, "Toward a Theory of Stakeholder Identification and Salience: The Principle of Who and What Really Counts," *Academy of Management Review* 22(4) (1997): 853–86.

2. Commission of the European Communities, *Communication from the Commission Concerning Corporate Social Responsibility: A Business Contribution to Sustainable Development* (Brussels: COM [2002]): 347 final, p. 3 (http://europa.eu.int/comm/employment_social/soc-dial/csr/csr_index.htm.)

3. S. Douma, H. Schreuder, *Economic Approaches to Organizations* (New York: Prentice Hall, 1991): 66.

4. J. Kay, *Foundations of Corporate Success* (Oxford: Oxford University Press, 1993): 8–9.

5. Compare C. W. Hill and T. M. Jones, "Stakeholder-Agency Theory," *Journal of Management Studies* 29 (1992): 145: "[O]bviously, the claims of different groups may conflict. . . . However, on a more general level, each group can be seen as having a stake in the continued existence of the firm." This passage is also quoted with approval in a recent article by R. Phillips, R. E. Freeman, and A. C. Wicks, "What Stakeholder Theory Is Not," *Business Ethics Quarterly* 13(4) (2003): 484.

6. L. Sharp Paine, Does Ethics Pay? *Business Ethics Quarterly* 10(1) (2000): 319–30.

7. S. P. Sethi and L. M. Sama, "Ethical Behavior as a Strategic Choice by Large Corporations: The Interactive Effect of Marketplace Competition, Industry Structure, and Firm Resources," *Business Ethics Quarterly* 8(1) (1998): 85–104.

8. R. Solomon, *Ethics and Excellence. Cooperation and Integrity in Business* (Oxford: Oxford University Press, 1992), 44.

9. P. Drucker, *Management: Tasks, Responsibilities, Practices* (New York: Harper & Row, 1974), 60.

10. H. Steinmann and A. Löhr, "Unternehmensethik: Ein republikanisches Programm in der Kritik," in *Markt und Moral: Die Diskussion um die Unternehmensethik,* ed. S. Blasche, W. Köhler, and P. Rohs (Bern: Haupt, 1994), 156.

11. Steinmann and Löhr, "Unternehmensethik," 147.

12. W. Baumol, "(Almost) Perfect Competition (Contestability) and Business Ethics," in W. Baumol and S. Batey Blackman, *Perfect Markets and Easy Virtues: Business Ethics and the Invisible Hand* (Cambridge, Mass.: Blackwell, 1991), 1–23; K. Homann and F. Blome-Drees, *Wirtschafts-und Unternehmensethik* (Göttingen: Vandenhoeck and Ruprecht, 1992), 42; Sethi and Sama, "Ethical Behavior as a Strategic Choice by Large Corporations," 90.

13. R. De George, *Competing with Integrity in International Business* (Oxford: Oxford University Press, 1993), 97.

14. Steinmann and Löhr, "Unternehmensethik," 170.

15. M. Friedman, *Capitalism and Freedom* (Chicago: University of Chicago Press, 1962), 120.

16. M. E. Porter, *Competitive Strategy: Techniques for Analyzing Industries and Competitors* (New York: Free Press, 1980); M. E. Porter, *Competitive Advantage: Creating and Sustaining Superior Performance* (New York: Free Press, 1985).

17. Porter, *Competitive Advantage,* 4.

18. Ibid., 7.

19. Porter, *Competitive Strategy,* 35.

20. A. Carroll, *Business and Society* (Boston: Little Brown, 1981); L. Sharp Paine, "Managing for Organizational Integrity," *Harvard Business Review* (March–April 1994): 106–17.

21. Sethi and Sama, "Ethical Behavior as a Strategic Choice by Large Corporations," 90.

22. One could object that bankruptcy might also mean that the interests of some stakeholders are protected. Although bankruptcy can be the best solution in the case of insolvency, it also means that the interests of the stakeholders are terminated. One could argue that this is not a moral problem, since after the bankruptcy, the assets will be put to more efficient use. Hence, total utility would benefit from bankruptcy. This argument, however, is built on the assumption that the market is efficient. This means, among other things,

that the rules governing the marketplace affect all the competitors in the same way. However, as we argued above, a lack of law enforcement punishes legal compliance and rewards noncompliance. In these circumstances, it may happen that an efficient and obedient firm goes bankrupt, while an inefficient disobedient firm survives. As a result, the social optimum will not be achieved.

23. M. Velasquez, *Business Ethics: Concepts and Cases,* 3rd ed. (Englewood Cliffs, N.J.: Prentice Hall, 1992), 40.

24. Fombrun and Rindova define corporate reputation as follows: "A corporate reputation is a collective representation of a firm's past actions and results that describes the firm's ability to deliver valued outcomes to multiple stakeholders. It gauges a firm's relative standing both internally with employees and externally with its stakeholders, in both its competitive and institutional environments." C. Fombrun and C. van Riel, "The Reputational Landscape," in *Revealing the Corporation. Perspectives on Identity, Image, Reputation, Corporate Branding, and Corporate-Level Marketing,* ed. J. Balmer and S. Greyser (London/New York: Routledge, 2003), 230.

25. Key, *Foundations of Corporate Success.*

26. Ibid., 66–86.

27. H. Steinmann and T. Olbrich, "Business Ethics in U.S. Corporations: Results from an Interview Series," in P. Ulrich and J. Wieland, *Unternehmensethik in der Praxis. Impulse aus den USA, Deutchland und der Schweiz,* (Bern: Haupt, 1998), 72.

28. Steinmann and Olbrich, "Business Ethics in U.S. Corporations," 75.

29. "We suggest that a theory of stakeholder identification and salience must somehow account for latent stakeholders if it is to be both comprehensive and useful, because such identification can, at a minimum, help organizations avoid problems and perhaps even enhance effectiveness." Mitchell, Agle, and Wood, "Toward a Theory of Stakeholder Identification and Salience," 859.

30. Kay, *Foundations of Corporate Success,* 87.

31. Ibid., 263.

32. N. Klein, *No Logo: No Space, No Choice, No Jobs: Taking Aim at the Brand Bullies* (London: Flamingo, 2000).

33. M. J. Sirgy and C. Su, "The Ethics of Consumer Sovereignty in an Age of High Tech," *Journal of Business Ethics* 28 (2000): 1–14, 2–9.

34. See, for example, the writings of John Entine, who has followed The Body Shop critically for a decade now: J. Entine, "The Body Shop: Truth and Consequences," *Drugs and Cosmetics Industry* (January 1995), 57–60; J. Entine, "Body Flop: Anita Roddick Proclaimed that Business Could be Caring as well as Capitalist. Today The Body Shop Is Struggling on Both Counts," *R.O.B.: Toronto Globe and Mail's Report on Business Magazine* (May 31, 2002).

The Ethics Commitment Process: Sustainability through Value-Based Ethics

Jacquelyn B. Gates
Soaring, LLC

Although most organizations in corporate America espouse to follow a formal ethics program, the recent headlines argue a much different case, carrying stories of widespread financial scandal and unethical business practices that make the term *business code of ethics* seem like an oxymoron.

The risk of shameful exposure seems to pale in comparison to the lure of immediate financial gain. The layers of cover-up and years of gradual deception speak of a fearless audacity by employees and executives alike. It is apparent that current business ethics strategies are ineffective. Furthermore, the general ethical health of the society at large seems to be in crisis. Is there a strength of individual conscience motivating employees to adhere to values and ethics—no matter what the cost?

In his book *The Cheating Culture*, David Callahan purports that Americans are cheating now, more than ever, to get ahead. Otherwise honest employees fall into the cheating trap when they become frustrated after trying to play by the rules and continually get beaten out by cheaters who are rarely or lightly punished. A sense that there is no true "equal opportunity" emerges and hence the need arises to cheat to get ahead. Callahan sites examples of corporate crooks "getting slapped on the wrist, while small-time criminals serve long mandatory sentences." Thus, he states, American cheaters are caught in one of two categories; a "Winning Class," which has enough money and influence to cheat without getting caught, and an "Anxious Class," which believes that not cheating will cost them an invaluable chance to achieve success.

The result? A pervasive cheating culture that creates its own ethical calculus—exchanging integrity for what seems to work. Callahan poses insightful questions, asking how workers, students, athletes, and the like will continue to do what is right if the only guarantee is that they will fall behind. What competitive high school student will tolerate a lower class ranking than other students who are getting ahead by cheating? What law firm associate hoping to make partner wants to bill honestly when others are padding their hours—and their way to making partner?

The issue of ineffective corporate ethics strategies seems to be darkly overshadowed by the need to revolutionize a winner-beats-all culture. More than reinventing ethics policies, programs, and penalties, American business must begin to do its part to instigate a behavior shift, a revolution of character, and a reintroduction of personal conscience, responsibility, and values.

A tall order? Not if corporate America partners with educators, government, and families in a broad-sweeping effort to inspire reform. Change needs to happen across the board, and a comprehensive collaboration is what is needed to unite against the demise of the "social trust" and "collective sacrifice" Callahan uses to describe a *pre-greed* America.

Reprinted from "The Ethics Commitment Process: Sustainability through Value-Based Ethics," Jacquelyn B. Gates, *Business and Society Review*, Vol. 109, No. 4 (December 2004), p. 493–505. Copyright © 2004 by Blackwell Publishing Ltd. Used by permission.

Businesses must start by looking inward and becoming actively introspective, asking hard questions and making bold changes. The very character of corporate America must center itself around long-abandoned values, integrating this thinking into all aspects of the organization.

Once a company has made the determination to join the fight against a "cheating culture," there are some basic steps the organization can take to refocus and reform. This paper will explore how organizations can cultivate a value-based ethics culture, build corporate reputation through character and trust, and increase market share through Ethics Value Added.

VALUES IN ACTION

In 1992, an entrepreneur named Rosemary Jordano set out to develop a model corporate emergency child-care facility. Her extensive research revealed a list of qualities that employer clients, parents, teachers, and children deemed the most important for providing the highest quality of care and service. These five qualities became the foundation of the "Human Qualities Initiative," an *"ongoing effort to bring greater clarity to who we are, whom we serve, and how we serve them. Our clients, children, parents and corporations see reflected in our centers not only well-honed professional skills but also the tangible manifestations of these human qualities essential to outstanding nurturing. Through our focus on these human qualities, we continue to enhance the way we serve each child and family."*[1]

In 1992, the ChildrenFirst company was launched in Boston, and has since grown to serve more than 260 clients in 32 centers. Throughout ChildrenFirst's history, the Human Qualities Initiative has been integrated into all facets of the business, from hiring to training, daily communications, local and regional meetings, conflict resolution, and performance/incentive standards. The Human Qualities[2] form the basis of all interaction and are the measure of true success within the company.

More than a code of conduct, the Human Qualities Initiative has inspired a sense of purpose, responsibility, and integrity within the ChildrenFirst organization. It forms a standard of behavior, but also empowers employees to think critically about how their actions affect themselves, their peers,

clients, and the children they serve. There is an expectation throughout the business environment that employees have a part in influencing the culture, and, without consistency, leave areas of dangerous vulnerability. There is a sense of ownership—a keen awareness that each employee "owns" a part of the overall culture of the business, with a responsibility to nurture, grow, and be accountable to his/her part in achieving the corporate vision.

ChildrenFirst's commitment to their proven values has inspired consistent, sustainable success.

MORE THAN A CODE

A mere compliance-based code of conduct does not have the energy or substance to produce a culture change. Alone, it has a stagnant authority that does not arouse analytical thinking on the part of the employee. The presence of the code of conduct suggests that simply complying with the rules is ethical behavior. But true ethical behavior is more than conformity to the law; it is understanding the value of the law and what it is trying to accomplish. The law is only a means to an end, and when a business bases its ethics strategies on the law rather than on the values behind the law, it will not produce a culture where personal responsibility drives critical thinking and decision making.

On the other hand, organizations that base their ethics process solely on a list of values will have the same problem. Even if the values are important to the leadership and to the success of the company, if leaders have done little to "flush out" how those values should manifest in everyday business, employees will be left to make fairly uninformed decisions with little or no accountability.

When the law (or compliance-based rules) and values are fused into a mutually influential set of principles, they become powerful tools that help to achieve greater understanding and accountability within the organization. A successful ethics program is the product of the proper marriage of the two principles.

The above diagram illustrates how values, compliance, and the synergy of the two working together create a successful program.

Triangle Point 1: Organizations are made up of people—employees who, by exemplifying shared

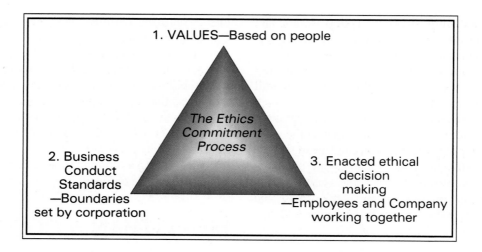

values, are the strongest demonstration of the company's worth and potential.

Triangle Point 2: The company's business standards should operate as "safe boundaries" that provide guidance in much the same way that medians on the highway guide cars as they move forward to their destination.

Triangle Point 3: As employees integrate the company's values into their daily business routines and adhere to the business standards of compliance, they will be better equipped to execute ethical decision making. The employees should commit to the company, and the company to its employees. Together, they should be (1) committed to consistently incorporating the values into every aspect of business, (2) committed to allowing autonomous decision-making power based on putting the values into action, and (3) committed to providing fair conduct standards with consistent reinforcement.

Any one of these elements without the other will produce an imbalanced perspective—either too much emphasis on the people without structure, or too much structure without giving employees a sense of empowerment and a chance to critically develop workable solutions to ethical dilemmas.

Together, the three elements—values, standards, and enacted ethical decision making—form an "Ethics Commitment Process." When all three parts are committed to working together to develop an ethical corporation, the company positions itself for long-term success.

This process is more than a trend, more than compliance, and more than a reactive effort. It is about achieving corporate excellence through the ethics process as an ongoing commitment to corporate and personal values. The values of trust, integrity, and quality are the foundation of showing stakeholders that a company is "doing the right thing." Eventually, trust will equal market share.

DIGGING DEEPER

An ethics system cannot influence change unless it is

- Motivated by an inspirational set of core values.
- Translated into continuous communications and training materials.
- Supported by a system of consistent rewards, incentives, and immediate penalties.

To begin the Ethics Commitment Process, a company must start by developing a core set of values. The values are the base—the foundation—of the process.

Tom Peters and Bob Waterman write in their book *In Search of Excellence*, "Every excellent company we studied is clear on what it stands for, and takes the process of value shaping seriously. In fact, we wonder whether it is possible to be an excellent company without clarity on values and without having the right sorts of values."

Values are characteristics of the organization that are visionary, clear, obtainable, and focused on the human element. They promote integrity, advocate respect for others, and revitalize a sense of community among workers.

Ethical decision making is based on making decisions that reflect the company's values. Choosing between two rights becomes a question of "which solution more closely reflects our values and gives us the most long-term sustainability?"

Soon, the values become the very character of the organization.

The word for character comes from the Greek word *charakter*, which means "engraving tool." This definition brings to life the notion that our experiences leave an indelible mark on our attitudes and life choices. They shape our character. In the same way, our character shapes and influences our actions, impacts our work, and affects decision making.

One of the most essential values is integrity. The word *integrity* is from the Latin origin "integer," meaning "whole" or "complete." It is the alignment of deeply held beliefs (i.e., values) and everyday actions and decisions. Integrity is the quality that bridges the gap from ideals to action and motivates employees to compliance.

In effect, organizations and individuals build character by exercising integrity.

As corporate values become the character of the organization, they will leave a mark on corporate reputation, leadership, employees, and stakeholders.

A corporate emphasis on values will foster an atmosphere of trust and empowerment within the organization. When employees feel as if they are serving a dictator, or a dictatorial set of rules, they are less productive, there is higher turnover, and there is less opportunity for creative conflict resolution.

THE ROLE OF LEADERSHIP

All businesses have missions—a statement or idea of *what* they desire to accomplish. Business values depict *how* the business will accomplish those goals and objectives.

In order to gain employee buy-in, foster a productive work environment, and build sustainability, leadership must exemplify and communicate the company's core values.

As leadership embodies the values—consistently and privately—employees will find security and accountability in knowing that there are fair expectations and clear standards across the board.

Leadership that motivates employees to be ethical helps employees to embrace the vision of the company as their own. When employees know their place and understand how their job contributes to the overall vision of the company, they are willing to accept the values and standards as a means to achieve a common "destiny." In this way, the values are not a distant set of ideals. Rather, employees "own" the vision and the values that make the vision credible!

ELEMENTS OF THE ETHICAL COMMITMENT PROCESS

A successful and visionary ethics process includes the following:

- A set of proven, shared values developed with all stakeholders in mind.
- Guiding principles that direct how the values will become operative.
- Standards of compliance and accountability.
- Critical thinking skills.
- "Moral autonomy"—being ethically reflective using the following thought pattern stop, think, ask, decide, act.
- A live form of support (i.e., hotline), preferably confidential and outsourced so employees are without fear of exposure or retribution.
- Training and discussion.
- Regular communications—values, principles, and standards should be "in the open," discussed regularly and integrated into interdepartmental as well as external communications.
- A leadership review of ethics-in-action within the company to demonstrate leadership's commitment to ethics (one of a number of ways, not the only one).
- An ethics risk assessment—a due diligence process means of evaluating consistency of business opportunities with values.
- A periodic sampling for effectiveness (i.e., surveys, focus groups). Ethics programs should have built-in flexibility and evolve with the company's size, scope, and purpose. Self-assessment should be objectively measured through the periodic help of a third party.

Organizations should start the process by having leadership develop a set of core values based on employee, customer, and stakeholder input. Gaining employee buy-in is key, and this is done by helping employees to see the corporate vision as their own— fostering a culture where they take ownership in an environment that values teamwork and accountability.

Buy-in is also facilitated over time through regular communications and consistent training. Training should not be viewed as a skill enhancement exercise alone, but as a behavioral shift, implemented by tested change methodologies.

Practical programs and policies are augmented by a powerful and strategic ethics organizational structure. There are a number of helpful elements, including a trusted and public ethics officer position that reports directly to senior leadership, preferably the CEO; public rewards and accountability measures; and strong interdepartmental partnerships, including Security, Legal, Human Resources, Labor Relations, Internal Auditing, and Safety, to name a few examples.

When these processes and structures are implemented consistently, companies position themselves to endure the long-term challenges of time and grow to be sustainable organizations.

SUSTAINABILITY: THE KEY TO LONG-TERM SUCCESS AND PROFITABILITY

There is a principle in nature called the Law of Sowing and Reaping which asserts that the kind of seed that is scattered today will bear a like fruit tomorrow.

There is a similar force at work in business; that which is determined, invested, organized, and implemented today will produce an analogous result at a future point. An organization can prepare itself to endure unforeseen challenges, ensure integrity in its promises, and secure a profitable future for its stakeholders by sowing attention and resources into the factors that will nurture long-term sustainability.

In 2002, PricewaterhouseCoopers (PwC) surveyed 140 large, U.S.-based companies to see how well American companies were responding to the challenge of increasing long-term sustainability.

PwC found that, in general, the respondents understood that (since the plethora of accounting scandals) the public now holds them "even more accountable for their environmental, social and economic activities—and their effects. But *less than 30%* had programs to systematically identify and evaluate these sustainability related risks."[3] Without these programs there is a significant risk and liability for the company.

In the fall of 1982, seven people on Chicago's West Side died because they had each ingested an Extra-Strength Tylenol capsule laced with cyanide. The news caused a massive, nationwide panic.

As soon as the connection between the deaths and the Tylenol was discovered, police began to drive through Chicago announcing the warning over loudspeakers. The national TV networks reported the deaths and, a day later, the Food and Drug Administration advised consumers to avoid the Tylenol capsules altogether. Soon copycat offenders tried to further compromise the over-the-counter drug.

Who would ever buy a bottle of Tylenol again?

In 1984, the Union Carbide chemical spill in Bhopal claimed more than 22,000 lives. At first, the company denied wrongdoing and was not forthright about the extent of the damage. Union Carbide never fully recovered from their financial troubles and the loss of public trust because of the way the incident was handled.

When Source Perrier found traces of benzene in their bottled water, they claimed that the contamination resulted from an isolated incident. It later became evident that this was based upon limited research into the event. As a result, they only recalled a few bottles of Perrier in North America. When benzene was found in Perrier bottled water in Europe, an embarrassed company then had to announce a worldwide recall. When consumers around the world found out they had been drinking contaminated water, the company was harshly attacked by the media. They were said to have had little integrity by disregarding public safety for their own concerns.

In 2000, Firestone had to recall 6.5 million tires that caused approximately 400 incidents, including 46 deaths. Firestone and Ford spent the first two weeks after the tire story broke arguing about whose fault it really was. Meanwhile, people were dying and families were losing loved ones. No one cared about whose fault it *wasn't*—they just wanted to know that solutions were in the making.

This critical time lost dealt a severe blow to the credibility of both companies. By the time Jacques Nasser, CEO of Ford, began making TV commercials to regain public approval, many said it was too little, too late. The continuing questions surrounding the automaker and tire maker still cloud their reputations.

In each of these incidents, warning signs emerged early enough for the companies to take preventive and corrective action. However, these signs were ignored, suppressed, or mishandled, causing terrible outcomes.

Further examination reveals that the businesses that survived had made decisions and laid groundwork before the crisis occurred. They shared a common priority: positioning themselves for the long term by establishing core values and processes and sticking by them at all costs.

In this way, they gained EVA . . . Ethical Value Added, adding to corporate reputation and bottom-line results by utilizing their ethics processes to guard against loss.

THE SUM OF SUCCESS: ETHICAL VALUE ADDED

Investing in EVA means building a strong ethics foundation within the organization. It is taking an honest look at what core beliefs, values, and responses are truly—not just seemingly—in operation within the organization, and working to mend loopholes. The resulting ideology is a set of basic objectives that serve as the base for all corporate activity—not just ethics and compliance issues, but business, marketing, PR, sourcing, finance, mergers, acquisitions, and so forth.

Companies that have weathered terrible storms have applied this principle with great purpose and effort. They have taken an honest look at their business values, improved them with the times of crisis in mind, and implemented them fully in the midst of the "storm," taking full advantage of the value of EVA.

The Johnson & Johnson Tylenol tragedy is a prime example. Early on, Robert Wood Johnson developed a document called "The Credo," setting forth the values by which J&J would always operate. The Credo became a part of everyday decision making as J&J integrated it into company communications. Employees were trained in its principles, and the leadership committed to embodying its values—publicly and privately.

During the Tylenol crisis, the makers of Tylenol openly admitted the problem and promised a replacement for every bottle returned by customers. In accordance with the Credo, leadership made the decision to make good on their promise to the customer; they went ahead with a $100 million recall of Tylenol products, and company stock value dropped 17 percent.

After launching a public relations program to help save the integrity of both their product and the corporation, J&J regained their share value—and surpassed it—within one month. Within three months, Tylenol had recaptured 95 percent of its market share.

That outcome was a defining—Ethical Value Added—moment, contributing to J&J's continued success. The EVA element was perhaps the greatest factor in their growth and long-term sustainability. The investment return of ethics-in-action is that EVA will almost certainly generate Economic Value Added when implemented consistently.

CHARACTER IN CRISIS

Ethically sound and sustainable companies thrive on the value of "discontent." Collins and Porras, authors of *Built to Last*, elaborate on this: "Visionary" companies understand that contentment leads to complacency, which inevitably leads to decline, and so they find a way to avoid it, remain self-disciplined, and continually improve how the organization runs and moves ahead. These types of organizations build in processes and methods to periodically sample or test for effectiveness of their business standards.

Collins and Porras call this a "discomfort mechanism," a way to combat the disease of complacency within a corporation. Visionary companies build in these discomfort mechanisms on purpose so that they do not become settled into business as usual or develop a laissez-faire attitude.

Visionary companies will speculate and attempt to see into the future—they imagine various scenarios that could occur in their facilities, with suppliers/vendors or employees, and scandals that could arise in the news, and so on. Of course it is impossible to foresee the future or to predict what exactly will happen. But the company that looks at potential pitfalls and ethical infringements can be more prepared to weather a crisis when—not if—it occurs.

WRAPPING IT UP

It is time that businesses began to lead the charge for a cultural reform and rebirth of ethical business practices. Institutional and individual behaviors must be transformed for true change to occur. Our actions in public are a reflection of deeply held private beliefs and practices, which, in light of the current headlines, demonstrate a powerful need for comprehensive reform.

What can businesses do? Externally, they can develop strong networks of collaboration to see that corporate thinking and character advance across the board. Corporate America must increase incentives for doing the right thing, and ensure parity of penalties for wrongdoing.

Internally, business must make an ongoing commitment to strengthening, communicating, enforcing, and rewarding corporate and personal values. The measure of effective ethics systems is the degree to which they influence change and inspire a behavior shift.

A successful ethics program builds corporate character from a set of core values and works as a contract between employer and employee. Together, the three elements—values, standards, and enacted ethical decision making—form an "Ethics Commitment Process," positioning the company for long-term success.

The Commitment Process facilitates corporate character building, seeking to mark actions and attitudes with integrity. Integrity motivates employees to comply with business standards and make ethical decisions because they have internalized the values and the importance of engaging them.

Leadership plays a key role in making an ethics process work. Their job is to help employees grab hold of the vision and the values and "own" them as their own. In this way, every decision is a personal choice to "do the right thing." Moments of crisis and competition are the two greatest mirrors for finding raw truth about an organization's true values and ethical standards. As visionary and sustainable companies build in "mechanisms of discontent," they will prepare, position, and pave the way for success even in the midst of a problem.

The bottom line is, it pays to be ethical. Long-term sustainability is built on the law of sowing and reaping—what a company builds today will determine its success tomorrow. Investment in the Ethical Value Added will almost always yield an economic return.

Committing to character in crisis is crucial to building and keeping stakeholder trust. Trust will improve corporate reputation and eventually increase market share. In the long run, *doing the right thing* will always reap a fruitful reward and pave the way for true change in generations to come.

Notes

1. http://www.childrenfirst.com/about/qualities.php.
2. The Human Qualities are perseverance, tolerance, optimism, commitment, and patience.
3. Savitz, A. "Sustainable Business Practices: Managing Risk and Opportunity." PricewaterhouseCoopers. www.pwcglobal.com/rebusiness.

Chapter 1

[1]Costas Markides, "What Is Strategy and How Do You Know If You Have One?" *Business Strategy Review* 15, no. 2 (Summer 2004), pp. 5–6.

[2]For a discussion of the different ways in which companies can position themselves in the marketplace, see Michael E. Porter, "What Is Strategy?" *Harvard Business Review* 74, no. 6 (November–December 1996), pp. 65–67.

[3]For an excellent treatment of the strategic challenges posed by high-velocity changes, see Shona L. Brown and Kathleen M. Eisenhardt, *Competing on the Edge: Strategy as Structured Chaos* (Boston: Harvard Business School Press, 1998), Chapter 1.

[4]See Henry Mintzberg and Joseph Lampel, "Reflecting on the Strategy Process, *Sloan Management Review* 40, no. 3 (Spring 1999), pp. 21–30; Henry Mintzberg and J. A. Waters, "Of Strategies, Deliberate and Emergent," *Strategic Management Journal* 6 (1985), pp. 257–72; Costas Markides, "Strategy as Balance: From 'Either-Or' to 'And,'" *Business Strategy Review* 12, no. 3 (September 2001), pp. 1–10; Henry Mintzberg, Bruce Ahlstrand, and Joseph Lampel, *Strategy Safari: A Guided Tour through the Wilds of Strategic Management* (New York: Free Press, 1998), 7; and C. K. Prahalad and Gary Hamel, "The Core Competence of the Corporation," *Harvard Business Review* 70, no. 3 (May–June 1990), pp. 79–93.

[5]Joseph L. Badaracco, "The Discipline of Building Character," *Harvard Business Review* 76, no. 2 (March–April 1998), pp. 115–24.

[6]Joan Magretta, "Why Business Models Matter," *Harvard Business Review* 80, no. 5 (May 2002), p. 87.

Chapter 2

[1]For a more in-depth discussion of the challenges of developing a well-conceived vision, as well as some good examples, see Hugh Davidson, *The Committed Enterprise: How to Make Vision and Values Work* (Oxford: Butterworth Heinemann, 2002), Chapter 2; W. Chan Kim and Renée Mauborgne, "Charting Your Company's Future," *Harvard Business Review* 80, no. 6 (June 2002), pp. 77–83; James C. Collins and Jerry I. Porras, "Building Your Company's Vision," *Harvard Business Review* 74, no. 5 (September–October 1996), pp. 65–77; James C. Collins and Jerry I. Porras, *Built to Last: Successful Habits of Visionary Companies* (New York: HarperCollins, 1994), Chapter 11; and Michel Robert, *Strategy Pure and Simple II* (New York: McGraw-Hill, 1998), Chapters 2, 3, and 6.

[2]Davidson, *Committed Enterprise,* pp. 20, 54.

[3]Ibid., pp. 36, 54.

[4]Jeffrey K. Liker, *The Toyota Way* (New York: McGraw-Hill, 2004), and Steve Hamm, "Taking a Page from Toyota's Playbook," *BusinessWeek,* August 22/29, 2005, p. 72.

[5]As quoted in Charles H. House and Raymond L. Price, "The Return Map: Tracking Product Teams," *Harvard Business Review* 60, no. 1 (January–February 1991), p. 93.

[6]Robert S. Kaplan and David P. Norton, *The Strategy-Focused Organization* (Boston: Harvard Business School Press, 2001), p. 3.

[7]Ibid., p. 7. Also, see Kevin B. Hendricks, Larry Menor, and Christine Wiedman, "The Balanced Scorecard: To Adopt or Not to Adopt," *Ivey Business Journal* 69, no. 2 (November–December 2004), pp. 1–7; and Sandy Richardson, "The Key Elements of Balanced Scorecard Success," *Ivey Business Journal* 69, no. 2 (November–December 2004), pp. 7–9.

[8]Information posted on the Web site of the Balanced Scorecard Institute, www.balancedscorecard.org (accessed August 22, 2005).

[9]Darrell Rigby, "Management Tools Survey 2003: Usage Up as Companies Strive to Make Headway in Tough Times," *Strategy & Leadership* 31, no. 5 (May 2003), p. 6.

[10]Information posted on the Web site of Balanced Scorecard Collaborative, www.bscol.com (accessed August 22, 2005). This Web site was created by the co-creators of the balanced scorecard concept, Professors Robert S. Kaplan and David P. Norton, Harvard Business School.

[11]The concept of strategic intent is described in more detail in Gary Hamel and C. K. Prahalad, "Strategic Intent," *Harvard Business Review* 89, no. 3 (May–June 1989), pp. 63–76; this section draws on their pioneering discussion. See also Michael A. Hitt, Beverly B. Tyler, Camilla Hardee, and Daewoo Park, "Understanding Strategic Intent in the Global Marketplace," *Academy of Management Executive* 9, no. 2 (May 1995), pp. 12–19.

[12]For a fuller discussion of strategy as an entrepreneurial process, see Henry Mintzberg, Bruce Ahlstrand, and Joseph Lampel, *Strategy Safari: A Guided Tour through the Wilds of Strategic Management,* (New York: Free Press, 1998), Chapter 5. Also see Bruce Barringer and Allen C. Bluedorn, "The Relationship Between Corporate Entrepreneurship and Strategic Management," *Strategic Management Journal* 20 (1999), pp. 421–444, and Jeffrey G. Covin and Morgan P. Miles, "Corporate Entrepreneurship and the Pursuit of Competitive Advantage," *Entrepreneurship: Theory and Practice* 23, no. 3 (Spring 1999), pp. 47–63.

[13]The strategy-making, strategy-implementing roles of middle managers are thoroughly discussed and documented in Steven W. Floyd and Bill Wooldridge, *The Strategic Middle Manager* (San Francisco: Jossey-Bass Publishers, 1996), Chapters 2 and 3.

[14]"Strategic Planning," *Business Week,* August 26, 1996, pp. 51–52.

[15]For an excellent discussion of why a strategic plan needs to be more than a list of bullet points and should in fact tell an engaging, insightful, stage-setting story that lays out the industry and competitive situation as well as the vision, objectives, and strategy, see Gordon Shaw, Robert Brown, and Philip Bromiley, "Strategic Stories: How 3M Is Rewriting Business Planning," *Harvard Business Review* 76, no. 3 (May–June 1998), pp. 41–50.

[16]For a discussion of what it takes for the corporate governance system to function properly, see David A. Nadler, "Building Better Boards," *Harvard Business Review* 82, no. 5 (May 2004), pp. 102–5; Cynthia A. Montgomery and Rhonda Kaufman, "The Board's Missing Link," *Harvard Business Review* 81, no. 3 (March 2003), pp. 86–93; and John Carver, "What Continues to Be Wrong with Corporate Governance and How to Fix It," *Ivey Business Journal* 68, no. 1 (September–October 2003), pp. 1–5. See also Gordon Donaldson, "A New Tool for Boards: The Strategic Audit," *Harvard Business Review* 73, no. 4 (July–August 1995), pp. 99–107.

Chapter 3

[1]There are a large number of studies of the size of the cost reductions associated with experience; the median cost reduction associated with a doubling of cumulative production volume is approximately 15 percent, but there is a wide variation from industry to industry. For a good discussion of the economies of experience and learning, see Pankaj Ghemawat, "Building Strategy on the Experience Curve," *Harvard Business Review* 64, no. 2 (March–April 1985), pp. 143–49.

[2]The five-forces model of competition is the creation of Professor Michael Porter of the Harvard Business School. For his original presentation of the model, see Michael E. Porter, "How Competitive Forces Shape Strategy," *Harvard Business Review* 57, no. 2

(March–April 1979), pp. 137–45. A more thorough discussion can be found in Michael E. Porter, *Competitive Strategy: Techniques for Analyzing Industries and Competitors* (New York: Free Press, 1980), Chapter 1.

[3]Many of these indicators of whether rivalry produces intense competitive pressures are based on Porter, *Competitive Strategy,* pp. 17–21.

[4]The role of entry barriers in shaping the strength of competition in a particular market has long been a standard topic in the literature of microeconomics. For a discussion of how entry barriers affect competitive pressures associated with potential entry, see J. S. Bain, *Barriers to New Competition* (Cambridge: Harvard University Press, 1956); F. M. Scherer, *Industrial Market Structure and Economic Performance* (Chicago: Rand McNally, 1971), pp. 216–20, 226–33; and Porter, *Competitive Strategy,* pp. 7–17.

[5]Porter, "How Competitive Forces Shape Strategy," p. 140, and Porter, *Competitive Strategy,* pp. 14–15.

[6]For a good discussion of this point, see George S. Yip, "Gateways to Entry," *Harvard Business Review* 60, no. 5 (September–October 1982), pp. 85–93.

[7]Porter, "How Competitive Forces Shape Strategy," p. 142, and Porter, *Competitive Strategy,* pp. 23–24.

[8]Porter, *Competitive Strategy,* p. 10.

[9]Ibid., pp. 27–28.

[10]Ibid., pp. 24–27.

[11]For a more extended discussion of the problems with the life-cycle hypothesis, see ibid., pp. 157–62.

[12]Ibid. p. 162.

[13]Most of the candidate driving forces described here are based on the discussion in ibid., pp. 164–83.

[14]Ibid., Chapter 7.

[15]Ibid., pp. 129–30.

[16]For an excellent discussion of how to identify the factors that define strategic groups, see Mary Ellen Gordon and George R. Milne, "Selecting the Dimensions That Define Strategic Groups: A Novel Market-Driven Approach," *Journal of Managerial Issues* 11, no. 2 (Summer 1999), pp. 213–33.

[17]Porter, *Competitive Strategy,* pp. 152–54.

[18]Strategic groups act as good reference points for predicting the evolution of an industry's competitive structure. See Avi Fiegenbaum and Howard Thomas, "Strategic Groups as Reference Groups: Theory, Modeling and Empirical Examination of Industry and Competitive Strategy," *Strategic Management Journal* 16 (1995), pp. 461–76. For a study of how strategic group analysis helps identify the variables that lead to sustainable competitive advantage, see S. Ade Olusoga, Michael P. Mokwa, and Charles H. Noble,

"Strategic Groups, Mobility Barriers, and Competitive Advantage," *Journal of Business Research* 33 (1995), pp. 153–64.

[19]Porter, *Competitive Strategy,* pp. 130, 132–38, and 154–55.

[20]For a discussion of legal and ethical ways of gathering competitive intelligence on rival companies, see Larry Kahaner, *Competitive Intelligence* (New York: Simon & Schuster, 1996).

[21]Ibid., pp. 84–85.

[22]Some experts dispute the strategy-making value of key success factors. Professor Pankaj Ghemawat has claimed that the "whole idea of identifying a success factor and then chasing it seems to have something in common with the ill-considered medieval hunt for the *philosopher's stone,* a substance which would transmute everything it touched into gold." Pankaj Ghemawat, *Commitment: The Dynamic of Strategy* (New York: Free Press, 1991), p. 11.

Chapter 4

[1]Many business organizations are coming to view cutting-edge knowledge and intellectual resources of company personnel as a valuable competitive asset and have concluded that explicitly managing these assets is an essential part of their strategy. See Michael H. Zack, "Developing a Knowledge Strategy," *California Management Review* 41, no. 3 (Spring 1999), pp. 125–45, and Shaker A. Zahra, Anders P. Nielsen, and William C. Bogner, "Corporate Entrepreneurship, Knowledge, and Competence Development," *Entrepreneurship Theory and Practice,* Spring 1999, pp. 169–89.

[2]In the past decade, there's been considerable research into the role a company's resources and competitive capabilities play in crafting strategy and in determining company profitability. The findings and conclusions have coalesced into what is called the resource-based view of the firm. Among the most insightful articles are Birger Wernerfelt, "A Resource-Based View of the Firm," *Strategic Management Journal,* September–October 1984, pp. 171–80; Jay Barney, "Firm Resources and Sustained Competitive Advantage," *Journal of Management* 17, no. 1 (1991), pp. 99–120; Margaret A. Peteraf, "The Cornerstones of Competitive Advantage: A Resource-Based View," *Strategic Management Journal,* March 1993, pp. 179–91; Birger Wernerfelt, "The Resource-Based View of the Firm: Ten Years After," *Strategic Management Journal* 16 (1995), pp. 171–74; Jay Barney, "Looking Inside for Competitive Advantage," *Academy of Management Executive* 9, no. 4 (November 1995), pp. 49–61; Christopher A. Bartlett and Sumantra Ghoshal, "Building Competitive Advantage through People,"

MIT Sloan Management Review 43, no 2, (Winter 2002), pp. 34–41; and Danny Miller, Russell Eisenstat, and Nathaniel Foote, "Strategy from the Inside Out: Building Capability-Creating Organizations," *California Management Review* 44, no. 3 (Spring 2002), pp. 37–54.

[3]George Stalk Jr. and Rob Lachenauer, "Hard Ball: Five Killer Strategies for Trouncing the Competition," *Harvard Business Review* 82, no. 4 (April 2004), p. 65.

[4]For a more extensive discussion of how to identify and evaluate the competitive power of a company's capabilities, see David W. Birchall and George Tovstiga, "The Strategic Potential of a Firm's Knowledge Portfolio," *Journal of General Management* 25, no. 1 (Autumn 1999), pp. 1–16, and Nick Bontis, Nicola C. Dragonetti, Kristine Jacobsen, and Goran Roos, "The Knowledge Toolbox: A Review of the Tools Available to Measure and Manage Intangible Resources," *European Management Journal* 17, no. 4 (August 1999), pp. 391–401. Also see David Teece, "Capturing Value from Knowledge Assets: The New Economy, Markets for Know-How, and Intangible Assets," *California Management Review* 40, no. 3 (Spring 1998), pp. 55–79.

[5]See Barney, "Firm Resources," pp. 105–9, and David J. Collis and Cynthia A. Montgomery, "Competing on Resources: Strategy in the 1990s," *Harvard Business Review* 73, no. 4 (July–August 1995), pp. 120–23.

[6]Donald Sull, "Strategy as Active Waiting," *Harvard Business Review* 83, no. 9 (September 2005), p. 121–122.

[7]Ibid., p. 122.

[8]Ibid., pp. 124–26.

[9]See Jack W. Duncan, Peter Ginter, and Linda E. Swayne, "Competitive Advantage and Internal Organizational Assessment," *Academy of Management Executive* 12, no. 3 (August 1998), pp. 6–16.

[10]The value chain concept was developed and articulated by Professor Michael Porter at the Harvard Business School and is described at greater length in Michael E. Porter, *Competitive Advantage* (New York: Free Press, 1985), Chapters 2 and 3.

[11]Ibid., p. 36.

[12]Ibid., p. 34.

[13]The strategic importance of effective supply chain management is discussed in Hau L. Lee, "The Triple-A Supply Chain," *Harvard Business Review* 82, no. 10 (October 2004), pp. 102–112.

[14]M. Hegert and D. Morris, "Accounting Data for Value Chain Analysis," *Strategic Management Journal* 10 (1989), p. 180; Robin Cooper and Robert S. Kaplan, "Measure Costs Right: Make the Right Decisions," *Harvard Business Review* 66, no. 5 (September–October, 1988), pp. 96–103; and John K. Shank and Vijay

Govindarajan, *Strategic Cost Management* (New York: Free Press, 1993), especially Chapters 2–6, 10.

[15]For more on how and why the clustering of suppliers and other support organizations matter to a company's costs and competitiveness, see Michael E. Porter, "Clusters and the New Economics of Competition," *Harvard Business Review* 76, no. 6 (November–December 1998), pp. 77–90.

[16]For discussions of the accounting challenges in calculating the costs of value chain activities, see Shank and Govindarajan, *Strategic Cost Management,* especially Chapters 2–6, 10, and 11; Cooper and Kaplan, "Measure Costs Right"; and Joseph A. Ness and Thomas G. Cucuzza, "Tapping the Full Potential of ABC," *Harvard Business Review* 73, no. 4 (July–August 1995), pp. 130–38.

[17]For more details, see Gregory H. Watson, *Strategic Benchmarking: How to Rate Your Company's Performance Against the World's Best* (New York: John Wiley, 1993); Robert C. Camp, *Benchmarking: The Search for Industry Best Practices That Lead to Superior Performance* (Milwaukee: ASQC Quality Press, 1989); Christopher E. Bogan and Michael J. English, *Benchmarking for Best Practices: Winning through Innovative Adaptation* (New York: McGraw-Hill, 1994); and Dawn Iacobucci and Christie Nordhielm, "Creative Benchmarking," *Harvard Business Review* 78 no. 6 (November–December 2000), pp. 24–25.

[18]Jeremy Main, "How to Steal the Best Ideas Around," *Fortune,* October 19, 1992, pp. 102–3.

[19]Shank and Govindarajan, *Strategic Cost Management,* p. 50.

[20]Some of these options are discussed in more detail in Porter, *Competitive Advantage,* Chapter 3.

[21]An example of how Whirlpool Corporation transformed its supply chain from a competitive liability to a competitive asset is discussed in Reuben E. Stone, "Leading a Supply Chain Turnaround," *Harvard Business Review* 82, no. 10 (October 2004), pp. 114–21.

[22]James Brian Quinn, *Intelligent Enterprise* (New York: Free Press, 1993), p. 54.

[23]Ibid., p. 34.

Chapter 5

[1]This classification scheme is an adaptation of a narrower three-strategy classification presented in Michael E. Porter, *Competitive Strategy: Techniques for Analyzing Industries and Competitors* (New York: Free Press, 1980), Chapter 2, especially pp. 35–40 and 44–46. For a discussion of the different ways in which companies can position themselves in the marketplace, see Michael E. Porter, "What Is Strategy?" *Harvard Business Review* 74, no. 6 (November–December 1996), pp. 65–67.

[2]Porter, *Competitive Advantage*, p. 97.

[3]Iowa Beef Packers' value chain revamping was first reported in ibid., p. 109. Since then the company has successfully extended its efforts to reconfigure the meat industry value chain, including an entry into the pork segment. IBP was acquired in 2001 by Tyson Foods after a heated bidding war with Smithfield Foods drove Tyson's acquisition price up to $14 billion. Tyson is now applying many of the same value chain revamping principles in chicken, beef, and pork.

[4]Ibid., pp. 135–38.

[5]For a more detailed discussion, see George Stalk, Philip Evans, and Lawrence E. Schulman, "Competing on Capabilities: The New Rules of Corporate Strategy," *Harvard Business Review* 70, no. 2 (March–April 1992), pp. 57–69.

[6]The relevance of perceived value and signaling is discussed in more detail in Porter, *Competitive Advantage,* pp. 138–42.

[7]Ibid., pp. 160–62.

[8]Gary Hamal, "Strategy as Revolution," *Harvard Business Review* 74, no. 4 (July–August 1996), p. 72.

Chapter 6

[1]Yves L. Doz and Gary Hamel, *Alliance Advantage: The Art of Creating Value through Partnering* (Boston: Harvard Business School Press, 1998), pp. xiii, xiv.

[2]Jason Wakeam, "The Five Factors of a Strategic Alliance," *Ivey Business Journal* 68, no. 3 (May–June 2003), pp. 1–4.

[3]Jeffrey H. Dyer, Prashant Kale, and Harbir Singh, "When to Ally and When to Acquire," *Harvard Business Review* 82, no. 7/8 (July–August 2004), p. 109.

[4]Salvatore Parise and Lisa Sasson, "Leveraging Knowledge Management across Strategic Alliances," *Ivey Business Journal* 66, no. 4 (March–April 2002), p. 42.

[5]David Ernst and James Bamford, "Your Alliances Are Too Stable," *Harvard Business Review* 83, no. 6 (June 2005), p. 133.

[6]An excellent discussion of the portfolio approach to managing multiple alliances and how to restructure a faltering alliance is presented in ibid., pp. 133–41.

[7]Michael E. Porter, *The Competitive Advantage of Nations* (New York: Free Press, 1990), p. 66. For a discussion of how to realize the advantages of strategic partnerships, see Nancy J. Kaplan and Jonathan Hurd, "Realizing the Promise of Partnerships," *Journal of Business Strategy* 23, no. 3 (May–June 2002), pp. 38–42; Parise and Sasson, "Leveraging Knowledge Management," pp. 41–47; and Ernst and Bamford, "Your Alliances Are Too Stable," pp. 133–41.

[8]A. Inkpen, "Learning, Knowledge Acquisition, and Strategic Alliances," *European Management Journal* 16, no. 2 (April 1998), pp. 223–29.

[9]For a discussion of how to raise the chances that a strategic alliance will produce strategically important outcomes, see M. Koza and A. Lewin, "Managing Partnerships and Strategic Alliances: Raising the Odds of Success," *European Management Journal* 18, no. 2 (April 2000), pp. 146–51.

[10]Doz and Hamel, *Alliance Advantage,* Chapters 4–8; Patricia Anslinger and Justin Jenk, "Creating Successful Alliances," *Journal of Business Strategy* 25, no. 2 (2004), pp. 18–23; Rosabeth Moss Kanter, "Collaborative Advantage: The Art of the Alliance," *Harvard Business Review* 72, no. 4 (July–August 1994), pp. 96–108; Joel Bleeke and David Ernst, "The Way to Win in Cross-Border Alliances," *Harvard Business Review* 69, no. 6 (November–December 1991), pp. 127–35 and Gary Hamel, Yves L. Doz, and C. K. Prahalad, "Collaborate with Your Competitors—and Win," *Harvard Business Review* 67, no. 1 (January–February 1989), pp. 133–39.

[11]This same 50 percent success rate for alliances was also cited in Ernst and Bamford, "Your Alliances Are Too Stable," p. 133; both co-authors of this *HBR* article were McKinsey personnel.

[12]Doz and Hamel, *Alliance Advantage,* pp. 16–18.

[13]Dyer, Kale, and Singh, "When to Ally and When to Acquire," p. 109.

[14]For an excellent discussion of the pros and cons of alliances versus acquisitions, see ibid., pp. 109–15.

[15]For an excellent review of the strategic objectives of various types of mergers and acquisitions and the managerial challenges that different kinds of mergers and acquisitions present, see Joseph L. Bower, "Not All M&As Are Alike—and That Matters," *Harvard Business Review* 79, no. 3 (March 2001), pp. 93–101.

[16]For a more expansive discussion, see Dyer, Kale, and Singh, "When to Ally and When to Acquire," pp. 109–10.

[17]See Kathryn R. Harrigan, "Matching Vertical Integration Strategies to Competitive Conditions," *Strategic Management Journal* 7, no. 6 (November–December 1986), pp. 535–56; for a more extensive discussion of the advantages and disadvantages of vertical integration, see John Stuckey and David White, "When and When Not to Vertically Integrate," *Sloan Management Review* (Spring 1993), pp. 71–83.

[18]The resilience of vertical integration strategies despite the disadvantages is discussed in

Thomas Osegowitsch and Anoop Madhok, "Vertical Integration Is Dead or Is It?" *Business Horizons* 46, no. 2 (March–April 2003), pp. 25–35.

19. This point is explored in greater detail in James Brian Quinn, "Strategic Outsourcing: Leveraging Knowledge Capabilities," *Sloan Management Review* 40, no. 4 (Summer 1999), pp. 9–21.

20. Dean Foust, "Big Brown's New Bag," *BusinessWeek,* July 19, 2004, pp. 54–55.

21. "The Internet Age," *BusinessWeek,* October 4, 1999, p. 104.

22. For a good discussion of the problems that can arise from outsourcing, see Jérôme Barthélemy, "The Seven Deadly Sins of Outsourcing," *Academy of Management Executive* 17, no. 2 (May 2003), pp. 87–100.

23. For an excellent discussion of aggressive offensive strategies, see George Stalk Jr. and Rob Lachenauer, "Hardball: Five Killer Strategies for Trouncing the Competition," *Harvard Business Review* 82, no. 4 (April 2004), pp. 62–71. A discussion of offensive strategies particularly suitable for industry leaders is presented in Richard D'Aveni, "The Empire Strikes Back: Counterrevolutionary Strategies for Industry Leaders," *Harvard Business Review* 80, no. 11 (November 2002), pp. 66–74.

24. George Stalk, "Playing Hardball: Why Strategy Still Matters," *Ivey Business Journal* 69, no. 2 (November–December 2004), pp. 1–2.

25. Ian C. MacMillan, "How Long Can You Sustain a Competitive Advantage?" in *The Strategic Planning Management Reader,* ed. Liam Fahey (Englewood Cliffs, NJ: Prentice Hall, 1989), pp. 23–24.

26. Ian C. MacMillan, Alexander B. van Putten, and Rita Gunther McGrath, "Global Gamesmanship," *Harvard Business Review* 81, no. 5 (May 2003), pp. 66–67; also, see Askay R. Rao, Mark E. Bergen, and Scott Davis, "How to Fight a Price War," *Harvard Business Review* 78, no. 2 (March–April, 2000), pp. 107–16.

27. Stalk and Lachenauer, "Hardball," p. 64.

28. Stalk, "Playing Hardball," p. 4.

29. Stalk and Lachenauer, "Hardball," p. 67.

30. For an interesting study of how small firms can successfully employ guerrilla-style tactics, see Ming-Jer Chen and Donald C. Hambrick, "Speed, Stealth, and Selective Attack: How Small Firms Differ from Large Firms in Competitive Behavior," *Academy of Management Journal* 38, no. 2 (April 1995), pp. 453–82. Other discussions of guerrilla offensives can be found in Ian MacMillan, "How Business Strategists Can Use Guerrilla Warfare Tactics," *Journal of Business Strategy* 1, no. 2 (Fall 1980), pp. 63–65; William E. Rothschild, "Surprise

and the Competitive Advantage," *Journal of Business Strategy* 4, no. 3 (Winter 1984), pp. 10–18; Kathryn R. Harrigan, *Strategic Flexibility* (Lexington, MA: Lexington Books, 1985), pp. 30–45; and Liam Fahey, "Guerrilla Strategy: The Hit-and-Run Attack," in *The Strategic Management Planning Reader,* ed. Liam Fahey (Englewood Cliffs, NJ: Prentice Hall, 1989), pp. 194–97.

31. The use of preemptive strike offensives is treated comprehensively in Ian MacMillan, "Preemptive Strategies," *Journal of Business Strategy* 14, no. 2 (Fall 1983), pp. 16–26.

32. W. Chan Kim and Renée Mauborgne, "Blue Ocean Strategy," *Harvard Business Review* 82, no. 10 (October 2004), pp. 76–84.

33. Philip Kotler, *Marketing Management,* 5th Edition (Englewood Cliffs, N.J.: Prentice Hall, 1984), p. 400.

34. Michael E. Porter, *Competitive Advantage* (New York: Free Press, 1985), p. 518.

35. For an excellent discussion of how to wage offensives against strong rivals, see David B. Yoffie and Mary Kwak, "Mastering Balance: How to Meet and Beat a Stronger Opponent," *California Management Review* 44, no. 2 (Winter 2002), pp. 8–24.

36. Stalk, "Playing Hardball," pp. 1–2.

37. Porter, *Competitive Advantage,* pp. 489–94.

38. Ibid., pp. 495–97. The list here is selective; Porter offers a greater number of options.

39. For a more extensive discussion of how the Internet impacts strategy, see Michael E. Porter, "Strategy and the Internet," *Harvard Business Review* 79, no. 3 (March 2001), pp. 63–78.

40. Porter, *Competitive Advantage,* pp. 232–33.

41. For research evidence on the effects of pioneering versus following, see Jeffrey G. Covin, Dennis P. Slevin, and Michael B. Heeley, "Pioneers and Followers: Competitive Tactics, Environment, and Growth," *Journal of Business Venturing* 15, no. 2 (March 1999), pp. 175–210 and Christopher A. Bartlett and Sumantra Ghoshal, "Going Global: Lessons from Late-Movers," *Harvard Business Review* 78, no. 2 (March–April 2000), pp. 132–45.

42. For a more extensive discussion of this point, see Fernando Suarez and Gianvito Lanzolla, "The Half-Truth of First-Mover Advantage," *Harvard Business Review* 83, no. 4 (April 2005), pp. 121–27.

43. Gary Hamel, "Smart Mover, Dumb Mover," *Fortune,* September 3, 2001, p. 195.

44. Ibid., p. 192.

45. Costas Markides and Paul A. Geroski, "Racing to be 2nd: Conquering the Industries of the Future," *Business Strategy Review* 15, no. 4 (Winter 2004), pp. 25–31.

Chapter 7

1. For an insightful discussion of how much significance these kinds of demographic and market differences have, see C. K. Prahalad and Kenneth Lieberthal, "The End of Corporate Imperialism," *Harvard Business Review* 76, no. 4 (July–August 1998), pp. 68–79.

2. Joseph Caron, "The Business of Doing Business with China: An Ambassador Reflects," *Ivey Business Journal* 69, no. 5 (May–June 2005), p. 2.

3. Extrapolated from 2002 statistics reported by the U.S. Department of Labor.

4. Michael E. Porter, *The Competitive Advantage of Nations* (New York: Free Press, 1990), pp. 53–54.

5. Ibid., p. 61.

6. For more details on the merits of and opportunities for cross-border transfer of successful strategy experiments, see C. A. Bartlett and S. Ghoshal, *Managing Across Borders: The Transnational Solution,* 2nd ed. (Boston: Harvard Business School Press, 1998), pp. 79–80 and Chapter 9.

7. H. Kurt Christensen, "Corporate Strategy: Managing a Set of Businesses," in *The Portable MBA in Strategy,* ed. Liam Fahey and Robert M. Randall (New York: Wiley, 2001), p. 42.

8. Porter, *Competitive Advantage,* pp. 53–55.

9. Ibid., pp. 55–58.

10. C. K. Prahalad and Yves L. Doz, *The Multinational Mission* (New York: Free Press, 1987), p. 60.

11. Porter, *Competitive Advantage,* p. 57.

12. Ibid., pp. 58–60.

13. Several other types of strategic offensives that companies have occasionally employed in select foreign market situations are discussed in Ian C. MacMillan, Alexander B. van Putten, and Rita Gunther McGrath, "Global Gamesmanship," *Harvard Business Review* 81, no. 5 (May 2003), pp. 63–68.

14. Canadian International Trade Tribunal, findings issued June 16, 2005 and posted at www.citttcce.gc.ca (accessed September 28, 2005).

15. George Stalk, "Playing Hardball: Why Strategy Still Matters," *Ivey Business Journal* 69, no. 2 (November–December 2004), pp. 1–2.

16. For two especially insightful studies of company experiences with cross-border alliances, see Joel Bleeke and David Ernst, "The Way to Win in Cross-Border Alliances," *Harvard Business Review* 69, no. 6 (November–December 1991), pp. 127–35, and Gary Hamel, Yves L. Doz, and C. K. Prahalad, "Collaborate with Your Competitors—and Win," *Harvard Business Review* 67, no. 1 (January–February 1989), pp. 133–39.

[17]See Yves L. Doz and Gary Hamel, *Alliance Advantage* (Boston, MA: Harvard Business School Press, 1998), especially Chapters 2–4; Bleeke and Ernst, "The Way to Win," pp. 127–33; Hamel, Doz, and Prahalad, "Collaborate with Your Competitors," pp. 134–35; and Porter, *Competitive Advantage,* p. 66.

[18]Christensen, "Corporate Strategy," p. 43.

[19]For an excellent presentation on the pros and cons of alliances versus acquisitions, see Jeffrey H. Dyer, Prashant Kale, and Harbir Singh, "When to Ally and When to Acquire," *Harvard Business Review* 82, no. 7/8 (July–August 2004), pp. 109–15.

[20]For additional discussion of company experiences with alliances and partnerships, see Doz and Hamel, *Alliance Advantage,* Chapters 2–7, and Rosabeth Moss Kanter, "Collaborative Advantage: The Art of the Alliance," *Harvard Business Review* 72, no. 4 (July–August 1994), pp. 96–108.

[21]Details are reported in Shawn Tully, "The Alliance from Hell," *Fortune,* June 24, 1996, pp. 64–72.

[22]Jeremy Main, "Making Global Alliances Work," *Fortune,* December 19, 1990, p. 125.

[23]Prahalad and Lieberthal, "The End of Corporate Imperialism," p. 77.

[24]Ibid.

[25]This point is discussed at greater length in Prahalad and Lieberthal, "The End of Corporate Imperialism," pp. 68–79; also see David J. Arnold and John A. Quelch, "New Strategies in Emerging Markets," *Sloan Management Review* 40, no. 1 (Fall 1998), pp. 7–20. For a more extensive discussion of strategy in emerging markets, see C. K. Prahalad, *The Fortune at the Bottom of the Pyramid: Eradicating Poverty through Profits* (Upper Saddle River, NJ: Wharton, 2005), especially Chapters 1–3.

[26]Brenda Cherry, "What China Eats (and Drinks and . . .)," *Fortune,* October 4, 2004, pp. 152–53.

[27]Prahalad and Lieberthal, "The End of Corporate Imperialism," pp. 72–73.

[28]Tarun Khanna, Krishna G. Palepu, and Jayant Sinha, "Strategies That Fit Emerging Markets," *Harvard Business Review* 83 no. 6 (June 2005), p. 63.

[29]Prahalad and Lieberthal, "The End of Corporate Imperialism," p. 72.

[30]Khanna, Palepu, and Sinha, "Strategies That Fit Emerging Markets," pp. 73–74.

[31]Ibid., p. 74.

[32]Ibid., p. 76.

[33]Niroj Dawar and Tony Frost, "Competing with Giants: Survival Strategies for Local Companies in Emerging Markets," *Harvard Business Review* 77, no. 1 (January–February 1999), p. 122; see also Guitz Ger, "Localizing in the Global Village: Local Firms Competing in Global Markets," *California Management Review* 41, no. 4 (Summer 1999), pp. 64–84.

[34]Dawar and Frost, "Competing with Giants," p. 124.

[35]Ibid., p. 125.

[36]Steve Hamm, "Tech's Future," *BusinessWeek,* September 27, 2004, p. 88.

[37]Dawar and Frost, "Competing with Giants," p. 126.

[38]Hamm, "Tech's Future," p. 89.

Chapter 8

[1]Michael E. Porter, *Competitive Strategy: Techniques for Analyzing Industries and Competitors* (New York: Free Press, 1980), pp. 216–23.

[2]Phillip Kotler, *Marketing Management,* 5th ed. (Englewood Cliffs, NJ: Prentice Hall, 1984), p. 366, and Porter, *Competitive Strategy,* Chapter 10.

[3]Several of these were pinpointed and discussed in Charles W. Hofer and Dan Schendel, *Strategy Formulation: Analytical Concepts* (St. Paul, MN: West, 1978), pp. 164–65.

[4]Ibid., pp. 164–65.

[5]Porter, *Competitive Strategy,* pp. 238–40.

[6]The following discussion draws on ibid., pp. 241–46.

[7]Kathryn R. Harrigan and Michael E. Porter, "End-Game Strategies for Declining Industries," *Harvard Business Review* 61, no. 4 (July–August 1983), pp. 112–13.

[8]R. G. Hamermesh and S. B. Silk, "How to Compete in Stagnant Industries," *Harvard Business Review* 57, no. 5 (September–October 1979), p. 161, and Kathryn R. Harrigan, *Strategies for Declining Businesses* (Lexington, MA: Heath, 1980).

[9]Hamermesh and Silk, "How to Compete," p. 162; Harrigan and Porter, "End-Game Strategies," p. 118.

[10]Hamermesh and Silk, "How to Compete," p. 165.

[11]Harrigan and Porter, "End-Game Strategies," pp. 111–21; Harrigan, *Strategies for Declining Businesses;* and Phillip Kotler, "Harvesting Strategies for Weak Products," *Business Horizons* 21, no. 5 (August 1978), pp. 17–18.

[12]The strategic issues companies must address in fast-changing market environments are thoroughly explored in Gary Hamel and Liisa Välikangas, "The Quest for Resilience," *Harvard Business Review* 81, no. 9 (September 2003), pp. 52–63; Shona L. Brown and Kathleen M. Eisenhardt, *Competing on the Edge: Strategy as Structured Chaos* (Boston: Harvard Business School Press, 1998); and Richard A. D'Aveni, *Hyper-Competition: Managing the Dynamics of Strategic Maneuvering* (New York: Free Press, 1994). See also Richard A. D'Aveni, "Coping with Hypercompetition: Utilizing the New 7S's Framework," *Academy of Management Executive* 9, no. 3 (August 1995), pp. 45–56, and Bala Chakravarthy, "A New Strategy Framework for Coping with Turbulence," *Sloan Management Review* (Winter 1997), pp. 69–82.

[13]Brown and Eisenhardt, *Competing on the Edge,* pp. 4–5.

[14]Ibid., p. 4.

[15]For deeper insight into building competitive advantage through R&D and technological innovation, see Shaker A. Zahra, Sarah Nash, and Deborah J. Bickford, "Transforming Technological Pioneering into Competitive Advantage," *Academy of Management Executive* 9, no. 1 (February 1995), pp. 32–41.

[16]Brown and Eisenhardt, *Competing on the Edge,* pp. 14–15. See also Kathleen M. Eisenhardt and Shona L. Brown, "Time Pacing: Competing in Markets That Won't Stand Still," *Harvard Business Review* 76, no. 2 (March–April 1998), pp. 59–69.

[17]The circumstances of competing in a fragmented industry are discussed at length in Porter, *Competitive Strategy,* Chapter 9; this section draws on Porter's treatment.

[18]What follows is based on the discussion in Eric D. Beinhocker, "Robust Adaptive Strategies," *Sloan Management Review* 40, no. 3 (Spring 1999), p. 101.

[19]Gary Hamel, "Bringing Silicon Valley Inside," *Harvard Business Review* 77, no. 5 (September–October 1999), p. 73.

[20]Beinhocker, "Robust Adaptive Strategies," p. 101.

[21]Kotler, *Marketing Management,* Chapter 23; Michael E. Porter, *Competitive Advantage* (New York: Free Press, 1985), Chapter 14; and Ian C. MacMillan, "Seizing Competitive Initiative," *Journal of Business Strategy* 2, no. 4 (Spring 1982), pp. 43–57. For a perspective on what industry leaders can do when confronted with revolutionary market changes, see Richard D'Aveni, "The Empire Strikes Back: Counterrevolutionary Strategies for Industry Leaders," *Harvard Business Review* 80, no. 11 (November 2002), pp. 66–74.

[22]The value of being a frequent first-mover and leading change is documented in Walter J. Ferrier, Ken G. Smith, and Curtis M. Grimm, "The Role of Competitive Action in Market Share Erosion and Industry Dethronement: A Study of Industry Leaders and Challengers," *Academy of Management Journal* 42, no. 4 (August 1999), pp. 372–88.

[23]George Stalk Jr. and Rob Lachenauer, "Five Killer Strategies for Trouncing the Competition," *Harvard Business Review* 82, no. 4 (April 2004), pp. 64–65.

[24]Ibid., pp. 67–68.

[25]For more details, see R. G. Hamermesh, M. J. Anderson, and J. E. Harris, "Strategies for Low Market Share Businesses," *Harvard Business Review* 56, no. 3 (May–June 1978), pp. 95–96.

[26]Porter, *Competitive Advantage*, p. 514.

[27]Some of these options are drawn from Kotler, *Marketing Management,* pp. 397–412; Hamermesh, Anderson, and Harris, "Strategies for Low Market Share Businesses," pp. 97–102; and Porter, *Competitive Advantage,* Chapter 15.

[28]William K. Hall, "Survival Strategies in a Hostile Environment," *Harvard Business Review* 58, no. 5 (September–October 1980), pp. 75–85. See also Frederick M. Zimmerman, *The Turnaround Experience: Real-World Lessons in Revitalizing Corporations* (New York: McGraw-Hill, 1991), and Gary J. Castrogiovanni, B. R. Baliga, and Roland E. Kidwell, "Curing Sick Businesses: Changing CEOs in Turnaround Efforts," *Academy of Management Executive* 6, no. 3 (August 1992), pp. 26–41.

[29]A study performed by Crest Advisors, a boutique investment firm and reported in Leigh Gallagher, "Avoiding the Pitfalls of Orphan Stocks," www.forbes.com, April 24, 2003.

[30]Phillip Kotler, "Harvesting Strategies for Weak Products," *Business Horizons* 21, no. 5 (August 1978), pp. 17–18.

Chapter 9

[1]For a further discussion of when diversification makes good strategic sense, see Constantinos C. Markides, "To Diversify or Not to Diversify," *Harvard Business Review* 75, no. 6 (November–December 1997), pp. 93–99.

[2]Michael E. Porter, "From Competitive Advantage to Corporate Strategy," *Harvard Business Review* 45, no. 3 (May–June 1987), pp. 46–49.

[3]Michael E. Porter, *Competitive Strategy: Techniques for Analyzing Industries and Competitors* (New York: Free Press, 1980), pp. 354–55.

[4]Ibid., pp. 344–45.

[5]Yves L. Doz and Gary Hamel, *Alliance Advantage: The Art of Creating Value through Partnering* (Boston: Harvard Business School Press, 1998), Chapters 1 and 2.

[6]Michael E. Porter, *Competitive Advantage* (New York: Free Press, 1985), pp. 318–19 and pp. 337–53, and Porter, "From Competitive Advantage," pp. 53–57. For an empirical study confirming that strategic fits are capable of enhancing performance (provided the resulting resource strengths are competitively valuable and difficult to duplicate by rivals), see Constantinos C. Markides and Peter J. Williamson, "Corporate Diversification and Organization Structure: A Resource-Based View," *Academy of Management Journal* 39, no. 2 (April 1996), pp. 340–67.

[7]For a discussion of the strategic significance of cross-business coordination of value chain activities and insight into how the process works, see Jeanne M. Liedtka, "Collaboration across Lines of Business for Competitive Advantage," *Academy of Management Executive* 10, no. 2 (May 1996), pp. 20–34.

[8]"Beyond Knowledge Management: How Companies Mobilize Experience," *Financial Times,* February 8, 1999, p. 5.

[9]For a discussion of what is involved in actually capturing strategic fit benefits, see Kathleen M. Eisenhardt and D. Charles Galunic, "Coevolving: At Last, a Way to Make Synergies Work," *Harvard Business Review* 78, no. 1 (January–February 2000), pp. 91–101. Adeptness at capturing cross-business strategic fits positively impacts performance; see Constantinos C. Markides and Peter J. Williamson, "Related Diversification, Core Competences and Corporate Performance," *Strategic Management Journal* 15 (Summer 1994), pp. 149–65.

[10]Peter Drucker, *Management: Tasks, Responsibilities, Practices* (New York: Harper & Row, 1974), pp. 692–93.

[11]While arguments that unrelated diversification are a superior way to diversify financial risk have logical appeal, there is research showing that related diversification is less risky from a financial perspective than is unrelated diversification; see Michael Lubatkin and Sayan Chatterjee, "Extending Modern Portfolio Theory into the Domain of Corporate Diversification: Does It Apply?" *Academy of Management Journal* 37, no. 1 (February 1994), pp. 109–36.

[12]For a review of the experiences of companies that have pursued unrelated diversification successfully, see Patricia L. Anslinger and Thomas E. Copeland, "Growth through Acquisitions: A Fresh Look," *Harvard Business Review* 74, no. 1 (January–February 1996), pp. 126–35.

[13]Of course, management may be willing to assume the risk that trouble will not strike before it has had time to learn the business well enough to bail it out of almost any difficulty. But there is research that shows this is very risky from a financial perspective; see, for example, Lubatkin and Chatterjee, "Extending Modern Portfolio Theory," pp. 132–33.

[14]For research evidence of the failure of broad diversification and trend of companies to focus their diversification efforts more narrowly, see Lawrence G. Franko, "The Death of Diversification? The Focusing of the World's Industrial Firms, 1980–2000," *Business Horizons* 47, no. 4 (July–August 2004), pp. 41–50.

[15]For an excellent discussion of what to look for in assessing these fits, see Andrew Campbell, Michael Gould, and Marcus Alexander, "Corporate Strategy: The Quest for Parenting Advantage," *Harvard Business Review* 73, no. 2 (March–April 1995), pp. 120–32.

[16]Ibid., p. 128.

[17]Ibid., p. 123.

[18]A good discussion of the importance of having adequate resources, and also the importance of upgrading corporate resources and capabilities, can be found in David J. Collis and Cynthia A. Montgomery, "Competing on Resources: Strategy in the 90s," *Harvard Business Review* 73, no. 4 (July–August 1995), pp. 118–28.

[19]Ibid., pp. 121–22.

[20]Drucker, *Management,* p. 709.

[21]See, for example, Constantinos C. Markides, "Diversification, Restructuring, and Economic Performance," *Strategic Management Journal* 16 (February 1995), pp. 101–18.

[22]For a discussion of why divestiture needs to be a standard part of any company's diversification strategy, see Lee Dranikoff, Tim Koller, and Antoon Schneider, "Divestiture: Strategy's Missing Link," *Harvard Business Review* 80, no. 5 (May 2002), pp. 74–83.

[23]Drucker, *Management,* p. 94.

[24]See David J. Collis and Cynthia A. Montgomery, "Creating Corporate Advantage," *Harvard Business Review* 76, no. 3 (May–June 1998), pp. 72–80.

[25]Drucker, *Management,* p. 719.

[26]Evidence that restructuring strategies tend to result in higher levels of performance is contained in Markides, "Diversification, Restructuring," pp. 101–18.

[27]Company press release, October 6, 2005.

[28]Dranikoff, Koller, and Schneider, "Divestiture," p. 76.

[29]C. K. Prahalad and Yves L. Doz, *The Multinational Mission* (New York: Free Press, 1987), p. 2.

[30]Ibid., p. 15.

[31]Ibid., pp. 62–63.

[32]For a fascinating discussion of the chess match in strategy that can unfold when two DMNC's go head-to-head in a global marketplace, see Ian C. MacMillan, Alexander B. van Putten, and Rita Gunther McGrath, "Global Gamesmanship," *Harvard Business Review* 81, no. 5 (May 2003), pp. 62–71.

Chapter 10

[1] James E. Post, Anne T. Lawrence, and James Weber, *Business and Society: Corporate Strategy, Public Policy, Ethics,* 10th ed. (Burr Ridge, IL: McGraw-Hill/Irwin, 2002), p. 103.

[2] For research on what are the universal moral values (six are identified—trustworthiness, respect, responsibility, fairness, caring, and citizenship), see Mark S. Schwartz, "Universal Moral Values for Corporate Codes of Ethics," *Journal of Business Ethics* 59, no. 1 (June 2005), pp. 27–44.

[3] See, for instance, Mark. S. Schwartz, "A Code of Ethics for Corporate Codes of Ethics," *Journal of Business Ethics* 41, nos. 1–2 (November–December 2002), pp. 27–43.

[4] For more discussion of this point, see ibid., pp. 29–30.

[5] T. L. Beauchamp and N. E. Bowie, *Ethical Theory and Business* (Upper Saddle River, NJ: Prentice Hall, 2001), p. 8.

[6] Based on information in U.S. Department of Labor, "The Department of Labor's 2002 Findings on the Worst Forms of Child Labor," www.dol.gov/ILAB/media/reports, 2003.

[7] ILO-IPEC (SIMPOC), *Every Child Counts: New Global Estimates on Child Labour,* www.ilo.org/public/english/standards/ipec/simpoc/others/globalest.pdf, April 2002. The estimate of the number of working children is based on the definition of the "economically active population," which restricts the labor force activity of children to "paid" or "unpaid" employment, military personnel, and the unemployed. The definition does not include children in informal work settings, non-economic activities, "hidden" forms of work, or work that is defined by ILO Convention 182 as the worst forms of child labor.

[8] W. M. Greenfield, "In the Name of Corporate Social Responsibility," *Business Horizons* 47, no. 1 (January–February 2004), p. 22.

[9] For a study of why such factors as low per capita income, lower disparities in income distribution, and various cultural factors are often associated with a higher incidence of bribery, see Rajib Sanyal, "Determinants of Bribery in International Business: The Cultural and Economic Factors," *Journal of Business Ethics* 59, no.1 (June 2005), pp. 139–45.

[10] For a study of bribe-paying frequency by country, see Transparency International, *2003 Global Corruption Report,* p. 267; this report can be accessed at www.globalcorruptionreport.org.

[11] Roger Chen and Chia-Pei Chen, "Chinese Professional Managers and the Issue of Ethical Behavior," *Ivey Business Journal* 69, no, 5 (May/June 2005), p.1.

[12] Thomas Donaldson and Thomas W. Dunfee, "When Ethics Travel: The Promise and Peril of Global Business Ethics," *California Management Review* 41, no. 4 (Summer 1999), p. 53.

[13] John Reed and Erik Portanger, "Bribery, Corruption Are Rampant in Eastern Europe, Survey Finds," *Wall Street Journal,* November 9, 1999, p. A21.

[14] See Transparency International, *Global Corruption Report* for 2003, 2004, and 2005; these reports can be accessed at www.globalcorruptionreport.org.

[15] For a study of "facilitating" payments to obtain a favor (such as expediting an administrative process, obtaining a permit or license, or avoiding an abuse of authority), which are sometimes condoned as unavoidable or are excused on grounds of low wages and lack of professionalism among public officials, see Antonio Argandoña, "Corruption and Companies: The Use of Facilitating Payments," *Journal of Business Ethics* 60, no. 3 (September 2005), pp. 251–64.

[16] Donaldson and Dunfee, "When Ethics Travel," p. 59.

[17] Thomas Donaldson and Thomas W. Dunfee, *Ties That Bind: A Social Contracts Approach to Business Ethics* (Boston: Harvard Business School Press, 1999), pp. 35, 83.

[18] Based on a report in M. J. Satchell, "Deadly Trade in Toxics," *U.S. News and World Report,* March 7, 1994 p. 64, cited in Donaldson and Dunfee, "When Ethics Travel," p. 46.

[19] Chen and Chen, "Chinese Professional Managers," p. 1.

[20] Two of the definitive treatments of integrated social contracts theory as applied to ethics are Thomas Donaldson and Thomas W. Dunfee, "Towards a Unified Conception of Business Ethics: Integrative Social Contracts Theory," *Academy of Management Review* 19, no. 2 (April 1994), pp. 252–84, and Donaldson and Dunfee, *Ties That Bind,* especially Chapters 3, 4, and 6. See also Andrew Spicer, Thomas W. Dunfee, and Wendy J. Bailey, "Does National Context Matter in Ethical Decision Making? An Empirical Test of Integrative Social Contracts Theory," *Academy of Management Journal* 47, no. 4 (August 2004), p. 610.

[21] P. M. Nichols, "Outlawing Transnational Bribery through the World Trade Organization," *Law and Policy in International Business* 28, no. 2 (1997), pp. 321–22.

[22] Donaldson and Dunfee, "When Ethics Travel," pp. 55–56.

[23] Archie B. Carroll, "Models of Management Morality for the New Millennium," *Business Ethics Quarterly* 11, no. 2 (April 2001), pp. 367–69.

[24] Ibid., pp. 369–70.

[25] John R. Wilke and Don Clark, "Samsung to Pay Fine for Price-Fixing," *The Wall Street Journal,* October 14, 2005, p. A3.

[26] For survey data on what managers say about why they sometimes behave unethically, see John F. Veiga, Timothy D. Golden, and Kathleen Dechant, "Why Managers Bend Company Rules," *Academy of Management Executive* 18, no. 2 (May 2004), pp. 84–89.

[27] For more details see Ronald R. Sims and Johannes Brinkmann, "Enron Ethics (Or: Culture Matters More Than Codes)," *Journal of Business Ethics* 45, no. 3 (July 2003), pp. 244–46.

[28] As reported in Gardiner Harris, "At Bristol-Myers, Ex-Executives Tell of Numbers Games," *The Wall Street Journal,* December 12, 2002, pp. A1, A13.

[29] Ibid., p. A13.

[30] Veiga, Golden, and Dechant, "Why Managers Bend the Rules," p. 36.

[31] The following account is based largely on the discussion and analysis in Sims and Brinkmann, "Enron Ethics," pp. 245–52. Perhaps the definitive book-length account of the corrupt Enron culture is Kurt Eichenwald, *Conspiracy of Fools: A True Story* (New York: Broadway Books, 2005).

[32] Chip Cummins and Almar Latour, "How Shell's Move to Revamp Culture Ended in Scandal," *The Wall Street Journal,* November 2, 2004, p. A14.

[33] Gedeon J. Rossouw and Leon J. van Vuuren, "Modes of Managing Morality: A Descriptive Model of Strategies for Managing Ethics," *Journal of Business Ethics,* 46, no. 4 (September 2003), pp. 389–400.

[34] Empirical evidence that an ethical culture approach produces better results than the compliance approach is presented in Terry Thomas, John R. Schermerhorn, and John W. Dienhart, "Strategic Leadership of Ethical Behavior," *Academy of Management Executive* 18, no. 2 (May 2004), p. 64.

[35] Anna Wilde Mathews and Barbara Martinez, "E-Mails Suggest Merck Knew Vioxx's Dangers at Early Stage," *The Wall Street Journal,* November 1, 2004, pp. A1 and A10.

[36] Archie B. Carroll, "The Four Faces of Corporate Citizenship," *Business and Society Review* 100/101 (September 1998), p. 6.

[37] Business Roundtable, "Statement on Corporate Responsibility," New York, October 1981, p. 9.

[38] Sarah Roberts, Justin Keeble, and David Brown, "The Business Case for Corporate Citizenship," a study for the World Economic Forum, www.weforum.org/corporatecitizenship, October 14, 2003, p. 3.

[39] N. Craig Smith, "Corporate Responsibility: Whether and How," *California Management Review* 45, no. 4 (Summer 2003), p. 63.

[40] Jeffrey Hollender, "What Matters Most: Corporate Values and Social Responsibility," *California Management Review* 46, no. 4 (Summer 2004), p. 112. For a study of the

corporate social responsibility reports of leading European companies, see Simon Knox, Stan Maklan, and Paul French, "Corporate Social Responsibility: Exploring Stakeholder Relationships and Program Reporting across Leading FTSE Companies," *Journal of Business Ethics* 61, no. 1 (September 2005), pp. 7–28.

[41]World Business Council for Sustainable Development, "Corporate Social Responsibility: Making Good Business Sense," www.wbscd.ch, January 2000 (accessed October 10, 2003), p. 7. For a discussion of how companies are connecting social initiatives to their core values, see David Hess, Nikolai Rogovsky, and Thomas W. Dunfee, "The Next Wave of Corporate Community Involvement: Corporate Social Initiatives," *California Management Review* 44, no. 2 (Winter 2002), pp. 110–25, and Susan Ariel Aaronson, "Corporate Responsibility in the Global Village: The British Role Model and the American Laggard," *Business and Society Review*, 108, no. 3 (September 2003), p. 323.

[42]www.chick-fil-a.com (accessed November 4, 2005).

[43]Smith, "Corporate Responsibility," p. 63. See also World Economic Forum, "Findings of a Survey on Global Corporate Leadership," www.weforum.org/corporatecitizenship, (accessed October 11, 2003).

[44]Roberts, Keeble, and Brown, "The Business Case," p. 6.

[45]Ibid., p. 3.

[46]Wallace N. Davidson, Abuzar El-Jelly, and Dan L. Worrell, "Influencing Managers to Change Unpopular Corporate Behavior through Boycotts and Divestitures: A Stock Market Test," *Business and Society*, 34, no. 2 (1995), pp. 171–196.

[47]Tom McCawley, "Racing to Improve Its Reputation: Nike Has Fought to Shed Its Image as an Exploiter of Third-World Labor, Yet It Is Still a Target of Activists," *Financial Times*, December 2000, p. 14, and Smith, "Corporate Social Responsibility," p. 61.

[48]Based on data in Amy Aronson, "Corporate Diversity, Integration, and Market Penetration," *BusinessWeek*, October 20, 2003, pp. 138 ff.

[49]Smith, "Corporate Social Responsibility," p. 62.

[50]See Social Investment Forum, *2001 Report on Socially Responsible Investing Trends in the United States* (Washington, DC: Social Investment Forum, 2001).

[51]Smith, "Corporate Social Responsibility," p. 63.

[52]See James C. Collins and Jerry I. Porras, *Built to Last: Successful Habits of Visionary Companies*, 3rd ed. (London: HarperBusiness, 2002); Roberts, Keeble, and Brown, "The Business Case," p. 4; and Smith, "Corporate Social Responsibility," p. 63.

[53]Roberts, Keeble, and Brown, "The Business Case," p. 4.

[54]Smith, "Corporate Social Responsibility," p. 65; Lee E. Preston and Douglas P. O'Bannon, "The Corporate Social-Financial Performance Relationship," *Business and Society* 36, no. 4 (December 1997), pp. 419–29; Ronald M. Roman, Sefa Hayibor, and Bradley R. Agle, "The Relationship between Social and Financial Performance: Repainting a Portrait," *Business and Society* 38, no. 1 (March 1999), pp. 109–25; and Joshua D. Margolis and James P. Walsh, *People and Profits* (Mahwah, NJ: Lawrence Erlbaum, 2001).

[55]Smith, "Corporate Social Responsibility," p. 71.

[56]Business Roundtable, "Statement on Corporate Governance," Washington, DC, September 1997, p. 3.

[57]Henry Mintzberg, Robert Simons, and Kunal Basu, "Beyond Selfishness," *MIT Sloan Management Review* 44, no. 1 (Fall 2002), p. 69.

[58]For a good discussion of the debate between maximizing shareholder value and balancing stakeholder interests, see H. Jeff Smith, "The Shareholders versus Stakeholders Debate," MIT *Sloan Management Review* 44, no. 4 (Summer 2003), pp. 85–91.

[59]Smith, "Corporate Social Responsibility," p. 70.

[60]Based on information in Edna Gundersen, "Rights Issue Rocks the Music World," *USA Today*, September 16, 2002, pp. D1, D2.

[61]This information is based on Charles Gasparino, "Salomon Probe Includes Senior Executives," *The Wall Street Journal*, September 3, 2002, p. C1; Randall Smith and Susan Pulliam, "How a Star Banker Pressed for IPOs," *The Wall Street Journal*, September 4, 2002, pp. C1, C14; Randall Smith and Susan Pulliam, "How a Technology-Banking Star Doled Out Shares of Hot IPOs," *The Wall Street Journal*, September 23; 2002, pp. A1, A10; and Randall Smith, "Goldman Sachs Faces Scrutiny for IPO-Allocation Practices," *The Wall Street Journal*, October 3, 2002, pp. A1, A6.

Chapter 11

[1]As quoted in Steven W. Floyd and Bill Wooldridge, "Managing Strategic Consensus: The Foundation of Effective Implementation," *Academy of Management Executive* 6, no. 4 (November 1992), p. 27.

[2]Jack Welch with Suzy Welch, *Winning* (New York: HarperBusiness, 2005), p. 135.

[3]For an excellent and very pragmatic discussion of this point, see Larry Bossidy and Ram Charan, *Execution: The Discipline of Getting Things Done* (New York: Crown Business, 2002), Chapter 1.

[4]For an insightful discussion of how important staffing an organization with the right people is, see Christopher A. Bartlett and Sumantra Ghoshal, "Building Competitive Advantage through People," *MIT Sloan Management Review* 43, no. 2 (Winter 2002), pp. 34–41.

[5]The importance of assembling an executive team with exceptional ability to see what needs to be done and an instinctive talent for figuring out how to get it done is discussed in Justin Menkes, "Hiring for Smarts," *Harvard Business Review* 83, no. 11 (November 2005), pp. 100–9 and Justin Menkes, *Executive Intelligence* (New York: HarperCollins, 2005), especially Chapters 1–4.

[6]Welch with Welch, *Winning*, p. 139.

[7]See Bossidy and Charan, *Execution: The Discipline of Getting Things Done*, Chapter 1.

[8]Menkes, *Executive Intelligence*, pp. 68, 76.

[9]Bossidy and Charan, *Execution*; Chapter 5.

[10]Welch with Welch, *Winning*, pp. 141–42.

[11]Menkes, *Executive Intelligence*, pp. 65–71.

[12]Jim Collins, *Good to Great* (New York: HarperBusiness, 2001), p. 44.

[13]John Byrne, "The Search for the Young and Gifted," *BusinessWeek*, October 4, 1999, p. 108.

[14]James Brian Quinn, *Intelligent Enterprise* (New York: Free Press, 1992), pp. 52–53, 55, 73–74, 76. Also see Christine Soo, Timothy Devinney, David Midgley, and Anne Deering, "Knowledge Management: Philosophy, Processes, and Pitfalls," *California Management Review* 44, no. 4 (Summer 2002), pp. 129–51, and Julian Birkinshaw, "Why Is Knowledge Management So Difficult?" *Business Strategy Review* 12, no. 1 (March 2001), pp. 11–18.

[15]Robert H. Hayes, Gary P. Pisano, and David M. Upton, *Strategic Operations: Competing through Capabilities* (New York: Free Press, 1996), pp. 503–7. Also see Jonas Ridderstråle, "Cashing in on Corporate Competencies," *Business Strategy Review* 14, no. 1 (Spring 2003), pp. 27–38, and Danny Miller, Russell Eisenstat, and Nathaniel Foote, "Strategy from the Inside Out: Building Capability-Creating Organizations," *California Management Review* 44, no. 3 (Spring 2002), pp. 37–55.

[16]Quinn, *Intelligent Enterprise*, p. 43.

[17]Quinn, *Intelligent Enterprise*, pp. 33, 89; James Brian Quinn and Frederick G. Hilmer, "Strategic Outsourcing," *Sloan Management Review* 35, no. 4 (Summer 1994), pp. 43–55; Jussi Heikkilä and Carlos Cordon, "Outsourcing: A Core or Non-Core Strategic Management Decision," *Strategic Change* 11, no. 3 (June–July 2002), pp. 183–93; and James Brian Quinn, "Strategic Outsourcing: Leveraging Knowledge Capabilities," *Sloan Management Review* 40, no. 4 (Summer 1999), pp. 9–22. A strong case for outsourcing is presented in

C. K. Prahalad, "The Art of Outsourcing," *The Wall Street Journal,* June 8, 2005, p. A13. For a discussion of why outsourcing initiatives fall short of expectations, see Jérôme Barthélemy, "The Seven Deadly Sins of Outsourcing," *Academy of Management Executive* 17, no. 2 (May 2003), pp. 87–98.

[18]Quinn, "Strategic Outsourcing," p. 17.

[19]For a more extensive discussion of the reasons for building cooperative, collaborative alliances and partnerships with other companies, see James F. Moore, *The Death of Competition* (New York: HarperBusiness, 1996), especially Chapter 3; Quinn and Hilmer, "Strategic Outsourcing"; and Quinn, "Strategic Outsourcing."

[20]Quinn, *Intelligent Enterprise,* pp. 39–40; also see Barthélemy, "The Seven Deadly Sins."

[21]The importance of matching organization design and structure to the particular needs of strategy was first brought to the forefront in a landmark study of 70 large corporations conducted by Professor Alfred Chandler of Harvard University. Chandler's research revealed that changes in an organization's strategy bring about new administrative problems that, in turn, require a new or refashioned structure for the new strategy to be successfully implemented. He found that structure tends to follow the growth strategy of the firm—but often not until inefficiency and internal operating problems provoke a structural adjustment. The experiences of these firms followed a consistent sequential pattern: new strategy creation, emergence of new administrative problems, a decline in profitability and performance, a shift to a more appropriate organizational structure, and then recovery to more profitable levels and improved strategy execution. See Alfred Chandler, *Strategy and Structure* (Cambridge, MA: MIT Press, 1962).

[22]The importance of empowering workers in executing strategy and the value of creating a great working environment are discussed in Stanley E. Fawcett, Gary K. Rhoads, and Phillip Burnah, "People as the Bridge to Competitiveness: Benchmarking the 'ABCs' of an Empowered Workforce," *Benchmarking: An International Journal* 11, no. 4 (2004), pp. 346–60.

[23]Iain Somerville and John Edward Mroz, "New Competencies for a New World," in *The Organization of the Future,* ed. Frances Hesselbein, Marshall Goldsmith, and Richard Beckard (San Francisco: Jossey-Bass, 1997), p. 70.

[24]Exercising adequate control over empowered employees is a serious issue. For example, a prominent Wall Street securities firm lost $350 million when a trader allegedly booked fictitious profits; Sears took a $60 million write-off after admitting that employees in its automobile service departments recommended unnecessary repairs to

customers. Several makers of memory chips paid fines of over $500 million when over a dozen of their employees conspired to fix prices and operate a global cartel—some of the guilty employees were sentenced to jail. For a discussion of the problems and possible solutions, see Robert Simons, "Control in an Age of Empowerment," *Harvard Business Review* 73 (March–April 1995), pp. 80–88.

[25]For a discussion of the importance of cross-business coordination, see Jeanne M. Liedtka, "Collaboration across Lines of Business for Competitive Advantage," *Academy of Management Executive* 10, no. 2 (May 1996), pp. 20–34.

[26]Michael Hammer and James Champy, *Reengineering the Corporation* (New York: HarperBusiness, 1993), pp. 26–27.

[27]Ibid. Although functional organization incorporates Adam Smith's division-of-labor principle (every person/department involved has specific responsibility for performing a clearly defined task) and allows for tight management control (everyone in the process is accountable to a functional department head for efficiency and adherence to procedures), *no one oversees the whole process and its result.*

[28]Rosabeth Moss Kanter, "Collaborative Advantage: The Art of the Alliance," *Harvard Business Review* 72, no. 4 (July–August 1994), pp. 105–6.

[29]For an excellent review of ways to effectively manage the relationship between alliance partners, see Kanter, "Collaborative Advantage," pp. 96–108.

Chapter 12

[1]For a discussion of the value of benchmarking in implementing strategy, see Christopher E. Bogan and Michael J. English, *Benchmarking for Best Practices: Winning Through Innovative Adaptation* (New York: McGraw-Hill, 1994), Chapters 2 and 6; Mustafa Ungan, "Factors Affecting the Adoption of Manufacturing Best Practices," *Benchmarking: An International Journal* 11, no. 5 (2004), pp. 504–20; and Paul Hyland and Ron Beckett, "Learning to Compete: The Value of Internal Benchmarking," *Benchmarking: An International Journal* 9, no. 3 (2002), pp. 293–304; and Yoshinobu Ohinata, "Benchmarking: The Japanese Experience," *Long-Range Planning* 27, no. 4 (August 1994), pp. 48–53.

[2]Michael Hammer and James Champy, *Reengineering the Corporation* (New York: HarperBusiness, 1993), pp. 26–27.

[3]Gene Hall, Jim Rosenthal, and Judy Wade, "How to Make Reengineering Really Work," *Harvard Business Review* 71, no. 6 (November–December 1993), pp. 119–131.

[4]For more information on business process reengineering and how well it has worked in

various companies, see James Brian Quinn, *Intelligent Enterprise* (New York: Free Press, 1992), p. 162; Ann Majchrzak and Qianwei Wang, "Breaking the Functional Mind-Set in Process Organizations," *Harvard Business Review* 74, no. 5 (September–October 1996), pp. 93–99; Stephen L. Walston, Lawton R. Burns, and John R. Kimberly, "Does Reengineering Really Work? An Examination of the Context and Outcomes of Hospital Reengineering Initiatives," *Health Services Research* 34, no. 6 (February 2000), pp. 1363–88; and Allessio Ascari, Melinda Rock, and Soumitra Dutta, "Reengineering and Organizational Change: Lessons from a Comparative Analysis of Company Experiences," *European Management Journal* 13, no. 1 (March 1995), pp. 1–13. For a review of why some company personnel embrace process reengineering and some don't, see Ronald J. Burke, "Process Reengineering: Who Embraces It and Why?" *TQM Magazine* 16, no. 2 (2004), pp. 114–19.

[5]For some of the seminal discussions of what TQM is and how it works written by ardent enthusiasts of the technique, see M. Walton, *The Deming Management Method* (New York: Pedigree, 1986); J. Juran, *Juran on Quality by Design* (New York: Free Press, 1992); Philip Crosby, *Quality Is Free: The Act of Making Quality Certain* (New York: McGraw-Hill, 1979); and S. George, *The Baldrige Quality System* (New York: Wiley, 1992). For a critique of TQM, see Mark J. Zbaracki, "The Rhetoric and Reality of Total Quality Management," *Administrative Science Quarterly* 43, no. 3 (September 1998), pp. 602–36.

[6]For a discussion of the shift in work environment and culture that TQM entails, see Robert T. Amsden, Thomas W. Ferratt, and Davida M. Amsden, "TQM: Core Paradigm Changes," *Business Horizons* 39, no. 6 (November–December 1996), pp. 6–14.

[7]For easy-to-understand overviews of Six Sigma, see Peter S. Pande and Larry Holpp, *What Is Six Sigma?* (New York: McGraw-Hill, 2002); Jiju Antony, "Some Pros and Cons of Six Sigma: An Academic Perspective," *TQM Magazine* 16, no. 4 (2004), pp. 303–6; Peter S. Pande, Robert P. Neuman, and Roland R. Cavanagh, *The Six Sigma Way: How GE, Motorola and Other Top Companies Are Honing Their Performance* (New York: McGraw-Hill, 2000); and Joseph Gordon and M. Joseph Gordon Jr., *Six Sigma Quality for Business and Manufacture* (New York: Elsevier, 2002). For how Six Sigma can be used in smaller companies, see Godecke Wessel and Peter Burcher, "Six Sigma for Small and Medium-sized Enterprises," *TQM Magazine* 16, no. 4 (2004), pp. 264–72.

[8]Based on information posted at www.isixsigma.com, November 4, 2002.

[9]Kennedy Smith, "Six Sigma for the Service Sector," *Quality Digest Magazine,* May 2003, posted at www.qualitydigest.com (accessed September 28, 2003).

[10]Del Jones, "Taking the Six Sigma Approach," *USA Today,* October 31, 2002, p. 5B.

[11]Pande, Neuman, and Cavanagh, *The Six Sigma Way,* pp. 5–6.

[12]Smith, "Six Sigma for the Service Sector."

[13]Jones, "Taking the Six Sigma Approach," p. 5B.

[14]Terry Nels Lee, Stanley E. Fawcett, and Jason Briscoe, "Benchmarking the Challenge to Quality Program Implementation," *Benchmarking: An International Journal* 9, no. 4 (2002), pp. 374–87.

[15]For a recent study documenting the imperatives of establishing a supportive culture, see Milan Ambroz, "Total Quality System as a Product of the Empowered Corporate Culture," *TQM Magazine,* 16, no. 2 (2004), pp. 93–104. Research confirming the factors that are important in making TQM programs successful in both Europe and the United States is presented in Nick A. Dayton, "The Demise of Total Quality Management," *TQM Magazine,* 15, no. 6 (2003), pp. 391–96.

[16]Judy D. Olian and Sara L. Rynes, "Making Total Quality Work: Aligning Organizational Processes, Performance Measures, and Stakeholders," *Human Resource Management* 30, no. 3 (Fall 1991), pp. 310–11, and Paul S. Goodman and Eric D. Darr, "Exchanging Best Practices Information through Computer-Aided Systems," *Academy of Management Executive* 10, no. 2 (May 1996), p. 7.

[17]Thomas C. Powell, "Total Quality Management as Competitive Advantage," *Strategic Management Journal* 16 (1995), pp. 15–37. See also Richard M. Hodgetts, "Quality Lessons from America's Baldrige Winners," *Business Horizons* 37, no. 4 (July–August 1994), pp. 74–79; and Richard Reed, David J. Lemak, and Joseph C. Montgomery, "Beyond Process: TQM Content and Firm Performance," *Academy of Management Review* 21, no. 1 (January 1996), pp. 173–202.

[18]Based on information at www.utc.com and www.otiselevator.com (accessed November 14, 2005).

[19]Fred Vogelstein, "Winning the Amazon Way," *Fortune,* May 26, 2003, pp. 70, 74.

[20]*BusinessWeek,* November 21, 2005, pp. 87–88.

[21]Such systems speed organizational learning by providing fast, efficient communication, creating an organizational memory for collecting and retaining best practice information, and permitting people all across the organization to exchange information and updated solutions. See Goodman and Darr, "Exchanging Best Practices Information," pp. 7–17.

[22]*BusinessWeek,* November 21, 2005, pp. 85–90.

[23]Vogelstein, "Winning the Amazon Way," p. 64.

[24]For a discussion of the need for putting appropriate boundaries on the actions of empowered employees and possible control and monitoring systems that can be used, see Robert Simons, "Control in an Age of Empowerment," *Harvard Business Review* 73 (March–April 1995), pp. 80–88.

[25]Ibid. Also see David C. Band and Gerald Scanlan, "Strategic Control through Core Competencies," *Long Range Planning* 28, no. 2 (April 1995), pp. 102–14.

[26]The importance of motivating and empowering workers so as to create a working environment that is highly conducive to good strategy execution is discussed in Stanley E. Fawcett, Gary K. Rhoads, and Phillip Burnah, "People as the Bridge to Competitiveness: Benchmarking the 'ABCs' of an Empowered Workforce," *Benchmarking: An International Journal* 11, no. 4 (2004), pp. 346–60.

[27]Jeffrey Pfeffer and John F. Veiga, "Putting People First for Organizational Success," *Academy of Management Executive* 13, no. 2 (May 1999), pp. 37–45; Linda K. Stroh and Paula M. Caliguiri, "Increasing Global Competitiveness through Effective People Management," *Journal of World Business* 33, no. 1 (Spring 1998), pp. 1–16; and articles in *Fortune* on the 100 best companies to work for (various issues).

[28]As quoted in John P. Kotter and James L. Heskett, *Corporate Culture and Performance* (New York: Free Press, 1992), p. 91.

[29]For a provocative discussion of why incentives and rewards are actually counterproductive, see Alfie Kohn, "Why Incentive Plans Cannot Work," *Harvard Business Review* 71, no. 6 (September–October 1993), pp. 54–63.

[30]See Steven Kerr, "On the Folly of Rewarding A While Hoping for B," *Academy of Management Executive* 9, no. 1 (February 1995), pp. 7–14; Steven Kerr, "Risky Business: The New Pay Game," *Fortune,* July 22, 1996, pp. 93–96; and Doran Twer, "Linking Pay to Business Objectives," *Journal of Business Strategy* 15, no. 4 (July–August 1994), pp. 15–18.

[31]Kerr, "Risky Business," p. 96.

Chapter 13

[1]Joanne Reid and Victoria Hubbell, "Creating a Performance Culture," *Ivey Business Journal* 69, no.4 (March–April 2005), p. 1.

[2]John P. Kotter and James L. Heskett, *Corporate Culture and Performance* (New York: Free Press, 1992), p. 7. See also Robert Goffee and Gareth Jones, *The Character of a Corporation* (New York: HarperCollins, 1998).

[3]Kotter and Heskett, *Corporate Culture and Performance,* pp. 7–8.

[4]Ibid., p. 5.

[5]John Alexander and Meena S. Wilson, "Leading across Cultures: Five Vital Capabilities," in *The Organization of the Future,* ed. Frances Hesselbein, Marshall Goldsmith, and Richard Beckard (San Francisco: Jossey-Bass, 1997), pp. 291–92.

[6]Terrence E. Deal and Allen A. Kennedy, *Corporate Cultures* (Reading, MA: Addison-Wesley, 1982), p. 22. See also Terrence E. Deal and Allen A. Kennedy, *The New Corporate Cultures: Revitalizing the Workplace after Downsizing, Mergers, and Reengineering* (Cambridge, MA: Perseus, 1999).

[7]Vijay Sathe, *Culture and Related Corporate Realities* (Homewood, IL: Richard D. Irwin, 1985).

[8]Kotter and Heskett, *Corporate Culture and Performance,* Chapter 6.

[9]See Kurt Eichenwald, *Conspiracy of Fools: A True Story* (New York: Broadways, 2005).

[10]Reid and Hubbell, "Creating a Performance Culture," pp. 2, 5.

[11]This section draws heavily on the discussion of Kotter and Heskett, *Corporate Culture and Performance,* Chapter 4.

[12]There's no inherent reason why new strategic initiatives should conflict with core values and business principles. While conflict is always possible, most strategy makers lean toward choosing strategic initiatives that are compatible with the company's character and culture and that don't go against ingrained values and beliefs. After all, the company's culture is usually something that strategy makers have had a hand in building and perpetuating, so they are not often anxious to undermine core values and business principles without serious soul searching and compelling business reasons.

[13]Kotter and Heskett, *Corporate Culture and Performance,* p. 52.

[14]Ibid., p. 5.

[15]Avan R. Jassawalla and Hemant C. Sashittal, "Cultures That Support Product-Innovation Processes," *Academy of Management Executive* 16, no. 3 (August 2002), pp. 42–54.

[16]Kotter and Heskett, *Corporate Culture and Performance,* pp. 15–16. Also see Jennifer A. Chatham and Sandra E. Cha, "Leading by Leveraging Culture," *California Management Review* 45, no. 4 (Summer 2003), pp. 20–34.

[17]Judy D. Olian and Sara L. Rynes, "Making Total Quality Work: Aligning Organizational Processes, Performance Measures, and Stakeholders," *Human Resource Management* 30, no. 3 (Fall 1991), p. 324.

[18]Information posted at www.dardenrestaurants. com (accessed November 25, 2005); for more specifics, see Robert C. Ford, "Darden Restaurants' CEO Joe Lee on the Importance of Core Values: Integrity and Fairness," *Academy of Management Executive* 16, no. 1 (February 2002), pp. 31–36.

[19]For several perspectives on the role and importance of core values and ethical behavior, see Joseph L. Badaracco, *Defining Moments: When Managers Must Choose between Right and Wrong* (Boston: Harvard Business School Press, 1997); Joe Badaracco and Allen P. Webb, "Business Ethics: A View from the Trenches," *California Management Review* 37, no. 2 (Winter 1995), pp. 8–28; Patrick E. Murphy, "Corporate Ethics Statements: Current Status and Future Prospects," *Journal of Business Ethics* 14 (1995), pp. 727–40; and Lynn Sharp Paine, "Managing for Organizational Integrity," *Harvard Business Review* 72, no. 2 (March–April 1994), pp. 106–17.

[20]For a study of the status of formal codes of ethics in large corporations, see Emily F. Carasco and Jang B. Singh, "The Content and Focus of the Codes of Ethics of the World's Largest Transnational Corporations," *Business and Society Review* 108, no. 1 (January 2003), pp. 71–94, and Murphy, "Corporate Ethics Statements." For a discussion of the strategic benefits of formal statements of corporate values, see John Humble, David Jackson, and Alan Thomson, "The Strategic Power of Corporate Values," *Long Range Planning* 27, no. 6 (December 1994), pp. 28–42. An excellent discussion of whether one should assume that company codes of ethics are always ethical is presented in Mark S. Schwartz, "A Code of Ethics for Corporate Codes of Ethics," *Journal of Business Ethics* 41, nos. 1–2 (November–December 2002), pp. 27–43.

[21]See Schwartz, "A Code of Ethics," p. 27.

[22]Ford, "Darden Restaurants' CEO Joe Lee."

[23]For excellent discussions of the problems and pitfalls in leading the transition to a new strategy and to fundamentally new ways of doing business, see Larry Bossidy and Ram Charan, *Confronting Reality: Doing What Matters to Get Things Right* (New York: Crown Business, 2004); Larry Bossidy and Ram Charan, *Execution: The Discipline of Getting Things Done* (New York: Crown Business, 2002), especially Chapters 3 and 5; John P. Kotter, "Leading Change: Why Transformation Efforts Fail," *Harvard Business Review* 73, no. 2 (March–April 1995), pp. 59–67; Thomas M. Hout and John C. Carter, "Getting It Done: New Roles for Senior Executives," *Harvard Business Review* 73, no. 6 (November–December 1995), pp. 133–45; and Sumantra Ghoshal and Christopher A. Bartlett, "Changing the Role of Top Management: Beyond Structure to Processes," *Harvard Business Review* 73, no. 1 (January–February 1995), pp. 86–96.

[24]For a pragmatic, cut-to-the-chase treatment of why some leaders succeed and others fail in executing strategy, especially in a period of rapid market change or organizational crisis, see Bossidy and Charan, *Confronting Reality.*

[25]Fred Vogelstein, "Winning the Amazon Way," *Fortune,* May 26, 2003, p. 64.

[26]For a more in-depth discussion of the leader's role in creating a results-oriented culture that nurtures success, see Benjamin Schneider, Sarah K. Gunnarson, and Kathryn Niles-Jolly, "Creating the Climate and Culture of Success," *Organizational Dynamics,* Summer 1994, pp. 17–29.

[27]Jeffrey Pfeffer, "Producing Sustainable Competitive Advantage through the Effective Management of People," *Academy of Management Executive* 9, no.1 (February 1995), pp. 55–69.

[28]For some cautions in implementing ethics compliance, see Robert J. Rafalko, "A

Caution about Trends in Ethics Compliance Programs," *Business and Society Review* 108, no. 1 (January 2003), pp. 115–26. A good discussion of the failures of ethics compliance programs can be found in Megan Barry, "Why Ethics and Compliance Programs Can Fail," *Journal of Business Strategy* 26, no. 6 (November–December 2002), pp. 37–40.

[29]For documentation of cross-country differences in what is considered ethical, see Robert D. Hirsch, Branko Bucar, and Sevgi Oztark, "A Cross-Cultural Comparison of Business Ethics: Cases of Russia, Slovenia, Turkey, and United States," *Cross Cultural Management* 10, no. 1 (2003), pp. 3–28, and P. Maria Joseph Christie, Ik-Whan G. Kwan, Philipp A. Stoeberl, and Raymond Baumhart, "A Cross-Cultural Comparison of Ethical Attitudes of Business Managers: India, Korea, and the United States," *Journal of Business Ethics* 46, no. 3 (September 2003), pp. 263–87.

[30]James Brian Quinn, *Strategies for Change: Logical Incrementalism* (Homewood, IL: Richard D. Irwin, 1980), pp. 20–22.

[31]Ibid., p. 146.

[32]For a good discussion of the challenges, see Daniel Goleman, "What Makes a Leader," *Harvard Business Review* 76, no. 6 (November–December 1998), pp. 92–102; Ronald A. Heifetz and Donald L. Laurie, "The Work of Leadership," *Harvard Business Review* 75, no. 1 (January–February 1997), pp. 124–34; and Charles M. Farkas and Suzy Wetlaufer, "The Ways Chief Executive Officers Lead," *Harvard Business Review* 74, no. 3 (May–June 1996), pp. 110–22. See also Michael E. Porter, Jay W. Lorsch, and Nitin Nohria, "Seven Surprises for New CEOs," *Harvard Business Review* 82, no. 10 (October 2004), pp. 62–72.

INDEXES

ORGANIZATION

A. J. Gallaher & Company, 329
A. T. Kearney, 117
A&E network, 314
A&W restaurants, 247
ABB, 593
ABC network, 148, 314
ABC Outdoor, 170
Abercrombie & Fitch, 193
Accenture, 117, 167, 219
Accuvue, 277
ACE Ltd., 329
Acer, 244
Ackerley Group, 170
Adelphia Communications, 11, 327, 328, 424, 449, 596
Adidas, 33
Advanced Micro Devices, 56–57, 178, 253–254, 509
Aerospatiale, 219, 375
AES, 420
Agilent Technologies, 303
AIG, 329, 449
Airborne Express, 401
Airbus Industrie, 219
Alberto-Culver, 416, 417, 432, 433
Albertson's, 103
Alcan Aluminum, 240, 397
Alcatel, 219
Aliant Inc., 475
Allied Signal, 397, 538, 546, 571
Altria Group, 298, 305, 333
Amazon.com, 6, 103, 110, 185, 186, 188, 193, 248, 366, 367, 401–402, 403, 407, 426, 440, 487, 510
AMC, 180
American Airlines, 166
American Association of Retired People, 47
American Express, 176
American Productivity and Quality Center, 117, 118, 395
American Standard, 281
American Tobacco, 256
America Online, 169, 171, 188
AmeriHost, 305
Amersham, 307
AM-FM Inc., 170
Amgen, 407
Amoco, 563, 568
AmSouth, 104
Anaheim Angels, 314
Anheuser-Busch Companies, 71, 251
Animal Planet, 152
AOL-Time Warner, 171
Aon Corporation, 329

Apple Computer, 59, 103, 112, 128, 256, 259, 326, 532
Arco, 563
Arsenal Digital Solutions, 219
Arthur Andersen, 29, 339, 594
Asahi Glass, 240
AST Computer, 514
AT&T, 64, 269, 297, 510, 513, 514
AT&T Broadband, 5
AT&T Canada, 32
Audi, 103, 152, 165, 471
Aveda, 500
Avid Technology, 152
Avis, 305
Avon Products, 13, 36, 85, 128–131, 147, 196

Baccarat, 256
Bahama Breeze, 277, 434
Bain & Company, 475
Bajaj Auto, 225
Balanced Scorecard Collaborative, 475
Bally shoes, 256
Banana Republic Inc., 83, 513
Bandag, 152
Band-Aids, 277
B&Q (UK), 344
Bank of America, 104, 168–169, 170
Bank One, 409, 454
Barclays Capital, 552, 555–556, 559
Barnes & Noble, 64
Barney's, 598
Batesville Casket, 498
BB&T Insurance Services, 104, 329
BEA, 166, 219
Beaird-Poulan, 143, 275
Bell companies, 190, 331
Bell Labs, 304
Bellsouth, 64
Belvedere, 500
Ben & Jerry's Homemade, 93, 101, 155, 240, 301, 348
Benchmark Exchange, 117, 395
BenchNet, 117, 395
Berkshire Hathaway, 315
Berol, 314
Bertelsmann, 354
Best Buy, 70, 171
Bestfoods, 302
Best Practices LLC, 117, 395
Bic, 143
Biotherm, 277
Birkenstock, 176

BitTorrent, 138
Black & Decker, 143, 251, 275
Blockbuster Entertainment, 24, 112, 185
Blue Diamond, 256
Blue Ice, 314
BMW Group, 6, 25, 32, 103, 145, 152, 159, 165, 171, 196, 219, 232, 397
Body Shop, 348, 507, 610
Boeing Commercial Airplanes, 559
Boeing Company, 219, 375
Bombardier, 275
Borders Bookstores, 303
BP Amoco, 202
BP Connect, 568
Braun, 301
Bravo, 307
Bridgestone, 112–113
Bridgestone/Firestone, 70
Briggs & Stratton, 143
Bristol-Myers Squibb, 327, 331
British Aerospace, 219
British Petroleum, 403, 473, 562–563, 564, 565, 567, 568
British Telecom, 269, 344, 609
Broadcom, 376
Brute, 314
BTR, 297, 540–545, 548–549
Budget Rent-a-Car, 305
Buffalo Sabres, 328
Buick, 206
Bulova, 531
Burberry, 498
Business Roundtable, 342, 350
Buy.com, 185, 187

CableLabs, 190
Cadillac, 103, 152
California Pizza Kitchen, 303
Callaway Golf, 251, 500
Calphalon, 314
Campbell's Soup, 145, 251, 302
Canada Life, 479, 480
Cannondale, 152, 256
Canon, 33, 153, 273, 455, 529–530, 531
Carefree, 277
Carlyle Group, 549
Carmike Cinema, 483
Carrefour, 122, 213, 251, 500
Carrier heating, 281
Cartier, 147
Casella Wines, 504–505
Castrol, 202, 206, 563
Caterpillar Inc., 23, 47, 145, 199, 228, 397, 513

CBS network, 148
Cdigix, 128
CDW Computer Centers, 441
Cendant, 305–306
Century 21, 305
CGA Inc., 152
Chanel, 6, 83, 84, 153
Charles Schwab, 26, 145, 187
Charmin, 275
Cheap Tickets, 305
Chemical Bank, 32
Chevron, 238, 375
Chicago Cutlery, 256
Chick-Fil-A, 346
ChildrenFirst, 615
Chrysler Corporation, 168, 171, 498, 503
Chubb fire detection, 281
Ciba Specialty Chemicals, 368
CIGNA, 32
Circuit City, 64, 184
Cirque du Soleil, 180
Cisco Systems, 169, 177, 196, 219, 226, 302, 366, 367, 376, 426, 529, 552, 557–558
Citibank, 104
Citicorp, 327
Citigroup, 301, 354, 356
Citizen watches, 531
Classic Sports Network, 314
Clear Channel Communications, 170
Clear Channel Worldwide, 170
CNBC, 7, 307
CNN, 147
Coca-Cola Company, 25, 58, 103, 145, 169, 209, 221, 222, 238, 298, 303, 344, 350, 508
Coldwell Banker, 305
Comcast, 4–5, 17, 252
Comcast Digital Voice, 5
Community Coffee, 151–152
Community Pride Food Stores, 346
Compaq Computer, 171, 225, 244, 484, 513
Compass, 104
Conference Board, 460
Conrad Hotels, 156
Continental Airlines, 166, 403, 410–411
Continental tires, 70
Cookware Europe, 314
Coors, 71
Corel, 171
Costco Wholesale Corporation, 13, 509
Courtyard by Marriott, 156

Note: Page numbers in *italics* indicate material in illustrations; page numbers followed by t indicate tables; page numbers followed by n indicate notes.

Covent Garden Soup, 240
Craftsman, 63
Cray Computer, 370
Credit Suisse First Boston, 330, 354, 356–357
Crest toothbrush, 240
Cuddledown, 256
CVS Pharmacies, 246

Daimler-Benz, 168, 171
Daimler-Benz Aerospace, 219
DaimlerChrysler, 32, 71, 165–166, 168, 206, 219, 232, 373
Danaher Corporation, 546, 571
Darden Restaurants, 277, 434–435
Dasani, 169
Days Inn, 247, 305
Dean Foods, 509
Dell Inc., 13, 68, 71–72, 119, 121, 142, 164, 177, 179, 196, 206, 207, 219, 222, 225, 226, 244, 275, 326, 367, 368, 373, 375, 426, 449, 484, 513, 528–529, 532
Deloitte & Touche, 211
Delta Air Lines, 166, 401
Diageo, 520
DiaSorin, 281
Digital Equipment Corporation, 484
Dillard's, 83
DirecTV, 5, 252
Disney Channel, 314
Disney Cruise Line, 314
Disney Radio, 314
Dollar General, 256, 510
Domino's Pizza Inc., 110, 152, 246, 510
Doubletree Hotels, 156
Dover, 546
Dow Chemical, 552, 558
Dow Jones & Company, 315, 373
Dowty Group, 549
Dr Pepper, 145, 256
Dry Idea, 301
Drypers, 509
Duke Children's Hospital, 32
Dunkin' Donuts, 66
DuPont Corporation, 28, 32, 397
Duracell, 275, 301

E. & J. Gallo Winery, 374
Eagle Snacks, 497
Eastman Kodak, 28, 103, 375, 376, 423, 455, 531
easyJet, 103
eBay, 7, 23, 36, 155, 180, 185, 188, 357, 402, 426
Eberhard Faber, 314
EBSCO, 387
EchoStar, 5
Econo Lodge, 247
Economist Intelligence Unit, 552
eDonkey, 128

Edward Jones, 441
Electronic Arts, 209, 252
Electronic Data Systems, 37, 366
Eller Media Company, 170
E-Loan, 186
eMachines Inc., 512
Embassy Suite Hotels, 156
EMC Corporation, 440, 508
Emerson Electric, 275, 397
EMI/Virgin, 354
E! network, 314
Enron Corporation, 11, 29, 327, 328, 330, 332–333, 339, 354, 424, 594, 597
Enterprise Rent-a-Car, 152
Epson, 13, 153
ERA, 305
Ernst & Young, 211, 346, 355
E*Service, 401
ESPN, 252, 314
ESPN: The Magazine, 252
ESPN Motion, 252
ESPN360, 252
eToys, 188, 472
Exertris Interactive Bikes, 248, 265
Expedia, 166
ExxonMobil, 32, 202, 375

Fairfield Inn, 156
Fanta, 169
Federal Express, 7, 139, 145, 149, 181, 373, 401, 418
Federal Mogul, 498
Fendi, 83, 84
Firestone, 618
First Automotive Works, 219
Fleet Boston Financial, 169
Flextronics, 376
Foamy, 301
Folgers Coffee, 275
Ford Motor Company, 20, 24, 33, 71, 145, 171, 219, 221, 232, 265, 357, 373, 375, 498, 500, 503, 573, 578, 619
Four Seasons, 7, 256
Fox Broadcasting, 252
Fox Network, 148, 307
Fox News, 147, 169
Fox Sports, 169
Fox Studios, 169
Frito-Lay, 303, 418, 497
Fuji-Xerox, 116–117
FX, 169

Gap, Inc., 83
Gardenia, 314
Garner, 277
Gateway Computer, 244
Gatorade, 169
Genentech, 164
General Electric, 36, 143, 263, 275, 281, 296, 307, 314, 366, 395, 397, 406, 416, 420, 440, 442, 475, 500, 531, 537–538,

540–546, 550, 571, 584, 585, 586, 592
General Electric Capital Mortgage, 397
General Electric Healthcare, 307
General Electric Medical Systems, 307
General Mills, 302, 346
General Motors, 33, 165–166, 193, 206, 207, 219, 226, 232, 237, 256, 265, 371, 373, 423, 459, 470–472, 487, 498, 500, 510
Genworth Financial, 307
Gerber, 251
Gillette Company, 13, 275, 301
Giorgio Armani, 277
GlaxoSmithKline, 120, 344, 587–588
Godiva Chocolates, 153
Gol Airlines, 140
Goldman Sachs, 330, 354, 356, 357, 562
Goodyear Tire & Rubber Company, 70, 112–113, 147, 193
Goody hair accessories, 314
Google Inc., 24, 152, 155, 192, 238, 366, 367, 407, 413, 416, 417, 426, 449
Google Scholar, 387, 413
Graco strollers, 314
Granite Construction, 392, 441
Graymont Inc., 511–512
Green Mountain Coffee Roasters, 345
Greenpeace, 26
Grey Goose, 500
Grocerygateway.com, 501
Grokster, 128
Gucci, 83, 84, 147, 153

H. J. Heinz Company, 23, 28, 33, 47, 71, 513
Häagen-Dazs, 6, 93, 153, 240
Hain, 256
Hamilton Sunstrand, 281
Hampton Inns, 66, 156
Handy Dan Home Improvement, 179
Hanson PLC, 307
Hanson Trust, 538, 540, 542–545, 548–549
Harley-Davidson, 6, 571
Harris Corporation, 390
Harrison Drape, 314
Head & Shoulders, 275
HealthSouth, 11, 327, 424, 449
Health Valley, 256
Heineken, 607, 609
Helena Rubenstein, 277
Hellman's, 302
Herman Miller Company, 448
Hero Group, 225, 228
Hewitt Associates, 582
Hewlett-Packard, 13, 29, 142, 153, 164, 166, 171, 177, 179, 219, 225, 226, 251, 303, 326, 393, 508, 513, 520, 532

Hi-C, 169
Hillenbrand, 179
Hilton Garden Inns, 156
Hilton Hotels Corporation, 23, 156, 202, 204
HIPPY USA, 462
History Channel, 152
Hitachi, 73
Hollinger International, 424
Home Depot, 13, 28, 70, 104, 138, 145, 179, 180, 193, 223, 344, 387, 501, 510
Homewood Suites, 156
Honda lawn mowers, 213
Honda Motors, 63, 71, 145, 219, 232, 273, 310, 370, 371, 471, 591
Honeywell, 546
Hotel.com, 186
Hotmail, 189
Howard Johnson, 305
Huawei, 226
Huffy Corporation, 514
Hummer, 256
Hynix Semiconductor, 326

IBM, 7, 73, 164, 176, 177, 219, 225, 226, 402, 423, 455, 484, 508, 509, 530–531, 532
IBM Global Services, 530
IDEO, 588, 589, 590–591, 592
IHC Carland, 607
Ikea, 529–530, 607
IMC Global, 240
ImClone, 596
Infineon Technologies, 326
InfoTrac, 387
Intel Corporation, 26, 27, 57, 66, 164, 169, 178, 198, 249, 253–254, 366, 368, 426, 461, 532, 591, 592
Interbrand Corporation, 562
Internet Security Systems, 219
Iowa Beef Packers, 140–142
Iridium, 598
Isuzu, 471
Ivory soap, 275

J. D. Power & Associates, 152
J. M. Smucker, 37
J. W. Marriott Hotels, 156
Jaguar, 171
Jani-King International, 204
JCPenney, 71
Jeep Grand Cherokee, 206
JetBlue Airways, 103, 509
Jif, 275
Jiffy Lube International, 7, 510
JM Family Enterprises, 407
John Crane Group, 549
John Deere, 63
Johnson & Johnson, 6, 145, 166, 277, 302, 303, 343, 344, 448, 520, 595, 619

Jollibee Foods, 225
JPMorgan Chase, 104, 409

Kaiser Permanente, 402
Karastan, 145
Kazaa, 128
KBToys, 472
Kellogg, 222, 508
Kentucky Fried Chicken, 204, 247, 303
Kerastase Paris, 277
Keybank, 104
Kidder Peabody, 544
Kiehl's, 277
Kimberly Clark, 315
Kinko's, 441
Kirsch, 314
KLM Royal Dutch Airlines, 218
Kmart, 6, 83, 84, 171, 275, 303, 500
Knights Inn, 305
Knorr's, 302
Kohlberg Kravis Roberts Company, 549
Kohl's, 83
Komatsu Ltd., 199, 513
KPMG, 211, 355, 424
Kraft Foods, 169, 256, 298, 302, 305
Krispy Kreme Doughnuts, 172
Kroger, 66, 70, 103, 141

L. L. Bean, 6, 71, 147, 256
Lan & Spar Bank, 454
Lancaster Colony, 281
Lancôme, 277
Lands' End, 256
La Roche-Posay, 277
Lenovo, 226
Lenscrafters, 441
Levi Strauss & Company, 17, 25, 251
Levolor, 314
Lexmark, 13, 138, 153
Lexus, 103, 151, 152, 171
Lifetime network, 314
Lincoln automobile, 84, 103, 152
Lincoln Electric, 143, 407
Linux, 238
Liquid Paper, 314
Listerine, 145
Little Tikes toys, 314
Loews, 535, 538
Long John Silver's, 247
Lord & Taylor, 514
L'Oréal, 277
Lowe's, 104
Lucent Technologies, 303, 304, 321
Lucent Worldwide Services, 304

Macy's Department Stores, 71, 83
Magnavox, 212
Marakon Associates, 552
Marks & Spencer, 298
Marriott Hotels, 156, 202
Marriott International, 441
Marriott Residence Inns, 156

Marsh & McLennan Companies Inc., 327, 329, 339, 354, 424
Maruti-Suzuki, 221
Mary Kay Cosmetics, 85, 147, 193, 256, 432, 442
Match.com, 152
Matrix, 277
Mattel, 596–597, 598
Maxwell House, 152
Maybelline, 277
May Department Stores, 514
Mayo Clinic, 26
Maytag, 164
Mazda, 578
Mazola, 302
MBNA, 169–170
McAfee, 7
McDonald's, 12, 25, 33, 66, 104, 204, 213, 222, 223, 225, 251, 343, 375, 392, 441, 442
MCI Communications, 64, 330, 331, 513
McKinsey & Company, 167, 250, 308, 366, 367, 406, 456
McWane, 424
Media Play, 171
Medtronic, 487
Men's Wearhouse, 509
Mercedes, 145, 152, 171, 206, 500
Mercedes-Benz, 6, 84, 103
Mercer Consulting, 329
Merck & Company, 166, 339, 405
Merrill Lynch, 354, 375, 471, 562
MGM, 5
Michelin Tires, 70, 112–113, 145
Micron Technology, 326
Microsoft Corporation, 13, 14, 17, 24, 33, 58, 63, 66, 128, 147, 164, 166, 188, 219, 225, 238, 251, 253, 309, 343, 366, 367, 371, 390, 418, 452, 453, 520, 532, 589, 591, 592
Microsoft Office, 145, 171
Microsoft Windows, 145
Microsoft Word, 171
Microsoft Xbox, 178
Mighty Ducks, 314
Miller Brewing, 298
Mills Corporation, 513
Minit Lube Ltd., 508, 510
Minute Maid, 169
Mitsubishi, 164
Mitsubishi Motors, 500
Mobile ESPN, 252
Molson Inc., 475
Monistat, 277
Monsanto, 589
Moody's Investor Services, 259
More Group, 170
Motel 6, 154
Motorola, Inc., 32, 145, 164, 225, 397, 500, 520, 571, 572, 573, 595, 598, 609
Motrin, 277
Mr. Coffee, 275

MSNBC, 307
Musicland, 112, 171
Musicmatch, 128
Mylanta, 277

Nabisco Foods, 305
Napster, 128
NASCAR, 209
National Basketball Association, 209
National Football League, 209
National Tyre Services, 297
NationsBank, 169
NatWest, 564
NBC network, 148, 307
NBC Universal, 281
Neiman Marcus, 83, 84
Nestlé, 169, 196, 256, 302, 309
Netscape Communications, 592
Neutrogena, 277
Newell Rubbermaid, 314
New Line Cimema, 487
News Corporation, 169, 252, 315
Nike, Inc., 25, 33, 184, 213, 348, 351, 366, 376, 528–529, 531, 607, 609
Nikki, 202
Nintendo, 25, 63, 309, 311
Nissan Design International, 590
Nissan Motors, 33, 110, 145, 219
Nokia Corporation, 25, 145, 164, 196, 225, 397, 426, 500, 529, 562, 564, 565, 566, 567, 568, 569, 588, 591, 592
Nordstrom, 83, 392–393, 407, 416, 418
Nortel, 529
North Carolina National Bank, 169
Northwest Airlines, 166, 218, 401
Northwest Water (UK), 395–396
Nova Scotia Power Inc., 32, 475
Novell, 171
NRT, 305
NTT Communications, 219, 269
Nucor Corporation, 77, 121, 135, 136, 240, 409, 410–411, 431, 509, 586

Occidental Petroleum, 416
Odwalla, 169
Office Depot, 77, 185, 186
Office Max, 77, 185, 186, 303
Oldsmobile, 237
Olive Garden, 277, 434
Omega-3, 256
On Cue, 171
1-800-CONTACTS, 512
OnStar division of General Motors, 470–472, 487
Oracle Corporation, 166, 219, 484
Oral-B toothbrush, 275, 301
Orbitz, 166, 305
Orvis, 256
Otis Elevator, 281, 401
OtisLine, 401

Overstock.com, 185
Owens Corning, 397

Packard Bell, 514
Palm Inc., 305
PalmPilot, 305
Panasonic, 259
Panera Bread, 187
Papa John's International, 246
Paper Mate, 314
Parker Pens, 314
Parmalat, 327, 424
Patagonia, 256
Paxton Communications, 170
PC Compustat, 477
Peapod, 188
Pemex, 327
Pennzoil, 202
Penske truck leasing, 281
People PC, 512
Pep Boys, 30
Pepcid AC, 166, 277
PepsiCo, 58, 103, 145, 169, 221, 277, 298, 303, 350, 366
PerkinElmer, 307
Perrigo Company, 509, 512
Pfizer, Inc., 344, 405
Philadelphia 76ers, 252
Philip Morris USA, 298, 305, 333, 334
Philips Electronics, 207, 212
Pirelli, 70
Pixar Studios, 167
Pizza Hut, 66, 204, 246, 247, 303
PlayStation, 178, 273, 309, 310
PNC, 104
Polaroid Corporation, 376
Polo Ralph Lauren, 83, 93
Porsche, 152, 165
PotashCorp, 240
Powerade, 169
PowerPoint, 8
Powerwave Technologies, 510
Pratt & Whitney, 281
Premier Oil, 607
Priceline.com, 185, 188
PricewaterhouseCoopers, 211, 355, 618
Procter and Gamble, 25, 71, 110, 141, 169, 240, 251, 275, 301, 302, 366, 368, 513, 587–588, 592
Progressive Insurance, 154, 155
Providian Financial Corporation, 330
Prudential Securities, 330, 354
Publix Supermarkets, 441
Putnam Investments, 329

Quaker Oats, 169, 277, 599
Quaker State, 202
Qualcomm, 448
Qualserve Benchmarking Clearinghouse, 117, 118
Qwest Communications, 64, 331, 424

R. J. Reynolds Tobacco, 305, 333
Ralcorp Holdings, 509
Ralph Lauren, 145, 147, 277
Ramada motels, 305
Real Networks, 253
Recording Artists' Coalition, 354
Recording Industry
    Association, 128
Red Hat Linux, 13, 14, 17, 23, 58
Redken, 277
Red Lobster, 277, 434
Refco, 424
Renault, 219
Renault-Nissan, 219
Right Guard, 301
Ringling Brothers and Barnum and
    Bailey, 180
Rite Aid, 246, 327, 424
Ritz-Carlton, 7
Roche, 552, 558
Rockwell Automation, 164
Rolex, 6, 84, 145, 147
Rolls-Royce, 147, 153
Ronald McDonald House
    program, 343–344
Roto-Rooter, 204
Roughneck storage, 314
Royal Ahold, 70, 297
Royal Bank of Canada, 475
Royal Bank of Scotland, 562, 564,
    565, 566, 567, 568, 569
Royal Dutch/Shell, 249, 327, 333,
    345, 348, 424
Rubbermaid, 594, 596
Ryanair, 103, 140, 179, 529–530

Saab, 237
Saatchi & Saatchi, 32
Safety Components
    International, 240
Safeway, 66, 70, 103, 141
Safeway United Kingdom, 473
Saks Fifth Avenue, 83, 84
Sally Beauty Company, 416
Salomon Brothers, 514
Salomon Smith Barney, 301,
    330, 357
Sam Goody, 171
Sammina-SCI Corporation,
    529, 531
Sam's American Choice, 71
Samsung Electronics, 145, 164,
    225, 259, 309, 326, 531, 595
Samuel Adams, 256
Sanford highlighters, 314
SAP, 166, 219
SAS, 219
Saturn Motors, 193
SBC Communications, 190
Schwinn Bicycle, 594
Sci-Fi Channel, 307
Seagate Technology, 33
Sears, Roebuck, 32, 64, 83, 171,
    423, 452, 510
Sears/Kmart, 84

Seasons restaurants, 434
Sega, 309, 311
Sematech, 486
7-Eleven Stores, 204, 483
SFX Entertainment, 170
SGI, 177
Shareasa, 128
Sharp, 259
Sharpie markers, 314
Shaw Group Inc., 512
Shell Oil, 25, 202, 424, 607, 609
Sheraton Hotels, 202
Sherwin-Williams, 171
Shu Uemura, 277
Siebel, 166
Siemens, 32, 309
Sikorsky Helicopters, 281
Silicon Graphics, 177
Sirius Satellite Radio, 84, 473
Six Sigma Academy, 396
Skippy peanut butter, 302
SlimFast, 301
Smiths Group, 546
Smokey Bones Barbecue
    & Grill, 434
Snapple, 63, 599
Snicker's, 275
Soft & Dry, 301
Soft Sheen/Carson, 277
Solectron, 376, 529
Sony Corporation, 5, 63, 110, 128,
    142, 164, 184, 196, 206, 251,
    259, 265, 273, 308–309, 310,
    311, 354, 355, 487, 589
Sotheby's International, 305
Source Perrier, 618
Southwest Airlines, 6, 103, 117,
    121, 138, 140, 142, 179, 366,
    367, 401, 419
Sports Authority, 303
Sports Ilustrated, 252
Sprint, 510, 513
Stain Shield, 314
Standard & Poor's, 259, 460
Staples, 70, 77, 185, 186, 510
Starbucks Corporation, 7, 33,
    36, 102, 110, 145, 152, 177,
    235–236, 251, 345, 347, 380,
    441, 500
Starbucks Foundation, 345
STAR satellite TV, 223
State Street, 104
Stayfree, 277
Stonyfield Farm, 346, 348
Strategic Planning Institute's
    Council on Benchmarking, 117
Stride Rite, 143
Subaru, 84, 471
Subway, 104
Summers Group, 297
Sunbeam, 275
Suncoast, 171
Sundaram Fasteners, 226
Sun Microsystems, 219, 465, 597
Super 8 motels, 247

Sure & Natural, 277
Suzuki, 223
Swish, 314
Sylvan Learning Centers, 66
Synovus, 407

T. J. Maxx, 83
Taco Bell, 104, 204, 247, 303, 375
Taiwan Semiconductor, 376
TakeAlongs, 314
Target Stores, 6, 13, 83, 84, 275,
    303, 402
Televisa, 225
Tennessee Valley Authority, 32
Tesco, 473, 501
Texas Instruments, 376
Textron, 558
3Com, 305
3M Corporation, 33, 101, 145, 245,
    442, 455, 538, 540–543, 545,
    546, 548, 552, 559, 588, 590,
    591, 592
    Dental Products Division, 23
Tide, 275
Tiffany, 147, 256
TI Group, 538, 540–546, 549
Time Warner, 169, 170, 171, 297,
    307, 354
Timex, 84
Tomkins, 549
Tommy Hilfiger USA, 424
Toon Disney, 314
Toro, 63
Toshiba, 36, 142
Towers Perrin, 117
Toyota Motors Corporation, 7, 28,
    33, 102, 122, 145, 151, 152,
    164, 177, 179, 196, 206, 219,
    265, 368, 371, 372, 373, 407,
    471, 498, 561
Toyota Production System,
    372, 574
Toys "R" Us, 346, 402, 510
Trader Joe's, 24, 153–154, 483
Trane furnaces, 281
Transparency International,
    320, 325
Travelers Group, 301
Travelocity, 166
Travelodge, 305
Tree of Life, 256
Trio cable channel, 307
Tupperware, 442
Twentieth Century Fox, 169
Tyco International, 11, 263,
    302–303, 327, 330, 424, 538,
    545, 556, 594, 595–596, 597
Tylenol, 277
Tyson Foods, 140

UBS, 562
Ukrop Super Markets, 407
Unilever, 101, 169, 222, 256, 301,
    302, 463
Union Carbide, 618

United Airlines, 166
United Parcel Service, 32, 149,
    176, 401
United States Postal Service, 78, 401
United Technologies, 281
Universal Outdoor, 170
Universal Studios, 307, 354
UPS Store, 204
USA Network, 307
USA Today, 193

Verio, 219
Verizon Communications, 190, 352,
    375, 445
Viacom, 307
Viacom/CBS, 170
Vichy Laboratories, 277
Viking stoves, 500
Vist, 225
Vivendi Universal
    Entertainment, 307
Volkswagen, 145, 165, 219, 373,
    397, 471
Volkswagen-Porsche, 232

W. L. Gore and Associates, 37, 153,
    407, 441
Wachovia, 104, 169
Walgreen's, 185, 246
Wall Street Journal, 465, 582
Wal-Mart Stores Inc., 6, 12–13, 66,
    70, 71, 83, 84, 103, 121, 138,
    140, 141, 143, 177, 184, 196,
    211–212, 251, 275, 303, 333,
    397, 415–416, 431, 440, 441,
    500–501, 509, 587
Walt Disney Company, 7, 164, 167,
    170, 252, 307, 314, 368, 441
Wasau Paper, 499
Wassall, 549
Waterman pens, 314
Weather Channel, 7, 180
Webvan Group Inc., 188, 512, 598
Wells Fargo, 23, 32, 104, 168, 329
Wendy's International, 32, 104, 461
Western Digital, 33
Whirlpool, 143, 207, 211, 213, 397,
    398, 517
White Rain, 301
Whole Foods Market, 7, 103, 345,
    348, 405
Windows Media Player, 253
WordPerfect, 171
WorldCom, 11, 29, 330, 331, 354,
    356, 424, 594
Wyndam motels, 305

Xerox Corporation, 33, 116–117,
    188, 397, 455, 592
Xilinx, 407
XM Satellite Radio, 84, 473

Yahoo!, 29, 30, 164, 185, 187, 188,
    265, 357, 367, 473
Yum! Brands, 204

NAME INDEX

Aaronson, Susan Ariel, EN-8
Abraham, Stan, 482, 488n
Ackatcherian, Carol, 488n
Adekola, Ade, 590
Afuah, A., 474
Agle, Bradley R., 609, 612n, 613n, EN-8
Ahlstrand, Bruce, EN-1
Ala-Pietilä, Pekka, 568
Alexander, John, EN-10
Alexander, Marcus, 266, EN-6
Aleyne, Adrian, 115
Ambroz, Milan, EN-10
Amit, R., 474
Amsden, Davida M., EN-9
Amsden, Robert T., EN-9
Anderson, M. J., EN-6
Anné, D. C., 576, 581
Anslinger, Patricia L., EN-3, EN-6
Ansoff, H. Igor, 458
Antony, Jiju, EN-9
Argandoña, Antonio, EN-7
Arnheiter, Edward D., 571
Arnold, David J., EN-5
Aronson, Amy, EN-8
Ascari, Allessio, EN-9
Ashish, N., 592, 593

Badaracco, Joseph L., EN-1, EN-11
Bailey, Wendy J., EN-7
Bain, J. S., EN-2
Baliga, B. R., EN-6
Balmer, J., 613n
Bamford, James, EN-3
Band, David C., EN-10
Bannon, L., 472, 474
Barabba, V., 470, 474
Barad, Jill, 596–597, 598
Barnevik, Percy, 593
Barney, J. B., 570n
Barney, Jay, EN-2
Barrett, Amy, 302
Barringer, Bruce, EN-1
Barron, A., 593
Barron, F., 589, 593
Barry, Megan, EN-11
Barthélemy, Jérome, EN-4, EN-9
Bartlett, Christopher A., 588, 592, 593, EN-2, EN-4, EN-8, EN-11
Basu, Kunal, 316, EN-8
Baumhart, Raymond, EN-11
Baumol, William, 612n
Beauchamp, T. L., EN-7
Beckard, Richard, EN-9, EN-10
Beckett, Ron, EN-9
Beinhocker, Eric D., 250, EN-5
Bellman, Eric, 221
Bennis, Warren, 590, 593
Bergen, Mark E., EN-4
Berkeley, G., 495
Bernick, Carol Lavin, 433
Bezos, Jeff, 403, 440

Bhide, Amar, 160, 414
Bickford, Deborah J., EN-5
Biederman, P., 590, 593
Birchall, David W., EN-2
Birinyi, Laszlo, 48
Birkenshaw, Julian, EN-8
Black, S. J., 489, 495
Blackman, S. Batey, 612n
Blank, Arthur, 179
Blasche, S., 612n
Bleeke, Joel, EN-3, EN-4, EN-5
Blome-Drees, F., 612n
Bluedorn, Allen C., EN-1
Bly, R., 590, 593
Bogan, Christopher E., EN-3, EN-9
Bogner, William C., EN-2
Bontis, Nick, EN-2
Bossidy, Lawrence, 358, 388, EN-8, EN-11
Bower, Joseph L., 543, 550, EN-3
Bowie, N. E., 612n, EN-7
Boyston, A., 593
Brandenburger, Adam M., 160
Bravo, Rose Marie, 497
Breen, Ed, 556
Brin, Sergey, 417
Brinkman, Johannes, EN-7
Briscoe, Jason, EN-10
Bromiley, Philip, EN-1
Brown, David, EN-7, EN-8
Brown, J. S., 592, 593
Brown, Michael E., 316
Brown, Robert, EN-1
Brown, Shona L., 243, EN-1, EN-5
Browne, John, 562, 565, 567, 568, 569, 570n
Bucar, Branko, EN-11
Buckley, N., 587, 593
Burcher, Peter, EN-9
Burgmans, Antony, 463
Burke, Ronald J., 577, 581, EN-9
Burnah, Phillip, EN-9, EN-10
Burns, Lawton R., EN-9
Byrne, John A., 366, EN-8
Byrnes, Nanette, 334

Caliguiri, Paula M., EN-10
Callahan, David, 614
Cameron, Johnny, 568
Camo, Robert C., EN-3
Campbell, Andrew, 266, 550, EN-6
Campbell, Lewis, 558
Campbell, R., 538
Cantrell, S., 466, 474
Caron, Joseph, EN-4
Carroll, A., 612n
Carroll, Archie B., EN-7
Carter, John C., EN-11
Carver, John, EN-1
Castrogiovanni, Gary J., EN-6
Cavanagh, Roland R., EN-9, EN-10

Caves, Richard, 526, 527
Cha, Sandra E., EN-10
Chakravarthy, Bala, EN-5
Chambers, John, 557
Champy, James, EN-9
Chandler, Alfred, EN-9
Charan, Ram, 358, EN-8, EN-11
Chase, Rodney, 569
Chatham, Jennifer A., EN-10
Chatterjee, Sayan, EN-6
Chen, Chia-Pei, EN-7
Chen, Ming-Jer, EN-4
Chen, Roger, EN-7
Chen, S., 469, 474
Chenhall, Robert H., 477
Cherry, Brenda, EN-5
Chesbrough, H., 474
Chisholm, Shirley, 316
Christensen, Clayton M., 488n, 532, 533n
Christensen, H. Kurt, EN-4, EN-5
Christie, P. Maria Joseph, EN-11
Chu, K., 586n
Clark, Don, EN-7
Clark, K., 570n
Clyde-Smith, D., 520n
Cohen, Ben, 155
Collins, James C., 358, 392, 619, EN-1, EN-8
Collins, John, 230
Collis, David J., EN-2, EN-6
Cooke, F., 474
Cooper, Peter, EN-3
Cooper, Robin, EN-2
Copeland, Thomas E., EN-6
Cordon, Carlos, EN-8
Coulter, M., 494, 495
Coutu, D., 590, 593
Covin, Jeffrey G., EN-1, EN-4
Cox, B., 472, 474
Crawford, R. J., 588, 593
Crosby, Philip, EN-9
Csikszentmihalyi, Mihaly, 570n, 590, 592, 593
Cucuzza, Thomas G., EN-3
Cummins, Chip, EN-7
Cusamano, Michael A., 230

Darr, Eric D., EN-10
D'Aveni, Richard A., EN-4, EN-5
Davenport, T. H., 592, 593
Davidson, Hugh, 22, EN-1
Davidson, Wallace N., EN-8
Davis, R. D., 581
Davis, Scott, EN-4
Dawar, Niraj, 194, 224, EN-5
Dayton, Nick A., EN-10
Deal, Terrence E., 570n, EN-10
Dechant, Kathleen, EN-7
Deering, Anne, EN-8
De George, R., 602, 612n
De Geus, A., 588, 593

Delbridge, R., 570n
Deming, W. Edwards, 576–577
De Pree, M., 593
Devinney, Timothy, EN-8
Devore, J. L., 572, 581
Diamond, Bob, 555, 557, 559
Dienhart, John W., 339, EN-7
Dixie Chicks, 355
Donaldson, Alison, 570
Donaldson, Gordon, EN-1
Donaldson, Thomas, 612n, EN-7
Donnan, S., 520n
Doornik, K., 588, 593
Douma, S., 612n
Doz, Yves L., 219, 520n, EN-3, EN-4, EN-5, EN-6
Dragonetti, Nicola C., EN-2
Dranikoff, Lee, 544, 550, EN-6
Drucker, Peter F., 470, 492, 495, 589, 593, 602, 612n, EN-6
Dubosson-Torbay, M., 474
Duguid, P., 592, 593
Duncan, Jack W., EN-2
Dunfee, Thomas W., EN-7, EN-8
Dunn, Frank, 529
Durroch, James, 534
Dutta, Soumitra, EN-9
Dyer, Jeffrey H., EN-3, EN-5

Ebbers, Bernard, 356
Eichenwald, Kurt, EN-7, EN-10
Eisenhardt, Kathleen M., 243, 570n, EN-1, EN-5, EN-6
Eisenstat, Russell, EN-2, EN-8
Eklind, Elisabet, 461–462
Elgin, B., 473, 474
El-Jelly, Abuzar, EN-8
Emerson, Ralph Waldo, 16
Emiliani, M. L., 576, 581
English, Michael J., EN-3, EN-9
Enrico, Roger, 497
Entine, John, 613n
Ernst, David, EN-3, EN-4, EN-5
Evan, W. M., 612n
Evans, Philip, EN-3

Fahey, Liam, 484, 488n, 533n, EN-4
Farkas, Charles M., EN-11
Fastow, Andrew, 328
Fauber, Bernard, 160
Fawcett, Stanley E., EN-9, EN-10
Ferratt, Thomas W., EN-9
Fiegenbaum, Avi, EN-2
Finkelstein, Sydney, 594
Fischer, B., 593
Fisher, L. M., 532n
Fitzgerald, Niall, 463
Flinn, Polly, 568
Flowers, Betty S., 488n
Floyd, Steven W., EN-1, EN-8
Flynn, L. J., 473, 474
Fombrun, C., 613n

Note: Page numbers in *italics* indicate material in illustrations; page numbers followed by t indicate tables; page numbers followed by n indicates notes; page numbers preceded by EN- indicate material in endnotes.

Foote, Nathaniel, EN-2, EN-8
Ford, Henry, 20, 503, 525, 574
Ford, Robert C., EN-11
Foust, Dean, EN-4
Fox, J., 588, 593
Francis, Theo, 329
Franko, Lawrence G., EN-6
Freeman, E., 612n
Freeman, R. E., 612n
French, Paul, EN-8
French, Ted, 558
Friedman, Milton, 316, 603, 612n
Friedman, S., 576, 581
Frost, Tony, 194, 224, EN-5
Fujimoto, T., 570n

Galban, Tony, 596
Gallagher, Leigh, EN-6
Galunic, D. Charles, EN-6
Gasparino, Charles, EN-8
Gates, Bill, 589, 591
Gates, Jacquelyn B., 614
George, S., EN-9
Ger, Guitz, EN-5
Geroski, Paul A., 521, 527, EN-4
Gerstner, Louis V., 530, 532n
Ghemawat, Pankaj, EN-1, EN-2
Ghoshal, Sumantra, 561, 570n,
    EN-2, EN-4, EN-8, EN-11
Gilbert, D., 612n
Ginter, Peter, EN-2
Goffee, Robert, EN-10
Golden, Thomas D., EN-7
Goldsmith, Marshall, EN-9, EN-10
Goleman, Daniel, EN-11
Gomez, Alain, 194
Goodman, Paul S., EN-10
Goodwin, Fred, 568, 569
Goold, Michael, 266, 538,
    550, EN-6
Gordon, Joseph, EN-9
Gordon, M. Joseph, Jr., EN-9
Gordon, Mary Ellen, EN-2
Govindarajan, Vijay, EN-2 to EN-3
Graham, Jefferson, 407
Grant, J. H., 494, 495
Grant, Peter, 190
Gratton, Lynda, 561, 570n
Green, Owen, 548
Greenberg, Jeffrey, 329
Greenfield, Jerry, 155
Greenfield, W. M., EN-7
Gregersen, H. B., 489, 495
Greyser, S., 613n
Grimm, Curtis M., EN-5
Grove, Andrew S., 26, 27, 194,
    461, 592
Grover, R., 473, 474
Grubman, Jack, 356
Gundersen, Edna, EN-8
Gundling, E., 588, 593
Gunnarson, Sarah K., EN-11
Gunter, B., 578, 581
Gunter, Marc, 5
Gupta, Anil K., 48

Hagel, J., 532n
Hall, Gene, EN-9
Hall, William K., EN-6
Hambrick, Donald C., EN-4
Hamel, Gary, 132, 219, 230, 452,
    469, 474, EN-1, EN-3, EN-4,
    EN-5, EN-6
Hamermesh, R. G., EN-5, EN-6
Hamm, Steve, EN-1, EN-5
Hammer, Michael, 388, EN-9
Hammond, J. H., 579, 581
Hansen, M. T., 570n
Hanson, James, 548
Hardee, Camilla, EN-1
Hargadon, Andrew, 589, 592, 593
Harrigan, Kathryn R., EN-3,
    EN-4, EN-5
Harris, Gardiner, EN-7
Harris, J. E., EN-6
Harrison, J. S., 493, 494, 495
Harry, M., 572, 581
Hayes, Robert H., 94, EN-8
Hayibor, Sefa, EN-8
Hedman, J., 474
Heeley, Michael B., EN-4
Hegert, M., EN-2
Heifetz, Ronald A., EN-11
Heikkilä, Jussi, EN-8
Hendricks, Kevin B., 475, EN-1
Herbold, Robert, 592, 593
Herzberg, Frederick, 388
Heskett, James L., EN-10
Hess, David, EN-8
Hesselbein, Frances, EN-9, EN-10
Hilhorst, R., 474
Hill, C. W. L., 489, 492, 495,
    612n
Hill, Ronald Paul, 343
Hilmer, Frederick G., EN-8, EN-9
Hirsch, Robert D., EN-11
Hirschberg, Jerry, 590–591, 593
Hitt, Michael A., EN-1
Hodgetts, Richard M., EN-10
Hofer, Charles W., EN-5
Hofstede, Geert, 570n
Hollender, Jeffrey, EN-7
Holpp, Larry, EN-9
Homann, K., 612n
Hopp, W. J., 574, 581
Hoque, F., 474
House, Charles H., EN-1
Hout, Thomas M., EN-11
Hubbell, Victoria, EN-10
Huber, C., 474
Humble, John, EN-11
Humer, Franz, 558
Hurd, Jonathan, EN-3
Hyland, Paul, EN-9

Iacobucci, Dawn, EN-3
Iansiti, Marco, 141
Immelt, Jeffrey R., 36, 307, 316,
    414, 592
Inkpen, A., EN-3
Inman, R. R., 574, 581

Ireland, Norman, 548
Ittner, Christopher D., 476

Jack, A., 587, 593
Jacobsen, Kristine, EN-2
Jassawalla, Avan R., EN-10
Jaworski, B. J., 474
Jenk, Justin, EN-3
Jensen, Michael, 583, 586n
Jeurissen, Ronald, 600
Johnson, Mark W., 488n
Johnson, Robert Wood, 619
Johnson, William R., 47
Jones, D. T., 575, 581
Jones, Del, EN-10
Jones, G. R., 489, 492, 495
Jones, Gareth, EN-10
Jones, T. M., 612n
Jordano, Rosemary, 615
Jung, Andrea, 36
Juran, J., EN-9

Kageyama, Yuri, 259
Kahaner, Larry, EN-2
Kahn, Gabriel, 221
Kale, Prashant, EN-3, EN-5
Kalling, T., 474
Kami, Michael, 2
Kaminsky, F. C., 581
Kamprad, Ingvar, 530
Kant, Emmanuel, 601
Kanter, Rosabeth Moss, EN-3,
    EN-5, EN-9
Kaplan, Nancy J., EN-3
Kaplan, Robert S., 475, 476, 479,
    502, EN-1, EN-2, EN-3
Kaufman, Rhonda, EN-1
Kay, John, 601, 608, 609,
    612n, 613n
Keeble, Justin, EN-7, EN-8
Kennedy, Allen A., 570n, EN-10
Keogh, John, 596
Kerr, Gerry, 534
Kerr, Steven, 411, 584, 586n,
    EN-10
Khanna, Tarun, EN-5
Kidwell, Roland E., EN-6
Killing, J. Peter, 488n
Kim, W. Chan, 94, 502, EN-1, EN-4
Kimberly, John R., EN-9
King, W. R., 494, 495
Kipling, Rudyard, 316
Klein, N., 613n
Knight, Phil, 348
Knox, Simon, EN-8
Köhler, W., 612n
Kohn, Alfie, EN-10
Koller, Tim, 544, 550, EN-6
Kosonen, Mikko, 569
Kotler, Philip, EN-4, EN-5, EN-6
Kotter, John P., 22, EN-10, EN-11
Kovacevich, Richard M., 358
Koza, M., EN-3
Kozlowski, Dennis, 595, 597
Kress, Donald, 94

Kwak, Mary, EN-4
Kwan, Ik-Whan G., EN-11

Lachenauer, Rob, 132, EN-2,
    EN-4, EN-6
Lampel, Joseph, EN-1
Landauer, 584
Langley, Monica, 329
Lanzolla, Gianvito, EN-4
Larcker, David F., 476
Latham, Gary, 582, 584
Latour, Almar, EN-7
Laurent, A., 570n
Laurie, Donald L., EN-11
Law, Andy, 590
Lawrence, Anne T., EN-7
Leavy, Brian, 528, 587
Lee, Hau L., EN-2
Lee, Kun-Hee, 595
Lee, Terry Nels, EN-10
Lei, D., 533n
Leibowitz, Mitchell, 30
Lemak, David J., EN-10
Leonard, Wayne, 414
Lester, M. A., 576, 581
Leuchter, Miriam, 366
Lev, Baruch, 478
Levering, Robert, 392
Levien, Roy, 141
Lewin, A., EN-3
Lewis, D. A., 579, 581
Lieberthal, Kenneth, EN-4,
    EN-5
Liedtka, Jeanne M., EN-6, EN-9
Liker, Jeffrey K., EN-1
Lincoln, Abraham, 18
Linder, Jane C., 465, 466, 474
Lipton, Mark, 459
Liveris, Andrew, 558–559
Locke, Edwin A., 582
Löhr, A., 612n
Lombardi, Vince, 358
Lorek, Laura, 186
Lorsch, Jay W., EN-11
Lowe, J., 570n, 592, 593
Lowry, Tom, 252
Lubatkin, Michael, EN-6

MacMillan, Ian C., EN-4,
    EN-5, EN-6
Madhok, Anoop, EN-4
Magaziner, I. C., 533n
Magretta, Joan, 474, EN-1
Main, Jeremy, EN-3, EN-5
Majchrzak, Ann, EN-9
Maklan, Stan, EN-8
Malayeff, John, 571, 579, 581
Mankins, Michael C., 551
Marcus, Bernie, 179
Margolis, Joshua D., EN-8
Markides, Costas C., 2, 94, 230,
    358, 452, 458, 521, 527, EN-1,
    EN-4, EN-6
Martin, J. A., 570n
Martinez, Barbara, EN-7

Maslow, Abraham, 518
Mason, David, 488n
Mathews, Anna Wilde, EN-7
Mauborgne, Renée, 502, EN-1, EN-4
Mays, Lowry, 170
McCawley, Tom, EN-8
McCombs, Joe, 170
McDonald, Ian, 329
McFadden, F. R., 573, 581
McGrath, Rita Gunther, 132, 155, EN-4, EN-6
McMillan, Ian C., 132, 155
McNerney, James, 546, 559, 592
Mehta, Stephanie N., 5
Menkes, Justin, EN-8
Menor, Larry, 475, EN-1
Midgley, David, EN-8
Miles, Morgan P., EN-1
Miles, Raymond E., 477
Miller, Danny, EN-2, EN-8
Millett, Stephen M., 488n
Milne, A. A., 358
Milne, George R., EN-2
Mintzberg, Henry, 316, 458, 462, 469, 474, EN-1, EN-8
Mitchell, R. K., 609, 612n, 613n
Mody, A., 520n
Moffatt, Bob, 533n
Mohammed, A., 321, 588, 593
Mokwa, Michael P., EN-2
Monteiro, Felipe, 570
Montgomery, Cynthia A., EN-1, EN-2, EN-6
Montgomery, Joseph C., EN-10
Montuori, A., 593
Moore, Gordon, 27
Moore, James F., EN-9
Morita, Akio, 589
Morris, D., EN-2
Morris, Donald, 489
Moskowitz, Milton, 392
Mroz, John Edward, EN-9
Mulally, Alan, 559
Murdoch, Rupert, 252
Murphy, Patrick E., EN-11

Nadler, David A., 458, EN-1
Nalebuff, Barry J., 160
Nash, Sarah, EN-5
Nasser, Jacques, 619
Nathan, J., 593
Negisji, S., 520n
Neman, Robert P., EN-10
Ness, Joseph A., EN-3
Neuman, Robert P., EN-9
Nichols, P. M., EN-7
Nicholson, David, 548
Nielsen, Anders P., EN-2
Nietzsche, Friedrich, 589
Niles-Jolly, Kathryn, EN-11
Nimgade, A., 588, 593
Noble, Charles H., EN-2
Nohria, Nitin, EN-11
Nordheim, Christie, EN-3

Norton, David P., 475, 476, 479, EN-1
Nouguier, S., 474
Nussbaum, B., 588, 593

O'Bannon, Douglas P., EN-8
O'Connell, Maurice, 533n
Oetinger, B. V., 570n
Ohga, Noria, 589
Ohinata, Yoshinobu, EN-9
Ohmae, Kenichi, 48
Ohno, Taiichi, 372, 574
Olbrich, T., 613n
Olian, Judy D., EN-10
Oliver, N., 570n
Ollila, Jorma, 529, 562, 569
Olusaga, S. Ade, EN-2
Osegowitsch, Thomas, EN-4
Oster, Christopher, 329
Oster, Sharon, 2
Osterwalder, A., 474
Ott, E. R., 579, 581
Oztark, Sevgi, EN-11

Page, Larry, 417
Paich, M., 474
Paine, Lynn Sharp, 601, 605, 612n, EN-11
Palepu, Krishna G., EN-5
Palmisano, Sam, 530
Pande, Peter S., EN-9, EN-10
Par, Terence P., 116
Parise, Salvatore, EN-3
Park, Daewoo, EN-1
Patinkin, M., 533n
Pauling, Linus, 591
Pekár, Peter, 485
Peter, Thomas J., 616
Peteraf, Margaret A., EN-2
Pfeffer, Jeffrey, EN-10, EN-11
Phillips, R., 612n
Picasso, Pablo, 526
Pigneur, V., 474
Pisano, Gary P., 94, EN-8
Pond, Randy, 557
Porras, Jerry I., 619, EN-1, EN-8
Portanger, Erik, EN-7
Porter, Michael E., 55, 111, 114, 132, 134, 452, 469, 474, 482, 488n, 535, 550, 557, 603, 612n, EN-1, EN-2, EN-3, EN-4, EN-5, EN-6, EN-11
Post, James E., EN-7
Potter, Don, 508
Powell, Dennis, 557
Powell, Thomas C., EN-10
Prahalad, C. K., 132, 487, 488n, 533n, EN-1, EN-3, EN-4, EN-6, EN-9
Pressman, Bob, 598
Preston, Lee E., 612n, EN-8
Price, Raymond L., EN-1
Prokesch, S. E., 570n
Propokoff, Ilya, 590
Prusak, L., 593

Pulliam, Susan, EN-8
Pyzdek, T., 466, 474

Quelch, John A., EN-5
Quinn, James Brian, EN-3, EN-4, EN-8, EN-9, EN-11

Rafalko, Robert J., EN-11
Ramaswamy, Venkat, 487, 488n
Randall, Robert M., 533n, EN-4
Rao, Askay R., EN-4
Raynor, M. E., 532n, 533n
Rayport, J. F., 474
Reed, John, EN-7
Reed, Richard, EN-10
Reid, Joanne, EN-10
Renick, S., 581
Rhoads, Gary K., EN-9, EN-10
Richardson, Sandy, 479, 480, EN-1
Ridderstråle, Jonas, EN-8
Rigby, Darrell K., 475, 488n, EN-1
Robert, Michel, 22, 160, EN-1
Roberts, A. E. P., 581
Roberts, J., 588, 593
Roberts, Sarah, EN-7, EN-8
Rock, John, 459
Rock, Melinda, EN-9
Rogan, Michelle, 570
Rogovsky, Nikolai, EN-8
Rohs, P., 612n
Roman, Ronald M., EN-8
Roos, Goran, EN-2
Rosenthal, Jim, EN-9
Ross, Joel, 2
Rothschild, William E., EN-4
Roussouw, Gedeon J., 335, EN-7
Rumelt, R., 535, 550
Rynes, Sara L., EN-10

St. John, C. H., 493, 494, 495
Salterio, Steven, 476
Salvia, A. A., 579, 581
Sama, L. M., 612n
Santos, J., 520n
Sanyal, Rajib, EN-7
Sapsford, Jathon, 219
Saro-Wiwa, Ken, 609
Sashittal, Hemant C., EN-10
Sasson, Lisa, EN-3
Satchell, M. J., EN-7
Sathe, Vijay, EN-10
Savitz, A., 619
Savoie, M. J., 581
Scanlan, Gerald, EN-10
Schein, Edgar, 570n
Schendel, Dan, EN-5
Scherer, F. M., EN-2
Schermerhorn, John R., 339, EN-7
Schilling, E. G., 579, 581
Schlender, B., 592, 593
Schmitt, Wolfgang, 596, 597
Schneider, Antoon, 544, 550, EN-6
Schneider, Benjamin, EN-11
Schneiderman, Howard A., 589, 593

Schreuder, H., 612n
Schroeder, R., 572, 581
Schulman, Lawrence E., EN-3
Schultz, Howard, 36
Schwartz, Mark S., EN-7, EN-11
Schwartz, Peter, 488n
Selby, Richard W., 230
Semel, Terry S., 473
Semple, Tom, 590
Sethi, S. P., 601, 612n
Shafer, Scott M., 465
Shaheen, George, 598
Shank, John K., EN-2, EN-3
Shaw, Gordon, EN-1
Sheridan, J. H., 571, 574, 581
Shingo, Shigeo, 574, 575, 581
Shirouzu, Norihiko, 219
Shuen, A., 570n
Silk, S. B., EN-5
Simons, Robert, 316, EN-8, EN-9, EN-10
Sims, Ronald R., EN-7
Singer, M., 532n
Singh, Harbir, EN-3, EN-5
Singh, Jang B., EN-11
Sinha, Jayant, EN-5
Sirgy, M. J., 613n
Skilling, Jeffrey, 597
Slevin, Dennis P., EN-4
Slocum, J. W., 533n
Slywotzky, Adrian J., 458
Smircich, L., 550
Smith, Adam, EN-9
Smith, H. Jeff, 465, EN-8
Smith, Iain, 343
Smith, J., 474
Smith, Kennedy G., EN-5, EN-10
Smith, N. Craig, EN-7, EN-8
Smith, Randall, EN-8
Snow, Charles C., 477
Solomon, R., 602, 612n
Sommerville, Iain, EN-9
Soo, Christine, EN-8
Sower, V. E., 572, 581
Spearman, M. L., 574, 581
Stalk, George, Jr., 132, 496, EN-2, EN-3, EN-4, EN-6
Stavropoulos, Bill, 558
Steele, Richard, 551
Steinbock, D., 588, 593
Steinmann, H., 612n, 613n
Stephens, Debra, 343
Stoeberl, Phillip A., EN-11
Stone, Reuben E., EN-3
Storr, A., 589, 593
Strickland, A. J., III, 491, 492, 493, 494, 495
Stringer, Howard, 259
Stroh, Linda K., EN-10
Stross, R. E., 589, 593
Stuckey, John, EN-3
Su, C., 613n
Suarez, Fernando, EN-4
Sull, Donald, EN-2
Sun Zi, 414

Sutton, Robert, 589
Swayne, Linda E., EN-2

Tam, P.-W., 474
Teece, David J., 570n, EN-2
Teets, John W., 18
Terry, Robert J., 266
Thomas, Dave, 461
Thomas, Howard, EN-2
Thomas, Terry, 339, EN-7
Thomke, S., 588, 593
Thompson, Arthur A., Jr., 491, 492, 493, 494, 495
Thomson, Alan, EN-11
Tichy, Noel, 414
Timmers, P., 474
Torvalds, Linus, 14
Tovstiga, George, EN-2
Treacy, M., 532n
Treviño, Linda K., 316
Truby, M., 573, 581
Tucci, C. L., 474
Tucci, Joe, 440
Tully, Shawn, EN-5
Tushman, Michael, 458

Twer, Doran, EN-10
Tyler, Beverly B., EN-1

Ungan, Mustafa, EN-9
Upton, David M., 94, EN-8

Välikangas, Lissa, 230, EN-5
Van Der Vorst, J. G. A. J., 474
Van de Ven, Bert, 600
Van Dongen, S., 474
Van Gogh, Vincent, 526
Van Putten, Alexander B., 155, EN-4, EN-6
Van Riel, C., 613n
Van Vuuren, Leon J., 335, EN-7
Veiga, John R., EN-7, EN-10
Velasquez, M., 606, 613n
Very, Philippe, 266
Vickers, Marcia, 329
Vitale, M. R., 469, 474
Vogelstein, Fred, 407, EN-10, EN-11

Wade, Judy, EN-9
Waleam, Jason, EN-3
Walsh, James P., EN-8

Walston, Stephen L., EN-9
Walton, M., EN-9
Walton, Sam, 440
Wambold, Richard, 266
Wang, Qianwei, EN-9
Waterman, Robert H., Jr., 616
Waters, J. A., EN-1
Watson, Gregory H., EN-3
Watts, Reid McRae, 526, 527
Webb, Alan, 476
Webb, Allen P., EN-11
Weber, James, EN-7
Webster, David, 589
Weick, K., 545, 550
Weill, P., 469, 474
Welch, Jack, 2, 266, 307, 316, 366, 388, 440, 542, 544, 545, 550, 585, 592, EN-8
Welch, Suzy, EN-8
Wernerfelt, Birger, EN-2
Wessel, Godecke, EN-9
Wetlaufer, Suzy, EN-11
White, David, EN-3
White, Gordon, 548
Whitman, Meg, 36

Wicks, A., 612n
Wiedman, Christine, 475
Wiersema, F., 532n
Wilke, John R., EN-7
Williamson, Peter J., 94, 515, 520n, EN-6
Wilson, H. J., 593
Wilson, Meena S., EN-10
Womack, J. P., 575, 581
Wong, A., 579, 581
Wood, D. J., 609, 612n, 613n
Woods, Tiger, 368–369
Woolridge, Bill, EN-1, EN-8
Worrell, Dan L., EN-8

Yip, George S., EN-2
Yoffie, David B., EN-4
Young, Shawn, 190, 304

Zack, Michael H., EN-2
Zahra, Shaker A., EN-2, EN-5
Zbaracki, Mark J., EN-9
Zimmerman, Frederick M., EN-6
Zott, C., 474

SUBJECT INDEX

Ability, developing, 369, 385
Access to information, 487
Accountancy services, 609
Accounting; see also Sarbanes-
    Oxley Act
    activity-based vs. traditional, 116t
    Big Four firms, 211
Accounting scandals, 327–332, 424
Accretion strategy, 535, 537,
    538t, 539
    example, 549
Achievement, 100, 408–410, 441
Acid-test ratio, 98t
Acquisitions; see Mergers and
    acquisitions
Action agenda; see also Strategic
    actions
    for changing problem cultures,
        428–432
    for embedding values and
        ethics, 436
    for implementing strategy, 42–43
    for strategy execution, 361,
        362–363
Action plan, 3–4
Activist groups, 347–348
Activities sharing, 540–541
Activity-based accounting, 112,
    114–115
    compared to traditional
        accounting, 116t
Activity ratios, 99t
Actual value, 147
Adaptation, 564–565
Adaptive corporate cultures,
    425–426
Added-value tests for
    diversification, 270
Administrative expenses, 136
Administrative support activities,
    in value chain, 111
Administrative support functions
    outsourcing, 374, 375
    strategic fit in, 276
Advertising costs, low-cost
    providers, 137–138
Advertising manager, 40
Affinity diagram, 466, 469
African American buying
    power, 348
Agents of change, 394
Aggressive moves, 262
Alliances; see Strategic alliances
Amoral managers, 324, 334–336,
    338, 352–353
Analyzer strategy, 478
Anomalies, exploiting, 498
Anti-Bribery Convention, 320
Anticorruption legislation, 338
Antitrust action, 252, 253
Asian American buying power, 348

Asian environment
    future of, 520
    shifts in
        China factor, 516–517
        decay of "me-too" strategies,
            517–518
        demise of asset speculators,
            515–516
        end of economic baronies, 517
    strategic responses to, 518–521
        brand building, 519
        cross-border synergies,
            518–520
        driving consolidation, 518–520
        innovation, 520
        new productivity drive, 521
        service equity, 519
Asian financial crisis, 515, 516
Assets
    competitive, 98–100, 290
    selling off, 257
    stranded, 500
Asset speculators, 515–516
Attention-seeking executives, 598
Attractiveness strength matrix,
    292–294, 293t
Audit committee, 45
Authoritarian structure, 379,
    383–384
Authority
    delegation of, 378–381
    placing limits on, 380–381
Automobile industry, blue ocean
    strategy and, 503–504
Automobile insurance
    business, 155
Average collection period, 99t
Awards and celebrations
    as incentive, 407
    national awards, 392, 433
    for operational excellence, 442
    in results-oriented climate, 442
    role in corporate culture, 432, 433

Backward integration, 68, 71, 171,
    172–173
Balanced scorecard, 475–481
    benefits, 475–476
    business strategy and, 477–478
    contingency factors, 476–477
    current use of, 475–476
    diagram, 476
    environmental uncertainty, 478
    financial performance and, 479
    firm size and, 478
    intangible assets and, 478–479
    key elements of success, 480
    scoring on, 476–481
Balanced scorecard approach
    example, 33
    financial/strategic objectives, 31

Balanced scorecard
    approach—Cont.
    long- and near-term objectives, 32
    performance measures, 31–32
    strategic intent, 32–34
    team effort, 34
    top-down objective setting, 34–35
    users of, 32
Balanced scorecard management,
    479–481
Bargaining leverage, 290
Bargaining power
    of buyers, 69–72, 603
    company vs. suppliers, 138
    to lower prices, 143
    from outsourcing, 175
    of suppliers, 66–68, 603
Barriers to entry
    capital requirements, 62
    cost/resource disadvantages, 61
    customer loyalty, 62
    distribution channel challenges, 62
    diversification and, 270
    economies of scale, 60–61
    in emerging industries, 232–233
    high vs. low, 63
    incumbent obstacles, 62–63
    regulatory policies, 62
    rising or falling, 63–64
    strong brand preferences, 62
    supply-side fragmentation
        and, 246
    trade restrictions, 62
Batch-and-queue techniques,
    574, 576
Believing-doing gap, 459–464
Benchmarking, 116–118
    competitive strengths, 122
    consulting organizations, 117
    for continuous improvement, 393,
        394–395, 400
    corporate culture and, 423
    cost disadvantages and, 117–120
    ethics and, 118
    for operational excellence, 442
    on workforce diversity, 347
Benefits, increasing level of, 513
Best-cost provider strategies, 157t
    compared to low-cost
        providers, 150
    competitive advantage, 150–151
    contrasted with other strategies,
        156–158
    example, 152
    key points, 159
    optimum conditions for,
        150–151
    risks of, 151
    target market for, 151
Best practices, 43, 238
    and benchmarking, 116

Best practices—Cont.
    continuous improvement
        programs for
        benefits of initiatives, 399–401
        business process
            reengineering, 395–396
        identifying best practices,
            393–395
        Six Sigma quality control,
            396–399
        total quality management,
            396, 399
    contrasted with signature
        processes, 561–564
    corporate culture and, 423
    cultural climate for, 438
    definition, 393–394
    development by adaptation,
        564–565
    origin in external research, 564
    origin of, 561
    shared knowledge, 565
    versus signature processes,
        561–562
Better-off test, 270
Big Four accounting firms, 211
Blue ocean strategy, 180–181, 192,
    502–507
    competition and, 502
    creating, 504–505
    dynamic process, 507
    expansion of, 506
    importance of, 506
    market universe, 505–506
    maximizing opportunity, 507
    minimizing risk, 507
    performance consequences, 503
    principles, 507
    profit growth consequences, 504
    strategic moves, 503–504
Blue Ocean Strategy (Kim &
    Mauborgne), 506, 507
Board of directors
    and chief executive officers,
        44–45
    independence of, 45–46
    negligence by, 45
    role in crafting strategy, 44–46, 47
Bonus plans
    effective, 586
    linear goal setting and, 583–584
    multiple goal levels and, 583
    stretch goals and, 582–583
Bottom-up objective setting, 34–35
Boundaryless company, 366
Brand building, 519
Brand image/reputation, 290
    ethical reporting, 609–610
Brand loyalty, 59, 233
Brand name, exploiting, 273
Brand preferences, 62

Note: Page numbers in *italics* indicate material in illustrations; page numbers followed by t indicate tables; page numbers followed by n indicate notes.

Brands
  global, 609–610
  strategic functions, 609
Brand switching, 58–59
Brazil, 199–200
Bribery, 606
  ethical relativism and, 319–320
  in global business, 325–327
  Global Corruption Report,
    326t, 327t
Brick-and-click strategies,
    184–185, 186
Brick-and-mortar operations,
    75, 185
Broadband service, 190
Broad differentiation strategies; *see*
  Differentiation strategies
Broadly diversified companies, 284
Budget
  reallocation, 390
  strategy-driven, 389
Budget-conscious buyers, 151
Built to Last (Collins & Porras), 619
Bureaucracies, 374, 375
  change-resistant, 423
Business base
  expanding, 300–303
  narrowing, 303–306
Business Builder Awards, 433
Business case
  for ethical strategy, 338–341
  for social responsibility, 347–349,
    353–354
Business environment
  changes and hardball competition,
    499–501
  changes in, 489
  competent analysis of, 92–93
  competitive forces, 51, 52,
    54–74, 55, 91
    profitability and, 72–74
    rivalry among sellers,
      55–60, 57
    seller–buyer relationships,
      69–71
    substitute products, 64–65, 65
    supplier–seller relationships,
      66–69
    threat of new entrants,
      60–64, 61
  competitive intelligence, 85, 92
    monitoring rivals, 85–86
    predicting rivals' moves,
      86–87
  conglomerates and, 535–539
  diagnosis for strategy making, 49
  dominant economic features,
    52–54, 53t, 90–91
  driving forces, 52, 91
    assessing impact of, 80–81
    concept, 74
    identifying, 74–79
    link with strategy, 81
    most common forces, 80t

Business environment—*Cont.*
  evolution of, 506
  factors influencing, 49–50
  fast-changing, 426
  in foreign markets, 198–199
  industry outlook, 52, 89–90, 92
  key success factors, 52, 87–89,
    88t, 92
  macroenvironment, 49–51, 51
  market position, 52, 81–84,
    91–92
    evaluating strategic group
      maps, 83–84
    rivalry effect, 56
    strategic group mapping,
      81–83, 83
  strategically relevant
    components, 49–51
  strategy corrections, 43–44
  thinking strategically about, 50,
    51–52
  uncertainty in, 478
Business ethics, 316–342, 352–353;
  see also Ethical *entries;* Social
  responsibility
  in benchmarking, 118
  business case for, 338–341
  codes of ethics, 434t, 435
    on bribes/kickbacks, 320
    genuineness of, 341–342
    worldwide enforcement, 323
  commitment process, 616–619
  company approaches,
    333–338, 335t
    compliance approach,
      336–337
    damage control
      approach, 336
    ethical culture approach, 337
    reasons for changing, 338
    unconcerned/nonissue
      approach, 334–336
  company strategies, 327–338
  compliance and enforcement,
    443–444
  core values and, 27–29
  corporate culture and, 434–437
  definition, 317
  drivers of unethical strategies
    company culture, 332–333
    earnings targets, 330–332
    pursuit of personal gain,
      328–330
  leadership in, 443–444
  management morality
    amoral managers, 324–325
    immoral managers, 324
    moral managers, 323
  managerial immorality in global
    markets, 325–327
  moral case for, 338
  more than codes, 615–616
  in product differentiation, 610
  recent scandals, 327–332

Business ethics—*Cont.*
  schools of thought
    ethical relativism, 319–322
    ethical universalism, 318
    integrative social contracts
      theory, 322–323
  strategy and, 10–12
  strategy/core values and, 341–342
  test of, 340
  universal vs. local norms,
    321–322
  value-based, 614–620
Business goals, untangling
  confusion in, 493
Business model, 12–13
  affinity diagram, 466, 469
  characteristics, 465–466
  components, 467–468
  definitions and terms for, 466–469
  for emerging markets, 225–226
  example, 14
  identity crisis of, 466–469
  outsourcing strategies, 528–531
  problems
    core logic flawed assumptions,
      471–472
    flawed value network
      assumptions, 473
    limitations in choices, 472
    value creation/capture
      misunderstandings,
      472–473
  strategy related to, 469–471
  to test strategic choices, 470–471
Business-performance management
  process, 480
Business principles, 416
Business process reengineering,
    395–396, 442
Business purpose, 24
Business risk
  first movers, 191
  industry attractiveness and, 287
  of multiple strategy horizons,
    250–251
  in outsourcing, 177
  reduced by outsourcing, 176
  reduction in, 79
  unrelated diversification, 280
  from vertical integration,
    173–174
Business Roundtable, 342, 350
Business standards, 616
Business strategy, 38, 39, 267; *see*
  also Strategy *entries*
  balanced scorecard and, 477–478
  definition, 601
  and organization structure,
    377–378
  single-business enterprise, 40,
    95–97, 96
  strategy cohesion, 41
  in strategy-making hierarchy,
    37–40, 39

Business-to-business markets, 607
Business-to-business relationships,
    71–72
Business units
  competitive strength
    calculating scores,
      289–291, 291t
    interpreting scores, 291–292
    nine-cell matrix, 292–294, 293t
  in conglomerates, 539–541
  cross-business strategic fits, 381
  cross-unit coordination,
    381–383
  degree of authority in, 378–381
  performance targets, 408
  ranking performance prospects,
    298–299, 299t
  strategy execution and, 377–378
BusinessWeek Global 1000,
    534–535
Buyer bargaining power, 69–72, 72,
    143, 603
Buyer demand, 76
  fall-off in, 58
  increase in, 57–58
  seasonal or cyclical, 287
  slow-down, 236
Buyer demographics, 76
Buyer diversity, 151
Buyer needs and requirements
  differentiation strategies and, 148
  product use, 143
Buyer perceptions, 147, 148
Buyer preferences; *see also*
  Customers
  competitive advantage and, 6
  dealing with cross-country
    variations, 205
  diverse, 148
  as driving force, 78–79
  in foreign markets, 197–198
  in fragmented industries, 246
  outsourcing and, 176
  supply-side fragmentation
    and, 246
Buyer-related activities, dispersed,
    210–211
Buyers; *see also* Customers
  best-cost provider strategy
    and, 151
  budget-conscious, 151
  competitive pressure on sellers,
    69–72, 72
  number of, 53t
  price-sensitive, 135
  seller–buyer partnerships, 71–72
  social responsibility and,
    347–348
  switching brands, 58–59
  value-conscious, 151
  view of product attributes, 149
Buyer segments, 153, 156
Buyers' market, 70
Buying power, 348

Cable television industry, 5
Capability-related KSFs, 88t
Capacity-matching problems, 174
Capacity utilization, 137
Capital-intensive business, 137
Capital investment
  fortify-and-defend strategy,
    252–253
  priorities, 268
  unrelated diversification,
    279–280
Capital requirements
  barrier to entry, 62
  for export strategy, 203
  technological requirements
    and, 77
Carbon-copy strategies, 4
Cash cows, 294–296
Cash flow
  differences in, 294–296
  generating, 260
Cash hogs, 294–296
Catalysts, 491
  confused with opportunities,
    492–493
  definition, 491–492
Category killers, 510, 513
Caution zone, 497
Census Bureau, 506
Centralized decision making,
    378–379, 378t
Champions, 441
Change; see also Resistance to
    change
  adapting to, 261
  in adaptive cultures, 425–426
  anticipating, 242
  driving forces, 74–81
  in high-velocity markets, 241–245
  in industry environment, 9
  leading, 242
  reacting to, 242
Change-resistant cultures, 422
Channel conflict, avoiding, 183–184
Channel stuffing, 331
Character
  in crisis, 619–620
  flawed, 596
  meaning of, 617
Charitable contributions,
    343–344, 351
Cheating Culture (Callahan), 614
Chief executive officer, 36
  and board of directors, 44–45
  compensation of, 352
  ethical leadership, 443
  leading culture change, 429, 430
  reasons for failure, 594–599
  role in crafting strategy, 35–36
  as role model, 583
  social responsibility
    initiatives, 445
  vision myopia, 462
Chief financial officer, 45

Child labor, 319
China
  as emerging market, 221
  factor in Asia competitiveness,
    516–517
  hardball strategy and, 499–500
  partnership agreements, 165
Choice, 490
Codes of ethical conduct, 614
  bribes/kickbacks and, 320
  corporate culture and, 434t, 435
  culture-building role, 435–436
  genuineness, 341–342
  value-based ethics and, 615–616
  worldwide enforcement, 323
Cognitive overload, 585
Collaboration in crafting
    strategy, 37
Collaborative partnerships, 68–69,
    161, 191
  advantages, 164–166
  capturing benefits of, 166–167
  dangers of relying on, 167–168
  definition, 163
  examples, 164
  factors in making, 163
  in foreign markets, 217–220
  kinds of, 485–487
  picking a good partner, 166
  with suppliers, 383
  with suppliers/buyers, 290
  unstable, 167
Combination strategies
  in diversification, 284–285
  turnaround strategies, 259
Command-and-control paradigm,
    379, 383–384
Commitment
  to innovation, 588
  in strategic alliances, 166
Commoditization, 506
Commodity products, 143
Communicating strategic vision
  motivational value, 25
  payoffs, 26
  resistance to change and, 25
  in slogans, 25–26
  strategic inflection points, 26, 27
  by top-level executives, 41
Community service endeavors, 343
Companies, 14
  business model, 12–13
  changes in environment, 26, 27
  coping with rapid change, 242
  evaluating business prospects, 3
  evolution of strategy, 8–9
  indicators of strategy, 7–8
  innovative, 590
  managing ethical conduct, 335t
    compliance approach, 335t,
      336–337
    damage control approach, 336
    ethical culture approach,
      335t, 337

Companies—Cont.
  managing ethical conduct—Cont.
    reasons for changing
      approaches, 338
    unconcerned/nonissue
      approach, 333–338, 335t
  menu of strategy options, 162
  moral value of survival, 610
  size of, 478
  strategic intent, 32–34
  strategy choices, 4
  strategy effectiveness, 95–97, 96
  strategy-focused, 15
  strategy-making hierarchy, 37–40
  visionary, 619–620
  winning strategies for, 13
Company culture; see Corporate
    culture
Company opportunity, 106
Company reputation (image)
  CEO obsession with, 597
  rehabilitating, 339–340
  social responsibility and,
    347–348, 606–608
Company-specific history, 566
Company subcultures, 419–420
Company values, 27–29
Company Web sites; see Web site
    strategies
  brick-and-click strategies,
    184–185, 186
  of manufacturers, 75
  minor distribution channel, 184
  online enterprises, 184–187
  outsourcing design of, 375
  for price comparisons, 70–71
  product information only, 183–184
Company-wide objectives, 34
Compensation
  bonus plans, 582–584
  culture change and, 431
  designing systems of,
    410–411, 412
  of executives, 44–45, 352
  fringe benefits, 405
  nonmonetary rewards, 404–405
  pay for performance, 584
  team-based system, 136
  for top executives, 409
Compensation committee, 45
Competencies, 165; see also Core
    competencies; Distinctive
    competence
  compared to core competence, 102
  in conglomerates, 542
  cross-border transfer, 211–212
  definition, 100–101
  differentiation strategies and, 147
  shared, 486
  SWOT analysis, 100–102
Competition; see also Five-forces
    model of competition;
    Hardball competition
  blue ocean strategy, 502–507

Competition—Cont.
  building a picture of, 54–55
  contending on global level, 226
  extremes of, 496
  fierce, 604–608
  from foreign markets, 196
  in fragmented industries, 246–247
  globalization and, 75
  global vs. international, 196
  key success factors, 87–89,
    88t, 92
  in maturing industries, 236
  multicountry vs. global, 201–202
  perfect, 602–603
  from product innovation, 76
  profit sanctuaries and, 213–215
  social responsibility and,
    602–603
  strong, 608–610
  from substitute products,
    64–65, 65
  threat of new entrants, 60–64, 61t
  weak, 610–611
Competitive advantage, 496
  best-cost provider strategy,
    150–151
  from blue ocean strategy,
    180–181, 502–507
  building core competencies, 386
  from core competencies, 373
  in cross-business
    opportunities, 268
  of cross-business strategic fits,
    294, 295t
  differentiation-based, 172–173
  in differentiation strategies, 144
  focused differentiation strategy,
    153–154
  focused low-cost strategy, 153
  in foreign markets, 227
    cross-border coordination,
      212–213
    cross-border transfers,
      211–212
    locational advantages,
      198–199, 209–211
  hardball competition and,
    496–497
  key success factors, 89
  of multinational corporations,
    308–311
  from offensive strategies,
    177–182
  online enterprises, 185
  outsourcing and, 176
  in related diversification,
    276–277
    economies of scope, 277
    shareholder value, 277
  with Six Sigma lean
    management, 580t
  stranded assets from, 500
  strategy and, 6–7, 13
  sustainable, 6, 13, 604

Competitive advantage—*Cont.*
  unrelated diversification, 284
  from value chain analysis,
    120–122, *121*
Competitive assets, 100–102,
  104, 290
Competitive attack
  choosing basis for, 181-182
  choosing rivals for, 181
Competitive capabilities, 363,
    385, 386
  access from merger or
    acquisition, 169
  from backward integration,
    172–173
  building
    competitive advantage,
      372, 373
    cross-functional work
      groups, 369
    customer needs, 370
    emergence of, 369–370
    employee training, 371–373
    role of leadership, 442–443
    three-stage development,
      368–371
  of business units, 290
  costly to emulate, 373
  cross-border transfer, 211–212
  from cross-unit collaboration,
    381–382
  differentiation strategies and, 147
  examples, 368
  from forward integration, 173
  identifying, 105t
  lost by outsourcing, 531
  of mature industries, 238
  mergers and acquisitions for,
    370–371
  outsourcing, 370
  resource fit and, 297
  strengthening, 108
  SWOT analysis, 97–104
  traits, 369–370
  updating and remodeling, 371
Competitive conditions, 370
  fairness of, 606
Competitive deficiencies,
    identifying, 104, 105t
Competitive disadvantages, 606
Competitive edge, 56, 373
Competitive environment, 51–52
Competitive forces; *see also* Five-
    forces model of competition
  in Asian environment, 515–520
  social responsibility and,
    600–601
    competitive strategies,
      603–604
    conclusions on, 611–612
    with fierce competition,
      604–608
    intensity of competition,
      602–603

Competitive forces—*Cont.*
  social responsibility and—*Cont.*
    with strong competition,
      608–610
    with weak competition,
      610–611
Competitive intelligence
  on foreign markets, 165
  monitoring rivals, 85–86
  predicting moves of rivals, 86–87
Competitive liabilities, 104
  reducing, 108
Competitive position, 95–96, 201,
    244, 261
  strengthened by
    diversification, 268
Competitive power of resource
    strengths, 102–104
Competitive pressures, *55,* 84
  buyer bargaining power, 69–72
  in five-forces model, 54
  jockeying among rival sellers,
    55–60
  new entrant threat, 60–64
  profitability and, 72–74
  from substitute products, 64–65
  supplier bargaining power, 66–69
Competitive rivalry; *see also* Five-
    forces model of competition
  among competing sellers, 55–60,
    55t, 63t
  among industry leaders, 251–254
  cross-group rivalry, 84
  cutthroat or brutal, 60
  in declining industries, 239–241
  in emerging markets, 231–234
  factors influencing, 56–60
  in fragmented industries, 245–249
  in high-velocity markets, 241–245
  in macro environment, 53t
  in maturing industries, 236–239
  moderate, 60
  in rapid-growth businesses,
    249–251
  in rapidly growing markets,
    234–235
  runner-up firms and, 254–257
  scope of, 53t
  threat of new entrants, 60–64, 61t
  weak, 60
  weak/crisis-ridden businesses,
    257–261
  weakened, 58
  weapons in, 56, 57t
Competitive rivals
  commodity products, 143
  competitive advantage and,
    6–7, 370
  cross-border rivals, 60
  defensive strategies against, 182
  few differentiators among, 148
  global vs. multicountry
    competition, 201–202
  identifying strategies of, 85–86

Competitive rivals—*Cont.*
  maneuvering by, 369–370
  market position of, 81–82,
    91–92
  number of, 53t
  offensive strategies against,
    177–182
  predicting next moves of, 86–87
  price competition, 143
  resource strengths of, 103
  resource strengths/weaknesses,
    85–86
  strategy choices, 4
  strengths or weaknesses versus,
    122–125
  underestimating, 262
  value chain differences, 112–113
Competitive scope, 95–96
Competitive strategies, 132–159,
    134, 157t
  best-cost provider strategies,
    150–151
  competitive forces and, 603–604
  contrasting features, 156–158
  definition and purpose, 133
  differentiation strategies, 144–150
  for emerging industries, 233–234
  five distinct approaches, 134–135
  focused (market niche) strategies,
    151–156
  in foreign markets, 204–209, *208*
  functional-area strategy for, 187
  key points, 158–159
  low-cost provider strategies,
    135–144
  multibrand strategies, 156
  stuck-in-the-middle strategies
    versus, 158
Competitive strength, 262
  relative market share, 289–290
Competitive strength assessment,
    122–125, 123t, 127
  of business units
    measures, 289–292
    nine-cell matrix for,
      292–294, 293t
  interpreting, 124–125
  unweighted rating system,
    122–124, 123t
  weighted rating system, 123t, 124
Competitive superiority,
    101–102, 103
Competitive weakness, 262
  attacking, 179
Competitive weapons, 56, 57t
Competitors
  costs of, 290
  enticed into retreat, 498–499
  identifying strategy of, 85–86
  increase in diversity of, 59–60
  increase in number of, 56–57
  leapfrogging, 178
  low-end, 508–514
  price cuts and, 59

Competitors—*Cont.*
  quantitative strength ratings, 122
  weakened rivalry, 58
Complementary strategic
    options, *162*
Compliance
  with ethical standards, 443–444
  under fierce competition,
    605–606
  legal loopholes and, 606
  with spirit of law, 608
  under weak competition, 610–611
Compliance approach, 335t,
    336–337
Compromises, 499
Compromise strategies, 262
Conglomerates, 534–550
  answering demands of, 546–547
  cross-functional teams, 556
  influence of headquarters, 540
    means of control, 542
    resources and
      competencies, 542
  management of, 545–546, 547t
  multi-industry firms, 536–537
  portfolio management, 541t
    building the portfolio,
      543–544
    criteria for content, 543
    divestiture and restructuring,
      544–545
  profile of, 534–353
  relationship among units, 539
    activities sharing, 540–541
    sharing /coordination, 541–542
    skills transfer, 540–541
    structure, 540
  strategies
    mixed strategies, 537–539
    portfolio strategy, 535
    propagation strategy, 535–537
    restructuring and accretion
      strategies, 537
  strategy archetypes, 538
  strategy examples, 547–550
  strategy framework, 534
Conservative strategies, 4
Consolidated financial statements,
    129–131
Consolidation, 519–520, 524–525
Consumerism in Asia, 518
Consumer tastes, 202
Content follower strategy, 256–257
Continuous improvement programs
  benchmarking for, 393, 394–395
  benefits of, 399–401
  business process reengineering,
    395–396
  comparison of, 399
  for operational excellence, 442
  Six Sigma quality control, 366,
    396–399
  total quality management,
    396, 399

Control
in conglomerates, 539–542
in decentralized structure, 380–381
over empowered employees, 403–404
information systems for, 402–403
Six Sigma program, 395, 396–399, 412
total quality management, 396
Convenience, 509
Core competencies, 363, 385, 386
attacking, 217
building
competitive advantage, 372, 373
employee training, 371–373
role of leadership, 442–443
three-stage development, 368–371
compared to competencies, 102
as competitive advantage, 120–121
costly to emulate, 373
from cross-unit collaboration, 381–382
definition, 101
examples, 368
foreign markets and, 196
mergers and acquisitions for, 370–371
outsourcing and, 370, 374–375
traits, 369–370
updating and remodeling, 371
Core logic, 466
flawed assumptions in, 471–472
Core values
versus actual practice, 29
in company subcultures, 419–420
in corporate culture, 416, 447–448
example of, 615
grounding culture in
benefits, 436–437, 437t
codes of ethics, 434t
cultural norms, 436
culture-building role of values, 435–436
linked to strategy, 341–342
linking vision with, 27–29, 30
signature processes from, 568–569
strategy–culture fit and, 427
in strong-culture companies, 420–421
in weak-culture companies, 421–422
Corporate culture, 416–438, 447–448
adaptive, 425–426
as ally or obstacle, 426–428
change approaches, 428–432, 429t
making case for change, 429–430

Corporate culture—Cont.
change approaches—Cont.
substantive actions, 430–431
symbolic actions, 431–432
time factor, 432
in conglomerates, 542
definition, 415
ethical, 337
ethical failures and, 332–333
evolution of, 419
examples, 417, 433
grounded in core values/ethics, 434–437
benefits of cultural norms, 426–427, 437t
culture-building role, 435–436
transforming values and ethics, 436
high-performance, 424–425
identifying key features, 416–420
multinational strategy–culture fit, 437–438
perpetuating, 418–419
psyche of, 415–416
results-oriented, 438
role of stories, 418
strategy execution and, 43
perils of strategy–culture conflict, 428
promoting better execution, 426–428
strong vs. weak
strong-culture company, 420–421
weak-culture company, 421–422
subcultures, 419
supporting strategy, 456–457
unhealthy
change-resistant culture, 422–423
insular/inwardly focused, 423–424
politicized culture, 422
unethical/greed-driven culture, 424
values-based, 438
Corporate downsizing, 168, 384
Corporate governance, 44–46, 47
Corporate intrapreneurship, 37
Corporate restructuring; see Restructuring
Corporate social responsibility (CSR); see Social responsibility
Corporate strategy, 38, 39, 267
single-business enterprise, 40
strategy cohesion, 41
Corrective adjustments, 19, 43–44, 47
leadership in making, 445–446
process, 446
Corruption Perception Index, 325t

Cost advantages, 61
of direct selling, 139
economies of scope, 278
focused low-cost strategy, 153
in foreign markets, 198
in low-cost provider strategies
cost-efficient value chain, 137–139
example, 140–142
revamping value chain, 139–140
of online technology, 139–140
of outsourcing, 138
pitfalls, 144
of price cutting, 178, 262
steel industry, 136
of vertical integration, 138
Cost-based competitive advantage, 6
Cost changes, 78
Cost cutting
in declining industries, 240
fixation on, 144
by low-cost providers, 137–138
in rapidly growing markets, 235
revenue-increasing turnaround strategy, 248
by runner-up companies, 255
Cost disadvantages
from forward channel allies, 119–120
internal, 119
remedying, 117–120
supplier-related, 119
Cost efficiency
from mergers, 168
in value chain analysis, 121–122
Cost-efficient management of value chain activities, 137–139
Cost estimates, 115
Cost-of-entry test, 270
Costs
competitive, 109–122, 127
versus competitor costs, 290
of ethical failure, 338–340, 339t
expense categories, 114–115
locational advantages, 211
trimming, 238
Cost-saving efficiencies, 67
Cost structure, high, 514
Coverage ratio, 99t
Crafting strategy; see Strategy crafting; Strategy making
Creative Destruction (Foster & Kaplan), 502
Creative talent, attracting and retaining, 589–591
Credit rating, 297
Crisis-ridden businesses; see Weak businesses
Cross-border alliances, 217–220
Cross-border coordination, 212–213

Cross-border cultural change, 437–438
Cross-border markets, transfer of expertise to, 225
Cross-border rivals, 60
Cross-border synergies, 519–520
Cross-border transfer, 211–212
Cross-business collaboration, 273, 310
Cross-business economies of scope, 308–309
Cross-business strategic fit, 274–278, 294, 295t, 381
example, 302
Cross-business subsidization, 311
Cross-business value chain relationships, 268
Cross-country collaboration, 310
Cross-country differences
competing in foreign markets, 197–201
customization vs. standardization, 197–198
host government policies, 200–201
locational advantages, 198–199
market growth rates, 197
multicountry vs. global strategy, 204–209, 205, 208
product design, 197
risk of exchange rate changes, 199–200
in cross-border alliances, 218–220
Cross-country subsidization, 311
Cross-functional teams, 556
Cross-functional work groups, 369, 395
Cross-group competitive rivalry, 84
Cross-industry strategic fits, 287
Cross-market subsidization, 214–215, 227–228
Cross-subsidization tactics, 311–312
Cultural differences, 197
in cross-border alliances, 218–220
sensitivity to, 166
Cultural fit, 304–305
Cultural imperatives, 433
Cultural norms, 421, 430
grounded in core values, 436–437
strictly enforced, 436
Cultural values, 569
Culture and lifestyle
compensation and, 410
cross-cultural variability, 320–321
in global community, 325–327
incentive pay, 411–412
multinational operations and, 419–420

Culture-changing actions, 428–432, 429t, 447
  example, 433
  leadership factor, 429, 430
  making case for, 429–430
  substantive actions, 430–431
  symbolic actions, 431–432
  time factor, 432
Culture of underperformance, 555
Cultures
  ethical relativism in, 319–322
  moral agreement across, 318
Culture training, 438
Current ratio, 98t
Customer loyalty, 62
Customer needs, changes in, 370
Customers; see also Buyers
  in Asia, 517–518
  bargaining leverage with, 290
  collaboration with, 487–488
  company reputation and, 607–608
  cultural differences, 197
  feedback from, 382
  in foreign markets, 196
  increasing sales to, 238
  Internet use, 75
  pressuring, 253
  suggestions from, 484
  tapping new sources of, 512–513
  value chain, 113
Customer satisfaction, short-pay policy, 392
Customer service activities
  for Asian consumers, 519
  in best-cost provider strategy, 150
  in differentiation strategies, 146, 148
  in distinctive-image strategy, 256
  in maturing industries, 238
  personalized, 253
  Six Sigma analysis, 399
Customer type specialization, 247–248
Cycle time, 375
Cyclical factors, 287

Damage control approach, 335t, 336
DART practices, 487
Data sharing, 138
Days of inventory ratio, 99t
Debt overload, 257
Debt-to-assets ratio, 98t
Debt-to-equity ratio, 99t
Decentralized decision making, 379–380
Decentralized organization
  capturing strategic fits, 381
  decision-making authority, 379–380
  maintaining control in, 380–381
  trends to, 383–384

Decision making
  centralized vs. decentralized, 378–381
  speeding up, 375
  in strategic alliances, 166
  on strategy options, 454–455
Declining industries
  decline in demand and, 239
  end-game strategies
    fast exit, 241
    slow exit, 241
  strategy alternatives, 240–241
  strategy choices, 239–240
Defects-free products, 572–573
Defender strategy, 478
Defensive strategies, 125, 192
  blocking challengers, 182
  for emerging markets
    contending on global level, 226
    home-field advantages, 224–225
    new business models, 225–226
    transfer of expertise, 225
  signaling retaliation, 182–183
Delivery agenda, 558
Demand
  decline in, 239
  seasonal or cyclical, 287
Demand conditions, 53t
Demographic differences, 197
Department of Defense, 523
Departments, 377
Deregulation, 79
Dialog, 487
Differentiation-based competitive advantage, 172–173
Differentiation strategies, 6, 144–150, 157t, 262
  buyer preferences and, 78–79
  contrasted with other strategies, 156–158
  in declining industries, 240
  definition, 134
  easy-to-copy features and, 145
  example of, 483
  focused, 153–156
  key points, 158
  means of, 604
  mistakes in, 149–150
  optimum conditions for, 148
  perceived value, 147
  pitfalls, 148–150
  in rapidly growing markets, 235
  reward systems, 408
  routes to competitive advantage, 146–147
  by runner-up companies, 255
  signaling value, 147
  successful, 144–145
  types of themes, 145
  value chain activities, 145–146
Digital subscriber line, 190
Direct attack strategy, 497
Direct selling, 139

Disruptive innovation, 529–530
Distinctive capabilities, 608, 609
Distinctive competence, 101–102, 104, 120–121, 147, 369, 370, 374–375, 385
Distinctive image, 262
Distinctive-image strategy, 256
Distinctive strategic position, 453, 455
Distribution activities
  collaborative partnerships, 383
  in differentiation strategies, 146
  strategic fit in, 275
  in value chain, 111
Distribution channels
  as barrier to entry, 62
  Internet use
    brick-and-click strategies, 184–185, 186
    minor distribution channel, 184
    online enterprises, 185–187
    product information only, 183–184
  low-cost, 139
  in rapidly growing markets, 235
  in search of products, 513–514
Distribution-related KSFs, 88t
Diverse strategy portfolio, 249–251
Diversification, 266–315; see also Related diversification; Unrelated diversification
  added-value tests
    better-off test, 270
    cost-of-entry test, 270
    industry attractiveness test, 270
  building shareholder value, 269–270
  candidates for, 268
  combination strategies, 284–285
  key points, 312–313
  post-diversification strategies
    broadening business base, 300–303, 301t
    divestiture strategies, 303–306
    multinational diversification, 308–312
    restructuring, 306–308
  related vs. unrelated, 272
  strategic alternatives, 273
  strategic analysis, 285–300, 312–313
    business-unit competitive strengths, 289–294
    cross-business strategic fits, 294
    industry attractiveness, 286–289
    new strategic moves, 299–300
    performance prospects, 298–299
    resource allocation priorities, 298–299, 299t
    resource fit, 294–298

Diversification—Cont.
  strategies for, 270–272
    acquisition, 271
    internal start-up, 271
    joint ventures, 271–272
    strategy-making facets, 267–268
    when to diversify, 269
Diversified companies
  building blocks of, 377–378
  cross-business strategic fits, 381
  decentralized decision making, 379
  identifying strategy of, 285
  strategy-making authority, 267–268
  strategy options, 301t
    broader business base, 300–303
    divestiture, 303–306
    multinational diversification, 308–312
    restructuring, 306–308
Diversified multinational corporations, 308–312
Divestiture
  aimed at retrenching, 303–306
  candidates for, 303, 306–307
  of cash hogs, 296
  in conglomerates, 543–544
  cultural fit and, 304–305
  of marginal businesses, 299
  selling or spinning off, 305–306
Divided-self notion, 590
Dividend payout ratio, 99t
Dividend yield on common stock, 99t
Divisional structure, 540–541
Divisional units, 377
DMADV Six Sigma process, 396
DMAIC Six Sigma process, 396–399
  components, 397
  example, 398
  for performance variations, 399
"Do-good" executives, 349–351
Domestic companies
  basic offensive strategies, 177–181
  basis of competitive attack, 181–182
  choosing rivals to attack, 181
  cross-market subsidization, 214–217
  defensive strategies, 182–183
  profit sanctuary potential, 214, 215
  strategies for emerging markets, 224–226
    contending on global level, 226
    home-field advantages, 224–225
    new business markets, 225–226
    transferring expertise, 225
Domestic-only companies, 214

Dominant-business enterprises, 284
Dominant design, 525–526
Dominant technology, 233
Dot-com enterprises, 185–187
Dot-com era, 472
  boom and bust, 496
Dow Jones Global Index, 348
Downsizing, 168, 384
Driving forces
  assessing impact of, 80–81
  concept, 74
  identifying, 74–80
  most common, 80t
  for outsourcing, 175
  strategic group mapping, 84
  strategy and impact of, 81
  technological innovation, 275
Dumping, 512
Dumping strategies, 216

Earnings management, 331
Earnings per share, 98t
Earnings targets, 330–332
Easy-to-copy features, 145
E-commerce, 183–187, 192, 383
  boom and bust, 496
Economic conditions, goal changes
    to meet, 586
Economies of scale, 53t
  as barrier to entry, 60–61
  compared to economies
      of scope, 277
  locational advantages, 210
  of low-cost providers, 137
  in multinational
      diversification, 308
  from outsourcing, 176
  product standardization and, 198
  supply-side fragmentation
      and, 246
Economies of scope
  in multinational diversification,
      308–309
  in related diversification, 277
Edge, 366
Efficiency
  balanced with innovation,
      591–593
  changes, 78
Electronic scorecards, 403
E-mail, 75
Emerging industries, 79
  strategic hurdles, 234
  strategies for competing in,
      231–234
  strategy options, 233–234
  unique characteristics, 232–233
Emerging markets, 220–226, 228
  local company strategies
    contending on global level, 226
    home-field advantages,
        224–225
    new business models, 225–226
    transferring expertise, 225

Emerging markets—Cont.
  market growth rates, 197
  opportunities in, 220–221
  strategy options for, 222–223, 224
  tailoring products for, 221–222
Emerging threats; see Threats
Employees; see also Workforce
  buy-in to ethics, 618
  child labor issue, 319
  commitment to values, 616
  constructive pressure on, 441–442
  creative talent, 589–591
  degree of authority, 378–381
  in high-performance cultures,
      424–425
  of high-tech companies, 367
  as intellectual capital, 367–368
  interaction with managers, 416
  linked to performance, 408–411
  performance tracking, 402–403
  recruitment and retention, 347,
      365–368
  rewards and incentives
    balancing rewards and
        punishments, 406–408
    motivational practices,
        404–406, 407
  screening job applicants,
      418–419
  sharing information with,
      405–406
  social responsibility and, 347
  strategy execution by, 359–360
  in strong-culture companies,
      420–421
  in weak-culture companies,
      421–422
  work environment, 344, 346
  workforce diversity, 344–345
Employee suggestions, 405
Employee training, 392, 441
  costs of, 347
  culture training, 438
  in ethics and values, 444
  leadership development,
      364–365, 366
  for strategy execution, 367–368,
      371–373
Empowered employees, 372
  agents of change, 394
  in decentralized decision making,
      379–380
  exercising control over, 403–404
  policies and procedures and, 393
  for quality improvement, 400
  work teams, 379–380
End-game strategy, 241, 257
Energy, 366
Enforcement of ethical standards,
    443–444
Enterprise resource planning, 138
Entrepreneurship, 35
  emulation of, 483–484
  multi-industry firms, 527–539

Entry barriers; see Barriers to entry
Entry of major firms, 77
Entry of new competitors, 312
  from innovation, 524
  means of entry, 267, 270–272
  shareholder value tests, 270
  unrelated diversification, 280
Environmental issues
  industry attractiveness and, 287
  social responsibility and, 344,
      346, 348, 445, 607
Environmental protection, 344
Ethical culture approach,
    335t, 337
Ethical displacement, 605
Ethical failures, 11–12; see also
    Business ethics
  accounting scandals, 424
  business costs, 338–340, 339t
  and core values, 29
  drivers of unethical strategies
    company culture, 332–333
    earnings targets, 330–332
    pursuit of personal gain,
        328–330
    responses to, 333–336
  in ethical relativism
    bribes and kickbacks, 319–320
    child labor, 319
    multiple ethical standards,
        320–321
    rudderless ethics, 321–322
  Global Corruption Report,
      325–327
  managerial immorality in global
      business, 325–327
  recent scandals, 327–332
  reporting infractions, 444
Ethical norms, 321–322
Ethical relativism, 352
  breakdown of, 321–322
  bribery and kickbacks, 319–320
  child labor issue, 319
  definition, 319
  multiple ethical standards,
      320–321
Ethical reporting, 609–610
Ethical standards, 416; see also
    Business ethics
  core values and, 341–342
  multiple sets of, 320–321
  origin of, 319–323
  rudderless, 321–322
  schools of thought, 352
Ethical strategy
  business case for, 338–340
  moral case for, 338
Ethical universalism, 318, 352
Ethical value added, 619
Ethics; see Business ethics
Ethics commitment process,
    616–617
  elements of, 617–618
Excess capacity, 58

Exchange rate fluctuations, 199–200
Execution, 366
Execution capabilities, 559–560
Executive compensation, 409
  linked to social responsibility, 352
  top-level executives, 409
Executive departures, 597
Exercise equipment industry, 248
Exit of major firms, 77
Expense categories, 114–115
Experience curve effects; see
    Learning curve effects
Expertise, 7, 99–100, 101
  in diversification, 310
  transfer of, 225
  tranfers in diversification, 272
Export strategies, 203
External environment; see
    Macroenvironment

Facilities
  appealing, 406
  foreign markets
    concentrated, 209–210
    dispersed, 210–211
  formula facilities, 247
  relocating, 140
  topping-out problem, 236
Fairness of competitive
    conditions, 606
Fallacy of composition, 494
Fast-exit strategy, 241, 257
Fast Second (Markides &
    Geroski), 520
Federal Communications
    Commission, 170
Fierce competition, 604–608, 611
Financial accounting practices, 45
Financial incentives, 404–405
Financial objectives
  achieving, 35
  kinds of, 31
  success indicators, 96–97
Financial performance, 31–32
  balanced scorecard and, 479
Financial projections, 556–557
Financial ratios, 98t–99t
Financial reporting practices, 45
Financial resources
  allocation options, 299t
  cash hogs vs. cash cows,
      294–296
  credit rating, 297
  resource fit and, 294–296
  star businesses, 296
  unrelated diversification and, 280
Finished goods, 490
Firm size, 478
First-follower advantage, 188
First-mover advantage, 188–191
  decisions about, 189–191
  example of, 190
  versus late-mover advantage, 189
  for runner-up companies, 255

First-mover advantage—*Cont*
  sustaining the advantage, 188
  timing of, 188
Five-forces model of competition,
  54–74, 55t, 91, 603, 604–605,
  610–611
  buyer bargaining power, 69–72
  competitive pressures in, 54
  jockeying among rival sellers,
    55–60
  picturing competition, 54
  profitability and, 72–74
  sellers of substitute products,
    64–65
  supplier bargaining power,
    66–69
  threat of new entrants, 60–64
Five whys root cause analysis, 579
Focus, 244
Focused (market niche) strategies,
  6–7, 151–156
  attractiveness of, 154–155
  contrasted with other strategies,
    151–152, 156–158
  in declining industries, 240
  definition, 135
  differentiation strategy,
    153–154, 157t
  example, 155
  key points, 159
  low-cost strategy, 153, 157t
  premise of, 604
  risks, 156
Focusing resources, 528–529
Forbes, 594
Forecasts
  versus assumptions, 556–557
  resource deployment and,
    557–558
  versus results, 552–553
Foreign Corrupt Practices Act,
  320, 606
Foreign markets
  cross-country differences,
    197–201
  buyer preferences, 197–198
  in cross-border alliances,
    218–220
  gaining competitive advantage,
    198–199
  global vs. multicountry
    strategies, 204–209,
    205, 208
  host government policies, 200
  market differences, 198
  risks of exchange rate changes,
    199–200
  cross-market subsidization,
    214–215, 227–228
  emerging market strategies,
    220–226
  defending against global
    giants, *224,* 224–226
  example of, 221

Foreign markets—*Cont.*
  emerging market strategies—*Cont.*
    local company strategies, *224,*
      224–226
    strategy options, 222–223
    tailoring products for, 221–222
  entry into, 79
  expansion into
    by mature industries, 238
    reasons for, 196
    by strategic alliances, 165
  international vs. global
    competition, 196
  key points, 226–228
  multicountry vs. global
    competition, 200–201
  offensive strategies, 215–217
  profit sanctuaries, 213–214, 227
  purchasing power variations,
    197, 221–222
  quest for competitive advantage,
    209–213
    cross-border coordination,
      212–213
    cross-border transfers, 211–212
    locational advantages, 209–211
  strategic alliances, 217–220
    examples, 219
    motivations for, 217–218
    questionable need for, 220
    risks of, 218–220
  strategic issues, 195, 226
  strategy options, 202–209, *205*
    examples, 209
    export strategies, 203
    franchising strategies, 204
    licensing strategies, 203–204
    localized vs. global,
      204–209, *208*
Formula facilities, 247
Fortify-and-defend strategy,
  252–253, 257
Fortune, 392, 594, 596
Forward channel allies
  cost disadvantages from, 119–120
  value chains of, 113
Forward integration, 171, 173
Fragmented industries
  competitive conditions, 246–247
  examples, 245
  illustration of, 248
  strategy options, 247–249
  supply-side fragmentation, 245–246
Franchising strategies, 204
Frills-free products, 140
Fringe benefits, 405
Full-capacity operation, 137
Full integration, 171–172
Function, 508–509
  improvements in, 513
Functional-area strategies, 38–40,
  39, 162, 192
  choosing, 187–188
  strategy cohesion, 41

Functional organization
  structure, 377
  weaknesses, 382
Funding, 389
Future of Competition (Prahalad &
  Ramaswamy), 487–488
Future orientation, 484–485
Futures research methods, 484

General administration, *111*
Generally accepted accounting
  principles, 45
Generic competitive options, *162*
Geographic coverage
  in fragmented industries,
    248–249
  from mergers and acquisitions,
    168–169
  in rapidly growing markets, 235
  supply-side fragmentation
    and, 246
Geographic organizational
  units, 377
Global brands, 609–610
Global companies, *214*
  strategy–culture fit, 437–438
  subcultures in, 419–420
Global competition, 227; *see also*
    International competition
  versus international
    competition, 196
  versus multicountry competition,
    201–202
Global Corruption Report, 320,
    325–327, 325t–326t
Globalization
  as driving force, 75
  strategic alliances and, 163
  strategy options from, 225–226
  technology transfer and, 78
Global market leadership
  illustration of, 170
  strategic alliances for, 163, 165
Global markets, 201
  ethical relativism and, 321–322
  management immorality in,
    325–327
Global strategy, 204–209
Goal integration, 585
Goals; *see also* Objectives
  activities set by, 584–585
  with changing conditions,
    585–586
  effective incentive systems
    for, 586
  linear system, 583–584
  multiple goals with
    bonuses, 583
  number of, 585
  pay for performance and, 584
  stretch goals with bonuses,
    582–583
Goal-setting theory, 582
Government policies, 200–201

Government regulation
  as barrier to entry, 62
  as driving force, 79
  against dumping, 216
  Foreign Corrupt Practices Act,
    320, 606
  foreign markets and, 200–201
  industry attractiveness and, 287
  Sarbanes-Oxley Act, 338, 341
Greed-driven cultures, 424
Gross profit margin, 98t
Growth
  by acquisition, 255
  from blue ocean strategy, 504
  slowing rate of, 236–237
Growth development leaders, 433
Growth rate potential, 286
Growth strategies
  earnings targets, 330–332
  for rapid company growth,
    249–251
  scaling without mass, 529
Guerrilla offensive, 179

Hardball competition
  business environment changes
    and, 499–501
  caution zone, 497
  classical approaches
    borrowing ideas, 498
    break compromises, 499
    entice competitors into retreat,
      498–499
    exploiting anomalies, 498
    overwhelming force, 497
    threat to profit sanctuaries, 498
  mergers and acquisitions and, 499
  mindset, 501
  principles of, 496–497
Harvard Business Review, 452
Harvesting strategies, 260–261
High-definition television, 5
High-end differentiators, 151
High-performance cultures,
  424–425
High-tech companies, 367
High-velocity change, 9
High-velocity markets, 241–245
  coping with rapid change, 242
  strategy options, 242–245, *243*
Hispanic buying power, 348
Hit-and-run warfare, 179
Home-field advantages, 224–225
Host government policies, 200–201
Human assets, 100
Human resource management, *111*
  in conglomerates, 541–542
Human rights activists, 348
Hype, 598

Idea borrowing, 498
Idea generation, 453–454
Immoral managers, 324,
  334–336, 352

Incentive programs, 404–411; *see also* Rewards and incentives
Industries; *see also* Declining industries; Emerging industries; Fragmented industries; Maturing industries
competitive attractiveness, 73
convergence of, 169
diversification strategy-making, 267–268
emerging, 79
future, 525–527
global competition, 201–202
key success factors, 87–89, 88t, 92
learning/experience curve effects, 54
multicountry competition, 201
in rapidly growing markets, 234–235
strategic alliances, 164
strategic groups, 82
topping-out problem, 236
types of market space, 180
value chain system, 113–*114*
Industry attractiveness
competitive conditions, 73
conditions for, 89–90, 92
in diversification
calculating scores, 277t, 286–288
difficulties in scoring, 288–289
interpreting scores, 288
measures of, 286–287
nine-cell matrix for, 292–294, 293t
performance prospects and, 298
Industry attractiveness test
attractiveness-strength matrix, 292–294, 293t
for diversification, 270
Industry conditions, 53t
buyer bargaining power, 69–72
competitive forces, 54–74
dominant economic features, 52–54
driving forces, 74–81
fluctuating, 502–503
goal changes to meet, 586
market position of rivals, 81–84, 91–92
monitoring rivals, 85–87
need for strategy changes and, 457–458
outlook, 89–90, 92
producing opportunities, 494
rivalry indicators, 56
supplier bargaining power, 66–68
supply-side fragmentation, 245–246
threat of new entrants, 60–64, 61t
union vs. nonunion, 66–67
Industry consolidation, 519–520
Industry demand, 260

Industry environment; *see also* Business environment
changing circumstances, 9
for focused (market niche) strategies, 154–155
relative attractiveness, 89–90, 92
strategic thinking about, 51–52
strategy flexibility and, 456
strategy options in, 263
Industry growth rate, 53t, 75–76
Industry leaders
examples, 251
illustration of, 252
inevitability of low-end attack, 513–514
insular corporate culture, 423–424
kinds of strategic retreats, 514
low-end attack on, 508
predators on, 509–510
reacting to low-end competitors
acquiring, 512
adding new price point, 512–513
blocking, 512
dropping prices, 513
ignoring, 511–512
increasing benefits, 513
strategies for, 251–254
structural/cultural inertia, 457–458
Industry life cycle, 74
Industry newcomers, 143–144
Industry opportunity, 106
Industry position, 263
Industry pricing, 513
Industry profitability, 287
Industry structure, social responsibility
under fierce competition, 604–608
under strong competition, 608–610
under weak competition, 610–611
Industry uncertainty, 287
reduction in, 79
Information
access to, 487
for benchmarking, 117
for leadership, 439–440
rapid dissemination of, 383
shared with employees, 405–406
statistical, 403
Information systems
areas covered by, 402
for control over empowered employees, 403–404
installing, 401–404
performance tracking, 402–403
real-time, 403
Innovation; *see also* Product innovation; Technological innovation
in Asia, 520
balanced with efficiency, 591–593
commitment to, 588
creative talent and, 589

Innovation—*Cont.*
disruptive, 529–530
in industries of the future, 525–527
new markets created by, 523
radical, 522–523
strategic, 458
supply-push, 523–525
types of, 522
Innovation culture
balancing innovation and efficiency, 591–593
creative talent, 589–591
right climate for, 587–589
Innovative companies, 590
Inputs, 67
lower specifications, 138–139
substitutes, 138
In Search of Excellence (Peters & Waterman), 502, 616
Insular/inwardly-focused cultures, 423–424
Intangible assets, 100, 478–479
Integrative social contracts theory, 322–323, 352
Integrity, 617
Intellectual capital, 100, 101, 367, 370
Internal cash flow, 99t
Internal cost disadvantage, 119
Internal cross-unit coordination, 381–383
Internal start-up, 271
Internal weaknesses, 104
International competition, 196; *see also* Global competition; Multinational corporations/enterprises
global vs. multicountry, 201–202
in maturing industries, 236
International expansion, 238
International Labor Organization, 319
International trade among Asian nations, 517
International Trade Commission, 512
Internet
conducting business via, 382
development of, 523
as driving force, 74–75, 91
for price comparisons, 70–71
Web site strategies, 192
brick-and-click strategies, 184–185, 186
minor distribution channel, 184
online enterprises, 185–187
product information only, 183–184
Internet-based phone networks, 76–77
Internet retailers, 501
Internet technology applications, 235
broadband service, 5, 190
direct selling, 139

Internet technology applications—*Cont.*
e-commerce, 383
supply chain management, 139–140
Voice over Internet Protocol, 5, 74–75, 76–77, 231–233, 327
Intrapreneurship, 37
Inventory, 490
Inventory turnover, 99t
Invest-and-expand strategy, 296
Investment
in intangible assets, 478–479
priorities, 268

Job applicant screening, 418–419
Joint marketing agreements, 165
Joint ventures, 486
for diversification, 271–272
in foreign markets, 217–220
Just-in-time systems, 140, 574

Kaizen, 396, 575, 579
Key performance indicators, 558
Key success factors, 87–89
in balanced scorecard, 480
common types, 88t
competitive strength assessment, 122–124, 123t
identifying, 89
resource fit and, 297
value-based ethics, 618–619
Kickbacks, 319–320, 326
Know-it-all executives, 596
Knowledge diffusion, 78
Knowledge sharing, 565
KSFs; *see* Key success factors

Labor costs
in foreign markets, 198
national differences, 75
union vs. nonunion, 66–67
Labor-saving operating methods, 138
Lagging indicators, 31–32
Late-mover advantages, 189
Leadership; *see also* Global market leadership; Industry leaders; Market leaders
in balanced scorecard management, 480
by board of directors, 44–46
in changing corporate culture, 429, 430
by example, 431–432, 443
growth development leaders, 441–442
by local managers, 438
reasons for failure, 594–599
role in value-based ethics, 617
strategic vision and, 461–462
in strategy execution, 359–360, 448
characteristics, 439

Leadership—*Cont.*
  in strategy execution—*Cont.*
    constructive pressure,
      441–442
    development of competencies,
      442–443
    ethics, 443–444
    focus on excellence, 441–442
    information sources for,
      439–440
    internal leadership, 43
    making corrective adjustments,
      445–446
    managing by walking
      wround, 440
    social responsibility, 445
    tests of leadership, 446–447
Leadership development
  programs, 366
Leading indicators, 31–32
Lean management
  integrating Six Sigma, 577–581
  misconceptions regarding,
    575–576
  origin of, 571
  overview, 574–575
Lean Sigma, 571
Leapfrogging competitors, 178
Learning curve effects, 53t, 54
  in emerging industries, 233
  locational advantages, 210
  of low-cost providers, 137
  in multinational
    diversification, 308
  product standardization and, 198
Legal compliance; *see* Compliance
Leverage ratios, 98t–99t
Licensing, 486
Licensing strategies, 203–204
Lifestyle changes, 79–80
Lifestyle differences, 197
Liquidation of weak business, 261
Liquidity ratios, 98t
Local circumstances
  accommodating, 222–223
  unacceptable, 223
Local content rules, 200
Local firms, 181
Localized multicountry strategies,
  204–209
Locational advantages in foreign
  markets, 198–199, 209–211
"Long-jump" strategic initiatives,
  249, *250*
Long-term debt-to-equity
  ratio, 99t
Long-term objectives, 32
Low-cost leadership, 6
  in declining industries, 240
  in foreign markets, 210
  industry leadership and, 251
  keys to achieving, 142–143
Low-cost provider strategies, 6,
  135–144, 157t

Low-cost provider strategies—*Cont.*
  achieving cost advantages with,
    135–142
  cost efficient management of
    value chain, 137–139
  examples, 140–142
  illustration of, 136
  revamping value chain,
    139–140
  company options, 135
  compared to best-cost
    providers, 150
  compared to focused low-cost
    strategy, 153
  contrasted with other strategies,
    156–158
  definition, 134
  focused (market niche), 153,
    154–156
  in foreign markets, 210
  in fragmented industries, 247
  goal of, 604
  key points, 158
  keys to success, 142–143
  optimum conditions for, 143–144
  pitfalls, 144
  reward systems, 408
Low-end competitors
  benefits reduced by
    convenience, 509
    function, 508–509
    reliability, 509
  dynamics of attack by, 508–511
  game plan against
    ride out the challenge, 511–512
    srengthen value proposition,
      512–513
  inevitability of attack by, 513–514
  predators, 509–510
  reformers, 510
  strategic retreats from, 514
  strippers, 509
  transformers, 510–511
  vulnerabilities, 511

Macroenvironment, 49–51, *51*
  competitive environment, 51–52
  competitive forces, 54–74
  industry attractiveness, 89–90
  industry changes, 75–81
  industry environment, 51–52
  industry's economic features, 52–54
  ket success factors, 87–89
  key points, 90–93
  market position of rivals, 81–84
  relevant components, 49–*51*
  strategic moves by rivals, 85–87
Make-to-order production, 574
Make-to-stock production, 575
Malcolm Baldrige National Quality
  Award, 392
Management
  action plan, 3–4
  of conglomerates, 545–547

Management—*Cont.*
  of ethical conduct, 333–338
  lean management, 571–581
  signature processes championed
    by, 567–568
  in unrelated diversification,
    283–284
  values, principles, and
    standards, 416
Management demands on, 496
Management morality, 323–325
  amoral managers, 324
  immorality in global business,
    325–327
  immoral managers, 324
  moral managers, 323
Management team
  at General Electric, 366
  staffing, 364–365, 366
  strategic choices, 470–471
  for strategy execution, 360
Management tools, 475
Managerial requirements, 283–284
Managerial skills, 359–360, 361
Managers
  business strategy role, 38
  crafting and executing strategy,
    15–16
  ethics and, 10–12
  four Es of, 366
  functional-area strategies,
    38–40
  grading of, 366
  interaction with employees, 416
  internal transfer, 366
  local, 438
  proactive vs. reactive, 9–10
  role in crafting strategy, 35–37
  strategic fit, 276
  strategic issues and problems,
    125–126
  strategy execution tasks,
    359–360, 361
  unified strategic moves, 40–41
  winning strategies, 13
Managing by walking around, 440
Manufacturers
  backward integration, 71
  buyer bargaining power and,
    70–71
  export strategies, 203
  franchising strategies, 204
  licensing strategies, 203–204
  online buying groups, 71
  power over retailers, 66
  revamping value chain, 139–142
  strategic alliances by, 165–166
  supplier bargaining power, 67–68
  value chain cost efficiency,
    137–139
  Web sites, 75
Manufacturing activities
  batch-and-queue techniques,
    574, 576

Manufacturing activities—*Cont.*
  business process reengineering,
    395–396, 412
  concentrated, 209–210
  cross-border coordination,
    212–213
  cycle time, 375
  in differentiation strategies, 146
  dispersed, 210–211
  exchange rate fluctuations and,
    199–200
  in foreign markets, 198–199
  innovation in, 76–77
  with lean management, 574–575
  make-to-order production, 574
  self-manufacturing, 68
  Six Sigma program, 396–399,
    412, 572–574
  strategic fit in, 275
  total quality management, 396,
    399, 412
  vertical integration drawbacks,
    173–174
Manufacturing costs, 198,
  209–210
Manufacturing executive system
  software, 138
Manufacturing lead time, 579
Manufacturing-related
  KSFs, 88t
Market(s); *see also* Foreign markets
  as competitive battlefield, 55–56
  high-velocity, 241–245
  new, 521–527
  rapidly growing, 234–235
  slow- vs. fast-growing, 57–58
Market advantage, 100
Market base, 196
Market conditions
  adapting to changes in, 261
  dealing with cross-country
    variations, *205*
  fierce competition, 604–608
  in foreign markets, 197–201
  future, 106
  perfect competition, 602–603
  with slowing growth, 236–237
  strategy flexibility and, 456
  strong competition, 608–610
  volatility, 106
  weak competition, 610–611
Market demand, 239
Market growth, 197, 234
Marketing activities
  in differentiation strategies, 146
  innovation in, 77
  online enterprises, 187
  strategic fit in, 276
  in value chain, *111*
Marketing-related KSFs, 88t
Marketing strategy, 38
Market leaders, 169–170, 254,
  295–296
  vulnerable, 181

Market niche, for emerging markets, 225–226
Market niche strategies; see Focused (market niche) strategies
Market opportunities
identifying, 104–106, 105t
priority, 109
Market-penetration curve, 189
Market position
in business environment, 81–84
cash cows and, 295–296
key success factors, 89, 92
nine-cell matrix, 293t
from offensive strategies, 177–182
from product innovation, 76
rivalry and, 58
strategic group mapping, 81–84, 83, 91–92
strengthening, 301–302
Market power, 610
Market reconnaissance, 106
Market segments
blue ocean strategy, 180
offensive strategies for, 179
Market share
antitrust policy and, 252, 253
exchange rates and, 199
in fortify-and-defend strategy, 252–253
from guerrilla offensive, 179
head-to-head competition for, 236
from potent brand name, 273
from product innovation, 178
in rapidly growing markets, 234–235
relative, 289–290
small, 254
strategies to build, 254–255
Market shocks, 107
Market size, 53t, 286
Market space, types of, 180
Market territory, uncontested, 179
Market universe, 505–506
Massive and overwhelming force, 497
Maturing industries
definition, 236
from slow growth, 236–237
strategic pitfalls, 238–239
strategies for, 237–238
Measurement of objectives, 29–30; see also Performance measures
Media companies, 170
"Medium-jump" strategic initiatives, 249, 250
Mergers and acquisitions, 161, 168–171, 191
access to competitive capabilities, 169
access to new technologies, 169
accretion strategy, 537
bargain-prices, 238
buying out challengers, 512

Mergers and acquisitions—Cont.
company subcultures and, 419–420
conglomerates, 534–550
cost-efficient, 168
definition, 168
for diversification, 271
examples, 169–171
to expand geographic coverage, 168–169
failures, 171
fast-exit strategy and, 241
in financial industry, 301
to get core competencies, 370–371
hardball competition and, 499
to invent new industry, 169
for market leadership, 60
in maturing industries, 237
new product categories from, 169
number of, 168
partial acquisition, 486
portfolio management, 543–544
restructuring strategy, 537
by runner-up companies, 255
as strategic issue, 486–487
in target industry, 302–303
Me-too strategies, 517–518
Mission statements, 23–25
Mixed strategies, 535, 537–539
example, 550
Modular structure, 566
Monetary rewards, 404–405
Moral case
for ethical strategy, 338
for social responsibility, 346–347, 353
Moral managers, 323, 336–337, 352
Moral scrutiny, 10–12
Moral standards, 318
Motivation; see also Rewards and incentives
of creative people, 589–590
for strategic alliances, 217–218
in strategic vision, 25
in strategy execution, 43
Mover-and-shaker offensives, 255
Multibrand strategies, 156
Multicountry companies, 214
Multicountry competition, 201–202, 227
Multicountry strategies, 204–209, 205, 208
Multicultural companies, 419–420
Multi-industry firms, 536–537
Multinational competition, 195
Multinational corporations/enterprises
in Asia, 515
changing local markets, 223
company subcultures and, 419–420
ethical relations in, 321–323
lack of need for alliances, 220

Multinational corporations/enterprises—Cont.
performance-based incentives in, 411–412
post-diversification strategies
appeal of, 308–309
combined effects of, 311–312
global scope of, 308–309
strategy–culture fit, 437–438
winning in Asia, 518–520
Multinational diversification strategies
appeal of, 308–311
characteristics, 308
combined effect of, 311–312
Multiple strategy horizons, 250–251
Multiyear results, 552–553
Muscle-flexing strategy, 253–254
Mutual funds, 350

Narrowly diversified companies, 284
National economic baronies, 517
Near-term objectives, 32
Net competitive advantage, 122
Net competitive disadvantage, 124
Net profit margin, 98t
Net return on sales, 98t
New entrants, threat of, 60–61, 61t
New markets
creation of, 521–523
industries of the future, 525–527
supply-push innovation and, 523–525
New product categories, 169
New product development committees, 484
New product introduction, 382
Next-generation products, 56, 375
Next-generation technology, 178
No-layoff policy, 392
Nonconforming parts per million (NCPRM), 572, 573, 577
Nongovernmental organizations, 607, 609
Nonissue approach, 334–336, 335t
Nonmonetary rewards, 405, 411, 412
Nonunion workforce, 66–67, 136
North American Industry Classification Standard, 506

Objectives, 19, 29–35; see also Goals
examples, 33
financial, 31
quantifiable, 29
short- vs. long-term, 32
strategic, 31
and strategic plan, 41–42
Objective setting, 46
balanced scorecard approach
company-wide objectives, 34
examples, 33

Objective setting—Cont.
balanced scorecard approach—Cont.
financial vs. strategic objectives, 31
performance measures, 31–32
short-term vs. long-term objectives, 32
strategic intent, 32–34
top down vs. bottom-up, 34–35
nature of objectives, 20–30
for sales, 34–35
in strategy making, 29–35
stretch objectives, 30–31
Occupational Safety and Health Administration, 24
Offensive strategies, 4, 125, 177–182, 192
basis for attack, 181–182
behaviors and principles, 177–178
blue ocean strategy, 180–181, 502–507
to build market share, 254–255
choosing targets, 181
against competitive strengths, 178
cross-market subsidization, 214–215
for foreign markets, 215–217
hardball competition, 496–501
mover-and-shaker offensives, 255
stay-on-the-offense strategy, 251–252
time needed for, 178
types of, 178–180
Office supply industry, 186
Online buying groups, 71
Online enterprises, 185–187
Online marketing, 77
Online technology, 139–140
Operating efficiencies
eliminating unnecessary work, 140
labor-saving methods, 138
outsourcing, 138
software for, 138
vertical integration, 138
Operating excellence, 441–442
Operating profit margin, 98t
Operating strategies, 39, 40
strategy cohesion, 41
Operating systems
installing, 401–404
streamlining, 375
Operations activities, in value chain, 111
Opportunities for defects, 572–573, 578
Opportunity, 106
versus catalysts, 492–493
context, 490
cross-business, 268
definition, 489–490
elements of, 490–491
emerging, 286
maximizing, 507
versus options, 493
sources of, 494

Opportunity-finding
    mechanism, 484
Opportunity model, 489–495
    application of, 491
    avoiding SWOT confusion, 495
    catalysts vs. opportunities,
        492–493
    elements, 491
    options vs. opportunities, 493
    SWOT analysis in, 491–492
    untangling SWOT confusion,
        493–494
Order-filling, 382
Order fulfillment activities, 186–187
Organizational assets, 100
Organizational bridge-building, 383
Organizational building blocks, 377
Organizational design tools, 384
Organizational environment,
    appropriate, 456–457
Organizational flexibility, 176
Organizational learning
    competitive advantage and, 120
    internal universities, 371–373
Organizational mission, 490
Organization building
    collaboration with suppliers, 383
    competitive capabilities, 363,
        368–373
    core competencies, 363, 368–373
    current trends, 383–384
    internal cross-unit coordination,
        381–383
    staffing, 363, 364–368
    for strategy execution, 363–364
    structure and work effort, 363,
        373–381
Organization climate for innovation,
    587–589
Organization for Economic
    Cooperation and Development,
    Anti-Bribery Convention, 320
Organization structure, 385
    centralized vs. decentralized,
        378–379, 378t
    of conglomerates, 540–542
    current trends in, 383–384
    divisional, 540–541
    to fit strategy, 363
    flattening, 375
    modified to fit strategy, 377–378
    signature process and, 566
    strategy-critical activities,
        376–378
    strategy execution and, 373–383
        collaboration and alliances, 383
        cross-unit coordination,
            381–383
        delegating authority, 378–381
        strategy-critical activities,
            376–378
        value chain activities, 373–376
    streamlining, 384
    supply chain management in, 383

Outsourcing, 192, 486
    advantages, 175–177
    of core competencies, 370
    cost advantages, 138
    dangers of
        bad timing, 531–532
        losing skills and capabilities,
            531
    definition, 175
    drivers of, 175
    in high-velocity markets, 244
    order fulfillment, 186
    protests against, 348
    risks of, 177
    by subcontracting, 525–526
    supply chain management and, 175
    of value chain activities
        benefits, 374–375
        dangers of excess in, 376
        versus internal performance,
            373–376
        partnering, 375
Outsourcing strategies
    disruptive innovation, 529–530
    by focusing resources, 528–529
    potential of, 532
    scaling without mass, 529
    strategic repositioning, 520–531
Overdifferentiation, 149
Overtime hours, 578

Pareto principle, 577
Partial acquisition, 486
Partial integration, 171–172
Partial ownership, 305
Partnerships, 375
Patent and trademark law, 512
Pay for performance, 584
Payoffs of vision statement, 26
Peer assist policy, 562–563, 568
Peer pressure
    in corporate culture, 416
    for ethical standards, 337
People management policies,
    406, 416
Perceived value, 147
Perfect competition situation,
    602–603
Performance; see also Strategy-to-
        performance gap
    from blue ocean strategy, 503
    consistent, 369
    key indicators, 558
    near- or long-term, 32
    outclassing rivals, 374–375
    strategy turned into, 551–560
Performance bottlenecks, 555
Performance contracts, 558
Performance evaluation, 19,
    43–44, 47
Performance indicators
    lagging vs. leading, 31–32
    strategy and, 13
    tracking, 403

Performance loss, 553–555
Performance measurement
    return on sales, 479
    return on assets, 479
Performance measures, 29–30
    financial ratios, 98t–99t
    stock prices, 348–349
    strategic vs. financial, 31–32
    SWOT analysis, 97–109
Performance monitoring, 558–559
Performance outcomes
    goal-setting for, 584–585
    linked to rewards, 407–410
        compensation system design,
            410–411
        example of, 409
        importance of results, 408–410
        in multinational
            enterprises, 411
Performance prospects, 298–299,
    299t, 313
Performance targets, 29–30
    companywide, 35
    in continuous improvement
        programs, 400–401
    heavy pressure to meet, 330–332
    linked to compensation, 408–410
    versus multiyear results, 552–553
    resource fit and, 296
    shortfalls, 96–97
    social responsibility and, 345
    strategic moves to achieve,
        299–300
    in strategic plan, 42
    unmet, 551–552
Performance tracking, 402–403, 552
Perks, 405
Personal computer industry, 164
Personal gain, 328–330
Personal preeminence illusion, 595
Physical assets, 100
Plant manager, 40
Policies and procedures for strategy
        execution, 390–393, 391, 412
    consistency, 391
    example, 392
    top-down guidance, 391
    work climate, 391–393
Politicized corporate cultures, 422
Portfolio management, 541t
    building the portfolio, 543–544
    criteria for content, 543
    divestiture and restructuring,
        544–545
Portfolio restructuring by unrelated
    diversification, 280
Portfolio strategy, 535, 538t, 539
Preemptive strike, 179–180
Pressure groups, 347–348
Price competition, 56
    commodity products, 143
    in emerging markets, 222
    by industry newcomers, 143–144
    low-end competitors and, 513

Price competition—Cont.
    in mature market, 238
    obstacles to, 514
    substitute products, 64–65
Price-cost comparisons,
    109–122, 127
    activity-based costing, 114–116
    assessing cost competitiveness,
        114–116
    benchmarking value chain costs,
        116–117, 118
    components of cost structure,
        110–112
    industry value chain, 113–114
    need for, 109–110
    remedying cost disadvantages,
        117–120
    translating performance into
        competitive advantage,
        120–122, 121
    value chain concept,
        110–112, 111
    value chain variations, 112–113
Price cutting
    aggressive, 144
    by competitors, 59
    cost advantages and, 262
    by dumping, 216
    by industry newcomers, 143–144
    in low-cost provider strategies, 135
    low-end competitors and, 513
    offensive strategy, 178
Price/earnings ratio, 99t
Price-fixing, 326
Price premium, 149
Primary value chain activities, 111,
    111–112
Priorities, clearly identified, 558
Private-empire mentality, 595–596
Private-label brands, 71, 153
Proactive (intended) strategy, 9–10
Problem, 490
Process departments, 377, 382
Product(s)
    broad or narrow offering, 186
    competitor imitation of, 148–149
    convenience, 509
    customization versus
        standardization, 197–198
    easy-to-copy features, 145
    frills-free, 140
    function, 508–509
    next-generation, 178
    noneconomic features, 147
    overdifferentiated, 149
    pruning, 237
    reliability, 509
    standardized vs. differentiated,
        78–79
    substitutes, 64–65
    supply-side fragmentation
        and, 245
    tailored for emerging markets,
        221–222

Product(s)—*Cont.*
tie-in, 244
user applications
in emerging industries,
232–233
in maturing industries, 236
in rapidly growing
markets, 235
in runner-up firms, 256
user requirements, 143
Product attributes, 146, 149, 232
matching or beating, 290
Product boycotts, 347–348
Product design for foreign markets,
197–198
Product development strategy, 38
Product differentiation, 53t, 59,
143; *see also* Differentiation
strategies
ethics in, 610
strong competition and, 608
weak vs. strong, 149–150
Product information, 183–184
Product innovation, 53t; *see also*
Innovation
in declining industries, 240
as driving force, 76
in maturing industries, 236
new product categories, 169
as offensive strategy, 178
in rapidly growing markets, 235
Production activities, globalization
and, 75
Production procedures; *see*
Manufacturing activities
Productivity drive, 519
Product line
expansion of, 235
limited, 140
Product modifications, 382
Product performance, 146
Product quality, improving, 382
Product research and
development, *111*
Product standardization, 59
buyer preferences and, 78–79
versus customization, 197–198
Product type specialization, 247
Profit, 25
from blue ocean strategy, 504
in cost-of-entry test, 270
overall prospects, 90
Profitability
backward integration and,
172–173
business model and, 12–13
of business units, 290
competitive advantage and, 7
erosion in differentiation
strategy, 149
five competitive forces for, 72–74
in five-forces model, 72–74
identifying threats to, 106–107
industry attractiveness and, 287

Profitability—*Cont.*
in maturing industries, 237
related diversification and, 278
in unrelated diversification, 282
from value-based ethics, 618–619
Profitability ratios, 98t
Profit sanctuaries, 213–215, *214,*
227, 311
threatening, 498
Promotion from within, 405
Propagation strategy, 535–537,
538t, 539
example, 548
Proprietary technology, 232
Prospector strategy, 478
Punishment, rewards and, 406–408
Purchasing power variations, 197,
221–222

Quality control
nonconforming parts per million,
572, 573, 577
opportunities for defects and, 578
Six Sigma program, 396–399,
412, 571–581
statistical process control, 575
total quality management, 396,
399, 412, 572, 573
zero quality control concept, 575,
577, 578–579
Quality of life, 344
Quantifiable objectives, 29–30
Quick ratio, 98t
Quick-response capability, 244

Rapid company growth
danger of multiple strategies,
250–251
strategic initiatives, 249–250
sustaining, 249–251
Rapidly growing markets, 234–235
Reaction strategy, 478
Reactive (adaptive) strategy, 9–10
in high-velocity markets, 242
Real-time information systems, 403
Reformers, 510
Regional firms, 181
Regret, 491
Related diversification, 312
case for, 272–278
competitive advantage and,
277–278
cautions on, 278
economies of scope, 278
profitability, 278
shareholder value, 278
cross-business strategic fits
in administrative support, 276
in distribution, 275
examples, 277
in manufacturing, 275
R&D and technology, 274–275
in sales and marketing, 276
in supply chain activities, 275

Related diversification—*Cont.*
strategic appeal, 274
strategic fit
characteristics, 272–274, *274*
competitive advantage,
277–278
economies of scope, 277–278
identifying, 274–277
profitability, 278
shareholder value, 278
strategy options, *273*
versus unrelated
diversification, 272
with unrelated diversification,
284–285
Relationship managers, 383
Relative market share, 289–290
Reliability, 509
Religions, 323
Reputation protection, 606–608
Research and development, *111*
consumer testing of, 487
costs of, 137–138
in differentiation strategies,
145–146
in high-velocity markets,
243–244
outsourcing, 486
shared resources, 486
strategic fit in, 274–275
Research and development
departments, 381
Resistance to change
communicating strategic vision
and, 26
in corporate culture, 422–424
Resource advantages, 61
Resource allocation, 42,
298–299, 299t
Resource fit
caution on resource transfer, 298
competitive capabilities, 297
credit rating, 297
definition, 294
financial resources, 294–296
managerial resources, 297–298
performance targets, 296
Resource requirements, 287
Resources; *see also* Financial
resources
of conglomerates, 542
deployment of, 557–558
focusing strategy, 528–529
shared, 486
for strategy execution, 389–390
Resource strengths, 313
combinations of, 104
competencies, 100–102
competitive power of, 102–104
of competitive rivals, 85–86
cornerstone of strategy, 109
cross-border transfer, 211–212
forms of, 97–100
in high-velocity markets, 244

Resource strengths—*Cont.*
identifying, 105t
locational advantages, 210
resource fit and, 297
specialist strategy, 256
strategy based on, 7
SWOT analysis, 97–104
Resource weaknesses
of competitive rivals, 85–86
identifying, 104, 105t
Respect, lack of, 595
Restructuring, reasons for, 306–308
Restructuring strategy, 537, 538t,
539, 543–544
example, 548–549
Results-oriented corporate
culture, 438
Results-oriented work climate,
441–442
Retail channels, 62
Retailers
online buying groups, 71
online vs. brick-and-mortar,
184–185
private-label brands, 71
Retaliation, 182–183
Retrenchment, 258, 303–306
Return on assets, 479
Return on sales, 98t, 479
Return on stockholders' equity, 98t
Return on total assets, 98t
Revenue-increasing turnaround
strategy, 248
Rewards and incentives,
404–411, 412
balancing rewards and
punishments, 406–408
effective, 586
examples, 407
execution capabilities, 559–560
ideal, 585
ideas for designing, 582
linked to performance
design of compensation
system, 410–411
importance of results, 408–410
in multinational
enterprises, 411
as management tool, 408
for operational excellence, 442
in strategy execution, 43
strategy-facilitating motivational
practices, 404–406, 407
Rise and Fall of Strategic Planning
(Mintzberg), 462, 469
Risk, 491
Risk assessment, 487
Risk-averse companies, 4
Risk minimization, 507
Rivalry; *see* Competitive rivalry
Rivals; *see* Competitive rivals
Runner-up firms, 181, 254–257
market share strategies, 254–255
obstacles for, 254

Runner-up firms—*Cont.*
  strategic approaches, 255–257
    content follower strategy,
      256–257
    distinctive-image strategy, 256
    growth by acquisition, 255
    specialist strategy, 256
    superior product strategy, 256
    vacant-niche strategy, 256

Sacrifice, 491
Safety concerns, 79–80
Sales
  brick-and-click strategies,
    184–185, 186
  in differentiation strategies, 146
  direct to customers, 139
  e-stores, 184
  in mature market, 238
  online enterprises, 185–187
  setting objectives, 34–35
  stagnating, 76
  strategic fit in, 276
Sales and marketing activities, *111*
Sales volume, 137–138
Sarbanes-Oxley Act, 338, 341
Scaling without mass, 529
Scenario planning, 484–485
Screening applicants, 418–419
Seasonal factors, 287
Secondary value chain activities,
  110–112, *111*
Securities and Exchange
  Commission, 330, 341, 424
Selfish interests, 328–330
Self-manufacturing, 68
Seller–buyer relationships
  collaboration, 383
  competitive pressures from,
    68–72
Sellers' market, 70
Selling businesses, 305–306
Selling costs, low-cost providers,
  137–138
Sell-out-quickly strategy, 241
Service activities, *111*
Service quality, 519
Shareholder interests, 44–45
Shareholders, 350
Shareholder value
  diversification and, 272
    related diversification, 278
    tests for, 269–270
    unrelated diversification,
      282–283
  social responsibility and,
    348–349, 351
Shoppertainment, 513
"Short-jump" strategic initiatives,
  249, *250*
Short-pay policy, 392
Short-term objectives, 32
Signaling value, 147

Signature processes, 561–570
  contrasted with best practices,
    561–564
  evolution of, 565–569, 567t
    championed by executives,
      567–568
    company core values, 568–569
    company-specific history, 566
    executive role in, 569–570
  origin of, 561
Single-business enterprise, 40
  business strategy-making, 267
  strategic action plan, 263–264
  strategy effectiveness, 95–97, *96*
Six Sigma quality control, 366, 395,
  396–399, 412
  bonuses for goals, 585
  capturing benefits of, 399–301
  DMADV process, 396
  DMAIC process, 396–399
  five whys root cause analysis, 579
  integrating lean management,
    577–581
  and lean management, 571–581
  misconceptions regarding,
    576–577
  for operational excellence, 442
  overview of, 572–574
Skills, 99–100, 101, 165, 174,
  369–370, 531
Skills-related KSFs, 88t
Skills transfer, 540–541
Slingshot Syndrome (Watts), 526
Slogans, 25–26
Slow-exit strategy, 241, 257
Small firms, 181
Social causes, 351
Social conscience
  components, 342–345, 343t
  demonstrating, 345–346
Social contract, 322–323, 352
Social factors, 287
Social forces, 79–80
Social responsibility, 342–354,
  600–612
  actions and behaviors for, 353
  business case for
    buyer patronage, 347–348
    internal benefits, 347
    shareholder value, 348–349
  business strategy and, 601
  charitable contributions,
    343–344, 351
  competitive conditions and,
    600–601
  competitive forces/strategies,
    603–604
  competitive strategy and, 601–602
  conclusions on, 611–612
  crafting strategy for, 345–346
  "do-good" executives and,
    349–351
  environmental protection, 344

Social responsibility—*Cont.*
  evading social harms and, 349
  extent of, 351
  with fierce competition, 604–608
    ethical displacement, 605
    legal compliance, 605–606
    reputation protection, 606–608
  Friedman's view, 603
  intensity of competition and,
    602–603
  leading initiatives in, 445
  linked to executive
    compensation, 352
  meaning of, 342–345
  moral case for, 346, 353–354
  origin of concept, 342
  shareholder value and, 342, 351
  social causes, 351
  social conscience and, 342–345
  in stakeholder terms, 600–602
  with strong competition
    brand reputation, 609–610
    compliance with spirit of
      law, 608
    ethical product
      differentiation, 610
    ethical reporting, 609–610
    stakeholder management,
      608–609
  with weak competition, 610–611
  work environment, 344
  workforce diversity, 344–345
Social responsibility strategy,
  345–346
Software companies, 14
Specialists, 175–176
Specialist strategy, 256
Specialization strategy
  customer type, 247–248
  in high-velocity markets, 244
  product type, 247
Spinning off businesses, 305–306
SS *United States,* 321
Staffing, 42, 363, 385
  capable employees, 365–368
  management team, 360,
    364–365, 366
Stagnant industries, 239–241
Stakeholder interests, 44–45,
  346–347, 417–418,
  425–426, 434
  social responsibility and, 350
Stakeholder management,
  608–609
Stakeholder theory
  continuation of firms, 611
  social responsibility and,
    600–602, 608–609
Standard Industrial Classification
  System, 506
Standardized products; *see* Product
  standardization
Star businesses, 296

Start-up companies
  emerging industries, 231–234
  internal start-up, 271
Statement on Corporate
  Responsibility, 342
Statistical information, 403
Statistical process control, 575
Stay-on-the-offense strategy,
  251–252
Stock prices, 348–349
Stock trading, 350
Stories, in corporate culture, 418
Stranded assets, 500
Strategic action plan format,
  263–264
Strategic actions, 161; *see also*
  Competitive strategies
  decisions about, 161
  defensive strategies
    blocking avenues, 182
    signaling retaliation, 182–183
  for emerging industries, 233–234
  ethical standards and, 341–342
  ethics of, 10–12
  first-mover advantages, 188–191
  functional-area strategies, 161,
    187–188
  to improve performance, 299–300
  key points, 191–192
  late-mover advantages, 189
  for maturing industries, 237–238
  mergers and acquisitions, 161,
    168–171
  offensive strategies, 161, 177–182
    basis for competitive attack,
      181–182
    blue ocean strategy, 180–181
    choosing rivals to attack, 181
    principles and behaviors,
      177–178
    types of, 178–180
  outsourcing strategies
    advantages, 175–177
    definition, 175
    risks, 177
  predicting, 86–87
  principles of, 456
  questions for, 263
  for rapid-growth companies,
    249–251
  for runner-up firms, 254–257
  strategic alliances, 161, 163–168
    advantages, 164–166
    capturing benefits of, 166–167
    dangers of relying on, 167–168
    definition, 163
    factors in making, 163
    unstable, 167
  from SWOT analysis, 108–109
  vertical integration
    advantages, 172–173
    backward, 172–173
    definition, 171

Strategic actions—*Cont.*
  vertical integration—*Cont.*
    disadvantages, 173–174
    forward, 173
    partial vs. full, 171–172
    pros and cons, 175
  Web site strategies
    brick-and-click strategies,
      184–185, 186
    e-stores, 184
    online enterprises, 185–187
    product information only,
      183–184
Strategic alliances, 100, 191
  advantages, 164–166
  capturing benefits of, 166–167
  dangers of relying on, 167–168
  definition, 163
  for diversification, 271–272
  in emerging industries, 233
  examples, 164
  factors in making, 163
  in foreign markets, 227
    examples, 219
    motivation for, 217–218
    questionable need for, 220
    risks of, 218–220
  for global market leadership, 165
  in high-velocity markets, 244
  for industry position, 165–166
  kinds of, 485–487
  organizational bridge-
    building, 383
  picking a good partner, 166
  with suppliers/buyers, 290
  unstable, 167
Strategic analysis, opportunity
  model, 489–495
Strategic analysis of diversification,
  285–300, 312–313
  business-unit competitive strength
    calculating scores, 289–391
    interpreting scores, 291–292
    nine-cell matrix, 292–294, 293t
  cross-business strategic fit,
    294, 295t
  industry attractiveness
    calculating scores, 288–296
    difficulties of calculating
      scores, 288–289
    interpreting scores, 288
  new strategic moves, 299–300
  performance prospects, 298–299
  resource fit
    cautions, 298
    competitive capabilities, 297
    credit rating, 297
    financial resources,
      294–296, 299t
    managerial resources,
      297–298
    performance targets, 296
Strategic balance sheet, 104

Strategic choices, 466
  limitations in considering, 472
  well-grounded, 471–472
Strategic coordination, 310
Strategic fit, 313
  of business units, 290
  competitive advantage and,
    294, 295t
  in conglomerates, 534
  cross-business, 381
  cross-industry, 287
  in decentralized organization, 381
  example, 302
  with flexibility, 456
  in related diversification
    administrative support, 276
    characteristics of, 272–274,
      273, 274
    competitive advantage and,
      277–278
    in distribution, 275
    examples, 277
    in manufacturing, 275
    in research and development,
      274–275
    in sales and marketing, 276
    in supply chain activities, 275
    in technology, 274–275
Strategic group, 82
Strategic group mapping, 81–84,
  *83, *91–92
  construction of map, 82–83
  learning from, 83–84
Strategic ideas, 453–454
Strategic inflection points, 26,
  27, 189
Strategic initiatives, portfolio of,
  249–250
Strategic innovation, 458
Strategic intent, 32–34
Strategic issues
  about foreign markets, 195, 226
  for online enterprises, 185–187
  "worry list," 125–126, 127
Strategic mistakes, 238–239
Strategic moves, 503–504
Strategic objectives
  achieving, 35
  kinds of, 31
  success indicators, 96–97
Strategic partnerships, 68–69
Strategic performance, 31–32,
  95–97, *96*
Strategic plan, 47
  action agenda for, 42–43
  development of, 41–42
  forecasts vs. assumptions,
    556–557
  rigorous framework for, 551
  tracking performance against, 552
Strategic position, 453, 455, 457
Strategic repositioning, 530–531
Strategic retreats, 514

Strategic thinking, 482–488
  approaches to, 482
  collaboration with customers, 487
  continuous process, 488
  by differentiation strategies,
    482–483
  emulating entrepreneurs,
    483–484
  examples of, 483
  finding new opportunities, 484
  scenario planning, 484–485
  spectrum of strategic alliances,
    485–487
Strategic value loss, 553–555
Strategic vision, 19, 46
  appetite for, 460–462
  believing-doing gap, 459–464
  characteristics, 21–23
  common shortcomings, 22
  communicating, 25–27
  definition, 20
  developing, 20–39
  distinctive and specific, 20–21
  emotional dissonance on,
    462–464
  examples, 23, 461
  external/internal
    considerations, 21
  failure from myopia, 462
  as incentive, 405
  linked with company values,
    27–29, 30
  as managerial tool, 21
  versus mission statements, 23–25
  positive impact of, 460
  reasons for failure, 459–464
  reliance on past, 598–599
  resistance to change and, 25
  and strategic plan, 41–42
  understating obstacles to, 598
  well-conceptualized, 464
Strategy, 2–17; *see also* Competitive
  strategies
  being different by, 482–483
  business model and, 12–13, 14
  combining choices, 455–456
  competitive advantage and, 6–7
  of competitive rivals, 85–86
  confusion in meaning of, 452
  in conglomerates, 534, 535–539
  crafting and executing, 15–16
  criteria for judging, 13
  definition, 3–4
  drivers of unethical behaviors,
    330–333
  effectiveness, 95–97, *96*
  ethics and, 10–12
  evolution, 8–9
  example of, 5
  fit and flexibility, 456
  hardball competition, 496–501
  identifying, 7–8
  key components, 95–97, *96*

Strategy—*Cont.*
  key points, 16–17
  linked to ethics and core values,
    340–341
  matched to competitive
    conditions, 73–74
  military roots of, 502
  of multinational diversification,
    311–312
  offensive vs. conservative, 4
  organizational environment,
    456–457
  parameters
    decision makers, 454–455
    idea generation, 453–454
  proactive vs. reactive, 9–10
  related to business model,
    470–471
  resource strengths and, 109
  results of changes in, 390
  simple and concrete, 555–556
  for social responsibility,
    345–346
  steps in crafting, 35
  and strategic plan, 41–42
  success factors, 4, 7
  tailored to circumstances
    commandments for success,
      261–262
    emerging industries, 231–234
    fragmented industries, 245–249
    high-velocity markets, 241–245
    industry leaders, 251–254
    key points, 262–264
    maturing industries, 236–239
    rapid-growth companies,
      249–251
    rapidly growing markets,
      234–235
    runner-up firms, 254–257
    stagnant/declining industries,
      239–241
    weak/crisis-ridden businesses,
      257–261
  temporary and fluid, 9
  transience of, 457–458
  turned into performance,
    551–560
  typology of, 478
  for unrelated diversification, 280
  winning strategy, 13, 17
Strategy cohesion, 41
Strategy crafting; *see also* Strategy
  making
  delegating authority, 37
  importance of, 15–16
  participants, 35–37
  phases, 19–20
  process, 35–42
  strategic plan, 41–42
  strategy-making hierarchy, 37–40
  uniting strategy-making effort,
    40–41

Strategy-critical activities, 376–378, 385
  cross-unit collaboration, 382
  dangers of outsourcing, 376
  examples, 376–377
  functional departments, 377
  geographic units, 377
  internal performance, 374–376
  organizational building blocks, 377
Strategy–culture clash, 421
Strategy–culture fit, 421, 426–428, 447
  core values and, 427
  for multinational enterprises, 437–438
Strategy execution, *20,* 358–387, 388–412; *see also* Corporate culture
  benchmarking for, 394–395
  capabilities, 559–560
  in conglomerates, 547–550
  continuous improvement programs
    benefits of initiatives, 399–401
    business process reengineering, 395–396
    identifying best practices, 393–395
    Six Sigma quality control, 396–399
    total quality management, 396
  core competencies and competitive advantage, 372, 373
  employee training, 371–373
  three-stage development, 368–371
  corporate governance and, 44–46
  corrective adjustments, 43–44, 47
  failure in, 472
  framework for, 361
  implementation phase, 42–43
  importance of, 15–16
  information and operating systems, 401–404
  key points, 46–47
  leadership in, 439–447
    constructive pressure, 441–442
    developing competencies, 442–443
    ethics, 443–444
    focus on excellence, 441–442
    information sources for, 439–440
    making corrective adjustments, 445–446
    social responsibility, 445
  long-term, 261
  management skills for, 359–360
  management team for, 360
  managerial components, 262–263, *362*

Strategy execution—*Cont.*
  marshaling resources for, 389–390
  organization building for, 363–364
  organizing work effort, 373–383, 374t
    collaboration and alliances, 383
    cross-unit collaboration, 382
    delegating authority, 378–381
    internal cross-unit coordination, 381–383
    strategy-critical activities, 376–378
    value chain activities, 373–376
  performance evaluation, 43–44, 47
  phases, 19–20
  policies and procedures, 390–393
  principal aspects, 42–43
  rewards and incentives for, 404–411
  staffing for
    employee recruitment and retention, 365–368
    management team, 364–365, 366
  in weak-culture companies, 422
Strategy-facilitating motivational practices, 404–406
Strategy-focused enterprise, 15
Strategy horizons for rapid growth
  kinds of, 249, *250*
  risks of, 250–251
Strategy implementation
  challenge of, 360
  as companywide crusade, 361
  first steps, 361
  low-cost leadership, 6
Strategy makers, 35
Strategy making, *20*
  corporate governance and, 44–46
  crafting strategy, 35–42
  developing strategic vision, 20–29
  for diversified companies, 267–268
  driving forces and, 81
  ethical, 338–340
  example, 564–565
  in foreign marketing, *208*
    think-global, act-global, 206–207
    think-global, act-local, 207–209
    think-local, act-local, 204–206
  implementation phase, 42–43
  key points, 46–47
  key success factors, 89, 92
  phases, 19–20
  role of intrapreneurship, 37
  setting objectives, 29–35
  uniting, 40–41
Strategy-making hierarchy, 37–40, *39*
  business strategy, 38, *39*
  corporate strategy, 38, *39*

Strategy-making hierarchy—*Cont.*
  functional-area strategies, 38–40, *39*
  operating strategies, *39,* 40
Strategy management process
  and corporate governance, 44–46
  corrective adjustments, 43–44
  crafting strategy, 35–42
  implementation phase, 42–43
  key points, 46–47
  performance evaluation, 43–44
  setting objectives, 29–35
  strategic vision, 20–29
  strategy-making hierarchy, 37–40
Strategy options
  company menu of, *162*
  for competitors, 4
  complementary, *162*
  decision making about, 454–455
  for declining industries, 240–241
  for diversification, 270–272
    acquisition, 271
    internal start-up, 271
    joint venture, 271–282
  of diversified companies, 301t
    broader business base, 300–303
    divestiture, 303–306
    multinational diversification, 308–312
    restructuring, 306–308
  for emerging industries, 233–234
  emerging markets
    avoiding some markets, 223
    changing local markets, 223
    local circumstances, 222–223
    price competition, 222
  example, 470–471
  in foreign markets, 227
    dealing with cross-country variations, *205*
    exporting, 203
    franchising, 204
    generic strategies, 202–203
    licensing, 203–204
    localized or global, 204–209
  for fragmented industries, 247–249
  generic, *162*
  from globalization pressures, 225–226
  in high-velocity markets, 242–245, *243*
  to improve corporate performance, 299–300
  pitfalls to avoid, 263
  for resource allocation, 299t
  for winning in Asia, 518–520
Strategy revision, 258
Strategy road maps, 565
Strategy-to-performance gap closing
    debating assumptions, 556–557

Strategy-to-performance gap—*Cont.*
  closing—*Cont.*
    identifying priorities, 558
    monitoring performance, 558–559
    resource deployments, 557–558
    reworking execution capabilities, 559–560
    rigorous framework, 557
    simple and concrete strategy, 555–556
  culture of underperformance, 555
  multiyear results vs. projections, 552–553
  performance bottlenecks, 555
  tracking performance, 552
  value loss, 553–555
Strengths; *see* Resource strengths; SWOT analysis
Stretch objectives, 30–31, 406, 442
Strippers, 509
  predators, 509–510
Strong competition, 608–610, 611
Strong-culture companies, 420–421
Structural and cultural inertia, 457–458
Struggling enterprises, 181
Stuck-in-the-middle strategy, 158, 239, 500
Subcontracting, 525–526
Subcultures, 419–420
Substantive culture-changing actions, 430–431
Substitute inputs, 138
Substitute products, 64–65
Sudden-death threat, 107
Superior product strategy, 256
Supplier bargaining power, 66–69, *69,* 603
Supplier-related cost disadvantage, 119
Suppliers, 67–68
  bargaining leverage with, 290
  collaboration with, 383
  company bargaining power and, 138
  outsourcing and, 175
  relocating facilities, 140
  strategic partnerships with, 68–69, 244
  to Wal-Mart, 501
Supplier–seller relationships
  creating competitive pressures
    examples, 66–67
    seller–supplier partnerships, 68–69
    supplier bargaining power, 66–68
  vertical integration and, 173–174
Supply chain activities
  in differentiation strategies, 145
  strategic fit in, 275

Supply chain management, *111*
  cross-unit collaboration, 382
  improving efficiency, 138
  with Internet, 139–140
  in organization structure, 383
  outsourcing and, 175
  remedying cost
    disadvantages, 119
  vertical integration and, 174
Supply conditions, 53t
Supply-push innovation, 523–525
Supply-side fragmentation, 245–246
Support activities
  strategic fit in, *274*
  in value chain, 110, *111*
Sustainable competitive
    advantage, 604
  outsourcing and, 176
  significance of, 261–262
  strategy for, 6–7, 13
Switching costs
  alternative suppliers, 67
  barrier to entry, 62
  buyer bargaining power and, 70
  low, 143
  product differentiation and, 59
  rivalry and, 58–59
  substitute products and, 64–65, *65*
SWOT analysis, 97–109,
    126–127, 489
  competitive deficiencies, 104, 105t
  on competitive strengths, 122
  drawing conclusions from,
    107–109, *108*
  identifying market opportunities,
    104–106, 105t
  identifying threats to profitability,
    106–107
  implications for strategic action,
    108–109
  key financial ratios, 98t–99t
  in opportunity model, 491–495
  questions for, 107–108
  resource strengths and
    capabilities, 97–104
    competencies and capabilities,
      100–102
    power of resource strengths,
      102–104
  resource weaknesses, 104, 105t
  untangling confusion in, 493–495
Symbolic culture-changing actions,
    431–432
Systems development, *111*

Target market
  best-cost provider strategy,
    150–151
  competitive strategies for,
    134–135
  focused low-cost strategy, 153
Tariffs, 62
Tax burdens, 200

Team-based incentive compensation
    system, 136
Team effort, 34, 36, 360
Technical know-how, 78
Technological innovation
  differentiation strategies and, 148
  driver of diversification, 275
  as driving force, 76–77
  in high-velocity markets, 243–244
  improved by outsourcing, 176
  pace of, 53t
  reason for strategic alliances,
    164–165
  restructuring and, 306
  by runner-up companies, 255
Technology
  access from merger or
    acquisition, 169
  in diversification, 272
  dominant, 233
  dominant design, 525–526
  franchising strategies, 204
  licensing strategies, 203–204
  next-generation, 178
  proprietary, 232
  strategic fit in, 274–275
  in value chain, *111*
Technology branching, 246
Technology-related KSFs, 88t
Technology sharing, 167
Technology transfer, 78
Telematics industry, 470
Ten commandments for strategy,
    261–262
Terrorist attack of 2001, 107
Think-global, act-global strategy
    making, 206–207
Think-global, act-local strategy
    making, 207–209
Think-local, act-local strategy
    making, 204–206
Threat of new entrants, 60–64, 61t
Threats, external; *see also* SWOT
    analysis
  emerging threats, 286
  identifying, 106–107
Three-sigma rule, 572
Tie-in products, 244
Time constraint, 490, 491
Timeliness of outsourcing, 531–532
Times interest earned, 99t
Timing of strategic actions, 102
  first movers, 188, 189
  offensive strategies, 178
Top-down guidance, 391
Top-down objective setting, 34–35
Top-level executives
  action agenda, 362–363
  and company values, 29
  compensation, 409
  corporate strategy role, 38
  crafting diversification strategy,
    267–268

Top-level executives—*Cont.*
  decentralized decision
    making, 380
  directing strategy execution,
    359–360, 384–385
  ethical leadership, 443
  leading culture change, 429, 430
  managing ethical conduct,
    333–338
  performance bottlenecks and, 555
  role in crafting strategy, 35–36
  role in signature processes,
    569–570
  setting objectives, 34–35
  signature processes championed
    by, 567–568
  social responsibility and,
    349–351
  social responsibility
    initiatives, 445
  strategic vision, 20
  strategy cohesion, 41
  strategy–culture fit and, 427–428
  strategy decisions, 454–455
  unsuccessful, 594–599
    distrust of other officers,
      496–497
    illusion of preeminence, 595
    know-it-all types, 596
    obsession with company
      image, 597–598
    private empire mentality,
      595–596
    reliance on past, 598–599
    underestimating obstacles, 598
  weak, 364–365
Topping-out problem, 236
Total quality management, 399,
    442, 572, 573, 577
  capturing benefits of, 399–401
  characteristics, 395, 396
Trade restrictions, 62
Traditional accounting, 114, 116t
Traditional functional
    departments, 377
Traditions, company, 417
Transformers, 510–511
Transparency, 487
Turnaround strategies, 59
  in unrelated diversification, 282
  for weak businesses, 257–258
Tylenol crisis, 618, 619

Uncertainty, 79
Unconcerned approach,
    334–336, 335t
Underage labor, 319
Underperformance, 555
Underpricing competitors, 135
Unethical behavior; *see* Ethical
    failures
Unethical/greed-driven
    cultures, 424

Unhealthy corporate cultures,
    422–424
Unions, 66–67
Unit costs, 290
Unrelated diversification,
    279–284, 312
  basic premise, 279
  criteria for, 279–280
  drawbacks
    demands on management,
      283–284
    limited competitive
      advantage, 284
  examples, 281
  mergers and acquisitions, 280
  merits of
    general merits, 280–282
    shareholder value, 282–283
  portfolio building, 280
  versus related diversification, 272
  with related diversification,
    284–285
  strategy options, *273*
Unweighted rating system,
    122–124, 123t
Up-and-out policy, 406

Vacant-niche strategy, 256
Value, 490
  in best-cost provider strategy, 150
  buyer perceptions, 148
  created for buyers, 110
  perceived vs. actual, 147
  signaling, 147
Value-added time, 579
Value-based ethics, 614–620
  elements of commitment, 618–619
  influencing change, 616–618
  key to long-term success, 618–619
  leadership role, 618
  more than codes, 615–616
Value capture, 466–469
  misunderstandings about, 472–473
Value chain
  concept, 110–112, *111*
  cross-business relationships, 268
  for entire industry, 113–*114*
  reinventing, 237
  supply-side fragmentation
    and, 246
  system for entire industry,
    171–175
  variations in, 112–113
  in vertical integration, 377
Value chain activities, 385
  benchmarking costs, 116–117
  competitive advantage,
    120–122, *121*
  cost disadvantages and, 117–120
  cost efficiency in performing,
    121–122
  dangers of excessive
    outsourcing, 376

Value chain activities—*Cont.*
  in differentiation strategies,
      145–146
  expense categories, 114–115
  in-house, 175
  internal vs. outsourced, 373–376
  linked, 113–*114*
  in low-cost provider strategies
      cost-management of, 137–139
      examples of revamped
          activities, 140–142
      revamping, 139–140
  in organizing work effort,
      373–376
  primary, 110–112, *111*, 114
  reengineering, 396
  related diversification, 273
  secondary, 110–112, *111*
  strategic fit and, 273, *274*, 274–278
  support activities, 110, *111*
  unrelated diversification, 279
Value-conscious buyers, 151
Value creation, 466–469
  misunderstandings about, 472–473
  success in, 487
Value innovation, 502–507
Value network, 473
Value proposition, strengthening
  adding new price point, 512–513
  dropping prices, 513
  increasing benefits, 513
Values; *see* Core values
Venetian blinds of business,
  552–553

Vertical integration, 53t, 161,
    171–175, 191–192
  advantages, 172–173
  backward, 171, 172–173
  cost advantages, 138
  disadvantages, 173–174
  divisional units, 377
  forward, 171, 173
  full vs. partial, 171–172
  pros and cons, 175
Videoconferencing, 75
Video-on-demand, 5
Vision framework, 463
Vision statements, 21; *see also*
    Mission statements
  common shortcomings, 22
Voice over Internet Protocol, 5,
    74–75, 76–77, 231–233, 235

Wall Street Journal, 319–320
Weak businesses
  harvesting strategies, 260–261
  liquidation of, 261
  strategies for, 257–261
  turnaround strategies, 258–259
    boosting revenues, 258
    chances of success, 259
    combination efforts, 259
    cutting costs, 258
    example, 259
    selling off assets, 258
    strategy revision, 258
Weak competition, 610–611
Weak-culture companies, 421–422

Weak executives, 364–365
Weaknesses; *see* Resource
    weaknesses; SWOT analysis
Web site strategies
  avoiding channel conflict,
      183–184
  brick-and-click strategies,
      184–185, 186
  minor distribution channel, 184
  online enterprises, 185–187
  product information only,
      183–184
Weighted competitive strength
    scores, 291t
Weighted industry attractiveness
    scores, 288t, 289
Weighted rating system, 123t, 124
Wholesale channels, 62
Winning strategy, 13, 17
Women, buying power, 348
Work climate
  corporate culture and, 416
  politicized, 424
  results-oriented, 441–442
  for strategy execution, 391–393
Work effort, 363, 385
  organizing, 373–383, 374t, 386
    collaboration and alliances, 383
    delegating authority, 378–381
    internal cross-unit
        coordination, 381–383
    strategy-critical activities,
        376–378
    value chain activities, 373–376

Work effort—*Cont.*
  overtime hours, 578
  reengineering, 395
Work environment
  high-energy, 346
  as incentive, 405
  monitoring, 351
  quality of life and, 344
  Toyota Production System, 372
Workforce; *see also* Employees;
    Labor *entries*
  child labor issue, 319
  nonunion, 66–67, 136
  people-first strategy, 346
Workforce diversity, 344–345, 347
Workforce retention, 347
Working capital, 98t
Work-in-process, 490
Work-in-process inventory, 579
Workout process, 366
Work teams
  empowerment, 379–380
  management team, 360,
      364–365, 366
World Trade Organization,
    200, 216
Worry list, 126, 127

Zero quality control concept,
    575, 577, 578–579

CGSD LIBRARY

32116183